1968

This book may be kept

FOURTEEN DAYS

A fine will be charged for each day the book is kept overtime.

GAYLORD 142			PRINTED IN U.S.A.

SOCIAL AND CULTURAL DYNAMICS

Social and Cultural Dynamics

VOLUME TWO

Fluctuation of Systems of Truth, Ethics, and Law

BY PITIRIM A. SOROKIN

The Bedminster Press
New York
1962

This book was printed in 1962 in the United
States of America. The text is identical with
that of the original edition in 1937.

PREFACE

Are there different systems of truth — the truth of faith, the truth of reason, the truth of the senses — and do they fluctuate in their influence and acceptability in the course of time? During which periods in the history of the Graeco-Roman and Western cultures from 600 B.C. to the present has each of these systems risen to importance or suffered decline? What is the dominant contemporary system of truth and how has it come to be dominant?

What has been the movement of discoveries in the natural sciences and of technological invention from 600 B.C. to the present? Which periods have been particularly fertile and which sterile in these respects, and why? Is the movement of discoveries and inventions connected with the rise and fall of the main systems of truth?

Have the main categories of human thought and the "first principles" of science, philosophy, and religion been fluctuating in acceptability and prestige during these twenty-five hundred years; and, if they have, which periods are marked by the domination of which of these categories and principles, and in what form? What is the reason for such dominance? How have the content and meaning of such categories as Causality, Space, Time, and Number been changing, and in which direction is the modification? Have concepts such as Idealism and Materialism, Eternalism and Temporalism, Being and Becoming, Realism and Nominalism, Universalism and Singularism, Determinism and Indeterminism, and many others that lie at the foundation of scientific, philosophical, and other theories, varied in their influence, now one, say Idealism, rising, now its opposite, Materialism, becoming dominant? And if they have varied in influence, when exactly did this take place and why? Have other general scientific and philosophical theories, such as cosmogonic hypotheses, Atomism, Vitalism, Mechanism, also been fluctuating with regard to their acceptability?

Do the main ethical systems, such as that of Absolute Principles, of Hedonism, Utilitarianism, Eudaemonism, fluctuate also in their comparative prestige and currency? If they do, when during the twenty-five hundred years under consideration was each of these systems dominant, and why? Similarly, do the moral codes and mores as they are incorporated in law, particularly in criminal law, also change?

v

These are the problems dealt with as the first object of this volume. The existence and the nature of long-time fluctuations are studied in the fields of the philosophy, religion, science, ethics, and law of the Graeco-Roman and Western cultures from about the year 600 B.C. Do such waves or fluctuations indeed occur? Which periods during these twenty-five hundred years have been marked by the rise or decline of the various main systems of truth, main competitive principles of science, philosophy, religion, ethics, and law? Is there in these fluctuations any steady tendency toward the disappearance of one of the currents, say of the truth of faith, or idealism, and toward an increase of some other, say of the truth of the senses, or materialism? Or does each of the competitive principles simply fluctuate, now rising, now declining, without any linear trend? Are these fluctuations periodical? The elucidation of these problems is the first task of the present volume.

The second object is to inquire, in conformity with the central idea of the entire work, whether the fluctuations in one compartment of the Graeco-Roman and Western cultures during the centuries involved are connected with fluctuations in their other compartments. Is a change in the system of truth always followed by changes in all the essential principles and theories of science, philosophy, religion, and ethics? Is it followed by analogous transformation in law; in painting, sculpture, architecture, music, literature (see Volume One); in the forms of social relationship, political and economic organization, and in the movement of wars and internal disturbances (see Volume Three)? Is culture a unified system in which a change in one compartment is accompanied by change in all the others? If it is, are all the modifications in all the compartments synchronous? Are they closely bound together? Or do they occur nonsynchronously? If they do not coincide in time, which compartment leads in the change and which lags behind? Is there any uniformity in the time and order of change in the various compartments of culture? What are the reasons for, and factors bringing about (*ratio sive causa*), all these fluctuations? These problems constitute the second task with which the present volume is concerned. And to this extent it deals with the sociology of cultural change, particularly in the fields of philosophy, religion, science, ethics, and law.

In the third place the volume inquires how all these fluctuations are related to the central idea of the whole work, namely, to the fluctuations of Ideational, Mixed, and Sensate types of culture. It aims to show that most of the fluctuations in all the main compartments of culture are but manifestations and component parts of deeper, all-embracing transformations of culture from one type to the others. When a culture passes from, say, the Ideational to the Sensate type, or vice versa, all its art, philosophy, religion, science, ethics, and law undergo the same profound transformation. From this standpoint the volume attempts to demonstrate that what a given society regards as true or false, scientific or unscientific, right or wrong, lawful or unlawful, beautiful or ugly, is conditioned fundamentally by the nature of the dominant culture. In the Ideational culture, Ideational science, philosophy, religion, law, ethics, and art triumph, and their Sensate forms are rejected as false, wrong, unlawful, sinful, heretical, and blasphemous. Contrariwise, in a dominant Sensate culture — such as we are now living in — Sensate forms of science, philosophy, religion, ethics, law, and art become dominant; and their Ideational forms are branded as superstition, prejudice, ignorance, and the like. In this aspect the volume represents a treatise in *Wissenssoziologie*, considered in its basic forms and principles.

The method, the material, the qualifications and reservations, remain the same here as in Volume One, to which the reader is referred for a discussion of them.

The importance of all these matters is evident. I have tried to avoid dealing with them flippantly, casually, fragmentarily, or in spectacular fashion. This volume, and the entire work of which it is a part, contributes something, I hope, to an understanding of the fundamental problems of social thought.

PITIRIM A. SOROKIN

Cambridge — Winchester

CONTENTS

PART ONE

FLUCTUATION OF IDEATIONAL, IDEALISTIC, AND SENSATE SYSTEMS OF TRUTH AND KNOWLEDGE (*WISSENSSOZIOLOGIE*)

I. Ideational, Idealistic, and Sensate systems of truth. Logically Ideational, Idealistic, and Sensate mentalities, to be consistent with their major premises, must have different systems of truth: Ideational, the truth of faith; Idealistic, the truth of reason, organically unified with truth of faith and truth of senses; Sensate, the truth of senses. Factually, all these and many Mixed systems of truth have functioned in the mental history of mankind. So-called "scientific system of truth" is largely the truth of senses; as such, it has not been either a unique or even predominant system of truth. These systems of truth are profoundly different in their nature, subject matter, interests, method, and evidence. II. Fluctuation of the main systems of truth: empiricism, religious and Idealistic rationalism, mysticism, skepticism, fideism in the Graeco-Roman and European cultures from 580 B.C. to A.D. 1920. Are the foregoing propositions corroborated by the relevant facts? Have the main systems of truth fluctuated in influence? Have the periods of domination of Ideational culture been those of truth of faith; of Idealistic culture, those of truth of reason; of Sensate culture, those of truth of senses? Translating these systems of truth into the respective categories of: religious rationalism, Idealistic rationalism, empiricism, criticism, mysticism, fideism, and skepticism, the chapter traces quantitatively the fluctuation of the influence of each of these systems of truth from 580 B.C. to A.D. 1920. Methodological and explanatory preliminaries. Reservations and qualifications. III. Main results. During this period each of these systems of truth has been dominant. Why? Mental spectrum of each period. Comparative power of each of these systems of truth. Truth of faith and atheism. Predominant system of truth of the present time. IV. Corroboration of the propositions in social space. V. Summary.

Quantitative results of Chapter One are clarified and amplified by a concise qualitative analysis of the dominant systems of truth in each of the main periods studied. I. Ideational phase of Greek mentality. II. Idealistic phase of Greek thought: Socrates, Plato, Aristotle, and other thinkers of the period. III. Mixed phase of Graeco-Roman mentality. IV. The rising tide of Ideational truth of faith. The greatest mental revolution. System of truth of Christianity. Its struggle against the truth of senses and other Mixed systems of truth. V. Truth of faith triumphant. Its characteristics and its monopolistic domination during the Middle Ages. Middle Ages as an age of certainty. VI. The Idealistic phase: the end of the eleventh, twelfth, and thirteenth centuries. This period is not so much a climax of the medieval system of truth, as a fundamental deviation from it. Truth of Albertus Magnus, St. Thomas Aquinas, and of great Scholastics as Idealistic system of truth. VII. The crisis of the fourteenth and the fifteenth centuries and the *crescendo, forte,* and *fortissimo* of the empirical system of truth from the sixteenth to the twentieth century. VIII. Truth of senses triumphant. Its characteristics. Scientism, quantitativism, objectivism, mechanisticism, cult of technique, imitation of the natural sciences, mentality of the "as if" (*als ob*) illusionism. IX. Forebodings. Why and how truth of senses is self-destructive. First signs of its crisis.

I. Methodological preliminaries. From the nature of each main type of culture it follows that in Ideational culture natural sciences and inventions are likely to show little progress, while in Sensate culture they should show marked progress, Idealistic culture occupying an intermediary position. Are these logical expectations corroborated by the relevant facts? Materials, sources, and method of the study of the movement of scientific discoveries and inventions from 800 B.C. to the present time. II. General character of the movement of scientific discoveries and inventions. III. Main results. Systems of truth and scientific discoveries. In which branches of science has the increase of discoveries in the Western European world been most marked? Erratically parabolic direction of the movement of discoveries in the life process of a single culture. Erratically undulating movement of discoveries in the world at large, with a rapid rise for the last five centuries. Development in more recent times. Decrease in the rate of increase of discoveries and inventions. Symptoms of fatigue of the present time. Number and qualitative estimation of discoveries and inventions. IV. Summary.

I. Preliminaries. Since the main systems of truth fluctuate in their influence, the first principles of all branches of human knowledge should be expected to fluctuate in their acceptability and influence with the fluctuation of the systems of truth and of the corresponding types of culture. II. Fluctuation in the influence of Idealism, Materialism, and Mixed theories from 580 B.C. to A.D. 1920. III. Main results. Correlation with Ideational and Sensate culture. Is there a linear trend? periodicity? Comparative strength of each current. Variations in patterns of fluctuation. Diversity

of rhythms and beats. Contemporary situation. Rising tide of materialism and Sensate interpretation of man and culture. IV. Corroboration in
social space.

ethics and affairs.   Dominant singularism of contemporary sociology and of the social sciences.   Contemporary crisis of nominalistic singularism in science and social conduct.

I. Main types of conceptions.   The problem as a more restricted variety of the general problem of realism and nominalism, universalism and singularism.   Its practical importance.   II. Fluctuation of the domination of the main conceptions.   Greece.   Rome.   The Middle Ages.   Transitional period.   After the thirteenth century.   The nineteenth and twentieth centuries.   Relationship to sociological universalism and singularism.   III. Main conclusions.

I. Determinism and indeterminism.   Theoretical and practical importance of the problem.   Its perennial character.   Its relationship to the main systems of truth and culture.   Fluctuation of the influence of each mentality (580 B.C. to A.D. 1920).   II. Main results.   As other "First Principles," determinism and indeterminism fluctuate in their influence according to the dominant type of culture.   Contemporary situation.   Weakening of deterministic conceptions at the present time.

I. Introductory.   The answer to "Whither mankind?" seems also to have been conditioned by the dominant type of culture.   II. Domination of the cyclical and trendlessly undulating theories in the Hindu and Chinese (and Babylonian) cultures.   III. Fluctuation of the main conceptions in Graeco-Roman and Western cultures.   In which periods was each conception dominant and why?   Evolutionary linearism in physicochemical, biological, and social sciences of modern times as a consequence of the dominant Sensate culture.   IV. The beginning of reaction.   Contemporary crisis of "linearism" in science generally and in the social sciences particularly.   V. Conclusion.

I. Introductory.   If the main thesis of this work is correct, we should expect that, with the fluctuation of the main types of culture, not only would the systems of truth and the "First Principles" fluctuate in their influence and credibility, but also the basic categories of human thought, such as causality, space, time, number. II. Fluctuation of Ideational, Idealistic, and Sensate conceptions of causality. This category is in a sense common to all mentalities, but in its meaning and content it is fundamentally different in Ideational, Sensate, and Mixed mentalities. Mixed idea of causality among primitive peoples. Chinese Mixed Causality. Hindu Ideational conception of causality. Fluctuation of the conceptions in Graeco-Roman and Western mentalities (580 B.C. to A.D. 1920). Contemporary situation. Crisis of Sensate conception of causality at the present time. Its suicidal immanent trend. III. Fluctuation of Ideational and Sensate conceptions of time. *Aeternitas, aevum,* and *tempus.* Periods of domination of each conception from 580 B.C. to A.D. 1920. Modern times. Domination of Sensate temporalistic *tempus,* the mechanistic clock time of modern culture. Its contemporary crisis. IV. Ideational and Sensate categories of space. Their fluctuation in acceptability and credibility. Contemporary crisis of Sensate category of space. V. Ideational and Sensate conceptions of number. Fluctuation of the influence of each conception.

If the systems of truth, "First Principles," and basic categories of human thought fluctuate in their acceptability and influence according to the rise and decline of the main types of culture, various scientific theories of a more or less general nature should fluctuate all the more in credibility and prestige. Each of these should be, like fashion, generally accepted today and rejected tomorrow. The proposition is validated by a study of fluctuation of the influence of several typical theories in the field of the natural and social sciences. I. Fluctuation of atomistic theories (580 B.C. to A.D. 1920). Relationship to the dominant types of culture and systems of truth. Modern materialism, empiricism, nominalism, singularism, and atomism. Contemporary crisis. II. Fluctuation of vitalism and mechanism in biology. III. Fluctuation in the theory of abiogenesis. IV. Oscillations of the theories concerning the nature of light. V. Fluctuation of cosmogonic theories. VI. Some general remarks on the long- and short-time fluctuations of prestige of the natural-science theories. VII. Fluctuation of the influence of Prout's theory. VIII. Fluctuation of theories in the social sciences and humanities. IX. Concluding remarks.

PART TWO

FLUCTUATION OF IDEATIONAL AND SENSATE FORMS OF ETHICAL AND JURIDICAL CULTURE MENTALITY (DYNAMICS OF ETHICAL VALUES)

I. Preliminaries. Every culture has a set of ethical values, though not all reach the stage of development of consistent ethical systems. II. Ideational, Idealistic, and Sensate systems of ethics. Ethics of absolute principles is implied in Ideational mentality, while the relativistic ethics of happiness in its hedonistic, utilitarian, and eudaemonistic varieties is logically demanded by the Sensate mentality. Idealistic mentality occupies an intermediary position. III. Fluctuation of the influence of Ideational, Idealistic, and Sensate systems of ethics (580 B.C. to A.D. 1920). Periods of domination of each system. Its reasons. Growth of ethics of happiness with the rise of the Sensate culture. Ethical Ideationalism of despair and Epicureanism of despair. Contemporary hedonistic-utilitarian ethical mentality, its characteristics and satellites: utility as the supreme category pervading all cultural values from God to science and art; hedonism; money madness; wealth as the measure of all values; contemporary leadership; rule by force and coercion; overestimation of the specious present. Its immanent self-destruction. Signs of reaction against it. IV. Main results.

I. Pulsation of the influence of absolutism and relativism. Contemporary relativistic mentality. Its relationship to Sensate culture. Its characteristics, by-products, and self-destruction. Revolt against relativism. II. Pulsation of optimism and pessimism. Their Ideational and Sensate forms.

I. Introduction. Law and criminal law as the best reflectors of the changes in mores and ethicojuridical mentality on its daily routine level. Reservations and qualifications. The reasons why criminal law is subjected to detailed study. Method of procedure: 104 forms of actions and relationships as the main fund of criminal actions. Material and codes studied: France, Germany, Austria, Italy, Russia. II. Fluctuations in the size of the class of criminal actions. Number of types of actions qualified as criminal in the Barbaric codes, in the Canon law, and in all the subsequent codes of the countries studied. What are the main changes in this respect from each code to the subsequent code in each country? Connection with the dominant type of culture and ethical mentality. Changes in the postwar criminal codes of Soviet Russia, Fascist Italy, and of the Third Reich. Meaning of these changes. Summary. III. Which types of actions are criminal in all codes studied and which are variable? and to what extent? "Absolute crimes." Their relationship to the "natural law." Underestimation of the uniformity, and overestimation of ethical and juridical relativity, in contemporary theory and practice. IV. Fluctuation of intensity of punishment, from the Barbaric codes to the postwar criminal codes. Does severity of punishment tend to decrease? The data and the answer. Which periods and codes were particularly stern and in regard to what crimes? Why? Summary. v. Fluctuation of extension and severity of punishment in social life. Law codes do not give an adequate answer to this problem. The main hypothesis and its corroborations. Relationship to the main types of culture and of ethical mentality. Other factors. When and where the severity and quantity of punishment increase and why. Contemporary situation viewed in the light of the hypothesis suggested. Its sinister and promising aspects. Summary. vi. Entr'acte: coefficients of correlation between the variables.

LIST OF TABLES

LIST OF FIGURES

PART ONE

Fluctuation of Ideational, Idealistic, and Sensate Systems of Truth and Knowledge (Wissenssoziologie)

Chapter One

FLUCTUATION OF IDEATIONAL, IDEALISTIC, AND SENSATE SYSTEMS OF TRUTH AND KNOWLEDGE (QUANTITATIVE) [1]

I. IDEATIONAL, IDEALISTIC, AND SENSATE SYSTEMS OF TRUTH

From Art we pass now to the next fundamental "compartment" of culture — to its *System of Truth and Knowledge*. This system, in integrated or unintegrated form, is embodied in what is loosely styled *Religious, Philosophical, and Scientific Thought* of a given culture. Contrary to the common procedure that begins with an attempt to distinguish the differences between the religious, philosophical, and scientific thought as such and from these differences tries to define their systems of truth and knowledge, we shall reverse the method and start with the delineation of the main types of systems of truth and knowledge, and from this delineation arrive at some conclusions concerning the differences between the religious, the philosophical, and the scientific thought. The reason is clear : If there is a fundamental difference between these forms of thought, it is due mainly to the difference in the systems of truth accepted by religion, philosophy, or science. If their systems of truth are identical, any essential difference between them disappears, and religion-science-philosophy become one and the same form of thought in all their essential traits. Under such conditions any logical distinction between them becomes impossible ; and any attempt to define them is doomed to fail, as evidenced by the great number of unsuccessful definitions of religion and science which have been presented. This explains why we shall proceed with the systems of truth as such and analyze them regardless of whether the problems involved belong to religion or science or philosophy in one of the hundreds of various meanings given to these terms in vernacular use. In the study of the categories of Truth and Knowledge we shall employ a method similar to that used in the study of the forms of art in Volume One. What are the main systems of truth and knowledge? Are the categories Ideational, Idealistic, and Sensate applicable to truth generally? If they are, what are the meanings of Ideational, Idealistic, and

[1] In co-operation with N. O. Lossky and I. I. Lapshin.

Sensate systems of truth and knowledge? What are the important characteristics of each of these systems of truth? Are such systems actually given in the historically existing cultures? Do they fluctuate in their domination in the life history of culture generally and of the cultures studied here specifically? If so, which have been the periods in the history of the Graeco-Roman and the Western cultures when each of these systems of truth dominated? How does the fluctuation of the system of truth reflect upon hundreds of various general and special theories of philosophy, religion, and science, beginning with the comparatively general theories of idealism-materialism, determinism-indeterminism, realism-nominalism, and ending with the categories of Time, Space, Number, Causality, and with the narrow problems of science like the theories of atomism, light, cosmogony, and hundreds of physio-psycho-sociological problems? Are the fluctuations in the field of truth and knowledge associated with those in the field of art? If they are, how — positively, or negatively? Have the "art and the truth compartments" of the Graeco-Roman-Western culture been integrated not only logically but also causally?

Such are the problems to be dealt with now. On first glance they appear few and sound abstract. In fact their study involves a large number of the most important problems of human knowledge and will lead us to an investigation of not only general and abstract problems but also of special and very concrete problems in this field.

Let us ask ourselves, first, Can the system of truth and knowledge with the criteria of what is and is not true be the same for Ideational and Sensate mentality and in predominantly Ideational and Sensate cultures respectively? In spite of the prevalence at the present time of the opinion that there is and can be only one system of truth and knowledge — that incorporated in science, outside of which any theory is supposed to be "unscientific" or fallacious — in spite of the popularity of such an opinion, mere logical deduction from the major premises of Ideational and Sensate mentality suggests a negative answer to the question. Deductively we must expect that the system of truth and knowledge — the subject matter of knowledge and the criteria and evidences of true and false — must differ for the groups and persons who have Ideational and Sensate mentality and live in Ideational and Sensate cultures respectively. The reasons for such a deduction are evident. If the bearers of Ideational mentality do not try to adapt themselves to the sensory, fleeting, and ever-changing milieu; if they consider it an illusion and mirage; if, correspondingly, they view the "telegrams" brought by the organs of senses as mere reflections of the shadow of the true reality and not as accurate "messages" of the eternal and true reality, then such a mentality can hardly make the organs of senses and their testimony the main evidences, main judges, and main criteria of what is true and what is false. Quite consistently with its major premises, such a mentality (in such an adaptation and culture) has to view the organs of senses as incompetent witnesses and still less competent judges of the true and the untrue, and incapable of grasping the true reality. Therefore, their testimony has little value, little certainty, and little validity. Such has to be the attitude of the bearers of Ideational mentality toward a sensualistic system of truth based upon the evidences of our organs of senses, an attitude which quite logically follows from the major premises of that mentality. The truth of organs of senses cannot be expected to play a dominant or important part in an Ideational culture. Some other system of truth based upon a criterion of validity different from the evidence of our senses has to be dominant in such a society. This dominant system has to be either the system of *truth of faith* — based upon some kind of non- or superempirical source revealed by personal or impersonal God, deity, or mana — in the way of revelation, divine inspiration, intuition, mystic experience, and the like — or the system of *truth of reason and logic of human mind* viewed as a source independent of the organs of senses.

For a purely Ideational culture mentality, the truth of faith has to appear more infallible than human reason and logic. Therefore, we should expect that in predominantly Ideational culture the dominant system of truth must be mainly "revelation" (the religious or magical system of truth) in a supersensory and even superlogical way "revealed," "granted," "inspired" by superempirical agency or power or source, be it personal or impersonal. Based upon the revealed truth of God, absolute, perfect, and omniscient, the truth is also believed to be absolutely certain in its validity. Such is the deduction that follows from the very nature of the major premises of the Ideational mentality and culture.

In a Sensate society and culture the Sensate system of truth based upon the testimony of the organs of senses has to be dominant. Since for the bearers of a Sensate mentality and culture there is no reality behind and except the sensory reality of Becoming; and since this sensory reality is "signaled" to us through our organs of senses, through what we see, touch, hear, etc., these senses must become the main and almost the only judges of what is true and what is false. If we see or hear a given empirical phenomenon in exactly the same way in which it is described by a given theory, the theory is valid and "scientific." If the testimony of these organs contradicts it, the theory is wrong and "unscientific." Such has to be the Sensate system of truth and knowledge. Just as for an Ideationalist the testimony of the organs of senses is practically worthless, so for a Sensatist the belief in a revealed truth is nonsense, gross superstition, and a mark of profound ignorance. In other words, we shall expect that in a predominantly Ideational culture (and periods) the dominant system of truth has to be the truth of faith (religious-magico-mystical), while in a predominantly Sensate culture it has to be the truth of senses. Such have to be the "correlations" deductively.

If now we consider the Idealistic mentality and culture, its underlying system of truth must be one between the supersensory revelation and sensory evidence; one in which both these systems are organically united. The system of truth which meets these requirements is the truth of human reason and logic, the *idealistically rationalistic system of truth of the medieval Scholastics* of the twelfth to the fourteenth centuries. In that system the main judge is human reason and logic itself with its own laws of the true and false. This judge, however, is not reluctant to hear the testimony of the organs of senses and is willing to use their information to transform it and to sanction it as true, and is also not reluctant to accept the truth of revelation when it appears to be reasonable and reconcilable with the logical laws of the human mind which itself, in a sense, has a vein of divine nature. Thus the idealistically rationalistic system of truth has in itself the elements of the revealed and Sensate system of truth in an organic synthesis, and for this reason corresponds to and is better adapted to the nature of this "Mixed type" of mentality and culture. As such, it is different from supposed "pure rationalism" as a truth of reason only, exemplified by the system of truth of Descartes and other "rationalists" of the seventeenth century. Their system is, however, not a "pure rationalism," but truth of reason, plus truth of senses, as we shall see further. Other "Mixed" mentalities and cultures require also a combination of truth of faith and of truth of senses, but the mixture is not necessarily a consistent synthesis, since these "mixed" mentalities are not integrated internally. The truth of faith and of senses may coexist mechanically, undigested and unintegrated. Finally, in the *passive and cynical forms of Sensate mentality*, the *system of skepticism, incapable of believing in any system of truth,* is by deduction the one most consistent with such a mentality and culture. Likewise, for the *Ideationalists of despair* the most consistent system of truth must be one "of a desperate will to believe" by those who, like Apostle Thomas, wish to but cannot believe without great difficulty.

Such are the deductive expectations which logically follow from the major premises of each of the types of culture mentality. For the sake of clarity an outline of these expected associations is given below.

TYPE OF PREDOMINANT MENTALITY AND CULTURE	TYPE OF PREDOMINANT SYSTEM OF TRUTH TO BE EXPECTED IN EACH OF THESE
Ideational (pure)	Revealed truth of religion, magics, mystic experience. "Truth of faith." Based upon superempirical, supersensory, and super-rational or logical word of God, or other supersensory and superlogical sources.
Sensate	"Scientific" system of truth, empirico-Sensate, based upon the evidence and testimony of organs of senses (with telescopes, microscopes, and other instruments as extensions of these sensory receptors).
Mixed Idealistic	The idealistically rationalistic system of human reason and logic, based upon the laws of mind itself, with subsidiary admission of the sensory as well as of the revealed truths if they are reconcilable with human reason. Inconsistent mixture of truth of faith, of reason, of senses.
Passive Sensate and Cynical	Skepticism as a belief in the impossibility for man to obtain an adequate, certain, and valid truth.
Ideational desperate	Fideism: a desperate will to believe by those who are disbelievers.

This outline does not bring about all the shadings and gradations which in reality exist. Being concerned, however, with the main classes, we shall pass the minor classes by, stressing that such shadings and intermediary combinations are to be expected, but for the sake of economy of effort are left unanalyzed.

From the very nature of each of these main systems of truth and knowledge several further characteristics follow. Their subject matter as well as the method of verification of any statement about the subject matter has to be profoundly different in each of these systems. In a concise way the following outline sums up the essentials of each of these systems as to the subject matter of their study as well as the method of proving the validity of each statement or theory about this subject matter.

SYSTEM OF IDEATIONAL TRUTH OF FAITH	SYSTEM OF IDEALISTIC TRUTH OF REASON	SYSTEM OF SENSATE TRUTH OF SENSES
Subject Matter	*Subject Matter*	*Subject Matter*

Mainly the supersensory, and superrational "subjects" and "realities." God, devil, angels, spirits; soul, immortality, salvation; sin; redemption; resurrection; paradise, purgatory, inferno; and so on, with an enormous number of other subproblems of the same kind, like St. Augustine's problem. Can angels use devils as their messengers? What is the estate of angels? Are the hellish pains proportional to crimes and so on? [2]

The sensory and empirical phenomena are studied only incidentally and even then not for their own sake but merely as "visible signs of the invisible world," as symbols of the supersensory reality. The supreme discipline in such a system of truth is always theology as a science of the supersensory realities. The exposition of the truth is apodictic and symbolic.

Partly supersensory, partly sensory-empirical. Each for its own sake, but the value of the knowledge about the sensory phenomena is subordinated to that of the supersensory "realities."

The total system of knowledge here incorporates, usually in the form of idealistically rationalistic philosophy ("Scholasticism" of Plato and Aristotle, of Albertus Magnus and St. Thomas Aquinas; or "Scholasticism" of the Upanishads and other Idealistic philosophies based upon the Vedas in India), reasoning and empirical knowledge in the sense of the contemporary science. The ultimate reality is thought of as knowable. The exposition of the truth is dialectic and deductive.

Mainly the world of the sensory perception, like the phenomena studied in the natural sciences. When, for instance, in the field of psychology, culture, and "values," the phenomena seem to have an aspect not easily reducible to the sensory-material forms, science concentrates mainly at their sensory aspect and either disregards the "nonmaterial" aspect or treats it as a subsidiary and tries to "measure them" through the measurement of the sensory-external phenomenal forms. Hence, the tendency to "objectivism," "behaviorism," "quantitativism," "mechanisticism." The supersensory realities are declared either nonexistent, or irrelevant, or "unknowable" (criticism, agnosticism, positivism). The natural sciences become the leaders as the most perfect, exact sciences, and are copied by philosophy and by even abortive pseudotheology which tries in the period of domination of the truth of senses to create "scientific religion." Exposition of the truth is "inductive" and especially "experimental."

[2] See St. Augustine, *The City of God*, Bks. XVI–XVIII *et passim*. This is, of course, an example of such problems. They may be concretely different but regardless of what religion

SYSTEM OF IDEATIONAL TRUTH OF FAITH	SYSTEM OF IDEALISTIC TRUTH OF REASON	SYSTEM OF SENSATE TRUTH OF SENSES
Method of Validation	*Method of Validation*	*Method of Validation*

Mainly reference to the Sacred Source, to the Scripture (revealed) in the form of quotations from it which would show that the statement perfectly agrees with the Scripture. If a new "truth" is claimed, the method of demonstration is to show that it is due to the same "divine inspiration" to which the Scripture is due. Purely logical reasoning and the testimony of the organs of senses have only a subsidiary role, and only in so far as they do not contradict the truth of the revealed Scripture. Otherwise they are unhesitatingly rejected as invalid or even inspired by the devil (heresy, blasphemy, black magic, etc.)

Intermediary between the methods of the other two systems. Mainly the method of logical reasoning ("Scholastic" method) but also reference to the testimony of the organs of senses. Both these methods are always "covered" and given an ultimate support by the proper reference to the Scripture and the revealed truth. Hence, concretely in the works which embody this system of truth one always finds the dialectical method, reference to the organs of senses and their data, and quotations from the Scripture or a source equivalent to it.[3] All these references to the three sources of truth tend to show that their testimony is unanimous and that they do not contradict one another. It is the method in which the evidence of Scripture, of logic, and of the senses is perfectly harmonious.

Mainly the reference to the testimony of the organs of senses (often reinforced by their extensions — telescopes, microscopes, etc.), supplemented by the logical reasoning, especially in the form of the mathematical reasoning. But even the well-reasoned theory remains in the stage of pure hypothesis, unproved until it is tested by the sensory facts; and it is unhesitatingly rejected if these "facts" contradict it. The truth of faith and its "Scriptures" do not play any role in the system and are not regarded as "evidence." If anything they most often are regarded as mere "superstitions." In the cases where some pious or hypocritical reference to the Scripture is given (often merely for practical reasons) it usually does not play any important part and is mostly superfluous. The truth of faith has as little value by itself in this system of truth as the testimony of senses in the system of truth of faith.

---

and theology the system of truth of faith incorporates, it always would have the same problems as the subject matter of its "study."

[3] Read from this standpoint, for instance, Plato's *Dialogues*, St. Thomas Aquinas's *Summa Theologica*, or the *Summa contra Gentiles;* or Ibn-Khaldun's *Prolégomènes*, and many other works belonging to the same type. See the details and the quotations given in a later part of this chapter and in Chapter Two.

This schematic characterization shows that each of these systems is quite consistent within itself and with the major premises of the respective mentality; that the character and "contents" of each of the systems of truth, from the standpoint of their subject matter, as well as the method of testing the truth, are profoundly different, and therefore the mentality incorporated in each of these systems differs again profoundly from that of any other.   If these conclusions are found accurate, and if the respective cultures are logically integrated, other corollaries will follow from them.

A. If various cultures coexisting in social space differ from one another — some more nearly approximating the Ideational, some the Mixed-Idealistic, and some the Sensate types — their systems of truth and knowledge must differ also, and each culture will have a dominant system of truth typical of it.

B. If and when a given culture passes from its predominantly Ideational to Idealistic or Sensate form, or vice versa, its system of truth and knowledge has to undergo a transformation; a system of truth corresponding to Ideational culture has to decline and that corresponding to the Mixed Idealistic or Sensate culture has to rise and become dominant. In other words, if the culture has recurrent fluctuations in its forms, similar fluctuations and "cycles" have to be experienced by its system of truth and knowledge.[4]

C. In the cultures and periods dominated either by the truth of faith or by that of senses, there always has to be either a nearly complete subordination of one of the truths, or, if the less powerful truth has considerable strength, some latent or actual antagonism between the system of truth of faith and that of senses will result.   Inasmuch as the truth of faith has mostly been incorporated in what is called religion and the truth of senses in what is called science, religion and science in such cultures either combat or absorb each other.   There is rarely, if ever, close co-operation between them.   In Idealistic cultures and periods the three main systems of truth can be expected to exist in perfect harmony with one another; therefore only such cultures and periods are marked by a real, "cordial alliance" of religion, philosophy, and science.[5]

D. "Scientific truth and knowledge" represent mainly the empirico-Sensate system of truth based upon the evidence of our organs of senses; especially upon the evidence not only of one individual but also of several

[4] Compare G. B. Vico, *Principj di una scienze nuova*, Vol. V of his *Opere* (Milan, 1854), pp. 39–49 and Bk. IV. L. Weber, *Le rythme du progrès* (Paris, 1913), chap. vii *et passim*. K. Jöel, *Wandlungen der Weltanschauung*, 3 vols. (Tübingen, 1928–1932).

[5] Compare with Saint-Simon's "critical" and "organic" periods. *Œuvres de Saint-Simon et l'Enfantin* (Paris, 1877), Vol. XLI, pp. 170 ff.

individuals or of a group (collective sensory experience).[6] *Science with its truth and discoveries has to experience the same ups and downs which are experienced by the empirico-Sensate system of truth.* More specifically:

(1) Science and the scientific system of truth have to be the dominant system and must have supreme prestige in a predominantly Sensate culture and society; but in a predominantly Ideational culture

[6] Many possibly do not realize that the system of truth and knowledge of what is called contemporary science is only one of the three main systems of truth which have functioned, have been believed in, and accepted by individuals, groups, and cultures. The main evidence of what is true and false in contemporary science is the testimony of our organs of senses. If a given scientific theory describes a given phenomenon or relationship in the form which is found accurate by our eyes, ears, and other organs of senses, the theory is scientific. If the testimony of our organs of senses contradicts the theory, it is unscientific or fallacious. "Observation," "experiment," and "inductions" are the main procedures by which science tries to study its phenomena, but the same organs of senses (with which we observe the natural set of the phenomena or the artificially selected set in the experiment) made the supreme judges of true and false. This empirico-Sensate "scientific" system of truth is almost free from the "truth of faith" and is openly inimical to it. It possesses some of the elements of the rationalistic system of truth in various forms; in the forms of the laws of logic which are obligatory for scientists and which are hardly mere results of the sensory experience; in that of deductions, which are incorporated in the queen of these sciences, mathematics; of many conceptual elements in form of the fundamental concepts and principles of the sciences; and in several other forms. However, being present in the scientific system of truth, these elements of the rationalistic system are mainly the tools and methods used for an accurate description of empirical phenomena as they are given by the organs of senses or are the mere framework for ordering the material given by these senses. Final judgment as to whether a given description or theory is true is practically always decided by the organs of senses. Until such a test is made any theory dealing with the empirical phenomena — physical, chemical, biological, and what not — is always in the stage of tentative hypothesis only. Likewise a purely logico-mathematical theory, like that of relativity, is subjected, for its scientific verification, to the test of the organs of senses: the observation of light, of eclipses, and so on, which are deciding its scientific fate. Telescopes, microscopes, laboratory instruments, and thousands of other scientific tools are but an extension and sharpening of the organs of senses. For these reasons the scientific system of truth is merely another name for the empirico-Sensate system of truth. All that has been said of it has a bearing on science and vice versa. Subsequently the terms "scientific" and "Sensate" systems of truth and knowledge will be used interchangeably as practically identical.

I have not the slightest doubt that to persons not acquainted with the problems of epistemology, logic, methodology, philosophy, history of science, and so on, these statements seem strange. As will be shown in this and the next two chapters, since we are living in a period of domination of the empirico-Sensate system of truth — in a period of scientism — we are prone to believe that scientific system of truth is the only system of truth and that all that is outside of it is "unscientific," in the sense of being untrue, fallacious, wrong, superstitious. However commendable is such a belief, an impartial investigator of sociocultural phenomena and the phenomena of mentality must state that exactly the same is the belief of the partisans of systems of truth other than the scientific. That the wisdom of this world (scientific truth) is foolishness with God was believed by St. Paul and other partisans of the truth of faith. We shall see this in detail. Therefore, however surprised a contemporary partisan of scientism may be at my impartiality in "observing and ascribing" the existence of various systems

and society, this system must occupy a much lower position and have much less prestige than, for example, truth of faith based upon revelation or its substitutes. This means that in this "mundane world," as Machiavelli used to say, even science and its system of truth is not exempt from fluctuations.

(2) Since the Scientific system of truth is to be supreme in the Sensate and secondary in the Ideational society, it can be expected that Ideational cultures and periods are to be marked by fewer important scientific discoveries; and since the mentality of Ideational culture is turned away from the world of senses toward the ultimate reality of everlasting Being, it is neither interested in an investigation of this empirical world nor in making various scientific (that is empirico-Sensate) discoveries concerning it. Since there is neither great interest nor great appreciation of such scientific studies and discoveries, comparatively little progress will result in science, especially in the field of material phenomena dealing with natural sciences, discoveries, and technical inventions. In Sensate culture and periods the situation must be reversed for the same reasons. Sensate mentality turns to the Sensate reality and is eager to study it, and either does not recognize any other reality or is not interested in it. For these reasons it is to be expected that such periods and cultures are to be marked by comparatively greater progress in science, scientific discoveries, and technological inventions in the field of the natural and technological sciences.

(3) If the last two expected regularities are valid, then not only the system of truth has to change with the change in the character of culture, particularly the relative position of "scientific system of truth" among other systems and its comparative blossoming, but even within the scientific system of truth several fundamental theories also have to change. General principles and categories of science — space, time, number, and the like; the cosmogony and theory of the universe; atomistic theory and theory of matter; mechanistic and vitalistic principles; theory of causation; fundamental principles of biology or evolution; and the like — also have to be expected to change when a given culture passes from one of its fundamental forms to another. In the terms of contemporary scientific jargon this means that many scientific theories are dependent for their acceptance and recognition (as accurate and scientific)

---

of truth and of their change, transformation, rise and decline, together with their causes, he has to countenance it because they are empirical facts witnessed by the testimony of our organs of senses, as will be demonstrated further. In other words, in my study I shall intentionally follow the "empirical system of truth" which must be convincing to such a partisan of "scientism."

upon the kind of culture in which they appear.   Theories about the class of phenomena A, which are easily accepted, for instance, in Ideational culture and are recognized by its thinkers as true, are likely to meet severest criticism and rejection from the scientists in Sensate culture; and vice versa.

(4) It also can be expected that even within the scientific system of truth of senses the main topics which would be worked out in Sensate and Ideational cultures would also considerably differ.   The "scientists" of Ideational cultures are likely to concentrate their attention on one group of Sensate phenomena as the most important, while scientists of Sensate culture may find these problems unimportant and may concentrate on another class of phenomena having little interest for the scientists of Ideational culture.   We may, for instance, assume that the scientists of Ideational culture would be more interested in the study of spiritual, mental, and psychological phenomena, problems of the soul, its mortality or immortality, psychological processes (especially specific ones, like ecstasy), modification of the human mind, and generally such phenomena as are closely allied to the Ideational world.   Scientists of Sensate culture would probably be more interested in the purely material phenomena, and especially in their mastery and control.

The above expectations and inferences mean, if they are valid, that even such primordial values as truth and knowledge, so far as their content, criteria, and evidences are concerned, in sociocultural actuality (but not in Plato's world of ideas) depend greatly upon the type of culture of which they are a part.   In other words, what appears to be true and what is not, what appears to be scientific and what is not, what is a valid criterion of truth and what is not, are, in the statistico-mathematical language, in a considerable degree a "function" of the sociocultural variable.   If this be found valid, then the sociologist should have his say also in the problems of epistemology and logic, in so far as there is a place — and a large one — for what the Germans call *Wissenssoziologie*.[7]   Adequately understood, it composes one of the most important parts of sociology of culture. Subsequent chapters are but a *Wissenssoziologie* applied to the fundamental problems of truth and knowledge.

The preceding pages show that our main categories are applicable to the field of truth and knowledge.   Without effort the various systems of

[7] K. Mannheim, "*Wissenssoziologie*" in *Handwörterbuch der Soziologie*, pp. 659–680 (Berlin, 1931).   See the literature there.   The author, however, gives it a too Marxian interpretation, which narrows unduly its field and makes it somewhat one-sided.   M. Scheler, *Die Wissensformen und die Gesellschaft* (Leipzig, 1926); W. Ziegenfuss, *Versuch über das Wesen der Gesellschaft* (Leipzig, 1935).

truth fall easily into the Ideational, Mixed, and Sensate classes. Likewise the categories permit deductions concerning the essential characteristics of each of the main systems of truth as well as a presentation of important propositions concerning their distribution in social time and space, their fluctuation, and the fluctuation of their constituent elements.

Let us turn now to an empirical verification of these deductions. If the cultures studied are logically integrated, it will be found that these deductions are corroborated by the empirical data. Such a corroboration would demonstrate again, on the one hand, the heuristic value of the "logico-meaningful" method and, on the other, that within the "compartment of truth and knowledge" these cultures also are integrated "causally." Besides these points, the actual study of the relevant data will possibly disclose several other "truths." Let us then enter the dark and slippery cave of the relevant facts concerning the movement of the main epistemological, ontological, logical, and philosophical systems: scientific discoveries and technological inventions during the last twenty-five hundred years. The journey may turn out to be laborious; but it may show us facts that are not quite platitudinous even for the specialists in these fields.

II. Fluctuation of the Main Systems of Truth: Empiricism, Religious and Idealistic Rationalism, Mysticism, Skepticism, Fideism in the Graeco-Roman and European Cultures from 580 b.c. to a.d. 1920

I. METHODOLOGICAL AND EXPLANATORY PRELIMINARIES

Since we plan to study now the quantitative fluctuation of the comparative influence and acceptability of the main systems of truth during some twenty-five hundred years; since such an approach is comparatively rare; and since the same problem will confront us many times, it is advisable to outline here concisely the material, the methodological procedure, the main assumptions, and other problems involved in such a study, What will be said here will be applicable subsequently to many problems discussed. Omitting many secondary technical reservations and limitations understood by every competent investigator without special mention, the main points to be considered are as follows.

The purpose of the study of this fluctuation is not to discuss the truth or error of the main systems of truth, nor is it to take sides concerning them. My objective is very different. Assuming the position of a perfectly impartial observer, and taking the systems involved as the factual datum, I am going to inquire whether in the life history of the Graeco-Roman and Western cultures the comparative influence and popularity of each of these systems of truth have been constant or variable in the mentality of the *leading thinkers* in the field. If variable, has there been in the course of time a linear trend of continuous increase in the influence and acceptance of one of these systems at the expense of the others, or has such a trend been absent? If such a trend exists, then what is its nature or, to use favorite terms of the nineteenth century, what has been its line of "progress" or its "historical tendency"? Has its direction been one of greater and better truth of faith, of reason, or of senses? If there be no such linear trend, then how have the rise and fall of these currents fluctuated? Have there been definite "cycles" and "periodicities" in these fluctuations, or only nonperiodic "ups and downs" of each of these currents, without any uniform tempo and rhythm? If the same themes recur, but each time with new variations, then is it possible to indicate with reasonable accuracy at which periods from about 580 B.C. to A.D. 1920 each of these systems of truth rose and declined, and to what extent? Finally, if the preceding questions are answered, what are the reasons (or the "causes" and "factors") of such fluctuations?

Several qualifications, reservations, and technical explanations are necessary before any answers to the above questions are given. They are made, briefly, in the following paragraphs.

II. RESERVATIONS AND QUALIFICATIONS

A. The fluctuations of the influence of the truth of faith, of reason, and of senses are studied only within the Graeco-Roman and Western cultures, from about 580 B.C. up to A.D. 1920. Other cultures and their respective streams of thought will be mentioned briefly later.

B. The study does not pretend to give a description and "measurement" of the fluctuations in the mentality of *the entire Graeco-Roman and European populations*, from generation to generation, during this period. Such a task would be impossible for the obvious reason that no one knows what every Greek or Roman, or the average man of the eighth, fifteenth, or twentieth centuries thought in this field, or if the great majority of these people thought anything at all about the problem.

C. The study roughly estimates the increase and decrease of the comparative acceptability and influence of each of these currents of thought, as they are represented, first, by the *number* of their partisans among the majority of prominent thinkers in the field, in each twenty-year period, and in each one-hundred-year period from 580 B.C. to A.D. 1920;

second, by the comparative "weight" or influence of these partisans in each of these periods.

Practically all the names of the great thinkers in the field of this problem were selected. For the last three or four centuries, when the number of scholars increased greatly, only the names of the most prominent philosophers and scientists who contributed to the problem were included. But the samples are so large that in all probability they are representative for these centuries. In this way Tables 1 and 2 and Figure 1 are based upon material far larger than any study of this problem hitherto made.

Respectively, two sets of data were computed. First, for each period, was computed the number of partisans to each of these currents among the total number of thinkers in the field, in that period, whose names are preserved in the annals of history. Turned into percentages, these numbers indicate the main changes in the comparative strength of each current from period to period, as manifested by changes in the number and percentage of its partisans. Second, for each period, data are given concerning the *comparative weight or influence* of each current in each period among the same group of thinkers; whereas, from the point of view of the number of partisans in each period, each of the thinkers is assigned the same value of influence, namely, one. In the "weight" data each of them is assigned different values of influence on a scale of one to twelve. Those thinkers who, like Plato, Aristotle, Plotinus, St. Augustine, St. Thomas Aquinas, or Kant, obviously exerted much greater influence than many others, are given the highest weight of influence, namely twelve. Those whose influence seems to have been noticeable (or their names would not be preserved in the annals of history), but seemingly the smallest in comparison with the influence of the other thinkers, are given the value of one. The rest of the thinkers are assigned values intermediary between one and twelve proportionately to their appraised influence.

The assignment of these values to each thinker is a difficult but not an impossible problem, if it does not pretend to be more than roughly accurate, and if several conditions are present. Given a thorough knowledge of the field of the problem, of the works of all the contributors of each period, of the proportion of the partisans of a given current among them, of the role of each contributor in the literature of the age, as well as of the subsequent ages, of the value of one specialist checked and compared with that of others, and of a few additional conditions which are to be mentioned further — given all these, it should be possible to prepare an approximately valid grading of the proportional influence played by a given contributor and a given creed in the total epistemological mentality of the given age.   By making such an evaluation for several periods one can obtain an index of the fluctuation of this influence in the course of time.   It will not be entirely adequate, but it is not probable that it will be entirely misleading.

Guided by these considerations, and following the above conditions, Professors N. O. Lossky and I. I. Lapshin and I have assigned the appropriate value to each of the contributors (in their influence) in the following way.[8]

As objective criteria of the comparative influence of each of the philosophers — the following data were selected :

(1) The number of special monographs devoted to a philosopher.

(2) The approximate frequency with which the philosopher's name has been mentioned, not only in the works of his contemporaries but also in those of the subsequent thinkers in this field.

(3) Whether he was a founder of a school of philosophic thought.

(4) Whether his name is mentioned even in the most elementary texts of history, epistemology, and theory of knowledge.

(5) The number of his avowed disciples and followers among the thinkers in the field.

(6) Whether his works have been translated into foreign languages.

(7) Whether his works have been republished again and again in spite of the length of time that had elapsed since his death.

(8) Whether he was a creator of an original and complete system of philosophy and epistemology.

From the above criteria one can see that almost all the relevant data have been considered.   On the basis of these criteria the following number of units of influence and the corresponding scale of grades were constructed : We started with the number of special monographs devoted to the thinker and distributed them into twelve classes, from zero to 2560 and more monographic studies.   Beginning with five the number doubles in each subsequent class.   In the second row the value of influence assigned increases by one unit, giving a scale of values from one to twelve. Then the number of monographic studies has been corrected by other considerations mentioned previously.   Weighting all these carefully, we assigned to each thinker in the field the value between one and twelve which appeared to be most adequate.

[8] The profound knowledge of philosophy possessed by Professors Lossky and Lapshin has been indispensable in the preparation of the problem involved.   Both were formerly of the University of St. Petersburg.   Both men are leading professors of philosophy in Russia, and both are notable in international philosophy.

Number of Monographs on a Philosopher	Units of Value Given
0	1
1	2
5	3
10	4
20	5
40	6
80	7
160	8
320	9
640	10
1280	11
2560 and more	12

In this way the elemental subjectivity in assigning the influence value to the thinkers has been reduced as much as it is humanly possible. The names of the thinkers and the values assigned to each one are given in the Appendix to this chapter. Any specialist in the field would probably give a similar weight to those values presented in the list. Even though a few discrepancies might occur, they would not change the result in any tangible degree when the total weight of all the partisans of each period has been grouped and summed up, providing the scale of values remains not very different from one to twelve. The weight of all the partisans of a given current in each period is summed up; from these figures percentages are computed which indicate roughly the main changes in the increase and decrease of the influence of each current from period to period. This is the rough but systematic method used to estimate the movement of each of the currents of thought, in the course of time, as embodied in Tables 1 and 2 and Figure 1.

As stated before, these results from the points of view of both number and weight cannot pretend to reflect the changes in the mentality of the whole population from period to period. But it is probable that, in both [9] cases, they indicate, at least roughly, the main changes in the mentality of the leading thinkers. In so far as the totality of the leading thinkers in a given field of a given period embodies the mentality of a given culture in that field, *upon its highest, or leading, or logically integrated level, the*

[9] "Both," because, as the reader can check for himself, the essential movements of the curves based on mere number and on "weight" are similar, the only difference being that the amplitude of the fluctuations of the "weight curve" is slightly wider. In hundreds of further studies the same result has been found. If the scale of weight is not very wide, the "weight curve" moves similarly to the "number curve." For the sake of economy, in subsequent chapters only "weight curves" and tables will be given. But the reader can assume that the mere "number tables" and "curves" deviate very little from the "weight tables and curves."

above results possibly reflect the main changes of the respective mentality of the Graeco-Roman and the European cultures upon this level in each of the specified periods.

Such are the bases upon which Tables 1 and 2 are built and they include several arbitrary assumptions. The main assumptions are found in the scale of "weight" from one to twelve, and in the assignment of a specific value to each thinker within this scale. No claim is made that instead of the scale from one to twelve, a scale from one to three, from one to a million, or any other cannot be used. Those who wish to use a different scale may, and we shall be most interested in the results. The considerations which governed our choice of scale are as follows.

Since we try to appraise *the influence* and not the scientific, nor any other, value of the thinker, the amplitude of the scale should not be too wide, say one million to one. In that case the results would often be such that though a given system of truth is represented by only one person it will appear more powerful than the systems represented by all the other thinkers of the period. Such a situation is self-contradictory. It claims influence where there are but few followers and denies influence to the stream followed or supported by the majority. If a given single person be really influential, his influence would have to be exerted upon the other thinkers, and his current would thereby be represented by many, or by the majority, of the thinkers of the period. If, however, he stands alone, without followers, this would mean that he did not influence the other thinkers or that his actual influence was small. In that case a value of influence equal to one million is quite contradictory to the facts. On the other hand, if a great and influential thinker such as Plato, or Aristotle, be given the highest mark, and it be only twelve, his influence is reflected not only in this value but also in the total values of all his followers and the thinkers of the same current. As a result, the stream will be represented in its real power with reasonable adequacy. At the same time the self-contradiction involved in the use of too wide a scale will be avoided. Neither is such a scale guilty of a false assumption of equal influence for all thinkers.

The reasonableness of our scale is attested, among other things, by the fact that the curves constructed upon a basis of weight and the curves constructed upon the basis of number, in which an equal value of one is given to each thinker, agree in their essential movements. This means that, all in all, the scale conforms to the principle that the greater the influence of a thinker in any given period, the greater is the proportion of thinkers who followed the same stream of thought, and vice versa.

The proposition may be said to contain three interdependent terms:
the influence of a given thinker, the number of thinkers in a given movement of thought, and the strength of the movement.[10]

As additional evidence of the approximate validity of the procedure
described, it can be mentioned that the movement of the empirical system
of truth (of senses) constructed according to the above method agrees
notably with the movement of the discoveries in the natural sciences and
of technological inventions (see Chapter Three) constructed upon quite a
different method. It must be evident, without further explanation, that
the empirical system of truth is the system of truth of the natural sciences;
if one grows, the other must grow; if one declines, the other must decline.
These curves are based upon radically different items and sources: one
upon the *number of the discoveries and inventions in the natural sciences*
computed from Darmstaedter's work; the other upon the systematic
registration of all the known or all the important known thinkers who are
mentioned in the histories of philosophy, epistemology, logic, and science.
The items and the sources were entirely different and the computations
were made by different persons who were not aware of the work of the
other computers. (Professors Lossky and Lapshin had no knowledge of
my study, and Dr. Merton, who made the computation of the scientific
discoveries, was unaware not only of my study but also of the computations made by Professors Lossky and Lapshin.) Under the circumstances, the agreement between the curve of the scientific discoveries and
inventions (Figure 3) and the curve of the fluctuations of the influence
of the system of truth of senses (Figure 1) is particularly strong evidence that the results obtained in both cases are neither incidental nor
misleading.

Not to mention other considerations, the preceding statements explain
why we selected the above procedure and scale. In any case the reader

---

[10] In passing, one may note that in a great many other social fields where rating or estimate
is involved the scales used are limited in their amplitude. In the schools we grade the
pupils (except for the failures) by the scale A, B, C, D, or by marks from 3 to 5, or 6 to 12;
the ranks of the instructors and professors (as well as their salaries) are only four or five in
number, and rarely exceed, even in salary, from the highest to the lowest, by more than from
two to ten or twelve times. Similar is the situation among the "elite" of other official ranks
and social gradations generally. One has to keep in mind that our scale estimates not the
comparative influence of men, from the man in the street to the greatest genius, nor even the
influence of all the persons who have thought about the problems, nor even the influence of
all the professors who have written about or taught the problems, but the comparative influence of a much more highly selected elite: the most prominent contributors to the problem,
whose distinction has been so great that their names are preserved in the annals of history.
To mark the difference in influence of various members of this most eminent elite by the
scale from one to twelve does not seem to be unduly conservative per se.

now knows the scale or the "measuring stick" being used. In a sense it is arbitrary, but even the geometry of Euclid or that of Lobachevski; the mechanics of Newton, or those of Einstein; the Roman or the Arabic system of numbers; the computation of weeks, months, years, or the altitude, latitude, and longitude of a certain place — all are arbitrary because the fundamental assumptions, or the frame of reference, upon which these geometries, mechanics, arithmetics, time reckonings, or geographical locations are based are also arbitrary. This is true in any field of human knowledge. The arbitrariness per se does not invalidate the study, if the fundamental principles are not unsound, if they help to organize the material, and if, out of several possible arbitrary principles, the one accepted appears to be as satisfactory as any other, under the circumstances.

If it be maintained, especially by the historians, that no quantitative appraisal is possible in this field, and therefore any scale is inadmissible, the answer is simple: *Medice cura te ipsum*. The point is that there is scarcely any historical work, whether in this or in any other field, where, explicitly or implicitly, quantitative judgments are not given in verbal form. What historians of ideas, human thought, science, religion, art styles, political systems, or economic processes do not use quantitative expressions like the following: "The period was marked by an *increase* of riots, revolts, and disorders," "The period was marked by a *decline* of idealism and religion," "Kant was one of the *greatest* philosophers," "It was the epoch of the *rise and triumph* of materialism, nominalism, the Gothic style, or socialistic doctrine," and so on? Statements like these, in many forms, are met in practically all historical works. They are but a variety of quantitative statements aimed to measure a comparative influence, popularity, magnitude, value, size, frequency; or an increase or decrease, growth or decline, rise or fall, of this or that cultural phenomenon. It is scarcely necessary to add that such statements are quite unavoidable in most sociocultural, humanitarian, and historical studies.

All these phenomena, as well as any process, have among their other aspects or directions the quantitative aspects or directions also. This has been explained in Chapter Four of Volume One of this work. Thus the question is one which is concerned not only with the use of quantitative statements but also with a comparison of the two varieties of quantitative description — verbal and numerical. The above quotations and thousands of other statements of historians and social scientists are quantitative and also *verbal quantitative*. The procedure used here is *numerical quantitative*. The first makes quantitative statements but in an indefinite verbal form without the use of figures or numerical indicators. The second describes the quantitative changes with the help of figures. Which method is preferable, verbal or numerically quantitative? That is the question. To that question my answer is decidedly in favor of numerical quantitative description.

In the first place, the numerical method proposed is much more concise and economical. On a table of two or three pages it sums up the rise and fall of influence for a period of twenty-five hundred years, while the purely verbal quantitative description would require at least several dozens, if not hundreds, of pages to describe the same variations without the use of figures. This in itself is by no means a negligible advantage.

In the second place, verbal quantitativism has a very limited number of gradations: "bad," "worse," "the worst"; "good," "better," "the best"; "big," "bigger," "the biggest"; and so on. The reason is that language has normally only from three to six comparative terms. With such limited gradations verbal quantitativists cannot describe any curve of movement of a social process in its numerous increases and decreases, "ups" and "downs"; or any series of quantitative values far more numerous than six. If they tried, the procedure would be very comical — like a chain of statements: "increase," "further increase," "still further increase," "still larger increase," and so on. When one has to denote dozens and dozens, often hundreds, of quantitative gradations, verbal quantitativism becomes utterly useless. Meanwhile in the social studies one often meets with a series of quantitative gradations or values amounting to a hundred and more.

In the third place, the method proposed makes clear to any reader its foundation, its bases, and its measuring stick. The yardstick used is uniform for all the periods compared, and these periods are all systematically taken and studied from this same standpoint. This claim can hardly be made for "increase," "decrease," and their equivalents used in most quantitative verbal judgments, where the bases, the nature of the measuring stick and its application remain unknown, or are often the result of intuitive guesswork. This does not mean necessarily that the great historians are at fault; sometimes they are, but more often they are not. It means that, by and large, they have no ground either to regard themselves as free from the "sin" of "quantitativization," or to be proud of their verbal quantitativism in comparison with procedures like those proposed here.

The arbitrariness in ascribing a certain value to each thinker in the field on the scale of one to twelve is very small. The criteria used scarcely allow room for personal bias, or at least it would be so small that it would exert little, if any, influence upon the summary results for each twenty- and one-hundred-year period.[11] Any specialist in the field who, in analyzing our list of names in the Appendix to this chapter, decides that in some cases the value given to a thinker should be changed, and proceeds competently to change them on the same scale of one to twelve, would find that the results for twenty- and one-hundred-year periods will differ very little from our results.

Thus, while it is contended that Tables 1 and 2, constructed upon the above basis, reflect roughly the changes in the mentality of the leading thinkers in the field from period to period, and give an idea of the comparative rise and decline of the influence of each system of truth, it is not maintained that the figures *measure* these changes exactly. They are aimed not so much to measure as to indicate the main periods of triumph and of greatest decline in the influence of each current. For minor, short-time fluctuations the figures and curves may be inadequate; but in all probability the major ups and downs in the curves of each current of thought reflect the change in the "high-level mentality" fairly accurately.

Tables 1 and 2 and their results have several other defects besides. For the earliest periods there are known too few names upon which to base conclusions of a general character. For many of these periods probably not all the names of the prominent thinkers are preserved, and furthermore it is probable that several of the known names were overlooked inadvertently. For the most recent periods a somewhat arbitrary selection of names had to be made owing to their enormous number; therefore, only those professors who have proved to be eminent and prominent have been included. There are several other defects well known to the investigators, which, for reasons of economy of space, cannot be enumerated here. In spite of these inadequacies it is hoped, however, that the results obtained are valid in their essentials.

III. EMPIRICISM, RATIONALISM, MYSTICISM, SKEPTICISM, FIDEISM, CRITICISM

Let us now turn to our main task, *i.e.*, a study of the fluctuation of the main systems of truth in the life history of the Graeco-Roman and the Western cultures. The nature of the relevant material requires a slight

---

[11] In this work, I have used similar estimates made by different authors in various fields of culture. Often some differences in regard to the number of names and the values given by them were found. However, when the results of each estimate are summed up by twenty-, fifty-, and one-hundred-year periods, the differences do not exert any appreciable influence upon the results, which appear to be very similar and frequently almost identical.

modification of the three systems of truth. Instead of a direct study of the rise and decline of the truth of faith, of reason, and of senses, we shall follow the fluctuation of the influence of the six main epistemological currents in the mentality of the Graeco-Roman and European cultures; empiricism, religious or ideational rationalism and idealistic rationalism, mysticism, skepticism, fideism, and criticism. *Of these, ideational or religious rationalism, mysticism, and fideism incorporate mainly the truth of faith; the idealistic rationalism, mainly the truth of reason; empiricism, mainly the truth of senses.* Skepticism is a purely negative system of "cynical" and "passive" Sensate mentality; criticism a specific mixture of skepticism, empiricism, and rationalism. The last two are important symptoms of specific cultural conditions and are discussed below. Following the fluctuation of the influence of these currents of thought from 580 B.C. to A.D. 1920, we shall obtain the fluctuation of influence of the three main systems of truth, translated into the above epistemological currents. Before beginning the study of these fluctuations, however, we shall present a brief characterization of each of these currents which will give only a rough outline of each of these systems of truth. Since we plan to attack the problem quantitatively, we shall have to leave out many shadings and delicate details. These delicate shadings have to be obtained from the special works in the history of epistemology, logic, philosophy, and science.

A. *Empiricism.* This theory corresponds to the truth of senses. The only source of knowledge and truth, according to empiricism, is the sensory perception of the singular objects and events separated in time and space. It gives us our exterior or interior experience. Logical and a priori principles are but mere associations of these experiences, mere "routine of perceptions." In Tables 1 and 2 and Figure 1 the data on empiricism are fairly adequate measures of the movement — expansion and contraction — of the system of truth of senses.

B. *Rationalism.* This term covers two essentially different systems of truth which have a common generic trait but which are profoundly different in their *differentia specifica*, namely, the *ideational rationalism* and the *idealistic rationalism*. Both subclasses assert that truth is knowable and that the reality can be known with certitude because both of them give a more or less important role to the mind or thought and its nonsensory categories and concepts. Both regard the truth of reason, of logical and mathematical inferences, more valid than the truth of senses. Likewise they both give some place to the truth of faith and truth of senses. In this respect they represent a system which blends together all the three forms of truth. These similarities in the generic traits force the union of both these systems into one generic class of rationalism. However, the characteristics of their subclasses are so profoundly heterogeneous that in their extreme forms these subclasses differ rather than agree.

(1) *The ideational* or *religious rationalism* in its extreme form is merely what is styled the *truth of faith.* Supersensory and sometimes superlogical revelation or its varieties is really its main truth. The truth of reason holds but a subsidiary role in the truth of faith and is entirely subordinated to it. It cannot independently disagree with the truth of faith. If it does it becomes invalid, even sinful, heretical, or blasphemous. In brief, the Religious Rationalism is a system of truth of faith and in this respect is similar to Mysticism, which is another form of the truth of faith. It differs from it, however, by its calmer, less exotic, and more rational "level headedness." Both religious rationalism and mysticism, especially the less emotional variety, are embodiments of the truth of faith in this study.

(2) *Idealistic Rationalism.* This second type of rationalism notably differs from the ideational rationalism. Its main difference is that idealistic rationalism gives (in fact, often contrary to the declarations of its authors) the main role to reason, to intellect, and to its categories as such. It also gives a more prominent role to the truth of senses than does religious rationalism. For these reasons idealistic rationalism is a blend of all the three forms of truth, each being given an important role, though the superior knowledge is still reserved for the truth of faith. While in religious rationalism the truth of faith plays an all-important — almost monopolistic — role, in idealistic rationalism all truths are harmoniously united into one and, factually, in spite of the declared supremacy of the truth of faith, the real power is the truth of reason. Dialectics and logic are used here to prove the validity and the possibility of the revealed truth. Like a constitutional monarch it nominally reigns, but does not rule; the real ruler in the idealistic rationalism is the logic of the human mind, its laws, categories, and concepts. In religious rationalism the truth of reason is purely subservient to the reigning and ruling truth of faith. Though in Tables 1 and 2 and Figure 1 both these different subclasses of rationalism are united into one class, subsequent comments will show which part of the curve of rationalism represents the ideational (truth of faith) and which represents the idealistic (blended system of all the three forms of truth). Idealistic rationalism is indeed a system of truth which deserves the above differentiation. Of course the rationalistic

theories of knowledge of various thinkers offer many intermediary shadings between the above types. Sometimes the theory of knowledge of
the same thinkers, for instance of Plato, experiences a passage from one
type to the other. (Plato's later system of truth more closely approximates
religious rationalism and mysticism than his earlier system, which was
similar to idealistic rationalism.) But as in any classification the "pure
types" of any class must be stressed with the understanding that there
always are many shadings and intermediary forms between the clear-
cut pure types.

C. *Mysticism.* Like religious rationalism, mysticism also contends
that the supreme source of truth and real knowledge is supersensory and
superlogical intuition or revelation. The truth of senses and that of
reason as such can give but the pseudo knowledge of the surface or of
mere appearance of the phenomena. They cannot penetrate to the ultimate reality and to the absolute truth. In this sense mysticism is also
mainly the system of *truth of faith*. From religious rationalism it differs,
however, by several secondary characteristics; such as stressing that the
"mystic way" of obtaining truth almost always assumes a form of esoteric
trances, and the like; that it requires a special training in that direction.
Mysticism generally values and uses the truth of reason, the laws and
categories of thought, and the rational principles of mind much less than
rationalism generally; it is a less rational and more esoteric brand of the
truth of faith than religious rationalism.[12]

Mysticism has several forms. In a schematic way we shall distinguish
two. First, the remotest from religious rationalism can be styled *mysticism of despair*. It is a mysticism par excellence. Visions, trances, ecsta-
sies, and similar "pathologies" play a particularly conspicuous role in
it. In hundreds of ways it shows its "antirationalism and irrationalism."
This variety of mysticism prevailed in the fifteenth and subsequent centuries. Second, there is the type of mysticism which differs little from
religious rationalism. For the present it is enough to stress that together
with religious rationalism, mysticism embodies mainly the truth of faith.
More detailed shadings of mysticism can be left to the qualitative charac-
terizations of the next chapter.

D. *Skepticism* is a systematic and methodical doubting of the possibility of valid knowledge. "We cannot know anything with certainty;
if we can, we cannot express it adequately; if we can express it others
cannot understand it; therefore abstain from any judgments." This is
the motto of skepticism. A diluted variety of it is agnosticism: it also

---

[12] See the works on mysticism quoted in Chapter Three of Volume One.

denies a possibility of knowledge of the ultimate reality. It even doubts its existence and is not interested in it but is different from a "straight skepticism" in that it believes in the possibility of knowing in the empirico-sensory world.

E. *Fideism* is logically connected with skepticism. Fideism, agreeing with skepticism that the truth of the most important principles and facts — like the existence of the external world, of God, of mind and psychical "self," psychical experiences of the others and so on — cannot be obtained through mere cognition, empirical or rational, believes further that the certainty of such most important truths can be obtained only through the act of volition, will to believe, or instinct, or natural suggestion, and the like. In this sense it stresses the element of volition and belief as noncognitive factors in obtaining and ascertaining the most important truths or fundamental knowledge. In this respect fideism is related in a sense to mysticism and often they merge imperceptibly into each other. If we view it as a positive system of truth, not merely a negative theory like skepticism, then fideism is mainly a desperate form of the truth of faith.

F. Finally, *criticism* or *agnosticism* is a theory which contends that only the phenomenal or empirical world is accessible to our knowledge, while the ultimate or transcendental reality — whether it exists or not — is inaccessible and does not need to be known. Differing from the other theories, it admits empiric as well as rationalistic elements in our cognitive activity and tries to tie them together and to make them corelated, codependent, and mutually conditioned. Criticism, therefore, occupies a somewhat middle position between empiricism, rationalism, and skepticism but more likely approximates empiricism.

Since we are mainly interested in the problem of fluctuation in the three systems of truth — of faith, of reason, and of senses — Tables 1 and 2 and Figure 1, given in the terms of these six systems of truth and knowledge, have to be translated into the terms of the truth of faith, of reason, and of senses according to the previous explanation or "legend." The results of the study of the fluctuation of the comparative influence of each of these epistemological currents during twenty-five hundred years are summed up in the two tables and the figure that follow.[13]

[13] Main sources for the list of the philosophers and contributors to the problem for each period were as follows. Other sources are mentioned in the footnotes throughout this work.

E. Zeller, *Die Philosophie der Griechen*, 6 vols. (Leipzig, 1919–1923); F. Ueberweg, *Grundriss der Geschichte der Philosophie*, 5 vols., re-edited by M. Heinze and T. Oesterreich (Berlin, 1926–1928); T. Gomperz, *Griechische Denker*, 3 vols. (Leipzig, 1896–1909); Pauly-Wissowa, *Realenzyklopädie der klassischen Altertumswissenschaft*, 16 vols. (Stuttgart, 1894–1936);

Table 1 gives the numerical indicators of the comparative influence of each current by periods of twenty years from 580 B.C. to A.D. 1920. It is the table constructed on the "weighted" basis of the different values of influence of the thinkers enumerated on the scale from one to twelve.

Table 2 gives the numerical indicators of the influence of each current by periods of one hundred years with the different values of influence on the same scale.

Figure 1 delineates the fluctuation of the influence by one-hundred-year periods, as it is given by Table 2.[14]

Finally, in the Appendix to this chapter the complete list of the thinkers in the field, with the weight of influence for each, is given. In this list it may be noticed that sometimes the same name is found in two systems. This indicates that the philosopher contributed to both systems and therefore has to be placed in both. Further on, a few thinkers may be placed not in the current in which they appear in our list but in the one nearest to it. This indicates that the theories of such thinkers are somewhat intermediary between the two currents, and therefore they may be

---

R. Eisler, *Philosophen — Lexikon* (Berlin, 1912); K. Joël, *Wandlungen der Weltanschauung*, 2 vols. (Tübingen, 1928-1934); O. Willmann, *Geschichte des Idealismus*, 3 vols. (Braunschweig, 1894-1897); F. A. Lange, *Geschichte des Materialismus*, 2 vols. (Leipzig, 1902); E. V. Hartmann, *Geschichte der Metaphysik*, 2 vols. (Leipzig, 1899-1900); R. Richter, *Der Skepticismus in der Philosophie*, 2 vols. (Leipzig, 1904-1908); G. L. Fonsegrive, *Essai sur le libre arbitre, se théorie et son histoire* (Paris, 1887); H. Hurter, *Nomenclator Litterarius Theologiae Catholicae*, 3d ed., 3 vols. (Oeniponte, 1871-1886); G. V. Florovsky, *Eastern Fathers of the IV Century* (in Russian) (Prague, 1921) and *Eastern Fathers of the V to VIII Centuries* (in Russian) (Prague, 1933); L. Karsavin, *Saint Fathers and Teachers of the Church* (in Russian) (Berlin); A. von Harnack, *Lehrbuch der Dogmengeschichte*, 3 vols. (Freiburg, 1894-1897); M. Grabmann, *Geschichte der Scholastischen Methode*, 2 vols. (Freiburg, 1909-1911); C. Hahn, *Geschichte der Ketzer in Mittelalter*, 3 vols. (Stuttgart, 1845-1850); Charles Guignebert, *Le Christianisme, mèdieval et moderne* (Paris, 1922); W. Riley, *American Thought* (New York, 1915); V. Parrington, *Main Currents in American Thought*, 3 vols. (New York, 1927-1930); J. Muirhead, *Contemporary British Philosophy*, 2 vols. (New York, 1924).

[14] The figures by century periods is not a mere summary of the five twenty-year periods of a respective century. Each name in century periods figures only once, while the same name figures often in two or three twenty-year periods of the same century. This remark concerns all the subsequent tables. I have at my disposal tables by twenty- and one-hundred-year periods constructed on the basis of equal value of influence of all the thinkers, the value of one. In other words they give the number and percentage of the partisans of each current at each period among all the thinkers and contributors to the problem in each period. As mentioned before (and in two cases it will be shown further in this volume), the results of the tables based upon the different and equal value of the influence of each thinker are practically the same. For this reason, and for the other reasons of economy of space and expense, the tables and figures constructed upon the basis of equal value of influence are not given in the work. Any reader can check them, using the data (number of the representatives of each current) given in Tables 1 and 2. This note pertains to all the subsequent tables in the subsequent chapters of this volume, unless otherwise stated.

placed in either one. However, even if such thinkers are shifted to the adjacent current, the results would not be changed to any significant degree. Finally, the value of influence of the living philosophers and thinkers in the field, namely, those of the period 1900–1920, are not given in the list for obvious reasons.

TABLE 1. INDICATORS OF FLUCTUATION OF THE INFLUENCE IN MAIN SYSTEMS OF TRUTH BY 20-YEAR PERIODS

(on the basis of *different values* of influence given from 1 to 12)

PERIOD	Empiricism		Rationalism		Mysticism		Criticism		Skepticism		Fideism		Total	
	No.	Per cent	No.	Per cent	No.	Per cent	No.	Per cent	No.	Per cent	No.	Per cent	No.	Per cent
580–560 B.C.	4	100	0	0	0	0	0	0	0	0	0	0	4	100
560–540	4	28.6	10	71.4	0	0	0	0	0	0	0	0	14	100
540–520	2	10.0	18	90.0	0	0	0	0	0	0	0	0	20	100
520–500	2	9.1	20	90.9	0	0	0	0	0	0	0	0	22	100
500–480	2	6.9	27	93.1	0	0	0	0	0	0	0	0	29	100
480–460	2	9.1	20	90.9	0	0	0	0	0	0	0	0	22	100
460–440	11	26.8	17	41.5	0	0	0	0	13	31.7	0	0	41	100
440–420	13	27.1	22	45.8	0	0	0	0	13	27.1	0	0	48	100
420–400	18	23.7	22	28.9	0	0	0	0	36	47.4	0	0	76	100
400–380	9	12.3	30	41.1	0	0	0	0	29	39.7	5	6.9	73	100
380–360	16	26.2	24	39.4	0	0	0	0	16	26.2	5	8.2	61	100
360–340	9	13.6	23	34.9	15	22.7	0	0	14	21.2	5	7.6	66	100
340–320	1	2.2	31	66.0	5	10.6	0	0	5	10.6	5	10.6	47	100
320–300	14	16.7	38	45.3	5	6.0	0	0	16	19.0	11	13.0	84	100
300–280	24	29.0	23	27.8	1	1.2	0	0	15	18.0	20	24.0	83	100
280–260	16	22.8	11	15.9	1	1.4	0	0	18	25.7	24	34.2	70	100
260–240	4	11.1	3	8.3	1	2.8	0	0	6	16.7	22	61.1	36	100
240–220	7	11.5	4	6.6	1	1.6	0	0	9	14.7	40	65.6	61	100
220–200	3	7.7	8	20.5	1	2.5	0	0	7	18.0	20	51.3	39	100
200–180	4	17.4	9	39.1	1	4.4	0	0	3	13.0	6	26.1	23	100
180–160	2	9.5	6	28.6	1	4.7	0	0	6	28.6	6	28.6	21	100
160–140	3	13.6	5	22.7	1	4.6	0	0	7	31.8	6	27.3	22	100
140–120	2	10.0	2	10.0	1	5.0	0	0	9	45.0	6	30.0	20	100
120–100	4	21.1	2	10.5	1	5.2	0	0	4	21.1	8	42.1	19	100
100–80	7	26.0	5	18.5	1	3.7	0	0	2	7.4	12	44.4	27	100
80–60	5	13.9	16	44.4	1	2.7	0	0	0	0	14	39.0	36	100
60–40	18	27.0	10	15.0	4	6.0	0	0	5	7.4	30	44.6	67	100
40–20	10	22.2	12	26.7	1	2.2	0	0	5	11.1	17	37.8	45	100
20–0	1	5.0	7	35.0	2	10.0	0	0	5	25.0	5	25.0	20	100
0–20 A.D.	1	4.4	9	39.1	8	34.8	0	0	0	0	5	21.7	23	100
20–40	1	4.4	5	21.8	11	47.8	0	0	0	0	6	26.0	23	100
40–60	1	3.3	2	6.7	11	36.7	0	0	0	0	16	53.3	30	100
60–80	1	2.6	2	5.3	8	21.0	0	0	0	0	27	71.1	38	100
80–100	1	2.7	2	5.4	16	43.2	0	0	0	0	18	48.7	37	100
100–120	1	2.3	12	27.9	16	37.2	0	0	2	4.7	12	27.9	43	100
120–140	2	3.1	8	12.3	32	49.2	0	0	6	9.2	17	26.2	65	100
140–160	3	4.4	14	20.6	31	45.6	0	0	6	8.8	14	20.6	68	100
160–180	10	13.7	15	20.6	31	42.5	0	0	6	8.2	11	15.0	73	100
180–200	12	12.8	26	27.6	42	44.7	0	0	6	6.4	8	8.5	94	100
200–220	20	27.4	13	17.8	33	45.2	0	0	6	8.2	1	1.4	73	100
220–240	12	23.5	9	17.6	29	56.9	0	0	0	0	1	2.0	51	100
240–260	11	21.6	3	5.9	36	70.6	0	0	0	0	1	1.9	51	100
260–280	13	32.5	3	7.5	23	57.5	0	0	0	0	1	2.5	40	100
280–300	9	34.6	2	7.7	15	57.7	0	0	0	0	0	0	26	100
300–320	7	26.9	4	15.4	15	57.7	0	0	0	0	0	0	26	100
320–340	9	21.4	16	38.1	17	40.5	0	0	0	0	0	0	42	100
340–360	6	20.7	12	41.4	11	37.9	0	0	0	0	0	0	29	100
360–380	3	5.1	16	27.1	40	67.8	0	0	0	0	0	0	59	100
380–400	9	16.4	16	29.1	30	54.5	0	0	0	0	0	0	55	100
400–420	8	16.0	20	40.0	22	44.0	0	0	0	0	0	0	50	100
420–440	6	13.1	22	47.8	18	39.1	0	0	0	0	0	0	46	100
440–460	4	12.9	14	45.2	13	41.9	0	0	0	0	0	0	31	100
460–480	4	14.3	11	39.3	13	46.4	0	0	0	0	0	0	28	100
480–500	1	3.9	11	42.3	14	53.8	0	0	0	0	0	0	26	100
500–520	1	3.2	16	51.6	14	45.2	0	0	0	0	0	0	31	100
520–540	1	2.6	24	61.5	14	35.9	0	0	0	0	0	0	39	100
540–560	0	0	17	73.9	6	26.1	0	0	0	0	0	0	23	100

TABLE 1. INDICATORS OF FLUCTUATION OF THE INFLUENCE IN MAIN SYSTEMS OF TRUTH BY 20-YEAR PERIODS — *continued*

(on the basis of *different values* of influence given from 1 to 12)

PERIOD	Empiricism		Rationalism		Mysticism		Criticism		Skepticism		Fideism		Total	
	No.	Per cent	No.	Per cent	No.	Per cent	No.	Per cent	No.	Per cent	No.	Per cent	No.	Per cent
560–580 A.D.	0	0	6	85.7	1	14.3	0	0	0	0	0	0	7	100
580–600	0	0	8	100	0	0	0	0	0	0	0	0	8	100
600–620	0	0	10	90.9	1	9.1	0	0	0	0	0	0	11	100
620–640	0	0	6	50.0	6	50.0	0	0	0	0	0	0	12	100
640–660	0	0	3	33.3	6	66.7	0	0	0	0	0	0	9	100
660–680	0	0	2	25.0	6	75.0	0	0	0	0	0	0	8	100
680–700	0	0	2	100	0	0	0	0	0	0	0	0	2	100
700–720	0	0	3	100	0	0	0	0	0	0	0	0	3	100
720–740	0	0	8	100	0	0	0	0	0	0	0	0	8	100
740–760	0	0	5	100	0	0	0	0	0	0	0	0	5	100
760–780	0	0	1	100	0	0	0	0	0	0	0	0	1	100
780–800	0	0	4	100	0	0	0	0	0	0	0	0	4	100
800–820	0	0	6	100	0	0	0	0	0	0	0	0	6	100
820–840	0	0	8	100	0	0	0	0	0	0	0	0	8	100
840–860	0	0	8	50.0	8	50.0	0	0	0	0	0	0	16	100
860–880	0	0	9	52.9	8	47.1	0	0	0	0	0	0	17	100
880–900	0	0	3	60.0	2	40.0	0	0	0	0	0	0	5	100
900–920	0	0	2	50.0	2	50.0	0	0	0	0	0	0	4	100
920–940	0	0	2	100	0	0	0	0	0	0	0	0	2	100
940–960	0	0	1	100	0	0	0	0	0	0	0	0	1	100
960–980	0	0	1	100	0	0	0	0	0	0	0	0	1	100
980–1000	0	0	3	100	0	0	0	0	0	0	0	0	3	100
1000–1020	0	0	6	100	0	0	0	0	0	0	0	0	6	100
1020–1040	0	0	3	100	0	0	0	0	0	0	0	0	3	100
1040–1060	0	0	8	61.5	0	0	0	0	0	0	5	38.5	13	100
1060–1080	0	0	11	40.7	11	40.7	0	0	0	0	5	18.6	27	100
1080–1100	3	11.5	9	34.7	11	42.3	0	0	0	0	3	11.5	26	100
1100–1120	3	15.0	7	35.0	7	35.0	0	0	0	0	3	15.0	20	100
1120–1140	3	9.4	17	53.1	12	37.5	0	0	0	0	0	0	32	100
1140–1160	3	7.5	21	52.5	16	40.0	0	0	0	0	0	0	40	100
1160–1180	3	10.7	17	60.7	8	28.6	0	0	0	0	0	0	28	100
1180–1200	7	30.4	6	26.1	10	43.5	0	0	0	0	0	0	23	100
1200–1220	4	13.8	15	51.7	10	34.5	0	0	0	0	0	0	29	100
1220–1240	4	17.4	17	73.9	2	8.7	0	0	0	0	0	0	23	100
1240–1260	4	11.8	29	85.3	1	2.9	0	0	0	0	0	0	34	100
1260–1280	10	16.1	44	71.0	8	12.9	0	0	0	0	0	0	62	100
1280–1300	9	12.5	56	77.8	7	9.7	0	0	0	0	0	0	72	100
1300–1320	5	6.9	53	72.6	12	16.4	0	0	3	4.1	0	0	73	100
1320–1340	12	20.3	30	50.8	10	17.0	0	0	7	11.9	0	0	59	100
1340–1360	16	27.6	13	22.4	25	43.1	0	0	4	6.9	0	0	58	100
1360–1380	7	18.9	4	10.8	26	70.3	0	0	0	0	0	0	37	100
1380–1400	4	20.0	4	20.0	8	40.0	0	0	0	0	4	20.0	20	100
1400–1420	0	0	2	20.0	4	40.0	0	0	0	0	4	40.0	10	100
1420–1440	0	0	9	53.0	4	23.5	0	0	0	0	4	23.5	17	100
1440–1460	0	0	9	42.9	12	57.1	0	0	0	0	0	0	21	100
1460–1480	3	13.6	3	13.6	16	72.8	0	0	0	0	0	0	22	100
1480–1500	3	50.0	3	50.0	0	0	0	0	0	0	0	0	6	100
1500–1520	3	20.0	4	26.8	6	40.0	0	0	1	6.6	1	6.6	15	100
1520–1540	8	27.6	4	13.8	11	37.9	0	0	4	13.8	2	6.9	29	100
1540–1560	8	21.6	4	10.8	13	35.2	0	0	2	5.4	10	27.0	37	100
1560–1580	8	13.3	14	23.4	22	36.7	0	0	8	13.3	8	13.3	60	100
1580–1600	9	14.5	20	32.3	24	38.7	0	0	8	12.9	1	1.6	62	100
1600–1620	18	21.7	39	47.0	17	20.5	0	0	8	9.6	1	1.2	83	100
1620–1640	24	31.2	39	50.6	12	15.6	0	0	1	1.3	1	1.3	77	100
1640–1660	31	31.6	42	42.9	17	17.3	0	0	1	1.0	7	7.2	98	100
1660–1680	32	20.4	74	47.2	42	26.7	0	0	2	1.3	7	4.4	157	100
1680–1700	50	26.3	84	44.2	44	23.2	0	0	11	5.8	1	0.5	190	100
1700–1720	35	24.1	63	43.4	39	27.0	0	0	7	4.8	1	0.7	145	100
1720–1740	30	35.7	35	41.7	16	19.0	0	0	1	1.2	2	2.4	84	100
1740–1760	65	37.8	73	42.4	14	8.2	0	0	19	11.0	1	0.6	172	100
1760–1780	80	43.5	53	28.8	26	14.1	0	0	19	10.3	6	3.3	184	100
1780–1800	79	29.9	68	25.7	58	22.0	41	15.5	2	0.8	16	6.1	264	100
1800–1820	58	21.9	78	29.4	61	23.0	36	13.6	3	1.1	29	11.0	265	100
1820–1840	64	29.0	78	35.3	65	29.4	8	3.6	1	0.4	5	2.3	221	100
1840–1860	102	31.4	97	29.9	93	28.6	11	3.4	18	5.5	4	1.2	325	100
1860–1880	187	46.0	80	19.6	74	18.2	25	6.1	20	4.9	21	5.2	407	100
1880–1900	304	47.1	90	13.9	94	14.6	100	15.5	21	3.2	37	5.7	646	100
1900–1920	439	53.0	107	12.9	101	12.2	121	14.6	36	4.4	24	2.9	828	100

TABLE 2. INDICATORS OF FLUCTUATION OF INFLUENCE IN MAIN SYSTEMS
OF TRUTH BY CENTURY PERIODS

(on the basis of *different values* given from 1 to 12)

PERIOD	Empiricism		Rationalism		Mysticism		Criticism		Skepticism		Fideism		Total	
	No.	Per cent	No.	Per cent	No.	Per cent	No.	Per cent	No.	Per cent	No.	Per cent	No.	Per cent
600–500 B.C.	6	19.4	25	80.6	0	0	0	0	0	0	0	0	31	100
500–400	23	19.2	61	50.8	0	0	0	0	36	30.0	0	0	120	100
400–300	31	14.6	89	42.0	17	8.0	0	0	54	25.4	21	10.0	212	100
300–200	34	21.7	34	21.7	1	0.6	0	0	28	17.8	60	38.2	157	100
200–100	11	19.6	16	28.6	1	1.8	0	0	12	21.4	16	28.6	56	100
100–0	26	24.3	26	24.3	7	6.5	0	0	7	6.5	41	38.4	107	100
0–100 A.D.	2	2.3	13	14.6	27	30.3	0	0	0	0	47	52.8	89	100
100–200	13	6.7	45	23.0	90	46.0	0	0	16	8.0	32	16.3	196	100
200–300	33	24.8	17	12.8	76	57.1	0	0	6	4.5	1	0.8	133	100
300–400	19	15.2	43	34.4	63	50.4	0	0	0	0	0	0	125	100
400–500	11	11.7	42	44.7	41	43.6	0	0	0	0	0	0	94	100
500–600	1	1.6	45	72.6	16	25.8	0	0	0	0	0	0	62	100
600–700	0	0	13	65.0	7	35.0	0	0	0	0	0	0	20	100
700–800	0	0	13	100	0	0	0	0	0	0	0	0	13	100
800–900	0	0	21	67.7	10	32.3	0	0	0	0	0	0	31	100
900–1000	0	0	6	75.0	2	25.0	0	0	0	0	0	0	8	100
1000–1100	3	7.7	17	43.6	11	28.2	0	0	0	0	8	20.5	39	100
1100–1200	13	14.3	38	41.8	37	40.7	0	0	0	0	3	3.2	91	100
1200–1300	21	12.8	117	71.4	26	15.8	0	0	0	0	0	0	164	100
1300–1400	28	17.2	83	51.3	40	24.7	0	0	7	4.3	4	2.5	162	100
1400–1500	3	7.2	15	35.7	20	47.6	0	0	0	0	4	9.5	42	100
1500–1600	24	15.8	44	29.0	51	33.6	0	0	21	13.8	12	7.8	152	100
1600–1700	132	29.6	179	40.1	104	23.3	0	0	21	4.7	10	2.3	446	100
1700–1800	260	37.5	212	30.6	131	18.9	41	6.0	29	4.0	20	3.0	693	100
1800–1900	644	42.6	320	21.1	261	17.2	156	10.3	42	2.8	90	6.0	1513	100

III. Main Results of the Study

The figures suggest the following conclusions.

A. *Trendless Fluctuation instead of Linear Trend.*   A mere glance at
Tables 1 and 2 and Figure 1 is sufficient to indicate that within the
period of some twenty-five hundred years there has been no continuous
linear trend of any kind.   None of the main systems has tended steadily
to increase or decrease or remain constant throughout all the period, but
each system has fluctuated, now rising in its influence, now declining, or
remaining for a time comparatively constant.   The popular and almost
commonly accepted opinion that there exists a linear trend in this field,
and that the linear trend consists in a progressive increase of the empirical
truth of senses at the expense of a progressively declining truth of faith
(religious rationalism, mysticism, and fideism) or the truth of reason
(idealistic rationalism) is contradicted by the data.   During the last five
centuries empiricism or the truth of senses has been rising very rapidly.[15]

[15] This situation is responsible for the popularity and acceptability of the belief in the ever-
increasing triumph of the truth of senses (science) over the truth of faith and of reason, with
an expectation that eventually "scientific truth of senses" will drive out entirely all the
"superstitions" and "ignorance" of the truth of faith and the "sterile speculations" of the
truth of reason.

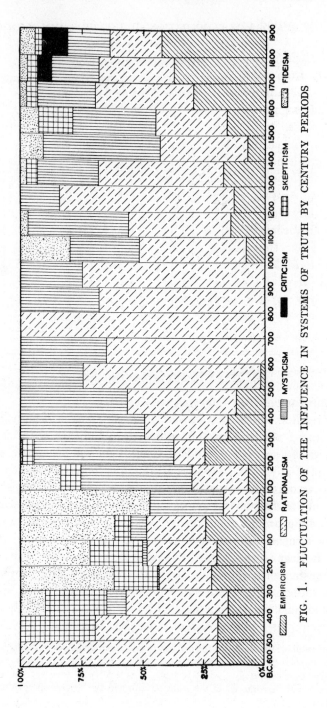

FIG. 1. FLUCTUATION OF THE INFLUENCE IN SYSTEMS OF TRUTH BY CENTURY PERIODS

If the whole period of twenty-five hundred years is considered, however, no such trend exists. To the contrary, after a fairly powerful period of influence from the sixth to the third centuries B.C., empiricism declined and from the fifth to the eleventh centuries A.D. remained almost nonexistent. No perpetual trend of any of the other currents is shown. This is more significant because we are dealing not with uneducated, illiterate masses incapable of logical thinking, but with the leading thinkers of the cultures studied. If among them there is no steady trend toward a progressive increase of one of the systems of truth and a decline of the others, all the theories supporting the existence of a linear trend of growth of the "scientific truth of senses" have to be declared unwarranted. Hundreds of thinkers of the past as well as of recent times believed in such a trend and most of the scholars and scientists of our time subscribe to it. In multifarious variations they repeat the formulas of Turgot, Condorcet, August Comte, Saint-Simon, particularly that of Comte — that in the course of time mankind as a whole passes from the theological to the metaphysical and then to the positive stage of its mentality. Stated in our terms this law of the three states indicates a passage from the truth of faith, to that of reason, and from the truth of reason to that of senses.[16] It is apparent that the formula is wrong. Thomas Huxley might have said that this beautiful generalization was killed by a set of ugly facts. The data presented support the theories of G. B. Vico and others on trendless fluctuation rather than the theories of other scholars on the linear trend of growth.[17]

Contemporary belief in the insured future progress of the empirical system of truth (and science) is, as we shall see, a mere reflection of the sociocultural fact that we are living at the high tide of this form of truth. In similar circumstances in the past such opinions also were held, as we shall see; but in due course of time the empirical system declined instead of perpetually growing. However improbable it may seem, it is possible that in some future time the present empirical system of truth also will decline. It is at least as probable as the belief that in the future the empirical system of truth will grow perpetually. The creative recurrent conception of sociocultural processes (see Chapter Four of Volume One) is supported, and likewise my contention that there have been different

---

[16] See A. Comte, *Positive Philosophy*, trans. by Martineau (New York, 1855), Vol. I, pp. 1–33 *et passim;* Vol. II, pp. 1–51, 68–110, 127–180. L. Lévy-Bruhl, *The Philosophy of A. Comte* (New York, 1903), pp. 36 ff.

[17] See G. B. Vico, *op. cit.*, Vol. V, *passim,* and particularly Bks. IV and V. Also his *Principj di una scienza nuova d'intorno alla comune natura delle nazioni, Opere* (Milano, 1853), Vol. IV, Bks. II to V.

systems of truth which have fluctuated without leading to the "final" predominance of any one of them is well corroborated by the data.

B. *No Spencerian Evolution.* There was no perpetual Spencerian "evolution" from the less differentiated and integrated to the more differentiated and integrated status. Before the fifth century B.C. there was a relative simplicity of systems; then, however, an increasing complication was manifested by a multiplication of the divers systems of truth and knowledge (mysticism, skepticism, fideism, and criticism). This stage was then followed by a recession to simplicity indicated by the disappearance of all these systems, except those of rationalism and mysticism, during the Middle Ages.

During the Middle Ages, as in the earliest period, only two systems of truth existed. The unanimity and simplicity of systems were as great as in the days of Thales. Then, step by step, the tide of differentiation appeared and grew again, and from the fifteenth century up to the present time all the systems of truth with all their varieties have been existing and multiplying. It is scarcely probable that the systems of truth will tend toward ever-increasing differentiation. Sooner or later it will probably reach its limit and will be replaced by simplicity and homogeneity. Simplification and differentiation, or homogeneity and heterogeneity, alternate without any perpetual linear trend.

Now let us examine Tables 1 and 2 and Figure 1, particularly from the standpoint of the periods in which each of the main systems has had its high and low points of influence and acceptability.

C. *Fluctuation of the Truth of Senses (Empiricism).* Turning to the tables and the figure, we note the following fluctuations of the truth of senses in so far as it is embodied in empiricism. The period from 580 to 560 B.C. opens with the absolute domination of empiricism. This conclusion is not reliable, however, because it is based on the contributions of only one man, Thales, whose theories were mildly empirical and who is known to us only through insignificant fragments. Formally Thales had to be put into a category of empiricism and hylozoism. According to the existing fragments, however, Thales identified God with the mind of the universe and regarded the universe as animated and even filled with demons. His conception of nature was, like that of other Ionian nature philosophers, permeated by ethiconormative elements and invested with a quasi-religious sanctity.[18]

---

[18] A. O. Lovejoy and others, *Primitivism and Related Ideas in Antiquity* (Baltimore, 1935), Vol. I, p. 109. Also J. W. Beardslee, *The Use of Φύσις in the Fifth Century Greek Literature* (1918).

In other words he, like most of the nature philosophers of the sixth and even the fifth centuries, being formally empiricist, hylozoist, and determinist, was in fact very similar to the religious rationalists, idealists, and believers in a divine providential control of the universe. We must not forget that even such materialists and atomists as Democritus regarded Fire as a soul substance, the divine fire being the soul of the world, and he seems even to have believed in the gods of traditional religion. For these reasons Thales can be placed among the idealists and religious rationalists more justifiably than among the empiricists, as has been done here, for formal reasons.

Other evidences we have clearly indicate that the dominant mentality at that time was strongly religious and was permeated by the *truth of faith* and by religious and magical revelations which dominated the empirical evidence and distorted its meaning according to its own nature.[19] For these reasons the percentage of one hundred allocated to empiricism for the years 580–560 B.C. has to be discounted. This is justified by the data of the next period, 560–540 B.C., when empiricism falls sharply to 28.6 per cent and continues its decline in the subsequent period, 540 to 480 B.C., when it reaches a low of 6 per cent. This means practically that up to *the beginning of the* fifth century B.C. the predominant mentality was not empiricism but mainly religious rationalism.

The truth of faith, represented by the ideational or religious rationalism, until about 460 B.C. amounted in our system of indicators to about 90 per cent of all the systems of truth. It was only after 460 B.C. that the truth of senses (empiricism) began notably to rise and grow with minor fluctuations. It remained comparatively strong until 20 B.C., when it

[19] Before the fifth century, as in Europe before the twelfth century, a serene and calm faith, questioning nothing, dominated. In all the local cults of Greece " there was a natural organic piety and no element of . . . tenseness of religious emotion. . . . Piety lay in a calm performance of traditional rites and in a faithful observance of traditional standards." In so far as specific dramatic sects like Orphism, or Pythagoreanism, and the like, are concerned, they again were idealistic, mystic, but not empirical. A. D. Nock, *Conversion,* (Oxford, 1933), p. 18 and chap. iii.

Likewise no atheism, free thinking, skepticism, or criticism existed before the fifth century. A. B. Drachmann, *Atheism in Pagan Antiquity* (Gyldenotal, 1922), pp. 5–8, 21, *et passim.* The enormous role played by "the mantic art, *i.e.,* the ability to predict the future by signs from the gods or direct divine inspiration," manifesting itself in the national institutions of the oracles, like the Delphic Oracle and others, is further testimony of the same domination of the truth of faith. *Ibid.,* pp. 27–28.

Finally, "Gods were there" and their existence was unquestioned. In the sixth century B.C. the change in the beliefs in gods consisted in their separation from the empirical nature rather than the opposite tendency. U. von Wilamowitz-Muellendorff, *Der Glaube der Hellenen* (Berlin, 1931), Vol. I, p. 17; (1932), Vol. II, 81 ff. *et passim.* See also O. Gruppe, *Geschichte der Klassischen Mythologie und Religionsgeschichte* (Leipzig, 1921).

weakened again, and was low up to about A.D. 160, when it flared up again and stayed comparatively high until about A.D. 480. After that date it sharply declined and after A.D. 540 disappeared from the "highway" of the thought, being submerged by the rising truth of faith of Christianity. It remained hidden until about 1100, roughly some six centuries, then emerged again and began, with minor fluctuations, to climb; and in the twelfth, thirteenth, and the fourteenth centuries again attained considerable influence, notable but not dominant, somewhat approaching its influence in the fifth and the fourth centuries B.C. in Greece. In the fifteenth century, for some sixty years it disappeared again (1400–1460), then re-emerged and rose rapidly, and with minor fluctuations grew steadily up to the present time, reaching in the nineteenth century the extraordinary and unique indicator of 42 per cent (for the whole century) and for the twentieth century a still higher indicator of some 53 per cent! For the last four centuries we have thus had a rising tide of the truth of senses, the contemporary scientific truth. This extraordinary domination of this system of truth at the present time explains why we are inclined to identify truth generally with the truth of senses, why other truths appear to us as "superstitions," why we believe that from now on the truth of senses is destined to grow further and further until it will eliminate forever all the other systems of truth. Such a mentality is but natural for this period. The periods in which empiricism attained a large percentage of influence follow.

(1) 460–400 B.C. The period of the "nature philosophers," like Empedocles and Democritus; the period of the Sophists and others; and also the period of a great development of the natural sciences in Greece.[20]

(2) 320–260 B.C. The period of the Epicureans; of the disciples of Democritus; of the Peripatetic scholars like Strato, Demetrius, and others. This period was also notable for its great progress in the Greek natural sciences.

(3) 120–20 B.C. The time of Lucretius and of the Graeco-Roman materialists and Epicureans. This period was marked by a great rise in the number of the discoveries in the natural sciences in Rome.[21]

(4) A.D. 200–360. The time of blossoming of the Epicureans, of Gallienus, of the Peripatetics, and of some empirically inclined of the Church Fathers and of the Manichaeans. It was marked in the fourth century by a notable increase of natural and scientific discoveries in

[20] See the number of the scientific discoveries in Tables 3 and 8.
[21] See Tables 3 and 8 of the discoveries for Rome.

Rome, but it was the last flaring up before a rapid decline took place and then became stagnant for a number of centuries. After that period both empiricism and the number of scientific discoveries rapidly declined to almost zero for a long period of about six centuries.

(5) Empiricism reappears at the end of the eleventh century, after which with strong fluctuations (especially in the fifteenth century) its rising trend is continued up to the present time. Of the relatively notable shorter waves upward the following periods may be noted: around 1100 (Roscellinus and others); 1180 (John of Salisbury, Alfredus Anglicus, Alexander Neckham); 1220 (Rolandus Cremonensis, Michael Scotus, etc.); 1260 (Roger Bacon, Bartholomeus Anglicus, Thomas Chantimpré, etc.); 1320–1400 (William Ockham, Durandus de S. Porciano, Buridanus, Nicolaus of Oresme, Albertus of Saxony, Peter Aureoli, Joannes de Mirecuria, etc.); 1460–1500 (Gabriele Biel, etc.). If one glances at Table 3 of the scientific discoveries, one can see that their curve begins to rise about one century later, at the end of the twelfth, and then in its essential fluctuations follows the upward trend of empiricism up to the present time.

(6) Seventeenth century. The century of greatest progress of natural sciences was also a century of the influential growth in empiricism ; natural science is in a way a child of empiricism and vice versa ; empiricism is nourished by this child when it is grown up.

(7) Since that time empiricism, with comparatively temporary recesses, has been steadily growing — absolutely and relatively. This growth has been especially rapid and great during the second half of the nineteenth century and in the present century. The main trend of the discoveries in the natural sciences has been similar.

The low points of empiricism occurred mainly during the following periods :

(a) Up to the beginning of the fifth century B.C.

(b) 260–200 B.C.

(c) 20 B.C.–A.D. 160.

(d) From the beginning of the sixth century A.D. up to the end of the eleventh century it disappeared from the highway of philosophical thought, and different, practically opposite, systems of truth dominated the field during that period.

(e) It was low in the fifteenth century ; then it had slight recessions in the second half of the sixteenth, in part of the seventeenth, and at the beginning of the nineteenth century. These recessions were, however, slight, short, and minor movements in the main trend of a rising tide of empiricism from the twelfth century on, and especially from the sixteenth century on.

D. *Movements of Truth of Senses and of Discoveries and Inventions in the Natural and Technological Sciences.* Previously it was mentioned that an additional criterion of the approximate validity of the quantitative indicators of the absolute and relative changes in the expansion and contraction of the systems of truth in the course of time is the essential agreement of the curve of the discoveries in the natural sciences and technological inventions with the curve of empiricism. Let us place the data and the curves of both movements side by side in order to verify this statement. The century indicators for both movements are shown in Table 3.

Although the data on empiricism and the scientific discoveries are not comparable because, on the one hand, we have the number of the discoveries, on the other, the percentage of the influence of empiricism among all the systems of truth or the weighted indicator of its representatives, nevertheless the three series are somewhat instructive. They show naturally many minor divergencies from century to century, and yet, when the most essential long-time waves of the discoveries and of the percentage of the influence of empiricism are taken, their remarkable agreement cannot fail to be noticed. Beginning with the twelfth century both grow from century to century. Through the period from the sixth to the twelfth century A.D. both are practically on zero line. In Greece both are comparatively high in the period from the sixth to the second century B.C.

Unfortunately the names of the various philosophers in the field for the eighth and the seventh centuries B.C. are not known. Therefore it is not possible to compute the influence of empiricism among other systems of truth for these centuries. Inasmuch as the truth of faith seems to have dominated greatly during these centuries, it is probable that empiricism was either nonexistent or had little influence. If this be so, then the small number of the discoveries in the eighth and the seventh centuries B.C. agrees with that assumption and supports the relation discussed. Another unfortunate circumstance is that after the end of the second century B.C. it is impossible clearly to separate the Greek philosophers from the Roman, because many Greek and Oriental (Egyptian, Syrian, and other) thinkers were Roman subjects and many of them lived in Rome; on the other hand, several thinkers of Roman extraction lived in one of the Roman provinces. It is impossible, therefore, to compare the movement of Greek discoveries with that of Greek empiricism; the

TABLE 3

	NO. OF SCIENTIFIC DISCOVERIES AND INVENTIONS			INDICATORS OF EMPIRICISM	
CENTURY				WEIGHT (ABSOLUTE FIGURES)	PERCENTAGE OF THE INFLUENCE OF EMPIRICISM AMONG ALL SYSTEMS OF TRUTH
	Greece	*Rome*	*Greece and Rome*	*Greece*	*Greece*
8 B.C.	6	0	6	0	0
7	3	2	5	?	?
6	26	5	31	6	19.4
5	39	1	40	23	19.2
4	52	5	57	31	14.6
3	42	3	45	34	21.7
2	14	3	17	11	19.6
				Greece and Rome	*Greece and Rome*
1	12	20	32	26	24.3
1 A.D.	25	35	60	2	2.3
2	5	13	18	13	6.7
3	0	6	6	33	24.8
4	1	15	16	19	15.2
5	0	4	4	11	11.7
6	3	1	4	1	1.6
	Western Christian Europe			*Western Christian Europe*	
7		4		0	0
8		4		0	0
9		6		0	0
10		7		0	0
11		8		3	7.7
12		12		13	14.3
13		53		21	12.8
14		65		28	17.2
15		127		3	7.2
16		429		24	14.8
17		691		132	29.6
18		1574		260	37.5
19		8527		644	42.6[1]

[1] The data of the discoveries and inventions are taken from the tables of Chapter Three. See the sources in that chapter.

movement of Roman discoveries with that of Roman empiricism. Nevertheless, from the first century B.C. to the fourth century A.D. it can be observed that the trend of the Graeco-Roman discoveries and of the Graeco-Roman empiricism was again upward, but after the fifth century A.D. both decline and remain almost on the zero line during the next six or seven centuries.

Thus the big movements of both variables are essentially parallel. It is to be expected for several reasons that discrepancies will occur from century to century, but they in no way annul the parallel, long-time tides of both variables. The minor discrepancies are due : first, to the incomparability of the data ; second, to their incompleteness (it is not probable that all the discoveries and the names of all the thinkers are preserved) ; third, to the incomplete integration of the two streams : that of the discoveries, and epistemological and philosophical thought. Both streams can influence each other although there is no reason to expect that the influence is *extremely close or instantaneous*. As was briefly mentioned in the first chapter of this work, and as will be developed later on, if science is a system and philosophy-epistemology is a system, then each has to have a margin of autonomy in its development, self-regulation, and other external conditions. For this reason, as in the relationships of the cultural variables generally, an integration is to be expected, but it is not to be instantaneous or close.[22] Therefore, while in one century the discoveries may rise in number and the influence of the empirical system may lag, or may increase in the next century when the number of discoveries may show no increase or may even decrease, in another century the philosophico-epistemological thought experiencing a notable change may exert, but with some lag, an influence upon the movement of the discoveries. Both variables may influence each other constantly without manifesting this in a synchronistic parallelism of their fluctuations in all periods. The parallelism of the main tides of empiricism and discoveries shows their interrelations. Partial discrepancies in their movements from century to century support the expectation of an imperfect causal integration of the variables of a culture. Thus, in the life process of culture these two processes, *i.e.*, the movement of the scientific discoveries and inventions and the epistemological and philosophical mentality — as it manifests itself specifically in empiricism, as a theory of truth and knowledge — are associated, and the movements of their major and long-time trends are essentially parallel. There are discrepancies in the minor movements of the two processes, but these discrepancies in no way annul the essential concord of their long-time tides. Sometimes the rise of empiricism precedes the rise or decline of the discoveries, sometimes discoveries precede the respective movements of the curve of empiricism. This does not indicate that science is the cause of the respective changes in the field of the philosophical systems of truth and knowledge, nor that the philosophical mentality is the cause

---

[22] We have seen this in Volume One in our discussion of the fluctuation in the main styles of various arts; they all fluctuated tangibly together, in a positive association, with the exception of music, for instance, which moved more slowly than the other arts in its transition from the Idealistic to the Sensate form.

of the increase or decrease, progress or stagnation, of scientific discoveries, but it means that both these processes are manifestations of the respective changes experienced by the whole culture given. This subject will be discussed later.

Now let us turn to the other systems of truth and comment briefly on the essential points of their highs and lows.

E. *Fluctuation of the Truth of Faith. Ideational Rationalism, Mysticism, and Fideism.* Although in Tables 1 and 2 and Figure 1 ideational rationalism is not separated from idealistic rationalism, as the truth of reason, or as the system of Scholastic intellectualism, as Grabmann calls it, nevertheless there is little difficulty in separating these forms of rationalism from each other in the theories of truth of the main periods studied. As mentioned previously the truth of faith is represented by religious or ideational rationalism, by mysticism, and by fideism. The latter two are esoteric and desperate forms of the truth of faith, while religious rationalism is the expression of a mentality free from any doubt or questioning of the truth of faith.[23]

Understood, then, as an ensemble of religious rationalism, mysticism, and fideism, the truth of faith has had, within the period studied, the following periods of domination over the other two systems of truth.

(1) Before the fifth century B.C. in Greece, by one-hundred-year periods, religious rationalism was given a value of 80.6 per cent, and a value of 71 to 90.9 per cent in the indicators by twenty-year periods. The whole field of the systems of truth was held by religious rationalism and by a minor stream of empiricism.

(2) The period from the beginning of our era to the end of the fifth century A.D., when these three currents of the truth of faith give the indicators: 97.7 per cent for the first century; 85.3 per cent for the second; 70.7 per cent for the third; 84.8 per cent for the fourth; 88.3 per cent for the fifth. But qualitatively this period was very different from that before the fifth century B.C. because mysticism and fideism were most powerful and dominated the truth of faith. This means it

---

[23] That this is so is shown by the fact that mysticism and fideism emerge and grow simultaneously, or after the emergence and growth of skepticism and empiricism. These are currents which either radically deny a possibility of any valid knowledge and truth (skepticism) or question, doubt, and deny the validity of the truth of faith (empiricism). In this sense mysticism and fideism are an esoteric and desperate reaction against these currents. Meanwhile, during the periods when such doubts and questionings are either lacking or are very minor, religious rationalism usually dominates. For this reason it is serene, calm, and absolutely certain in its truth of faith without any desperate efforts. In Chapter Two this subject will be treated more substantially. For the present, the reader by examining the Tables 1 and 2 and Figure 1 can see this easily for himself.

was not a period of a serene faith, untroubled by doubt, but it was a period of a desperate "will to believe" assailed and attacked by empiricism and skepticism.

(3) The centuries from the sixth to the twelfth. These centuries were periods of monopolistic domination of the truth of faith over the truth of senses and the truth of reason. The truth of faith occupied 100 per cent of the field. Qualitatively religious rationalism was the dominant current (rating from 65 to 100 per cent). Side by side with it in some centuries the truth of faith was represented by mysticism but, as will be mentioned in the next chapter, the mysticism of that period was very similar to religious rationalism, since it was almost free from any "despair," or any stressed "will to believe" similar to St. Thomas's "I believe, O Lord; help me in my disbelief." For these reasons the whole period can be regarded as one of the monopolistic domination of ideational or religious rationalism, as the truth of faith absolutely free from any doubt and questioning.

(4) The fifteenth century. All the three systems of truth of faith were given a total value of 92.8 per cent. Here again the main currents of the truth of faith are represented mainly by the desperate forms of mysticism and fideism, but not by religious rationalism.

It impresses us as being the last desperate effort of the truth of faith to maintain its influence before its inexorable decline for several subsequent centuries up to the present time. This decline is shown in Tables 1 and 2 by the indicators of hundred- as well as of twenty-year periods. Beginning with the sixteenth century the truth of faith in all its forms declined more and more, giving the dominant position to other systems of truth, particularly to that of truth of senses.

Throughout all the centuries studied mysticism and fideism, because of their somewhat esoteric or sophisticated nature, have been less powerful than religious rationalism. The difficult nature of an esoteric mystical experience makes it inaccessible to most people and therefore renders the mystical truth unconvincing and incomprehensible because its force is in the mystical experience itself and not in the testimony of the senses, not in logical reasoning, nor in a simple, unquestioning, spontaneous belief. Therefore, except for a few periods, mysticism has had a lesser power and emerged comparatively late as compared with religious rationalism.

Fideism presupposes the previous or simultaneous existence of highly skeptical, sophisticated, and analytical thought, full of doubts and questionings in regard either to truth of senses or truth of reason or even to the unsophisticated faith. Therefore it emerges late, after the appearance of skepticism, and represents in a sense a highly artificial and intentional self-hypnotism. As such it has little chance of being accessible and understandable to the masses. For this reason, with the exception of very few periods, it has been a comparatively minor current in the main systems of truth.

The following periods of the minor upward movements of each of these two currents of the truth of faith can be noted.

For Mysticism: (1) At the debut of mysticism, about the middle of the fourth century B.C. (Plato after 385, Xenocrates, and others). (2) Around the beginning of the Christian era (Philo, Thrasyllus, and others). (3) With slight oscillations it rose from the second to the end of the fourth centuries (up to A.D. 370); remained generally high throughout the fifth, sixth, and seventh centuries; and then disappeared, being merged into religious rationalism. It appeared again in the ninth century and reached a high point in the twelfth century (Erigena, Maxim Confessor, and others). (4) In the thirteenth it was low. It rose again in the fourteenth and reached its climax in the fifteenth century. In the sixteenth century it stayed high, though much lower than in the fifteenth. (5) There were slight crescendos from 1660 to 1720 and from 1780 to 1840. Since 1840 it has steadily declined up to recent times.

Fideism's highs have been: 280–240 B.C.; the first century B.C.; the first and second centuries A.D.; from the third to the eleventh centuries it was submerged, emerged for a brief period, disappeared again until the fourteenth century. Since that time, however, it has continually existed but as a current of even less importance than skepticism. Immediately after the French and other revolutions at the end of the eighteenth century it jumped up temporarily, but it soon receded and has remained at this low level up to the present time.

F. *Inverse Movement of Truth of Faith and Atheism.* It is to be logically expected that the essential movement of the curve of the truth of faith goes on inversely with the curve of the rise and decline of atheism, as the denial of God (or gods) and supersensory and superhuman intelligence, and that atheism's curve runs parallel with the truth of senses (empiricism and its allies: materialism, ethics of happiness, nominalism, temporalism, and so on). Though A. B. Drachmann in his *Atheism in Pagan Antiquity* studies the rise and fall of atheism only in the sense of "the point of view which denies the existence of the ancient gods,"[24] the essentials of the rise and decline of such a narrow form of atheism, according to Drachmann's results, follow inversely our curve of the movement of

[24] A. B. Drachmann, *op. cit.*, p. 1.

truth of faith and other curves (idealism, eternalism, ethics of the absolute principles, ontological realism) associated with it. Up to the fifth century B.C. we scarcely have a single case of atheism among the known thinkers, and no criminal prosecution of it.[25] In the second part of the fifth century a decline of religion becomes noticeable and atheism as well as criminal condemnation for impiety appear (Anaxagoras, Diogenes of Apollonia, Hippo of Rhegium, Protagoras, Critias, even Socrates, and others).[26] These streams grow in the fourth, in the third, and partly in the second centuries B.C.[27] With the beginning of the second century A.D., if not earlier, we witness definite signs of a decrease of atheism and an increase of religiosity in the sense of a system of beliefs and practices posited in a supersensory world; beginning with God (or gods) and other transcendental values.[28] During subsequent centuries — the third and the fourth — atheism declined and practically disappeared during all the centuries of the Middle Ages. Thus, this "variable" — a mere detail of the main variables dealt with in my work — moves in the way which can easily be deduced from the essentials of the theory of Ideational and Sensate cultures. (See some other details in the qualitative historical works of Cumont, Lake, Nock, Gruppe, Jackson, quoted in this work.) It is hardly necessary to add that parallel with the decline of the truth of faith at the end of the Middle Ages, atheism in various forms has been rising up to the present time, with minor setbacks.

G. *Fluctuation of the Truth of Reason. Idealistic Rationalism.* In the sense of the harmonious synthesis of the truth of reason, of faith, and of senses, with the truth of independent reason dominant (if not *de jure* then *de facto*), there were, so far, only two periods when this system of truth of Scholastic intellectualism was dominant. The first of these periods was about the fifth and the fourth centuries B.C. in Greece, and the second period was from the end of the twelfth to the second part of the fourteenth century with the thirteenth century as the climax. The rationalism of these periods (qualitatively not separated in Tables 1 and 2 from the religious rationalism) was idealistic rationalism. In the next chapter the qualitative analysis of the systems of truth will be given.

The upward movements of idealistic rationalism during the following periods may be mentioned.

(1) 540–450 B.C.: Pythagoreanism, Herakleitos, the Eleatian School.

---

[25] *Ibid.*, p. 21.   [26] *Ibid.*, p. 13.
[27] *Ibid.*, pp. 60 ff. and 75 ff.   [28] *Ibid.*, pp. 120 ff.

(2) Second half of the fifth and the first half of the fourth century B.C. (its climax in Greece). Socrates, Plato, Aristotle, the Meharians, and others.

(3) About 200 B.C.

(4) About 80 B.C.

(5) The twelfth, the thirteenth, and the first half of the fourteenth centuries (its climax in the history of the Western culture).

(6) The first half of the fifteenth century.

(7) The sixteenth and the first half of the seventeenth centuries.

(8) The end of the eighteenth and the beginning of the nineteenth centuries. After which time the trend has been downward.

H. *Pulsation of Skepticism and Criticism.* Skepticism, as a denial of possibility of any truth, is not a constructive part of the systems of truth. Nevertheless such a mentality is symptomatic in many respects, and its fluctuations deserve to be followed at least briefly. Like mysticism and fideism it emerged comparatively late in the history of the Greek mentality (about the middle of the fifth century B.C.). The late appearance of this stream of thought as well as its comparatively lesser power is comprehensible. Great progress of analytical and sophisticated thought and failure of the constructive systems of truth are necessary in order that such a "desperately nihilistic" system can emerge and gather power. Being negative and sophisticated, it can hardly appeal to a large number of thinkers and is little comprehended by the mass mentality.

Skepticism reached its high points in the periods from 460 to 380 B.C., 180–120 B.C., about 20 B.C., and then in the second century A.D. when it flared up for the last time in the Graeco-Roman world. After the third century A.D., when the era of the truth of faith was ushered in, there was no place for skepticism and it disappeared until the fourteenth century, when it emerged for a short time. Disappearing again in the fifteenth century (the century of mysticism and fideism), it reappeared in the sixteenth century and since that time has existed only as a minor stream of thought. Since the sixteenth century the periods 1520–1540, 1560–1600, 1740–1780 were marked by increases in the influence of skepticism.

By examining its trends it can be observed that skepticism emerges usually when the truth of faith declines and when truth of reason and especially truth of senses begin to grow. In this sense it is a satellite of the first phases of growth of empiricism because of its relativistic and agnostic tendencies. However, when empiricism triumphs, skepticism retreats, although it does not disappear as it does in the periods when truth of faith dominates.

It can be observed, also, that the periods of a flaring up of skepticism have usually been those either immediately preceding or coinciding with the periods in which great social upheavals and calamities occurred: the Peloponnesian War and subsequent calamities; the great civil wars in Rome of the first and the second triumvirates; the Black Plague; the emergence of Christianity; the Reformation; the religious wars of the Reformation and of the League; and the great French Revolution. With one or two exceptions some connection seems to have existed between the growth of skepticism and the appearance of social upheavals.

The third fact to be noted is that as soon as skepticism rises its emergence or rise is almost immediately followed by emergence and rise of fideism as a desperate reaction against it.

Finally, *criticism* (in a specific sense a critical philosophy) is a special rivulet which emerged at the end of the eighteenth century mainly through the works of Hume and Kant. It appeared comparatively strong at once. After about 1810, however, it experienced, like several currents of thought, a sharp decline in strength as a result of the reaction against the ideologies of the Revolution. After 1860 it reassumed its growth, and at the end of the nineteenth century and at the present time has become, next to empiricism, the most powerful current. From the figures one can see that its movements are almost opposite to that of skepticism. This suggests that in a sense it is a diluted form of it and fulfills in a much milder way the functions of skepticism which in a pure form cannot function under the given psychosocial conditions. Such are the important fluctuations of the main systems of truth which have occurred during the period of some twenty-five hundred years studied.

I. *Total Mental Spectrum of the Main Periods.* We shall now concentrate on the total mentality of the main parts of the period under investigation. The following inferences are warranted by the character of the "mental spectrum" of these parts.

(1) The total spectrum of mentality (in the field studied) of Greece before the fifth century B.C. appeared to be predominantly Ideational. The system of the religious rationalism was overwhelmingly dominant, and empiricism only as a minor force was present; neither skepticism, mysticism, fideism, criticism, nor even idealistic rationalism existed. It was the period of certitude in the Greek mentality, the age of the certitude of faith; the age of calm serenity and untroubled simplicity.

(2) The fifth century, especially its second part and also the first two-thirds of the fourth century B.C. were marked by the domination of the *idealistic rationalism* or the *truth of reason*. The system of truth of

"scholastic intellectualism" (the truth of the autonomous and dialectic reason in contradistinction to religious rationalism) occupied about 40 per cent of the field; truth of faith was still recognized in the form of Plato's "divine madness" or Aristotle's theology (see Chapter Two of this volume); empiricism was not only present but was also comparatively strong; even skepticism, mysticism, and fideism existed, although each was comparatively weak.

All the three truths harmoniously coexisted, and more than that, all were organically blended into one system of truth; namely, idealistic rationalism, giving *suum cuique* to the truth of faith, of reason, of senses. The main governor, if not *de jure* then *de facto*, was dialectics, through which and upon which was based the evidential power of even the truth of faith. The mental spectrum was marvelously balanced and free from any extremism. None of the negative or desperate current (skepticism, fideism, mysticism) tended to be dominant. All these characteristics are evidences of the domination of truth of reason in that period. It was also an age of certitude based upon reason, and also partly upon "divine madness" and the auxiliary but important role of the organs of senses (especially in the Aristotelian system).

In the light of such a spectrum of the Idealistic system of truth, and in the light of the data concerning all the main branches of art of the fifth and fourth centuries, their culture and mentality appear to be idealistic. This means that the contended correlation between the main types of cultures and the respective main types of the dominant systems of truth (Ideational culture and truth of faith; Idealistic, and the truth of reason; Sensate and the empirical system of truth) is so far well supported by the data.

(3) In the subsequent centuries — the third, the second, and the first B.C. — the tide of empiricism grew and became as strong as rationalism. Rationalism of both types greatly declined and the negative and desperate forms of truth flourished. The above correlations indicated a rising tide of the Sensate culture and a decline of the Ideational and the Idealistic cultures in their strong and balanced forms; and a growth of the esoteric, exotic, and desperate mentality in the field; or a great mental disturbance, disorganization, and upheaval. As we shall see from the data of other branches of the cultures, Hellenistic culture of that period became progressively more and more Sensate, less and less Idealistic and Ideational. Subsequent centuries — from the first B.C. to the third A.D. — were stamped by the entrance of the Romans into the field. The indicators given in Tables 1 and 2 are the joint products of thought of the

Romanized Greeks as well as of the Hellenized Romans, and also the Orientals. In addition, in the first and the second centuries A.D. Christianity with its thinkers appeared. The spectrum of the mentality in the field of truth in these centuries is very interesting and peculiar. In reference to the Pagan mentality (data have been computed separately for the Christian and for the Pagan thinkers of these centuries) empiricism and rationalism (in the sense of the truth of reason) declined; in their places, skepticism, mysticism, and fideism grew, indicating a disturbed mentality and a great transition from one form of culture and truth to another fundamentally different. The dominant system of the period is either cynical skepticism, purely negative in its cynicism, or esoteric and desperate systems of mysticism and fideism. In a sense such a mentality is a mixture of Ideationalism, partly Idealism and partly Sensate truth. It bears some resemblance to Idealism but merely imitates it because the real Idealism is harmonious idealistic rationalism. From the analysis of the forms of art we have seen that the period was indeed pseudo Idealistic, on the one hand, and cynically Sensate, on the other. It bears the marks of the confused mixture of artificial pseudo Idealism with cynicism, so typical for the periods foreboding a decline of a Sensate form of culture and a transition to the Ideational form.

The Christian mentality represented, since the second century, only two currents : desperate and militant mysticism and religious rationalism. Mysticism, however, was about twice as powerful as religious rationalism (the indicators of religious rationalism being thirty-two for the second century, and that of mysticism sixty-one for the Christian thinkers). This means that the Christian thinkers rejected entirely the empirico-Sensate (scientific) system of truth, and embraced mainly an admixture of the truth of faith and the truth of subservient reason. We shall see that a detailed qualitative study entirely corroborates this statement.

The total indicators of Tables 1 and 2 for these two centuries thus represent a mixture of these two widely different mentalities of the Pagan thought with a very dissimilar Christian truth of faith. The Pagan thought was thrown out of balance by the tragic circumstances of the preceding period and somewhat lost its faith in the truth of the senses as well as in that of independent reason and turned, instead, either to cynicism and skepticism or to fideism, as the artificial will to believe, and to mysticism, as the desperate truth of faith. The Christian thought broke completely with the truth of senses and turned to a belief in the truth of the Gospel, in revelation, and in mystical experience, slightly supported by the truth of logic in so far as it did not contradict the creed and could be used for its purpose. Here, then, was a great shattering of the empirical and idealistically rationalistic systems of truth which were dominant before.

(4) When the indicators of the spectrum of mentality of the next two centuries — the third and the fourth — are examined, the first impression is that the mental balance shattered previously has been somewhat regained; skepticism and fideism practically disappeared; among the Pagans empiricism had a revival (even a few Christian thinkers shared it); rationalism grew also, mainly among the Christian thinkers; but mysticism gained especially great influence with the Pagan as well as with the Christian contributors. In other words some stabilization was apparent in the sense that the nihilistic and fideistic forms of mentality in the field were discarded: for the Pagans in the sense that there was a revival of their belief in the truth of senses; for the Christians, as well as for a great number of Pagans, because there was a growing belief in the esoteric truth of faith (mysticism). All in all the period was one of transition; as such it indicated the opposing currents, with the truth of faith gaining and the truth of the senses decreasing in power.

(5) We are at the end of the empirico-rationalistic system of truth and at the beginning of the domination of the truth of faith, with the truth of reason assuming a subsidiary role. Within one century or a little more this became clear; empiricism declined and disappeared. The truth of faith became dominant and clothed itself in the solid and confident form of the religious rationalism; as such it was stabilized and from that time needed no extreme and desperate forms, like fideism or esoteric mysticism. We are ushered into the age of faith which questioned nothing in the Gospel and in God's truth. We are in the age of a new great ideationalism of the Middle Ages, in the monopolistic domination of the truth of faith with its "handmaid" human reason (not questioning but only justifying and serving faith). The indicators show that such a situation continued for about six centuries. A miracle of human confidence in the truth of faith! A marvelously happy age of certitude and peace of mind! A miraculous disdain toward organs of senses as the source of truth! "An age of profound regression and stark mental stupor," the partisans of liberal and Sensate progress would say. What qualifications are used — vituperative or glorifying — are unimportant. What is certain is that it is an Ideational age not only on the basis of the dominant truth of faith, of the dominant Ideational art, but also upon the basis of data given subsequently. If at any period in the history of the Western mentality the philosophers and the people as a whole felt that

they were in the possession of truth, the whole truth, and nothing but truth, it was in these centuries. There was no skepticism, no questioning, no doubt, no relativity, no hesitation, no reservation. They had the truth of faith and believed in it absolutely. The age was very similar to that of Greece before the fifth century.

(6) Then in the eleventh century empiricism reappeared after many centuries. Weak at the beginning, it doubled its strength in the twelfth century, especially at its end, and stabilized itself in the thirteenth and fourteenth centuries. Thus in these centuries the monopolistic domination of the truth of faith with its subordinate, the truth of reason, was ended. The mental spectrum changed; it became a harmonious blending of empiricism and of mysticism with the dominant truth of independent rationalism different from religious rationalism of the previous period. Now it was not a mere tool of the truth of faith but its independent partner on its own initiative, in its own right questioning everything in the truth of faith. This questioning led it, however, not to a contradiction but to a reinforcement of faith by dialectic of reason. The harmonious blending of all these truths of faith, of senses (empiricism), and of reason gave the idealistic rationalism of the great Scholastics of the twelfth and the thirteenth centuries the dominant position in that period. In it *suum cuique* is given to all these sources and to all the criteria of truth and knowledge. It united them all harmoniously into one organic unity where faith, senses, and reason did not fight one another, but all were co-operating in the great service to God, to truth, and to man's real happiness, in building the full and complete truth, real wisdom and knowledge not narrowed to one vista and not reduced to one source. A wonderful and happy age! An age in which science did not fight religion, and vice versa; in which the organs of senses did not disdainfully reason: "*Nihil esse in intellectu quod non fuerit prius in sensu*," or reason did not consider the senses as the foolish and incompetent registers of the shadows of reality, but respected them and accepted their testimony within certain limits in the fields where they were thought to be competent. The age of Idealistic system of truth. It was the European replica of the Greek Idealistic mentality of the fifth and fourth centuries B.C. This result will be strongly corroborated by the data from other branches of the culture of these centuries which unmistakably showed its idealistic nature.

In the second part of the fourteenth and in the fifteenth centuries the Idealistic system was shattered and a desperate and esoteric kind of mysticism prevailed. Its wave swept over Western society. During the second part of the sixteenth century, and especially in the seventeenth, however, mysticism subsided, and empiricism gained in strength, which with very slight fluctuations has persisted up to the present time. The system of faith, as well as rationalism, and the truth of reason also lost ground and the truth of senses became triumphant. At the end of the nineteenth and in the twentieth century (at least up to the prewar time) its influence has grown to unprecedented heights. Verily we are living in the age of scientism! This means our culture is Sensate culture par excellence! As a result, the other systems of truth have been constantly degraded to a lower level of sterile speculation, fantastic and unscientific and unverified purely logical derivations — in regard to the truth of reason; and to mere superstition and ignorance so far as the truth of faith is concerned. Discord between these systems of truth marks this period. Scientific truth leads the offensive in an effort to exterminate entirely the other systems of truth, and they in turn are fighting for their existence. So far the offensive of the empirical system of truth has been successful and has driven the other systems from the vast territory which they occupied before the seventeenth and especially the fourteenth centuries. It has weakened also their inner strength and confidence in themselves and their validity. It has forced them to imitate — even in the question of pure theology and logic — the weapons, the tactics, and the strategy of the triumphant scientific truth of senses. Hence scientism as a cult; hence the commonly accepted opinion that there is only one truth and knowledge — the scientific; hence the belief that in the future these other systems of truth will be entirely eliminated from human mentality as useless survivals of ignorance and superstition; hence all the other similar phenomena and beliefs of that kind. On the other hand, our age being resplendent in the variety of its scintillating colors has, at the same time, something of "the devil's spectrum," if one may say so figuratively. Its spectrum is exceedingly complex. *It believes less than almost any other age in reason, in nonsensory sources of truth, in thought itself;* in anything and anybody that cannot be seen, heard, tasted, smelled, touched, and sensed generally. In this sense it is the age which looks for truth only in "the empirical bank" of senses, investing a greater part of its mental capital in it (in contradistinction to the Middle Ages particularly). As this bank has had many difficulties, however, investors cannot have complete confidence in its integrity or in the safety of their too little diversified investments. For these reasons the undercurrents of skepticism and criticism flow unhindered and destroy the serenity, faith, and sense of security in the truth of senses. We try to convince ourselves that our investments are safe and that we are happy, but only for a moment, as our feeling of insecurity never vanishes but tends rather to grow more and more. Skepticism and criticism compose about 20 per cent (for the years 1880–1900 and 1900–1920) of all systems of truth — an unusually high percentage, indicating a growing crisis of our Bank of the Truth of Senses!

This and other symptoms make the future of the "Bank of Empirical Truth" uncertain. There are already many indications of the coming crisis of the scientific system of truth (as the truth of senses) and of its decline. Any system of truth that is dominant begins to be undermined from within the system itself. For instance the truth of faith of the Middle Ages began to be disorganized from within by the theologians themselves. In the course of time many discrepancies among the various dogmas and interpretations of the Scriptures appeared. Each referred to the revealed truth; thus several irreconcilable revealed truths came to light. They began a struggle with one another which tended to undermine the truth of faith itself, and in this struggle they were forced to use more logical and sensory evidences. As a result, truth of faith gave way to the logical and empirical truths. A similar process begins to go on within the contemporary empirical truth and contemporary science. One of the symptoms of its weakening is a decreasing rate of creativeness in contemporary science, as is shown in Chapter Three.

Another symptom is a multiplication of various contradictory theories within its field which make the certainty of scientific truth less and less possible and which respectively undermine the very faith in its validity. This is especially important in regard to the main principles and laws of science, like the Newtonian or classical mechanics or similar fundamentals of the scientific disciplines. As a result, skepticism, fideism, and criticism, like wolves, are already waiting for empirical truth to weaken further so that it can be attacked more violently and vigorously. Relativity and doubts of the possibility of a scientific study of the problems which cannot exactly and directly be put under microscopes or manipulated in a laboratory seem to be increasing. Criticism as a diluted substitute for skepticism has grown from the end of the nineteenth century up to the present time. The feeling of confidence in science has begun to wane as it waned in the system of faith at the end of the Middle Ages. In philosophy various intuitivistic and mystical theories of knowledge, beginning with Bergsonism, begin to rise. There are many other symptoms examined elsewhere in this work. For these and many other reasons it appears improbable to me that the trend of growth of empiricism and scientism will continue, but sooner or later the trend will probably change and possibly even be reversed. As a matter of fact the systems of truth concerning the social, political, moral, and spiritual matters, in several Western countries like Communist Russia, Nazi Germany, and Fascist Italy, have changed considerably already. Many empirical truths of the social sciences and humanities, sufficiently corroborated by empirical data, have already been declared untrue, treasonable, and heretical, and have been replaced by the truths, faiths, credos, dogmas, and revelations of the Communist, Hitlerite, or Mussolinian. The pronunciamento of the dictators or the chiefs is the supreme truth, evidence, and source. What they say is true; what they reject is untrue.

No further empirical evidence is necessary. In milder forms the same is growing everywhere. The words on the wall are beginning to be written; and they forebode the coming decline (perhaps temporarily, perhaps for a long time) of the triumphant empiricism. Possibly in its triumph it has gone beyond the element of truth and has begun to be overcome by pseudo truth. When such a condition occurs in any system of truth, it is headed for a crisis and for a temporary decline.

J. *Principle of Limit and of Self-regulation of Sociocultural Processes.* If the closest rivals among these systems are selected and studied for three separate periods, and also for the entire period, the total sums of the indicators of each of the rival currents are shown in Table 4.

TABLE 4.   SUMS OF THE INDICATORS OF SOCIOCULTURAL
PROCESSES

Periods	Fideism	Skepticism	Empiricism	Rationalism
580 B.C. to A.D. 100	185	137	133	264
100 to 1500	52	29	145	515
1500 to 1900	132	113	1060	755
Total	369	279	1338	1534

No arithmetical and mechanical balances are sought in this or in any other social process; nevertheless, considering the fact that the length of the total period studied is about twenty-five hundred years, and that all these indices have been made without any idea of an arithmetical balance, one must confess that the sums of the indices for fideism-skepticism and empiricism-rationalism are strikingly close. It suggests that in the sociocultural life and sociomental processes there seems to be present some factor which, in the long run, does not permit any single or extreme current to absorb all the other systems for any length of time and thus to narrow the richness and many-colored completeness of truth. Sooner or later the prejudices and limitations of any single current call forth ever-increasing criticism and result in the reappearance of its rivals, their growth, and the overthrow of the dominant current.

These figures give a concrete idea of the principle of immanent self-regulation of sociocultural processes. This immanent self-regulation is manifested, however, by our data in a different form. This method of manifestation is, perhaps, not so impressive as the preceding figures, but it is more important in its bearing. By going carefully through the vertical rows of the figures in Tables 1, 2, and 4, the reader, if he is well versed in the philosophies of each of the periods, will find the picture given by such an examination still more complete and convincing.

The unfolding of the course of the currents studied starts with a mild empiricism which almost simultaneously is balanced by a mild rationalism. Action of empiricism, so to speak, is followed almost immediately by counterreaction of rationalism. When one is moderate the other is moderate also.

Then, in the process of differentiation, skepticism appears; and almost immediately it is counterbalanced by the appearance of fideism and partly by mysticism. Again action is followed by counterreaction. Those who know the character of the philosophies of each of the periods can scarcely fail to see that if one current becomes more extreme in its accentuation of its own truth and in its denial of the truth of its rival, the competing philosophies usually become also more sharp and extreme.

Further on, it can be seen again that when skepticism disappears from the highway of the philosophical mentality, fideism, as its closest rival, disappears also, and later on when one reappears the other soon reappears.

Empiricism and rationalism, selected as closest rivals, show considerable deviations from the line of balance, especially during the Middle Ages. Yet, the data show that all in all even these great deviations are but temporary phenomena and over a longer period of time seem to be corrected, if not quantitatively then quantitatively-qualitatively, and to be brought close to the line of the quantitative-qualitative balance. Perhaps if there had been more accurate and more complete data at our disposal, the balance might have been much closer. For instance, if during the Middle Ages empiricism was eliminated, the rising tide of empiricism during the last four centuries is perhaps a counterbalance or a counteraction to this medieval one-sidedness.

Based on the available data, a relatively close quantitative and still closer qualitative balancing of the rival currents seems to remain. The conclusion is reinforced also by the subsequent data.

For the whole period considered the total sums of the indicators for each of these currents and the respective systems of truth are as follows:

Fideism	369	*Truth of faith*	1650 [29]
Skepticism	279	*Truth of reason*	1292 [30]
Mysticism	1039	*Truth of senses*	1338 [31]
Criticism	197	*Skepticism and Criticism*	476
Empiricism	1338		
Rationalism	1534		

These figures show that in the cultures studied the religious and the idealistic rationalism has been so far the most powerful system of truth. Then next in importance was empiricism, then mysticism, then fideism, then skepticism and criticism. Interpreted in another way, in reference to the system of truth, the total sums of the indicators of power of all the systems of truth are fairly close, giving a slight edge to the truth of faith. This demonstrates once more the principle of immanent self-regulation of sociocultural processes and their autonomous tendency to balance one another, sometimes quantitatively, sometimes qualitatively, sometimes quantitatively and qualitatively. The data suggest, also, that possibly each form of truth has its own important function in the psychosocial life of mankind and is equally necessary. Otherwise this unexpected balance would hardly have been possible.[32] Perhaps, indeed, the devil in one of Anatole France's novels was after all not so wrong in saying that the absolute and whole truth is "white," meaning by white a color which represents a blending of all the colors of the spectrum. Perhaps the whole and absolute truth is indeed the truth which embraces in some way all the three forms of truth, each of which is therefore only a "partial truth." However this may be, these results are interesting and as such deserve to be mentioned.

[29] Composed of mysticism, fideism, and religious rationalism made up of the indicators of rationalism for the centuries before the fifth century B.C., from the third century A.D. to the twelfth century.

[30] Composed of the indicators of rationalism for the centuries from the fifth B.C. to second century A.D., inclusive; and from the twelfth to the twentieth centuries, because the rationalistic theories of these periods were mainly logico-dialectic.

[31] Composed of empiricism.

[32] Though the arithmetic or numerological balance is by no means the only or the most important form of balance in my opinion, proportional or qualitative balance, whose examples will be discussed in the subsequent ten chapters, is generally more important.

IV. CORROBORATION OF THE PROPOSITIONS IN SOCIAL SPACE
(IN OTHER CULTURES)

The preceding discussion shows that in the course of some twenty-five hundred years, the periods of domination of Ideational art were also those of Ideational truth; the periods of domination of Sensate art those of Sensate truth; the moments of domination of Idealistic art were also those of domination of the Idealistic system of truth. The long-time pulsations in these two compartments of culture have been essentially parallel. This means that in the compartments of art and truth the cultures studied have been integrated logically and causally; it gives also a direct inductive corroboration to the propositions formulated at the beginning of this chapter. Among these propositions there is the statement that the predominantly Ideational cultures have to exhibit domination of the truth of faith, while predominantly Sensate or Mixed culture mentalities exhibit respectively the domination of the Sensate and the Mixed systems of truth and knowledge — no matter where and when such cultures exist or existed. The only important condition is that the cultures have to be logically consistent and integrated. This proposition has not as yet been discussed.

Therefore, let us pause to indicate that the material given in Volume One of this work is sufficient to corroborate the principle to a considerable extent. In Chapter Three it was shown that in the Hinduist-Brahmanist, Buddhist, Jainist, Taoist, Tibetan, and other Ideational mentalities the system of truth of faith has been dominant. All the essential earmarks of the truth of faith are found in these culture mentalities. Their real truth and knowledge is believed to be derived from the superempirical source through ecstatic experience, supersensory intuition, divine revelation, divine inspiration, and other supersensory ways. Their truth and knowledge is holy and sacred. It is based upon the divine source — "Scripture" — be it the Bible and the Gospel, the Vedas, or the like. As such it is believed to be absolute and unquestionably valid. The testimony of the organs of senses is given little, if any, cognitive value in all their systems. It is regarded as even a liability, "foolishness of this world," deserving only to be rejected by those who want to obtain the true and real knowledge. All these systems of truth are primarily systems of theology concerned mainly with a cognition of the supersensory reality: God, soul, immortality, and the like. They are little occupied with the study of the sensory reality, its physicochemical, biological, and other sensory aspects, and as such they use the Scripture as the main source of validation of the truth of this or that statement and theory. They all are highly symbolical in their language and their logic. In brief, the Ideational nature of their system of truth and knowledge is unquestionable. A minimum of quotations from the main sources was given in Chapter Three of Volume One and need not be repeated here. Instead of additional long quotations which would not change the conclusion it is perhaps more advisable to mention, especially in relation to the Vedic-Brahmanic-Hindu culture with their Protestant variations (Buddhism and Jainism), that even those systems of truth which have been set forth in the Hindu culture by various thinkers as opposite and supposedly Sensate and rationalistic factually are as little empirical or Sensate as are the systems of truth of Plato, Aristotle, or of St. Thomas Aquinas. Except for a very few materialistic and Sensate systems of thought (connected with half-legendary names of the two Brihaspati, Chārvākā and Nastika, and the Lokayata system of thought generally [33]

[33] The materialistic stream of thought, whether expressed in the Sensate theory of truth or hedonistic system of ethics, has certainly existed in India, but almost all the Indian and European investigators of the problem (like M. Müller, L. de la Valle Poussin, R. Garbe, Rhys Davids, and many others) unanimously stress that the materialistic thought never gained any important place in the literature of India, except in the legendary, pre-Aryan period, before 2000 to 4000 B.C., of which nothing is known and which did not have as yet the Vedic culture (see some suppositions in A. K. Mazumdar, *The Hindu History* (Dacca, 1920), pp. 127–160, 256–262, 326, 430–432, and 555), nor crystallized into a real school of thought, nor if it existed as such had any great influence. Even K. V. Krishna, who greatly helped me in this connection, and who wanted by all means to overestimate its influence (due to his materialistic, anti-Brahmanic, and somewhat Marxian-Communistic sympathies), has not been able to prove it. Even taking his version, as the most extreme, the Lokayata (materialist) system of thought was in fact, in the period 1200–700 B.C., a mere natural philosophy, the type of the early Greek nature philosophers, which was neither materialistic, nor hedonistic, but merely questioned several Vedic dogmas. Only later on there appeared purely materialistic and hedonistic theories (after the systematization of the earlier Brihaspati's thoughts by Chārvākā and by the second Brihaspati), but even then it had a comparatively unimportant place in the philosophic thought of India. Its influence became somewhat noticeable during the periods of transition and crisis in Hindu culture, but even then it hardly ever became a strong or dominant force. It used to disappear after the transitional period like the materialistic and hedonistic theories in the Middle Ages of European culture. See besides K. V. Krishna's unpublished work prepared in my seminar: *Some Hindu Materialists: Brihaspati and Charvaka;* Dakshinaranjan Shastri, *Charvaka System* (Calcutta, n. d.), with a foreword by B. K. Shastri; H. H. Wilson, "A Sketch of the Religious Sects of the Hindus," in his *Collected Works*, Vol. I (London, 1862); H. T. Colebrooke, *Miscellaneous Essays*, 2 vols. (London, 1875); E. B. Cowell, "The Charvaka System of Philosophy," in the *Journal of the Asiatic Society of Bengal*, Vol. XXXXI (1862); J. Muir, "Indian Materialists," in *Journal of the Royal Asiatic Society*, new series (1862), article 11; A. Hildebrandt, *Alt-Indien, Kulturgeschichtliche Skizzen* (Breslau, 1899); M. Müller, *Six Systems of Indian Philosophy* (London, 1899), pp. 123 ff.; A M. Pizzagalli, *Nastika Carvaka e Lokayatica* (Pisa, 1907); R. Garbe, "Lokayata," in *Encyclopedia of Religion and Ethics*, Vol. VIII (1916); A. B. Keith, *A History of Sanskrit Literature* (Oxford, 1928), pp. 498 ff.; A. A. Macdonell, *A*

which, except during the legendary pre-Aryan period, apparently was the creed of a very limited group in the Hindu thought and culture, all the other systems which most radically tend to deviate from the Vedic system are, at the most, the systems of idealistic rationalism and do not go beyond it.   Such is the Sankhya System of Philosophy.   Its four main forms are the Pure Sankhya (Nirishwara), the Theistic Sankhya (Seshwara), the Yoga of Pantanjali, and the Karma Yoga of *Bhagavad-gitā;* the first one the most Sensate (connected with the name of Kapila about 500 B.C., though the dates as given by different investigators vary) is but idealistic rationalism, very similar in its system of truth to the Aristotelian and St. Thomas Aquinas systems.   The last three are ideationally idealistic in their system of truth.   In no way is it either atheistic, materialistic, or empiristic, as some investigators desired to style it.   In it we find, combined into one system, as the sources of truth: the senses, reason, and revelation, or tradition.   When perception and inference fail, one must turn to revelation and tradition.[34]

What is said of Kapila's system can be said even more about other systems of Sankhya, mentioned previously, and about practically all the works which deviate from the orthodox Ideationalism of the main stem-

---

History of Sanskrit Literature (London, 1900), pp. 406 ff.; S. Das Gupta, *A History of Indian Philosophy* (Cambridge, 1928), Vol. I, pp. 79 ff.; S. Radhakrishnan, *Indian Philosophy* (London, 1929), Vol. I, pp. 278–283; L. de la Valle Poussin, "Materialism" in the *Encyclopedia of Religion and Ethics*, Vol. VIII; S. Das Gupta, *Yoga Philosophy* (Calcutta, 1930).

The very fact that all these investigators have had great difficulty in picking up some threads of the materialistic and hedonistic writings from all the existing sources, and the fact that most of the information obtained has been gathered mainly from the Brahmanic, Vedic, and generally ideational sources, and that little of the materialistic writings is extant, testify also that the stream has been uninfluential in Hindu thought throughout the three thousand years.   About the relative rise of such a stream in the periods of transition, see Belvelkar and Ranade, *History of Indian Philosophy* (Poona, 1927), Vol. II, pp. 77–78 and 443–465.   A. K. Mazumdar's work quoted, Santosh Kumar Das, *The Economic History of Ancient India* (Howrah, 1925).

[34] See R. G. Bhandarkar, *Collected Works* (Calcutta, 1933), Vol. I.; F. C. Thompson, *Bhagavad-gitā*, chapter on Sankhya; A. B. Keith, *The Sankhya System* (London, 1918); J. Davies, *Sankhya Karika of Iswara Krishna* (London, 1881).

Generally for the corroboration of all the above statements see: S. Radhakrishnan, *op. cit.,* especially Vol. I; P. Deussen, *The System of the Vedanta* (Chicago, 1912); R. Garbe, *The Philosophy of Ancient India* (Chicago, 1897); Max Müller, *Six Systems of Indian Philosophy* (London, 1899); S. Das Gupta, *A History of Indian Philosophy* (Cambridge, 1928), Vol. I; P. Masson-Oursel, *Esquisse d'une histoire de la philosophy indienne* (Paris, 1923).

I am very grateful for the great assistance given to me in this special subject by K. V. Krishna, who prepared several excellent papers for my seminar in sociology.   I am indebted to him for his outline and analysis of several untranslated texts.   Likewise, his study of the history of Hindu Materialism, especially of the Lokayata system, and his research on Brihaspati and Chārvākā were a great help.   Some help was given also by J. V. Boldyreff by his bibliographical work.

Vedic-Brahmanic-Hindu of the Hindu thought. Even in such seemingly purely secular works as the great Hindu treatise on politics, the *Artha-Shastra* ascribed to Kautilya, we do not find a purely secular, empirical, and morally cynical standpoint so pronounced as in many Western works beginning with Machiavelli's *Prince*. The standpoint of the *Artha-Shastra* is Sensatism mitigated by pure Ideationalism; that is, it is idealistically rationalistic in its epistemology as well as in its ethics and politics.[35]

Some slight fluctuations of the Sensate system of Truth seem to have occurred, especially in the periods of crisis of the Hindu culture,[36] but they hardly ever led to the domination of the empirical system of truth. This allows us to conclude that the association discussed has far wider validity than the purely Graeco-Roman and Western cultures.

The same can be said of the Mixed types of culture mentality and their dominant systems of truth. Whether exemplified by the Egyptian or Confucianist systems of mentality, or by any other Mixed system, the dominant system of truth in such culture mentalities is found to be Mixed also. The concrete forms of this mixture may greatly vary; but it combines the elements of the truth of faith with those of the truth of senses — sometimes consistently, sometimes mechanically and incoherently united.

Finally in a conspicuously Sensate mentality and culture — no matter where or when it exists — the truth of senses is dominant. Some exceptions to this rule undoubtedly exist because not all human groups and persons think logically even in an elementary way. Nevertheless in application to the great historical cultures the generalization fits well.

If many contemporary groups and persons are analyzed on the basis of such material, the rule will be corroborated quite tangibly. The real ideationalists among us (though they are very few) will be found to be the bearers of some system of truth of faith; real Sensatists, of the truth of senses;[37] the Mixed type persons, of the Mixed system of truth.

---

[35] For literature on it see especially N. C. Bandhopadhya, *Kautilya or Exposition of His Social and Political Theory* (Calcutta, 1927). B. K. Sarkar, *Political Institutions and Theories of the Hindus* (Leipzig, 1912); *Kautilya's Artha-Shastra*, trans. by R. D. Shama Sastry (Bangalore, 1923).

[36] All our attempts to trace this problem from historical material have failed because of the nonexistence of any reliable material and dates.

[37] Just as the Chārvākās, Lokayatas, and other Sensate and materialistic currents, which at various times have appeared in Hindu and Chinese cultures, in most cases have professed the empirical systems of truth — the truth of senses — as the supreme and sometimes the only source of truth and knowledge. Respectively they derided the truth of faith, revelation, mysticism, the sacred texts, be they the Vedas or some other Bible and Gospel, with their supersensory theory of truth and knowledge.

All in all, therefore, the association established is corroborated not only in time series but in the space series also. It is not claimed that the rule is universal, but it seems to be existing as a tangible uniformity of a fairly general nature.

V. SUMMARY

Thus, the material presented seems to support well the hypothetical propositions with which this part of the work was concerned. We have observed: (1) that the systems of truth have been fluctuating; (2) that empirical truth has been only one of these systems and by no means the most influential; (3) that the empirical system of truth and the movement of the scientific discoveries go hand in hand, as is to be expected; (4) that the subject matter of the study of each of these systems and the method of verification are such as have been deductively characterized above; (5) that when we know which of these systems is dominant in a given period we can, with a reasonable degree of certainty, foresee what will be the dominant mentality of the period in relation to the progress of scientific discoveries, to the subjects and problems which will be studied mainly, and to the method of testing the validity of the theories presented; (6) that the dominant systems of truth correspond to the respective forms of the dominant type of the culture: truth of faith to the Ideational, truth of reason to the Idealistic, and truth of senses to the Sensate cultures, providing that after further study of the cultural forms of the period studied the Greek culture before the fifth century is found to be predominantly Ideational; that of the fifth and the fourth centuries predominantly Idealistic; that of the subsequent centuries predominantly Sensate or, from the beginning of the Christian era to the end of the fourth century, transitional; that the culture from the fifth to the twelfth centuries will be found predominantly Ideational again; the culture from the twelfth to the fourteenth centuries predominantly Idealistic; and the culture from the sixteenth to the twentieth centuries predominantly Sensate. Subsequent study of the other main compartments of the Graeco-Roman and Western cultures within the period considered will show whether these expectations are corroborated.

Chapter Two

QUALITATIVE CLARIFICATION OF THE FLUCTUATION OF THE SYSTEMS OF TRUTH AND KNOWLEDGE

For many readers who are not familiar with epistemology, philosophy, and the theory of science, the data as well as the conclusions of the previous chapter may appear less significant and convincing than they are. Partly for this reason and partly as a further substantiation and corroboration of the theory set forth previously, it is advisable to show, as concisely as possible, that a shift from one system of truth to another means the greatest revolution of human mentality and culture, and that these revolutions have occurred several times during the periods and centuries marked by the above tables.

I. IDEATIONAL PHASE OF GREEK MENTALITY

Before the fifth century B.C., the theory of truth which dominated in Greece was the religious and magical truth of faith, supplemented by subservient reason, and by the truth of senses. Such was the truth mentality of Homeric Greece, of the Hesiodic *Theogony* and *Work and Days;* and, as was shown, by the Greek religion of the period; by many "truth institutions" of Greece, such as the oracles, prophets, seers, priests; by many religious and magic practices, agencies, and institutions as the mouthpieces of the divinely inspired and revealed truth which was unconcerned with the testimony of the organs of senses.[1]

II. IDEALISTIC PHASE OF GREEK THOUGHT

The indicators for the fifth and fourth centuries B.C. show a considerable change in the spectrum of the epistemological mentality which is now the spectrum of the Idealistic theory of truth.

If rationalism, the most powerful of all the currents of the period, is considered separately, it can be seen that it preserves all the earmarks of the Idealistic system of truth. The systems of truth of Anaximendros,

[1] See the preceding chapter and Wilamowitz-Moellendorff, *Der Glaube der Hellenen* (Berlin, 1931), and the works of others quoted.

Pythagoras, Xenophanes, Herakleitos, Parmenides, Hippasos, Zenon, Anaxagoras, Archytas, Archelaos, Philolaos, Aeschines, Kratilos, Melissos, Eukleidos, and others (see the Appendix to Chapter One for the list of the representatives of rationalism in these centuries) have these earmarks. In them all, in various forms, the elements of all the three systems of truth are incorporated, giving a rationalistic system of truth which is neither truth of senses only, nor truth of faith only, nor truth of reason only, but which embraces all these elements in one system.   Naturally this comes in a most perfect form in the systems of truth of the greatest leaders of the period, namely, Socrates (469–399 B.C.) and his greatest pupil, Plato (427–347 B.C.).   Though Plato's system of truth tended somewhat, during the later period of his life, toward a greater and greater accentuation of mysticism, nevertheless, in its essentials, it did not change.

What are its essential traits from the standpoint of our problem? Reduced to a brief formula they are as follows: There are three degrees of knowledge and truth, three sources and ways of cognition: first, through the organs of senses is obtained a knowledge of the ever-changing empirical world and phenomena which gives a very uncertain truth.   All the empirical sciences based on observation through organs of senses give this inferior and unlasting truth.   Plato disdainfully terms such a knowledge mere "opinion."   The second form or degree of knowledge is based partly upon the data of the organs of senses and partly upon the logical laws of human intelligence which uses and fashions the raw material of the organs of senses according to its own laws; for example, mathematics, geometry, and human logic itself.   Their verities are mainly those of the human mind or intelligence, and their certainties are much greater than those of the truths of senses.   Finally, the third and the most sublime form of knowledge is "divine intuition," or "divine contemplation," or "divine madness," which in an act of pure and sublime contemplation, divine inspiration, or mystic experience and revelation, goes beyond the empirical appearances, beyond even human logic, to the everlasting ultimate reality — the eternal Being — identifies itself with it and merges into it, not only from without but from within, and thus achieves complete, eternal, and certain knowledge — the supreme and absolute truth.[2]   This sublime, divine, or mystic form of truth cannot be

----

[2] See Plato, *Republic*, Bks. VI, VII, *et passim.   Timaeus, Phaedo, Phaedrus*, and practically all of Plato's *Dialogues*.   In them all he touches the problem (*e.g.*, in the *Symposium*, the *Ion*, the *Meno*, the *Gorgias*, the *Protagoras*) and with various shadings and accentuations gives essentially the same answer he himself asserts in the *Phaedo* that "I am now saying nothing new, but what I have always at other times never ceased to say."   *Phaedo*, in Everyman's Library ed., p. 180.

imparted by teaching or training because it is the gift of the gods, and only those who have this spark can grasp it.[3] From this standpoint Pierre Duhem [4] is right in saying that for Plato there were three categories of sciences: (1) theology as the most sublime, which deals with the eternal, ultimate, and unchangeable reality; (2) mathematics, as Mixed-empirical-intelligible form of knowledge which deals with the Mixed-eternal and changeable aspects of reality; (3) the most inferior form of knowledge or "opinion" — the empirical sciences which deal, on the basis of the perception, with the perishable and ever-changing empirical world of an incessant "corruption and generation."

It is not incidental also that for an allusion of the most sublime verities, Plato uses — and is forced to use, as an Ideationalist — a poetic-symbolic language, images, and terms. The Platonic system of truth and knowledge, then, embraces all the three main forms of truth — the truth of "divine madness or revelation," the truth of reason or intelligence, and the truth of senses. It also combines them, giving *suum quique*, into one coherent whole, in which empiricism is assigned an unimportant but a real place and divine contemplation is given the highest place. All this is shaped through and by the finest dialectic of human mind. Such a system is *idealistically rationalistic*, par excellence. It is neither pure empiricism, pure religious truth, nor even pure truth of intellect, but it is a combination of all dominated by the nonempirical forms of truth. The truth of faith still remains in it, but it is blended with other truths in such a way that it becomes radically different from the mere religious and magical credo of the preceding time as evidenced by and through logic of intelligence. It is not given as a mere *fiat* or *Credo quia absurdum*.[5]

---

[3] This is what Plato meant in his letter to Dionysius, who asked him for a short exposition of philosophy. "I have one thing to say about all writers, past or future, who claim to understand my philosophy. . . . All such claimants stand convicted of charlatanism on my showing. At any rate there is no written work of my own on my philosophy, and there never will be. *For this philosophy cannot possibly be put into words as other sciences can.*" Plato's *Letters*, No. 7, 341 B–E. And Plato means the same when in the *Republic* he, in explaining this highest knowledge at the request of Glauco not to omit the smallest matter in the explanation of it, says, "There will be a great deal omitted," in spite of his desire not to omit anything. In other words, such a sublime knowledge cannot be conveyed by words or taught. This is what all the mystics say. See the *Republic*, last part of the Bk. VI and Bk. VII. In Everyman's Library ed., pp. 217 ff.

[4] Pierre Duhem, *Le système du monde. Histoire des doctrines cosmologiques de Platon à Copernic* (Paris, 1913), Vol. I, pp. 133 ff.

[5] "In the tremendous achievement of Plato's philosophy . . . the antique power of myth-making was imbued with the fructifying logical intelligence to an unprecedented degree," rightly says W. Jaeger, *Aristotle* (Oxford, 1934), p. 372; Cf. Wilamowitz-Moellendorff, *op. cit.*, Vol. I, p. ii; Vol. II, pp. 246–258.

II — 6

Though the idealistically rationalistic theories of the other thinkers of the time differed from Plato's in many concrete forms, nevertheless they practically all represent a blending of the elements of all the three systems of truth and all claim their validity by and through logic of intelligence. In so far as the tone of this predominant system of truth of the fifth and the fourth centuries is already notably different from the tone of the un-questioning *truth of faith* of the preceding period, a different mental atmosphere exists. Though no detailed enumeration can explain the difference, we feel it as clearly as we feel the difference between two essentially different physical atmospheres or, likewise, between the tone of the Gregorian chants and the *Mass in B minor* by Bach or the *Missa solemnis* by Beethoven. We feel and know that the atmospheres of the systems of truth before the fifth century and that of the fifth and partly of the fourth centuries in Greece are very different. The term "idealistic rationalism" in the above sense, contrasted with the term "truth of faith," used here, imperfectly alludes to the great change that took place. Thus the period, as shown by an analysis of the dominant current based on the philosophical theory of its greatest representatives, corroborates this conclusion.

Besides Plato and the Platonic school, not to mention other rationalists of the period studied, idealistic rationalism was professed also by the other powerful school, the Peripatetic, whose great leader was Aristotle (384–322 B.C.). In spite of the fact that the elements of the truth of senses played a much larger part in the Aristotelian theory of truth than in the Platonic (that is also significant as an expression of the further increase of scientific discoveries and inventions and of a growing "sensualization" of the Greek culture as we pass from the fifth to the fourth centuries B.C. and from the first part of the fourth century to its second part), as a whole the Aristotelian theory of truth is a variety of the same idealistic rational-ism, embracing in its organic synthesis the elements of all the three systems of truth. The truth of the senses is given much more importance than in Plato's system; the truth of reason or logic, with its categories and the Noûs (though here lies one of the dark points of the Aristotelian logics), is not derived from perceptions but organizes perceptions of the senses into knowledge; and finally, the truth of theology or metaphysics is the ultimate and supreme knowledge with God, to which it leads and whose existence it states. All these three systems of truth are woven into one idealistically rationalistic system (in the sense given to this term in this work on page 6) which was in its essence more similar, so far as the aspect discussed is concerned, to the system of Plato, in spite of all the frequent criticism of the great teacher by his great disciple.[6]

These two schools were the great schools of the time and as such typify the dominant system of truth of that period. Though Aristotle's system tries to descend from the heavenly heights of Plato's idealism to the empirical reality, it is still in the same supersensible world of the idealistic essence, "the Form," "the Universals," "The Being and Eternal," "that which causes motion without itself being moved," "that is God" as the final cause and the end of the Universe.

In the field of the thought they both can be styled the Phidias and the Praxiteles. They possess the same traits, play the same role, and give the same type of creations as Phidias and Praxiteles in sculpture; as Polygnotus in drawing; as Pindar, Aeschylus, and Sophocles in literature and music. All are, to a somewhat different degree, the masters of idealistic cultural creations, similar in spirit, in style, in their whole *Weltanschauung*. Other rationalistic thinkers of the period (see the names in the Appendix to Chapter One) gave their own variations, but these were of the same idealistic rationalism. To be sure, there were other systems of truth (see the indicators of Tables 1 and 2), but they were not the most powerful ones.

Let us glance at the subsequent "confused" period. So far as Greek natural science is concerned, the fourth century produced fifty-two discoveries; the third century forty-two — a very high number of discoveries and inventions — but nevertheless lower than in the fourth century; the number then rapidly falls in the second and the first centuries B.C. to fourteen and twelve respectively. The indicators of the movements of the systems of truth unfortunately combine the Greek and the Roman streams. We may reasonably assume, however (see the names of the thinkers for the third and second centuries B.C. in the Appendix to Chapter One), that, up to the end of the second century B.C., the role of the Roman thinkers was practically insignificant and that the indicators show mainly the changes in the mentality of the Greek thinkers up to the end of the second century B.C.

[6] See particularly Aristotle, *Metaphysics, passim,* and in J. M'Mahon's translation, Bohn ed. (London, 1857), Bks. I, VI, VII, VIII, IX, and — about God — XI, chaps. vi ff.; Aristotle, *De anima, De caelo, De generatione et corruptione,* and his *Physics.* See also W. Jaeger, *op. cit., passim,* and Zeller, *Aristotle and the Earlier Peripatetics* (New York, 1897), trans. from Zeller, *Die Philosophie der Griechen,* particularly Vol. I, chaps. v–vii; A. Kazanski, *Aristotle's Theory of the Role of Experience in Cognition* (in Russian) (Odessa, 1891); A. E. Taylor, *Aristotle* (London, 1919); P. Duhem, *op. cit.,* Vol. I, chap. iv, and practically any competent study of the epistemology and metaphysics of Aristotle.

With this in mind, what spectrum of mentality is shown by the third and the second century B.C.? Compared with the spectrum of the fifth and the fourth centuries, it is the mentality of a further progressed Sensate system of truth which reached rapidly its zenith and was quickly permeated by the currents foreboding its decline. This is evidenced by a great decline of idealistic rationalism; by a comparative increase of empiricism; and especially by a great growth of fideism and skepticism. Thus a situation existed very similar to that which was encountered in the field of the Hellenistic art. In both cases from the end of the fourth to the end of the second centuries the progression was more and more toward Sensate mentality, and at the same time there were signs of the beginning of its end, so far as Greece was concerned.

When one remembers the main sociopolitical and cultural changes of the period (for Greece) and the main philosophical streams of thought that embody the above systems of truth — *cynicism, Stoicism, Epicureanism, and skepticism* — the above diagnosis of the spectrum becomes still more valid. During the third century Hellenistic Greece continued successfully its scientific work, as shown by the number of discoveries and inventions. Likewise, the mature Sensate culture continued to scintillate, spreading far and wide. Hence, a comparatively high level of empiricism. And yet at the same time shadows of the coming decline of this culture and empiricism quickly grew. After the Peloponnesian War (431–404 B.C.)

Greece was in all respects in a hopeless state of decline. . . . The old morality and propriety of conduct disappeared. . . . The old belief in the Gods was gone. Art could no longer compare with the excellence of the strictly classic period. The government became more ineffectual. Destitute of a political center of gravity, the Greeks drifted into a disgraceful dependence on the now declining Persian empire. . . . With the decline of civil order the well-being and martial prowess of the nation declined also.[7]

Each party as it gained the supremacy, in turn massacred the prominent members of the opposition. Tyrants in name or in reality; foreign adventurers in search of power or pleasure; mercenary troops with no national ties and respect for law, morality, or religion; exiles saturated with the gathered hatred of the years. These and similar inflammable conditions throughout Greece made the life of a peaceful inhabitant impossible. With no security for life and property, poverty and lawlessness spread apace; and the young not infrequently grew up indifferent to their country, sceptical of their religion, bent

[7] E. Zeller, *The Stoics, Epicureans, and Sceptics* (London, 1870), p. 12.

upon enjoyment, and seasoning sensuality with a dash of literary or philosophic cultivation. . . . Such was Greece in the beginning of the third century.[8]

About one hundred and thirty-five years elapsed from the time of Pericles to the organization of the Stoic school.   During this period occurred the Peloponnesian War (431–404) which ruined Greece; the collapse of Sparta before the Thebans at Leuctra (371); the subjection of Greece to Macedonia after Chaeronea (338).   Before the Peloponnesian War "superficial prosperity let loose a mood of recklessness and this, in turn, gave rise to the domineering selfishness that wrecked the generous co-operation of the citizens.   The moral tone slackened and irresponsibility led to factions.[9]

Whatever were the reasons, one thing is clear, that adaptation through a successful alteration of the exterior (social, biological, and cosmic) world became more and more difficult for Greek society after the end of the fourth century and especially after the third century B.C.   In spite of the progress of science and technique, failure tended to become more and more frequent.   Certainty and security tended to decrease; the seemingly solid foundation turned out to be fragile, and prosperity, glory, old religious and moral foundations disappeared.   "If all that faded into an empty dream, man found himself left naked to fortune."   Fear of insecurity and uncertainty grasped him.   Several schemes, plans, and theories were offered to free him from this insecurity, but in vain. "The result was not happiness. . . .   Mankind seemed to be driven hither and thither in a sea of contrary desires; one impulse overrode and frustrated another. . . .   The Fear became one of the constituents of human misery." [10]

Truth of faith and unquestioning religion were gone and could not serve as the basis of certainty and security.   Idealistic rationalism declined.   Empiricism and science remained as the only hopeful way of conquering these obstacles; but since empiricism was dying and insecurity was growing, skepticism and fideism appeared: skepticism as an indication of the hopelessness and the *vanitas vanitatum* of all the Sensate efforts of sincere skeptics and cynics, and as the beautifying "rationalization" for the sensual and nihilistic *Carpe diem* of (in my terminology) all the

[8] W. Wallace, *Epicureanism* (London, 1880), p. 34.   For a detailed description of this period see any of the important historical works on Greece, like Ferguson's *Hellenistic Athens*, quoted, R. P. Pohlmann, *Geschichte der sozialen Frage und des Sozialismus in der antiken Welt* (München, 1912); Wilamowitz-Moellendorff, *op. cit.*, Vol. II, pp. 261–427.

[9] R. M. Wenley, *Stoicism and Its Influence* (New York, 1927), p. 7.   See many important details in C. E. Robinson, *The Days of Alkibiades* (London, 1916).

[10] Edwin Bevan, *Stoics and Sceptics* (Oxford, 1913), p. 28.

passive and cynical Sensatists; fideism (and partly mysticism) as an artificial cocktail to brace up the desperate will to believe where serene and spontaneous belief was no more.   The four main currents of thought of the period — cynicism, skepticism, stoicism, and Epicureanism — were bearers of the most powerful systems of truth of the period — empiricism, skepticism, and fideism — and they all, in a sense, were the rationalization of the outlined status of the Greek culture.

In spite of their other differences, all these currents have one trait in common; namely, a tendency to turn away from the sensate reality — imperturbability (ataraxia) of Pyrrho and other Skeptics; freedom of body from pain and of mind from disturbance achieved through inner tranquillity of the Epicureans; a complete contempt for external environment by the Cynics; and the apathy and concentration on the inner self of many of the Stoics.   They all are similar and all advocate the achievement of happiness, equilibrium, peace of mind, even partly truth, or physical and mental adaptation, not so much through modification of the external environment as through modification of man himself and his mind.   Even empirical Epicureanism was not free from this trait.   Dr. Zeller rightly says:

The Epicurean imperturbability is akin to the imperturbability of the sceptics; both resemble the Stoic apathy.   All three Schools (also the Cynics, it may be added) are agreed that the only way to happiness consists in peace of mind and in avoiding all disturbances — disturbances sometimes arising from the external causes, at other times from internal emotions; they are only divided as to the means by which peace of mind may be secured.[11]

"If Pyrrhonism was the expression of weariness, of disgust with the endless strife of tongues, of the relief found in mere ceasing from effort and stagnation"[12] (ataraxia — not to bother oneself with anything external, even with knowledge or a care for knowledge), stoicism, cynicism, and even Epicureanism were also an attempt to escape from the sensate reality to an inner world of mind, vaguely conceived and self-suggested through a desperate will to believe.

To stem the tide of deterioration, and, if possible, to produce in men a healthy robust moral nature which would be able to resist the temptations to degeneracy and which would yield inward and abiding peace in the midst of the exceptional difficulties and trials that were inseparable from the exigencies

[11] E. Zeller, op. cit., p. 22; see also pp. 449, 457, 470, 492, et passim.   About the Skeptics see Mary Mills Patrick, The Greek Sceptics (New York, 1929).

[12] E. Bevan, op. cit., p. 125.

of the times, was one great object that Stoicism served, and for the accomplishment of which it was consciously called into existence.[13]

This drift from the sensate reality is quite conspicuous in their moral and ethical teachings;[14] in a less conspicuous form it is also present in their theory of truth and knowledge. In their positive program they did not reach Ideationalism; in their negative attitude to the sensate reality they all show, even the most sensate Epicureans, this tendency. Hence fideism and skepticism increased during this period. As a result the spectrum of mentality is one of overripe Sensate culture whose zenith is over.

III. MIXED PHASE OF GRAECO-ROMAN MENTALITY

Let us pass now to the mental spectrum of the next centuries. Beginning with the first century B.C. the Romans — meaning by the Romans not only the Romans by nationality but all the thinkers in the orbit of the Roman Empire — entered the field. Many of these were of Egyptian, Syrian, or of other Oriental extraction. The mental spectrum of these centuries was not a natural development of the previous Roman mentality but a violent transformation of it through the most effective influence of Hellenistic mentality complicated further by Oriental influences.[15] This heterogeneous factor is responsible in a great degree for the spectrum of the first century B.C. and the next centuries. Since Greek influence assumed the form of the Hellenistic mentality in the third and the second centuries B.C., it is not to be wondered at that the spectrum of the mentality in the first century B.C. was in a way a replica of the Hellenistic mentality in the third and the second centuries.

An examination of the diagram will show that in the first century B.C. almost all the field is occupied by a somewhat reinforced Epicurean empiricism, fideism, skepticism, mysticism, and a still less influential idealistic rationalism. Here, as in the field of art (see Volume One),

[13] W. L. Davidson, *The Stoic Creed* (Edinburgh, 1907), pp. 21–22. See also R. D. Hicks, *Stoic and Epicurean* (New York, 1910); A. Bonhöffer, *Epiktet und die Stoa;* Walter Pater, *Marius, the Epicurean*, 2 vols. (New York, 1920); E. Bignone, *Epicuro* (Bari, 1920).

[14] See the works mentioned.

[15] After the conquest of the Greek cities like Tarentum, Syracuse, and others, their art treasures began to be imported by conquerors in Rome (Fabius Maximus, Marcellus, and others). Beginning with the end of the second century the Hellenistic influence upon, especially, the intelligentsia and the upper classes became enormous in spite of the apprehension of the Roman Puritans of the deleterious effects of that influence. Many of the censors, beginning with Cato the Elder and ending with Cicero, Varro, Livy, Sallust, Plutarch, Seneca, and others, admired, imitated, and facilitated the spread of this influence.

the Roman intelligentsia imitated the overripe stage of the Hellenistic systems of truth. New strength, however, was given to the empirical system of truth by reinforcing it epistemologically as well as scientifically, through new discoveries and inventions. The number increased from three in both the third and second centuries B.C. to twenty during the first century B.C.

There was, then, not only a continuation of the development of the Hellenistic mentality, refreshed and reinforced in its empiricism, but also a parallel growth of empiricism and scientific discoveries. Perhaps, if the general constellation of Roman culture and society had been free from the tragic events of the first century B.C., empiricism would have continued to grow and would have kept the Roman system of truth on the level of balanced empiricism, free from the desperate forms of extreme skepticism, fideism, and mysticism. Such an expectation would have been justified because of the fact that the natural sciences progressed rapidly in the first century A.D. (there were thirty-five discoveries for the century — the maximum ever attained by Rome).

The total sociocultural constellation of the first centuries B.C. and A.D., with their tragic events, prevented such a development and resulted in the most *desperate and tragic spectrum of the Roman truth mentality of the first century* A.D. (See Tables 1 and 2 and Figure 1 in Chapter One.) Of all the twenty-five centuries it had the smallest percentage of idealistic rationalism; the lowest percentage of empiricism (with the exception of the medieval centuries), and more than 80 per cent of it was taken up by fideism and mysticism. Tragic and desperate spectrum indeed! And, yet, when the relevant factors are considered, such a spectrum is but natural. Why? First of all, so far as the role of the Hellenistic mentality of truth is concerned, we have seen that it itself was a mentality of the overripe Sensate culture devoid of certainty, wearied, and disillusioned. So far as it was imitated it could not give any solid certainty, security, faith. Its fragility and desperation were now enormously increased by the tragic events of the period, which destroyed temporarily even the balancing power of sound empiricism. It is enough to point out the main tragedies of the centuries considered in order to comprehend the inevitability of this tragic spectrum.

Roughly, from the end of the second century B.C., the first signs of a decline of the successful Sensate adaptation appeared. Outwardly Rome was still victorious and continued to mold the other societies into its own body, and it continued to grow. Inwardly conditions changed. Inner class struggles started and resulted in a series of riots, revolts, and the great civil wars of the first and the second triumvirates, which lasted, with short intervals of interruption, about one century.

During this period (the end of the second and the first centuries B.C.) life became exceedingly difficult. First, security of life was gone. Mass terror and mass slaughtering of the opponents of the temporarily victorious faction made security of life impossible. Incessant mass confiscations of property of the defeated faction reduced to zero the sacred right of property and material security. Farmers and peasants were dispossessed of their land and were turned into the urban proletariat. The proletariat itself — mental and intellectual — was placed in the position of a homeless, lawless, and propertyless parasite, poorly fed and poorly amused at the cost of the state. It became the bearer of the spirit of restlessness and destruction at the hands of the demagogues and politicians. Previous prosperity led to a development of sensuality and materialism; traditional rustic mores vanished. The result was a general demoralization. "Daily life had developed peculiar reasons for uncertainty." [16] Neither princes, nor senators, nor anybody felt secure. The riots of the subjugated countries, the invasions of the enemies, the revolts of the slaves, cessation of a further notable expansion of the Empire and consequently a decrease in the possibility of the exploitation of the newly subjected countries (*predia populi Romani*), and hundreds of other unfavorable circumstances aggravated the position of the Empire and its population enormously. From the economic, the political, psychological, and every other standpoint, conditions were going now from bad to worse.

The time of Augustus and a few other periods showed temporary improvement, but even then "a nameless unease, amounting to fear, sometimes assailed men. . . . A mist of unshed tears seems to haunt the stream of Virgil's genius . . . majestic in its sadness at the doubtful doom of human kind." [17] Similar presentiment is noticeable in Lucretius.[18] Among the masses the idea of the end of the world began to spread.[19]

After the first century, with a few breathing spells, the decline of the Roman Sensate culture, with its economic comfort, security, sentient pleasures, and so on, resumed its course and led to the so-called "Fall of the Roman Empire."

[16] R. M. Wenley, *op. cit.*, p. 45.   [17] *Ibid.*, pp. 40–41.

[18] Lucretius, *De rerum natura*, II, 1170 ff.

[19] See E. Renan, *L'Antéchrist* (Paris, 1873), pp. 444 ff.; *Les Évangiles* (Paris, 1877) pp. 358 ff.; *Philostorge* (Paris, 1866), pp. cxv and 137.

Let us expand a little the main points of this situation, as mentioned above.   The mental effects of such a desperate situation are almost always an enormous growth of the apocalyptic fideism and mysticism on the one hand and, on the other, cynical and nihilistic skepticism and *Carpe diem* sensualism.   This is what is reflected in our tables and what factually took place.

Since the active Sensate adaptation through change and improvement of the external world proved itself more and more helpless, a part of the people and thinkers began to turn more and more to the Ideational world in their ethical mentality as well as in their quest for truth and knowledge. The turning, however, was made in despair.   Therefore, it assumed not the form of calm and serene Ideational rationalism but that of fideism and mysticism — desperate and militant.

In order to understand this catastrophic psychology one has to bear in mind the situation of the social reality during the first and subsequent centuries of the Christian era.   The following lines from Ernest Renan's work perhaps make the picture as vivid as any other description.

When one reads the Apocalypse without knowing the date and the key to it, the book would appear to be the work of a most capricious and individualistic imagination; but when its strange vision is replaced by the picture of the period between Nero and Vespasian, when the Roman Empire experienced its most acute crisis, the Apocalypse will be found in marvelous accord with the state of the people's minds during the period; [20] even with that of the world because it appeared to be mad with miracles; never before had there been such a preoccupation with admonitions.   God seemed to have hidden his face and all kinds of impure larvae and monstrosities seemed to have been wandering in the air.   They believed themselves at the threshold of some catastrophe.   The belief in signs and miracles was universal. . . .   Meteors, comets, stars, and many other phenomena were given the most sinister and ominous interpretations. . . .   They talked but of showers of blood, astounding effects of lightning, the rivers swelling over their banks and streams full of blood. . . .   The "whips of the time" justified, however, to a certain degree these follies.   Blood was indeed flowing everywhere.   Nero's death opened the period of the civil wars.   The struggle of the legions in Gallia was horrible.   Galilee was the arena of an extraordinary extermination; the war with the Parthians was extraordinarily homicidal.   The cruelty of the military and civil mores banished any pity from the world.   Retreated, terrified and quivering, into their asylums the Christians undoubtedly were already repeating the words ascribed to Christ: "And when ye shall hear of wars and rumours of wars, be ye not troubled: for such things must needs be; but the end shall not be yet.   For

[20] See also Tacitus, *Histories*, I, 3, 18; *Annals*, XV, 47.

nation shall rise against nation, and kingdom against kingdom: and there shall be earthquakes in divers places, and there shall be famines, and troubles: these are the beginnings of sorrows." [21]

Famine joined the massacres. In the year 68 the supplies of Alexandria were insufficient. In March, 69, the inundation of the Tiber was exceedingly disastrous. Misery was extreme. A sudden flood from the sea covered mourning Lycia. In 65 a horrible pestilence afflicted Rome; in the fall there were thirty thousands dead. In the same year a terrible conflagration destroyed Lyon; Campania was ravaged by typhoons and cyclones whose devastations spread to the gates of Rome. The natural order appeared to be reversed; thunderstorms spread terror throughout the country. What, however, created the greatest terror were earthquakes. The earth was experiencing a convulsion similar to that of the moral world and mankind appeared to be suffering from fever. . . There was the terrible eruption of Vesuvius in 79. On February 5, 63, Pompeii was almost ruined by the trembling of the earth. . . .

And so on. Under these conditions, the expectation that the world would end and

the moral situation of the country [are] not surprising. . . . And so it was not only in Italy but in the whole Mediterranean region. For two centuries Asia Minor was in a state of perpetual terrestrial tremblings. The cities were incessantly being rebuilt; certain areas like Philadelphia experienced almost daily shocks. In the year A.D. 17, fourteen cities were demolished. . . . The years 23, 33, 37, 46, 51, 53 there were again similar misfortunes in Greece, Italy, Asia. . . . Beginning with the year 59, almost every year was marked by a great disaster. . . .

All this created a sort of a sombre atmosphere in which the imagination of the Christians found the strongest excitation. How, in view of this derangement of the physical and social world, could the believers help not crying with a greater assurance than before — *Maran atha! Maran atha!* Our Saviour has come! Our Saviour has come! The earth appeared to them to be falling down and already they believed that they saw the kings, the powerful, the rich in flight crying: "Mountains! fall upon us; hills! hide us."

A passage from Joel gave as symptoms of the coming of this great day (of the end of the world) certain signs in the heaven and on the earth, the rising of the prophets from all parts; the streams of blood, fire, the sun-eclipse, the bloody moon. They believed also that Jesus had announced the earthquakes, the famines, the pestilences as the overture to the great sufferings; and the eclipses, the obscured moon; the stars falling from the firmament; the whole skies trembling; the seas coming out of their borders; the population fleeing

[21] Mark xiii. 7–9; Luke xxi. 9–11; Matthew xxiv. 6–8.

lost in terror and not knowing which way was perdition and which was the salvation.[22]

Under these conditions the catastrophic and apocalyptic mentality was natural. Inevitable, also, was the firm belief in the approaching end of the world. We have more than enough evidence showing the widespread belief in this end by Christians, Jews, Gnostics, Roman Stoics, Neo-Platonists, Neo-Pythagoreanists.[23]

This belief persisted during the next centuries as the calamities continued. Studies of Parmentier, Mercati, Franz Cumont, Boissier, De Labriolle, and many others make it clear that since the first century of the Christian era

they regarded the end of the world as quite near. And these beliefs continued to grow toward the fifth century amidst the calamities which accompanied the invasions of the barbarians and the collapse of the Empire. In the Occident this belief grew stronger as the floods, invasions, and disasters accumulated. It finds especially strong expression and was often mentioned by Gregory the Great (604 A.D.). In the Orient destruction of the world was expected to take place during the first years of the sixth century, but these apprehensions did not survive the restoration of the Empire by Justinian.[24]

Relaxation of the mores at the beginning of the Christian Era has often been exaggerated, but it was real. Many unsound symptoms testify to a profound moral anarchy. As the end of the Empire approached the wills of the people seem to have been softened and the temperaments enervated. There was less and less of the robust soundness of character; greater became the diffusion of degeneration and deterioration which follow the orgies of the passions; the same weakness which led to crime was responsible for the attempts to find absolution in the practice of asceticism and the people went to the priests of the oriental religions, as to the physicians of soul, demanding spiritual remedies. . . . [Subsequently] the evils of the period caused enormous sufferings; during this violent and tormenting period there were so many undeserved ruins, so much unpunished crime that the people tried to find refuge in a better existence (after death) where all the iniquities of this world would be repaid. No earthly

[22] E. Renan, *L'Antéchrist* (Paris, 1873), pp. 325–339.

[23] See also E. Renan, *Les Évangiles* (Paris, 1877), pp. 356 ff. The end of the world and the last Judgment were believed in not only by the followers of Christianity, but also of several other religions, including many Romans and Hebrews.

[24] Franz Cumont in *Revue de Philologie* (1897), Vol. XXI, pp. 152–153. See also Boissier, *La fin du paganism* (Paris, 1891), Vol. II, pp. 452 ff. Pierre de Labriolle, *Histoire de la littérature latine chrétienne* (Paris, 1919), Introduction and *passim*. P. Gardner, *The Growth of Christianity*, Lecture III (London, 1907). St. Paul's I Corinthians xv. 51; I Thessalonians; *The Apocalypse of Baruch*, clxxxv. *The Ezra Apocalypse*, iv. 22–37; *The Epistle of Barnabas*. *Hermetica* (Oxford, 1924), 2 vols. trans. by W. Scott.

hope then illuminated life. The tyranny of corrupted bureaucracy suffocated any possibility of political progress. Stagnant sciences no longer rebelled at any more unknown verities. Arts, stamped by sterility, could only unskillfully reproduce the creations of the past. Progressive impoverishment discouraged every spirit of enterprise. More and more successfully spread the conviction that mankind approached irremediable decay, and that the end of the world was near. . . . In the stifling atmosphere of oppression and impotency the oppressed souls aspired, with an invincible ardour, to escape to the radiant horizon of the heaven.[25]

There was universal lust for gold; riches were the one ornament and stay of life. And yet a great fortune was only a splendid servitude. It had to be guarded amid perpetual peril and envy. Human life became a scene of cruel and selfish egotism; a ferocious struggle of beasts of prey, eager for rapine, and heedless of those who went down in the obscene struggle. It is little wonder that on such lives an utter weariness should settle the disgust of oversated appetite. . . . Yet these jaded souls were tortured by an aimless restlessness. . . . Oppressive terror and a thick atmosphere of gloom and foreboding seem to stifle us [26] [says a contemporary].

Such was the atmosphere among the aristocracy. Among the lower classes it was still gloomier. In all fields of creative activities the decline was setting in.

After Hadrian's reign (117–138) pure Roman literature, in any worthy sense, was extinct. There was no great historian after Tacitus; there was no great poet after Statius and Juvenal until the meteor-like apparition of Claudian in the ominous reign of Honorius. . . . The glory of classic art almost vanished.[27]

Only the material life, in short, spurting periods, revived and reached an outward splendor, but its foundations were fragile and the periods were short in this "age of the cities when engineers and architects turned villages into cities and built cities in the desert." [28]

It would be a miracle if in such an atmosphere mysticism and fideism would not develop, especially if the influence of the Hellenistic mentality

[25] F. Cumont, *Les religious orientales dans le paganisme romain* (Paris, 1929), pp. 38–40.

[26] S. Dill, *Roman Society from Nero to Marcus Aurelius* (London, 1925), pp. 10–22. See the whole book.

[27] *Ibid.*, pp. 3 and 4.

[28] *Ibid.*, p. 4. See about that part of Roman history in: M. I. Rostovtzeff, *Social and Economic History of the Roman Empire* (Oxford, 1926); S. Dill, *op. cit.*, and also, *Roman Society in the Last Century of the Western Empire* (London, 1919); J. P. Waltzing, *Étude historique sur les corporations professionelles chez les Romains* (Bruxelles, 1896); R. Pöhlmann, *Geschichte der soziale Frage*, quoted (München, 1912); Wilamovitz-Moellendorff, *op. cit.*, Vol. II, pp. 432–532; M. I. Rostovtzeff, *Mystic Italy* (New Haven, 1927).

and the decay of a spontaneous belief in the traditional gods and in religion among the upper Roman classes and the Graeco-Roman intelligentsia are considered.   Hence, there was an enormous increase of these desperate forms of the truth of faith in the first and subsequent centuries of the Christian era, which resulted in the temporary impotency (in the first century) of a balanced empiricism and of the large number of the scientific discoveries.

On the other hand, such a catastrophic constellation favored also a development of nihilism, cynical skepticism, or passive and cynical Epicureanism.   In the first century of the Christian era it did not manifest itself among the thinkers — conditions were too catastrophic; but among the rank and file of the middle classes and among the thinkers of the second and the third centuries it appeared.   As often happens, its beginnings in the form of a noble and moderate Epicureanism similar to that of Epicurus, with its imperturbability, prevailed among the intelligentsia in the first century B.C.

In the time of Lucretius (c. 95–55 B.C.) it had already found excellent expression in his *De rerum natura* and had spread considerably within the Roman intellectual circles.   "Its adepts in Cicero's circles were numerous, including Cassius, the murderer of Caesar. . . .   Men of science, in particular, were attracted by these theories." [29]

Subsequently its diffusion among the majority of the population began. At an earlier stage in Rome its influence was very moderate and the notes of cynicism and despair consisted mainly of a quite philosophic denial of any existence after death and in the appraisal of death as an eternal rest and way out from sorrows and worries.   It did not advocate *Carpe diem* behavior in any great degree.   Only balanced enjoyment, a short life — from nothing to nothing — was advocated by Lucretius, Sallust (86–34 B.C.), Horace (65–8 B.C.), Ovid (43 B.C.–A.D. 17), Pliny the Elder (A.D. 23–79), and many others.

For Lucretius death was "a blessed calm, the perfect quietude, or ataraxia."   For Sallust it was "the rest from torment which dispels the ills which afflict mankind."   For Pliny the Elder it was "the greatest boon which belongs to our nature," the "tranquillity" of which there is nothing to be afraid of.[30]   For an unknown man it was also a boon; "horror does not seize me when I think of the putrefaction of my body, nothing further touches us," as was written on a tombstone.[31]   And many other unknown citizens left similar epitaphs on their tombstones that testified

---

[29] F. Cumont, *After Life in Roman Paganism* (New Haven, 1922), p. 8.
[30] *Ibid.*, pp. 8–9.   [31] *Ibid.*, pp. 10–11.

to the considerable diffusion of such an attitude of life and adaptation. "I was; I am not; I do not care." "I paid my debt to nature and have departed," wrote many. "What remains of man, my bones, rests sweetly here. I no longer have the fear of starvation; I am exempt from attacks of gout; my body is no longer pledged for my rent; and I enjoy free and perpetual hospitality," and so on.

In all this there was a note of weariness of life, disillusionment, cynicism, and skepticism. Later on, and with the great masses of people, it changed into the desperate tone of the *Carpe diem*, and bitter and cynical disappointment became extreme.

Summing up the epitaphs on the tombs of the Romans, Dr. Cumont says:

Often a grosser Epicureanism recommends that we make profit of our earthly passage since the fatal term (death) deprives us forever of the pleasures which are the sovereign good. "*Es bibe lude veni*" — "Eat, drink, play, come hither" is advice which is several times repeated. Not uncommonly, variations occur, inspired by the famous epitaph which was on the alleged tomb of Sardanapalus and is resumed in the admonition: "Indulge in voluptuousness, for only this pleasure wilt thou carry away with thee!" or as it is expressed in the Epistle to the Corinthians, "Let us eat and drink, for tomorrow we die." So we read on a stone found near Beneventum: "What I have eaten and what I have drunk; that is all that belongs to me." A well-known distich states that "Baths, wine, and love impair our bodies, but baths, wine, and love make life"; and a veteran of the army had advice based on his own example engraved on his tomb: "While I lived, I drank willingly; drink, ye who live." The exhortation to enjoy a life soon to be interrupted by death is a traditional theme which has lent itself to many developments in ancient and modern poetry. Some silver goblets, found in Boscoreale near Pompeii, indicate that philosophers and poets were among the dead, and inscriptions urging man to rejoice while he lives, since no man is certain of the morrow. Epicurus appears in person, his hand stretching towards a cake on a table; and between his legs is a little pig lifting his feet and snout to the cake to take his share of it. Above the cake are the Greek words: "The supreme end is pleasure." Horace, when he advises us to live from day to day without poisoning the passing hour with hopes or fears for the future, speaks of himself, jestingly, as a fat "hog of Epicurus' herd." It was thus that the vulgar interpreted the precepts of him who had in reality preached moderation and renunciation as the means of reaching true happiness.[32]

It is difficult to find a more extreme expression of the Epicureanism of despair. This philosophy, during the period of Rome's decline, affected

[32] *Ibid.*, pp. 11–12. See also M. Rostovtzeff, *History of the Ancient World*, Vol. II, p. 206. *Social and Economic History of the Roman Empire*, pp. 75–77.

not only the uneducated but the intellectuals as well, like Lucian (A.D. 120–200), who wrote: "The altars of Zeus are as cold as Chrysippus. Religion is absurd, philosophy vacuous, therefore, let us enjoy the moment, eschewing enthusiasms." [33]   For a short time society can believe in such a *Carpe diem*, but it cannot continue to do so indefinitely.   An examination of Tables 1 and 2 and Figure 1 discloses that after the third century this Epicurean skepticism and nihilism disappeared.

IV. The Rising Tide of Ideational Truth of Faith

Stoics, Neo-Platonists, Neo-Pythagoreans, Gnostics, even some of the real Epicureans (see the Appendix to Chapter One) among the Pagans, all more and more began to subscribe to mysticism and fideism as the desperate forms of the rising Ideational system of truth. The partisans of various esoteric and mystic religions and sects, with which the Roman culture began to be flooded, did likewise.   Finally, the Christians, who were destined to absorb all these rivulets, became the main bearers of the rising Ideational truth and the main destroyers of the truth of senses and even of pure reason (for these first centuries of the Christian era).   Though during the second and especially the third centuries A.D. the empirical system of truth rose again — after its depression in the first century — and though scientific discoveries continued during these centuries, amounting to eighteen, six, sixteen in the Graeco-Roman world for the second, third, and fourth centuries respectively, the last flaring up of the Graeco-Roman empiricism and science before its long-time sleep took place.   After the third century empiricism rapidly waned and in the sixth century disappeared; likewise, the number of scientific discoveries decreased to only four in the fifth, sixth, and seventh centuries.   The Sensate culture mentality and system of truth declined and the new Ideational mentality and truth rose in influence.   During the first centuries of its growth, Ideational truth assumed the desperate form of mysticism and fideism on account of sociocultural conditions and its struggle for existence and growth.   After the fifth century A.D., when its victory was secured, mysticism and fideism gave place to Ideational rationalism as the serene and confident system of truth of faith.

In the light of the preceding conditions it must be obvious that the *first five or six centuries of the Christian era were periods in which one of the greatest mental revolutions occurred.*   During these centuries the Graeco-Roman and then the Western mentality changed from the predominant

[33] Wenley, *op. cit.*, p. 69. See also P. Gardner-Smith, *The Church in the Roman Empire* (Cambridge, 1932), pp. 9 ff.

system of truth of senses to that of truth of faith. It was accomplished, as is any great mental revolution, not without bitter mental and moral clashes of the radically different systems of truth. The partisans (the Christians) of the rising Ideational truth realized fully its incompatibility with the truth of senses and of reason and were fully aware of what they were doing when they pitilessly attacked the truth of senses and the truth of reason. The partisans (the scholars, intellectuals, scientists, and philosophers) of the declining truth of senses and of reason seem not to have understood, especially at the beginning of the struggle, the gravity of the situation and the mortal danger in which their system of truth and knowledge was placed. Like many contemporary scientists and scholars, they regarded the Christian, as well as other Ideational systems of truth, as mere superstition or ignorance, destined to disappear with increasing knowledge and incapable of menacing science, and still less capable of growing and becoming the monopolistic system of truth for the next thousand years. Like ourselves they believed that after the brilliant progress of science and philosophy their further progress and growth were secured.

And yet, contrary to their firm belief,[34] the truth of an unquestioning and professedly illogical, irrational, un-Sensate, or, to use the current jargon, "an unscientific, blind, superstitious," truth of faith came and

[34] Not only generally in regard to the truth of faith, but in regard to Christianity, the attitude of the Roman "intelligentsia" was identical with the above and the majority of them considered it but superstition and ignorance and did not expect that it was destined to triumph over their science and enlightened philosophy. Pliny's and Tacitus's attitudes are typical. For Tacitus Christianity was but "a dangerous superstition," belonging to the class of "infamous and abominable" currents that flow into the city of Rome "from all quarters of the world." Tacitus, *Annals*, XV, 44 (Everyman's Library ed., pp. 486–487). Likewise for Pliny it was "nothing but a debased superstition carried to great length." Pliny, *Epistles*, X, xcvi, 8. Not very different was the attitude of many Pagan intellectuals and the "educated and sophisticated Romans." For Marcus Aurelius (XI, 3) Christianity was merely an unreasoned, intemperate, and theatrical spirit of opposition. For Celsus Christians were "like folk who put an illogical faith in those who collect alms for the Great Mother and in examiners of portents. . . . They will not give or hear reason about their faith, but stick to *Ask no question but believe* and *Thy faith shall save thee* and *The wisdom in the world is a bad thing and the foolishness a good.*" In brief, ignoramuses, charlatans, presti-digitators, and the like. Suetonius (in *Nero*, XVI, 2) brands Christianity as a "novel and maleficent superstition." See some interesting details also in A. D. Nock, *Conversion* (1933), chaps. xiii and xiv. Also A. Drachmann: *Atheism*, chap. vii, and the works of Lake, Cumont, Renan, and Jackson, quoted. When I hear nowadays similar statements about the progress of the human mind, about the present and the future progress of science, about the vanishing forever of the age of faith and superstition, and all similar statements of scholars, scientists, journalists, politicians, preachers, teachers, talkers before women's and men's clubs, and so on and so forth, I often have an impulse to style them as "unteachable fellows" who have learned nothing and who know little about such matters.

was monopolistic for almost nine centuries in the form of the system of truth of the Christian Faith.

One of the greatest and deepest mental transformations in the history of mankind — the revolution in the very foundations of truth, knowledge, wisdom, upon which depend and by which are conditioned all the superstructures of all the theories and opinions about everything, in any field of culture and in any compartment of the mental activity, in the sciences, in the arts, in philosophy, in ethics and law, and what not — took place.

Its essence was a complete shift from the truth of senses and that of the reason, and from the vagaries of skepticism, fideism, and other systems of mental weariness and disillusionment, to the fiat, dogmatic, superrational, supersensible, superskeptical, superfideistic *truth of pure faith*, openly negligent and disdainful of all other sources of truth and knowledge *except faith and divine revelation*. Yes, it was a triumphant revolt of faith against empirical science and logical philosophy which ended in the dictatorship of the truth of faith over all its rivals.

Such in brief was the essence of this great mental revolution. Many, even among authorities, seem not to realize this clearly and perhaps will consider my characterization exaggerated. Others may believe that such a fundamental change occurred but that the men of the time, especially the Christian thinkers, the Apostles, the Church Fathers, were unconscious that such a revolution was taking place; and that, in any event, they did not intentionally strive for it. In order to point out fallacies of such opinions and also to get a closer insight into the great transformation of the system of truth and of the whole mentality, it would be advisable to pause at this time in order to obtain a better comprehension of the mentality of the Christian thinkers and also of the Pagan thinkers of the period because, as mentioned previously, the trend of thought of some Pagan thinkers was essentially in the same direction as that of the Christian thinkers, expressed, however, not so radically. A mere glance through their writings shows at once that they fully realized the fundamentally different nature of their truth from that of the previous centuries and conscientiously strove to repudiate the truth of senses and the truth of reason as independent from faith, and to secure and to propagate the Divine Gospel of Faith and Revelation. Using the simile of the current language, we may say that, like the contemporary revolutionists against social order, they *expressis verbis* proclaimed that they were overthrowing the regime of the bourgeois empiricism and that of the liberal reason, and that they were striving for the dictatorship of the faith. A cursory survey of the "speech reactions" and a few quotations of the early Christians are sufficient to show that these statements are true.

Already the Apostles, who had absolute confidence in the truth of the Gospel, revelation, and prophetic gift, clearly and unequivocally expressed this negative attitude toward empirical science, the empirical system of truth, and logical reason.

"They turn not to science and philosophy but to prophecy for demonstration" of many of their truths, like the tragedy of the cross and other messages of the Gospel.   For instance, "All the prophets as the mouthpieces of God's will have foreshown that Christ should suffer, and in his death these prophecies have been fulfilled." [35]

Likewise, divine inspiration of the Holy Spirit is another source and absolute criterion of truth — the source and criterion perfectly unacceptable to empiricism. The scene on Pentecost day,[36] when the Holy Spirit "hath poured forth this," is a familiar instance of this belief.

Likewise the Gospel itself, as *the glad tidings* about Jesus, does not pretend to prove its truths by empirical tests, but by faith and creed. The Apostles, including St. Paul, do not teach the gospel of empirical experience but the "Gospel of God," "the word of the Lord," "the word of faith," or "the truth." [37]

"We preach not ourselves, but Christ Jesus," says St. Paul.[38]   And in the Epistle to the Galatians he definitely states that he received this Gospel or the word of faith not from man but through direct revelation from Christ.[39]   Naturally, on the basis of this truth of faith the Apostles asserted and believed in the existence of the devil, angels, demons, and other nonempirical or superempirical creatures. In harmony with it they asserted and believed in miracles and in many things which the empirical system of truth denies and rejects. In brief, in its constructive aspect the system of truth of early Christianity is one of the purest militant forms of the truth of faith, diametrically opposite to the truth of senses and reason, to science and logic,[40] which prevailed before and at the beginning of Christianity.

[35] James Mackinnon, *The Gospel in the Early Church, A Study of the Early Development of Christian Thought* (London and New York, 1933), p. 5. See I Peter i. 10–11; Luke xxiv. 25 f. and 46; Acts iii. 18.

[36] Acts i. 16 and 33.

[37] I Thessalonians i. 6 and 8; Romans x. 8.

[38] II Corinthians iv. 5.

[39] Galatians i. 12.

[40] See many details in K. Lake, *The Beginnings of Christianity* (London, 1920–1926), 3 vols.

Quite consistently, therefore, the early Christian thinkers unequivocally rejected *expressis verbis* the empirico-Sensate and even rationalistic systems of truth.

Paul has a profound contempt for Philosophy [and still greater for the empirical science, one can add] or "the wisdom of this world," "the wisdom of men," as he calls it. He depreciates reason and the exercise of reason, as exemplified by the philosophers, in the search of God and the good. . . . Saving knowledge in his sense, knowledge of God in Christ — the only knowledge that matters is a thing solely of revelation.[41]

From this standpoint "the wisdom of this world is foolishness with God." [42] Similar, perhaps even more forceful, language is used by the early Christian thinkers and Church Fathers in their radical rejection of the testimony of the organs of senses or of reason (respectively empirical and rationalistic systems of truth) as the criteria of truth. Here are a few examples out of the many with which their writings are filled.[43]

In the *Epistle to Diognetus* (c. A.D. 140) of St. Polycarp (A.D. 110–156) we read:

Their knowledge (that of the Christians) has not been discovered by the thought and effort of inquisitive men; they are not champions of a human doctrine. . . . God himself in very truth . . . planted among men and established in their hearts the Truth and the holy teaching which surpasseth the wit of man.[44]

In Justin's *Dialogue with Trypho* (c. A.D. 160) it is said:

There once lived men called Prophets, who were the predecessors of any of those who are considered philosophers, and who were blessed, just, and beloved by God. These spoke of the Holy Ghost. And they alone knew and taught the truth. . . . Whoever reads them will derive much instruction about the

[41] James Mackinnon, *op. cit.*, pp. 139–140.

[42] I Corinthians iii. 18–19. See also I Corinthians i. 20 f. and ii. 5.

[43] It is to be noted that among the Pagan thinkers of these centuries, a similar process was taking place: empiricism and its system of truth was losing prestige, and the truth of faith (not Christian) was gaining ground. In varied concrete form the change in the mentality of truth was moving in the same direction as the change in the mentality of the Christians; *i.e.*, from the truth of senses and logic to the truth of faith and revelation. This applies to the Gnostics, the Neo-Platonists, and a large number of "schools and sects" in the period. See W. Bousset, *Hauptprobleme der Gnosis* (Tübingen, 1907): S. Angus, *The Mystery Religion and Christianity* (London, 1925); F. Cumont, *Les religions orientales dans le paganisme romain;* M. de Wulf, *History of Medieval Philosophy* (London, 1909), 70 ff.; J. F. Toutain, *Les cultes paiens dans l'empire romain* (Paris, 1907–1920), 3 vols.; P. Gardner-Smith, *op. cit.*, 64 ff.; F. J. Foakes Jackson, *An Introduction to the History of Christianity* (New York, 1921).

[44] I am quoting from B. J. Kidd (ed.), *Documents Illustrating the History of the Church,* (New York, 1920), Vol. I, pp. 55 ff.

first principles. . . . They have not indeed given demonstration in their writings, for they are in fact above all demonstration as faithful witnesses of the truth. . . . Do you above all things pray that the gates of light may be opened to you; for these things are not to be seen or comprehended except of him to whom God and His Christ give the grace of understanding.[45]

Already in these two excerpts the whole theory of the truth of the pure faith is excellently formulated and unflinchingly set forth. Let us read carefully the sayings of other Christian leaders of the period discussed. In the *Legatio pro Christianis* of Athenagoras (*c.* A.D. 177) we read:

Poets and philosophers . . . have not been found competent fully to apprehend the truth, because they thought fit to learn, not from God concerning God, but each one from himself; hence they came each one to his own conclusion respecting God, matter, forms, and the world. But we have for witnesses of the things we apprehend and believe, prophets, men . . . guided by the spirit of God. [Therefore] it would be irrational for us to cease to believe in the spirit of God . . . and to give heed to mere human opinions.[46]

In the *Octavius* of Minucius Felix (*c.* A.D. 180) the note of contempt toward human knowledge, science, and philosophy (empiricism and rationalism) is still more conspicuous.

Everything in human affairs is doubtful, uncertain, undecided, and probable rather than true. . . . Surely all (intellectuals) must feel grieved and indignant at the thought that certain people (Christians) — people, too, ignorant of learning, unlettered, and unacquainted even with the meanest arts — should pronounce definitely upon the universe and the supreme power, which, after all these ages, still form the subjects of the deliberations of the philosophers and their numerous schools. And this is only natural, since human insignificance is quite incapable of investigating things divine.[47]

When we pass to the writings of Irenaeus (*Adv. haereses, c.* 185), of Clement of Alexandria (*Stromateis, c.* 200), of Origen (185–254), (*Philocalia*), especially of Tertullian (*Apology, c.* 197), then of St. Jerome (*Epistles, c.* 384), of Athanasius (*Ad monachos, c.* 358–360); of St. Basil of Caesarea (*Epistles, c.* 370–379), of Gregory of Nazianus (*Orations, d.* 390), and, omitting other names, of St. Augustine, the same motives and statements are reiterated still more powerfully and the negatively

---

[45] *Ibid.*, Vol. I., pp. 79–80. See also "documents" on pp. 64–65, where again and again St. Paul's (I Corinthians ii. 9) pronouncement of the Christian truth, "neither hath ear heard nor eye seen," is reiterated.

[46] *Ibid.*, Vol. I, p. 107. See similar statements in the *Ad Autolycum*, pp. 111–112.

[47] *Ibid.*, Vol. I, pp. 112–113.

contemptuous estimation of human knowledge — empirical or rational — becomes still sharper and still more emphatic.[48]

For Origen "Scriptures were written by the Spirit of God" and are infinitely more true than science and philosophy, which at best only in some points approach the truth.[49]

Temperamental Tertullian was especially wild in his denunciation of the worldly wisdom. Philosophers (including scientists) are for him but "patriarchs of heresy." "Philosophy is the theme of worldly wisdom, that rash interpreter of the Divine Nature and Order. And in fact, heresies are themselves equipped by philosophy." He further cites that the heretic theory of "aeons" of Valentinus is taken from Plato; "the better God" of Marcion, from the Stoics. "And the soul is affirmed to perish" — a tenet that is taken from the Epicureans. Similarly he criticizes the theories of Zeno, Herakleitos, and then Aristotle. Here is his evaluation of him.

Wretched Aristotle! who established . . . the dialectic art, so ingenious . . . so crafty . . . so inflexible . . . so damaging even to itself, always reconsidering everything, so that nothing is treated thoroughly.

And in contrast to this he asserts "the Rule of Faith." "This Rule, taught by Christ, admits no questioning amongst us." In his *De Anima* he reiterates: "We acknowledge spiritual charismata or gifts" to see the truth, to converse with angels, etc. "O testimony of a soul, by nature Christian!" which knows God and the Truth directly.[50]

Still more emphatically he asserts:

What is there in common between Athens and Jerusalem, between the Academy and the Church? . . . The worse for those who talk of the Stoic, Platonic, and Dialectic Christianity. For us we do not have any curiosity after Jesus Christ, nor any research after the Gospel. . . . *Hesterni sumus, et vestra omnia implevimus* ("We are men of yesterday and yet we have filled your world"),

proudly says he.

As the climax of this denunciation of any form of knowledge and truth except the truth of Christian Faith is his famous masterpiece:

Crucifixus est Dei Filius; non pudet, quia pudendum est. Et mortuus est Dei Filius; prorsus credibile est, quia ineptum est. Et sepultus resurrexit; certum est, quia impossible est. Credo quia absurdum.

---

[48] *Ibid.*, Vols. I and II of the work quoted.
[49] *Ibid.*, Vol. I, pp. 175 and 182.
[50] *Ibid.*, pp. 141. See especially his *Apologeticus adversus gentes.*

(The Son of God is crucified; that is not shameful because it is shameful. And the Son of God died; that is credible because it is absurd. And He rose from the dead; that is quite certain because it is impossible. . . . I believe because it is absurd.)[51]

It would be difficult to denunciate more sarcastically and powerfully all empirical knowledge as well as all the logic of human intelligence.

Other Church Fathers like Origen and Clement of Alexandria were not so "bolshevistic" as Tertullian toward empirical science and philosophy. "Faith, then, is a compendious knowledge of the essentials. . . . Before the Advent of the Lord, philosophy was necessary to the Greeks for righteousness. And now it becomes conducive to piety." [52]

In spite of a touching note, in St. Jerome's letter, of his vision, the final outcome of his great devotion to the Graeco-Roman science and philosophy was also harshly negative. He tells us that he lived in a comfortable house, had an excellent classical library consisting of the works of Cicero, Plautus, and others, and that even after his conversion to Christianity he could not cease to enjoy reading and studying these works; and that when he became sick, he had a vision in which he heard a voice reproaching him. "Thou liest, thou art a follower of Cicero, not of Christ." After that he gave up his "Ciceronism" and vowed:

Lord, if ever again I possess worldly books, or if ever again I read such, I have denied Thee! . . . Thenceforth I read the books of God with a zeal greater than I have previously given to the books of men.[53]

Somewhat similar is the confession and the attitude of Basil the Great.

Much time had I spent in vanity and had wasted nearly all my youth in vain labour . . . in acquiring the wisdom made foolish by God. Then . . . I turned my eyes to the marvelous light of the Truth of the Gospel, and I perceived the uselessness of "the princes of the world that come to naught."

He visited the hermits and wrote:

I admired their consistency in living, and their endurance in toil; I was amazed at their persistency in prayer, and at their triumphing over sleep; subdued by no natural necessity, ever keeping their soul's purpose high and free, in hunger, in thirst, in cold, in nakedness, they never yielded to the body.[54]

And finally, St. Augustine, who, like St. Jerome and St. Basil, was before his conversion one of the leading intellectuals of his age, well

[51] See Pierre de Labriolle, op. cit., pp. 23 ff., and the Introduction.
[52] Kidd, op. cit., Vol. I, pp. 159-160.
[53] Ibid., Vol. II, pp. 181.
[54] Ibid., Vol. II, pp. 90-91.

versed in Graeco-Roman science and philosophy, expressed all this in a still more emphatic and temperamental form, similar to the "bolshe-vistic" denunciation of all Human Wisdom and all systems of Truth, except that of the Gospel, by Tertullian.[55]

After St. Augustine's conversion to Christianity his attitude toward the whole Graeco-Roman culture and social world was purely "bolshe-vistic." Rhetoricians, scientists, and philosophers are for him "the buyers and sellers of grammar rules," [56] "the deceivers and babblers," [57] "full of deceits and tricks"; Roman history and culture are nothing but a tale of "slaughtering, bloodshed, inhumanity, riot, rapine," and so on; [58] the Roman religion and others are but vile inventions of "the unjust and devil-like princes" for the exploitation of the people; [59] Homer and the whole art and literature are "immodest fables"; [60] law is but the art of deception and injustice.[61] In brief, the whole Roman and Greek and generally the non-Christian science, philosophy, and culture, and also, the values, institutions, and external social world are denounced, reviled, and rejected.

Augustine's positive program is the pure truth of the Christian faith, divinely revealed, and as such, being supersensible, superrational, super-logical, is directed toward the ultimate reality which is God. *Deum et animam scire cupio. Nihilne plus? Nihil omnino*, such is his motto.

O, thou supreme, most powerful, most merciful, most just, most secret, most present, most beautiful, most mighty; most constant and incomprehensible; immutable, yet changing all things; never new and never old, yet renewing all things, and drawing such as are proud into decay, although they mark it not. Ever in action, and ever quiet; heaping up, yet needing nothing; upholding, filling and protecting, creating, nourishing and perfecting all things. . . . Thou art Truth indeed, wherein there is no change, no shadow of alteration. . . . God is a spirit who has no parts either of length or of breadth and has no bulk . . . incorruptible, and inviolable, and unchange-able.[62]

When Desiderius, Archbishop of Vienna, wanted to revive a study of the ancient authors, he was severely reproved by Gregory the Great (the Pope, *d.* 604). Likewise, under Charlemagne, Alcuin, though he

---

[55] About animosity of the Fathers toward Pagan astronomy, physics, and natural science, see especially P. Duhem, *Le système du monde* (Paris, 1914), Vol. II, pp. 393–408.

[56] St. Augustine, *Confessions*, trans. by Sir Tobie Mathews (London, 1923), p. 25.

[57] *Ibid.*, pp. 146 and 177.

[58] St. Augustine, *The City of God*, trans. by John Healy (n. d.), Vol. I, p. 37.

[59] *Ibid.*, p. 212.   [60] St. Augustine, *Confessions*, pp. 21 ff.

[61] *Ibid.*, p. 48.   [62] *Ibid.*, pp. 6, 9, 55, and 144.

had an excellent library of the ancient philosophers, strongly reproved a monk who wanted to study Virgil, styling him as "Virgilian" (similar to St. Jerome's "Ciceronianus"), saying that "the sacred poets are enough for you."

It is unnecessary to continue these quotations. Practically the same position was taken by almost all the Christian thinkers.

It is proved that during the first centuries of our era in the Orient as well as in the Occident, there was a large number of Christians who were the enemies of the ancient culture and who, being content with their single faith and with the single book, the Bible, voluntarily rejected — without any distinction and specification — the intellectual heritage of the ancient world.

Most of them

proclaimed that the whole of the *doctrina saecularis literaturae* is stupid in the eyes of God; that the philosophers (including scientists and scholars) were "the traders in wisdom and eloquence" and saw in dialectics invented by the "pitiful Aristotle" the mother of the heresies.[63]

Such a mental revolution, as mentioned, was not limited to the Christian thinkers of the period. A similar trend toward rejection of empirical and rationalistic systems of truth prevailed also among the Pagan thinkers, which was shown previously by my indicators. Qualitatively the main currents of the period like Neo-Platonism, Gnosticism, Donatism, Neo-Pythagoreanism, Pythagorean Platonism, Graeco-Judaic philosophy (Philo and others), not to mention other currents, shared with Christianity a negative attitude toward the empirical and purely rationalistic systems of truth and knowledge.

All these systems became theurgic and religious.

The most striking feature of Neo-Platonism is religious mysticism. Man must conquer his sense-feelings by struggling against them; he must draw near to God by a series of steps or stages, and unite himself to the Infinite by employing aids of religious nature.[64]

[63] De Labriolle, *op. cit.*, pp. 25–26. See many details in this and other quoted works. See in addition: R. L. Poole, *Mediaeval Thought and Learning*, 2d ed., pp. 7 ff.; H. M. Gwatkin, *Early Church History to 313*, 2 vols. (London, 1909); Monsignor Duchesne, *Early History of the Christian Church* (New York, 1924), Vol. III; G. G. Coulton (Cambridge, 1930), *The Mediaeval Scene*, pp. 13 ff., and the well-known works of H. O. Taylor, *Mediaeval Mind*, 2 vols. (London, 1922); K. Lake, *The Apostolic Fathers*, 2 vols. (New York, 1912–1913); C. T. Cruttwell, *A Literary History of Early Christianity* (London, 1893), 2 vols.; F. J. Foakes-Jackson, *An Introduction to the History of Christianity* (New York, 1921), and others, quoted, further.

[64] Maurice de Wulf, *History of Medieval Philosophy* (London and New York, 1909), pp. 70 ff.

Plotinus, the greatest thinker of the period, had the same negative and contemptuous attitude toward empirical and rationalized knowledge as did the Christian Church Fathers.

Thus, during these six centuries from the beginning of our era this supposedly superstitious and ignorant system of truth of faith emerged and grew, and, contrary to the expectations and beliefs of many intellectuals of these first few centuries of our era, the empirical and rationalistic systems of truth were conquered and driven out, with all the infinitely great and numerous changes of mentality which such a transformation involved.

V. Truth of Faith Triumphant

As my tables show, after the sixth century the victory of the truth of faith was complete and during the next six or seven centuries it dominated the mentality. (See Tables 1 and 2 and Figure 1.) The truth of reason as such ceased to exist; the logic of reason was, of course, employed to some extent, but only in a subservient role of a "handmaid" to theology and only in so far as it could serve without the slightest contradiction to the truth of faith.[65] *Credo ut intellegam* and *intelligo ut credam*, such is its essence.

"There were theologians who would not be philosophers; so far as we know, there were no philosophers who were not theologians." [66] "The thought of the Middle Ages was essentially theocentric and the great Medieval thinkers were one and all of them theologians; as soon as this ceased to be, the Renaissance may be said to have begun." [67]

We shall see elsewhere that it has in all its fundamental principles the earmarks of the system of truth of faith. And not because of fear or other motives, but spontaneously, the thought of the thinkers from about the sixth to the twelfth centuries turned to this system with almost no attempt to assert the right of the truth of the senses or that of the reason. Even the systems of a few of the greatest thinkers of the period (like that of John Scotus Erigena, ninth century), for example, which were condemned as unorthodox, were thoroughly permeated by the truth of faith, and reason was merely subservient.

Possibly merely the novelty of some of the rationalistic considera-

[65] In Tables 1 and 2 and Figure 1 it can be seen that during this period there was an almost complete domination of rationalism. It is to be understood, however, that this rationalism was not an independent or idealistic rationalism, but was theology or the truth of faith.

[66] Maurice de Wulf, *History of Medieval Philosophy* (New York, 1909), pp. 70 ff.; C. Guignebert, *Christianity, Past and Present* (New York, 1927), pp. 208 ff.

[67] C. R. S. Harris, "Philosophy" in the *Legacy of the Middle Ages*, cited, p. 227.

tions was responsible for their condemnation as heresy, a fact which in itself is eloquent evidence of the "monolithic" mentality and unlimited domination of the truth of faith in the period discussed.[68]

With such a change in the very system of truth all the other traits of mentality in the field of knowledge and even of education also had to be changed. Experimentation and observation as the instrumentalities of the organs of senses as well as of pure reason, unrestrained by the truth of faith, disappeared or were relegated to a secondary position.

Even later on in the twelfth and the thirteenth centuries, in the age of the Scholastic thought, when, as we shall see, a notable change in the system of truth took place, nevertheless

Scholastic philosophy is almost always confounded with scholastic theology, which, in its dogmatic aspect, is a body of doctrines received through a positive revelation from God. . . . Servant or handmaid for some, *philosophia ancilla theologiae*, Scholasticism is conceived by all as philosophy under the direction and control of Catholic theology.[69]

The medieval thinking is marked, first, by a great *development of theological dialectics* [70] at the cost of observation and of independent logic unrestrained by creed. Since the medieval thought was little interested in the problems of the external and Sensate world, which can be studied mainly through observation and experimentation, these methods were undeveloped, while theological logics and dialectics, with the main argument in the form of quotation of the Holy Writ, as the ultimate and absolute authority, were developed brilliantly.

The Middle Ages professed an altogether undue esteem for dialectics and the principal manuals in use in the schools tended to aggravate this exclusive attachment to [theological] logic. . . . Among the branches [of philosophy]

---

[68] Indeed, for Erigena the visible and sensible world is mere appearance or a congeries of accidents which come and go; a study of these accidents through the organs of senses is fruitless and useless; the ultimate and eternal reality is God, the only real reality of the four classes of realities given by Erigena. The source and the foundation of the genuine knowledge of the reality is, after all, faith and divine revelation. And so on. See Erigena's *De divisione naturae* (Oxonii, 1681).

[69] De Wulf, *op. cit.*, pp. 101 and 110. Alcuin's definition is typical; philosophy is "Naturarum Inquisitio, rerum divinarum humanorumque cognitio, quantum possibile est homini aestimare." Alcuini, *Opera omnia*, Vol. II, in Migne, *Patrologia Latina*, t. 101, col. 952, A.

[70] I have to insert "theological" because otherwise these characteristics are inaccurate. The medieval logic and dialectics before the end of the twelfth century were not free formal logic and dialectics but theological: their final argument was always the Scripture, but not observation or syllogism. When the proper quotation from the Scripture was given, it was deciding the problem absolutely, without any appeal to logic or facts. Dialectics was used mainly in connection with controversial interpretation of the Scripture's quotations. Only after the eleventh century the independent logic and dialectics emerged.

[theological] dialectics was the only one then taught as such. . . . The liberal arts and philosophy were regarded as a preparation for theology.[71]

Hence, when even some information about the external world (physics, geometry, mathematics, astronomy, which composed the so-called *Quadrivium* or the second part of the teaching, the main part being composed of the *Trivium* — grammar, dialectics, and rhetoric) was touched or given, it always represented "the intermixture of matters and [72] arguments in philosophy with theological questions and arguments."

Or as another author puts it :

Theology is the queen of the sciences, the end of all knowledge being God. . . . [Peter of Lombard says: "The object of our happiness is God."] Natural science is consequently only of secondary importance if it administers to mere utility, or to the comfort and convenience of the human race. Astronomy, for example, is not primarily intended to aid us in navigating ships, or forecasting the seasons but to raise our minds to the contemplation of Eternal Truths. Christian philosophy . . . assumes a revelation which places the Truth within our reach. The believer has in the Scriptures, in the Sacraments, and in the Church a means of access to God. He possesses a body of irrefrangible truth, and it is his duty to align himself with this divine knowledge.[73]

The study of the Scripture was of all studies the most congenial to Christian sentiment. The principal texts studied by the clerics were "The Divine letters — the Scripture and the patristic writings," and those by the common people were the Lord's Prayer, the Creed, the "Hail! Mary," Psalms, and so on.

The main textbooks of even the *Trivium* and the *Quadrivium*, as mentioned, dealt with mathematics and what is called the natural sciences, but they occupied a secondary place and were entirely "theologized," or, as Rabanus says in his *De universo*, they treat not "only . . . the nature of the things and properties of words, but especially . . . the *mystic* significance of these things and words." [74]

This is equally true of the texts like *The Lay Folk's Mass*, the *Primer*, the *Psalter*, Isidore of Seville's *Encyclopedia; De Mirabilibus* of Augustine of Hibernia; *De ordine*, of pseudo Isidore; Bede's *History; De Universo* of Rabanus Maurus; Strabo's *Glossary;* Honorius's *De imagine*

---

[71] De Wulf, *op. cit.*, p. 127.
[72] *Ibid.*, p. 137. Compare F. J. F. Jackson, *op. cit.*, pp. 230 ff.
[73] Jackson, *op. cit.*, p. 232.
[74] B. Rabanai Mauri, *Opera omnia*, t. 5, col. 12, in Migne's *Patrologia Latina*, Vol. CXI.

mundi; the *Summulae of Petrius Hispanus, Nuptials of Philology and Mercury,* Donatus's text, *Sentences* of Peter Lombardus, the *Consolations* of Boethius, several grammars and other texts widely used, many for several centuries without any change, like those of Isidore of Seville. This fact in itself is very significant.[75]   Only in a mentality which ignores the ever-changing sensible world and which is directed to the super-sensible, eternal, and unchangeable ultimate reality is such a fact possible. Nowadays each text, even the most authoritative in any field, is practically "old" at the moment of its publication: in the short period elapsing between the composition of the work and its printing, new conditions usually occur which require a change, and now after a few years any text is hopelessly obsolete.

In a logical consistency with the dominant truth of faith stands the *exceedingly small number of discoveries in the natural sciences and of technological inventions.*   For the seventh, eighth, ninth, tenth, and eleventh centuries, the total number of the discoveries and inventions was respectively only four, four, six, seven, eight.   As the mentality turned to the supersensory world little interest was shown in the study of the sensory world — physicochemical and biological sciences.   Hence little progress was made by the natural sciences during these centuries of domination of the Ideational truth.[76]

Another trait of this medieval mentality was its *symbolism.*   That characteristic has been pointed out previously in Volume One, which is devoted to art.   It is enough to point out in this connection that its symbolism was not incidental.   Since the reality (God) is supersensible and immaterial, it cannot be described otherwise but through use of symbols as "the sensible or visible signs of the invisible and supersensible world."   Hence it is inevitable that any system of knowledge based upon the truth of faith has to be symbolic.[77]

---

[75] See J. W. Adamson, "Education," in the *Legacy of the Middle Ages,* pp. 255–287, especially P. Duhem, *op. cit.,* Vol. II, pp. 393–503, and Vol. III, *passim.*

[76] See some details in L. Thorndike, *History of Magic and Experimental Science,* 2 vols. (New York, 1929) ; L. Thorndike, *Science and Thought in the 15th Century* (New York, 1932). Compare L. Weber, *Le rythme du progrès* (Paris, 1913).   See the next chapter of this volume.

[77] From this standpoint even such brilliant scholars of the medieval mind as H. O. Taylor in his *Mediaeval Mind* emphasize too much the practical and utilitarian motives of this symbolism, *i.e.,* the necessity of the "ennoblement and beautification" of many indecent Biblical stories and contradictions, and stress too little the real, inevitable reason for the symbolism of the medieval mentality as based upon the truth of faith. I am afraid that these scholars in their interpretations are unduly influenced by our own culture and mentality, in which symbolism is unnecessary (in the medieval form), and are inclined, therefore, to stress utilitarian and political motives where they appear.

Many other traits of the medieval mentality likewise follow and become perfectly comprehensible when the thesis discussed is adequately interpreted, namely, the system of knowledge based upon the truth of faith.

Thus the truth of faith reigned supreme for about six or seven centuries. When in the fifth and sixth centuries it became dominant, empiricism, skepticism, and fideism were almost entirely eliminated. Now that this truth became triumphant and unquestionable, there was no need for them. The truth of faith was now firmly entrenched and was certain, absolute. As any ruler under such conditions, it became calm, serene, free from any elements of despair, from any exotic quality, from extremism, from any "emergency way out." Therefore, these currents disappeared. Even mysticism, though tangible in some centuries of this period, in other centuries was practically nonexistent, as Tables 1 and 2 and Figure 1 show. More than that, even in the centuries like the seventh and the ninth, when it was tangible, this mysticism had little of the mysticism of despair which we met at the beginning of our era, and meet in the fourteenth, the fifteenth, and the sixteenth, and also later centuries. Then it was in many respects a mysticism of despair combined, so to speak, with artificially managed (upon the basis of the scientific and empirical experience) technique of its creation and training, and even used for political, utilitarian, and other empirical purposes of this empirical world — from the mysticism of St. Ignatius and the Jesuit Society up to that of Mrs. Eddy and Christian Science.

In contradistinction to that "mysticism of despair," "of scientific technique," and "of empirico-utilitarian application," mysticism from the seventh to the thirteenth centuries was free from all these traits typical of the age of the waning truth of faith in these later centuries. It was again serene, calm, and perfectly confident in itself — a slight variation of the same all-powerful truth of faith. Nothing pathetic, exotic, extreme, or desperate marked it. Its tone was radically different from the mysticism of either St. Francis or St. Ignatius Loyola, St. Teresa, St. Catherine of Siena, or even of Meister Eckhart, not to mention many other mystics, like Savonarola, St. Thomas à Kempis, Giacomo of Flora, Heinrich Suso, Lois de Granada, St. John of Cross, Lois de Leon, and others; [78] and still more different was it from the so-called mysticism of recent times from the revivalists to the Christian Scientists. In the

---

[78] In addition, the mysticism of the later centuries, like that recommended by Loyola's *Spiritual Exercises*, is a "scientifically managed — stimulated and developed — mysticism, where the external technique (very scientific) plays an enormous role.

mysticism of Maximus Confessor, or Erigena, or Anselmus, or Remigius one does not discover anything from either despair, abnormal supersensibility, overelaborated reasoning, superstrenuous ecstasy, utilitarian aims, mystical sexuality, scientism, or from political exploitation with which the mysticisms of the later centuries was marked. The mysticism of the early Middle Ages was so balanced, moderate, and normal that without any particular difficulty these mystics could be put into the main current of the theological rationalism of the Middle Ages. In which case, mysticism would be almost nonexistent in that period.

When these qualifications are considered, the monolithic unanimity and uniformity of the system of truth and of the mentality of the period from the sixth to the twelfth centuries stand out particularly clearly. It was indeed the age of unshakable, unquestioning, absolutely confident faith. There was no doubt, no uncertainty, no inner disharmony, and no mental conflict. There was no dualism between religion, science, and philosophy, because science and philosophy were banished and faith reigned supreme. Living in an age of uncertainty par excellence; in an age of science which by its very nature is relative, uncertain, and can give at the best only some propositions more or less probable; in an age of a multitude of theories and convictions each fighting with the others; in an age of tacit and open conflict between religion and science, religion and philosophy, science and philosophy, between the truth of faith, of reason, and of senses; in this anarchy and confusion, especially now when the confusion has grown menacingly large and the agreement dangerously small — in such circumstances one, at least by moments, can but admire and envy this "Age of Certainty." In its own way it was a marvelous and great age. So-called liberal thinkers — journalists, historians, sociologists, philosophers, moralists, and the like — can style it "the Dark Age," "the Age of Superstition and Ignorance," and so forth, as they have been doing for the last four centuries, but by so doing they only show their "intellectual lilliputianism," measuring the immense and infinite universe of human Mind with their minute yardstick which, in their shortsightedness, they view as an infinite rod.

They also repeat the recurrent story of the partisans of the truth of senses who scorn all the other systems of truth. Who except Almighty and Omniscient God can decide which of these three main truths is the real truth? Inasmuch as all three have been functioning in human history since time immemorial, and the empirical truth has by no means been the strongest, it can hardly be claimed that the other systems of truth are in their entirety mere superstition and mere ignorance. If they were such, then according to the popular mainstay of the present empirical science — its theory of evolution and survival of the fittest — such ignorance and superstition should have been eliminated long ago from the history of human mentality. It has not been eliminated and shows no sign of such a trend, in spite of the rising tide of empiricism for the last few centuries.

Ergo, even from this scientific standpoint we are by no means entitled to regard either the truth of faith or that of reason as ignorance, superstition, and the like. They probably have and probably will continue to perform some very vital functions in social and cultural life — of which a serious student of sociocultural phenomena is perfectly aware. Still less are we entitled to dub them contemptuously "the Age of Superstition" because of the creation of great sociocultural values under the regime of this truth of faith. Yes, the age was great in its own way and was indeed enviable, at least, in its peace of mind and certainty.

This, however, is a deviation. Returning to the topic, let us now state that the same period from the sixth to the twelfth centuries shows itself in the compartment of art as predominantly Ideational; thus art and truth compartments here are again logically and factually integrated: both are Ideational.

Further, my second proposition is again well corroborated: that in the period of domination of the Ideational truth of faith, when the truth of senses is low or nonexistent, the progress of scientific discoveries and inventions becomes either much slower, or stops, or even regresses. It can be seen that the proposition is well sustained by the facts.

Third, if we shall find out that, besides the Art and Truth compartments, other compartments of the culture of the period were Ideational, then we have a corroboration of the third proposition; that with a passage of a culture from the predominantly Sensate to Idealistic or Ideational type or vice versa, its system of truth also changes, each type of culture giving the upper hand to the system of truth which logically is consistent with it. Now we see — and see rather strikingly well — the validity of this proposition. With the passage of the Graeco-Roman Sensate culture of the Hellenistic and Graeco-Roman period of the first two centuries of the Empire to the more and more Ideational type (as we shall see), the dominant system of truth underwent a similar and strikingly deep transformation, until in the centuries from the sixth to the twelfth it became quite Ideational and opposite to the type which was dominant before. Thus, so far, the expectations deduced are well sustained by the facts.

Now we can continue further to trace the transformation of the systems of truth during the subsequent centuries.

VI. THE IDEALISTIC PHASE: THE END OF THE ELEVENTH, TWELFTH, AND THIRTEENTH CENTURIES

Glancing at Tables 5 to 12 and Figures 2 to 8, on the movement of the scientific discoveries and inventions (see Chapter Three), we see that after several centuries of stagnation, about the end of the eleventh century, their curve begins to rise, then rises more rapidly in the twelfth and thirteenth centuries. The rising is quite notable and steady, though it is as yet in its initial stage; the spirit of the scientific inquiry reawakens but is not as yet in full swing.

Glancing at Tables 1 and 2 and Figure 1, on the movement of the main systems of truth, we see also that beginning with the same period, the end of the eleventh century, the curve of the empirical system of truth reappears and begins to rise also; religious rationalism declines and fideism reappears. This means first the reawakening of the spirit of empiricism — a datum which is in complete agreement with what is shown by the curve of the scientific discoveries and is therefore hardly misleading; it means also that some new and important change took place in the system of truth and also in the whole mentality of the period, compared with the preceding one. From the standpoint of our present problem, in what did this change consist?

Many historians of the medieval mentality often pass over this change by merely saying that the Scholastic philosophy of the thirteenth century was the highest development of medieval philosophy, assuming thus that it was a mere development of it and did not have any new and fundamentally different element.[79]

Such an opinion is rather fallacious. In the period under consideration the system of truth (and of mentality) was not a mere continuation of the preceding period but was a new phase as different from it as the Ideational truth of faith is different from the Idealistic truth of independent reason, as the system of truth in Greece before the fifth century was different from that of the fifth and of the fourth centuries B.C. In other words, the *centuries from the end of the eleventh to the fourteenth are the Age of the Idealistic Rationalism, quite similar to that of the age in Greece of the fifth and the fourth centuries, but not a continuation of the*

[79] For instance, even such a careful and excellent investigator of the medieval philosophy as M. de Wulf says: "Scholastic philosophy, which represents medieval philosophy par excellence." *Op. cit.*, pp. 101 and 110.

preceding system of the truth of faith with mere subservient truth of reason.
We are now in a very different mental atmosphere and this atmosphere
is that of the idealistic rationalism in the sense given to that term above.
The *Scholastic philosophy of these centuries with its climax in the thirteenth
is not a system of truth of faith but that of idealistic rationalism as a harmonious blending together, into one system, of the truths of faith, of reason,
and of senses.* It is similar in that respect to the idealistic rationalism of
Plato and Aristotle. Such is the thesis contended.

What are its evidences? There are many, but at this time I shall
point out only a few taken directly from the data in this part of the
work. First, we saw that in art it was Idealistic; second, in the way
of anticipation of what will be demonstrated herein, the other compartments of culture of this period also show clearly all the earmarks of the
Idealistic culture. Next, the curves of the movement of scientific discoveries and of empiricism show that they reappeared again and began to
grow. Since the truth of faith and that of reason are present also, all
the three systems are now on the stage, functioning together. Before
the appearance of empiricism on the stage, the system of idealistic
rationalism could not be created simply because one of its elements,
empiricism, was lacking. Now that it was present on the stage, however, a possibility of the blending of the system of the idealistic rationalism was given in *potentia*. It can be seen, further, from Tables 1 and 2 and
Figure 1, that the curve of the truth of faith began to descend while
the curve of the truth of senses began to ascend. Moving so, they had
to meet, so to speak, and blend together in some system similar to idealistic rationalism. Moreover, since empiricism was just beginning to
climb, it was, as yet, neither the most powerful system, nor more powerful than the systems of truth of faith and of reason. When it is too
powerful, *ex definitio*, it hinders the domination of the Idealistic system.
When it is weaker than the truth of faith and of reason, the Ideational
elements are stronger than empiricism; therefore the Idealistic system
of truth is possible.

These considerations are sufficient to indicate why this age is a new
and different phase in the movement of the systems of truth, as is
shown by the quantitative data.

Are these contentions corroborated by the qualitative examination
of the dominant systems of truth of the period? They are, because
the quantitative curves of the main systems of truth given are based
not upon a chance classification of the thinkers of the period into one of
the classes of the systems of truth but upon the qualitative study of their

systems. An additional examination, however, of the systems of truth
of the dominant thinkers of the period will support further the validity
of the claim and will make possible a more concrete and comprehensive
understanding of the situation in the field. For these reasons a concise
and brief characterization of the leading system of truth, as it is given by
the greatest thinkers of the period, is advisable.

Everyone who is acquainted with the Scholastic philosophy of the
period — and the Scholastic philosophy existed only in that period,
neither before, nor later when we have, at the best, only a somewhat
diluted and degenerated pseudo-Scholastic system, as it is given in its
greatest creators like Albertus Magnus (c. 1193–1280) and his still greater
disciple St. Thomas Aquinas (1225–1274) (a remarkable similitude of
the greatest Greek philosophers of idealistic rationalism, Plato and his
pupil Aristotle) — cannot fail to observe that the Scholastic system
of truth was exactly the system of idealistic rationalism. To confirm
this it is enough to examine St. Thomas's theory of knowledge.

That it belongs to the idealistic rationalism in the above sense is shown
first of all by the fact that he follows closely "the Philosopher" (as he
writes); that is Aristotle, in all his essential principles, but naturally
"Platonized" and Christianized.[80]

Second, even St. Thomas's manner of writing shows that his theory
embraces all the three forms of truth : in his demonstration, he uses the
testimony of the organs of senses, the logic of reason, and, as a final
evidence, he does not fail to quote this or that statement from the Scripture and the Church Fathers. In almost every problem this method is
followed.

Third, and naturally the most important evidence, is given by the
character of his theory of truth and knowledge. Its essential tenets are :
there are practically the three kinds of knowledge — sensory, intellectual,
and superintellectual or divine. Any cognition begins with the sensory
perception (as with Aristotle), but to become knowledge and truth as
adequatio rei et intellectus [81] the sensory data are, so to speak, transformed
by the intellect, which has a power to render a material object immaterial,
and especially by the active intellect which brings out the universal or
the intelligible in the object or thing perceived.[82] Thus (omitting many

[80] About Platonization of Aristotle by St. Thomas and Scholasticism, G. Truc rightly says :
"Scholasticism borrowed its arms from Aristotle but it had the soul of Plato." *La pensée
de Saint Thomas d'Aquin* (Paris, 1924), Introduction, p. 3.

[81] Per conformitatem intellectus et rei, veritas definitur. St. Thomas, *Summa theologica*,
I, 1, q. 16, a. 2.

[82] St. Thomas, *De veritate*, q. 13, a. 3 ; *Summa theologica*, I, i, q. 57, a. 2.

details already presented) the co-operation of both sources and forms of truth — the sensory and the intellectual — is evident.   For a knowledge of most of the empirical phenomena these two forms of truth and of sources are sufficient.   But there are the superempirical phenomena which cannot be perceived either by the senses directly or cannot be apprehended by human reason and logic.   They can be known only by the grace of God, who reveals such truths to mankind through prophets and in other ways.   This form of truth is the most supreme and sublime of all forms of knowledge.

This brief outline of the theory of knowledge of St. Thomas shows clearly its idealistic rationalism.   As a detailed analysis of the theory is not a part of this work, I shall but quote a few passages which outline clearly and authentically the essentials of the theory of the Angelic Doctor.

The sense always apprehends the thing as it is, except there be an impediment in the organ or in the medium.   [It can do so because] sensible objects exist actually outside the soul.[83]

Sensory cognition is occupied with external, sensible qualities, but intellectual knowledge penetrates to the very essence of the things.[84]

Certitude of knowledge varies in various natures. . . .   Because man forms a sure judgment about a truth by the discursive process of his reason: and so human knowledge is acquired by means of demonstrative reasoning. . . .[85]

As to the divine knowledge or the truth of faith, practically almost the whole of the *Summa contra Gentiles* and also many parts of the *Summa theologica* — particularly the latter section of the second part devoted to Faith, and to the Gratuitous Graces as well as the many other parts — are but a systematic development of the theory of the existence of such a truth.   Here is its essence.

In the things which we hold about God there is truth in two ways.   For certain things that are true about God wholly surpass the capability of human reason; for instance that God is three and one; while there are certain things to which even natural reason can attain, for instance, that God is, that God is one, and others like these, which even the philosophers proved demonstratively of God, being guided by the light of natural reason. . . .   That certain divine truths wholly surpass the capability of human reason is most clearly evident . . . since our intellect's knowledge originates from the senses: so that things which are not objects of sense cannot be comprehended by the

[83] St. Thomas, *De veritate*, q. 1, a. 11.   *Summa theologica*, I, 1, q. 79, a. 3, ad. 1.
[84] *Summa theologica*, II, q. 8, a. 7.   See also II, q. 9.
[85] *Ibid.*, II, q. 9, a. i, ad. 1.

human intellect, except in so far as knowledge of them is gathered from sensibles. . . . Accordingly some divine truths are attainable by human reason, while others altogether surpass the power of human reason.[86]

In the next chapters St. Thomas demonstrates

that those things which cannot be investigated by reason are fittingly proposed to man as an object of faith.   Divine Wisdom Himself, Who knows all things most fully, deigned to reveal to man the *secrets of God's wisdom* . . . the truth of His doctrine and inspiration, [foretold by] the manifold oracles of the prophets.[87]

In the *Summa theologica* this truth of faith he styles exactly by this term "truth of faith"; and under the name "wisdom" separates it from intellectual-sensible knowledge, indicating again and again that this "divine wisdom" or "truth of faith" has much greater certitude than knowledge of intellect and is supreme in comparison with it.[88]

From the foregoing discussion, the skeleton of St. Thomas's theory of knowledge is clear and there is no doubt but that it is idealistic rationalism in my meaning of the term.   The three forms of truth are all harmoniously blended.   Not to leave any uncertainty, St. Thomas again and again stresses that this "truth of faith" in no way contradicts the sensory-intellectual truth but supplements it and leads it to the higher level of the divine wisdom.

It is impossible for the aforesaid truth of faith to be contrary to those principles which reason knows naturally.

And vice versa:

Those things which are naturally instilled in human reason cannot be opposed to this truth [of Christian faith].   The truth of reason is not in opposition to the truth of the Christian Faith.[89]

As a matter of fact, a considerable part of the works of St. Thomas is devoted to the demonstration of that proposition and to a marvelous display of the truth of reason (which by definition implies the truth of senses) used to demonstrate, by its own power, the truth of faith.   There is no conflict, no antagonism, no opposition between these three truths. They are not and cannot be opposed to one another; "the false alone is opposed to the true."[90]

Such is this system of the idealistic rationalism.   It is a European variety of the system of the Platonic-Aristotelian idealistic rationalism.

---

[86] St. Thomas, *Summa contra Gentiles* (London, 1924), Bk. I, chap. iii.

[87] *Summa contra Gentiles*, Bk. I, chaps. v and vi.

[88] *Summa theologica*, II, ii, q. 9, a. 2, ad. 1.   *Summa contra Gentiles*, Bk. I, chaps. iii ff.

[89] *Summa contra Gentiles*, Bk. I, chap. vii.   [90] *Ibid.*, Bk. I, chap. vii.

As such it itself shows exactly what is to be anticipated on the basis of the expectation derived from the nature of the Idealistic culture if the culture of Europe of the twelfth and thirteenth centuries was Idealistic, as we shall see throughout this work.

As mentioned, this system of truth was very different from the dominant system of the preceding period up to the end of the eleventh century. That system was practically the Ideational system of pure faith which drove out the truth of senses and truth of reason, and admitted them, not as free and independent comrades, but as mere serfs. Here the total or the organically whole system of rationalism is composed of all these three truths inseparable from one another and harmoniously united organs of one and the same whole truth. This is one of the profoundest differences, and there are many others.

In the preceding period the truth of faith did not condescend to a minor role which could be damaged or needed support of the "truth of natural reason and senses." It was an unlimited monarch who could occasionally make use of these "humble subjects" but whose power and authority in no way were dependent upon positive or negative testimony of the truth of natural reason and of that of senses. If necessary, as Tertullian marvelously put it, it could declare and indeed often proudly declared: *Credo quia absurdum:* because it looks absurd from the standpoint of the truth of senses and reason, it must be true. Now a very different mentality — that of harmonious blending of all these truths — exists. And more than that, the accent is now put upon the sensory-intellectual truth of natural reason rather than upon the sublime truth of faith. Like a revered constitutional monarch who reigns but rules rather nominally, this faith is solemnly proclaimed the sovereign, but the prime minister and the real ruler in this rationalistic constitution of truth is rather the sensory-intellectual truth of reason. As in the preceding period, it is used to support the truth of faith instead of being supported by the truth of faith. And studying carefully the Scholastic philosophy, from this standpoint one finds ample corroboration in St. Thomas, Albertus Magnus, and other Scholastics who, consciously or not, stated the matter clearly again and again.

Here are two examples of their beliefs which are repeated many times.

Although matters of faith are Divine and eternal, yet faith itself is something temporal in the mind of the believer. Hence to know what one ought to believe, belongs to the gift of [sensory-intellectual] knowledge.[91]

[91] *Summa theologica,* II, ii, q. 9, a. 2, ad. 1, English trans. (London, 1917), pp. 114–115.

Or

Because some . . . like the Mohammedans and Pagans, do not agree with us as to the authority of any Scripture whereby they may be convinced [because they do not accept the Scripture as the true revelation of Divine Wisdom]. . . . Whereby it is necessary to have recourse to natural reason, to which all are compelled to assent.[92]

Hence the objective of the *Summa contra Gentiles* is to show "how demonstrable truth is in agreement with the faith of the Christian religion."

These passages show what I mean by the simile that in the Scholastic system of truth, the truth of faith reigns but in a lesser degree than the sensory-intellectual truth of reason. Here the latter supports the former rather than the reverse, as was the case in the preceding period. This brings out another profound difference of this system of truth from the system of dictatorship of the truth of faith of the preceding period. These two fundamental differences are sufficient to prove that the Scholastic philosophy of this period was not a mere refinement of the preceding system of truth but a new form, profoundly different from it.[93]

Thus, this concise examination of the greatest and also most influential theory of truth of the period under consideration well corroborates the expectation and thereby the propositions which are set forth at the beginning of this part of the work: that the systems of truth change; that the change takes place with a change in the whole character of the culture; that in this sense the system of truth, so far as its acceptance and domination are concerned, is conditioned by the sociocultural milieu and in this sense is its function (though, in usual terminology, being part of it through its change it conditions the other parts of the given culture); that indeed the predominantly Idealistic culture (and we shall see that the culture of the twelfth and thirteenth centuries was such) gives domination to the idealistically rationalistic system of truth, in the above sense and respectively to the idealistic-rationalistic mentality; that such a system, as a dominant one, comes usually in a period when scientific discoveries and inventions, on the one hand, and empiricism as the system of truth, on the other hand, reawaken and begin to rise, while the system

[92] *Summa contra Gentiles*, Bk. I, chap. ii.

[93] For the system of truth of St. Thomas and Scholasticism see, besides the works quoted: K. Werner, *Der heilige Thomas von Aquino* (Regensburg, 1889), 3 vols.; E. Gilson, *Le Thomisme* (Strasburg, 1920); A. D. Sertillanges, *Saint Thomas d'Aquin*, 2 vols., 3d ed. (Paris, 1922); G. Truc, *Le retour à la scholastique* (Paris, 1919); M. Schumacher, *The Knowableness of God, Its Relation to the Theory of Knowledge in St. Thomas* (Notre Dame Press, 1905).

of truth of faith (religious rationalism) begins to show the first signs of its quantitative decline and qualitative "softening."

So it was in Greece in the fifth and the fourth centuries B.C. and in Europe in the twelfth, thirteenth, and part of the fourteenth centuries. The dominant systems of truth in both cases were essentially similar. Not incidental, therefore, was the fact that Platonized Aristotle became *the* Philosopher, *the* authority, and *the* guide. It is probably incidental that the pair, Plato and Aristotle, as the teacher and disciple, both supreme masters, was repeated here also in a similar pair, Albertus Magnus and St. Thomas. But the fact deserves to be mentioned.

We have seen in art and shall further see that these periods in Grecian culture and in European culture show many other — neither incidental, nor superficial — similarities in the sense that both are Idealistic in all the main compartments of their culture.

Taking their systems of truth, the scholar and thoughtful scientist of our days can hardly fail to notice its marvelous completeness in the sense of organic blending of all the three main kinds of truth; its inner harmony in which none of the three truths struggles with the other but all co-operate as the parts of one healthy organism co-operate and function together. Here again an age of certainty prevails, but it is different from the preceding kind of certainty of unquestioning and uninquiring faith. Now it is questioning and inquiring; but the ordeal is passed through successfully by the certainty of the truth of the idealistic rationalism. All and everything was answered and answered definitely, without doubts either of the later critical philosophy, Kantianism, and Neo-Kantianism, or of the later skepticism, agnosticism, positivism, relativism, "conditionalism," pragmatism, and "fictionism" (the theory of "as if," or of *als ob*) of our times.

The firm and simple "*adequatio rei et intellectus*" of St. Thomas sounds often, in our age of uncertainty and relativity in any knowledge, like Maeterlinck's *Blue Bird*, beautiful but lost. One cannot help envying again, at least occasionally, the idealistic-rationalistic age of certainty and also its ability to create and to believe in a complete system of truth where the truth of senses, of reason, and of faith find place and where all are in harmony and all are unity in plurality. Our predominant system of empiricism is much narrower; it does not want to and cannot give place to the other truths, but it fights them and expels them as "superstition" and "unscientific speculation," which it must do because such is its nature (like the dictatorial system of pure faith). Only in this idealistic rationalism is real tolerance and co-operation of the different systems of truth possible.   This, perhaps, is one of the reasons why many of our thinkers, tired of the narrowness, uncertainty, and intolerance of the dominating empiricism, skepticism, criticism, and relativism, begin to look for a revival of Neo-Scholasticism.   I am in sympathy with them. But as we shall see, the Idealistic culture hardly ever follows directly the Sensate culture, nor does the idealistic-rationalistic system of truth follow immediately the empirico-skeptical age.

In the Graeco-Roman culture the age of domination of the empirico-skeptical systems of truth was followed not by the idealistic rationalism of the thirteenth century but for six or more centuries by the dictatorship of the truth of faith.   Only after that did the idealistic rationalism come. This suggests that if our system of truth of senses is going to decline, its successor will probably not be the system of idealistic rationalism but a kind of dictatorial system of faith.   This, of course, is not certain in any way but is at least as probable "inductively and deductively" as the expectations of the Neo-Scholastics and the Neo-Thomists.   If and when our system of truth of the "*nihil esse in intellectu quod prius non fuerit in sensu*" crumbles, its place is likely to be taken not by the "*per conformitatem intellectus et rei, veritas definitur*" [94] but rather by some kind of the "*Credo quia absurdum*" — be it of the Christian Science type, of the Communist, of the Hitlerite, or of some Neo-Mystic and Neo-Gnostic type, or of a return to the mentality of the Christian system of unquestioning faith of the early Middle Ages.   This is, however, a guess and a deviation from my course; therefore, let us continue our journey along the trail blazed by the systems of truth in the subsequent centuries.

VII. THE CRISIS OF THE FOURTEENTH AND THE FIFTEENTH CENTURIES AND THE CRESCENDO, FORTE, AND FORTISSIMO OF THE EMPIRICAL SYSTEM OF TRUTH FROM THE SIXTEENTH TO THE TWENTIETH CENTURY

The Idealistic culture, with the Idealistic forms of its main aspects, comes usually when the Sensate culture begins to rise and the Ideational culture begins to decline.   When these two processes, one descending and the other rising, meet at their optimum point, the meeting leads to their blending and gives some form — marvelous or primitive — of the Idealistic culture with its Idealistic system of truth, of art, of ethics, of philosophy, and a form of all the other important compartments of culture.

[94] *Summa theologica*, I, i, q. 16, a. 2.

Emerging in such circumstances, Idealistic culture is, therefore, by its nature, transitory and as a point of "equilibrium" can hardly last for any length of time in the incessantly fluctuating forces of Ideational and Sensate culture. When one of these streams becomes too strong, the equilibrium is broken and the Idealistic culture begins to crumble. Since it comes at the earlier phases of the long-time trend of the ascending Sensate culture, it usually disintegrates as a result of a further growth of the Sensate stream and a further decline of the Ideational stream.

This was true in the Greek culture, and also in the history of the Western culture, when the Idealistic phase lasted hardly more than about one hundred and fifty years. Toward the second part of the fourteenth century, in most of its main compartments it was already broken and, since the new Sensate culture was only in the state of potential shaping, and not as yet established, the result was confusion — mental, moral, and social. It was similar to a building scene when the solid and centuries-old Ideational house, remodeled already into the Idealistic form, is demolished, and when the new modern house of Sensate culture was not as yet built; perhaps only the cellar was excavated, and the foundation was in part laid. Such a stage of building is a picture of disorder and confusion; where the remnants of the old house, its stones, bricks, beams, tiles, pipes, pieces of decoration, and so on, are scattered everywhere and new material is dumped here and there near by; as a whole the scene is neither orderly, beautiful, nor comfortable for the members of such a house. In the periods of transformation of culture its population cannot go to any other house or to a hotel, to live there while the new house is built, but they must stay on the place, under the sky, and endure all the inclemencies of the weather, and the discomforts of the ruins.

Such seems to have been the period which we enter, as it is shown, in the field of the system of truth and mentality generally, by Tables 1 and 2 and Figure 1. A glance at these shows at once the essential traits of the mental conditions of the second part of the fourteenth, and the fifteenth centuries. Its spectrum is decidedly that of sharp instability, profound confusion, mental crisis, and extremism, not unlike the spectrum of the after-Idealistic centuries, third and later in the Graeco-Roman culture. Indeed the indicators show that all in all the line of idealistic rationalism sharply declines (as usual with minor fluctuations); likewise even the line of empiricism temporarily drops also at the end of the fourteenth and at the beginning of the fifteenth centuries; thus these two most balanced forms of truth greatly weaken. On the other hand, the "exotic" and "extreme" systems — fideism and skepticism — reappear again while mysticism grows enormously.

Any investigator of the mentality of that period knows how the high tide of mysticism swept over the whole European culture at that time. We met it in the field of art. It was indeed a "Time of Trouble" and, in a sense, of despair; wars, the Black Death, and hundreds of other most tragic events [95] battered the population. Whatever were the causes or the reasons for such a wave of mysticism and fideism (see Chapter One of this volume, Chapter Nine of Volume One, and subsequent chapters of this volume and Volume Three), the existence of these waves is unquestionable.

What is still more important is that the mysticism of that period is very different from that of the Ideational medieval period. There, as mentioned, it was free from any desperate sensitivity, and, if I am permitted to say, emotional and pathetic exhibitionism. Then there was a complete disregard of the sensory reality, complete confidence in the revelation or in divinely inspired truth and in the supersensory Kingdom of

[95] Calamities of the period, like other great calamities, stimulated simultaneously "Epicureanism of despair" as well as "Ideationalism of despair." The familiar example of stimulation of the *Carpe diem* mentality and conduct by the Black Plague is given by Boccaccio in his familiar *Decameron*. The chronicles of the period do not fail to note this effect. The observations of the contemporaries — like Guy of Chauliac, physician of Pope Clement VI, in 1348, of John of Reading in 1349, of two archbishops of Canterbury in 1350, 1362, and 1378; of Felix Fabri, Rudolph of Saxony, and of many others — all stress an increase of lawlessness, lewdness, unrighteousness, demoralization, heresy, and vice and a "great decline of all religions in the pestilence." See some of the statements in A. M. Campbell, *The Black Death and Men of Learning* (New York, 1931), pp. 3, 129, 134, 138, and 142–143; in Huizinga, *op. cit.*, 103.

On the other hand, the contemporaries stress also that such catastrophes called forth repentance, religiosity, ideationality, and the desperate forms of Ideational mentality and conduct. The scenes of repentance and religious revivals after such calamities are familiar. "The epidemic of religious revivals (in the Middle Ages) was due to general public calamities, or to dread of such. The Crusades and the Flagellant revival are instances." So it was in Perugia after the tragic events of the fall of Ezzelino, and in 1310 and 1334; in Bologna when the plague came in 1457; at Siena in 1496; in Milan in 1529; in Ferrara in 1496, and so on. "Terrible crises had still power of reawakening the glow of mediaeval penitence and the conscience-stricken people sought to move the pity of Heaven by wailings, scourgings, by fasts, processions, and moral enactments." J. Burckhardt, *The Civilization of the Renaissance in Italy* (London, 1909), 467 ff. and 485 ff. These effects of the calamities — a splitting of the population stricken into extreme sensualist Epicureans of despair and the stoics of despair — seem to result in a fairly general uniformity repeated in almost all the societies of all times under the conditions of a calamity. When Sensate culture is ascending, the extreme Epicureanism is possibly stronger than extreme Ideationalism of despair. When the Ideational culture is ascending, the Ideationalism of despair is possibly stronger than the Epicureanism of despair. In the light of this it is comprehensible why in the truth mentality of the fourteenth century the balanced idealistic rationalism was shattered and why, especially in the second part of the fourteenth century, fideism, skepticism, and mysticism greatly gained.

God. Even among the Christian martyrs is not found much of the pathetic exhibitionism of the type of St. Francis or many mystics of the period.

Here mysticism has these traits conspicuously. It is pathetic; it is empirically oversentimental and oversensitive; it is macabre, as we saw already in the field of art; it broods and centers on such images as death, as the wounds of Christ, as corpses, as tortures, Hell, and other most terrifying events and objects. Through all this it shows that it could not reach the sublime ataraxia in regard to the empirical reality, as it was reached formerly by the unquestioning certitude of faith. It is not spontaneous and organic; it is a self-torturing mysticism of intentional self-hypnotization. The spontaneous ataraxia toward the empirical world is lacking. Its bearers madly try to "fly from the empirical reality" to the Kingdom of God; but they do not succeed — without ecstasy, trances, hallucinations, exotic visions, and "training" — in accomplishing it easily and spontaneously; hence its exotic, exhibitionistic, overemotional, and sensitive character. For this reason it is extreme and is a sign of a lost certitude of faith.[96]

The same characteristics have to be attributed to fideism. Finally there reappeared the usual satellite of any crisis of the truth of faith — the demon of skepticism — the *alter ego* of mysticism and fideism of despair, the phantom of the lost certitude. Skepticism has a cynical mask; the others (mysticism and fideism), a pathetic one; but all three are the creatures which appear in periods of deep mental crisis. They now become more powerful than the more balanced rationalism and empiricism. Both of these strongly recede in the fifteenth century. In that century the truth of faith tries desperately to take its stand and to regain the place taken by the growing truth of senses. Temporarily it succeeds, to a small extent, but only in the form of its desperate varieties. With the end of that century it is driven back by the rising tide of empiricism and purely cerebral rationalism (mixed with empiricism) of the type of Descartes, Spinoza, and other rationalists of the seventeenth century, with their *Cogito, ergo sum*. This rationalism was, however, a merely passing stage from the truth of Faith and of Idealism, to that of the senses (see Chapter Eleven).

In the field of truth such was the spectrum of the mind of these cen-

---

[96] See the data on the life, psychology, and teachings of the mystics of the period in the quoted works of Underhill, Angus, and others. See particularly E. A. Peers, *Spanish Mysticism* (New York, 1924); D. Knowles, *The English Mystics* (London, 1927); Dom E. C. Butler, *Western Mysticism* (London, 1922).

turies; it was the spectrum of the deep mental crisis existing after the truth of faith and of idealistic reason, which endured for a thousand years, began to crumble before the inroads of the new force of empirical truth.

This building, however, was progressing. The curve of the discoveries and inventions of the empirical science continued to move upwards. For the period considered, although the rising was steady, it was not, as yet, sufficiently spectacular to be perceived and felt by all the thinkers.

It would take some time for the fruits of scientism and empiricism to become visible and tangible to all. Toward the end of the fifteenth and the beginning of the sixteenth centuries the fruits of scientific discoveries grew to such an extent that in the debris of the previous crumbling systems of truth, the truth of senses became the only possible foundation upon which a new house of truth could be built. Discoveries and also empiricism now begin to increase very rapidly. We are at the beginning of the age of domination of the truth of senses; in an era of scientism and empiricism; at a stage of vigorous growth of the greatest Sensate culture the world has ever known; a new phase, and a new fundamental turn in the endless fluctuation of the systems of truth in the life history of culture.

Toward the end of the fifteenth century the curves of the scientific discoveries and of empiricism strongly flared up, and, with minor fluctuations, have continued to grow, up until the present time (see Chapter Three). To the leading minds — scientific or philosophical — this rise became evident in the sixteenth century; in the great seventeenth century it reached such a level that even the "blind" had to reckon with it. When this new mooring was found and had proved itself to be capable, rapidly growing, and able to create theoretical and practical "miracles," the old and, for the time being, worn-out dress of the truth of faith and of reason became more and more obsolete. It continued naturally to have its partisans and its streams still flowed, but these partisans became less powerful and the streams became increasingly dry. The power and effervescence of life were not there. They more and more centered in and around science and the empirical system of truth.

From Tables 1, 2, and 3, it can be seen how rapidly both were growing and again confirming the validity of the proposition that they are associated and that in the period of rapid rise and domination of empiricism the curve of scientific discoveries mounts rapidly, and vice versa. The periods of rapid progress of science are marked by the rise and domination of empiricism as the system of truth. Now John Locke's "*Nihil esse in intellectu quod non fuerit in sensu*" became in a sense a motto.

Such a situation naturally called forth several consequences in the mentality concerned with truth. It had to, and did indeed, inspire the thinkers with pride, enthusiasm, and confidence in the truth of senses and science. It had to, and did, fill them with the firm conviction that only now has real progress of the human mind begun and is assured in the future; it had to, and did, lead them to think of the past, and its systems of truth of faith and of reason, very condescendingly as childish, immature, and "unscientific," or even as mere superstition. These "motives," started by the "Pre-Humanists and the "Humanists," appear at that period clearly — implicitly or explicitly — in the works of the scientists and scholars of the Renaissance and the Reformation, not to mention the popularizers, and have continued up to the present time.

The truth of faith, of reason, and of senses organically united into one body in the system of the idealistic rationalism now began to disintegrate and disassociate. Disassociation led to their independent existence and to antagonisms and conflicts. *Since that time it has been less and less an age of the co-operation of science, religion, and philosophy than an age of their warfare — explicit and implicit.* When we have truce, it is like that of two belligerent states: not cordial, nor permanent. Many truths of faith are regarded by science as mere superstition and many truths of reason are regarded as sterile speculation, and vice versa. Religion has branded many scientific theories as "atheism," "dangerous heresy," "indecency, "and so on. Likewise philosophy has often styled the truths of science as superficial appearances which miss the reality entirely.

Side by side with these tendencies other ones had to appear, only slightly at the beginning, but later more and more clearly. The point is that empiricism and the truth of senses by its very nature, and on testimony of the senses themselves, cannot have a certitude of the truth of faith or of idealistic rationalism. The testimony of the organs of senses is conditioned by their anatomy and their functions: for the blind in the empirical world there are practically no colors; for the deaf, no sounds; the perception of the same object by the senses of man and of ant are probably different. The real nature of the empirical world, therefore, *as it is, für und an sich,* is practically inaccessible or at least not certain in its adequate knowableness; hence the doubt, skepticism, relativism, criticism, conditionality, conventionality, and general uncertainty — at the best only a conditional probability of the verity of the truths of science and of organs of senses. At the "springtime" of rising empiricism in the period considered, these motives were not particularly strong, but their seeds were there and they had to grow.

A few quotations from the prominent leaders of thought of the period will show clearly these tendencies.   Pride, confidence, and intoxication with the progress of science and empirical truth were shared by many thinkers.   Here are a few examples.[97]

Campanella (1568–1639):

Our century has more history in its hundred years than had the whole world in the previous four thousand years; more books have been published in the last century than in the five thousand years before it; for it has profited by the recent inventions of typography, cannon, and the marine's compass.[98]

Leibnitz (1646–1716):

We have raised up a truly philosophical age, in which the deepest recesses of nature are laid open, in which splendid arts, noble aids to convenient living, a supply of innumerable instruments and machines, and even the hidden secrets of our bodies are discovered; not to mention the new light daily thrown upon antiquity.[99]

Huygens (1629–1695):

I hope that in time all nations, even the less civilized, will embrace each other as dear comrades, and will join forces, both intellectual and material, to banish ignorance and to make true and useful philosophy regnant.

Francis Bacon (1561–1626):

No age hath been more happy in liberty of enquiry than this.

Dryden (1631–1700):

In these last hundred years . . . almost a new Nature has been revealed to us — more errors of the schools have been detected, more useful experiments in philosophy have been made, more noble secrets in optics, medicine, anatomy and astronomy have been discovered than in all these doting and credulous ages from Aristotle to us.

Even Luther (1483–1546) in 1521:

Whoever reads these chronicles will find that from the birth of Christ on, the whole history of the world in these hundreds of years is unparalleled, in every way.   Such building and planting have never been in the whole world, such fine and varied eating and drinking so common as they are now.   Clothing, too, has become so splendid that it cannot become finer.   Who, moreover, has ever seen such trading as now journeys round and swallows up the whole world.

[97] Quoted from P. Smith, *A History of Modern Culture* (New York, 1930), Vol. I, pp. 147 ff.
[98] *De Civitate Solis.*
[99] *Samtliche Schriften* (1669), Vol. I, p. 30.

And so on. We hear and read these statements every day in almost any newspaper, in any address of a politician, lecture of a professor, or sermon of a minister, and practically everywhere.

The following excerpts give a typical picture of the superior attitude of the scientific truths to other truths, their mutual tacit or open animosity, their explicit or implicit warfare.

Descartes (1596–1650) who is far from being extreme or atheistic:

And although religion teaches us much on this subject (the nature of our souls and their immortality), nevertheless I confess in myself an infirmity which seems to be common to the greater part of mankind; namely that though we wish to believe and even think we believe strongly all that religion teaches us, yet are we not usually so touched by it as by what has been brought home to us by natural and clear reason.[100]

The testimony of such witnesses (biased, but in this instance, just because of the bias, it is particularly trustworthy) as Bossuet (1627–1704) gives the picture of the objective results of the scientific truth upon the religious truth of faith. The scientists factually were

denying the work of creation and that of redemption, annihilating hell, abolishing immortality, stripping Christianity of all its mysteries and changing it into a philosophical sect agreeable to sense, by which all religions are made the same. The foundation of faith attacked, Scripture directly assailed, and the path opened to Deism, which is disguised Atheism.[101]

In another place he exclaims:

How I hate these philosophers who, measuring the designs of God by their own thought, make of him nothing but the author of a certain general order, from which the rest develops as it can.[102]

Even in the testimony of Huygens some of the thinkers, like Hobbes, were violently warfaring against religion.

Our Leviathan is furiously attacking and destroying our universities and especially ministers and clergy and all religion, as though the Christian world had no sound knowledge, none that was not ridiculous either in philosophy or religion. [And he qualified Hobbes's theories as] arrogance which will vomit poisonous filth against us.[103]

Besides, the purely objective results of a certain theory, unforeseen often by the author and perhaps even unwanted by him, frequently have

---

[100] *Correspondence of Descartes and Huygens*, p. 182 and *op. cit.*, p. 193.

[101] P. Smith, *Correspondence*, p. 421.

[102] *Correspondance de Bossuet*, Vol. II, p. 383.

[103] Jan. 1, 1659. Huygens, *Œuvres*, Vol. II, p. 296. See also R. Boyle, *Works*, Vol. I, p. 186.

CLARIFICATION OF SYSTEMS OF TRUTH

happened to be unfavorable to the truth of faith and of reason. An example of this is well pointed out by one of the eighteenth-century critics of such supposedly "religious" or moderate theory as that of Descartes.

The Cartesian [philosophy] with its Corpuscularian Hypothesis, attempts to explain all the phenomena of nature by matter and motion; requiring only that God should create a sufficient quantity of each, just enough to set him [Descartes] on work, and then pretends to do business without his further aid . . . this hypothesis, I say, which on the one hand contributed so much to free philosophy from the nonsense and tyranny of the Schools, yet, on the other produced, while it was in vogue, many rank and irreligious materialists.[104]

Bossuet again remarks: "I see that under the name of Cartesianism a great battle against the Church is preparing."[105]

In brief now from the victor (empiricism) the truth of faith began to receive "the rough treatment" which it itself gave to the truth of senses at the moment of its victory from the period of early Christianity to that of idealistic rationalism. If nowadays one often hears about the persecution by and intolerance of religion in regard to science, it must not be forgotten that the scientific truth is just as intolerant toward, and as persecutory of, the truth of faith as religion is of the truth of senses. Each of these extreme forms of truth is intolerant and has to war with the other. Now empiricism reacted toward religion as religion previously did toward empiricism.

There is no doubt that many scientists like Kepler, Newton, and others were religious, but the objective results of their scientific works often proved detrimental themselves or were used by others injuriously against the truth of faith and of reason, contrary to the desire of the scientists, as was the case with Newton (who wrote his great *Principia*, on which is based the "classical mechanics and physics," and *Commentary on Apocalypse*).

As to doubts and skepticisms, their germs reappeared simultaneously with the beginning of the decline of the idealistic rationalism, and then, after a brief disappearance, they emerged almost simultaneously with a big upward swing of empiricism around the beginning of the sixteenth century. Since that time they have been with us up to the present moment. The inner reason for the lack of certitude in empiricism was mentioned previously.

This reason, as well as the uncertainties and doubts, was felt and understood fully by the delicate and refined minds of the sixteenth and

[104] W. Warburton (an Anglican bishop), *Divine Legation of Moses* (London, 1788), Vol. III, p. 330.   [105] *Correspondance de Bossuet*, Vol. III, p. 370.

the seventeenth centuries. Pascal (1623–1662) can serve as an example of that.

I look on all sides and I find everywhere nothing but obscurity. Nature offers nothing which is not a subject of doubt and disquietude; if I saw nowhere any sign of a Deity I should decide in the negative; if I saw everywhere the signs of a Creator, I should rest in peace in my faith; but, seeing too much to deny and too little confidently to affirm, I am in a pitiable state, and I have longed a hundred times that, if a God sustained nature, nature should show it without ambiguity, or that, if the signs of a God are fallacious, nature should suppress them altogether. Let her say the whole truth or nothing, so that I may see what side I ought to take.[106]

A little later, thinkers like Montaigne (1533–1592) and Peter Bayle (1647–1706) developed this seed of skepticism much further and tried to show that though neither religious nor scientific truth is certain, it is unimportant because from the practical standpoint the certain truth is not more useful than error.

'Tis therefore certain, that the discovery of errors is not important or useful to the prosperity of the State, or of private persons. . . . The faith of mankind does not depend upon them (errors). A narrative abounding with the grossest ignorance is as proper to move the passions, as historical exactness.[107]

Having started with the burning of the truth of religion, skepticism could not stop there but tended to burn science and everything which was taken as a new refuge of certainty. This is exactly what happened. After religion, the certainty of the reason and science itself was also doubted. "Men have tried everything and sounded everything, but have found in this mass of science . . . nothing solid and firm, but all variety," is the motto of Michel de Montaigne.[108] Religion is uncertain; our reason is uncertain; science as well as philosophy is full of fantastic follies which come and go as fashion; truth is a neighbor of falsehood; even probability is hard to obtain in knowledge. "Is there anything that can be proposed unto you, either to allow or to refute, that cannot be considered as ambiguous or doubtful?"

Then Kant (1724–1804) with his criticism contributed something to its further development in so far, at least, as he demonstrated that the true reality in itself and for itself was unknowable, was even somewhat uncertain whether or not it existed, and in this way prepared the ground for

---

[106] Pascal, *Pensées*, 229. Later on he found the certitude in mysticism and truth of faith.
[107] P. Bayle, *Historical and Critical Dictionary*, 2d ed. (London, 1734), Vol. I, Preface and pp. 1–2.
[108] See especially Vol. I, chap. xxvi and Vol. III, chap. xiii of his *Essays*.

agnosticism, positivism, "fictitionism" ("as if," *als ob*), conventionalism (the framework of science is conditional and conventional), relativism, and finally for pragmatism and illusionism.

Such a stream had to call its "counterpoison," *fideism*, and it can be seen that it appeared only a short time after the reappearance of skepticism, and since that time has remained in the open, being almost equal in power to skepticism, its *alter ego*, and has repeated fairly regularly, with a slight lag, the fluctuations of skepticism as its "counteraction."

VIII. TRUTH OF SENSES TRIUMPHANT

These tendencies, however, have been secondary. The main trend has been the rising tide of empiricism quite parallel to the rising tide of the scientific discoveries. There have been some minor fluctuations in this ascendance: temporary declines at the end of the sixteenth and at the beginning of the seventeenth centuries (the period of the Counter-Reformation and of Ascetic Protestantism); at the beginning of the eighteenth and of the nineteenth centuries (reaction against the mentality of the Enlightened Philosophy and the Revolution, at the beginning of the nineteenth century), but these down-swings were secondary and temporary. The trend for the last four centuries has been for empiricism to rise steadily until, at the beginning of the twentieth century, it reached a unique, unprecedented level, making about 53 per cent of all the systems of truth. There was also a unique and unprecedented multiplication and increase of important discoveries and inventions in the sciences. Thus we truly live in the age of the truth of senses, of a magnitude, depth, and brilliancy hardly witnessed in other cultures and periods. Scientism is in truth the most prominent and most important mark of our mentality.

In the light of that it is comprehensible why we are prone to think that there is only one system of truth, the scientific truth; and that everything outside it, particularly the truth of faith or of reason, is either "superstition" or "baseless speculation"; why many ministers of God now try to make "scientific religion" and to remodel their nominally Christian creed along the lines of science — so much so, that in their "scientific religion" or "liberal Christianity" there often remains little if anything from Christianity and its dogmas; why the center of the intellectual life shifted from the church pulpit to the university laboratory or classroom; why we look mainly and often exclusively to science as the only agency to solve our individual and social difficulties; and why science is regarded by many as powerful a panacea as God in the eyes of the believers. Just as in the age of the truth of faith God's name was everywhere, so in our time Science is on everyone's mind and lips, from quacks and salesmen to scientists and scholars themselves.　If something is qualified "scientific," even soap, face powder, car grease, or dog biscuits, it sounds to us as great as the word "orthodox" in an age of faith.　"Unscientific," on the contrary, sounds as bad as the words "heretic," "sacrilegious," and "blasphemous" in the period of the early Middle Ages.

Many other traits follow from, and are indeed mere logical elements of, this dominant system of truth.　As mentioned previously, the domination of the truth of faith logically and immanently leads to a neglect of the study of the empirico-sensory world and therefore to stagnation or even regression of the natural sciences and technology.

For empiricism the situation is radically different.　From the very nature of the truth of senses, it logically follows that science should and can study only the empirico-sensory phenomena, and first of all the material phenomena — inorganic, organic, and biological; hence the concentration of attention on the phenomena of the natural sciences; hence an intensive work and effort and study of their objects; hence the rapid progress of the scientific discoveries and technical inventions; hence a lack of interest and unwillingness, often even animosity and rebellion, to waste one's good mind in a study of what hardly exists, is in any event problematical and probably most superstitious, namely, the problems of supersensory God, soul, angels, virtue, justice, salvation, sin, saintliness, and so on.　Just as the mentality dominated by faith feels and views the sensory world as a kind of illusion, so the empirical mentality views and feels the supersensory world as a mere delusion. Only the insane can and will study the phantasmagorias of delusion. The sane minds can and will study only the empirical world.　This is the reason (and not necessarily that scientists have better minds or better talents than those of men of the truth of faith) why the natural sciences make rapid progress in such a period.

Just as the mentality of the *truth of faith spiritualizes everything*, even the inorganic material phenomena and their motions or happenings (see Chapters Four and Eleven), so the mentality of the *truth of senses*, which by definition perceives, and can perceive, only the material phenomena, *materializes everything, even the spiritual phenomena*, like the human soul; seeks for the material substratum, the material motive in everything, and reduces man to the class of the inorganic, or merely organic, material phenomena.　As we shall see, empiricism, materialism, mechanisticism, and determinism are positively associated and go together, while the truth of faith, idealism, indeterminism, and nonmechanisticism or animism (in the sense of seeing spiritual agents behind the sensory material phenomena, not in the sense necessarily of the animism of primitive groups) also go together.

This explains why, in a period when empiricism dominates, there is a tendency even to interpret man's mind, psychology, ideas, feelings, beliefs, and likewise the immaterial culture itself "mechanistically," "materialistically," "deterministically," "behavioristically," "physiologically," "reflexologically," "endocrinologically," "psychoanalytically," and why all such "mechanistic" interpretations of man and culture, which leave in man nothing divine or spiritual, or non-reflexo-animal, prosper in such an age and are viewed as particularly, and the only, "scientific." Whether it will be "economic interpretation of history," or "mechanistic interpretation" of social events, or "endocrinological, psychoanalytical" interpretation of man as a mere bag filled with filthy sex (Freud), or sex hunger plus excretion reflex (some other psychoanalysts), or a mere plaything of this or that gland and its secretions, or whether it will be "behavioristic" interpretation along exactly the same line of mechanism of reflexes which govern paramecia and rats, or some other variety of the "physiodirty" theory, they all bear the marks of materialism, mechanisticism, determinism, and sensorism and all prosper and are viewed as "scientific" in such an age of the truth of senses. In a culture in which such a system of truth dominates, it cannot be otherwise; hence the virtues and the sins of all such theories. In an age of faith they can hardly appear; if they do appear, they will scarcely have any following, and it will be still more impossible for them to acquire prestige. They probably will be stamped as blasphemy, "the utter and most shameless indecency," the product of insanity and of mental and moral idiocy, and so on.

In an age when the truth of sense dominates they have been and are recurrently haloed and praised as great scientific discoveries, as new steps in the progress of the scientific study of man and culture, as a great achievement, and so on; and their inventors will obtain honors, prestige, authority, and all the other tokens of social appreciation and recognition of their great achievements in the enrichment of human knowledge concerning man and his behavior.

All this is familiar to us from what we have now; all this appeared at the beginning of the period under investigation and was repeated before, on a smaller scale, in the Graeco-Roman culture in the period of growth of the empirical system of truth. And it all logically follows from the very principle of the truth of senses.

Not all these traits only, but also hundreds and hundreds of others of our mentality, are easily apprehended in the light of the present dominating system of truth. In the discovery of truth itself and the scientific methodology such conspicuous characteristics of the "scientific method," as *quantitative approach and measurement* of everything, including even what cannot be measured : intelligence, mind, qualitative values, and so on. It was not incidental that the seventeenth century created "social physics," wherein all the spiritual, cultural, and other immaterial phenomena were studied *modo mathematico sive geometrico* in exactly the same manner and with the same principles with which physics studied matter.[109]

Since that time *the transportation of the methods of the physicochemical and mathematical sciences into* the field of psychology, sociology, history, religion, culture, art, and so on, has been incessant and indefatigable and has continued up to this day. For a scientific study of anything and the discovery of truth, the role of thought as such has been considered less and less important. Instead, the *role of "technique" is regarded paramount.* If the "technique" applied is right, even an idiot can make a contribution; such is the situation suggested by the incessant talk of scientific and other technique which is going on now and has been going on for these four centuries. Respectively, the role of "speculation," in the sense of the analytical and synthesizing work of thought as such, has fallen into disrepute.

In other fields of social life the satellites of such a mentality have been multitudinous, as indicated by the enormous expenditures of money for schools, universities, laboratories, and research; by the elevated position of scientists and researchers, up to the countless "experts" and "brain trusters" as the real power in political, social, or any other control. But this will be discussed in Chapter Three of this work.

IX. FOREBODINGS

Such, then, is the system of truth which now dominates and with which we have breathed and lived since the beginning of our conscious life. What is the future? Shall we expect, as most of the scholars and scientists in these centuries and especially in the nineteenth century assured us, that this trend of bigger and better empiricism will continue forever and ever? Should we think that, since it is the only "scientific system of truth," this truth, since it is discovered, cannot fail in the future and give

---

[109] See E. Spektorsky, *The Problems of Social Physics in the Seventeenth Century,* 2 vols. (in Russian) (Warsaw, 1910, and Kiev, 1917). P. Sorokin, *Contemporary Sociological Theories,* chap. i.

place again to superstitions and speculation? Should we subscribe, then, that from now on the progress of the human mind will forever run along the track of the empirical system of truth and that the other truths do not have any chance for a recapture of domination and are doomed to die out?

Such has been the belief of most of the scientists and scholars in the preceding centuries, and such is the belief at the present time. Any forecasting of the future in such a matter must be a guess; but with this reservation one can say that this dominant belief is hardly probable. Since in the past there have occurred fluctuations from one system to another and from the empirical to the Ideational truth, there is no guarantee that such a shift cannot happen in the future. If, furthermore, empiricism as a system of truth rises and falls in its main tides parallel with those of the discoveries in the natural sciences, a slackening of the rate of their progress will probably lead to a decline of the truth of senses. We shall see in the next chapter some symptoms of a slowing down in the progress of the scientific discoveries and inventions in recent times. If it is continued, in all probability the truth of senses will suffer a decline, proportional to the decline in science. More than that, in conformity with the principle of "immanent causation" empiricism in its development must have a limit after which it has to "turn its direction" from ascendance to stagnation or decline. Without interference from external factors, it bears, like any other system of truth, the germs of its self-destruction or decline for some time.

And an attentive observer of the modern times and the modern science can possibly already notice several signs of such a self-destruction. Few may be mentioned here. Their inner importance is not spectacular, but for thoughtful thinkers they are pregnant with a number of most important consequences.

Empiricism and empirical science in the process of its developments have quite unexpectedly themselves brought us to a strange result: to the illusionary and visionary nature of the "reality" with which they deal. Since they recognize only the sensory reality, logically, with the progress of their study of it, this reality has been found more and more conditional, subjective, refracted, diffracted, and modified by the organs of senses, their variety, their changes, their modifications by the environment, and respectively by the contradictory results given by persons and groups who either had sensory or cultural differences or differences in the instruments and in the technique of their empirical study. The result has been agnosticism, positivism, pragmatism (what is pleasant is true, what does not help eudaemonistically or hedonistically or pragmatically is untrue: if the idea of God helps one to enjoy life, God exists; if it does not help, He does not exist.   Quite an elastic theory of truth!) ; relativism, *and illusionary impressionism in science — the mentality of "as if"* (formulated by Vaihinger and other Neo-Kantians).

The first and safe world of matter has already disappeared.   It has become a mere "possibility of perception."   The material things themselves became but "routine of perception" (in the terminology of K. Pearson) ; even the firm laws of science, still believed in the nineteenth century, have lost somewhat their certitude, definiteness, and have become mere probabilities.   The reality has been changing into something less and less real, more and more dreamy and illusionistic.   Even atoms and solid matter, together with the solid laws of mechanics, are shattered.   As a result the science itself in its immanent course has brought us to something very indefinite, very nebulous, quite uncertain, conditional, relativistic, and illusionistic.   A similar illusionism we met in the modern art. We shall see that in other compartments of the present-day culture a similar illusionism is also paramount.   Considering this, one may venture to say that such a picture of reality as an illusion can hardly satisfy mankind forever, especially since this illusion is fairly dull, mechanistic, and devoid of the spiritual and interesting agents from the gnomes, ghosts, good and bad spirits, up to angels, devils, God, and Satan.   If one has to choose between a dull and an enchanting illusion, one would prefer rather the enchanting one if for no other reason than an aesthetic one.[110]   The "illusions" of the age of faith and of idealistic rationalism, especially, were at least less dull, more inspiring, ennobling, elevating, and romantic than the illusionism of the abstract "as if" constructions and principles.

Not only illusion but science also in the process of its development, especially in the last fifty years, has been bringing more and more uncertainty.   More and more discrepancies between various hypotheses began to crop out.   Faster and faster (as we shall see) the fundamental principles and theories began to change and today's "generally accepted" theory will be found inadequate tomorrow and will be replaced by a new order (only new the day after tomorrow), which in turn will be replaced by a

[110] *Cf.* B. Russell, " The Revolt against Reason," in *Atlantic Monthly* (1935), pp. 222–232 ; L. Hogben, *The Retreat from Reason* (London, 1936) ; K. Singer, " *Die geistesgeschichtliche Bedeutung des Faschismus,*" in *Schmollers Jahrbuch* (1932), Vol. II, pp. 1203–1221 ; L. Rougier, " *Les mystiques politiques contemporaines* " (Paris, 1935) ; K. Mannheim, " The Crisis of Culture," in *The Sociological Review* (1934) ; E. Spranger, *Der Sinn der Voraussetzungslosigkeit in den Geisteswissenschaften* (Berlin, 1929) ; W. Inge, *God and the Astronomer* (New York, 1933).

"new new" theory, and so on. It was only a short time ago that Darwinian, Mendelian, Newtonian, and many other theories were held to be eternal, but now there remain much less of them than a few decades ago. Such a rapid change robs man more and more of his certitude. Factually we are already living in an Age of Incertitude. It is true that some scholars who are not up to date still talk about the method and trend of "successive approximation" to a greater and better knowledge of this or that phenomenon; but it would be difficult for them to show, indeed, the existence of such a successive approximation, especially in the last few decades, unless they accept their own views as the most "successive approximation" (again a variety of linear conception). What we have had in these decades in many fields has been not a successive approximation but "permanent revolutions" in which a given theory has been overthrown by quite a different one; and this in turn has been often overthrown by a variety of the defeated theory. In such an overthrow there is little of the successive approximation, but there is instead a rather erratic shift from one theory to another, which is different and sometimes contrary to it. Perhaps someone is willing to style such an erratic walk as an approximation, but in most cases it is not, and the walker often lands in a place far from his destination.

One can turn to any field of science now and find first of all a multitude of different theories and sometimes even opposite hypotheses fighting one another for "recognition" as true theory. Such an opulence of contradictions and mutual criticism does not permit any certitude, especially concerning the most important principles, and therefore fosters more and more uncertainty. Nowadays in any science scarcely a fundamental principle exists concerning the empirical world, as well as the laws of logic, which is uncontested and "universally accepted."

If such a situation continues — and empiricism, as long as it is dominant, cannot help continuing it — the incertitude will increase. Its increase will more and more obliterate the difference between "the scientific truth" of one group of scientists with their "as if" and the blatant offhand crass ignorance of another group that also can say this "as if" for their stand. The boundary lines between knowledge and nonknowledge thus are bound to become less and less clear. When this situation approaches, man is likely to prefer out of two *als ob*'s the one which gives him firmer certitude and the one which happens to be more fascinating, more ennobling, more elevating, and more imaginative, or better adapted to the emotional status. In such circumstances the truth of senses can easily give way to a truth of faith.

In other words, neither doubt, nor uncertainty, nor changeability of the scientific theories can be pushed too far without destroying science itself and its truth.   Contemporary science has already possibly gone too far in that direction and therefore is already exposed to danger.

Then we must not forget the "*primum vivere deinde philosophare.*" Life, in order to be decently possible, needs many other values besides science: for instance, the decent behavior of its members; several virtues, beginning with a readiness to make sacrifices; some altruism, willingness to perform duty, and many other values.   If empirical truth is placed above all these and given an unlimited liberty for its development, it may prove itself exceedingly injurious to many "illusions" which are necessary for the existence of such values in a group.   As a matter of fact it has already injured many of them, beginning with the religious and ending with the moral, political, and many other values.   By its very nature the standpoint of empirical science is totally amoral, areligious, asocial.   Good and bad, sacred and profane, sinful and virtuous, harmful and beneficial, these and similar categories are perfectly heterogeneous to it and are outside of it.   It studies with "the same objectivity" the saint and the criminal, the moral and unmoral, the sacred and the vulgar phenomena.   As a matter of fact even these qualifications, strictly speaking, are unscientific because they involve some evaluation different from that of the scientific.   If, therefore, science drives out the other truths within which such categories are natural, the result may be amoralism, asociality, and similar phenomena which make decent social life impossible.   Suppose someone should discover a simple but terrific explosive which could easily destroy a considerable part of our planet.   Scientifically, it would be the greatest discovery, but socially the most dangerous for the very existence of mankind, because out of 1,800,000,000 human beings there certainly would be a few individuals who, being "scientifically minded," would like to test the explosive and as a result would destroy our planet.   Such an explosion would be a great triumph of science, but it would lead to the destruction of mankind.   This half-fantastic example shows that there must be limitations of science imposed by the reasons which are outside it, and these reasons usually come from the truth of faith and that of reason.

In conclusion, the above gives an allusion to the immanent consequences of science itself, which come with its excessive development and begin to inhibit it in its further progress and in its excessive domination over the other truths.   Regardless of any exterior factors, these immanent consequences are sufficient to slow down or even to stop for some time the growth of this domination and to call forth a revival of the other forms of truth.

The truth of senses in this respect is not in an exclusive position.   The same is true of the other forms of truth : their excessive domination is also followed by immanent consequences which inhibit internally their further development and lead to their decline for some time, regardless of the interference of the external factors.   Thus the domination of the truth of faith slowed down and then declined not so much because of the interference of external factors but because of the internal development of this system of truth itself.

With the progress of Christian faith there began to appear one after another somewhat discordant but purely theological "interpretations" of the creed and dogmas.   One kind of a divine revelation was followed by another divine revelation which was different from the first, and sometimes contrary to it.   One interpretation of the words of the Scripture was followed by another, but different, interpretation.   For instance, such discordant sects and factions appeared in Christianity very early, almost simultaneously with its emergence.   In the fourth and the fifth centuries the theological discordance was already terrific and necessitated the all-Christian Councils of Nicaea and others with all the clash of the opinions and struggle of the factions (Arian, Monophysitic, Nestorian, and other "heresies").   No creed is exempt from the appearance of such conflicts of interpretations, dogmas, and principles, though they all claim to be the truths of faith.   As a result, it is merely a matter of time before they begin their mutual struggle and are forced to resort to reason, logic, and sensory experience to prove the point of each faction.

The very multiplicity of the discordant revelations or truths of faith lead naturally to a conclusion that something, somewhere, must be wrong since all the opposite contentions pretend to be the absolute truth of faith. Eventually the very belief in such a truth begins to weaken.   Skepticism, inquiry, questioning, doubt in these truths of faith and in the truth of faith generally appear.   To settle it, logic and experience have to be called forth.   Idealistic rationalism is in fact the consequence of such a situation and phase when the doubted truth of faith calls to logic and empirical experience for help.   When these are called, they have to, and in fact do, grow out of the servant role to that of the independent person and then to that of the master.   In that way the truth of faith has also a limit in its development and domination and immanently calls forth its own decline for some period of time.   This is also true of idealistic rationalism.   All the forms of truth are subject to this "dialectical destiny" and are hardly exempt from a self-preparation of their own decline in the course of their development. The whole question is merely one of the length of time necessary for such a "cycle" to run. There is hardly any regular periodicity in the span of time during which each form of truth dominates. So far as the period of twenty-five hundred years studied and several cases in the history of other cultures — the Chinese, Hindu, and, in part, Arabian — show, the periods of the domination of the truth of faith seems to have been all in all longer than those of the other forms of truth and the period of domination of the idealistic rationalism the shortest of all.

In the light of these considerations it is probable that the present domination of the truth of senses will hardly continue forever. Probably in some near or remote future its domination will decline also and after the transitory period of reorganization of the system of truth, the truth of faith — whatever is its form — will rise again and will again be dominant. Then again it will find its span of time at an end and will decline, giving place probably to some kind of idealistic rationalism; then the truth of senses will rise again and so on, forever and ever as long as the history of the *homo sapiens* is continued.

The sequential order of these alternations in most of the cases is probably such as described, but it is not to be assumed that in some cases the sequence cannot be different. However improbable it seems for the present domination of the truth of senses to be followed by that of the truth of reason, or the truth of faith to be followed directly by that of senses, I would not swear that it has never taken place and never will. Though the typical, or the most frequent, sequence is the one that I have described, exceptions are to be found in every rule of history, and they might be found in this instance also.

Whatever is going to be the future system of truth, the foregoing shows that the systems of truth truly fluctuate in their domination and in the increase and decrease of their power in the course of time. Perhaps the deepest reason for such a fluctuation is that none of these three systems contains the whole truth, the truth of a really omniscient mind. Each of them has, perhaps, only a part of truth and side by side with it a part of falsity. When falsity begins to take the upper hand over the truth which the system has, it begins to decline and the other form of truth accentuates that part of the Whole Truth which was deficient in the preceding system. Then in its turn it repeats the same "cycle." In these "accentuations" of different aspects of the Whole Truth its manifoldness, richness, inexhaustibility, and infinity are demonstrated. This Whole Truth of the

Omniscient Mind seems to be far greater and deeper and many-sided than the narrow truth either of faith only, or of reason only, or of senses only. This inference is, of course, not a truth of senses but rather one of idealistic rationalism.   As such it appears to me probable and also beautiful.   Therefore, as metaphysics it is quite acceptable to me and, anyhow, more so than the identification of the Whole Truth with one of the three systems of it.   Such an identification is much more contradicted by the "facts" and by "logic" than the above "metaphysics."

The preceding shows also that the main propositions set forth at the beginning of this volume are well corroborated by the quantitative as well as the qualitative data.

So much about that fundamental problem. We will not stop here, however, for we have to go still further in our study of the fluctuations of the contents of the systems of truth.   Of the propositions formulated in the preceding chapter there still remain undemonstrated the proposition about the relationship between the systems of truth and the movement of the scientific discoveries and inventions and the statement that with the fluctuation of the systems of truth many of the leading principles, dogmas, and theories of science and philosophy fluctuate in their influence and acceptability in accordance with the dominant type of truth and culture. So we turn now to a substantial study of the movement of the scientific discoveries and technological inventions.

Chapter Three

MOVEMENT OF SCIENTIFIC DISCOVERIES AND TECHNO-LOGICAL INVENTIONS[1]

I. METHODOLOGICAL PRELIMINARIES

It was stated in the two preceding chapters that the movement of scientific discoveries and inventions is associated with the type of culture and its prevalent system of truth. The rate of scientific development tends to become slow, stationary, even regressive in Ideational cultures (in which there is a complete domination of the truth of faith), becoming rapid and growing apace in Sensate cultures (wherein the truth of senses dominates). For the elaboration of this proposition, and for the elucidation of the many important problems involved in a sociological study of the movement of discoveries and inventions, there will now be presented an analysis of the development and fluctuations of the natural sciences and technology.[2]

Neither vague generalities concerning scientific progress from the time of the supposedly ignorant prehistoric man to the *homo sapiens* of the "Century of Progress" nor occasional fragmentary illustrations can answer the questions adequately. Likewise are purely verbal quantitative descriptions unsatisfactory for reasons indicated in Chapter One of this volume. On the other hand it is equally evident that a perfect device for the measurement of the comparative progress of science at various periods is also unavailable. Under these circumstances, one must rest temporarily content with the best available barometer of the comparative progress or regress of science. *This index is comprised of the number of scientific discoveries and technological inventions made in each of the periods compared.* If within two periods of equal duration — say, twenty-five years — were produced twenty-five and two discoveries, respectively, it is reasonable to maintain that scientific

---

[1] In co-operation with R. K. Merton and J. W. Boldyreff.

[2] For the sake of brevity, the elliptical terms, "science," "sciences," "inventions," will be used for the more precise terms, "natural and physical sciences," and technological inventions.

progress was, at least quantitatively, greater in the first period than in the second.

The shortcomings of such a barometer are obvious. In the first place, not only the number but the *quality* of the discoveries should be considered. One important discovery may outweigh hundreds, even thousands, of less important achievements. Hence a more adequate barometer would register not only the number but also the qualitative importance of each discovery or invention. To effect such differentiations, each discovery must be assigned a certain numerical value ranging, let us say, from 1 for the least important to 10, 1000, or 1,000,000 for the most important. Summing up the assigned values of all the discoveries for each period, the total figure would provide a more adequate quantitative-qualitative index than that based merely upon the number of discoveries.

Unfortunately, however, this index cannot be constructed because of the difficulty, at present insurmountable, of qualitatively grading all known discoveries and inventions by assigning to each of them a certain numerical value. For if there is some difficulty involved in indicating a few of the greatest discoveries, it is an insuperable task accurately to rank thousands of less important discoveries. Moreover, the scale or range of values adopted, whether from 1 to 3, or from 1 to 15, or from 1 to 1,000,000 is arbitrary. For these and similar reasons such a hypothetically precise barometer is unattainable.

Achievable, however, is the index showing the movement of the number of discoveries and inventions in each of the periods compared. It provides at least a reliable approximation to the quantitative aspect of such a movement. However imperfect, it is certainly better than mere speculative generalities or fragmentary, unsystematically selected facts. Furthermore, it can be improved. Once the "quantitative basis" is obtained, it is possible to correct and to supplement it by data (not necessarily numerical) which give an approximate idea of the qualitative importance of the most fruitful discoveries in each period.

Moreover, a recent investigation [3] has demonstrated that there is *synchronous* movement of indices of scientific and scholarly achievement based respectively upon (1) the equal evaluation of individuals, (2) differentiation, according to importance, on a scale ranging from 1 to 3, (3) differentiation ranging from 1 to 15 "points." It can be seen from Figure 2 that the curves derived from evaluation on these three bases vary concurrently (save in minor details). The essential difference is found in

[3] P. A. Sorokin and R. K. Merton, "The Course of Arabian Intellectual Development, 700–1300 A.D.," in *Isis*, Vol. XXII (1935), pp. 516–524.

the amplitude of the several "waves" of development. The same is demonstrated by all the subsequent tables and figures: the movements of curves where the thinkers are given an equal value of one, and where they are given different values from 1 to 12, are essentially similar, almost

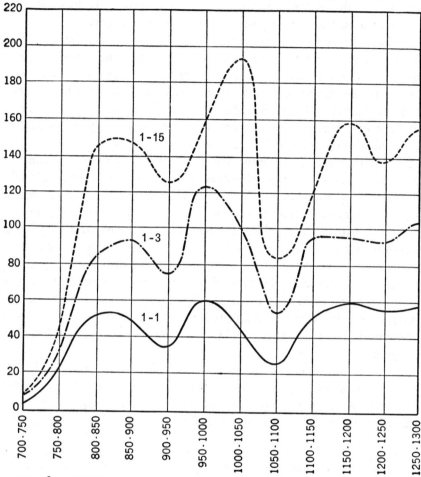

FIG. 2. COMPARATIVE INTELLECTUAL DEVELOPMENT OF ARABIAN CIVILIZATION, A.D. 700–1300

identical (see Chapters One to Seven). It would seem a legitimate inference from the essential similarity of the course of development pictured by these curves that an index based exclusively upon the *number* of discoveries and inventions is not misleading and that it reflects actual movements in so far as these are accurately described by the historian of science.

The reason for this is at hand. A discovery is deemed fundamentally important when it opens new fields and new possibilities for further developments. When such a pathfinding discovery is made, it is followed by a legion of other discoveries which "flow" from it. The relatively unimportant discovery is, on the contrary, unfruitful. It does not open any, or at least many, new possibilities for further discoveries and hence is not likely to be followed by a host of new scientific conquests. These almost axiomatic considerations explain largely why the periods of great discoveries are also periods of a large number of discoveries, and vice versa. If the importance of a great discovery is appreciated at once it will be followed almost immediately by an increase in the number of auxiliary discoveries. In such cases, periods wherein *great* discoveries occur will also be periods of large *numbers* of discoveries.

Sometimes, however, the importance of a great discovery is not immediately recognized; an interval elapses before such appreciation is forthcoming. In such instances, the period of an increase in the *number* of discoveries may lag behind the period of the great discovery (or discoveries). But, with few exceptions, the period of lag is comparatively short. Therefore, in a rough way, the periods of great increases in the number of discoveries and inventions, or the periods immediately following them, are, as a rule, those of the great discoveries and inventions.[4] A few exceptions to this rule have occurred; but they were exceptions. These remarks explain why the quantitative barometer of discoveries and inventions is, in a sense, also a qualitative barometer; why, therefore, it is not grossly misleading.

Such an index is not misleading, however, only on the condition that all the discoveries and inventions for all the periods compared are registered completely or with an equal comparative completeness. If a study deals with long periods of time separated by intervals of several centuries,

---

[4] The mathematical inventions of the essential elements of calculus may serve as a "large-scale" example of this phenomenon. The basic innovations were those of Kepler (1615), Cavalieri (1598–1647), Descartes (1637), Leibnitz (1684), and Newton (1687). These major contributions opened the way for many minor ones which led to an amazing increase in the number of mathematical discoveries during the seventeenth and first part of the eighteenth century (see Table 5). In similar fashion, the Darwinian theory and associated discoveries are in no small degree responsible for an enormous increase in the number of biological discoveries during the interval 1850–1875, and somewhat later, in the number of medical discoveries. The curve of discoveries and of scientific literature pertaining to nitrogen fixation after the basic discovery by Hellriegel and Wilfarth in 1886 serves as a more restricted illustration of this same phenomenon. On this latter case, see P. W. Wilson and E. B. Fred, "The Growth Curve of a Scientific Literature," in *Scientific Monthly* (September, 1935), pp. 245–250.

or even longer, this condition is absent. Due to the obliterating role of time, as well as to failures in recording many discoveries, *it is highly probable that the discoveries and inventions of relatively recent times are registered in the annals of the history of science much more completely than, for instance, the discoveries made several hundreds or thousands of years ago.* As we shall see from the data based upon several of the most authoritative sources, the number of scientific discoveries made, for example, in Ancient Egypt, Ancient Assyria, Babylonia, India, China, and other great Oriental cultures of the past appears in these sources as incredibly small. The very fact that these ancient cultures possessed great cultural achievements makes it improbable that they were so nearly sterile in discoveries. It does not seem likely that they were so backward in this respect, in view of the fact that they constructed great buildings, performed marvelous engineering feats, successfully treated (as we now know, after several recent archeological findings) many ailments and maladies, possessed medical and biological treatises, surprisingly accurate calendars, and the like. In brief, due to the effacing role of time and other circumstances, we do not have as complete a record of their discoveries as of those in recent centuries. Therefore, the more remote the period, the more markedly do our data underestimate the number of discoveries. In this sense, they are unavoidably biased.

For the same reasons, the *number of discoveries cannot serve as a quantitative-qualitative barometer when the periods compared are relatively recent and several centuries removed, respectively.* In so far the subsequent data in this respect have to be taken *cum grano salis.* They are, if not unreliable, reliable only in a small degree and need a great deal of correction. On the other hand, if one compares either the consecutive periods within recent times or consecutive periods in the more distant past — for instance, discoveries of the ninth, tenth, and eleventh centuries A.D., or of the sixth, fifth, and fourth centuries B.C. — the difference in the completeness of the registration of the discoveries of the contiguous centuries is probably slight. There is no apparent reason to suppose that the discoveries of the fifth century B.C. are recorded less completely than those of the fourth or second century B.C. In other words, the obliterating role of time and other differential circumstances (among which the relatively late invention and spread of printing and the type — Ideational or Sensate — of culture may be specifically mentioned) make comparisons between more recent and more remote periods of dubious value. But in reference to periods prior to the last five or six centuries these factors cease to play a particularly important role in this respect. For these earlier periods the obliterating role of time remains, so to speak, constant, though not, of course, entirely so; the discoveries of the periods from 1000 to 4000 B.C. are almost certainly recorded less completely than those of the period between 600 B.C. and A.D. 1500. However, for all practical purposes, the completeness of the registration for consecutive centuries of, say, the same millennium may be assumed to be more or less equal; equally complete or incomplete, so far as the effacing role of time is concerned. For this reason, the data pertaining to such centuries may fruitfully be compared.

The degree of completeness in the recording of discoveries in our sources is not uniform in yet another respect: in regard to discoveries made in the several countries. Western historiography has, up to recent times, neglected the history of non-European countries. It has devoted relatively few pages to Ancient Egypt, Babylonia, Assyria, India, and China, while dealing with Occidental or with recent history in great detail. As Spengler aptly remarks:

The nineteenth century A.D. seems to us infinitely fuller and more important than, say, the nineteenth century B.C.; but the moon, too, seems to us bigger than Jupiter or Saturn. The physicist has long ago freed himself from prepossessions as to relative distance; the historian not so.[5]

This "prepossession" concerns not only remoteness in time but also the degree of congeniality of the cultures and their spatial adjacency. Even contemporary events of considerable importance in Oriental history are noted and recorded to a much smaller extent than "provincial" events in our own or neighboring country.

Similarly do our main sources, Darmstaedter's work and the ninth edition of the *Encyclopaedia Britannica* suffer from the same bias and prejudice. Written by Western scholars and scientists, these sources in all probability record the discoveries of Greece, Rome, and of the European countries including the United States and the British dominions much more fully than the discoveries of the countries outside this orbit, especially of the Oriental countries. Moreover, the *Encyclopaedia Britannica* is apparently partial even in regard to the several European countries: as J. W. Boldyreff's data show, it records more fully and devotes much more space to British science, art, philosophy, scholarship, statesmanship, and other achievements of British culture, than to achievements in these fields by other nationals. Furthermore, in respect to these other countries, the accounts of the discoveries, inventions, and of

[5] O. Spengler, *The Decline of the West* (New York, 1926), Vol. I, p. 94.

the cultural achievements generally of the Slavic, the Latin American, and the several other contemporary countries are appreciably less complete than those of the major European countries, such as France, Germany, etc.

For these reasons comparisons of the number of the discoveries made in different countries even during recent times, as recorded in these sources, must be made *cum grano salis*. This caution concerns the *Encyclopaedia Britannica* to a greater extent, perhaps, than the Darmstaedter work. Fortunately, with but few exceptions, there is virtually no need for making such comparisons for the purposes of this study.

The net consequences of these considerations and admonitions may be briefly summarized. The data concerning the number of discoveries and inventions compiled from the best available sources require considerable correction in the sense of increasing the number for the remote centuries of the past and thus decreasing somewhat the contrast between the number for recent centuries (especially after the invention of printing) and for centuries prior to the fourteenth. So far as centuries prior to the last five or six are concerned, there is doubtless lacking completely uniform and equally adequate registration of discoveries, but such discrepancies between intervals from about 600 B.C. to A.D. 1300 (for Graeco-Roman and Western cultures) are probably not extremely great. For the centuries between these limits and for these cultures, the existing data concerning the number of discoveries and inventions may be taken as fairly reliable and approximately indicative. The registration is incomplete, but the incompleteness is more or less constant for all these past centuries. Therefore the data are roughly comparable.

With these reservations, the proposition that the movement of the number of the discoveries from period to period is also roughly indicative of the importance of the discoveries may be accepted. The proposed index or "barometer" is still imperfect, but it is probably as accurate as any and is possibly the best available. To avoid over-nice discussion, other reservations and qualifications, obvious to author and reader alike, are omitted.

We may now proceed with the study of the movement itself. First to be considered is the general movement of discoveries and inventions in the various historical cultures, with a more detailed consideration of discoveries in Graeco-Roman and Western culture. Subsequently, the study is narrowed to several specific problems. Let it be said at the outset that only a few fundamental tables and charts are herewith presented, though many more specific tables have been computed (and are in my, as well as J. W. Boldyreff's, possession). For the purpose of economizing space they are not presented here, though many subsequent statements and data are based upon these special tables and computations.

But first, a few words about the chief sources from which the data were derived and the tables computed. The principal source is Ludwig Darmstaedter's *Handbuch zur Geschichte der Naturwissenschaften und der Technik*,[6] which is the co-operative work of twenty-six German specialists. This chronological survey probably affords the most comprehensive account available. It includes "not only the pioneering creations and fundamental achievements but also the separate individual steps necessary for a successful production. . . ." By and large we may say that all the important discoveries of science and technology are included along with a less comprehensive list of those less significant developments which were necessary for the final achievement. For the medical sciences, a more detailed work, F. H. Garrison's *An Introduction to the History of Medicine*,[7] was used as an additional source.

In Tables 5 to 9 discoveries and inventions are classified according to the period and country of origin and the field to which they pertain.

In all these fields, each unit corresponds to a discovery or development listed in the *Handbuch*. Similar discoveries, which are simultaneous but made independently by two or more individuals, are counted as separate items. The same discovery made co-operatively by more than one individual is counted as one unit.

In the field of mathematics are included arithmetic, algebra, geometry, trigonometry, and statistics. Innovations in the calendar and studies of menology as well as discoveries concerning stellar systems, astrophysics, etc., are placed in the field of astronomy. Biology includes zoology, botany, physical anthropology, and paleontology. The medical sciences embrace anatomy, surgery (phlebotomy, gynecology, ophthalmology), physiology, haematoscopy, bacteriology, and therapeutics (pharmacology except when it entails a discovery of new chemical materials). Physics is held to include studies of mechanics (except when used in practical application), optics, electricity, light, etc. Geology refers to seismology, stratigraphy, systematic geography, and physiography, but *not* geographical explorations, which are listed separately. The technology category includes applied science and technological inventions.

As previously suggested, it is not supposed that the source as well as the tables computed from it do not have shortcomings. But it is none

[6] Berlin, 1908.   [7] Philadelphia and London, 1929.

the less probable that both the original compilation and the subsequent tabulations comprise the closest approximation to the actual development of science and technology which is at present possible.

II. General Character of the Movement of Scientific Discoveries and Inventions

An answer to this problem is provided by Tables 5 to 9 and Figures 3 to 9. Table 5 — the basic table — comprises a tabulation of the number of discoveries and inventions by 100-, 50-, and 25-year periods from 3500 B.C. to A.D. 1908.[8]

Up to roughly the sixth century A.D., the figures refer to practically the whole world with the exception of China, India, and a few other Oriental countries. However, their share, due to the above incompleteness of recording, is small and does not materially change the situation. After that time, the figures concern only the Western World (European-American). This means that for the seventh to fourteenth centuries A.D. the share of the discoveries of Arabia — the only important contributor in the field for that period — is not included in Tables 5 and 6.[9] Table 5 includes the total figures for all the discoveries and inventions and explorations listed in Darmstaedter as well as for each main field of science. Table 6 comprises the movement of discoveries and inventions from 1400 to 1900, by decennia. Figures 3 to 6 depict the general movement of discoveries and inventions by 100-, 20-, and 10-year periods, and by special fields of science, and Figure 7 indicates the spread of discoveries and inventions by countries.

---

[8] A large number of tables by special fields and by countries are not included here because of their complicated and cumbersome nature. Some materials discussed herein and not found in the main table are taken from these omitted tables and additional computations.

[9] This is the main reason for the discrepancy between the figures given in Table 5 and those computed from the same source and given by B. Weinberg in his *"Les lois d'évolution des découvertes de l'humanité,"* in *Revue générale des sciences* (1926), No. 2. He includes all the countries.

Differences in the manner of computing Darmstaedter's data — for instance, counting as different items the same discovery made independently by two or more persons, counting a discovery made by several co-operating persons as one discovery, regarding auxiliary discoveries as separate units — are responsible for discrepancies between the figures in Table 5, those of Weinberg, and those of W. F. Ogburn and S. C. Gilfillan (*Recent Social Trends*, New York, 1933, p. 126). The figures given in Table 5 occupy an intermediary position between the most "liberal" computation of Weinberg and most "conservative" computation of Ogburn and Gilfillan. Another reason for these minor discrepancies is that the periodization differs: for instance, in my tables, 1501–1525, 1526–1550, and so on; in Ogburn-Gilfillan's computation they are: 1499–1524, 1525–1549, and so on. However, discrepancies are comparatively small and do not affect the results and conclusions in any appreciable way.

TABLE 5. WESTERN WORLD OUTPUT OF NATURAL SCIENCE, TECHNOLOGICAL, AND GEOGRAPHICAL DISCOVERIES AND INVENTIONS, BY 100-, 50-, AND 25-YEAR PERIODS

Period	Mathematics	Astronomy	Biology	Medical Science	Chemistry	Physics	Geology	Total (Science)	Technology	Geographical Discoveries	Grand Total	Boldyreff's Geometric Averages
3500–801 B.C.	1	2	—	—	2	—	—	5	17	—	22	—
800–701	—	3	—	—	—	—	—	3	6	—	9	—
700–601	2	—	—	—	—	—	—	2	5	—	7	—
600–501	3	7	2	3	3	1	1	20	10	1	31	17.9
500–401	8	8	2	8	1	6	1	34	5	1	40	14.7
400–301	7	5	14	8	4	8	—	46	12	2	60	64.5
300–201	2	9	2	4	5	11	—	33	12	—	45	12.9
200–101	—	2	4	2	2	4	—	14	2	1	17	30.7
100–0	1	2	1	6	2	2	—	14	17	1	32	22.5
1–100 A.D.	1	5	6	15	2	10	—	39	21	1	61	49.0
101–200	2	7	3	9	—	2	—	23	4	—	27	4.3
201–300	2	—	—	2	—	1	—	5	3	—	8	24.4
301–400	2	—	—	4	1	1	—	8	8	—	16	0.0
401–500	—	—	—	1	—	1	—	2	2	—	4	12.1
501–600	—	2	—	4	1	1	—	8	5	—	13	4.1
601–700	—	—	—	2	—	—	—	2	2	—	4	0.0^2
701–800	—	—	1	—	1	1	—	3	1	—	4	0.0^2
801–900	—	—	1	—	—	—	—	1	5	—	6	0.0^2
901–1000	—	—	1	—	—	—	—	1	5	1	7	0.0^2
1001–1050	—	—	—	—	—	—	—	—	3	2	5	0.0^2
1051–1100	—	—	—	—	—	—	—	—	2	1	3	0.0^2
1101–1150	—	—	—	2	—	1	—	3	5	—	8	0.0^2
1151–1200	—	—	—	3	1	—	—	4	—	—	4	0.0^2
1201–1250	1	1	5	4	3	1	—	15	3	2	20	12.2^2
1251–1300	1	—	5	3	12	3	—	24	6	3	33	13.2^2
1301–1350	3	1	3	5	1	6	1	20	12	4	36	8.8^2
1351–1400	—	1	3	2	2	1	2	11	13	5	29	5.8^2
1401–1450	1	2	1	1 (2)[1]	3	3	1	12	17	10	39	0.0^2
1451–1500	10	4	2	5 (29)[1]	4	1	7	33	32	23	88	12.1

Period												
1501–1525	3	3	1	7	3	7	—	24	27	26	77	96.3
1526–1550	7	5	4	40 } 48[1]	10	4	6	76	28	17	121	
1551–1575	3	13	10	25 } 68[1]	4	2	3	60	28	6	94	187.0
1576–1600	14	24	13	17	8	9	—	85	38	14	137	
1601–1625	14	31	3	13 } 66[1]	19	6	3	86	31	12	129	295.0
1626–1650	28	13	3	10	24	16	3	97	32	5	134	
1651–1675	23	24	16	56 } 112[1]	34	14	1	170	53	6	229	420.7
1676–1700	21	24	30	22	23	18	1	139	53	7	199	
1701–1725	12	19	9	16 } 107[1]	33	21	6	111	47	2	160	451.0
1726–1750	46	25	30	73	40	29	5	249	90	1	340	
1751–1775	21	20	32	58 } 165[1]	83	39	7	258	121	4	383	
1776–1800	24	26	37	64	191	67	21	416	261	14	691	1318.0
1801–1825	19	34	113	82 } 269[1]	307	110	39	686	378	26	1090	
1826–1850	22	42	231	137	478	242	27	1191	803	27	2021	2042.2
1851–1875	19	37	382	178 } 455[1]	489	311	32	1443	1073	39	2555	
1876–1900	7	55	371	263	459	430	32	1617	1223	21	2861	
1901–1908	—	15	77	114	216	123	7	552	309	1	862	
Total	329	478	1415	1268	2469	1511	175	7645	4830	286	12,761	

[1] Figures taken from F. H. Garrison, *An Introduction to the History of Medicine* (1929).
[2] Without Arabia and Persia.

TABLE 6. NUMBER OF IMPORTANT SCIENTIFIC, TECHNOLOGIC, AND
GEOGRAPHIC DISCOVERIES AND INVENTIONS, BY 10-YEAR PERIODS,
1401–1900 [1]

Years	Science	Technology	Geographic Discoveries	Total
1401–1410	—	3	1	4
1411–1420	—	4	1	5
1421–1430	—	2	—	2
1431–1440	7	6	3	16
1441–1450	5	2	5	12
1451–1460	6	3	3	12
1461–1470	3	6	—	9
1471–1480	8	10	2	20
1481–1490	9	4	2	15
1491–1500	7	9	16	32
1501–1510	6	13	11	30
1511–1520	15	11	11	37
1521–1530	13	7	8	28
1531–1540	26	11	9	46
1541–1550	40	13	4	57
1551–1560	25	13	3	41
1561–1570	21	11	3	35
1571–1580	29	16	4	49
1581–1590	39	10	7	56
1591–1600	31	16	3	50
1601–1610	33	14	7	54
1611–1620	44	11	5	60
1621–1630	23	13	—	36
1631–1640	35	11	2	48
1641–1650	48	14	3	65
1651–1660	35	17	2	54
1661–1670	79	28	2	109
1671–1680	90	16	3	109
1681–1690	68	28	5	101
1691–1700	37	17	1	55
1701–1710	46	20	—	66
1711–1720	48	22	—	70
1721–1730	69	18	2	89
1731–1740	76	25	1	102
1741–1750	121	52	—	173
1751–1760	108	33	—	141
1761–1770	69	53	3	125
1771–1780	165	74	3	242
1781–1790	183	109	5	297
1791–1800	149	113	7	269
1801–1810	228	128	6	362
1811–1820	286	157	13	456
1821–1830	388	227	16	631
1831–1840	441	313	9	763
1841–1850	534	356	9	899
1851–1860	584	423	13	1020
1861–1870	553	424	15	992
1871–1880	635	490	17	1142
1881–1890	663	477	13	1153
1891–1900	625	482	2	1109

[1] Computed from Ludwig Darmstaedter, *Handbuch zur Geschichte der Naturwissenschaften und der Technik.*

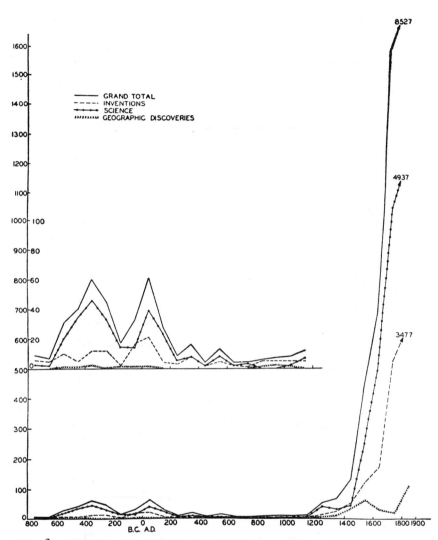

FIG. 3.   NUMBER OF SCIENTIFIC DISCOVERIES AND INVENTIONS FROM
800 B.C. TO A.D. 1900, BY CENTURIES

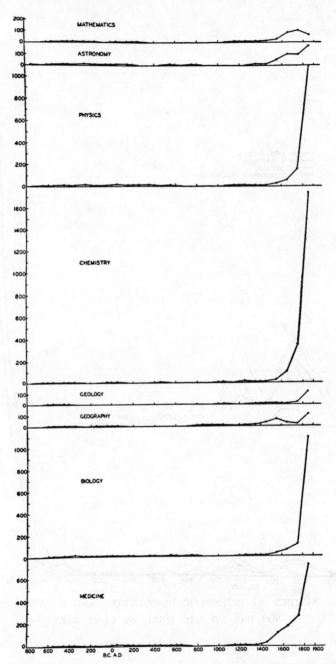

FIG. 4.   NUMBER OF SCIENTIFIC DISCOVERIES AND INVENTIONS FROM
800 B.C. TO A.D. 1900 BY CENTURIES

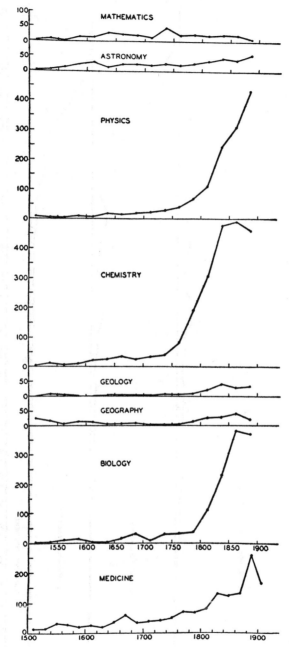

FIG. 5. NUMBER OF SCIENTIFIC DISCOVERIES AND INVENTIONS FROM 1500 TO 1900 BY 20-YEAR PERIODS

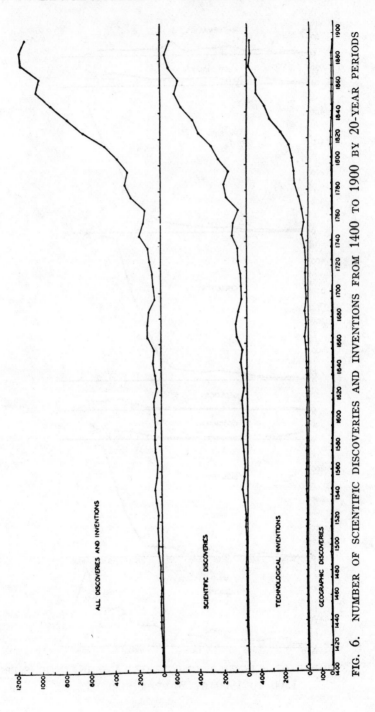

FIG. 6. NUMBER OF SCIENTIFIC DISCOVERIES AND INVENTIONS FROM 1400 TO 1900 BY 20-YEAR PERIODS

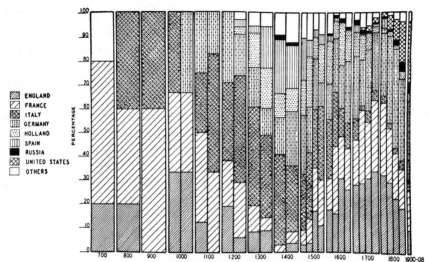

FIG. 7. IMPORTANT DISCOVERIES AND INVENTIONS FROM 700 TO 1908
DISTRIBUTED BY COUNTRY OF ORIGIN

Before discussing the conclusions suggested by the tables, let us confront the tables computed from Darmstaedter's work with a set of data which, though not quite comparable, nevertheless concerns the same problem. This second set of data (Table 7) was kindly given to me by J. W. Boldyreff, who collected them for his Ph.D. thesis (unpublished) in the Department of Sociology of Harvard University. The source of his data is the ninth edition of the *Encyclopaedia Britannica*, one of the most authoritative epitomes of the history of science as well as of human culture. For purposes of his dissertation, Mr. Boldyreff tabulated and classified all the names of persons mentioned in the *Encyclopaedia* and counted the number of lines devoted to each name. He classified these names (and lines) in periods, countries, and in ten main classes of cultural activities; namely, religion, state, literature, scholarship (humanistic and social sciences), science and technology, philosophy, business, fine arts, music, and miscellaneous. (In his detailed studies by countries his classifications are still more detailed.)

In this way, among many other results, he obtained the number of scientists mentioned in the *Encyclopaedia* for periods from the "beginning" of human history to the present time. Classifying them by 50-year periods he obtained the number of the scientists (note: number of the *scientists*, but not of *discoveries*) for each period, for mankind generally as well as for each of the main countries separately. Realizing that the number of prominent scientists is not a satisfactory barometer of the state of science for each period, he computed the number of lines devoted to each of the scientists. His assumption that, all in all, the more important the scientist the more space devoted to him in the *Encyclopaedia*, is essentially sound though not, perhaps, quite perfect. It results in making his barometer quantitative-qualitative. For each period he then took the geometric averages of the total sum of the lines devoted to all the scientists of the given period multiplied by the number of the scientists (square root), and treated this as the index of the status of scientific thought at a given period. The series of such geometric averages for all the periods in consideration serves as an index of the movement of science and technology from period to period. Such was the source and the procedure used by him in obtaining his indicators of the movement of science from 500 B.C. up to the middle of the nineteenth century. The same procedure is followed by him in respect to religion and other fields of sociocultural creativeness of man.

From this outline it is clear that his tables are based upon quite different sources from mine; they comprise the number of scientists and the space devoted to them, but not the number of the discoveries as is the case with my tables. Again, the use of the geometric average differs from my direct computation of the number of discoveries. In view of this, it would not be surprising if the two sets of data were to show wide discrepancies. Nevertheless, when confronted (see the totaling columns in Table 5) they show a notable agreement in their main movements. First, the typical range of maxima and minima for all the main periods (500 B.C. to A.D. 400; A.D. 400 to 1200; finally from 1200 to 1850) is practically the same for the two sets of material. When the share of Arabia and Persia in the period from 700 to 1450 is subtracted, their movement by 100- and 50-year periods is parallel in 24 such periods out of 30, and opposed in only 6. Both curves are comparatively high in the period from the fifth century B.C. to the second A.D.; both remain low during the centuries from the third A.D. to the thirteenth; and from the fifteenth century to 1850 the similarity is so marked that the curves are almost coincident. The greatest discrepancy is found for the periods from 1250 to 1300, 1350 to 1400, and for four periods in the fifth and fourth centuries B.C., and about the beginning of our era.

Considering the differences in the sources, material, and methods of computation; considering further differences of opinion concerning the precise time at which a scientist made a given discovery, to say nothing of the occasional difficulty of "dating" some scientists themselves, these minor discrepancies are to be expected. More striking and significant than these discrepancies is the remarkable similarity in movement of the two curves. Such agreement constitutes impressive additional evidence that both barometers are roughly reliable so far as the main tides in the movement of discoveries are concerned. The periods when they move parallel may be accepted as reliable even in minor points.

The 6 periods out of 30 where they disagree in minor movements are more questionable. In these instances, the Darmstaedter material is probably preferable, since this deals directly with the number of discoveries and not merely the number of scientists. Moreover, the Darmstaedter data are more complete than those contained in the tables based on the *Encyclopaedia*, since those discoveries of which the discoverers are not known are not, in the very nature of the case, included in Boldyreff's compilations (which deal with persons, rather than with discoveries). Finally Darmstaedter's data do not involve the amount of space devoted to the scientists which, though generally a fairly sound criterion of the importance of a scientist, is not such in all cases. The sympathies and biases of the editors of the *Encyclopaedia* or any other work of this sort frequently lead to differences in the amount of space devoted to various individuals which are not congruent with the differences in importance or merit.[10] For these and similar reasons, in instances of

TABLE 7. SPACE DEVOTED BY ENCYCLOPAEDIA BRITANNICA[1] TO CULTURAL ACHIEVEMENTS OF VARIOUS COUNTRIES FOR 1800–1849[2]

Country	Religion	Literature	Scholarship	Science	Philosophy	Fine Arts	Music
England	407.9	1346.3	784.5	869.6	116.9	739.5	80.9
Germany	313.1	341.8	477.4	458.8	198.7	189.9	103.8
France	53.9	435.3	405.4	415.5	132.8	292.0	57.9
U.S.A.	82.4	176.4	74.9	125.0	0.0	31.1	0.0
Austria, Hungary, and Bohemia	12.5	99.2	62.9	12.0	5.2	13.4	52.8
Russia and Poland	5.3	82.3	43.2	6.4	0.0	0.0	19.5
Belgium and Holland	0.0	16.2	13.8	7.4	0.0	0.0	6.0
China and India	10.5	0.0	9.7	0.0	0.0	0.0	0.0

[1] Ninth edition.

[2] Without presenting data for other countries these figures speak for themselves. With all due respect for the achievements of England in these fields during 1800–1849, a neutral, competent analyst would hardly maintain that the superiority of English cultural achievement was as marked as is suggested by these figures. As these data are the composite result of two variables, the number of persons in each field mentioned in the *Encyclopaedia* and the number of lines devoted to each of these persons, it is evident that British nationals are recorded more nearly completely and are given more space than the non-British. If there is in this respect an unquestionable bias in the *Encyclopaedia* for 1800–1849 (a bias quite comprehensible), a similar prepossession may be found in the amount of space devoted to different persons in the past. See further Table 9, which definitely indicates this bias in the *Encyclopaedia*.

[10] This tendency is demonstrated by the fact that the British are, all in all, assigned a greater amount of space than the non-British Europeans. The period 1800–1849 may serve as a typical example. Table 7 shows the geometric averages for that period for the specified countries in the several fields of cultural achievement.

minor discrepancies between the two sets of data, the Darmstaedter material is to be preferred.

III. Main Results

A. *Systems of Truth and Movement of Discoveries and Inventions.* We are now in a more advantageous position for checking the propositions that the domination of truth of faith is negatively, and that of truth of senses positively, correlated with a high rate of discovery and invention, or, in other words, with the progress of science and technology. Confronting the movement of empiricism (in Figure 1) with the contour of fluctuations in the number of discoveries and inventions, we find a virtual coincidence, not in all the minor oscillations, but in the ebb and flow of the principal tides of both currents. The curve of discoveries has two main crests in the Graeco-Roman world: one rising in the sixth century, climbing higher in the fifth, and reaching its peak in the fourth century B.C.,[11] thereafter declining in the third and the second centuries B.C.; the other, based chiefly upon the Roman achievements in science, finding a turn upward in the first century B.C., and reaching its summit in the first century A.D., subsequently declining irregularly. (In Boldyreff's index the first peak is attained in the third century B.C., instead of the fourth; and the second peak in the second century A.D., instead of the first A.D.)

In the growth curve of empiricism there also occur two waves from the sixth B.C. to the fifth century A.D. However, since this curve is consti-

---

[11] It is not incidental, therefore, that in Greece, and particularly in Athens of the fifth and the first part of the fourth century B.C., "technique and scientific engineering of everything became as great a vogue as it has been with us for the last few centuries."

"The influence of the ideas associated with τέχνη [most fashionable term of the period in Greece] cannot be adequately illustrated by a limited collection of texts; it is to be seen rather, on the one hand, in the general aim and presuppositions of the activity of many Sophists, and, on the other, in the copious production of technological writings on all manner of subjects, of most of which only the titles remain to us. The claim of many of the Sophistic teachers was the ability to impart a new, nontraditional *technique* — a technique ostensibly based upon special knowledge or original reflection — in one or another practical activity, a novel and more intelligent way of doing things. . . . There were 'professors' of politics, oratory, the art of writing, medicine, mental healing, education, the improvement of the memory, painting, agriculture, pharmacology, household economics, boat-designing, as well as of the general art of life." Even Socrates did the same in his own way. In brief, the period was "scientifically minded," and techniques which lay claim to being scientific were as fashionable as they are at present among the group of "brain-trusters" who engage in supposedly "scientific social engineering." The basic variables being the same, the total picture is likewise similar. A. O. Lovejoy and G. Boas, *Primitivism and Related Ideas in Antiquity* (Baltimore, 1935), Vol. I, pp. 194–195. See the details in Abel Rey, *La science dans l'antiquité* (Paris, 1933–1936), Vols. II and III. A. Espinas, *Les origines de la technologie* (Paris, 1897).

tuted by percentages of all the systems of truth, it cannot be expected to move identically with the curve based upon the *absolute* number of discoveries and inventions. Once this is understood, it may be observed that the curve of empiricism rises in the sixth century and, with slight fluctuations, continues at a high level up to the end of the first century B.C., when it rapidly declines; while the second wave begins to rise in the second century A.D., reaches a climax in the third A.D., and then declines in the fourth, fifth, and the sixth (disappearing entirely in the sixth century). The percentual maxima and minima of both waves of empiricism do not fall precisely within the same centuries as the maxima and minima of the two waves in the number of the discoveries. However, this discrepancy is a minor point. A more important consideration is that the curves representing both "variables" describe (with varying, sometimes alternating periods of lag) two waves during the same centuries; that both reach a comparatively high level during these centuries; and that both subsequently decline after the third century A.D. Then, in the second medieval phase, both curves remain practically at the zero line (or consistently very low, so far as the discoveries are concerned) from the seventh A.D. to the end of the eleventh century A.D. For this period the curves are synchronous. Finally, beginning with the twelfth century both start their upward movement and with slight fluctuations continue this trend up to the present time, reaching an unprecedented height. In this third phase they again move almost concurrently, so far as century periods are concerned.

On the other hand, confronting the curve of discoveries with that of the truth of faith (Ideational rationalism, mysticism, fideism), we see that all in all they fluctuate inversely. To this extent, then, the propositions which logically follow from the concepts of Ideational and Sensate truth as well as Ideational and Sensate cultures are sustained, in essentials, by the relevant facts.[12] The two variables develop independently (to some degree) in their minor movements. But this is to be expected

---

[12] These propositions are also corroborated in social space. The predominantly Ideational mentality and system of truth of India, Tibet, and Taoist China contribute little to the increase of discoveries and inventions. In this respect they remained comparatively as unproductive as was the Western World prior to the sixteenth century. Great discoveries in mathematics, astronomy, and other natural sciences were made in India and China, but they were probably made in the periods of the relative weakening of truth of faith, or by partisans of the truth of reason and senses. Even so, the discoveries cannot even remotely compete with those of the Western World for the last four centuries. See Benoy Kumar Sarkar, *Hindu Achievements in Exact Sciences* (London, 1918), also his *Political Institutions and Theories of the Hindus* (Leipzig, 1922); Abel Rey, *op. cit.*, Vol. I, and *La science orientale avant les Grecs* (Paris, 1931).

since the causal-functional integration of divers cultural compartments, in so far as each of them constitutes a system, cannot be perfect, for such absolute integration would run counter to the autonomy possessed by any system. Each cultural system-variable must have by definition, and factually does have, some margin of autonomy in its functioning and destiny. Hence, even when it is factually integrated with the other system-variables with which, logically considered, it should be integrated, the integration is never perfect and always permits some "independent movements" for each system. This is precisely the case in this instance. Integration of the systems of truth with scientific development is demonstrated by the tangible association between the basic movements of the two, while, by virtue of the autonomy of the systems, minor oscillations occasionally occur independently.

Several more specific bases for corroboration of the propositions under consideration are reserved for discussion in subsequent chapters and in Volume Four. For the present we may consider other results furnished by our tabulations.

B. *In Which Branches of Science Has the Increase of Discoveries in the West-European World Been Most Marked?* A glance at Table 5 and Figures 3 to 7 suffices to disclose two significant facts. First, considering the discoveries in the Graeco-Roman world from about 800 B.C. to A.D. 700, it is evident that there is no consistent or permanent tendency for increases in some fields of science to occur more rapidly than in others. The number of discoveries in each discipline varies trendlessly throughout the centuries, with a notable concentration occurring in a few centuries. None of the disciplines tends to manifest a progressive increase in the number of discoveries, thus outdistancing the other sciences.

But examining the information on the number of discoveries in the Western World from about A.D. 800 to 1900 it is equally evident that the increases in the various sciences do not proceed at the same rate. Consequently, the number of discoveries in the several fields are far from being equal. The total number of the discoveries listed in Darmstaedter's work as made in the Western World from 800 to 1908 are : in mathematics, 301 ; astronomy, 426 ; biology, 1378 ; medicine, 1200 ; chemistry, 2447 ; physics, 1469 ; geology, 173 ; geography, 279 ; and technology, 4698. Thus the greatest number is in the field of technological inventions, becoming progressively less in chemistry, physics, biology, and medicine, with the fewest in astronomy, mathematics, geography, and geology. Furthermore, it appears that, passing from A.D. 800 to the present time, the rate of increase has been more rapidly accelerated in the disciplines with the greatest number of discoveries (technology, chemistry, physics, etc.) than in the disciplines with the smaller number of discoveries. Some of these latter disciplines, for example mathematics, after the few first centuries, have not presented any steady and notable rate of increase, while in some others, such as astronomy, it is very slight. Moreover, in the last two centuries, the rate of increase of technological inventions has been greater than that of discoveries in all the sciences combined.

Thus, these data are seen to provide a clear-cut description of the differential cultivation of the various fields of science and of the different rates of achievement within these fields. Moreover, this material sheds some light on the relationship between scientific development and systems of truth. Mathematics is a branch of logic. As such it is, in contrast to technology, physics, and medicine, concerned but little with sensory and empirical phenomena. The fact that these more Sensate and empirical disciplines have been developed more rapidly with the increasing prevalence of the truth of senses represents a significant detail corroborating the propositions discussed in the last section.

C. *"Erratically Parabolic" Direction of the Movement of Discoveries in the Life Process of a Single Culture.* The linear conception of sociohistorical processes was exceedingly widespread in the nineteenth century, and to some extent subsists even today. In reference to this field it was maintained that moving from the earlier to the later periods in the history of a given culture the number of discoveries and inventions tends to increase more and more and the natural sciences tend to develop more rapidly and more successfully. Is such a belief corroborated by the available data? It is definitely not, in so far as one considers a single culture and the number of *new* discoveries and inventions made in each successive period.[13]

For answering the question involved in this conception we have at our disposal relatively adequate data concerning at least three cultures: the Greek, the Roman, and the Arabian. Table 8 provides a conspectus of the curve of scientific development in each of these cultures as we pass from the earlier to the later centuries of their history.

[13]This should not be confused with the question of the cumulative nature of science, which holds that every successive generation has at its disposal an ever-increasing capital of discoveries and inventions as a result of the progressive cumulation of all the previous discoveries and progressively increased by the discoveries — no matter how few — of each succeeding generation. This is a different problem and as such it will be discussed in another context. For the present, I am concerned only with the more restricted problem.

TABLE 8. CURVE OF SCIENTIFIC DEVELOPMENT FROM 800 B.C. TO A.D. 700 BY CENTURIES

PERIOD	GREECE [1]	ROME [1]	GREECE AND ROME (total)
800–701 B.C.	6	—	6
700–601	3	2	5
600–501	26	5	31
500–401	39	1	40
400–301	52	5	57
300–201	42	3	45
200–101	14	3	17
100–0	12	20	32
1–100 A.D.	25	35	60
101–200	5	13	18
201–300	—	6	6
301–400	1	15	16
401–500	—	4	4
501–600	3	1	4
601–700	4	—	4

ARABIA [2]

Period	Mathematics	Physics	Chemistry	Natural History	Medicine	Geography	Humanistics	Total
700–750	18	—	7	1	4	—	6	6
750–800	61	7	1	4	16	—	15	45
800–850	72	7	6	6	25	6	47	142
850–900	33	6	1	2	11	3	28	147
900–950	52	—	9	8	29	35	35	123
950–1000	48	21	5	5	43	9	49	156
1000–1050	27	2	—	3	7	18	56	196
1050–1100	25	14	1	5	23	6	37	82
1100–1150	23	2	1	18	26	11	40	119
1150–1200	18	4	3	12	17	22	67	159
1200–1250	25	14	5	10	19	20	64	138
1250–1300						26	58	157

[1] Computed from Darmstaedter's work.

[2] Derived from the previously cited paper by P. A. Sorokin and R. K. Merton. The sources and the procedure of deriving these figures are fully described therein. It should be noted that, whereas the figures for Greece and Rome refer to the number of *discoveries* (listed by Darmstaedter), those for the Arabian culture refer to the number of *scientists* of sufficient importance to be discussed by G. Sarton, in his *Introduction to the History of Science*, 2 vols. (Baltimore, 1927–1931).

It is evident from these figures that the movement of scientific achievements is irregular and somewhat erratic, inasmuch as there was no perpetual linear trend throughout the life history of these cultures. If anything, the curve describes an uneven parabola. For Greece, from the period prior to 800 B.C. to the fourth century B.C. inclusive, the curve rises, with irregular fluctuations, reaching its climax in the period, 400 to 301 B.C.; thereafter, from the third century B.C. to the seventh A.D. it declines, again with slight fluctuations. (It need hardly be mentioned that at that time Greece existed as neither an independent body politic — after 146 B.C. — nor as a Greek culture, discoveries in this latter period being those made by persons of Greek origin.) Similar was the movement in Rome. From about the fifth century B.C. there was a trend of increase up to the first century A.D. which was followed by a decline with minor erratic fluctuations. No trace of an ever-progressing or ever-regressing linear movement of discoveries throughout the life history of these cultures is noticeable. Finally, in Arabia the curve rises with fluctuations from 700 to 1050 and then tends to decline, also with irregular oscillations. Thus in the case of these three cultures for which fairly reliable data exist, it does not appear that the rate of scientific discovery and invention tends to increase with the passage of time.

Unfortunately, we do not have even remotely adequate information about the movement of scientific discoveries and inventions in other great cultures of the distant past which have run the full course of their life span. A few fragmentary data pertaining to Ancient Egypt or Assyria are available but are too incomplete to be significant for this type of analysis. Darmstaedter's work lists 14 important discoveries and inventions for Egypt from 3500 to 801 B.C.; 2 items for 700–601 B.C.; 1 for 400–301 B.C.; 1 for A.D. 0–100; and 8 for A.D. 101–200. For Assyria are listed 2 discoveries for the period 800–701 B.C.; for Babylonia 6 between 3500 and 801 B.C. Such manifestly scattered data do not warrant any conclusion. However, those cultures which have completed the full gamut of their history, and for which fairly adequate information is present, seem to have encompassed an "erratically parabolic" development of science.

The data concerning "living" cultures are not as suitable for the present analysis, precisely because their history is not yet complete, and extrapolation of contemporary trends is scarcely warranted. However, with this reservation in mind, one may make use of the pertinent information. As may be seen from Table 9, the curve of development

TABLE 9. IMPORTANT DISCOVERIES AND INVENTIONS, DISTRIBUTED BY COUNTRY OF ORIGIN

PERIOD	England No.	England Per cent	France No.	France Per cent	Italy No.	Italy Per cent	Germany No.	Germany Per cent	Holland No.	Holland Per cent	Switzerland No.	Switzerland Per cent	Spain No.	Spain Per cent	Scandinavia No.	Scandinavia Per cent	Portugal No.	Portugal Per cent	United States No.	United States Per cent	Russia No.	Russia Per cent	Total No.	Total Per cent
701–800 A.D.	1	20	3	60	0	0	0	0	0	0	0	0	0	0	0	0	0	0	0	0	0	0	5	100
801–900	1	20	2	40	2	40	0	0	0	0	0	0	0	0	0	0	0	0	0	0	0	0	5	100
901–1000	0	0	3	60	2	40	0	0	0	0	0	0	0	0	0	0	0	0	0	0	0	0	5	100
1001–1050	1	33.3	1	33.3	1	33.4	1	33.4	0	0	0	0	0	0	0	0	0	0	0	0	0	0	3	100
1051–1100	1	33.3	1	33.3	0	0	2	25	0	0	0	0	0	0	0	0	0	0	0	0	0	0	3	100
1101–1150	1	12.5	3	37.5	2	25	1	17	0	0	0	0	0	0	0	0	0	0	0	0	0	0	8	100
1151–1200	0	0	2	33.2	3	49.8	6	17	0	0	0	0	0	0	0	0	0	0	0	0	0	0	6	100
1201–1250	4	19	4	19	7	33	6	17	1	3	0	0	1	3	0	0	1	3	0	0	0	0	21	100
1251–1300	2	5.6	8	23	16	45	6	16.6	5	14	0	0	1	3	0	0	2	5.5	0	0	0	0	35	100
1301–1350	3	8.3	4	11.4	15	41.6	4	11.4	6	17	0	0	1	3	0	0	2	5.7	0	0	0	0	36	100
1351–1400	3	8.6	2	5.7	12	34.6	6	15.5	6	17	0	0	13	17	0	0	5	9	0	0	1	2	35	100
1401–1450	0	0	2		22	38	4		8	10	1	1.2	15	22.5	0	0	9	11	0	0	1	1.2	58	100
1451–1500	3	3.6	4	4.8	23	27.6	9		10	9.6	2	3	12	18	5	4.5	5	7.3	0	0	0	0	83	100
1501–1526	3	3	4	5.9	16	23.5	19		23	14.7	5	4.6	12	17.6	5	3	1	1	0	0	0	0	68	100
1526–1555	4	3.7	11	10	31	28	17	9	9	21	4	4	8	7	10	7	0	0	0	0	1		109	100
1551–1575	17	17	18	18	25	25	21	19.2	22	16	1	1	3	3	2	1.5	1	1	0	0	1	1	100	100
1576–1600	15	11	25	19	42	31	21	21	23	17.7	9	7	5	4	3	0.7	0	0	0	0	1	0.7	135	100
1601–1625	23	17.7	17	13	32	25	14	10	9	7	7	0.7	3	2.3	10	1.3	1	1	0	0	1	1.7	129	100
1626–1650	21	16	38	28.5	30	22.5	19	14.8	40	17.3	9	0.9	2	1.5	2	0.7	0	0	0	0	4	1	133	100
1651–1675	70	30.7	41	17.7	28	12	42	18	25	12.8	5	2.6	1	0.4	3	1.3	0	0	0	0	2	1	231	100
1676–1700	51	26	34	17.4	21	10.7	51	26	16	10	3	3	1	0.5	6	3	0	0	0	0	2		196	100
1701–1725	45	28	31	19	15	9	42	26	35	10.4	13	4	4	3	5	3	0	0	0	0	3	2	161	100
1726–1750	96	28.7	103	30.7	6	2	65	19.1	24	6.7	13	3.7	2	0.5	6	1.8	0	0	4	1.1	5	1.5	335	100
1751–1775	109	30.7	85	24	16	4.5	91	25.5	18	2.6	9	1.3	1	0.3	7	2	0	0	7	2	3	0.8	355	100
1776–1800	232	33.6	205	30	28	4	166	24	26	2	10		5	1	6	1	0	0	13	2	4	0.5	687	100
1801–1825	359	32	341	30.5	36	3	295	26	38	2	10	0.5	0	4	13	1	1	0.1	22	2	11	1	1119	100
1826–1850	584	29	460	23	46	2.2	731	36	37	1.8	15		6	0.2	16	0.8	0	0	115	5.7	19	1	2019	100
1851–1875	581	22.3	482	19	63	2.5	1067	41.4	98	1.5	47	1.7	5	0.2	29	2.1	2	0.1	232	9.1	42	2	2554	100
1876–1900	503	18.2	453	16.4	83	3	957	34.7	98	3.6	47	1.7	6	0.2	59	2.1	2	0.1	453	16.4	99	3.6	2759	100
1901–1908	83	9.6	140	16.2	32	3.7	290	33.6	30	3.5	20	2.3	1	0.1	17	2	0	0	219	25.3	32	3.7	864	100

during the past is such as to corroborate our hypothesis of erratically fluctuating movement.[14]

Table 9 presents the number of important discoveries in the natural sciences and technological inventions listed by Darmstaedter as having been made during each specified period in each specified country in Europe (as well as the United States) and the proportional contribution of each nation. The figures show that in the course of time the *number* as well as the *percentages* in each country fluctuate without any continuous linear trend, when the whole period from the eighth to the twentieth century is considered. Even during the period from the fifteenth century on, though marked by a general trend of increase, there occurred several interruptions of the linear trend of increase in practically every country. In some countries, such as Italy, Spain, Scandinavia, and partly Holland, the series do not manifest a linear trend at all or only for the last century and a half. To this extent, then, the data support the hypothesis that even in these instances the movement of discoveries and inventions in a single country does not exhibit any continuous or constant linearity.

A number of other significant points are disclosed by the tabulated figures. First, in some countries — such as Spain and Portugal — the highest rate of scientific achievement occurred not in the most recent period but during the period of their great political power (thirteenth to sixteenth century). Second, of the countries which contributed most to scientific development, it is precisely those — France, England, and Germany — which began their contribution relatively early which manifest, at the end of the nineteenth century (1876–1900), some recession not only in the proportion but even in the absolute number of their discoveries and inventions. Other countries — such as Russia, the United States, Switzerland, and Scandinavia — which entered the field later, do not evidence such recession at all. It would seem that the countries which have engaged in scientific discovery for a long time have, as it were, exhausted their potentialities in this respect and, temporarily or protractedly, have decreased their scientific output. In the mean-

---

[14] The total figures in the last column of this table deviate slightly from the total figures in Table 5. The reason is that here those discoveries which were made independently in two or more countries are credited to each country; likewise, discoveries made co-operatively by two or more scientists belonging to different countries are also credited to each country. This explains why the totals for some periods are greater in Table 9 than in Table 5. On the other hand, where the total figure in Table 9 is slightly less than in Table 5, the explanation is that the former does not include all the countries (Belgium, Poland, Greece, and others). This explains the few discrepancies, which are, however, very slight.

time, the "newcomers" have taken up the task. The contribution made by the United States indicates that it is one of the more vigorous of these newcomers. The political and economic growth of the United States was followed by the growth of its scientific and technical achievement. In studying the movement of art styles, it was frequently evident that Russia lagged some one hundred and fifty years behind most of the European countries. In the field of science is found a similar lag. Russia begins its scientific contribution (excepting a few sporadic discoveries) in the seventeenth century — later than all the other European countries. But after these initial achievements it progressed markedly.

Due to these changes, the proportionate contribution of each country varies considerably. At the very end of the nineteenth century, the first place was attained by Germany, then by England, France, and the United States [15] (in the period 1901–1908 the United States occupied second place). From the second half of the seventeenth to the first quarter of the nineteenth century, the first two places were occupied by England and France. The long period from the eleventh to the second half of the seventeenth century was one of Italian, and partly, of Spanish pre-eminence.[16] Holland's greatest proportion (not the absolute num-

---

[15] These data show, by the way, with especial clarity, the one-sided attention given to different countries in the *Encyclopaedia Britannica*. For the period 1800–1849, twice as much space was devoted to the British scientists as to German or French. Our data show for the same period that the largest number of the discoveries was made by Germany and that the number of French discoveries was only slightly less than that of the English. There is a similar tendency manifested in reference to other periods. It need hardly be added that the Darmstaedter data may also involve a "national bias," but this does not seem to be pronounced, since nations other than Germany have been accorded considerable attention. In many periods, discoveries made in non-German areas are listed more frequently than German discoveries. Moreover, since this constitutes a list of *scientific discoveries*, not *scientists*, there is not so much opportunity for such "national biases" to find expression.

[16] These data, as well as the total character of Table 9, well refute Max Weber's contention that Protestantism was the cause of the growth of rationalism, scientism, technology, and so on. We see that long before the emergence of Protestantism discoveries began to increase in Catholic countries (Italy, Spain, Portugal); that even after its emergence during the sixteenth and the first half of the seventeenth centuries the scientific contribution of the Catholic Italians was higher than that of any other country. Only during the eighteenth and the nineteenth centuries did hegemony pass to Protestant countries. All this constitutes a strong refutation of the direct causal relationship between Protestantism and scientism which Max Weber and some of his followers have attempted to establish. Attempts to support this theory by indicating scientific hegemony of the Protestant countries in the eighteenth and the nineteenth centuries are repudiated by the data on Holland, which, though Protestant, nevertheless, like Catholic Italy, decreased its percentual share and even its absolute number of discoveries after 1750. Likewise, Russia, though not a Protestant country, nevertheless experienced an increase of its scientific output greater than any other European country. Since Catholic Italy and Protestant Holland manifested a similar decline in scien-

ber) of discoveries occurred during the period from the fourteenth to the end of the seventeenth century.

We find from these data that in general each country makes its most notable scientific contribution during the period of its greatest social and cultural blossoming.   Thus Italy, which was the sociocultural center of Europe from the twelfth to the seventeenth century, was contemporaneously superior to the other countries in science as well.   And, in turn, when France, England, and Germany became centers of sociocultural achievement, they likewise attained scientific hegemony at the same time.   When the United States began to secure greater and greater world power during the nineteenth century, its growth was reflected also in a rapid progress of its science and technology.   The climax of the scientific contributions of Spain occurred at the height of the Spanish Empire, in the fifteenth and at the beginning of the sixteenth century. Likewise the greatest proportion of discoveries of the Netherlands was found in the fifteenth, sixteenth, and seventeenth centuries — at the climax of their social, economic, and political power.[17]

For the time being, it suffices to present these conclusions, though we shall have occasion to refer to these data in connection with other problems.   With the reservation previously mentioned, the data support the statement that there is no linear trend of the movement of science in the life history of a single country.

Finally, in concluding this section it is to be noted that in Greece and Rome the curves of discoveries and of the empirical system of truth are parallel, as has been indicated previously.   As for Arabia, the incompleteness of records and the limited knowledge of the author do not permit a definite statement to the same effect.   In a tentative way, however, it may be suggested that some positive association between the system of truth and the movement of discoveries seems to be tangible here as well.   Table 8, pertaining to Arabia, presents three important

---

tific output during the period 1700–1850, the reason would seem to be not in Protestantism and Catholicism but in some other factor.   The precise character of this factor will be discussed subsequently.   For the time being it is enough to call attention to the fact of the contradiction between these data and the theory of Max Weber.   The basic error in his doctrine lay in assuming that in considering an organism passing from one stage to another in the course of which many anatomical, physiological, and psychological traits are changing, one may take one of the traits, say, the appearance of a mustache, for the cause of muscular, glandular, and mental changes experienced by the organism.   Protestantism as the cause of capitalism, scientism, and many similar developments is precisely a case of the "mustache" being taken for the cause of all the other changes.

[17] In passing, it may be noted that Table 9 again agrees in essentials with Boldyreff's data concerning the movement of science in these countries.

points in this respect.   There is observable first, the fact that important
contributions in humanistics emerge earlier than in the natural sciences;
second, a relative lack of discoveries and inventions prior to A.D. 750–
800; and third, that the courses of the contributions in humanistics and
in most of the natural sciences are different.   These three points may
be interpreted in the following way.

In the early period of the Arabian culture (after Mohammed up to
750) the dominant system of truth was almost exclusively a religious
Koranic system of revelation fused with the previous tribal, magico-
religious beliefs.   Under such a system of truth there was hardly any
place for great scientific development.   This is logically to be expected
and is precisely what is actually found (note dearth of discoveries prior
to 750).   Subsequently, after some two hundred years of the extraordinary victorious expansion of Mohammedanism, with an unavoidable
secularization and Epicureanization of the population, and with admixture of the non-Arabian population in the conquered cities and regions,
the Arabian culture experienced a change toward greater and greater
sensualization.[18]

About 750–800 the change of culture and mentality in that direction
manifested itself also in the first definite signs of the transformation of
the system of truth of that culture: the empirico-Sensate truth made
its appearance in the form of discoveries in the natural sciences.   The
process continued subsequently without, however, disruption of the
main previous system of the revealed truth.   During the next two centuries it still remained dominant among the Arabs (excepting non-
Arabian elements of the population).[19]   The natural sciences (and to
some extent the humanitarian disciplines which may be predominantly
either Ideational or Sensate) progressed without entering into open
conflict with the religious system of truth.   In this respect, the Arabian
situation in the ninth and the tenth centuries seems to have been somewhat similar to that which obtained in Europe from the twelfth to the

[18] See the excellent analysis in the works of Ibn-Khaldun (1332–1406): *Histoire des Ber-
bères*, trans. by le Baron le Slane (Paris, 1925), Vol. I, pp. 4 ff.; *Prolégomènes historique*, in
Notices et extraits des manuscrits de Bibliothèque Impérial (Paris, 1862–68), Vols. XIX, XX,
and XXI, particularly Vol. XIX.

[19] Ibn-Khaldun stresses the fact that the majority of the Arabian scientists are not Arabs
but foreigners who happened to live in the cities conquered by Arabs.   They are mainly
the bearers of science and empiricism, while the Arabs remain still more religious than these
non-Arabian scientists and scholars.   *Prolégomènes*, in *Notices*, Vol. XXI, pp. 296 ff.   In
this connection it should be noted that those who comprised our tabulation of Arabian intellectual development were Arabic-speaking persons.   Many of these were *not* Moslems or of
Arabian blood.   *Cf.* Sorokin and Merton, *op. cit.*

fifteenth century. It was a type of Idealistic system of truth not unlike the rationalistic system of truth of European Scholasticism.

In the eleventh century science and empirical truth continue to grow, but Ideational and Idealistic truth are still alive. Such a situation manifested itself, among other ways, in the most successful and harmonious development of the humanities and natural sciences roughly from about 950 to 1050. There then occurred a short-time decline of both fields of intellectual endeavor, possibly due to a revival of the purely religious system of truth, instead of the rationalistic and scientific systems which had been growing at its cost. Thereafter, the rationalistic and empirical systems of truth seem to have regained their prior dominance but with a difference. The humanities developed more and more apart from the natural sciences and attracted a larger number of highly competent persons than did the sciences. The rate of development in the natural sciences progressively declined.

The "story" told by our data ends in this indefinite situation. Whatever the specific incidents of subsequent development, the great climax of of Arabian science (and humanities) was over. The Arabic-speaking peoples have never again attained the resplendence which was theirs in the eleventh century. On the other hand, up to the thirteenth century, the scientific or even rationalistic systems of truth did not supplant the religious system, which remained, if not monopolistic as prior to the eighth century, as powerful as any of these systems.[20]

[20] In reading the major works of the great Arabian thinkers of even the fourteenth century, such as Ibn-Khaldun's *Universal History*, especially its *Prolégomènes*, one finds a typical picture of the mentality involved in the rationalistic system of truth. Reading in Ibn-Khaldun's work one detects a perspicuous observer of empirical facts which are clearly described and used as evidence sustaining his theories. It is significant that after such a discussion every paragraph is completed by Ibn-Khaldun (and the same is true of many Moslem thinkers of these centuries) with a quotation from the Koran which often appears to have no bearing upon the matter under consideration. The present-day reader may be surprised at the peculiar mixture of what we term "real science" and of magico-religious topics and problems. In the greater part of his *Prolégomènes* or his *History of the Berbers*, Ibn-Khaldun strikes a modern note and his work impresses one as being quite as scientific as any modern work in sociology, philosophy of history, anthropology, or history. But here and there, quite unexpectedly after such scientific chapters, there is discussed, with the same sincerity and seriousness, the nature of superhuman beings, their forms, classes, properties, and characteristics — chapters which seem quite different, as though they had been written by some necromancer or believer in magic.

This character of the greatest work of the late Arabian thinkers shows clearly that the religious system of truth was still considerably diffused and was still existing side by side with the scientific and rationalistic systems. These facts indicate that the mentality of even the leading thinkers of Arabian culture never reached the stage of abandonment of the rationalistic and the religious systems of truth as occurred partly in Graeco-Roman and especially in the

In the whole development of the Arabian culture, from the foundation of Islam practically up to the present time, the religious system of truth has been, all in all, the principal system.   But it has experienced several oscillations in its scope and degree of influence, becoming less powerful at times when the empirical and the rationalistic systems became more widespread.   The periods from the eighth century to about 1050 and, in a less degree, from about 1150 to 1300 were such periods of its comparative weakening in favor of the truth of senses.   In the history of the Arabian societies these centuries were also much more "Epicurean" than either the preceding or the subsequent period (after the decay of the Arabian caliphates and decline of their empires as well as of their privileged position as conquerors).   Hence, the history of Arabian culture does not seem to constitute an exception to the proposition under consideration.

D. *Erratically Undulating Movement of Discoveries in the World at Large, with a Rapid and Consistent Rise for the Last Five Centuries.*   It is more difficult to determine whether or not the movement of discoveries in the world at large has evidenced any linear trend.   The most adequate and accurate conclusion, whether based upon developments from 3500 B.C. or from 600 B.C., to the present time, would seem to be that, in so far as the data in Table 5 are concerned, one cannot claim any linearity in the movement of new discoveries (construing linearity as progressive increase in subsequent periods of time).   It becomes clear from the figures in the "grand total" column of Table 5 which indicate the number of

---

Western cultures. After the fourteenth century, the scientific system of truth among the Arabs receded and the religious system recovered a great deal of its previous, almost monopolistic domination. Compare particularly most of Vol. I with most of Vols. II and III of the *Prolégomènes* to observe the contrasts in Ibn-Khaldun's thought. Or see several chapters in each volume: the impression is that these chapters were written by different persons. Ibn-Khaldun himself stresses, *expressis verbis*, that scientific truth is neither sufficient nor more important than religious revelation. His theory of truth is in essentials similar to those of Plato and of St. Thomas Aquinas. The supreme form of truth is the religious truth of faith which provides the absolute truth of ultimate reality. It is revealed to the human soul in those exceptional moments when "it divests itself of its human nature and transforms itself into the nature of angels and really becomes an angel for a single instant of time — a moment which comes and goes as quickly as the twinkling of an eye " — Vol. XX of the *Notices*, p. 437. Without such a knowledge, even the truth of reason or the truth of philosophy "is vain in itself and harmful in its application " — Vol. XXI of the *Notices*, p. 227. Still less certain and vain in itself, without these truths of faith and of reason, is the empirical truth of senses, which in the form of empirical science is no more than "an accident of urban civilization " — Vol. XXI, pp. 228 ff. Moreover, he criticizes Aristotle for having attributed too much positive epistemological significance to the empirical aspects of his theory of knowledge — Vol. XXI, pp. 228–240. In brief, in its essentials the theory is the idealistic rationalism quite similar to that of Plato and of St. Thomas and of great Scholastics. See further the *Notices*, Vol. XIX, pp. 324 ff., and Vol. XXI *passim*.

most important discoveries and inventions of practically the whole of civilized mankind [21] from 3500 B.C. to A.D. 1908, that the rate of development over a very long period of time is marked by an undulatory character. The curve is very low from 3500 B.C. to 600 B.C., rising notably for the period from 600 B.C. to about A.D. 200. But from A.D. 200 to 900 it declines once again. The decline is arrested if the Arabian contributions during the interval 900 to 1100 are included, but if (as in Table 5) these discoveries are omitted, the curve continues consistently low for almost a millennium (c. A.D. 200 to 1200). After 1200 the curve begins a slow ascent, but from about 1500 it rises more and more rapidly as it approaches the twentieth century.

As previously suggested, it may be granted that the discoveries and inventions of the more distant past are not recorded very fully and are therefore underestimated; while, contrariwise, the discoveries of more recent times may be comparatively overestimated. Despite this and other similar differential factors, several trends and tendencies may be reasonably summarized. First, that after the period prior to 600 B.C., which was relatively sterile in respect to science, there ensued an interval of some 800 years which was comparatively highly productive. Second, that instead of further acceleration and ascent, this movement ceased and was replaced again by a period of very low productivity which lasted some 900 to 1000 years. This unfruitful period was in turn succeeded by one of unprecedented progress in science which, thus far, has lasted some 700 years, gaining ever-increasing momentum as it moved from the thirteenth to the twentieth century.

This means that *the direction of this process has not been linear in any form, but rather has fluctuated erratically, despite the unprecedented height of the curve attained in the last seven centuries.* Another impression derived from Table 5 is that, besides short-time erratic fluctuations, there have been long-time waves comprised by high and low levels in the rate of scientific discovery. *The time span of these waves has been roughly about 700 to 1000 years.* In view of these facts, the linear conception of the movement of science appears unjustified. One may hardly maintain that there has been linear scientific advance simply because science has

---

[21] Though Table 5, as previously mentioned, does not include discoveries made in all countries (especially omitting China, India, and Arabia), the inclusion of these discoveries (see the appropriate data in Weinberg's work, *op. cit.*) does not change in any appreciable way the curve of the discoveries as it is in the table. The slight changes resulting from an inclusion of these discoveries are, first, a slight increase in the number of units for the period prior to our era and, second, for the period from A.D. 700 to 1400, the Arabian contributions lead to a notable ascent (especially marked for the eleventh century).

been developing rapidly for the last six or seven centuries. It should be remembered that prior to this recent epochal development, there is no trace of linearity for a period of some two thousand years. Hence, one may not denote the trend of scientific development as permanently unilinear.

Moreover, there is no certainty that the recent rising trend of these discoveries and inventions will continue permanently in the future. It should be borne in mind that our data indicate great waves of rise and decline which endured for some 700 to 1000 years. The trend of increasing discovery has thus far lasted some 600 or 700 years. Perhaps, after one or some centuries, it will also be replaced by a trend of decline as has happened before. This conjecture is prefaced with the word "perhaps" because none can pretend to any exact prediction concerning this matter. It is true that the predominant belief at the present time is a firm conviction that the rising trend toward bigger, better, and more numerous discoveries will be continued indefinitely. Thus, a typically optimistic prognostication reads:

More and more inventions are made every year, and there is no reason to think that technological development will ever stop. On the contrary, there is every reason to expect that more inventions will be made in the future than in the past. [Darmstaedter's material demonstrates] not only an increasing number of inventions (and discoveries) but since there are more inventions per unit of time, it shows an increasing rapidity in their occurrence.[22]

However, when such beliefs are scrutinized, they appear no more justified than those which involve the expectation of a decline in the future. In the first place, the five centuries of most marked increasing rapidity of discovery constitute too short a period in comparison with the prior several thousand years during which such a trend was lacking. Second, if exceedingly long periods are considered, proponents of the opposite (nonoptimistic) view may suggest that scientific decline is inevitable since, with the cooling of the sun, predicted by the astrophysicists, not only science and art but terrestrial life itself is destined to disappear. In that case, the whole curve of human achievement will describe a long-time irregular parabola. Others, such as Boris Weinberg, introduce additional considerations. According to him, there have thus far occurred four successive waves in the history of discovery and invention, each subsequent wave superimposing its effects upon the preced-

---

[22] W. F. Ogburn and S. C. Gilfillan, "The Influence of Inventions," in *Recent Social Trends*, pp. xxv and 127. See also E. Thomas: "Computing Progress in Chemistry," in *Science* (February 14, 1936), pp. 159–161.

ing one. The first, from 3500 B.C. with its climax about 1500 B.C., had its source in "intuition." In the second, from about 900 B.C., discoveries were derived principally from Graeco-Roman "rationality." The third, from 1450 to the eighteenth century, was the period in which discoveries were made mainly through "experience and observation." The fourth, from 1780 onwards, is the period of discoveries mainly in the field of "mechanical power." This fourth wave is to be the last because of the universal dissipation of energy and the gradual exhaustion of coal, iron, and other natural resources. In some few centuries, mankind will have reached the limits of material culture and discoveries, and will then enter upon a period of decline.[23] He presents the following figures of annual production of discoveries, the first column derived from the data of Darmstaedter; the second calculated according to his formula of development.

Period	Observed	Calculated
1500 A.D.	3.1	1.2
1600	5.8	6.8
1700	8.2	8.1
1750	13.	10.
1800	31.	35.
1850	95.	92.
1900	114.	125.
1950		128.
2000		110.
2100		90.
2200		20.
2400		5.

These and similar considerations may not be conclusive, but they have some serious bearing upon the problem. Third, we have seen that within a separate culture the trend of discovery has been one not of linear increase but rather of parabolic development. The development within a single culture may be repeated, over a longer period of time, in all of human culture. Fourth, the movement of discoveries in any special field of the natural sciences, as the data of Table 5 indicate, has been undulating, with short- and long-time movements of advance and recession.[24] Since

[23] Weinberg, op. cit., pp. 44–45.
[24] On the undulating character of scientific development, see also T. Rainoff, "Wave-like Fluctuation of Creative Productivity," in Isis, Vol. XII (1929), p. 292; F. Mentré, "L'attribution et le baptême des inventions," in Revue scientifique, series 5, Vol. III; H. Thompson, Age of Invention (New Haven, 1921), p. 124; W. H. Doolittle, Inventions in the Nineteenth Century (Philadelphia, 1915); S. C. Gilfillan, The Sociology of Invention (Chicago, 1935), pp. 17 ff.

recessions have occurred in the past, they may recur in the future.   In any case, there is manifestly no evidence clearly bespeaking the contrary. Since such declines have occurred in the history of separate cultures, they may occur likewise in the history of man generally.   Not only a decline in the number and value of new discoveries but a decrease of the currently existing knowledge has occurred in the past.   For instance, "Egyptian medicine, like Egyptian art, was fated to go backward as the centuries advanced. . . .   Egyptian medicine actually improves in worth as we move backward in time." [25]

These and many similar considerations are mentioned not for the purpose of predicting an inevitable decline of science but merely to suggest that the claims of the "optimists" are no more probable than those of the "pessimists."   The dogmatic assertions of optimist and pessimist alike are frequently manifestations of their wishes rather than their knowledge.

In any event, the recent movement of the discoveries and inventions in all the natural sciences seems to suggest that the optimistic forecasts are in no way more strongly warranted than the opposed predictions.   It is advisable to analyze our data to see what light they cast upon the more recent development of science and technology.   This may help us to determine our bearings in reference to the long historical road of mankind whose beginning is lost in the past and whose future is hidden by the veil of Destiny.   Moreover, these data are relevant to the problem of the direction of sociocultural processes.   Let us then look at these data.

E.   *Developments in More Recent Times.*   Table 6 and Figures 5 and 6 depict, by ten- and twenty-year periods, the movement of discoveries and inventions from A.D. 1401 to 1900.   These indicate an unmistakable retardation in the *rate* of increase during the last years of the nineteenth century and the first eight years of the twentieth.   Not only has the *rate* evidenced such retardation, but even the *absolute number* of discoveries has been less in some decades than in those immediately preceding.   For example, there are fewer discoveries listed for the decennium 1861–1870 than for 1851–1860; and fewer for 1891–1900 than for either of the two immediately anterior decades.   This indicates, then, that during the last forty years of the nineteenth century, in contrast to the uninterrupted and most intensive rise of the curve from 1791, and only quite insignificantly interrupted rise from 1691, the number of the discoveries and inventions not only did not continue to rise but involved a recession. This may be but a short-time fluctuation, to be followed again by a continuation of the rising trend.   On the other hand, it may possibly

[25] Hans Much, quoted by F. H. Garrison, *op. cit.*, pp. 53 and 59.

constitute the first sign of a reversal of the trend and the beginning of a long-time decline, similar to that found in the case of the Greek, the Roman, and the Arabian civilizations. Whichever of these opposite interpretations is justified by the future, one thing is certain: the data definitely do not demonstrate an "increasing rapidity in the occurrence" of inventions and discoveries.[26] Whatever the causes of such retardation,[27] the fact itself seems certain, in so far as the Darmstaedter source is reliable for this purpose.[28] This is reinforced also by the data concerning the quarter-century period in which the greatest number of discoveries in the principal natural sciences were made. The data summarized in Table 5 and Figures 4 to 6 show that the peak quarter century was:

For mathematics	1726–1750
For astronomy	1876–1900 (also very high in the period 1901–1908)
For chemistry	1851–1875 (also very high in the period 1901–1908)
For geology	1826–1850
For biology	1851–1875
For medicine	1880–1899 [29]
For geography	1851–1875

In other fields, physics and technology, the number continued to increase up to the final period included in the compilation (1901–1908). To these fields may be added astronomy and chemistry, since the number of discoveries in these disciplines was such in 1901–1908 that if the same rate

[26] W. F. Ogburn and S. C. Gilfillan, op. cit., p. 127. My conclusion is also supported by the number of discoveries for the period 1901 to 1908 (last years included in Darmstaedter's work). For these eight years the total is 862, while for the previous twenty-five years it was 2861. If the number of discoveries for the period from 1909 to 1925 continued at the same rate as for the years 1901–1908, then the figure for the period 1901–1925 would be 2694, i.e., lower than that for the previous quarter-century.

[27] One of these may be technical in the sense that some of the discoveries made at the very end of the nineteenth century were not sufficiently appreciated to be included in Darmstaedter's compilation. Granting this (though this would scarcely apply, to any significant degree, to the period in which the decline was first marked — 1861–1870) for the forty to fifty years prior to 1908, most of the significant discoveries certainly became "facts," and in all likelihood were properly appreciated and registered in Darmstaedter's work. In any event, only some required a longer time for their "appreciation" and "registration," and were consequently not included. But these would hardly change the results, especially since this "technical" basis for nonregistration of some of the new inventions may have been completely offset by the tendency to register more fully the more recent discoveries.

[28] Boldyreff's data show that the rate of increase in scientific advance was considerably less in 1800–1849 than in the preceding half-century. His figures (geometric averages) are: 451.0 for 1700–1749; 1318.0 for 1750–1799; and 2042.2 for 1800–1849. His data do not extend beyond the last period.

[29] According to Garrison's data: by 20-year periods, the number of important discoveries in medicine was: 79 for 1800–1819; 129 for 1820–1839; 124 for 1840–1859; 132 for 1860–1879; 260 for 1880–1899; 217 for 1900–1919; and 43 for 1920–1928.

were maintained up to 1925, the peak quarter century would be the latest period, that is 1901–1925. Making these allowances there are, nevertheless, the fields of mathematics, biology, medicine, geology, and geography, where, according to the Darmstaedter compilation, the peak period was not the last, but one of the earlier quarter-century periods in the nineteenth century or, in the case of mathematics, was found in the eighteenth century.[30] Thus these data show also that not only the rate of increase of discoveries decreased at the end of the nineteenth century in practically all the natural sciences, but that in several of them the absolute number of the discoveries also declined. In the light of these data one may hardly maintain that an acceleration in the rate of discovery has continued throughout the last century. Some "breakdown" in science and technology — whether temporary or not remains to be seen — seems to have occurred at the end of the nineteenth century.

These data extend only to 1900–1908. They disclose nothing concerning more recent developments in the twentieth century, from 1900 (or 1908) to 1937. Only in regard to medicine are data available up to 1928, and these data, if reliable, indicate a rapid decrease: 123 important discoveries in 1900–1909; 94 in 1910–1919; and 43 in 1920–1928 (according to Garrison's work).

There is no source similar to Darmstaedter's work for the most recent period in the twentieth century. There are, however, some data showing the situation at least in one field: technological invention. It is commonly held that the number of inventions grows and will continue to grow with increasing rapidity. The best available source for "measurement" of the movement of the number of inventions is constituted by the statistics concerning patents issued to inventors. Such statistical information pertaining to patents issued in Great Britain is available for a long period. These data as well as the patent statistics of the United States may well be considered in connection with our problem.

It is understood that invention and patent are of course not identical units; that statistics of patents issued represent an imperfect reflection of

[30] In passing, it is interesting to note that in Arabia the recession of the number of discoveries in mathematics also began somewhat earlier than in the other sciences. There, the peak half-century for mathematics was either A.D. 800–850 or 850–900, while for all the natural sciences the peak occurs later: for physics, 1000–1050; chemistry, 950–1000; medicine, 900–1000; natural history, 1150–1200. See P. Sorokin and R. Merton's paper, *op. cit.* Our data are based upon the most complete and reliable general source in the field of Arabian science, namely, George Sarton, *Introduction to the History of Science*, 2 vols. (Baltimore, 1927 and 1931). Also in Greece, the peak century for mathematical discoveries is one of the earliest and the recession also occurs earlier than in several other (though not all) natural sciences.

the actual movement of inventions; and consequently that, especially in reference to a short period of time, patent statistics may be misleading. The difficulties involved in the use of patent statistics have been so often indicated and are so obvious that we need not enter into a detailed discussion of this matter.[31] Yet, despite these shortcomings, there is no more adequate index of the movement of inventions than these patent statistics. As an approximate measuring device it may serve more effectively than any other now at hand.

Moreover, the biases and shortcomings tend to inflate rather than deflate the number of the most recent patented inventions as compared with the number for preceding decades or centuries. One reason for this is that in the past a greater proportion of inventions remained unpatented than in the most recent decades. During these decades patenting — most of which is done by various great corporations with facilities for such purposes — has become one of the principal means of safeguarding financial returns for the corporations which employ a corps of technicians and professional inventors. In any event, there is little reason to suppose that there is any marked tendency for inventions to be less frequently patented than they were in the past. Hence, there is probably no increase in the discrepancy between the actual movement of inventions and that of patents.[32] If one may not say that a greater proportion of inventions tends to be patented in recent decades, one may still less contend that the proportion is becoming less.

After these preliminary remarks let us glance at Table 10, on the statistics of patents issued in the United States and in Great Britain. In order not to encumber the text, only the principal data are included. More detailed data will be briefly summed up in the ensuing discussion.

In the United States the data arranged by intervals of five years show that throughout the whole period, from 1840 to 1930, the number of patents was steadily increasing, with the exception of one period (1890–1895). The peak was attained in 1930. The movement in Great Britain has been similar; with a continuous increase save for the period 1911–1921.

[31] See the discussion in S. C. Gilfillan, *op. cit.*; S. S. Kuznets, *Secular Movements in Production and Prices* (Boston, 1930); J. Rossman, *The Psychology of the Inventor*, rev. ed. (Washington, 1931); F. L. Vaughan, *Economics of Our Patent System* (New York, 1925). W. Kaempffert, *A Popular History of American Invention*, 2 vols. (New York, 1924).

[32] See the discussion of the problem and the arguments in Gilfillan, *op. cit.*, chap. vi. Compare the conclusions of the author with his conclusion in the same chapter (p. 12) on a declining native ability as one of the causes of decline of inventions. See the bibliography in Gilfillan's work.

TABLE 10. NUMBER OF PATENTS ISSUED IN U. S. AND GREAT BRITAIN

UNITED STATES [1]		GREAT BRITAIN [2]	
Period Ending	Number of Patents	Period Ending	Number of Patents
1840	1,922	1761	100
1845	2,425	1771	234
1850	3,517	1781	309
1855	6,143	1791	535
1860	16,997	1801	722
1865	20,779	1811	947
1870	58,833	1821	1,119
1875	61,024	1831	1,576
1880	64,496	1841	3,002
1885	97,357	1851	4,679
1890	110,493	1861	19,188
1895	108,465	1871	22,356
1900	112,325	1881	33,495
1905	143,791	1891	87,623
1910	171,560	1901	130,197
1915	186,241	1911	160,386
1920	197,644	1921	138,909
1925	203,977	1931	182,782
1930	219,384		
1931	51,771		
1932	53,519		
1933	48,819		
1934	48,523		

[1] From the *Annual Reports of the Commissioner of Patents.* See also *Statistical Abstracts* (Washington, 1928), p. 811; (1908), p. 202; (1888), p. 230.

[2] Taken from Ogburn and Gilfillan, *op. cit.,* p. 126, and E. W. Hulme, *Statistical Bibliography in Relation to the Growth of Modern Civilization* (London, 1923).

Turning to the *rate of increase* of patents, however, there is evidence of a retardation, as may be seen from Table 11.

TABLE 11. AVERAGE ANNUAL RATE OF INCREASE OF PATENTING IN THE UNITED STATES, 1841–1930

Period	Average Annual Increase	Period	Average Annual Increase
1841–1845	100	1886–1890	2627
1846–1850	218	1891–1895	− 396 [1]
1851–1855	525	1896–1900	762
1856–1860	2170	1901–1905	6293
1861–1865	757	1906–1910	5554
1866–1870	7611	1911–1915	2936
1871–1875	438	1916–1920	2281
1876–1880	694	1921–1925	1259
1881–1885	6571	1926–1930	3089

[1] Represents decrease.

The greatest *rates of increase* are found in the periods 1866–1870, 1881–1885, and 1901–1910, after which there was a notable decline. Likewise, if we compute the number of times greater the patents of each decennium in Great Britain were than the patents in the preceding decennium, the results are as follows: 2.3 for 1771 in relation to 1761; subsequent figures for each decennium are: 1.3, 1.4, 1.3, 1.3, 1.2, 1.4, 1.9, 1.5, 4.1, 1.2, 1.5, 2.6, 1.5, 1.2, − (minus) 0.8, 1.3. From these figures one may not justifiably conclude that this retardation will necessarily be continued, just as a similar prediction is dubious for the movement of scientific discoveries. But the decreased or stationary rate of increase, quite similar to that found for scientific discoveries at the end of the nineteenth century, does not provide any foundation for optimistic contentions of an ever-increasing rate and number of patented inventions. The decrease or stationary status of the rate (and a decrease even in the number) of scientific discoveries at the end of the nineteenth century and a similar decrease or stationary state of the rate of increase of patented inventions in the United States and Great Britain in the twentieth century, especially after 1910, indicate clearly a slackening of the prior trends.[33] This slowing up of the rate in recent times becomes much more evident in more restricted fields of invention. Tables 12 and 13 demonstrate this clearly. Moreover, they manifest not only a decreasing rate of increase of the patented inventions in recent years (up to 1930), but in almost all these fields which comprise some of the main fields of invention there is also found a decrease in the absolute number of inventions.

It is manifest from a glance at these figures that in the old as well as in quite recently established fields of invention (automobile, airplane) not only the rate but even the absolute number of patented inventions tends to decrease. The one exception is the field of radio. Similar situations are encountered in many other important fields. For instance, in the field of steam engines the average annual number of patents was

---

[33] This is found irrespective of the increase of population. If the rate of patenting is computed per capita of population, then the situation appears even less optimistic. "Since about 1885 American patents have been increasing only in proportion to the population — no faster, despite all the incitements from increasing industrialism and civilization. We were granting a patent yearly for each 2675 inhabitants in 1883–1887, and 1 per 2691 in 1925–1929, since when the depression has reduced applications by a third. . . . In England patents have been decreasing rapidly since 1910. German patents per capita increased at 24 per cent per decade in 1877–1913, 17.5 per cent per decade in 1913–1926, and 17.2 per cent per decade along the straight-line trend of 1920–1933. In all countries, Dr. Sanders tells me, except a few like Greece, which have not yet attained industrialism, the same slowing up of the patenting rate is to be seen. This internationality of the phenomenon rules out one possibility, that the check to patents might be due to arbitrary changes in patent legislation." Gilfillan, *op. cit.*, p. 109. See other details in the same work.

TABLE 12. NUMBER OF PATENTS ISSUED IN VARIOUS FIELDS IN UNITED STATES FROM 1846 TO 1930

Years	Cotton Machinery	Weaving Machinery	Spinning Machinery	Telegraphy	Telephony	Automobile	Airplane	Radio
1846–1850	50	52	16	12				
1851–1855	55	64	18	14				
1856–1860	87	55	20	26				
1861–1865	47	139	66	48				
1866–1870	187	397	142	130				
1871–1875	266	398	192	368				
1876–1880	253	281	183	294	220			
1881–1885	356	283	193	652	760			
1886–1890	313	594	340	436	525			
1891–1895	277	632	227	261	506			
1896–1900	262	783	222	182	699	61		
1901–1905	276	989	285	526	976	265	44	
1906–1910	486	1053	251	457	1335	572	206	
1911–1915	484	766	283	363	1211	1329	840	
1916–1920	351	684	154	316	1630	3294	878	50
1921–1925	317	834	207	267	1316	3803	965	443
1926–1930	266	923	178	288	1348	1589	786	1061

in each five-year period, beginning with 1881–1885 and ending with 1926–1930: 22.0, 44.4, 36.2, 26.0, 23.8, 11.8, 13.6, 7.6, 5.2, 7.4.

Thus, in these fields, so selected as to represent important fields of invention and, at the same time, to provide samples of relatively older fields, such as the steam engine, loom, cotton machinery; relatively new fields, such as the telephone and telegraph; and finally, quite recent fields, such as the airplane, radio, automobile — in all these fields do we see the same slackening in the rate of patented invention. In addition to this retarded rate of increase of patented inventions, there is evidenced a decrease, after 1881–1890, of the absolute number of inventions in the older fields, in more recent fields after the beginning of this century, and in most recent fields after the second decade of this century. Finally, so far as these fields are concerned, it has been suggested that the basic inventions were made in the earlier, not in the later part of their development. Though these obviously do not embrace all the fields of invention, being basic fields, they probably provide a typical picture which accentuates and supports the conclusion derived from the curve of all the patented inventions and is in turn supported by it.

Thus, the movement of the number of technological inventions in the United States, in so far as it is roughly indexed by patent statistics, manifests not only a retardation of the rate of increase from the end of the nineteenth century, but also a sort of hesitation even in the increase of the absolute number of inventions. After a brilliant period of rapid climbing the process of invention has begun, as it were, to become tired and has slackened its pace. These data well agree, then, with the movement of discoveries and inventions derived from Darmstaedter's compilation.

The statistics of patented inventions in Great Britain present results essentially similar to those for the United States. For economy of space the more detailed tabulations will be omitted. The summary, Table 10, for the period 1761–1931 was included in an earlier discussion. An additional graph, Figure 8, taken from E. Wyndham Hulme's work,[34] gives some conception of the movement of patents from 1449 to 1921. Extending over a much longer period than patent statistics in the United States, the British data show several erratic waves in the number of inventions. We see that after an increase from 1612–1620, there occurs a decline until about 1632; which is followed by another and higher rise succeeded after 1638 by a great decline up to about 1690. During the next few years the number increases markedly only to decrease

[34] E. W. Hulme, *Statistical Bibliography in Relation to the Growth of Modern Civilization* (London, 1923).

again during the period from 1700 to about 1740. Beginning at this point, patents begin (with temporary slight fluctuations) a persistent and rapid rise; the ascent (of absolute number, not of rate) becoming

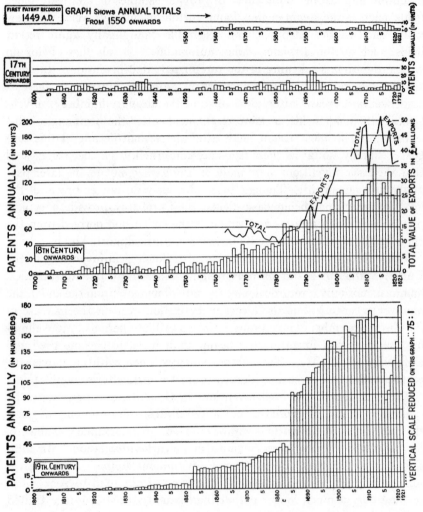

FIG. 8.   NUMBER OF BRITISH PATENTS GRANTED ANNUALLY FROM 1449 TO 1921

extremely great from about 1852 to 1885. But this is only a prelude to an enormous increase from 1885 to 1911, which suddenly declines, reaching its lowest position in 1915. This is followed by yet another ascent which surpasses the peak of 1911.

Thus after a practically uninterrupted ascent for more than one hundred and fifty years, the number of the patented inventions first manifested a *sharp decline* in the decade 1911–1920. It is evident that the decline occurred during the World War period. But there are several observations to be made in this connection. This coincidence of war and decline of invention does not make the decline any less real, or incidental. Nor is there any certainty that the future will not witness further war and associated declines in invention. Any such decline must have *some* cause or causes, but for the time being we are not primarily concerned with the causation, but only with the fact, of decline. The curve of inventions began once again to ascend in the decade subsequent to 1911–1920, but the rate of increase for the entire period from about 1898 has been notably slower than in the foregoing interval. In this sense, the British data are in agreement with those of the movement of scientific discoveries and inventions generally and with the patent statistics for the United States. They all, as far as sheer *number* of discoveries is concerned, show "increasing fatigue" and even "stumbling" in scientific and technological progress at the end of the nineteenth and in the twentieth century. No precise information concerning the most recent developments in science is available, but the probabilities are that the symptoms of "fatigue" which marked scientific advance at the end of the nineteenth century have continued in the twentieth.

It is quite probable that the movement of technological inventions is typical for the totality of the natural sciences. Indeed, technological inventions have in a sense comprised the most productive and basic field of our modern culture. Technological progress (as measured by numerical increase of inventions) has been more rapid, for the last two centuries, than scientific advance. Indeed, the number of important discoveries in the sciences increased from 111 in 1701–1725 to 1617 in 1876–1900, that is, about fifteen times; the number of inventions for these two periods respectively was 47 and 1223, representing an increase of about twenty-six times. The number of significant scientific discoveries in 1876–1900 was about 2.3 times as great as that in 1801–1825; the number of technological inventions, however, was about 3.2 times as great in the latter period. This indicates an increase of technological inventions more rapid than that of scientific discoveries. Hence, if in the twentieth century there is a slackening in the numerical increase of inventions, it is highly probable that this slackening is as pronounced, or perhaps even more marked, in the natural sciences.

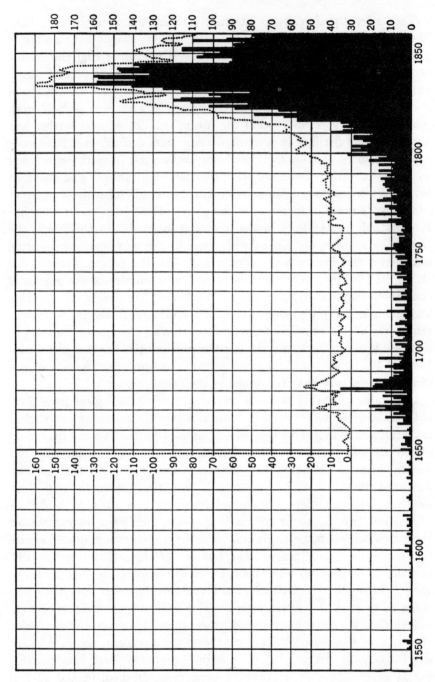

FIG. 9.   COLE-EALES DATA ON LITERATURE OF ANATOMY

That this conclusion is valid is suggested also by additional materials. First, the data concerning discoveries in medicine (see Table 5 and Figure 5) show that the peak period here was 1880–1889 (147 discoveries); during the subsequent decades the respective figures are: 117 for 1890–1899; 123 for 1900–1909; 94 for 1910–1919; and 43 for 1920–1928. All in all, there is evidenced a marked sharp downward movement.[35]

A second additional, though not very reliable, source of evidence is provided by Hulme. Computing the quantitative output (with some qualitative consideration) of the total scientific literature for 1900–1913, on the basis of *The International Catalogue of Scientific Literature*, he obtains the following figures for the years 1901 to 1913, respectively: 43,440; 49,896; 49,264; 50,741; 73,034; 74,877; 74,327; 75,034; 70,030; 85,519; 74,773; 69,323; 62,799.[36] Thus, after the bumper year 1910, the total output of scientific literature (including all the sciences — mathematics, mechanics, physics, chemistry, astronomy, meteorology, mineralogy, geology, geography, paleontology, biology, botany, zoology, anatomy, anthropology, physiology, bacteriology, serology) for some reason declines, even prior to the war, thus evidencing a movement similar to that of inventions in the United States and Great Britain, to the movement of literature in comparative anatomy, and finally to that of discoveries from 1900 to 1908 as derived from Darmstaedter's work. Hulme's data are, however, of little significance per se. Thus, if one were to judge solely on the basis of number of publications,

[35] In passing, it is to be noted that the movement of discoveries in medicine as derived from the compilations of Darmstaedter and of Garrison agrees in essentials with the movement of the literature on comparative anatomy from 1550 to 1860, as presented by F. J. Cole and N. B. Eales in their "Statistical Analysis of the Literature of Comparative Anatomy" in *Science Progress* (April, 1917), quoted by Hulme. A confrontation of the two appropriate charts (Figures 8 and 9) suffices to indicate the resemblance. The Cole-Eales data and charts are based upon the number of publications in this field from 1550 to 1860. The results show: "At first, the research work in comparative anatomy is intermittent — but from 1650 to 1700 a period of increased activity is shown — reaching its maximum output about 1683. The first half of the eighteenth century is uneventful; the second half is again a period of revival — between 1815 and 1835 the tide is flowing strongly — flood tide being reached in the latter year. . . . The steep decline after 1835 can only be explained as an admirable example of that rhythm which underlies all the activities of the living world." The data cannot describe the situation subsequent to 1860, but their study of the problem leads the authors to the following conclusion. "Our records do not extend beyond the year 1860, but we believe that bottom was reached soon after that time and was followed by another rise. That in its turn gave place to the current depression of which all students of the literature of comparative anatomy have been conscious for several years." Quoted by Hulme, *op. cit.*, pp. 31–32.

[36] *Ibid.*, p. 44, which includes a detailed and careful analysis.

it would seem that our contemporary literature, natural science, humanities, newspapers, social sciences, and religion were all in a stage of hitherto unequaled efflorescence, with genius run rampant, and accomplishment a commonplace. And yet, such a conclusion would be premature, for it identifies the fact of an abundance of paper, availability of printing presses and of hack writers with discovery, invention, creative achievement, and genius — an identification which is utterly fallacious.[37]

Without introducing other symptomatic data which likewise indicate a sort of fatigue in the movement of scientific discoveries, it may be held that the materials already discussed warrant the modest conclusion that toward the close of the nineteenth and during the twentieth century there has occurred a slackening in the rate of increase and, in some periods and in some sciences, even a stationary state or decline in the absolute number of discoveries and inventions. This conclusion seems more adequately supported by the facts than overenthusiastic assertions of an ever-increasing number and an ever-accelerating rate of increase in discovery and invention. At this juncture, one cannot say whether this slackening is simply a minor, short-time fluctuation or the prelude to a long-time decline of science and technology. In either event, the fact of retardation remains.

As we have seen and shall see further, the field of science and technology does not stand alone in this respect, for one may observe a similar reversal in other compartments of our culture since the end of the nineteenth century. These "trends of reversal" seem to be bound together, logically and causally. The complex of such changes indicates some transformation of our culture within the last half century or so — a transformation infinitely more profound than is commonly realized.

F. *Number and Qualitative Estimation of Discoveries and Inventions.* Now, from the number we shall turn to the *qualitative importance of discoveries and inventions.* It has been indicated several times that it would indeed be imprudent to base even tentative conclusions concerning the progress or regress of science and technology solely upon changes in the *number* of innovations. Clearly, the qualitative aspect demands considerable attention.

On the other hand, there does not exist any purely objective basis for an estimation of the qualitative importance of a discovery or invention.

[37] Little need be said, therefore, of such measurements of scientific progress as, for instance, the number of abstracts of articles published in the *Chemical Abstracts* or in any journal of abstracts in physics, biology, or the social sciences. The mere number of abstracted articles means little in this respect. As an example of such measurement see E. Thomas, *op. cit.* The data and analysis of P. W. Wilson and E. Fred. *op. cit.*, are far more valid.

The only relatively objective, and relatively valid, criterion is constituted by the opinions of the specialists in the field, when such opinions are more or less unanimous and when they are not limited to one or two generations but have been maintained by many *generations of specialists*. Such an opinion, based upon the intrinsic importance of the scientific or inventive work of a person, is a relatively satisfactory criterion of importance — as adequate as any basis thus far vouchsafed to mortals. Many, very many, generations of scholars and philosophers have thought of Plato and Aristotle as thinkers of the first order. This justifies our regarding them likewise. Similarly, have Pythagoras and Archimedes, or Copernicus, Galileo, and Newton withstood this test. Ergo, their discoveries and inventions were of great importance. When such a basis is supplemented by additional criteria, such as the number of monographs written about these scientists, their role in initiating a new movement, the appearance of their names in the most elementary texts, and the like, there results an integrated and compounded criterion which is the best available.

This method enables us to discriminate between the *greatest* scientists and discoveries, but unfortunately it does not facilitate the differentiation of the bulk of them. The majority of discoveries and inventions have never been evaluated on the basis of this or any other criterion. Moreover, even unanimity of opinion among specialists does not denote infallibility, for such estimations, being greatly influenced by social and cultural conditions, change from age to age. Shakespeare's work was less esteemed by his contemporaries than it was some hundred or hundred and fifty years later. G. B. Vico was not appreciated by his contemporaries at all. Achievements of the masters of Gothic style were sharply deprecated by specialists in art and architecture during the sixteenth, seventeenth, and, partly, eighteenth centuries. Yet subsequently the Gothic style was once again most enthusiastically praised and imitated. And so it goes, in virtually every field, including science. We have already noted such reversals of opinion not only about this person or that discovery, but about all achievements based on one or another system of truth. We shall see subsequently that even within science itself the appraisal of this or that basic theory, such as atomism, vitalism-mechanisticism, various cosmogonies, Darwinism, Mendelianism, etc., varies considerably. In other words, the opinion of specialists, during one or but few generations, is subject to very considerable, sometimes mercurial, changes and reversals.

There is an added difficulty with regard to recent discoveries and inventions. Many of the more important of these frequently require some time for their culmination. A relatively insignificant discovery or invention, the effects of which are instantaneously felt, may readily appear much more important than another which needs a much longer period for its maturation. In this way one can easily be so misled as to overestimate a "sensational" discovery, accounts of which appear in newspapers and magazines, and, on the other hand, to minimize the importance of a discovery, unheralded, unpublicized, but eventually found to be fundamental. When these and many similar considerations are recognized, one sees at once the extreme difficulty of an adequate qualitative estimation of discoveries and inventions.

Nevertheless, since such estimates are made every day, whether in the selection and appointment of scholars, inventors, technicians, etc., or in historical research where judgments (often implicit) of relative importance determine the choice of historical persons and achievements to be discussed, it is probable that a more systematically derived set of qualitative estimates will be of some value. Though this may not provide an "absolute measure of importance," it may possibly constitute an improvement over more informal procedures.

Viewing discoveries and inventions from this standpoint, one must conclude that *the greatest discoveries have been scattered throughout the past as well as the present.* Such achievements as the use of fire; use of language; discovery of the principle of the lever, the wheel, and the plow; utilization of wind and animal power; the domestication and breeding of animals; cultivation of land; discrimination between poisonous and edible plants; construction of shelters and boats; fashioning of tools and weapons; the institution of social organizations; rudiments of the various arts and sciences — all these represent innovations and accomplishments of the very first order. Yet the origins of these and many others are lost in time immemorial and have since served as the very foundation of our activities and culture. On the other hand, the achievements of the less distant past require no apology. It is a needless, and almost endless, task to enumerate the foremost discoveries of more recent eras.

However, though these scientific discoveries and technological inventions have occurred in both the distant and recent past, their distribution in time has been uneven. Even a superficial glance at the history of science and technology suffices to disclose this fact. European culture from the fourth to the twelfth century A.D., almost completely sterile as far as great discoveries and inventions are concerned, stands in striking contrast to the grandeur of achievement which marked the period from the end of the sixteenth to the beginning of the eighteenth century. Within some two hundred years, natural science and, less notably, technology were refashioned. This brilliant efflorescence had been anticipated by the hardly inconsiderable achievements of the prior two centuries. The following list, perforce most brief, barely taps the contributions of the fourteenth and fifteenth centuries: perfection of the mariner's compass, invention of the rudder, great improvements in the construction of ships (two-masted and three-masted), invention of heavy artillery, introduction of the blast furnace (with draft created by water power) making cast iron possible, invention and rapid diffusion of modern printing, division of hours and minutes into sixties, perfected mechanical clock, scientific cartography, foundations of trigonometry (Regiomontanus), great geographical discoveries, great progress in surgery and medical knowledge.[38]

The movement gained momentum and by the close of the seventeenth century the principles basic to much of subsequent science had been formulated. Professor Whitehead succinctly summarized the situation, saying that European science has "been living upon the accumulated capital of ideas provided for them by the genius of the seventeenth century." [39] This extraordinary progress manifested itself perhaps most clearly in mechanics. During some one hundred and seventy years almost all the fundamental principles of mechanics and physics generally found expression through the efforts of the following "scientific giants": Leonardo da Vinci (1451–1519), Simon Stevin (1548–1620), Kepler (1571–1630), Galileo (1564–1642), Descartes (1596–1650), Leibnitz (1646–1716), Roberval (1602–1675), Torricelli (1608–1647), Pascal (1623–1662), Huygens (1629–1695), Wallis (1616–1703), Mariotte (1620–1684), and Newton (1642–1727).[40]

The contributions of these individuals comprise the bulk of our knowledge in this field. If we include the achievements of these persons and some of their contemporaries, the same may be said of the disciplines of mathematics, astronomy, and anatomy. Among these may be mentioned Copernicus (1473–1543), Jerome Cardan (1501–1576), Tycho de Brahe (1546–1601), Cavalieri (1598–1637), Agricola (1490–1555), Gesner (1516–1565), Paracelsus (1493–1541), Gilbert (1540–1603), Napier (1550–1617), Glauber (1604–1668), Otto von Guericke (1602–1686), G. B. della

[38] L. Thorndike, *Science and Thought in the Fifteenth Century* (New York, 1929), 18 ff. *et passim*.

[39] A. N. Whitehead, *Science and the Modern World* (New York, 1925), 55 ff.

[40] L. Lecornu, *La mécanique*, 60 ff.

Porta (1543–1615), J. B. van Helmont (1577–1644), Robert Boyle (1627–1691), Fermat (1601–1665), Briggs (1561–1631), and many others.

Exclude the contributions of these individuals from our contemporary knowledge in these fields and you exclude practically all of their basic principles and laws and the greater part of their content. Clearly, then, during these two centuries there appeared an extraordinary galaxy of great scientists in these fields and a concentration of those cardinal discoveries which are the greatest pride of the Western mind. The intensified concentration of scientific development is commented upon by Professor Smith.

Neither Rome nor medieval Europe added anything of importance to pure science. And then suddenly, within two years, appeared three of the most momentous works of science that the world has ever seen, Copernicus, *On the Revolutions of the Heavenly Orbs* (1543), Vesalius, *On the Structure of the Human Body* (1543), and Cardan's *The Great Art* (his treatise on algebra, 1545).[41]

In other fields, namely, in the biological sciences, progress was not so pronounced, but in its purely material, anatomical, and physiological aspects, it was considerable. Andreas Vesalius (1514–1564) with his cardinal treatise *On the Structure of the Human Body* (1543) — an epoch-making work in anatomy; Eustacchi, Fallopia, Volcher Coiter, and Marc' Aurelio Severino continued his work and laid the foundations of comparative morphology. Michael Servetus (burned at the stake by Calvin in 1553) was aware of the lesser, and William Harvey (1578–1657) discovered the greater, circulation of the blood; while Marcello Malpighi (in 1660–1661) and Jan Swammerdam (*c.* 1667) discovered the capillary circulation. Leeuwenhoek (1632–1723) laid the foundations of microscopy, and Cirolamo Frascatoro, Thomas Sydenham, Jan Heurnius of Leyden, and others promoted the clinical and experimental investigation of vital phenomena. As a result, these two centuries represent a period unique in the history of mankind, precisely because of the unparalleled development of the natural sciences which deal with the Sensate environment of man — the milieu which must be known if it is to be modified for the satisfaction of human needs — in accordance with the Sensate manner of adaptation.

In the history of the Greek, Roman, and Arabian cultures, there is similarly manifested an unevenness in the distribution of the great dis-

---

[41] Preserved Smith, *A History of Modern Culture* (New York, 1930), Vol. I, p. 18. For a survey of the scientific progress between 1543–1687, *passim*, compare my *Contemporary Sociological Theories*, chap. i, on the Mechanistic School. For a detailed list of discoveries during this period see Darmstaedter's work.

coveries and inventions.   In these three cultures, as previously indicated, the movement of the number of discoveries and inventions is, in a rough way, an index of qualitative variations : all in all, the periods of a notable ascending movement of the curve were likewise the periods of the greatest discoveries and inventions.   Conversely, the periods which are represented by an exceedingly low level of the curve were also the periods of comparative sterility in respect to great discoveries and inventions. The reasons for such correlations have been presented at the beginning of this chapter.

On the basis of this induction, it is, perhaps, justifiable to assume that the same correlation is found, with one important correction, in our culture.   Since we have a curve approximately representing the number of discoveries and inventions in our culture, and since in these other three cultures such a curve is roughly indicative of the qualitative progress of science and technology as well, it is not unwarrantable that we judge the qualitative progress of science and technology in our culture on the basis of the quantitative curve.   We know that from the third and the fourth century A.D. up to about the twelfth century there was practically no important discovery and invention introduced.   The quantitative curve denotes the same, being very low and remaining stationary almost on the zero line.   We know that from about the fourteenth century scientific progress was more marked ; the curve shows that also.   Hence, with but one correction which is to be discussed, the quantitative curve may be held to reflect, in a rough way, the curve of qualitative progress or regress of science and technology.

The required correction pertains to the last two or three centuries. It is reasonable to assume that the more recent discoveries are likely to be registered in the annals of history generally and in history of science specifically, with fewer omissions than in the case of earlier periods. These later achievements are better remembered ; there has not been so much opportunity for the elimination of the less significant discoveries (which appear great to contemporaries) nor for the rigorous sifting of them.   For these and similar reasons it is probable that the curve representing the number of the items tends to exaggerate recent contributions considerably and to depreciate those of the past, with the exaggeration probably becoming more pronounced the more recent the period.   In the cases of the Greek, Roman, and Arabian cultures this does not occur. The entire course of their cultural development was run during, relatively speaking, such an early period that the time perspective remains virtually unchanged.   Whether one considers the fifth century B.C.

or the fourth century A.D., in both cases there has elapsed ample time for the less important discoveries to be cast into oblivion. But in comparing the scientific contributions of the eighteenth, nineteenth, and twentieth centuries with those of the eleventh and twelfth, or even the sixteenth and seventeenth, the time factor and (at least in the earliest period) invention of printing make a considerable difference. For these reasons, the section of the quantitative curve pertaining to the last two centuries or less must be somewhat discounted, if it is to be used as an index of qualitative progress or regress. Then, in lieu of any other, this curve may serve as a rough index of the qualitative progress of science.

Used as an index of qualitative variation, the curve describes, subsequent to a stationary period of some nine to ten centuries, a notable ascent since approximately the fourteenth century. In the sixteenth and seventeenth centuries this upward movement becomes extremely marked : the curve begins to rise almost vertically. These centuries, as we have seen, were indeed the great period of qualitative progress in science and technology. In the eighteenth and the nineteenth centuries, the slope of the curve becomes more steep and more "stratospheric" than even in the seventeenth century. However, making the requisite correction, it is found that the ascent of the curve continues very steep, but possibly not notably more than in the seventeenth century. Finally, and this is particularly important, even without this correction, the curve at the end of the nineteenth and possibly in the twentieth century becomes less steep, almost stationary, with even a temporary decline. If such is the situation, without introducing any correction, this may serve as a fairly reliable indication that the qualitative progress of some of the natural sciences has slackened. If the necessary correction is made, the signs of "fatigue" during this most recent period would be even more conspicuous.

However enthusiastic we may be about the "unparalleled" progress of science and invention in our time; however great the publicity accorded many of its achievements — such as the theory of relativity — it may be possible that, in this field as well as others, a long-time perspective is necessary for unbiased judgments. It is precisely this perspective which is afforded by our chart. Therefore, its indications are worthy of some consideration and attention. And when one observes how quickly some of the supposedly great discoveries of our day, such as Darwinian and Mendelian laws, the theory of relativity, or "intelligence tests," have been subjected to severe criticism, and how limitations and inadequacies have been disclosed, one's enthusiasm for contemporary scientific advance tends to cool.

The same is to be said of the qualitative aspects of technological inventions. However proud we may be of our achievements in this sphere, their importance should not be exaggerated. Thus, if the comparatively careful appraisal made by the editors of the *Scientific American* of the outstanding inventions produced in the United States be at all indicative, there is no marked tendency for an increase in basic innovation. (See Table 13.)

TABLE 13. NUMBER OF FUNDAMENTAL INVENTIONS [1] IN THE UNITED STATES FROM 1846 TO 1915

Years	Number
1846–1855	25
1856–1865	24
1866–1875	20
1876–1885	16
1886–1895	13
1896–1905	15
1906–1915	10

[1] " Seventy-five Years of Innovation," in *Scientific American*, Vol. CXXIII, No. 14, pp. 323–325.

It is to be noted that the number of important inventions decreases continuously with but one exception. This decrease may be due to the fact that many inventions appearing in the latter periods have not been sufficiently exploited to be ranked as important or revolutionary. However this may be, there does not appear to be any increase in the number of basic inventions. This accords with the conclusions derived from the quantitative curve (Table 11 and Figure 6). The practical conclusion from the foregoing is that if we must keep the pace, we need not less, but more, discoveries and inventions. Otherwise, we would be moving not upward, but downward.

IV. SUMMARY

For the present we may bring to an end our discussion of the development of the natural sciences and technology. Several allied problems will be considered subsequently. Meanwhile, the net results of our analysis may be briefly summarized. (1) The cultivation of natural sciences seems indeed to be associated positively with the truth of senses and negatively with that of faith, the neutral position being occupied by the truth of reason. (2) The development of the natural sciences, like the empirical system of truth, is subject to fluctuations, at times manifesting rapid advance, at others stagnating. No linear trend is noticeable either in the life history of single cultures or in the life history of mankind generally. (3) The empirical system of truth and the natural sciences have both had an unprecedented growth during the last four or five centuries. This development is at present continuing vigorously in both fields. (4) However, scrutiny of the recent development of the natural sciences discloses a slowing up in the rate of progress and signs of "fatigue." At this juncture it cannot be said whether it is a purely temporary and short-time "relaxation" or the beginning of a long-time decline. (5) Moreover, this "fatigue" at the close of the nineteenth and the twentieth century accords with similar departures from the over-ripe Sensate culture, which our culture displays in most of its compartments. To this extent it is not an isolated "sign" but merely one of the many mutually related symptoms of a — short-time or long-time — transformation experienced by our culture in this period. (6) As the direction of movement in this field is likewise away from the reality of the senses, this means that even in this most recent period our culture shows itself (in the compartments thus far examined) not only logically but also causally integrated to a tangible extent.

Chapter Four

FLUCTUATION OF "FIRST PRINCIPLES": I. FLUCTUATION OF
IDEALISM AND MATERIALISM[1]

I. Preliminaries

It was stated in Chapter One that the change of a culture from the
Sensate to the Ideational type, or vice versa, involved changes not only
in its system of truth, science, and technology, but also in many of its
general principles and basic ideas concerning *the* reality. The three
preceding chapters have thus far demonstrated the occurrence of changes
of the systems of truth and of fluctuations in the rate of scientific advance. In this and subsequent chapters, an attempt will be made to
indicate the changes in the general principles and basic ideas of reality
which explicitly or implicitly underlie every philosophy, science, and
important theory.

Every scientist and scholar has some sort of philosophy and some set
of "first principles," whether his assumptions in this respect are explicit
or implicit, whether his position is adopted advisedly or whether, as
Molière's hero, he talks prose without being aware of it. Likewise, the
total philosophico-scientific mentality of the various cultural periods
studied has invariably involved some type of "first principles" basic to
the complex "superstructure" comprised by the numerous, more
restricted philosophical and scientific theories of the time. For instance,
first principles relating to the nature of the ultimate reality, determinism
and indeterminism, absolutism and relativism, eternalism and temporalism, nominalism and realism, and the like, have always been fundamental to this superstructure. In similar fashion, such categories and
fundamental concepts as those of time, space, relation, causation, number, structure of matter, vitalism, mechanisticism, structure of the universe, and so on, have, in some form or other, comprised the basic framework of reference — a framework which served to put in order an immense
number of "facts," and to organize all concrete data. Without such a
framework no systematization, classification, or even apprehension of

[1] In co-operation with N. O. Lossky and I. I. Lapshin.

the facts would have been possible. Clearly, some form of such first principles must be assumed if the more detailed theories in various fields are to be coherently organized.

If these first principles have always been present in some form, a study of their fluctuation manifestly involves an investigation of the nature of the "content" with which each of them has been "filled." Since the main forms of this content have been few, our investigation resolves itself into a study of the undulations in the acceptance or influence of each of these forms in the course of time (as well as in social space). Hence, the following discussion is devoted to the study of the fluctuations in the influence (acceptance as truth) of several of these first principles.

The nature of reality, particularly of the ultimate reality, has always constituted one of these first principles. Beginning with the earliest mythologies of preliterate and historical peoples and ending with contemporary science, philosophy, and religion, everywhere and always has this question been raised and, in some way, answered. These answers can be grouped into three main classes: Idealism, Materialism, and a Mixed class comprised by those theories which do not fall into either of the other classes.

It is not our intention to discuss the truth or error of these theories, nor to adopt any of them, but rather to study the rise and decline in influence of each of these three currents of thought in the life history of the Graeco-Roman and Western cultures. Other problems as well as the method, qualifications, reservations, and specifications of the study now in hand are precisely the same as those laid down at the beginning of Chapter One (pertaining to the fluctuations in influence of empiricism, rationalism, and other systems of truth). Hence, they need not be repeated here.

Our first task is a definition and elaboration of the terms Idealism, Materialism, and Mixed mentality. In addition to this, will be found at the end of the book a list of the names of the thinkers classified in the three classes, and the values (indices of influence ranging from 1 to 12) assigned to each (see the Appendix to this chapter). Here again, for economy of space, are omitted the tables based upon an equal evaluation of all the thinkers.[2] However, Figure 10 shows clearly that the curves constructed on the basis of equal values for all the thinkers and on the

---

[2] These tables are presented in my article: "The Fluctuation of Idealism and Materialism in the Graeco-Roman and European Cultures from 600 B.C. to 1920 A.D.," in the *Festschrift Tönnies* (Leipzig, 1936), pp. 38–78.

basis of values varying from 1 to 12 vary concomitantly and are almost identical.

II. FLUCTUATION IN THE INFLUENCE OF IDEALISM, MATERIALISM, AND MIXED THEORIES

By *Idealism* as philosophy, metaphysics, or mentality is meant a system of ideology which maintains that the ultimate, or true, reality is spiritual, in the sense of God, of Platonic ideas, of immaterial spirit, of soul, or of psychical reality. The several varieties of Idealism can be reduced to two fundamental classes: monistic and pluralistic Idealism. *Monistic* idealism holds that all the individual and separate systems of the immaterial, spiritual, and psychical reality are but temporary manifestations or emanations of One Principle or One Ultimate, All-Embracing, Spiritual Being, be it God, Absolute Idea, Absolute Mind, Absolute Spirit, or the like. In contradistinction to this, *pluralistic* idealism contends that there exists a multitude of independent centers or systems of spiritual and psychical realities — such as souls, spirits, monads, and other spiritual-immaterial entities — which constitute the ultimate reality.

By *Materialism* is meant that philosophy which holds that the ultimate reality is matter, and that spiritual or immaterial phenomena are but a manifestation of it, are simply the result of the motion of particles of matter. Of the many varieties of Materialism, there are two which are most important. *Hylozoistic* materialism ascribes a species of life to matter, and maintains that the ultimate reality is living matter which possesses sensation, conation, and, in a sense, consciousness. Materiality or corporeality and spirituality are inseparable. Hylozoism is similar to what is frequently termed "monism." *Mechanistic* materialism, on the other hand, is much more "materialistic" than hylozoism. While the latter is a sort of Pan-Somatism [3] which does not radically deny the spiritual principle but claims that it is always incorporated corporeally or somatically, mechanistic materialism maintains that matter is the *only* reality and that spiritual or immaterial phenomena, if they exist, are nothing but a purely passive product of matter and of purely mechanistic motions of material particles.

Each of these forms of Idealism and Materialism has many varieties and shadings, but since we are concerned with the fluctuation of only the main forms of Idealistic and Materialistic mentality, these minor variations are not considered.

[3] Concerning this point, see N. Lossky, "The Metaphysics of the Stoics," in *Journal of Philosophical Studies*, Vol. IV, No. 16 (1929).

Idealism and Materialism constitute the major categories with which we are concerned. The third, the Mixed category, includes all those intermediary doctrines pertaining to the nature of the ultimate reality which cannot be classified as Idealistic or Materialistic; and also such systems as skepticism, agnosticism, critical philosophy, and the like.

Hence, these three currents of thought relating to this problem include all the relevant systems in all cultures at all times. The classification of thinkers and the "weights" ascribed to each are presented in the Appendix to this chapter. At this juncture it is advisable to note that several names — for example, Kant — are found not in one, but in two classes (*e.g.*, Idealism and Mixed). This is due to the fact that such thinkers either hold different positions in their several works, or their respective systems are so clearly marginal that they can be classified in two adjacent categories. The number of such names, however, is small.

It may now be considered whether or not the relative influence of each of these currents remains constant and, if not, how and when it fluctuates. The method of setting up the scale of indicators, it will be remembered, is explained in Chapter One. As previously suggested, the mere tabulation of the number and proportion of representatives of each current of thought is omitted for the purpose of economizing space. Only the tables based upon an attribution of differential significance to the various thinkers are presented here, one by 20-year periods, the other by 100-year periods. The "weights," ranging from 1 to 12, represent the total number of points of influence exercised by all the representatives of a given current of thought in a given period.[4] The absolute weights and the percentages of the total weight of each of the three currents, both of which are presented in Tables 14 and 15 and depicted in Figures 10 and 11, permit ready comparisons and analysis. Those who wish to examine in detail the representatives of Idealism, Materialism, and the Mixed systems should turn to the list of names appended to the study (see the Appendix to this chapter). Since this list includes the names of all the persons dealt with, as well as their respective weights (both arranged by 20-year intervals), it presents all the details necessary for criticism and analysis of the tabulations. Tables 14 and 15 and Figures 10 and 11 follow.

---

[4] Since most of the thinkers included in the period 1900–1920 are still in the ranks of the living, the specific weight assigned each of them is not recorded separately. It may be mentioned, however, that the independent rankings made by three specialists in this field were markedly consistent.

TABLE 14. INDICATORS OF FLUCTUATION OF IDEALISM, MATERIALISM, AND THE MIXED SYSTEMS,[1] BY 20-YEAR PERIODS, FROM 580 B.C. TO A.D. 1920

PERIOD	MATERIALISM						IDEALISM						MIXED		GRAND TOTAL	
	Pluralistic		Monistic		Total		Hylozoistic		Mechanistic		Total					
	No. of points of weight	Per cent	No. of points of weight	Per cent	No. of points of weight	Per cent	No. of points of weight	Per cent	No. of points of weight	Per cent	No. of points of weight	Per cent	No. of points of weight	Per cent	No. of points of weight	Per cent
580–560 B.C.	0	0	0	0	0	0	4	100.0	0	0	4	100.0	0	0	4	100
560–540	0	0	5	35.7	5	35.7	9	64.3	0	0	9	64.3	0	0	14	100
540–520	8	40.0	5	25.0	13	65.0	7	35.0	0	0	7	35.0	0	0	20	100
520–500	8	36.4	5	22.7	13	59.1	9	40.9	0	0	9	40.9	0	0	22	100
500–480	10	34.5	12	41.4	22	75.9	7	24.1	0	0	7	24.1	0	0	29	100
480–460	2	9.1	12	54.6	14	63.7	8	36.3	0	0	8	36.3	0	0	22	100
460–440	1	5.3	8	42.1	9	47.4	10	52.6	0	0	10	52.6	0	0	19	100
440–420	8	15.7	8	15.7	16	31.4	20	39.2	2	3.9	22	43.1	13	25.5	51	100
420–400	19	24.1	3	3.7	22	27.8	11	14.0	10	12.6	21	26.6	36	45.6	79	100
400–380	25	33.3	5	6.7	30	40.0	7	9.3	9	12.0	16	21.3	29	38.7	75	100
380–360	25	41.2	6	9.8	31	51.0	5	8.2	9	14.8	14	23.0	16	26.0	61	100
360–340	42	63.7	3	4.5	45	68.2	5	7.6	2	3.0	7	10.6	14	21.2	66	100
340–320	21	42.2	17	34.7	38	76.9	5	10.9	1	2.0	6	12.9	5	10.2	49	100
320–300	15	18.5	35	43.2	50	61.7	11	13.5	4	5.0	15	18.5	16	19.8	81	100
300–280	7	8.3	30	35.7	37	44.0	20	23.8	12	14.3	32	38.1	15	17.9	84	100
280–260	7	9.5	14	18.9	21	28.4	24	32.3	11	15.0	35	47.3	18	24.3	74	100
260–240	1	3.0	3	8.1	4	11.1	22	61.1	4	11.1	26	72.2	6	16.7	36	100
240–220	1	1.7	4	6.5	5	8.2	40	65.5	7	11.5	47	77.0	9	14.8	61	100
220–200	1	3.0	8	23.5	9	26.5	15	44.1	3	8.8	18	52.9	7	20.6	34	100
200–180	1	4.4	9	39.1	10	43.5	6	26.1	4	17.4	10	43.5	3	13.0	23	100
180–160	1	4.8	6	28.5	7	33.3	6	28.6	2	9.5	8	38.1	6	28.6	21	100
160–140	1	4.6	5	22.7	6	27.3	6	27.3	3	13.6	9	40.9	7	31.8	22	100
140–120	1	4.6	4	18.1	5	22.7	6	27.3	2	9.1	8	36.4	9	40.9	22	100
120–100	1	4.9	4	19.0	5	23.9	8	38.1	4	19.0	12	57.1	4	19.0	21	100
100–80	3	11.5	2	7.7	5	19.2	12	42.7	7	30.4	19	73.1	2	7.7	26	100
80–60	12	34.3	4	11.4	16	45.7	14	40.0	5	14.3	19	54.3	0	0	35	100
60–40	18	27.0	4	5.8	22	32.8	22	32.7	18	27.0	40	59.7	5	7.5	67	100
40–20	16	36.3	5	11.4	21	47.7	9	20.5	9	20.4	18	40.9	5	11.4	44	100
20–0	4	19.0	6	28.6	10	47.6	5	23.8	1	4.8	6	28.6	5	23.8	21	100
0–20 A.D.	8	33.3	10	41.7	18	75.0	5	20.8	1	4.2	6	25.0	0	0	24	100
20–40	11	45.8	6	25.0	17	70.8	6	25.0	1	4.2	7	29.2	0	0	24	100
40–60	11	36.7	2	6.7	13	43.4	16	53.3	1	3.3	17	56.6	0	0	30	100
60–80	8	21.1	2	5.3	10	26.4	27	71.0	1	2.6	28	73.6	0	0	38	100
80–100	16	43.3	2	5.4	18	48.7	18	48.6	1	2.7	19	51.3	0	0	37	100
100–120	19	43.2	10	22.7	29	65.9	12	27.2	1	2.3	13	29.5	2	4.6	44	100
120–140	31	47.0	10	15.1	41	62.1	17	25.8	2	3.0	19	28.8	6	9.1	66	100
140–160	35	49.3	13	18.3	48	67.6	14	19.8	3	4.2	17	24.0	6	8.4	71	100

[1] On the basis of different values given from 1 to 12.

TABLE 14. INDICATORS OF FLUCTUATION OF IDEALISM, MATERIALISM, AND THE MIXED SYSTEMS,[1] BY 20-YEAR PERIODS, FROM 580 B.C. TO A.D. 1920 — continued

PERIOD	IDEALISM						MATERIALISM						MIXED		GRAND TOTAL	
	Pluralistic		Monistic		Total		Hylozoistic		Mechanistic		Total					
	No. of points of weight	Per cent	No. of points of weight	Per cent	No. of points of weight	Per cent	No. of points of weight	Per cent	No. of points of weight	Per cent	No. of points of weight	Per cent	No. of points of weight	Per cent	No. of points of weight	Per cent
160–180 A.D.	42	53.2	17	21.5	59	74.7	11	13.9	3	3.8	14	17.7	6	7.6	79	100
180–200	58	58.0	23	23.0	81	81.0	8	8.0	5	5.0	13	13.0	6	6.0	100	100
200–220	41	56.2	16	21.9	57	78.1	7	9.6	3	4.1	10	13.7	6	8.2	73	100
220–240	35	66.0	10	18.9	45	84.9	7	13.2	1	1.9	8	15.1	0	0	53	100
240–260	44	80.0	5	9.1	49	89.1	5	9.1	1	1.8	6	10.9	0	0	55	100
260–280	32	75.4	5	11.6	37	86.0	5	11.7	1	2.3	6	14.0	0	0	43	100
280–300	19	76.0	1	4.0	20	80.0	4	16.0	1	4.0	5	20.0	0	0	25	100
300–320	24	92.3	0	0	24	91.3	1	3.8	1	3.9	2	7.7	0	0	26	100
320–340	37	88.1	0	0	37	88.1	4	9.5	1	2.4	5	11.9	0	0	42	100
340–360	26	78.8	0	0	26	78.8	6	18.2	1	3.0	7	21.2	0	0	33	100
360–380	59	90.8	0	0	59	90.8	6	9.2	0	0	6	9.2	0	0	65	100
380–400	52	88.0	0	0	52	88.0	7	12.0	0	0	7	12.0	0	0	59	100
400–420	45	84.9	0	0	45	84.9	8	15.1	0	0	8	15.1	0	0	53	100
420–440	43	82.7	0	0	43	82.7	9	17.3	0	0	9	17.3	0	0	52	100
440–460	32	97.0	0	0	32	97.0	1	3.0	0	0	1	3.0	0	0	33	100
460–480	27	90.0	0	0	27	90.0	3	10.0	0	0	3	10.0	0	0	30	100
480–500	24	88.9	0	0	24	88.9	3	11.1	0	0	3	11.1	0	0	27	100
500–520	30	97.0	0	0	30	97.0	1	3.0	0	0	1	3.0	0	0	31	100
520–540	38	97.4	0	0	38	97.4	1	2.6	0	0	1	2.6	0	0	39	100
540–560	25	100.0	0	0	25	100.0	0	0	0	0	0	0	0	0	25	100
560–580	8	100.0	0	0	8	100.0	0	0	0	0	0	0	0	0	8	100
580–600	8	100.0	0	0	8	100.0	0	0	0	0	0	0	0	0	8	100
600–620	12	100.0	0	0	12	100.0	0	0	0	0	0	0	0	0	12	100
620–640	14	100.0	0	0	14	100.0	0	0	0	0	0	0	0	0	14	100
640–660	9	100.0	0	0	9	100.0	0	0	0	0	0	0	0	0	9	100
660–680	8	100.0	0	0	8	100.0	0	0	0	0	0	0	0	0	8	100
680–700	2	100.0	0	0	2	100.0	0	0	0	0	0	0	0	0	2	100
700–720	3	100.0	0	0	3	100.0	0	0	0	0	0	0	0	0	3	100
720–740	8	100.0	0	0	8	100.0	0	0	0	0	0	0	0	0	8	100
740–760	6	100.0	0	0	6	100.0	0	0	0	0	0	0	0	0	6	100
760–780	1	100.0	0	0	1	100.0	0	0	0	0	0	0	0	0	1	100
780–800	4	100.0	0	0	4	100.0	0	0	0	0	0	0	0	0	4	100
800–820	6	100.0	0	0	6	100.0	0	0	0	0	0	0	0	0	6	100
820–840	10	100.0	0	0	10	100.0	0	0	0	0	0	0	0	0	10	100
840–860	18	100.0	0	0	18	100.0	0	0	0	0	0	0	0	0	18	100
860–880	21	100.0	0	0	21	100.0	0	0	0	0	0	0	0	0	21	100
880–900	9	100.0	0	0	9	100.0	0	0	0	0	0	0	0	0	9	100
900–920	4	100.0	0	0	4	100.0	0	0	0	0	0	0	0	0	4	100

Date																
920–940 A.D.	100	2	0	0	0	0	0	0	0	0	100.0	2	0	0	100.0	2
940–960	100	1	0	0	0	0	0	0	0	0	100.0	1	0	0	100.0	1
960–980	100	1	0	0	0	0	0	0	0	0	100.0	1	0	0	100.0	1
980–1000	100	3	0	0	0	0	0	0	0	0	100.0	3	0	0	100.0	3
1000–1020	100	8	0	0	0	0	0	0	0	0	100.0	8	0	0	100.0	8
1020–1040	100	5	0	0	0	0	0	0	0	0	100.0	5	0	0	100.0	13
1040–1060	100	13	0	0	0	0	0	0	0	0	100.0	13	0	0	100.0	31
1060–1080	100	31	0	0	0	0	0	0	0	0	100.0	31	0	0	100.0	32
1080–1100	100	32	0	0	0	0	0	0	0	0	100.0	32	0	0	100.0	22
1100–1120	100	22	0	0	0	0	0	0	0	0	100.0	22	0	0	100.0	36
1120–1140	100	36	0	0	0	0	0	0	0	0	100.0	36	0	0	100.0	42
1140–1160	100	42	0	0	0	0	0	0	0	0	100.0	42	0	0	100.0	28
1160–1180	100	28	0	0	0	0	0	0	0	0	100.0	28	0	0	100.0	25
1180–1200	100	25	0	0	0	0	0	0	0	0	100.0	25	0	0	100.0	36
1200–1220	100	30	0	0	0	0	0	0	0	0	100.0	30	20.0	6	80.0	24
1220–1240	100	24	0	0	0	0	0	0	0	0	100.0	24	0	0	100.0	24
1240–1260	100	42	0	0	0	0	0	0	0	0	100.0	42	0	0	100.0	42
1260–1280	100	70	3.4	3	11.6	8	0	0	11.6	8	96.6	70	8.6	6	91.4	64
1280–1300	100	80	10.1	7	18.8	13	0	0	18.8	13	78.3	84	7.5	1	92.5	74
1300–1320	100	87	5.9	4	10.6	5	0	0	10.6	5	75.3	54	1.1	2	95.5	83
1320–1340	100	69	0	0	0	0	0	0	0	0	89.4	52	3.0	3	75.3	52
1340–1360	100	69	16.6	4	0	0	0	0	0	0	83.4	42	4.3	1	71.0	49
1360–1380	100	47	0	0	0	0	0	0	0	0	100.0	20	2.1	1	87.3	41
1380–1400	100	24	0	0	0	0	0	0	0	0	100.0	10	4.1	1	79.3	19
1400–1420	100	10	0	0	0	0	0	0	0	0	100.0	17	20.0	2	80.0	8
1420–1440	100	17	0	0	0	0	0	0	0	0	100.0	21	11.8	2	88.2	15
1440–1460	100	21	0	0	0	0	0	0	0	0	100.0	2	9.5	2	90.5	19
1460–1480	100	22	0	0	0	0	0	0	0	0	100.0	28	9.1	2	90.9	20
1480–1500	100	8	0	0	0	0	0	0	0	0	100.0	21	37.5	3	62.5	5
1500–1520	100	24	0	1	8.3	2	4.1	0	4.2	1	87.5	42	25.0	6	62.5	15
1520–1540	100	54	4.2	10	3.7	2	1.9	1	1.9	1	77.8	47	14.8	8	63.0	34
1540–1560	100	57	18.5	8	4.0	2	2.0	1	2.0	1	82.0	55	19.0	11	63.0	36
1560–1580	100	71	14.0	14	2.8	2	1.4	1	1.4	1	77.5	82	8.5	6	69.0	49
1580–1600	100	99	19.7	12	5.0	5	4.0	4	1.0	1	83.0	99	10.0	10	73.0	72
1600–1620	100	125	12.0	19	5.6	7	0.8	1	4.8	6	79.4	119	10.4	13	69.0	86
1620–1640	100	143	15.0	15	6.3	9	0.7	1	5.6	8	83.2	98	0.7	1	82.5	118
1640–1660	100	129	10.5	8	17.9	23	10.1	13	7.8	10	75.9	122	6.2	8	69.7	90
1660–1680	100	156	6.2	10	15.0	24	7.0	11	8.0	13	78.6	147	9.6	15	69.0	107
1680–1700	100	208	6.4	45	7.7	16	5.3	11	2.4	5	70.6	108	9.1	19	61.5	128
1700–1720	100	150	21.6	37	3.5	5	2.7	4	0.7	1	71.9	74	6.7	10	65.2	98
1720–1740	100	104	24.7	22	3.7	8	6.7	7	1.0	1	71.1	98	11.5	12	59.6	62
1740–1760	100	182	21.2	46	20.7	38	9.2	17	11.5	21	54.0	80	3.0	5	51.0	93
1760–1780	100	171	25.3	38	30.9	53	21.6	37	9.2	16	47.0	104	3.0	5	44.0	75
1780–1800	100	215	33.5	72	18.1	39	14.1	30	4.0	9	48.4	160	6.5	14	42.0	90
1800–1820	100	251	31.4	79	5.5	12	4.4	11	0.4	1	63.8	196	15.2	38	48.6	122
1820–1840	100	269	23.4	63	3.7	10	1.5	4	2.2	6	72.9	226	9.7	26	63.2	170
1840–1860	100	348	25.9	90	9.2	32	8.9	31	0.3	17	64.9	253	6.0	21	58.9	205
1860–1880	100	485	30.7	149	17.1	83	13.6	66	3.5	95	52.2	382	9.5	46	42.7	207
1880–1900	100	783	33.3	261	17.9	140	5.7	45	12.2	98	48.8	363	12.5	98	36.3	284
1900–1920	100	901	36.4	328	23.3	210	12.2	110	11.1	100	40.3	—	12.2	110	28.1	253

¹On the basis of different values given from 1 to 12.

TABLE 15. MOVEMENT OF IDEALISM, MATERIALISM, AND THE MIXED SYSTEMS, BY 100-YEAR PERIODS, FROM 600 B.C. TO A.D. 1900

PERIOD	IDEALISM						MATERIALISM						MIXED		GRAND TOTAL	
	Pluralistic		Monistic		Total		Hylozoistic		Mechanistic		Total					
	No. of points of weight	Per cent	No. of points of weight	Per cent	No. of points of weight	Per cent	No. of points of weight	Per cent	No. of points of weight	Per cent	No. of points of weight	Per cent	No. of points of weight	Per cent	No. of points of weight	Per cent
600–500 B.C.	8	25.8	5	16.1	13	41.9	18	58.1	0	0	18	58.1	0	0	31	100
500–400	30	25.4	20	17.0	50	42.4	28	23.7	10	8.5	38	32.2	30	25.4	118	100
400–300	67	34.9	41	21.4	108	56.3	23	12.0	14	7.3	37	19.3	47	24.4	192	100
300–200	8	4.1	41	24.3	49	28.4	61	36.7	24	14.2	85	50.9	35	20.7	169	100
200–100	1	1.4	18	25.4	19	26.8	21	29.6	11	15.5	32	45.1	20	28.1	71	100
100–0	30	27.3	12	10.9	42	38.2	32	29.1	26	23.6	58	52.7	10	9.1	110	100
0–100 A.D.	27	35.1	14	18.1	41	53.2	35	45.5	1	1.3	36	46.8	0	0	77	100
100–200	129	57.7	37	16.6	166	74.3	32	14.3	6	2.9	38	17.2	19	8.5	223	100
200–300	94	71.3	21	15.9	115	87.2	11	8.3	4	3.0	15	11.3	2	1.5	132	100
300–400	102	90.2	0	0	102	90.2	10	8.9	1	0.9	11	9.8	0	0	113	100
400–500	88	88.9	0	0	88	88.9	11	11.1	0	0	11	11.1	0	0	99	100
500–600	63	100	0	0	63	100	0	0	0	0	0	0	0	0	63	100
600–700	21	100	0	0	21	100	0	0	0	0	0	0	0	0	21	100
700–800	13	100	0	0	13	100	0	0	0	0	0	0	0	0	13	100
800–900	39	100	0	0	39	100	0	0	0	0	0	0	0	0	39	100
900–1000	9	100	0	0	9	100	0	0	0	0	0	0	0	0	9	100
1000–1100	47	100	0	0	47	100	0	0	0	0	0	0	0	0	47	100
1100–1200	93	100	0	0	93	100	0	0	0	0	0	0	0	0	93	100
1200–1300	171	93.4	12	6.6	183	100	0	0	0	0	0	0	0	0	183	100
1300–1400	155	81.5	5	2.7	160	84.2	18	9.5	0	0	18	9.5	12	6.3	190	100
1400–1500	37	84.1	7	15.9	44	100	0	0	0	0	0	0	0	0	44	100
1500–1600	159	67.4	35	14.8	194	82.2	5	2.1	8	3.4	13	5.5	29	12.3	236	100
1600–1700	385	71.7	37	6.9	422	78.6	28	5.2	15	2.8	43	8.0	72	13.4	537	100
1700–1800	309	53.0	35	6.0	344	59.0	25	4.3	58	9.9	83	14.2	156	26.8	583	100
1800–1900	715	45.3	167	10.6	882	55.9	102	6.5	98	6.2	200	12.7	496	31.4	1578	100

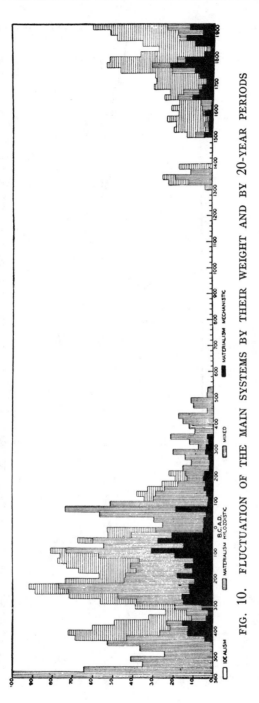

FIG. 10. FLUCTUATION OF THE MAIN SYSTEMS BY THEIR WEIGHT AND BY 20-YEAR PERIODS

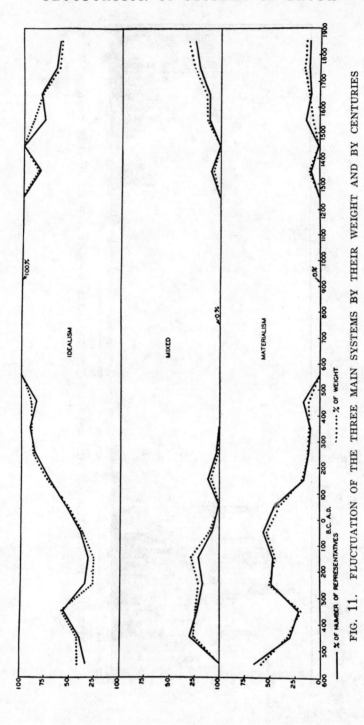

FIG. 11. FLUCTUATION OF THE THREE MAIN SYSTEMS BY THEIR WEIGHT AND BY CENTURIES

These statistics summarize concisely a number of important details. First of all, let us indicate the most important periods of rise and decline of each of the three mentalities.

A. *Idealism*. (1) The figures for 580–540 B.C. require qualification. At their face value the indicators for 580–560 B.C. show 100 per cent hylozoistic materialism, and no idealism. However, this fact cannot be interpreted as meaning that this was purely or even essentially a materialistic period. Hylozoism is almost as closely related to idealism as it is to materialism. Furthermore, 100 per cent hylozoism in this period is due to a "statistical incident" — to the fact that only one name, Thales, is known to us. Similarly only two thinkers, Thales and Anaximander, are included in the period 560–540 B.C. Moreover, their systems were so "idealistically hylozoistic" that they could be readily classified in the Mixed category, or as Idealism, almost as well as Materialism. They represent a monistic identification of the Idealistic principle with nature. Their unity had not yet become divided or differentiated; God and matter represented an undifferentiated oneness. Therefore the period was really Idealistic rather than Materialistic, in spite of the formal reason for classifying these systems under the hylozoistic variety of materialism. With this qualification the mentality of the period is seen to be essentially Mixed, rather than Materialistic. The same must be said of the next period, 560–540 B.C. Though the indicators constitute 35.7 per cent monistic idealism, and 64.3 per cent hylozoism, the nature of the theories classified as hylozoism in this period was such that they were either Mixed or idealistic materialism, if such an expression is not "*contradictio in adjecto.*" In brief, the whole period 580–540 B.C. was the age of an undifferentiated "somatic idealism" or "idealistic materialism" with a current of true idealism beginning in the period 560–540 B.C. Together they give an idealistic rather than a materialistic color to the period.

(2) Such an interpretation is supported by the indicators for the subsequent periods, from 540 to 460 B.C. when the undifferentiated oneness of God and nature began to be divided, and the division showed immediately the predominance of Idealistic mentality over mild hylozoistic materialism. Even this latter was free from true mechanistic materialism, which is still totally absent. In other words we are justified in viewing the mentality of the sixth century B.C. in Greece and of the first part of the fifth century (up to 450 B.C.) as predominantly Idealistic.

(3) After 460 B.C. there was a relative weakening of Idealism, paralleled by the relative growth of a Materialist current. The weakening continues up to 400 B.C., the duration of the decline being about sixty years.

(4) From 400 to 320 B.C. (duration *c.* 80 years) there was again a rising tide of Idealism due to Philolaos, Socrates, Plato, the Academicians. Aristotle, the Peripatetics, and others.

(5) From 320 to 220 B.C. (duration *c.* 100 years) Idealism was again declining, whatever the causes may have been.

(6) From 220 to 180 B.C. there was a relatively slight and short-lived rise of Idealism (duration *c.* 40 years).

(7) From 180 to 80 B.C. (duration *c.* 100 years) Idealism declined once again.

(8) Then, with the exception of a brief decline, *c.* 40 B.C., Idealism again rose until the beginning of our era. This rise was due to the New Academy, Antiochus of Ascalon, Philo of Larissa, Varro, Cicero, Nigidius, and other philosophers, mainly, though not entirely, of Roman stock, The decline, *c.* 40 B.C., may be explained by a sudden blossoming of the mechanistic materialism of Lucretius, Asclepiades, Philodemus, and others (duration *c.* 80 years).

(9) From the beginning of our era until A.D. 80 (duration *c.* 60 years) Idealism was on the decline.

(10) From that time on, with a few fluctuations it rose steadily for about 500 years, at the end of which period it was the only mentality which existed on a high plane of culture. It then monopolized and ab-solutely dominated the whole religio-philosophical and scientific thought (100 per cent) for about 750 years (up to 1300). Including the period of ascent, the whole span of its domination extends over an exceptionally long period of about 1200 years. This advance during the first five centuries of our era was due, on the one hand, to the Pagan Idealistic philosophies of the Peripatetics, the Neo-Pythagoreans, the Middle and the Neo-Platonists; and on the other, to the Idealistic philosophy of Christianity. This second source was actually of greater importance than was the Pagan Idealism. However, the trend was the same, in both the Pagan and the Christian mentalities. From the beginning of the seventh century, Christian philosophy absorbed this Pagan Idealism, as well as the other philosophies of the time, resulting in the monopoly of Christian Idealism up to the thirteenth century.

(11) About A.D. 1140 the first tiny stream of an idealism different from the official Church idealism began to appear. (These data are not presented in the tables, but they are in my possession.) It was the first sign of a break in the monopolistic and monolithic idealism of the Church, and of the whole medieval culture; the "first swallow of the coming spring of differentiation of the religio-philosophical mentality," which

first divided into a few, and later on, into many separate currents.   And indeed, about 160 years later the monopoly of Idealism was generally ended.   The Mixed philosophies reappeared on the highway of mentality about A.D. 1300.   At the outset they were only a tiny rivulet (4 per cent); then they grew, simultaneously with materialism, which first appeared from "underground" about A.D. 1320–1340, where it had lain dormant for more than 700 years.

(12) Thus the fourteenth century was a period of the end of the monolithic idealism of the Middle Ages, a slight decline in Idealism and of a reappearance of the rivals of Idealism on the open road of culture.

(13) In the fifteenth century, however, Idealism revenged itself and again drove its opponents underground; it regained its monopoly and maintained it for about a century.

(14) About 1500, this utter domination was again lost and has not been regained up to the present day.   There has been a long-time *downward* trend of Idealism, in spite of various minor fluctuations, a trend which has continued for almost 450 years.

Of the minor fluctuations within this secular trend there are to be noted:

(a) During the period from about 1500 to 1740 Idealism, though deprived of its previous monopoly, continued to be quite dominant, maintaining itself as high as 70 or 80 per cent of the total stream.

(b) The eighteenth century witnessed a catastrophic decrease in the influence of Idealism (from 71 per cent in 1700 to 48 per cent in 1780–1800).

(c) At the end of the eighteenth century and the beginning of the nineteenth (up to 1830) there was a strong but short-lived reaction to the materialistic philosophy of the Enlightenment.

(d) Finally, the century from about 1830 to the present time has been a period of a steady and enormous decline in Idealism.   During 1900–1920 it reached one of its lowest levels in the whole 2500 years under consideration.   This fact is well worth noting, though its precise significance is not to be discussed here.

Such, in brief, have been the long and short fluctuations of Idealistic mentality in the Graeco-Roman and Western cultures during the period of approximately 2500 years.   The course of pluralistic and monistic idealisms may now be considered.   As has been stated, the former contends that the fundamental or ultimate reality consists in a multitude of eternal, primeval centers of spiritual or nonmaterial actualities: ideas, souls, spirits, or monads.   In most systems of pluralistic idealism these numerous centers of psychical and spiritual actualities are crowned by one Over Soul (God, etc.), but in a number of such systems the Over Soul is absent, or is even denied. The philosophies of Pythagoras, Socrates, Plato, and many others may be cited as examples of pluralistic idealism.

Monistic idealism (*e.g.*, Aristotle's conceptions and many other pantheistic philosophies) views the individual systems of spiritual or psychical reality as mere temporary emanations, or manifestations, of one spiritual principle of Being which embraces all of them. The immortality of any separate spiritual center, such as an individual human soul, follows from the fundamental principle of pluralistic idealism; its finite existence is one of the conclusions which follows from the fundamental principle of monistic idealism.

The indicators of each of these forms of Idealism in the course of 2500 years show that, all in all, pluralistic idealism has been a more powerful current than monistic idealism. The latter played a relatively important part about 560 B.C. (Xenophanes); in the period from 500 to 440 B.C. (Parmenides, Zeno of Elea, Melissos); from 340 to 280 B.C. (Aristotle, the Peripatetics, and others); from about 220 to 100 B.C. (the Peripatetics like Ariston, Satyros, Kritolaos, and others); from A.D. 100 to about the beginning of the third century (the Peripatetics, Ptolemaios Chennos, Aspasios, Adrastos, Galenus, Alexander of Aphrodisias, and some of the Christian philosophers and Church Fathers). After that, it disappeared, being submerged by the pluralistic philosophy of Neo-Platonism and Christianity. Only after a lapse of about a thousand years did it reappear (*c.* A.D. 1200), having thus remained quite an insignificant stream of thought for a very long period. About A.D. 1480 (Achilline, Nifus, Pomponazzi, and others) it became relatively strong, but up to the nineteenth century it continued to be comparatively unimportant. In the nineteenth and twentieth centuries it became somewhat stronger, but even then it remained a minor movement as compared with the much more powerful current of pluralistic idealism.

During the long period, maxima of influence have been reached by monistic idealism in the following periods: (1) around 1480–1500; (2) 1540–1560; (3) around 1580–1620 (Giordano Bruno, Vanini, and others); (4) 1800–1820 (young Schelling, Hegel, Lamarck, Cabanis — wrongly regarded as a materialist, young Schopenhauer, and others); (5) in our day (H. Bergson, Tolstoi, Schopenhauer, R. Wagner, Hartmann, and others). (See the list of names in the Appendix to this chapter.)

The periods of its minimum influence were: (1) 1620–1640, the period following the burning of G. Bruno and Vanini, and in general the period of the Catholic Counter-Reformation; (2) 1740–1780, the period of the greatest blossoming of materialism; and (3) 1840–1860.

The periods of maximum and minimum influence of Pluralistic Idealism are as follows.

Maxima	*Minima*
(Periods when it is comparatively strong)	(Periods when it is comparatively weak)
1. *c.* 540 B.C.	1. 580–540 B.C.
2. 420–320	2. 480–440
3. 80–20	3. 300–100
4. 100–1480 A.D. (From 540 to 1260 it dominates absolutely.)	4. 20–0
5. 1560 to 1720	5. 60–80 A.D.
6. 1800 to 1860	6. 1480–1560
	7. 1720–1800
	8. 1860–1920

The significance of these data will be analyzed later, but meanwhile let us turn to Materialism.

B. *Materialism.* Taken as a whole, in both of its major forms, the main oscillations of Materialism occurred during the following periods.

Maxima	*Minima*
1. 460–400 B.C.	1. 540–460 B.C.
2. 280–60 (especially strong *c.* 260–200, and *c.* 100	2. 400–280
	3. 40 B.C.–40 A.D.
3. 40–80 A.D.	4. 100 A.D.
4. 1320–1380 (weaker than Idealism but a notable increase in influence)	5. 540 to 1320 and 1380 to 1500 (complete disappearance)
5. 1640–1680 (weaker, but notable increase)	6. 1520–1640 (very low)
6. 1730–1790 (weaker, but notable increase)	7. 1680–1720 (very low)
7. 1860–1920 (notable increase)	8. 1800–1840 (very low)

(1) *Hylozoistic and Mechanistic Materialism.* Of these two main forms hylozoistic materialism, or monism, has been much more powerful than mechanistic materialism in the great majority of the periods under consideration. As has been mentioned, the former is not a pure materialism. In a sense it is a mixture of Materialism and Idealism, since it does not deny the spiritual principle but regards it as inseparable from matter, and as nonexistent in independence from it. Nor is it purely mechanistic in the sense of trying to reduce all vital and spiritual phenomena to a mere resultant of the motions of particles of matter in the form of pressure and shock, according to purely mechanistic laws. Mechanistic materialism is a much more purified and more genuine form of Materialism. As such it has rarely been more powerful than the hylozoistic current. Excep-

tions to this general situation, when it has been stronger than, or at least equal to, the hylozoistic current, include the following periods: 400–380 and 40 B.C.; A.D. 300, 1500–1580, and 1680–1920. For the time being, enough of figures! Let us turn to the tales they tell.

III. Main Results

A. *Correlation with Ideational and Sensate Cultures.* Having outlined the main fluctuations of Materialism and Idealism, we may attempt to depict the spectrum of the whole mentality in this field during the various periods studied.

(1) We begin our analysis with the sixth century B.C. For the reasons mentioned above it is to be regarded, in spite of the formal "hylozoistic" domination, as essentially monistic idealistic, where "nature" is inseparably united with the spiritual principle. It was the period of a simple, undifferentiated, and undivided mentality, without any clash of decidedly different streams of thought. Idealism and Materialism were very similar, and no Mixed theories are yet to be found.

(2) The fifth and the fourth centuries were predominantly Idealistic. Idealism became more pronounced and more conspicuous in its nature, as did *also* Materialism. In addition, several Mixed theories appeared. The whole period was one of differentiation of the previous undifferentiated and uniform mentality; each of the main streams began to separate from the preceding undifferentiated "oneness." But of these streams Idealism was the most powerful. In this sense the field under consideration is found to be similar to the other compartments of the culture during this period. Being idealistico-rationalistic in ontological mentality, the period is also found to be idealistico-rationalistic in its system of truth, in its art, and in other compartments of culture.

(3) Our indicators (by 20-year, as well as by 100-year periods) show further a decrease in Idealism, an increase in Materialism, and especially in mechanistic materialism, in the centuries from the third B.C. to the beginning of our era. This means that the increase in Materialism, and the decrease in Idealism proceeded hand in hand with an increase in the empirical system of truth (the truth of the senses), and a decrease in idealistic rationalism. Both of these factors mean an increase in Sensate culture.

(4) From the beginning of our era up to the sixth century A.D. may be observed (especially in the indicators by century periods) a new rising tide of Idealism (among the Christian as well as the Pagan thinkers). At the same time, however, the opposite current, and especially the extreme

types of materialism, became even more extreme. In the process of their decline they showed temporary, short-lived flarings. For instance, mechanistic materialism, having fallen from 23.6 in the first century B.C., and to 1.3 in the first century A.D., then rose to 2.9 in the second and to 3 in the third century A.D. Idealism also became more extreme; in the main, extreme pluralistic idealism grew at the cost of Materialism as well as of monistic idealism. In brief, the data show that these centuries were the period of a sharp struggle between Materialistic and Idealistic mentalities, and though Idealism was progressing victoriously, its progress was not without desperate opposition by its chief opponent.

The spectrum of mentality in the field of the system of truth is in a sense highly consistent with the spectrum of mentality outlined above. In the systems of truth, the period was marked by a growing trend toward the truth of faith at the cost of the other truths (of reason and of the senses). But the truth of faith, as in the case of Idealistic philosophy, was growing mainly in its more extreme forms, the forms of mysticism and fideism (especially in the first, second, and the third centuries A.D.). With a temporary increase in empiricism in the third century A.D. there was even a corresponding increase in mechanistic materialism, though the amplitude of the increase in the latter was much more narrow than in the case of empiricism.

(5) The period from the sixth to the eleventh centuries A.D., in the field of the forms of truth, as well as in the field of the problem studied, again appears to be perfectly uniform and similar: monopolistic idealism in the latter case, and a monopolistic domination of the truth of faith in the former. Idealism and the truth of faith were again very closely related.

(6) The monopoly of the truth of faith ended in the twelfth century, whereas the monopoly of Idealism did not end until the fourteenth century, a lag of about two hundred years. However, if the Idealistic systems of the twelfth and thirteenth centuries be studied from a qualitative point of view, it will be seen that they began to differ from the simple, purely religious, idealism of the previous centuries. The idealism of the twelfth and the thirteenth centuries became more and more "intellectualistic" and "dialectical." This fact cannot be detected by the quantitative indicators, but is evident from a qualitative study. Therefore, here again we see a positive association of the truth of reason with dialectical idealism, a situation somewhat similar to that in the fifth and the fourth centuries B.C. in Greece.

(7) In the fourteenth century both the truth of senses and Materialism again increased in importance. During the fifteenth century

they both underwent a marked diminution in influence; then, beginning with the sixteenth century, they have both been on the increase up to the present time (though Materialism gave an index for the nineteenth century slightly lower than for the eighteenth century, but the Mixed systems, some of which are but a diluted form of Materialism, grew systematically up to the twentieth century). Thus again we have positive association between the empirical system of truth and Materialism. On the other hand these four centuries have been marked by a decrease in the truths of faith and of reason, and by a systematic decrease in Idealism. These "variables," then, are positively associated and change in a parallel manner.

When these data are properly considered, they justify the following conclusions.

(a) If not in all the minor fluctuations, then at least in the main waves, the empirical system of truth of senses shows itself positively associated with Materialism, the truth of faith with Idealism, especially in its pluralistic form, and the truth of reason with less religious and more dialectical idealism, especially with monistic idealism. (Note that it reappears in the thirteenth century.)

(b) In so far as the empirical system of truth showed itself tangibly associated with the movement of scientific discoveries and inventions, the above proposition means that the empirical system of truth, Materialism, and scientific discoveries are tangibly associated with one another.

(c) In so far as the truth of faith showed itself negatively associated with the movement of scientific discoveries, this means that the truth of faith, and pluralistic idealism, on the one hand, and scientific discoveries and empirism on the other hand, are negatively related.

These propositions do not hold for all the minor fluctuations, but they do hold in regard to the main upward and downward long-time waves. Such associations are to be expected logically, from the very nature of Idealism and the truth of faith, Materialism and the truth of senses; logical expectations are indeed borne out by the factual data. Here again the logically expected integration is realized, to a tangible degree, by the causal-functional integration.

(d) In so far as Idealism is a trait of Ideational and of Idealistic culture (in accordance with the character of the Idealistic theory) and Materialism is a trait of Sensate culture, the above spectra of mentality in this field, as well as in the field of art, of systems of truth, and of the movement of the natural sciences, suggest the following inferences. The predominant form of culture in Greece in the sixth, fifth, and fourth centuries B.C. was mainly Ideational and Idealistic; in the centuries from the third to the beginning of our era it was mainly Sensate; from the first to the sixth centuries A.D. it was transitory, in the sense of a decline in the Sensate culture and a rise in the Ideational; from the sixth to the twelfth centuries it was monopolistically Ideational; the twelfth and the thirteenth and fourteenth centuries were mainly Idealistic, but with a rising tide of Sensate culture; in the fifteenth century there was a desperate reaction against this tide; but beginning with the sixteenth century, the rising tide of the Sensate culture was resumed and, with minor fluctuations, has been on the increase to the present time. We have seen and shall also see that similar "spectra of the forms of culture" will be given by data concerning other compartments of culture, and particularly by data in the field of art (Volume One). This means that the above indicators also have some value in diagnosing the type of the predominant culture.

This discussion may now turn to a brief characterization of other "tales" told by Tables 14 and 15 and Figures 10 and 11.

B. *No Continuous Linear Trend.* The next, and hardly questionable, conclusion suggested by these tabulations is that, for this period of about twenty-five hundred years, there is no indication of any perpetual *linear* trend for any of these three main currents. From 580 B.C. to A.D. 1920 there is no tendency toward a continuous increase, decrease, or constancy of Idealism, Materialism, or the Mixed current. For a given period, any of these currents rises at the cost of the others, but sooner or later the ascent ceases, is replaced by a downward movement, and the other current begins its "crescendo." This does not exclude the possibility of a monopolistic domination for a time by one of these currents and sometimes even for a long period, as is witnessed by the interval of about seven hundred years of an exclusive domination of Idealism, about A.D. 540 to about 1280. All traces of Materialism and other currents seem to have disappeared during that period. And yet, this domination came to an end, the opposite currents of Materialism or Mixed ontologies again reappeared, developed, and during several periods even became dominant.

For those of us who are followers of Idealism, Materialism, or the Mixed philosophies, and therefore maintain, as some popular writers would have it, that "the opposite philosophy has been disproved once and forever" and that "the future belongs entirely to the philosophy we hold," these data should inspire a more cautious attitude. It is nothing but a mere wish, and it is by no means warranted by the facts.

C. *Principle of Limits and of Self-regulation.* Thirdly, these statistical data provide clear-cut illustrations of the "principle of limits"[5] and the principle of the "immanent" or, as Professor I. Lapshin puts it, "dialectic" self-regulation of sociocultural processes. One of the ontological currents increases for a given period, attains its limit in this direction, changes its course, and reverses itself. This limit varies for the different periods: at times, the upper limit of a given current is but 30 per cent, sometimes as much as 80 per cent or even 100 per cent. But some limit is invariably found and inevitably leads to a turn in the direction of the stream of philosophical thought. Speaking figuratively, the course of the stream is uneven, and ever deviates from a "line of equilibrium." But these deviations do not stray irrevocably from this line; subsequent to a marked deviation, the action of certain forces leads to the reversal of movement with a reversion to the line of equilibrium. The reversion occurs in the form of a reappearance and reinforcement of the opposite current of thought.

D. *Comparative Strength of Each Current of Thought.* Which of the three currents has been most influential throughout the period studied? Which, during certain specific periods? Table 16 provides the answer to these queries.

TABLE 16. RELATIVE INFLUENCE OF THE THREE MAJOR SYSTEMS

Period	All Idealisms (weighted indices)	All Materialisms (weighted indices)	The Mixed Theories (weighted indices)
580 B.C. —A.D. 100	322	304	142
100–600	534	75	21
600–1500	609	18	12
1500–1900	1842	339	753
1900–1920	363	210	329
Total	3670	946	1257

The figures show that, by and large, the Idealistic theories have been most influential, with the Mixed less, and the Materialistic system least, influential. The prevalence of the Idealistic current has actually been about four times as marked as the Materialistic. This may perhaps be interpreted as an indication that, all in all, a certain predominance of Idealism over Materialism is necessary for the continued existence of human culture and society and that a balance of the Mixed-Idealistic-Materialistic systems is still more indispensable than pure, otherworldly Ideationalism

[5] See P. A. Sorokin, "The Principle of Limits Applied to Problems of Causal Relationship and of the Direction of Social Processes," in *Publications of the American Sociological Society,* Vol. XXVI (1932).

and Idealism. It is hardly incidental that Materialism has been at all times a relatively insignificant philosophical system; there was not a single period within a span of twenty-five hundred years when it was monopolistic or even clearly dominant. Contrariwise, for almost a thousand years our culture adhered virtually exclusively to an idealistic philosophy.

These facts make one ponder whether any culture can subsist with only materialism, and especially with mechanistic materialism! It seems that a considerable proportion of idealism is a prime requisite for the durable existence of society. This implication is reinforced by a study of the character of the periods in which the tide of materialism rose. It almost always occurred before or during crises, hard times, social disintegration, demoralization, and other phenomena of this kind.[6]

However that may be, the data seem to show clearly that Materialistic mentality has been a much less influential current than the Idealistic or Mixed, in spite of the fact that hylozoism is also included in materialism. Table 16 also summarizes the specific spectrum of the mentality of each of the long periods. It indicates that the period from A.D. 100 to 1500 was characterized almost exclusively by Idealism and the Mixed mentality. The period from 1900 to 1920 was dominated by an excessive reinforcement of the Materialistic current in comparison with its strength in all other periods, save that from 580 B.C. to A.D. 100.

E. *No Mechanical Periodicity.* The fifth tale told by the data involves a repudiation of numerous mechanical theories which claim the occurrence of certain periodicities in many social processes and their fluctuations, in business cycles, political processes, etc.[7] One of the recent theories in the field of philosophy which claims an approximate hundred-year periodicity in the pulsation of philosophical theories, particularly those of individualism and collectivism, "binding and loosening," is developed by Karl L. Joël in a thoughtful and excellent work.[8] Without dealing specifically with Joël's theory, it suffices to indicate that our data concerning ontological mentality here, as well as those concerning science, art, and other compartments of culture, do not show this or any other regular periodicity. Rising and falling tides of any one of the main currents have occurred within very different spans of time, varying from

[6] See Chapter Thirteen of Volume Three on the Movement of Internal Disturbances.

[7] A history and survey of these theories of periodicity will be presented in Volume Four. See also Chapter Ten of this volume, and Chapters Ten to Fourteen of Volume Three.

[8] See K. Joël, *Wandlungen des Weltanschauung*, Vol. I, pp. 42 ff. and 60 ff. His rhythms of "Losung und Bindung," of Tyranny and Freedom, Differentiation and Integration, which have one, three, and six hundred years of duration, are based on "generation-periodicity."

some 20 and 40 years to almost 1000 years. Frequently, they evidence a duration of about 60 or 80, or even 100 years, but this is by no means an invariable or even a clearly predominant duration. Therefore, to insist upon the occurrence of any uniform mechanical periodicity in these crescendos and diminuendos is to impose upon reality a uniformity which it does not possess. History repeats itself, but its themes recur in variations ever new — with changes not only in content, but also in rhythm and tempo. As a great artist, history provides creative, not monotonously mechanical, variations.

F. *Variations in Patterns of Fluctuation.* The sixth tale told by the data is that the rise and fall of the tides of Materialism and Idealism have different patterns in different times. In some instances, the fluctuation is sharp; in others, constituting the more general pattern, the curves of rise and decline are more or less gradual and relatively smooth, but even in these cases there is considerable variation in period. This variation probably derives in part from the inadequacy and incompleteness of the data. In all probability, the greater part of this variation is due to an actual diversity of these patterns, a diversity which again indicates the "erratic or creative" character of historical processes. There is repetition in so far as these rises and declines formally recur, but each repetition is a new variation of the same theme.

G. *Long- and Short-time Waves.* A glance at Figure 11 suffices to demonstrate that there are both small, short-time — in a sense incidental — oscillations, and large, long-time, secular trends; the former are ripples and wavelets, and the latter waves and tides. The manifest import of this is that a study of merely short-time fluctuations in any field of culture is insufficient. The longer trends, or tides, are of great importance, not only in and of themselves, but also for an adequate understanding of the shorter fluctuations. Thus, finding that the index of Materialism increased from 10.09 in A.D. 240 to 14 in 260, and to 20 in 280, one might conclude that there was a rising tide of materialism; our data show, however, that this constituted a mere ripple upon an ebbing long-time tide of Materialism. Similar considerations apply to many other cases. Contemporary research in various fields of social phenomena has been virtually restricted to relatively short trends; economics especially has been limited by the study of almost exclusively short-time business cycles. Only quite recently have appeared some scattered attempts to study somewhat longer fluctuations, but they are still very few and the periods rarely extend beyond some twenty-five to sixty years, periods of comparatively brief duration. Despite the difficulties inherent in the study of long-time trends, such research is indispensable, for otherwise even the most careful study of short-time fluctuations is likely to lead to many theoretical and practical blunders, as has often occurred, particularly within the last few years. The past few years have convincingly disproved the "business forecastings" presented prior to 1929, which were based on the study of short-time business fluctuations.

H. *Diversity of Rhythms and "Beats."* The data also lead to a correction of the Hegelian, or similar, "dialectical" formula, concerning the type of rhythm and the number of "beats" in recurring processes. The famous formula of a three-beat rhythm, "thesis-antithesis–synthesis," to which, it is maintained, all processes can be reduced, is not universally applicable. In its rigid sense, it is hardly applicable at all to the phenomena studied here. The point is that in most cases thesis and antithesis (Materialism and Idealism) exist contemporaneously in the same culture. Sometimes they are well balanced, in other cases one of them is now slightly, now greatly, predominant, or even monopolistic. Under such circumstances it is difficult to say where and when the thesis has ended, where and when the antithesis has begun, or finally where and when there is a synthesis. The formula oversimplifies the variety of the real processes and imposes upon them a nonexistent monotonous uniformity. Instead, an admission of plurality of the various phases, rhythms, and beats in each wave is much nearer to the truth, and once again supports the thesis of the "creative-erratic" nature of the whole historical process. Hegel's formula describes only one of many varieties of rhythms and the number and character of the beats constituting various waves. It exceeds legitimate generalization.

I. *Alternation of Periods of Complication-Differentiation and of Simplification-Uniformization.* Now let us glance at some of the psychosocial meanings of the data, and at their mutual relationships. Greek philosophy opened with a monolithic domination of hylozoism, or more properly, monistic idealistic materialism. There was only one stream of thought with no dissension or difference — a serene and balanced idealistic naturalism, indicating a unanimity of ideology and mind. Soon, however, the unanimity was disrupted: in 560 B.C. the stream of philosophy was divided into two currents, Idealistic and Materialistic; in 540 B.C. Idealism itself split into two subcurrents, pluralistic and monistic; and in 440 B.C. we find not only that Materialism and Idealism split into their main subclasses, but also that several Mixed philosophies appeared and occupied an important place. Thus as time goes on, and the Greek culture develops, we witness an increasing differentiation, as Spencer would say.   It means a division in the previous unanimity of philosophical thought and ideology, the growth of various schools and factions, and their mutual struggle and antagonism.

This differentiation, though not necessarily increasing in its complexity and sharpness, continued to exist.   This was the case up to our era, especially from 80 B.C. to *anno Domini*.   By the first century B.C. the Mixed theories had begun to show signs of recession, and by the beginning of our era they had disappeared.   In this way a step toward unification was made — a step, note, quite opposite to the previous trend of differentiation.   The Mixed theories reappeared, for but a century, as the last sigh of a dying movement.   By A.D. 220 they had completely disappeared, not to return for a thousand years.

The fate of the Mixed theories was followed, with a lag, by Materialism. Materialism began to die about A.D. 100; the "agony" lasted for some four hundred years, after which Materialism was nonexistent on the "front page of culture" for almost eight hundred years.   In this way the second fundamental step toward an involution, or decrease of differentiation and increase of unanimity, was made.   Simultaneously with the decline of Materialism, Idealism itself showed in part the same tendency; by A.D. 300 the monistic stream of idealism had dried up, and only one, the pluralistic, stream remained.   Toward the beginning of the sixth century of our era, there was again a monolithic unanimity of philosophical thought, as simple as at the beginning of its history in Greece.   If its beginning corroborates Spencer's formula of progress-evolution, the subsequent development contradicts it utterly.   Instead of ever-increasing differentiation and integration the Graeco-Roman philosophical thought, after its initial stages, began to fluctuate indefinitely in this respect, made a definite move toward a decreasing differentiation, and finally returned to its initial simplicity and monolithic unanimity.   These ugly facts, like many others, serve to kill Spencer's beautiful generalization, as well as most of the linear conceptions of evolution in whatever form they be given.

The story discussed does not end here.   Subsequent indices show that after a long, but happy, sleep during the Middle Ages — when the mentality was undivided, faith was firm and free from any deep uncertainties, and there was a wonderful age of unanimity of mind, soul, and conscience — the devil of diversity and differentiation reappeared.   First he was modest and hesitant, even temporarily withdrawing; then he became more and more audacious, potent, and relentless.   After 1500 the soul of our culture was again divided into various streams of different philosophical thought, each with its vanity and glory, its dissensions and creations. If we would judge the movement toward differentiation by the percentage of the Mixed theories, then the century from 1680 to 1780, the end of the nineteenth century, and the present day may be considered the times when unanimity of philosophical mind is particularly low, with, it may be said, "as many philosophies as philosophers." In brief, instead of a calm and serene unanimity, the philosophical soul of these times has been rent into many dissenting ideologies; differentiation, or even atomization, has been rampant. This is especially true of the twentieth century, a period of factions, of a multitude of various currents, each strong enough to leave its stamp upon the culture, but yet too weak to subsume and dominate the others, and to give the public an authoritative, unquestioned guidance.

Such is the tale told by the data in this respect. When the whole series for twenty-five hundred years is taken, it demonstrates the existence of long-time waves, or recurrences, of increasing differentiation and decreasing unanimity in the philosophical thought, and opposite waves of an increasing unanimity and decreasing diversity. Thus, quite unexpectedly, the long row of figures has disclosed to us a peculiar, though rarely mentioned or seriously studied, alternation of the trend to diversity with the trend to unanimity and similarity. The rhythm of these waves has a bearing on Spencer's formula, but in the sense of demonstrating its faultiness. After any differentiation and complication, sooner or later there come simplification and uniformization, and after any simplification sooner or later there comes the opposite trend toward differentiation. Such is our formula. It tells a quite different story from Spencer's concept of linear evolution-progress. It again points to the validity of our *principle of limits* and of the immanent self-regulation of various trends, and their directions, in the field of philosophy (as in all the other sociocultural processes).

If these principles are valid it may be predicted that the present trend toward differentiation, in the field studied, cannot go on forever. Sooner or later it will be replaced by the opposite trend. One after another many of the existing currents are destined to dry up, and one of the main currents (who can say which?) is destined to grow and to dominate the others. And then, as at the beginning of the Middle Ages, it will become monopolistic; philosophical mind will become one and unanimous, calm, simple, serene, and believing, instead of being questioning, skeptical, sophistic, cynical, and disbelieving. Such a unanimous philosophy will be, at the same time, religion, as it was at the dawn of Greek philosophy and at the beginning of our culture. When its time elapses, it is destined to be rent in its turn into partial currents.   The phases of differentiation and unanimity will continue to alternate as long as the culture itself exists.

J. *Contemporary Situation.*   In some of the other compartments of culture studied — art, system of truth, and science — we discovered that at the end of the nineteenth and in the twentieth century there appeared the symptoms of revolt against the dominant tendencies of the overripe Sensate culture.   In ontology we do not find a similar rebellion (just as we did not find it in the field of empiricism) during the period 1900–1920.   But the previous period, 1880–1900, is also marked by a considerable decline of mechanistic materialism (from 13.6 in 1840–1860 to 5.7 in 1880–1900). Moreover, the indices of mechanistic materialism for the nineteenth century generally are lower than those for the eighteenth century.   This decline should perhaps be taken as a manifestation of revolt against an overripe Sensatism, a revolt much more pronounced in other fields of culture (especially art).   Though, in accordance with the previously established uniformity of increased Materialism during periods of socio-cultural crisis, the indices of Materialism during 1900–1920 were higher than hitherto, the possibility that the twentieth century, regarded as a whole, may experience a recession of Materialism is not excluded.   In a word, in this field, as in others, there are symptoms of revolt at the close of the nineteenth century, though they are neither pronounced nor definite.   In this respect, they are similar to recent developments in the field of the natural sciences: signs of fatigue were met there also, but thus far they are not extremely marked or conspicuous.

K. *Rising Tide of Materialism and the Sensual Interpretation of Man and Culture.*   It has been suggested in previous pages that the recent tendency in science to interpret man, culture, and history mechanistically, materialistically, "reflexologically," "endocrinologically," "behavioristically," "psychoanalytically," "economically," etc., is but a reflection of our overripe Sensate mentality.   Here again, we find added verification of this proposition.   Since scientists and scholars of the last four centuries have been living in an atmosphere of a rapid rise in Materialism, and decline in Idealism, their progressive inability to see "the idealistic," "divine," "spiritual" aspects and forces of man and culture becomes readily understandable.   More and more they have been led to see there principally the material, sensory, external, mechanistic, and other sensual aspects and forces.   Hence the increasing fashionableness of materialistic, reflexological, endocrinological, biological, psychoanalytic (man viewed as an entity of largely superphysiological sex), and other anti-idealistic interpretations of history, culture, and man. Such theories have been more and more popular; more and more accredited as "scientific"; more and more readily and widely adopted as the "last word of science." The continued successful diffusion of these doctrines among the lay public has developed to the point where, at the present moment, virtually every aspect of sociocultural reality is being interpreted almost exclusively in terms of these "sensual variables."

It is not my task to censure or praise this vogue. My function is to indicate that it stands in the closest relationship with the predominant system of truth and the swelling tide of Materialism, just as the predominantly Idealistic interpretation of man and culture in the Middle Ages, during the domination of the Ideational mentality, was clearly harmonious with that mentality. This observation should provide abundant warning to the partisans of the "sensual" or "idealistic" interpretation of man; it should lead these theorists to disavow the claim that their doctrines constitute "the last word of science," that they incorporate the whole truth, and only the truth. The data show that both "sensual" and "idealistic" positions are conditional and highly subject to fluctuation. Both positions probably contain a part of truth, but only a part. Either interpretation in extreme forms may involve more "un-truth" than truth. Consequently, these extreme views are bound to be confronted, sooner or later, with a reaction against their misleading pseudo truth.

The "sensual" mode of present-day "scientific" theories regarding man and culture seems to have exceeded the legitimate bounds of truth and to have moved a considerable distance from the secure ground of verified hypothesis. It will not be surprising, then, if in the future this position is confronted with a rapidly and unexpectedly increasing reaction in the form of Idealistic interpretations. Whether this conjecture is fulfilled is of secondary importance. The basic point at this juncture is that contemporary "sensual" interpretations of man are a reflection of the rising tide of Materialism, just as the predominantly Idealistic interpretation of man in the Middle Ages (man as a creation of God, endowed with free will, as an incarnation of the divine plan, divine mind, and law) was conditioned by the domination of Idealism (and other elements of the Ideational-Idealistic mentality) in that period. Here we see once again how that which is accepted as truth and verity in a certain period is conditioned by the dominant mentality of the given culture.[9]

---

[9] "In no case do we rest assured that what is absolute in science to-day will remain absolute for all time. . . . The absolute can never finally be grasped by the researcher. The absolute represents an ideal goal which is always ahead of us and which we can never reach. . . . The

IV. Corroboration in Social Space

The observed association of the truth of faith and partly of reason with Idealism and with a low productivity in the natural sciences, and of the truth of senses with Materialism and with a high level of science, is found also in several other great cultures. We have seen that the predominant system of truth in the Hindu culture was that of faith and partly of idealistic reason. The expectation, based on uniform associations in other instances, that Idealism would consequently have been the predominant system of ontology is well fulfilled indeed.

The overwhelmingly dominant metaphysics of India from the Vedic period up to the present has certainly been Idealism of various types. Detailed data concerning this subject were presented in Chapter One, where the role of Materialism in Hindu thought was concisely and adequately outlined. In that discussion, it was found that the domination of Idealism was so complete that only through a considerable amount of intensive research has it been possible to find any traces of Materialism in the higher levels of Indian thought. It is true that there are some slight traces in Vedic and post-Vedic India, but the very sparsity of Materialism suggests that it had virtually no influence. Moreover, materialistic allusions are found almost solely in the works of idealistic writers engaged in attempts to refute such ideas.[10] Two Brihaspati and the school of Chārvākā and of Nastika are virtually the only materialists. But even these are mentioned mainly in the works of their idealistic critics — such as Krishna Misra's *Probodha Chandrodaya*, or *Rise of the Moon of Intellect* — or occasionally in the Brahmanic texts or in the essentially idealistic literary works (*e.g.*, *Vemana*, c. A.D. 1400) or in some political writings (*e.g.*, *Artha-Shastra*). Such facts are eloquent testimony to the pronounced dominance of Idealism in the Indian culture and furthermore verify the thesis that an Ideational culture comprises the truth

---

value of the journey is not in the journey's end but in the journey itself." M. Planck, *Where Is Science Going?* (New York, 1932), pp. 199–200. This view is applicable to our problem. It may be indicated further that the metaphysical assumptions basic to my research do not exclude either of these positions. It is my position that neither Idealism nor Materialism is totally divorced from reality but that each of these systems declines when its claims exceed justifiable bounds. Moreover, such fluctuations do not in any way lead to a relativistic or skeptical position, since the validity of the fundamental laws of logic rests assured in both systems. In this sense, these laws are absolute and continue to be absolute. There is fluctuation, not in the validity of logical laws, but in the existential premises to which they are applied.

[10] See A. A. Macdonell, *A History of Sanskrit Literature* (1900), pp. 366 ff.; A. B. Keith, *The Sanskrit Drama* (1924). Further literature was cited in Chapter One, pp. 56–59.

of faith and Idealistic ontology and that these are associated with but slight developments in science and technology.

What has been said of India likewise applies not only to Buddhism, Jainism, etc., but also to the Taoist culture and its metaphysics. We have seen that its truth is principally that of faith and it may now be added that its ontology is predominantly Idealistic. Even a cursory examination of Taoist texts permits the conclusion that Materialism occupies little if any place in its philosophy. Moreover, in this instance as well, is found a close association of truth of faith, Idealism, and a low level of the natural sciences.

Chapter Five

FLUCTUATION OF "FIRST PRINCIPLES": II. FLUCTUATION OF ETERNALISTIC AND TEMPORALISTIC MENTALITY[1]

I. ETERNALISM, TEMPORALISM, AND MIXED THEORIES

A further general principle which underlies — implicitly or explicitly — many scientific, philosophical, religious, and ethical theories, and which likewise conditions a number of more special ideologies, beliefs, and convictions, is the principle of Eternalism as against Temporalism.

In the preceding chapters devoted to the definition of Process and to the preliminary definition of the main types of mentality and culture, the problem of Being and Becoming, of Permanency and Change, has been treated. It was indicated that the Ideational culture mentality perceives and believes in the unchangeable or eternal Being as the true reality, while the Sensate culture mentality principally considers Becoming, the ever-changing process, as the essence of the ultimate reality. The Idealistic and the intermediary types of culture mentality attempt eclectically or organically to reconcile both. It was also suggested that in the course of time the influence and acceptability of the philosophies of Being and Becoming do not remain constant, but fluctuate. One philosophy rises and becomes dominant in the integrated mentality of the given culture, then declines and gives way to its rival.[2] The purpose of this chapter is to show how and when these fluctuations occurred in the life history of the Graeco-Roman and the Western cultures. The method of collection and classification of the names of the thinkers in this field, the construction of the tables, their groupings by 20- and 100-year periods, remain the same as before. The list of the names of each authority current in the field is given in the Appendix to this chapter at the end of this volume.

---

[1] In co-operation with N. O. Lossky and I. I. Lapshin.

[2] In this chapter the problem of eternalism and temporalism is considered only in outline. Its complication by the theories of space and time is omitted. See Chapter Eleven for space and time. See the changes in the meanings of space and time in P. Duhem's work, *Le système du monde*, 5 vols. (Paris, 1913–1915), and in W. Gent, *Die Philosophie des Raumes und der Zeit* (Bonn, 1926).

As to the classification of the main solutions of the problem, the three main classes into which all the solutions fall are : (1) The *ideology of Being*, or *eternalism*, which stresses that the true ultimate reality is an unchangeable super- or all-time Being.   Any change or any Becoming is either pure illusion or something secondary.   (2) The *ideology of Becoming*, or *temporalism*, according to which the true reality is an incessant change, a never-ceasing flux, where any moment differs from another, with its "earlier-later," "before-after," and other time references.   (3) *Synthesis*, or *reconciliation of both eternalism and temporalism*, according to which the true reality has both these aspects.   These are the main classes into which practically all the answers to, and theories in, the field of this problem fall.   A few additional comments on each of these "philosophies" and on their variations are not out of place, before proceeding with the study of their fluctuations.   The comments would show, among other things, that the categories of Being and Becoming are indeed the basic principles that underlie hundreds of more specific theories in science, philosophy, and religion.   As mentioned, eternalistic mentality, or *philosophy of Being*, tries to reduce the category of Becoming or change or process to that of an unchangeable or eternal Being.   Eternal and unchangeable reality does not imply time and is free from it.   It does not have, therefore, "before-after," or "earlier-later."   It remains permanent both in its supertemporality and unchangeability throughout infinite duration or throughout all times.[3]   The reduction of change to Being has consisted in attempts to show that Becoming (or its equivalents) is either nonexistent or unreal, or represents nothing but a specific aspect of Being. The predominant thought of Brahmanic India, the Taoism of China, many a theological concept of God, many an "ultimate reality" of several philosophical systems, Parmenides's and Zeno's philosophies of the true reality, and Zeno's famous proofs of the nonexistence of movement — all these give an example of this philosophy.   Here are a few typical formulas of it.   "The really existing is neither this nor that, is neither effect nor cause ; is neither past nor future." . . .   " It is without sound, without touch, without form, without decay, without taste, without smell, without beginning, without end, eternal, beyond the Great and un-

[3] I am putting the idea in these three forms because, as Professor I. I. Lapshin rightly points out, the idea of eternity meant with some thinkers something supertemporal; to others, an infinitely lasting duration; finally, the third group of thinkers stressed it as something that remains the same throughout all times (and all spaces).   In spite of a difference between these three meanings of eternity (or Being), they all have to be regarded as branches of the philosophy of Being.   The same is true of the conceptions like Augustine's conception of the world created *with* time but not in time.   See Chapter Eleven of this volume.

changeable." . . . "It sprang from nothing, nothing sprang from it."
. . . "The ancient is unborn, eternal, everlasting." Such is one of the
best formulas of Being ever offered in the history of human thought.
Many centuries before our era it was formulated in Ancient India.[4]

Along the same lines run other philosophies of Being. Here is the
formula of Taoism, almost identical with the Hindu formula.

There was something, undifferentiated and yet perfect, before heaven and
earth came into being. So still, so incorporeal! *It alone abides and changes
not.* It pervades all, but is not endangered. It may be regarded as the mother
of all things. I know not its name; if I must designate it, I call it Tao.[5]

The Greek theories of Parmenides and Zeno are too well known to be
quoted here extensively. We are familiar with the skillful and logical
reasoning of Zeno and his four famous arguments, the Dichotomy, the
Achilles, the Arrow, and the Stadium, in which he tried to prove that there
is no movement or motion or change in this world. When, later on, other
formulas of God or ultimate reality are given, they often present it as a
form of Unchangeable Being. St. Augustine's formula may serve as an
example: *"Quid es ergo, Deus meus?"* "Thou art truth indeed, *wherein
no change, no shadow of alteration* . . . most constant and incomprehensible . . . immutable . . . never new and never old . . . still the
same." [6]

In many variations, this philosophy of Being, either in its application
to true reality generally, or to the ultimate reality only, has been going on
throughout the whole history of philosophy and human thought from the
remotest past to the present time.[7]

[4] The Upanishads, *The Sacred Books of the East* (Oxford, 1884), Vol. XV, 1, 2, 4–20; 11,
4, 6. This philosophy of Being permeates all the ancient Hindu thought and is equally domi-
nant in Buddhism. See, for instance, the Vedānta Sutras, *The Sacred Books of the East*, Vols.
XXXIV and XXXVIII; the *Dhammapada*, in *The World's Great Classics* (New York, n. d.).
See also F. Max Müller, *The Six Systems of Indian Philosophy* (New York, 1899), pp. 159 ff.
Asvagosha Bodhisattva, *Life of Buddha*, trans. by Samuel Beal (New York, n. d.).

[5] *Tao-Teh-King*, 6. See the Texts of Taoism, *The Sacred Books of the East* (Oxford, 1891),
Vol. XI. Again this philosophy of Being pervades the whole theoretical and practical —
moral and social — system of Lao-tse and Taoism.

[6] St. Augustine, *Confessions*, trans. by Sir Tobie Matthew (London, 1923), Bk. I, chap.
iv; Bk. III, chap. vii; Bk. VII, chap. i, pp. 5, 6, 10, 55, 144, *et passim*.

[7] As it is not my purpose to give in this chapter a history of the philosophy of Being and
Becoming, but merely to give its concrete types, I limit myself to a few examples. Those
who are desirous of knowing its history must turn to the courses on the history of philosophy
or to special works devoted to the history of time concepts and ultimate reality, as, for instance,
the excellent work of P. Duhem, *op. cit.* (Paris, 1913–1915), especially Vol. I. A slight
introduction to the problem is given in G. Simmel, *Hauptprobleme der Philosophie* (1911),
chap. ii; and in E. Underhill's *Mysticism*, 12th ed., chap. ii. See further Chapter Eleven
of this volume.

The opposite effort, to reduce the category of Being to that of Becoming, is represented by the philosophy of *Becoming*. It claims that everything is in the state of incessant Becoming, change, flux; that Becoming or process is the only reality, and there is no unchangeable and everlasting permanency whatsoever. At the best, a Being is nothing but a slow Becoming, viewed statically, and nonexistent in reality. This stream also flows throughout the whole history of human thought, from the remotest past to the present time. Herakleitos's famous: "All things are born through opposition and all are in flux like a river. . . . Reality is a condition of unrest" [8] is one sample of this conception; Zend-Avesta's somewhat similar conception of reality as an incessant strife and change of the two opposite forces, Ahura-Mazda and Angra Mainyu, until the final victory of Ahura-Mazda is secured, is another.[9]

Nearer to our time is the Hegelian conception of reality and, in our own day, that of A. N. Whitehead.[10] Finally, we have the writings of a crowd of modern professors and journalists,[11] who again and again stress—intentionally or not—that only process, change, Becoming are existing reality.

The third solution of the problem has been to give direct or indirect recognition to both categories, and an allotment of some room to each. The forms of this solution have been divers. *One* of them, connected with the names of Leukippos and Democritus, found it in an *atomistic* theory; the atoms or the last particles of the reality are unchangeable; they represent Being; their combinations are ever changing; they give process, Becoming. Replace the atoms by electrons, protons, or by the still smaller elements, and you will have arrived at most of the contemporary theories of reality of the same type. *Another form* of this solution is given by the theories of *aeternitas*, *aevum*, and *tempus* of Plato, the Neo-Platonists, partly of the Peripatetic School, by most of the medieval thinkers (from Augustine, St. Thomas, the Scholastics up to Spinoza) and by many others, where the realm of Being is allotted to the ultimate or supreme reality; the realm of Becoming to the empirical reality of our sense perception where "generation and corruption," change and process, the beginning and the end, reign supreme.[12] In some of the theories there

---

[8] Herakleitos, *Fragmenta*, 46, 84; and Diogenes Laertius, *Lives*, IX, 7–9.

[9] See the Zend-Avesta, in *The Sacred Books of the East*, Vol. 4, pp. lvi ff.

[10] See A. N. Whitehead, *Process and Reality* (New York, 1929). See also studies by S. C. Pepper, V. F. Lenzen, G. P. Adams in *The Problem of Time* (Berkeley, 1935).

[11] Especially the writings of many sociologists and political scientists, not to mention biologists and various adepts in evolution.

[12] See Plato's *Republic*, II, 381, the end of VI, and the beginning of VII; *Timaeus, passim*, particularly 27 and 51–52. Aristotle, *Metaphysics*, VII, VIII, IX; *De generatione et corrup-*

is a gradation of reality in three and four classes, with an increasing Being and a decreasing Becoming, as we pass from the lower to the higher forms of existence. A *third* variation of this solution is given by an enormous number of both the old and the modern theories which claim that the concrete things are changeable (are in process), but that the relationships between the things and the laws which govern the changes are constant and immutable. The former are in the realm of Becoming, the latter in that of Being.[13] This idea is predominant in the nineteenth-century conception of "evolution," according to which everything incessantly changes, but the causal laws of this change are supposed to be constant and everlasting. The usual conception of the existence of invariable scientific laws and uniform relationships between the ever-changing phenomena; the very essence of a causal relationship according to which A is invariably connected with B in this ever-changing universe; the very essence of any scientifically true concept or definition which is supposed to be true forever (otherwise it is not true and not scientific, according to the prevalent opinion), but which describes ever-changing reality — these and dozens of similar theories and beliefs are all merely variations of this third solution. In one way or another, all of them — explicitly or implicitly — allot a place for Becoming and another for Being (sometimes contrary to their own contentions). The *fourth* variety is represented by those theories, in all fields of science and philosophy, which claim that the "form" of a class of phenomena is constant while the content is ever changing. Here the form is in the realm of Being, the content in that of Becoming. Still another diluted example of the same is given by the fundamental concepts of the natural sciences. Whether or not scientists want fixed and — hypothetically or factually — immovable points of reference in their study of phenomena in flux, they are

---

tione, passim; see also his *De coelo* and his *Physics.* With a variation, the same theory is found in the works of most of the Peripatetics and Neo-Platonists. See, for instance, Plotinus's *Enneades,* and the works of Jamblicus, L. Apuleius, Proclus, and others. See Chapter Eleven.

[13] For instance, "A change of the laws of the world and its perdition mean almost the same; the world which would not have any more laws (known to us) would not be any more our world; it would be another world." H. Poincaré, *Dernière pensées* (Paris, 1913), p. 11. See also his *Science et méthode* (Paris, 1920), pp. 8 ff.; E. Mach, *The Science of Mechanics* (Chicago, 1902), pp. 5 ff., 77–78; A. Comte, *System of Positive Polity* (London, 1875), Vol. I, pp. 18–21 and 343–345. See further about belief in the immutable scientific laws in the works of the methodologists of modern science, in A. A. Tschuproff, *Ocherki po teorii statistiki* (in Russian) (St. Petersburg, 1909), pp. 95–138.

Montesquieu's formula of causal laws as "the necessary relations arising from the nature of things" and their supposed immutability is another variation of the same type of intentional or unintentional reconciliation of Being and Becoming.

forced to assume, to admit, to postulate, such fixed and for the time being invariable framework of reference. Even in the study of the simplest motions of a material point, there is necessary a fixed and immovable system of vector as a point of reference. The same is also true of the study of more complex forms of motion.

By a system of references or a system of comparison is meant an *invariable* system in relation to which a motion is studied. Thus when they say that a train is moving, that a stone, left to itself, falls along the vertical, that the sun rises and goes down, they take the earth as a system of reference. In astronomy and celestial mechanics, the movements of the earth, the planets, the sun are studied in reference to an ensemble of the stars called fixed by definition.[14]

In the Newtonian mechanics, absolute space is taken as ever identical with itself and immovable. Even the opponents of the absolute space theory, like Mach, have to admit the fixed points of reference by definition.[15] Here, then, the outlet for Being is found, besides the laws, uniformities, causal or functional and logical relations, which are assumed to be eternal and immutable, in the system of reference invariable either by definition ("as if") or by nature.

In the special field of human relations, there are hundreds of concrete examples of the same solution. The Greeks viewed "nature" as the realm of immutability, and man-made norm as that of change.[16] When the Romans thought that the *jus civile, jus Quiritum,* and *jus honorarium* were all changeable, while *jus naturale* and *aequitas*[17] were unchangeable, eternal, immutable, valid for all times and for all peoples, they again gave *suum cuique* to Being as well as to Becoming.

With a slight variation and under the name of either "the eternal law" (St. Thomas Aquinas and others) or "natural law" or "divine law," almost all theorizers about law and morals have admitted or stressed the unchangeable and everlasting Being in this field in contradistinction to the "positive law" and concrete codes of laws, mores, prescriptions, which are changing in time and in space.[18]

[14] P. Appel et S. Dautherville, *Précis de méchanique rationnelle* (Paris, 1924), p. 39. See also J. C. Maxwell, *Matter and Motion* (London, 1882), chaps. i and ii; L. Lecornu, *La méchanique, Les idées et les faits* (Paris, 1918), *passim.*

[15] E. Mach, *The Science of Mechanics* (Chicago, 1902), pp. 229–230.

[16] See J. W. Beardslee, Jr., *The Use of* Φύσις *in the Fifth-Century Greek Literature.*

[17] *Jus naturale* is " *quod natura omnia animalia docuit.*" In Cicero's formulation it is " *aeturnum quiddam, quod universum mundum regeret imperandi prohibendique sapientia* "; it incorporates " *ratio recta summi Jovis.*" See I. Pokrovsky, *A History of Roman Law* (in Russian) (Riga, 1924), pp. 130 ff.

[18] See R. W. and A. J. Carlyle, *A History of Mediaeval Political Theory in the West,* 5 vols. (New York, 1903–1922), *passim;* R. B. Vaughn, *The Life and Labors of St. Thomas*

The same concept has been given, in a slightly different form, as applied to all human relationships and institutions. As an example of this, the physiocratic concept of the natural order and natural law can well serve. While admitting that the concrete set of mores, laws, social relationships, and institutions is ever changing, François Quesnay and other leaders of the physiocrats claimed that side by side with these there exists an immutable *"l'ordre naturel"* and *"le droit naturel"* different from *"le droit légitime."* This natural order and natural law are eternal, "immutable," everlasting, and unchangeable.[19]

In a somewhat different form, essentially the same method of the reconciliation of the Being and Becoming in human affairs is presented by all the numerous theories which, admitting and stressing the ever-changing character of human behavior, relationships, laws, mores, institutions, historical destinies, and what not, at the same time claim that in all these changes there are the *uniformities, the regularities, the causal relationships, and the laws* according to which these changes proceed, and that these uniformities, regularities, and causal laws are themselves immutable, constant, unchangeable; and that the task of science consists essentially in the discovery and formulation of these immutable uniformities, causal laws, and regularities. This means that in this case the refuge of the immutable Being becomes the science itself, with its discovery of the supposed immutable causal laws and uniformities and functional relationships. And this is equally applicable to the social as well as to the natural science of the past as well as of the present day. An example of this in the field of social theory is given by either G. B. Vico's or Montesquieu's formulations of the causal laws and uniformities. Vico said that the main task of his famous work was

not an explanation of a temporary and particular (and in this sense changeable and incidental) history of Greece or Rome (or any other country) but the ideal, universal and eternal laws along which proceed all nations in the cycles of their appearance, development, decadence and end. Through the diversity of the external forms we grasp the identity of the substance of all particular histories.[20]

Aquinas, 3 vols. (London, 1871); J. M. Littlejohn, *The Political Theories of the Schoolmen and Grotius* (Columbia University thesis, 1896).

[19] See F. Quesnay, "Le Droit Naturel," in *Physiocrates* (Paris, 1846), Vol. I, pp. 99, 42 ff., xii ff. Mercier de la Rivière, "*L'ordre naturel et essentiel des sociétés politiques*," in *ibid.*, *passim* and pp. 607–608.

[20] G. B. Vico, *Principes de la philosophie de l'histoire traduit de la Scienza par J. Michelet* (Bruxelles, 1835), p. 392 and Bk. IV, chap. i.

These examples give a sufficiently clear idea of the variety of the third solution where, explicitly or implicitly, neither of these categories is absorbed by the other.

Having outlined these solutions, I must note that all the attempts to reduce one of these categories to another, in the way of exclusion of the other category, have failed, with hardly any exception.   This means that these theories in a disguised form have had to give place to the other principle, and in fact, though contrary to the claims of their authors, represent also a variation of the third solution.   When a Hindu, Brahman, or Taoist, a Zeno or St. Augustine, or any other philosopher of Being, unchangeable, everlasting reality, has to give a meaning to the concept of Being, he can do it only by invoking Becoming and its equivalents.   Only by contrasting their Being to Becoming, *aeternitas* to *tempus*, could they give to it any sense.   More than that; the changeableness of the empirical reality is such an undeniable dictum that they could not deny its existence and had to recognize it.   All that they could do was to qualify it as inferior, less real, more illusionary; or, having expelled it from the realm of reality, return it as one of its properties.   We shall not quarrel with their evaluation of what is superior and what is inferior reality, it does not concern us here; what does concern us is that, whether in the form of inferior or superior reality, they have admitted it, and were unable to reduce it to nothing, or let it be merged into Being.   That is exactly what they did.   In other cases, after expelling it from the realm of reality, they put it back there secretly.   What I mean by that is well shown by a continuation of the quotation from St. Augustine given above. Note it attentively.   "Thou art truth indeed, wherein no change, no shadow of alteration; most constant and incomprehensible; *immutable, yet changing all things; never new and never old, yet renewing all things*" . . . and so on.[21]

The italicized statements show how Becoming is clandestinely reintroduced into the realm of reality.[22]

Mutatis mutandis, the same is to be said of the philosophers of Becom-

---

[21] St. Augustine, *Confessions*, quoted, pp. 5, 6, 10, 55, 144, *et passim*.   See also his *The City of God*, where the domain of Becoming is the empirical world; the domain of Being is "the celestial city which is eternal; no man is born in it because no man dies in it"; it is "the kingdom of which there is no end" — *The City of God*, trans. by John Healy, Bk. V, chap. vii, p. 230 and Bk. XVIII, chap. xviii.

[22] As to the attempts of Zeno and others to show nonexistence of motion or movement or change in the reality, while giving all due admiration to the exquisite and most subtle logic of Zeno, one can detect flaws in this wonderful lace of reasoning.   From many demonstrations of the flaws, one example is given in H. Bergson's *Matter and Memory*.

ing. To make meaningful their concept of Process, they have to recur to that of Being. Having expelled Being from reality, they have to reintroduce it, either in the form of "the ultimate reality" (A. N. Whitehead), the transcendental, the *ding an sich und für sich*, matter, energy, cosmic rays, Universal Spirit, Will, Herakleitos's *One* or *Fire*,[23] God, the Unknowable, "Conation," World's Mind, Brahma, or any other ultimate entity, which is in process, and which, in spite of that, has to remain identical with itself. Otherwise, there is no logical subject which is in process, and no possibility of talking of a process, as indicated in Chapter Four of Volume One. Or, in a still more disguised form, invariability and unchangeability of the relationships between the processes and the "things" is considered as a constant bunch of processes — a more subtle reintroduction of Being. Even the simplest form of Becoming or Change — a motion of a material point — cannot be described without an admission of points of reference, because, as Bergson rightly said, "every movement is a passage from rest to rest."[24] Being and Becoming, or the unchangeable and the changeable, have never been reduced to either one of them, and all such attempts have failed.

This difficulty of reduction of one of these categories to the other explains why the number of the pure eternalists and the pure temporalists has been small during the twenty-five hundred years studied. It makes it also advisable to differentiate our three classes a little more exactly, namely, to separate them into five classes. The point is that, as mentioned, the absolute and pure eternalism and the partly pure temporalism are met very rarely. Explicitly or implicitly, most of the thinkers in the field have had to admit, in some form and to some degree, both aspects: eternal and temporal, Being and Becoming. In this sense, the majority of the theories would have been of the intermediary type, if the thinkers had stressed equally both aspects, or if they had not attempted (contradicting themselves) to stress one of the aspects to such an extent that the other is left in a shadow or forgotten. Meanwhile, there are numerous theories which belong exactly to that type; though implicitly they admit both aspects, in fact they stress one of them to such an extent that the other becomes insignificant. Some do it in favor of Being, or eternal permanency, at the cost of the temporal or changing aspect; others take the opposite stand. As a result, we have a large number of theories which

---

[23] Herakleitos gives us an illustration of that. After asserting that "reality is a condition of unrest" he had to admit the Unchanging One — God — fire, which remains identical with itself, in spite of an incessant change of aspect.

[24] H. Bergson, *Matter and Memory* (London, 1919), pp. 246 ff.

cannot be classed as either pure eternalism or pure temporalism, but which greatly stress one or the other of these aspects. In view of this, it appears advisable to classify the theories into five classes: (1) *pure eternalism;* (2) *eternalism-temporalism, where the aspect of Becoming is present but is greatly overshadowed by the aspect of permanent Being;* (3) *pure temporalism;* (4) *temporalism-eternalism, where the aspect of Becoming is much more stressed than that of Being;* (5) finally, the theories of *equilibrium of eternalism-temporalism, where are found only those concepts which give equal importance to both aspects and regard them as equally important modes of reality.* Subsequently this study is made along the line of this fivefold as well as the threefold classification. In the threefold classification are united pure and preponderant eternalism and pure and preponderant temporalism; the third section is made up of the "equilibrium" theories.

Some thinkers placed in a certain class in the Appendix to this chapter may well be put into the next congenial class also, because their theories permit them to be placed in one class as well as in the other. However, the number of such thinkers composes a small minority in the total number studied; even if they are put into another class than the one in which they are listed, such a shift would not have any appreciable effect upon the tables of 20-year as well as 100-year periods. The results would be about the same as those reached in this study. In Tables 17 and 18 are given the number of the representatives of each theory in each period (in other words, each thinker is given the same value — one) as well as the indicators of their weight; here the thinkers are given different values, from one to twelve, according to their importance and influence. The percentages are computed upon the basis of the "weight." However, computed upon the basis of the number, the results would not be very different, so far as the essential fluctuations are concerned.

II. Fluctuation of the Influence of Eternalism, of Temporalism, and of the Intermediate Mentality

Table 17 shows by 20-year periods the main ups and downs of the influence of each of the five, as well as the three, main streams of thought in the field.

Table 18 gives the same by century periods. Figure 12 depicts the movement by century periods.[25]

---

[25] The last column of Table 17 gives the percentages for 1900–1920. See the list of the names in the Appendix to this chapter.

TABLE 17. FLUCTUATION OF ETERNALISM AND TEMPORALISM FROM 560 B.C. TO A.D. 1920 BY 20-YEAR PERIODS

PERIOD	Eternalism Number of representatives	Eternalism Their weight	Eternalism Percentage of the total	Temporalism Number of representatives	Temporalism Their weight	Temporalism Percentage of the total	Eternalism-Temporalism Number of representatives	Eternalism-Temporalism Their weight	Eternalism-Temporalism Percentage of the total	Temporalism-Eternalism Number of representatives	Temporalism-Eternalism Their weight	Temporalism-Eternalism Percentage of the total	Equilibrium of Both Number of representatives	Equilibrium of Both Their weight	Equilibrium of Both Percentage of the total	PERCENTAGE OF ALL ETERNALISM	PERCENTAGE OF ALL TEMPORALISM	PERCENTAGE OF THE EQUILIBRIUM OF BOTH
560–540 B.C.	0	0	0	0	0	0	2	10	100	0	0	0	0	0	0	100	0	0
540–520	0	0	0	0	0	0	2	10	50	1	2	10	1	8	40	50	10	40
520–500	1	7	24	1	7	32	1	5	23	1	2	9	1	8	36	23	41	36
500–480	2	12	50	1	7	24	1	5	17	1	2	7	1	8	28	41	31	28
480–460	2	8	38	1	7	29	1	1	4	2	3	13	1	1	4	54	42	4
460–440	2	8	18	1	1	5	1	1	5	4	10	47	1	1	5	43	52	5
440–420	1	3	4	2	10	22	1	2	2	7	20	45	2	6	13	20	67	13
420–400	1	3	4	8	29	40	1	1	1	4	18	25	6	21	29	5	65	29
400–380	1	3	6	7	27	39	2	2	3	3	11	16	9	26	38	7	55	38
380–360	0	0	0	3	15	28	4	14	26	3	16	30	3	5	10	32	58	10
360–340	0	0	0	6	18	29	4	20	33	5	15	25	6	8	13	33	54	13
340–320	0	0	0	5	9	20	3	10	22	5	10	22	6	17	36	22	42	36
320–300	0	0	0	8	17	24	3	6	8	7	13	18	11	35	50	8	42	50
300–280	0	0	0	9	18	26	4	9	13	6	17	24	6	26	37	13	50	37
280–260	0	0	0	7	16	26	3	7	12	4	13	21	7	25	41	12	47	41
260–240	0	0	0	4	14	40	0	0	0	2	4	11	7	17	49	0	51	49
240–220	0	0	0	8	27	45	0	0	0	4	7	12	10	26	43	0	57	43
220–200	0	0	0	5	14	42	0	0	0	2	3	9	6	16	49	0	51	49
200–180	0	0	0	2	3	14	0	0	0	3	4	18	7	15	68	0	32	68
180–160	0	0	0	2	6	30	0	0	0	2	3	10	5	12	60	0	40	60
160–140	0	0	0	3	7	33	0	0	0	1	2	14	5	11	53	0	47	53
140–120	0	0	0	2	9	43	0	0	0	2	4	10	5	10	47	0	53	47
120–100	0	0	0	2	4	20	0	0	0	4	7	20	7	12	60	0	40	60
100–80	0	0	0	1	4	15	0	0	0	3	5	27	7	15	58	0	42	58
80–60	0	0	0	1	2	6	1	4	6	4	18	14	10	28	80	6	20	80
60–40	0	0	0	1	5	7	1	2	5	3	10	27	17	40	60	5	34	60
40–20	0	0	0	1	5	11	2	4	19	2	2	23	11	27	61	19	34	61
20–0	0	0	0	1	5	24				2		10	5	10	47			47

TABLE 17. FLUCTUATION OF ETERNALISM AND TEMPORALISM BY 20-YEAR PERIODS — continued

PERIOD	Eternalism			Temporalism			Eternalism-Temporalism			Temporalism-Eternalism			Equilibrium of Both			PERCENTAGE OF ALL ETERNALISM	PERCENTAGE OF ALL TEMPORALISM	PERCENTAGE OF THE EQUILIBRIUM OF BOTH
	Number of representatives	Their weight	Percentage of the total	Number of representatives	Their weight	Percentage of the total	Number of representatives	Their weight	Percentage of the total	Number of representatives	Their weight	Percentage of the Total	Number of representatives	Their weight	Percentage of the total			
0–20 A.D.	0	0	0	1	1	4	1	8	32	2	2	8	9	14	56	32	12	56
20–40	0	0	0	1	1	5	1	8	40	1	1	5	7	10	50	40	10	50
40–60	0	0	0	2	2	8	1	8	31	1	1	4	4	15	57	31	12	57
60–80	0	0	0	2	2	5	2	8	21	1	1	3	7	28	71	21	8	71
80–100	0	0	0	2	7	19	2	8	22	1	1	3	4	21	56	22	22	56
100–120	0	0	0	3	8	20	2	6	15	1	1	2	7	26	63	15	22	63
120–140	0	0	0	3	7	12	6	17	28	1	1	2	12	35	58	28	14	58
140–160	0	0	0	3	7	15	8	21	35	2	2	3	14	30	50	35	15	50
160–180	0	0	0	3	12	12	8	23	28	2	2	2	14	45	55	28	17	55
180–200	0	0	0	1	12	10	9	21	21	2	4	4	17	63	63	21	16	63
200–220	0	0	0	0	6	0	6	22	37	1	3	5	8	29	48	37	15	48
220–240	0	0	0	0	0	0	4	20	51	1	1	3	4	18	46	51	3	46
240–260	0	0	0	0	0	0	4	15	33	1	1	2	7	30	65	33	2	65
260–280	0	0	0	0	0	0	3	10	29	1	1	3	6	24	68	29	3	68
280–300	0	0	0	0	0	0	3	13	69	1	1	5	3	5	26	69	5	26
300–320	0	0	0	0	0	0	3	15	63	1	1	4	4	8	33	63	4	33
320–340	0	0	0	0	0	0	6	18	49	1	1	2	6	18	49	49	2	49
340–360	0	0	0	0	0	0	7	14	48	1	1	4	4	14	48	48	4	48
360–380	0	0	0	0	0	0	9	20	32	0	0	0	10	42	68	32	0	68
380–400	0	0	0	0	0	0	7	22	37	0	0	0	9	37	63	37	0	63
400–420	0	0	0	0	0	0	5	16	33	0	0	0	12	33	67	33	0	67
420–440	0	0	0	0	0	0	5	16	37	0	0	0	11	27	63	37	0	63
440–460	0	0	0	0	0	0	3	12	52	0	0	0	4	11	48	52	0	48
460–480	0	0	0	0	0	0	3	12	48	0	0	0	7	13	52	48	0	52
480–500	0	0	0	0	0	0	4	12	55	0	0	0	7	10	45	55	0	45
500–520	0	0	0	0	0	0	4	14	50	0	0	0	6	14	50	50	0	50
520–540	0	0	0	0	0	0	4	14	38	0	0	0	6	23	62	38	0	62
540–560	0	0	0	0	0	0	2	5	23	0	0	0	5	17	77	23	0	77

Period	1	2	3	4	5	6	7	8	9	10	11	12	13	14	15	16	17	18
560–580 A.D.	83	0	17	83	5	2	0	0	0	17	1	1	0	0	0	0	0	0
580–600	50	0	50	50	4	2	0	0	0	50	4	1	0	0	0	0	0	0
600–620	67	0	33	67	8	3	0	0	0	33	4	1	0	0	0	0	0	0
620–640	57	0	43	57	8	3	0	0	0	43	6	1	0	0	0	0	0	0
640–660	33	0	67	33	3	2	0	0	0	67	6	1	0	0	0	0	0	0
660–680	25	0	75	25	2	1	0	0	0	75	6	1	0	0	0	0	0	0
680–700	100	0	0	100	2	1	0	0	0	0	0	0	0	0	0	0	0	0
700–720	100	0	0	100	3	1	0	0	0	0	0	0	0	0	0	0	0	0
720–740	100	0	0	100	8	1	0	0	0	0	0	0	0	0	0	0	0	0
740–760	100	0	0	100	6	2	0	0	0	0	0	0	0	0	0	0	0	0
760–780	100	0	0	100	1	2	0	0	0	0	0	0	0	0	0	0	0	0
780–800	100	0	0	100	4	1	0	0	0	0	0	0	0	0	0	0	0	0
800–820	80	0	20	80	6	1	0	0	0	20	2	1	0	0	0	0	0	0
820–840	78	0	22	78	8	2	0	0	0	22	4	2	0	0	0	0	0	0
840–860	71	0	29	71	14	3	0	0	0	29	6	3	0	0	0	0	0	0
860–880	100	0	0	100	15	3	0	0	0	0	0	0	0	0	0	0	0	0
880–900	100	0	0	100	9	4	0	0	0	0	0	0	0	0	0	0	0	0
900–920	100	0	0	100	4	4	0	0	0	0	0	0	0	0	0	0	0	0
920–940	100	0	0	100	2	2	0	0	0	0	0	0	0	0	0	0	0	0
940–960	100	0	0	100	1	1	0	0	0	0	0	0	0	0	0	0	0	0
960–980	100	0	0	100	1	1	0	0	0	0	0	0	0	0	0	0	0	0
980–1000	62	0	38	62	3	3	0	0	0	38	5	2	0	0	0	0	0	0
1000–1020	48	0	52	48	8	2	0	0	0	52	16	4	0	0	0	0	0	0
1020–1040	56	0	44	56	5	3	0	0	0	44	14	3	0	0	0	0	0	0
1040–1060	35	0	65	35	8	6	0	0	0	65	15	5	0	0	0	0	0	0
1060–1080	42	0	58	42	15	7	0	0	0	58	21	7	0	0	0	0	0	0
1080–1100	39	0	61	39	18	4	0	0	0	61	25	7	0	0	0	0	0	0
1100–1120	27	0	73	27	8	6	0	0	0	73	19	6	0	0	0	0	0	0
1120–1140	36	0	64	36	15	7	0	0	0	64	14	9	0	0	0	0	0	0
1140–1160	45	0	55	45	16	4	0	0	0	55	17	8	0	0	0	0	0	0
1160–1180	33	0	67	33	7	4	0	0	0	67	16	11	0	0	0	0	0	0
1180–1200	45	0	55	45	8	6	0	0	0	55	18	15	0	0	0	0	0	0
1200–1220	42	0	58	42	14	3	0	0	0	58	37	13	0	0	0	0	0	0
1220–1240	50	0	50	50	8	4	0	0	0	50	36		0	0	0	0	0	0
1240–1260	63	0	37	63	15	8	0	0	0	37	30		0	0	0	0	0	0
1260–1280		0			26	11	0	0	0				0	0	0	0	0	0
1280–1300		0			36	15	0	0	0				0	0	0	0	0	0
1300–1320		0			50		0	0	0				0	0	0	0	0	0

TABLE 17.   FLUCTUATION OF ETERNALISM AND TEMPORALISM BY 20-YEAR PERIODS — continued

PERIOD	Eternalism			Temporalism			Eternalism-Temporalism			Temporalism-Eternalism			Equilibrium of Both			PERCENTAGE OF ALL ETERNALISM	PERCENTAGE OF ALL TEMPORALISM	PERCENTAGE OF THE EQUILIBRIUM OF THE BOTH
	Number of representatives	Their weight	Percentage of the total	Number of representatives	Their weight	Percentage of the total	Number of representatives	Their weight	Percentage of the total	Number of representatives	Their weight	Percentage of the total	Number of representatives	Their weight	Percentage of the total			
1320–1340 A.D.	0	0	0	0	0	0	7	14	22	1	4	6	16	47	72	22	6	72
1340–1360	0	0	0	0	0	0	11	30	45	1	4	6	11	33	49	45	6	49
1360–1380	0	0	0	0	0	0	6	24	51	0	0	0	8	23	49	51	0	49
1380–1400	0	0	0	0	0	0	2	6	32	0	0	0	5	13	68	32	0	68
1400–1420	0	0	0	0	0	0	1	4	40	0	0	0	2	6	60	40	0	60
1420–1440	0	0	0	0	0	0	2	7	44	0	0	0	3	9	56	44	0	56
1440–1460	0	0	0	0	0	0	2	7	33	0	0	0	4	14	67	33	0	67
1460–1480	0	0	0	0	0	0	2	9	41	0	0	0	3	13	59	41	0	59
1480–1500	0	0	0	0	0	0	3	3	30	1	6	11	4	7	70	30	0	70
1500–1520	2	5	7	1	4	7	13	36	67	1	6	11	1	8	15	67	18	15
1520–1540	2	5	9	1	4	5	15	53	71	2	12	16	1	1	1	78	21	1
1540–1560	1	1	1	1	2	4	10	39	74	1	6	11	1	2	2	83	15	2
1560–1580	1	1	1	2	8	10	24	57	69	3	15	12	2	16	19	70	11	19
1580–1600	2	8	5	3	12	9	34	84	66	7	32	21	2	16	12	67	21	12
1600–1620	7	12	8	3	12	8	25	66	43	5	27	19	6	34	22	48	24	22
1620–1640	1	34	24	1	1	1	23	65	45	6	23	16	7	38	27	53	20	27
1640–1660	1	7	6	3	6	5	17	46	33	7	27	21	6	36	26	57	17	26
1660–1680	1	1	1	4	10	6	19	63	50	13	49	28	8	23	18	56	26	18
1680–1700	1	1	1	3	11	8	36	89	48	10	39	26	7	26	15	51	34	15
1700–1720	1	1	1	1	3	2	29	71	41	11	48	37	5	25	17	49	34	17
1720–1740	3	4	2	3	20	11	18	53	31	17	60	35	11	23	18	32	39	18
1740–1760	1	1	0.5	3	20	10	14	54	30	20	82	39	8	39	22	32	46	22
1760–1780	3	21	9	1	2	0.5	18	64	37	18	75	35.5	8	39	19	37.5	49	19
1780–1800	6	28	10	2	1	3	24	78	37	14	56	23.5	14	55	26	46	36.5	26
1800–1820	5	30	8	5	7	7	30	88	53	10	50	19	9	71	15	63	24	15
1820–1840	10	53	11	5	25	5	46	141	57	17	71	20	8	40	8	65	22	8
1840–1860	7	40	6	5	25	4	72	204	37	36	179	36	9	29	11	48	27	11
1860–1880	10	53	11	5	26	5	62	187	37	55	242	39	30	53	17	41	41	17
1880–1900	7	40	6	5	26	4	72	207	34	55	242	39	30	103	17	40	43	17
1900–1920	10	47	6	11	37	4	100	268	32	97	382	45	34	109	13	38	49	13

TABLE 18. FLUCTUATION OF ETERNALISM AND TEMPORALISM FROM 600 B.C. TO A.D. 1900 BY 100-YEAR PERIODS

PERIOD	Eternalism			Temporalism			Eternalism-Temporalism			Temporalism-Eternalism			Equilibrium of Both			PERCENTAGE OF ALL ETERNALISM	PERCENTAGE OF ALL TEMPORALISM	PERCENTAGE OF THE EQUILIBRIUM OF BOTH
	Number of representatives	Their weight	Percentage of the total	Number of representatives	Their weight	Percentage of the total	Number of representatives	Their weight	Percentage of the total	Number of representatives	Their weight	Percentage of the total	Number of representatives	Their weight	Percentage of the total			
600–500 B.C.	0	0	0	1	7	26	2	10	37	1	2	7	1	8	30	37	33	30
500–400	3	15	13	10	37	31	2	6	5	9	30	25	9	31	26	18	56	26
400–300	1	3	2	21	57	31	7	26	14	13	35	19	20	61	34	16	50	34
300–200	0	0	0	19	49	34	4	9	7	12	27	19	18	56	40	7	53	40
200–100	0	0	0	5	12	21	0	0	0	7	11	19	18	34	60	0	40	60
100–0	0	0	0	3	9	8	3	8	7	10	27	24	33	68	61	7	32	61
0–100 A.D.	0	0	0	3	8	9	3	16	18	4	4	5	20	59	68	18	14	68
100–200	0	0	0	6	23	12	19	49	25	4	6	3	35	115	60	25	15	60
200–300	0	0	0	1	6	5	11	41	36	2	4	3	18	64	56	36	8	56
300–400	0	0	0	0	0	0	18	53	42	1	1	1	20	71	57	42	1	57
400–500	0	0	0	0	0	0	9	31	36	0	0	0	25	55	64	36	0	64
500–600	0	0	0	0	0	0	7	20	36	0	0	0	13	36	64	36	0	64
600–700	0	0	0	0	0	0	2	10	48	0	0	0	5	11	52	48	0	52
700–800	0	0	0	0	0	0	0	0	0	0	0	0	4	13	100	0	0	100
800–900	0	0	0	0	0	0	4	8	21	0	0	0	10	31	79	21	0	79
900–1000	0	0	0	0	0	0	0	0	0	0	0	0	4	8	100	0	0	100
1000–1100	0	0	0	0	0	0	5	19	41	0	0	0	11	28	59	41	0	59
1100–1200	0	0	0	0	0	0	21	60	64	0	0	0	16	34	36	64	0	36
1200–1300	0	0	0	0	0	0	42	103	60	0	0	0	25	68	40	60	0	40
1300–1400	0	0	0	0	0	0	27	66	38	1	4	2	37	104	60	38	2	60
1400–1500	0	0	0	0	0	0	6	18	40	0	0	0	10	27	60	40	0	60
1500–1600	3	6	2	6	24	8	69	192	66	6	28	10	6	41	14	68	18	14
1600–1700	10	49	9	8	19	4	101	265	52	27	104	20	19	76	15	61	24	15
1700–1800	4	5	1	8	36	6	85	240	38	57	215	35	37	127	20	39	41	20
1800–1900	19	89	6	11	52	4	233	640	45	102	420	29	68	237	16	51	33	16

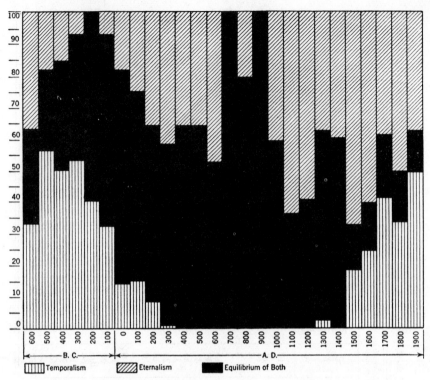

FIG. 12.   TEMPORALISM, ETERNALISM, EQUILIBRIUM OF BOTH

III. Main Results

A. As in all other similar tables, no perpetual linear trend and no increasing differentiation — complication or the opposite, simplification, uniformization — are shown by the data.   Instead of any linear trend, the currents rise and fall, fluctuating without any continuous tendency in the course of time.

B. A glance through either the 20-year or 100-year periods shows at once that the *current of eternalism* (philosophy of Being) *is indeed closely associated with the Ideational culture and its various aspects, while the mentality of temporalism is allied with the Sensate culture and its variables.* The century-periods table shows:

(1) In the sixth century B.C. — the Ideational century according to the earmarks of other aspects of its culture — eternalism is the highest, comparatively;   then it tends to decrease from the fifth to the first century B.C., the period of the rise of the Sensate culture, as is shown by the other aspects of that culture.   On the other hand, during these

centuries temporalism rises (from the sixth to the fifth B.C.) and stays up to the beginning of our era very high and powerful. Such a movement of these rivals is a direct corroboration of the expectation that follows from the very nature of the Ideational and Sensate cultures.

(2) After the first century A.D. temporalism begins to decline rapidly and disappears entirely after the fourth century A.D. — again a result in perfect agreement with the movement of the Ideational and Sensate curves in all the other compartments of culture. Thus throughout the Middle Ages, up to the fourteenth century, temporalism remains underground, as it were; materialism, empiricism, natural sciences, visual art, and, as we shall see, ethics of happiness, nominalism, singularism, and other variables of the culture studied here also remain underground, or of very low value. The Middle Ages emerge as the period of the monopolistic Ideationalism, with its mentality turned not to the temporal and fleeting aspects of reality, but to its eternal aspects; not to Becoming, process, change, progress, Evolution, but to Being, permanency, *aeternitas* and *aevum*, everlasting reality. This tallies very well with the movement of the Ideational and Sensate curves in practically all the important aspects of these cultures. On the other hand, this medieval period is marked by a rise of eternalism and by a high level of the synthetic current of the "equilibrium" permeated greatly by eternalistic elements (see Chapter Eleven on the *aevum* of the medieval thinkers). These two currents share all the field.

(3) The fourteenth and fifteenth centuries are marked by a notable decline of eternalism and the re-emergence of temporalism, with the "equilibrium current" present. Thus this period appears again as "synthetic" or "idealistic" in the sense of a harmonious and partly eclectic mixture of all the currents, and with a particularly strong rise of the "equilibrium current." Though slightly later than painting and a few other variables of culture which gave the Idealistic phase in the thirteenth and fourteenth centuries, this period, from the thirteenth to the fifteenth century inclusive, stands out here also as a "mixture" or Idealistic phase.

(4) Having re-emerged in the fourteenth century, temporalism, with a short-time recess in the fifteenth century (again similar to many recesses met in other variables), rapidly and steadily grows from the fourteenth (only 2 per cent there) to the eighteenth century, where it reaches 41 per cent and then slightly recedes to 33 per cent in the nineteenth century and soars up again to 49 per cent in 1900–1920 (the last column in Table 17). Thus it grows in this period, as all the other

curves of the Sensate culture in all its compartments have been growing during the centuries from the sixteenth to the twentieth.

Thus the movement of the curves studied testifies that the mentality of eternalism and that of temporalism is indeed an element in the integrated Ideational or Sensate cultures; that the mentality of the Ideational culture is turned mainly toward the unchangeable (or relatively lasting *aevum*) aspects of reality, while that of the Sensate culture is turned to the temporal aspects from the fleeting "*Carpe diem*," "Love, drink and eat, for tomorrow is uncertain," to the ideologies of change, evolution, progress, and, generally, of Becoming.

C. The 20-year period data show several short-time flare-ups of pure eternalism and of pure temporalism. Studying the periods of the respective flare-ups, we notice that here again, as in the case of skepticism and fideism, *these extreme mentalities tend to flare up together*, the pure temporalism of the *Carpe diem* rising a little earlier and being followed by the extreme eternalism as its counterirritant. In this sense they counterbalance each other and show the phenomenon of "action reaction," and of self-regulation of sociocultural processes. Farther on we notice that pure eternalism flared up, besides its rise in the sixth century B.C., in the periods 1520–1560, 1600–1660, 1800–1840. Pure temporalism rose, besides the sixth century B.C., in almost the same periods — 1500–1560, 1580–1640, 1760–1840. The only difference is that it started its rise somewhat earlier than did pure eternalism. Here, then, we see a replica of the movement of skepticism and fideism. Looking at the periods of the short-time flares of these two extreme currents, we notice at once that they are the periods of short-time but sharp social crises; the Reformation, peasant, and other wars and revolutions; religious wars, including the Thirty Years' War; the prerevolutionary license, revolutionary crises, and postrevolutionary reactions. This suggests, as in the flarings of skepticism, mysticism, fideism, and in the case of the extreme ascetic and hedonistic mentalities (see Chapters One and Thirteen), *that such sharp crises, with their insecurity, instability, anxiety, and sufferings, split human beings into the two opposite extreme types. Some of them are turned into pure eternalists* who try to *anchor human existence* to something solid, lasting, capable of withstanding all the storms of the empirical reality; *others are turned into the extreme sensual temporalists* of the *Carpe diem* type, with their tendency to catch the pleasure of the moment for "tomorrow is uncertain " ("*di doman no c'e certezza !*"). Which psychological types are turning into the one, and which into the other is unimportant just now. What is important is the fact of such a split, under catastrophic sociocultural conditions, into the extreme mentality of "eternalism, asceticism, and mysticism of despair," on the one hand, and into that of "temporalism, sensualism, and skepticism of despair," on the other. We have met and shall meet this phenomenon of splitting several times. It seems to be of fairly general nature.

There is no doubt that there are other "factors" which condition the short-time flare-ups of each of these currents, but a detailed analysis of them is outside the scope of this work.

D. In regard to the spectrum of the nineteenth and twentieth centuries in this respect, Table 17 tells us that since 1860 the mentality of our culture has been marked by a decline of eternalism — 65, 48, 40, 38, respectively, for each 20-year period from 1840 to 1920; by an increase of temporalism — 27, 41, 43, 49, respectively; and by a relatively small role played by the equilibrium theories — 8, 11, 17, 13 per cent, respectively. These dry figures tell in their own way several significant things. They show that *our mentality has been becoming more and more "temporalistic,"* seeing less and less the eternal or lasting aspect of the reality and more and more its fleeting and passing qualities. The first consequence of this has been an enormous growth of *dynamic viewpoint* in our mentality. All things began to be viewed more and more in their dynamic aspects, as something incessantly moving, changing, never being in the state of rest or unchangeableness. Everything is regarded as in a state of flux. It is not incidental that as a crowning touch to this tendency even the "immutable points of reference" in cosmogony and mechanics were in danger of being eliminated in the twentieth century by the removal of the Newtonian theory of absolute space and time (Poincaré, Mach, and others) and by the appearance of the special and general theory of relativity, promulgated by Einstein and others.[26]

[26] See H. Poincaré, *Dernière pensées*, p. 38. "Thus not only we cannot know the absolute position of an object in space . . . but the expression: 'absolute position of object' does not have any sense. . . . Likewise the expressions: 'absolute magnitude of an object' . . . 'absolute distance between two points' do not have any sense " — Poincaré, *Science et méthode*, p. 96. "Whoever talks of absolute space uses a word devoid of any meaning." The same in regard to time. The role of the relativity theory is, from the standpoint discussed, double. On the one hand it attempts to take from time and space any absolute character, whether as Newtonian reality or Kantian category of mind. They, and all the "fixed" points, like the "fixed stars," are declared arbitrary, relative, unfixed. In this sense it is the last finishing touch of temporalistic and relativistic mentality. On the other hand, so far as it tries to set forth absolute standards of reference independent of arbitrary thought in the form of the "four-dimensional manifold welding time and space into one continuum," it "by no means gets rid of the absolute, but, on the contrary, it has brought out the absolute into sharper definition" — Max Planck, *Where Science Is Going*, pp. 197–198. In this aspect it is one of the "swallows" of the revolt against the Sensate mentality observed in other fields of our culture.

This theory removed from the physical world even such "fixed" or immovable points as the remnants of the eternalistic Being.   The other fields of human science have been invaded and overwhelmingly flooded by this dynamic viewpoint.   In regard to any phenomenon studied, we do not ask what it is as such.   Instead we ask how it (and what that *it* is we do not care) originated ;   how it developed ;   through what stages it passed ; what are the factors responsible for these incessant modifications.   If we can answer these questions, we think we know all that there is to know about the phenomenon.   This procedure is used also in biology, sociology, psychology, anthropology, and in all the humanistic and social sciences.

The eternalistic or, in Husserl's terminology, "phenomenological" (though Husserl's and Heidegger's term is not quite the same as the eternalistic)[27] viewpoint that asks what a given phenomenon is as such, regardless of its modifications and transformations ; what is its "essence," its everlasting nature that remains unchangeable in all the transformations — this viewpoint has almost disappeared.   The very terms "essence" and "unchangeable nature" are viewed suspiciously and branded as "scholastic" and "metaphysics."   So-called *"Biologismus"* and *"Psychologismus"* invaded the field of epistemology, logic, philosophy, and attempted to destroy the category of immutable truth, with its absolute validity. An effort was made to reduce truth and validity [28] to mere biological "reflexes," and useful "adaptation" (most of the biologists) ; to psychological "associations," "routine of perception," "conditioned responses," or "to the utility of the principle of the most economical line of least resistance" (E. Mach, K. Pearson, R. Avenarius, H. Poincaré, Maxwell, P. Duhem, W. James, and other pragmatists), and the like. All such "epistemologies" tended to destroy the categories of truth and cognitive validity and to replace them by a somewhat incidental, temporary "convention," due either to a mere biological survival-adaptation value ; or to an economic or other Sensate utility ; or to incidental "associations," "routines of perception," "combination of the unconditioned and conditioned stimuli responses," and the like.

At the end of the nineteenth century, the position of the leading scientists in the field of the most exact — mathematical and physicochemical — sciences assumed an almost skeptical position in regard to truth,

---

[27] For an adequate understanding of this and subsequent statements, one has to know something about the epistemology in the second part of the nineteenth century and of the twentieth century.   For a meaning of the term "phenomenological," see Husserl's work, quoted; also the works of M. Heidegger and other contemporary "phenomenologists."

[28] Again for an adequate meaning of the term *Psychologismus* used here, see E. Husserl, *Logische Untersuchungen*, 3 vols. (Halle, 1922) and his *Ideas*, quoted.

knowledge, validity, and verity. According to the theories of these scientists:

A scientist is never placed by nature in the presence of a decisive alternative between the true and the false. Consequently the very word " verity " — in the categorical meaning that hitherto made a value of it — tended to disappear from the scientific vocabulary and to be replaced by the terms of convention and convenience.[29]

The validity of the laws of nature (in physics and mechanics and other branches of the natural sciences) was made more and more conditional and relativistic. If the Copernican system was regarded as more acceptable than the Ptolemaic, the reason was only that the first "is more convenient"[30] or better fitted to the present convention. From this standpoint the laws of nature were put on the same level of conventionality with the conventional civil laws.[31]

But then the decisive question arose as to whether this [relativization and conventionalization] did not result in ruining the very idea of the distinction of the [eternal] order of nature from the conventional order, between φύσις and νόμος. . . . If the φύσις disappears, then everything becomes νόμος; everything is conventional up to the full sense of the term: convention itself. . . . On the other hand, since the principles of mechanics and physics and science generally are mere conventions, the facts, so far as they are applied to the principles, are not submitted any more to a discrimination of the true and false.[32]

Summing up his history and analysis of the theories of science, causality, and validity in the physicomathematical sciences of the nineteenth century, and of the beginning of the twentieth, Brunschvicg characterizes the recent situation in the following way.

Thus the 19th century, so famous as the century of science, ended in an unexpected crisis of scientific scepticism. The earlier physicist dreamed of basing the necessity of the causal relationship simultaneously upon the intelligible purity of the mathematical demonstrations that make its conclusion irrefutable for a mind; and upon the evidence of the facts which experimental demonstration imposes upon it. The two conditions of scientific necessity whose union was consecrated by the classical mechanics, resolved themselves finally into a double contingency. The principles of the rational deduction

[29] L. Brunschvicg, *L'expérience humaine* (Paris, 1922), p. 446.

[30] H. Poincaré, *La science et l'hypothèse*, p. 141.

[31] Brunschvicg, *op. cit.*, p. 448.

[32] *Ibid.*, pp. 448–449. See there the factual history of the theories of causality and truth in the mathematical, mechanical, physical theories of the nineteenth century, pp. 298–453.

and the factual evidence supplied by the experimental technique, between which mechanics proposed to exercise mediating functions, became plastic in their own turn. The whole system of human knowledge began to be menaced, to liquefy and to slip from the hands that were believed to have grasped it; so much so, that in the generation that precedes us immediately, not only the interpretation of the physical causality was put into jeopardy, but . . . the value of science itself.[33]

In such temporalistic "truths" there remains nothing of the absolute ever-valid truth. It is replaced by fleeting, conventional, relativistic shadows. In this way, the temporalistic mentality attempted to destroy even this "last stand" of eternalism in our world and mentality. If truth and validity are but mere incidental and relativistic and ever-changing associations and routines, then there remains nothing immovable, un-changeable, absolute. The whole world, including the world of our mentality, with its categories, becomes an eerie and phantasmagoric complex (I cannot even say "space," or "realm," or "universe") of ever-fleeting, ever-changing, ever-passing shadows of events, objects, persons, values, and what not. There remains nothing "firm," no "fixed point of reference," no eternal and absolute boundary line between the true and untrue, right and wrong, and so forth.

And indeed, what happened to truth and validity happened still more to "the right and wrong," "good and bad," "beautiful and ugly," "great and small," "positive and negative value." "Right and wrong" became a mere species of the "mores" and "conventions." Now and here the custom A is "right"; now and there it is "wrong." So we proceeded earnestly with the collection of the ethnographic and anthropological "mores" and beliefs and traditions and tastes among all the primitive tribes, from the methods of sexual copulation up to their magic and religious beliefs and convictions. We found that there was a most diverse variety and had to conclude that here also everything was changing; nothing was absolute; everything was local, conditional, temporary. Hence, the "fixed points" between the right and wrong, beautiful and ugly, noble and ignoble, sacred and profane, were removed. And so in all fields of our culture and our mentality. We literally returned to the dynamic quality of the sophists — Protagoras, Kritias, Thrasymachos, and others — with their "everything is relative in the world; man (the singularistic individual) is the measure of all things"; truth and right and beauty are mere conventions invented by the minority for the exploita-tion of the majority. They change, as everything changes in this world.

[33] *Ibid.*, p. 450.

Another aspect of this temporalistic and dynamic viewpoint was *an extraordinary rise, especially since the end of the eighteenth and the beginning of the nineteenth century, of various theories of Becoming, from the theory of the biological evolution of Lamarck-Spencer-Darwin-Huxley-Heckel and the biologists, to the theories of social dynamics, social evolution, cultural change, social progress of Turgot-Condorcet-August Comte, and a vast legion of sociologists, anthropologists, historians, economists, political and social scientists generally.*

The category of Becoming — of change, of process, of evolution, of flux, of transformation, of mutation, of revolution — has become the fundamental category of our mentality, the specific glass through which more and more the Western society has been seeing the reality. It has been becoming blinder and blinder to the eternal or lasting aspects of it. At the present moment even the mentality of the masses is permeated by this category of change and shift. Everybody, from the layman and minister up to the journalist and politician, is talking of change only and thinking mainly in that term. It is taken for granted that everything and all values — seemingly without any exception whatsoever — shift, change, come and go. Of religion, God, truth, art, mores, ethical values — including the law, the family, property, the political organization — in brief, of anything and everything we say, as a mere matter of fact : "Well, they change ; and there is no reason to deplore it. What was sacred yesterday is today profane. Our task consists in moving and changing as times change. We must make the necessary 'adjustment of the maladjustments' caused by this change." In millions of forms we repeat : *"tempora mutantur, et nos mutamur in illis"* and *tempus fugit* and *tempus edax rerum* — statements coined also in the period of a high level of temporal mentality.

From the nature of the temporalistic mentality, it follows that astronomical or watch time plays a particularly great role in it. Time is the basic category of any Becoming. And Becoming is a succession of stages in time. Such a succession is *history*. Hence, the development of historical-mentality in our culture. It is in this sense evolutionary-historical mentality par excellence. *Historismus* is a category of the Sensate-temporalistic mentality, while it plays only a modest role in the Ideational-eternalistic mentality. In Chapter Eleven and Volume One, page 616, it is pointed out that the Middle Ages had a very blurred sense of time. In the literature of the Middle Ages the past, present, and future were hopelessly mixed. Likewise, no real history and no successful development of history should be expected or could occur. For the

Ideational-eternalistic mentality, the empirical time as a marking system separating one empirical event from another is perfectly superfluous, because these events are superfluous. A. A. Macdonell puts the idea clearly in application to the Hindu Ideational mentality:

> The Brahmins . . . had early embraced the doctrine that all actions and existence are positive evil, and could therefore have felt but little inclination to chronicle historical events. . . . Nothing can be more confused, nothing more imperfect than the chronology of the Indians; no people which has attained to culture in astronomy, mathematics, is as incapable of history; in it they have neither stability nor coherence.[34]

"The historical sense being lacking, the difference between reality and mythology became obliterated. So history became mythologised." [35]

In contradistinction to this, the Sensate-temporalistic mentality is immersed in the time sequence of events, and has to mark it and chronicle it. Hence, development of history, historical bent of mind, and historical — that is time-sequential — narrative of events. For these reasons, it is not incidental that in Greece the history as history (Herodotus, Thucydides, and others) did not emerge until the fifth century. It is not incidental that in European culture history emerged only in the fourteenth or thirteenth century (Joinville, Froissart, and a few others), and reached its climax in the nineteenth century. In a larger sense, *Historismus* permeates our mentality, beginning with endless genealogical histories of this or that family, memoirs, personal diaries, biographies, reporters' narratives of events and scandals in the newspapers, and ending with tremendous archives, collections of documents, multitudes of courses in history, and an unembraceable literature of history. We cannot help viewing everything historically. The standpoint of "origin and development and evolution" is our main standpoint in studying anything, from religion to the stock market. It has rooted itself in our mind so deeply that many of us cannot even conceive of any other — nonhistorical, or nonevolutionary, or nondevelopmental — approach to the study of any phenomenon.

Another aspect of this supreme role of time category in our mentality is the *mechanistic timing of everything*, the use of time units as the marking system for the punctuation of events, phenomena, processes, and the subjecting of our whole life to time control. It is not incidental that the mechanical clock was invented in the early stages of the rising tide of the

---

[34] A. A. Macdonell, *A History of Sanskrit Literature*, cited, p. 11.

[35] F. E. Pargiter, *Ancient Indian Historical Tradition* (London, 1922), pp. 67 and 63; see also pp. 20 and 58–77. See further Chapter Eleven, on fluctuation of time conception.

temporalistic mentality (in the fourteenth century), and with the progress of this rise, more and more perfected watches and watch time were developing in our culture. At the present, this wonderfully perfected watch time most tyrannically controls our whole existence. We cannot live without a watch. We go to bed winding it; we get up at the command of the hands or alarm of a clock; we move, work, act, eat, sleep, love, quarrel, study, pray, live, by a watch and controlled by watch time.[36] Watch-time category is the supreme ruler of our mentality, action, life. Not so much the necessary length of this or that activity determines the span of time to be given to it as the mechanically imposed units of watch time, which alone determine how long the activity shall last. We are so accustomed to this that we do not often notice its peculiarity. When, however, we can put ourselves into the different time atmosphere of the Ideational mentality and culture, all the enormous peculiarity of this watch-time tyranny in our lives becomes noticeable. Overripe temporalistic mentality has to be the victim of this tyranny, and it is indeed.

Therefore, it is not incidental that we coined our famous phrase, "*Time is money.*" Where the reality is viewed temporally, the reality of our own existence is so viewed also. As such it is short and is limited in the span of its existence. Time becomes a precious commodity which, like anything scarce, becomes valuable. Another aspect of it is the *particular stress upon the present moment* in contradistinction to the past and the future. By definition, temporalism is centered in the present. Remote past is over; remote future is uncertain. Only the present moment of the endless flux is real, only it exists and only it has value. Hence our stress of the present. We are unwilling to sacrifice it for a remote future. If we are forced to make a concession in regard to the near future, we require some compensation for such a sacrifice, be it interest on our savings, be it "profit" on our invested capital.[37]

[36] Besides watch time, there are many varieties of social time; see Volume Four, of this work, in the chapter on Social Time. See also P. Sorokin and R. K. Merton, "Social Time," in *American Journal of Sociology* (March, 1937).

[37] From this, one can see that even such seemingly theoretical and detailed currents in our scientific mentality as Senior's "theory of abstinence" as the source of profit, that appeared in the thirties of the nineteenth century, are not incidental. Likewise not incidental is the medieval negative attitude toward a profit generally, and especially profit and interest, as a legitimate reward for sacrifice of the immediate enjoyment of capital in favor of the future. It signifies a profoundly different evaluation of the present and the future, compared with that of the temporalistic mentality. To the latter the present is the only reality, while the future is uncertainty and quasi reality. For the Ideational mentality, lasting eternity, the lasting eternity of the future, is the primary and true reality. Such a mentality viewed the whole human life as a mere insignificant episode in the lasting eternity of future salvation. For that it sacrificed not only the present *moment*, but the whole present life.

We live in and appreciate mainly the present.   In the field of our practical activity this temporalism manifests itself in hundreds of different ways, so familiar to us and so strange to an Ideational mentality, from "get rich quick" (no matter how: through the stock market, kidnaping, racketeering, or any productive activity); "wine, women, and song"; from the "maximum of happiness" in a given moment; from thrills and pleasures, to our politics and our policies — financial, social, and otherwise — that look for immediate effects and care little for the long-time consequences.   In almost all fields of our activities we inflate the present, use all kinds of "stimulants" (inflation, relief, and what not) to remedy the present evils, and remedy them quickly, without any consideration of the future effects of the "social drugs" upon society and culture. *The "short-time" attitude* prevails and permeates our mentality in all its fields.   To make a "sensation," to "create a hit," to have an "instantaneous success" — in movies, in music, in literature, in science, in business, in politics — that is our motto, our supreme ambition, our paramount dream.   "Time is money" is indeed one of the most characteristic formulas of our time.

The next consequence of the temporalism discussed is the *ever-quickening tempo of our life and the ever-faster rhythm of social change.*   Tempo of change has increased already to a maddening speed in the turnover of all our values, from the changing models of our cars, radios, clothing, buildings, to the turnover in husbands and wives, mores, best sellers, art styles, scientific theories, philosophies, beliefs, and economic and political structures.   In this rush our temporalistic time begins to devour its own children.   Before a new "model" has time to settle and become rooted, it is swept away or torn down by a still newer "model," or "fashion," or "pattern."   Not incidental, therefore, is the discovery of the sociologists of the nineteenth century that the "mode" and "fashion" are the lawgivers of our culture. *Fashion is indeed the most intimate child of our temporalistic mentality, while the "lasting tradition" is the child of the more eternalistic culture.*   Who does not know that "fashion" and "mode" rule our life?   And who does not know that the tempo of their

---

Therefore, it could not expect to be given a premium (profit, interest, etc.) just because the immediate enjoyment of the values was postponed.   It was no sacrifice for such a mentality. For the temporalistic mentality the situation is reversed.   Hence the difference in this particular point.   All this means that the *temporalistic and eternalistic mentalities evaluate very differently the past, the present, and the future movements of time and the various phenomena of life.*   This is a problem of great significance, which has been studied little, if at all.   I hope that sometime some really thoughtful scholar will give it the deep and systematic study which it fully deserves.

change is ever increasing? We are already half crazy in our desire to be "most modern," to have "the newest and the latest" model of everything. These are for us the best, regardless of whether they are rotten or good.

Nothing has sufficient time to crystallize. Everything is in a liquid state. Nothing has a chance to be tested for its good or bad qualities. We really do not know which of the incessantly changing "models" and values are good and which are poor. Therefore *the whole social life and the whole mentality are also in a liquid state, formless, shapeless, foggy, like a primeval protoplasm or a crowd of fleeting shadows.* One would look in vain, in this fog of shadows, for clear-cut boundary lines between the sinister and the benevolent, the good and bad, the true and false, the beautiful and ugly, the wholesome and harmful, right and wrong. The shadow values are so crowded, so foggy, they come and go so fast, that no such lines can be established. Hence the supreme reign of relativism in our mentality and culture — relativism of everything. *Hence a lack of any certainty, stability, and security in our mental and social life.* In this atmosphere of queer, dancing shadow values nobody can feel secure; nobody can have firm ground under his feet. We try our best to "adjust" ourselves to this continuous change. A hopeless task, more hopeless than that of Sisyphus. The only result of this desperate "adjustment of maladjustments" is exhaustion, fatigue, and the senseless state of "being busy doing nothing." How *can* we "adjust the maladjustments" increasingly created by an ever-increasing tempo of change? Our whole life becomes more and more maladjusted, and more and more human derelicts and wrecks are thrown on the shore of history by the rushing current of our temporalistic times. Instability is increasing everywhere, from the mind to the family, the church, industry, and the State.[38]

[38] In the light of these statements, the hopelessness and utter illogicality of the popular theory of maladjustments and the means of their elimination must be evident, even to the most thoughtless. It sees the source of social maladjustments in the lagging of the immaterial culture from the material, in the process of cultural change. It further contends that this lagging is the general law of social change. In addition, it claims that as time goes on the tempo of change of the material culture becomes progressively faster, and from this it concludes that the best and indeed the only way of adjustment of the maladjustments consists in an elimination of the lagging of the immaterial culture from the material in the process of change. It must be clear that if the lagging of the immaterial culture from the material is a general law, it will continue, in the present and in the future. Therefore the maladjustments will continue; therefore they cannot be eliminated; consequently, the attempt to eliminate them is doomed to failure. On the other hand, if the lagging can be eliminated, this means that the law of the lagging is not a law at all; that it is not even a prevalent uniformity; therefore the theory contradicts itself. In a word, it is remarkable in its sheer illogicality and self-contradiction, and one can but wonder how it could become the basic

The high tide of wars and revolutions of our time, of the multitude of internal and external disturbances that overcrowd it (see Chapters Ten to Thirteen of Volume Three of this work), is but one of the numerous manifestations of this instability, inseparable from temporalistic culture. Since everything is in flux and supposedly should be in the flux of the temporalistic deity of Evolution and Progress, social structures and organizations should be in flux also. Since we indefatigably build and tear down our steel and concrete skyscrapers, why not do the same to any social structure? Hence, one social shock follows another; one explosion after another occurs before our eyes. Nothing lasting or eternal is found in these conditions. Everybody is supposed to be entitled to make a revolution, a reconstruction, a reorganization, and almost everybody does. The result is a triumphant instability, a fleeting change of regimes, gluttonous competition, forever new and ever bolder social "experiments," with inevitable anarchy on the one hand and a rule of the boldest coercion on the other. The experimenters are permeated by the same temporalistic mentality: "Though short, my hour of triumph!" "Though short-lived, what an adventure and what a thrill!"

And all this is accompanied by the "*for tomorrow is uncertain*" creed. Yes, almost everybody now feels that in various forms. Certainty and certitude, the safety which is based upon it, the security which demands it — all is evaporating. Hardly anyone nowadays, from the dictator to the unemployed, feels any certainty of the morrow. No new scientific theory is expected to live for long; even when it appears, it does not claim either certainty or certitude; it is regarded as "the first approximation," "a mere hypothesis," and any cautious scientist and scholar expects, of course, that soon it will be blasted by a still newer theory. Science has also become "fleeting" and is changing more and more rapidly. Still less certainty exists in the philosophical and religious beliefs. Relativity of the ethical values is triumphant. They are expected to change, as a mere matter of fact, and any moral command is expected to be reversed. There is still less certainty in economic life; from the rich to the poor, nobody feels sure that tomorrow they will not be confronted with ruin or unemployment, or some other catastrophe. Still less does one feel secure of the safety of his life from dictators, racketeers, and other vicious forces, and of the inviolability of his "inalienable rights as man and citizen." Friends are not certain of the everlasting contin-

theory in the semiofficial *Recent Social Trends* and how it could be subscribed to by a large number of sociologists, social workers, and social scientists. See W. F. Ogburn's *Social Change* and *Recent Social Trends*, Vol. I.

uation of their friendships. Instead of one "sweetheart," lovers expect to have dozens. Among wives and husbands divorce becomes more and more fashionable. Like a branch in a wild torrent each of us is carried on by the whirlpool of social life, knocked about, tossed and thrown, regardless of our wishes and efforts. We have little chance of being left quietly on the shore to take a breath and to take stock of where and what we are, what we are doing, and where we want to go. Instead, we are more and more "busy," more and more in a rush, more and more greedy to live faster and faster, "for tomorrow is uncertain." We forget entirely the wisdom that "doing nothing is better than to be busy doing nothing." "Business" — in both the narrow and wide meaning of this term — is our motto; and it means but an incessant Sisyphean "reconstruction," "readjustment," "change," "remodeling," tearing down and building up, no matter whether in the field of industry, of education, or in science, religion, art, philosophy, law, or what not.

We are prisoners of this curse of temporalism where, using Maltus's terminology, maladjustments grow in geometric ratio while our adjustments grow only in arithmetical ratio.

Thus our temporalistic culture grinds its values into a more and more relativistic dust; robs them of their lasting nature; reduces them constantly to the decreasing value of the ever-shorter "present moment." In this way it depreciates them, immanently, by its own hand and by its own destiny. Likewise, by its own immanent development — through its increasing tempo of change — it devours itself and prepares its own destruction. Steadily it makes itself more and more impossible, poisonous, deadly. In this way it paves the way for its own decline and for an ascendance of the eternalistic mentality, with its unhurried life, its rest, quiet repose, and static contemplation of eternal verities, or what is believed to be such.

E. If we glance at the spectrum of the mentality in the field by long periods, and attempt to ascertain the comparative strength of each of the five groups generally, and in each of the long periods, an answer is given by Table 19.

A glance at these figures shows that of the five currents of thought, mixed eternalism has been the most influential; next in order come the equilibrium current, mixed temporalism, and then pure temporalism and pure eternalism. Glancing at the totals of each of the three united currents, we see that the *eternalistic current has been the strongest throughout the whole period studied; then comes temporalistic and close to it the equilibrium current.* However, the comparative strength of the rivals

TABLE 19. COMPARATIVE STRENGTH OF ALL ETERNALISMS AND
ALL TEMPORALISMS

PERIOD	Eternalisms		Temporalisms		EQUILIB-RIUMS
	Pure	Mixed	Pure	Mixed	
600 B.C.–A.D. 100	18	75	179	136	317
100–600	0	194	29	11	341
600–1500	0	284	0	4	324
1500–1900	149	1337	131	767	481
1900–1920	47	268	37	382	109
Total	214	2158	376	1300	1572

All eternalisms, 2372   *All temporalisms*, 1676   *Equilibriums*, 1572

is not strikingly different; with some preponderance of eternalism, their strength has been fairly close to one another. Even the totals for pure temporalism and pure eternalism are not far different from each other. Considered that the periods studied are, in a sense, taken incidentally, such an approach of the total points of each of the three currents to one another is again suggestive of the principle of self-regulation of cultural processes. Forces hardly lending themselves to a detailed analysis somehow control the swings of the mentality in such a way that in the long run each of the currents gets its own prominence and approaches arithmetically to another in their comparative strength. If eternalism in its mild form is somewhat preponderant, perhaps the very essence of life and culture demands such a preponderance from the cultures that live and endure and create. Just as in the study of idealism and materialism we found out that idealism prevails over materialism, and that such a prevalence is perhaps necessary for the lasting existence of a creative culture, a phenomenon of the same kind seems to be met here. However it may be, the comparative similarity of the strength as well as the principle of balance and self-regulation are suggested again here.

When we take the figures for the specific periods, we find deep contrasts and differences from period to period. The spectrum of the period A.D. 600 to 1500 and then from A.D. 100 to 600 is decidedly eternalistic; the spectrum of the periods 440 B.C. to A.D. 100, 1900 to 1920, and then 1500 to 1900 is either predominantly temporalistic or temporalistic in a degree much greater than the spectrum of the first groups of the periods.

F. Finally, the preceding data and comments teach us again that what appears to be truth fluctuates; in the predominantly eternalistic times the eternalistic theories receive the credit of being truth, and are believed in; in the temporalistic mentality the theories of change-evolution-progress acquire an infective and convincing power. Studying these fluctuations, we see again that they have been going on hand in hand with those of the three main systems of truth, which in their turn are but one of the elements or aspects of the rise and fall of the Ideational, Idealistic, and Sensate cultures.

As a practical moral to be drawn from that, the following words can be addressed to the partisans of eternalism, temporalism, and equilibrium: "If the temporalists are now in the saddle, they have reason to rejoice; their creed is dominant, and any domination is inducive to rejoicing. But let their joy, as well as the regret of the eternalists, be not too great; sooner or later, temporalism will decline and eternalism will become triumphant again. If eternalism today is subdued, this means that it will be dominant tomorrow. So it has been, and so it probably will be in the future. For this reason the factions should not necessarily war with each other and should perhaps be inclined to believe that not all the truth is in their own credo and not all the credo of their adversary is error and blunder. The pure truth and the whole truth is possibly "white" and contains in itself the eternal as well as the temporal aspects: Being and Becoming, permanence and flux, eternity and moment. This, however, is only my personal credo and metaphysics; therefore it is not obligatory for anybody else to accept it. What may be obligatory is the fact of the fluctuation of these mentalities and their logical and functional integration with Ideational and Sensate cultures.

G. That this association is not limited to the Graeco-Roman and the Western cultures has briefly been shown already. The Ideational mentality of the Hindu, the Taoist, the Tibetan cultures has certainly been predominantly eternalistic in its conception of the true reality; of the true value — ethical, intellectual, and any other; of slow tempo in the change of their cultures and in all the other earmarks of these cultures. This statement appears to be so obvious and certain that there is hardly any need for its detailed corroboration. When the comparative decline of the Ideational mentality occurred, it led also to the decline of the eternalistic mentality; in this sense their fluctuation seems to show the same association.

Chapter Six

FLUCTUATION OF "FIRST PRINCIPLES": III. FLUCTUATION OF THE INFLUENCE OF REALISM, CONCEPTUALISM, AND NOMINALISM [1]

I. PRELIMINARIES

For many the inclusion of this topic may appear somewhat strange. If they have any idea of what these terms mean, they may ask : Why, in a sociological work, deal with such a topic, which is seemingly too specific and (some may add) superannuated and already decided once and forever. Why revive this favorite problem of the Scholastics in our "scientific age"? Is it not certain that, beginning with W. Ockham, the medieval *universalia* are discarded and may have now, at the best, only a purely historical interest? These and similar questions may arise in the mind of many a reader. My answer to these is that even granted that the problem has now only a purely historical interest, one can afford to study the course of these three streams of thought for the sake of mere curiosity, just as we study the change and fluctuation of various beliefs, mores, convictions, ideologies. However, there are many other and much more important reasons. The struggle of these currents is in no way ended, explicitly or implicitly. One of these three principles is assumed and lies at the foundation of many scientific, philosophical, and religious conceptions of the present time. The problem is not dead at all, but is living a full-blooded life. It makes one of the most basic principles of science and mentality. Upon an assumption of one of these rival streams depend a great many theories and intellectual constructions of a specific character. Like idealism-materialism, empiricism-rationalism-mysticism, determinism-indeterminism, and a few other principles, the theory of realism-nominalism is one of the most general and contains fundamental principles which compose a framework for the system of truth and knowledge of a given period. More than that. Many an actual problem of the social sciences, especially such as individualism-collectivism, society and the individual, universalism and singularism, are most closely tied

[1] In co-operation with N. O. Lossky and I. I. Lapshin.

243

up with this problem and can hardly be studied fruitfully without its preliminary investigation.   Moreover, the real movement of these currents is rather different from what we read in many a work on the history of philosophy.   Finally, we shall inquire into the relationship between these two currents of thought and our types of culture.   Is there any connection between them, and if there is, what is it?   These reasons are sufficient to explain why the problem is introduced here and why a considerable amount of work is given to its elucidation.   Now for a few explanatory definitions.

By *logico-ontological realism* is meant a system of thought which claims that in all singularistic objects or subjects of the same class, which exist singularistically at different points of space — for instance, horses or dogs or stars — there is, besides their specifically individual differences, some essence or element which is common to all of them and which composes, so to speak, their essence or their *universalia*.   Horse A may be white, horse B brown, but besides this and other differences, A and B have an element, say "horsiness," which is the same in both and in all horses, and without which A and B cannot exist; neither could we style A and B as "horses," put them into one class, and have a concept or definition of a horse generally if they lacked this element.   Just because such an identical, generic element or, better, a superspatial and supertimely essence universal to all horses exists objectively outside our minds, we are able to create a general concept of a horse, and this concept is not something which exists only in our minds but is something that corresponds to the transsubjective reality, be it transcendental or immanent.   In this sense, such generic concepts, such *universalia*, are neither a mere fiction nor a mere idea of our minds, but in a sense they are the "holy of holies," the very essence of reality itself, not to mention the fact that they are the heart and soul of our knowledge.   In brief, logico-ontological realism insists that the generic concept — be it of a triangle generally, a man generally, a horse, atom, number, society, organism, a social class generally — exists really in our mind as well as outside of it in the transsubjective world, in the forms of the *universalia*.

This general essence, the *universalia*, the "horsiness" in our case, is what Plato called the *idea* (εἶδος) of a given singular individual; it composes, not the individual, but the generic essence of it, the essence which is superspatial and supertimely.   As such, in our example, it is given in both and in all horses, though not in the space occupied by either horse A or horse B.   This means that realism contends that the *identity* of the essence of all the singular phenomena of the same class is embraced by the same generic or general concept. Plato's *idea*, Aristotle's *form*, Christianity's concept of the identity of the members of the Holy Trinity (the Father, the Son, the Holy Spirit), Plotinus's *Logos* (Noûs), the ultimate realities of many philosophers, are examples of such a realism. In this, as well as in many other respects, it has several variations. Logico-ontological realism may be, for instance, *transcendental or immanent* or *transcendental-immanent*. When a realist claims that ideas which exist in the Divine Mind and compose the Kingdom of Ideas are transcendental to the objects learned through experience, we have *transcendental realism*. In this sense, many a philosopher has interpreted, for instance, the philosophy of Plato.[2]

For a transcendental realism, the abstract generic concepts exist *ante rem* only, but neither *in re* nor *post rem*. The immanent realism contends that the ideas in the sense of the realistic *universalia* are immanent to the phenomenal world of the singular objects. It claims that the *universalia* exist *in re*. Aristotle's theory is an example of such an immanent realism. Others, like Plotinus, teach that the *universalia* exist in the mind of God (Noûs) as well as *in re;* that is, they are, at the same time, immanent to the empirical world of singular objects. In other words, they claim that the *universalia* exist *ante rem* and *in re*. Such a theory is a synthesis of *transcendental as well as immanent realism*. In addition to this, many a philosopher says that our *knowledge* about the *universalia ante rem* and *in re* is obtained through experience and other forms of intellectual activity (abstraction, comparison, etc.); for this reason the *universalia* exist also *post rem*. In such case, exemplified for instance by St. Thomas Aquinas, the *universalia* exist *ante rem, in re,* and *post rem*. Of these varieties, the realism which claims the reality of the *universalia in re* (*in re* only; *ante rem* and *in re; ante rem, in re,* and *post rem; in re* and *post rem*) is possibly the most genuine logico-ontological realism. It insists that all the singular objects or phenomena which belong to the same class have an identical generic essence, which is present in all of them and without which their singular qualities cannot constitute what they are. The purely transcendental realism, which contends that the *universalia* exist in the Divine Mind only, *ante rem*, and are transcendental to empirical objects, may be regarded in a sense as a pseudo realism: since the ideas exist only in the transcendental kingdom or in the Divine Mind, and God creates the empirico-singular objects,

[2] Professor Lossky and some other philosophers contend, not without reason, that such an interpretation of Plato's philosophy underestimates his theory of the "participation" of phenomenal objects in the world of ideas.

according to these ideas (concepts), but each object as a singular individuality, separated ontologically from other individualities of the same class, these individualities can have only a *similarity* to another one, but not an *identity* of essence.[3]

Such a similarity deviates from the very core of realism, namely, that the singular objects of the same class have the identity of their essence and therefore the generic concepts of such classes correspond to that reality and as such are real themselves.

Likewise realism which accepts the existence of the *universalia* or generic concepts only *post rem* but not *in re* is conceptualism rather than a genuine realism. The latter becomes void as soon as the thesis that the *universalia* exist *in re* is neglected. At the same time it is to be noted that in the Appendix classification of the thinkers into realists, nominalists, and conceptualists, we put into the class of the realists all those who, according to their own opinions, regarded themselves as realists and were opposed to nominalism and conceptualism, though somewhat neglecting the existence of the *universalia in re* as the central point of realism.

Besides this difference, realists differ in several other respects from one another. For instance, some of them regard the *universalia* as substance (*e.g.*, Clarenbaldus, Bernard of Chartres, and others); the singular individuals of the same genus or species are for them but a mere modality of one and the same substance common to all of them and identical in all of them. Such "modalists" are the extreme realists. The other realists consider the *universalia* as a sum of characteristics or statuses identical in all the singular individuals of the same genus or species or class (the *Status-Lehre* in the terminology of many German investigators). Theories of Walter of Montagne or Gualterus of Mauretania are examples of that. Evidently such a realism is moderate.

These and other secondary differences among the realists do not, however, play any role in our classification and computation. The extreme as well as the moderate, the transcendental as well as the immanent and mixed realists, all are put into the class of the realists and computed as such.

[3] Such, for instance, is Leibnitz's monadology: each monad is so absolutely separated ontologically from all the others that no interaction is possible between them; their activities are co-ordinated with one another only through the pre-established harmony ordered by God. In such a conception, singular monads have only ontological similarity, but not identity with one another. This, perhaps, is the reason why Leibnitz regarded himself as a nominalist, though all his system, with its theory of the unborn ideas, with the divine plan of the world, with eternal verities in God, with the world considered as a realization of the divine plan — *Cum Deus cogitat et cogitationem exercet, fit mundus* — such a system is certainly not nominalistic, and is either realistic or conceptualistic. Some of the historians of philosophy regard him as a realist, the others, conceptualist.

The second fundamental current in this field is *conceptualism*. In contradistinction to realism, it states that in the transsubjective world there exist only singular or individual objects — horse A, horse B, horse S, each occupying a different position in space and time. They may be similar in regard to various properties, but they are neither identical nor quantitatively the same. In other words, in the transsubjective world there is no "horsiness." The cognizant subject perceives only the singular and individual impressions of things and objects and cannot perceive any *universalia*. However, in our mind these impressions and perceptions of the singular objects undergo a process of transformation into the general and generic concepts, the *universalia*. In the process of our thinking about the general, a special nonsensory (not supersensory) cognition of it enters in and transforms the singular impressions and images into an abstract concept. Many conceptualists explain such a transformation by a comparison of various singular impressions from similar objects, the retention from these impressions of those traits which are similar in all the compared objects, and the rejection of the traits that are dissimilar. Out of the similar traits we create the generic concept, which becomes in our mind a substitute for each of the singular objects compared.

These concepts exist in our mind as concepts; we think with them; we operate with them. Thus conceptualism occupies an intermediary position between realism and nominalism. With realism it agrees in that the general concepts exist in our mind, but disagrees in that the *universalia* exist in the *transsubjective* world. With nominalism it agrees in that there are no *universalia* in the transsubjective world, but disagrees in admission of the reality of the *universalia* in our mind — which is denied by nominalism.

Like realism, conceptualism has several varieties. For our purposes here it is unnecessary to enter into their description.

Finally *nominalism* is the opposite pole to realism. It contends that there are no *universalia* either in the transsubjective or subjective worlds. In *rerum natura, extra nos et praeter nos* there exists nothing which corresponds to any concept or *universalia*. Outside us only the singular objects are given. In our mind also there are only singular images and impressions, but no real concepts. What is regarded as concept is practically a mere word or symbol which we use, but, using it, we always think in terms of a singular object — horse A or horse B, in our case. We do not and cannot think about any "horsiness" or "horse generally." Thus it claims that the generic essences are nonexistent in the transsubjective as well as subjective worlds. A simulacrum of a concept in our mind is a kind of illusion, due to a mere association of various singular impressions with the same *word or symbol*. Using the word "horse" for A, B, C, we are prone to believe that the identity of the word in all such cases means the existence of the identity of the objects compared, or the concept. Meanwhile, it is mainly an identity of the word used, and nothing more. From this it is comprehensible why the current is styled by the name of nominalism (*universalia sunt nomina*).

Like the rival currents, nominalism has also many varieties. Some — the extreme nominalists — claim that when thinking about a generic class we have in our mind merely a word and nothing more. Others, less extreme, admit that besides the word we have at that moment also singular images of various individuals of the class. Others, like Berkeley, go so far as to approach imperceptibly conceptualism in this respect. Likewise the explanations of how and why we are prone to take a mere word and symbol for a real concept differ from nominalist to nominalist. But again these secondary points are unessential for our purposes and therefore can be omitted.

Such are the main currents in the field of this fundamental problem. As mentioned before, its fundamentality must be obvious to every person who is not a total stranger either to science or to thought generally. What are all the concepts and definitions and generalizations of science, from mathematics to sociology? Are they mere fictions or artificial images in our mind to which nothing corresponds in the *rerum natura?* Are they, in this sense, a kind of illusion with which we build an illusionary world which may last for some time but which sooner or later is bound to vanish and disappear? Or are they something which exists in our mind as well as in the reality outside it? As soon as the question is put in that form, it becomes axiomatic that the problem of nominalism-realism did not originate in the Middle Ages (though the terms did) but began with the conscientious thought of man, and continues to this day. It exists today and will exist as long as human thought. And indeed, from the earliest date at which our quantitative study begins it is present, is discussed, and answered. On the other hand, when a contemporary physicist or chemist or mathematician — not to mention the social scientist — creates his definition of number, space, time, force, matter, atom, "species" (in taxonomy), religion, social class, demand and supply, economic phenomenon, State, law, culture, cause and effect, and so on, any such scientist or scholar is confronted with the problem; he cannot escape it and gives — explicitly or implicitly, conscientiously or not —

his answer to it. More than that: giving the answer, he gives it along one of the currents outlined here. With a reasonable degree of certainty, one may say that all the definitions and solutions of the problem which have been given, say, during the last few decades, fell within one of the variations of these three currents, and did not and cannot introduce anything fundamentally new which could be classified outside nominalism, conceptualism, and realism.

It is true that many scientists and scholars, especially those who, knowing little about Scholasticism, like to express their contempt for it and for the Middle Ages generally, remind one often of Molière's hero, who, talking prose, was unaware that he was talking prose. Similarly, many such a scientist and scholar, factually giving his finished solution of the problem, is unaware that he is doing — and often rather poorly — exactly what the medieval Scholastics — who are blamed so much for their "silly and sterile Scholasticism" — did in their day. The problem is eternal and unescapable at any time, regardless of whether we want to solve it or not. A study of the fluctuation of thought in that field is a study of one of the most fundamental and eternal problems of human thought, human science, and system of truth.

The next question to be asked is: What relationship does it bear to the main systems of truth and to the Ideational and Sensate types of culture respectively? Is there any connection between one of the systems of truth and culture, and one of the three currents in the field studied? If there is, what is it?

Deductively, we seem to be justified in expecting a certain relationship. Logically, *domination of the system of the truth of faith has to be followed by that of realism, the system of truth of senses by that of nominalism; and the system of truth of reason by that of conceptualism, followed by the currents of diluted realism as well as diluted nominalism.* The reasons for such an association are: since the truth of faith aims at eternal reality and since it is meant to be supersensory, the *universalia* of realism are the eternal reality sought for by the truth of faith. Also the world of Plato's ideas, Aristotle's forms, and the ultimate realities of various thinkers are the reality sought for by the truth of faith. Likewise, even in this phenomenal or empirical world, the reality of the generic "essences" or "concepts" or "*universalia*" is more important to the truth of faith than the reality of the singularistic empirical phenomena. In brief, logico-ontological realism and truth of faith are logically consistent and congenial; therefore, if human mentality in history is logical to some extent, it has to show this correlation and association. Similarly, truth of the senses (empiricism) and nominalism are twins in their logical nature. Both claim that we can know only the world of the senses. Both contend that in the world of the senses only singular objects can be perceived and no *universalia* are given. Both deny the autonomous creative function of human thought as such, the thought which transforms the singular impressions and images into the generic concepts. For both, *nihil esse in intellectu quod non fuerit prius in sensu.* For both, finally, simulacrum of concepts is a result of associations and combinations of singular images hypostatized with the help of a *nomen* (word) or symbol or "conditioned stimulus," but nonexistent as such. Therefore, if the thinkers of the period studied are logical, to some tangible extent parallelism in the movement of the curves of nominalism and empiricism is to be expected.

Finally, so far as the truth of reason is in a sense a blending of both extreme systems of truth, and so far as conceptualism occupies also an intermediary position between nominalism and realism and is in this sense their blend also, some association between the two has to be expected. So far as each of these systems of truth is an expression of the mentality of the Ideational, Idealistic, and Sensate cultures, the respective association of realism, conceptualism, and nominalism is to be expected, if the mentality of these cultures is logical.

Such, then, is the logical connection of these currents with the main types of cultures studied. Whether or not the expectation is corroborated by facts we shall see later.

After these preliminaries we can pass to the study of the fluctuations of these currents within the period investigated. The method and all the details of the study remain the same as in previous similar studies. The list of names in the Appendix to this chapter classified as realists, conceptualists, and nominalists gives an account of the material upon which Figure 13, Tables 20 and 21 are constructed. It is necessary to repeat here one remark. As has been mentioned, the existence of various gradations and variations of realism, conceptualism, and nominalism makes some thinkers' positions such that they can be classed, with some reason, either as realists or conceptualists, as nominalists or conceptualists. In other words, their position is not perfectly clear and definite. For instance, even such a prominent thinker as Abelard is classed usually as a conceptualist; meanwhile J. Reiners, in his *Der Nominalismus in der Frühscholastik*,[4] indicates, and not without reason, that he should be regarded as a nominalist rather than as a conceptualist. On the other hand, William Ockham almost unanimously is regarded as the initiator of

---

[4] Münster, 1910, pp. 41–59.

nominalism, as its main and earliest supporter. However, in more recent times, several investigators (like Ueberweg[5] and Gilson[6]) are inclined to class him as a conceptualist rather than as a nominalist. These examples show what is meant by the "indefinite cases." Such a situation forced us to make our own decision as to the class in which such thinkers would better be put. Such a decision involved some amount of subjectivity. However, it is to be noted that in such a mass study as ours, such a subjectivity can hardly exert any important effect upon the results; if all these indefinite thinkers were put into the next congenial class instead, it would change little the essential movement of the curves of these three currents.

Now turn to the study of the fluctuation. Tables 20 and 21 and Figure 13 give the results by 20-year and by 100-year periods, indicating the number as well as the weight of the representatives of each current in each period.[7]

II. MAIN RESULTS

The main results given by Tables 20 and 21 can be summed up as follows.

A. If the whole period from 540 B.C. to A.D. 1920 is taken, there is no perpetual trend of a continuous increase or decrease of any of these currents in the course of time, whether by 20-year or 100-year periods. Instead, we have trendless fluctuation, increase and decrease of each of these currents. The same is true in regard to either Graeco-Roman or Western culture, taken separately.

B. Measured by the presence or absence of each of these currents there is no progress of Spencerian differentiation and integration in this field of thought in the course of time. The series opens with a monopolistic domination of realism. Subsequently conceptualism (460–440 B.C.) and then nominalism appear. The field becomes thus progressively differentiated. But beginning with A.D. 280–300, one of the streams,

[5] B. Geyer, *Die Patristische und Scholastische Philosophie*, in Ueberweg's *Geschichte der Philosophie* (Berlin, 1928), pt. ii, p. 575.

[6] E. Gilson, *La philosophie au moyen âge* (Paris, 1922), Vol. II, pp. 97 ff.

[7] Besides the works quoted before and in later chapters, the following additional works were used for the study of this fluctuation.

K. von Prantl, *Geschichte der Logik im Abendlande*, 4 vols. (Leipzig, 1855–1885); F. Exner, *Ueber Nominalismus und Realismus* (Leipzig, 1842); J. Loewe, *Der Kampf zwischen dem Realismus und Nominalismus* (Stuttgart, 1876); M. Offner, *Nominalismus und Realismus* (Berlin, 1919); J. Reiners, *op. cit.* (*Beiträge zur Geschichte der Philosophie des Mittelalters*); A. K. Kühtmann, *Zur Geschichte des Terminismus* (Leipzig, 1911); A. Dempf, *Die Hauptform Mittelalterischer Weltanschauung* (München and Berlin, 1925).

TABLE 20.   MOVEMENT OF NOMINALISM, CONCEPTUALISM, AND REALISM FROM 540 B.C. TO A.D. 1920 BY 20-YEAR PERIODS

PERIOD	Number of Representatives			Indicators of Weight			Comparative Weight in Percentages		
	Nominalism	Conceptualism	Realism	Nominalism	Conceptualism	Realism	Nominalism	Conceptualism	Realism
540–520 B.C.	0	0	1	0	0	8	0	0	100
520–500	0	0	1	0	0	8	0	0	100
500–480	0	0	2	0	0	15	0	0	100
480–460	0	0	3	0	0	13	0	0	100
460–440	0	1	3	0	5	9	0	36	64
440–420	1	2	4	8	11	14	24	33	42
420–400	7	2	4	27	14	21	43.5	22.5	34
400–380	6	1	7	25	8	27	42	13	45
380–360	3	1	5	15	8	21	34	18	48
360–340	7	1	5	19	1	23	44	2	54
340–320	6	1	3	10	1	18	34	3	62
320–300	8	1	6	15	1	29	33	2	64
300–280	9	1	6	23	8	19	46	16	38
280–260	7	2	3	23	13	7	54	30	16
260–240	5	1	1	17	5	1	74	22	4
240–220	9	3	2	28	13	2	65	30	5
220–200	3	2	2	8	8	4	40	40	20
200–180	3	3	1	4	6	3	31	46	23
180–160	2	2	1	2	6	2	20	60	20
160–140	2	2	1	3	6	2	27	55	18
140–120	1	2	1	2	6	1	22	67	11
120–100	1	4	1	2	8	1	18	73	9
100–80	5	4	1	9	10	1	45	50	5
80–60	4	4	2	7	12	9	25	43	32
60–40	4	11	3	18	22	17	31.5	38.5	30
40–20	2	6	2	9	9	13	29	29	42
20–0	1	3	3	1	6	5	8	50	42
0–20 A.D.	1	2	3	1	3	11	7	20	73
20–40	1	1	2	1	1	10	8	8	84
40–60	1	2	2	1	12	10	4	52	44
60–80	1	4	2	1	19	5	4	76	20
80–100	2	2	2	7	11	11	24	38	38
100–120	1	1	7	6	6	21	18	18	64
120–140	3	4	8	6	12	25	14	28	58
140–160	4	3	12	7	6	32	15	13	71
160–180	3	1	12	4	6	36	9	13	78
180–200	3	2	15	6	12	48	9	18	72
200–220	2	2	8	9	7	32	19	15	66
220–240	2	2	4	7	7	21	20	20	60
240–260	2	1	8	2	1	37	5	2.5	92.5
260–280	3	1	6	4	1	22	15	4	81
280–300	3	0	3	5	0	10	33	0	67
300–320	2	0	4	3	0	18	14	0	86
320–340	5	0	5	13	0	19	41	0	59
340–360	2	0	4	5	0	12	29	0	71
360–380	2	0	6	2	0	34	6	0	94
380–400	2	0	5	6	0	28	18	0	82
400–420	1	0	5	5	0	19	21	0	79
420–440	1	0	5	3	0	20	13	0	87
440–460	2	0	3	6	0	13	32	0	68
460–480	1	0	3	3	0	14	18	0	82

TABLE 20. MOVEMENT OF NOMINALISM, CONCEPTUALISM, AND REALISM FROM 540 B.C. TO A.D. 1920 BY 20-YEAR PERIODS — *continued*

PERIOD	Number of Representatives			Indicators of Weight			Comparative Weight in Percentages		
	Nominalism	*Conceptualism*	*Realism*	*Nominalism*	*Conceptualism*	*Realism*	*Nominalism*	*Conceptualism*	*Realism*
480–500 A.D.	1	0	3	1	0	13	7	0	93
500–520	1	0	6	1	0	21	5	0	95
520–540	2	0	6	5	0	28	15	0	85
540–560	1	0	5	4	0	16	20	0	80
560–580	0	0	1	0	0	2	0	0	100
580–600	0	0	1	0	0	4	0	0	100
600–620	0	0	1	0	0	4	0	0	100
620–640	0	0	1	0	0	6	0	0	100
640–660	0	0	1	0	0	6	0	0	100
660–680	0	0	2	0	0	8	0	0	100
680–700	0	0	1	0	0	2	0	0	100
700–720	0	0	1	0	0	3	0	0	100
720–740	0	0	2	0	0	8	0	0	100
740–760	0	0	1	0	0	5	0	0	100
760–780	0	0	1	0	0	1	0	0	100
780–800	0	0	1	0	0	4	0	0	100
800–820	0	0	2	0	0	6	0	0	100
820–840	0	0	2	0	0	6	0	0	100
840–860	0	0	2	0	0	12	0	0	100
860–880	0	0	2	0	0	11	0	0	100
880–900	0	0	2	0	0	5	0	0	100
900–920	0	0	2	0	0	4	0	0	100
920–940	0	0	1	0	0	2	0	0	100
940–960	0	0	1	0	0	1	0	0	100
960–980	0	0	1	0	0	1	0	0	100
980–1000	0	0	1	0	0	3	0	0	100
1000–1020	0	0	2	0	0	5	0	0	100
1020–1040	0	0	1	0	0	2	0	0	100
1040–1060	0	0	2	0	0	5	0	0	100
1060–1080	0	0	5	0	0	19	0	0	100
1080–1100	1	0	4	3	0	17	15	0	85
1100–1120	2	0	5	4	0	14	22	0	78
1120–1140	2	0	10	7	0	27	21	0	79
1140–1160	1	0	13	4	0	34	10.5	0	89.5
1160–1180	0	0	7	0	0	15	0	0	100
1180–1200	0	0	6	0	0	12	0	0	100
1200–1220	0	0	12	0	0	24	0	0	100
1220–1240	0	0	8	0	0	19	0	0	100
1240–1260	0	0	11	0	0	30	0	0	100
1260–1280	1	0	14	6	0	52	10	0	90
1280–1300	1	0	19	9	0	52	15	0	85
1300–1320	1	0	17	3	0	51	6	0	94
1320–1340	4	0	14	16	0	32	33	0	67
1340–1360	8	0	8	22	0	18	55	0	45
1360–1380	7	0	2	13	0	8	62	0	38
1380–1400	4	0	1	10	0	3	77	0	23
1400–1420	1	0	1	4	0	4	50	0	50
1420–1440	1	0	4	4	0	11	27	0	73
1440–1460	1	0	5	1	0	19	5	0	95
1460–1480	1	0	3	3	0	13	19	0	81
1480–1500	1	0	2	3	0	2	60	0	40

TABLE 20.   MOVEMENT OF NOMINALISM, CONCEPTUALISM, AND REALISM
FROM 540 B.C. TO A.D. 1920 BY 20-YEAR PERIODS — *continued*

PERIOD	Number of Representatives				Indicators of Weight				Comparative Weight in Percentages			
			Realism				Realism				Realism	
	Nominalism	*Conceptualism*	*Secular*	*Secular and Religious*	*Nominalism*	*Conceptualism*	*Secular*	*Secular and Religious*	*Nominalism*	*Conceptualism*	*Secular*	*Secular and Religious*
1500–1520	1	3	6	10	6	10	16	26	14	24	38	62
1520–1540	3	2	10	15	18	11	34	46	24	15	45	61
1540–1560	1	3	5	10	2	15	15	35	4	29	29	67
1560–1580	2	1	16	25	8	4	43	70	10	5	52	85
1580–1600	6	1	23	38	28	4	61	108	20	3	43.5	77
1600–1620	9	1	14	31	32	1	45	95	25	1	35	74
1620–1640	5	3	13	31	27	19	50	99	19	13	34	68
1640–1660	6	4	11	22	23	26	39	68	20	22	33	58
1660–1680	10	9	15	26	36	39	47	85	22	24	29	53
1680–1700	19	3	29	48	69	15	87	133	32	7	40	61
1700–1720	14	4	19	39	54	29	51	94	31	16	29	53
1720–1740	12	12	7	18	51	26	26	50	40	20	20	39
1740–1760	20	10	8	12	82	45	34	46	47	26	20	27
1760–1780	24	12	5	12	106	57	22	38	53	28	11	19
1780–1800	21	19	14	22	83	69	53	70	37	31	24	32
1800–1820	17	30	28	36	55	88	90	112	22	34	35	44
1820–1840	17	15	32	52	69	55	120	167	24	19	41	57
1840–1860	29	9	55	78	117	31	175	227	31	8	47	61
1860–1880	49	17	36	57	239	68	142	186	49	14	29	37
1880–1900	66	43	37	82	275	157	160	254	40	23	23	37
1900–1920	80	46	44	90	322	173	186	276	42	22	24	36

conceptualism, disappears, and then, after A.D. 560, nominalism disappears also.   Thus, instead of further differentiation, we have the opposite movement, from the more to the less differentiated and a return to the initial simplicity.   After A.D. 1080 the opposite direction — toward increasing differentiation — again appears and continues practically up to the present time.   Here again, then, we have a result similar to those obtained in many fields before.

C. Studying the ups and downs of each of the currents, we see a tangible, factual corroboration of the logical deductions concerning the correlation of realism with the truth of faith and Ideational culture; of nominalism with the truth of the senses and Sensate culture; and, to a less degree, of conceptualism with the truth of reason and Idealistic culture.   The sixth century B.C. — the period of the domination of the truth of faith and Ideational culture — appears monopolistically realistic. The fifth and fourth centuries represent a balance of realism and nominalism, about fifty-fifty, with an admixture of conceptualism.   Though the fourth century gives the per cent of realism as slightly higher than

TABLE 21. MOVEMENT OF NOMINALISM, CONCEPTUALISM, AND REALISM FROM 600 B.C. TO A.D. 1900 BY 100-YEAR PERIODS

PERIOD	Number of Representatives			Indicators of Weight			Comparative Weight in Percentages		
	Nominalism	Conceptualism	Realism	Nominalism	Conceptualism	Realism	Nominalism	Conceptualism	Realism
600–500 B.C.	0	0	1	0	0	8	0	0	100
500–400	7	3	8	27	19	42	31	22	47
400–300	20	2	15	53	9	71	40	7	53
300–200	19	4	9	56	21	24	55	21	24
200–100	6	8	3	9	16	6	29	52	19
100–0	10	18	8	28	32	27	32	37	31
0–100 A.D.	3	8	6	8	29	24	13	48	39
100–200	6	6	29	17	24	90	13	18	69
200–300	6	2	18	15	7	72	16	7	77
300–400	9	0	13	22	0	62	26	0	74
400–500	4	0	11	12	0	40	23	0	77
500–600	2	0	11	5	0	38	12	0	88
600–700	0	0	3	0	0	12	0	0	100
700–800	0	0	3	0	0	12	0	0	100
800–900	0	0	6	0	0	23	0	0	100
900–1000	0	0	3	0	0	7	0	0	100
1000–1100	1	0	7	3	0	24	11	0	89
1100–1200	3	0	27	8	0	66	11	0	89
1200–1300	2	0	50	9	0	131	6	0	94
1300–1400	15	0	29	39	0	82	32	0	68
1400–1500	3	0	9	8	0	26	24	0	76

PERIOD	Nominalism	Conceptualism	Realism		Nominalism	Conceptualism	Realism		Nominalism	Conceptualism	Realism	
			Secular	Secular and Religious			Secular	Secular and Religious			Secular	Secular and Religious
1500–1600	11	5	44	74	54	20	127	215	19	7	44	74
1600–1700	35	13	59	128	120	54	173	364	22	10	32	68
1700–1800	67	43	46	92	258	158	156	256	38	24	23	38
1800–1900	137	91	144	244	531	301	376	577	38	21	27	41

that of the fifth (53 and 47 per cent respectively), in the fourth century B.C. the nominalism is also reinforced at the cost of the milder conceptualism, and gained even more than did realism. Subsequent centuries, the third and the second B.C., give a decisive decrease of realism in favor of nominalism and conceptualism. Thus, in the history of Greek and Hellenistic culture we see a quite unmistakable association of the movement of these currents with their logical "partners." The same result is obtained if one takes 20-year periods instead of century periods.

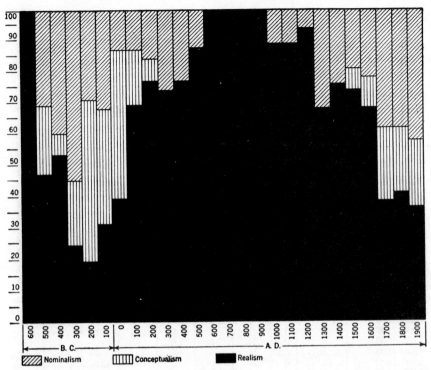

FIG. 13.   MOVEMENTS OF NOMINALISM, CONCEPTUALISM, AND REALISM

Association continues to be quite tangible in the subsequent period. Beginning with the second century A.D., realism starts to grow again and its rivals begin to decline.   After the fifth century A.D., realism, like the truth of faith and other earmarks of the Ideational culture, becomes monopolistic and reigns supreme up to the twelfth century.   Then nominalism emerges again, but during the first few centuries remains a small rivulet.   We saw the same change occur in regard to the re-emergence of the truth of reason and the senses, and the other earmarks of the Idealistic and Sensate cultures.   The parallelism is not exactly perfect, but quite evident.   Even most of the minor fluctuations are parallel. For instance, in the fifteenth century, in the field of the system of truth as well as in that of eternalism and other compartments of culture, we have noticed a temporary reaction toward Ideationalism.   We see the same reaction here in favor of realism.

Finally, after the thirteenth century, notwithstanding these minor reactions, we witness a steady trend of a rising tide of nominalism, and especially of conceptualism, at the cost of the retreating tide of realism.

So far we have again a complete agreement of the logical expectations and the actual data. Again, logically, due integration is followed by the causal-functional. Accordingly, we are justified in our contention that increase or decrease of an influence of one of the systems of truth is an ingredient of the growth or decline of the respective types of culture. In its turn, the fluctuation of the systems of truth involves a fluctuation of the acceptance and rejection of many theories in different fields of human thought — among them realism, conceptualism, and nominalism. Increase or decrease of their influence, their acceptability, and their "convincingness" or "scientific validity" is thus due not so much to their logical validity per se as to the type of the rising culture. When the Sensate culture rises, nominalism begins to appear more and more "scientific" and "true" to the leading minds and thinkers of the period. When the Ideational tide is rising, realism appears to be more and more "scientifically valid." In this sense, "validity" of each of these currents is a function of the type of culture which rises and declines. So we have again a corroboration of the claim that truth, or what appears to be truth to the human mind, is in a great degree a reflection of the transformation of the whole culture. In other words, human truth is a sociological category, in a great degree, and cannot be understood without a consideration of the culture in which it lives and functions. As stressed, this does not make illogical any of these cultures. By the same logic, they all are logical within their major premises, but their premises are different. Such a difference in premises does not prevent me from being an absolutist in the field of the complete truth. But such a whole truth is never given in full to our minds and exists only in the Divine Mind or is a goal toward which mankind eternally strives; at any given moment one grasps some part or aspect or approximation of it, but never the whole truth and the only truth.[8]

[8] That the association studied is not incidental and is not limited by the cultures studied is shown by verification of the associations in "social space," in the mentality of other logically integrated cultures. We know already that the Brahmanic culture of India and the Taoist culture of China are Ideational in all their essential characteristics. If the association holds beyond the cultures studied, we shall expect that the predominant current in these cultures will be realism. Even a superficial study of the Hindu and Taoist thought is sufficient to show that the dominant solution of the problem by the Hindu and Taoist thought was indeed realistic, with an admixture of a mild conceptualism and with slight flurries of nominalistic conceptions, mainly in the insignificant rivulets of materialism and sensualism, which once in a while become noticeable in the history of these cultures, but which have always been purely secondary and unimportant. (See above.) Such a testimony is an indication that the associations claimed are neither incidental nor purely local nor confined to the Graeco-Roman and Western cultures.

D. Coming to the time we live in, we see that the eighteenth, nineteenth, and twentieth centuries have been the period when realism has been at its lowest. One has to retreat to the third, second, and first centuries B.C. to find as low an influence of realism. These centuries were the period of the domination of nominalism and especially conceptualism. However, beginning with about 1860, the further decline of realism is practically halted; likewise a further rise of nominalism (after 1880) and conceptualism is stopped. Whether this fact is one of the numerous short-time "flurries," after which the trend of the decline of realism is to be continued, or whether it is the beginning of the coming trend of rising realism, nobody can tell. What is important is that this symptom agrees with many similar "twists and turns" and "revolts" in most of the compartments of culture which we see at the end of the nineteenth and in the twentieth century. Here again our data are in agreement with the others and once more testify to the integrated character of our culture.

E. However high is the correlation outlined, it is not absolute. The movements of the curves of the systems of truth and of the currents studied are not identical. There are numerous secondary deviations, as can be seen from the curves of Figures 19 and 20. Similar secondary discrepancies we have seen in the relationship of the other sociocultural variables studied here. This fact means two things important to us.

(1) In the integrated cultures, the sociocultural mentality is *logical* to a very considerable degree; facts as they stand in our study are indeed close to the logical deductions from the nature of each of the variables considered. The thinkers who stress particularly the illogicality of human mentality are somewhat overshooting the mark, so far as the mentality of the cultures studied is concerned.

(2) The deviations signify that the mentality of the cultures and of the thinkers who embody it is not entirely logical; if the deviations were absent, it would have been; since the deviations are given, their existence and the degree of the discrepancy between the perfect correlation which logically follows and the tangible but imperfect association factually given, between the cultural variables studied, is an evidence and, in a sense, a measure of the amount of the illogicality of the mentality of the integrated cultures. Even the integrated cultures, in the field of their mentality, are in a degree illogical. So far as we deal with the logical integration, even within the compartments of various forms of social thought, the integration logically due is not perfectly followed by the causal one. The main reason for this, as explained above, is the

margin of immunity and autonomy which every system, including the system of thought, has. It permits it to live its own life, within a certain margin of autonomy. Incompleteness of data may be responsible for that also.

F. Of the other results given by the data, few deserve to be mentioned. In the courses on history of philosophy and science, it is customary to read that nominalism was started by W. Ockham; that it is, in contradistinction to realism, the only scientific standpoint in the field of the problem; that with the progress of science, nominalism has also been progressing; that the whole problem was started by the medieval Scholastics and represents a purely medieval phenomenon. In the light of the data given, we see that the problem is eternal, existed long before the Middle Ages, has existed in modern times, and will exist in the future. Next, we see that the nominalistic current re-emerged much earlier than is usually supposed: already in 1080–1100 nominalism composed 15 per cent of the total 100 per cent of all the three currents. Later, the data show that nominalism, empiricism, and scientific discoveries have advanced together, though the connection is far from being perfect. And what is still more important is that after the fifteenth century conceptualism grew much faster than nominalism and represented a current notably more powerful than it is customary to admit.[9]

G. Finally, if we sum up the number of the representatives, as well as the weight of each current, for the whole period studied, as well as for its main parts, we obtain the results shown in Table 22.

TABLE 22. CURRENTS IN NOMINALISM, CONCEPTUALISM, AND REALISM

PERIOD	NUMBER OF REPRESENTATIVES			INDICATORS OF WEIGHT		
	Nominalism	Conceptualism	Realism	Nominalism	Conceptualism	Realism
540 B.C.–A.D. 100	65	43	50	181	126	202
100–600	27	8	82	71	31	302
600–1500	24	0	137	67	0	383
1500–1900	250	152	538[1]	963	533	1412[1]
1900–1920	80	46	44	322	173	276
Total	446	249	851	1604	863	2575

[1] Both secular and religious realism.

[9] Therefore the customary qualification of nominalism as "progressive" and "scientific" and of realism or conceptualism as "reactionary" is also inaccurate. As a matter of fact, many a first-rate scientist and scholar, like Copernicus, Galileo, Harvey, Kepler, and more recently Hegel, Schelling, Galois, Cantor, Duhem, Mendel, were realists; the others, like Leibnitz, Descartes, were half realists.

These figures are interesting in several respects. We see that of the three currents, the most powerful has been realism, whether we take the number or the weight. This is a good warning to the too ardent partisans of nominalism not to overestimate it. If, however, we unite nominalism and conceptualism, then we get a curious equilibrium of the two currents for the whole period; by the number, nominalism and conceptualism taken together give 695 and realism 851; by the weight, the first two give 2467, while realism gives 2575. In both cases, we have a curious equality or counterbalancing of each of the currents by the other. As the period is not chosen specifically but is taken, so to speak, incidentally, such a balance suggests that each current embodies in itself a part of the truth and represents an aspect of the true reality; as such, each seems to perform an important function in the mental life of a culture, and as such is immortal in the history of human thought. It points again to what is styled here the principle of limit and a kind of an autonomous self-regulation of sociocultural processes in the field of the mentality of a given culture. Considering further that the influence of these currents in each of the subperiods is not even, the data suggest that for some periods one of the currents can grow at the expense of the others; but sooner or later in this process it is liable to reach the limit beyond which it cannot grow and has to recede and give way to the growth of its rival. So here again we meet with the phenomenon with which we have met many times already and which we shall meet many times again.

Another service of Table 22 is that in a concise way it gives the mental spectrum of each of the periods in regard to the problem studied. We see that the most even distribution of all of the three currents occurred in the periods 540 B.C. to A.D. 100 and 1900 to 1920; the most realistic period was 600 to A.D. 1500. So much for main conclusions. Now we can pass to a specific aspect of the problem of realism-nominalism in its sociological application. This problem has never been abstract and "academic" and has always been very concrete and important, though many a social thinker has not been aware of that. One of the purposes of the next chapter is to show that fact convincingly.[10]

---

[10] Here I can pay the promissory note given in Chapter Two of Volume One. Introducing the term "culture mentality" there, I pointed out a possible protest against it by the partisans of nominalism, who think that it is the only "scientific" and "valid" standpoint. Now we see that it is only one of three — and not the most powerful — standpoints. In the light of the above, the pretensions of the nominalists, especially in the social sciences, can easily be denied. They do not have any claim to be the exclusive trustees of truth and knowledge. This will be still clearer after a study of the next two chapters.

Chapter Seven

FLUCTUATION OF "FIRST PRINCIPLES": IV. FLUCTUATION OF
THE INFLUENCE OF SOCIOLOGICAL UNIVERSALISM AND
SINGULARISM[1]

I. MAIN CURRENTS IN THE FIELD

That the problem of realism-nominalism is an eternal and basic problem
has been shown in the preceding chapter. That it is not merely an
"academic" problem and has a direct bearing upon many an important
practical question is evidenced by the movements of such basic social
problems as that of sociological universalism and singularism, society and
the individual, collectivism and individualism, and still more by the
fluctuation of the purely juridical conceptions of juridical personality,
corporation, and the like. The problems: What is society? Is it a
reality that exists per se as a true reality, different from the mere sum of
its members (sociological realism), or is it a mere fiction, to which nothing
corresponds in the transsubjective or in the subjective world of mind, and
which is no more than a mere word, mere phantasma (sociological nominalism)? Or is it something that does not exist as reality in the transsubjective world but exists as a real concept in our mind (sociological
conceptualism)? Similar questions arise in regard to "social group,"
"real collectivity," "juridical personality," "corporation," "the State,"
and the like. These problems of *the ontological social reality are closely
connected with the socioethical aspect of these problems.* Which is the
supreme or the higher value, the individual or society? Which of
these is to be subordinated to the other? Or are they equal and inseparable? Shall social and political order be organized in such a way that the
individual and his values — life, liberty, creativeness, comfort, and the
like — be dominant and not restrained by any social considerations;
or, on the contrary, shall the *salus populi* be the *suprema lex*, and, for
the sake of the welfare of society, is the individual to be sacrificed
and restrained as much as the considerations of the *salus populi* may
demand?

[1] In co-operation with I. I. Lapshin, N. O. Lossky, N. S. Timasheff, and Peter B. Struve.

From this short outline it becomes evident at once that the problems of nominalism and realism are very concrete, very vital, and have an immediate bearing upon practical affairs. This is witnessed by the endless and most vivid discussions of these problems in the past and in the present; by the existence of the sociopolitical currents, from anarchism and individualism up to the liberal, communist, corporative, totalitarian states, Plato's Republic, absolutistic *Polizei-Staat;* by universalistic or singularistic principles used as the basis of thousands of practical policies; by enacted laws; by political and social revolutions for the sake and in the name of either *salus populi suprema lex* or the "inalienable rights of Man and Citizen." Thousands of lives have been sacrificed, and hundreds of thousands mutilated in the name and for the sake of one of such principles. Finally, even a social scientist who advertises his "antiphilosophical" standpoint cannot avoid being either a conceptualist or a nominalist or a realist, however enthusiastic he may be in his aversion to "all these scholastics"; as soon as he begins to define society, interaction, collective unity, or as soon as he starts an unavoidable discussion of the value of the individual and society, he becomes — explicitly or implicitly — either a nominalist or a realist or a conceptualist.[2] The same is true of most of the moralists, politicians, social workers, and "uplifters." They all are one of these, no matter whether they are aware or not of their nominalistic or realistic assumptions.

The purpose of this chapter is not to take sides with one of these solutions, but, as before, to classify numerous solutions and theories into a few main classes; then to inquire how, in the history of the Graeco-Roman and the Western cultures, each of these classes fared; which of them has been dominant in its influence, and during which period. Finally, what has been the reason for the fluctuations, and have they been tangibly connected with the fluctuations of the main types of culture studied here?

When one considers the respective theories, one can see at once that they present the problem mainly in two aspects: *the ontological and the ethical.* The ontological setting consists of an inquiry as to which of the two — the individual or society — is the primary and true reality. The answers given fall into three classes: the individual is the primary and true reality, while society is something either derivative or a mere sum of individuals (ontological singularism); society is the true and primary reality, while

---

[2] If one takes most texts and treatises in sociology and social science one can see this clearly. Many an anti-"metaphysical" sociologist talks either realistic, or conceptualistic, or nominalistic prose, like Monsieur Jourdain, without being aware of what he is talking.

the individual is the derivative phenomenon (ontological universalism) ; finally, the two are inseparable and represent two different aspects of the same reality (ontological "harmonism"). When the problem is taken ethically, it presents the question : Which of the two is the supreme value? Such a query leads also to three main answers : the individual is of supreme value, and society should be a mere means for the richer and ampler realization of the singularistic values of an individual — his safety, happiness, pleasures, etc. (ethical singularism) ; society is the primary value and the individual or singularistic interests should be subordinated to it (ethical universalism) ; finally, the singularistic and social interests are two aspects of the same value, therefore they are harmonious and in this sense equivalent (ethical harmonism). In this way, all the theories and answers to the problem could be divided into the three main classes of ontological and the three classes of ethical setting. If the respective thinkers were quite consistent, there would be practically only three main classes, in each of which the ontological and the ethical settings would coincide, namely, *ethico-ontological-singularism-individualism;* [3] *ethico-ontological-universalism-societalism; and ethico-ontological "harmonism."*

However, here, as in practically many other fields, such a logical consistency of the thinkers is not always to be found. It is a fairly frequent case when a thinker is universalist ontologically and singularist ethically, or vice versa. Not infrequently still more complex and fanciful combinations of the ethical and ontological aspects are given. Farther on, a series of thinkers subscribe to one of the solutions in one work and to a very different one in another. For these and similar reasons, the classification has to be somewhat modified in order to make it better fit the existing theories. Subsequently, all the theories in the field are classified into the following classes: (1) sociological singularism; (2) sociological universalism; (3) sociological mystic unity of individuals. A few commentaries follow to clear the meaning of each class.

A. *Sociological Singularism.* By this is meant any theory which claims that ontologically any society is a mere sum of its members and, apart from that, does not have any true reality per se. It is a sociological variety of nominalism. Like the latter, it contends that in the trans-

[3] The terms "singularism-universalism" were used by P. Struve in his article about the fundamental philosophical motives in the development of economic thought, in *Logos* (1910–1911), Bk. I; and in his book, *Khosiastvo i zena (Economy and Price)* (Moscow, 1913). He took them from Goethe's *"Sprüche"* in *"Prosa I. Ueber Naturwissenschaft,"* in *Einzelne Betrachtungen und Aphorismen,* and Goethe took them from the medieval Scholastic terminology which in its turn took them from Aristotle.

subjective social world there exist only individuals; that the existence of each individual is separate from the existence of other individuals; that they are not permeated existentially and ontologically by any identical entity; at the best they may be only singularistically similar, and therefore they are not parts of one organic and ontologically united whole. It is a kind of atomistic conception of society as an aggregate of singularistic individuals, behind and beyond which there is no ontological entity called society. Such being the general characteristics of sociological singularism, it gives further several varieties, due especially to the combination of the ontological with the ethical principles. Main subclasses of it are as follows.

(1) *Extreme or Consistent Sociological Singularism.* This states that the individual is the only social reality ontologically, and also that he is the supreme ethical value. It is atomistic-singularistic, not only in its sociological ontology, but also in its system of values; all its primary values are those of singularistic existence; security and safety of the individual, his happiness, pleasures, comfort, liberty, etc. The superindividual and supersingularistic or social values are, in this system, at the best purely derivative and aimed to be the means to the singularistic values : society is of value only in so far as it serves the purpose of securing the life and happiness of the individual. In such a setting, the ethical system of the extreme singularism is almost always a system of the ethics of happiness in its hedonistic or eudaemonistic or utilitarian variety (see Chapter Thirteen). It is natural, therefore, that the curves of the extreme singularism and the ethics of happiness should go hand in hand to quite a perceptible degree. This current embraces a large variety of the thinkers, from the extreme hedonists of the *Carpe diem,* or the *après moi le deluge* types, up to the anarchists and moral individualists of the kind of Stirner and many others. It is ontological as well as ethical singularism or sociological nominalism.

(2) *Moderate Sociological Singularism.* Like the extreme form of singularism, it assumes the ontological reality of the singularistic individuals; but in its ethical aspect it insists that for any given individual not only he himself is the supreme value, but all the other individuals and society, as a sum of the individuals, are also the supreme values. So far, on its ethical side it is a deviation from the singularistic ethics to the social or universalistic ethics, interpreted atomistically as the sum of individuals or, in the familiar motto of utilitarianism, "the maximum of happiness for the maximum of the individuals." Ethically it is also connected with the moderate and sensible-eudaemonistic or utilitarian-

ethical systems. The liberalism of the nineteenth century, with its rights of man and citizen, with its maximum of happiness and liberty, and its rugged or soft individualism moderated by the equal interests of other individuals, is one of the best examples of this moderate singularism.

(3) *Collectivistic Sociological Singularism.* In its ontological aspect that society is a sum of the individuals, it has the same singularistic position as singularism generally, but in its ethical aspect it claims the priority and superiority of the value of the collectivity compared with that of the individual. It contends, therefore, that the individual and his interests should be subordinated to the social welfare and interests of the collectivity, that the individual should be dissolved, so to speak, in the collectivity. This peculiar combination of ontological singularism with ethical "regimentation" of the individual — often his complete suppression as a value — is due logically, among other things, to its empirico-materialistic conception of reality generally and social reality in particular. As for materialistic or hylozoistic empiricists, its partisans do not see any superempirical or ideal reality. Therefore, in contra-distinction to ontological universalists and mystics, they cannot postulate any reality of society apart and independent of that of its members. On the other hand, for various practical reasons, they do not want to recog-nize the individual as the supreme social and ethical value : for various reasons their "residues" require that the individual or certain classes of individuals are to be subordinated to some kind of collectivity of the individuals of which the authors are the partisans : the proletarian class ; the Communist Party ; the Fascist or Hitlerite group ; the nobility ; the religious collectivity, the given state, and so on. Hence, their col-lectivistic singularism : the *salus populi* (of the group which they extol) becomes the *suprema lex.* All the individuals that oppose it can and should be subordinated, restrained, muzzled, even exterminated, if necessary ; but being collectivistic in this sense, they remain ontologically singularists : all this subordination and extermination is done for the glory of their collectivity, which is still an aggregate of the interacting individuals, each existentially separate from the others and each repre-senting an atom beyond whose aggregation there is no social reality and no other entity. Ethically again, it is connected with one of the varieties of the ethics of happiness, often with the rudest, purely materialistically hedonistic form of it.

These three branches embrace almost all the varieties of the sociological singularism.

B. *Sociological Universalism.* In contradistinction to the sociological singularism, the sociological universalism states that society is much more than a mere number of individuals — interacting or not; that ontologically, like the claim of realism in regard to the *universalia* and concepts, there is an ontological social entity which embraces all the individuals externally as well as permeates them internally. Like the *universalia* in the world generally, there is a social reality *sui generis* irreducible to the individuals — no matter whether they are isolated or related. This social reality is sociological *universalia* existing in the transsubjective social world as well as in our mind. From these premises it naturally follows that society is a superindividual and supersingularistic system, which lives its own organic (but not organismic)[4] life and has its own existential modus, irreducible to the existence of the individuals. This shows that, ontologically, sociological universalism is a special case of ontological realism generally, just as sociological singularism is a special case of either ontological nominalism or conceptualism. From this ontological position of the sociological universalism, it logically follows that ethically society is of neither secondary nor derivative value, but a supreme value which — regardless of the singularistic values — should be guarded, cared for, and promoted. The main varieties of sociological universalism can be divided into two classes.

(1) *Extreme Sociological Universalism.* It regards the individual as a mere part, a toe of a foot, so to speak, of the societal whole; as a mere organ or even as a part of an organ which, as such, does not have any ontological autonomous existence. Ethically, it considers him as a value of a mere part much inferior to the value of society as a whole.

(2) *Moderate Sociological Universalism.* Sharing in the fundamental principles of universalism, it concedes some independent reality to the individual as well as his value. Sometimes, some of the representatives of this branch treat the reality and value of the individual as equal to that of society. Such representatives imperceptibly merge with the group of the partisans of the mystic unity of individuals.

It is to be expected, and the expectation is well corroborated by the

---

[4] Organicism of sociological universalism should not be mixed with most of the bio-organismic theories. These latter, even when they insist on the existence of some bio-organismic or mechanistic bonds between the individuals, are mostly singularistic in their ontological standpoint. For them society is a kind of machine or system where various parts *are adjusted* into one system mechanically but where there is no ontological entity which permeates them all. For the universalist, such an entity is the main thing. Individuals compose a society not because they are interacting, but first of all because the ontological social reality is already present in every individual.

facts, that most of the universalists are in agreement, ethically, with the ethics of the absolute principles (see Chapter Thirteen). For a justification of a given political or religious or social order, and of the restraint of an individual, they usually refer to the absolute principles — religious, moral, philosophical, and others — and on this basis demand a subordination of the individual, limitation of his appetites and liberties, and sacrifice of his life. Often they declare that the singularistic values, including the life of the individual, matter little in comparison with the demand and the imperatives of the absolute ethical principles enacted by God, or government, or dictator, or Pope, or any other authority. On this point they often meet closely with the partisans of the collectivistic singularism. Both are not opposed to the regimentation imposed by their authority. Both cling to the *salus populi suprema lex*, whether they are members of the Communist Party, of the Inquisition, of theocracy, of the autocratic dictators, or what not.

The moderate universalists show often some "softness" on this point and sometimes ally themselves with the moderate singularists in protection of the rights of the individual. Nevertheless, they do this, as a rule, upon the basis of the absolutistic principles but not upon that of hedonistic, eudaemonistic, or utilitarian relativistic ethics. Only a few of the universalists, like some of the Jesuits, unite their universalistic position with the ethics of happiness.

C. *Sociological Mystic Integralism.* The third current in the field is mystic integralism. In many respects it is near to a moderate form of universalism as well as of singularism. Nevertheless, it does not coincide with either one and has several specific accents which entitle it to be regarded as the third current of *sui generis*. It attempts to give a harmonious synthesis of individualistic singularism with universalism. Ontologically, it thinks that society and the individual both are real; the individual is the singularistic incarnation of the societal reality; society is the *universalia* of all the individuals, permeating all of them; it is the condition without which the individual is impossible. Like entelechy it permeates all of them and is the generic essence of every individual. Therefore the synthesis of individualism and universalism is achieved by this current, not mechanically, not through addition of the value or reality of the individual to that of society, but intimately, mystically, internally, in the sense that the genuine realization of the individuality of every singular person is obtained through free creative effort of the person, the effort which aims to realize the absolute and universal values for their own sake, for the pure love of them. Since these absolute and universal values are incorporated in superindividual culture and society, their realization is at the same time realization of the aims of society and of its values.   When the individual makes such an effort, he expresses through it the societal *universalia* and objectivizes the reality as well as the value of society.   Such a harmony or coexistence of the individual and societal reality is somewhat mystic in its nature. It is not the result of a mere mechanical subjection of an individual to the authority or the result of the machinatory adjustments of the "sensible individuals" or of their "interaction."   It is all inner.   As such, it mystically pre-exists the individual, as a singularistic person.   Such is the essence of the ontological position of the mystic integralism.   Ethically, it logically claims that both the societal and the individual values are inseparable; that they are the same but represent two different aspects of the same value; that, consequently, both the individual and society are the absolute value and this value is the same; therefore neither the individual nor society can be relegated to a secondary or derivative value, and neither of them can be used as the mere means for some other purpose.

In this harmonious and ideal form, the mystic integralism attempts to solve the difficult problem.   The above outline has several not quite clear points in the characterization of this mystic integralism.   However, these dark points are not so much a fault of mine as of the nature of the current itself: if in an emotional-psychological aspect the nature of the current is conspicuously different from that of the preceding currents, analytically and scientifically its theory has hardly been clarified sufficiently in distinct details.   It still waits such an elaboration.   Each of us feels clearly a profound difference in the position on the question of St. Francis of Assisi and of Gregory VII, or of the creators of the singularistic liberalism with its rights of man and citizen.   Though all the three currents seemingly plead for a harmony between society (even mankind) and the individual, yet the position, the psychology, the whole mentality of St. Francis here is as different from the representatives of universalism, or of moderate or collectivistic singularism, as it can be. In other words, there is hardly any doubt that the mystic integralism is a current profoundly different from universalism and singularism; but to indicate the difference clearly in analytical terms is not easy, but almost impossible.   Hence, the relative darkness of the above characterization of integralism.   It indicates, however, several traits sufficient to distinguish it from the other two currents.   In view of the specific difficult traits and mentality of this integralism — which, like mysticism generally, is accessible only to relatively few persons — its representatives have been less numerous and the current less ample than those of its two other rivals. Mystic integralism has also several diverse shadings in the writings of its various representatives. But as these shadings are also somewhat "elusive" for an analytical characterization, no attempt is made to subdivide it.

Such, then, are the main classes of the theories set forth in this field as the solution of the problem. As a classification, this unites into one group or class the theories similar in the above essential traits. But this does not mean that all the theories put into one class are identical with one another in all traits, just as putting into a class of the *vertebra* many species and subspecies does not mean that all are identical in all their traits. Theories of the same class, say singularism, sometimes differ from one another profoundly in their secondary traits. Epicurus's singularism is very different from that of J. J. Rousseau (as the author of the *Discours*) ; both are different from Tolstoi's and all from Nietzsche's or Stirner's. The same is true of universalism and mystic integralism. Each theory of the same class represents the same theme, but each has its own variations. A careful study of these "variations" is in itself a fascinating task, but it is outside the purpose of this work. Only very brief remarks of that kind can be given hereafter. They will give an allusion to the most conspicuous qualitative change of the same current from period to period, but that is all. I am not writing a qualitative history of universalism and singularism, but merely tracing the main course of the quantitative fluctuation of their ups and downs; and even this task — though hardly ever touched systematically — is but a mere "case" in the main theories developed here.

II. FLUCTUATION OF THE INFLUENCE OF SINGULARISM, UNIVERSALISM, AND MYSTIC INTEGRALISM

Tables 23 and 24 and Figure 14 indicate the essential oscillations in the relative influence of each of these currents within the period studied, from about 560 B.C. up to the present time. (The last column of Figure 14 depicts the period 1901–1920.) The method of their construction is essentially the same as that of the preceding tables. The tables give the number of the representatives as well as their weight by each period.[5]

[5] Besides the works mentioned in other chapters of this work — the general histories of philosophy and science and a series of special monographs — the following additional works were used for construction of Tables 23 and 24.

E. Troeltsch, *Die Sociallehren der Christlichen Kirchen und Gruppen*, cited — there is an English translation of it; O. Schilling, *Christliche Gesellschaftslehre* and *Naturrecht und Staat nach der Lehre der alten Kirche* (Freiburg, 1914) ; R. W. and A. J. Carlyle, *A History of*

The names of the representatives of each current and their weight are given in the Appendix to this chapter in order that the specialist and the reader can check to what extent the list is representative.

Besides the usual limitations and qualifications outlined before, in Chapter One, two additional reservations need to be made here. Peter Struve stresses rightly that in a study of this kind we shall distinguish the rise and decline of each of these currents in the *theories* of the thinkers from those in the *mores and customs and sociopolitical phe-*

Medieval Political Theory in the West, cited, 5 vols.; K. Krumbacher, *Geschichte der Byzantinischen Literatur* (München, 1891); G. Ostrogorsky, *Relationship of the Church and the State in Byzantium* (in Russian), Vol. IV of the *Sborniki Kondakovskago Instituta* (Prague, 1931); H. von Arnim, *Die politischen Theorien des Altertums* (Wien, 1910); M. Pohlenz, *Staatsgedanke und Staatslehre der Griechen* (Leipzig, 1923); R. Pöhlmann, *Geschichte der Sozialen Frage und des Socialismus in der antiken Welt*, 2 vols. (München, 1912); H. Leisegang, *Die Gnosis* (Leipzig, 1924); P. Janet, *Histoire de la science politique*, 3 vols. (Paris, 1887); B. Tchicherin, *A History of Political Doctrines* (in Russian), 5 vols.; P. Elzbacher, *Anarchismus* (Berlin, 1900); G. Gooch, *History of Democratic Ideas in England in XVIIth Century* (Cambridge, 1903); E. Spektorsky, *A History of Political Theories* (Ljubljani, 1932); C. H. McIlwain, *The Growth of Political Thought in the West* (New York, 1932); L. Proal, "L'anarchisme au XVIII siècle," in *Revue Philosophique* (1916); W. Sombart, *Der Proletarische Socialismus* (Jena, 1924); J. Jaures, *La Convention* (Paris, 1904); P. Barth, *Philosophie der Geschichte als Soziologie* (Leipzig, 1922); A. I. Tschuproff, *A History of Political Economy* (in Russian); N. Kareev, *Human Personality and History* (in Russian); R. Verrier, *E. De Roberty, Le positivisme russ et la fondation de la sociologie* (Paris, 1934); A. von Kirchenheim, *Schlaraffia politica* (Leipzig, 1892); E. Albee, *A History of English Utilitarianism* (1902); P. Sakulin, *A History of Socialism in Russia* (in Russian); F. Dostoievsky, *The Diary of a Publicist, 1873–1880* (in Russian).

Encyclopedias: Brokhouse and Ephron, and the *Soviet Encyclopedia* (in Russian); *Larousse* (in French); *Britannica* (in English); Otto Slovnik, *Cyclopedia of Masaryk* (in Czech).

P. Struve, *Economy and Price* (in Russian) (1913); L. Robin, "Sur la conception aristotélienne de la causalité," *Archiv für Geschichte der Philosophie*, Vol. XXIII, pt. i (1909); pt. ii (1910); L. Robin, *Sur la théorie platonicienne des idées et des nombres d'après Aristote* (Paris, 1908); S. Trubetzkoi, *Metaphysics of Ancient Greece* (in Russian) (1890); K. Holl, *Der Kirchenbegriff des Paulus in seinem Verhaltniss zu der Urgemeinden* (Tübingen, 1921) and *Gesammelte Aufsätze zur Kirchengeschichte*, 3 vols. (Tübingen, 1921–1928); H. Denifle, *Luther und Luthertum*, 2 vols. (Mainz, 1904–1909); R. Seeberg, *Lehrbuch der Dogmengeschichte*, 4 vols. (Leipzig, 1908–1920); A. von Harnack, *Lehrbuch der Dogmengeschichte*, 3 vols. (Freiburg, 1894–1897); M. Weber, *Gesammelte Aufsätze zur Religionssoziologie*, 3 vols. (Tübingen, 1921–1922); C. Beudant, *Le droit individuel et l'État* (Paris, 1920); J. K. Bluntschli, *Geschichte der neueren Staatswissenschaft* (München, 1886); W. H. Dunning, *A History of Political Theories from Rousseau to Spencer* (New York, 1920); O. von Gierke, *Deutsches Genossenschaftrecht*, Vols. III and IV (Berlin, 1881 and 1913); G. Gurvitch, *L'idée du droit social* (Paris, 1932); H. Michel, *L'idée de l'État* (Paris, 1898); R. von Mohl, *Die Geschichte und Literatur der Staatswissenschaften*, Vol. I (Erlangen, 1855); K. Pribram, *Die Entstehung der individualistischen Sozialphilosophie* (Leipzig, 1912); G. de Ruggieri, *Storia del liberalismo europeo* (Bari, 1925); P. Sorokin, *Contemporary Sociological Theories;* E. Halévy, *La formation du radicalisme philosophique*, 3 vols. (Paris, 1901–1904); P. Novgorodzeff, *Social Ideal* (in Russian) (Berlin, 1924).

nomena of the same society. The reason for such a distinction is that not always are the movements in theory and social practice, so to speak, quite parallel. Some tangible connection between these two — theoretical and practical — currents there is, and we shall notice that in Volume Three, Chapter Fifteen. But there are minor periods and currents when, in the social practice, universalistic tendency is rising, while in the theory, the singularistic tendency grows, and vice versa. Such dissonances of the theory and practice are, it is true, the exceptions rather than the rule. But once in a while they seem to occur, though we should not exaggerate them.[6] This means that here, as in other compartments,

---

[6] For instance, P. Struve points out that the European Middle Ages display almost monopolistic domination of universalism in the theory and a feudal singularism in social practice and organization! He himself, however, indicates that the medieval social reality had such gigantic bodies social as the Roman Catholic Church and the Holy Roman Empire. In addition, it can be said that the feudal singularism is more than relative : it also represented not so much singularism and individualism as an almost all-embracing universalism, but on the narrower scale of the localized relationship between the medieval estates and other bodies social. As is shown in the chapters on the fluctuation of the forms of social relationships in Volume Three, the medieval society generally and the texture of the feudal relationships specifically, had little element of singularism or individualism, either in ethical or ontological aspects. Its fundamental relationship, the *fidelitas*, is universalistic in its nature, though often contractual in origin; it is singularistic in the forms of its establishment, like the marriage bond, which in its nature (in good marriages) is *consortium omnis vitae*, in which the individual parties are merged into one unity, though the origin of the establishment of such a marital relationship is often contractual. (See the details in Chapters One to Eight in Volume Three.)

Another important case of such a discrepancy between the theory and social practice indicated by P. Struve concerns the growth of the national empires at the end of the Middle Ages, which growth was paralleled not by an increase of the universalistic ideologies, but by that of the singularistic ones. This confrontation is again hardly complete and therefore convincing. Yet, after the *Unam Sanctam*, such a growth of the National States manifested itself clearly; likewise, it was followed by a somewhat similar growth of the national religious Church organizations. If the picture were exhausted by these phenomena, the discordance between the theory and practice would be striking indeed. However, one must not forget that these national States and national Church organizations did not grow where before was purely singularistic social reality, but grew where before was the *Universal Christian Church*, the Universal *corpus mysticum*, without any division of its universal unity into the parcels of the national churches. The national State likewise grew where before were several States and in addition the Universal Holy Roman Empire, which in several forms embraced the national States in one unity. With the end of the Middle Ages, these Leviathans disappeared. They were parceled, so to speak, into several unities. Therefore, the whole picture is not an increase of universalism in social practice, but rather its decrease. The same increase of singularism in practice is shown by the replacement of the medieval *fidelitas* by the individualistic and singularistic contractual relationships, in the modern sense of the word. For these and similar reasons, one can hardly take the beginning of the modern period after the end of the Middle Ages as an evidence of the discrepancy between the trend in the social ideologies and social practice. If anything, both tendencies were moving in the same direction. But minor discordances between these tendencies in thought and practice are possible.

we do not find a perfect integration of thought and practice, as the elements of the sociocultural world. It means also that the subsequent results and curves attempt to reflect the waves and swings in the sphere of thought primarily, and only secondarily those in the field of its sociocultural practice.

One more remark. In studying Tables 23 and 24, Figure 14, and the list of the names in the Appendix to this chapter the reader may notice: first, that collectivistic singularism appears as a separate class, only beginning with A.D. 1500 This does not mean that such a stream did not exist before; but it means that the clear-cut representatives of this current before A.D. 1500 were few, while many others who might have been collectivistic singularists expressed their position in the problem so unclearly or fragmentarily that one could not be sure that they were really collectivistic singularists. Their statements and theories were coined in such terms that they appear to be nearer to the other currents. Hence, the explanation of why this stream appears in the tables only after 1500.

Another technical detail is that some of the names will be found not in one but in two currents; for instance, Thomas Morus or G. Bruno are placed in the class of Mystic Integralism as well as in Universalism. The reason for such a double placing is that such thinkers either assumed different positions in their different works or their theories were such that they can be placed in either one of the two adjacent currents. When a thinker shows some amount of difference in his total works in the field, but one of these is evidently dominant, such a thinker — for instance, Luther — is placed in only one current. In two currents are placed all those who show a difference in their position in the field, but in whom one cannot be sure which of the two tendencies predominate, for instance, Machiavelli, as an author of the *Prince* and of the *Discorsi*. This, plus some indefiniteness of several theories, makes it possible to place such thinkers in either one of two adjacent currents. However, as mentioned, most of the names clearly belong to the class where they are placed; and the few names which by other investigators may be placed in a different class do not affect notably the results. As a matter of fact, three lists were made independently, one by Professors Lossky and Lapshin; another by Professor Timasheff; the third by Professor P. Struve. The completeness of the three lists was different. Likewise several names

---

In their essential movements, these two "variables" move together, however. One of the reasons for that is that singularism in social practice and that in social mentality are "the functions" of the same main variable — the type of the dominant culture, as is shown further. See Chapter Fifteen in Volume Three of this work.

were put into different classes.[7]   When, however, the names were grouped and summed up by periods, the essential movements of all the three curves happened to be similar, almost identical.   This is additional, a posteriori, evidence of the validity of the results and of the relative harmlessness of the above "indefinite" or "double" cases discussed.   So much for the explanatory notes.   Now Tables 23 and 24, by 20-year and 100-year periods, follow.   Figure 14 gives the movement of the currents in a visual form.

III. MAIN RESULTS

A.   Whether we take the fivefold division of the main currents in the field or the unified threefold division, we do not find any continuous trend during the whole period studied, by 20-year or by the 100-year period. Instead, we see a trendless fluctuation, now one of the currents rising, now the others.   This result is similar to those found in other fields.

B.   The rise and fall of the main rival currents, universalism and singularism in all their varieties, show again a quite tangible correlation with the rise and fall of realism and nominalism; with the system of truth of faith and of the senses; with eternalism and temporalism; Ideational and visual art; and, finally, with the main waves of the Ideational and Sensate cultures.

(1) The sixth century appears to be the period of decisive domination of universalism.   However great are the differences between the various philosophical systems of the time, all the thinkers in this field (see the names in the list in the Appendix to this chapter) — even Herakleitos, whose metaphysics can easily lead to singularistic conclusions — professed themselves universalists.   Such a uniformity of thought in

[7] For instance, in P. Struve's list: Antisthenes is put in the class of the extreme singularists; early and middle Stoicism generally is put into the singularistic current also; Luther is considered primarily a singularist, and so on.   In the list appended, Antisthenes is put into the class Singularism-Universalism; early and the middle Stoicism into the class of the Moderate Universalism (Universalism-Singularism), while thinkers of the late Stoicism (Marcus Aurelius, Seneca, Epictetus) are classed as the Mystic Integralists; Luther is put into the class of the Universalists.   Here Struve's as well as Lapshin and Lossky's classification of these names can be justified.   Yet, Luther was in several senses a singularist and perhaps one of the great singularists.   But Luther was at the same time one of the great universalists, especially in the later period of his activity.   Of course, Stoics denied in a sense the national State and therefore can be regarded as singularists; but they denied it in favor of the universal State and therefore, not to mention the other reasons, they can be regarded as universalists.   However, in spite of these differences in the "pigeonholing" of a number of thinkers, when the names are taken in mass and grouped by the 20- and 100-year periods, such discrepancies do not exert any important effects upon the movement of the curves of these currents from period to period.   The results are, in all three variants mentioned, essentially the same. Similar things have been and will be met in this work several times.

TABLE 23. MOVEMENT OF SINGULARISM, UNIVERSALISM, AND MYSTIC UNITY BY 20-YEAR PERIODS, 580 B.C.—A.D. 1920

PERIOD	Extreme Singularism-Individualism			Singularism-Universalism			Universalism-Singularism			Universalism			Mystic Unity of Singularistic Persons			All Varieties of Singularism			All Varieties of Universalism			Mystic Unity		
	N of representatives	Their weight	Percentage of the total	N of representatives	Their weight	Percentage of the total	N of representatives	Their weight	Percentage of the total	N of representatives	Their weight	Percentage of the total	N of representatives	Their weight	Percentage of the total	N of representatives	Their weight	Percentage of the total	N of representatives	Their weight	Percentage of the total	N of representatives	Their weight	Percentage of the total
580–560 B.C.	0	0	0	0	0	0	0	0	0	0	0	0	0	0	0	0	0	0	0	0	0	0	0	0
560–540	0	0	0	0	0	0	0	0	0	1	5	100	0	0	0	0	0	0	1	5	100	0	0	0
540–520	0	0	0	0	0	0	1	8	62	1	5	38	0	0	0	0	0	0	2	13	100	0	0	0
520–500	0	0	0	0	0	0	2	15	94	1	1	6	0	0	0	0	0	0	3	16	100	0	0	0
500–480	0	0	0	0	0	0	2	15	68	1	7	32	0	0	0	0	0	0	3	22	100	0	0	0
480–460	0	0	0	0	0	0	1	6	37	2	12	63	0	0	0	0	0	0	3	19	74	0	0	0
460–440	0	0	0	1	5	26	1	11	32	2	8	42	0	0	0	1	5	26	3	14	52	0	0	0
440–420	4	8	14	3	19	47.5	2	9	27.5	3	10	25	0	0	0	3	19	48	5	21	19	0	0	0
420–400	4	10	17	7	48	66.5	2	10	12.5	2	5	7	0	0	0	11	58	81	4	12	18	0	0	0
400–380	3	11	13	7	42	65	3	9	15	1	2	3	0	0	0	10	53	82	4	17	37	0	0	0
380–360	1	6	17	4	23	50	3	10	11	0	0	0	0	0	0	5	29	63	3	24	46	0	0	0
360–340	4	9	11	4	19	37	3	10	19	2	12	26	0	0	0	8	28	54	5	32	63	0	0	0
340–320	4	4	8	3	10	26	4	22	58	1	14	27	0	0	0	7	14	37	5	24	64	0	0	0
320–300	2	12	21	7	14	28	7	32	54	1	2	5	0	0	0	9	18	36	7	30	54	0	0	0
300–280	3	15	32.5	2	3	25	8	30	64	0	0	0	0	0	0	6	26	46	8	28	60	0	0	0
280–260	4	12	50	1	4	6.5	7	28	61	0	0	0	0	0	0	5	18	40	7	18	42	0	0	0
260–240	4	23	51	1	3	8	2	10	42	0	0	0	0	0	0	5	14	58	2	10	40	0	0	0
240–220	8	4	38	2	4	9	4	18	45	0	0	0	0	0	0	4	27	48	4	18	52	0	0	0
220–200	3	4	28	2	2	10	3	11	52	0	0	0	0	0	0	4	10	35	3	11	45	0	0	0
200–180	3	2	13	1	1	7	3	8	64	0	0	0	0	0	0	3	5	47	3	8	53	0	0	0
180–160	2	3	13.5	1	5	33	4	12	53	0	0	0	0	0	0	3	7	45	4	12	55	0	0	0
160–140	1	2	10	2	7	31.5	4	12	57	0	0	0	0	0	0	3	10	45	4	12	57	0	0	0
140–120	2	4	20	1	7	33	5	14	70	0	0	0	0	0	0	3	9	30	6	14	70	0	0	0
120–100	2	7	32	2	5	10	4	10	45	0	0	0	0	0	0	6	6	55	4	10	45	0	0	0
100–80	3	5	16	1	5	23	6	21	68	0	0	0	1	8	12	7	12	32	6	21	68	1	8	12
80–60	3	9	28	1	1	16	6	37	58	0	0	0	1	8	15	5	19	30	14	37	58	1	8	15
60–40	2	18	17	2	8	2	14	28	53	0	0	0	0	0	0	4	17	32	9	28	53	0	0	0
40–20	2	9	0	4	15	15	9	19	56	0	0	0	0	0	0	4	15	35	5	19	56	0	0	0
20–0	1	½	1	2	0	44	5	17	87.5	0	0	0	1	8	31	2	13	13	4	17	65	1	8	31
0–20 A.D.	1	½	1	3	2	12.5	4	14	65	1	1	3	1	8	32	2	2	4	5	14	87	1	8	32
20–40	1	½	1	1	1	4	5	17	65	0	0	0	2	14	48	3	1½	4	4	17	65	2	14	48
40–60	1	½	1	1	1	24	5	16	64	0	0	0	2	14	45	3	1½	19	5	16	64	2	14	45
60–80	1	½	1	1	1	19	2	8	28	0	0	0	3	16	33	2	7½	24	2	8	28	3	16	33
80–100	1	1	1	2	7	32	3	10	32	1	1	3	2	14		3	6½	19	4	11	36	2	14	
100–120	1		1	1	6	19	3	10	32	0	0	0	2	14		2	6	12	2	8		2	14	
120–140	2	1	2	2	5	10	8	21	44	2	5	10	3	16	33	3	6		10	26	54	3	16	33

140–160 A.D.	2	2	5	2	5	12	11	27	64	3	6	14	1	2	5	4	7	17	14	33	78	1	2	5
160–180	3	6	11	1	2	4	10	31	56	1	1	2	3	15	27	4	8	15	11	32	58	3	15	27
180–200	3	8	11	2	8	11	16	49	64	1	1	1	2	10	13	10	16	22	17	50	65	2	10	13
200–220	1	3	6	1	6	11.5	10	32	61	1	6	11.5	1	5	10	2	9	17.5	11	38	72.5	1	5	10
220–240	1	½	1	1	6	17	3	11	30	1	6	17	2	13	36	2	6½	17	4	17	47	2	13	36
240–260	1	½	1	0	0	0	4	13	30	2	8	19	3	22	51	1	½	1	6	21	49	3	22	51
260–280	1	½	1	0	0	0	4	9	29	2	8	26	2	14	45	1	½	1	6	17	55	2	14	45
280–300	1	½	1	0	0	0	3	6	33	1	4	22	2	8	44	1	½	1	4	10	56	2	8	44
300–320	1	½	1	0	0	0	2	4	17	1	1	4	4	18	78	1	½	1	3	5	21	4	18	78
320–340	1	½	1	0	0	0	4	11	39	1	1	4	4	16	57	1	½	1	5	12	43	4	16	57
340–360	1	½	1	0	0	0	3	9	50	2	4	22	2	5	28	1	½	1	5	13	72	2	5	28
360–380	0	0	0	0	0	0	4	13	28	2	4	8	5	30	64	0	0	0	6	17	36	5	30	64
380–400	0	0	0	0	0	0	2	6	13	2	11	24	5	28	62	0	0	0	4	17	37	5	28	62
400–420	0	0	0	0	0	0	4	10	31	2	11	34	3	11	34	0	0	0	6	21	65	3	11	34
420–440	0	0	0	0	0	0	5	12	40	2	11	37	2	7	23	0	0	0	7	23	77	2	7	23
440–460	0	0	0	0	0	0	2	5	29	1	1	6	2	11	64	0	0	0	3	6	35	2	11	64
460–480	0	0	0	0	0	0	2	6	33	1	1	6	2	11	61	0	0	0	3	7	39	2	11	61
480–500	0	0	0	0	0	0	2	4	27	1	1	7	2	10	66	0	0	0	3	5	34	2	10	66
500–520	0	0	0	0	0	0	4	17	71	1	1	4	2	6	25	0	0	0	5	18	75	2	6	25
520–540	0	0	0	0	0	0	5	21	62	1	1	3	3	12	35	0	0	0	6	22	65	3	12	35
540–560	0	0	0	0	0	0	4	14	67	0	0	0	2	7	33	0	0	0	4	14	67	2	7	33
560–580	0	0	0	0	0	0	2	5	50	0	0	0	2	5	50	0	0	0	2	5	50	2	5	50
580–600	0	0	0	0	0	0	2	6	75	0	0	0	1	2	25	0	0	0	2	6	75	1	2	25
600–620	0	0	0	0	0	0	2	8	100	0	0	0	0	0	0	0	0	0	2	8	100	0	0	0
620–640	0	0	0	0	0	0	1	4	40	0	0	0	1	6	60	0	0	0	1	4	40	1	6	60
640–660	0	0	0	0	0	0	1	1	14	0	0	0	1	6	86	0	0	0	1	1	14	1	6	86
660–680	0	0	0	0	0	0	1	2	25	0	0	0	1	6	75	0	0	0	1	2	25	1	6	75
680–700	0	0	0	0	0	0	1	2	100	0	0	0	0	0	0	0	0	0	1	2	100	0	0	0
700–720	0	0	0	0	0	0	1	3	100	0	0	0	0	0	0	0	0	0	1	3	100	0	0	0
720–740	0	0	0	0	0	0	1	3	37.5	0	0	0	1	5	62.5	0	0	0	1	3	37.5	1	5	62.5
740–760	0	0	0	0	0	0	1	1	17	0	0	0	1	5	83	0	0	0	1	1	17	1	5	83
760–780	0	0	0	0	0	0	1	1	100	0	0	0	0	0	0	0	0	0	1	1	100	0	0	0
780–800	0	0	0	0	0	0	1	4	100	0	0	0	0	0	0	0	0	0	1	4	100	0	0	0
800–820	0	0	0	0	0	0	2	5	100	0	0	0	0	0	0	0	0	0	2	5	100	0	0	0
820–840	0	0	0	0	0	0	3	6	100	0	0	0	0	0	0	0	0	0	3	6	100	0	0	0
840–860	0	0	0	0	0	0	3	6	43	0	0	0	1	8	57	0	0	0	3	6	43	1	8	57
860–880	0	0	0	0	0	0	2	4	25	2	4	25	1	8	50	0	0	0	4	8	50	1	8	50
880–900	0	0	0	0	0	0	1	3	60	1	2	40	0	0	0	0	0	0	2	5	100	0	0	0
900–920	0	0	0	0	0	0	1	2	100	0	0	0	0	0	0	0	0	0	1	2	100	0	0	0
920–940	0	0	0	0	0	0	1	2	100	0	0	0	0	0	0	0	0	0	1	2	100	0	0	0
940–960	0	0	0	0	0	0	1	2	100	0	0	0	0	0	0	0	0	0	1	2	100	0	0	0
960–980	0	0	0	0	0	0	1	2	100	0	0	0	0	0	0	0	0	0	1	2	100	0	0	0
980–1000	0	0	0	0	0	0	1	3	100	0	0	0	0	0	0	0	0	0	1	3	100	0	0	0
1000–1020	0	0	0	0	0	0	2	5	83	1	1	17	0	0	0	0	0	0	3	6	100	0	0	0
1020–1040	0	0	0	0	0	0	1	2	100	0	0	0	0	0	0	0	0	0	1	2	100	0	0	0
1040–1060	0	0	0	0	0	0	1	3	37.5	2	5	62.5	0	0	0	0	0	0	3	8	100	0	0	0
1060–1080	0	0	0	0	0	0	2	6	27	3	12	55	1	4	18	0	0	0	5	18	82	1	4	18
1080–1100	0	0	0	0	0	0	3	8	27	4	18	60	1	4	13	0	0	0	7	26	87	1	4	13
1100–1120	0	0	0	0	0	0	2	4	22	4	14	78	0	0	0	0	0	0	6	18	100	0	0	0
1120–1140	0	0	0	0	0	0	5	12	50	2	7	29	1	5	21	0	0	0	7	19	79	1	5	21
1140–1160	0	0	0	0	0	0	5	12	40	3	13	43	1	5	17	0	0	0	8	25	83	1	5	17
1160–1180	0	0	0	0	0	0	2	4	16	7	21	84	0	0	0	0	0	0	9	25	100	0	0	0

TABLE 23. MOVEMENT OF SINGULARISM, UNIVERSALISM, AND MYSTIC UNITY BY 20-YEAR PERIODS — *continued*

PERIOD	Extreme Singularism-Individualism			Singularism-Universalism			Universalism-Singularism			Universalism			Mystic Unity of Singularistic Persons			All Varieties of Singularism			All Varieties of Universalism			Mystic Unity		
	Number of representatives	Their weight	Percentage of the total	Number of representatives	Their weight	Percentage of the total	Number of representatives	Their weight	Percentage of the total	Number of representatives	Their weight	Percentage of the total	Number of representatives	Their weight	Percentage of the total	Number of representatives	Their weight	Percentage of the total	Number of representatives	Their weight	Percentage of the total	Number of representatives	Their weight	Percentage of the total
1180-1200 A.D.	0	0	0	0	0	0	2	3	15	6	14	70	1	3	15	0	0	0	8	17	85	1	3	15
1200-1220	0	0	0	0	0	0	3	5	26	3	11	58	1	3	16	0	0	0	6	16	84	1	3	16
1220-1240	0	0	0	0	0	0	2	4	21	3	9	47	1	6	32	0	0	0	5	13	68	1	6	32
1240-1260	0	0	0	0	0	0	2	4	15	6	22	85	0	0	0	0	0	0	8	26	100	0	0	0
1260-1280	0	0	0	0	0	0	2	8	19	7	35	81	0	0	0	0	0	0	9	43	100	0	0	0
1280-1300	0	0	0	0	0	0	3	11	29	9	27	71	0	0	0	0	0	0	12	38	100	0	0	0
1300-1320	0	0	0	1	3	5	6	19	31	10	31	51	1	8	13	1	3	5	16	50	82	1	8	13
1320-1340	0	0	0	3	11	19	8	18	31	8	21	36	1	8	14	3	11	19	14	39	67	1	8	14
1340-1360	0	0	0	2	8	14	7	22	39	4	7	13	4	19	34	2	8	14	12	29	52	4	19	34
1360-1380	0	0	0	0	0	0	6	16	41	2	4	10	4	19	49	0	0	0	9	20	51	4	19	49
1380-1400	0	0	0	0	0	0	4	15	71	1	2	10	1	4	19	0	0	0	7	17	81	1	4	19
1400-1420	0	0	0	0	0	0	4	11	69	1	2	12.5	1	3	18.5	0	0	0	5	13	81.5	1	3	18.5
1420-1440	0	0	0	0	0	0	4	12	63	3	7	37	0	0	0	0	0	0	7	19	100	0	0	0
1440-1460	0	0	0	1	2	8	4	10	38	2	6	23	1	8	31	1	2	8	6	16	61	1	8	31
1460-1480	0	0	0	0	0	0	7	15	55.5	3	4	15	1	8	29.5	0	0	0	10	19	70.5	1	8	29.5
1480-1500	0	0	0	0	0	0	6	12	63	2	3	16	1	4	21	0	0	0	8	15	79	1	4	21

PERIOD	Extreme Singularism-Individualism			Singularistic Collectivism			Singularism-Universalism			Universalism-Singularism			Universalism			Mystic Unity of Singularistic Persons			All Varieties of Singularism			All Varieties of Universalism			Mystic Unity		
	Number of representatives	Their weight	Percentage of the total	Number of representatives	Their weight	Percentage of the total	Number of representatives	Their weight	Percentage of the total	Number of representatives	Their weight	Percentage of the total	Number of representatives	Their weight	Percentage of the total	Number of representatives	Their weight	Percentage of the total	Number of representatives	Their weight	Percentage of the total	Number of representatives	Their weight	Percentage of the total	Number of representatives	Their weight	Percentage of the total
1500–1520 A.D.	1	4	9	1	6	14	1	1	2	3	10	23	2	12	28	2	10	23	3	11	25	5	22	51	2	10	23
1520–1540	2	6	10	2	8	14	1	6	10	2	10	17	5	25	42	1	4	7	5	20	34	7	35	59	1	4	7
1540–1560	1	2	5	2	2	5	0	0	0	3	14	36	3	21	54	0	0	0	3	4	10	6	35	90	0	0	0
1560–1580	2	6	6	1	1	2	1	1	2	8	25	51	5	19	51.4	0	0	0	4	5	10	8	44	90	0	0	0
1580–1600	1	3	3.4	1	1	1.4	1	1	1.4	5	22	31.4	9	36	39	1	8	11	3	4	6.2	13	58	82.8	1	8	11
1600–1620	1	2	6	1	6	8	1	1	1	4	18	35	10	42	51.4	0	0	0	5	11	15	14	60	84	0	0	0
1620–1640	1	4	2	3	7	13	1	2	2	3	17	32	4	20	38	1	7	13	3	9	17	7	37	70	1	7	13
1640–1660	1	1	1	1	4	6	2	8	3	9	35	51	3	14	20	2	13	19	6	7	10	12	49	71	2	13	19
1660–1680	1	1	1	3	2	3	3	16	13	3	13	20	8	31	50	1	7	11	5	11	18	11	44	72	1	7	11
1680–1700	1	1	1	1	6	7	3	16	20	3	24	17	12	45	55	0	0	0	6	23	28	15	59	60	0	0	0
1700–1720	2	4	9	1	1	2	4	19	18	4	17	20	8	35	40	1	5	6	6	30	34	12	52	59	1	5	6
1720–1740	1	1	4	1	7	6	0	47	35	2	8	15	6	24	44	0	0	0	6	22	41	8	32	30	0	0	0
1740–1760	3	8	6	2	6	4	9	91	41	1	12	10	5	23	23	1	8	7	14	73	63	7	35	24	1	8	7
1760–1780	2	7	16	2	8	5	2	47	54	6	24	14	8	17	20	2	20	12	16	107	64	14	41	42	2	20	12
1780–1800	2	19	6	3	8	4	0	39	32	7	38	26	9	23	10	2	20	13	11	67	45	16	61	65	2	20	13
1800–1820	1	10	8	1	4	2	11	70	22	8	46	26	24	71	39	1	12	7	17	51	28	32	117	61	1	12	7
1820–1840	1	12	2	1	2	8	9	64	33	11	43	21	21	83	40	1	5	2	28	78	37	41	126	56	1	5	2
1840–1860	7	4	1	5	8	10	15	80	22	12	55	19	29	107	37	2	5	2	30	120	42	46	162	54	2	5	2
1860–1880	5	33	12	9	23	19	16	139	24	24	103	30	22	83	24	1	12	3.5	41	142	42.5	31	186	34	1	12	3.5
1880–1900	10	29	8.5	22	75	19	16	111	36	22	89	23	9	42	11	1	7	2	69	251	64	46	131	34	1	7	2
1900–1920	8	37	9	31	80	19	37		27	33	134	33	15	50	12	0	0	0	70	228	55	48	184	45	0	0	0

TABLE 24. MOVEMENT OF SINGULARISM, UNIVERSALISM, AND MYSTIC UNITY BY CENTURY PERIODS

PERIOD	Extreme Singularism-Individualism			Singularistic Collectivism			Singularism-Universalism			Universalism-Singularism			Universalism			Mystic Unity of Singularistic Persons			All Varieties of Singularism			All Varieties of Universalism			Mystic Unity		
	N	Their weight	% of total	N	Their weight	% of total	N	Their weight	% of total	N	Their weight	% of total	N	Their weight	% of total	N	Their weight	% of total	N	Their weight	% of total	N	Their weight	% of total	N	Their weight	% of total
600–500 B.C.	0	0	0	0	0	0	0	0	0	2	15	71	2	6	29	0	0	0	0	0	0	4	21	100	0	0	0
500–400	4	10	9	0	0	0	8	53	48	5	30	27	4	17	16	0	0	0	12	63	57	9	47	43	0	0	0
400–300	9	19	12	0	0	0	17	72	46	12	49	31	3	16	11	0	0	0	26	91	58	15	65	42	0	0	0
300–200	11	35	34	0	0	0	9	18	17	13	51	49	0	0	0	0	0	0	20	53	51	13	51	49	0	0	0
200–100	7	11	24	0	0	0	3	8	17	12	27	59	0	0	0	0	0	0	10	19	41	12	27	59	0	0	0
100–0	8	25	22	0	0	0	6	20	17	23	63	54	0	0	0	1	8	7	14	45	39	23	63	54	1	8	7
0–100 A.D.	1	1	1	0	0	0	5	16	21	11	36	48	4	7	4	3	22	30	6	17	22	11	36	48	3	22	30
100–200	6	10	7	0	0	0	4	17	11	28	83	57	3	14	12	6	31	21	10	27	18	32	90	61	6	31	21
200–300	2	3½	3	0	0	0	1	6	6	18	51	47	4	15	15	6	35	32	3	9½	9	21	65	59	6	35	32
300–400	1	0	1	0	0	0	0	0	0	9	25	25	2	11	19	2	59	59	1	½	1	11	40	40	2	59	59
400–500	0	0	0	0	0	0	0	0	0	9	22	39	1	0	2	6	24	42	0	0	0	11	33	58	6	24	42
500–600	0	0	0	0	0	0	0	0	0	9	24	57	0	0	0	5	17	41	0	0	0	10	25	59	5	17	41
600–700	0	0	0	0	0	0	0	0	0	4	11	65	0	0	0	1	6	35	0	0	0	4	11	65	1	6	35
700–800	0	0	0	0	0	0	0	0	0	3	8	61	0	0	0	1	5	39	0	0	0	3	8	61	1	5	39
800–900	0	0	0	0	0	0	0	0	0	6	14	71	0	0	0	1	8	29	0	0	0	9	20	71	1	8	29
900–1000	0	0	0	0	0	0	0	0	0	5	7	100	3	0	0	0	0	0	0	0	0	3	7	100	0	0	0
1000–1100	0	0	0	0	0	0	0	0	0	8	13	32	7	24	58	1	4	10	0	0	0	12	37	90	1	4	10
1100–1200	0	0	0	0	0	0	0	0	0	21	23	30	15	45	59	2	8	11	0	0	0	26	68	89	2	8	11
1200–1300	0	0	0	0	0	0	0	0	0	19	20	19	21	75	72	2	9	9	0	0	0	29	95	91	2	9	9
1300–1400	0	0	0	0	0	0	0	0	0	19	57	40	19	46	33	5	27	19	0	0	0	40	103	73	5	27	19
1400–1500	0	0	0	5	11	6	3	11	8	16	36	53	8	15	22	3	15	22	3	11	8	24	51	75	3	15	22
1500–1600	5	12	6	9	25	11	1	2	5	17	61	33	15	67	37	4	22	12	13	31	18	32	128	70	4	22	12
1600–1700	5	12	7	7	20	5	3	8	8	18	76	32	27	101	42	2	13	5	16	48	21	45	177	74	2	13	5
1700–1800	9	44	2	33	111	10	5	18	36	16	77	19	23	86	21	4	33	8	48	208	52	39	163	40	4	33	8
1800–1900	17	68	11				32	144	29	57	246	24	70	288	28	4	29	3	124	479	45	127	534	52	4	29	3

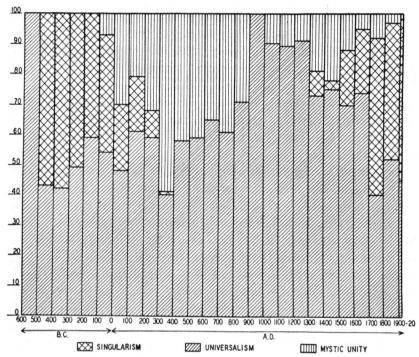

FIG. 14. MOVEMENT OF SINGULARISM, UNIVERSALISM, AND MYSTIC UNITY

this respect is particularly significant and is in perfect accord with the Ideational forms which dominated all the main compartments of the grand culture of this century. The fact that, in spite of a great difference in the systems of thought of the period, all of the thinkers happen to have universalistic positions (as well as Ideational positions in other relevant fields) is a conspicuous evidence that the Ideational or Sensate forms of the dominant culture condition many fundamental modes of thought in the relevant problems, regardless of whether the respective solution is in the best logical accord with the rest of the theory of the respective author. Here we see again that, regardless of other agencies, the nature of the dominant culture makes true and valid what is in accord with its nature. The fact evidences also the existence of the close integration between the nature of the dominant culture and the specific solution of this or other general problems.

(2) Beginning with the fifth century B.C., the monopolistic domination of universalism is broken, and singularism emerges in its extreme form. In so far we have coexistence of both main currents almost equally

balanced, with a slight predomination of both forms of singularism over universalism, giving respectively 57 and 43 as the comparative weight of the currents. Considering, however, that the extreme universalism is almost twice as strong as the extreme singularism, this decreases the slight domination of singularism and makes the period almost ideally balanced in this respect. This is a direct evidence of the idealistic character of the century, according to the meaning of the term in this work, and supports the idealistic earmarks of it found in other compartments of this century.

The stream of singularism at this period appears with many of the sophists. (See the Appendix to this chapter for the names.) Even Socrates, with some of his principles, somewhat paved the way for the subsequent conclusions of singularistic nature, though he himself did not draw such conclusions. It is in that period that the confrontation of the man-made norm ($\nu\acute{o}\mu os$) with the law of nature ($\phi\acute{v}\sigma\iota s$) emerges.[8] From this premise the early sophists seem not to have made the extreme singularistic conclusions; but the later sophists of the second half of the fifth century B.C. made it and created the above powerful current of singularism. In the field of sociopolitical facts, this second half was disastrous and unhappy for Greece in many respects, especially the period of the greatest expansion of singularism, 420–380 B.C.: the activities of Alcibiades, the Peloponnesian War, the intervention of the Persians in Greek affairs, the loss of political independence of Greek colonies in Asia Minor; factual loss of independence in Europe; and so on.

(3) The fourth, the third, and the second centuries B.C. are marked, in spite of minor fluctuations, by a decided recession of extreme universalism, which disappears after the fourth century, and by a notable rise of extreme singularism (with a rivulet of the collectivistic singularism not given in Table 24). This, again, well supports the rising tide of the Sensate culture in this period, evidenced by the rise of the Sensate forms in other compartments of the Greek culture.

The great tide of singularism in the period from 420 to 380 B.C. called forth a temporary reaction against it, led by the standard-bearers of universalism: Plato and Aristotle, with their followers. Plato's universalism, like that of Xenophanes, is colored by Spartan sympathies; Aristotelian universalism is more abstract; but both schools were universalistic, in spite of their other differences. Both regarded the State as the supreme and sublime value, outside of which there is no place for the social individual; outside of which there is no human personality,

[8] See J. W. Beardslee, Jr., and Lovejoy and G. Boas's (chap. iii) works, quoted.

but only human animalism. The State, the society, is ontologically and ethically the supreme value and the indispensable condition for the individual, in regard to his social, cultural, and moral being.

These two powerful schools are responsible for the temporary recession of singularism in its mainly moderate form in the second and the third quarters of the fourth century B.C. But even they were unable to check the extreme singularism and to reduce the moderate singularism to a small rivulet. Singularism continued to be a strong current — almost as strong as universalism, even, during this period. At the end of the fourth and in the third and in the first centuries B.C. the singularistic tide, especially in the form of the extreme singularism, grows definitely,[9] asserting the temporary nature of the Plato-Aristotelian universalism. Especially great is the success of singularism generally, and of its extreme form particularly, in the period from about 300 to 200 B.C. Pure universalism as well as mystic unity are absent and do not counterbalance the extreme singularism. The only opposition to it is the moderate universalism-singularism. It is a powerful current but it is, after all, only slightly more universalistic than singularistic. Here we are in a singularistic-individualistic age. Epicurus, the Epicureans, and some of the Stoics assume definitely singularistic positions. Some of them go to its extreme (see the list of the names of the singularists of the period in the Appendix). It is the time of rapid disintegration of the Greek states, with their sovereignty lost, with their former power gone, with their previous forms of social ties (of the clan, of the state, of the family) and strongly integrated social bodies disorganized, with the previously strong "familistic relations" replaced by the individualistic contractual.[10] The rising tide of singularism in the ideology thus reflected the loosening of the super-

---

[9] Its growth would appear still greater if the Stoics were put into the singularistic class. As mentioned above, there are some reasons which would not make such a qualification of Stoics entirely unjustifiable. On the other hand, there are other, slightly more important reasons, which forced us to class them with moderate universalists.

[10] See the chapters on social relationship in Volume Three. See also W. S. Ferguson, *Hellenistic Athens* (London, 1911), pp. 216 ff. "There had been a time in Athens when . . . the primordial *phratries*, or brotherhoods, had, indeed, meant more to men than citizenship itself. . . . During the fifth and early fourth centuries B.C., the State came to include so completely the ideal interests of the citizens that many found it useless expense to enter a brotherhood." Now they were replaced mainly by the clubs as associations of specific interests of the members, with free entrance and exodus. . . . "The relaxation of the imperious interests in state or municipal affairs was accompanied in Athens, as in the Roman Empire, by the growth of private associations" (of an individualistic-contractual character, instead of the previous familistic or the state ones). See also G. Glotz, *La solidarité de la famille dans le droit criminel en Grèce* (Paris, 1904); E. Weiss, *Griechisches Privatrecht* (Leipzig, 1923), Vol. I.

individual social bonds that previously united the Greeks into strongly integrated bodies social, and an increasing "liberty" of the "roving and independent" individuals, who supposedly could choose their associations and their preferences. The Epicurean current went far in this direction, some of the Epicureans quite turning their back on the whole social world, its groups and cultures and states and organizations, and trying to center their lives either around the *Carpe diem* or singularistic ataraxia. Likewise, as mentioned, in Stoicism the singularistic motives were also strong, though not so strong perhaps as the universalistic ideas with which they tried to unite singularism.

(4) Beginning with the end of the first century B.C., and then with the first century A.D., the tide turns in the opposite direction: singularism, especially its extreme form, begins to recede, followed by a rise of universalism. If the latter rises more slowly than singularism recedes, the reason is the emergence and then the rapid rise of mystic integralism, which is nearer to universalism than to singularism. Antisingularistic reaction thus assumes two forms: universalism and its, so to speak, desperate form, mystic integralism. This trend continues up to the fifth century A.D. In that century it reaches the point of the disappearance of singularism entirely from the "highway" of the mentality of the culture of the period. We are ushered, in the fifth century, into the era of monopolistic or dualistic domination of universalism and mystic integralism, without any share of singularism. Here, then, singularism as a component of the Sensate culture disappears like temporalism by about a century earlier than its other components (nominalism, empiricism, and others).

This trend in the period studied is manifest among the Christian as well as the Pagan thinkers. Except for several external points of difference, the mentality of the Christian and the Pagan universalists and of the Christian and the Pagan integralists is similar in many essential points. It is different from the preceding universalism of either the sixth century B.C. or of even Plato and Aristotle. There the empirical universalist State was at the same time the reality permeated by the divine or sublime value: the supreme good. No dualism, in the form of aspiring to the universalist ideal City of God or the ideal State, and at the same time despising or considering the real State as the least of the evils, existed there. Now this dualism appeared and assumed a conspicuous form. The empirical bodies social were regarded at the best as the least of the evils, though the ideal State or "the City of God" was blessed and aspired to. Already in the middle Stoicism this dualism had appeared and in the late Stoicism of Marcus Aurelius, Seneca, and Epictetus it came out quite clearly. The same is true of the Neo-Platonism of these centuries, as expressed by Plotinus, Jamblich, Proclus, and later Julian the Apostate. The same is still more true of the Christian thinkers. Like the Stoics they were clearly universalists or mystic integralists, but during the first four centuries of our era, before the legalization of the Christian Church, they had a reluctant, often quite negative, sometimes revolutionary attitude toward the real State and the other real bodies social (except the Christian Church itself). At the same time they aspired to the universalist or mystic City of God. In such a setting the problem of singularism and universalism was complicated by the intrusion of this dualism and assumed specific forms of mystic integralism, which now emerged and became practically the most powerful current. Its peculiarity consisted not in the mere attempt to harmonize society and the individual — but in the manner in which the solution of the task was sought. It did not assume the form of the so familiar and somewhat flat discussion that the individual and society were two inseparable aspects of the same reality ; that the individual could become a personality only through society, and society could exist only through the individuals ; that, therefore, what was good for the one was good for the other, and so forth — the discussions given and repeated in almost any elementary text on sociology. The solution of the mystic integralism and of the transcendental universalism (Christian and Pagan) of the period consisted, on the one hand, in treating the empirical bodies social as something of low order ; in toleration of them as the least of the evils ; in estimation of the empirical, political, and social activities as something of low order also. On the other hand, in the positive assertion that the supreme goodness is union with God (or with some other transcendental absolute value) ; that, respectively, the peak of human existence is the state of ecstasy in which man frees himself from the tenets of the empirical world and enters into union with the infinitive Divine. In such a union there is no individuality, no singularity ; all become dissolved in God and God's kingdom, and all are united into oneness in the City of God. Thus universalism and mystic integralism assume here transcendental forms of the salvation of the soul in God, an all-embracing universe where unity and plurality, oneness and multiplicity, are inseparable and coexistent in one whole.

This specific dualism and mystic "twist" explain why the antisingularism assumed now not so much the form of universalism as that of mystic integralism : the harmonization of the part and the whole, the singular and the general, the individual and the society in the transcendental world

of Divineness — for Christians as well as for Pagans.[11]   Such was the new
note, as P. Struve calls it rightly, brought by the Pagan (Neo-Platonic)
and the Christian thought of the period into the problem.   It sharply separated the realm of the empirical reality from that of the transcendental
kingdom ; it "invested" all the universalism in this transcendental universe of God as a real *coincidentia oppositorum*, in which the singular is
dissolved in the infinity ; and it turned away from the empirical reality
in its universalistic and singularistic aspects as the inferior and unimportant appearance, which, as such, one has to bear but which one should not
take too seriously.   If one is confronted with it, one should follow the
path dictated by the salvation of the soul ; at the most to tolerate it and
to give to Caesar what is Caesar's.

(5) After the legalization of the Christian Church and subsequent
"institutionalization" of it, the "desperate" mood and the firm conviction in the end of this world begin to pass.   This expresses itself in a
liquidation of singularism in the fifth century A.D. and in an increase of
more balanced and less desperate universalism at the cost of mystic
integralism.   Note here that the singularism disappears around the fifth
century — the period when we have met liquidation of several variables
of the Sensate culture in various compartments of the culture studied,
while all the other Sensate variables disappeared a few decades later
(in the sixth century).

This confirms the validity of each of the "curves," based upon quite
different material and collected by quite different persons, who did not
know either the objective of this investigation for which they were doing
the spade work or about the work of one another.

The centuries from the fifth to the thirteenth appear as the period of
ideational or transcendental universalism and of mystic integralism
without any sign of singularism whatsoever.   In this respect, the result
is strikingly similar to those obtained in other compartments of culture
studied.   We are in an age of all-powerful Ideationalism.

Continuing the dualism brought by the previous period, this period
stands under the banner of Christ and Christianized Plato and Aristotle.
The two dominant currents of the period — the transcendental universalism and transcendental mystic integralism — gave a Christian
synthesis of an absolute individualism in the sense of the salvation of the

---

[11] P. Struve rightly stresses in his *Economy and Price*, as well as in his materials, that
Marcus Aurelius, Julian the Apostate, and Constantine the Great all were in this stream,
though not all equally deeply and conscientiously felt it.   Julian the Apostate — the Neo-
Platonist, partly mystic, at the same time anti-Christian, and, like Marcus Aurelius, a ruler
— represents a particularly interesting figure from this standpoint.

individual soul, with an absolute universalism and integralism in the sense that the indispensable condition of such a salvation is not only unlimited faith but unlimited fusion with God, which is Love itself. In this love of God and of every neighbor, the individualism dissolves entirely and becomes an absolute transcendental universalism or integralism. Through this transcendental medium of unification, each individual Christian is entirely fused with all the others, with "neighbors." The singular empirical individual is turned into the "soul" as a ray of God or of the same absolute and infinite value.

Concretely, therefore, the main tasks are now: salvation of the individual soul in Christ and through Christ, and communion with other souls in the Church, as the earthly embodiment of the City of God.

In the first centuries of Christianity the Christian Church seems to have been thought not so much an institution (*Anstalt*) [12] as a purely spiritual community of souls united in God — a kind of "pneumatic or charismatic [13] democracy," as Harnack puts it. Subsequently, after its legalization, it became more and more institutionalized.[14] With its institutionalization the purely transcendental conception of the Church was more and more supplemented with an empirical manifestation of it in the form of the institution of the Church with the obligatory laws, authorities, rights and duties, use of compulsion, and other earmarks of an empirical body social.

This process of the empirical institutionalization of the Church has been followed by the growth of universalism, at the cost of mystic integralism, after the fifth century A.D. In the subsequent centuries the latter flares up only sporadically and convulsively, while universalism becomes the main and almost monopolistic ideology up to the re-emergence of singular-

[12] "Die Kirche des Paulus ist keine unsichtbare, sondern eine sichtbare: sichtbar in allen Menschen, die Gott beruft und die 'in Christus' sind; aber sie ist keine Anstalt und hat keine rechtlichen Merkmale. Sie steht also noch jenseits des Protestantismus wie Katholizismus. Sie ist nicht gekennzeichnet doch irgendeine Verfassung; Gott hat ihr wohl 'Charismata,' Begabungen für ihre Dienst gegeben (I Kor. 12, 28) und Menschen die freiwillig arbeiteten und freiwillig Gehorsam fanden (I Kor. 16, 15), aber nicht Beamte und Priester." H. Weinel, in *Religion in Geschichte und Gegenwart*[2], "Kirche," Vol. II, p. 5.

See also Karl Holl's *Die Kirchenbegriff des Paulus*, quoted, and his *Gesammelte Aufsätze* (Tübingen, 1927), Vol. II, pp. 44–67.

[13] "Die Gemeinden stehen unter dem Worte Gottes und unter der väterlichen Zucht des Apostels, der sie begründet hat, aber sofern der Geist, sie regiert, ist dieser Geist der Gemeinde als Ganzes und als einer Einheit geschenkt, und auch die Amts- und Ehrenpersonen stehen als Glieder in dieser Einheit und nicht über ihr." A. von Harnack, "*Verfassung, kirchliche und kirchliches Recht im 1 und 2 Jahrhundert*," Herzog-Hauck, *Real encyklopädie für Protestantische Theologie und Kirche* (1908), Vol. XX, pp. 519–520.

[14] "Doch beginnt langsam das Anstaltliche zu wachsen."

ism in the fourteenth century. This universalism remains still transcendental, but it is more and more permeated by the worldly empirical motives, and the individual is required now to submit himself to the Church in its visible form, as an empirical or worldly institution.

In other words, not only the proportion of mystic integralism and universalism changes during these centuries, but each of them undergoes a qualitative transformation. Instead of the charismatic and mystic conception of the Church as Christ's Bride, the growing universalism more and more has the Church in view as the Universal Leviathan, a vast empirical organization with enormous power, in the face of which the individual as individual feels a mere *quantité negligeable* and is so handled to a considerable degree. We are in an age of a *theocratic universalism*, so far as its specific nature is concerned.

(6) The fourteenth century is marked by the re-emergence of singularism.

This component of Sensate culture reappears thus synchronously with a few other components and somewhat later than the majority of other Sensate components reappeared. However, considering that possibly not all the thinkers are recorded in the annals of history and happen to be in our list; and considering also that the difference of a quarter of a century or even of a whole century is a relatively short period in the system of the long-time waves studied here; and finally remembering my thesis that even the best integrated cultures are never perfectly integrated and admit of some amount of nonsynchronous turns in their variables; such a lag is unimportant in itself.[15] What *is* important is that the re-emergence of singularism at the beginning of the fourteenth century was followed by its rapid growth during the subsequent centuries. For this reason, its movement during these centuries, followed by a recession of universalism and mystic integralism, is in complete accordance with the rising tide of

---

[15] Even in such highly integrated concrete unities as a plant or animal organism, there is always present some nonsimultaneousness of appearance of the various characteristics of passage of the organism from one stage to another, as well as some variation from organism to organism, from species to species. For instance, some of the plants passing from the winter "slumbering" to the reawakening of the spring, show it first in flowering and then in opening their leaves; other plants proceed in the opposite way, while still others develop synchronously flowers as well as leaves. When an organism passes from the stage of childhood to puberty, not all the anatomical and physiological and other signs of puberty take place simultaneously. In addition, in some organisms of even the same species one set of traits appears earlier, while in others the process is reversed. For instance, some babies develop speech earlier than the ability to walk, while others have the reverse sequence in the development of these two traits. There is no reason to expect that the integration of cultures shall be — in regard to time — more rigid than that of the organisms.

the Sensate culture and all its cultural variables. By the century period, the highest level of singularism is given in the eighteenth and nineteenth centuries. This shows again that these centuries were indeed the period of the triumphant individualism and singularism, as is shown by other compartments of the culture of these centuries. Especially high was singularism in 1880–1900 (64 per cent) and in 1900–1920 (55 per cent), though in this period it slightly receded. The end of the nineteenth and the first twenty years of the twentieth centuries were further marked by a rapid rise of the singularistic collectivism which has been during the last sixty or seventy years the main gainer of all the five currents.

Thus, here again the essential movements of the main currents are in tangible agreement with those of practically all the variables or components of the Ideational and Sensate cultures. This shows once more the integrated character of the culture studied, as well as the validity of the theory developed here that when the integrated culture passes from one form — Ideational or Sensate — to the other, all its main compartments change also.

It is needless to add that the movement of universalism and singularism shows close association with that of realism and nominalism, with the respective system of truth, with eternalism and temporalism, idealism and materialism, Ideational and Sensate art, and so on.

So far as the qualitative transformations of each of the three main currents during these centuries from the fourteenth to the twentieth are concerned, they have been considerable. Each of the currents has experienced, as in the preceding centuries, several modifications of form and shading. It is superfluous here to try to characterize all these perambulations. It is enough to say that the main trend of the qualitative transformation of universalism during this period consisted, a few short-time flarings excepted, in a further weakening of its previous transcendental character and in its secularization. As we approach our own time, the transcendental universalism, in the sense of subordination of the singular to the transcendental, God or the like, more and more evaporated. Its place has been increasingly occupied by empirical universalism, which maintains the inferiority or derivativeness of the singular in regard to the *empirical* universals : the State, the class, the order, the family, the union, the party, and so on, and for empirical reasons. As a sign of that, in social life has come a weakening of the power of the Christian Church and the Spiritual Power itself, after the climax of the *Unam Sanctam* (November 8, 1302) at the very beginning of the fourteenth century. The general trend of secularization and the growth of empiricism and similar earmarks of the

Sensate culture point in the same direction. The place of the Church or the *corpus mysticum* began more and more to be occupied by the State (which, beginning with the thirteenth century, manifested itself in the ever-growing trend of the theories which maintain the superiority of the secular power over the spiritual),[16] by mankind, by class (proletarian and others), by syndicate, by association generally, and by other bodies social viewed not transcendentally but empirically.

Similarly, the re-emerged singularism has undergone several changes during these centuries and has consisted of diverse rivulets of different colors : singularism spiritual, singularism liberal, singularism anarchistic, singularism of the Stirner type, of the Ibsen type, of the "bourgeois type," with its rights of man and citizen, and prosaic "live and let live."   The general trend of singularism for the centuries has possibly consisted of an evaporation of the transcendental motives of the Christian singularism of man as a pure soul, and in its progressive replacement by the "behavior-istic individual," consisting of "anatomy and physiology," plus "reflexes and habits," psychoanalytical "libido" and similar "complexes," with ever more doubted "mind" and "soul," "conscience and consciousness." Ontologically and ethically singularism tended to become more and more "anatomo-physiological," material, bodily, and therefore progressively eudaemonistic, hedonistic, utilitarian, and behavioristic.   Not the salva-tion or damnation of his "soul" but "the greatest happiness" of the individual — of myself only or of the "greatest number" of the indi-viduals — becomes now the goal of singularism.

As mentioned, of various rivulets of singularism, the particular growth of the collectivistic singularism or singularistic collectivism, has been an especially conspicuous trait of these centuries.

Thus the above data show clearly that the fluctuation of universalism and singularism is indeed connected with that of the Ideational and Sensate cultures and is one of its components as well as its signs.

C. If one wants to know which 20-year periods have been par-ticularly singularistic or individualistic and which particularly universal-

---

[16] Treatises of Walter von der Vogelweide (d. 1230); Wolfram von Eschenbach (d. 1220); Hartmann von der Aue (d. 1220); Henry of Isernia (d. 1270); Gottfried von Strassburg (d. 1230); Roger Bacon (d. 1292); Henry of Ghent (d. 1293); Niccolo of Pisano (d. 1280); Giovanni Pisano (d. 1328); a little later, those of Pierre du Bois (b. 1255); partly Dante (1265–1321), as far as he opposed in his *De monarchia* the supremacy of the spiritual power; Marsilio of Padua (b. 1270); John of Paris (his treatise, *The Authority of the King and Pope* in 1302); Peter Flotte (*Antequam esset clerici*), William Nogaret, William Durant, and a number of other both well-known and anonymous authors. See A. C. Flick, *The Decline of the Medieval Church* (London, 1930), Vol. I. See also the quoted works of O. von Gierke, Carlyle, McIlwain, Hearnshaw.

istic, one can turn to the table and find an answer there. So far as the extreme singularism-individualism is concerned, its golden days were: generally the period from 420 B.C. to 40–20 B.C., then A.D. 160–200, then 1520–1540, 1740–1760, and 1840–1920. Extreme universalism blossomed in the sixth century B.C.; then in the periods 260–300 A.D., 380–440, then throughout the centuries from the eleventh to the fifteenth, then sporadically it flared up in 1520–1640, 1660–1700, 1800–1840. Finally, the mystic integralism blossomed in the first six centuries of our era; and then sporadically flared up at different periods, especially throughout the fourteenth and the fifteenth centuries; then in the periods 1620–1680, 1760–1820.

A mere glance at these minor fluctuations in the shorter periods shows that the extreme and moderate universalism tended to flare up, in minor fluctuations, besides its general connection with the rise and the domination of the Ideational culture, in *the periods either of the existence of strongly integrated*, powerful groups, like tribes and other — mainly kinship — groups, as in Greece before the fifth century; or in the period of building the vast bodies social, like the State and the Church, the crystallization of their organization, the concentration of their power, and the expansion of their controlling functions. Such were the periods 260–300 and 380–440, and generally the third, the fourth, and the fifth centuries A.D., when we have the expansion of the regimentation of the Roman Empire, the complete power of the Emperor now *legibus solutus est;* when the State Socialism, not unlike the contemporary regimes of the Communist, Fascist, Hitlerite regimentation, became triumphant; when, especially in the fourth century, the Christian Church began to build itself into an institution (*Anstalt*) whose function, power, and empire commenced to grow rapidly.

Not incidental perhaps are even such seemingly sporadic flare-ups of universalism as its jump from 75 per cent at the end of the sixth century to 100 per cent in the period of 600–620: it is the period of Gregory the Great and possibly the most decisive period of crystallization and final organization of the papacy as well as of the whole of the Christian Church as a world institution and as the future world empire. Not incidental, perhaps, is also the flaring up of universalism in the period from 760 to 840: it is the period of growth and climax of the Carlovingian Empire. Hardly incidental, also, is the almost monopolistic domination of universalism throughout the centuries from the tenth to the thirteenth (inclusive); it is the climax of the expansion and power of the Roman Catholic See. It became the World Empire; the power of the Pope became practically absolute. Face to face with such force, the individual was nothing—factually, ontologically, and ethically. In perfect agreement with the hypothesis are further short-time flarings of universalism generally, in the period from 1540 to 1620, and of the extreme universalism in the periods 1580–1620 and 1660–1700. These periods were marked by the climax of the power of the Holy Roman Empire and the Spanish, All-Catholic World Monarchy of Charles V, and then of Philip II; by the crystallization and consolidation of the great national empires; by the Catholic Counter-Reformation and the religious wars, in which the churches as well as the empires were reorganized and consolidated; finally, the later period was that of the Absolute *Polizei-Staat* of Louis XIV (before the beginning of the decline of his "luck"), that is, of the great autocrat and king, *legibus solutus*, juridically as well as factually. The French, as well as several other empires and their rulers, became again the Leviathans — vast, powerful, autocratic, and busy with the universal control of the individual, from his economic affairs up to his religion and esthetic tastes.

Subsequent revivals of the extreme and of the partly moderate universalism occurred again in the period of the Napoleonic Empire, with its vast governmental regulation; of the restoration of the State and of the monarchies overturned by the French and other revolutions in Europe, in the period from 1800 to 1860.

Finally, the slight but unmistakable rise of universalism in the period from 1900 to 1920 (practically before the Communist Leviathan, the Fascist Corporative State, the Third Reich, most of the contemporary dictatorships from Pilsudsky to the mild Rooseveltian regime) reflects the absolutization of the State and of its power during the World War and after it. Though these states have a great deal of collectivistic singularism, they have also a great deal of a rude universalism. If the investigation were extended to 1937, the rise of universalism would have been much more conspicuous than is shown by the period of 1900–1920. Numerous, and sharpest, forms of absolutization of the State and the state dictators; of extension of the regulative and regimentative functions of the State in almost all the countries of Europe, the Anglo-Saxon countries not excluded, have come after 1920. It is enough to be lightly acquainted with the Fascist and pro-Fascist, with the Communist and the pro-Communist, with the Hitlerite and the pro-Hitlerite, with the N R A, regimes, with laws enacted and doctrines taught, in order to see an enormous swing toward, if not a pure and consistent universalism, then at least a rude form of it as opposed to singularism in all its forms, except, perhaps, the collectivistic one. In the chapters devoted to the study of the fluctuations in the criminal, civil, and constitutional law, we shall see something of that. For the present, a mere reminder of this fact is enough to make the last case unquestionable. This "turn" is again a variety of the "revolt" against the Sensate culture at the end of the nineteenth and beginning of the twentieth century that we met in art and in most of the compartments of our culture. Like "cubism" in painting, it is definite in its negativeness to that Sensate culture; but it is not, as yet, a real universalism of the Ideational culture. Its consistency with the anti-Sensate revolts in other fields deserves to be mentioned. Taken together, they show that this "revolt" is real indeed, and is spread over almost all the compartments of our culture. These cases give a reasonable corroboration to the hypothesis offered, namely, that the minor flare-ups of universalism usually occur in the period of building, crystallization, and consolidation of the vast bodies social, like the State, the Church, and some others; and especially, in the period of an expansion of their controlling, regimentative, and regulatory functions.

Logically, such a hypothesis is easily comprehensible. When such vast bodies social emerge with their powerful and all-controlling government, the factual power of individuals as individuals and of their free and voluntary association decreases. If they are opposed to the Leviathan and to its government, they are pitilessly crushed. If they support it, their support increases the power and the authority of the autocrat. In both cases, the individual becomes a *quantité négligeable* in the social reality. It is natural that social thought should reflect this situation, and this reflection cannot help becoming as universalistic or more universalistic than in the periods of the "rights of man and citizen," "inalienable rights of the individual," his guarantees and liberties, on the one hand; in the period when governments are mild, elective, constitutional, liberal, limited in their power and functions, control and interference, on the other.

When these considerations are developed in detail, the above a posteriori uniformity becomes not only comprehensible but in a sense the only condition possible. So much about the minor fluctuations of universalism and the reason ("the cause or the factor" or the "independent variable") of it.

As to the periods of ascendancy of mystical integralism, it seems to tend to rise, besides its fundamental connection with the domination of Ideational culture, in the periods of great social calamities and catastrophes, and generally in the periods when the existing sociocultural system was upset — when its shattering, its decline, preceded the estab-

lishment of a new and solid sociocultural order. At least, its prolonged
blossoming in the first six centuries of our era generally and its minor
rises during this period well agree with that hypothesis. We see its first
flare-up in the period from about 60 to 20 B.C. We know that this was
the time of the greatest civil wars of the first and the second triumvirates
in Rome and of the deepest crisis of the Roman Empire and culture:
the end of Republican Rome and the beginning of the transition to
the monarchical Roman Empire. Besides, at that time there began the
deepest inner crisis of the Graeco-Roman culture, the beginning of the
end of its Sensate form and the first emergence of the future Ideational
culture. Likewise, its re-emergence in the period beginning with A.D. 40
and the subsequent strong position it held during the first six or seven centuries of our era is also in agreement with the hypothesis. We know the
expectation of the end of the world and the catastrophic psychology of the
first few centuries of our era. Elsewhere in this work they are described
more fully. It is evident also that these centuries were, as we have seen
from all the tables in this work, the period of transition from the dying
Sensate culture to the new Ideational Christian culture. Not only the
external sociopolitical order was changing and unsettled, but the whole
mentality and culture of the period was unsettled from the top to the
bottom, from science, philosophy, religion, and art up to the ethical,
juridical, economic, and other aspects of the culture. According to the
hypothesis, in such circumstances mysticism generally, and the mystic
integralism specifically, have to rise. And they flared up indeed. Omitting a few other flare-ups of this current — like the periods 720 to 760 and
840 to 880, the first, among other things, being a transition from the
Merovingian to the Carolingian orders, the second being the period of the
beginning of the end of the Carolingian order, filled with many internal
troubles and disputes of the members of the dynasty — omitting these
and a few other short-time risings of the current, its subsequent prolonged
conspicuousness in the fourteenth and the fifteenth and the beginning
of the sixteenth centuries is again in agreement with the hypothesis.
We know already that these centuries were the transition period of a
new and deeper crisis of culture: its transition from the Ideational to the
Sensate form. There was again the psychology of catastrophe, of pessimism, of the macabre; the waves of various calamities, from the Black
Death to the end of the medieval order. Elsewhere it is concisely described how the wave of mysticism generally, as a "desperate form" of
Ideationalism, swept over the whole of Western Europe; how various
calamities and catastrophes and crises contributed to its reinforcement.

In brief, here the facts support the hypothesis very well. Finally, of the short subsequent rises of mystic integralism in the periods 1620–1680 and 1760–1820, it is enough to remember that the first period was that of the acutest religious wars and the Thirty Years' War, of the English Revolution and Civil War, with the many terrible satellites of these troubles. As to the second period, it embraces the great crisis at the end of the eighteenth century centered around the French Revolution, but factually spread over the whole of Europe — the crisis which shook again the socioeconomic, political, mental, and moral order of Europe.

If the study were continued up to the present time, one would be reasonably certain to find some revival of mystic integralism and mysticism generally, after the postwar period of incessant crises and especially after the general depression of 1929 and the subsequent years. In the countries which experienced especially great catastrophes, like Russia, the flaring up of mysticism generally and of mystic integralism specifically seems to be certain (though it is not on the surface and little noticeable to superficial observers).

Thus, these confrontations of the facts with the hypothesis seem to vindicate it well. It is reinforced also by similar uniformity, met several times before. There is hardly a doubt that the reason indicated is not the only one for these minor flares (the major movements of it are "conditioned" by the type of culture), but of these "factors" the reason indicated is probably one of the most important. And for a sociologist it is particularly important, because it is purely sociological in its nature.

Finally, as to the minor or short-time ups and downs of singularism (its major movements being the "function" of the type of the dominant culture), their main "factors" or causes are generally opposite to those of universalism and mystic integralism, though in the ups and downs of extreme singularism the factors of "despair" and calamity may also play some part. As we saw, such calamities tend to make some persons "stoics" and "mystics"; others "epicureans" of a vulgar type of the hedonistic *Carpe diem*. In the field studied, especially when the dominant culture is of the Sensate type, calamities of the sociocultural and political order tend to reinforce the motives of extreme singularism in such persons and groups: since the State, or the society, or culture, or any superindividual order and body and value are at a crisis and do not secure or supply the maximum of pleasure, away with them; let them go to the devil! And let the clever or wise persons center their lives around themselves and the individual generally. When such bodies social in addition "pinch" the individual, put some acutely felt restraints upon him, they have still less reason to be cherished and all the more reason to be sent to the dogs. Such is the psychology and sociology of extreme singularism — anarchistic or other type — in its connection with the crises of the bodies social, in the period of a domination of the Sensate culture. In the period of domination of Ideational culture, most of these are turned into mystics. Therefore it is hardly surprising that some of the minor rises of extreme singularism-individualism occurred in the periods of crises, like the flare-up in the period 420–380 B.C. (the Peloponnesian War and the beginning of the decline of Greece generally; of its Idealistic culture; the period of incessant social and political revolutions and warfares; of the ten and the thirty tyrants, and so on); and 260–200 B.C.; again the period of incessant crises in the life of the Greek states. If the crises and calamities after the beginning of our era did not lead to similar flare-ups of extreme singularism, the reason is that these centuries were the time of the ascendancy of the Ideational culture, and for this reason, in this period as well as during the domination of Ideational culture in the Middle Ages, such calamities tended to reinforce the stream of mysticism but not extreme singularism. It flares up again in the periods 1500–1540, 1740–1760, 1840–1860, and 1880–1920. I leave it to the reader to remember the main events of these periods; if the period 1880–1900 was quiet and orderly and prosperous, the other periods were full of crises and calamities.

So far, a tangible, but neither universal nor close, connection exists between the minor ups of extreme singularism and the sociocultural calamities. The very word *anarchism*, as one of the forms of extreme singularism, implies either nonexistence or weak existence of the super-individual social bonds and structures; and such weak existence they always have in a period of crisis.

Extreme singularism may be bred also by a prolonged, comfortable epicurean prosperity. In their search for excitement and thrill, the people, bored with their quiet existence in the confines of the state or other social body, can easily be induced to fancy singularism as one of the unusual forms of thrill. The relatively high level of extreme singularism in the period 1880–1900 is an example of that: the comfortable and orderly and prosperous Victorian Age bred in a number of the "bored" intellectuals such tendencies and inclinations, especially in the intellectuals well situated and belonging to the upper or rich middle classes, as did the majority of the theorizers on anarchism and the extreme singularism of that period.

As to the moderate forms of singularism, they are satellites of the comparatively prosperous and comfortable and balanced Sensate culture, before its disintegration and sensualization, or of the Idealistic culture where it shares and mixes with the forms of the moderate universalism.

This explains its minor flare-ups in the fifth and in the fourth centuries B.C.; in the first part of the first century A.D. — the pacific and prosperous Augustan Age; in the period from A.D. 80–160, which was again comparatively prosperous and blossoming; and then in 1740–1780, and 1860–1900. These periods were, all in all, in spite of some minor crises, orderly and comparatively comfortable, for the groups from which the thinkers came; and in a sense well balanced and "sensible" in their Sensatism.

Finally the *minor flare-ups of the collectivistic singularism* also seem to occur more frequently in the periods of crises, especially of crises of a deeper kind, when the previously existing culture and order rapidly declines. At least, the periods 1500–1540 and 1880–1920 fit this theory. Historical knowledge testifies also that in the history of Greece and Rome, the flare-ups of this current occurred mainly in such periods.[17]

Likewise in the Middle Ages, in the centuries twelfth to fifteenth, before 1500, the occurrences of the diluted collectivistic singularism-mysticism represented by various sects,[18] like some of the Arnoldists, the Poor Brethren of Lyon, the Utraquists, the Patarini, the Catharists, the Valdenses, the "Spirituals," the Bohemian Brethren, the "Flagellants," the Taborites, the "Millenarians," "Conventuals," "Brothers of Free Spirits," and others, took place in the transitory period from the Ideational to the Sensate culture, not to mention that some of these sects and their "ideology" were born in the years and in the circumstances of a catastrophic and calamitous character. In this sense the collectivistic singularism-mysticism, like the mystic integralism and partly the extreme singularism, is a "desperate form" of singularism, which tries to pull itself out of the difficulties through resorting to a simulacrum of universalism or mystic unity, but without its inner content and value. Respectively it leads to violent or half-violent redistribution of the mainly material values; to increase but not decrease of singularistic greediness; and especially to an ample use of rude force in its dealings with individual groups. As such it almost always is the phenomenon of crisis and transition, but rarely, if ever, the constructive current which builds a new social body, united inwardly, and a new social order which stands by the virtue of its

[17] See especially R. Pöhlmann, *op. cit.*

[18] See particularly L. Karsavin, *Studies of Religious Life in Italy in the 12th and the 13th Centuries* (in Russian) (St. Petersburg, 1912), pp. 5, 22, 52, 216, *et passim;* A. C. Flick, *op. cit.*; B. Jarrett, *Medieval Socialism* (London), chaps. iv-vi; C. Guignebert, *Christianity; Past and Present* (New York, 1927), pt. ii, chap. xv.

inner value, without a superabundant use of the cement of a rudest coercion and force. However, as a sign of "revolt" against Sensate culture, it is symptomatic and, through its destruction, it possibly paves the way for the advent of real universalism with not external but inner — "familistic" — fusion and unification of individuals into real unity approaching that of good members of a strong family. This role it possibly plays at the present time of dissolution of the singularistic contractual ties in our society.[19]

So much for the minor fluctuations of the currents studied and their causes (factors).

D. The movement of the currents shows again that there is no trend to a continuous increase of differentiation and heterogeneity at the cost of homogeneity.

E. If we inquire which of these currents has been more powerful generally, and what has been the "spectrum" of the main periods in regard to the respective mentality, the answer is given by the summary of the weight points for the whole period studied as well as for the main subperiods (see Table 25).

TABLE 25. CURRENTS IN SINGULARISM, UNIVERSALISM, AND INTEGRALISM

Period	All Singularisms	All Universalisms	Mystic Integralism
600 B.C.–100 A.D.	288	300	30
100–600	37	253	166
600–1500	13	400	82
1500–1900	766	1002	97
1900–1920	228	184	0
Total	1332	2139	375

The figures show that the most powerful current throughout the whole period has been universalism. It is almost twice as powerful as singularism. Only in the period 1900–1920 was singularism slightly more powerful than universalism, and both were about equal in the period from 600 B.C. to A.D. 100. Especially universalistic was the period from A.D. 100 to 1500. These figures give a concise spectrum of the mentality of each period; at the same time they suggest that both of these currents seem to reflect two different aspects of the transsubjective reality; that probably neither one of them is totally wrong or totally right, totally

[19] For a proper understanding of this statement and also the terms "familistic" and "contractual," see Chapters One to Eight of Volume Three of this work — on fluctuation of social relationships.

true or totally false; therefore, it is not likely that one of them can drive out the other forever. Temporary swings toward a domination of one of them have occurred and probably will occur, but not forever.

The data seem to suggest again that for a lasting culture and social system the universalist current will be stronger than the singularist one. At least, so it was in the past. The possible reason is somewhat similar to that in the case of idealism and materialism, namely, that the universalist ideology and mentality are necessary, to a degree, for the maintenance of social cohesion and solidarity. As a cohesive agent they are more needed than the singularist ideology, which fosters the centrifugal forces of society and, if much more powerful than the universalist, leads, in conjunction with other factors, to the disruption of social ties, and makes social life, with its authority and government, with its free or forced sacrifices of the individual, impossible. Just as for the living who want to live, some surplus of optimism over pessimism is natural and necessary, so in this case, for a society which lives and wants to live as an integrated system, some excess of universalism over singularism is unavoidable. Otherwise, if the members of such a society would not become *homo homini lupus*, they are likely to become too egotistic and singularistic to make possible any real co-operation, any sacrifice, any government, and any functioning of the society as a whole.

This means that the above figures also show the "proportionate balance" of the main rival currents and therefore the spontaneous self-regulation of sociocultural processes. In this sense, they exhibit once more the validity of the "principle of limit" and other principles emphasized in this work.

F. The above results, together with the next chapter, have an important bearing upon the theories of many sociologists and social scientists busy with a study and definition of such terms as society, group, social phenomenon, and the like. The data show that the period from 1880 to 1920 was one of the few periods (next in the past is the period of the atomistic mentality of the Encyclopedists and the Enlighteners of 1740–1780) when the singularist stream was more powerful than the universalist one. Confront this datum with the dominant definition of society, whether in sociology or in social-science treatises of that period, or in the treatises, texts, and political platforms dealing with the comparative value of the individual and society; confront these two, and the result is interesting in a number of ways. The definitions of society or group or collective unity given in a great majority of sociology courses and in other

texts for the period 1880–1920 [20] are almost invariably singularistic, either
in the form of the extreme or — more often — a moderate singularism.
In a majority of such definitions the individuals, the members, are taken
as the primary reality; not the society.   Society as an entity, independent of or primary to the individuals, is rejected.   An admission of such an
entity is almost unanimously branded as "metaphysical" and "unscientific."   Some of the definitions identify society with a mere sum of the
individuals;   the others — the majority — with the individuals interacting with one another; being in contact, co-operation, united by
common aim (or aims) and interests, and so on; but still the individuals
compose the true and primary reality.   In these definitions society, as a
rule, is defined as a derivative and still singularistic conglomeration of
interacting individuals who give a somewhat different picture from that
of the same individuals isolated.   In both and in other varieties, the
standpoint remains essentially singularistic.   No social *corpus mysticum*,
no society as the primary reality, no social entity as fundamentally
irreducible and inexpressible in the terms of the individuals — interacting or not — is admitted.[21]   Similarly in socioethical valuation of
culture and the individual, the individual is made the measure of all
things, no matter whether the smaller or the greater collection of them.
The value of the society or culture as something superindividual, not
related to, and independent from, the interests, welfare, and happiness
of the greatest number of individuals, is mentioned rarely.   Hedonism,
utilitarianism, eudaemonism, dominant in recent times (as is shown in
Chapters Thirteen to Fifteen), are all more or less singularistic and can
hardly help being so.

Thus this particular standpoint of our texts in the social sciences and
politics and ethics once more supports the accuracy of the picture given
by our data.   I mention this, however, in order to emphasize once more
the principle carried through this work and in this part particularly,
namely, that what appears to be true or scientific — and most of the social
scientists of this period regarded their standpoint as scientific and the
universalistic standpoint as metaphysical — is in a greater part, for each
given period, a reflection of the nature of the culture then predominant.
The domination of the Sensate culture favors sociological singularism

[20] See P. Sorokin, *Contemporary Sociological Theories*, *passim*, and chap. viii, particularly
pp. 456 ff.

[21] Some mild and diluted forms of universalism mixed with singularistic collectivism began
to grow at the end of the nineteenth and in the twentieth centuries (the Sociologistic school;
Marxian, and other collectivist theories) but even these are still far from an undiluted universalism.

appearing and being considered "scientific"; while the domination of the Ideational or Idealistic culture leads to the universalistic or mystic integralist ideology being credited as true or "scientific." Here again social conditions interfere with human epistemology, methodology, logics, and observation of the "facts." They "fool" the scientists and scholars in what appears to them scientific or true and what is not. Most of the writers of sociology texts and treatises have hardly thought that they were "fooled" by the contemporary Sensate culture. Writing their singularistic-nominalistic texts and treatises on society, they proudly thought they were formulating the eternal verity: "perfectly scientific," "free from any metaphysics," based only upon "logic and observation," carried out with the "perfect scientific technique." They believed their objectivity and science; when they were contemptuously treating various "metaphysicians" of the past with their hypostatization of "social entities." Helas! I am afraid they were in the same boat in which were most of the writers, especially from A.D. 400 to 1400, who also were convinced of the existence of the primary social reality; society, be it the Church, the State, the order, or any body social; who did not try to reduce it to the interacting or not of individuals; who regarded it as more real than the individuals and more valuable than the members. They were convinced of the verity of their universalism as the present-time singularistic-nominalistic sociologists are convinced of the eternal verity of their "interacting individuals." Both were the instruments of the dominant culture in which they lived: by their thought, hand, and mouth the dominant culture has been speaking, rather than they themselves. The same dominant culture with its system of truth dictated what was to appear as "true" and "scientific," and what was not. The scientific nature of the modern singularism in sociology and social sciences generally is, from this standpoint, neither more nor less scientific than the nature of the universalistic theories. It appears to be "scientific" and is credited as such (more than are universalistic theories) just because the dominant Sensate culture makes it look so; if the dominant culture be Ideational, singularism will lose its charm and will be branded as metaphysical or superficial.

The complete and absolute and eternal truth in this field is also "white" in a sense of being a synthesis of both and of something else. So much about this aspect of the "sociology of sociology texts and treatises."

There is another aspect of this contemporary sociology and the social sciences. It consists in what is styled the "fact-finding" character of these sciences, for the end of the nineteenth and the twentieth centuries.

There is hardly any doubt that this fact-finding trait stamps these social disciplines in the period mentioned.[22]

We have been a generation of fact finders. Fact finding has been our pride. We proclaimed a revolt against "speculation," "theorizing," "synthesizing," and "subjectivity," meaning by it anything that cannot be observed as a transsubjective phenomenon. We made our motto: "No theory; let facts speak for themselves." We believed in the "objective method," in "quantitative measurement," "reflexes," and "overt behaviorism." Whether or not we found many new "facts," the fact-finding style of the social sciences during the prewar and postwar period stamped our research and our study with a series of typical characteristics.

By its very nature the fact-finding study is unfavorable to a broad generalization, to an original synthesis, or to a dazzling originality. Instead, it calls for "caution" and "factualness," "solidity," and "reliability." In such an atmosphere any self-respecting scholar tends to avoid a large synthesis and the large vistas as he would the worst plague. If he is even inclined toward these, he has to abstain in order not to endanger his reputation. In this way, the very aspiration toward synthetic, theoretical generalizing and analytical—"universalistic," "eternalistic," and "realistic" — studies is chilled to death by the "fact-finding mode." It is the only legitimate child of the prevalent nominalistic, singularistic, temporalistic, and anti-Idealistic mentality of our times.

The aspiration and habit of being "objective" and "quantitative" lead to a similar result. When all one's hopes are placed in the "objectivity" of a questionnaire, in tabulating machinery, or in other mechanical procedures and "techniques," one finds that such operations are not conducive to abstract analytical thinking or to the construction of a vast lasting and "realistic" (versus nominalistic) synthetic theory. On the contrary, they are adverse to them and tend to inhibit them. The place of penetrating and concentrated thought is taken by these mechanical operations; pure thought, "dialectic," and "meditation" are regarded suspiciously, while the tabulating machine, the coefficient of correlation, or a "mental test" are believed to be the patented ways to the kingdom of truth. In addition, all these operations take so much time and energy that there is little left for just thinking itself. Hence, an outstanding lack of skill and a childish innocence of theoretical thinking is charac-

<hr>

[22] See for a development of this point P. Sorokin, "Some of the Basic Factors in the Improvement of Scholarship among American Students of Social Science" in *Social Science* (March, 1936).

teristic of present-day sociology, and possibly of the other social sciences as well.   Hence, their sterility in production of vast generalizations.

The fact-finding style leads to the same result in another way.   However paradoxical it may sound, it is true that the fact-finding periods are marked by far fewer findings of *new* and *relevant* facts than are the synthetic periods.   Since a fact finder wants to be "objective," "behavioristic," "quantitative," and even "experimental," he can take for his study only such problems as can be studied along these lines : that is, only those that already have reliable statistical data ; only those singular phenomena that can be put under experimental conditions ; and only those local, temporary, and singular that can easily be observed "objectively," on a small scale, in a limited span of time and space.   Meanwhile, as a rule, only the best-known and most routine types of phenomena have reliable quantitative data ; only the simplest, most singular and limited in time and space, and therefore the best-known, sociocultural phenomena can be studied under experimental or pseudo-experimental conditions ; only the simplest and the best-known phenomena again can be studied "overtly" or "objectively."   The more complex phenomena, often the more important and significant, especially if they are taken on a large scale in time and space, with a broad perspective, and in all their real intricacy and lasting nature, do not have the necessary statistics ; they cannot be studied in a laboratory under experimental or pseudo-experimental conditions, nor can they be reduced to a mere "overtness." Even the very grasp of these phenomena demands a large background, developed analytical thinking, and many other qualities.   *Hence the nemesis of the fact finders :* they find usually only such facts as are already well known ; their study of these is often but a "painful elaboration of the obvious."   They rarely find *new relevant* facts.   Another aspect of their procedure is an ever-increasing neglect of the phenomena which cannot be studied by means of the dominant singularistic-nominalistic approaches and techniques.   As all such phenomena and relationships come to be more and more neglected, the result is the famous "knowing more and more about less and less."   All this leads to a progressive narrowing of the mental vistas ; to an increasing singularistic, nominalistic, and temporalistic fragmentariness of our studies, our treatises, and our texts on the one hand ; and to their more and more mechanical standardization of routine and "technique."   Look through most of our texts.   They are rich in conglomeration of the empirical, fragmentary data about this and that, from A to Z.   They are full of "cases" and "field-work studies"; they are inflated by the data pertaining to this or that singular phenomenon. They use mainly cases and the "case or statistical methods" (this latter being but collectivistic singularism, par excellence). On the other hand, how utterly lacking they are in any inner integration; in any inner system; in any long-time and large-vista perspectives. There is almost nothing in them from the "eternalistic," "realistic," and "universalistic" principles and viewpoints. They do not care for these and therefore they do not have them. The singularistic fragmentariness is so great that in most of the texts the only bond between their chapters is but the binding of the book. This makes it urgently necessary to introduce some form of standardization. Having no system of thought and no real synthesis, they cannot order the fragmentary material organically, inwardly, by the logic of the system, synthesis, uniting, and integrating principles. Therefore they order it in the only way which is available—in the mechanical way of sequence of chapters, of topics to be treated, and the size of the book and the terminology. When we turn to so-called "research in the social sciences," it is marked by the same singularistic, temporalistic, and nominalistic earmarks. Most of the topics are "local," of "present-day interest," aimed to be "practically useful" — singularistic and temporary fragments of the social world, incidentally taken, incidentally studied, without any time-and-space background or any reference to their bearing on the fundamental problems involved or the fundamental studies made previously.

The training of "researchers" (and who is not a "researcher" now?) is also quite typical for the ends of the fact-finding science in any special period; the art of thinking, the logic, epistemology, and methodology of the social sciences, as well as their history, are terribly neglected. Instead, a training is given in the so-called "technique" of social investigation, be it the "technique of how to use the formula of correlation" (without any serious study of the principles underlying it); or "how to use the technique of interviewing," or the "technique of case study in field work" and that of the "field study in case work"; not to mention hundreds of techniques of this and that test, of this and that "approach." In other words, we have trained ourselves well in the technique of mixing paints, cleaning brushes, testing the quality of the canvas, and in the technique of knowing the various paint firms; but, alas, we have forgotten to train ourselves to paint as artists paint. Shall we wonder that no durable and great masterpieces have come from our efforts, in spite of the enormous quantity of paint used and the number of painters at work (from "researchers" from the P W A unemployed to any clerk in any retail store)?

At the starting phase of this "fact finding," we firmly believed in an unlimited accumulation of "facts" — singularistic and quite temporalistic "facts" — as the "first-hand data." We were hopeful that the more we accumulated, the fuller, completer, and more adequate would be our knowledge. So a mad rush was started to collect historical documents, statistical data, observations, "cases" — any singularistic fact which would "speak for itself." We established archives, libraries, laboratories, to collect them; started compendiums, digests, and bibliographies of the facts. Our efforts were highly successful. We collected so many singularistic facts that at the present moment we are lost in their multitude; we are drowned in them; and do not know what to do with them and still less do we know what they mean and what knowledge they contain. Courageously we continue to compile them; to list them in bibliographies; in the "bibliography of bibliographies" and in the "bibliography of bibliographies of bibliographies." But no human being can grasp all this infinite collection of singularistic-fragmentary facts; no one can read even a small part of the publications on these facts; we have reached a stage when hardly many can read even the mere titles of the works listed in endless bibliographies; and the bibliographies become also more and more useless, because they do not separate real works from trash; and because no bibliography can be complete and list the infinite number of the fact-finding studies. Hence, we are now not relieved by the enormous collection of "facts" but overburdened with them and lost in them. We are lost so much that we even do not know what fact is indeed relevant fact, and what is not. The more they accumulated, the more they contradicted one another — the more "uniformities" and "causal generalizations" evaporated and were found to be fallacious. As a result, we are now more lost than we were before the accumulations of all these fragmentary facts.

Immanently and imperceptibly, here, as in many other fields, the fact-finding, singularistic, nominalistic, and temporalistic science begins to prepare its own funeral and self-destruction, or more accurately, its "drowsiness and sleep" for some time. In this immanent manner it begins to pave the way for the coming ascendance of the "synthesizing," "speculative," "thoughtful" phase of the social sciences, concentrated mainly upon the lasting, general, universalistic, realistic, and eternalistic aspects of the phenomena studied; with little interest in a study of the coefficient of the correlation between the number of windows in tenant-farmer houses (whose tenants have an income of $1150 to $1200) of village A, of the county B, in the winter of 1935, and the number of toilets with and without running water, or "what exactly was the size of and the number of the nails in the shoes of Danton at the moment of his execution," or "what was the exact income of merchant X, in Venice, in July, 1224," and the like. "Universalistic" or less singularistic sociology may use such "facts," but their finding as well as their value will always be secondary for such a science. In contradistinction to the "fact-finding" science, attention is turned to the universal, general, eternal, "essential," or "real" aspects of the phenomena studied, and also to the particular phenomena which are important from this standpoint.

This means that the fact-finding character of our social sciences and their texts and books is again not an incidental trait of our culture, but one of its inherent traits. It is another term for the singularistic, nominalistic, and temporalistic science, a logical component of Sensate mentality and culture. In Ideational mentality and culture, the science becomes less "fact finding," more "speculative," more confident in regard to thought, more eternalistic, realistic, and universalistic. *This means that there is an alternation of the domination of the fact-finding and "scholastic" or synthesizing periods in the social sciences also.* The first is dominant in the Sensate, the second in the *Idealistic and Ideational periods*.

For the present these conclusions suffice. Some others are to be added in the next chapter, where the same topic is taken up but in the still more specific and narrow form.

Starting with nominalism and realism, we narrowed the topic to singularism and universalism as its social forms; and now we are going to narrow it still more, to a study of the juridico-analytical conceptions of the juridical personality, throughout the same period of the same cultures.[23]

[23] I do not want to go into a detailed analysis of universalism and singularism and their fluctuations in the life history of other great cultures, like the Hindu and the Chinese. I can, however, state that so far as the Hindu (Brahmanic) culture, the Taoist culture of China, the Buddhist culture (modified) of several countries like Tibet have also been predominantly Ideational, the expectation that they will exhibit the respective domination of universalism or mystic integralism seems to be well corroborated by the sociophilosophical history of their thought and ideologies. To be sure, as has been shown in greater detail in the preceding chapters, tiny and sporadic rivulets of singularism have not been absent from these histories, but they have been very minor streams in the wide and ample river of universalism and integralism in the thought of these cultures. We hear rarely, and only after a painstaking research and exploration, of the individualistic and singularistic motives — ontologically and ethically — there. So far I can contend that the validity of the conclusions given in this chapter goes beyond the cultures studied: it is corroborated in time as well as in space.

Still further, so far as the Confucian culture of China occupies an intermediary position between the Ideationalism and Sensate culture types, we shall not wonder that the position of Confucianism in this question is also intermediary; it can be styled as a mixture of singularism and universalism.

Chapter Eight

FLUCTUATION OF "FIRST PRINCIPLES": V. FLUCTUATION OF
REALISTIC, NOMINALISTIC, AND MIXED CONCEPTIONS OF THE
REALITY OF THE JURIDICAL PERSONALITY: CORPORATIONS
(*Universitas Personarum* or *Collegia Personalia*) AND INSTITUTIONS
(*Universitas Bonorum* or *Collegia Realia*).[1]

I. Main Types of Conceptions

The preceding chapters have shown that the predominant Ideational
or Sensate mentality manifests itself not only in the respective predominance of general realistic or nominalistic mentality but also in a
predominance of sociological universalism or singularism. In this
chapter I am going to show that this Ideational or Sensate culture mentality determines the dominant theories or ideologies, even in such a
specific field as the problem of the reality of so-called juridical personality.
Upon this or that solution of this problem have depended often the life,
property, and liberty of thousands of persons. This means that the
problem has not only a theoretical but also a paramount, practical importance. Subsequent pages are intended to show that in this field we
have had a fluctuation of the domination of the "realistic" and the
"nominalistic" interpretations of the reality and the nature of the
"juridical personality" or its equivalents; that these waves have followed
in tangible associations with those of general realism and nominalism,
and therefore of the Ideational and Sensate mentalities; that, respectively, in the period of the domination of the Ideational mentality, the
theories or beliefs in the true reality of the juridical personality tend to
dominate and to be considered "true" or "scientific," while in the period
of domination of the Sensate and nominalistic-singularistic mentalities the
nominalistic theories are likely to be believed to be "true" and "scientific."

By juridical personality in law is meant *any body consisting of one or
more individuals treated by the law as a unit, and usually endowed with
the right to perpetual succession and to act as a single person.* Since the
Roman Law, two main forms of the juridical personality have been dis-

---

[1] In co-operation with N. S. Timasheff.

tinguished : (1) Corporations (*universitas personarum*, or the medieval *collegia personalia*), where the union of the members as persons is stressed — such are most of the various corporations, incorporated societies, firms, etc. (2) Institutions (*universitas bonorum* or the medieval *collegia realia*) as a complex of property with a specific purpose, endowed by the law to act as a single person, such as various universities, asylums, etc. (3) Mixed juridical personalities, intermediary between the two (*collegia mixta*).[2]

If the general juridical concept of the juridical personality seems to be clear and simple (though in fact it is not ; see especially Petrajitsky's criticism of it), the problem of its nature and its reality has caused unspeakable difficulties and hardships to the jurists. What is the juridical personality : is it a true reality of the transsubjective social world, different from that of its individual members, or is it a mere fiction, which does not have any transsubjective reality beyond that of its members, but which, for practical purposes, may artificially be treated as if it had a reality similar to that of a single person? (Note here this famous "as if," *als ob*). Such, in brief, is the crux of the problem.

An enormous number of theories have attempted to solve it in a simple or complicated, flat or ingenious manner, with hundreds of thinkers and jurists and lawyers exerting their imagination, logic, observation, intuition in any way they could. Omitting secondary differences, these theories can easily be classed in three main groups : Realistic, Nominalistic, and Mixed, with several subdivisions within each of the groups.

A. *Realistic Conception.* According to it, juridical personality is a transsubjective and superindividual reality, which truly exists in the social world. This reality is neither secondary to nor derivative from the reality of its members, nor coincides with it. It exists side by side and above it. It is neither fiction, nor mere artificial device, intentionally set forth for practical convenience. In no way is it less real than the singular individual. Such being the general conception of realism in the field, in other — more specific — details, realistic theories differ from one another. Some of the more important subclasses of realism are as follows.

(1) *Transcendental realism* of juridical personality sees its reality in some supersensory or transcendental "essence" or "entity." An example of it is given, for instance, in the "charismatic conception" of

[2] See besides the works quoted further, Suvorov, *Juridical Personalities According to the Roman Law* (in Russian) (1900) ; L. Petrajitsky, *Theory of Law and State* (in Russian) (St. Petersburg, 1910), Vol. II, pp. 388-421 ; J. Pokrovsky, *History of the Roman Law* (in Russian) (Riga, 1924), pp. 312 ff. ; D. Grimm, *Dogma of the Roman Law* (in Russian) (Riga, 1924), chap. ii.

the early Christian Church, where all and everything Christian is united and dissolved in God. Instead of God, any other transcendental reality may serve.

(2) *Empirico-organismic realism*, which views the juridical personality as a real organism of superindividual character, with its own body and its own system, partly corporeal, partly psychological. Such are, for example, the conceptions of many of the eminent representatives of the Germanic School in Jurisprudence, like Beseler, Bluntschli, Gierke (partly), and of a few even of the Romance School of Law, like Baron, Regelsberger, and others.[3]

Over the human individuals there continue to exist the human collective unities of diverse order and rank. They are real creatures of historical existence, the social organisms with heads and other organs, of which organisms each participates in its proper place in the life of the whole.[4]

(3) *Psychological realism*, whose partisans see the reality of the juridical personality mainly in some superindividual psychological essence or substratum, like "public opinion," "group mind," "common will," and so on. In the juridical literature specifically (in general sociological literature such a current is very common; see the quoted chapter of my *Theories*), the detailed theory of "will," "corporeal and uncorporeal," was developed especially by Zitelmann. Other theorizers use "group interest," "group aims," and so on, instead of the "will." In all such theories all these psychological essences are viewed as sorts of real entities, which exist outside and above the individual wills, interests, aims, being united with them either corporeally or incorporeally. Persons like Gierke see, side by side with the corporeal reality of the juridical personality, also this superindividual psychological reality.

Corporation is a union with its own autonomous personality; its soul is one common will; its body is a united organism. Institution (*Anstalt*) is a unity with the personality ingrafted on it from outside; its soul is the will of the founder; its body the organic adaptation through which the individuals incessantly serve the will.[5]

Further on, Gierke states that the will of the corporations is immanent, while that of the institutions is transcendental. Thus Gierke unites several varieties of the realism discussed.

[3] See the details of these theories in M. Schwabe, *Rechtssubject* (1901).
[4] O. von Gierke, *Deutsches Privatrecht* (1895), Vol. I, p. 468. Still more organismic is the theory of Bluntschli. See also P. Sorokin, *Contemporary Sociological Theories*, chap. iv, on Bio-Organic School in Sociology.
[5] *Ibid.*, Vol. I, p. 474.

(4) *Functional or naïve realism* bases its belief in the reality of the juridical personality upon its functional unity, which sensorily appears as a reality of *sui generis*, different from that of its members. Such a theory may be more or less sophisticated, more or less extreme, the moderate forms merging imperceptibly into the kind of theories intermediary between realism and nominalism.

The idea of the juridical personality (not being a fiction) assumes the real phenomenon under the adequate concept. The idea of community, for instance, associated with land and persons who are in certain relationships between themselves, corresponds to the reality. It is not a result of a phantasy, as some think, but of common sense.[6]

Such is one of the sophisticated formulations of this standpoint by one of the eminent jurists.

Less sophisticated — and this is important for our subsequent analysis — are all the conceptions, beliefs, ideas which take the reality of a collective unity as a sensory datum based upon its functional and corporeal unity and — reflectively or even spontaneously — believe in its unity and superindividual reality, seeing it in the property, building, persons who are involved in it, and its unified existence and functioning. Such seems to be the conception of the reality of the tribe, of the clan, of the kinship between many primitive collectivistic groups. The tribe or the kinship group is perceived not as a mere sum of its members, or a mere conglomeration of the sensory objects (territory, buildings, property of the tribe), or as something derivative from these components, but as a primary reality in its own right. It often makes derivative the reality of the individual members of the tribe or clan or family. Hence such phenomena as "the collective or indivisible" responsibility or "collective and indivisible" honor of the group, as different from that of its individual members. In such a situation the group comes first and the individuals second.[7]

---

[6] H. Dernburg, *Pandekten* (Berlin, 1903), Vol. I, p. 59. In passing, it is to be noted that these purely juridical theories are special replicas of the theories of sociologists concerning the problem of reality of society generally. Those representatives of the "special" sciences who often accuse sociologists for their vague discussion of many general topics can well see that they themselves discuss the same topics, often not being aware of that, and discuss them not always either better or more clearly than sociologists. If one confronts any of these juridical theories with the theories of sociologists, one can easily find the same varieties of realism and nominalism in regard to the reality of society that we find here, in application to the juridical personality.

[7] See any good description of many a primitive people. Summary is given in R. Thurnwald's *Die menschliche Gesellschaft* (Berlin, 1935), Vol. IV, chaps. i–iii. As concrete examples

In this naïve-realistic conception, in contradistinction to the transcendental, the juridical personality, or the collective unity, is perceived as a semisensory or sensory entity, with its own ontological reality. Finally, there may be and are the realistic conceptions representing a mixture of all these varieties, the transcendental and the naïve-realistic or sensory types. When the Christian Church began to be institutionalized and to appear in a double aspect (as a charismatic transcendental unity in God and as the earthly Bride of Christ represented by the Church as the Institution — *Anstalt*), its reality was perceived partly as transcendental, partly as sensory. In the practical psychology of primitive as well as of civilized people, the reality of the collective unity as a juridical personality often belongs to that type; it rarely occurs that the reality of the primitive tribe or family is perceived (by the realists) either as purely sensory or purely transcendental; besides the symbolic material incarnations of its home, territory, property, building, name, members, etc., there is almost always present a complex of the nonsensory "intangibles": "honor," traditions, mores, beliefs, feelings; magic, moral, and other "values" which play an important part in the perception of the reality of such a unity.

B. *Nominalistic Conception.* It is opposite to the realistic. For its partisans there is no reality of the juridical personality different from that of its members, either in the transsubjective social world or even in our thought. The only real elements in it are its individual members and various sensory objects attached to it artificially. The juridical personality is a *fiction* created artificially for specific practical needs and conditionally treated "as if" (*als ob!*) it were a unity or reality,[8] though in fact it is not. It is merely convenient and serviceable fiction.[9] Again

---

may serve M. Kovalevsky, *Coutume contemporaine et loi ancienne* (Paris, 1893); E. Westermarck, *The Origin and Development of Moral Ideas* (London, 1908); G. Glotz, *La solidarité de la famille dans le droit criminel en Grèce* (Paris, 1904); Sorokin, Zimmerman, and Galpin, *Systematic Source Book in Rural Sociology*, Vol. II, chap. x.

[8] This category of the *als ob* or "as if" of the fiction is one of the fundamental categories of the empirical system of truth and of contemporary science generally. In a sense, it is all based upon a series of fictions or "as ifs." So nominalism, in the problem of the juridical personality, is a specific case of the same general category.

[9] The same is exactly the argument of the Neo-Kantians, Pragmatists, and empiricists in contemporary science, in regard to their "science" and knowledge. If a belief in God is helpful, God exists; if it is not, He does not exist; this pragmatic fiction in a rough but conspicuous form gives an idea of this "fictitious character" of the empirical science. G. Vahinger, then E. Mach, H. Poincaré, K. Pearson, R. Avenarius, and many leading methodologists of contemporary empirical science generally, and V. Pareto and others in sociology particularly, have been indefatigable in repetition and drilling in that "as if" as the important and valuable fundamental principle of the empirical science.

the nominalist conception of the juridical personality has several varieties, ranging from the extreme nominalism which sees in it a pure fiction to which nothing corresponds in reality and which is nothing more than the mere sum of the individuals — its members and the singularistic complexes of material objects — up to the moderate nominalism, which is ready to admit that though the juridical personality does not have any reality independent and different from that of its singularistic members, the specific combination of these members creates a reality different from what they possess as a mere collection of individuals not united by juridical and other interrelationships.

In the field of juridical literature this nominalistic conception was possibly predominant up to the end of the nineteenth century. Many names (given in detail, pages 330 to 335) are connected with it. Almost the whole Romance School of Jurisprudence stands upon this platform. An especially great role was played in the elaboration of the juridical personality as a mere fiction by Pope Innocence IV, the great jurist of the thirteenth century (c. 1245) and more recently by Savigni. For the theory of the fiction, according to Innocence IV, the juridical personality is a mere concept to which nothing corresponds in the reality: it is mere *nomina juris et non personarum, nomina intellectualis*. In a sense, this theory of fiction is a conceptualistic rather than a purely nominalistic conception of the juridical personality. Other jurists go still farther and are inclined to deny not only the transsubjective reality of the juridical personality but its reality as a concept different from singular images. In other words, these theories go still farther in their nominalism than the theory of fiction. For instance, Brinz, in 1857, flatly stated that there is nothing real in the juridical personality, that it generally does not exist, and that the term itself has to be eliminated. Instead, we have to distinguish not two forms of the personality, physical and juridical, but simply two forms of property: *Personenvermögen* — property owned by a certain individual — and *Zweckvermögen* — property which belongs to no individual but exists for a certain purpose. This sensory complex of the property for a certain purpose is what is improperly called juridical personality. Others, like Jhering, also denied its reality, contending that the only reality which is in the juridical personality is that of the members of the corporations and of the persons whom a given complex of property serves: the sick in the hospitals, the poor in the philanthropic institutions, the members of the firm in the corporation, and so on.

In diverse forms, the standpoint of extreme nominalism has been set forth by many an eminent and noneminent jurist and lawyer.

C. *Mixed Conception.* Between the realistic and nominalistic conceptions there are many intermediary conceptions which are composed of eclectic, sometimes inconsistent, sometimes systematic, combinations of various characteristics of both conceptions. One of the important forms of these intermediary theories is the conceptual. Like the conceptualism in ontology, it contends that in the transsubjective social world there is no reality of *sui generis* of the juridical personality which is not derived from that of its individuals and their possessions. In this sense, it is near to nominalistic conception. But to our mind, there is a concept of the juridical personality which is different from the mere sum of its members; which has its own existence as a conceptual reality; is different from the concept of the mere collection of its members. According to the conceptual theory, the juridical personality exists as a reality of *sui generis* in our mind, though it does not exist in the outside social world. In this it is near to the realistic conception of the juridical personality. This theory has again several shadings, some of which imperceptibly pass into the moderate forms of the realistic, others into those of the nominalistic conceptions. Such intermediary theories are those that depict society or a corporation as a functional system of the "as if" type (Pareto and others); which contend that though it consists of individuals and cannot have any reality independent from them, through the process of co-operation, association, contact, and so on, or through the process of incorporation, such a collectivity of individuals gives a reality different from that of the same individuals in isolation, or not subjected to these modes of interaction (the majority of the contemporary sociologists from Pareto to Durkheim and others).[10]

Such are the main types of the conceptions of the nature and reality of the juridical personality and collective unity generally. As we see, they represent but a special case of the problem of realism, conceptualism, and nominalism generally and of universalism and singularism specifically.

It is not my purpose to enter into a discussion of which of these theories is true and which is wrong. From the standpoint of an impartial observer of the dynamics of cultural processes, my task is quite different: it consists in finding out whether, in the course of the life history of the culture studied, there are fluctuations in the domination of each of these conceptions; if there are, when approximately each of them dominated and declined. Then, are these ups and downs of each of these currents connected with the ups and downs of nominalism and realism, universalism

---

[10] See my *Contemporary Sociological Theories,* chaps. iii, viii, *et passim.*

and singularism, and generally with the Sensate and Ideational cultures and their systems of truth?

In the light of such a setting — the really, and the only, observational and impartial — the attempt to argue in favor of the validity of one of these conceptions becomes superfluous. If the above problems are answered positively, the question of validity or invalidity of any of these conceptions receives a definite and quite unexpected solution. It runs: none of these conceptions is absolutely true or false per se; none of them can convince the others of its own adequacy and of the inadequacy of the opponent. But each of them may rise in the period of the domination of its respective type of culture and decline when the uncongenial type of culture rises. Each of them has a "popularity" and is believed to be true and "scientific" in the period of domination of its congenial type of culture mentality and becomes "false" when this culture mentality declines. In other words, we come to the same conclusion here as in other fields studied: what is true or appears to be true and scientific and valid depends greatly upon the dominant type of culture and its respective mentality.

This explains why I need not enter into the discussion of which of these theories is valid, and why such an attempt in the above setting is superfluous. I can leave the matter to all those who have a taste for the production of such "derivations" and who are urged to it by the existing "shining lights" of the sociocultural world they live in.[11]

Before passing to the actual tracing of the ups and downs of each of these currents, several remarks are necessary to indicate the diagnostic signs which show to which of these currents a certain theory or belief in the field belongs. Specification of these "diagnostic signs" is prompted not only by the fact that many a theory in the field contains elements so diverse that it is not easy at once to say to which of these currents it belongs, but especially by the appearance of the specific theories concerning the juridical personality much later than the existence and functioning of such bodies social in the real social life. The Greek and the Roman juridical thought throughout the history of these cultures had only in the late stages of their history some simulacrum of the theories of the juridical personality. Meanwhile, in the real social life, a large number of corporations and collective bodies had functioned practically since the

---

[11] Again I shall add that such a sociologistic theory of knowledge does not mean a position of skepticism. It means that the whole and the pure truth is hardly ever given to us; but a part of it always is in our possession: each of these conceptions has possibly an element of truth. When it is inflated too much and deviates more and more from the line of the pure truth, it receives — sooner or later — a setback, and declines, giving place to its opponents. And so the story goes on.

earliest stages of the culture. And a similar thing is applicable to almost all the other cultures: a reasoned theory of the juridical personality in almost any culture appears late, while the social phenomenon (corporations and institutions) corresponding to the juridical personality appears at the earliest stages of its history. From the lateness of the appearance of a reflective and more or less systematic conception of the juridical personality, it does not follow that the existence of such superindividual collective unities is equally late. Since they existed, in some way they were thought of, and if not an analytical and reflective then an "unreasoned" and "intuitive or habitual" mental attitude nearest to one of the three currents must also have existed, even in the early stages. Using various sayings, laws, and other related evidences, one can roughly reconstruct this attitude and mentality, and tentatively define to which of the three main currents it was nearest. Even in regard to the later stages, such diagnostic signs are necessary also. The point is that some of the characteristics stressed by the jurist as a sign of the realistic conception of the juridical personality are not such at all, in many cases. For instance, some of the investigators of the problem say that when law recognizes the juridical personality as such, and clearly separates its rights, duties, and property from those of the members of the corporation, they take such recognition as sign of evidence of the realistic conception of the juridical personality.

From this standpoint, the following statements of the classic jurists in Rome were often interpreted as evidence of a realistic conception in the field: "*In decurionibus vel aliis universitatibus nihil refert, utrum omnes idem maneant, an pars maneat, vel omnes immutati sint.*" [12] "*Si quid universitati debetur, singulis non debetur, nec quod debet universitas, singuli debent.*" [13] A slave belonging to the corporation is not "*servus plurium, sed corporis.*" [14]

On the other hand, some of the theorizers interpreted as an evidence of nominalistic conception the facts that in a given *sodalitas* or *collegia* a separation of the property of the association as such from that of its members is not made; that the outsiders do not deal with a given association as such but only with its singular members, and so on. From this standpoint, they have to interpret as nominalistic the mentality and the attitude of the law of early Rome in regard to most of the collectivities and corporations (*sodalitates, collegia sodalicia*), because at that period the above separation of the rights and duties and property of the *sodalitates* as such from those of their individual members did not exist.

[12] Fr. 7.2.D.3.4.   [13] Fr. 7.1.D.3.4.   [14] Fr. 16.D.50.16

Such an interpretation appears to me fallacious. And for a very simple reason : only when singularism and individualistic nominalism progress far enough; when the collective unity becomes a mere contractual and comparatively superficial merging together of a part of the activities, personalities, and interests of its members,[15] only under such circumstances does it become important and urgent to separate the responsibilities, rights, and property of the corporation from those of its individual members. On the one hand, their singularity and individuality and the artificially nominalistic mentality in regard to the collective unity is excellently evidenced by this very fact — that the individuals are aware of their "independence" from the unity, that they are not and do not want to be absorbed in it, that they keep their singularism, and that they invest as singular individuals only a portion of their personality, property, and interests in the artificial "common pot." When, on the other hand, the personality of the individual members of a unity — say the early Roman family — are entirely fused together and merged in the unity; when the interests of the collectivity coincide with those of its members entirely; when outside of the collectivity the individual is amounting to nothing; when, in contemporary terms, the singular individuals "invest" all they have — not only their property but their very life, honor, dignity, social status, and personality — in the "bank of the given collective unity" — be it tribe, the agnatic family, the phratry, or the like — then the separation of the rights and duties of the unity from those of its individual members becomes superfluous and unnecessary. There the collective and the singular are inseparable. Under such conditions, the above : "*Si quid universitati debetur, singulis non debetur*" becomes quite out of place, a useless and meaningless superfluity, like an attempt in one organism to separate the "interests" of the organism as such from that of its organs. If the whole goes on the rocks, every member goes on the rocks; and vice versa.

For these and similar considerations, our diagnostic signs can and should deviate from those which have been set forth by some (not by the majority nor even the greatest) jurists.

After these remarks, let me indicate some of the signs which help to diagnose the somewhat indefinite theories as to the class to which they belong. Of these diagnostic signs the following can be mentioned.

---

[15] See, for a proper understanding of this statement, Chapters One to Eight of Volume Three, devoted to an analysis of the fluctuation of the compulsory, contractual, and familistic forms of social relationships.

(1) Is the reality of the juridical personality viewed as primary to, or derivative from, the reality of its singularistic members? Theories or beliefs or opinions answering that question positively, in the sense of "primary to," are in most of the cases realistic; those answering in the sense of "derivative from " are either nominalistic or conceptualistic.

(2) Is the sanction of the State or of any other social body regarded as absolutely indispensable for the establishment and functioning of the juridical personality? The theories which answer the question positively view juridical personality as an artificial — fictional — creation and therefore in most of the cases they are nominalistic or conceptualistic. The theories which claim that juridical personality originates "naturally," that no sanction or permission of the State or any other agency is necessary for its origin, and that at the most the positive law of the State only regulates its functioning, are likely to be, in most of the cases, realistic.

(3) The degree of the fusion of the individual members — their personality, interests, rights, duties, property, dignity, etc. — with one another in the collective unity, or the degree of the identification of the whole personality of the members — all their values — with the collectivity. If and when it is unrestrained, unspecified and complete, or approaching to it, such an attitude is near to the realistic; while when it is limited and specified and "superficial," such an attitude and the respective mentality is likely to be nominalistic or conceptualistic.[16]

From this standpoint most of the groups where the main form of the relationships among the members is "familistic" are likely to be viewed by its members and contemporaries realistically.

Most of the groups with contractual relationships predominant are likely to be viewed nominalistically or conceptualistically. (Note that this statement means the *nature* of the existing relationship but not the *mode of its origin:* a familistic form of relationship may originate "contractually"; for instance, the marriage, which often in the strong family leads to an establishment of the familistic relationship between husband and wife and parents and children, originates often contractually; and vice versa, several spontaneously born relationships sometimes turn into contractual ones. The nature of the relationship and the mode of its establishment are different things and should not be confused.) [17]

In such "fused" and familistic collectivities, viewed realistically, no need exists for a separation of the rights and duties of the whole from those

[16] See the chapters devoted to the study of the contractual, familistic, and compulsory forms of social relationship.

[17] See Chapters One to Eight of Volume Three.

of the singular members. *Pater familias* or any other member is an incarnation of it, and acting as an individual he acts as an instrument of the group. There, "*si quid universitati debetur, singulis debetur; quod debet universitas, singuli debent.*"

Hence, so-called "collective honor," collective responsibility, and generally collective functioning of the group are inseparable from that of its members, and vice versa. Crime committed by a member becomes the crime of the group, that is, of all other members. Heroic action of a member is heroic action of the group, belongs to it as a whole and to all its members respectively.

When the merger of the personalities and values of the members is quantitatively and qualitatively limited and shallow, and assumes the form of a specific "contractual" relationship (with its "no more and no less"), the separation of the "merger's" rights and duties from those of the individual members becomes necessary. The merger or the group becomes a mere derivative unity, with which only a little part of the personalities and values of each member is identified, and which is entirely derivative in its "reality" from the primary reality of the individuals. In such conditions, no real collective responsibility of all the members in the above sense is possible. Each of them has its own — singular — rights and duties separate from those of other members and the collectivity; only in a specified and limited form has the association as such its own rights and duties, quite separate from those of its members. It has not a collective responsibility in the above sense, but just the responsibility of the total sum of shares contributed by each member and managed by a special manager.

(4) Generally, when the dominant mentality is Ideational, its nature is conducive to surveying the collective unity realistically; when the mentality is Sensate, it facilitates the nominalistic outlook upon such collective bodies.

Such are some of the diagnostic signs which may be helpful in the cases of somewhat indefinite theories and beliefs in the field.

Now we can turn to a study of the problem of the quantitative-qualitative fluctuation, rise, and decline of these conceptions in the life history of the Graeco-Roman and the Western civilizations. Here, however, we shall satisfy ourselves with a descriptive characterization of the main waves with only a partial help from the "quantitative indicators" used before: our attempt to do that in this field met insuperable difficulties which forced us to abandon the procedure in its main parts. The subsequent outline is based, therefore, upon the best and the most authoritative sources, which permit us to say roughly which of these three conceptions has been particularly strong and dominant in a given period and how their domination fluctuated in the course of time.[18]

II. Fluctuation of the Domination of the Main Conceptions

A. *Greece.* Our knowledge of the fluctuation of the conceptions studied in the history of Greek culture is very unsatisfactory; the existing sources give only fragments and glimpses of the matter and do not supply any satisfactory material from which to construct a continuous history of the mentality in the field. On the basis of the existing fragments, it is possible to make the following statements.

Though the Greek philosophy and jurisprudence, especially before the fifth century B.C., had hardly any explicit theory of the juridical personality, nevertheless the dominant mentality here was realistic. This follows from the generally assumed principle of the period that the individual is entitled to rights only in so far as he is a member either of the State or other social body and all the rights of an individual belong to him only as to a part of the whole body social. Outside of that he is an "outlaw," a nonsocial, or rather asocial, being. This means that in such a conception, individual rights are considered derivative from the rights of the whole social body;[19] it is a definite symptom of the realistic nature of the respective opinions and convictions. This agrees well with the domination of realism and universalism in that period of Greek culture mentality. It is also supported by the fact that the Greek law recognizes the rights — especially the property rights — and considers as juridical subjects such collective bodies as the phyle and phratry, as well as the religious body, whose property is conceded to belong to the gods.[20]

Furthermore, various associations and collective corporations did not need the special permission of the State to be started and to become juridical subjects with rights and duties.[21]

Finally, as is shown elsewhere, the predominance of the "familistic relations" in the texture of social relationships of the period also points to the same realistic conception of the collective bodies in that period.

Whether later on, beginning with the second part of the fifth century, an essential change took place in that respect, we can but guess. The

[18] The main sources used here are indicated in the subsequent footnotes.
[19] See the details in O. von Gierke, *Das deutsche Genossenschaftsrecht*, Vol. III, pp. 11 ff.
[20] See the details in E. Weiss, *Griechisches Privatrecht* (Leipzig, 1923), Vol. I, pp. 155 ff.
[21] See P. Foucart, *Les associations religieuses chez les Grecs* (Paris, 1873), pp. 47–49.

fragmentary evidences suggest that such a change did take place in the direction of a conceptualistic or nominalistic mentality. One of these fragmentary evidences is the appearance of dualism between Nature and man-made institutions and laws, started by the later sophists (Hyppias, Critias, Thrasymachos, and others).[22]   Since the man-made institutions and laws were now viewed as a purely artificial device of the stronger for the exploitation of the weaker, not only the reality of the juridical personality but the reality of the social institutions generally and of "law" as an expression of the "justice" of the body social or politic was challenged. They were interpreted as inventions of the singularistic individuals; their reality was reduced to that of the dominating individuals; and any other collectivistic reality was practically denied as reality and asserted to be fictitious.

Such a change is an evidence of the nominalistic interpretation of the juridical personality as well as of the reality of any collective unity.

Another evidence of a nominalistic swing is the growth of nominalism in philosophy and singularism, including the extreme one, in the problem of the individual and the society. (See the two preceding chapters.) These, and a few other evidences, however fragmentary, indicate that such a nominalistic trend probably appeared in the fifth century B.C. If the assumption be valid, then in this field the Greek thought changed parallel with respective transitions from the Ideational to the Idealistic and the Sensate culture.

B. *Rome.*   Like other early laws, the early *jus quiritium* does not operate with the term of juridical personality. But it applies to numerous social bodies or collective corporations — public and private — which are similar in their nature to the corporation or juridical personality. Such were the Roman State itself, *ager publicus,* and other state corporations or institutions. Such were also the *gens,* with their subdivisions; *res sacrae, res religiosae, res sanctae,* and other religious associations; and property, which were the *res divini juris.*   In all such cases, these forms of property were regarded as belonging to a collectivity; either to the *populus Romanus,* or to the *gens,* or to the *gods* and the religious institutions.   Side by side with such public bodies, there was a multitude of private corporations: those of religious character (*sodalitates, collegia sodalicia*), trade unions of the artisans (*collegia pistorum, fabrorum*), of the officials (*apparitorum*), and so on.   Later on, to these were added

---

[22] See here A. O. Lovejoy and others, *Primitivism and Related Ideas in Antiquity,* Vol. I, chap. iii; J. W. Beardslee, Jr., *The Use of φύσις in the Fifth Century of Greek Literature* (New York, 1918); E. Barker, *Greek Political Theory* (London, 1918), pp. 64–77.

many others : municipalities, *civitates* with *suffragio* and without *suffragio*, and others.

It is of little importance for our purposes that the protection of the rights of the public collectivities (as *res extra commercium*) was carried on through a processual system of law different from that applied to private persons. What is important is that the Roman population was organized into a large number of corporations, unions, associations, and other collective bodies. Now the problem arises : Were these bodies regarded realistically or nominalistically? However scanty are the direct evidences, the indirect data suggest an answer in favor of a moderate, simple realism of partly transcendental and partly "naïve-realistic" kind. The reasons in brief are as follows.

For the establishment and existence of these bodies, no permission or sanction of the State was required, according to the testimony of Gaius. The unity within the collectivities was so great that no question could arise as to their reality or fictitiousness : membership in the same *sodalitas* was called *cognatio*, indicating thus the closest and the familistic nature of the bonds, amounting to kinship; a member of the *sodalitas* could not be an accuser or persecutor of another member of the same *sodalitas;* their members had common funerals, common meals, common religious ceremonies. *A nostro collegio dolus malus* (among the members) *abesto*, such is the situation. In brief, they were as closely bound together as any kinship or familistic group; they functioned as a real unity and as such were thought of, recognized, and treated.[23]

The whole social structure of the early Roman society was such that the individual's status, position, personality were decisively dependent upon the groups to which he belonged. Outside of the collectivity, the individual as an individual amounted to little, almost to nothing. In these conditions, it is hardly probable that the reality of the collectivities could be questioned or thought of as mere "fiction" or as entirely nonexistent. As mentioned, just because such was the situation, it was useless to try to separate the responsibility and property of the members from that of the corporation.

Such a "naïve-realistic" conception existed up to about the middle of the first century B.C. — more exactly up to 64 B.C. In that year was enacted the *senatus consultum*, which ended all the *collegia* and the

[23] See O. Karlowa, *Romische Rechtsgeschichte* (Leipzig, 1892), Vol. II, pp. 60–66 ; W. Liebenam, *Zur Geschichte und Organization des Romisches Vereinswesens* (Leipzig, 1890), pp. 1, 160, 225, 258–263, and 185 ; R. Saleilles, *De la personalité juridique* (Paris, 1910), p. 58 ; V. Eliashevitch, *Juridical Personality, Its Origin and Functions in the Roman Private Law* (in Russian) (St. Petersburg, 1910).

associations.   Then, under Augustus, was enacted the *lex Julia de collegiis*, which required the special permission of the State (the Senate or the Emperor) for the establishment of any association or corporation.[24] This was followed by further enactments which introduced the separation of the rights and property of the sanctioned corporation from those of its members.   Thus both enactments are a definite diagnostic sign of the swing of the law toward the nominalistic conception of the juridical personality.

A similar swing appears in the juridical doctrine.   In the second century A.D., it already is viewed nominalistically, as a fiction expedient for practical purposes.   With it appears the term so typical of the "fiction" theory: styling the corporation "as if a personality." [25]

In brief, there appear all the signs of the nominalistic conception in the law as well as in the juridical doctrine.   F. C. Savigny [26] and then Gierke painstakingly studied the problem and, as Gierke says, none of the later investigations disproved the conclusion of Savigny that the Imperial jurisprudence of the period of Principatus and the Imperial period of Rome had a nominalistic position in the question.[27]   The law up to the *Corpus juris civilis* of Justinian (sixth century A.D.) remains, in essentials, at that nominalistic position.

Parallel with the development of the Roman law was going on the development of the Christian doctrine and theology.   Here, in application to the Church and the religious corporations, re-emerged the realistic conception, at the beginning in the form of the transcendental realism ("charismatic" reality in God, outlined above), and, after the legalization of the Church, in a mixed — partly transcendental, partly empirical — form.   In this way, the realistic current reappears in the Ideational mentality of early Christianity.   Though it seems to have influenced the positive law little during the first few centuries of our era,[28] its reappearance in the Christian doctrine and mentality seems to be as unquestionable as is its later synthesis with the early Teutonic law, which

[24] Neque societas, neque collegium, neque huiusmodi corpus passim omnibus haberi conceditur, nam et legibus, et senatus consultis, et principalibus constitutionibus ea res coercetur (and so on). I, 1, pr. D. quod cuiusqumque universit, 3 and 4.

[25] The famous text of Florentinus: quia hereditas jacens *personae vice* fungitur, sicut municipium, decuria, societas. L. 22 D. 46. 1.

[26] F. C. Savigny, *System des Romischen Rechts*, 8 vols. (Berlin, 1840–1849).

[27] See Gierke, *Das deutsche Genossenschaftsrecht*, Vol. III, pp. 131 ; also 101–103 and 134–135.

[28] *Ibid.*, Vol. III, pp. 108 and 111–113.   However, under the Christian emperors, many corporations and institutions of especially religious character — churches, monasteries, institutions for the poor (*ptochotrophia*), hospitals (*nosocomia*), and others — appeared and began to increase.

led to the rise and domination of realism during the first part of the Middle Ages.

This "curve" of domination of the realistic conception before the first century B.C., its subsequent decline, and then the domination of the nominalistic conception after the beginning of our era up to about the sixth century, is supported also, indirectly, by our data from other compartments of Roman culture and mentality. Before the first century B.C. the collective-familistic type of social relationship was dominant; individualism and singularism had not developed greatly as yet; other earmarks of the Sensate mentality and culture were also little developed. With the first century B.C., these earmarks appeared in practically almost all the compartments of Roman culture. And they dominated it up to about the third, fourth, and fifth centuries A.D., after which the Sensate culture disappeared. The above outline of the movement of realism and nominalism in the special field studied tallies with this general movement of the Ideational and Sensate cultures very well. What is still more important is that the curve of the fluctuations of the main conception of the juridical personality given above is based not upon my own data but mainly upon the studies and conclusions of the best investigators in the field, who naturally did not have the slightest idea of the theory of the fluctuation of the Ideational and Sensate cultures set forth in this work.

C. *The Middle Ages.* When the realistic stream of Christian thought united itself with the naïve-realistic conception of the early Teutonic law in regard to collective bodies, the result was a decline of the nominalistic conception and the rise and domination of the realistic one in its various forms — partly transcendental, partly naïve-realistic and functional.

The early Teutonic law did not have a formal conception of the juridical personality. However, the strong collective bonds which united the members of many a collectivity, from the tribe and the family up to the brotherhoods, *compagnonnage* and other unions; the predominance of the familistic type of relationship between their members;[29] the most intensive functioning of these collectivities and the engulfment of the individual by these unities — all this forced the people to look at the collectivities as the real unities, and nothing could suggest the nominalistic view to them. The position of the Germanic law here is similar to that of the early stages of the Roman law; the existence of a real

---

[29] See Chapters One to Eight, on the fluctuation of the familistic and contractual types of social relationship in Volume Three.

collectivity as a sensory unit, or multitude of members merged into one body with which their personality and their property were identified and inseparable.[30]   As such, it was perceived and thought of realistically.

According to Gierke, at that period the common will of the collectivity was a complex volitional action of the members.   (As mentioned before, Gierke contends that the collective bodies have their own body and will, different from those of the members.)   Disagreement of separate members they tried to eliminate through preliminary discussion.   The unanimous decision, *mit eine Munde*, was the rule at the large meetings. If there was no such unanimity or overwhelming majority, the decision could not be made.[31]

The decisions often bound not only the living members but their descendants also, through an oath.   Here is a typical form of the decision in behalf of such a collectivity or juridical personality: "*Schulthess und meyer auch gemeine huber und stulgenossen . . . für sich und für alle ihre nachkomen, vereinbart entschlassen und zu rechte erkannt.*"   Likewise the same naïve-realistic conception manifests itself in the identification of the union with its members, especially with its head: for instance, state property with that of the king, *res fisci quae sunt res regis*.[32]

Side by side with this naïve-realistic current, the current of transcendental and empirical realism continued to flow in the Christian Church. It continued to regard the Church as a real unity, partly transcendental, partly empirical.   In the documents of the eighth and ninth and tenth centuries, we find terminological as well as conceptual and "operational" manifestations of that.   For instance in the document of 812 we read, "*ecclesia villis dotata.*"   Church institutions and groupings were regarded as unities and treated so, whether in positive or punitive measures.

Later on, as Gierke shows, the transcendental realism tended to fade and the Christian thought became more and more engulfed by the naïve-realistic mentality of the Germanic peoples.[33]

But this means only the replacement of one form of realism with another.

---

[30] See Saleilles, *op. cit.*, pp. 161–164; also F. Ferrara, *Teoria delle persone giuridiche* (Napoli, 1915), p. 44.

[31] Gierke, *Das deutsche Genossenschaftsrecht*, Vol. II, pp. 476–480.

[32] *Ibid.*, Vol. III, p. 189, No. 2.   See in this unrivaled and unexcelled work the details. One of the main contentions in the work of Gierke is that the realistic conception of the juridical personality and collectivities has always been the most typical trait of the Germanic law.   See his *Deutsches Privatrecht*, Vol. 1, p. 468.

[33] Gierke, *Das deutsche Genossenschaftsrecht*, Vol. II, p. 549.

Other diagnostic signs point to the same conclusion. No permission or sanction of the State was necessary for the origin and the functioning of the collective unities;[34] no separation of the responsibility and property of the union from that of its members. The familistic relationship predominated in the social relationships of the members of the collectivities.[35] Singularism and individualism had little existence. The real unities of social reality were the various collectivities, rather than singularistic individuals: the family, the tribe, the kinship groups, the neighborhood group, and others. The singularistic individual was, so to speak, dissolved in them, engulfed by them, and therefore figured and functioned little on the front page of historical reality.

This means that the period from the sixth to the twelfth centuries was dominated by various forms of realistic mentality. This tallies well with the domination of general realism, of universalism, of the truth of faith, and other marks of the Ideational culture.

D. *Transitional Period.* The situation changes in the twelfth and thirteenth centuries, as the works of the glossators on the civil and canon law show. Glossators attempt to unite mechanically the Roman "fiction" conceptions with the naïve-realistic conceptions of the Germanic law, without any real attempt to think the problem through logically.[36] For instance, in the *glossa ordinaria* of Accursius (1182–1258) we read: "*Universitas nihil aliud est nisi singuli homines qui ibi sunt*"; and at the same time: "*quod universitatis est non singulorum.*"

This indicates a change, an intrusion of nonintended nominalism in the field, and as a result, a mechanical mixture of the declining realistic stream with the incoming nominalistic stream. Now the permission of the State is necessary for the starting and functioning of corporations; all corporations which do not have it are regarded as unlawful.[37] Other signs of nominalism are not lacking. But it only begins to emerge, therefore the realistic stream continues to flow strongly, and many Roman-law texts are interpreted realistically, either through the addition of some words or through other means. Thus, for instance, according to the Roman law, the corporation as such is capable of having rights but incapable of acting as a single person : "*universitas consentire non potest.*" Glossators insert the word *facile*, and make the corporation capable in this respect. According to the Roman text, "*universitas delinquere non*

---

[34] Saleilles, *op. cit.*, p. 203. Gierke, *Das deutsche Genossenschaftsrecht*, Vol. II, p. 522.
[35] See Chapters One to Eight of Volume Three, on the fluctuation of these relationships.
[36] Gierke, *op. cit.*, Vol. III, pp. 191, 208, and 204–205.
[37] Gierke, *Das deutsche Genossenschaftsrecht*, Vol. III, p. 206.

potest"; glossators add again the word *facile* and thus make it capable of committing crime.[38]

All this mechanical mixture is highly significant from our standpoint. It shows clearly the beginning of the turn toward nominalism and Sensate culture, which we have in practically all the compartments of the Western culture of that period.

In this mixture the naïve-realism still predominates. Glossators habitually say that the corporation is *corpus unum* (*e.g.*, Pillius, d. 1207); the members of the corporation are compared with the organs of the human body, and so on.[39]   But side by side with that, the nominalistic motives are also given : "*collegium est personarum plurium in corpus unum quasi conjunctio*" (Pillius), and the like.

As to the commentators on the canon law, they show the same eclectic mixture with somewhat stronger nominalistic trend than the glossators of the civil law.

They more definitely stress the difference of the *universitas* from the *singuli;* the independent juridical nature of the corporations ; they apply the terms : *persona universitates, collegii, municipii;* the comparison of the corporation with the *persona: ecclesia vicem personae*, and so on (Durantis and others).   This nominalistic trend finds its culmination for the period in the famous theory of "fiction" of the corporations classically developed by Innocence IV in his main work (1245).   With his work conceptualism and (partly) nominalism become well established and formulated and powerful.

For Innocence IV the corporation is a noncorporeal phenomenon of a purely conceptual character : "*persona non vere, sed representata*" ; respectively, the collectivity as such cannot be responsible for crime : "*impossibile est quod universitas delinquent.*" [40]

If the theory of Innocence IV is conceptualistic rather than purely nominalistic, his disciples, especially Petruccius Serrensis (d. 1343), develop it into a clear nominalism, using the principles of nominalistic philosophy and metaphysics for its foundation.   For the subsequent canonists, the corporation becomes a purely artificial device : it cannot as such commit crime ; it cannot act as such, and only its singularistic representatives can do that ; it does not have either a soul which can be condemned or a body which can be punished ; it cannot be either godfather or godmother ; it needs the permission of the Church or the state

---

[38] *Ibid.*, Vol. III, pp. 218 and 234.
[39] *Ibid.*, Vol. III, p. 203.
[40] *Ibid.*, Vol. III, pp. 243 ff.

authorities for its establishment and functioning, *tacitum vel expressum consensum*, and other nominalistic ideas are included.

However, realism still lingers and finds its expression in several transcendental and bio-organic conceptions and comparisons of the corporation with the body or unity; many canonists refused to follow Innocence IV in the theory that the corporation is incapable of crime and cannot be punished, and in other nominalistic traits given to it by him.[41] Thus here we have also the eclectic mixture of both currents.

Similar eclecticism dominates practical life and everyday formulas. These manifest a coexistence of the realistic and nominalistic conception.[42]

E. *After the Thirteenth Century.* Subsequent centuries, up to the emergence of the School of Natural Law, show a somewhat similar eclecticism with an increasing nominalistic tendency. Post-glossators (the end of the thirteenth and fourteenth centuries) follow the canonists. The corporations are styled regularly *persona*, but more and more frequently *persona representata, ficta*. Possibly the most prominent jurist of the period, Bartolus (1314-1357), states that *"secundum fictionem juris universitas aliud est quam homines universitates"*; that it is a phenomenon without soul or body. Others follow him, deviating from him in only secondary points, like Oldradus, who claims that on account of the fiction we shall also ascribe fictitiously soul and body to the *universitas*. Bartolus and others, assuming the attitude of philosophical nominalism, claim that in reality *universitas* is equal to the sum of its members, but in law it is different from the sum. The nature of the fiction is understood in two ways: some mean by it a fictitious creation of a *persona sui generis* above the sum of the members; others, the fictitious identification of a plurality as a unity. Later, the corporations as *persona representata* need the permission or sanction of either the State or of the *jus gentium* and *jus civile*.

Side by side with these nominalistic tendencies are the elements of the realistic conception, like the conviction that a corporation can be capable of crime, and the like.

In the fifteenth century the theory of fiction closely connected with the rising general nominalism becomes still more conspicuous and influential. But it continues to be mixed eclectically with heterogeneous conceptions. We read formulas like: *"totum non differt realiter a suis partibus; etiam*

[41] See the details in *ibid.*, Vol. III, pp. 281-345.

[42] See the examples of the formulas in Gierke's work, quoted, Vol. II, pp. 549, 779-780, and 822.

universitas est nihil aliud quam homines universitates."   But this is immediately followed by : " *secundum fictionem juris aliud est universitas et
aliud personae de universitate.*"   Bartholomeus (d. 1412), J. de Anania
(1457), Panormitanus (1453), M. Socinus (1401–1457), and others support
such an opinion and call the corporation : " *persona ficta et representata,*"
or " *improprie persona.*"   Differing in details, such as : Can a corporation
exist, having one member in a noninhabited place? and so on, similar
theories are shared by J. de Imola (d. 1436), F. Sandacus (1444–1503),
A. Tartagnus (1423–1477), and others.   The jurists, like Baldus (1327–
1400), Bartholomeus, Paulus de Castro (d. 1441), Zabarella (1375–1417),
and others, share the theory of fiction, but like to use bio-organismic
analogies, comparing the corporation with an organism and its members
with its organs.

As before, some realistic elements are mixed with the nominalistic
conception.[43]

Not different is the picture of the sixteenth century.   Similar formulas
are repeated, like Ulrich Zapius's (1461–1535) that : "*universitas vere et
realiter non est a personis universitatis separata*"; but on account of the
fictio juris it receives an autonomous existence.   *Universitates* are "*personae quae intellectu juris per rationem hominis praesentantur*"; they are
"*personae fictae, non verae.*"   Others add, "*fungitur vice persona sed
persona ficta et imaginaria.*"

Side by side with this, the theory, and especially the juridical practice,
do not now insist strictly on the permission of the State for the establishment of a corporation ; likewise they admit that the corporation is capable of crime and is responsible for it, and some other elements of the
realistic conception.   Most of the German doctors in law stand at this
position : Zapius, H. Golde (d. 1521), N. Everarbus (d. 1553), H. Schürff,
J. Oldendorf (d. 1561), A. Gerl (d. 1587), Hotomanus, J. Cujacius, and
others.[44]

Not much different was the situation in England, Italy, and France.
There also the theory of fiction dominated.   If, according to Saleilles,
in the thirteenth century in France, the old Teutonic realistic conceptions still dominated, in the sixteenth century the domination of the
theory of fiction was unquestionable.[45]

English law and doctrine early accepted the theory of fiction of Innocence IV.   Already in 1376, a law was enacted that no corporation could

[43] See details in Gierke's work, quoted, Vol. III, pp. 425–497.
[44] *Op. cit.*, Vol. III, pp. 672–681 and Vol. IV, p. 183.
[45] Saleilles, *op. cit.*, pp. 222–223.

exist without the king's consent. The doctrine overwhelmingly states that the corporation is an artificial, incorporeal, immortal person. As such, it is incapable of crime, but that does not release it from responsibility for a damage caused by its representative.[46]

F. *The Seventeenth and Eighteenth Centuries.* So far as the juridical doctrine and law are concerned, the seventeenth and eighteenth centuries continue the conceptions of the preceding period. The predominant theory of the juridical personality remains nominalistic or conceptualistic, mainly in the form of the theory of fiction in France and England, and an eclectic theory — though mainly nominalistic — in Italy and Germany. The works of Losaeus: *De jure universitatum* (1601); of Bruningus: *De variis universitatum speciebus* (1609); of Faber, de Luce, Griacus, and others — all have mainly the position of the theory of fiction.[47] In France, the juridical part of the *Encyclopédie*, the works of R. J. Pothier (1699–1772), of Jousse, Le Bret, M. de Vouglans, and others take the same position, while the *ordonnances* of 1659, 1666, and 1749 continue to demand the permission of the State for corporations.[48]

The following fragments are typical.

Les corps et corporations établies selon les lois du royaume sont considérés dans l'État comme tenant lieu des personnes. Ces corps sont des êtres intellectuels différents et distincts de toutes les personnes qui les composent. . . . Les communautés sont des personnes qui n'existent que dans l'intellect ou des êtres intellectuels.[49]

Similar is the position of the Dutch law and doctrine, as it is shown by commentaries of G. Voet (1589–1676) and other works of the period, as well as by the laws themselves.[50] In other words, the law and the practical juridical doctrine of the period continue the predominantly nominalistic-conceptualistic position of the previous period, with still stronger stress on nominalism.

In philosophy and theoretical jurisprudence, the situation is considerably different, however. The period under consideration is marked by the emergence and great success of the so-called doctrine of natural law.

---

[46] G. Schirrmeister, *Das Bürgerliche Recht Englands* (Berlin, 1905), Vol. I, p. 59; A. Grant, *A Practical Treatise on the Law of Corporation* (London, 1850), pp. 1 and 4.

[47] See the details in Gierke, *op. cit.*, Vol. III, pp. 682 ff. and Vol. IV (1913), pp. 63–75 and 185–187; Ferrara, *op. cit.*, pp. 91–92.

[48] See E. Michaud, *La théorie de la personnalité morale* (Paris, 1924), Vol. I, p. 408; Saleilles, *op. cit.*, pp. 241 ff.

[49] R. J. Pothier, *Traité des personnes et des choses. De la propriété*, in his *Œuvres*, Vol. VIII (Paris, 1827). See also Le Bret, *Traité de la souveraineté du roi* (Paris, 1682), Bk. I, chap. xv.

[50] Ferrara, *op. cit.*, p. 88.

A long series of brilliant names of this period stand out as the proponents of this doctrine: H. Donellus (1527–1591), J. Althusius (1557–1638), Thomas Hobbes (1588–1679), J. Locke (1632–1704), S. Pufendorf (1632–1694), G. Grotius (1583–1645), C. Thomasius (1655–1728), J. H. Boehmer (1634–1719), C. Wolf (1679–1754), J. J. Rousseau (1712–1774), C. Nettelbladt (1719–1795), G. W. Leibnitz (1646–1716), C. L. Montesquieu (1689–1755), Bossuet (1627–1700), Fénélon (1651–1715), Horn (1620–1670), and many others. This galaxy of names embraces practically, an overwhelming part of the intellectual leaders of the period — the most influential and the most "modern." If not at once, then eventually, the doctrine of natural law, promoted by such a galaxy, was bound to exert a strong influence upon the positive law and practical juridical doctrine. As a matter of fact, in the second part of the eighteenth century this influence became very strong.

What is the position of the school of natural law in the field of our problem? In a sense it is ambiguous; partly extremely nominalistic, partly realistic. The extreme nominalism manifests itself in the fact that most of the representatives of the doctrine of natural law drop the theory of fiction and explicitly state that any corporation or collectivity is a mere collection of individuals (*homines conjuncti* of Althusius), and its rights and duties are purely derivative from the individuals, as a mere result of the sum of their volitions and their contractual or other agreements. Almost all of them start with the singularistic individual and view any collectivity as either the mere sum or derivation of the existence and activities and contractual agreements of these individuals. Such is the position from Donellus, Althusius, and Hobbes to Montesquieu and most of the others in the school. Some of them, like Horn, stand exclusively at this extremely nominalistic position, claiming that any society is only "*multitudo singulorum, quasi-corpus per analogiam et similitudinem.*"

Side by side with this nominalistic position, many of them, beginning with Althusius,[51] added, logically or not — it does not matter here — that through this conjunction of the *singuli* is created a superindividual *persona* of a real character, and therefore responsible for its actions.[52]

Likewise, Hobbes's *Leviathan*, derived from the singularistic atoms, becomes an appalling, all-powerful reality. Even the conceptions of

---

[51] It is the reason why Gierke, the most prominent representative of the realistic conception in the nineteenth and twentieth centuries, devoted a special monograph to him.

[52] See the characterization of the period and of Althusius in Gierke, *Das deutsche Genossenschaftsrecht*, Vol. IV, pp. 191 ff. and 353 ff.

other social physicists of the seventeenth and eighteenth centuries, who characterized collectivities as an astronomical or functional system composed of individuals — their attractions and repulsions — did not reduce them to mere fiction or *persona representata*.[53]

Likewise, statements similar to the following one from Rousseau, but in different wording, set forth by many partisans of natural law, point to the same element of realistic conception. Talking about the results of the contract of individuals, Rousseau says :

À l'instant au lieu de la personne particulière de chaque contractant cet acte d'association produit un corps moral et collectif composé d'autant de membres que l'assemblée a de voix, lequel recoit de ce même acte son unité, son moi commun, sa vie et sa volonté.[54]

Similar elements of realistic conception are found in Pufendorf's concept of *societas* (the term used now, instead of the previous *universitas*) as *persona moralis composita*, misunderstood by his disciples; or in Montesquieu's conception of the State; [55] and factually, in the theories of the enormous majority of the theorizers about natural law, with the exception of a very few like Horn, who were consistent nominalists in the field.[56]

This explains why I styled the position of the doctrine of natural law ambiguous. Being nominalistic and singularistic, it had nevertheless some elements of an empirical realism in the theories of its partisans. Pointing this out, at the same time I shall stress that whether in its practical effects upon law or in its application to social life, the nominalistic-singularistic part of the doctrine was incomparably more powerful than the realistic part. In most cases, the latter was entirely swallowed by the former, and the former assumed the very sensory, very empirical and singularistic form of a corporeal individual, viewed almost materialistically and behavioristically. For this reason, the school of natural law was not so much a mitigation of the domination of the nominalistic-singularistic conception — and in spite of the realistic elements — as an extremization of this domination. Shall we wonder that the establishment and existence of societies were conditioned by the permission of the State, according to the partisans of the doctrine; that in conformity with it, the nominalistic decrees, like that of August 7, 1791, prohibiting

[53] See P. Sorokin, *op. cit.*, chap. i; E. Spektorsky, *The Problems of Social Physics in the Seventeenth Century*, 2 vols. (in Russian) (Warsaw, 1910, and Kiev, 1917).

[54] Rousseau, *Contrat social*, Bk. I, chap. vi.

[55] Montesquieu, *L'esprit des lois*, Bk. I, chap. iii.

[56] See many details in Gierke, *Das deutsche Genossenschaftsrecht*, Vol. IV, pp. 415 ff.

all corporations, were issued; that the new codes, like the *Preussische Landrecht* (1794), based upon the principles of natural law, showed a similar nominalistic conception.[57]

To sum up: not only the positive law and the juridical doctrine, but even the doctrine of the natural law, continued the predominant nominalistic trend of the previous centuries and somewhat even reinforced it in the seventeenth and eighteenth centuries. And this in spite of the presence of some realistic elements in the doctrine of natural law. These elements remain undeveloped and were suppressed by the nominalistic current — so congenial to the awakened "atomism," "singularism," and "individualism" of the period.

G. *The Nineteenth and Twentieth Centuries.* In the first part of the nineteenth century there continued to be a domination of nominalistic and conceptualistic conceptions of the juridical personality in law, in juridical doctrine, and in juridical philosophy. In a sense, during this period, nominalism and conceptualism possibly reached their climax. Subsequently nominalism began to show some signs of weakening and realism some signs of reawakening, especially in the twentieth century; but we are still far from a domination of realistic conception.

The conceptualistic-nominalistic trend of the preceding centuries, colored by the principles of natural law, became the basis of Napoleonic legislation which influenced that of a considerable part of Europe. In this legislation, the nominalistic conception is dominant; the right of citizens to create associations is subject to the supervision of the State; the permission of an association by the government does not make it as yet a juridical person; for that, a special authorization — so to speak, a second permission — is necessary, and this is given only to the associations recognized as having "*utilité publique.*" [58]

Accordingly, only commercial and a few other associations were granted the right of the juridical personality. Subsequently, a series of civil associations (after the law of 1891), trade unions, agricultural co-operative organizations, and so on, were included in this class. Only in the law of April 4, 1884, was the term *Personne civile* introduced. It is to be mentioned also that the authorization of the State was considered as an act of creation of the juridical personality, not merely a registration of what already existed — a trait so typical of the nominalistic conception.

[57] See H. Dernburg, *Preussisches Privatrecht* (Halle, 1875), Vol. I, pp. 83–85; O. von Gierke, *Deutsches Privatrecht*, Vol. I, p. 462.
[58] See M. Planiol, *Traité de droit civil* (Paris, 1925), Vol. I, Nos. 3005–3011. Ferrara, *op. cit.*, pp. 95–97.

The Italian Civil Code (June 25, 1865) followed the Napoleonic legislation in its early, particularly nominalistic phase.[59]

Similar to the French legislation was the standpoint of the Belgian laws. In England, as mentioned, the nominalistic theory in the variety of the "fiction" conception continued to dominate. In Germany, the particular laws of various states (before the Civil Code of 1900) also followed the French lead. Thus the law of Europe, of the first half of the nineteenth century, was unquestionably nominalistic conceptualistic.

Similar was the position of the predominant current of the juridical doctrine. Though in the general social philosophy of the post-revolutionary period of "reaction" (J. de Maistre, De Bonald, Galler, and others) the realistic conception of the nature of social collectivities was stressed strongly, it hardly exerted a tangible influence upon the juridical doctrine. It remained mainly nominalistic conceptualistic.[60] Being such, in 1840 it found its "superclassical" expression in the theory of Savigny, published in Volume Two of his *System des römischen Rechts* (1840), which restored in systematic form the nominalistic theory of the fiction of the Roman Imperial Law, and polished the fiction theory of Innocence IV. It was put so simply, and at the same time had so much common sense, that it did not fail to appeal to jurists, and soon became a generally accepted conception, almost monopolistic up to the end of the nineteenth century. It argued that the law exists for human beings and therefore only human beings in the sense of individuals can be subjects of law. However, for practical convenience, sometimes it is expedient to ascribe rights and duties to the collectivities or even to the property complexes. Law considers this expediency and uses for it one of its usual methods: fiction. In the way of fiction, it views such collectivities as similar to the physical or singular individuals. All this sounded so reasonable in the nominalistic-singularistic atmosphere, so scientific, so logical, that one can hardly wonder that Savigny's conception became *communis opinio* of lawyers, jurists, and theorizers on juridical personality and collectivities. Up to the end of the nineteenth century it dominated law and doctrine and theory. In Germany, Savigny, Puchta, J. F. Kierulff, A. Arndts, F. Roth, B. Pfeiffer, P. Laband, E. R. Bierling; in France, Laurent, G. Beaudry, T. Ducrocq, A. Esmein, C. Aubry, and R. A. Weiss, A. Tissier, Cassagnade; in Italy, G. Bianchi, Tedeschi, E.

[59] See Ferrara, *op. cit.*, pp. 794 ff. and 870.

[60] Typical and influential examples are given in the treatises of A. F. J. Thibaut, *System des Pandekten Rechts*, in English trans. (London, 1855); A. Schweppe, *Das römische Recht* (Göttingen, 1828); K. A. Mittermaier, *Grundsätze des gemeinen deutschen Privatrechts* (Berlin, 1824).

Pacifici-Mazzoni, P. Fiore, F. Ferrara — these are a few of the leading names that represented this current of thought.

The realistic voices were of course not absent; but they were in the decided minority and their voices were "crying in the nominalistic wilderness." Three years after the publication of Savigny's work, Beseler, in 1843, set forth a theory with a realistic bent; in 1847 Weiske, later on G. S. Kuntze, then Sulkowsky followed; a few others joined the movement. But it was still a minority current. About 1870, O. von Gierke joined it and made it the main theme of his scientific work.[61] If, at the beginning of his studies, he clothed his realistic theory in the bio-organismic form and analogies, in the process of his work he overcame these tendencies, and finally shaped his theory in a form free from these analogies and similitudes. He has shown that the Germanistic conception of the collectivities was, in contrast to the Romanistic, always realistic; that the early Germanic law viewed them as natural and originating naturally as any reality, but not artificially created by the State in the way of fiction. The juridical personality, according to him, is not an organism similar to a biological organism; it is an organic (in contrast to a mechanical) structure or a concrete system. As such it consists (1) of singular members who maintain their independence; (2) of a superindividual unity different from the sum of the members; (3) of specific organic relationships between them, irreducible to juridical or any other concepts — which organic unity is not a fiction; it is as real as, say, electricity in the network of the wires; (4) as such a concrete system, it originates and functions naturally, but it is not created by the State. The State can but somewhat regulate its functions as it can regulate also the conduct of an individual, but such a regulation neither creates it nor makes it fictitious. Such is the essential nature of Gierke's theory.[62]

In general sociology the second half of the nineteenth century was also marked by the appearance of various mixed conceptualistic-universalistic or mild realistic-collectivistic theories: August Comte's conception of mankind as a Supreme Being; Spencer's bio-organismic theories (inconsistently matched with his singularism and Man versus State); other organismic theories of Schäffle, Lilienfeld, Novicow, Worms; the

---

[61] His main works are the above quoted *Das deutsche Genossenschaftsrecht; Deutsches Privatrecht; Der Entwurf eines BGB* (1889); *Die Genossenschaftstheorie und die deutsche Rechtssprechung* (1887); *Johannes Althusius* (1887). See about Gierke in G. Gurvitch, "*O. von Gierke als Rechtsphilosoph*," *Logos* (Tübingen, 1922–1923), Vol. II, pp. 86–132.

[62] It is easy to see that it is very near to the "Sociologistic Theories" in the field of general sociology. See about these theories in P. Sorokin, *op. cit.*, chaps. viii, ix, and x.

neopositivistic theories of E. De Roberty, then of Durkheim and his school; and generally by the emergence and growth of the "Sociologistic School" in sociology and social sciences, the school which gives, if not a quite consistent, and not very conspicuous, theory, still some form of a mixed conceptualistic-realistic formula of collectivities, not greatly different from that of Gierke.

In the field of social sciences and sociology where there were no specific obstacles, the respective moderately realistic theories (though still mixed with collectivistic singularism and nominalism) began to spread. In the field of jurisprudence the obstacles were much greater. Therefore Gierke's theory did not have an immediate success at the beginning of its career. Only a few jurists followed him, like E. Zitelmann (*Begriff und Wesen der juristischen Person*, 1873) Bolze (*Der Begriff der juristischen Person*, 1879), C. Meurer (*Begriff und Eigentümer der heiligen Sachen*), Regelsberger, partly (*Pandekten*), H. Preuss, and a few others.

At that time the order of the day was the preparation and enactment of the new German Civil Code. Gierke came out with the most powerful criticism of its first project, which was based upon nominalistic principles regarded by Gierke as contrary to the whole spirit of the Germanic law. His protest had a success and the Civil Code of 1900 incorporated some of his realistic principles.[63]

In accordance with these the BGB requires a registration (not permission) of corporations of the type of the juridical personality; it makes them responsible for the debts of their members. These and other novelties of the Code are, as Tuhr rightly says, the results of the realistic-organic theory put at the basis of the BGB.[64]

This success began to turn the current. After the enactment of the Code, the juridical doctrine of the twentieth century, as well as the law, began to move more and more away from the nominalistic-conceptualistic conception toward, if not a full-blooded realism, then at least a mild variety, in Germany, Italy, France, and other countries, with the exception of the Anglo-Saxon ones. If, up to the postwar period, one cannot say that the realistic theory (still inconsistent and diluted) was already dominant, one can say, at least, that it became much more powerful than in the preceding few centuries, and almost as strong as the nominalistic conceptions. In Germany its partisans included such "stars" as F. Endemann, G. von Bülow, H. Dernburg, F. Klingsmüller; in France,

---

[63] A. von Tuhr rightly says that it is based upon the organic-realistic principles of Beseler-Gierke. Tuhr, *Der allgemeine Teil des deutschen BGB* (Leipzig, 1910), Vol. I, pp. 372–373.

[64] *Ibid.*, pp. 467, 539, and 541.

R. Saleilles, B. Terrat, Mestre, M. Hauriou, L. Michaud, J. Bonnecasse; in Italy, G. Amades, E. Giantures, to mention but a few names.

The opposite currents — more or less nominalistic and negativistic toward realism — have not been absent and have had a still larger number of representatives among the eminent jurists. A small group continues to claim that the juridical personality does not have any reality except that of its singularistic members, and that its property is nothing but that of the members (M. Planiol, E. Thaller, L. Lacour). Another group contends that the juridical personality does not exist; instead there exist the complexes of property with a special purpose; it belongs not to "whom," but to "what" (*Zweckvermogen* theory of Brinz, shared by E. E. Bekker, Bolze, J. Bonelli, partly by O. Karlowa, L. Duguit, G. Jèze, G. Rümelin). The others, following Jhering's theory, view the juridical personality merely as complexes of property which serve and belong to the receivers of it, that is, to those persons whom it serves: the patients in hospitals, the poor who use it, and so on (Jhering, C. Bornhak, and others). Another group claims that the so-called property of the juridical persons is nothing but the property belonging to its "organs" — to its managers (Hölder, Binder, and others).

However, these nominalistic currents had their golden days in the nineteenth century. At its end and in the twentieth century they hardly have grown or recruited many followers or created brilliant theories. They exist but do not grow.

In the postwar period, we are confronted by the Communist conception of the State and collectivities; with the Fascist conception of the Corporative State; with the Hitler conception of the Third Reich; with other dictatorial regimes having somewhat similar conceptions. All these new regimes have a common element, namely, a conception of collectivity versus the singular individual. We have the rise of a collectivistic singularism as depicted in the previous chapter. As was shown before, it is not a genuine realism, nevertheless it is a continuation of the prewar trend of movement away from the purely nominalistic conception of the group, collectivity, corporation, association, society, and juridical personality. Like cubism in painting, it is a revolt against nominalism and individualistic singularism. In the laws of the postwar period, in the doctrines of these regimes, in their theories, the reality of the collectivity (though still set forth in a singularistic mode) is stressed and overstressed. Whether the Communist State or the Communist Party, or the Corporative State, or the Third Reich, or any other collectivity, they are thought of as real ontologically, to some extent, and superior ethically — at least the special collectivities to which the partisans of these regimes belong — to the individual. This distorted and twisted realism, mixed with collectivistic singularism, pervades the mentality of the present in almost all the Western countries. It is in the air; it is exceedingly strong; it is even more antinominalistic than the theories of Gierke or the other partisans of the mild realism of the prewar time. As we shall see in other parts of this work it is not incidental that all these regimes canceled individualism, the "rights of man and citizen," and other manifestations of atomistic nominalism-singularism. Whether we like it or not, the trend of "collectivization" and of the realistic conception is unmistakable.

In this respect, at the end of the nineteenth and in the twentieth century, we are confronted with a revolt against nominalism and with a turn of the curve toward realism — a turn quite consistent with that toward the sociological universalism in the twentieth century, and partly (but rather vaguely) toward the general philosophical realism which was shown in the preceding chapters. Though the sources and material upon which are built these three curves of general realism, of sociological realism, and of realism in relation to the nature of the juridical person are different, and the data were gathered and compiled from different sources and by different scholars, the total result is rather consistent.

In all three curves we see in the twentieth century either a cessation of the further growth of, or a turn away from, general nominalism, singularism, and juridical nominalism, toward general realism, universalism, and juridical realism. Such is the "sign of our time" in these fields. This "sign" is a variety of "revolt" against the Sensate culture met by us in practically all the compartments of the Western culture at the end of the nineteenth and in the twentieth centuries.

III. Main Conclusions

A. No perpetual trend, only short and long-time fluctuations.

B. Ups and downs of the realistic conception of the juridical person go tangibly together with those of the general philosophical realism, with sociological universalism — mystic unity — with the truth of faith, and, partly, of reason, with eternalism and generally with the rise and decline of the Ideational culture. Ups and downs of juristic nominalism move with philosophic nominalism, sociological singularism, the truth of the senses, temporalism, and of the Sensate culture generally.

Finally, mixed, eclectic, and conceptualistic theories crop out and dominate in the period of the mixed, partly Idealistic, culture and its respective variables.[65]

C. This association means also that even such seemingly special problems as that of the juridical person enter as an organic component into an integrated culture and live and change as such a culture changes.

D. It means, further, that the rise and decline of the main conceptions in the field are, like all the other special phenomena studied, incomprehensible without considering them in the light of the much larger perspective and much broader and more embracing "variable" — the culture — of which it is a part. Without such a setting, one can hardly account intelligently for the fluctuations and would have either to take them as a mere riddle, or tie them to some special variable (economic factor, religion, science, or what not, up to sunspots) which can hardly yield any valid result. Here, then, once more we find a reason for the use of the larger perspectives and "totalitarian" approach. Too narrow a specialization and perspective can never grasp the logic of these changes nor even the mere fact of the long-time fluctuations. Like a microscope it may show well many details of an infinitesimally small particle of reality; but the whole wide world is infinitely larger and richer and more colorful than this particle, and to know something of the universe we need a telescope no less than a miscroscope. *Sapienti sat!*

E. The above gives additional support to the conditioning by the type of culture of what appears to be true and "scientific." A nominalistic theory in the field cannot be dominant and given as "true" and "scientific" in a blooming Ideational culture; and vice versa, a realistic, especially a transcendentally realistic — theory has little chance of being accepted as "scientific" and "true" by the majority of the leading scientists in a period of the blooming of the Sensate culture. The above shows that. Therefore, in the light of this result, I can but humorously take the most enthusiastic defense, or a criticism by a sociologist, social scientist, or anybody, of one of these theories as perfectly "scientific," "true," "observational," "logico-experimental," "proved forever,"

---

[65] Again I am not in a position to enter here into a detailed study of this association between the conception of the reality of the group or collectivity and the Ideational Sensate culture, in other cultures. However, a preliminary knowledge of the situation in the Brahmanic, Taoist, and Tibetan cultures which have predominantly been Ideational, seems to show that the association holds also in social space: the predominant mentality of these cultures in the problem discussed seems to have been also realistic, mainly transcendentally realistic. If this tentative conclusion is found, after a special study, to be valid, then the association of these "variables" goes far beyond the Graeco-Roman and the Western cultures.

while other theories may be styled "unscientific," "meaningless," "metaphysical," false, and so on.[66]

Such overenthusiastic and not too well-informed debaters may be reasonably assured that, even if their theory is generally accepted today, tomorrow, if another type of culture comes, it will be generally rejected. These "ricorsi" have been repeated many times and will probably be repeated many times more in the future.

[66] As a recent example of this, the heated, enthusiastic dispute between F. H. Allport's nominalism and that of his opponents who tried to defend a mild form of realism can be cited. Those who have followed that dispute have seen in it all the above characteristics. On my part, I took it humorously; no argument was given by either party which had not been set forth many times, centuries before; the arguments that were given were far less refined than many found in the theories of either the juridical person or of the collectivity. Neither party showed an understanding of the cultural relativity of the "truth" defended by it. On the contrary, they argued without any consideration of the nature of the culture in which the groups exist and act, and without any consideration of the cultural conditioning of the system of truth generally and of the "validity" of the problem discussed specifically. See literature on this point in P. Sorokin, *Contemporary Sociological Theories*, pp. 457–458.

Chapter Nine

FLUCTUATION OF "FIRST PRINCIPLES": VI. FLUCTUATION OF THE INFLUENCE OF DETERMINISTIC AND INDETERMINISTIC MENTALITIES [1]

I. Determinism and Indeterminism

The next general principles underlying most of the scientific and philosophical and ethical theories are the principles of indeterminism and determinism. Again, explicitly or implicitly, theoretically or practically, they lie at the basis of most of such theories. In this sense one of them is a basic principle of science, philosophy, religion, ethics, politics, and practical activity. All the respective theories in the field represent either a deterministic or an indeterminate or a mixed standpoint. By *determinism* in a broad sense is meant a theory that everything in the world, including man and his mind and actions, are causally conditioned, subject to the principle of the uniform and necessary relationship, and that each cause A has invariably the same effect B and therefore is invariably connected with it. More specifically, it contends that no free will exists as a factor in human behavior. Man is determined as rigidly as any other phenomenon.

Indeterminism is a theory opposite to determinism, especially in application to man. Generally, it denies the existence of invariable causal relationship between the phenomena; it admits a potentiality of variation there: either through the will of God or Providence, or any supreme intelligent power; or through "incidental" or "creative" variations; or as a possibility of several and diverse effects, B, C, D, of the same cause, or variable, A. In brief, it denies the category of the uniform and specific and invariable necessary relationship between the phenomena generally. In regard to man, it contends for the existence of either free will, or free choice, or, in a diluted form, several diverse potentialities in steering his behavior and mind. Here particularly it denies the rigid and invariable and imposed conditioning of his behavior in the same fixed course as that of the motion of inorganic bodies.

[1] In co-operation with N. O. Lossky and I. I. Lapshin.

Such being the general characteristics of determinism and indeterminism, each of them has an enormous variety of concrete forms and shadings. There is a whole gradation of more or less rigid determinisms and more or less free indeterminisms, as they have been given in various theories. In some of the deterministic theories man's behavior is considered as rigidly conditioned as is the motion of a stone falling. In others its conditioned character is qualified by so many reservations, exemptions, and limitations that such a deterministic theory almost imperceptibly merges into indeterminism. *Mutatis mutandis*, the same can be said of various conceptions of indeterminism, which range from almost absolute freedom of man, or anything else from any external conditioning except man's free will, to such diluted indeterminisms as are on the border line between determinism and indeterminism.

By dozens of other characteristics, the theories in the field differ from one another in their conceptions. Some philosophers, like Kant, contend that man's behavior in this phenomenal world is absolutely determined, and if we knew all the circumstances, it could be predicted as accurately as an eclipse of the sun or the moon ; on the other hand, as an "intelligible" and "noumenal" being (in contradistinction to man as an empirical phenomenon) he is quite free from any external conditioning. In other theories determinism amounts almost to fatalism; in several theories the clear-cutness of the concepts is complicated by the introduction of such factors as destiny, Providence, predestination, God's will ; by consideration of the moral responsibility of man for his actions; by distinction between actual and potential freedom, between absolute and relative freedom ; by the introduction of a gradation of forms of conditioning and of freedom, and by hundreds of other circumstances. There are few problems in which so many of the most vital interests of man are involved. Theologians, educators, lawyers, moralizers, politicians, statesmen, scientists, teachers, social reformers, and even the "forgotten man" — each one and everybody is confronted with it, theoretically or practically, and has to give to it some theoretical or practical solution. As their needs and interests are different, each, so to speak, has to cut it to fit his own particular requirements. Therefore an enormous variety of forms, shadings, accentuations, reservations, and qualifications have been injected into the problem and have resulted in a most intricate diversity of concepts of determinism and indeterminism. The complications have gone so far that it is not a rare phenomenon to meet a thinker who in a way is an indeterminist and in a way a determinist. The cases of Cicero or Plutarch or Kant or Melanchthon or of Epicurus and the Epicureans, with whose basic theories their indeterminism is in contradiction, are examples of that. Cicero and Plutarch are quite deterministic in most of their works; on the other hand, they objected to the fatalistic determinism of the stars claimed by the astrological theories of the "Grand Year." Similar contradictions are found in other mentioned and unmentioned cases.

The same motives are given by one group of thinkers as the reason for determinism as by the other group for indeterminism.

I mention all these complexities in order to indicate that this study is made with a full awareness of them and confronts them at its very beginning in its work of classifying the thinkers under one head or another. Almost at once appeared the cases of those thinkers who were indeterministic in some of their works, deterministic in some others: the cases where the theory of a philosopher was such that in one respect it belonged to the indeterministic class, in another to the deterministic. All such cases in our classification were put either into both classes, or into a Mixed class (not shown in Tables 26 and 27 or in Figure 15), where the whole system was undifferentiated, or into the class to which the thinker belongs by reason of his main position. Thinkers who have not made any serious contribution in this field — though they may have made important contributions in other fields of philosophical or scientific thought — were naturally excluded. The method of constructing the tables remains the same as before. The indicators give only the quantitative fluctuations of the influence of the currents. For an adequate knowledge of the real situation, these indicators need to be supplemented by at least a qualitative study of the theories involved. This study is naturally· omitted here. Such a qualitative shading is especially important for some of the periods like 540–320 B.C., or A.D. 1900–1920 and others. When it is done, the meaning of the figures in Tables 26 to 28, and of Figure 15 would change somewhat. As before, it is understood that the indicators are but rough approximations, that the figures for several of the 20-year periods are probably erratic and inadequate; that "zero" in the table does not necessarily mean that the corresponding current disappeared absolutely, but means only that it weakened so much that it is difficult to find any thinker who was representing it at that period. All the other reservations mentioned before apply also to these tables and the list of names in the Appendix to this chapter.[2]

[2] Besides the works mentioned, L. Brunschvicg's *L'expérience humaine et la causalité physique* (Paris, 1922), as well as the works quoted in Chapter Eleven, were consulted. In Figure 15 the Mixed class is not shown for the period 540–340 B.C.

TABLE 26. INDICATORS OF THE FLUCTUATION OF DETERMINISM AND
INDETERMINISM FROM 540 B.C. TO A.D. 1920 BY 20-YEAR PERIODS
(on the basis of different values given from 1 to 12)

PERIOD	Determinism		Mixed		Indeterminism		Total	
	No.	Per cent	No.	Per cent	No.	Per cent	No.	Per cent
540–520 B.C.			8	100			8	100
520–500			15	100			15	100
500–480			15	100			15	100
480–460			7	100			7	100
460–440			1	100			1	100
440–420			9	100			9	100
420–400			29	100			29	100
400–380			41	100			41	100
380–360			42	100			42	100
360–340			47	100			47	100
340–320	30	71.0			12	29.0	42	100
320–300	34	62.0			21	38.0	55	100
300–280	37	69.0			17	31.0	54	100
280–260	37	77.0			11	23.0	48	100
260–240	22	76.0			7	24.0	29	100
240–220	40	78.0			11	22.0	51	100
220–200	20	65.0			11	35.0	31	100
200–180	6	68.0			13	32.0	19	100
180–160	6	43.0			8	57.0	14	100
160–140	6	46.0			7	54.0	13	100
140–120	8	67.0			4	33.0	12	100
120–100	10	62.0			6	38.0	16	100
100–80	12	57.0			9	43.0	21	100
80–60	23	72.0			9	28.0	32	100
60–40	40	65.0			22	35.0	62	100
40–20	24	67.0			12	33.0	36	100
20–0	10	91.0			1	9.0	11	100
0–20 A.D.	12	57.0			9	43.0	21	100
20–40	15	65.0			8	35.0	23	100
40–60	19	66.0			10	34.0	29	100
60–80	27	93.0			2	7.0	29	100
80–100	26	93.0			2	7.0	28	100
100–120	23	64.0			13	36.0	36	100
120–140	47	78.0			13	22.0	60	100
140–160	38	63.0			22	37.0	60	100
160–180	31	46.0			36	54.0	67	100
180–200	34	40.0			50	60.0	84	100
200–220	9	18.0			40	82.0	49	100
220–240	5	16.0			27	84.0	32	100
240–260	15	37.0			25	63.0	40	100
260–280	13	37.0			22	63.0	35	100
280–300	4	33.3			8	66.7	12	100
300–320	1	12.0			22	88.0	23	100
320–340	1	4.0			27	96.0	28	100
340–360	2	9.0			20	91.0	22	100
360–380	2	5.0			36	95.0	38	100
380–400	3	7.0			41	93.0	44	100
400–420	3	8.0			33	92.0	36	100
420–440	3	7.9			35	92.1	38	100
440–460	1	4.0			24	96.0	25	100
460–480	1	5.0			18	95.0	19	100
480–500	1	8.0			12	92.0	13	100
500–520	1	13.0			7	87.0	8	100

TABLE 26. INDICATORS OF THE FLUCTUATION OF DETERMINISM AND IN-
DETERMINISM FROM 540 B.C. TO A.D. 1920 BY 20-YEAR PERIODS — *continued*

(on the basis of different values given from 1 to 12)

PERIOD	Determinism		Mixed		Indeterminism		Total	
	No.	*Per cent*	*No.*	*Per cent*	*No.*	*Per cent*	*No.*	*Per cent*
520–540 A.D.	1	6.0			16	94.0	17	100
540–560	0	0			11	100.0	11	100
560–580	0	0			3	100.0	3	100
580–600	0	0			4	100.0	4	100
600–620	0	0			4	100.0	4	100
620–640	0	0			6	100.0	6	100
640–660	0	0			6	100.0	6	100
660–680	0	0			8	100.0	8	100
680–700	0	0			2	100.0	2	100
700–720	0	0			1	100.0	1	100
720–740	0	0			5	100.0	5	100
740–760	0	0			5	100.0	5	100
760–780	0	0			0	0	0	0
780–800	0	0			4	100.0	4	100
800–820	0	0			4	100.0	4	100
820–840	0	0			4	100.0	4	100
840–860	0	0			14	100.0	14	100
860–880	0	0			15	100.0	15	100
880–900	0	0			5	100.0	5	100
900–920	0	0			2	100.0	2	100
920–940	0	0			2	100.0	2	100
940–960	0	0			0	0	0	0
960–980	0	0			0	0	0	0
980–1000	0	0			0	0	0	0
1000–1020	0	0			0	0	0	0
1020–1040	0	0			0	0	0	0
1040–1060	0	0			0	0	0	0
1060–1080	0	0			14	100.0	14	100
1080–1100	0	0			21	100.0	21	100
1100–1120	0	0			12	100.0	12	100
1120–1140	0	0			21	100.0	21	100
1140–1160	0	0			27	100.0	27	100
1160–1180	0	0			19	100.0	19	100
1180–1200	0	0			16	100.0	16	100
1200–1220	0	0			13	100.0	13	100
1220–1240	3	18.0			14	82.0	17	100
1240–1260	3	15.0			17	85.0	20	100
1260–1280	6	16.0			31	84.0	37	100
1280–1300	9	19.0			39	81.0	48	100
1300–1320	6	10.0			54	90.0	60	100
1320–1340	8	18.0			36	82.0	44	100
1340–1360	12	37.0			20	63.0	32	100
1360–1380	6	30.0			14	70.0	20	100
1380–1400	5	71.0			2	29.0	7	100
1400–1420	2	33.0			4	67.0	6	100
1420–1440	2	15.0			11	85.0	13	100
1440–1460	2	12.0			14	88.0	16	100
1460–1480	2	15.0			11	85.0	13	100
1480–1500	7	64.0			4	36.0	11	100
1500–1520	8	40.0			12	60.0	20	100
1520–1540	19	54.0			16	46.0	35	100
1540–1560	38	66.0			20	34.0	58	100
1560–1580	22	44.0			28	56.0	50	100

TABLE 26. INDICATORS OF THE FLUCTUATION OF DETERMINISM AND IN-
DETERMINISM FROM 540 B.C. TO A.D. 1920 BY 20-YEAR PERIODS — *continued*

(on the basis of different values given from 1 to 12)

PERIOD	Determinism		Mixed		Indeterminism		Total	
	No.	Per cent	No.	Per cent	No.	Per cent	No.	Per cent
1580–1600 A.D.	24	39.0			37	61.0	61	100
1600–1620	27	47.0			30	53.0	57	100
1620–1640	30	52.0			28	48.0	58	100
1640–1660	42	61.0			27	39.0	69	100
1660–1680	38	43.0			51	57.0	89	100
1680–1700	36	33.0			73	67.0	109	100
1700–1720	31	35.0			57	65.0	88	100
1720–1740	27	40.0			42	60.0	69	100
1740–1760	40	40.0			60	60.0	100	100
1760–1780	59	56.0			47	44.0	106	100
1780–1800	52	39.0			80	61.0	132	100
1800–1820	79	47.0			90	53.0	169	100
1820–1840	76	49.0			80	51.0	156	100
1840–1860	100	47.0			114	53.0	214	100
1860–1880	163	61.0			105	39.0	268	100
1880–1900	186	54.0			157	46.0	343	100
1900–1920	205	53.0			185	47.0	390	100

TABLE 27. INDICATORS OF THE FLUCTUATION OF DETERMINISM AND
INDETERMINISM FROM 600 B.C. TO A.D. 1900 BY CENTURY PERIODS

(on the basis of different values given from 1 to 12)

PERIOD	Determinism		Mixed		Indeterminism		Total	
	No.	Per cent	No.	Per cent	No.	Per cent	No.	Per cent
600–500 B.C.			15	100			15	100
500–400			44	100			44	100
400–300	110	84.0			21	16.0	131	100
300–200	75	66.4			38	33.6	113	100
200–100	18	41.9			25	58.1	43	100
100–0	60	62.5			36	37.5	96	100
0–100 A.D.	65	83.3			13	16.7	78	100
100–200	96	55.2			78	44.8	174	100
200–300	25	24.8			76	75.2	101	100
300–400	6	6.5			86	93.5	92	100
400–500	4	6.3			59	93.7	63	100
500–600	1	4.2			23	95.8	24	100
600–700	0	0			12	100.0	12	100
700–800	0	0			10	100.0	10	100
800–900	0	0			23	100.0	23	100
900–1000	0	0			2	100.0	2	100
1000–1100	0	0			21	100.0	21	100
1100–1200	0	0			61	100.0	61	100
1200–1300	12	12.6			83	87.4	95	100
1300–1400	22	19.3			92	80.7	114	100
1400–1500	11	32.3			23	67.7	34	100
1500–1600	75	45.5			90	54.5	165	100
1600–1700	89	35.7			160	64.3	249	100
1700–1800	137	41.5			193	58.5	330	100
1800–1900	395	48.3			423	51.7	818	100

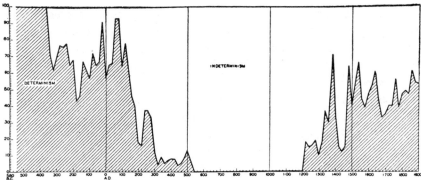

FIG. 15.   FLUCTUATION OF DETERMINISM AND INDETERMINISM

II. MAIN RESULTS

After the commentaries on the tables in preceding chapters, it is unnecessary to comment at length on Tables 26 and 27 and Figure 15. It is enough to say that all the conclusions suggested and warranted by them are sustained by these: fallacy of the linear conception of historical processes; fallacy of an existence of evolutionary linear tendency; fallacy of the Spencerian formula of evolution; fallacy of the belief of the partisans of determinism and indeterminism that their case is "finally and irrevocably" proved, that the fallacy of the rival theory "once and forever" is exposed, that the future is insured for their theory and theirs only. Tables 26 and 27 and the reality they represent can but furnish a laugh at these "ever-recurrent" naïve beliefs.

The next point which needs to be mentioned is the bearing which Table 28 has on the problem of the immanent self-regulation of the currents in the course of time. The total sum of the indices for each of the currents for the total and the specified periods is given in Table 28.

TABLE 28.   INDICES FOR DETERMINISM AND INDETERMINISM

Period	Determinism	Indeterminism
580 B.C.–A.D. 100	678	212
100–540	239	557
540–1500	73	519
1500–1920	1302	1339
Total	2292	2627

Again it is worthy of mention that in spite of a long course of time — 2500 years — and in spite of the fact that the indices are made regardless of their possible quantitative balance, this balance is there, and all in all is rather surprisingly close. For each short period, or even for the longer periods given in the above figures, there is a considerable quantitative difference in the strength of the rival currents; but for the total period, or even for the period of the last 420 years, they fairly closely balance each other. In the light of this, the "ever-recurrent" foolish assurances that one of the currents would disappear forever becomes particularly childish as a scientific statement.

So far as the highs and lows of each of the currents in Figure 15 are concerned, the most conspicuous periods in these respects are as follows.

The period from 540 to 380 B.C. is that of the domination of a kind of Mixed form represented by a belief in Destiny, God, *Fatum*, Μοῖρα, and εἱμαρ μένη, the Pythagorean belief in the mystic, quantitative relationship between phenomena, etc. In a sense, it is a kind of determinism, but a determinism very different from the purely mechanical determinism of the later period. No less can it be styled indeterminism, because the determination here is near to "God's will," or *logos*, indeterministic in its nature. The period is a mixture of both, so typical of the Idealistic culture. A similar situation was met before in the systems of Truth and of Idealism-Materialism. The real blossoming of determinism in Greece and Rome is the period beginning with the second half of the fourth century B.C. and ending with the first century A.D., with its climaxes in the fourth century B.C. and the first century A.D. Since the second century A.D. it has rapidly declined and after the sixth century it becomes "unnoticeable."

Now comes the turn of the domination of indeterminism. It becomes monopolistic from the sixth to the thirteenth century. In the thirteenth century (note again, the century of the Idealistic culture), determinism reappears and rapidly grows, reaching a climax in the sixteenth century; then it recedes slightly in the seventeenth and resumes its rise in the eighteenth and nineteenth centuries.

During the last four centuries both streams have been almost equal in their strength, determinism having its relative jumps in the periods around 1540–1560, 1620–1660, 1760–1780, and 1860–1920, indeterminism retaliating by crescendos in the periods around 1500, 1560–1600, 1680–1740, 1780–1860. The rise of determinism for the last sixty years is to be noted specifically, though the period 1880–1920 shows a slight recession.

The next point to be mentioned is that when the Graeco-Roman culture split into the Pagan and the Christian streams — approximately from A.D. 100 to the sixth century when the Christian stream absorbed the Pagan — the Pagan as well as the Christian philosophical thought had in this (as well as in other respects considered above) practically the same course of direction. We find the Pagan as well as Christian thinkers split between these two currents; in both groups, after the second century, appeared almost simultaneously the trend of reinforcement of indeterminism, and after the third century a rapid weakening of determinism. Thus, the "turn of the direction" which appears in a given culture involves equally all the sects or factions of that culture, in spite of all their dissensions, and each of them contributes to that pending "turn," even though its members do not want to facilitate it.[3] A similar thing has been shown by preceding tables.

A glance at the figures shows, further, that the patterns of the fluctuations are neither uniform nor periodical in time. They exhibit a wonderful diversity in both respects.

As to the why of these crescendoes and diminuendoes, generally determinism fluctuates parallel with the variables of the Sensate culture (truth of senses, materialism, increase of discoveries, temporalism, nominalism, visual art, and so on); indeterminism with those of the Ideational culture (truth of faith, ideational art, realism, idealism, and so on).

Finally, the Mixed indeterminism-determinism — mixed in the theories and mixed in the sense of a coexistence of both currents — seems to be typical of the Idealistic culture.

The dominant current in the field in Greece of the fifth and of the first half of the fourth century B.C., as well as in the Western culture of the thirteenth and fourteenth centuries, was "indeterministic determinism" in the sense of God or Destiny or some other superempirical power running the universe, but running it along "orderly lines," like a clock made and started by power. Such is the dominant conception of the Schoolmen of the thirteenth and fourteenth centuries, as well as of the Greek thinkers of the centuries mentioned. And such a parallelism is not incidental. We have seen that these periods resemble one another in the systems of truth, in idealism-materialism, in their art styles, and now they show similarity in this point also.

[3] Just as in our day the capitalists, the propertied classes, and other beneficiaries and avowed partisans of the capitalist regime contribute to the destruction of this regime — through their abuses, mishandling, misuse of their privileges, neglect of their duties; through their greediness, cynicism, loans to a Communist government, propaganda for its recognition, subsidies for radical, socialist, and similar movements, etc. — by all these they contribute to the decay of their own regime much more than all the Communist propaganda taken together. Paradoxical as it may sound, most of the regimes — economic or political — have been destroyed mainly by the bearers and beneficiaries and "aristocracies" of those regimes.

Concerning the recent period, 1880–1920, we see a slight recession of determinism (quantitatively). It seems to have been followed by a qualitative recession. If, around the middle of the nineteenth century, the scientists and thinkers believed in a kind of "iron determinism," inexorable, invariable, rigid, and unavoidable in its necessity, in the twentieth century such an "iron determinism" has greatly softened: the inexorable, invariable, and necessary relationships have been more and more replaced by the standpoint of a mere probability that implies little, if any, "necessity," "inexorability," or even invariability. "Uniformity of relationship" between A and B, viewed from the standpoint of probability, is an enormous shift from the "rugged determinism" to its very liberal brand, which is quite close to a "conservative indeterminism." That is the standpoint of the majority of the leading scientists and thinkers of the present time.[4]

This quantitative recession and qualitative softening of determinism is a sign of a mild "reaction" against the rugged determinism of the Sensate culture.[5] It is a variety of revolt against the Sensate forms and variables, which we have met in practically all the variables studied at the end of the nineteenth and in the twentieth century. It reinforces the

[4] As examples of this greatly diluted determinism, often amounting almost to indeterminism, may serve Max Planck's concept of causation: "dynamic" and "statistical," with the region of "ego" and "free will" exempted from it, and practically exempted also the field of social relationships. See Max Planck, *Where Science Is Going* (New York, 1932), chaps. iv and v, particularly pp. 145–169. For W. Heisenberg's "principle of indeterminacy," see his *The Physical Principles of the Quantum Theory* (Chicago, 1930), chaps. ii and iii; also his *Wandlungen in den Grundlagen der Naturwissenschaft* (Leipzig, 1935). See other changes in P. W. Bridgman's "The Recent Change of Attitude toward the Law of Cause and Effect," in *Science*, Vol. LXXIII (1931), pp. 539–547; also his *The Logics of Modern Physics* (New York, 1932). Likewise shift the meaning of cause and effect to that of the total space-time configuration, where the specific antecedent determinant becomes a mere part of the configuration, and besides the configuration itself is viewed not so much externalistically as internalistically; or a reduction of causality to K. Pearson's, E. Mach's, H. Poincaré's mere "routine of perception" and "associationism"; or to a mere probability as a result of an endless intercrossing of endless causal chains. These and many other variants of the contemporary meaning of causation manifest the qualitative dilution or mitigation of the older determinism of the middle of the nineteenth century. For the changes during the nineteenth and in the first part of the twentieth century see L. Brunschvicg, *op. cit.*, pp. 297–614. For further details see Chapter Eleven of this work. Also A. A. Tschuproff, *Ocherki po teorii statistiki*, chaps. i–iii; Borel, *Le hasard* (Paris, 1914), p. 153.

[5] Brunschvicg pointedly says that while "the rationalism of the eighteenth century demanded that the civil laws be elevated to the intrinsic level of the (axiomatic) rational law," now "the principles of mechanics are reduced to simple conventions of the subjective synthesis, where the civil laws are placed." In this way "a complete reversal of the relationship between the laws of nature and the civil laws is found at the beginning of the twentieth century, compared with the eighteenth or the first part of the nineteenth." Brunschvicg, *op. cit.*, p. 448.

reality of the revolt in other compartments of culture and is sustained by these revolts in its own reality.[6]

[6] Again, the association of determinism with Sensate culture and of indeterminism with Ideational culture seems to be found also in the Hindu, the Tibetan, the Buddhist, and Taoist cultures. Their mentality is little impressed by determinism in the proper sense of the word. They all regard the universe and man as controlled by a supreme intelligent — personal or impersonal — power (Brahma, Tao, "self," etc.), and they particularly stress the spiritual, supersensory potentialities of man: his will, volition, mind, "self," as the supreme "factor" (in our sense) of man's destiny and conduct. So far the association seems to go much beyond the cultures studied.

Chapter Ten

FLUCTUATION OF "FIRST PRINCIPLES": VII. FLUCTUATION OF THE LINEAR, CYCLICAL, AND MIXED CONCEPTIONS OF THE COSMIC, BIOLOGICAL, AND SOCIOCULTURAL PROCESSES

I. INTRODUCTORY

"Whither Mankind?" and "Whither the World?" Whence did they start and where are they going? These questions have also been among the oldest and most basic problems of human thought. Many answers have been given. As shown in Chapter Four of Volume One, all these answers, from the standpoint of the problem, "whence and whither," can be grouped into the classes: (1) Linear, (2) Cyclical, and (3) Mixed, including in the Mixed also the erratically or variationally recurring conception. An explicit or implicit answer to these questions conditions the nature of thousands of theories in the more specific problems of science and human knowledge. In this sense it lies at the foundation of a multitude of scientific and philosophic theories of so-called "purely factual" character. Therefore the fundamental theory in this field is one of the "First Principles" of science and human knowledge.

The appearance and success of the Darwinian and general linear theory of evolution in biology quite definitely determined the trend, the character, the solutions, and the whole orientation of the research and theories in thousands of very specific biological problems. Likewise, the similar success of the linear theory of social evolution and progress, especially after its formulation by Auguste Comte and Herbert Spencer, stamped quite definitely the whole field of the social sciences, oriented uncounted special theories along the linear principles of social evolution and progress, conditioned their nature and their application, and at one time threatened to reduce almost all sociology and most of the social sciences to an endless variation of the same theme of social evolution and progress, its stages, its trend, the traits of each stage, the level reached by this or that people, and so on, with the monotonous refrain: Glory to evolution and progress that leads mankind to never-ceasing betterment and perfection. If we imagine for a moment that such a conception had not risen, or had not been successful, we can rest assured that three quarters of the works, problems, and theories produced in the social sciences after Auguste Comte would never have appeared.

It is not my purpose to give in this chapter a detailed history of the fluctuation of the influence of each of the three main conceptions in this field. Space and time do not permit it, however fascinating the subject is, and however much I should like to do the work.[1] Instead, in a very succinct form, I shall draw the most important lines of the "distribution in space," as well as swings in time, of each of the main conceptions. The main propositions relevant to the main topic of this work can be summed up as follows.

A. The linear, the cyclical, and the mixed conceptions fluctuate in their influence in the course of existence of the Graeco-Roman and the Western cultures.

B. These fluctuations are dependent, in a tangible degree, upon the fluctuation of the Ideational, Idealistic, and Sensate types of culture.

(1) The progressively linear conception of the course of the world, and especially of mankind, tends to rise with the rise of the Sensate culture. When it begins to be overripe and to decline, the progressively linear conception tends to be replaced by partly regressively linear or cyclical or trendlessly undulating, or various mixed theories.

(2) Certain types of cyclical, trendlessly undulating, and eschatological conceptions, with two or one "terminal" points of perfection, tend to be dominant in the periods and cultures of the mainly Ideational type. Namely, the types where the cycles and fluctuations are viewed not mechanically but as manifestations of the inner transformations experienced by the ultimate or true spiritual reality (God, Brahma, Providence, Tao, and the like). This means that not all the cyclical and undulating conceptions are claimed to have such an association. The theories that claim cycles and revolutions to be purely mechanical uniformities, similar to the revolutions of a motor, are not necessarily to be associated with the Ideational culture. Such theories are congenial either to the declining phase of Sensate culture or to the Mixed cultures generally.

(3) Finally, in the periods and culture of predominantly mixed type, all these theories, as well as theories mixed in their character, coexist and tend to be dominant.

---

[1] As a matter of fact, I have almost ready a little monograph on the history of this problem, especially of the cyclical conceptions. For the present, I shall very concisely outline the main swings, on the basis of this material. For the sake of economy, I give references only to general sources, with few exceptions, instead of to all the works of the thinkers mentioned.

Interpreted not too rigidly, with a number of exceptions admitted, these propositions seem to describe the "laws" of the distribution in social space and of pulsation in time of the conceptions discussed with rough accuracy. The minimum of commentaries and references to the relevant data follow.[2]

II. Domination of the Cyclical and Trendlessly Undulating Theories in the Hindu and Chinese (and Babylonian) Cultures

A. *Hindu Culture Mentality.* Whatever temporary declines of the Ideational and rises of the Sensate types are to be found in the history of Hindu culture, it has been predominantly Ideational, as we have seen. Whatever have been the streams of the linear conception of the course of the universe and mankind in Hindu thought (though there are very scarce traces of the existence of such a conception), the overwhelmingly dominant conception has been cyclical or endlessly recurring. More than that. These cycles and recurrences are the manifestations of the transformations which the ultimate — spiritual — reality, say, Brahma or Vishnu, endlessly undergoes. In accordance with the nature of the transformation of the Ideational ultimate reality, the empirical cycles have a respective duration and character. In this characteristic the connection of the Ideational mentality with the cyclical-undulating conceptions comes out with particular clearness. There are several variations of this conception in various Hindu sources; but the above general character is found in all of them.

A typical and one of the most developed variants is given in the *Vishnu Puránâ*. Here are a few excerpts from it.

Time effects the production and dissolution of all creatures. . . . At the period of creation, the god of gods creates; in that of duration, he preserves; and at the end (of all) he is mighty to annihilate.[3]

This creation and dissolution is incessantly repeated.

The dissolution of everything is of four kinds: "occasional" (Naimittika); "elemental" (Prakritika); "absolute" (Atyantika); "perpetual" (Nitya). The first occurs when the sovereign of the world (Brahma) reclines in sleep. In the second, the mundane egg resolves into the primary elements whence it was

[2] The data, that is the theories themselves, except a few, as well as the references to all the works concerned, are not given. But the minimum of the references where the theories are to be found, and the main conclusions that follow from their study, are indicated.

[3] *The Vishnu Puránâ*, trans. by H. H. Wilson, 5 vols. (London, 1864–1877), Vol. V, pp. 162–163.

derived. "Absolute" nonexistence of the world is the absorption of the sage (Yogin), through knowledge, into supreme spirit. "Perpetual" destruction is the constant disappearance, day and night, of all that are born.[4]

More specifically: "Occasional" destruction takes place endlessly at the end of Brahma's day; it is the destruction of singularistic forms and creatures, but not of the substance of the world. "Elemental" means a periodic general resolution of the elements into their primary source or prakriti, and occurs at the end of Brahma's life. "Perpetual" is the imperceptible change that all things suffer in the various stages of growth and decay, life and death, produced by the irresistible stream of time taking everything away. Finally, the "absolute" destruction concerns the individual and his annihilation in the form of dissolution of the individual stage in the supreme spirit or ultimate reality. It is Moksha, exemption forever from future existence.[5] "Occasional" dissolution occurs at the end of every Kalpa or Brahma's day. It is equal to 4,320,000,000 mortal years.[6]

At the end [of Kalpa] the earth is exhausted. A total dearth then ensues . . . and all beings perish. [The whole world in its concrete or sensory forms is also destroyed.] The world is now enveloped in darkness; and all things — animate and inanimate — having perished, the clouds continue to pour down their water for more than a hundred years. . . . When the universal spirit wakes [after its slumber], the world revives.[7]

The "elemental" dissolution or cycle occurs at the end of Brahma's life. In it every element of the world — space, smell, color, form, flavor, sound, ether, matter, and all its properties; self, consciousness, mind, and all its properties — all is resolved. The true reality becomes Pure Supreme Spirit, "that spirit which is other than embodied spirit, in which there are no attributes of name, species or like, which is one with all wisdom, and is to be understood as sole existence." [8]

It occurs once in 311,040,000,000,000 mortal years.[9]

[4] *Ibid.*, Vol. I, pp. 114 ff.

[5] *Ibid.*, Vol. V, p. 186. The Buddhist's Nirvana. Only in this individual form there is present an element of the eschatological conception; with the final "terminal" point of arrival.

[6] According to this source. As a matter of fact, even there is found some discrepancy in the figures. In other sources the figures for the different kinds of cycles are varying. See here some inconsistencies: Vol. V, p. 47; Vol. I, pp. 46 ff.; Vol. V, pp. 190 ff. For a shorter interpretation of each of these, as well as other cycles, see V. G. Aiyer, *The Chronology of Ancient India* (Madras, 1901); S. N. Pradham, *Chronology of Ancient India* (Calcutta, 1927); Z. A. Ragozin, *The Story of Vedic India* (New York, 1895).

[7] *Vishnu Purâná*, Vol. V, pp. 195 ff.

[8] *Ibid.*, Vol. V, Bk. VI, chaps. iii and iv.

[9] In other sources the figures vary.

After this period of dissolution, The Pure Spirit again creates and incarnates itself into the material form, and so the cycles go on.[10]

As to the course of mankind within these large periodicities of world cycles, it has shorter periodicities and cycles that endlessly continue. Within the shortest time span in the world pulsation, 4,320,000 mortal years, there are four ages that incessantly repeat themselves in the same sequence: the Krita Yuga (1,728,000 mortal years); the Treta Yuga (1,296,000 mortal years); the Dwapara Yuga (864,000 years); and the Kali Yuga (432,000 years).[11]

The creation of the world takes place always in the Krita age, while its dissolution comes in the Kali age. The worst of these ages — the age of decline — is the Kali age. According to the *Vishnu Puráná*, beginning with about the fourteenth century B.C. the history of mankind entered the Kali age.[12]

Here are a few characteristics of this age, so far as human culture is concerned.

The observance of caste, order, and institutes will not prevail in the Kali age [that is everything that is inconvenient and uncomfortable to the sensate individual] nor will that of the ceremonies [of religion]. Marriages, in this age will not be conformable to the ritual. . . . The laws that regulate the conduct of husband and wife will be disregarded; and oblations to the gods with fire no longer be offered. In whatever family he may be born, a powerful and rich man will be held entitled to espouse maidens of every tribe. [Religion will be disregarded.] Every text will be scripture, that people choose to think so . . . all gods will be gods to them that would like to worship them; and all orders of life will be common alike to all persons. . . . Wives will desert their husbands when they lose their property; and they only who are wealthy will be considered by women as their lords. He who gives away much money

---

[10] As we see, the ancient Hindus were as liberal in operation with gigantic figures as most of the contemporary astrophysicists, like Sir James Jeans or Sir Arthur Eddington. When the latter assures us that in every 1,500,000,000 years, the universe, turned into a "ball of radiation," would double its radius; or when it is asserted that the age of the universe is "ten million times a million years" (Sir James Jeans), or, according to Dr. B. J. Bok, that it is five hundred times shorter than that estimate; or when they contend that the material universe is passing away and the end of the world is to come, after a large, large number of years, after all, the theories seem to differ little from that of the ancient Hindus. The only difference is in the figures used; but since the widest difference exists in the estimates of the contemporary scientists, which estimate is correct (if any) nobody can tell. The other difference is that the Hindu theory meets the ends; while the theories of the contemporary astrophysicists leave in the dark either the beginning of the universe or its finite and infinite character, and what is meant by finity and infinity; or, especially, what is meant by "the end of the universe" and what is comparable to what is to come after "the end of the world."

[11] *Vishnu Puráná*, Vol. I, pp. 48 ff. and Vol. V, pp. 170 ff.

[12] *Ibid.*, Vol. IV, pp. 232 ff.

will be master of men; and family descent will no longer be a title of supremacy.
. . . Accumulated treasures will be expended on ostentatious dwellings.
The mind of men will be wholly occupied in acquiring wealth; and wealth
will be spent solely on selfish gratifications. Women will follow their inclinations, and be ever fond of pleasures. Men will fix their desires upon riches,
even though dishonestly acquired. . . . Men of all degrees will conceit themselves to be equal with Brahmins. . . . There will never be abundance in
the Kali age and men will never enjoy pleasure and happiness. . . . [Men
will be effeminated. They] will possess little sense, vigor or virtue. . . .
[There will be growth of heresies, irreligiosity, and so on. Duration of life
will decrease.] [13]

[The rulers will be] of churlish spirit, violent temper, and ever addicted to
falsehood and wickedness. They will inflict death on women, children, and
cows; they will seize the property of their subjects; they will be of limited
power and will rapidly rise and fall . . . their lives will be short; their desires
insatiable; and they will display but little piety. The people of various
countries intermingling with them will follow their example; and the barbarians
being powerful, whilst the purer tribes are neglected, the people will perish. . . .
Wealth and piety will decrease day by day, until the world will be wholly
depraved. . . . Then property alone will confer rank; wealth will be the
only source of devotion; passion will be the sole bond of union between the
sexes; falsehood will be the only means of success in litigation; and women
will be objects merely of sensual gratification. . . . Earth will be venerated
but for its mineral treasures. . . . Dishonesty will be the universal means
of subsistence . . . menace and presumption will be substituted for learning
. . . mutual assent will be marriage; fine clothes will be dignity. . . . No
man's life will exceed three and twenty years. . . . Thus, in the Kali age,
shall decay constantly proceed, until the human race approaches its annihilation. . . .[14]

At its end there will appear a Brahman with superhuman faculties.
He will destroy "all thieves and all those whose minds are devoted to
iniquity. He will then reestablish righteousness upon earth." Then
purified and awakened men "shall give birth to a race who shall follow
the laws of the Krita age (or age of purity)." In this way the cycle
returns again to the Krita age and then it is revolved again and again.
Finally the sources indicate a short-time — five-year — period in which
various political and religious events are repeated.

There are also several other periodicities given in various Puránas,
and particularly in Hari Vamsa.[15]

---

[13] *Ibid.*, Vol. V, pp. 170 ff.   [14] *Ibid.*, Vol. IV, pp. 224 ff.   [15] *Ibid.*, Vol. I, p. 54.

With some variations, this conception of the direction of the world's history, as well as of human history, goes, from the earliest to the later times, throughout the history of Hindu thought.[16]

The whole conception is cyclical. Only within the long-time cycles there are shorter phases (like the four ages) during which there is a temporary linear trend, like the trend of creation and purity in the age of Krita, or degeneration and decline in the age of Kali.[17] But these are temporary phases of the ever-repeated larger cycles, ending with the largest "elemental" cycle of dissolution of the whole material world into the immaterial spirit, the rematerialization of the spirit into the sensate form.

So far then, in the case of the Hindu (and also of the Buddhist and Jainist) culture, the formulated association of the Ideational culture mentality with the domination of the cyclical or endlessly undulating conception of the course of the world and mankind's history is well corroborated.

B. *Chinese Culture Mentality.* This, being partly Ideational (the ancient Chinese and the Taoist stream) and partly Mixed (the Confucianist stream), presents us with the coexistence of the cyclical or trendlessly recurrent and undulating conception with one partly linear and even progressively linear. The cyclical and endlessly undulating conception of the world course as well as of human history is represented, first of all, in the most basic theory of *eternal rhythm of the Yin and Yang*, and then in the prevalent, almost habitual, "cyclical" standpoint of Chinese traditional history in regard to the rise and fall of its various dynasties; the rhythm of integration and disintegration of China; the rise and decline of its prosperity and depression, its blossoming and decay, order and disorder, peace and war, and so on. All these and many other fluctuating processes are, after all, but special varieties of the eternal rhythm of the Yin and Yang. It stamps the Chinese historiography, philosophy of history, cosmogony, and all the relevant fields of Chinese thought: science, philosophy, religion, and ethics.

It would be superfluous to attempt to characterize here the complex and manifold meaning of the Yin and the Yang and of their rhythm.

---

[16] See, for instance, the Vedanta Sutras, in *The Sacred Books of the East*, Vol. XXXIV, pp. xxvi ff., 211 ff., 382 ff.; Vol. XXXVIII, pp. 47, 371, and 392. The theories of the Vedantas and the Puránás are based, of course, upon the oldest sacred sources of Hindu thought.

[17] In such a phase there is also repeatedly given "the Fall" from the wise and virtuous status of mankind into the depraved and sinful status. See the ever-repeated statements of the Fall (similar to the Biblical version) in *Apastamba*, *Gautama*, the *Laws of Manu*, and in other law books of India, in *The Sacred Books of the East*, Vols. VII, XV, and others.

The antithesis of the Yin and the Yang is neither that of two opposed Substances, nor two Forces, nor two Principles.   It is simply the antithesis of two Emblems, more rich in their suggestive power than all of these.[18]

Being such, they are opposed to and, at the same time, inseparable from one another.   One calls forth, immanently, the other ; engenders it.

The absolute moves and engenders Yang [fire, the sun disk, and other symbols].   The movement having reached its climax, rest ensues.   From rest springs Yin [coiling clouds over the sun, water, and other symbols] ; and when rest has reached its utmost limit, again movement follows.   Thus we have alternately now movement, now rest.[19]

The Ultimate Principle has operated through all eternity.   This process is represented as pulsative, as a succession of active expansive and passive intensive states ; which succession never had a beginning.   The Ultimate Principle, in its active expansive operation, constitutes and produces the Yang or Positive Essence ; in its passive intensive operation it constitutes and produces the Yin or Negative Essence.   When the active expansive phase has reached its extreme limit, the operation becomes passive and intensive (and vice versa).   Each phase roots in the other.   [A principle akin to the Hegelian "thesis antitheses" and to what I style in this work "immanent self-regulation" and the "principle of limit."]. . . .   All existences [originated] and do now subsist in virtue of the same process, operating in ceaseless repetition.[20]

The conviction that the whole universe (le Tout) and each of the totalities which compose it have a cyclical nature and resolve into alternations dominates so much the Chinese thought that the idea of succession is always dominated by that of interdependence.[21]

From this the all-embracing and universal nature of these symbol categories is comprehensible.

At least beginning with the period of the fifth century B.C. the symbols Yin and Yang are found to be used by theorizers of the most diverse orientation. This exceedingly wide use gives an impression that these two symbols signal the notions inspiring a most vast ensemble of technique and doctrines.[22]

In the light of this it is now comprehensible how and why this primordial symbol category permeates all the compartments of Chinese thought and gives to it a "cyclical" or endlessly alternating rhythmical

[18] M. Granet, La pensée chinoise (Paris, 1934), p. 124.
[19] A. Forke, The World Conception of the Chinese (London, 1925), pp. 110, 64, 200 ff. See also H. Maspero, La Chine antique (Paris, 1927).
[20] T. T. Meadows, The Chinese and Their Rebellions (London, 1856), p. 343.
[21] M. Granet, op. cit., p. 330.   [22] Ibid., p. 117.

character; and why, therefore, the course of the world and of mankind's history is viewed also "cyclically" and "trendlessly rhythmically." As Granet rightly remarks in regard to the rise and fall of dynasties, of culture, of integration disintegration, and most of the sociocultural processes, this "cyclical" conception became even stereotyped in Chinese historiography and social philosophy.[23] According to this traditional formula of Chinese historico-philosophical standpoint:

The power of every dynasty springs from a Virtue or a Prestige which passes through a time of fullness, then declines, and after an ephemeral resurrection becomes exhausted and is extinguished. The dynasty *ought* then to be extinguished for it no longer has heaven on its side. . . . This investiture, this heavenly mandate, is always temporary. Heaven is changeable and inexorable. Its favor is lost and wears away. The Great Happiness does not come twice [for the same dynasty].[24]

"Dynasties are founded, attain their zenith, decline, disappear. . . . History assigns the same causes to the same effects." Parallel with this cycle of a dynasty, the people are virtuous and happy when the dynasty is rising and attaining its zenith; and they become violent and degenerated when it declines. And so does the whole culture and sociocultural life.

Yao and Shun [founders of respective dynasties] practiced virtue; their subjects were humane and lived to be old. The last of the Hsia and the last of the Yin practiced violence; their subjects were barbarians and died prematurely." . . .
This traditional history, then, "is engaged in noting in successive cycles the infallible repetitions." [25]

These lines characterize well the cyclico-undulating standpoint of traditional Chinese history and social philosophy, their ethics and their whole mentality in the field of our problem. The conception is but a special case of the general principle of endless alternation of the Yin and Yang. Regardless of the Taoist stream, it corroborates the expectation that follows from the general diagnosis of Chinese culture as Mixed, in our terms.

The expectation seems to be sustained also in regard to the Linear and Mixed conceptions that are to be expected from the Confucianist and other more Sensate streams in Chinese culture. The Confucianist theory of the three stages in the interpretation of many is indeed the

[23] See M. Granet, *Chinese Civilization* (New York, 1930), pp. 14 ff.
[24] *Ibid.*, p. 14.   [25] *Ibid.*, pp. 46–47.

linear theory of progressive evolution. According to it, mankind passes through three main stages in the course of time: the *Disorderly Stage*, with its anarchy, continuous warfare, primitive conditions, lack of efficient social control and other traits of a "primitive society"; the *Stage of Small Tranquillity*, characterized by the institutions of the family, private property, egotism, social instability, and other traits of a "capitalist society"; the *Stage of Great Similarity*, marked by social order, almost common property, mutual benevolence, and reverence.[26]

Thus our expectation is well corroborated, considering the power of the stream of Confucianist thought in the cultural history of China and in Chinese mentality.

C. *Babylonian Culture Mentality*. The history and the nature of the Babylonian culture mentality is too little known for us to venture to apply this hypothesis to it. With this reservation, it is possible to note the fact that the cyclical conception of the course of world history seems to have been dominant there also. The fact itself being reasonably assured, it is somewhat uncertain as to whether these cycles were viewed mechanically, as a mere uniformity of the astrologico-astronomical nature, or were regarded also as the manifestation of the spiritual ultimate reality. If the first hypothesis be accurate, then such a conception alludes to the Mixed character of the Assyro-Babylonian culture mentality, which allusion seems to be in harmony with the Mixed (with a good deal of the Sensate or Visual) character of Babylonian painting and sculpture; with a similar tone that permeates the main literary documents of this culture: *The Code of Hammurabi*, the famous epic, *Gilgamesh*, the Babylonian story of the Flood, or the legends centered around Sargon of Agade. In the *Code of Hammurabi*, who styles himself a demigod, the spirit of pride in earthly achievements — victories, annihilation of enemies, in "making the fame of Babylon great, in filling the city of Ur with plenty, in making the city of Borsippa beautiful"[27] — is more than prominent, as the spirit of preoccupation with "earthly values" (regulation of land possession, tenancy, landmarks, water chan-

---

[26] Li-Ki, Bk. VII, *The Sacred Books of the East*, Vol. XXVII, pp. 364 ff. In this translation, the meaning is that these three stages are repeated, in this sequence. Meanwhile a number of Chinese scholars translate and interpret these stages in the linear sense. See, for instance, Chen Huan Chang, *The Economic Principles of Confucius and His School* (New York, 1911), pp. 16–19. So Leonard Hsu, in his work on Confucius and Confucianism and many others. In my inquiries as to the right translation, I am told that the text permits either the linear or cyclical translation. If this be so, then it is still more typical of the Mixed Confucianist mentality.

[27] See *The Code of Hammurabi*, trans. by R. F. Harper (Chicago, 1904). Prologue, *et passim*.

nels, commerce, etc.) is more than conspicuous. There is little of the otherworldly mood in the whole Code. The same has to be said of the legends about Sargon,[28] or the *Gilgamesh*, with its violent demigod king, oppressor and active Epicurean, and with the half-savage hero, Enkidu; [29] while in the story of the Flood it is explicitly stated that the city of Shuruppak was destroyed because of the wickedness of its people.[30] In all this, as well as in other sources, there is little of otherworldliness or pure Ideationalism. The Sensate spirit, mixed with and moderated by religion, with its stern, somewhat cruel and "very active" Bel and other deities, permeates it. For these reasons, this alternative seems to be more probable than the alternative of an interpretation of the Babylonian cyclic theories in the Ideational sense. This conclusion is supported also by the nature of the theories which are based mainly upon purely astrological-astronomical foundations and depict the cycles (so far as the sources permit that to be said) as an immanent uniformity of the heavenly bodies and of the Sensate world as such. Here it is little stressed that the cycles are manifestations of the inner changes experienced by Bel or the ultimate spiritual principle of the reality, as is the case with the Hindu and partly Taoist conceptions.

The essentials of the old Babylonian cyclical conceptions concerning the course of the world in its existence are known to us mainly from Graeco-Roman sources, through the work of Berosos. He was a Babylonian priest of Bel (born around 350 or 340 B.C.) who migrated and settled in the Greek island state of Cos, opened a school there, and became, according to Pliny, so famous for his astronomo-astrologic teachings and prognostications that the Athenians erected a statue in his honor. Transmitting the ancient theories of the Babylonian priesthood (which was at that time the main body of scientists), Berosos claims that for his *Babylonian History* he "used the notes and sources 480,000 years old, which cover the period of 2,150,000 years." Of these 2,150,000 years, about 2,000,000 belong to the period preceding the universal flood recorded in the history of Babylonia (and also in the Bible).[31]

---

[28] See Rawlinson's translation in the *Athenaeum* (September 7, 1867); G. Smith's text in the *Transactions of the Society of Biblical Archeology*, Vol. I, pp. 46 ff.; E. A. Wallis Budge, *Babylonian Life and History*, 2d ed., pp. 23-25.

[29] See *Das Gilgamesch-epos* (Göttingen, 1911).

[30] Wallis Budge, *op. cit.*, p. 8.

[31] See P. Schnabel, *Berosos* (Leipzig, 1923), pp. 175-176. See also Bidez, "*Bérose et la grand année*," in *Mélanges Paul Fredericq* (Bruxelles, 1904), pp. 9 ff.; W. Gundel, *Sterne und Sternbilder* (Bonn, 1928); F. Boll and C. Bezold, *Sternglaube und Sterndeutung* (Berlin, 1920). These figures show again, by the way, that the ancients regarded the earth as old, and were as well acquainted with large figures as contemporary astrophysicists.

Main theories set forth by the old Babylonians in the field studied are as follows: First of all the theory of *annus magnus*, "the world's year" cycle in the life of the universe as well as of mankind. Its essence is thus described by F. Cumont.[32]

The existence of the universe is formed out of a series of "the great years," each having its summer and winter. Their summer comes when all the planets are in conjunction in the same point of Cancer, and it leads to a general conflagration; their winter arrives when all the planets are reunited in Capricornus, and it results in a universal flood. Each of these cosmic cycles, whose duration, according to the most authoritative computation, has been 432,000 years,[33] is an exact reproduction of the preceding ones.

The stars reassuming the same position must act in the same way. This Babylonian theory being an anticipation of that of "the eternal return of the things," whose discovery Nietzsche was so proud of, enjoyed a durable favor in antiquity and was transmitted in various forms up to the time of the Renaissance.[34]

[32] Here is Seneca's statement on it. "Quidam existimant terram quoque concuti et dirupto solo nova fluminum capita detegere, quae amplius ut e pleno profundant. Berosos, qui Belum interpretatus ist, ait ista cursu siderum fieri; adeo quidem affirmat, ut conflagrationi atque diluvio tempus assignet; arsura enim terrena contendit, quandoque omnia sidera, quae nun diversos agunt cursus, in Cancrum convenerit; inundationem futuram, cum eadem siderum turba in Capricornum convenerit. Illic solstitium, hic bruma conficitur; magnae potentiae signa, quando in ipsa mutatione anni momenta sunt." Seneca, *Naturales quaestiones*, III, 29, 1. See also enthusiastic comments on Berosos by Vitruvius, *The Ten Books on Architecture*, trans. by M. H. Morgan, Bk. IX, chap. ii, p. 1; chap. vi, p. 2; chap. viii, p. 1; Bk. V, chap. vi.

[33] As to the duration of this Berosos cycle, the ancient sources somewhat differ. Cicero, criticizing the theory of the *annus magnus*, mentions a 470,000-year cycle. "Condemnemus etiam Babylonios et eos qui e Caucaso caeli signa servantes numeris et modis stellerum cursus prosequuntur; condemnemus, inquam, hos aut stultitiae aut vanitatis aut impudentiae, qui quadraginta septuaginta milia annorum, ut ipsi dicunt, monumentis comprehensa continent." Cicero, *De divinatione*, i, 19, § 36.

Other ancient authors, like Diodorus, give 473,000 years as the length of the *annus magnus* of the Chaldeans. Some others, like Pliny, say that the Berosos great cycle is 480,000 years "E diverso Epigenes apud Babylonios DCCXX annorum observationes siderum coctilibus laterculis inscriptas docet, gravis auctor in primis; qui minimum, Berosus et Critodemus, CCCCLXXX. Ex quo apparet aeturnus litterarum usus. Pliny, *Naturalis historia*, VIII, 193. Still other authors ascribe to the Chaldeans 490,000 years as the length of the great cycle. Finally, if Herakleitos has in view also the Chaldean *annus magnus*, its length, according to him, is 10,800 years. See the details of this problem in P. Schnabel, *op. cit.*, *passim*, and pp. 94–95, 106–107, 117–118, 175–176, 183, and 266; Bidez, *op. cit.;* Boll and Bezold, *op. cit.*, 3d ed., pp. 78 ff. and 200 ff.; F. Cumont, *Astrology and Religion among the Greeks and Romans* (New York, 1912), pp. 15–19, 30 ff., 44 ff., and 67–68; L. Thorndike, *History of Magic and Experimental Science* (New York, 1929), Vol. 1, p. 95; P. Tannery, *Mémoires scientifiques* (Paris, 1912), Vol. II, pp. 345–366.

[34] F. Cumont, *Les religions orientales* (1929), p. 164. See also his *Astrology and Religion among the Greeks and Romans* (New York, 1912), pp. 19 ff.

Whatever was the actual length of Berosos's *annus magnus*, the ancient Babylonians seem to have believed in such a great cycle, with its dissolution of the world through flood and conflagration, with its eternal return of the same things.

Besides this great cycle they marked shorter cycles of 2484 years, 500 years, 59, 54, 19, and 8 years.[35]

Since these conceptions assumed the dependence of human affairs upon the movement of stars and constellations, it follows that each of these cycles marks also a cycle in the course of mankind. And in the cuneiform library of Assurbanipal such correlations of human affairs with the stars are mentioned several times.[36]

Partly by reason of this, partly by inference from the astrological postulate of these theories, the course of human history seems to have been considered cyclically by the Babylonians also, though there is preserved little, if anything, from the sociological theories of this people.

If, then, this interpretation be admitted, the Mixed character of the Babylonian culture mentality is associated with the "mechanico-astrological" cyclical conceptions of the direction of the world processes, and possibly of the processes of mankind's existence. There is little, if anything (at least, I have not come across anything), of the linear conception in this field. With these reservations, the case of this culture seemingly does not contradict the propositions of this chapter.[37]

III. FLUCTUATION OF THE MAIN CONCEPTIONS IN GRAECO-ROMAN AND WESTERN CULTURES

A. The earliest Greek conception in the field known to us is Hesiod's regressively linear (though not quite that) theory of the succession of the Golden, the Silver, the Bronze, the Heroic, and the Iron ages.[38]

Likewise, in Homer, there is a passage that depicts the past as better than the present.[39]

[35] See Tannery, *op. cit.*, Vol. II, pp. 344–346; Schnabel, *op. cit.*, pp. 94 ff., 117–118, 175 ff.; Cumont, *Astrology and Religion*, p. 44.

[36] Boll and Bezold, *op. cit.*, p. 2.

[37] The famous formula of the ever-repeated cycles of Ecclesiastes (1 : 2–11) stands somewhat fragmentarily and incidentally in the whole conception of the Bible, with Paradise at the starting point of history and the eschatological terminal Paradise at its end. As such, it is not typical. As a fragment, it is a manifestation of the weariness of an overripe Sensate culture mentality, and as such fits the above proposition. With its *vanitas vanitatum* free from Ideationality, it is a product of the declining Sensate culture.

[38] See Hesiod's *Works and Days*.

[39] The *Iliad*, I, 260–268. For the sake of economy, here again I give, with few exceptions, references to only a few general works, instead of referring to all the works of the

Since the exact time when either Homer or Hesiod lived is unknown; and since the exact relationship between the Creto-Mycenaean and the Greek culture is also not quite certain, it is not possible to say anything definite about the relationship of these theories and the types of culture in which they (especially Hesiod's theory) were produced. If, however, Hesiod's time is somewhere between the eleventh and eighth centuries B.C., and if that period was the transitional period from the "overripe Sensate Creto-Mycenaean" to the Ideational culture of the centuries from the eighth to the sixth, then the regressive linear theory of Hesiod fits well the proposition made at the beginning of this chapter about some congeniality between such a transitory stage from the Sensate to the Ideational culture and the regressive linear conception of historical process.

B. The theories of the sixth and the first part of the fifth centuries are almost uniformly "cyclical" and most of them not only mechanically but "ideationally cyclical," viewing the endless rhythm behind these cycles as a manifestation of either spiritual or animated ultimate reality in the Sensate world and Sensate human history.

Such are the conceptions of Pythagoras and the Pythagoreans; of Alcmeon of Crotona, Oenopides of Chio, Philolaos, and others; of Herakleitos, Empedocles, Anaximander, Anaximenes, and practically almost all the theorists of the period in the field discussed. Almost no linear theory (except the repetition of Hesiod's theory) is known in that period. The idea of periodicity, long- and short-time cycles in which identically the same world and any element in it recurs ("numerically" or quite identical to it, if not exactly the same), seems to have been quite dominant.[40] There is hardly any single fragment from that period that pleads the cause of the linear progressive conception. So far as the sixth and the beginning of the fifth centuries were predominantly Ideational (in the compartments we examined), the association of the Ideational mentality with the cyclical (nonmechanical) conception seems to be well sustained. Giving different formulation to the cyclical conceptions, the thinkers also give different numerical lengths for the span of various cycles, beginning with the longest (*annus magnus*) and ending with the shorter one. According to Censorinus's *De Die Natali* (probably in the third century A.D.) and the *Placita* of pseudo Plutarch, the great cycle of

persons mentioned. Many of the Graeco-Roman relevant excerpts are given in Lovejoy and Boas, *Primitivism*, quoted. Much more systematic and analytical along special lines is P. Duhem's work quoted, Vol. I.

[40] See particularly P. Duhem, *Le système du monde* (Paris, 1913), Vol. I, pp. 70 ff. See there the sources, the quotations, and analysis.

the *annus magnus* was, according to Aretas, 5552 years; Herakleitos, 18,000 years; Dion of Naples, 10,884 years; Orpheus, 100,020 years; according to others either of shorter or much longer periods.[41]

C. As we proceed along the fifth and then to the fourth century, the cyclical conceptions still are prominent. Plato and Aristotle and their followers are still the bearers, in spite of the somewhat complicated character of the theories of both, and especially of Plato.[42] Some change, however, is taking place. First, the regressive linear conceptions of Hesiodic type seem to have lost their prestige greatly and become the object of attack and satire on the part of many Greek comic poets and writers, from Aristophanes to Cratinus and Pherecrates.[43]

On the other hand, the progressively linear conceptions or, perhaps, motives, begin to appear; not in the clear-cut form of a systematic theory, but in more negativistic description of the earliest stages of mankind, of the progress of arts and sciences, of marvels of technique, of better adaptation of man, and, once in a while, in an expression of hope of further improvement. Now the present is favorably compared with the past, in contradistinction to the prevalent theories of regressive linearism of the centuries before the sixth. In various forms these "progressive" motives are found in the funeral oration of Pericles,[44] in some of the tragedies of Aeschylus, in Euripides, in the fragments of Anaxagoras, in the Hippocratic writings, in Archelaus, Democritus, Protagoras, Critias, Timotheus, Philemon, and others.[45] The outlook on human history becomes somewhat more optimistic and more "progressively linear," at least so far as comparison of the present with the past is concerned.

So far, in these centuries of the prevalent Idealistic culture, we see coexistence of the cyclical with the undeveloped (as yet) progressively linear, and with the remnants of the regressively linear beliefs. Such a mixture, together with the inner mixture of the elements of these conceptions in several theories, seems to agree with the statement made at the beginning of this chapter.

[41] See the details in Censorinus, *De Die Natali* (Paris, 1843), chap. xviii, in the *second série de la bibliothèque latin-française*, published by C. L. F. Panckoucke. Pseudo Plutarch's figures differ. See "Why the Oracles Cease," in Plutarch's *Morals*, ed. by W. Goodwin, Vol. IV, pp. 15–16 (Boston, 1870), Vol. III, pp. 147–148. See about the question in P. Tannery, *op. cit.*, Vol. II, pp. 363 and 345 ff.; also P. Duhem's *op. cit.*, Vol. I, *passim*.

[42] See the analysis in Duhem, *op. cit.*, Vol. I, chaps. ii, iii, *et passim;* also Lovejoy and Boas, *op. cit.*, chaps. v and vi.

[43] See on this the excerpts in Lovejoy and Boas, *op. cit.*, pp. 38 ff.

[44] Thucydides, *History of the Peloponnesian War*, Bk. II, chap. vi.

[45] See the excerpts in Lovejoy and Boas, *op. cit.*, chap. vii.

D. The third and the subsequent centuries B.C. and the first three centuries A.D. give here, as in other compartments of culture, a checkered picture, due partly to the rise of the Hellenistic centers, with Alexandria as the scientific one, the decline of Continental Greece and then the entrance of the Roman stream into the picture. As a result, we have a continuation of the undeveloped "progressively linear" conceptions and a revival of the cyclical or trendlessly undulating theories by the Stoics, Neo-Platonists, and others. At the same time, partly regressive, partly catastrophic theories of the end of the world began to emerge. Finally the Christian conception complicated the picture still more. Among the Greeks, the "eclectic progressively linear" statements continued to circulate (Philemon, Moschion, Athenio, Polybius, Diodorus Siculus, and others). Among the Romans rose the somewhat similar eclectic theories of Lucretius, Cicero, Varro, Virgil (partly), Horace, Cratius Faliscus, Vitruvius, Manilius, Pliny the Elder, Galenus, Celsus, and others. With the exception of Pliny the Elder, who expressed the linear progressive theory clearly by his famous: "Let no one lose hope that the ages will always grow better," [46] none of these thinkers developed any consistent theory of progressive linearism. All were eclectic and in a sense inconsistent. Nevertheless, all of them, comparing the present with the earliest past, extolled the progress of arts and sciences, of forms of social life, of culture. So far they viewed the trend of the movement from the past to the present as an ascending line.[47] Only, in viewing the remote future, they admitted the possibility of a senescence of the world and the decay of mankind (e.g., Lucretius, Cicero, and others). At the same time, the course of many social processes they viewed cyclically, like Polybius's cycle of the forms of government. This stream continued to flow after the beginning of our era, up to at least the fourth century A.D. (Macrobius and others). It seems to have been an expression of the optimistically Sensate mentality of the period.

The second stream that ran side by side with it was the revived (not without a diffusion of the astrology of the Orient), and step-by-step spiritualized, cyclical conception. It found its partisans among the Stoics and Neo-Platonists, the Neo-Pythagoreans, and some of the Gnostics (Zeno, Cleanthes, Chrysippus, Posidonius, Seneca, and later Stoics; Plutarch, Plotinus, Porphyry, Nigidius, Apuleus, Proclus, Asclepius, Nemesius, Manilius, Censorinus, Celsus, Philo, Claudius Ptolemy, Galenus, Julius Firmicus Maternus, Timon Magnus, Barde-

---

[46] *Naturalis historia*, II, 15, 62.
[47] See Lovejoy and Boas, *op. cit.*, chaps. 7, 8, 9, 10, and 12.

sanes, and others).[48] All of these believed also in the existence of the Grand Year Cycle, as well as several shorter cycles. It is to be noted, however, that as we pass from the third century B.C. to the first centuries of our era, the cyclical conception tends to assume more and more spiritual forms [49] until in the theories of Plotinus and other Neo-Platonists and Gnostics, the cycles of the sensory universe become mere manifestations of the Soul of the World, or its Intelligence.[50]

In other words, the growth of the cyclical theories with the decline of the Sensate culture and the rise of the Ideational was not only a quantitative growth, but at the same time a qualitative change toward the Ideational nature of the theories.

The third current, not very noticeable in the third and second centuries B.C., was an "eclectic regressive" theory of the pending or actual decay of mankind. It assumed mainly the form of an unfavorable comparison of the present with the past, particularly with the remotest past, viewing the road taken by mankind as a downward one. Some admitted the hope of a future upgrade movement; but this was a secondary theme in their "music." Hyginus, Ovid, Tibullus, Statius, Juvenal, Trogus, Tacitus, Philo, Pliny the Younger, Seneca, Lucretius, the Hermetic Corpus, Asclepius,[51] and others are the representatives of this theory.

The early Christians, with their Apocalyptic and catastrophic beliefs in the end of the world, and an unbearable present, were perhaps the extreme upholders of this conception, with the difference that they added to it their eschatological belief in the coming of Christ and Christ's City of God.

Thus, in the transitory centuries, especially from the second B.C. to the fourth A.D., we find the coexistence of these three currents: one expressing the still lingering optimism of the decaying Sensate culture, especially from the third century B.C. to the first A.D., when the decay had progressed little as yet; another, the premonition and pessimism of its decline; the third — the cyclical — the generation and growth of the coming Ideational culture.

---

[48] See Duhem, op. cit., Vol. I, pp. 251-296. Thorndike, op. cit., Vol. I, pp. 178 ff., chap. xv, pp. 455-456; Vol. II, chaps. xiii-xiv.

[49] According to the testimony of Philo (20 B.C.–A.D. 54), many before and about his time interpreted the universe and its cycles absolutely atheistically, mechanically, and fatalistically.

De Migratione Abrahami, chap. xxxii. Manilius's Astronomicon, written about that time, is one example of it.

[50] See about that in Duhem, op. cit., Vol. II, pp. 303-344.

[51] Hermetica, trans. by W. Scott (Oxford, 1926).

E. With the triumph of Christianity, we enter, after the fourth century A.D., the Ideational phase of European culture. The main changes in the field studied are: (1) *the rise of a specific eschatological conception of the world's and mankind's history;* (2) *the disappearance almost entirely of the linear — regressive as well as progressive — conception;* (3) *the domination of cyclical concepts of the course of mundane affairs between the two terminal points of the world's and mankind's existence, marked by the eschatological conception.* So far as the complete history of the world and of mankind is concerned, the Christian conception of it assumed a specific form. First, the empirical world and its duration in time, as well as time itself, was regarded as finite, having a beginning (Tertullian's *natum et factum*) and destined to have an end.[52] Second, the initial point of this history and the final terminal point were both viewed as perfect: the Eden of Adam and Eve at the beginning and the City of God at the end, after the Last Judgment. The intermediate link, that is, practically the whole of human history, that lasts between the Fall and the Last Judgment, was viewed as something infinitely more degraded than the initial and the final terminal points. In this sinful and degraded *continuum*, there were admitted to be relative ups and downs, certain decisive and "progressive" points, like the origin of Christianity itself; nevertheless, no linear trend — progressive or regressive — that persists throughout all this period between the terminal points was contended or claimed. Of all the conceptions, the linear one is the least noticeable throughout the Middle Ages. A few mentions of a temporary linearity by Tertullian, St. Augustine, Cyril of Alexandria, Vincent of Lerins, Orosius and others, and then mainly for polemical reasons when the Christian thinkers were strongly pressed by their adversaries, could be found, of course.[53] But that is all, and this is quite secondary, even, in the main conceptions of the Christian thinkers who mention it. For instance, there can hardly be any doubt that St. Augustine viewed the whole empirical history of the world and mankind that lies between the two terminal points in an indefinite way, mainly as cyclically or trendlessly undulating.

This whole history of "the City of Man" is purely temporary. It "totters through the one transitory instability."[54] "*All earthly things*

---

[52] Tertullian, *Apologeticus contra gentes*, chap. xi. St. Augustine's "Proculdubio, non est mundus factus in tempore, sed cum tempore," *De Civitate Dei*, Bk. XI, chap. vi. See his analysis of this problem and of time in Bks. XI, XII, of his *Confessions*.

[53] See R. S. Crane, "Anglican Apologetics and the Idea of Progress," in *Modern Philology*, Vol. XXXI (1934), pp. 274–278. J. Delvaille, *Essai sur l'historie de l'idée de progrès* (Paris, 1910), pp. 82 ff.   [54] *The City of God*, trans. by John Healy, Vol. I, chap. i.

have their changes, revolutions, and dissolutions." [55] No happiness is possible in their pursuit. Wealth does not give it. "He that is good is free, though he be a slave, and he that is evil, a slave though he be a king." Earthly kingdoms are "but fair thievish purchases"; great empires are but a piracy on a large scale; kings are but pirates and sword players.[56] True Christians in this world are but pilgrims. Their permanent place is "the City of God."

That city is eternal: no man is born in it because no man dies in it. Felicity is there fully, but no goddess, but a god's gift; of this habitation have we promise by faith, as long as we are here in pilgrimage on earth, and long for that rest above. The sun arises not there both upon good and bad, but the Sun of righteousness shines only over the good. . . .[57]

Cain built a city, but Abel was a pilgrim, and built none. For the city of the saints is above, though it have citizens upon earth, wherein they live as pilgrims until the time of the kingdom come, and then it gathers all the citizens together in the resurrection of the body and gives them a kingdom to reign in with their king, forever and ever.[58]

This is "the end without end. For what other thing is our end, but to come to that kingdom of which there is no end. Amen."[59]

Such is the main conception of Christianity that persisted throughout the Middle Ages. To such an eschatological mentality the whole empirical history of mankind and of the world was of comparatively little importance, as a passing, purely temporary thing; therefore, the holders of this conception were not particularly interested to study its course and direction, whether linear, or cyclical, or trendlessly undulating, or what. This explains why they did not work over the problem systematically and why their statements in this field were, in a sense, casual. However, judged by these casual remarks, the predominant conception of this empirical history was trendlessly undulating, now on the downward curve, becoming more and more sinful and calling this or that catastrophe, the punishment of God for this sinfulness; now, after correction, improving and curving upward until a new sinful trend comes, and so undulating between these relative "ups and downs," marked and punctuated by catastrophes as signs of the wrath of God, without any continuous and

---

[55] *Ibid.*, Vol. I, p. 166. His reference and quotations from Apuleius's *De Mundo* here is also significant. *Cf.* also Orosius, *Seven Books of History against the Pagans*, trans. by J. Raymond (New York, 1936).

[56] *Ibid.*, Vol. I, pp. 168 ff.

[57] *Ibid.*, Vol. I, p. 230.

[58] *Ibid.*, Vol. II, p. 40.

[59] *Ibid.*, Vol. II, pp. 266-267.

persistent linear trend in either direction.[60] That is the all-embracing scheme of the course of the world and man.

Side by side and partly combined with it, so far as the empirical history between the terminal points is concerned, there flowed another current which interpreted the course of the mundane world as mainly cyclical or as trendlessly undulating. In a sense it continued the old astrological and cyclical conceptions.

The early Church Fathers well understood the incompatibility of the Christian *credo* with the eternal return of things, the eternal dissolution and rebirth of the universe and of everything in it, claimed by the theories of the *annus magnus*. They also understood well the incompatibility of astrology, with its absolute determination of man's conduct and all human history. Therefore, whether St. Basil, or Origen, or St. Gregory, or St. Augustine, they all were opposed to both, and took great pains to refute the cyclical theory of the Grand Year, as well as the astrological claim of the absolute dependence of man upon the heavenly bodies and their constellations.[61]

And yet, even St. Augustine admitted the influence of the sun and the heavenly bodies upon the bodily aspects of man. Likewise, if not the return of the identical things, and the endless recurrence of the identical dissolution and recreation of the world, then, within the span of time and the empirical world (which are coextensive and finite), nonidentical recurrence of things, nonidentical cycles, were admitted. Some of the Church Fathers, like St. Clement of Alexandria, Minucius Felix, Arnobius, even Origen (partly), Bishop Theodoret, and a few others seem to have accepted from the previous astrological cyclical conceptions even more than this.[62] Subsequently this stream continued, partly in the form of the nonastrological conception of cycles and periodicities; partly associ-

---

[60] This conception manifested itself also in the Christian periodization of human history. From the time of Claudius Ptolemy, a more or less generally accepted periodization was the division of the history of mankind into the four periods of the four world empires: (1) Assyro-Babylonian, (2) Mede-Persian, (3) Graeco-Macedonian, (4) Roman. In the fourth century A.D., Hieronymus connected it with the Bible and Daniel's vision and turned the fourth period into the period that shall last up to the Last Judgment, thus making the greater part of history fall in one period. In the fifth century Orosius modified it into the periods Babylonian, Macedonian, African, and Roman, before the Christian era. His division became popular during the Middle Ages. See Orosius, *op. cit.* See also H. Spangenberg, "*Die Perioden der Weltgeschichte*," in *Historische Zeitschrift*, Vol. CXXVII (1922), pp. 7 ff. Also E. Bernheim, *Lehrbuch der Historischen Methode* (Leipzig, 1908), pp. 74 ff.

[61] See, for instance, Augustine, *The City of God*, Bk. XII, chaps. x–xiii and Bk. V. See the details in Duhem, *op. cit.*, Vol. II, pp. 446–460.

[62] See the details in Duhem, *op. cit.*, Vol. II, pp. 404 ff. and 447–478.

ated with it and tangibly permeated by the astrological theories of the *annus magnus* and other — shorter — periodicities. A number of the Christian thinkers who condemned astrology and the astrological cycles were in fact permeated by these conceptions and tried to set them forth in a form compatible with the main principles of the Christian *credo*.

The *Pseudo Clementines* and its Latin version the *Recognitiones; De mirabilibus Sacrae Scripturae* of Augustine of Hibernia (*c.* A.D. 660); John Chrysostom, Peter Abelard, Erigena (partly), Hugh of St. Victor, Roger Bacon, Adelard of Bath, William of Conches, Bernard Sylvester, Daniel of Morley, Roger of Hereford, Alexander Neckam (with his *annus magnus* of 36,000 years), the influential spurious works like *Theology, Book of Judgment*, and one of the "best sellers" of the Middle Ages, the *Secret of Secrets*, and many others shared this cyclical astrological conception.[63]

As we come to the scholars of the thirteenth and the next two or three centuries, the astrologico-cyclical theories, influenced by the theories of some of the Arabian thinkers,[64] tend to become more and more elaborated, and attempts are made to establish more and more correlations of human affairs with the cosmic and geographic (astrologico-astronomical) factors and respective periodicities along the lines not unlike the theories set forth by C. Ptolemy in his famous *Tetrabiblos* [65] (in the second century A.D.). Scholars like Michael Scot, William of Auvergne, Thomas of Cantimpré, Bartholomew of England, Robert Grosseteste, Gilbert, Albertus Magnus, Dante (in his *Convivio* [66]), St. Thomas Aquinas, Roger Bacon, Siger of Brabant, Peter of Abano, William Ockham, Nicolas of Bonet, and many others, in various ways subscribed to the theory that these cycles and periodicities in the history of the world, as well as in human history, were caused by the influence of the heavenly bodies and their conjunctions, operating either as the instruments of God's will or — and this tendency becomes more and more prominent — immanently, at the virtue of their own uniformities.[67]

---

[63] See F. Cumont, *Les religions orientales*, pp. 151 ff., 166–167, 284 ff., and 290. Thorndike, *op. cit.*, Vol. I, chap. xv, pp. 455 ff., and chaps. xix–xxvii.

[64] See about that in Duhem, *op. cit.*, Vol. V, pp. 223 ff. The real history of the idea of progress and of the main conceptions discussed throughout the Middle Ages is not written yet. Works like J. B. Bury's *The Idea of Progress*, or Delvaille's work, quoted, only most superficially touch the problem. The same is to be said of other works in the field.

[65] See Ptolemy's *Tetrabiblos* or *Quadripartite*, trans. by Ashmand (London, 1822, reprinted in 1896).

[66] Bk. II, chap. xiv.

[67] See L. Thorndike, *op. cit.*, Vol. II, pp. 12, 40, 55–56, 103–104, 177, 183–185, 203, 211, 254, 267 ff., 325, 369, 393, 416–419, 485–487, 581–583, and 608 ff. See there the details and the literature. Duhem, *op. cit.*, Vol. V, pp. 225, *et passim*.

In this way, a number of periodicities and fluctuations were set forth in the movement of vital processes (births, deaths, marriages, epidemics, health), forms of government, war and peace, catastrophes and happy periods, prosperity and depression, revolutions, and other social processes.[68]

Thus, summing up the main features of the Ideational medieval period, we see that the eschatological (with the two "terminal perfect points") conception and the cyclical or endlessly undulating conceptions occupied the field. Little, if any, attention was paid to the linear conception, of either regressive or progressive variety. So far, the propositions set forth seem to be corroborated by this period also.

F. As we move from the thirteenth to the next three centuries, these two streams — the eschatological and the cyclical or trendlessly undulating — continue to occupy almost the whole field. There appear, however, several changes, slight and not spectacular, but nevertheless quite tangible. First, no clear-cut linear theory appeared; none the less, the linear — progressive — motive, especially in regard to the progress of arts and sciences and technique, began to sound more distinctly and more frequently, beginning with the twelfth century. In the works of Hugh St. Victor, then St. Thomas [69] and Albertus Magnus, Joachim de Floris, Roger Bacon, Vincent de Beauvais, and several others, these motives are already quite noticeable. Some of them were like Joachim's; he set forth in his theory of the Eternal Gospel, something like a progressively linear law of the "three stages of Humanity": the stage of the Old Testament, of the New, and of the Eternal Gospel, each stage being more perfect than the preceding one : the first being the stage of law and fear or intimidation ; the second that of grace and faith ; the third that of love.[70]

This fact is important for us because it shows once more the Idealistic character of the mentality of these centuries which we have met several times in other compartments of its culture. The progressively linear ideas, as an ingredient of the Sensate mentality, appear here and give to it Idealistic color. Nevertheless, though these motives become unmis-

---

[68] In passing, it is to be noted that this large literature, and particularly the astrological literature of these and subsequent centuries, is still almost entirely ignored by historians of various geographic and climatic theories of the causation of human affairs; meanwhile, many of the theories differ little in their nature from supposedly "scientific geographic-climatic" theories; and some of them are perhaps even more sound — and anyhow more interesting — than many theories of sunspots and other climatic factors of business and other sociocultural phenomena.

[69] *Summa theologica*, i–ii, q. 98, 106, and 107.

[70] See Joachim de Floris, *L'évangile éternel*, French trans., 2 vols. (Paris, 1928).

takable now, they are still only quite minor themes amidst the eschatological and cyclical main motives.

The next change is in the internal character of these eschatological
and cyclical conceptions, compared with that of the earlier period. The
eschatological theories began to decrease in popularity, while the factual
course of human history and that of the world began to attract greater
attention. The cyclical and trendlessly undulating theories tended to be
elaborated more and more, and, as mentioned, the cycles, the periodicities,
the fluctuations and recurrences began to be interpreted more and more
"immanently"; as a manifestation of the properties of the universe and
heavenly bodies as such, or of that of the empirical qualities of man and
society. Movements and revolutions and conjunctions of the heavenly
bodies are still regarded as the result of God's will and creation, but such
mentions become more and more a kind of pious *façon de parler* mainly.
The center of the theories is shifted to the study, description, and interpretation of these movements and revolutions and cycles and periodicities
and "correlations" as such: occurring immanently and due to the properties of the universe or of its parts. These changes mean a shift from
the Ideational conceptions toward more Sensate theories, though formally
both streams — eschatological and cyclical (or undulating) — remain the
same in this period as before.

Now treatises on astrology — enormous volumes — were flourishing
and being published in great numbers. Their authors — usually
"teachers of mathematiks and astrology" — explained all "mutations"
of social life — political, religious, literary, scientific, etc. — as occurring
mainly through the influence of the heavenly bodies. They repeated
the earlier theories of periodicities in human history; computed and
forecasted them; predicted the future of an individual and group; in
brief, with slight variation and with indefatigable energy, they repeated
what had been said many times before and is known to us from the above.
As is well known, among these astrologers there were several great
scientists, like Tycho Brahe, Kepler, Cardanus, not to mention other
names. The following brief excerpts from the astrological treatises of the
seventeenth century are typical and show the bearing of astrology upon
the interpretation of social mutations, cycles, and periodicities.

It hath been the Divine Will of the Creator,[71] from the foundation of the
World, that all things below the Moon should be subject to *Change*, and that
their *Mutations* should be govern'd by a cause above them, which are the

---

[71] The reference to the Divine Will of the Creator, in order to reconcile astrology with
the teachings of Christianity, is also typical, as mentioned.

Celestial Bodies, they being set in a due order from their creation, and to keep their courses in the several stations. . . . Great have been the Mutations of the World . . . among which are reckoned many great Monarchies or Empires, that have been erected and continued for several hundreds of years; but yet at the last, had their time of Destruction, by whose Fall there were new ones erected: as, for example, 1258 years before the coming of Christ, is said to begin the Persian Monarchy; and that was under the influence of the conjunction of Saturn and Jupiter in Virgo: that conjunction happening the same year; and this monarchy continued in its ebbing and flowing 810 years; at which time began the Grecian Monarchy; and seven years before the beginning of the Grecian Monarchy there was a conjunction of Saturn and Jupiter in Taurus; and this Monarchy continued in its ebbing and flowing near 505 years; at which time there did happen a conjunction of Saturn and Jupiter in Scorpio, which did destroy the Grecian and lay the foundation of the Roman Monarchy. . . . But that which is worth our taking notice of is that the next time that Saturn and Jupiter made their conjunction in Gemini, the Bishops of Rome claimed themselves the unlimited title of supremacy, it being the same time that Mahomet established his opinions, and as they had their rise together, so will they have their Fall. [Generally] All Families, Cities, and other Things that had a Beginning have been subject to Mutations, and at last to Dissolution.[72]

Further, the author gives a list of the years of conjunction of Jupiter and Saturn since 3958 B.C. and also a list of the years of the comets' appearances, and makes a causal timing of these years with the extraordinary events in human history. For instance, the year 1402 was marked by the appearance of a comet and . . . Tamerlane; in 1558 there was a comet and . . . the death of Charles V, three kings, two queens, two Dukes, fifteen cardinals, and many other princes. Then he forecasts future events.

When we approach the end of the fifteenth and enter the sixteenth century, we notice that the cyclical and trendlessly undulating theories continue to have the front-stage position, some of them detached from the astrological basis; at the same time, new progressively linear motives begin to be heard in crescendo, continuing and enlarging their beginnings of the twelfth and thirteenth, and their stream of the fourteenth and fifteenth century. Thinkers like Machiavelli (1460–1527) are in the

[72] *Catastrophe Mundi:* or *Europe's Many Mutations until the Year 1701*, by John Holwell, Philomat (London, 1682), pp. 1 and 10–11; *An Appendix to Holwell's Catastrophe Mundi*, by John Holwell, teacher of mathematiks and astrology (London, 1683), Proeme and p. A2. See also John Russel, *Astrological Predictions on the Affairs of the English Commonwealth* (London, 1659); E. Sibley, *A Complete Illustration of the Celestial Science of Astrology*, etc. (London, 1788). See also J. Friedrich, *Astrologie und Reformation* (München, 1864).

cyclical stream still, but detached from the astrological basis. Others, like J. Bodin (1530–1596), G. Bruno, Campanella (1568–1629), G. Botero (1540–1617), are also in that stream, but they introduce, to a notable extent, the elements of the progressively linear conception. Though things move in cycles, in the series of the undulations there is an ascending trend of progressive improvement of the arts and sciences, of humanity generally. Others, like Francis Bacon (1561–1626), Pascal (in the early period), stressed this progressive linearism still more. The nearer we come to the second part of the sixteenth and then to the seventeenth century, the louder and more dominant becomes the progressive linear conception. In Chapter Two, a number of the leading scientists and thinkers of these centuries, like Luther, Descartes, Huygens, Leibnitz, and others are quoted in optimistic statements about the enormous progress made and the possibility of an infinite or great progress in the future.

G. Beginning with the seventeenth century, we are in a rapidly rising tide of the progressively linear conception of human history — Fontenelle, L'abbé de Saint-Pierre, Montesquieu, Voltaire, Turgo, Shaftesbury, Mandeville, G. P. Turnbull, D. Hartley, Hume, A. Ferguson, A. Smith, Price, Priestley, Paley, the Encyclopedists, Condorcet, Lessing, Herder, Kant, and others. In hundreds of forms this conception begins to rise : in literature, science, philosophy, political writings, social theories. A few, and perhaps the greatest voices, still continue to advocate the cyclical conceptions, like G. B. Vico and some others ; nevertheless, the day of cyclical, trendlessly undulating, regressive linear theories, and of Christian eschatological conceptions, was over. These concepts all begin the course of decline. The rising sun is the sun of progressive linearism.[73]

This period and the rising tide of progressive linear conception are comparatively well known and are diligently studied ; and the trend itself, from the seventeenth to the twentieth century, is so well established that there is no need either to insist upon it or outline it in detail.[74]

---

[73] It manifested itself also in the new periodization of the history of mankind. Quasi-linear division of history into the ancient, medieval, and modern emerges in the fifteenth century. *"Media aetas"* begins to be used in this century, and in the seventeenth century the threefold division *antiquitas, media aetas, recens aetas* becomes common. See Spangenberg, *op. cit.*

[74] See about that period in Jules Delvaille, *Essai sur l'histoire de l'idée de progrès jusqu'à la fin du XVIIIe siècle;* J. B. Bury's *Idea of Progress*, quoted; W. Wallis, *Culture and Progress*, chaps. xvi–xviii; C. L. Becker, "The Uses of Posterity" in his *The Heavenly City of the Eighteenth Century Philosophers* (New Haven, 1932); R. Crane's *Anglican Apologetics*, quoted; L. Whitney's *Primitivism and the Idea of Progress*, quoted; E. Halevy's work, quoted; G. de Greef, *Le transformisme social* (Bruxelles, 1895); R. Mathis, *La loi des trois états* (Nancy, 1924).

After Turgot, Lamarck, Condorcet, and then Saint-Simon and Auguste Comte in France; Lessing, Kant, and Herder in Germany; the English Deists, Spencer, Darwin, and other prominent thinkers, the idea of linear evolution progress (or uniform sequence of stages arranged linearly) was the dominant category in the mentality of the eighteenth and especially of the nineteenth century.[75]

This conception became especially dominant in the field of biological and social and humanistic sciences and theories. In biology, after Lamarck, Milne, Edwards, Spencer, and Darwin, the linear conception of the direction of the life process in unilinear, fluctuating, spiral, or branching varieties (see Chapter Four of Volume One) became almost unanimously accepted, under the name of evolution of life or biological evolution. It continues to be dominant up to the present time.

If one were to try to sum up the essential characteristics of what is meant by biological evolution by most of the biologists (just in the aspect discussed), then evolutionary process would seem to possess the following characteristics.[76]

(1) It has linear direction in one of its main varieties: for a few it is rectilinear; for others it is fluctuating linear; for some, spirally linear; for many, branchingly linear.

(2) The linear trend consists seemingly in a passage from the less complex organisms to more complex organisms, or in a progressively increasing differentiation and integration of the Spencerian formula of evolution.

(3) Like Spencer, most of the thinkers explicitly or implicitly identify such evolution with progress; the main path of evolution is viewed as that of bigger and better progress: of improvement, per-

[75] Of course, the cyclical and trendlessly undulating or even the regressively linear conceptions were not lacking in that period; but they were an uninfluential minority.

[76] See *Creation by Evolution*, ed. by F. Mason, and consisting of the studies of A. J. Thompson, J. Huxley, C. L. Morgan, H. H. Newman, H. Jennings, and others (New York, 1928); a similar symposium in the *Evolution in the Light of Modern Knowledge* (London, 1925); E. G. Conklin, *The Direction of Human Evolution* (New York, 1925); W. M. Wheeler, *Emergent Evolution* (Boston, 1918); H. H. Newman (ed.), *The Nature of the World and of Man* (Chicago, 1926); H. H. Newman, *The Gist of Evolution* (Chicago, 1926); R. S. Lull, *Organic Evolution* (New York, 1917); W. B. Scott, *The Theory of Organic Evolution* (New York, 1917); A. N. Whitehead, *Science and the Modern World* (New York, 1928); C. Lloyd Morgan, *Emergent Evolution* (London, 1923); S. Alexander, *Space, Time and Deity* (London, 1920); J. C. Smuts, *Holism and Evolution* (London, 1926); G. P. Conger, *New Views of Evolution* (New York, 1929). Other literature is given in the two volumes quoted: *Creation by Evolution* and *Evolution in the Light of Modern Knowledge*. See also G. Richard, *L'idée d'évolution dans la nature et l'histoire* (Paris, 1903); G. Spiller, *The Origin and Nature of Man* (London, 1935).

fection, ascendance, from "the lower to the higher" (species, levels, values). Here biologists who supposedly have nothing to do with so-called evaluations and evaluative judgments have "bootlegged" these judgments into their theories to such an extent that the "bootlegged" evaluations have become almost as dominant as the whole conception of the supposedly nonevaluative evolution. Some of them went along this line so far that they made out of evolution a kind of wise, merciful, omnipresent, omnipotent, marvelous Providence, which sponsors for these biologists even their liberal or socialist platforms, the League of Nations, or the Third International.[77]

(4) It is finite, so far as its beginning is concerned, because life is supposed to appear, at least on this planet, at a later stage of the earth's existence; its first stages were devoid of life.

(5) Most of the theorizers about evolution are somewhat vague as to its finiteness or infiniteness in the future. Some of them are often self-contradictory on this point.

(6) Only the minority seem to stress rather rhythmical and recurring processes in this whole evolution, and the changing and diverse direction of its processes, the diversity of their paths and the existence of limits in the process of any particular line of evolution; and this minority does not bind itself to any quite clearly expressed belief in the existence of a main, perpetual, and linear trend.

(7) Many of them mention "continuous," "orderly," "gradual," "systematic," and similar characteristics, but leave these terms unexplained and practically vague or meaningless.

(8) Most of them use the terms "advance," "upward," "from the lower to the higher," and so on; but again they do not specify the meaning of these terms and abuse them greatly. As a rule, they inject, through

[77] " Evolution has progressed from amoeba to man; from reflexes to . . . intelligence and reason; from the solitary individual [??] to the family, the modern State, in spite of narrow-minded and reactionary politicians [???]; we or our descendants will yet see the whole human race brought together into a Society of Nations." Farther on, we are promised Paradise in all respects. Conklin, *op. cit.*, pp. 75–78. [It is really pleasant to have such a nice evolution; it looks exactly like the old-fashioned Benevolent Guardian Angel.] See similar effusions in the papers of A. J. Thompson, in the *Creation by Evolution*, pp. 20–22; of J. Huxley, *ibid.*, pp. 327–339. Reading the biological literature on evolution from this standpoint, one has to confess that this is the realm of science where the persecuted evaluative judgments and subjectivity and political and personal tastes of the scientist-authors have found the best refuge in the nineteenth and twentieth centuries. According to the taste, evolution is leading us to order or mutation, orderly or revolutionarily; to conservative rugged individualism or collectivism; to liberalism or Toryism; to religion or irreligiosity; to democracy or anarchism or monarchism; in brief, to everything that the sense or the non-sense of the author and his tastes dictate.

these expressions, into a supposedly objective scientific description of the processes a purely subjective and morally, socially, aesthetically evaluative judgment. They do the same in their identification of evolution with progress.

(9) The meaning of the main trend seems to be the cumulative meaning of the time direction (from the past to the present and future), quantitative direction (increase of complexity and differentiation), and qualitative direction (from qualitatively lower to qualitatively higher forms of life, from a qualitative lower level to the qualitative higher level; from reflex to intelligence, from a lesser knowledge, beauty, adaptation, self-control, morality, and sociality to the qualitatively better forms of all these values).

(10) The velocity of the process is assumed to be not constant; it is at one period quicker, at another slower. As mentioned, this linear conception of evolution has been unquestionably dominant, beginning especially with the second part of the nineteenth century.

Similar linear conceptions have been dominant also in the field of the social, humanistic, and other sciences dealing with man and his culture. The linearism in these theories assumed either the form of some main trend of progress in a certain field, with minor temporary deviations and setbacks, or a uniform sequence of stages in certain fields arranged again in a linear progressive way, like Comte's three states. Anthropologists, sociologists, historians, economists, political scientists, social philosophers, even theologians of the eighteenth and nineteenth and twentieth centuries, have indefatigably been manufacturing by dozens these theories of progress "from caveman or ape or even amoeba to modern man," seeing it as a progress from ignorance to science; instinct to reason; disorderliness to order; wretchedness to the "three-car-per-family" standard of living; fetishism to monotheism; promiscuity to monogamy (or vice versa, according to the preferences of an author); despotism to liberty; the *Gemeinschaft* to *Gesellschaft;* "mechanical to organic solidarity"; from imperfectly revealed religion to more fully revealed; inequality to equality; and so on and so forth. Or in the form of various "laws of stages": three, four, five, six, seven, or more, through which mankind as a whole, or its knowledge, or its economic organization, or its family, or its art or what not, have supposedly been passing and are destined to pass. These linear — and mostly progressively linear — conceptions flooded the social and humanitarian sciences; became their chief topic, their main ordering principle; the main perspective in which everything else and all the "facts" have been viewed. "Progress" and its derivatives became the main category of these sciences in the nineteenth century particularly.

All this is so well known and is so unquestionable that there is no need to give quotations and references.

To sum up, *in so far as the period from the fifteenth to the twentieth century has been that of the rise and triumph of the Sensate mentality and culture, the parallel rise and triumph of the progressively linear conception in the evolution of life and mankind well supports the proposition as to the association of progressive linearism with rising Sensate culture.*

IV. The Beginning of Reaction

As we approach the end of the nineteenth and pass into the twentieth century, we notice a slight, perhaps, but hardly doubtful, tendency of re-emergence and then growth of the cyclical and trendlessly undulating conceptions, partly in regard to the direction of the life processes, and especially in regard to that of sociocultural processes. In the field of biology, the tendency manifested itself in an increasing criticism and rejection of many previously unquestioned traits of the Darwinian evolution theory, meaning by this not only Darwin's, but that of the powerful current that made Darwinism its flag and symbol. Survival of the "fittest" began to be interpreted more and more critically in the sense that those who survive are not necessarily the best and fittest ; that therefore the line of evolution is not necessarily so linear, especially the progress line ; that there are many reversals, deviations, and other byways that make the linear route not so certain ; that the whole theory has many points that are not so settled as they first appeared to be ; that even the ancestral line and "tree of life evolution" is a conjecture rather than an ascertained fact, and so on. Likewise, the basic points of the theory began to be more and more questioned : the role of the struggle for life ; the mechanical ways of variation ; their fixation by heredity ; the role of heredity and environment ; and hundreds of other points. To sum up : the net results have been, so far, an increasing criticism of an ever-growing number of the facets of the theory of evolution ; an increasing questioning of its linearity and its identification with progress. Parallel with that, an interest began to grow in the theory of short- and long-time cycles in the diverse vital processes, beginning with the "cycles of epidemics" and "latent and kinetic" stages of various micro-organisms, and ending with the life cycles of vital processes among many species. In other words, in the biology of the end of the nineteenth and of the early twentieth centuries, there seems to have appeared a slight tendency toward the weakening of the previous linear conception of life evolution and an increase of interest toward the recurrent, cyclical, and trendlessly undulating pulsations of life phenomena.

In the field of the social and humanitarian sciences, this tendency has expressed itself more clearly and conspicuously than in biology. The end of the nineteenth and the beginning of the twentieth centuries are marked by a *definite decline of the theories of the uniform sequences of stages through which various societies pass in their life process.* This theory at the present moment is practically dead ; neither sociologists nor anthropologists nor respectable social scientists of the present moment, in an overwhelming majority, subscribe to this variety of the linear conception, so popular in the nineteenth century (it probably had its zenith around 1860–1900). Its decline means the decline of various linear conceptions.

The second symptom of the same decline is the progressively increasing attention of the social scientists to the "cyclical," "recurrent," "fluctuating," and "undulating" aspects of the sociocultural processes. If the economists of the nineteenth century were very busy with the "economic stages of development" (Roscher, Hildebrand, Bücher, Schmoller, and others), at the present time economists are mainly busy with business "cycles, fluctuations, oscillations," and recurrences. The situation is similar in almost all the social and humanitarian sciences. At the present moment there are few, if any, of the leading specialists in anthropology, sociology, law, ethics, political science, psychology, history, social philosophy, or history of religion who are devoting their main time and energy to works in which they aim to formulate the respective "uniform sequence of stages" through which, by the order of evolution progress, all societies and cultures supposedly pass in the course of time. That was the main business of the scholars and scientists busy with "social dynamics and progress" in the nineteenth century. Instead, the "cyclical" or "fluctuating" aspect of these processes is beginning to attract their attention more and more. In brief, linearism in this form is also fading.

The third symptom is *the emergence and rapid growth of the literature and theories that try to formulate the nonlinear conceptions of sociocultural processes and, what is still more important, the success which such theories are beginning to have.*

The meaning of the second part of this statement is illustrated by the attention which Nietzsche's enunciation of the theory of the eternal cycles at the end of the nineteenth century received, and by the success which works like Spengler's *Decline of the West* had, as well as by the impression it made. Hardly any single work along the lines of the linear evolution-progress theory published after 1914, or even perhaps in the twentieth century, has had as much influence. (Note that I do not say anything about the scientific or nonscientific *nature* of the works; I point only to their influence.) On the other hand, almost all the works along the old-fashioned linear conception — some of them not bad at all — pass unnoticed, regardless of their intrinsic worth. From this standpoint, there is hardly any doubt that (in postwar Europe particularly) linearism in the social sciences, with its evolution progress and stages of development and all the other traits, is dead, for the time being. In journalistic and popular literature it still lingers, but in the "path-finding, scholastic, and scientific and thinking groups" it is either dead or is viewed as a nice, old, old grandmother, with old-fashioned notions, is viewed by a modern "flapper."

As to the increase of the literature that stands for the cyclical, or trendlessly undulating, and generally nonlinear conception of the course of sociocultural processes, this is hardly questionable. As a matter of fact, beginning with the second half of the nineteenth century, it has already grown to such an extent that a special monograph is needed to enumerate it and to give a brief account of the theories involved.[78]

---

[78] In no way pretending to give a complete bibliography or even a greater part of these works, I would mention just a few samples. Such are, besides the works of O. Spengler, F. Petrie, P. Ligeti, O. Crawford, K. Joël, J. Ferrari, E. Gay, W. Deonna, H. Wölfflin, F. Cornelius, H. Schneider, E. Bovet, F. Chambers, C. Lalo, L. Weber, K. Scheffler, H. Schäfer, H. Krauss, and many others quoted in this work, S. Bodnar, *Mikrokosmos* (1898); G. Weissner, *Der Pulsschlag deutscher Stilgeschichte* (1929); W. Pinder, *Das Problem der Generation* (1927); H. von Müller, *Zehn Generationen deutscher Dichter und Denker* (1928); O. Lorenz, *Die Geschichtswissenschaft in ihren Hauptrichtungen und Aufgaben* (1886) and his *L. von Ranke* (1891); Richard von Kralik, *Die Weltgeschichte nach Menschenaltern* (1903); W. Vogel, *Ueber Rhythmus im geschichtlichen Leben*, in *Historische Zeitschrift* (1924); K. G. Schneider, *Die Periodizität des Lebens und der Kultur* (1926); H. Schlieper, *Der Rhythmus des Lebendigen* (largely biological) (1914); W. Fliess, *Vom Leben und Tod* (largely biological) (1923); R. Mewes, *Kriegs und Geistesperioden im Völkerleben* (1896; 2d ed. 1922); F. Stromer-Reichenbach, *Was ist Weltgeschichte?* (1919) and other works of this author, unavailable for me, especially his *Historionomie*; F. Noetling, *Die kosmische Zahlen* (1921). (Mewes, Noetling, and Reichenbach's works, as a few other works mentioned, belong to the type of "numerology" and partly "cosmic-astrological" literature, that is also rapidly growing.) L'Abbé Moreaux, "*Influence australes: la guerre te la paix*" in *Revue de l'Ouest* (October, 1920); E. Sasse, *Zahlengesetz der Volkerreizbarkeit* and *Plan zu einer allgemeine Statistik der Weltgeschichte*, in *Zeitschrift des König. Pres. Statist. Bureau* (1879); P. Choisnard, *Les précurseurs de l'astrologie scientifique* (1929); and his *L'Influence astral et les probabilités* (1924). (Add to this a large economic and other literature that tries to explain the long- and short-time cycles by the sunspots and other cosmic and astral influences, and this literature is enormous; see a part of it in my *Contemporary Sociological Theories*, pp. 120 ff.)

N. Berdyaev, *End of Our Time* (1934); R. Mayreder, *Der Typischen Verlauf sozialer Bewegungen* (1925); F. Kumer, *Deutsche Literaturgeschichte . . . nach Generationen dargestellt*

When all this is considered, the statement about the growth of the cyclical literature at the end of the nineteenth and in the twentieth centuries, and especially in the postwar period, would be acceptable. These three symptoms are sufficient to warrant a decline of the linear conceptions in the cultural and social sciences at this time.

Finally, even in the field of the physicochemical sciences, there seems to be present, in the form of a growth of a regressively linear conception, a symptom of the decline of the progressive-linear interpretation. I mean the principle of Carnot, set forth in 1824, enunciated in the second law of thermodynamics by Clausius in 1850 and steadily growing in its entropic interpretation as to the future course of the world. As we approach the end of the nineteenth century and the present era, more and more it is stressed that, as a consequence of this law, the universe has been tending steadily to a more and more equal distribution of the potentials of energy in it, and therefore to its death. If this principle was known among the specialists at the end of the nineteenth century, among the masses it did not begin to spread until the postwar period, and then only the popular works on the universe around us and its "whither" found a success and a large market. The works of James H. Jeans, A. S. Eddington, and the like, are examples of this. The theories propounded in these, as well as in

(1922); A. L. Kroeber, "On the Principle of Order in Civilization" in *American Anthropologist* (1919); L. Benloew, *Les lois de l'histoire* (1881); F. S. Chapin, *Cultural Evolution* (1928); C. Gini, "Cyclical Rise and Fall of Population," in *Population* (1930); also his *Patologia Economica* (1935); J. L. Lowes, *Convention and Revolt in Literature* (1926); E. Spranger, *Kulturzyklentheorie und das Problem des Kulturverfalls* (1926); W. Roscher, *Politik. Geschichtliche Naturlehre der Monarchie, Aristokratie und Demokratie* (1892); K. Breysig, *Der Weg der Menschheit* (1928) (spirally linear); F. Boll, *Die Lebensalter* (1913); J. Petersen, *Die Wesenbestimmung der Romantik* (1925); also his "*Die Literarische Generation,*" in E. Ermatingen (ed.), *Philosophie der Literaturwissenschaft* (1930); A. Rey, *Le retour éternel et la philosophie de la physique* (1927); O. Becker, "*Nietzsches Beweise für seine Lehre von der ewigen Wiederkunft,*" in *Blätter für deutsche Philosophie* (1935); G. Valois, *D'un siècle à l'autre* (1921); Danilevsky, *Russia and Slavhood* (1869); H. Adams, *The Degradation of the Democratic Dogma* (1919); E. von Lasaulx, *Neuer Versuch einer allein auf die Wahrheit der Tatsachen gegründeten Philosophie der Geschichte* (1857); R. Brück, *Manifeste du magnétism du globe* (1866) and *L'humanité, son development, et sa durée* (1866); U. von Wilamowitz-Moellendorff, "*Kulturperioden*" in his *Reden und Vorträge* (1901); A. J. Balfour, *Decadence* (1908); C. Dawson, "The Life of Civilizations," in *The Sociological Review* (1922); G. Milner, *The Problem of Decadence* (1931); A. J. Toynbee, *A Study of History,* Vol. III (problem of periodicity) (1935); A. B. Gough, "An Alleged Periodic Factor in History," in *The Sociological Review* (1936); E. Faure, *Histoire de l'art* (1924–1927); E. Lasbax, *La cité humaine* (1927) and *La France ira-t-elle à un 3ᵉ Empire* (1936). (Add to this the fairly large literature quoted in my *Contemporary Sociological Theories,* in sections devoted to a survey of the various theories of cycles and periodicities, pp. 728–741, none of which is mentioned above. Also many undulating theories are developed in special works in the history of art, science, philosophy, etc.)

many other astrophysical works of the present time (De Sitter, Lemaître, and others), are of this entropic type — the regressive linear running down, with the death of the universe as the terminal point.

The end of a star, and indeed, so far as we can see, of the whole material universe, is simple [!!!] — it is annihilation:

> Like the baseless fabric of this vision,
> The cloud-capped towers, the gorgeous palaces,
> The solemn temples, the great globe itself,
> Yea, all which it inherits, shall dissolve,

and either leave no rack behind, or, in so far as anything is left behind, it will be intangible radiation, travelling endlessly through space. [79]

This unexpected "funeral march," as a finale of the birthday hymn and wedding march of the linear evolution progress, and the popularity which it has had in our day is certainly a symptom of the weakening of the progressively linear mentality.[80]

Together with the other symptoms in biology and social sciences, it makes still more probable the claim that the end of the nineteenth and the early twentieth centuries show a weakening of the progressive linearism

[79] J. H. Jeans, " Cosmogony," in *Evolution in the Light of Modern Knowledge*, p. 20. See his other works, *The Mysterious Universe, Problems of Cosmogony,* and *Stellar Dynamics* (Cambridge, 1919); see also A. S. Eddington, *The Nature of the Physical World* (New York, 1929), p. 86.

[80] It is interesting to note the difference between these theories and the similar theory and principle that confronted Herbert Spencer and other scientists of his period some seventy years ago. In his *First Principles*, Spencer was also confronted with this principle of entropy, or inevitable equilibration to which the universe tends in the course of time. As a result, Spencer falls into the crudest self-contradiction between the death of the world in the future and the greatest happiness as the end of evolution. "The end of all the transformations (in the whole universe and in the human universe) is a state of quiescence" and "omnipresent death," "which brings Evolution, under all its forms, to a close."

Two pages further he assures us: "Evolution can end only in the establishment of the greatest perfection and the most complete happiness." Spencer, *First Principles* (London, 1870), pp. 514–517. Here we see clearly the "optimistic" phase of linearism when, in spite of an evident contradiction, Spencer and other devotees of this theory could assure themselves of the greatest happiness to which it leads. At the present moment, our astrophysicists are more logical, but have much less optimistic views on evolution. The contrast is typical from psychological and sociocultural standpoints. Very typical is also H. Adams's position in this problem. See his *The Degradation of the Democratic Dogma* (New York, 1919).

It is hardly necessary to say that if we add to these theories of the future death of the universe the next stage, namely, that after its dematerialized form it again rematerializes somehow, we find resurrected the old Babylonian, Hindu, Greek, and Roman theories of the *annus magnus*, with all their traits. The above theories of the death of the universe are but a step toward that end. And it is not improbable that in the near future some of the astrophysicists will make this new discovery.

and a reinforcement of the cyclical-undulating conception. If this be so, then this again is a variety of revolt against the overripe Sensate culture we met in other compartments of this period. Its fact is reinforced by the other facts of the revolt, and it reinforces them in its turn.

V. Conclusion

The above sketch is very concise but I hope it is roughly accurate in tracing the main swings and distributions in the field of this "First Principle." It makes reasonably certain three conclusions: (1) that the comparative influence of each of the main conceptions is different in different cultures; (2) that in the life history of the same culture this influence fluctuates; (3) that the influence or acceptability or creditability of each conception depends greatly upon the character of the dominant mentality of a given culture at a given period. Less certain, but hardly misleading, is the fourth proposition, namely, the tentative correlations established between the Ideational and Sensate cultures and between the types of the conceptions favored by each of these types of cultures, and therefore, tending to become influential in it. The factual study along the lines briefly outlined in this chapter plus several logical considerations seem to make these propositions probable. Thus validity or invalidity of each of these conceptions is, like the other First Principles mentioned above, a matter of the predominant type of culture. All the conclusions made in preceding chapters apply also to this "category" of human thought.

Chapter Eleven

FLUCTUATION OF THE BASIC CATEGORIES OF HUMAN THOUGHT: CAUSALITY, TIME, SPACE, NUMBER

I. INTRODUCTORY

Preceding chapters have shown that with the change of the main types of culture and their systems of truth, the "First Principles" of human thought — scientific and philosophical — change also in their influence, acceptability, and verity and prestige. In this chapter I am going to pursue this idea further. With the change of the type of culture, not only do the first principles change, but a deep transformation of their meaning is experienced also by the *basic categories of human thought* such as *time, space, number, causality,* that are indispensable for any cognition of any phenomena. Some of these transformations possibly are independent of our main variables — the types of culture and their systems of truth. Some others seem to have a tangible connection with the rise and fall of each type of culture and are, therefore, included in the thousands of details that undergo modification with the respective modification of the dominant type of culture. Space does not permit me to give here the factual history of these transformations as completely as it deserves to be described. Such a task would require a separate monograph. Thus, in this work, the only thing possible is to sum up the results which such a monographic study would probably give. Omitting, therefore, a rather large universe of relevant "facts" and "evidences" that have been accumulated in my studies, and reducing to the bare minimum the references to the works where the factual data can be found and the conclusions given can be verified, I simply give here a most concise summary of the results to which the study of the facts and the works has led me, together with a minimum of explanatory remarks to make these conclusions intelligible. In Volume Four I hope to develop more fully some of the propositions briefly stated here.

II. Fluctuation of Ideational and Sensate Conceptions of Causality

An unanalytical mind is inclined to think, when these terms, Time, Space, Number, Causation, and their derivatives are mentioned — in the past and in the present, in culture A and in B or C or D — that these terms in all such cases cover the same meaning, and that in their essentiality they always mean, for a thoughtful and logical mind, something identical. Such an assumption is the more legitimate in that, according to Kant and several other epistemological theories, these categories are not only a priori principles but the conditions of the possibility of any cognition, of any thinking, of any knowledge. In a sense they are, regardless of how they are derived and "planted" in the human mind. Some of these categories are "preconditions" to any coherent thinking, to any cognition of any, especially empirical, factualness. They have to be present in the mind in order that the mind can grasp anything and can know anything. But this does not preclude the possibility of a great difference in the *meaning* or "content" of the category of time, or that of space, or that of number or causality. The diversity may be even great, in spite of the identity of the term. And that is exactly what is to be found when the problem is studied from this standpoint. The "time" of the Ideational mentality is profoundly different from that of the Sensate; though Ideational and Sensate time both belong to the category of Time. The same is true of Ideational and Sensate space, number, causality, and several other categories. They are present in both mentalities, but they are profoundly different from one another. Their respective shells are similar; the content of the shells is greatly dissimilar.[1] Let us briefly elucidate that, beginning with the category of causality.

Ideational as well as Sensate mentality admits that *each fact or phenomenon has a cause or reason* for its existence. But as to what this cause is, and where, in the field of the supersensory or sensory phenomena, it is to be looked for, these mentalities differ greatly. Logically it is to be expected that the Ideational mentality will look for the cause or reason (*causa sive ratio*, as Descartes and others used to put it) in the Ideational world that lies behind or above the illusionary world of the senses, while

---

[1] In the chapter on Social Space and Social Time, in Volume Four of this work, it will be shown that the "contents" of each of these categories are different even in various cultures of the same type (Ideational or Sensate) in accordance with many purely empirical conditions. Here I am leaving these differences without any consideration, and concentrating only upon the difference connected with the main types of mentality. As a preliminary, see Sorokin and Merton's paper on "Social Time" quoted in *American Journal of Sociology* (1937).

the Sensate mentality has to seek the cause in the field of the sensory phenomena and nowhere else. Logically it is to be expected, further, that for the Sensate mentality the second principle of causation — "the same causes are followed by the same effects" — is in a sense inevitable; otherwise the causal relationship itself would be imperceptible and undistinguishable from the incidental *post hoc ergo propter hoc* or mere spatial or temporal contiguity and succession of the respective facts. For such a mentality an admission that the same cause A may now be followed by the effect B, now by C, now by D, would amount to a mere indeterminacy of the relationship between A and B and C and D. In brief, a denial of this principle for such a mentality means either pragmatic undistinguishability of the causal from the noncausal relationship or an explicit or implicit indeterminism.

Different is the situation in regard to the Ideational mentality. The supersensory nature of its cause (God, devil, Providence, Brahma, etc.) makes it unnecessary to claim that the same cause is to be followed by the same effects. "The will of the God is inscrutable"; the spiritual, creative, and free nature of the supersensory causative agent permits it to create an effect A and B and C and N — in brief, any effect. Here is an example, illustrating this.

In truth there is no other agent or efficient cause than *spirit* . . . or immediate hand of God. . . . "The Lord, he causeth the vapours to ascend; he maketh lightning with rain; he bringeth forth the wind out of his treasures." Jer. x:13. "He turneth the shadow of death into the morning, and maketh the day dark with night." Amos v:8. "He visiteth the earth, and maketh it soft with showers; he blesseth the springing thereof, and crowneth the year with his goodness, so that the pastures are clothed with flocks, and the valleys are covered over with corn." See Psalm lxv. But notwithstanding that this is the constant language of scripture; yet, we have I know not what aversion from believing that God concerns himself so nearly in our affairs. Fain would we suppose him at a great distance off, and substitute some blind unthinking deputy in his stead, though (if we may believe St. Paul) he be "not far from every one of us." [2]

The example shows the point clearly. Such a conception of causality amounts practically to indeterminism (and this is the reason why, in Chapter Nine, all such theories are put into the class of indeterminism or Mixed); but still it is a kind of causality and the moral of that is that the

[2] George Berkeley, *Principles of Human Knowledge* (Everyman's Library ed.), chaps. cii and cl, pp. 164 and 191–192. Just now it is unimportant for us that by God's will there are some laws in nature which, according to Berkeley, are created for "our guidance in the affairs of life."

concept of causality and those of determinism and indeterminism are not identical.   If the first principle of causality that everything has a cause or reason is acceptable to both the Ideational and Sensate mentality, the second principle of causality, invariability of the causal relationship between the cause and effect, is almost unavoidable for the Sensate and unnecessary for the Ideational conception of causality.

Several other differences can be expected logically in the Ideational and Sensate conceptions of causality.   For the sake of space, however, they have to be omitted here.[3]

When the problem of causality is studied from this standpoint, the essential results may be summed up in the form of the following propositions.

(1) *There have been two profoundly different conceptions of causality, Ideational and Sensate, with several intermediary types.*   The Ideational mentality looks for the cause in the supersensory world; the Sensate in the Sensate world; the Idealistic and the Mixed mentalities look for it in both the Ideational and Sensate domains.

(2) *These two different conceptions (plus the Intermediary ones) have been struggling with each other for domination in various cultures and in various periods of the life process of the same culture mentality.*

(3) *In essentials, in the dominant Ideational culture mentality, the Ideational conception of causality tends to be dominant; in the dominant Sensate culture mentality, the Sensate conceptions prevail; the dominant Idealistic mentality is marked by an intermediary or Mixed conception of causality.*

These deductions follow logically from the nature of the main types of mentality.   Are they corroborated factually?   An attentive study of the problem seems to answer the question positively.   A brief résumé of the relevant facts follows.

A. *Mixed Idea of Causality among Primitive Peoples.*   The works of anthropologists and sociologists, and especially of L. Lévy-Bruhl, have made it clear that a kind of Ideational conception of causality is widespread among them.   On the other hand, contrary to the one-sided claim of Lévy-Bruhl, the idea of the Sensate causality is also not absent among them.   Ideational conceptions come out in many forms, like the following ones.

[3] As mentioned, this topic. for its adequate treatment, requires a monographic work. This being impossible here, only the most essential points and only their most important fluctuations will be noted.   The results will be sufficient to allude to the nature of the problem and to the way in which it is connected with the Ideational and Sensate mentalities and their fluctuations.

[Australian aborigines] ignore the definite relationship that unites the fact of birth with the sexual act; they believe each conception is due to a sort of mystic fecundation.[4]

Often in the primitive societies the deaths, most "natural" in our eyes, are accounted for by mystic causes. . . . Thus . . . death by a poisonous snake's bite is generally considered due to the snake being influenced by a sorcerer. . . .[5]

[In these and numerous facts of this type] the mentality does not consent to be satisfied on the plan of the (sensory) experience. It goes beyond it in establishing the liaison between the visible (sensory) effect and invisible (supersensory) cause, rightly says Brunschvicg.[6]

The very existence of magic and supersensory religion among the "primitive" and "prehistorical" peoples, in the form of belief in this or that deity, or in the supersensory power; in ceremonies of religious and magical character; in forms of sorcery; in shamanism; even in such a specific system of evidences as ordeals in deciding the question of guilt and innocence; in divination; and in hundreds of similar mores, institutions, and customs widely diffused among practically all the "primitive," "prehistorical," and earlier stages of the "historical" peoples — all this is an incontestable evidence of the existence of a variety of the Ideational conception of causality.

On the other hand, it is erroneous to think that only this conception is known to these peoples, and that all of them are equally Ideational in this respect. However little the question is studied, two things seem to be clear: first, that all or most of these primitive and prehistoric peoples have also a Sensate form of causality applied to many daily experiences where the connection between the phenomena is explained sensately and "experientially" as a result of the "natural" properties of the "variables" involved;[7] second, that the relative influence of Ideational and Sensate conceptions varies from people to people and is not constant among all the

---

[4] E. Durkheim, *Les formes élémentaires de la vie religieuse* (Paris, 1912), p. 258.

[5] L. Lévy-Bruhl, *Les fonctions mentales dans les sociétés inférieures* (Paris, 1910), p. 325. See there, and in Lévy-Bruhl's *Mentalité primitive* (Paris, 1922), an enormous collection of facts of this kind.

[6] L. Brunschvicg, *L'expérience humaine et la causalité physique* (Paris, 1922), p. 96.

[7] This merely follows from an almost unanimous criticism of the one-sidedness of Lévy-Bruhl's theory of the alogical mentality and of the "law of participation" which he develops in his otherwise excellent works quoted. Anthropologists and sociologists have indicated a large category of facts where the logic of the primitive peoples is as "normal" as ours. See, for instance, R. Thurnwald, "*Psychologie des primitiven menschen,*" in *Handbuch für vergleichende Psychologie,* ed. by G. Kafka (1922).

groups.   So far as the culture mentality of most of the primitive peoples seems to be of Mixed type, such a coexistence of Ideational and Sensate conceptions, often poorly harmonized with each other, is in harmony with the logical expectations.   We have met before a similar coexistence of the elements of both mentalities in other compartments of the culture and mentality of the "primitive" and "prehistoric" peoples.

B. *Chinese Mixed Causality.*   Diagnosing Chinese culture mentality several times, we have diagnosed it as Mixed in the sense that it includes the two mentalities: Taoist (Ideational) and Confucianist (Mixed); and in the sense of the existence of theories and conceptions wherein Ideational and Sensate elements are mixed.   The same is the conclusion to which we must arrive in the question of causality conception.   Instead of a long analysis and many quotations, a few excerpts from the work of one of the most thoughtful investigators of the Chinese thought will suffice.   Though not written to corroborate my theory, they nevertheless exhibit clearly the Mixed nature of the Chinese conception of causality or of what is its substitute.

Mythical thought, and with it, the different techniques that are used for an appropriate control of the World, are penetrated by a belief that the realities are influenced (*suscitées*) by emblems.   Viewing Tao as the Principle of Order that rules equally the mental activity as well as the life of the World, they admit uniformly that the changes in the course of the realities (*choses*) are identical with the substitutions of symbols in the course of thought.   This axiom once admitted, neither the principles of causality nor that of contradiction can be invoked to take the role of the directive principles.   This is not because the Chinese thought enjoys confusion, but, on the contrary, because the idea of Order — and of the Order that is efficacious and totalitarian — dominates it, engulfing in itself the notion of causality and of class. . . .   Instead of register-ing the succession of the phenomena, they register the alternations of aspects. If two aspects appear to them related it is not a relation of cause and effect; they appear to them to be like the two sides of cloth; or sound and echo; or shadow and light. . . .   What they like to notice are not the causes and effects but (the order of the apparition being unimportant) the singular mani-festations that are offshoots of the same root.   Equally symptomatic, these manifestations appear to be substitutive (for one another).   River that dries up; mountain that slides down; man that changes into woman — these announce the approaching end of a dynasty.   Here we have four aspects of the same phenomenon: an order destined to disappear, giving place to a new order.   Each aspect deserves to be noted as the premonitory sign or a confirma-tion of a sign (or of a series of signs), but nothing invites us to seek for an efficient cause. . . .

When a *rapport* is established, they never care to measure the terms of a relationship. They consider neither the phenomena nor their order of magnitude. In these aspects they deal with the signs whose quantitative evaluation or dimension or frequency is of little importance. The most useful premonitory signs are those that are the most singular, most delicate, most rare, and most furtive. A bird that destroys its own nest furnishes a physical and moral indicator of the destruction of the Empire; its gravity is extreme, because the sentiment of the familial piety is lacking *even* among the humblest animals. . . . The slightest symptoms [appearances] thus deserve to be catalogued, and the most peculiar are more valuable than the most normal. The catalogues are not intended to discover the *sequences* but to disclose the *solidarities*. Instead of considering the course of affairs [*choses*] as a sequence of phenomena susceptible of being measured and then put in relationship, the Chinese see in the sensible realities but a mass of concrete signs. . . .[8]

All the changes of the emblems and realities are accounted for, not by causality or causes, but by Tao, and then by the derivative principles of the Yin and Yang.

These lines show a peculiarly Mixed conception of what serves in lieu of causality. This conception has a large part of the Ideational elements: mental emblems influencing or being in a mystical *rapport* with things and events; premonitory signs — mostly rare, queer, and physically unrelated to the phenomena — viewed, as related, most intimately; the supersensory Tao and the Yin and Yang as the responsible Total, whose expressions are these signs. These elements by their very nature are outside of the Sensate world in the proper sense of this term. On the other hand, we are told that:

These dispositions of their thought have not hindered the ancient Chinese from manifesting their great mechanical aptitudes. . . . The perfection of their arcs and their carriages is an evidence of that. . . . In its other aspect their thought is animated by a passion of empiricism which predisposes it to the minutest observation of the concrete that has led it to such fruitful results [discoveries in pharmacopoeia, chemistry, agriculture, etc.][9]

Without continuing this characterization, the above shows well two elements — Ideational and Sensate — in the Chinese conception of causality, Mixed in the sense of coexistence of both in their culture, and Mixed in a peculiar combination within the same theory or conception. So far the proposition seems to be not contradicted by the data.[10]

---

[8] M. Granet, *La pensée chinoise*, quoted, pp. 329-333. See there an elaboration of this concept that is not easy for a Western mind to grasp.

[9] *Ibid.*, pp. 334 and 338-339.

[10] A more detailed analysis of the problem permits us to substantiate the proposition greatly, up to many most conspicuous details.

C. *Hindu Ideational Conception of Causality.*   Being predominantly Ideational in all other compartments, the Hindu mentality is also predominantly Ideational in the field of the present problem.   The character of the Vedas, other sacred sources, and the dominant philosophy of India, beginning with the Upanishads and ending with other main currents of the philosophical thought, make this hardly questionable.   Real cause in all these sources is supersensory.   Even the course of nature, of the world, and of its great and small cycles are but manifestations of the supersensory power, be it Brahma or other such agency.   The rites and religious and magic ceremonies testify to the same.   Behind the illusionary appearance of the Sensate phenomena, there operate non-Sensate forces, whatever their names.[11]   They are the reality and the real causes or forces that rule the phenomenal world and control it.   And that in a much more real sense than, as we shall see, in the teachings of Descartes and Malebranche and other Western thinkers of the seventeenth and eighteenth centuries who postulated God, but relegated Him to a passive role behind the ruling forces of sensate nature.

D. *Fluctuation of the Conception of Causality in the Graeco-Roman and Western Thought.*   The main phases through which the conception passed may be summed up as follows.

(1) The Greek thought before the fifth century B.C. was dominated by a kind of Ideational conception of causality.   Destiny, and the gods, and other supersensory agencies determined and controlled the fate of men and groups, and the course of events of the phenomenal world.   Behind the happenings in the Sensate world there was a world of supersensory agents that "caused" and "controlled" them.   This is clear from the works of Homer and Hesiod [12] as well as from the character of the Greek religion, mythology, and magic.   It is supported also by Aristotle, who says that "those who lived in the most ancient times and who first formed schemes of theology . . . constituted both Oceanus and Tethis as the parents of generation, and water as the object of adjuration amongst

[11] Even the contemporary Hindu thought remains essentially in the same stream, in spite of some softening of the Ideational motive and a pantheistic tendency in it.   Read from this standpoint the teachings of Sri Ramakrishna, the Vedanta philosophy by Sridhar Majumdar, the commentaries on the Vedanta and the Upanishads by Sri Sankaracharya, the writings of Swami Vivekananda, of Sri Aurobindo, of Swami Brahmananda, of Swami Abhedananda, and others.   Somewhat typical in this respect is the main current of mentality expressed in such periodicals as *Prabuddha Bharata* (*Awakened India*).

[12] "First of all the deathless gods . . . made a golden race of mortal men. . . ."   Then, "Zeus, the father, made a third race," and so on.   *Works and Days*, pp. 109–201.   Similar is terminology of Theognis; see his *Elegies*, for instance A, 1135 ff.   See also Aristotle's *Metaphysics* (Bohn's ed.), Bk. I, chap. iv, p. 18.

the gods — called Styx." [13] Such were the primary causes in this ancient mentality. This period thus appears to be mainly Ideational here, just as it appeared to be in other compartments of the Greek culture.

(2) Beginning with the second half of the sixth, and throughout the fifth and the fourth centuries B.C., the Greek conception of causality becomes less Ideational, more Sensate, and assumes the form of the Mixed conception ; and among the Mixed, the Idealistic conception of causality becomes paramount.

This conclusion follows from the study of the causality or its substitutes in the Pythagorean stream of thought, in the works of Empedocles, Pindar, Aeschylus, Euripides, Aristophanes, Herodotus, Thucydides, and several other prominent thinkers of the period, and culminates in the Idealistic conception of Plato and Aristotle and their schools. Whatever are the differences between the conceptions of these thinkers, they all are similar in one respect, namely in their Mixed nature, in the terms of our classification. They neither ignore the empirical relationship of the phenomena studied, nor their uniformities and properties ; nor do they ignore the superempirical forces and agencies that exist side by side with the empirical phenomena and relationship or behind them.

The Ideational element is present there, first, in the form of an eternalistic Being that does not change, and therefore does not call forth even the problem of the cause of change ; or, in Aristotle's terms, the final cause. Such was the mentality of the early nature philosophers, like Thales and others.[14] Second, when the problem of final cause was put, most of the thinkers sought for it either in the mind or in such superempirical principles as the "love" of Hesiod and Parmenides ; "love and discord" of Empedocles ; in mystical nature and the power of numbers, of the Pythagoreans ; in similar principles of other philosophers of the period : Hermotimus, Alcmeon of Crotona, Anaxagoras, Anaximenes, Herakleitos and others.[15]

On the other hand, the theories of Leukippos and Democritus introduced the elements of a nearly Sensate, purely phenomenal, interpretation of causal relationships between the empirical phenomena.[16] Thus both elements are present in the coexistence of both types of theories, as well as in the mixture of both elements in the same theory.

The decisive evidence of the Mixed conception of the period is, however, the nature of the causality in Plato's and Aristotle's systems of thought,

---

[13] Aristotle, *Metaphysics*, Bohn's ed. (London, 1857), Bk. I, chap. iii, p. 14.
[14] *Ibid.*, Bk. I, chaps. iii and iv.   [15] *Ibid.*, Bk. I, chaps. iii, iv, and v.
[16] See Aristotle's characterization of their standpoint, *ibid.*, Bk. I, chap. iv, 7–8.

which were the culminating point of the efforts of these centuries in the field of this problem.   The Mixed (Idealistic) character of their conception follows directly from the dual character of Plato's causality and from the fourfold character of the Aristotelian concept.   Regardless of whether Plato succeeded in giving synthesis to his two kinds of causes — one empirical, the other supersensory — the very fact that these two forms of causality were advanced by Plato is hardly questionable, and they show the Mixed character of his conception.   The *Phaedo* and *Timaeus* are the dialogues where it is developed.

In *Phaedo* we have, on the one hand, an empirical explanation of "why a man grows" through eating and drinking," when from the food flesh is added to flesh, bone to bone, and so on," and other similar explanations where the causality seems to be viewed sensately; the phenomenon to be explained is Sensate and the cause of which it is effect is also of Sensate nature.   On the other hand, in the same dialogue Plato develops the inadequacy of such an explanation by taking, among other things, the case of Socrates, and asking why he sits in prison awaiting death instead of fleeing elsewhere.   He ironically points out that one of the apparent causes of his sitting there is that he has bones and sinews.

The bones, therefore, being suspended in their sockets, the nerves relaxing and tightening, enable me [Socrates] to bend my limbs as I now do, and from this cause I sit here bent up. . . .   But to call such things causes is too absurd. . . .   For this would be not to be able to distinguish that the real cause is one thing, and that another, without which a cause could not be a cause. [Developing his idea, he sums up, stating:]   I am now saying nothing new, but what I have always . . . never ceased to say. . . .   There is a certain *abstract* beauty, and goodness, and magnitude, and so of all other things. . . . I hope that I shall be able from these to explain the cause to you, and to discover that the soul is immortal. . . .   If there be anything else beautiful, besides the beauty itself, it is not beautiful for any other reason than because it partakes of that abstract beauty. . . .   By means of beauty, all beautiful things become beautiful. . . .   And that by magnitude great things become great. . . .[17]

In brief, the real cause is the Platonic supersensory idea.

In his *Timaeus, Phaedrus, Statesman*, and *Republic*, similar confrontations of two kinds of causality are also found.   For instance, in the *Statesman* God is taken as the real cause of what happens with and in the phenomenal world.

[17] *Phaedo*, in *Five Dialogues of Plato* (Everyman's Library ed.), pp. 175–181.   Lévy-Bruhl can style the whole logic of Plato here as a sample of the prelogical "*loi de participation.*"

There is a time when God goes round with the world, which he himself guides and helps to roll; and there is a time, on the completion of a certain cycle, when he lets go, and the world . . . turns around and revolves in the opposite direction. . . .[18]

Such a moment is marked by a great shock, destruction, and catastrophe of the whole world and mankind. When God takes his guidance again, the world and mankind are re-established in order, virtue, wisdom, and other values.

Similarly, in his *Republic*, the cause of the dissolution and reappearance of states and regimes is a supersensory mystical cycle of a certain period, whose completion leads through various empirical manifestations to the end of the given constitution.[19] A similar mystic cycle is postulated in *Timaeus*: "the perfect number of time completes the perfect year"; [20] also in his *Phaedrus*.[21]

These indications are sufficient to warrant the contention concerning the Mixed — and Idealistically Mixed — conception of Plato's causality, as a synthesis of the physicomechanistic and finalistic causality.[22]

The Idealistic character of Aristotle's conception comes out clearly in his doctrine of the four classes of causes: formal, efficient, material, and final.[23] If the material cause (or matter) and often the efficient cause belong to the Sensate world, the final and — partly at least — the formal cause belong to the Ideational world, especially the supreme final cause, or the first cause, God.[24] This theory of causality, together with the whole system of Aristotelian philosophy, attempts to unite organically the

---

[18] The *Dialogues of Plato*, trans. by B. Jowett (Oxford, 1921), Vol. III, 563 ff. and 587 ff.

[19] *Republic*, Bk. VIII, 546–547, in the *Dialogues*, trans. by B. Jowett (Oxford, 1921), Vol. II, pp. 380–382.

[20] *Timaeus*, 39, in the *Dialogues*, trans. by Jowett, Vol. II, p. 533.

[21] *Phaedrus*, 249, in the *Dialogues*, by Jowett, Vol. I, p. 583. What is this "perfect number" of Plato remains unknown, in spite of a large literature about the question and many hypotheses: 21,000 and 760,000 years (J. Dupuis); 2700 days (P. Tannery); 10,000 years (E. Zeller, J. Hunziker); 20,250, 7500, 4800, 3600, 6400 years, and several others were given to this Plato's mystical number. The very role which mysticism of number plays in the system of Plato is also an evidence of the Ideational aspect of his conception. See about this perfect number a long note in the French translation of the *Republic* by V. Cousin, Vol. X, of Plato's *Œuvres*, pp. 322 ff.; E. Zeller, *Philosophie der Griechen*, 4th ed., Vol. III, pp. 857–860; G. C. Young's "Nuptial Number of Plato," in the *Proceedings of the London Mathematical Society* (1924), Vol. XXIII, pp. 27–44.

[22] Aristotle also corroborates it, saying that "Plato employed two causes; namely, both the formal cause and the material cause." *Metaphysics*, Bk. I, chap. vi, 5. Compare Brunschvicg, *op. cit.*, chap. xi; A. Menzel, *Griechische Soziologie* (Wien, 1936), chaps. ii, iii, vi.

[23] See Aristotle, *Physics*, Bks. I and II. *Metaphysics*, Bk. I, chaps. iii, iv, v, and vi; Bk. IV, chap. ii (Bohn's ed., quoted).

[24] See especially Bk. XI, chaps. vii ff. of *Metaphysics*.

immanent reality with the transcendental; the Sensate world with the Ideational; mechanism with finalism. From this standpoint it, like Plato's conception, presents a conspicuous case of the Idealistic synthesis of both forms of causality. Here again, then, we meet the Mixed and Idealistic form which has been found before in other compartments of the Greek culture of the fifth and the first part of the fourth centuries B.C. So far the proposition of this chapter is well supported by the dominant form of causality of the period, its Mixed and partly Idealistic character.

E. *From the End of the Fourth Century* B.C. *to the Beginning of Our Era.* This period is marked by the Stoic and Epicurean schools which represented the most powerful currents of the philosophico-scientific thought (philosophy for that period still embraced in itself science). The Cynics, the Skeptics, and a few other groups were present; but they were either secondary in influence or, like the Skeptics, occupied a "nihilistic" position toward science generally and causality in particular; therefore they can be passed by. So far as the causality of the Stoics and Epicureans is concerned, they took from the two streams of Platonian-Aristotelian thought, Sensate and Ideational — mainly the first; therefore the period is to be regarded as showing a comparative increase of the influence of the Sensate causality at the cost of the Ideational.

[In their system] a being or object (*l'être*) is adequate in the aspect in which it manifests itself. As a result, the Aristotelian system of causes disappeared, driven out by the following dilemma: Either the denomination of cause is applicable to all the conditions without which a change cannot be accomplished, in which case the (fourfold) classification of causes by Aristotle is insufficient and shall embrace (as causes) such conditions as time, place, and so on, or if the term of cause shall be reserved only for that which is indeed determinant, in which case the enumeration of Aristotle is superabundant. Therefore, there is only one kind of cause — the efficient cause.[25]

This unique [efficient] cause of the Stoics [and I can add of the Epicureans] is corporeal because from the realistic standpoint assumed by the Stoics nothing exists that is not corporeal. To act and to react are the attributes of a body [corps]. A cause put in contact with a body devoid of quality impresses upon it a qualitative form.[26]

According to Zeno, "cause is 'by what' something is produced; reason,

---

[25] Haec, qua ab Aristotele et Platone ponitur turba causarum aut nimium multa aut nimium pauca. . . . Stoicis placet unam causam esse, id quod facit. Seneca, *Epistles*, ed. by Haase (Leipzig, 1886), Vol. III, p. 139. See also *Simplicius in Aristot. categ.*, in H. von Arnim, *Stoicorum veterum fragmenta* (Leipzig, 1903), Vol. II, p. 227. Plutarch, *de Stoicorum repugnantiis*, in H. von Arnim, *op. cit.*, Vol. II, chap. xliii. Plutarch, *De comm. noticii*, § 30, in *ibid.*

[26] Brunschvicg, *op. cit.*, p. 161.

for instance, is 'through what' knowledge is produced, soul is 'through what' life is produced." "All causes are corporeal." [27]

Similar are the statements of Chrysippus and other Stoics.

For them bodies are the only realities. Bodies are of two kinds: pneumatic and material. The pneumatic are active; the material passive. The first embrace the second; and the first, through pressure, impress and move the second. Thus, though the causes were reduced to the pneumatic bodies, to something suggesting soul, this soul was represented corporeally and is, at the best, a kind of a somatic spiritualism, as Professor Lossky styles it; [28] or a kind of a hylozoistic materialism, where the soul is interpreted in the sense of Anaxagoras's subtle fluid or Herakleitos's fire and the like. Taken as a whole, it remains much more in the realm of the Sensate reality than the Platonic or Aristotelian conceptions. Being empiricists and partly nominalists, they went along Sensate lines so far they were interpreted by some specialists as more empirical even than J. S. Mill.[29]

This Sensate trend is still more noticeable in the conception of causality by the Epicurean school.

In brief, the period is marked, in this special field, by some increase of the Sensate mentality. It also agrees with the proposition that the dominant conception of causality is conditioned by the dominant type of culture mentality of the period.

F. *From the Beginning of the First to the Fourth Century* A.D. The period from the beginning of our era up to the fourth century A.D. was here, as in other compartments of culture, transitory: most diverse conceptions — Ideational and Sensate and Mixed — existed side by side in the Stoic, Epicurean, Neo-Platonic, Neo-Pythagorean, and Christian currents of thought. The trend, however, was toward a rise of the Ideational causality, not only in the Christian but in Neo-Platonic (Plotinus, Jamblichus, Proclus, and others) and other currents.

G. *From the Beginning of the Fifth to the End of the Twelfth Century* A.D. Around the fifth century A.D. this rise ended in a complete victory of the Christian Ideational conception of causality that continued to dominate almost up to the end of the twelfth century. The essentials of this conception can be summed up in the following propositions.

[27] H. von Arnim, *Stoicorum veterum fragmenta* (Leipzig, 1900), No. 89, Vol. I, p. 25.

[28] See Lossky's paper, quoted; P. Duhem, Vol. I, pp. 301 ff.; also E. Bréhier, *La théorie des incorporels dans l'ancien Stoicism* (Paris, 1906); E. Zeller's *The Stoics, Epicureans, and Sceptics*, English trans.

[29] This is, of course, wrong, when to their somatic spiritualism their ethical tendencies, their belief in divination and astrology and the like, are added.

(1) The first and the last, the final and the efficient, in brief, the only real cause of anything is God.   Everything that happens or does not happen, exists or does not exist, is God's will, created by him, and controlled by him.

(2) God's will is, in application to man, to grant him free will and make him responsible for himself and his conduct.

(3) A number of nonmaterial and spiritual agencies, like angels and the like, are participating in the production and change of the phenomenal world, but as the agencies of God.

(4) The omnipotence of God precludes an impossibility of "miracles" or the necessity of achieving the same effects through the same causes.   Though He may will to establish an order in the phenomenal world and "natural laws" and "uniformities," they can be removed or replaced by quite different relationships if the inscrutable ways of God find it advisable.   Respectively, the very contrast between the "natural" and "the miracle" did not appear to that mentality as great a contrast as it did to the Sensate mentality.

Such a conception of causality is evidently profoundly different from the Sensate or that to which we are accustomed.   It reduces to almost nothing the immanent relationship of Sensate phenomena; does not consider it necessary; only in so far as this or that natural uniformity is established by God, has it a validity and reality.   Still less does it admit any mechanical determinism.   And for the mentality of this period, in contradistinction to the next one, the transcendental cause was not thought to be "retired" after establishing the order and the laws of nature. On the contrary, it was thought to be "active" all the time, ruling as well as reigning.   It was the king as well as the prime minister, commanding the vast legion of transcendental forces that control and guide the world.

This conception is found, with variations, in the works of the Church Fathers and Christian thinkers of the period.   It is enough to take St. Augustine's definition of God in order to see in it all the above characteristics.

What art Thou, then, my God? What, but the Lord God? . . . Most highest, most good, most potent, most omnipotent; most merciful, yet most just; most hidden, yet most present . . . unchangeable, yet all-changing . . . all-renewing, and bringing age upon the proud, and they know it not; ever working, ever at rest; . . . supporting, filling, and overspreading; creating, nourishing, and maturing; seeking, yet having all things. . . .[30]

[30] *Confessions*, Bk. I, iv. See also Bk. VII (against corporeal conception of God) and Bks. XI and XII about the problem of time and God.

In such a conception, the empirical phenomena, their relationships, even their uniformities, are considered but mere signs of the will of God. Even the astrological and astronomical phenomena were but signs of the sometime comprehensible, sometime inscrutable ways of the transcendental power.

Explicitly or implicitly, this conception is found in the works of Boethius, Isidore of Seville, Bede, Rhabanus Maurus, and others, up to Erigena. For Erigena also God is the cause of the Universe; He gives existence to it. And the Divine Logos is the indivisible unity of all things because it is all things itself. Being absolutely simple, the Divine Logos is at the same time infinitely multiple, present in all things, and these things subsist only because it is in them. . . . These eternal reasons

are the causes of all things, visible and invisible; in the whole universe of the natural things perceived by senses, or by reason or by intelligence, there is nothing which does not proceed from these causes and which does not subsist through them.[31]

From the pseudo *Areopagitae*, through the medieval versions of the "astronomical and cosmological" works of Macrobius, Chalcidius, M. Capella, up to the treatises on theology, the essentials of this conception of causality are common to all the thinkers of the period. In this sense the whole period is dominated by Ideational causality.[32]

H. *From the End of the Twelfth to the Fourteenth Century.* When we approach the end of the twelfth, and then pass to the thirteenth and the fourteenth centuries, a tangible change becomes noticeable. The penetra-

[31] Joannis Scoti Erigenae, *De divisione naturae liber tertius*, 8–14, in Migne's *Patrologiae latinae*, Vol. CXXII, col. 639–664.

[32] It comes out conspicuously also in the fairly common assumption of the thinkers of the period that the ways of God are often incomprehensible and that when we do not understand how this or that is possible, we shall believe — and they believed indeed — that for God all and everything is possible. Even such thinkers as William of Conches (1080-1150) and some others of the School of Chartres especially, who were very reluctant to assume such a position and who assailed it, nevertheless admitted it, after all due allowances to reason. "The miserables! William assails such believers. What may be more miserable indeed than to say: God can do a thing and at the same time not be able to explain what it is, or to give any reason for its existence and not to show any useful purpose which it serves. . . ." "They want us to believe in the manner of peasants, without seeking the reasons of anything. . . . We, on the contrary, pretend that in everything we shall search for the reason; but if the reason escapes us in a thing affirmed by the Holy Scripture, then only shall we confide ourselves to the Holy Spirit and Faith. . . . When we study a question concerning God and if we do not understand it, let us appeal for help to our neighbor; that is, to a person who stays in the same Catholic faith as ourselves. If neither he nor ourselves can comprehend the question, let us give ourselves to the ardent flames of the faith." Duhem, *op. cit.*, Vol. III, pp. 97-98.

tion of the influence of Arabian thinkers, plus the translation and circulation of many works of Aristotle previously little known, undoubtedly
contributed to it, though they were neither the only nor the main reason.
In few words, this change can be accurately characterized *as a replacement
of the Ideational conception of causality by the Mixed and, particularly,
Idealistic idea.* This follows merely from the fact that the dominant
conception now became the Aristotelian conception of the fourfold
causality, and partly the Platonic twofold conception of it. These two
conceptions, with some variations, came to be shared by almost all the
thinkers of this period.

Thierry de Chartres (twelfth century) in his treatise on the Creation of
the World according to *Genesis* writes :

The sovereign Trinity operates in matter which is an ensemble of the four
elements (fire, air, and so on). In so far as the Trinity is the efficient cause,
It creates this matter ; as a formal cause, It forms and unforms it ; as the final
cause, It cares for and governs it. Because the Father is the Efficient Cause ;
the Son is the Formal Cause ; and the Holy Spirit is the Final Cause, while
matter is the Material Cause.[33]

Here before us the Aristotelian theory of causality is laid down in all its
essential traits, adapted, however, to the terminology and concepts of the
Bible. Developing the thesis, the authors pay more and more attention
to the properties of material things as such. This tendency goes through
the works of Gilbert de la Porre, in his commentaries on *De Trinitate* of
Boethius, appears still more in the prohibited summaries of Aristotle's
Metaphysics by David de Dinant ; in the writings of Maurice the Span-
iard, Amalricus the Heretic, William of Auvergne, Alexander of Hales,
Robert Grosseteste, Roger Bacon, and many others ; ending with the
works of Siger of Brabant, Albertus Magnus, and St. Thomas Aquinas.
Individual variations are of course present in these works ; they differ
from one another in many secondary points. They criticize often this
or that point of Aristotle's and Plato's conceptions. And yet, the
Mixed or Idealistic character of their conceptions of causality is common
to practically all of them. Their conceptions run along the lines and
terms and theories of Aristotelian and Platonic constructions, colored by
St. Augustine and the Christian *credo*.[34]

---

[33] See B. Hauréau, "*Notice sur le numero 647 des manuscrits latins de la Bibliothèque
Nationale*," in *Notices et extraits des manuscrits de Bibliothèque Nationale*, Vol. XXXII,
pt. ii (1888), p. 173.
[34] See an analysis of their theories in Duhem, *op. cit.*, Vol. V, pp. 233 ff.

Comparing his opinion and that of Aristotle about the first cause and the creation of the world, Albertus Magnus sums up the situation in the following words.

Our opinions then differ only in this: The Peripatetics pretend that the firmaments emanate from the First Cause through the intermediary of the intelligences that occupy the first rank in the order of the creatures. We say, on the contrary, that the firmaments emanate directly (*absolute*) from the First Cause, by the choice of Its Volition. Neither of these opinions can be demonstrated; they may be supported only by the probable reasons.[35]

Somewhat similar is the situation in all the other questions connected with causality. Putting aside the dualism of Albertus Magnus as a theologian and as a philosopher, which often makes his own opinion uncertain,[36] his interpretation of causality runs all the time along the Peripatetic line, colored by the Arabian thinkers on the one hand, and by St. Augustine on the other.

"Truly Peripateticism conquered the reason of Albertus Magnus as with the help of Albertus it was going to conquer the greater part of the Latin Scholastics," rightly says Duhem.[37]

Peripateticism also conquered St. Thomas Aquinas.

As St. Thomas more and more profoundly meditated over the problems of Philosophy, the philosophy of Aristotle . . . exerted upon him the most powerful attraction. The greatest of the Latin Scholastics, he grasped indeed the spirit of this doctrine. He understood the power which it derived from the precision of definitions and rigorousness of reasoning. This pure and almost geometric beauty of the Peripatetic logical perfection . . . he preferred to the poetic abundance of the Neo-Platonic discourses. This clear and simple form, an enemy of ambiguity, he put in everything he wrote, even where he attempted to fight the teachings of the Stagerite. Through that he gave to the Scholastic discussions the habits which they guarded after St. Thomas. . . . Farther on, all the time when the Christian orthodoxy was not involved in the problem, St. Thomas excerpted from Aristotle not only the form of his argumentation but also the very source of his thought.[38]

In his theory of causality we find the Aristotelian four classes of causes: material (matter which is not an active principle), final, efficient, and

---

[35] Alberti Magni, *Physica*, Bk. VIII, tract. i, cap. xv, in *B. Alberti Magni Opera omnia*, Vol. III, (Paris, 1890).

[36] See about that dualism in Duhem, *op. cit.*, Vol. V, chap. xi.

[37] *Ibid.*, Vol. V, p. 440. See here Alberti Magni, *Metaphysica*, Bk. XI, tract. ii, cap. xi–xv, in *Opera*, quoted (Paris, 1890), Vol. VI.

[38] Duhem, *op. cit.*, Vol. V, p. 566.

formal causes.[39] In all three last causes God operates. He is the end, the agent, and the formal cause of everything. The causality descends from God into the world through an uninterrupted hierarchy of successive delegations. St. Thomas compares this hierarchy of the physical causes with that of the social world :

"Causa superior non continetur sub ordine causae inferioris, sed e converso. Cujus exemplum apparet in rebus humanis." [40]

Further, he divides the causes into several categories: univocal and equivocal and so on. Dealing with the empirical phenomena he, like Albertus Magnus, Siger of Brabant, and other thinkers of the period, points out many conditions, factors, and causes that approach to our own conception of causality.

In brief, here again we meet the same situation which we met in the theory of truth : the thirteenth and the fourteenth centuries reproduce here, as in many other fields, the Greek thought of the fifth and fourth centuries B.C. Both periods appear Idealistically minded.

I. *From the Fifteenth to the Twentieth Century.* When we come to the subsequent centuries, we find that their trend consists of a further decline of the Ideational conception of causality and a rise of Sensate conceptions. This trend realized itself in many ways. First, scientists began to press more and more the Sensate causality, as it is already shown by the famous Preface : *Ad lectorem, de hypothesibus hujus Operis* to Copernicus's *De revolutionibus orbium coelestium* (1543). Here the whole question about the validity of the hypothesis and the causes of the movement of the celestial bodies was put upon a mathematico-empirical basis : if the results of the mathematical calculation are corroborated by the data of observation, the hypothesis is valid. Through the works of Galileo, Gassendi, Pascal, Kepler, Newton, and other great scientists of the sixteenth, the seventeenth, and the subsequent centuries, the triumph of the Sensate causality was greatly facilitated.[41]

Secondly, the thinkers and philosophers moved in similar directions. The problem of the First Cause and transcendental causality generally began to receive less and less attention ; while the study of the empirical causality of the empirical phenomena began to acquire progressively increasing importance. Some of the thinkers, like Francis Bacon or Montaigne, if not in their accomplishments then at least in their aspi-

---

[39] *Summa Theologica*, I, i, q. 105, a. 5, concl.

[40] *Ibid.*, I, i, q. 105. Also I. i, q. 44, 45, and 104. See a brief résumé in Brunschvicg, *op. cit.*, pp. 166 ff.; Duhem, Vol. V, chap. xii.

[41] See Brunschvicg, *op. cit.*, chaps. xxv and xxvi.

rations,[42] tried to be empiricists free from any "Scholastic ideationalism." A few of them, like Thomas Hobbes or David Hume and others, in a sense carried this program indeed.   We read in Hobbes:

Science is the knowledge of consequences and dependence of one fact upon another: by which out of what we can presently do, we know how to do something else when we will, or the like, at another time. Because when we see how anything comes about, upon what causes, and by what manner; when the like causes come into our power, we see how to make it produce the like effects.[43]

When we read that we are in a mental atmosphere profoundly different from the preceding one, we are entirely in a Sensate world.   The same is still more true of great works like Hume's *A Treatise on Human Nature*, where not only the transcendental causality is brushed aside, but even the empirical causality in the sense of a necessary relationship between cause and effect, or any nonexperimental inferences, was subjected to doubt.   The whole problem was reduced to the sensately experiential "contiguity and succession" of the phenomena.   The contiguous and successive impressions, plus the idea of necessity which is not given in the observations of phenomena but added to them from our mind — that is causal relationship, according to Hume.

The idea of necessity arises from some impression.   There is no impression conveyed by our senses which can give rise to that idea.   It must, therefore, be derived from some internal impression. . . . Upon the whole, necessity is something that exists in the mind, not in objects. . . .   The efficacy or energy of causes is neither placed in the causes themselves, nor in the Deity, nor in the concurrence of these two principles; but belongs entirely to the soul, which considers the union of two or more objects in all past instances. . . .[44]

Here Hume opens the way for a further development of this empiristic causality that passes later on through the works of Main de Biran and J. S. Mill and ends with K. Pearson's causality as a mere "routine of perception."   It also paves the way for Kant's conception of causality as an a priori form of our mind.   This stream not only eliminates the Ideational causality but in a sense it contains a menace to the conception of the Sensate causality as a *necessary* relationship between cause and effect.

[42] Because, contrary to one-time popular opinion, thinkers like Francis Bacon, Roger Bacon, and some others heralded as great scientific revolutionaries, were not such in fact; and, aside from some of their aspirations, were little, if at all, less "metaphysical" than most of their contemporary thinkers.

[43] *Leviathan* (Everyman's Library ed.), pt. i, chap. 5, p. 21.

[44] Hume, *A Treatise on Human Nature* (Everyman's Library ed.), Vol. I, pp. 163–164. See also pp. 78–80, 152–153, *et passim*.

Other thinkers, beginning with Descartes, Malebranche, Spinoza, Leibnitz, or Berkeley, allowed the Ideational causes to stay but in fact relegated them to the position of a king who nominally reigns but does not rule. What rules in their system is the Sensate causality derived either through experience or pure reason.

Perhaps it is an exaggeration to state that with Descartes and Cartesianism a veritable revolution occurred in this field, as Brunschvicg says. But it is accurate to claim that with Descartes "the problem of movement and with it that of causality changed not only in solution but in meaning." [45]   Through his declaration that "motion is always in the movable thing, not in that which moves" [46] and that "once a body has it, it remains in it, if it is not taken out by some other cause," [47] he removed the necessity to look for the "mover" or First Mover or First Cause, which was necessary to the Aristotelian conception; and in this way "cause appeared on the same level and of the same order as effect. Effect is the (actual) motion of a body through space; cause is the motions of such and such bodies, each tending to move rectilinearly but, as a result of shocks and bumps, subjected to modifications of this course, and as a result giving the accountable effect." In this way, a quantitative equality was established between cause and effect as a symbol and consequence of their identity.[48]   God as a final cause was left only in the respectable position of a nominal ruler.

We must examine not the final but the efficient causes of created things. . . . We will not seek reasons for natural things from the end which God or nature proposed to himself in the creation [of the world, and we will entirely reject from our philosophy the search of final causes], for we ought not to presume so far as to think that we are sharers in the counsels of Deity; but, considering him as the efficient cause of all things, let us endeavor to discover by the natural light [faculty of reasoning] . . . what must be concluded regarding those effects we perceive by our senses . . .[49]

Thus, in most polite form, the whole transcendental or Ideational causality was dismissed and replaced by a purely Sensate one: the necessary relationship between the empirical phenomena "perceived by our senses."

However different in several points are the theories of Malebranche, Berkeley, or Leibnitz from Descartes's conception, and from one another's,

[45] Brunschvicg, *op. cit.*, pp. 183 ff.
[46] Descartes, *The Principles of Philosophy*, pt. ii, xxv, p. 211, in Everyman's Library ed.
[47] Letter to Mersenne, November 13, 1629.
[48] Brunschvicg, *op. cit.*, p. 186.   [49] Descartes, *op. cit.*, pt. i, xxviii, p. 176.

in this main point — respectful retirement of the Ideational cause to the position of an "Emeritus" and enthronement in its place of the Sensate causality — they all share equally. In Leibnitz's *Monadology*, "bodies [that is the whole sensate universe] act as though, *per impossibile*, there were no souls; and souls act as if there were no bodies."

Thus the empirical world was not only freed from any interference of any superempirical agency but was even declared to be subjected to purely mechanical laws. More than that, even the causation in the world of souls was greatly empiricized, in spite of the formal declaration to the contrary.

Souls act according to the laws of final causes by *appetitions, ends, and means*. Bodies act according to the laws of efficient causes by motions. And the two kingdoms, of efficient and of final causes, are in harmony with one another.[50]

These "appetitions, ends, and means" as the causes of souls' actions contain in themselves a great deal from empirical psychological processes. Again, God and the Ideational causality are relegated to the position of the beloved *Emeritus*. The same is true of Bishop Berkeley's system. In spite of his indefatigable assertion that the hand of God is behind any phenomenon, his conception of the natural laws is purely empirical, so far as their applications are concerned.

There are certain general laws that run through the whole chain of natural effects; these are learned by the observation and study of nature, and are by men applied (1) as well to the framing of artificial things for the use and ornament of life, as (2) to explaining the various phenomena, which explication consists only in showing the conformity any particular phenomenon has to the general laws of nature; or, which is the same thing, in discovering the *uniformity* there is in the production of natural effects. . . .[51]

In spite of his solipsism and ultimate theology, the working conception of causality and causal laws in his system is such that the above formulation can be accepted as that of some natural scientist of the nineteenth century. Likewise, putting aside transcendental elements in Malebranche's system, his working "occasionalism" amounts almost to positivism.

---

[50] Leibnitz, *Monadology*, 81 and 79; pp. 17–18 in Everyman's Library ed. See also his correspondence with Clarke, in the same volume. Here "as if" is also typical. Later on it is destined to play a fundamental role.

[51] Bishop Berkeley, *Of the Principles of Human Knowledge* (Everyman's Library ed.), lxii. See ccxlix and xxxi, pp. 143–144.

If positivism implies these two conditions: first, a systematic elimination of every speculation on cause as a cause; second, definition of laws as a functional relationship between the coefficients experimentally attributed to the phenomena, it is accurate to say that the occasionalism of Malebranche is already positivism.[52]

Finally, when Kant produced his cleansing criticism, his relegation of the category of causality to the class of "forms of our mind" represented a dilution of the transcendentalism of the "retired Emeritus" (before it was God and the like), and a complete justification of the purely empirical, purely Sensate causality.[53]

In these ways the tide of the Sensate causality was rapidly rising, especially after the sixteenth century; and at the end of the eighteenth century there was little left of the Ideational causality. In the nineteenth century it almost drove it entirely from the highway of scientific and philosophical thought. The conceptions of the Sensate mentality of the mathematicians, specialists in mechanics and natural science, positivists, and social scientists, methodologists of science, and finally philosophers, differed from one another on several points; but practically almost all their conceptions were basically Sensate, limited to the plane of the sensory world, and free from the assumption or admission of any supersensory agent in causality; also they did not seek the "first cause" along the line of Platonic, Aristotelian, Augustinian, or medieval thought. The Ideational stream was present, but it was a little rivulet compared with the big river of Sensate causality.

The general notion of the Sensate causality of the period studied is contained in the statement that always and everywhere, where A is given, B is given — either coexisting with A or following A. If the relationship of A and B is one-sided (A always precedes B) the causal relationship is one-sided; A is the cause and B the effect. If it is two-sided, A and B always are given together, but we cannot say which is the cause and which is the effect (for instance, a triangle and the sum of its angles equal to two straight angles, the example given by E. Mach; or when two bodies with different temperatures are put in contact and the result is the equalization of the temperatures of the bodies, in which we cannot say that this equalization is due to A or to B), the causal relationship there is two-sided; or, as they say, functional, meaning by this the causal relationship of a two-sided character.

The formulas that discover and describe such relationships are called the causal or functional formulas or causal and functional laws. Montes-

---

[52] Brunschvicg, *op. cit.*, p. 244.　　　[53] *Ibid.*, Bks. XI and XII.

quieu's definition that "Laws, in their most general signification, are the necessary relations arising from the nature of the things" [54] or Auguste Comte's definition of laws as "the invariable relations of succession and resemblance" [55] discovered through reasoning and observation, or the still more current formula of laws as "the uniformities," are samples of what is meant by causal-functional laws and relationships.

The further common characteristics of this Sensate causality have been : that A and B, between which the causal relationships are sought, are both Sensate phenomena; that the existence of such uniform relationship belongs also to the world of Sensate phenomena and does not need to invoke any supersensory agency or power; it is either purely empirical or immanent to the empirical world or represents a category of our mind with which it orders the chaos of the perceptional world; that the ways and means of discovery of such relationship are either pure — and especially mathematical — reasoning or observation (including induction, experiment, statistical technique, etc.) or both. The full-pledged causal law is that which passes the test of reasoning and of sensory experience. Almost all the shades of Sensate causality in the nineteenth century assumed that in the genuine causal or functional relationship the same cause A is followed by the same effect B, and cannot be followed now by B, now by C, now by D. In that case, the relationship would not be strictly causal, or would represent only a very remote and diluted form of causality, as a mere tendency to a loose association of A and B. The so-called principle of plurality or nonspecificity of causes is regarded as due to the incompleteness of our knowledge rather than to the nature of the causal relationship. The adequately known causal relationship is always specific, and the same cause has always the same effect. [56]

Finally, most of the causalists assume — explicitly or implicitly — the principle of coexistence of a multitude of parallelly developing causal

[54] Montesquieu, *The Spirit of Laws* (London, 1894), Vol. I, p. 1.

[55] A. Comte, *Positive Philosophy*, trans. by Martineau (New York, 1855), p. 26. With slight variations, this definition will be found in the courses on logic like J. S. Mill's, C. Sigwart; J. Venn; K. Pearson's *Grammar of Science* (London, 1900), chap. iii. The methodological works like the quoted works of A. Cournot, A. A. Tschuproff, H. Rickert, H. Poincaré, E. Mach, P. Duhem, up to Pareto and the statisticians.

[56] See the discussion of the problem in A. A. Tschuproff, *Ocherki*, pp. 97–161; J. Venn, *The Principles of Empirical or Inductive Logic* (London, 1907), pp. 62–64, 97 ff., and 423 ff.; A. Bain, *Logic* (London, 1873), Vol. II, p. 17; J. Venn, *The Logic of Chance* (London, 1876), pp. 229–230; J. S. Mill, *A System of Logic* (London, 1843), Inductive part; H. Poincaré, *La science et l'hypothèse*, p. 6; E. Durkheim, *Les règles de la méthode sociologique* (Paris, 1895), pp. 156–157; C. Sigwart, *Logik* (Tübingen, 1873), Vol. II, pp. 493 ff.

chains in the world. Each chain, like the genealogy of a family living among other families, though it often crosses the other chains of cause and effect, at the same time keeps, like the family, its own singularistic continuity and individuality without being dissolved in the totality of the other causal chains existing in the world. Without this assumption, the proper causal analysis would have been impossible; in that case, everything would be the cause of everything else. With this assumption

We pass from a given effect to its immediate cause; this cause in its turn is conceived as effect, and so on. . . . The actual effect becomes or can become in its turn a cause of the subsequent effect, and so *ad infinitum*. This . . . chain of the causes and effects which succeed . . . constitutes essentially a linear series. An infinity of parallel series can coexist in time; they may cross one another. . . . The bunches of concurrent lines in whose forms our imagination depicts the liaisons that bind the events by causal bonds become somewhat similar to the bunches of light-rays which mutually penetrate, separate, and converge, without any ruptures in their continuity.[57]

Such is the *"passeport"* of the Sensate causality as it has been circulated in the eighteenth, nineteenth, and twentieth centuries — the *passeport* accepted practically by almost all the factions of Sensate causality in this period. Its sensateness and profound difference from Ideational causality is clear from this *passeport*.

In other respects, various factions of Sensate causality have, however, differed greatly. First, *the nature of the causal bond has been represented differently*. By some, like Lagrange, Joseph Fourier, D. Bernoulli, Maxwell, K. Pearson, and most of the statisticians, it is considered purely *functionally or mathematically*, as a relationship capable of being expressed mathematically in the form of a differential equation or other mathematical formula of probability, without any further inquiry as to why it is so or what lies behind this purely quantitative uniform relationship.

Some, like the Cartesian school, Fresnel, and others, represented it purely *mechanistically* as a bond due to the *continuity of motion* resulting in a uniform relationship between cause and effect. Still others represented it *dynamically*, where the causal liaison implies the existence of forces (immanent or transcendental, but both in the sensate aspect) which bind the cause and effect into uniform unity: such is Leibnitz's conception (dynamism of forces, instead of dynamism of motion); the conception of Newton, Laplace, Poisson, Robert Mayer, and others, who account for the relationship through the forces of attraction and repul-

[57] A. Cournot, *Essai sur les fondements de nos connaissances* (Paris, 1851), Vol. I, pp. 49–51.

sion, or any other living force.[58] Neither the mechanistic nor dynamic conceptions exclude the quantitative description of the causal relationship; but, unlike the purely functional-mathematical conception, they go beyond a mere grasp of the quantitative uniformity, and question what lies behind it and can account for it, and respectively set forth either purely mechanistic or dynamic interpretations of its nature — the interpretation derived from some of the general principles — as in the Cartesian school — believed to be axiomatic. It is possible to note that as we move from the seventeenth to the twentieth century, *the functional-mathematical interpretation has tended to increase at the cost of the mechanistic or dynamic.* Due to development of positivism, agnosticism, criticism, empiricism, the problem of what lies behind the quantitative uniformity has been regarded as more and more "metaphysical," and the mere quantitative description of the relationship on the plane of the principle of probability has been thought of as the only task of science and the only aspect having scientific value. Hence, this tendency which, in connection with other tendencies to be mentioned further, has resulted in the contemporary reduction of the causality to probability, and to the mathematical calculation of it, from the loose "correlational" associations with the low coefficients of the correlations, up to the formulas with the high coefficient of probability and therefore more perfect association of the variables. Why the association is loose or close — this question is not set forth, no attempt is made to answer it, and it is regarded as "metaphysical."

The Sensate conceptions of causality differ also in regard to the assumption or nonassumption of the category of *necessity* as an element of the causal relationship. For many, beginning with Descartes, Newton, Leibnitz, and most of the thinkers of the seventeenth, eighteenth, and of the first part of the nineteenth centuries, including even such "occasionalists, solipsists, and associationalists" as Malebranche and Hume, as well as Kant and the Kantian criticism, mere "association" or "correlation" or, in the excellent terms of Hume, mere "contiguity and succession" of A and B is not enough to elevate such an association into the causal relationship. In addition, this association has to be a *necessary*[59]

---

[58] In recent sociology, Durkheim's conception is an example of it. "What is implied first of all in the notion of causal relation is the idea of efficacy, of productive power, of active force. By cause is usually meant that which is susceptible of producing a determined change. Effect is the same power, but actualized." Durkheim, *Les formes elementaires de la vie religieuse*, p. 519.

[59] As Hume puts it: "An object may be contiguous and prior to another, without being considered as its cause. There is a *necessary connection* to be taken into consideration; and that relation is of much greater importance than any of the other two mentioned." *A Treatise on Human Nature* (Everyman's Library ed.), Vol. I, p. 80.

connection.   Without it, every *post hoc* would be *propter hoc*, the causal relations would be undistinguishable from incidental associations. Therefore, this current causal relationship is defined by the *necessary* relationships arising either "from the nature of the things" as Montesquieu says; or from the Cartesian general and self-evident principles of "mechanistic and automatic" functioning of the universe; or from that of the general principles of gravitation — repulsion as the source of this invariability and necessity; and the like.   Most of those who agree to the above mechanistic or dynamic interpretation of causality regard the necessity as the main element of causal relationship.

Others — and such are many of the functional-mathematical interpreters and, of course, most of the contemporary statisticians and most of the pure "empiricists" and "positivists" — do not demand the category of necessity as an element of causal relationship.   For these such a category is also bad metaphysics, not given in our sensory experience, unobservable, and introducing only a speculative entity into the "scientific concepts."   Remaining on the plane of probability, they distinguish only the uniformities with a high and low degree of probability; and respectively, express it through the value of the coefficient of probability or correlation on a scale from o to 1, one being the highest probability, zero being an index of the lack of any association between the variables. The reasons for such a position are different with different partisans of this faction, but the trait is common to many.   As a matter of fact, *as we move from the seventeenth to the twentieth century, this second conception of causality, devoid of an implication of necessity and reduced to high probability association, has been more and more driving out the first one, especially beginning with the second half of the nineteenth century.*   This transformation has been proceeding parallel with the growth of the above functional-mathematical understanding of a causal bond; and naturally parallel with the growth of empiricism, positivism, neo-positivism, agnosticism (of Spencerian type); empirio-criticism, pragmatism, and epistemological and ontological relativism.   (Positivists, beginning with Comte, Poincaré, Mach, R. Avenarius, K. Pearson, Cournot, Maxwell, Pareto, Planck, Heisenberg, Einstein, most of the statisticians, and others.)   In this sense, this purely empiristic conception is purged even from such diluted Ideational abstractions as the category of necessity and reduced to either a purely observational association of our perceptions (for the solipsists and empiricists of the Pearsonian type with his "routine of perceptions") or of the empirical phenomena, or to a combined quantitatively calculated and observationally supported association.

In Chapter Nine, on the fluctuation of determinism and indeterminism, the great contrast between the causal conception of the eighteenth century and that of the end of the nineteenth was pointed out. Then, as the formula of Montesquieu shows, even the civil laws were considered as "the necessary relations arising from the nature of things"; now even the laws of nature are considered as mere associations.[60] This is the reason why, in that chapter, I indicated that the end of the nineteenth and the twentieth centuries is not only marked with a quantitative decrease of determinism, but by its qualitative softening. There is a great difference between the causal relationship and causal law understood as *necessary* and the causal relationship and law understood as a mere association with higher and lower probability, more or less frequently met, but devoid of anything related to the idea of necessity. Such a causality is fundamentally different from the "necessary causality," is much more liberal, less rigid, less uniform, less exacting. Respectively, causal laws and their verity as a criterion of science also become softened. The difference between the true and false also becomes relative. The system of Ptolemy and of Copernicus; of Euclid, of Lobachevsky; or Rieman's or the Minkovsky-Einstein theory of space and geometry are neither true nor false per se. The best of them is that which is more convenient, more expedient, more useful for us. Poincaré says:

The statement *the earth turns*, does not have any sense, because no experiment permits us to verify it. . . . In other words, these two propositions, *the earth turns around* and *it is more convenient to suppose that the earth turns around*, have the same sense; there is nothing more in one than in the other.[61]

[60] The well-known conception of K. Pearson's *Grammar of Science*, chap. iii, is a typical example of it.

[61] Poincaré, *La science et l'hypothèse*, p. 141; also *Science et méthode*, pp. 95 ff. *Dernières pensées*, pp. 38 ff. and 14 ff. It is curious to note, on the other hand, a startling inconsistency of Poincaré — again typical of most of the "relativists" — when side by side with this relativism the same Poincaré says: "To perish or to change the laws (causal) is about the same; the world which would have no more the laws of ours would not be any more our world; it would be another world." *Dernières pensées*, p. 11. If the laws are just a kind of contingent association devoid of necessity, and very relativistic and often unsusceptible of being properly grasped and easily replaceable since the difference between different laws is a relative matter of convenience and a supposition of the "as if" and *als ob* type, such a world is a totality of an enormous number of various probabilities and potentialities with many-sided relativistic laws. A slight replacement of a less convenient by a more convenient law in the potential possibility of many such replacements does not logically amount to the perdition of the world. It is just a slight variation in our preference and taste for convenience and expediency. To identify any such fancy with the perdition of the world is to go too far and to contradict all the other relativistic and associational principles.

In this "half-free causality" we have the extremest form of the Sensate causality that throws out everything except the data of observation and sensory perception.[62]   In this sense it corresponds to extreme impressionism in painting; empiricism in theory of knowledge; temporalism in the conception of reality; relativism in science and ethics.   Like these, it turns the world and reality into something liquid, frameless, uncertain, indeterminate, and fantastic.   The boundary line between causal and accidental or "occasional" disappears.   In brief, it is flesh from flesh of the overripe Sensate mentality.   As such, here as elsewhere, it finally begins to dig its own grave and "eat itself up."

If any causal relationship is but a "routine of perception" to which nobody knows whether anything corresponds in reality; if the given causal law is better than any other only because it is more expedient; then any, even the most foolish, routine of perception can pretend to be causal law, because it is such in the perception of a given person or persons; then any dogma imposed by a dictatorial government — be it Marxian *credo* or Aryan *credo* — is science because it is found to be more convenient, under the circumstances, by the dictators or the majority of the taxpayers.   In brief, the boundary line between science and non-science; true and false; causal and incidental, disappears.   The scientific or natural law is identified with convention and convenience, its validity is destroyed, not to mention the fact that since everything is conventional, the terms "convention," or "utility," or "convenience" lose all meaning.   As a result, all is plunged into chaos and darkness. This would be the result of such an attitude; and such indeed it is.   The development of this conception has led to a skepticism in science, in empiricism, in the very foundations of our knowledge at the end of the nineteenth and in the twentieth century.   Before our eyes this current is putting the finishing touches to its own strangulation and self-destruction.[63]

Even some of the relativistic-empiristic conceptions of causality begin to show their longing for a more definite, rigid, absolutistic causality, at

[62] " *Les lois sont obtenue par l'expérience,*" Poincaré, *Dernières pensées*, p. 11.

[63] It is not my purpose to enter here on any substantial criticism of this extremely sensate conception of causality; of its premises; its assumptions; its self-contradictions. It is enough to say that it is no less — possibly much more — vulnerable than almost any other conception of causality. The above statements are mentioned only in order to indicate its logical congeniality with the Sensate mentality and also to give a few allusions to the reasons of its contemporary crisis. For its criticism the reader is referred to any good course on epistemology and to a series of monographic studies on causality. Some criticism will be found in Brunschvicg's work, quoted, though the "progressively linear" bias of the author makes him err in many important points.

least in the field of nature, with the exception of man's will and mind.[64] Such a reaction is to be expected because this extreme form of Sensate causality is neither determinism nor indeterminism; speaking in terms of Poincaré himself, it gives only inconveniences without the conveniences of free will and God's guidance, as well as of a definite and firm uniformity that makes this world less liquid and phantasmagoric than it appears in this extreme conception. Reaction against it looms on the horizon.

The foregoing concise sketch of the main transformations of the conception of causality and of the rise and fall of the influence of the Ideational and Sensate forms of it, shows that such fluctuation has indeed been going on; that the predominantly Ideational cultures and periods create Ideational causality; in the predominantly Sensate, the Sensate conception becomes dominant; while in the Mixed and Idealistic mentalities, the Mixed and Idealistic causality rises. So far the propositions of this chapter as well as of the preceding chapters are corroborated by the facts. We see once more that even such a fundamental category of human thought as causality, so far as its influence and acceptability are concerned, is not exempt from the influence of the total predominant mentality and the respective type of culture.

Our *Wissenssoziologie* touches now the last and the most primordial categories of human thought. Since they seem to be dependent upon the prevailing type of culture mentality, still more dependent must be such superficial and comparatively unimportant political or other opinions and "ideologies" with which the *Wissenssoziologie* has hitherto dealt. More than that: even the kind of *Wissenssoziologie* itself (mainly of a Marxian type) that has been prevalent recently is but a reflection of the present-day overripe Sensate mentality. Our *Wissenssoziologie* makes the current *Wissenssoziologie* itself a mere object of its study and easily explains its contemporary character. In other words, the theory developed here is a *Wissenssoziologie* of the contemporary *Wissenssoziologie*.

III. FLUCTUATION OF IDEATIONAL AND SENSATE CONCEPTIONS OF TIME

What is said of causality can be said of another category of our thought, *time*. In regard to it we all can repeat St. Augustine's: *Quid est ergo tempus? Si nemo ex me querat, scio; si quaerenti explicare velim, nescio.* "What then is time? If no one asks me, I know; if I wish to explain it to one that asketh, I know not."[65] For my purposes, however, it is

---

[64] The case of Max Planck is typical. See his work, quoted.

[65] *Confessions*, Bk. XI, chap. xiv. The same was repeated by Pascal and by Lagrange.

enough to indicate that *there have been two different conceptions of time: Ideational and Sensate; that their comparative influence fluctuated; and that the Ideational conception of time tends to dominate in the cultures and periods mainly Ideational, while the Sensate conception does so in the cultures and periods mainly Sensate.*

What is meant by Ideational and Sensate conceptions of time? Without any reference to my theory, P. Duhem in his so often referred to — and unexcelled — work did not fail to put his finger upon one of the profoundest differences between these conceptions.

The theories of Time . . . can be classified into two categories: the theories of the first category look for absolute time in a world different from this world of our sense perception. The others make out of time a phenomenon relative to the movements of the sensible world.[66]

Connected with this fundamental difference are a few other differences. (1) If Ideational time is an emanation or manifestation of the supersensory reality and its "movements" (God, the Soul of the World, Brahma, Cronos, and so on), *the unit* of time is determined by the "pulsations" of this reality but not by the movement of sensory things as such, as it is determined in the Sensate time. (2) This *unit of time* in the Ideational conception is not infinitely divisible, while in the Sensate time it is, and the division is often purely mechanical and quantitative. (3) The Ideational time unit, if measured in terms of the units of Sensate time (year, month, day, hour, minute, second, and so on), is much *longer* than the unit of the Sensate time. (4) The Ideational sequence of time, viewed sensately, is either no sequence at all, being an eternity where the past, present, and future do not exist or exist "simultaneously"; or it appears blurred, with "past, present, and future" mixed and with no — or a hopelessly confused — "chronology" of dates that fix the time sequence or synchronism of the sensory events. (5) Ideational time tends to be always *qualitative*, rather denoting the changes in the supersensory reality from which it emanates, than purely quantitative and sensately numerical (I have to say "sensately numerical" because, as we shall see, the conception of Number is also profoundly different in Ideational and Sensate mentalities).

Such are the main differences. For persons who have never studied the problem they may appear unimportant. As a matter of fact, they make Ideational and Sensate time something radically different from

---

[66] Duhem, *op. cit.*, Vol. I, p. 244.

each other.[67] Respectively they lead to the profoundest difference in all the conceptions and ideas where the time element is involved. As it enters into an enormous portion of the sum total of ideas of human thought, the fundamental difference between these conceptions of time conditions the difference in all such ideas.

A sample of Ideational time we have already seen in the Hindu conception of time (Chapters Five and Ten) as a manifestation of the changes in Brahma (or ultimate reality): Brahma's day, Brahma's night, Brahma's dematerialization and materialization. Each such change in Brahma manifests itself in the form of one of the "periods" and "cycles" in the life of the world and of all its parts. These periods are exceedingly long in the terms of mortal years: the unit of time — *kalpa* — is 4,320,000 mortal years; the smallest unit being 432,000 years, the period of the Kali-Yuga. No "chronology of dates" even remotely satisfactory from the Sensate standpoint was developed there: the time perspective in the Sensate sense was hopelessly blurred and undeveloped. Likewise, history as a narrative of the sequence of sensory events in time was undeveloped in the Hindu mentality. In brief, all the earmarks of the Ideational time were present in Ideational Hindu mentality. This, among other things, confirms the proposition that predominantly Ideational culture mentalities have the predominantly Ideational conception of time.

If we would analyze from this standpoint the conception of time of Ancient China (Mixed culture mentality) we would see that it was Mixed also, showing a coexistence in it of the Ideational and Sensate streams, and the mixture of the elements of both conceptions.[68]

If we pass to our main field, the Graeco-Roman and the Western European cultures, we see the fluctuation of the domination of each conception from 600 B.C. to the present time, and this fluctuation seems to have run somewhat parallel with the main waves of the Sensate and Ideational cultures. Here is a summary of the main phases of this fluctuation.

Before the sixth century B.C., mythological, religious, Homeric, and Hesiodic time appears essentially Ideational. Time manifests the activity of Cronos or Zeus or some other supersensory reality. Sequence

[67] Within the Sensate time there are many varieties; but just now they are not discussed. For that see the chapter on Social Time in Volume Four and Sorokin and Merton's paper, quoted.

[68] Read from this standpoint M. Granet's analysis of time conception of Ancient China, *op. cit.*, pp. 86–148. Reading of it would show, first, how great is the difference of our time conception from that of the Chinese; second, his analysis gives essentially what, in my terminology, would be a *Mixed* conception of time.

of periods (Golden, Silver, and so on) in the life of mankind and of the whole universe simply denotes what Cronos or Zeus did, now creating the Golden race, now destroying it and replacing it by the Silver, and so on. The periods (time units) are exceedingly long. They are unequal quantitatively and time is mainly qualitative. No Sensate chronology and dates are given in the Sensate units of time. The time perspective is quite blurred, whether in the time sequence of events (for instance, whether Cronos or Zeus were earlier is not clear: in some fragments Cronos, in others Zeus was earlier) or in time apprehension and reckoning. In brief, all the marks of Ideational time are present there.[69]

In the sixth century we have the Pythagorean conception of time, which is "mystic" and Ideational, par excellence. In the fifth and the first part of the fourth century, we have the domination of the Pythagorean time, then its variety, the conception by Architas of Tarent and by Plato and then Zeno-Parmenides's timeless time or eternity, all predominantly Ideational. Pythagorean-Architas-Plato's time is "an image" or "reflection" of the movement of the Soul of the World. Its unit, especially in the conception of Architas, is definite: it is coextensive with the movement of the Soul of the World, no more and no less. Movements of the Sensate phenomena cannot give a unit of time. For Zeno and Parmenides, the true Reality, Being, is timeless in its eternity as well as in any of its "moments." Respectively neither time nor movement exist for them. Pythagorean-Architas-Plato's unit of time is very long — expressed in the terms of the Sensate unit, mortal years. This unit is the unit of the Great Year (*annus magnus*) whose duration, as was mentioned above, is also very long (Plato's mystical number).

In brief, we have a conspicuously Ideational conception of time dominant in the Greek thought of the sixth and the fifth centuries B.C.[70]

---

[69] See some of the excerpts in Lovejoy and Boas's work, quoted, pp. 22–79. An additional evidence of the validity of this interpretation is the statement of Simplicius that the concept of time of Architas of Tarent (440–360 B.C.), which is clearly Ideational, as we shall see, "is in accordance with the teachings of the ancients." Simplicii, *In Aristotelis categorias commentarium*, ed. by C. Kalbfleisch (Berlin, 1907), p. 351. See also W. Gent, *Die Philosophie des Raumes und der Zeit* (Bonn, 1926), chap. i.

[70] See Simplicius's work, quoted, pp. 350 ff. Also Simplicii, *In Aristotelis physicorum libros quattuor commentaria*, ed. by H. Diels (Berlin, 1882), p. 758. For Plato, see his *Timaeus* and his *Republic*, mainly Bk. VIII; his *Statesman* and *Phaedrus*. An admirable analysis is given by Duhem, *op. cit.*, Vol. I, pp. 65–85, 180 ff., and 242–350; also Gent, *op. cit.*, chap. i. For those who are not acquainted with these theories, the above few lines would not give, of course, any satisfactory idea of the content of the time theories of these thinkers. Lack of space does not permit me to make quotations and to give a more substantial unfolding of the statements made. However, that cannot be helped. I am not writing here either a popular text or a monograph on this topic. Mere indication of the situation is sufficient

P. Duhem is quite right in saying these conceptions are exceedingly similar to the Hindu conception of time.

In this [Architas-Plato's] unit of time that rhythms the periodic life of the World, the analogy with the Hindu *kalpa* is striking; also with the Day of the *sindhind*, with the Day of the World, which manifests a day in the life of Brahma, and which brings the Universe to the same status [where it was before]. This *rapprochement* between the Hindu doctrine and Architas on the one hand, and of Plato's theory on the other, becomes still more conspicuous when one remembers the language which Plato used in the *Republic* before writing *Timaeus*.[71]

On my part I can but concur in this statement, and its nature shows also the conspicuous Ideationality of the fifth-century Greek time conception. This means that the sixth and the fifth centuries (and the beginning of the fourth) appear again as predominantly Ideational (the sixth century) or Ideationally Idealistic (the fifth and the beginning of the fourth century).

When we pass to the Aristotelian conception of time, it remains Idealistic, though less so than the conception of Architas and Plato. Aristotle starts with an almost empirical conception of time, defining it as a number or enumeration or indication relative to movement when it is considered as presenting a part that precedes and a part that follows. Movement cannot be separated from the notion of time. Where there is movement there is time and vice versa. We measure movement by time and time by movement. And every movement has time and can be measured and be a measure of time. So far the conception is empirical, posited in the sensory world.[72]

However, Aristotle's analysis does not stop there. The first step toward the Idealistic conception is his further statement that time exists objectively, outside of our mind. It exists in the same sense as a special category of objective number — *numerus numerabilis* — exists in any multitude of really existing things, in contradistinction to another (subjective) kind of number — *numerus numeratus* — that exists only in a mind when it enumerates or counts things. Farther on, Aristotle deduces that though every motion may be a measure of time, ultimately

---

for my purposes. It is accurate and those who want to go into the matter more deeply or to test the accuracy of my statements may go to the sources and works mentioned.

[71] Duhem, *op. cit.*, Vol. I, p. 83. (See *The Republic*, ed. cited, Bk. VIII, 546.)

[72] See Aristotle, *Physics*, Bk. IV, chaps. xi–xii. An excellent analysis is given in Duhem, *op. cit.*, Vol. I, pp. 180 ff. See also W. Gent, *op. cit.*, chaps. i and ii. Note, however, that for Aristotle time is the numerator of motion but motion is not the condition of time, as several extremely Sensate theories claim.

there is only one motion — the uniform and rotatory motion of the firmament, identical almost with immobility. It is the real measure of time. Time properly is its number. Considering the cosmology, physics, and finally metaphysics of Aristotle, one knows that his firmament is something different from the sky, or purely empirical universe. It is composed of layers of the concentric spheres inclosed in one another. Of these spheres the ultimate sphere of the fixed stars is the proper measure of time.[73] From this he takes a further step and finally comes to the conclusion that time is a measure of the movement of the "primary and eternal substance," or of the immobile First Mover, who imparts motion to everything else.[74]

This final conclusion goes far beyond the sensory world and represents practically Architas's and the Pythagorean "Soul of the World," somewhat diluted and given in an abstract form.

Thus the fifth and fourth centuries B.C. appear, as in other fields, Idealistic Ideational.

When we pass to the leading conceptions of the next centuries, of the Peripatetic, Stoic, Epicurean, and Skeptic schools (not to mention the Platonic), one can notice a further swing to the Sensate conception in comparison with the conceptions of the previous centuries. Of the immediate disciples of Aristotle, Theophrastus and Eudemus faithfully held to the Aristotelian conception, Strato already notably deviated from it in the direction of Sensate conception. Likewise, the conceptions of the Stoics and Epicureans were more Sensate than Aristotelian.[75] The Platonic conception seems to have been in the minority in this period. The Skeptics gave practically only the negative answer that time is neither corporeal nor uncorporeal, neither finite nor infinite, neither divisible nor indivisible, neither has a beginning nor will it have an end, and so on.[76]

Beginning with the second century A.D., the Peripatetics (Alexander Aphrodisiensis, second half of the second century A.D.) return to the Aristotelian concept and succeed in giving it popularity. This is the first sign of the return of an Idealistic-Ideational conception, after the preceding period (the end of the fourth century B.C. to the second century A.D.) when the movement was toward Sensate conception. What is still more important, in the second century the Neo-Platonic move-

---

[73] Aristotle, *Physics*, Bk. IV, chap. xiv.
[74] Aristotle, *Metaphysics* (ed. cited), Bk. XI, chap. viii.
[75] See Duhem, *op. cit.*, Vol. I, chap. v; Gent, *op. cit.*, chap. iii.
[76] See Gent, *op. cit.*, pp. 27–28.

ment rises in its power and gives us in the third and subsequent centuries a series of great thinkers and an almost purely Ideational conception of time — more Ideational, even, than Plato's. The remarkable theories of Plotinus, Jamblichos, Proclus, Asclepiodotus, Damascius (whose conception is very similar to Bergsonian time), Simplicius, and others, held time to be derived from a source more supersensory, and placed farther from the Sensate world and higher in the supersensory world than even Architas or Plato placed it.[77] One of the results of their analysis was the classification of time not into one or two but into three classes: one purely transcendental; *aeternitas*, eternal Being, changeless, and remaining the same; *aevum*, its derivation, still mainly transcendental; and finally *tempus*, empirical time as a mere manifestation of the preceding two more real times. This division played an important part in the medieval thought. Finally, the conception of Christian thinkers, of the Church Fathers, and then of Augustine was Ideational also. In brief, beginning with the second century A.D., we see an unmistakable rise of Ideational conceptions and toward the fifth century A.D. they become triumphant.[78] In other words, the swing here agrees with the Ideational swings met in other parts of the Graeco-Roman and Western culture of the period.

The conception of St. Augustine deviated in several points from that of the Pythagoreans, Plato, Architas, and Aristotle: in his rejection of eternal cycles — *annus magnus;* in his insistence that the world was created by God not *in* time, but *with* time (no time existing before the world was created, and time being created simultaneously with the world: *Proculdubio, non est Mundus factus in tempore sed cum tempore*) and several other points. In spite of that, his conception of time is greatly influenced by Neo-Platonism and Aristotle, and is *Ideational* par excellence.[79]

God created time together with the world. God is eternity. "Eternity ever still standing, neither past nor to come, uttereth the time past and to come." [80] These "never fixed times" uttered by "everfixed Eternity" are, however, in a sense unreal. They are a peculiar reflection of eternity in the human soul.

What now is clear and plain is that neither things to come nor past are. Nor is it properly said, "there be three times, past, present, and to come": yet perchance it may properly be said, "there be three times; a present of

---

[77] See Duhem, *op. cit.*, Vol. I, pp. 246 ff.; Gent, *op. cit.*, pp. 28–40.
[78] See Duhem, *op. cit.*, Vol. II, pp. 393–501; Gent, *op. cit.*, chap. iv.
[79] See St. Augustine, *Confessions* (ed. cited), Bk. XI.   [80] *Ibid.*, Bk. XI, chap. xi.

things past, a present of things present, and a present of things future." For these three do exist in some sort, in the soul, but otherwhere do I not see them; present of things past, memory; present of things present, sight; present of things future, expectation.[81]

[Respectively] time is not the motion of a body; [neither do] the motions of heavenly bodies constitute time [nor can they measure it].[82] It is in thee, my mind, that I measure time . . . the impression of the things passing by and contemplation of the things to come." [Such times with their past, present, and future, are due but to the limitations of the human mind. If it were] gifted with such vast knowledge and foreknowledge, as to know all things past and to come [for such a mind there would be no "times," or "times" would be equivalent to eternity].[83]

The Middle Ages continued the Ideational conception of time so far as the problem was touched at all, and such a conception dominated almost monopolistically up to the thirteenth or fourteenth centuries. Ideational is the conception found — at least in fragmentary allusions in the pseudo Dionysius, Gregory Nasiansis, and other Church Fathers. Ideational is also the conception of time developed by Erigena. It is a Neo-Platonic conception, somewhat modified by the Christian creed (Augustine) and by Aristotle. God as the true reality is unchangeable and eternal. He is the cause of the "universality of creations." They are primordial causes of all visible and invisible things. In the world of visible (Sensate) things separateness and change go on. For this world, time and space categories are indispensable. Both are created by God. "*Locus et tempus in numero eorum quae a Deo creata sunt.*"[84] Both are incorporeal and exist as categories of thought or definitions in the rational mind: "*Atque diffinitiones . . . non alibi nisi in anima rationabili sunt. . . . At si rationalis anima incorporea est . . . necessario quicquid in ea intelligitur, incorporeum esse manifestum est.*"[85]

Space and time are inseparable from each other and also from the things with which they are connected.

Impossibile est locum subtracto tempore intellegi, sicut neque tempus sine loci cointelligentia diffiniri potest. . . . Omnium itaque existentium essentia localis atque temporalis est; atque ideo nisi in loco et tempore et sub loco et sub tempore nullo modo cognoscitur.[86]

---

[81] *Ibid.*, Bk. XI, chap. xx.   [82] *Ibid.*, Bk. XI, chaps. xxiii–xxiv.

[83] *Ibid.*, Bk. XI, chaps. xxvii, xxx, and xxxi.

[84] J. S. Erigena, *De divisiones naturae* (Oxonian edition, 1681), 23.

[85] *Ibid.*, 21–24.

[86] *Ibid.*, 22. Gent in his work, quoted, rightly remarks that this thinker, probably the greatest of the Middle Ages (up to the great Scholastics) — far greater and more "revolu-

In stressing time and space as categories of thought that logically precede any cognition of any phenomena ("*praecedit omnia quae in eo sunt,*"
"*ante omnia quae sunt intelligendum,*" "*mensura omnium rerum, quae
creatae sunt, naturaliter conditionem earum ratione praecedit*"),[87] Erigena
was a forerunner of Kant.   In this time continuum the things pass from
sensate nonexistence to sensate existence, and then to sensate nonexistence again, which is the achievement of the end set for them and an
engulfment in the supersensate world of the universality, "*donec veniat
stabilis finis in quo immutabiliter omnia stabunt. . . . Quemadmodum
nil aliud est tempus nisi rerum per generationem ex non esse in esse
inchoatio.*" [88]

The Ideational remains essentially the time conception of Petrus
Lombardus, Witello, and other medieval thinkers,[89] though as we approach the twelfth and the thirteenth centuries, Ideationalism begins
to be penetrated by the elements of Sensate time.   This manifests itself
in the growing influence of the Aristotelian conception, in the time
theories of the great thinkers of these centuries.   Such a mixture results
in the Ideational-Idealistic theory.   This is perfectly clear in the time
conceptions of Siger of Brabant (*c.* 1280–1304), Albertus Magnus, St.
Thomas Aquinas, J. Duns Scotus, Petrus Aureolus, and then, a little
later, in those of Aegidius Romanus, Gregor of Rimini, Johannes Bacon,
Johannes Capreolus, and others.   Without attempting to outline their
theories of time, it is enough to say that in essentials they give a variation of the Aristotelian conception (departing from it here and there);
continue the classification of time into three categories: *aeternitas,
aevum,* and *tempus,* making *aeternitas* timeless eternity where no becoming exists; *aevum,* intermediary between transcendental eternity and
Sensate *tempus* with accidental change; and conceiving *tempus* as a
merely Sensate phenomenon bound with the motion and change of the
sensory phenomena and as such divisible into moments.   More than
that: in their analysis they pay more and more attention to the *tempus*
and stress more and more its ever-fleeing, ever-passing nature, as well
as its endless divisibility into moments.   For Siger of Brabant: "*De
tempore non est nisi instans*"; for Albertus Magnus: "*in tempore non
est nisi nunc fluens*"; for St. Thomas: "*nunc et tempus esse simul . . .*

tionary" than Roger Bacon (wrongly extolled by many) — in this part of his theory set out
the theory of "space-time-object-continuum" formulated in 1908 by Minkowski, and then
by Einstein in his special and general theory of relativity. See Gent, *op. cit.*, p. 51. Also
A. Einstein, *Specielle und allgemeine Relativitätstheorie* (Brunschweig, 1920), pp. 64 ff.; M.
Schlick, *Raum und Zeit in der gegenwärtigen Physik* (Berlin, 1920), pp. 37 and 64 ff.

[87] *Ibid.*, 25, 26, and 240.   [88] *Ibid.*, 23.   [89] See Gent, *op. cit.*, chaps. vii and viii.

nihil est praesens de tempore nisi nunc."   As such it is a series of changing moments inseparably bound with ever-changing empirical phenomena that come and pass, are born and disappear.[90]

In brief, here as in many other fields, we have the Ideational-Idealistic conception of time not unlike that of the dominant time conception of Greek thinkers of the fifth and the fourth centuries B.C.

As we move from the thinkers of the thirteenth century to the later ones, the empirical conception of time becomes more and more pronounced. *Aeternitas* and *aevum* more and more recede to backstage and *tempus* comes more and more to the front stage. This is clear already in the conception of William of Ockham (died *c.* 1349), Durandus, Nicolaus Cusanus, and other thinkers of the fourteenth and fifteenth centuries.

Ockham practically dismisses *aeternitas* and *aevum;* for him time is mainly *tempus* in the sense of motion of the sun; of the corporeal earthly things (two forms of "objective" or extramental time); and the registration or enumeration of these changes (*numerus numeratus* of Aristotle); and in the sense of movement of ideas and images (*motus imaginatus*) and our subjective enumeration of these changes (*numerus quo numerans*) — both being "intramental" or subjective forms of time.[91]

Subsequently, with some fluctuations, up to the sixteenth century inclusive, the Scholastic theories of time, often with the disquisition of *aeternitas, aevum,* and *tempus,* continue to linger in the conceptions of Nicolaus Cusanus (1401–1464), Carolus Bovillus, Hieronimus Cardanus, Julius Caesar Scaliger, Bernardino Telesio, Franciscus Patricius, Campanella, Giordano Bruno, Leonardo da Vinci, William Gilbert, and especially Franciscus Suarez, and others; but even in these conceptions the Ideational elements of time begin to fade in various forms and the Sensate elements begin to encroach more and more. Nicolaus Cusanus rejects the absolute time and attempts to introduce a mathematical concept; Bovillus gives a geometric conception to *aeternitas, aevum, tempus,* and *momentum.* Cardanus makes time a mere function of motion; so does Scaliger; Telesio replaces *aeternitas* and *aevum* with the theory of absolute time, not unlike the Newtonian absolute time, on the one hand; on the other, he makes time a mere satellite or function of motion. Patricius goes still farther and makes time a duration of the bodies (*duratio corporum rerumque*). Campanella sensualizes mathematics and logics themselves and does it still more in regard to time, making it a succession of day and night, warm and cold and other sensory things (*tempus est duratio successive rerum*).   G. Bruno rejects the motion

---

[90] *Ibid.,* chaps. ix, x, and xi.   [91] Gent, *op. cit.,* chaps. xvii and xviii.

of the firmament as *"primus motus"* and as the absolute measure of time; rejects absolute time generally; makes it relative to the standpoint of the observer and in this respect introduces plurality of empirical times (*tot sane erunt in universo tempora, quot sunt et astra*) and (*ubi est illud (tempus) sibi aequum, quod aliorum aequalitatem et inaequalitatem judicet?*); and, in contradistinction to Aristotle, makes motion the measure of time instead of time being the measure of motion.[92]

This de-Ideationalization and Sensatization of time marks a further step in a progressively increasing disregard of *aeternitas* and *aevum* and in a replacement of these by empirico-mathematical time, by the famous mathematical symbol t with its infinite divisibility into td — time differentials. In the works of Kepler, Galileo, and others, this "revolution" occurs. Time now is turned into mere quantity. As such it is "colorless"; as such it is infinitely divisible; it is mathematically and experientially related to empirico-mathematical space and motion. From the Ideational eternity and *aevum* and other constituents of Ideational time, there remains little. We are ushered into a new mental atmosphere: into the rationally Sensate era of time conception.[93]

The scientists and thinkers of the subsequent centuries, beginning with the seventeenth, follow this stream in an overwhelming majority. However great are the differences between them in their time conceptions and general philosophy; however sharp is the contrast between time understood as a purely subjective (intramental) conception and as existing objectively; time regarded as substance and as relation; time absolute and relative — in spite of these and other differences, most of the influential conceptions of time are, in their essential traits, Sensate.

For Descartes time is "the duration of things" and "the duration of a thing is a mode under which we conceive this thing, in so far as it continues to exist."

More specifically, duration is the attribute that exists in the things themselves, while time,

which we distinguish from duration taken in its generality, and call the measure of motion, is only a certain mode under which we think duration itself. . . . [Time is] a common measure [of duration of all things measured by] the greatest and most regular motion that gives rise to years and days. [As such it is] superadded to duration and exists only in our thought.[94]

Spinoza, distinguishing duration, time, and eternity, stresses eternity more than Descartes does, but gives to it a meaning somewhat remote

---

[92] See Gent, *op. cit.*, chaps. xx–xxix.   [93] See Gent, *op. cit.*, chaps. xxix–xxxi.
[94] Descartes, *The Principles of Philosophy*, ed. cited, xxi and lv–lvii, pp. 173 and 186–187.

from time; and so far as duration and time are concerned, gives to them meanings similar to Descartes's and almost completely quantitatively Sensate. Duration, for Spinoza, is "existence in so far as it is conceived as a certain form of quantity," or "indefinite continuance of existing." Time is a measurement of duration, and as for Descartes, it exists only in our thought (as an *ens rationis*).[95] In this there is nothing Ideational. This element enters only in his *Aeternitas*, as "an attribute under which we conceive the infinite existence of God. Duration is an attribute under which we conceive the existence of created things, in so far as they persevere in their actuality."[96] Eternity is "infinite existence" which coincides with the real substance of God, is attributable only to Him, and not to created things, even if they endure forever. Here the Ideational element is present but it is removed from the Sensate order and motion and movement entirely. For this "sublunar" world only purely Sensate time and duration are left to operate and to function.

Other great thinkers of these centuries deal mainly with the Sensate time. First of all Pierre Gassendi and then Hobbes. For both time is either a successive quantity, existing in connection with the motion of empirical things though independently from that (Gassendi), or a purely psychological phantasma as a reflection of the motion of Sensate phenomena (Hobbes). For Gassendi: *"tempus est extensio sive quantitas successiva vel fluens, incorporea,"* similar to space and extension.[97]

For Hobbes: *"Corpus motum motus sui phantasma in animo relinquit, nimirum ideam corporis, nunc per hoc, nunc per aliud spatium continua successione transeuntis. . . . Talis idea sive phantasma . . . appello tempus. . . ."*[98]

Time becomes purely empirical, a derivative of the motion or change of the empirical bodies, and existing either only in our mind or in the sensate world outside of it. This applies to Leibnitz, Locke, Berkeley, Hume, and other thinkers of the seventeenth and eighteenth centuries. For D. Hume:

The idea of time, being derived from the succession of our perceptions of every kind, ideas as well as impressions . . . will afford us an instance of an abstract idea. . . . Wherever we have no successive perception, we have no notion of time, even though there be a real succession in the objects. . . . Time cannot make its appearance to mind, either alone or attended with a

[95] Spinoza, *Ethics*, Bk. II, xlv, Sch.; Bk. II, Def. v. and *Cogitata Metaphysica*, Bk. I, iv. See also S. Alexander, *Spinoza and Time* (London, 1921); H. F. Hallett, *Aeternitas, A Spinozistic Study* (Oxford, 1930), pp. 4–6.

[96] Spinoza, *Cogitata Metaphysica*, Bk. I, iv; Hallett, *op. cit.*, pp. 43 ff.

[97] See Gent, *op. cit.*, chap. 35.   [98] Hobbes, *De corpore*, chap. vii.

steady unchangeable object, but is always discovered by some *perceivable* succession of changeable objects.[99]

Similarly sensate is Leibnitz's conception of time, "which presents to the mind nothing but an order among changes" . . . or "an order of successions." It cannot exist "apart from temporal things." As such it is an "ideal thing" existing in our mind, but not outside of it, except in the form of a succession of temporal or sensate things.[100]

Still more solipsistic and psychologico-empirical is Berkeley's conception :

For my own part, whenever I attempt to frame a simple idea of time, abstracted from the succession of ideas in my mind, which flows uniformly, and is participated in by all beings, I am lost and embrangled in inextricable difficulties. . . . Time therefore being nothing, abstracted from the succession of ideas in our minds. . . .[101]

The same goes for John Locke, and most of the prominent thinkers of the period.[102]

When we pass to Newton's conception we find his absolute and relative times. The absolute time bears upon itself a mark of supersensory time, not in the sense of the Ideational, however, but abstract and mathematical time, beyond and behind which there stands no Demiurge, no God, no other Ideational agency. It is something intermediary between Ideational and Sensate time — mathematical time, as Newton himself styles it. Here is this famous formula (abbreviated) :

Tempus absolutum, verum et mathematicum, in se et natura sua, sine relatione ad externum quodvis, aequabiliter fluit, alioque nomine dicitur duratio: relativum, apparens et vulgare est sensibilis et externa quaevis durationis per motum mensura (seu accurata seu inaequabilis) qua vulgus vice veri temporis utitur, ut hora, dies, mensis, annus.[103]

[99] D. Hume, *A Treatise on Human Nature* (Everyman's Library ed.), pp. 41 ff.

[100] Leibnitz, *The Philosophical Writings of Leibnitz* (Everyman's Library ed.), pp. 126, 199 ff., 215, and 223.

[101] Berkeley, *Principles of Human Knowledge*, ed. cited, xcviii, pp. 162 ff.

[102] See J. Locke, *An Essay Concerning Human Understanding*, II, 6, 12, 21.

[103] *Newtoni opera* (London, 1779), Vol. II, 6 and 7. "Absolute, true, and mathematical time, of itself, and by its own nature, flows uniformly on, without regard to anything external. It is also called duration. Relative, apparent, and common time is some sensible and external measure of absolute time (duration), estimated by the motions of bodies, whether accurate or inequable, and is commonly employed in place of true time; as an hour, a day, a month. . . . It may be that there is no equable motion, by which time can accurately be measured. All motions can be accelerated or retarded. But the flow of *absolute* time cannot be changed. Duration, or the persistent existence of things, is always the same, whether motions be swift or slow or null."

In his *Commentaries on the Apocalypse*, Newton went beyond this and postulated or admitted God and a duration of Ideàtional type; but his theology had little influence; and even of the absolute and relative times the relative time has played a much more important part in his mathematico-physical theories.

Kant's "critical" conception of time as an a priori form of our mind or of intuition left the reality of time per se (as a *ding an sich und für sich*) an open question and "justified" the empirical time as property of all temporal phenomena.[104]

Subsequently in scientific theories Newton's absolute time, as any other not purely Sensate time, fared more unsuccessfully than his relative time. The first has been declared unnecessary and useless many times,[105] while the second, the symbol t with its derivatives — and this t has always been mathematico-empirical — has been practically the only time that functioned. This means that even Newtonian absolute time has been dismissed by the later scientific and often philosophical theories and the main time of the eighteenth and the nineteenth centuries has been almost exclusively Sensate time, and, for the people generally, the watch or clock time specifically.[106] The process has gone so far that at the present time most of the Ideational and Idealistic conceptions of time, with their traits and characteristics, with their disquisitions of *Aeternitas*, *Aevum*, and *Tempus*, with their references to God, Demiurge, Brahma, and the like, sound strange and incomprehensible to most of us. More than that: "It is utterly beyond our power to measure the changes of things by time." We can measure time only through the changes of things.[107]

Thus not only Ideational but even Idealistic conceptions of time — for instance, Aristotle's, that made time a measure of motion and of changes — are rejected and reversed. Not only the supersensory time is rejected as absurd, but even the Sensate time is made a "poor dependent" of the

---

[104] "*Die Zeit nur die Form der Anschauung mithin der Gegenstände als Erscheinungen ist.*" I. Kant, *Kritik der reinen Vernunft* (Berlin, 1903), p. 102. See N. Kemp Smith, *A Commentary to Kant's Critique of Pure Reason* (London, 1918), pp. 240 ff.

[105] As an example Poincaré and E. Mach both find Newton's absolute time and space meaningless and useless. "That which cannot be measured cannot be the object of science. . . . Measurable time is essentially relative. . . . The properties of time are but those of the clocks, as the properties of space are but those of the instruments of measurement." H. Poincaré, *Dernières pensées*, pp. 41–42. Also his *Science et méthode*, pp. 95 ff. "This absolute time can be measured by comparison with no motion; it has therefore neither a practical nor a scientific value; and no one is justified in saying that he knows aught about it. It is an idle metaphysical conception." E. Mach, *The Science of Mechanics* (Chicago, 1902), p. 224.

[106] See the chapter on Social Time in Volume Four.

[107] Mach, *op. cit.*, p. 224.

purely Sensate phenomena of change without which it has no existence, no meaning, no use. Respectively, in mechanics, time is a measure of the motion of a material body (or point) in reference to the motion of another material body or point taken as a point of reference. Such a point of reference is the rotation of the earth around its axis. In social practice, such a point of reference at the present time is a clock and the motion of its hand (while in other societies some other empirical phenomena are used for that purpose; see Volume Four). As shown in Chapter Five, on fluctuation of eternalism and temporalism, this "clock time" tended to become atomized and divided into shorter and shorter units; more and more "temporary" and "momentary." In this sense time has become not only thoroughly Sensate, but its sensatism has been pushed to the extreme of its temporalism; so much so that "the long-time point of view" has been replaced in the conduct and in the world of values by shorter and shorter time viewpoints. In this mentality the past as well as the future tended to fade more and more, leaving only the present; and this present has tended to be reduced to shorter and shorter, fleeting, rushing moments. For scientific as well as practical purposes, the moments of the present were split not only into hours, but into minutes, seconds, and parts of seconds. And these seconds had been made the "watch-time seconds," quantitatively equal to one another; qualitatively — all of the same colorless quality — that of the motion of the watch hand over the same "distance" on the watch circle. The Sensate time reached its extreme limit — the limit in which time itself began to be destroyed by this Sensate extremism.

It is hardly surprising, therefore, that in the twentieth century some signs of reaction against this began to appear. One of them is the restoration of the *qualitative* time by Bergson and others, with the conceptions of time which contain elements heterogeneous to purely Sensate time and congenial to Ideational time.[108] Another is Minkowski-Einstein's "space-time continuum," which in a sense is also a revolt against the extreme Sensate time.[109] Several other conceptions deviating greatly from the purely sensate, colorless, quantitative, endlessly divisible and

---

[108] See Bergson's *Matter and Memory* (London, 1919), pp. 176–178, 272–280, *et passim*. See also S. Alexander, *Space, Time, Deity* (London, 1920); A. N. Whitehead, *An Enquiry Concerning the Principles of Natural Knowledge* (Cambridge, 1919) and *Adventures of Ideas* (New York, 1933), chap. xii; A. E. Taylor, *A Commentary on Plato's Timaeus* (Oxford, 1928).

[109] See A. Einstein, *Specielle und allgemeine Relativitätstheorie* (1920); for the changes in the concept of time in the exact sciences, see M. Schlick's *Raum und Zeit in der gegenwärtigen Physik* (Berlin, 1920). Also L. Brunschvicg, *op. cit.*, pp. 491–523; H. F. Hallett, *Aeternitas, op. cit.*, pt. iii.

homogeneous "clock time" are appearing. In this sense S. Alexander aptly said :

The most characteristic feature of the thought of the last twenty-five years [is] the discovery of Time. . . . I do not mean that we have waited until to-day to become familiar with Time ; I mean that we have only just begun ["again," I would like to add] to take Time seriously.[110]

This means that signs of "revolt" against Sensate time are not absent. This "revolt" is in harmony with other "revolts" against Sensate culture mentality at the end of the nineteenth and in the twentieth century in all the other compartments of culture, and speaks — even in this detail — of the dependence of the fundamental conceptions of science upon the transformation of the whole culture mentality. Thus, however short and sketchy this outline of the "history" of time conception is, it shows that there indeed are Ideational, Mixed (Idealistic), and Sensate conceptions of time ; that in their influence they fluctuate ; and that their fluctuations go hand in hand with the rise and decline of Ideational and Sensate culture mentalities.

IV. IDEATIONAL AND SENSATE CATEGORIES OF SPACE

There is no room to sketch similarly the fluctuations of the conception of space. It is possible, however, to contend — and the competent reader can check the contentions for himself — that the content covered by the same term, *space*, varies greatly from thinker to thinker, from culture to culture, and from period to period. These diverse conceptions of space fall easily into Ideational, Mixed, and Sensate conceptions of space (with further subdivisions within each of these classes). Ideational space is non-Sensate space and often derives nothing from the sensory space, with its extension, its three or more sensory dimensions, its mutual impenetrability, its spatial adjacency and situation. Ideational space is often thought of merely as a center of unspatial (sensorily) supersensory noumena — God, Soul, Mind, and the like — which do not have and do not need any sensory extension, sensory *locus*, sensory volume, form, dimension, or other attributes of the Sensate space. For this reason, Ideational space relations, viewed sensately, appear, as a rule, blurred and not clear, with one *locus* seemingly merging, covering, crossing, overlapping, and generally being mingled with the others. The "subject" of the judgment seems to be here and not here ; there and not there ; nowhere and everywhere. The distances and spatial positions

[110] S. Alexander, *Spinoza and Time*, p. 15.

seem to be equally undefined or outlined most queerly. Gods seem to exist on Mount Olympus but the *locus* of their habitation is at the same time not on Mount Olympus. They are there and not there. God is in heaven, but not in the heaven that is known to us as a sensory phenomenon. God is nowhere and everywhere. These allusions hint at the nature of Ideational space. It is devoid of almost all the traits of the sensory space. It is a kind of "reference system" which shows the coexisting relationship of the realities involved, say God, archangels, angels, and the rest of the hierarchy of supersensory beings; or, say, Paradise, Purgatory, and Inferno; or various categories of the realities. The reference system "locates" each of the realities in its coexisting relationship to other supersensory or sensory realities involved; and often it defines the relationship quite clearly; and yet, it does it in a form of reference that is devoid of any spatial properties of Sensate space. Respectively, Ideational space does not need any unit for its measurement, or the delineation of its dimensions: these may be one and millions; any specification of sensorily spatial distance, volume, size, extension; any clarification of spatial relationship of the realities involved: "above," "below," "to the left," "to the right," "so many miles," "altitude, longitude, latitude," and the like. Such a space is neither quantitative, nor uniform, nor infinitely divisible into identical units. If one asks the very familiar question: "Where is the spatial *locus* of human thought?" or "Where is Plato's system of philosophy?" one would get an imperfect idea of Ideational space. My thought or Plato's system of philosophy exists, and in a sense they occupy a definite place in an Ideational system of reference; but they are neither here nor there in any particular point of sensory space. We shall see in Volume Four that for the "location" of a large portion of sociocultural phenomena and values, sensory space is inadequate and, whether we want it or not, at least a kind of Mixed (Ideational-Sensate) spatial system is unavoidable.[111]

To many of my contemporaries who have been reared in an atmosphere of Sensate space; who are even unaware of the existence of Ideational space conception; and who try to locate everything — even mind, and thought, and sociocultural values like Plato's system of thought, a Beethoven symphony, Homer's *Iliad*, Euclid's geometry — in some sensory *locus*, in some Sensate place — be it the nervous system, or the symphony score, or the hall where the symphony is given, or the book in which the *Iliad* is printed, and other similar "places" — to these contemporaries with these hopeless and perfectly absurd attempts at "objec-

[111] See Volume Four. See also my *Social Mobility*, chap. i.

tive location" of these values, the very idea of Ideational space appears something strange and queer. And yet, after the above remarks, even they have to admit that such strange conceptions have existed. More than that. If they would try to acquaint themselves more seriously with a few conceptions of space in various cultures, say, ancient Chinese, they would see that these strange conceptions not only existed, but they were elaborated in great detail and appeared to the respective people or thinkers as clear and definite as our sensory three-dimensional space of the classical mechanics, with all its specific properties.

"None of the Chinese philosophers have found an interest in considering space as a simple extension resulting from the juxtaposition of homogeneous elements or as an extension all of whose parts are superposable. All prefer to view space as a complex of the domains, climates, and horizons (d'orients)." For them time and space "are not definite and distinct concepts but emblems rich in affinities." "Space in the first place has to be quadrangular. . . . Every surface is in its nature square. . . . The earth, being square, divides itself into squares. The external walls of principalities must form a square and the walls of the cities and the fields must do the same. . . . Each side of the earth corresponds to the Orient. Fields, fortifications, and cities must also be oriented. . . . The technique of division and management of space (surveyorship, urbanism, architecture, political geography) and the geometric speculation which they imply, are apparently attached to the public cult. The faithful (les fidèles) indeed make their formation in a square. The Sun Altar around which the great meetings usually take place is a square mount. . . . The sacred square represents the totality of the Empire. . . . One can see that the idea of the square earth, square space, is bound together with the ensemble of social rules." Farther on, space is neither infinite, nor uniform, nor existing everywhere, nor having many other purely sensory traits. On the contrary, it is represented as possessing many Ideational traits, qualities, properties, which as such are not given in sensory space.[112]

If in a similar way we try to analyze the conception of space of the Hindu, or ancient Greeks, or of the thinkers of various periods, we shall see that Ideational or Mixed conceptions of space have not been rarities and at some periods have even been dominant. The conceptions of space and its properties have been widely different — mainly Ideational — among the Greek thinkers of the period before the fifth and in the fifth century B.C. Ideationality decreased and the Sensate representations of space increased in the fourth, the third, the second, and the first centuries

[112] M. Granet, op. cit., pp. 86 ff. and 90 ff. See the whole chapter, Le temps et l'espace.

B.C. The triumph of Christianity led to a new rise of the Ideational conceptions of space that were dominant throughout the Middle Ages. After the fifteenth century Sensate conceptions began to rise, and the rising tide has continued up to the present time.[113] Such is the result of the preliminary study of the problem from this standpoint.

This fluctuation of Ideational and Sensate can be seen in the conceptions of space as such; and still more clearly in the cosmogonic theories of the universe and its spatial structure. When these cosmogonic pictures are taken, in their whole as well as in their specific parts, the contrast between Ideational and Sensate conceptions of the universe and its spatial structure comes out at once. Here are a few examples.

A. Contemporary Sensate conceptions of the spatial structure of the universe do not speak of the Soul of the World, or God, or the Central Fire (the Mind of the World), or Demiurge, or Jupiter, or any other supersensory agency as the center of the world, as the inalienable, nay, central part of the spatial structure of the universe. Likewise, they do not talk of special regions reserved for angels, saints, sinners, and various categories of such supersensory "population." Neither do we find in these theories a classification and division of the universe into regions of paradise, or purgatory, or inferno. They are free from all such supersensory "additions"; they talk and discuss the spatial aspect of the Universe without anything supersensory, no matter whether they claim finite or infinite space; empty or filled with ether or atoms or anything else — again sensory. Turn from these theories to the cosmogonic pictures of the universe, whether of Hesiod, Homer, Pythagoras, Philolaos, Plato, or even Aristotle. What a contrast! The "supersensory" elements of the spatial structure of the Universe not only are there but they are the central — absolutely inalienable — part of it, be it the Soul of the Universe and its *locus* in it; be it Jupiter; be it "the center of the Necessity"; be it the spiritualized Central Fire; or the like. This is true of almost all the cosmogonic theories of the centuries before the third in Greece. A famous place in Plato's *Republic* gives a sample of it.[114] When carefully read from this standpoint, the deep contrast of the Platonic (still mainly Ideational) representation of the spatial structure of the universe to any Sensate theory becomes striking. And this can be said of any Ideational conception of space. The same is true of the

---

[113] A study of the history of conceptions of space given in the quoted works of P. Duhem and Gent gives material and data for substantiation of this scheme.

[114] See Plato, *Republic* (Everyman's Library ed.), Bk. X, 616 ff., pp. 340 ff. See about other theories in the admirable analysis of Duhem, *op. cit.*, Vols. I, II, *et passim.*

medieval cosmogonic theories of the universe, preoccupied with the regions of souls, angels, saints, sinners, devils, and the like; with the qualitative properties of each respective region; with their "spatial relation"; with the most exacting attempts to give a picture of the universe and its space structure which will be in agreement with the Scripture and with some of its embarrassing statements, like the region of the "supercelestial waters." When one passes, after a study of the cosmogonic theories of the Greeks and the Romans, like Aristarchos of Samos or Claudius Ptolemy, to the study of the cosmogonies of the Church Fathers and the medieval cosmogonists (Isidore of Seville, Bede, Rhabanus, Walafrid Strabo, Honorius, Hugo St. Victor, Petrus Lombardus, and others), one cannot help being bewildered, even stunned with the change in this field. The whole mentality is altered and we are moved from one — considerably Sensate — atmosphere to something radically different — to the Ideational conception of space and the Universe.[115]

B. Enormous also is the contrast in many details of the spatial image of the universe in the theories of the cosmogonists who lived in predominantly Ideational and predominantly Sensate periods. We measure, for instance, the size and distances between various parts or stars of the universe with the help of purely empirical units of measure (whatever they are). Not so with the Ideational theories. Even on this seemingly very definite point they introduced units and relationships of a supersensory kind. Pythagoras and his school assumed that the spatial distances between "the center" of the universe and its specific parts are based on the mystical figure "3": 3 units of distance from the center to the antiearth, 9 to the earth, 27 to the moon, 81 to Mercury, and so on. With variations, we find a similar use of figures in Plato. They assumed further that there is a certain relation between musical notes and the celestial distances and spatial relationships (the so-called doctrine of "the Celestial Music" or the "harmony of the astral spheres"). Respectively they assumed that the distances between the stars correspond to the distances between certain musical chords; or to the length of the cords on a lyre.[116] Something similar is found in the cosmogonic theories of the Middle Ages and of any predominantly Ideational mentality.

The same can be said of many other details. And the blurred character (from the Sensate standpoint) of Ideational conceptions of space in the relationship of various spatial regions and of various realities in it, is again a common trait of most of such conceptions. The sensory and

---

[115] See Duhem, *op. cit.*, Vols. I, III, V, *et passim*.
[116] See the details in Duhem, *op. cit.*, Vol. II, pp. 8 ff.

supersensory are inextricably mixed together in these. The mentioned passage from Plato's *Republic*[117] gives a sample of it. The Chinese space image (page 430) gives another. If one studies the discussion of the medieval cosmologists about, for instance, "the supercelestial waters," one finds the third example.[118]

These pages give an idea of the profound difference between Ideational and Sensate conceptions. They also indicate that, when studied, the rise and decline of these conceptions agree with the respective rise and decline of Ideational and Sensate mentalities.[119]

V. Ideational and Sensate Conceptions of Number

Without attempting to outline a history of the conceptions of number here, I want merely to indicate that this term has covered conceptions which are fundamentally different from one another. Here also one can distinguish Ideational and Sensate conceptions. At the present time most of us think of number as a result of counting or of comparison of quantities with a standard unit. Number and quantity, number and magnitude, appear to us as inseparable from one another. Number as a number appears to us quantitative only and devoid of any qualities except the quantitative quality of the number itself (odd and even, rational and irrational, prime and composite, and so on). Comparative magnitude

[117] Book X.

[118] As it is said in the Holy Scripture, "there are waters above the firmament . . . these waters are, by the place they occupy, above any corporeal creature." (St. Isidore placed above these supercelestial waters still higher the region of the supreme heaven — the habitat of the blessed.) He continues, further, that according to some authorities, the role of these supercelestial waters is to serve, by the will of God, as a reserve fund for future floods; according to others, these waters come out from the clouds, like ordinary rain; according to others their role is to temper the heat of the fire that burns in luminary heavenly bodies. "Next to these waters in the order of the corporeal creatures comes, in the second place, the firmament, created on the second day (of the Creation). It separates the supercelestial and the undercelestial waters." Isidori Hispalensis Episcopi, *De ordine creaturarum liber*, chaps. iii–iv. Migne's *Patrologiae latinae*, t. LXXXIII, cols. 920–925, gives an example of the mixture of the Sensate space with the Ideational; of the blurred nature of the space representation and relationship. See further examples in the work of Duhem, *op. cit.*, Vols. III, IV, and V.

[119] The end of the nineteenth and the twentieth centuries manifest also some signs of "revolt" against the purely Sensate conception of space. It is shown by the construction of Minkowsky-Einstein's four-dimensional space-time continuum; by Bergsonian treatment of space as a relaxation of the *élan vital* resulting in its extension; the conception reminding us of several Ideational theories of the Hindus and others of materialization and extension as a phase of existence of the true reality in, so to speak, its relaxed state; by the appearance of the non-Euclidian (Lobachevsky, Riemann) geometries with the properties different from the three-dimensional space of Euclid; and several other symptoms. All these theories are not Ideational, as yet; but they contain many anti-Sensate elements.

again appears to us to be decided by the numerical magnitude of the numbers themselves: 6 as containing six units is greater than 4 or 5. These and others characteristics to which we are accustomed appear to us so clear and definite that no fundamentally different conception of number seems possible. Especially any conception where number is quality, rather than quantity, in which 4 may be greater than 6; where number functions not for a comparison of magnitude but for radically different purposes. To give an idea of one fundamentally different conception of number, however, let me quote again the case given by M. Granet.

The *Tso tchouan* tells of the debate of the (Chinese) council of war: Should they attack the enemy? The Chief is inclined to the idea of attack, but it is necessary that he should engage the responsibility of his subordinates and take their advice. Twelve generals, including himself, participate in the Council. The opinions are divided. Three generals refuse to engage in the battle; eight want to go to it. These eight are thus *majority* and they proclaim it. However, the opinion that unites 8 votes does not carry the opinion that unites 3 votes: 3 is [for the Chinese] almost *unanimity*, which is quite a different thing from a mere *majority*. The Chief will not fight. He changes his opinion. The opinion to which he adds his *unique* vote becomes the *unanimous* opinion.[120]

Here we have an example of how 3 may be greater than 8 and how a number may function not for a comparison of quantitative magnitudes but for making up *qualities and values* (unanimity and majority) and their hierarchical scale. It shows also that number may be viewed as containing in itself qualities and properties that have nothing to do with number as a quantitative category. After this the subsequent statements of M. Granet are comprehensible and introduce us more fully into what I style the Ideational or Mixed conception of number.

Idea of quantity does not play any role in the philosophical speculations of the Chinese. Numbers, however, passionately interest the sages of the ancient China. . . . One of the fundamental traits of the Chinese thought is an extreme indifference for any quantitative conception. . . . Each tries to manipulate numbers as they manipulate emblems: and for the Chinese, in fact, numbers are remarkable, like emblems, in their propitious polyvalence for efficient manipulations.[121]

Knowing, for instance, that for human species embryonic life lasts about ten months a philosopher reasons as follows. The Heaven signifies 1; the Earth, 2; Man, 3. 3 times 3 makes 9; 9 times 9 makes 81 [octant and 1]; 1 rules the Sun; the number of the Sun is [1 (ten)] 10; the Sun controls man;

[120] Granet, *op. cit.*, p. 299.   [121] *Ibid.*, pp. 149–150.

therefore man is born in the tenth month. [From this can be seen on the one hand a *symbolic equivalent* of *81* and *10*; *72* and *12*, while *63* and *54* signify *3* and *4*.] . . .

Numerical symbols command every sort of reality and symbol.

Side by side with their quantitative value they possess much more interesting symbolic value. . . . Numbers permit one to classify the things but not in a merely simple numerical order. . . . Chinese use numbers for the expression of the *qualities* of certain groupings, or for indication of a hierarchical scale.[122]

Numbers do not function to express magnitudes; they serve to adjust the concrete dimensions to the proportions of the Universe.[123]

The quotations give an allusion to a conception of number fundamentally different from what we are used to.[124] The Ideationally Mixed nature and functions of numbers in this case are clear.

Does this Chinese case represent something unique? By no means. The spread and persistence of the Ideational "numerology," to use E. T. Bell's expression,[125] is infinitely greater than in the Chinese case. Who, for instance, does not know about the Pythagorean numerological mysticism? In its nature, as Chavannes rightly remarks, Chinese numerology is a variety of Pythagorean numerology. For the Pythagoreans (including Philolaos), according to the preserved statement of Jamblichos,[126] "numbers are permanent causes of everything that occurs in the Universe. . . . Unity is the principle of numbers and of everything that exists and that is identical with God."

Similarly, to certain numbers like 10, 3, and some others are ascribed a mystical significance and power. In their qualitative functions the different numbers may be equivalent, quantitatively smaller numbers may be greater, and equal numbers (say 72 made by 8 multiplied by 9, and 72 made by 12 multiplied by 6) may be quite unequal.

This Ideational conception was the dominant conception in Greece before the fourth century; it is found developed in the Hesiodic calendar of the lucky and unlucky days: in every month the sixth day is unpropitious for the birth of a female; the thirteenth, for sowing; the sixteenth,

---

[122] *Ibid.*, pp. 150–151.   [123] *Ibid.*, p. 273.

[124] See the long and interesting analysis of Granet. It shows in a sense the most "bewildering" character of the conception of number in the thought of the ancient Chinese sages. *Ibid.*, pp. 149–299.

[125] See E. T. Bell, *Numerology* (Baltimore, 1933). What Bell calls numerology and satirizes is in a great part but a kind of Ideational conception of number.

[126] See Duhem, *op. cit.*, Vol. I, pp. 12 ff.

for planting; likewise the fifth, the fifteenth, the twenty-fifth are generally bad days; on the contrary, the fourth day is good for marriage; the ninth for begetting or birth of a child; and so on.[127]   It permeates the whole Pythagorean conception of number: beginning with the special numbers, like 10, endowed with a specific power, and ending with the mystical conception of number, the mystical relationship between numbers, music, and the harmony of the Universe.   We all know the large part which a similar Ideational conception of number plays in Plato's philosophy, beginning with Plato's "perfect number" and ending with numerous similar discussions of numbers.   The Pythagoreans and the Platonists followed this path.   Other Greek thinkers of the sixth and the fifth centuries shared in that Ideational conception.   This is shown by their theories of the *annus magnus* and other cycles repeated after a certain number of units of time and, often, just by the virtue of this number.   Alcmeon of Crotona, Herakleitos, Empedocles, Philolaos, Anaximenes, Aretas, Linus, Dion, pseudo Orpheus, and others, all ascribed to numbers certain qualities, and used numbers not so much as indicators of quantity, as for symbols and mystic agencies of qualities, events, hierarchies, and the like.[128]   Such a conception is held also by many Stoics, and other Greek and Roman thinkers.   It was current in the circles whose writings are known under the heading *Hermetica*.   It played a role in astrological numerology throughout the Middle Ages.

It is manifested *urbi et orbi* in the universal belief in the specific importance and mysterious power of certain numbers, like 3, 7, 9, 13, 81, and many others: in the Hebrew, the Hindu, the Mohammedan, the Christian, the Graeco-Roman, the Chinese, the Babylonian, and other culture mentalities.[129]   All this shows that such a conception of number has been something not exceptionally rare but something as diffused as the Sensate and "scientific" treatment of numbers.   More than that: sometimes the elements of some kind of Ideationalism crop up even in seemingly quite scientific — purely quantitative — conceptions of number.   At the present time, for instance, a belief is held by many that

[127] See Hesiod, *Works and Days, passim.* See also A. W. Maire's commentary on the Hesiodic Calendar in *Hesiod: the Poems and Fragments*, done into English by A. W. Maire (Oxford, 1908), pp. 162–166.

[128] See a summary of many of such theories in Censorinus, *De die natali;* also the *Placita* of pseudo Plutarch.

[129] It comes also in many theories of periodicity of this or that sociocultural phenomenon and the *annus magnus*.   In Volume Four I hope to give a history of the theories of periodicity where the details of such conceptions and all the variety of the mysterious numbers set forth will be shown.   See Chapter Ten in this volume.

only a quantitative knowledge is the real knowledge; that by manipulating quantities, whether in various statistical ways from the "mysterious" coefficient of the correlation up to other quantitative procedures, one is guaranteed to obtain the truth and real knowledge; these and many similar beliefs and conceptions up to the belief in the efficacy of mathematical formula and the sense of the mathematical irrational numbers, like the square root of minus one ($\sqrt{-1}$), contain elements of Ideational conception of number.

These remarks are possibly sufficient to show that there has been and indeed exist Ideational and Sensate conceptions of number most profoundly different from one another. This primary difference manifests itself in many derivative uses, computations, numerical manipulations, measurements, and other procedures where numbers are involved. Quantitativism or, more accurately, numerology and mathematics of the Ideational and Sensate conceptions are fundamentally different numerologies, mathematics, computations, and quantitativisms. He who does not realize that is liable to make a serious error, by accepting as identical what is quite different.

It is out of place here to give an outline of the rise and decline of the Ideational and Sensate conceptions of number from the sixth century B.C. up to the present time. So far as my preliminary study shows, each of these conceptions seem to have fluctuated tangibly parallel with the rise and decline of Ideational and Sensate mentalities, as is shown by the preceding and subsequent curves from various compartments of the cultures studied.

However brief and sketchy is the analysis and historical outline of the Ideational and Sensate fluctuations of the conception of causality, time, space, and number — as the fundamental categories of our thought — the above seems to be sufficient to demonstrate that each of these categories has indeed Ideational and Sensate forms; and that each of these forms rises and declines with the rise and decline of the respective culture mentalities.

Chapter Twelve

FLUCTUATION OF GENERAL AND SPECIAL SCIENTIFIC THEORIES [1]

Not only do the first principles and the categories of human thought fluctuate, but also almost all of the scientific theories of a more or less general nature.[2] Some of these fluctuations probably proceed independently from our main variables. The others seem to be connected with the rise and decline of our main types of culture mentality.

Perhaps only so-called facts remain unchanged, but any fact as a "routine of sense perception" is meaningless per se, if it is not put in some conceptual reference system or — what is the same — if it is not embraced by some kind of theory. Without this, no "fact" can exist as a relevant fact or can constitute knowledge in any sense.

As examples of the fluctuation discussed, I am taking cosmogonic theories, the atomistic theory, the mechanistic and vitalistic interpretation of life phenomena, the theory of light, and a few others. The tracing of their quantitative and qualitative fluctuations is very concise. But it is probably accurate in all the essential traits. The literature given in the footnotes makes it possible to check the accuracy of the outlines. We begin with the Atomistic theories.

I. Fluctuation of Atomistic Theories

The fluctuation of atomistic theories seems to have been tangibly associated with that of the main systems of truth. In so far as atomism

---

[1] In co-operation with R. K. Merton.

[2] "Philosophy goes through a cycle of forms by fashion. Even mathematics and science do the same, both as to method and as to concepts," W. G. Sumner, *Folkways* (Boston, 1907), p. 193. *Cf.* also John T. Merz, *A History of European Thought in the Nineteenth Century* (London, 1907), Vol. I, pp. 56, 312–314, and 385 ff. and Vol. II, p. 95; F. A. Lange, *History of Materialism*, trans. by E. C. Thomas (London, 1877), Vol. II, pp. 371–372; V. Pareto, *Traité de sociologie générale* (Paris, 1919), Vol. II, 1002–1003; J. Needham, *The Sceptical Biologist* (New York, 1930), pp. 88 and 107–108; Egon Friedell, *A Cultural History of the Modern Age* (New York, 1932), Vol. III, p. 189; E. N. daC. Andrade, *The Structure of the Atom* (New York, 1924), p. 2; F. C. S. Schiller, "Hypothesis," in *Studies in the History and Method of Science*, Chas. Singer ed. (Oxford, 1921), p. 437; J. H. Woodger, *Biological Principles* (London, 1929).

is connected with materialism, according to the opinion of the competent investigators of its history,[3] and in so far as materialism is associated with the truth of the senses, it follows that we should expect the curve of atomistic theories in its main upward and downward movements to go somewhat parallel with that of the empirical system of truth, and with mechanistic materialism. The survey of its main "ups and downs" corroborates this expectation.

In Greek tradition, the "atomical philosophy" appears first as a conception of the Phoenician Mochus, or Moschus (incidentally referred to by Boyle), who is held to have lived in the pre-Trojan era.[4] The first widespread promulgation of the atomic theory comes later in the fifth century, with the establishment by Leukippos at Abdera of the so-called Atomistic school, which was later consolidated by Democritus, one of the disciples, about 420 B.C. The atom was here conceived as indestructible, as the component of the single primary matter, and the theory also entailed the idea of a void or genuine vacuum.[5]

But, thirty years after Democritus, there remained almost no trace of his doctrine.[6] In the period between Democritus and Epicurus, atomism disappeared in the idealistic movement of reaction determined by Socrates, Plato, and Aristotle. Aristotle turns back to the Eleatic doctrines and definitely posits the notion of *continua*, the contiguous "one," and thus, of course, rejects the idea of atoms and vacuum as a fundamental condition of change.[7] Here, then, is completed one phase in the cycle: from the Eleatic continuum, through Leukippos and Democritus, to Aristotle, is a swing from nonacknowledgment to acceptance to banishment of the Atomic hypothesis.

At the close of the fourth and the opening of the third century, Epicurus revived the outcast theory with but few changes. The vacuum was admitted and the atom, indivisible in practice and divisible in theory, was given an essential weight.[8] But this revival was comparatively

[3] Lange, *op. cit.*, Vol. I, pp. 4 and 114–115.

[4] J. C. Gregory, *A Short History of Atomism* (London, 1931), Vol. I; L. Mabilleau, *Histoire de la philosophie atomistique* (Paris, 1895), pp. 430 and 237 ff.; W. T. Sedgwick and H. W. Tyler, *A Short History of Science* (New York, 1921), p. 61; H. Vaihinger, *The Philosophy of "As-If"* (London, 1924), pp. 138–139.

[5] George Sarton, *Introduction to the History of Science* (Baltimore, 1927), Vol. I, p. 88; Gregory, *op. cit.*, Vol. I; Leon Robin, *Greek Thought and the Origins of the Scientific Spirit* (New York, 1928), pp. 113–115; Sedgwick and Tyler, *op. cit.*, p. 62.

[6] Mabilleau, *op. cit.*, p. 267; W. C. D. Dampier-Whetham, *A History of Science* (Cambridge, 1929), p. 29.

[7] Robin, *op. cit.*, pp. 279–280.

[8] *Ibid.*, pp. 329 ff.; Gregory, *op. cit.*, pp. 4 ff.; Mabilleau, *op. cit.*, pp. 270 ff.

short-lived in Greece and, with the solitary exception of Asclepiades (the Greek physician who was the teacher of Lucretius) in the first century B.C., atomism was once again left to perish. This decline coincided with the increasing influence of the Stoics, who dismissed the concept of a vacuum and atoms.[9]

But, when Greek ideas found their way to Rome, atomism was among them, and the theory had its rebirth in the poem of T. Lucretius Carus (99–55 B.C.). Although the *De rerum natura* represents a rather faithful rendering of Epicurean Atomism, yet in holding the impossibility of infinite divisibility it harks back to the Democritean idea.[10] Though this represented the temporary return of the atom, it must not be assumed that Atomism held unquestioned sway in Rome during this period. Contemporary with Lucretius, Cicero criticized it severely, and in the following century Seneca and Plutarch were the popular exponents of similar opposition. This conflict presaged the approaching demise of the Atomic doctrine, and "the probable year of Galen's death, 200 A.D., marks, with the convenient arbitrariness of a single date, the exile of the atom." Galen's attacks found favor in a mental atmosphere so opposed to an atomically arranged universe, with its predominant role accorded to chance — "atoms were far too naked to be genuine framers of a world so richly clothed with qualities. . . ."[11] The virtual disappearance of the atomic theory in the Western World was to last almost a millennium.[12]

Although the atomic theory did not find any significant degree of credence until its revival by Galileo and Gassendi in the seventeenth century, it reappeared on the scene (note this!) in the twelfth century, and since that time has remained there, with slow — at the beginning — and then faster rising trend (after the sixteenth century). "There were sundry . . . hankerings after atoms in the twelfth century . . ." as can be seen by the works of Adelard of Bath or William of Conches.[13] In the

---

[9] Gregory, *op. cit.*, pp. 14 ff.

[10] "Lucretius supposed the atoms of a solid to be hooked so as to cling together. Hooked atoms were used in more recent times by John Bernoulli, and also by nineteenth-century chemists to explain chemical combination and valency." Florian Cajori, *A History of Physics* (New York, 1929), pp. 18–19. Boyle in 1666, John Mayow in 1674, and Lemery in 1675 all adopted this idea of hooking "branchy particles." Gregory, *op. cit.*, p. 26.

[11] Gregory, *op. cit.*, pp. 17 ff.

[12] In Arabia, however, where, according to one version, the Greek atomistic ideas may have come by way of Byzantine theologians, atomism reappears somewhat earlier. Al-Baqilani (died A.D. 1013) introduced the conception of atoms and vacuum into the Kalam. The belief in the discontinuity of time bears a close resemblance to the Hindu conception. Sarton, *op. cit.*, Vol. I, p. 706; Gregory, *op. cit.*, p. 22.

[13] Gregory, *op. cit.*, p. 22; Sarton, *op. cit.*, Vol. II, pp. 197–198.

thirteenth century, a few intrepid thinkers, such as Vincent of Beauvais
and Peter of Albano, dared oppose the dominance of Aristotelian
thought with a rather favorable consideration of the atomic conception.[14]
However, these were but isolated instances, and the prevailing attitude
toward atomism is best represented by the antagonism of Roger Bacon.
At Paris, in 1348, another solitary figure, Nicolaus de Autricuria, dared
present an atomic theory, but under strong pressure found that it was
advisable to recant.[15] "Atomism made gestures of return in philosophy
from 1418, when Poggio rediscovered Lucretius, to 1600, when Bruno was
burned at the stake, but it made little impression, and virtually none at
all upon science. . . ."[16] Indications of such adumbration of succeeding
theories of atomism can be found in the sixteenth century, in the works
of Titelman, Leonard Fuchs, Fernel, and Fracastor.[17]

With the opening of the seventeenth century, atomic theories begin to
come into their own. Though Kepler ignored atomism, Galileo accepted
the ancient idea.[18] In the works of Sala, Sennert, Berigard, Magnen,
and even of Van Helmont, atomism played a greater and greater role, as
the century proceeded.[19] Bacon held that without the assumption of
atoms, nature could not well be explained.[20] But it was Pierre Gassendi
who, having adopted the Epicurean conception almost *in toto*, attained
for atomism "a lasting importance, however much . . . [the theory] was
gradually modified as it passed through the hands of later inquirers.[21]

The Cartesian corpuscular mechanism varied somewhat from the
"classic" atomism : it denied the vacuum and held that the "corpuscles"
were divisible and deformable. After Descartes's death in 1650, his
theory was generally adopted for a period of about thirty-five years.[22]
Hobbes, Boyle (in the *Origine of Formes and Qualities*, 1666), Rohault
(*Traité de physique*, 1672), Nicholas Lémery (*Cours de chimie*, 1675), all
bear witness to the temporary vogue of the corpuscular thesis during the
greater part of the second half of the seventeenth century.[23] However,

---

[14] Gregory, *op. cit.*, pp. 22–23. [15] Lange, *op. cit.*, Vol. I, pp. 225–226.

[16] Gregory, *op. cit.*, p. 23.

[17] Kurd Lasswitz, *Geschichte der Atomistik* (Hamburg, 1890), Vol. I, p. 450.

[18] Dampier-Whetham, *op. cit.*, pp. 161 and 146–147.

[19] "In fact, shortly after Bacon, and in the very shape which Epikuros had given it, Atomism became the foundation of modern natural science." Lange, *op. cit.*, Vol. I, p. 15. Also, Gregory, *op. cit.*, p. 23 ; Mabilleau, *op. cit.*, p. 399.

[20] Lange, *op. cit.*, Vol. I, pp. 236 ff. ; Mabilleau, *op. cit.*, p. 428.

[21] Lange, *op. cit.*, Vol. I, pp. 255 and 125 ; Gregory, *op. cit.*, p. 31.

[22] Gregory, *op. cit.*, pp. 25 ff. ; Lange, *op. cit.*, Vol. I, pp. 269 and 277 ff. ; Dampier-Whetham, *op. cit.*, p. 150.

[23] Gregory, *op. cit.*, pp. 22 ff. ; Lange, Vol. I, pp. 304 ff. ; Lasswitz, Vol. II, p. 235.

the acceptance of the Epicurean-Gassendi conception of the atom and vacuum by Isaac Newton re-established the older version at the very close of the century.[24] Hartsoeker, between 1696 and 1712, also aided this "stiffening back" of the corpuscle into the atom.[25] With this sketchy outline in mind we may summarize the seventeenth-century development of the atomic theory in this wise: the theory of atoms was generally accepted throughout the course of the century, but under Cartesian influence there was a temporary tendency to deny the vacuum and to admit the infinite divisibility of atoms, which variation in turn gave way to the previous doctrine, as the century closed. Here is an instance of a "*cycle within a cycle*," an oscillation of the minor elements of the theory and a subsequent reversion to the previous type — a phenomenon which we shall have occasion to note again.

The atomic idea underwent a twofold change in the eighteenth century: it acquired forces and these were conceived as inherent in the atom.[26] In 1742, Desaguliers vaguely anticipated the developments of more than a century later by speculations concerning the electrically constituted atom.[27] Somewhat later appeared also the Boscovich force atom (in 1758).[28] (This latter conception, in somewhat modified form, appeared throughout the course of the following century, in the works of Robinson, Priestley, Wollaston, Ampère, Faraday, Gerhardt, and Clerk-Maxwell.)[29] It must not be supposed, however, that atomism moved steadily onward, for "a strain of scepticism appeared in the eighteenth century after the period of corpuscularian fervor, and Joseph Black (1728–1799) himself shared this distrust of hypothetical atoms."[30] But this apparently represented only a slight and casual interruption in the course of atomism, and in 1789 William Higgins antedated the Daltonian hypothesis concerning the weight of individual atoms.[31]

It should be noted that the modern chemical distinction between atom and molecule was only slowly confirmed after the middle of the nineteenth century.[32] (Epicurus had vaguely realized this molecular conception in speaking of "sets of atoms.") Also, in 1789, Lavoisierre marked that the "primitive particles" into which chemical agents divided bodies remained

[24] Dampier-Whetham, *op. cit.*, p. 196; Lange, *op. cit.*, Vol. II, pp. 352 ff.

[25] Gregory, *op. cit.*, p. 54.

[26] *Ibid.*, p. 30.

[27] *Ibid.*, pp. 166–167.

[28] *Ibid.*, pp. 89–90. According to Mabilleau, the Hindu Kanada anticipated the Boscovich theory in a general way. *Cf.* p. 19.

[29] *Ibid.*, pp. 90 ff.

[30] *Ibid.*, pp. 49 and 137.

[31] *Ibid.*, pp. 67 ff.; Merz, *op. cit.*, Vol. I, p. 398.

[32] Gregory, *op. cit.*, p. 56.

"perfectly constant in their specific forms." In 1808, John Dalton (followed, six months later, by Gay-Lussac) took over the Democritean-Newtonian atom and emphasized the idea of the weight of atoms.[33] "The Daltonian atom maintained itself to the end of the nineteenth century by sheer expository power. Then it succumbed, and the modern electrical structure, whatever its ultimate fate, has probably exiled the *atom* for ever."[34] (!)   This is to say that the modern atom is more like a Boscovich *force atom* than like a Democritean "solid billiard ball," for the modern atom is neither indivisible nor indestructible.

But such statements as the above should not be taken as a detailed description of the nineteenth-century treatment of the theme.   We could relate the various developments which were made by Avogadro, Prout, Faraday, Cannizzaro, Lord Kelvin, Mendeleeff Van't Hoff, Helmholtz, etc., etc., save that we are not fundamentally interested in the *differences* in the theory but in the constant repeated elements of it.   The nineteenth century was a peculiar compound of alternate acceptance and rejection of Atomism, in part and *in plenum*.[35]   In this century, running across the large wave of actual use of the atomic conceptions in science were numerous smaller fluctuations of refusal to accept such hypothetical scientific constructs; an attitude which, toward the end of the century, led to the positing of nonmaterial energy as the ultimate "reality" by Ostwald, Tait, and others.

The twentieth-century atom, with much variation in detail, represents a metamorphosis of the earlier one of about 1876.[36]   Moreover, just as at the end of the preceding century the atom was generally held to be a mere working hypothesis, a conceptual convenience (for example, Mach's view), so has this attitude reappeared in the last five years.   Thus, Eddington and Jeans, from 1928 on, do not hesitate to refer to atoms as merely symbolic conceptions,[37] in the same fashion as do Ruark and Urey (*Atoms, Molecules and Quanta*, 1930).   But this most recent attitude contrasts sharply with the generally adopted belief, in the interim from about 1910 to 1928, that atoms are physical realities.   Thus, Bray and Branch held in 1913, as did Sir William Bragg in 1920 and Aston in 1922, that "the atomic

[33] Merz, *op. cit.*, Vol. I, pp. 245–246 and 395.

[34] Gregory, *op. cit.*, p. 63.

[35] See Gregory, *op. cit.*, pp. 83 ff.; Merz, *op. cit.*, Vol. I, pp. 436–437; Sedgwick and Tyler, *op. cit.*, p. 362; Cajori, *op. cit.*, pp. 147–148.

[36] Gregory, *op. cit.*, p. 136.

[37] Sir Arthur S. Eddington, *The Nature of the Physical World* (New York, 1929); Sir James H. Jeans, *Atomicity and Quanta* (Cambridge, 1926), *The Mysterious Universe* (New York, 1930), and *Through Space and Time* (New York, 1934).

theory has been transformed from a convenient working hypothesis into a definite statement of fact"; Andrade and Bohr in 1923, Millikan in 1924, Desch in 1925, Bridgman in 1927: "now we are as convinced of the atom's physical existence as of our hands and feet."[38] But this certainty of the physical reality of the atom finds a denial in Eddington's statement in 1928 that "the physical atom . . . is a schedule of pointer readings." Moreover, the indeterminacy and the quantum jumps of the present-day atom are "startling modern analogues of casual swerves by Epicurean atoms." There is still some dissent from this conception of these spasms of indeterminacy, but modern physics is none the less distinctly inclined to drift away from determinism. "Science 'withdraws its moral opposition to freedom' in Eddington's 1928 exposition, as Lucretius affirmed that freedom in the first century, B.C."[39]

Bringing this account of the atomic theory up to date enables us to fulfill the original purpose of our investigation. First, we see that atomic theories have indeed fluctuated in the course of time studied. At some periods they rose and gathered a power impressive enough to be accepted as the "last word of science" by the leading scientists or thinkers of the period. At other periods they declined and sometimes practically disappeared. Such is the first conclusion reached by the above outline. Second, one can easily notice that, all in all, atomism appeared in the periods of the Idealistic culture (fifth century B.C.; thirteenth century A.D.); it grew in the period of Sensate culture (third and first centuries B.C. and first two centuries A.D.; then the centuries from the sixteenth to the twentieth); and disappeared almost completely in the periods of domination of the Ideational culture (before the fifth century B.C. and from the fourth to the twelfth centuries A.D.). In Greece atomism gathered its greatest momentum possibly in the third century B.C. (Epicurus and the Epicureans); in Rome, in the first century B.C., and the first A.D., that is, in the periods when the Greek and the Roman cultures were Sensate par excellence; while in the Western culture it has been rapidly growing, beginning especially with the sixteenth century, up to the end of the nineteenth century. These fluctuations show that atomism is positively associated with the empirical system of truth and the Sensate culture.

Here, then, we have a sample of one of the scientific theories which rises and declines in its "believability" or "scientific prestige" somewhat

---

[38] Gregory, op. cit., pp. 235–236; P. W. Bridgman, The Logic of Modern Physics (New York, 1927), p. 59; K. T. Compton, "The Electron," in Science, January 8, 1937, pp. 27–37.

[39] Gregory, op. cit., pp. 231–232; Compton, op. cit.

parallel with the main turns of the main systems of truth and their respective cultures. Logically, the reasons for such a connection are at hand. To the partisans of the supersensory and immaterial reality, matter itself, and consequently its atoms, are "unreal"; therefore such a mentality cannot be inclined toward any variety of atomistic theory. For the Mixed Idealistic mentality, to which in part matter is a reality, some admission of atomism is possible and logically admissive. To the sensory, empirical mentality, with matter (or its substitutes) as the main reality, atomism is not only acceptable but rather inevitable logically.

The "inductive" verification justifies this connection.

One more remark. The very "immaterialization" of the atom in the twentieth century also may not be incidental, and may be a sign of the "revolt" met several times in other compartments of our culture. Perhaps "the immaterialization" and "indeterminization" (quantum theory) and "disatomization" of the atom in the twentieth century (briefly outlined above) are symptoms of the passing of the atomistic-materialistic conceptions of our overripe Sensate culture. That may or may not be so. The fact anyhow is worth being noted. So much for the atomic theory.

II. FLUCTUATION OF VITALISM AND MECHANISM IN BIOLOGY

The next example of the fluctuation of scientific theories is given by the increase and decrease of the "scientific" prestige, and acceptance of the rival theories of mechanism and vitalism, in the field of biology. This case also shows that these fluctuations have a tangible association with the ups and downs of the respective systems of truth and the types of cultures to which each of these systems belongs.

Across the ever-recurring alternation of these theories, short-time fluctuations may also be perceived, though it is more rhetorical than accurate to say that "the magnificent Phoenix of biology, vitalism . . . rises from its ashes as regularly as clockwork every decade or so." [40] In speaking of cycles or rhythms or oscillations in the realm of scientific thought, one qualification must be made — a precaution which justifies our making the following rather long quotation.

When the progress of science is spoken of, we must bear in mind the two aspects of discovery and interpretation. Progress in the one by no means implies progress in the other. While we can unquestionably speak of serial

[40] Joseph Needham, *The Sceptical Biologist* (New York, 1930), pp. 88 and 107–108.

progress in the case of discovery, progress in interpretation has by no means been a simple serial affair, but a process better described as "oscillatory." That is clear from a moment's consideration of some of the traditional explanations which can be found in any branch of science but particularly in biology — now one and now another being in favour, without any decisive result being reached, and no ground being so sure as to be held as absolute and not liable some day to revision. If we run over our stock of fundamental explanatory notions we find that most of them have been "anticipated" speculatively in Greek thought. What I wish to suggest, therefore, is that we may be as mistaken as were the peripatetic philosophers of the Middle Ages if we suppose that we are in possession of infallible principles of interpretation.[41]

Thus, in dealing with the *theories* of mechanism and vitalism, that is, biological *interpretations*, we will attend to specific *discoveries* only in so far as they seem to affect the scientific attitude toward these two general conceptions which prevails at any given time. But before proceeding with our historical account, it would facilitate our task if we first defined the sense in which we use the terms "vitalism" and "mechanism." We do not attempt to differentiate the various types of mechanism and vitalism, though these are several and constituently different in details, but rather we lump together those theories which, in a first approximation, fall into one or the other of the two major categories.[42] One essential and commonly accepted criterion is used as a basis for classification: acknowledgment or denial of an essential difference between living and nonliving matter, between the organic and inorganic. It is convenient and logically consistent to classify as mechanistic those theories which maintain that the phenomena of life are simply special cases of the phenomena of matter, so that the organism is merely a dynamic structure which is subject to physicochemical principles without the significant intervention of any force or action which is not appropriate data for the investigations of physics and chemistry. The vitalistic doctrines, be they concerned with entelechy or holism or *anima sensitiva*, all possess one common characteristic: they state or imply that living matter entails some unique, inherently different principle from that of inanimate matter, which principle affects some or all of the activities of the organism in such fashion that the living body is not subject to the exclusive operation of physicochemical forces. The organism is thus, in varying degrees, differentiated from

[41] J. H. Woodger, *Biological Principles* (London, 1929), pp. 88 and 107-108. *Cf.* also, John T. Merz, *A History of European Thought in the Nineteenth Century*, 3 vols. (Edinburgh and London, 1907), Vol. II, p. 377.

[42] Woodger, *op. cit.*, chap. v, provides a summary of various mechanistic and vitalistic views.

nonliving matter.[43]   Almost needless to add, in this discussion we are not
concerned with the "validity" of either of these general views; we aim
simply to trace their historical oscillations.

The cyclical movement of these theories has been noted by many
thinkers, but to our knowledge no systematic account of these fluctuations
has been offered.   Thus, J. A. Thomson remarks: "Over and over again
in the history of biology the doctrine of a special vital force has arisen,
held sway for a time, and then disappeared." [44]

And from Dampier-Whetham we learn :

As thought has moved on from age to age, mechanical and spiritual theories
of the Universe have alternated with each other in recurring pulsations. . . .[45]
In the history of biology, vitalism and mechanism have alternated with each
other for the last 300 years.[46]

We begin our inquiry at a far frontier of the history of science : classical
Greece.   In the first part of the sixth century B.C. appears a well-defined
movement which finds the outstanding Greek thinkers on the road to a
mild mechanistic conception of becoming.   Thales and Anaximander
present the first symptoms of a trend in this direction — a trend which
finds explicit and emphatic expression in the following century.   Matter,
living and nonliving, is reduced to a single principle which suffices to
govern both realms.[47]   Anaxagoras and Parmenides are concerned with
the unity of being, an idea mildly related to mechanism.   Empedocles
of Agrigentum evidences a tendency to reduce all physical and psychical
phenomena to universal natural processes of the same order; barriers
between the organic and inorganic are declared nonexistent.[48]   "One of
the foremost figures in the Age of Pericles," Diogenes of Apollonia, is also
responsible for a mechanistic interpretation of all phenomena.[49]   In the
thought of Leukippos and of his disciple Democritus, as well as of Hip-
pocrates, the considerable influence of mechanism in the fifth century is

[43] P. C. Mitchell, *Materialism and Vitalism in Biology* (Oxford, 1930), pp. 10 and 26;
H. Elliott, *Modern Science and Materialism* (London, 1919), p. 106; Lancelot Hogben,
The Nature of Living Matter (London, 1930), p. 57.

[44] *The Science of Life* (Chicago and New York, 1899), p. 86.

[45] Dampier-Whetham, *op. cit.*, p. 339.

[46] *Ibid.*, pp. 369–370.   See also Needham, *op. cit.*, pp. 111 ff.; Erik Nordenskiöld, *The
History of Biology*, trans. from Swedish by L. B. Eyre (New York, 1928), pp. 268–269.

[47] Robin, *op. cit.*, p. 41.   Also Theodor Gomperz, *Greek Thinkers*, 4 vols. (London, 1913),
Vol. I, pp. 208 ff.; W. T. Sedgwick and H. W. Tyler, *op. cit.*, p. 61.

[48] Gomperz, *op. cit.*, Vol. I, pp. 236–237; M. de Wulf, *History of Medieval Philosophy*
(London, 1909), p. 9.

[49] Gomperz, *op. cit.*, Vol. I, pp. 375 ff.

noticeable.[50]   General acceptance of this view, it is interesting to note, is coeval with the vague anticipation by Democritus of the notions of conservation of matter and of energy.[51]   As we shall see later, when the idea of the conservation of energy reappears in more precise form, in the nineteenth century, it is again coincident with a wave of mechanistic theory.

The temporary reaction comes with the spreading Socratic influence toward the end of the fifth century, and the vitalistic notions, "undergoing various modifications in the systems of Plato and Aristotle, dominate the succeeding century." [52]   Aristotle, specifically, may be considered as the "first exponent of a scientific 'vitalism,'" and according to one of the most prominent of modern protagonists of vitalism, "Aristotle's statements have been confirmed by recent researches." [53]   In any case, the historical importance of Aristotle in this, as in many other fields, can scarcely be exaggerated,[54] for not only is he "a typical forerunner of all vitalistic theories until the most recent times" [55] but from his authority stems in large measure the general acceptance of the vitalistic doctrine throughout the greater part of the medieval period.

A reaction to the Aristotelian vitalism and a reversion to the previous mechanism is quick to follow at the end of the fourth century.   From the very school of Aristotle himself emerged thinkers with strong mechanistic leanings, men like Dikaearchos and Aristoxenos.   Straton of Lampsacus, nominal peripatetic disciple though he was, found that a modified atomism, a well-defined mechanism, was the only hypothesis by which many puzzling phenomena could be explained.[56]   Epicureanism reared its powerful head in the third century and championed the revived cause of mechanism.   But this trend did not go unchallenged.   Zenon and the Stoics in general espoused a mild form of vitalism.   This influence, however, though great, was not equal to the Epicurean at this time, and the whole of the third and the second and the first century B.C. (Asclepiades, Lucretius, and others) was marked by a general recrudescence of mechanistic modes of thought.[57]

[50] *Ibid.*, Vol. I, pp. 355 ff.; Robin, *op. cit.*, pp. 118–120; Sarton, *op. cit.*, Vol. I, p. 88.

[51] Sarton, *op. cit.*, Vol. I, p. 89.

[52] Lange, *op. cit.*, Vol. I, p. 93.

[53] Hans Driesch, *Geschichte des Vitalismus* (Leipzig, 1922), pp. 8 ff.

[54] Sarton, *op. cit.*, Vol. I, pp. 128–129; Gomperz, *op. cit.*, Vol. IV, p. 111.

[55] Driesch, *op. cit.*, p. 9.

[56] Gomperz, *op. cit.*, Vol. IV, pp. 501 ff.; Sarton, *op. cit.*, Vol. I, p. 152; Nordenskiöld, *op. cit.*, p. 45.

[57] Robin, *op. cit.*, pp. 329–356; Lange, *op. cit.*, Vol. I, pp. 93–94.

At the beginning of our era a reaction set in against it. It still lingers, but is on a decline. In the second century A.D. vitalism is already dominant (Galen, Adrastus, Alexander Aphrodisiensis, and others).

From the third century A.D., for more than a thousand years, the historical continuity of the mechanistic doctrine appears to have been practically effaced. Some semblance of natural history there was during this period, but biology, sufficiently developed to require consideration of the mechanism-vitalism wrangle, was, to all intents and purposes, lacking.[58]

The first symptoms of a revival of mechanism seem to have appeared in the thirteenth and the fourteenth centuries, and then, in a well-defined form, the theory emerged in the first half of the sixteenth century (Girolamo Fracastoro — 1483-1553 — Giordano Bruno, and others).[59]

Modern vitalism, "by a notable irony of history," finds its birth in the first biochemist of the Renaissance. Paracelsus, in 1527, first promulgated his brand of vitalism (with its hypothetical *archaei*); a theory which had a deep influence at that time.[60] This notion, with the *Archaeus* as the "smith" who bears within himself the image of what he has produced and what he will produce, has a resemblance to the Aristotelian doctrine. This idea was adopted almost completely by Paracelsus's disciple, Jean-Baptiste van Helmont, who, as is well known, exercised a great influence on the scientific thought of his time.[61]

The seventeenth century was definitely dominated, as far as its scientific attitude was concerned, by the great advance made in the field of mechanics, which, as Driesch puts it, "exercised its influence on the totality of all thought connected in any way with nature . . . the whole theory of nature is under the influence of mechanics and is mechanistic; and mechanistic becomes also the theory of life." [62] The thought of this century in all departments of science was truly a "mechanistic mechanism." [63]

It is difficult to overestimate the influence wielded by Descartes in favor of mechanism. "No philosopher has ever exercised so great an influence on purely scientific studies as has Descartes." [64] Under his

---

[58] Mitchell, *op. cit.*, pp. 26 ff.; Charles Singer, *From Magic to Science* (London, 1928), pp. 7–8 ff.

[59] Nordenskiöld, *op. cit.*, pp. 86–87.

[60] *Ibid.*, pp. 133–137; Needham, *op. cit.*, pp. 108–109.

[61] Driesch, *op. cit.*, pp. 22–23; Needham, *op. cit.*, p. 110.

[62] Driesch, *op. cit.*, pp. 19–20; Dampier-Whetham, *op. cit.*, p. 339; P. Sorokin, *Contemporary Sociological Theories*, chap. 1.

[63] A. N. Whitehead, *Science and the Modern World* (New York, 1931), pp. 60 and 74.

[64] Needham, *op. cit.*, p. 111.

influence and yet independently from it, the mechanistic interpretation of life became quite dominant (Franciscus Sylvius, W. Harvey, Robert Boyle, Hobbes, Steno, C. Perrault, O. Rudbeck, T. Willis, G. Bathurst, H. Boerhaave, and others).[65] The notion of a specific vital energy seemed practically buried in this mechanism.[66]

But a reaction toward vitalism, though incapable of breaking its domination, was not long in coming. Opposition to the Cartesian physiological mechanism was marked in the works of Francis Glisson and Ralph Cudworth of Cambridge.[67] In his *Theoria Medica* (1708), Georg Ernst Stahl leveled his argumentative guns at the mechanistic physiology which his precedessors had almost universally accepted. His conception of the *anima sensitiva* gained many followers and his influence was especially felt in the school of Montpellier and throughout France in general.[68] For a time, vitalism was considered by many — but hardly by a majority — as the most plausible means of explaining natural phenomena.

In turn, this vitalistic flurry gave way to the alternative conception, around the middle of the eighteenth century (Fontenelle, De la Mettrie, Voltaire, D'Alembert, Diderot, and others).[69]

Toward the latter part of the eighteenth century, however, there is a noticeable change. At first it was not that the mechanists had become so much fewer in number as the fact that the vitalists girded up their loins and intensified their pretensions to a "valid view of nature." Caspar Friedrich Wolff entered a preliminary wedge in 1759, with his vitalistic prototype, the *vis essentialis*.[70] Indeed, if we turn to Driesch's estimate, Wolff was the "clearest and most profound representative of vitalism since Aristotle."[71] Buffon added his criticism of Cartesianism and found as disciples Maupertuis, president of the Academy of Berlin, and Tuberville Needham.[72] The school of Montpellier, under the leadership of Theophile de Bordeu, took up a radically vitalistic position which harks back to Stahl, and disputed the mechanism which rested on the authority of Boerhaave.[73] P. J. Barthez, of the same Montpellier group, found it necessary to assume a special "life principle" to account for the behavior

[65] Nordenskiöld, *op. cit.*, pp. 118 ff. and 151 ff.; Driesch, *op. cit.*, pp. 23–27.

[66] Lange, *op. cit.*, Vol. I, p. 243; Harold Höffding, *A Brief History of Modern Philosophy* (New York, 1912), p. 52.

[67] Needham, *op. cit.*, p. 112.

[68] Dampier-Whetham, *op. cit.*, p. 202; Driesch, *op. cit.*, pp. 27–33; Nordenskiöld, *op. cit.*, pp. 178–183; Garrison, *History of Medicine* (Philadelphia, 1929), p. 313.

[69] Needham, *op. cit.*, p. 113; Merz, *op. cit.*, Vol. I, p. 144; Nordenskiöld, pp. 203–209 and 238–243.

[70] Mitchell, *op. cit.*, pp. 26–27.   [71] Driesch, *op. cit.*, pp. 43 ff.   [72] *Ibid.*, pp. 35 ff.

[73] Garrison, *op. cit.*, pp. 363–364; Nordenskiöld, *op. cit.*, p. 345.

of organisms.[74]   Under the same influence, Xavier Bichat evidenced a reaction "against those clumsy mechanical theories of life which were then being propounded by Lamarck and others,"[75] and formulated a completely vitalistic theory.[76]   Needham and J. F. Blumenbach accounted for organic growth by a "creative urge," *Bildungstrieb, nisus formativus*.[77]   Louis Dumas and J. C. Reil were influential representatives of the same camp.[78]   In short, the banner of vitalism was being carried aloft by a considerable group of outstanding scientists of the time.

However, mechanism had not died by any means and was hardly weaker than vitalism.   Felix Vicq d'Azyr was actively criticizing the vitalism of the period, Lamarck was maintaining that life itself was nothing but motion, that it was a purely mechanical phenomenon,[79] and Charles Bonnet, "in spite of his religious fanaticism," was a follower of the mechanistic viewpoint.[80]   In the same tradition was Holbach's *Système de la nature*.   Furthermore, all of the experimental researches of this time were tending in a mechanistic direction — Réaumur's earlier studies of enzymes, the work of that "inquisitive ecclesiastic," Abbé Spallanzani, the researches of Priestley in England, De Saussure in Geneva, Ingenhousz in Holland, Senebier in France.[81]

As the nineteenth century opened, vitalism had a number of partisans among the scientists and philosophers, like Humboldt, Cuvier, De Blainville, A. de Candolle, L. Oken, G. Treviranus, J. Müller, and others.[82] For all of them the notion of a "life force" was deemed an indispensable assumption.[83]

But now a series of convincing experiments was beginning to cast some doubt on the firmly entrenched vitalism.   In 1812, Legallois's location of the respiratory center in the spinal medulla had sufficient theoretical repercussions to lead to an occasional questioning of Stahlian conceptions.[84]   If any arbitrary date be set for the perceptible beginning of the swing from vitalism to mechanism, however, 1828, the year of Wöhler's

[74] Nordenskiöld, *op. cit.*, p. 346.

[75] *Ibid.*, p. 351.

[76] Merz, *op. cit.*, Vol. II, pp. 382–383.

[77] Mitchell, *op. cit.*, p. 28; Driesch, *op. cit.*, pp. 55 ff.

[78] Thomson, *op. cit.*, p. 87; Driesch, *op. cit.*, pp. 94–96.

[79] Nordenskiöld, *op. cit.*, pp. 304 ff.

[80] *Ibid.*, p. 347; Driesch, *op. cit.*, p. 51.

[81] Elliott, *Modern Science and Materialism*, pp. 116–117; Merz, *op. cit.*, Vol. II, pp. 389 ff.; Needham, *op. cit.*, p. 114; Nordenskiöld, *op. cit.*, p. 330.

[82] Nordenskiöld, *op. cit.*, pp. 344, 361, and 436; Driesch, *op. cit.*, pp. 92–103 and 110–114; Garrison, *op. cit.*, p. 452.

[83] Nordenskiöld, *op. cit.*, p. 406.   [84] Needham, *op. cit.*, p. 116.

synthesis of urea from inorganic substances, may most advisedly be chosen.[85] Organic from inorganic ! Reluctantly arose the belief that the conception of a hyperphysical life force was a gratuitous and superfluous assumption. "The pale spectre of a vital force could no more be seen." [86]

Thus began the upswing of the circle of mechanism, J. J. Berzelius and F. Magendie, M. J. Schleiden, J. Schwann, J. R. Mayer, Helmholtz, K. Ludwig, E. du Bois-Reymond, and many others contributed to it.[87] And a veritable tidal wave it was.

But beneath the crest of this pronounced mechanistic movement there was still a subdued vitalism. At this time F. Tiedemann, M. F. Autenrieth, and K. F. Burdach were outstanding representatives of the "dogmatic school" of vitalists which so influenced Karl von Baer that he took too a similar stand.[88] Comte adopted Blainville's brand of vitalism — life is "*composition et decomposition.*" [89] Elias Fries, the famous Swedish botanist, would not apply the laws of inorganic matter to living matter.[90] Wöhler, the man whose synthesis of urea had probably done more than any other single experiment to re-enforce the mechanism of the period, was an avowed vitalist.[91] Justus von Liebig, also, apart from his materialistic view of fermentation and putrefaction, was an "uncompromising vitalist." [92] Yet, although some of the leading scientists, such as those mentioned above, took up a vitalistic stand, the prevailing temper of the period was thoroughly mechanistic, and these instances of vitalistic thought are outstanding simply because they were opposed to the dominant current of scientific opinion. From the middle of the century on, after a period of preliminary struggle and debate, for several decades mechanism was in firm possession of the field of biological theory, and two such confirmed vitalists as Driesch and J. S. Haldane agree that vitalism was generally repudiated during this period.[93]

But once again a reaction was in the offing. ". . . a mistrust of the oversimplified idea of the phenomena of life . . . in certain quarters caused a return to that vitalistic biology that exact physiology imagined

[85] K. C. Schneider, *Vitalismus* (Leipzig, 1903), p. 2. Also Needham, *op. cit.*, p. 113.

[86] Du Bois-Reymond, quoted by Merz, *op. cit.*, Vol. I, pp. 217–218.

[87] Nordenskiöld, *op. cit.*, pp. 372 ff., 395–396, and 408; Merz, *op. cit.*, Vol. II, p. 419; Benjamin Ginzburg, *The Adventure of Science* (New York, 1930), pp. 264–265.

[88] Driesch, *op. cit.*, pp. 103–109.

[89] Nordenskiöld, *op. cit.*, p. 444.

[90] *Ibid.*, pp. 439–440.

[91] Merz, *op. cit.*, Vol. II, p. 405.

[92] Garrison, *op. cit.*, p. 473; Driesch, *op. cit.*, pp. 114–117.

[93] Driesch, *op. cit.*, p. 137; J. S. Haldane, *Mechanism, Life and Personality* (New York, 1914), pp. 41–42; *The Philosophical Basis of Biology* (Dublin, 1931), p. 12.

it had disposed of for all time." [94]   Needham describes the beginning of the transition in this fashion.

Possibly because of the nature of thought itself, the mechanistic viewpoint was not to be allowed to suppress all other conceptions.   There had always, even in the crests of the movement, been a small minority of the older type of vitalists, and late in the nineteenth century they found leaders in the persons of Hans Driesch and J. S. Haldane. . . .[95]

In 1894, the celebrated botanist, Kerner von Marilaun, could speak once more of a vital force.   Virchow, after having assisted in expelling "palaeovitalism," turned about and himself posited the principle of a life force.[96] Driesch informs us that "already in 1895 I had become convinced . . . of the necessity of vitalism."[97]   In the final year of the century, O. Hertwig warned of the "extreme which sees in vital processes nothing but chemicophysical and mechanical problems, and thinks it finds the true science of nature only in so far as it is possible to reduce phenomena to the motions of attracting and repelling atoms, and to submit them to calculation." [98]   "And so we find, even before the turn of the century, vitalistic theories of life of various kinds being produced, supported by representatives of no small importance, as regards both their numbers and their attainments." [99]   A brief catalogue of the names of those who found themselves under the vitalistic banner may serve to indicate this perceptible change: E. Albrecht, J. Reinke, P. Cossmann, F. Noll, Pauly, Rignano, E. S. Russell, J. A. Thomson, E. Radl, G. Bunge, Auerbach, Bechterew, Bell, Dreyer, Fischel, Gemelli, Hartog, Herbst, Japp, Lodge, Mackenzie, Morgan, Moskowski, R. Neumeister, Schmitz-Dumont, Strecker, and others.[100]

The situation in regard to mechanistic and vitalistic conceptions in the present century appears to be one of armed conflict.   Both conceptions seem to be existing side by side and both seem to be flourishing.[101]   In the first two decades of the century, the radical mechanisticism of Jacques Loeb is countered by the extreme vitalism of Hans Driesch — the tropism meets the entelechy; on the one side is the vitalism of Von Üexkull, in

---

[94] Nordenskiöld, *op. cit.*, p. 414.

[95] Needham, *op. cit.*, pp. 116 and 180; Garrison, *op. cit.*, p. 562.

[96] Merz, *op. cit.*, Vol. II, pp. 376–377; Nordenskiöld, *op. cit.*, p. 403.

[97] Driesch, *op. cit.*, p. 174.

[98] Quoted by Merz, *op. cit.*, Vol. II, p. 402.

[99] Nordenskiöld, *op. cit.*, p. 607.

[100] See Driesch, *op. cit.*, pp. 175 ff.; Needham, *op. cit.*, pp. 19 ff.; Nordenskiöld, *op. cit.*, pp. 610 ff.

[101] Nordenskiöld, *op. cit.*, p. 603.

the modified Neo-Lamarckian school, on the other, the mechanistic theory of Max Verworn based on the hypothetical "biogen."

The above outline demonstrates that in its main movements the curve of vitalism goes with that of idealism and the truth of faith and partly that of reason, while the curve of mechanism goes with that of materialism, atomism, and the truth of senses. Indeed, we do not meet mechanism before the end of the sixth century B.C. It appears in the fifth century, but in the whole configuration of the mentality of the period is neither dominant nor exclusive. It is a part of the Mixed Idealistic mentality of the period. After the fourth century it grows, reaching its climax in the third, for Greek thought, in the first century B.C. for the Roman; that is, in the periods of domination of the Sensate cultures in these countries. After the first century A.D. it weakens and then disappears until the thirteenth century, when it emerges again and becomes a constituent element of the Mixed mentality in the field which corresponds to the Idealistic type of culture. After that century it begins to crystallize more and more and in the sixteenth century becomes powerful, in the seventeenth dominant. Then, with secondary and temporary setbacks, it steadily grows up to the end of the nineteenth century, parallel with the growth of the Sensate culture. In the twentieth century vitalism revives and mechanism comparatively weakens. Thus in these essential movements the ups and downs of these rivals run closely parallel with the main rising and receding tides of the types of the cultures and of the respective systems of truth to which each of them logically and — after the above — factually belongs. Scientific theory thus is but an opinion made "creditable" and "fashionable" by the type of the prevalent culture.

Revival of vitalism in our time may be a temporary reaction, like several reactions before. But it may also be a symptom of the beginning of the decline of the Sensate mentality. Whichever of these possibilities is true it is to be said that we find again a "revolt" here, similar to the "revolts" against overripe Sensate culture at the end of the nineteenth and in the twentieth century in other compartments of culture. For this reason, it deserves to be noted.

III. FLUCTUATIONS IN THE THEORY OF ABIOGENESIS

As an example of a theory whose fluctuations cannot be expected logically to be connected with our main variables, the theory of abiogenesis is taken.

The notion of spontaneous generation (abiogenesis or *generatio aequivoca*), which conceives of life arising *sponte sua*, is a long-lived idea which has, however, suffered periods of rejection as well as of acceptance. It may be said summarily at the outset that virtually all of the thinkers of antiquity and the Middle Ages were firmly convinced of the validity of this conception.[102]   Not until the seventeenth century, most notably at first with Redi, was there any concerted serious questioning of the belief.   But ". . . the theories of the origin of life, from the time of the Italian Redi down to Pasteur, show how experiment and theory alternately supported and contradicted the doctrine that living matter could be formed out of not-living matter. . . ." [103]

In ancient Greece, Anaximander was "the first teacher of the doctrine of Abiogenesis"; [104] Anaximenes followed him implicity.[105]

Xenophanes, in a somewhat more guarded manner, held that the *ultimate* origin of life was spontaneously generated.[106]   But even in ancient times a critic of the doctrine was not wholly wanting, for it was the position of Pythagoras that ". . . animals are born from one another by seeds, and . . . it is impossible for there to be any spontaneous production by the earth." [107]   This criticism, however, did not succeed in exorcising the notion of abiogenesis, for Diogenes of Apollonia and Empedocles received it with favor.[108]   And it was as a participant in the prevalent mode of "scientific" thought that Aristotle spoke of the spontaneous origin of eels.[109]   As always in matters of scientific interest, Aristotle's opinions were important in influencing later ancient and medieval thought.

On throughout the Middle Ages, spontaneous generation was accepted as a fact, though the figure of Albertus Magnus stands forth prominently in the thirteenth century as one who dared to challenge the fast-held belief and refuted it explicitly (though not by experiment, of course).[110]

---

[102] J. A. Thomson, *The Science of Life* (Chicago and New York, 1899), p. 94; Henry Fairfield Osborn, *From the Greeks to Darwin* (New York, 1894), p. 23.

[103] Merz, *op. cit.*, Vol. II, p. 451.

[104] Osborn, *op. cit.*, p. 35.

[105] E. T. Brewster, *Creation: A History of Non-Evolutionary Theories* (Indianapolis, 1927), p. 70.

[106] Leon Robin, *op. cit.*, pp. 83–84.   *Cf.* the theoretical position of E. H. Haeckel and his followers.

[107] Quoted from Diogenes Laertius's summary of Pythagorean views by Henry S. Williams, *A History of Science*, 5 vols. (New York and London, 1904), Vol. I, p. 123.

[108] Osborn, *op. cit.*, p. 37.

[109] Sedgwick and Tyler, *op. cit.*, p. 382; L. L. Woodruff, "Biology" in *The Development of the Sciences* (Yale University Press, 1923), p. 250; Theodor Gomperz, *op. cit.*, Vol. IV, p. 476; Osborn, *op. cit.*, p. 60; Charles Singer, *op. cit.* (London, 1928), pp. 8–9; Thorndike, *A History of Magic and Experimental Science*, 2 vols. (New York, 1923), Vol. I, p. 543.

[110] Thorndike, *op. cit.* Vol. II, p. 543.

Passing over several centuries in which the restoration of the hardly faltering doctrine was complete, we come to the justly famed experiments of Francesco Redi in 1668. In refuting the Aristotelian conception, he proved that no grubs or maggots appeared in rotting meat when it was protected by a fine gauze from the eggs laid in it by insects.[111] "The good work begun by Redi was confirmed and extended by Swammerdam (1637–1681) and Vallisnieri (1661–1730) until the notion of the spontaneous generation of any form of life visible to the unaided eye was banished from the minds of scientific men." [112] The biologists of the later part of the seventeenth century definitely rejected the ancient spontaneous generation hypothesis, and "during the greater part of the eighteenth century" this kind of propagation was "held in discredit." [113]

About the middle of the eighteenth century, the doctrine of abiogenesis briefly returned to favor. Georges de Buffon accepted the doctrine with little hesitation.[114] So did Otto F. Müller, De la Mettrie, T. Needham, and others.[115] But this reaction toward ancient views soon fell into abeyance with the more carefully conducted experiments of the Abbé Spallanzani, in 1775 — experiments which were anticipations of modern sterilization and bacteriology.[116] These experiments "were regarded as conclusive in refuting the contention of Needham, Buffon, and others. . . ." [117] They "were generally regarded by the naturalists of that period as answering in the negative the question of the spontaneous generation of life." [118]

But again the pendulum swings back; and in the last decade or so of the eighteenth century and more emphatically in the first part of the following century, serious objections were raised against the decisiveness of Spallanzani's experiments, when it was clearly realized what an important part oxygen plays in the maintenance of life. K. E. von Baer, writing in 1864, states that between 1810 and 1830 there were probably few naturalists who "did not consider the generation without parents of inferior organisms as proved, or at least as highly probable" and he himself would not at that time (1828) "declare it to be non-existent." [119]

[111] Dampier-Whetham, *op. cit.*, p. 201; E. Friedell, *Cultural History of the Modern Age* (New York, 1932), Vol. III, p. 191; Brewster, *op. cit.*, pp. 102–103.

[112] W. A. Locy, *Biology and Its Makers*, 3d rev. ed. (New York, 1926), p. 279.

[113] Nordenskiöld, *op. cit.*, pp. 225–226 and 430–431.

[114] Nordenskiöld, *op. cit.*, pp. 245 and 427.

[115] Locy, *op. cit.*, pp. 281–282; Thomson, *op. cit.*, p. 96.

[116] Dampier-Whetham, *op. cit.*, p. 202.

[117] W. A. Locy, *The Growth of Biology* (New York, 1925), p. 445.

[118] Locy, *Biology and Its Makers*, p. 284.

[119] Quoted by Merz, *op. cit.*, Vol. II, p. 451.

The idea of spontaneous generation was supported by the knowledge of that time concerning fermentation,[120] and it was against a firmly rooted doctrine that a renewed assault began in the 1830's.   C. G. Ehrenberg and De Latour repeated their objections to the notion of abiogenesis,[121] and in 1836, Schulze and Schwann conducted a series of experiments intended to test the prevalent thesis.   In addition to boiling the infusions under examination, they admitted air which had first been passed through a red-hot tube; no animal life was found.[122]   Helmholtz, and later Schroeder and Dusch, elaborated these experiments with similar results.[123] But the leading chemists of that day — Berzelius, Wöhler, Liebig — still regarded Schwann's theories as chimeras.[124]   It was reserved for Pasteur, as victor in the famous controversy with Pouchet, to provide the decisive stroke.   The brilliant experiments of Pasteur were decisive in banishing the lingering doctrine of abiogenesis.[125]   And such seems to have been the prevailing attitude since Pasteur's epochal investigations.   True, there have been occasional protesting opinions, but they are in a minority. Perhaps an adequate statement of the general biological opinion toward the close of the last century and the opening of this is expressed in Locy's account of the history of biology, as first written in 1908 (though he did not find it necessary to make any change in the revised edition of 1926):

These experiments [of Pasteur, *et al.*] showed that under the conditions of the experiments no spontaneous generation of life takes place.   But while we must regard the hypothesis of spontaneous generation as thus having been disproved on an experimental basis, it is still adhered to from the theoretical standpoint by many naturalists; and there are also many who think that life arises spontaneously at the present time in ultra-microscopic particles.   Weismann's hypothetical "biophors," too minute for microscopic observation, are supposed to arise by spontaneous generation.   This phase of the question, however, not being amenable to scientific tests, is theoretical, and therefore, so far as the evidence goes, we may safely say that the spontaneous origin of life under present conditions is unknown.[126]

Thus, in spite of occasional yearnings for the doctrine of abiogenesis, we are justified in treating the period from Pasteur to the present as one of general rejection of the hypothesis.   It will be interesting to note whether this theory, which at present seems so definitely discarded, will arise again from its ashes, as it has so often done in the past.

---

[120] Nordenskiöld, *op. cit.*, p. 431.
[121] *Ibid.*, p. 428.
[122] Thomson, *op. cit.*, p. 97.
[123] Locy, *Biology and Its Makers*, p. 286.
[124] Nordenskiöld, *op. cit.*, pp. 431–435.
[125] Locy, *Biology and Its Makers*, pp. 290–292.
[126] *Ibid.*, pp. 292–293.

The very nature of this theory is such that logically it can be associated with any of the three systems of truth and, on the other side, it is not associated definitely with any of them. Indeed, nonacceptance of abiogenesis can mean admission of a miracle, which can fit well the Ideational system of truth. Acceptance of abiogenesis can also mean a miracle performed regularly by the mysterious supersensory forces. And the same is to be said of the relationship of abiogenesis to other systems of truth. Therefore it is perhaps to be expected that the fluctuations of the respective theories in the field should not necessarily show a definite association with the fluctuations of systems of truth and their respective cultures. In that case, the above sketch indicates that in this field also the respective theories have fluctuated and in all probability will continue to do so. We have here an example of the oscillations of the theories independently from the waves of the systems of truth and their cultures.

It is, however, to be added that at least in the history of the mentality of the Western culture, the Middle Ages were predominantly abiogenetic, while the last few centuries have been predominantly biogenetic. In so far as biogeneticism denies the possibility of spontaneous creation of life where it does not exist, it reflects perhaps the mechanistic mentality that without external force a body at rest cannot spontaneously generate motion, or vice versa. In this sense, the biogenetic theory is perhaps nearer to the mechanistic-empirical and Sensate mentality than the abiogenetic theory. If this be so, then the popularity of the biogenesis idea for the last few centuries may be interpreted as a reflection of the growing Sensate culture mentality. Considering that the biogenetic theory does not solve logically the problem of the origin of life (if it cannot be generated spontaneously), how and where did life originate? Was it pre-existent primordially? Was it created by some miracle? And so on, and considering that the main and perhaps the only argument in favor of biogenesis is experimental — that it is sensory par excellence — such an interpretation is possibly not wholly devoid of basis. If this be so, then the rise and decline of the acceptability of even these theories is also, to some extent, connected with the tides in the field of the systems of truth and their respective cultures.

IV. Oscillations of the Theories Concerning the Nature of Light

A further example is given by the theory of light. It can serve our purpose as a case where theories seemingly quite unrelated to our variables

are, in fact, connected with them.[127]   In this study, our primary interest
is in the historical oscillations of the two theories of light which have
finally found a place in modern thought, the *emission, corpuscular, or
emanation theory and the undulatory, vibratory, or wave theory;* but a survey
of ancient and medieval doctrines as to the nature of light must include a
third, the *visual-ray hypothesis.*[128]

Optical theory may be said to begin, for our purposes, in the sixth
century B.C., with Pythagoras and his school.[129]   Authorities differ as to
the exact theory held by this group.   In any event, it is generally agreed
that the later Pythagorean, Archytas of Tarentum, certainly adopted
the visual-ray hypothesis in the fourth century.   In the fifth century, the
wide influence of Empedocles, who maintained this theory, assured its
general acceptance.   However, toward the close of the century it was
temporarily subordinated to a corpuscular doctrine which, being promulgated in clear-cut fashion by Leukippos and Democritus, was generally
accepted by followers of the Atomistic school.[130]   The return of the visual-
ray notion was evidenced in the first part of the fourth century, in the
powerful influence of Plato and his school and the Pythagorean Archytas.[131]

Both of the preceding theories were criticized and discarded by Aristotle.   Light, for Aristotle, was an impulse propagated through a continuous medium which he called the "pellucid" or "diaphanes" (which
corresponds to the modern "luminiferous ether").[132]   Thus, before the
fourth century had run its course, three leading theories of light had been
advanced, two of which were destined to have an important role in the
optical thought of the last three hundred years.

At the outset of the third century, Euclid took up the visual-ray theory
and returned it to its former position of supremacy.[133]   But proponents

---

[127] For lack of space, I give only a summary of a much more detailed history of these
theories, competently prepared by Dr. Robert K. Merton.

[128] See Arthur E. Haas, *"Antike Lichttheorien,"* in *Archiv für Geschichte der Philosophie,*
N. F. 13 (1907), p. 354; August Heller, *Geschichte der Physik,* 2 vols. (Stuttgart, 1882–1884);
C. G. Vernon, *Light* (Cambridge, 1929); Thomas Preston, *The Theory of Light* (London,
1928); H. Buckley, *A Short History of Physics* (New York, 1928).

[129] Robin, *op. cit.,* p. 106; Sarton, *op. cit.,* Vol. I, p. 87.

[130] Ferdinand Rosenberger, *Die Geschichte der Physik,* 3 vols. (1882–1890), Vol. I, p. 13;
Otto Wiener, *"Entwicklung der Wellenlehre des Lichtes,"* in *Physik,* ed. by E. Warburg;
Die Kultur der Gegenwart (Leipzig and Berlin, 1915), p. 518.

[131] Wiener, *op. cit.,* p. 518; Buckley, *op. cit.,* p. 61.

[132] Emil Wilde, *Ueber die Optik der Griechen* (Berlin, 1832), p. 6.   See also D. N. Mallik,
Optical Theories (Cambridge, 1917), p. 4; Wiener, *op. cit.,* p. 518; Rosenberger, *op. cit.,*
Vol. I, p. 20; Dampier-Whetham, *op. cit.,* p. 161; Haas, *op. cit.,* p. 378.

[133] Wilde, *op. cit.,* p. 9; W. Whewell, *History of the Inductive Sciences,* 2 vols. (New York,
1874), Vol. I, p. 101; Rosenberger, *op. cit.,* Vol. I, pp. 30–31.

of the other two viewpoints were not wanting. Epicurus adopted the atomistic view that from the surfaces of all bodies in constant flow are detached particles which are impressed upon the eye.[134] Straton of Lampsacus, "the Physicist," was not inclined to make light immaterial but rather tended to the Epicurean corpuscular theory.[135] Thus, the third century found all three theories juxtaposed.

From this time on, there is a noticeable diminution of philosophical and quasi-scientific thought on the nature of light; though some few continued to support one or another of the outstanding theories.

There was not the slightest semblance of a unified theory of light in early Christian philosophy. In the third century Tertullian turned to the extra-mission (visual-ray) theory. Lactantius, and later St. Augustine, held a conception in which the Soul viewed the outer world through the eyes as through a window. This view was probably typical of the dominant mentality of the Middle Ages.[136] The Neo-Platonists — Plotinus, Porphyry, Prescianus — have a notion wherein light is conceived as a psychical interaction of the will and the outer world.

Thus the predominant theory of the nature of light in "antiquity," up to the beginning of the Middle Ages, was that of visual rays — light is believed to emanate from the eyes. Slight fluctuations in the dominance of this doctrine are afforded by the temporary intrusions of the other two theories. The emission hypothesis had a brief period of passing triumph with the flowering of the atomistic school in the latter part of the fifth century. And later, in the fourth century, with Aristotle and some of his immediate disciples, the wave theory found a measure of support. The third century found all three conceptions with some followers, but in this juxtaposition of rival theories the visual-ray notion was possibly predominant. Occasional flickerings of the wave and emission theories for many centuries afterwards are repeatedly repressed by the visual-ray theory which, through the medium of Ptolemy's *Almagest*, was accepted on and off far into the Middle Ages.[137]

Throughout the medieval era there are only casual expressions of physical theories of light, and mainly by the Arabian scholars. In Europe, up to the thirteenth century, the Platonic visual-ray theory, and especially the Augustinian theory of sight as window of the Soul, remained dominant. Beginning with the thirteenth century, the corpus-

[134] Haas, *op. cit.*, p. 364.
[135] Theodor Gomperz, *op. cit.*, Vol. IV, pp. 501 ff.
[136] Haas, *op. cit.*, pp. 384–385.
[137] Wiener, *op. cit.*, p. 518.

cular theory began to revive (Albertus Magnus, Witelo, and Giles of Rome).[138] The subsequent course of the theories can be summed up as follows. Casual flickerings of wave conceptions appear possibly with Roger Bacon and Leonardo da Vinci. In the later sixteenth and first part of the seventeenth century, the emission theory is in the ascendancy. From the middle of the seventeenth century for about four decades, the wave theory finds a number of protagonists, but as the movement reaches fruition in the brilliant conceptions of Huygens, the prestige of Newton, which is invoked in the service of the emission hypothesis, turns scientific thought from the undulatory theory for more than a century. Thus, the eighteenth century is completely dominated by the corpuscular hypothesis, which, despite the work of Young from 1801 on, is not subdued until the second and third decades of the nineteenth century. Then follows the control of the wave theory till the early part of the present century, when the corpuscular (*quantum*) theory arises. The contemporary situation is the anomalous one in which both — apparently opposed — views of light exist side by side, each doctrine being used to explain different light phenomena. Both theories are necessary to get a full description of light phenomena.[139] Physicists find it advisable to view light on some occasions as *quanta*, on others as waves. As Sir William Bragg waggishly puts it :

For the present we have to work on both theories. On Mondays, Wednesdays and Fridays we use the wave theory; on Tuesdays, Thursdays and Saturdays we think in streams of flying energy *quanta* or corpuscles.[140]

(And after such strenuous alternation, with Sunday, probably, a well-merited day of rest.) At any rate, if we are to describe contemporary scientific opinion in terms of our cyclical conception of scientific theories, we must say that neither theory — the corpuscular nor the wave — is predominant, but that both are equally in vogue.

However remote the theory of light may appear from the system of truth, idealism and materialism, determinism and indeterminism, and generally from the types of culture studied, we can see that in fact even such a specific theory is connected with these "variables" and their fluctuations. We notice that before the second half of the sixth century B.C. there was

[138] Lynn Thorndike, *op. cit.*, Vol. II, pp. 33, 440, 456, and 527 ; Sarton, *op. cit.*, Vol. II, p. 926.

[139] Max Planck, *The Universe in the Light of Modern Physics* (New York, 1931), p. 45 ; B. Ginzburg, *The Adventure of Science* (New York, 1930), pp. 443–444 ; Whitehead, *Science and the Modern World*, pp. 69–70.

[140] *Electrons and Ether Waves* (Oxford, 1921), p. 11.

neither corpuscular nor undulatory, nor even the visual-ray theory, just as none of these concepts in any definite forms were present throughout the Middle Ages from the sixth to the twelfth century. This means that the character of cultures during these periods — and we have mentioned that it was predominantly Ideational — made the very problem of the nature of light unimportant and therefore prevented a concentration of attention on it; it was considered along the line of the Ideational, St. Augustine's, or similar Neo-Platonic opinion, viewing the eyes and sight as windows of the soul, or the like.

The survey shows further that in the fifth and fourth centuries B.C., as well as in the thirteenth and the fourteenth A.D., the problem attracted attention and began to be studied and that in these — Idealistic — centuries we find a mixture and balance of the visual-ray theory, of the undulatory, and of the corpuscular, with the domination of the first two. These facts again are in a harmony with the supposed — Idealistic — character of the culture of the period and the Mixed system of truth.

Third, we see further that, in spite of temporary reactions, the period from the sixteenth to the twentieth centuries represented a decline of the somewhat more Ideational visual-ray theory and the ascendance of the undulatory and — especially — of the corpuscular theories, which by their very nature are more Sensate than even the visual-ray theory. Similar ascendance (though not to the same degree) is noted in the Graeco-Roman mentality after the fourth century B.C. and in Rome in the first century B.C. (closely associated with the ascendance of materialism and atomism). These periods have shown themselves as those of a comparative ascendance of the Sensate culture, with empiricism as their system of truth.

Thus, in the main movements, the rise and decline of the respective theories in this field show unexpected association with the main movements in the systems of truth and in the rise and decline of the main types of culture. In other words, even in this supposedly purely scientific problem, the theories in their ups and downs seemingly happen to be also conditioned by the nature of the dominant type of culture and its system of truth.

Finally let us emphasize again the change noticed in the theories in the twentieth century. In this respect we see again that, as in the preceding problems, the twentieth century gives a reaction against what was dominant in the nineteenth. We are once more confronted with a "revolt" met many times in other compartments of culture.

V. FLUCTUATIONS OF COSMOGONIC THEORIES

Like other scientific and philosophic theories, cosmogonic theories about the structure and the properties of the universe have also been fluctuating in the course of time. In these fluctuations, various and often opposite theories have been appearing, rising, receiving prestige as the last word in science, and then declining and giving place to other — often contradictory — theories, which, in their turn, have undergone the same course. Such have been the alternations of the geocentric, heliocentric, and other more complex concepts of the universe. In the history of the Graeco-Roman and the Western cultures, the "story" opens before the sixth century with the idea that the earth is a flat circular disk (Homer, Hesiod, Xenophanes), or is shaped like a nonspherical cylinder (Thales), being the center of the world.[141]

Then comes Pythagoras (between 570 and 470 B.C.) and his school, with the theory that the earth is spheric and immobile, in the center of the world, with the stars and the firmament rotating around it.[142]

But his disciple, Philolaos (the end of the fifth century B.C.), submits a different theory, which received a large acceptance and became dominant: namely, that in the center of the world is not the earth, but an immobile sphere of central fire, the locus of Jupiter's seat, and there is another sphere of supreme fire which surrounds the world. The earth is only one of the stars which, together with the other stars and the sky, revolves around the center of the world, thus producing day and night. This astronomy of Philolaos remained for a long time in favor with the school which followed Pythagorean traditions.[143] Thus the center of the world and the whole system of the universe was regarded as changed, in accordance with this theory.

However, in the fourth century B.C. there was a swing back to the idea of a world system similar in several respects to that of Pythagoras, with the earth as the center of the world, and with other characteristics taken partly from Pythagoras, partly from Philolaos. Such were the theories of Hicetas and Ecphantos of Syracuse, with a further modification accepted by Plato and by Aristotle. In other words, we have a new swing toward a geocentric system. At the time of Aristotle, "this transformation of Philolaos's system was already accomplished

---

[141] Sir Thomas Heath, *Aristarchus of Samos: the Ancient Copernicus* (Oxford, 1913), pp. 7–9, 19, and 58; P. Tannery, *La science Hellène* (Paris, 1930), p. 73; J. Sageret, *Le système du monde* (Paris, 1931), p. 16.

[142] P. Duhem, *Le système du monde*, Vol. I, pp. 8–10.

[143] *Ibid.*, pp. 12–21.

and the followers of Philolaos were considered as the backward persons." [144]

After Aristotle the geocentric system prevails generally, though becoming modified and varied in the hands of Theophrastus, Straton, Eudoxes of Gnidos, and others. But the heliocentric system was not quite dead, and had, partly through Heraclides of Pontos and especially through Aristarchus of Samos (c. 280 B.C.) a temporary revival, though it hardly became dominant. Aristarchus had several followers, the most prominent of whom was Seleucos the Babylonian (about the middle of the second century B.C.), but the shift to the geocentric system was all-powerful and

after Seleucos we do not find any person during the Graeco-Roman antiquity who held the heliocentric theory; it seems to have fallen into a profound oblivion from which, before Copernicus, nobody tried to extract it. [145]

Instead of the heliocentric system arose a system of eccentrics and epicycles, as a modification of the geocentric system. Hipparchus of Nicaea (c. 128 B.C.) and especially Claudius Ptolemy (c. A.D. 142) were particularly responsible for it. The Ptolemaic system dominated throughout the Middle Ages up to the appearance of Copernicus's helio-centric system. [146] During the Middle Ages there was revived also the theory of the flatness of the earth, though it hardly became dominant.

With the Copernican theory there began a new domination of the heliocentric system which has continued up to the present time. At the moment this theory is already greatly modified, even so far as the solar system is concerned, not to mention the new theories concerning the "mysterious universe" around us. At the same time the geocentric and the heliocentric standpoints are so interpreted that both of them, in a sense, with their respective points of reference, are correct. [147]

Thus we see oscillations in this field and a slight tendency toward a domination of the heliocentric system of the universe in the periods of

[144] *Ibid.*, Vol. I, pp. 22–26 and 219.

[145] *Ibid.*, Vol. I, p. 424.

[146] *Ibid.*, Vol. I, pp. 468 ff. For the Middle Ages, see the remaining four volumes of Duhem's work.

[147] "Nor is it quite proper, according to modern notions, to state that the heliocentric theory is 'correct' and the geocentric theory is 'wrong.' They are both correct, but represent different viewpoints. One refers motions in the solar system to the sun as a point of reference (origin of co-ordinates); the other refers these motions to the earth as a point of reference. The superiority of the first procedure over the second is that we find it more 'convenient' in describing the dynamics of the solar system." Cajori, *op. cit.*, p. 33. For a variety and multitude of the contemporary cosmogonic theories see Eddington's, Jeans's, Bragge's, De Sitter's, theories and works quoted.

domination of the Sensate culture and the empirical system of truth, and toward a preponderance of the geocentric system in the periods of domination of the Ideational culture. However, it would be incorrect to claim this association to be real. It does not follow logically from the concepts of the main cultures; and it is, in distinction from the atomism and other variables studied, not definitely supported by the data.

In a similar manner it is easy to show that in regard to many other aspects of the universe somewhat similar oscillations — but not necessarily connected with any certain type of culture and system of truth — have also been occurring. Whether we take such an aspect as the *finity or infinity* of the universe, or the *emptiness or nonemptiness of its space*, or its nature and dimensions, or its finite and infinite existence in time (together with the conception of time and space, see Chapter Eleven), we see somewhat similar "cycles" or oscillations of the theories. Each new "return" to domination of a certain theory has not been an exact repetition; each time it has appeared in a modified form; but not so much modified as not to show its central similarity with its predecessors, in the preceding occurrences.

Only the formal laws of logic and of its derivative — mathematics — have remained perhaps unchanged for the period studied. So far as "interpretation" of empirical reality is concerned, the ups and downs of such theories seem to have been a universal uniformity, with few, if any, exceptions. The old and oft-repeated statement that in the field of the empirical or sensory reality with which scientific theories deal primarily, nothing remains everlasting and unchangeable — the contentions of almost all the Hindu, the Chinese, the Greek, and other thinkers — seems to be justified.

Shall we, therefore, wonder that within the memory of present generations, dozens and dozens of theories in various fields of the natural sciences have risen, had a success, and then faded, being replaced by others? So it happened with many of the Darwinian principles and hypotheses; with the linear evolution and progress; with the enormous number of cosmogonic theories manufactured on a large scale up to the present time; with the unlimited faith in the all-important role of heredity or environment; with Mendelian laws in application to human heredity; with the belief in the adequacy of mental tests as indicating the original intelligence of man; with "behaviorism"; with the faith in the statistical formulas of correlations, especially partial and multiple; with the law of entropy; with the theories concerning the origin of life (not merely its transference through meteorites and the like to the earth from somewhere else) ; with the various systems of geometry ; even with the theory of relativity. Each of these hypotheses, taken at random, has experienced within the last fifty years many ups and downs in its "credibility" and scientific prestige. If some of them are still vigorous, the reason is probably that there has not been time enough to show their oscillations in prestige and credibility. Sufficient time given, one can predict they will follow the path of fluctuation.

In regard to some of these oscillations, one can note a tangible connection with those in the systems of truth and in the dominant types of culture; in other cases such a connection is intangible, and oscillations seem to have occurred independently of the waves in our main variables.[148]

VI. Some General Remarks on the Long- and Short-time Fluctuations of Prestige of the Natural-science Theories

The above examples, taken from the domain of the natural sciences, show that the scientific theories, like those in philosophy, and in other fields of thought have indeed fluctuated. They show also that the upward and downward movement of rival theories of a relatively broader character have been tangibly connected with the respective oscillations of the main systems of truth, and of the types of culture corresponding to each of them.

There is hardly any doubt that, as far as mere oscillation is concerned, there probably has been no scientific theory which has not undergone it, and, like a fashion, now has been heralded as the last word of science and now has fallen into disrepute. At least, for me it is exceedingly difficult, indeed practically impossible, to indicate any single comparatively broad theory in the whole field of natural sciences which has been free from such a vicissitude. I do not know of any single general theory which after being formulated has remained an unchanged truth in subsequent time, if that time has been sufficiently long. Some of the theories need a span of several centuries before being recognized as "the last word of science," or being discredited as erroneous and inadequate. Others require a much shorter time to undergo the cycle, and most of the theories

---

[148] As we have seen and shall see, in each compartment of culture there is a limited autonomy of functions and changes from those in the other compartments; and within each compartment many a secondary change occurs without any tangible connection with either the changes in the whole type of culture, or in any of its other compartments. Just as in an organism, in spite of its unity, many a secondary process can go on, in its various systems of organs, without any tangible connection with, or effect upon, the life and functions in other systems of organs in the same complex organism. One can cut his hair or shave his beard without any tangible effect upon the circulation of blood, or breathing, or any other bodily function.

just mentioned are examples of this type. A special illustration of these
is given further by Prout's hypothesis, and an outline of the course of this
and two other hypotheses is perhaps advisable.

VII. Fluctuation of the Influence of Prout's Theory

Here too the preliminary admission must be made that the conception
discussed — Prout's hypothesis — has not recurred in completely unchanged form, but none the less we shall see that the essence of this
hypothesis has been substantially revived from time to time, despite great
variation in its details.

We need not remark the resemblance of Prout's theory to that of the
Greeks, of Thales and Anaximenes in particular, as did Mabilleau,[149]
but we will begin with the conception as it first appeared anonymously
in 1815. In short, Prout held that since each element had a definite
combining number, all these numbers must be the multiple of the lowest
among them, the equivalent of atomic weight of hydrogen. Thomas
Thomson took the theory to his bosom and his energetic activities in its
behalf from 1819 to 1825 led to its attaining widespread credence. But
this acceptance of the doctrine was quite temporary, and the idea of an
Urstoff, of a "mother stuff," was apparently disproved by Turner in
England and by Berzelius in Germany, with the result that about 1830
the theory sank quietly into almost complete oblivion.

The trough of the cycle, however, was of short duration, and in 1840,
Dumas, with the assistance of his disciples, Laurent and Gerhardt, brought
the general conception back into favor. Stas accepted this then-prevail-
ing theory, but he reflected the general change of attitude when in 1860 he
turned against it and produced "accurate measurements" to prove its
falsity. But by the turn of the decade, this phase in the cycle was virtually brought to an end with the work of Lothar Meyer, and Mendeleef,
who successfully demonstrated a connection between the atomic weights
of the elements and their physical properties, although the latter refused
to recognize any tie between the periodic law and the idea of a unique
matter.[150] This work, however, paved the way for the revival of Prout's
hypothesis, and in 1886 Crookes originated the term *protyle* to refer to
the "prime element"; while in 1889, Ashe combined the term *dimidium*
for Prout's element with "half the combining weight of hydrogen."[151]

[149] Mabilleau, *op. cit.*, pp. 64 ff.
[150] Dampier-Whetham, *op. cit.*, p. 230.
[151] Gregory, *op. cit.*, p. 144; Merz, *op. cit.*, Vol. I, pp. 402–403.

The favorable attitude toward the theory was indicated by J. J. Thompson's acceptance of the general conception in 1897.[152]

In the first part of the current century there was little concern about this hypothesis, but the protons and electrons of today are almost the homologues of Prout's hydrogen conception and of Crookes's *protyle*.[153] Aston's work on isotopes in 1922 helped to clear up the slight discrepancy in Prout's hypothesis, and it may fairly be said that it now stands generally accepted.[154]

This sketchy outline of the history of Prout's hypothesis has revealed, first, that certain scientific theories are subject to short-time fluctuations of acceptance and rejection, and second, that the oscillation phases are not of equal duration.

Putting aside many purely sensational "soap-bubble" theories which continually come into the field of science, quickly gain credibility, and as quickly explode, many more serious theories in the field of natural science have a course similar to that of Prout's theory.

VIII. Fluctuation of Theories in the Social Sciences and Humanities

If the "First Principles," "categories of human thought," and the natural-science theories rise and decline in their acceptability, this is equally true of all the theories concerning man, culture, and social phenomena that compose the social sciences — including history, psychology, and anthropology — and the humanities, including philosophy, ethics, and law. The content, the subject matter, the internal structure, the methodology of these sciences are conditioned by the type of the dominant culture probably even more than are those of the natural sciences. Therefore, they fluctuate in all their essential traits possibly even more than do those theories dealing with inanimate and organic phenomena. As a matter of fact, the long-time, and especially the short-time, transformation of these theories is almost spectacular. Their whole "style" or "physiognomy" changes notably even within a few decades. Still more pronounced are their long-time transformations.

We have already seen the latter. The fluctuations of the First Principles studied are but the first corroboration of that. It must be evident that the social sciences and humanities of the predominantly

[152] Cajori, *op. cit.*, pp. 358–359.

[153] Gregory, *op. cit.*, p. 145; E. N. daC. Andrade, *The Structure of the Atom* (New York, 1924), p. 2; K. C. Compton, "The Electron," quoted, pp. 29 ff.

[154] Dampier-Whetham, *op. cit.*, p. 391; Gregory, *op. cit.*, pp. 213 ff.

Ideational or Idealistic period have to be and are, in fact, fundamentally different from those of the predominantly materialistic mentality. In the periods when rationalistic mentality is dominant, the social sciences and humanities are profoundly different from the aspect they present in the periods when empiricism is dominant. This point has been illustrated at some length by a study of the movements and relationship of general nominalism and realism and of sociological universalism and singularism and the conceptions of the juridical personality. We have seen that during the domination of ontological realism, the sociological and social theories acquire a universalistic character profoundly different from the singularistic character which they acquire in the periods of dominant nominalism. Even the current definition of what is "society" is entirely different in these two periods.

The same has been shown in regard to the theories of juridical personality and the linear and cyclical conceptions of sociocultural and historical processes. Likewise it has been shown that during the domination of materialism and Sensate mentality, the social sciences and humanities also become materialistic in their choice of subjects studied, in their content, and in their method. Man, the sociocultural world, and the world of values become in such times mainly "materialistic," "physiologic," "reflexo-logical," "endocrinological," "economical," "psychoanalytical," "behavioristic." Social sciences become blind toward almost anything in man and the sociocultural world that is a manifestation of "divineness," "idealism," "nonmaterial values," and the like. Instead, they concentrate mainly upon the material and half-animal aspects of humanity and its world; try to interpret everything through such factors, and causes and forces as instincts, reflexes, prepotent drives, sex, hunger, economic conditions, "residues," and other sensory-corporeal conditions, be they the density of the population, intensity of interaction, ecological area, heredity, struggle for existence, or so on. The nobler, higher, less material and less tangible forces, aspects, and agencies are disregarded, are ridiculed as "back numbers" and "ignorance." The whole world of the sociocultural values is dragged down to the level of the reflexes and pure physiology. Heroes as values are similarly "primitivized." The heroes of the social sciences and humanities of the Ideational periods are gods, saints, angels, and other supersensory and divine creatures. The heroes of the Idealistic social sciences are noble and great men and demigods. In a prevalently Sensate period the heroes are the "common people," "the labor classes," and especially the "negative" types: criminals, prostitutes, the mentally abnormal, social derelicts, and the like.[155] Here we have an exact replica of what we have met in the field of art, particularly in the field of portraiture and *genre*. There we have seen that with the progress of Sensate mentality, the "heroes" of painting and sculpture and literature become more and more "common people," the mediocrity, labor classes, and especially the socially pathological types. (See Part Two of Volume One, particularly Chapters Nine, Ten, and Thirteen.)

Similar is the situation in the social sciences and humanities. The history of the Ideational period is first of all, and most of all, a history of God's activities and of man as an incarnation of divinity guided by God. The history of the Idealistic period is that of the gods, saints, and great human heroes, be they kings, warriors, statesmen, religious, moral, scholastic, or other leaders. The history of the Sensate periods is that of the "common man," and of pathological groups, set forth in a prosaic and low configuration of social conditions (poverty, disease, dissatisfaction, the world mainly of physiology and "social sewers"). It gives little, if any, place to any hero. It becomes the "social history" of the nameless common masses and groups, interspersed with some sprinklings of pathological or subnormal individuals. Professor W. C. Abbott excellently puts this condition in his brilliant characterization of the "new history."

On every hand we have a multitude of books endeavoring to depict for us not the great figures and events and movements of the past but the way the ordinary man lived, what he did for a living, what he ate and drank and wore, how much of various commodities he produced, what he did for his amusement, and what things attracted his attention as he went his daily round. Whether it calls itself "social," or is concerned with "civilization," it has chiefly to do with what it describes as the "common man," that heir of the ages once called the "average man," one of whose incarnations Ricardo christened "economic man," the French revolutionaries "the man and citizen"; he whom Sinclair Lewis named "Babbitt," and the author of the morality play called "Everyman." He now replaces Caesar and Alexander and Shakespeare and George Washington as the hero of the "new" history. . . .[156]

In addition, this "new" history centers on social service, statistics of production, immorality, insane asylums, sex problems, and political corruption. . . ."

---

[155] G. B. Vico excellently formulated this, together with other sound generalizations. See his description of the Age of Gods, of Heroes, and of Common Man. Vico, "Principj di una scienza nuova," *Opere* (Milano, 1854), Vol. V, pp. 41 ff. and 462 ff.

[156] W. C. Abbott, *Adventures in Reputation* (Cambridge, Mass., 1935), pp 224–230. See the whole essay on "New History and Historians."

So it is with other social sciences and sociology and anthropology. They study "culture and civilization," not in the works of Homer, Plato, Aristotle, Phidias, Dante, Newton, Augustine, Bach, Beethoven, Kant, and Charlemagne; not in the finest creations of human genius; but mainly among the Ashantis and Trobrians, the Zulu and other primitive peoples; in the world of slums and gangs, in the "Middletowns" and prisons, and in the autobiographies of notorious criminals and the like, whose writings become more and more popular as treatises on sociology, criminology, psychology, anthropology, and political science. Not only gods and saints, but Tristan and Isolde, Lancelot and King Arthur, and, generally speaking, all heroes tend to disappear from the social literature of the Sensate period.

And even when such a hero is considered, be he Washington or Lincoln, Napoleon or Goethe, Christ or Mohammed, Caesar or Dante, by the biographers (all the Ludwigs and the Stracheys and other Sensate writers) they are so psychoanalyzed and "reflexologized" and sexualized and "physiologized" that the poor hero is stripped of anything heroic and debunked to the level of a mere physiological incarnation of sex or some similar complex. (See same data given on pages 651–652 of Chapter Thirteen of Volume One concerning the growth of the debunking biographies.)

This is only one of the innumerable traits in which the social sciences and the humanities of the predominant types of culture mentality profoundly differ from one another. In the preceding chapters many other differences have been pointed out. Generally, considered from the standpoint of the phenomena on which these sciences concentrate, their interrelation, their explanations (especially "factorial and causal analysis"), their methodology, the social sciences and humanities of the predominantly Ideational, Sensate, and Mixed periods differ from one another as much as can be. They look upon one another almost as strangers and are hardly on speaking terms. To the social sciences and humanities of the Ideational period, the social sciences of the Sensate period are the perverse disciplines, specializing in the reviling of God, man, and the world; a pitiful blasphemy; heresy; demoralizing and degrading instruments of deviltry. To the social sciences and humanities of the Sensate period, their counterparts of the Ideational period are but the eerie, queer, ignorant superstitions and phantasmas of the "uneducated and unillumined and unconditioned central nervous system of their bearers." They are so different that for Sensate social scientists the social sciences and humanities of the Ideational periods appear to be nonexistent. This is the reason why, for instance, in our courses and books on the history of social, political, economic, psychological, anthropological, and other theories, the Middle Ages are either barely mentioned, or only a few pages are devoted to several centuries, with the implicit or explicit assumption that there is nothing worth looking for along these lines, and that no social science existed then.[157] All this is so unquestionable and has been and will be factually indicated so many times on so many concrete points that it is unnecessary to discuss it further.

Side by side with the great transformations of these social and humanistic disciplines in connection with the rise and decline of the main types of culture mentality, each of them and their theories undergo almost incessant short-time transformations. Almost continually, a number of the theories or interpretations commonly accepted at a certain period are discarded and replaced by different ones. These undergo a similar cycle. The history of Greece by Winckelmann has little similarity with the history of Greece as it is given in the works of the leading historians of the middle of the nineteenth century; or this history with that of Greece of the twentieth century. Histories and treatises of the present time on the Middle Ages and the medieval culture are as different from those of the seventeenth and eighteenth and the first part of the nineteenth centuries as they can be.

The political science, or economics, of the Middle Ages has little in common with those of the eighteenth and nineteenth centuries, while these latter are declared outdated by the political science and economics of the twentieth century, especially in the Communistic, Fascistic and Hitlerite countries, and also in the New Deal regimes. The science of psychology of Albertus Magnus or St. Thomas Aquinas is profoundly different from that of the seventeenth century, be it a Descartian, a Hobbesian or a Lockian psychology; and these, in turn, are again quite different from the psychologies of the eighteenth and nineteenth centuries. Even those of the second part of the nineteenth century differ widely from those of the twentieth. Nay, even prewar psychologies are vastly unlike the postwar ones. Within the last ten years, several fashions (behaviorism, reflexology, psychoanalysis, mental tests, Gestaltism, and other brands) came, blossomed, and are already gone. Not different is the story with anthropology, theories of language, religion, art, law,

---

[157] Many a work, especially on political thought, devotes many chapters to the medieval political thought, like the controversy on the supremacy of the spiritual and secular powers, the moralizing on the institutions of property, government, slavery, and the like. All these theories are given, however, not as a brand of scientific theory, but mainly as a peculiar reflection of social conditions in the ignorant minds of their authors. Few scholars take them as a scientific theory on a level with the scientific theories of the present-day writers.

the mores, and philosophical systems.   Still more true is this "throbbing" in the field of sociology.   Within some seventy years after August Comte,[158] dozens and dozens of different theories and approaches and systems rushed into the field of sociology, had their heyday, and dwindled. Today's commonly accepted theory is discarded tomorrow.[159]

These remarks suffice for the present.   Whether we like it or not, the long- and short-time fluctuations in the social and humanitarian sciences, as well as the connection of their deep transformations with the rise and decline of the main types of culture mentalities can hardly be questioned.

IX. CONCLUDING REMARKS

Since I am not writing a history of scientific theories, the above examples are sufficient to show the relative validity of my first claim that in science, as in any other field of sociocultural mentality, the fact of oscillation of the acceptability and prestige of the theories cannot be questioned.

Also the above examples substantiate my second claim that even in the field of the natural sciences many of their broad and leading theories fluctuate in their prestige and acceptability in a tangible connection with the fluctuations of the systems of truth and the main types of culture.   As mentioned, it is not claimed that all scientific theories show, or must show such a connection; many of them can fluctuate independently of our main variables, within their limited sphere of autonomy and the immediate mental atmosphere of their compartment.

---

[158] See my *Contemporary Sociological Theories, passim.*

[159] One of the manifestations of this quick tempo of "scientific fashions" in the social and humanitarian — and also other — sciences is the short span of life of most of the texts and treatises published.   From one to ten years, rarely more, is about the duration of life of a contemporary work.   Often before they are published they are "antiquated."   In the field of sociology I can indicate hardly any single work out of all those published during the last fifteen years which is going to live longer.   For some, such a rapid turnover is a sign of the remarkable progress of science; a more valid interpretation is that it is a sign of a particularly rapid change of "scientific fashion."   Not every later fashion is necessarily better than the earlier ones.   For myself, I still prefer Bach or Mozart or Beethoven to all the most modern musical compositions, would not trade even one single work of these great masters for all the most modern music in the world.   The main works of Plato or Aristotle or St. Thomas or several other great social thinkers I would not exchange for all the textbooks on sociology of the postwar period taken together.   And so in other fields.   My tastes are not obligatory, but the tastes of the "progressives" and the "modernists" are also not obligatory.   Therefore, objectively, the discussed changes of these theories are neither progress nor regression, but just an exceedingly rapid change of scientific fashions.   Such is its objective characterization, independent of mine or anybody's tastes.

But many other theories and probably all of the "First Principles," "categories," and general principles of philosophy and science are conditioned in their credibility and scientific acceptability by the dominant system of truth and dominant system of culture.

The foregoing chapters show that therefore the second claim is now substantiated also. Whether or not we like it, a great deal that is styled scientific or philosophical theory and scientific or philosophical truth is greatly conditioned by the above variables. A theory harmonious with the given dominant system of truth is likely to be proclaimed by the scientists and philosophers as the last word of science. And the same theory, under a different system of truth dominant, is likely to be declared an error or mere superstition.

Insistence on such a relativity of scientific theories does not mean skepticism on my part. It simply means that the full and complete truth is "white" and is possibly accessible only to the Divine Mind. We can grasp but its approximation. Our efforts in this direction seem in most of the cases to go beyond the proper limit when we accept this or that theory as radically true and reject other theories as radically wrong. According to the principles of limit and immanent self-regulation of the sociocultural processes, when, in our eagerness, we go too far beyond the legitimate limit of a given theory, a reaction sets in and leads to its decline. But the new theory also goes too far, denying to its predecessor not only its value, but often the germ of truth which it contains. Hence, in its turn, it is destined also, after its period of domination, to be discarded for a new theory, which often is a modification of the one previously overthrown. And so it goes.

In these eternal oscillations there is a great value, a great fascination, and a great optimism. They mean that we are almost always in close touch with the ultimate reality, in spite of our inability to grasp it fully. This is something quite different from skepticism or its allies. It means also that the whole truth is infinite in its aspects and unfathomable in its depth. It is more worth our while to be in real touch with, and in partial possession of, such an infinite value than to be in complete possession of something which is entirely graspable, and therefore is limited and finite. At least, such is the preference of the writer. However, this is a matter of taste, and is not obligatory for anybody. What is obligatory is to realize that the fact of the oscillations discussed seems to be without doubt.

We have traversed a long and arduous road to this part of the work. Now we can look back and take stock of what we have seen.

(1) All four of the propositions with which this part is concerned and which follow logically from the nature of each of the main culture mentalities are corroborated inductively.

(2) The logically expected "integrations" happened to be integrated factually or causally. So far, the culture mentalities studied show themselves mainly logical, and not illogical or alogical as many claim. It is true that the causal and logical integrations are not perfect, but they are quite tangible. Due to the *Principle of Autonomy* of any really integrated system, each of the integrated currents of culture mentality studied should be expected to have some margin of this autonomy; therefore it should have some margin of an "independent movement" not completely related to the other currents and compartments of culture.

(3) The above shows also that our "main variables" or our key principles for a logical comprehension of the perceptional chaos of socio-cultural phenomena work well. They work well, not only as the "heuristic principles" that help to look for functional connections where otherwise the connections cannot even be suspected of existing, but as the principles analogous to "causal laws" which order the chaos of the millions of fragmentary phenomena into a system; which give a sense to what otherwise is meaningless; which put in their proper places thousands of fragments and make out of them a comprehensible whole. Yes, we see now the "hows and whys" of the rise and decline of all the "First Principles," "categories," theories studied; and the thousands of more detailed subcurrents embraced by each of these. In this sense, the theory of the Ideational, Idealistic, Sensate culture mentalities meets well the test of its validity; fits as well as any other theory this class of phenomena; explains them as well as any other heuristic concept does. Therefore it is entitled to claim as large a share of validity as any theory in the field studied.

PART TWO

---

*Fluctuation of Ideational and Sensate Forms of Ethical
and Juridical Culture Mentality (Dynamics of Ethical
Values)*

Chapter Thirteen

FLUCTUATION OF IDEATIONAL, SENSATE, AND MIXED SYSTEMS OF ETHICS IN THE GRAECO-ROMAN AND WESTERN CULTURES [1]

I. Preliminaries

We can pass now to the next compartment of culture : ethicojuridical. In this vast and complicated field we shall discuss the same problems that have been studied in the preceding compartments. A few introductory statements follow.

Every organized group and its culture has a set of ethical values. Even among the most primitive tribes or criminal gangs we invariably find it in the form of taboos of certain forms of conduct and objects and events, and in the permission or glorification of others as sacred, good, and recommended. In some form an ethical evaluation of "the right and wrong" is present in any culture and in any organized social group. In this sense the ethical mentality is a universal and permanent component of any culture mentality. The content of this mentality differs from society to society, from period to period, but its ethical forms are perennial.

Some of the cultures and their mentality may not develop this ethical mentality up to the level of the integrated ethicophilosophical systems. Other more integrated cultures develop it. In the former cultures, the division of the actions, relationships, objects, and events into right and wrong exists, but it is not welded into a consistent ethical system, with its principles, hierarchy of values, and their "justification." For such a step a high degree of analytical thought and a considerable degree of ethical controversy are necessary. These conditions may not be given in many simple societies. When they are given, the ethicophilosophical systems appear. In the case of the Graeco-Roman and the Western society, such systems are present.

For a sociologist and social psychologist, these ethicophilosophical systems have a specific interest. They are possibly the best manifesta-

[1] In co-operation with I. I. Lapshin and N. O. Lossky.

tion of the ethical ideals of a given culture, the sublime peaks of its ethical mentality. Therefore, a study of these systems is necessary in order to grasp the character of this mentality as such at its best and noblest, without any inference as to whether the *real* actions of the members correspond to it or not.

It goes without saying that the real behavior of the respective society, and even of the creator of a given ethical system, does not always coincide with the predominant ethical ideal accepted. Factually, as we shall see in Volume Three, there is always some discrepancy. For this reason one cannot infer from the dominant ethical ideal of a given society that the conduct of its members corresponds to it. On the other hand, some "affinity" between the ideal and certain aspects of behavior seems to exist. Many aspects of the actual conduct seem to be colored or permeated somehow by the predominant ethical system. In this sense they are in some agreement with it and receive from it their meaning — not in the sense that the noble ideals are always realized and that the negative taboos of the system are not transgressed. There are not many Christians who, on being slapped upon one side of the face, immediately offer the other side. Likewise, there are more than enough Christians who violate not only the supreme command to "love thy neighbor as thyself," but almost all of the "Ten Commandments." The "affinity" means a different correspondence: the ethical meaning or moral coloring of many aspects of the actual conduct by the nature of the predominant ethical system. If the predominant ethical system is utilitarianism, the atmosphere of utilitarian principles permeates the conduct and moral mentality of the members of the society, in spite of the fact that they fail to carry out its supreme prescriptions. If the predominant system is the System of Love, it again reflects itself in the actual conduct of such a society, and especially in its moral mentality, though the actual conduct may violate the command of such a system. In this sense, there is a degree of affinity between the dominant system of ethics and the actual moral conduct and mentality of the society.

Thus from these two standpoints, as the manifestation of the ethical mentality at its best, and for the significant light which they throw upon the inner meaning of real conduct, a study of the ethicophilosophical systems of a given culture is particularly important for a sociologist and for any scholar who wants to understand the ethical forms of the culture studied.

They, however, do not throw much light upon the actual moral behavior of the society's members in its lower and daily routine. The systems do not descend to these low levels. They remain in the heavens, and remaining there they do not supply us with any reliable information about this "routine, daily, factual, and — in this sense — real form" of the conduct of the members. For that we have to turn to other sources and material; first of all to law, and especially to the criminal law that deals with the lowest level of moral mentality and conduct.

The whole field of moral phenomena can be divided into two main classes: *the moral or ethical* in the narrow sense of the term, and the *juridical (or legal)*. As we shall see in the next chapter, the first are recommended but not required; the second are obligatory and enforced. The purely juridical norms and values represent in this sense the moral minimum of the society demanded from all its members.[2] The moral phenomena are only recommended, and left up to the good will of the members. The integrated ethical systems represent the peak of the "moral" mentality (in a narrow sense) of the society. The laws, and particularly the criminal laws, reflect its juridical mentality in its daily and prosaic routine (providing the laws are enforced and functioning). In this and the next chapters we shall study the fluctuation of the Graeco-Roman and the Western moral mentality at its loftiest and at its lowest levels. As material for the first task, their ethical systems are taken. As material for the second problem, their criminal codes are investigated. We shall begin our study with the moral mentality of the cultures investigated at its best, as this best is incorporated in their ethical systems. If one succeeds in showing the fact of their fluctuation and its hows and whys, this is sufficient for an acquisition of some knowledge concerning the modes and forms of change in this compartment of culture. If, in addition to this, we can elucidate, to some extent, the problem as to whether the fluctuations in these fields are associated with those in other compartments of these cultures and, if associated, how and to what extent, such an elucidation would add a great deal to our knowledge of the "dynamics" of moral values. At the same time, it will round out the problem of the fluctuation of the total mentality of the cultures.

II. IDEATIONAL, IDEALISTIC, AND SENSATE SYSTEMS OF ETHICS

A. From the nature of the Ideational mentality, the following characteristics of the Ideational ethical system follow.

[2] See G. Jellineck, *Socialethische Bedeutung von Recht, Unrecht und Strafe* (Wien, 1878). Definition of law as the social minimum of ethics is insufficient to distinguish the two classes. But it is important as one of the relevant traits. For a further elaboration of the distinction between the juridical and moral phenomena, see pages 523 to 527 and 596 to 597.

(1) It is not and cannot be intended merely to increase the sum of sensate happiness, comfort, pleasure, and utility. These are imaginary and therefore cannot be the end of the principles of Ideational ethics.

(2) The Ideational system of ethics must be and usually is absolute. Since it is intended to bring its followers into unity with the supreme and absolute value, its commands are also absolute. They are the supreme value that cannot be turned into a means for anything and anybody. Therefore relativism, expediency, and anything that limits them is heterogeneous to such ethics. *Fiat justitia et pereat (sensate) mundus* is their spirit.

(3) Its principles are considered as emanating from God or some other supersensory absolute value. In most cases, they are given as the Commandments of God (or gods).

B. The nature of the Sensate mentality determines the opposite characteristics of the Sensate ethical system.

(1) The aim of such a system of ethics can be only an increase of the total sum of a man's (or a group's) sensate happiness, comfort, utility, and pleasure. Since there is no reality except the sensory and no value except the sensory value, sensate happiness remains the only value which can be secured by Sensate ethics.

(2) Such a system can be but relativistic, because with the changing sensate conditions the ethical rules must change also; rules that serve the purpose in one set of conditions cease to serve it in different circumstances; therefore they can and should be replaced by rules that fit the new situation. Hence, relativism, expediency, and changeability of the rules of Sensate ethics.

(3) They always appear as man-made rules, having no other authority behind them. If they are reasonable and serve the purpose of happiness, they are useful. If they do not serve that purpose, they should be discarded.

C. Finally, the Idealistic ethical system occupies an intermediary position between these two systems.

(1) Its aims are simultaneously transcendental and earthly: service to God (the absolute ethical value), which leads, at the same time, to the real eudaemonistic happiness of those who do that.

(2) Its main principle is absolute; its subordinated commands are relative and therefore changeable.

(3) It gives its main principles as the commands of God or of some other supersensory supreme authority; its secondary principles as the commands of reason and of the human bearers of it.

These characteristics follow logically from the nature of each of these mentalities. Thus the classification of the numerous ethical systems into these three classes is quite proper. The enormous number and variety of ethical systems created by numerous thinkers quite naturally and easily fall into one of these classes. Once more, then, we find that our main categories are not only logically consistent constructs, but constructs that fit the reality of the ethical systems and easily consign them into the three classes of Ideational, Idealistic, and Sensate systems of ethics. Sensate ethics can be called the *ethics of happiness;* Ideational ethics, the system of *absolute principles.* Its specific variety, represented by the Christian ethical system, is *ethics of love.* It differs from other varieties of absolutistic ethics by several characteristics. Finally, Idealistic ethics is a class intermediary between these and is represented by the ethics of absolute principles somewhat diluted, mixed with the finest form of *eudaemonistic* ethics as a variety of the *ethics of happiness.* Let us clarify a little more each class of these three ethical systems.

To the Sensate ethics of happiness belong all ethical systems which regard sensate happiness as the supreme value and make everything else a means for its achievement and quantitative and qualitative increase. All that leads to that is good; all that hinders it is evil; such is the criterion and the supreme value of such systems.

Though similar in this respect, various systems of ethics of happiness differ from one another in several secondary specifications. According to these specifications they can be divided into three principal subclasses. First is the *eudaemonistic* subclass which considers, as the supreme objective, happiness of the *whole system of life*, in which pleasure and joy shall outweigh pain, suffering, and grief. Not happiness as a mere *Carpe diem*, as merely grasping as many singular and fragmentary pleasures as possible. In accordance with that, eudaemonism means by happiness not merely the sum total of sensual pleasures but also — and rather — nonsensual pleasures, more refined, more noble, more lasting, and less fragile. In this sense it is neither mainly nor predominantly sensual and carnal, nor is it aimed at the passing moment only. It has a longer perspective of time in its evaluation of pleasure, and for this reason views happiness as a conscientious system of living, and not as a mere hunt for transient enjoyment.

The *hedonistic* branch of the ethics of happiness differs from the eudaemonistic in that it views as the supreme objective of life separate or singular pleasures. The more such pleasures are caught, the greater the happiness, the greater the goodness of life.[3] Accentuating these pleasures, hedonism has to be and in fact is more "sensual" and carnal than eudaemonism. The ideal of the *"Carpe diem"* or "Wine, women, and song," cannot be styled eudaemonistic, though it is in agreement with the principles of hedonism and is one of its forms. It does not stress the continuance of the pleasures and happiness, and does not give any premium to long-time values as compared with short-time ones, as does, in a sense, eudaemonism.

Finally, *utilitarianism* is also a form of ethics of happiness. Being nearer to the eudaemonistic system than to the hedonistic, especially in the works of the English utilitarianists, it differs from both in that it puts an emphasis on the *means* of obtaining happiness (on what is useful for the achievement of happiness) rather than on what the happiness itself is.

Eudaemonism, hedonism, and utilitarianism can be either individualistic or egotistic, when the happiness of only a given individual is considered, regardless of its effects upon the others; or social, when not so much the happiness of a given individual as that of a group is regarded as the supreme objective. The social forms of the ethics of happiness can have also various — more broad and less broad — forms, according to whether the happiness of the nearest group (for instance, of a certain family only) or a larger group (possibly the whole nation) or a still larger group (for instance, the whole of mankind) is the objective. Farther on, as mentioned, various systems of eudaemonism, hedonism, and utilitarianism can be and are more or less carnal and sensual. Between the extremes there is always a series of the intermediary forms. Such are the main forms of the Sensate ethics of happiness.

According to the Ideational *ethics of absolute principles*, the supreme objective of life is a realization of the highest value — for instance, union with God, salvation of soul, truth, goodness, beauty, for their own sake, regardless of whether or not such a realization leads to an increase of happiness. Happiness may be the result of a life carried on in accordance with the ethics of principles, but it is not the objective of it; it is a mere by-product. If such a result is forthcoming, it is good; if it is not forthcoming, it is good also, and does not make any difference, because the ethics of principles does not consider happiness as the supreme objective. What values are taken as supreme by a given system of the ethics of absolute principles is a secondary matter. The main matter is an

---

[3] For this difference between eudaemonism and hedonism see H. Gomperz, *Die Lebensauffassung der griechischen Philosophen und das Ideal der inneren Freiheit* (Jena, 1904). Compare for instance *the hedonism of Aristippus and the eudaemonism of Epicurus.*

absolutization of the supreme value and of its realization regardless of anything else. This means that the ethics of principles takes its values as absolute — supreme and final. As such, they are always transcendental. All other values are but a means to these. In this sense, it is one of the currents of philosophical absolutism discussed in Chapter Fourteen.

Between the noblest systems of eudaemonism and that of the ethics of principles, the difference becomes often imperceptible. One is merged organically with the other, in the form of the Idealistic system of ethics, which is simultaneously absolutistic and — in part — relativistic, transcendental, and at the same time eudaemonistic.

Such are several ethical systems of the Greek and Scholastic philosophers, which can be classified as eudaemonistic as well as Ideational. Some investigators put them in the eudaemonistic, others in the absolutistic class. It is truer to regard them as Idealistic. These systems are those where happiness is given great value, but it is viewed as a mere result of a rightly set purpose in the form of the absolute ethical values.

Ethics of love, in a sense, is a variety of the *ethics of absolute principles*. Among and above all values it puts the value of infinite, unlimited, sacrificing love of God, and of all the concrete individual persons. Love in this sense includes all the other values. The genuine ethics of Jesus, St. Francis, and other Christians give examples of such ethics of love.[4]

Such are the differences between these main systems. It should be indicated that in diagnosing any given ethical system, one has to be careful not to be misled by appearances. For instance, some of the Greek systems look eudaemonistic while in fact they belong either to idealistic ethics or to the ethics of absolute principles. Other ethical systems sound like ethics of absolute principles; for instance, many which demand unconditional subjection to, and following of, the orders of the rulers, the popes, the Church, the party, the nation, etc. In most cases, such systems are but a variety of the eudaemonistic or utilitarian systems, and not a system of the ethics of principles.

---

[4] In the history of the Graeco-Roman and Western cultures, ethics of love is represented by Christianity, and is in a way its discovery. From eudaemonism it differs by rejection of happiness as the ultimate and supreme value. Though it also talks of happiness, it is not the empirical happiness of eudaemonism; it is a quite different transcendental happiness in the Kingdom of God, after the transfiguration of body and soul. Many theorizers of Christianity, like St. Thomas Aquinas, give a clear formulation of this system of ethics. Many Christian mystics, like St. Francis of Assisi and others, demonstrate it clearly in their conduct.

Like ethics of principles, it urges an entirely disinterested realization of the values but subordinates and includes all the values in the principle of infinite and unlimited Love of God and of all living creatures, for their own sake and for the sake of love itself.

III. Fluctuation of Systems of Ethics

In the subsequent pages, the results of the study of the fluctuation of these systems in the history of the Graeco-Roman and the Western cultures, so far as they have been reflected in their ethicophilosophical thought, are given.

The Idealistic class is not specifically differentiated in Tables 29 and 30. These theories are put in the nearer of the two classes. However, further comments will show in which periods such a class was comparatively strong. The method of the construction of the tables, the reservations and qualifications, are here the same as in the preceding chapters and as they are enumerated in Chapter One of this volume. Table 29 gives the movement of each of the main systems of ethics by 20-year periods; Table 30 by century periods.[5] Figure 16 furnishes a pictorial image of the fluctuation of the currents. The list of the names of the thinkers and their values is given in the Appendix to this chapter.

TABLE 29. INDICATORS OF THE FLUCTUATION OF THE INFLUENCE OF ETHICAL SYSTEMS AND MENTALITY BY 20-YEAR PERIODS, 580 B.C.—A.D. 1920

(on the basis of different values given from 1 to 12)

PERIOD	Ethics of Happiness (Eudaemonism, Hedonism, Utilitarianism)		Ethics of Principles		Ethics of Love		Total	
	No.	Per cent	No.	Per cent	No.	Per cent	No.	Per cent
580–560 B.C.	0	0	0	0	0	0	0	0
560–540	0	0	0	0	0	0	0	0
540–520	0	0	8	100	0	0	8	100
520–500	0	0	15	100	0	0	15	100
500–480	0	0	15	100	0	0	15	100
480–460	0	0	7	100	0	0	7	100
460–440	0	0	1	100	0	0	1	100
440–420	13	52.0	12	48.0	0	0	25	100
420–400	53	79.1	14	20.9	0	0	67	100
400–380	49	73.1	18	26.9	0	0	67	100
380–360	29	56.9	22	43.1	0	0	51	100
360–340	22	44.0	28	56.0	0	0	50	100
340–320	8	20.0	32	80.0	0	0	40	100
320–300	17	27.0	46	73.0	0	0	63	100
300–280	24	38.7	38	61.3	0	0	62	100
280–260	35	53.8	30	46.2	0	0	65	100
260–240	21	61.8	13	38.2	0	0	34	100
240–220	32	58.2	23	41.8	0	0	55	100
220–200	8	38.1	13	61.9	0	0	21	100

[5] Here again, as in all the preceding tables, the indicators for century periods are not a mere sum of the indicators of five 20-year periods of a given century. Each thinker in the century period is given his value only once, while by 20-year periods it figures often in two or even three 20-year periods of his life and activity. Hence the difference in the figures of Tables 29 and 30.

TABLE 29. INDICATORS OF THE FLUCTUATION OF THE INFLUENCE OF ETHICAL SYSTEMS AND MENTALITY BY 20-YEAR PERIODS — *continued*

(on the basis of different values given from 1 to 12)

PERIOD	Ethics of Happiness (Eudaemonism, Hedonism, Utilitarianism)		Ethics of Principles		Ethics of Love		Total	
	No.	Per cent	No.	Per cent	No.	Per cent	No.	Per cent
200–180 B.C.	4	30.8	9	69.2	0	0	13	100
180–160	7	46.7	8	53.3	0	0	15	100
160–140	10	55.6	8	44.4	0	0	18	100
140–120	9	50.0	9	50.0	0	0	18	100
120–100	6	35.3	11	64.7	0	0	17	100
100–80	7	30.4	16	69.6	0	0	23	100
80–60	5	15.1	28	84.9	0	0	33	100
60–40	23	38.3	37	61.7	0	0	60	100
40–20	14	48.3	15	51.7	0	0	29	100
20–0	6	37.5	10	62.5	0	0	16	100
0–20 A.D.	1	4.8	20	95.2	0	0	21	100
20–40	1	7.7	12	92.3	0	0	13	100
40–60	1	4.3	22	95.7	0	0	23	100
60–80	1	2.8	35	97.2	0	0	36	100
80–100	1	2.9	34	97.1	0	0	35	100
100–120	1	2.4	38	90.5	3	7.1	42	100
120–140	2	3.3	56	91.8	3	4.9	61	100
140–160	3	4.8	54	85.7	6	9.5	63	100
160–180	9	12.5	57	79.2	6	8.3	72	100
180–200	11	12.3	68	76.5	10	11.2	89	100
200–220	9	13.2	49	72.0	10	14.8	68	100
220–240	1	2.2	36	80.0	8	17.8	45	100
240–260	1	2.4	31	73.8	10	23.8	42	100
260–280	1	3.3	27	90.0	2	6.7	30	100
280–300	1	5.9	15	88.2	1	5.9	17	100
300–320	1	5.25	17	89.5	1	5.25	19	100
320–340	1	5.0	15	75.0	4	20.0	20	100
340–360	1	6.7	6	40.0	8	53.3	15	100
360–380	5	9.6	21	40.4	26	50.0	52	100
380–400	5	9.6	15	28.9	32	61.5	52	100
400–420	0	0	12	37.5	20	62.5	32	100
420–440	0	0	13	41.9	18	58.1	31	100
440–460	0	0	17	68.0	8	32.0	25	100
460–480	0	0	12	70.6	5	29.4	17	100
480–500	0	0	12	85.7	2	14.3	14	100
500–520	0	0	18	64.3	10	35.7	28	100
520–540	0	0	17	63.0	10	37.0	27	100
540–560	0	0	14	87.5	2	12.5	16	100
560–580	0	0	5	71.4	2	28.6	7	100
580–600	0	0	2	33.3	4	66.7	6	100
600–620	0	0	4	50.0	4	50.0	8	100
620–640	0	0	4	40.0	6	60.0	10	100
640–660	0	0	1	14.3	6	85.7	7	100
660–680	0	0	1	14.3	6	85.7	7	100
680–700	0	0	1	50.0	1	50.0	2	100
700–720	0	0	1	50.0	1	50.0	2	100
720–740	0	0	1	16.7	5	83.3	6	100
740–760	0	0	1	16.7	5	83.3	6	100
760–780	0	0	0.5	50.0	0.5	50.0	1	100
780–800	0	0	1	33.3	2	66.7	3	100
800–820	0	0	1	33.3	2	66.7	3	100
820–840	0	0	6	85.7	1	14.3	7	100
840–860	0	0	6	42.9	8	57.1	14	100

TABLE 29. INDICATORS OF THE FLUCTUATION OF THE INFLUENCE OF
ETHICAL SYSTEMS AND MENTALITY BY 20-YEAR PERIODS — *continued*

(on the basis of different values given from 1 to 12)

PERIOD	Ethics of Happiness (Eudaemonism, Hedonism, Utilitarianism)		Ethics of Principles		Ethics of Love		Total	
	No.	Per cent	No.	Per cent	No.	Per cent	No.	Per cent
860–880 A.D.	0	0	2	15.4	11	84.6	13	100
880–900	0	0	1	16.7	5	83.3	6	100
900–920	0	0	1	33.3	2	66.7	3	100
920–940	0	0	1	50.0	1	50.0	2	100
940–960	0	0	0.5	50.0	0.5	50.0	1	100
960–980	0	0	0.5	50.0	0.5	50.0	1	100
980–1000	0	0	1	50.0	1	50.0	2	100
1000–1020	0	0	1	33.3	2	66.7	3	100
1020–1040	0	0	1	33.3	2	66.7	3	100
1040–1060	0	0	5	62.5	3	37.5	8	100
1060–1080	0	0	5	22.7	17	77.3	22	100
1080–1100	0	0	6	26.1	17	73.9	23	100
1100–1120	0	0	3	20.0	12	80.0	15	100
1120–1140	0	0	5	21.7	18	78.3	23	100
1140–1160	0	0	2	9.1	20	90.9	22	100
1160–1180	0	0	2	16.7	10	83.3	12	100
1180–1200	0	0	2	16.7	10	83.3	12	100
1200–1220	0	0	2	20.0	8	80.0	10	100
1220–1240	0	0	4	44.4	5	55.6	9	100
1240–1260	0	0	4	26.8	11	73.2	15	100
1260–1280	0	0	10	26.3	28	73.7	38	100
1280–1300	0	0	12	21.1	45	78.9	57	100
1300–1320	0	0	3	4.9	58	95.1	61	100
1320–1340	0	0	4	11.8	30	88.2	34	100
1340–1360	0	0	9	24.3	28	75.7	37	100
1360–1380	0	0	6	18.8	26	81.2	32	100
1380–1400	0	0	1	11.1	8	88.9	9	100
1400–1420	0	0	2	33.3	4	66.7	6	100
1420–1440	0	0	2	15.4	11	84.6	13	100
1440–1460	3	13	2	8.7	18	78.3	23	100
1460–1480	0	0	2	10.5	17	89.5	19	100
1480–1500	0	0	1	33.3	2	66.7	3	100
1500–1520	10	23.3	32	74.4	1	2.3	43	100
1520–1540	17	18.3	45	80.6	1	1.1	63	100
1540–1560	16	33.3	31	64.6	1	2.1	48	100
1560–1580	28	41.8	35	52.2	4	6.0	67	100
1580–1600	45	52.3	27	31.4	14	16.3	86	100
1600–1620	56	48.4	48	41.3	12	10.3	116	100
1620–1640	35	35.7	54	55.1	9	9.2	98	100
1640–1660	34	39.1	46	52.9	7	8.0	87	100
1660–1680	32	29.1	71	64.5	7	6.4	110	100
1680–1700	30	23.2	94	72.9	5	3.9	129	100
1700–1720	33	28.4	78	67.3	5	4.3	116	100
1720–1740	35	34.0	64	62.1	4	3.9	103	100
1740–1760	56	35.9	88	56.4	12	7.7	156	100
1760–1780	82	52.6	60	38.5	14	8.9	156	100
1780–1800	61	35.0	93	53.5	20	11.5	174	100
1800–1820	54	28.5	102	54.0	33	17.5	189	100
1820–1840	60	29.4	108	52.9	36	17.7	204	100
1840–1860	127	40.3	150	47.6	38	12.1	315	100
1860–1880	138	38.3	166	46.1	56	15.6	360	100
1880–1900	188	42.8	187	42.6	64	14.6	439	100
1900–1920	200	43.0	191	41.0	74	16.0	465	100

TABLE 30. INDICATORS OF THE FLUCTUATION OF THE INFLUENCE OF ETHICAL SYSTEMS AND MENTALITY BY CENTURY PERIODS, 600 B.C.—A.D. 1900

(on the basis of different values given from 1 to 12)

PERIOD	Ethics of Happiness (Eudaemonism, Hedonism, Utilitarianism)		Ethics of Principles		Ethics of Love		Total	
	No.	Per cent	No.	Per cent	No.	Per cent	No.	Per cent
600–500 B.C.	0	0	15	100	0	0	15	100
500–400	53	63.9	30	36.1	0	0	83	100
400–300	72	46.2	84	53.8	0	0	156	100
300–200	64	50.0	64	50.0	0	0	128	100
200–100	18	42.9	24	57.1	0	0	42	100
100–0	31	33.0	63	67.0	0	0	94	100
0–100 A.D.	1	1.3	76	98.7	0	0	77	100
100–200	12	6.8	143	82.2	19	11.0	174	100
200–300	10	8.8	83	72.8	21	18.4	114	100
300–400	6	9.1	23	34.8	37	56.1	66	100
400–500	0	0	31	53.4	27	46.6	58	100
500–600	0	0	25	61.0	16	39.0	41	100
600–700	0	0	5	31.3	11	68.7	16	100
700–800	0	0	1.5	15.0	8.5	85.0	10	100
800–900	0	0	9	36.0	16	64.0	25	100
900–1000	0	0	1.5	30.0	3.5	70.0	5	100
1000–1100	0	0	9	29.0	22	71.0	31	100
1100–1200	0	0	7	13.2	46	86.8	53	100
1200–1300	0	0	18	18.9	77	81.1	95	100
1300–1400	0	0	15	13.8	94	86.2	109	100
1400–1500	3	8.7	5	13.5	29	77.8	37	100
1500–1600	100	43.5	109	47.4	21	9.1	230	100
1600–1700	129	38.4	181	53.9	26	7.7	336	100
1700–1800	175	36.3	272	56.4	35	7.3	482	100
1800–1900	395	38.0	499	48.0	146	14.0	1040	100

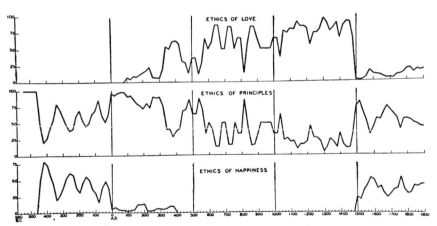

FIG. 16. FLUCTUATION OF ETHICAL CURRENTS

IV. Main Results

A. Table 29 and Figure 16 show that up to the second part of the fifth century B.C., the ethics of happiness did not play any role.   The whole field was occupied by the ethics of principles : religious and moral commands were viewed as absolute, without any regard to their bearing upon sensate happiness.   The moral values were held sacred, and their authority was transcendental gods, whose commands were neither doubted nor questioned.   This was not only the standpoint of thinkers like Pythagoras and others indicated in the list, but also of the poets and literary oracles of the centuries preceding the fifth and of the first part of the fifth century.

At him are gods and men wroth, who liveth in idleness. . . .   Justice followeth weeping . . . into the homes of men who drive her forth and deal with her crookedly. . . .   Zeus shall destroy [such a race]. . . .[6]

Hesiod's standpoint views the moral commands as established by Zeus and the gods as absolute values; without any questioning of the reasons or effects of their existence.   Even as late as the first part of the fifth century this standpoint is maintained by Pindar, Aeschylus, Sophocles, Herodotus, and other great writers of the period.   For all of these moral commands are absolute commands of the gods.   These commands are not questioned even when the gods punish men who seem to be not guilty at all from our standpoint.   Even in such cases a violation of the absolute moral order cannot continue without a restoration of the transcendental justice, no matter if the men who violated the moral order did it contrary to their own desire.   The tragedy of Oedipus falls upon him without any guilt on his part : he did all that one can do to avoid the crimes of parricide and marrying his mother, that destiny imposed upon him.   From our standpoint his punishment is quite undeserved.   Not so from the standpoint of Sophocles.   "His religious feeling even passionately demands that any attempt made by men to defy an undeserved fate like Oedipus's should be overborne." [7]   Likewise for Herodotus, who deals with many similar cases of the "arbitrariness of the gods," there is nothing painful nor unjust in such an arbitrariness.   On the contrary, "it is an edifying truth to which he clings with the fear and strength of religion."   For both

---

[6] Hesiod, *Works and Days*, trans. by A. W. Maire (Oxford, 1908), pp. 11–13 and 5–9.

[7] Svend Ranulf, *The Jealousy of the Gods and Criminal Law at Athens. A Contribution to the Sociology of Moral Indignation*, 2 vols. (London and Copenhagen, 1933–1934), Vol. I, pp. 32–49, 112, 148, *et passim*. See there the detailed analysis of the situation and of the literary works of the period. The analysis is good, though the explanatory hypothesis of the author is questionable. See also L. Gernet, *Recherches sur le développement de la pensée iuridique et moral en Grèce* (Paris, 1917).

of them all the Sensate values are pseudo values. Still more true that is of Aeschylus and Pindar. "Human happiness does not stay long," says Pindar. "Neither Peleus, nor Kadmos, the equal of the gods, was given a life of security, and yet the legend records that of all mortals they attained the highest happiness." "As long as we live, we are but vain and fleeting shades," reiterates Sophocles. All of them explain the misfortunes of the guiltless men by "the divine power" which has its own logic, often incomprehensible for us but never to be questioned and never to be criticized.

> The belief in this peculiar form of divine justice cannot have been inspired by any wish to protect the community against the consequences of crimes. . . . If the gods deter some, they force others (Oedipus, for instance) to continue, even against their will, in the path of crime,[8]

rightly states Ranulf, indicating that the usual utilitarian explanation of the criminal law and this kind of justice in ancient Athens does not explain the situation.

The real reason for it is the absolutistic conception of moral values and moral order. Since it is absolute and since it can be violated, it must be sustained; violated justice must be restored; the violation must not pass unpunished, no matter whether the violation was intentional or not; no matter whether we understand or not the will of the gods. It is assumed to be absolute and always right, even when we do not comprehend it. For any absolutistic system of ethics, any transgression of the absolute moral order cannot pass without its expiation, and without a restoration of the moral value itself. Such, in brief, is the moral mentality of Greek thinkers before and at the beginning of the fifth century B.C. It shows itself exceedingly Ideational — and in this respect happens to be in harmony with the Ideationalism dominant in other compartments of Greek culture of that period.

B. When we pass to the middle and then to the second half of the fifth and then to the fourth century B.C., the spectrum of the moral mentality changes — and changes greatly. First, the system of ethics of happiness emerges and rapidly grows, mainly in a noble eudaemonistic form. Second, more extreme Sensate systems of ethics of some of the

---

[8] See, for instance, G. M. Calhoun, *The Growth of Criminal Law in Ancient Greece* (Berkeley, 1927). Calhoun in his good work explains the early criminal law by "the fear of religious consequences to unpunished crime" and by the desire to avoid the pollution of the community. In this theory he inadvertently applied the so natural — for us — utilitarian motive to a situation fundamentally different from our mentality. See also K. Latte, "*Beiträge zum griechischen Strafrecht*," in *Hermes* (1931).

Sophists appear (see the list of names in the Appendix to this chapter). Third, the main theories of ethics, namely, of Plato and Aristotle and their followers, appear to be nearest to the Idealistic system. Such a spectrum means that the second part of the fifth and the fourth centuries show themselves here partly Mixed but mainly Idealistic. So far the fifth and the first part of the fourth centuries B.C. in this field have the Idealistic character met by us in practically all the compartments of Greek culture of that period. When one takes the "eudaemonistic" systems of Plato and Aristotle, they have all the earmarks of the Idealistic system rather than Ideational or Sensate. Plato's system is nearer to the Ideational, Aristotle's to the Sensate, but both are neither; both are Idealistic, in the above sense of the term.

A man ought to be confident about his soul, who during this life has disregarded all the pleasures and ornaments of the body as foreign from his nature, and who, having thought that they do more harm than good, has zealously applied himself to the acquirement of knowledge, and who having adorned his soul not with a foreign but its own proper ornament, temperance, justice, fortitude, freedom, and truth . . . is ready to depart whenever destiny shall summon him.[9]

Socrates teaches in the last minutes of his life, before drinking the poison :

If the company will be persuaded by me, accounting the soul immortal, and able to bear all evil and all good, we shall always hold the road which leads above. And justice with prudence we shall by all means pursue in order that we may be friends both to ourselves and to the gods, both while we remain here, and when we receive its rewards, like victors assembled together; and we shall both here, and in that thousand years' journey we have described, enjoy a happy life.[10]

These excerpts give an idea of Plato's moral system. As mentioned, it is antihedonistic and antiutilitarian; it is also not quite Ideational. It is Idealistic, with eudaemonism whose one foot is in the supersensory world of absolute values, the other in the noblest field of the sensory world — eudaemonistic happiness — as a consequence of the other aspect of the service to the gods, to the soul, or to the absolute moral value.

Idealistic also, though more "earthly," is Aristotle's system of ethics. His supreme *summum bonum*, the supreme end, is self-sufficiency, which is

[9] *Phaedo*, in *Five Dialogues of Plato* (Everyman's Library ed.), pp. 199 ff. See this dialogue *passim*, with its sarcastic criticism of any Sensate system of ethics.

[10] Plato, *Republic*, the end of Bk. X. With these words the *Republic* and the famous myth of the "after-death" is ended. See also Bk. IV of the *Republic*.

neither hedonistic nor utilitarian; it is again eudaemonistic and absolute. Concretely, it is described as a wise, contemplative life of the mind or soul which partakes of "the divine Principle." The eudaemonistic happiness follows, as a by-product, from such a *summum bonum*. But sensate happiness is neither the self-value, nor do sensate pleasures play an important part in such a happiness. A self-sufficient and perfectly happy life in the Aristotelian sense

will be higher than mere human nature, because a man will live thus, not in so far as he is man but in so far as there is in him a divine Principle: and in proportion as this Principle excels his composite nature so far does the Working thereof excel that in accordance with any other kind of Excellence: and therefore, if pure Intellect, as compared with human nature, is divine, so too will the life in accordance with it be divine compared with man's ordinary life.

Yet must we not give ear to those who bid one as man to mind only man's affairs, or as mortal only mortal things; but, so far as we can, make ourselves like immortals and do all with a view to living in accordance with the highest Principle in us; for small as it may be in bulk, yet in power and preciousness it far more excels all the others (than they it in bulk). In fact, this Principle would seem to constitute each man's "Self," since it is supreme and above all others in goodness: it *would* be absurd then for a man not to choose his own life but that of some other.[11]

Idealistic also is the position of the great writers of the second part of the fifth and of the first part of the fourth century: Euripides, Aristophanes (partly), Thucydides. Their moral systems are still rooted in the transcendental world of gods. But now their will is scrutinized, sometimes questioned, sometimes protested on the basis and for the sake of the eudaemonistic sensate values of man's life. Eudaemonistic and utilitarian principles enter as components of their moral standpoint.[12]

C. At the end of the fifth and the beginning of the fourth century B.C. (420 to 380), there is a great quantitative flaring of the ethics of happiness. It becomes dominant. It stays high throughout the fourth, the third, the second, and the first centuries B.C. So far it bears witness to the Sensate character of this period. Qualitatively, the moral mentality undergoes a still more important change. The noble eudaemonistic theories were more and more replaced by more primitive hedonistic and utilitarian branches of the Sensate ethics of happiness. As we have seen in Chapter Two, Sensate hedonism of a crude *Carpe diem* type seems to

[11] Aristotle, *Nicomachean Ethics* (Everyman's Library ed.), Bk. X, 1177*b*, 1178*a*, pp. 250 ff. For an understanding of Aristotle's system, see the whole of this work; also his *Magna Moralia* and *Politics*.

[12] See Ranulf, *op. cit., passim.*

have spread among the masses of that period and become much more powerful than it was before, in spite of the fact that according to our data it was about as strong as the ethics of principles.

D. With the beginning of our era, it begins to decline, and after the fourth century A.D. it goes underground. Here again its movement is similar to that of all the other Sensate variables of Graeco-Roman culture.

E. The period from the fifth century A.D. to the end of the fifteenth century appears again monolithic, entirely dominated by the ethics of principles. This period, up to at least the thirteenth century, appears to be Ideational here also, similar to its Ideationalism in all the other fields of Western culture. The ethical mentality of it was in a perfect agreement with the other variables of the culture studied. The perfectly Ideational, even ascetically Ideational character of the medieval moral mentality is well known. Moral commands are those of God. They are absolute. They are the supreme value. They do not have any regard for the value of sensate happiness at all. If anything, they are inimical to it.

> Fear not them that kill the body.

> *Memento, homo, quia pulvis es et in pulverem revertis.*

> *Quisquic amat Christum, mundum non diligit istum*
> *Sed quasi fetores spernit illius amores*
> *Aestimat obsoenum quod mundus credit amoenum*
> *Et sibi vilescit quod in orbe nitescit.*[13]

These are the mottoes, in millions of variations, that dominated the medieval moral mentality. The emergence and growth of monasticism testify to the same contempt toward all the earthly values. And its growth was parallel with the decline of Sensate and the growth of absolute moral mentality. It originated in the third and began rapidly to spread in the fourth century A.D.

Men fled from a half-heathen world to seek for God and wrestle against the powers of evil in the remotest wilderness. In the first decades of the fourth century, the monks had spread themselves throughout the deserts of Egypt. From this time the passion for monastic life spread throughout the Christian world. It appeared next in Syria. . . . By the opening of the fifth century there were monks throughout Gaul and in distant Britain. The movement was lay rather than clerical; it was an impulse which drove men into the solitude of the desert, which thousands were forced to obey. . . . Within little

---

[13] St. Bernard.

more than a century of its inception, the monastic life had come to be regarded as the consummation and flower of Christianity.[14]

It was by monks that the Christian religion was carried beyond the bounds of the Roman Empire (into Central Asia, Russia, Siberia, Ireland, British Isles, and so on). The Christianity of the new nations was . . . a monastic creed.[15]

The reasons for such a rapid diffusion of the Christian monasticism were the same as those for any other monasticism.

In a falling world, like that of the age which ushered in the Medieval period, men were impelled to take refuge in the desert, the cloister or the forest, that they might at least save their own souls from the impending destruction. Circumstances forced many to acknowledge the emptiness and misery of life on earth and to look for happiness outside the world. That those who did so were not all actuated by base and cowardly motives is proved by the services of the monks to mankind. . . . It is hardly too much to say that (by monasticism) Christianity was saved from being utterly overwhelmed by the constant inroad of the barbarians.[16]

Seclusion from the world, holiness, devotion of the whole life to God, the vows of obedience, poverty, chastity; contempt, often torture, of the flesh; suppression of carnal needs — these were the traits of monastic Ideational ethics, whether for hermits or for monks living in monasteries. (See the rules of Pachomius, St. Benedict, and others.)[17] Monasticism and asceticism compose the main pattern of the medieval ethics even outside of the monks.

Of the Middle Ages, it may be said that everybody was a monk at heart, in the sense that no man was so usefully employing his life for the benefit of others, but he acknowledged that the summons of the monastery or of the hermit's cell was a call to better things, and even sinners believed that repentance could most surely be found in the self-torture of solitary asceticism. To all men the monastic life represented the highest goal on this earth. In this way the Medieval ideal is quite distinct from the modern. . . . In the Middle

[14] F. J. Foakes Jackson, *An Introduction to the History of Christianity* (New York, 1921), pp. 5–6.

[15] *Ibid.*, p. 8. "The outskirts of the town became covered with hermitages, veritable dens; in these they [monks] lived the lives of savages, emaciated, unclean, and in rags." L. Duchesne, *Early History of the Christian Church* (New York, 1924), Vol. III, p. 23.

[16] Foakes Jackson, *op. cit.*, p. 9. See there *passim*. See also Cardinal Gasquet, *Monastic Life in the Middle Ages* (London, 1922); J. B. O'Connor, *Monasticism and Civilization* (New York, 1921); H. O. Taylor, *The Medieval Mind*, 2 vols. (London, 1927); A. von Harnack, *Monasticism* (New York, 1895); I. C. Hannan, *Christian Monasticism* (New York, 1925); Monsignor L. Duchesne, *Early History of the Christian Church*, 3 vols. (New York, 1924).

[17] See also G. G. Coulton, *The Medieval Scene* (Cambridge, 1930), pp. 74–78.

Ages it was held that the more a man devoted himself to meditation and sub-jugation of the flesh to the spirit, the more pleasing was he in the sight of God. Monasticism was the first characteristic of this long period.[18]

This Ideational mentality permeated the whole of life.

Medieval conceptions were founded upon religion and law. The theory of life at least was profoundly Christian. . . . Religion was not simply a part of man's life; it pervaded his every action. The Church was necessary for him in all he undertook; he could neither live nor die without its aid. The powers of evil swarmed around him; and but for the Church, the saints, the angels, he might be overwhelmed at any moment. . . . The great difference between modern and Medieval Christianity is that in theory at least, the reli-gion of the Middle Ages was uncompromising in its demand. It was grounded on the monastic idea of absolute surrender of all things for God.[19]

It is not surprising, therefore, that among the thinkers of these centu-ries from the fifth to the thirteenth, practically no name can be found that expounded a Sensate system of ethics.

F. In Table 29 we do not find any representative of such a system up to the end of the fifteenth century. Besides L. Valla a few other names can be mentioned, but they did not give any system of ethics. This, however, does not mean that *qualitatively* the ethical systems for all these centuries did not experience any change from the standpoint of our main categories. As a matter of fact, such a change becomes noticeable, especially beginning with the end of the twelfth and in the thirteenth and the fourteenth centuries. As late as the thirteenth and fourteenth centuries the main principle is still: "The perfect happiness of man cannot be other than the vision of the Divine essence"[20] or, as Dante puts it: the supreme end of humanity is "Glory to God in the heaven and peace be unto earth"; therefore its task is "to actualize continually the entire capacity of the possible intellect, primarily, speculation, then action for which purpose is necessary, peace and tranquillity."[21] For-mally, the ethical systems of these centuries are still religious, transcen-dental, and absolutistic. And yet, new notes begin to sound in them — a note of a sublime eudaemonism; a note somewhat reluctant to the previous monastic asceticism and torture of body; a note of admis-sibility and justification of the supreme eudaemonistic happiness in so far and inasmuch as it does not contradict the commands of God; and

---

[18] Jackson, *op. cit.*, p. 4.   [19] Jackson, *op. cit.*, pp. 376–378.
[20] St. Thomas Aquinas, *Summa Theologica*, II, i, q. 3, a. 8.
[21] Dante, *De Monarchia* (Boston, 1904), chaps. i–iv.

an additional note, to the effect that it does not contradict it often; therefore it is admissible, perhaps even desirable. These new notes sound in the works of the great Scholastics of the period as well as in those of the minor thinkers.

Peter Abelard, Hugo de St. Victor, Albertus Magnus, St. Thomas Aquinas, Walter of Brugges, Alexander of Halle, Roscelinus, Roger Bacon, Siger of Brabant, Dante, and others, not mentioning even such names as Petrarch; all these thinkers to some degree and in some forms introduced these "new notes" in their ethical systems. For this reason, the period appears not very unlike that of the fifth century B.C. in Greece. It is not incidental that the Platonized Aristotelian system of ethics is the ethics of St. Thomas, Albertus Magnus, Dante, and of many other Scholastics marked by the Idealistic stamp rather than by the purely Ideational form of the preceding centuries. The values of Sensate world "got some footing" in the ethical systems of these centuries and were now not regarded as absolutely valueless or negative.

As we have seen in Chapter Thirteen of Volume One, in the field of literature and among the works of the great writers of the period, the Sensate stream — in the literary content as well as in form — emerged in the twelfth century and became much more conspicuous. The ethical system of the *Roman de la Rose* and other great works of the period, with the exception of a few, was Idealistic, with a much stronger Sensate element. In the philosophicoethical and religious ethical systems, this element was more insignificant than in those expounded by literary works, but it was definitely present there. In this sense, the period was Mixed and Idealistic in its ethical mentality.

G. The growth of Sensate elements continues within the absolute systems of ethics of the next centuries, and culminates in an emergence of Sensate systems of ethics at the end of the fifteenth century, and their sudden enormous increase in the sixteenth century, up to 43 per cent of all the systems of ethics. Sensate (not Idealistic) eudaemonism, then hedonism, and utilitarianism re-emerge on the highway of the ethical thought of the Western society, and after that, with temporary fluctuations, rapidly grow. The expansion of this stream, or the trend toward the sensualization of ethics during the centuries from the sixteenth to the twentieth has proceeded in three ways: first, quantitatively, the ethics of happiness in all its three forms held during the last four centuries about 40 per cent of influence compared with 60 per cent of that held by the ethics of absolute principles. In the sixteenth century — the time of the Renaissance and the Reformation — quantitatively, Sensate ethics was the highest (43 per cent).[22]   In the next two centuries it fell slightly, but in the nineteenth and the twentieth century has rebounded.   The second form of the expansion of this stream manifested itself in a greater growth of its hedonistic and utilitarian branches at the cost of eudaemonistic variety.   With the exception of the Renaissance hedonism, which was sensual, the ethics-of-happiness system of the subsequent period had been becoming, with minor fluctuations, more and more hedonistic, less and less eudaemonistic, until it became predominantly utilitarian and hedonistic, especially in the moral mentality of the masses of the end of the nineteenth and in the twentieth century.   Finally, the growth of this current manifested itself also in a greater and greater contamination by Sensate elements of the systems of the ethics of principles of these centuries.   Formally many of these appear absolutistic and Ideational; factually, when one analyzes their content, one sees that many of them are rather Sensate than Ideational.   Formally, many of these theories are put, in Tables 29 and 30, in the class of the ethics of principles; factually, they deserve to be put into the class of the ethics of happiness.

A brief sketch of the ethics of Protestantism, the ascetic Protestantism not excluded, illustrates this point well.

As to Lutheranism and Luther himself, the presence of a large dose of Sensate elements in their ethical system and conduct is rather certain. In contradistinction to Calvinism and other branches of the ascetic Protestantism, Luther did not offer any systematic and new code of moral conduct.   His role was mainly in "liberating" people from a great many Ideational ascetic bonds inconvenient from the standpoint of economic expediency and worldly comfort.   His activity consisted mainly in the destruction or disruption of these bonds, and in clearing the ground for a flowering of Sensate mentality.   In this sense he was its "nurse" and preparer.   By his teachings and activities he helped greatly to eliminate asceticism, monasticism, celibacy (even for the monks, nuns, and priests), indissolubility and sacredness of marriage, even monogamy, so far as he admitted polygamy as lawful; domination of the Church and religion in social life; fastings; mendicants; unnecessary expenses and wastes connected with the cult of the saints and holy days; canon and medieval law, so far as they hindered utilitarianism, economism, and "reasonable" material comfort; and many other things inconvenient from the stand-

[22] This sudden growth is due especially to the Italian and then the French Renaissance. Its thinkers were notoriously sensual in their ethical systems as well as in their conduct. See J. Burckhardt, *The Civilization of the Renaissance in Italy* (London, 1909), *passim*, and pt. vi, pp. 432–547; R. Davidson, *Geschichte von Florence* (Berlin, 1922), Vol. IV, chap. i *et passim;* A. V. Martin, *Sociologie der Renaissance* (Stuttgart, 1932), pp. 1–5, 17–21, 27, and 45.

point of the reasonable enjoyment of life were undermined or eliminated by and through his activity. This is shown well by his motto : Let men "by all means use their Christian freedom as they pleased, how, when, and as long as matters seemed to indicate and require it." [23]

By this rather liberal formula the discussed role of Luther is shown to be unquestionable. His stress of the proper discharge of one's calling as the spiritual and virtuous task,[24] in which "to make shoes is as spiritual as to pray and preach," shows this role still more clearly.[25] More questionable was the character and role of the ethics of the ascetic branches of Protestantism : Calvinism, Pietism, Methodism, and the Baptist sects. The very word "ascetic" makes us think of these movements as predominantly Ideational in their nature. To the same conclusion we seem to be driven by the character of their apparent ethics [26] and by the fact that at their earlier stages they indeed made man's life orderly, puritan, and austere in suppression of the carnal weaknesses and lusts. All this cannot be denied [27] and so far these movements were, in their early stages (like the simultaneous Catholic Reformation), to a considerable degree an Ideational reaction against the loose mores and Sensate ethics of the end of the fifteenth and sixteenth centuries.

This being granted, there remains, nevertheless, something much more important concerning the main character, role, and particularly the real effects of these currents and systems. Notwithstanding their apparent ethical absolutism, the content and the role of these currents consisted

[23] H. Boehmer, *Luther* (New York, 1930), p. 235. See in his work — which is biased in favor of Luther — corroboration of these statements. A large group of the non-Protestant authors, especially the Roman-Catholic historians of Luther and Lutheranism (Denifle and others), draw his picture much more sharply and stress his destructive role much more conspicuously as that of "a glutton and drunkard of the worst sort, a bestial debauchee, a ribald brawler, a mountebank of the lowest order, a writer who surpassed Zola in obscenity, an impudent falsifier, liar and cheat, a man of crass ignorance," and so on.

[24] See about that Max Weber, *The Protestant Ethics and the Spirit of Capitalism* (New York, 1930), chap. iii; R. H. Tawney, *Religion and the Rise of Capitalism* (New York, 1926), pp. 92 ff.

[25] George Herbert expressed the same in the words :

> A servant with this clause
> Makes drudgery divine;
> Who sweeps a room as to Thy laws
> Makes that and the action fine.

[26] For instance : "What is the chief end of human life? [we read in the Genevan catechism of Calvin.] To know God, by whom we have been made human beings. What is the reason for saying that? Because He created us and placed us in this world that He might be glorified in us," and so on. "*Catechismus Ecclesiae Genevensis*," in J. C. G. Augusti, *Corpus librorum symbolicorum* (Erberfeld, 1827), pp. 464 ff.

[27] See the details in Tawney's and M. Weber's works, cited.

indeed in undermining the real Ideational ethics and in justifying, beautifying, and sanctifying the utilitarian sensate mode of life.   Max Weber,
R. H. Tawney, E. Troeltsch,[28] and many other investigators of these
movements claim that in a way they were the godfathers of the contemporary capitalism, pecuniarism, economism, utilitarianism, or the
rationalistic worldly epicureanism.   Their works permit me to be brief
and to use their studies for a corroboration of the above claim.[29]   Already

---

[28] See besides Tawney's and Weber's works, E. Troeltsch, *Die Soziallehren der christlichen Kirchen und Gruppen* (Tübingen, 1912).

[29] This does not mean at all that I am accepting the greater part of their theories.   On the contrary I am definitely rejecting them.   In my opinion, the very exceptional role ascribed to Protestantism in origination of the modern capitalism is wrong and unproved by Max Weber.   As it follows from all the above chapters, the growth of Protestantism, utilitarianism, "economism," "sensate rationalism," science, and other characteristics of Sensate culture — all these are the manifestations of one fundamental reason — the transformation of the Western culture from its Ideational phase into its Sensate phase, the process that began roughly around the end of the twelfth century and subsequently progressed *crescendo*.   In these circumstances to regard Protestantism as *the* cause of progress of science or capitalism is as fallacious as to regard a growth of whiskers in a male organism as *the* cause of hundreds of anatomical, physiological, and psychological changes that take place in such an organism as a result of its passage from the stage of childhood to that of puberty and maturity.   If we should style this transition of the Western culture from its Ideational to Sensate form, A; B, a change in art from Ideationalism to Visualism; C, growth of the natural sciences; D, change of the system of truth; E, growth of utilitarian and other branches of Sensate ethics; F, decline in Idealism; H, the Reformation; G, the Renaissance; M, the growth of capitalism, and so on; and then take H as the cause of B, C, D, E, F, G, M, it would be as childish as to take the growth of whiskers in the above case as the cause of growth of weight, of height, of glandular and muscular changes, of physiological and psychological transformations that occur in an organism in the transformation mentioned.   In the chapter on the movement of scientific discoveries, I have already pointed out the fact that their increase began a long time before Protestantism appeared; and began in the Catholic countries; and, even after the emergence of Protestantism, the Catholic countries like France — includ-
ing many Catholics who were the greatest of the scientists of the time, like Descartes, Pascal, and others — continued to grow.   The same is to be said of other "generalizations" of Max Weber in this field.   His thesis is corroborated little by the factual data.   Farther on, Weber, Troeltsch, Tawney, all are guilty of "modernization" of Protestant theories, according to the pattern of a sensate liberalism of the end of the nineteenth and of the beginning of the twentieth century.   Max Weber's analysis of the practical effects of the doctrine of predestination is perfectly arbitrary.   He does not give any serious evidence that it had to vitalize the industry and economic activity of the followers of this doctrine.   His concept of rationalism, and especially modern capitalism (which is derivative of this rationalism) is perfectly vague and ambiguous; his interpretation of the rationalism of other religions is sometimes mistaken.   His theory of the causal relationship between religious and economic factors is also defective.   In its essence it is shaped along the "functional" conception of causality of the end of the nineteenth century, outlined above in Chapter Eleven.   As such, it is the conception of the period of the crisis in the conception of causality.   Even within this brand of causality conception, his thesis is not proved.   In brief, I do not subscribe to the greater part of Weber's theory repeated in a diluted form by Tawney and many others.   See some of my criticisms in my *Contemporary Sociological Theories*, pp. 683–696.   In Vol-

the ideal of orderliness and asceticism of these movements is potentially Sensate in its heart and soul. A little later this "Epicureanism" came out clearly, while "the Ideational subterfuge" which masked it in the earliest stages of these movements faded and fell away from it. To put concisely what I mean by this, it is enough to compare the medieval attitude toward economic interests and values. In the moral theory as well as, to a considerable degree, in the practice of the Middle Ages, the economic conditions of life were regarded as entirely subordinated to the religious and moral values; the wealth as such was viewed, especially in the early Middle Ages, negatively, as a source of perdition, and the rich as the group for which it was more difficult to save their souls than for a camel to pass through a needle's eye. The reason of a pure economic expediency was unthinkable, and all the important economic questions were decided in conformity with the religious and moral ends. As soon as the economic expediency contradicted these ends it was repressed and rejected. The most fundamental difference between medieval and modern economic thought consists in the fact that, whereas the latter normally refers to economic expediency for the justification of any particular action, policy, or system of organization, the former starts from the position that there is a moral authority to which considerations of economic expediency must be subordinated.[30]

In regard to the economic interests and conditions the medieval

fundamental assumptions were two: that economic interests are subordinate to the real business of life, which is salvation, and that economic conduct is one aspect of personal conduct, upon which the rules of morality are binding. There is no place in medieval theory for economic activity which is not related to a moral end. [Therefore] at every turn there are limits, restrictions, warnings, against allowing economic interests to interfere with serious affairs.[31]

Such an attitude explains why seeking money or trying to make money and wealth beyond what is necessary for a modest living was regarded as an avarice and a great sin; why moneylending for interest was regarded in the same way and was punished by expulsion, excommunication, outlawing, and other severe measures, and was branded as *turpitudo* and *a pudendum* even in the thirteenth century when this negative attitude was considerably softened in the legislations of the Lateran

---

ume Four a much more substantial criticism will be given. However, their work permits me to use some of their analyses to illustrate the point I am discussing.

[30] Tawney, *op. cit.*, pp. 39–40.

[31] R. H. Tawney, *op. cit.*, pp. 31–32; Max Weber, *op. cit.*, pp. 72 ff.

Council (1175), of the Councils of Lyons (1274), of Vienna (1312), and others.[32]

Consequently, any economic interest and economic activity was regarded with the greatest suspicion and was tolerated only in so far as it was necessary for mere living. Beyond that it was outlawed and branded as sin and crime.

"*Summae periculosa est venditionis et emptionis negotiatio*" — such was the warning against the commercial and money-making professions. Any profit was "*turpe lucrum*"; usury and moneylending were put on a par with adultery, fornication, and other gravest crimes; even any man who would try to declare that usury was not a sin was punished as a heretic, and inquisitors proceeded against him "*tanquam contra diffamatos vel suspectos de haeresi.*" The clergy as well as civil authorities often made a special search to find out whether such a crime was committed. The rich generally were regarded as most likely candidates for hell. Anatole France correctly expresses this attitude in his statement: "*La miséricorde de Dieu est infinie: elle sauvera même un riche.*"[33] In such circumstances a man who would spend his life just in making money and, as such, would be respected and appreciated, was unthinkable. On the other hand, this whole atmosphere appears so strange to us that one has to make an effort and study it more substantially in order to be able to understand it.

Later on, after the twelfth and thirteenth centuries, this attitude began to be changed and, from being merely "soft-pedaled" at the beginning, was given a more and more "tolerant" interpretation, until after approximately the sixteenth and the seventeenth centuries it was forsaken, and the economic interests and values were raised to the level of the self-sufficing and almost the main value, to which all the others should be subordinated.[34]

The Calvinist and several other Protestant doctrines were one of the

---

[32] Of course similar was the attitude of most Christian thinkers of the earlier period of the Middle Ages. The very trade and commerce for making of profit was condemned (Gratian, *Decretum*, pt. i, dist. 88, cap. 11), *Corpus juris canonici*. Even private property was regarded either as a result of the Fall and the lesser evil or was rejected. See above that G. G. Coulton, *The Medieval Scene*, pp. 140–142; R. W. and A. J. Carlyle, *A History of Medieval Political Theory in the West*, Vol. I (New York, 1903), pp. 83 ff. and Vols. II–IV (New York, 1909–1923); R. Pöhlmann, *Geschichte der sozialen Frage und Sozialismus in der antiken Welt* (München, 1912), last chapters.

[33] See the details in Tawney, *op. cit.*, pp. 32 ff.; Weber, *op. cit.*, pp. 72 ff. See Bibliography in these works. Also Martin Saint-Leon, *Histoire des corporations de métiers* (Paris, 1922), p. 187; Thomas Aquinas, *Summa theologica*, II, i, q. 2, a. 1; q. 8, a. 8.

[34] See the details of this transition in the cited works of Weber and Tawney.

expressions (not the causes) of this transformation of the ethical mentality. For some of the followers, the Calvinist doctrine of predestination possibly helped the idea that if the Puritans were successful in their calling or business, this was a sign that they were among the elect in the state of grace, and for this reason they were required to exert all their energies in the successful management of their economic affairs, and to become the devotees of the economic values and their virtues.[35]

A concentration of the Puritans' energy and thought upon the commercial aspect of their activity, calling, and business, due to a series of other circumstances, was justified by such teachings. Business, money, economic success, and economic value became, in the early stages of Puritanism, the central interest of their lives, and the main guide of their activities. The religious phraseology was rather a mere — though sincere — "derivation," in Pareto's sense.

The usefulness of a calling, and thus its favor in the sight of God, is measured primarily in moral terms. . . . But a further, and in practice the most important, criterion is found in private profitableness. For if that God, whose hand the Puritan sees in all the occurrences of life, shows one of His elect a chance of profit, He must do it with a purpose. Hence, the faithful Christian must follow the call by taking advantage of the opportunity.[36]

This depicts well — and gracefully — the situation. Still more clearly is it expressed in the typical statements of the great ideologists of the Puritan movement.

[35] See Max Weber, *op. cit.*, pp. 112–116 ff., 162–163, and 172 ff. "God blessed His trade." "God shows one of His elect a chance of profit." These are expressions of this belief. This point of Weber that the doctrine of predestination was a cause of this transformation is open to criticism. The doctrine of predestination can as well lead to passivism and inactivity. Since there is no use to make an effort to get salvation by personal actions, is it not natural not to strive for anything? If you are predestined to be saved, you will be saved; if you are not, nothing and no virtuous life can help you. Such a practical conclusion is rather more natural than that made by Weber. Such a conclusion would be quite inevitable for those who failed in their enterprises; such a failure or lack of success would be simultaneously a sign that such men were not among the predestined to be saved, and evidence that their efforts would be useless against destiny. And as the number of unsuccessful men is always greater than the successful, such an effect would be more probable if the doctrine of predestination were the main factor in the game. The more so that, according to the Calvinist computation, no more than one person out of every hundred thousand (Pierre Demoulin's computation) was called to eternal bliss. In brief, here, as well as in many other points, Weber's explanations and interpretations are very questionable. Especially, since among the prosperous Protestants, a great many protested and rejected or modified this doctrine, which they found unethical. Vondel, Arminius, Latitudinarians, Milton, Barneveldt, the Remonstrants, and others.

[36] Weber, *op. cit.*, p. 162. See also Tawney, *op. cit.*, pp. 99 ff., 78, and 115 ff.

"The cultivation of tobacco brings money into the country, and is thus useful, hence not sinful," assures Spencer, in accordance with the other leading pietists.[37] "We must exhort all Christians to gain all they can and to save all they can, that is, in effect, to grow rich," preaches John Wesley.[38]

If God show you a way by which you may lawfully get more than in another way, if you refuse this and choose the less gainful way, you cross one of the ends of your calling, and you refuse to be God's steward and to accept His gifts [preaches Baxter].[39]

One can scarcely imagine a more convenient and justifying ideology for money-making and enriching oneself. It is indeed an easy way "to get a capital and to save one's soul." The whole asceticism of the Puritans appears permeated with economism and utilitarianism and is directed primarily toward economic wealth, while the asceticism itself is rather a mere "saving" and accumulation of wealth, instead of its immediate spending. It is not Ideational ethics and asceticism, but a mere thrift, parsimony, and a sensible enjoyment of money as the greatest value by a man who dearly loves and appreciates it. In brief, it is Sensate through and through. Dr. Tawney puts it in the following way.

Discarding the suspicion of economic motives (which was general for the Middle Ages), Puritanism added a halo of ethical sanctification to the appeal of economic expediency. It insisted that money-making, if not free from spiritual dangers, was not danger and nothing else, but that it could be, and ought to be, carried on for the greater glory of God.[40]

"The triumph of Presbyterianism swept away all traces of any restriction or guidance in the employment of money," says Cunningham.[41]

"On Sundays he (the Puritan) believes in God and Eternity; on week-days in the Stock Exchange. On Sundays the Bible is his ledger, and on week-days the ledger is his Bible." [42]

From this a series of the characteristic traits of Puritanism follows — the traits which show the same "commercial soul and heart" of it. Such

---

[37] Weber, op. cit., p. 266.

[38] Ibid., p. 175.

[39] Ibid., p. 162. See in Tawney's work quoted a prayer on p. 150.

[40] Tawney, op. cit., pp. 239–240. Such a commercial enthusiasm called forth the sneers of the contemporaries expressed in such phrases as "Presbyterian old usurer," "devout miser," "extorting Ishban," etc. Ibid., p. 252.

[41] W. Cunningham, The Moral Witness of the Church on the Investment of Money and the Use of Wealth (London, 1909), p. 25.

[42] E. Friedel, Cultural History of Modern Europe (New York, 1932), Vol. I, pp. 287–292; Vol. II, pp. 187–189.

are: unprofitable waste of time, because time is money; a regular book-keeping of one's good deeds, because bookkeeping is an important business procedure and because it provides a document useful for many purposes; utilitarianism of the Puritans; their individualism; their aversion to any waste of money and to anything which requires unnecessary expenses (like theaters, ostentatious objects, etc.); their prohibition of alms-giving philanthropy to beggars and mendicants, and, finally, their inexhaustible energy, diligence, and success in their commercial and economic pursuits, which notably transformed the social world of all mankind, a fact which in itself is excellent testimony to the Sensate nature of these movements.

In the course of time all these traits became quite clear when the draperies of the religious Ideational mentality were lost, or rather, having served their purpose, fell off as useless hindrances incapable of bringing any further commercial profit. Here is a description of this "undressing" of Puritanism.

Since asceticism undertook to remodel the world and to work out its ideals in the world, material goods have gained an increasing and finally an inexorable power over the lives of men, as at no previous period in history. To-day the spirit of religious asceticism — whether finally who knows? — has escaped from the cage. But victorious capitalism, since it rests on mechanical founda-tions, needs its support no longer. . . . In the field of its highest development, in the United States, the pursuit of wealth, stripped of all its religious and ethical meaning, tends to become associated with purely mundane passions, which actually often give it the character of sport. . . . Of the last stage of this cultural development it may be said: "Specialists without spirit, sensual-ists without heart; this nullity imagines that it has attained a level of civi-lization never before achieved." [43]

John Wesley described well this progressive commercialization of Puritanism in his terse sentences:

I fear, wherever riches have increased, the essence of religion has decreased in the same proportion. Therefore I do not see how it is possible, in the nature of things, for any revival of true religion to continue long. For religion must necessarily produce both industry and frugality, and these cannot but produce riches. But as riches increase, so will pride, anger and love of the world in all its branches. . . . So, although the form of religion remains, the spirit is swiftly vanishing away. [44]

Here we have one of the immanent transformations of a social process. Just as the ascetic medieval Church, due to its asceticism, attracted

<hr>

[43] Weber, *op. cit.*, pp. 181–182.   [44] *Ibid.*, p. 175.

wealth more and more and was changed, becoming the richest institution, so the commercial devotion of the ascetic Puritanism with its "limitation of consumption, its release of acquisitive activity led through this compulsory saving to accumulation of capital. And the greater it was, the greater became its grip and the more strongly it embraced Puritans in its tentacles," and dried out even those Ideational and noncommercial values which it had at the moment of its inception.[45]

Calvinism "had begun by being the very soul of authoritarian regimentation. It ended by being the vehicle of an almost utilitarian individualism." [46]

Out of an Anabaptist Puritanism was transformed into a company promoter and a mere businessman; out of a Christian kingdom of God into a social system which "is the negation of any system of thought or morals, which can, except by a metaphor, be described as Christian." [47]

In the seventeenth and the eighteenth centuries, economic interest and expediency became the supreme value and the criterion for evaluation of all the other (especially the noneconomic) values, including the religious and moral ones.

Honesty is useful because it assures credit; so are punctuality, industry, frugality, and that is the reason they are virtues. . . . Remember that time is money. . . . Remember that credit is money. . . . Remember that money is of prolific, generating nature.[48]

These statements of Benjamin Franklin in Weber's interpretation show as great a revolution in the moral values as there could be. From being censored, branded, punished, and persecuted in the Middle Ages, the economic values and interests now became the king and queen of all the other values. All that helps economic expediency is virtue; [49] all that hinders it is sin. In such a schematic way was this greatest moral revolution carried on by these "ascetic" movements.

These considerations illustrate the point that many apparently absolutistic systems of ethics of the sixteenth and subsequent centuries were in fact the vehicles of Sensate ethics — utilitarian and hedonistic — that grew within and contaminated more and more the Ideational systems of ethics of these cultures. When this is considered, the growth of Sensate ethics during these centuries becomes much greater than the percentages

[45] *Ibid.*, p. 172.   [46] Tawney, *op. cit.*, p. 227.   [47] *Ibid.*, p. 286.   [48] Weber, *op. cit.*, p. 52.
[49] Hence all these numerous tracts, like "Navigations Spiritualized," "Husbandry Spiritualized," "The Religious Weaver," etc. See P. Smith, *A History of Modern Culture* (New York, 1930), Vol. I, p. 377.

in Tables 29 and 30 show. Utilitarianism and hedonism, with their derivatives, also grew enormously and covered with their shadows the whole horizon of the social and moral world, and molded it according to their own ideals. So much for this point.

In a concrete, different form, the same transformation took place within the Catholic doctrines and moral teachings of these centuries.

H. During these four centuries, the ethics of happiness had its highs in the periods 1560–1620; then around 1760–1780; and finally, since 1880 up to the present time. We are living at the age of its high tide. This high tide would appear still greater if one considered the qualitative extreme of eudaemonism, hedonism, and utilitarianism which has been experienced during these last few centuries and especially during the above periods of their flare-ups, and the discussed "sensualization" of the ethics of Principles. Most of the Sensate systems have become more sensual, more relative, more earthly, and more carnal than, for instance, they were during the greater part of their Graeco-Roman history. As we shall see later, this "carnalization" of all the ethical values in the public mentality of the present time has gone exceedingly far and has reduced almost all the ethical values to those of mere bodily comfort and enjoyment; these have become the measuring sticks for the evaluation of ethical as well as other values.

I. So far as the relative ups and downs of the other systems of ethics are concerned, they naturally go inversely to those of the ethics of happiness. The ethics of principles and that of love (the variety of the first) dominated relatively in the periods before 440 B.C., 360–280 B.C., 220–160 B.C., around 120–40 B.C.; then, since the fifth century A.D., they almost monopolistically dominated for more than a thousand years. Throughout the Middle Ages they were the only systems which openly existed. This means that since approximately the beginning of our era the moral mentality has been experiencing a fundamental change opposite to that which took place at the end of the fifth century B.C. Then ethical values were humanized, made relative, conditional, and sensual; and atomization and disabsolutization of these values occurred; with them came an increase of variety of various ethical systems and principles: an increase of differentiation and heterogeneity. Now the process is reversed.

Now the "dehumanization," derelativization, desensualization of these values were started. They rapidly became more and more absolute and independent of the value of sensate happiness and especially of that of carnal pleasures, joys, and comforts. They became again sacred and absolute. Differentiation, variety, heterogeneity of moral codes, systems, convictions, tended to be reduced more and more to a uniform and unanimous simplicity.

After the end of the fourteenth century — factually earlier — the opposite process, similar to that at the end of the fifth century B.C. in Greece, took place. Relativization, humanization, sensualization, carnalization, differentiation, and all the other familiar tendencies reappeared. Ethical values became divested of their absolute and sacred veils; they were dragged down from the heavenly heights of the absolute to the earthly lows of the empirical joys and pleasures; they were deprived of any virtue of their own: for the ethics of happiness they are mere "moons" which do not shine by their own light and only reflect the shining of the sun of empirical happiness.

Since the absolute was overthrown, and the problem was reduced to the earthly values, it was inevitable that a multiplication and differentiation of these earthly systems had to take place. Liberated from the "slavery" of the sacred absolute, everybody could coin his own system, perfectly suited to his own needs, fancies, and whims; and there was no judge to decide why one man's fancies were less important than the fancies of another. In this way "atomization," "pulverization," "singularization" of the ethical values again reappeared. As anything is pulverized, it loses more and more of its value; therefore the ethical values as such have been more and more depreciated. At the present, the mottoes "unethical," "amoral," "unmoral," "evil," "perversion," and so on, sound as respectable as their opposites, and more attractive, fashionable, and profitable than the old-fashioned morality and all the ancient "Commandments" and other "nonsense." We are liberated and each of us tailors now his own system of ethics. If some of these systems unhappily land their representatives in prison, this is just "bad luck"; neither the criminals nor their judges always believe that the prisoner's code is worse than that of the nonprisoners. These are just out of luck and that is all. As Table 29 shows, these tendencies have been rising during the last few decades, giving respectively the indicators 38, 42.8, 43 for the 20-year periods from 1860 to 1920.

J. When these dry figures reveal the richness of their meaning, they throw a light upon a number of the dominant characteristics of contemporary mentality.

(1) Its predominantly utilitarian and hedonistic nature. *"Utility" in the Sensate meaning is the dominant trait of our moral mentality.* From science to religion we demand that everything be useful — mate-

rially useful and profitable. If A is useful, A is good. If not, though in a larger and deeper sense it may be much more important, it is no good. "Science is the most economic adaptation of man to environment, his thought to facts, and facts to one another." [50]

Truth is the most economical and convenient mode of thinking, and science is the most economic form of adaptation of man.[51]

"If belief in God is useful, God exists; if not, He does not." [52]

"What is the truth's cash value in the experiential terms?" [53]

These and dozens of other definitions of truth and science — "operational criteria of truth," "survival value of science," "science as the most efficient instrument for survival" — reflect this all-pervading utilitarian principle of our mentality. With proper modifications, the same is thought, asserted, and heralded in regard to any value. If God himself should come to us, His acceptance or rejection would depend upon whether He appears to us to be useful or not. If useful, we accept anything as God; if not, we reject Him. What is still more characteristic is that we demand to be shown quickly (in association with our temporalistic mentality) the useful effects of anything. When a church or university or any other agency starts its "financial drive," the main argument, the main convincing reason, of the solicitors is the argument of utility. The same is true of anything else. As a detail, the category of utility is the central principle of economics, and economics is the central discipline of all the social sciences. Under this banner of utility, plenty of the most scandalous and detrimental enterprises and drives and movements parade and circulate in the social life; specialists in "inventions of utility arguments" thrive and prosper in all the social groups, from ministers and politicians to professors and salesmen. And yet, all this is in accordance with the style of our moral mentality.

(2) *Its second fundamental category is hedonism.* Whether in its sensible or reckless form, it again pervades our moral mentality, from the daily, "Unhappy? Buy a New Car," "Want to Be Happy? Buy A Brand Ham or Refrigerator," or "Listen to Rudy Vallee's Band" to our "We immensely *enjoyed* the Sunday sermon" or "the lecture," or anything else. The term "enjoyment" bears the Sensate connotation, and we do not even notice how awkward it is in its application to the values that do not need, and do not seek, "enjoyment" in order to be

---

[50] E. Mach, *The Science of Mechanics* (Chicago 1902), p. 2 ff.

[51] H. Poincaré, *Science et méthode* (Paris, 1920), pp. 8-12.

[52] One of the formulas of pragmatism.

[53] William James, *Pragmatism* (New York, 1914), p. 200.

values. If somebody starts to claim nowadays that many values are not sensually enjoyable and still are most important values, his voice will likely be the voice crying in the wilderness. Everything is viewed by us from this hedonistic standpoint. It is demanded that sermons, lectures, philanthropic actions, even execution and murder be enjoyable and entertaining. This psychology is so omnipresent, so habitual, so common, from the gangster and profligate to the "heroes" of our days, that it is unnecessary to dwell upon it further. Anything that does not contain in itself at least a promise of sensate pleasure has little chance of being appreciated in our times. Such plants do not blossom in our culture except as rare exceptions.

(3) The third category, derivative from that, is *our money madness*. It manifests itself in thousands of forms. Nowadays we strive to turn almost anything into a profit-making business. Titles, religious preaching, quintuplets, quadruplets, notoriety received at a kidnaping trial, participation in a murder case, fame in the scientific field, in a war, in a baseball game, in politics — all is sought to be turned into profit. Almost all such "heroes" sooner or later land either on the vaudeville stage, or on a Hollywood stage, or in the pages of a sensational paper, or on the board of directors of a bank or insurance company, turning their reputation into money.

(4) Its next form is *the contemporary leadership*. Who are our leaders? First of all, successful money-makers. It matters little how the money is made. With few exceptions, they are at the top of "society"; they are granted scientific degrees, with all their alphabets; they are trustees of everything; they are political leaders; they control this, that, and the other. Some of them, no doubt, deserve such prominence. The others — and they are the majority — hardly. Some certainly not. The money-makers are our heroes, from the Rothschilds to the lucky "wolf of Wall Street." Shall it be added that, in harmony with this, almost everything is for sale in our culture? Money buys all, from saintliness to "beauty." Old Jugurtha's *urbem venalem* is as applicable to us as it was to the culture of Sensate Rome. The main desire, ambition, dream, of most of our contemporaries is to be rich; to have "all that money can buy." Many are obsessed by this mania to such an extent that they enter the "business of crime" as the most promising. Others are more sensible and keep less dangerous paths, but dream no less of becoming rich. Money is our main and supreme value, the criterion for all other values. And this is conspicuously shown by those who, like socialists and communists and anarchists, attack and denounce

this phase of our culture. In spite of all this denouncing, if one tries to find the positive objective of their activity, it is the same money, the same "standard of living" of the rich, the same desire "to have all that money can buy"; but claimed for larger social groups; for masses; and, of course, for the denouncers themselves. That is the whole difference. They do not reject the Sensate standards and morality; on the contrary, they eulogize them even more than do the rich. Only they want it to be diffused *urbi et orbi;* for all and everybody. This means that they appreciate it to such an extent in fact that they want to make it universal.

(5) Its fifth trait is *"moral atomism, relativism, nihilism."* We hardly have any moral value now that is absolute or sacred. By the way of hypocritical inertia, individuals and groups, when they try to defend their existence, or their robbery of existence from others, continue to issue appeals "in the name of humanity," "to the public opinion," "to the sense of justice," and the like; but few except the hopelessly naïve people believe in these appeals and these so-called principles and values. Where and what can be an absolute categorical imperative for communists and their victims, for Hitlerites and Jews, for Italians and Ethiopians, for atheists and believers, for the "moderns" and the "old fashioned," for rich and poor, for the oppressed and the oppressors, and the like! Since the absolute principles are rejected and the moral and other values are reduced to sensual "pain and pleasure"; since no common principle binds, such opposite factions can exist. One faction is trying to increase "the total sum of its pleasures and utility" at the cost of the other; and the other does the same at the cost of the former, or some other group. The result is moral anarchy; moral singularism; moral atomism. Everyone is — and under these conditions is entitled to be — his own moral legislator. And many of us factually are that. Such an *anomie,* to use Durkheim's term, is inevitable when the absolute standards are rejected. It is a mere matter of time when the relativistic ethics of happiness, in the immanent process of its development, comes to this *anomie.* Our culture seems to have reached it. Therefore, we should not be surprised at such phenomena as kidnaping and murdering babies, for the sake of making money; as using them to counteract a possible persecution; as surrender of the state government to the threats of the kidnapers and murderers; as the mailing of bombs by parcel post; as the excellently organized business of crime industry on a large scale, managed with scientific technique, and the like.

The next consequence of it is the *rule of force and coercion* in our social life, in interindividual as well as intergroup relationships. When there are no absolute moral standards, the only guarantee for everybody is either hypocrisy and profit or force. As the profit is desired by all, force becomes the only means of self-protection or of coercion of the others to comply with our demands. Postwar periods have demonstrated clearly that international treaties and obligations do not mean anything; they are just scraps of papers aimed to deceive the naïve. Therefore, at the present moment nobody but the naïve believes in them; any states-man who is not hopelessly stupid does not rely, and cannot rely, upon contracts and treaties. The only means of reliance is force. Hence an enormous increase of its role in international and intergroup relationships. Since neither God, nor moral values, nor promises, nor contracts, can be relied upon, one is forced to rely upon his own rude force or that of his own group. Hence, use of force by every state that feels it can use it safely, be it Japan, Italy, Germany, Russia, or any other country. Hence, an enormous increase of armaments; military budgets; more and more destructive inventions as means to international, interclass, inter-group, interindividual wars. Force has become the supreme arbiter. We have approached very near to the Hobbesian hypothetical "war of everybody with everybody."

Such a rise of force to the position of the supreme moral arbiter is but an immanent result of the excessive development of the hedonistic and utilitarian moral mentality of our days. If this mentality is going to progress further, the role of force will be still more increased until it makes a social life impossible. Then the reaction is to be expected. And this reaction would mean, even has to be preceded by, a decline of the Sensate morality and rise of the ethics of absolute principles. Signs of such a reaction are absent, as yet. But we all feel sharply enough the "carnal inconveniency" of overripe Sensate morality: it has robbed us of our security of life, of our comfort, of our sensate well-being, of our position, of our self-respect, of our dignity, of almost everything. With a further movement in this direction, this "uncomfortable feeling" is likely to increase until it reaches the stage when a shift to the absolute moral standard becomes unavoidable, and with it, the reaction to these "con-stituents" of the overdeveloped ethics of happiness will set in. Then the curve of the ethics of principles will rise again while that of the Sensate ethics will decline once more. So it has been, and so it will go.

Hundreds of other characteristics of our moral mentality are revealed by the above figures; but their enumeration and connection with the variable of the overdeveloped Sensate morality of our days are left to the reader.

K. The data support all the main conclusions derived from Tables 29 and 30 as to the invalidity of any linear conception in this field; as to the principle of limits; Spencer's formula of evolution; the childish character of belief in a final victory of one of the systems over all the others and so on.

L. As to the comparative quantitative strength and balance of these systems, the picture at various periods and for the total period considered is given in Table 31.

TABLE 31. SUM OF INDICES FOR EACH SYSTEM FOR THE SPECIFIED PERIOD

Periods	Ethics of Happiness	Ethics of Principles	Ethics of Love
540 B.C.–A.D. 100	239	356	—
100–600	28	305	120
600–1500	3	71	307
1500–1900	799	1061	228
Total	1069	1793	655

Thus the first period was that of relatively close balance between the ethics of happiness and that of principles. In the second and third periods the balance was entirely broken and the ethics of principles prevailed almost absolutely. The fourth period is again a period of somewhat closer balance between the ethics of happiness and that of principles and of love. When the totals of both of these systems of ethics of principles and of love is taken for the whole period, the sum is 2448, which is more than twice as great as the total sum for the ethics of happiness. This may be interpreted in the sense that, all in all, social existence of man requires that in the relationship between the ethics of principles and that of happiness, the former must be generally much stronger than the latter. And perhaps such a conclusion would not appear strange to anyone who realizes that some degree of sacrifice and altruism is always necessary, and that the ethics of principles stimulates these forms of relationship much more than the ethics of happiness, which is more prone to slip into the egotistic, individualistic sensualism or into a debasing "commercial utilitarianism" which leads sooner or later to a flat — open or masked — moral philistinism, egotism, and rule of force. Later on we shall see that this interpretation is not entirely baseless.

Another thing revealed by the figures in Table 31 is that these numerous "modern" writers on ethics, who assure us that the days of any authoritative system of ethics are over, and that from now on the future belongs entirely to the "scientifically calculated" moral engineering of a purely utilitarian or eudaemonistic or hedonistic type, are but poor victims of their flat imagination and limited knowledge. The probability of a realization of their predictions and expectations is almost nil in the light of these figures and of other reasons developed in this work.

Chapter Fourteen

FLUCTUATION OF ABSOLUTISM AND RELATIVISM, OPTIMISM AND PESSIMISM, IN ETHICOPHILOSOPHICAL THOUGHT

I. Pulsation of Absolutism and Relativism

Are the values absolute or relative? and Which of the values, positive or negative, predominates in the world and its history? — such have been important among the problems of ethicophilosophical thought. From the preceding chapter we see that the answers given to the first problem fall into two fundamental classes: absolutism and relativism. Likewise, the answers given to the second problem fall into two main classes: pessimism and optimism.

Ethicophilosophical *optimism* contends that in the history of the world, the positive values predominate over the negative ones. Ethicophilosophical *pessimism's* contentions are the opposite. Farther on we shall see that optimism and pessimism have two different forms: Ideational and Sensate. Absolute and pure optimism or pessimism hardly exists. Practically all the philosophies are partly and in a sense optimistic, and partly and in a sense pessimistic. For instance, according to Christianity, the empirical world "lies in evil," and sin predominates in it. But the empirical world is only a small part of the ultimate reality, of the Kingdom of God, which is perfect and where only the positive values exist and will exist forever. In this way, Christianity contains both currents: pessimistic and optimistic, but the optimistic current predominates. Putting the matter in the words of St. Augustine, the absolute evil does not and cannot exist, while the absolute Goodness, God, exists and uses the relative evils for the sake of goodness.

In different forms the same coexistence of both currents is given in other predominantly optimistic ethicophilosophical theories. In other theories pessimism is stressed as predominant.

In view of this, each of the ethicophilosophical systems is put in either one of these classes, according to whether optimistic or pessimistic currents predominate in it.

Such is the meaning of the terms pessimism and optimism in this study.

It is to be stressed here especially that in view of the above duplicity and the vagueness of most of the theories in the field, a very considerable amount of subjectivity is unavoidable in classifying the theories.   Therefore, in regard to Tables 33 and 34, my feeling of uncertainty as to how accurately they reflect the reality is especially strong.   It need not be mentioned that the pessimism and optimism studied here concern only the purely intellectual aspect of these outlooks, without any relationship to the pessimistic or optimistic emotional tone and life feeling.   We know there are many persons intellectually pessimistic and very cheerful and optimistic in their emotional moods and in their "life tonality," and vice versa.   For this reason, the subsequent data do not and cannot be taken at all as the indicators of this aspect of pessimism and optimism.

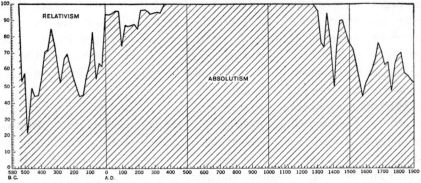

FIGURE 17.   MOVEMENT OF RELATIVISM AND ABSOLUTISM

As far as the curves of absolutism and relativism are concerned, as Figure 17 shows, their movements in essentials coincide with the movements of the curve of the ethics of absolute principles and of love (the curve of absolutism) and with that of ethics of happiness (the curve of relativism).[1]   Such a parallelism is comprehensible.

For the sake of economy, I shall not repeat all the conclusions suggested by the data and Figure 17; it is sufficient to say that they bear out all the facts derived from previous tables, and as outlined above.

[1] For this reason I omit here the tables and the list of the thinkers.   In essentials they reproduce the respective data concerning the movements and the representatives of the main ethical systems given in the preceding chapter.   The principal differences are two: several eudaemonistic theories — consistently or not does not matter here — have been much nearer to absolutism than to relativism.   Therefore they are put into the class of absolutism. On the other hand, the curve of relativism is also somewhat changed by the inclusion of an additional number of the representatives of purely individualistic and egotistic philosophies, ethics and literature, who were not included in the curve of the systems of ethics (because as creators of systems of ethics they have not amounted to anything notable).   These reasons explain why the parallelism of the curves discussed is not quite perfect.

From Figure 17 we see that the period before the very end of the sixth century in Greece is the period free from relativism and its satellites. It is the time of firm convictions and unshakable beliefs.   The fifth century here again is the Idealistic century of balance between *absolutism and relativism; belief and criticism; faith and doubt.*   In the fourth century we see a moderate reaction against too vigorous relativism which in its youthful stage is often too energetic and efficient.   The fourth century somewhat cools its vigor.   In the third and second and first centuries B.C. relativism revives (except for a few short drawbacks).   Beginning with the end of the first century B.C., it undergoes a strong decline, temporarily checked in the second century A.D.; in the third century its decline is decisive and toward the middle of the fourth century it practically becomes *quantité négligeable* and stays underground for some nine hundred years.

Here again the medieval mentality appears monolithic in its absolutism; in its unbounded faith in absolute and unconditioned values.

In the fourteenth century relativism reappears and then, with some fluctuations, reaches a power little below that of absolutism during the subsequent centuries.   These relative ups and downs are shown by the chart.   The *prerevolutionary period of the eighteenth century* is marked by its flare-up; postrevolutionary reaction weakens it, but since 1840 it has steadily risen, up to the present time, and it reached one of its highest peaks in 1900–1920 (53 per cent for 1760–1780, and then respectively for each subsequent 20-year period: 36.2, 31.5, 29.4, 42.2, 43.4, 46.0, 48.6 (in 1900–1920)).   This means that our ethical (and other mentality) is predominantly relativistic and atomistic.   No unanimity, no uniformity of mind or conscience.   Therefore, no uniform public opinion and uniform social reaction to the "right" and "wrong" behavior. What is right for one person or group is wrong for another, and vice versa. Such a relativization of moral and other values means a state of moral anarchy.   In these circumstances, one cannot expect a low rate of violation of the rules of the official moral conduct, for the simple reason that such rules uniformly recognized by the whole society are lacking. Hence, the high rate of so-called criminality, and the impotence of the more delicate and refined means of social control to maintain even the minimum of morality and sociality.   Their place is taken — and has to be taken — by a physical coercion, a strong police aided by the most up-to-date technical means (police radio, signals, etc.) in order to apprehend the man who formally is a criminal and has to be punished, but who often considers his own code to be quite as good as the "official" code.

We have seen that relativism is found in many other fields, scientific, religious, philosophical, artistic, up to Einstein's general and special theory of relativity.   It is one of the most important traits of contemporary mentality.

Table 32 gives the sum of the indicators of relativism and absolutism for separate eras, as well as for the entire period considered.

TABLE 32.   SUM OF INDICES FOR RELATIVISM AND ABSOLUTISM FOR
THE SPECIFIED PERIODS

Period	Absolutism	Relativism
580 B.C.–A.D. 100	694	345
100–560	916	52
560–1500	927	53
1500–1920	2187	1518
Total	4724	1968

Here we do not have an arithmetical balance of the two currents.   But here such a balance should hardly be expected.   The point is that relativism contains a germ of egotistical moral and social anarchy.   This, when strongly developed, makes decent social life, and safety, and sociality hardly possible.   Therefore, if relativistic ethics were as strong as absolutistic, the chances of moral anarchy and therefore the incessant conflicts of individual with individual, of group with group, would be rather unavoidable.   Even a social suppression of so-called crimes would be hardly possible, because under such moral individualistic singularism no generally recognized division of conduct into criminal and noncriminal, right and wrong, just and unjust, is possible; everybody is his own moral legislator.

In view of these and other considerations, it is perhaps comprehensible that absolutism, even from the standpoint of social welfare, has to be much stronger than relativism; and it has to be especially strong in the stern, difficult, and catastrophic conditions, while in the conditions of comfort, when "everything goes all right," one can afford — and is inclined — to indulge in relativism which tends to lead, in its turn, to stern and catastrophic conditions which would check their own "breeder." This explains, perhaps, why in the periods from the third century A.D. and throughout the Middle Ages up to the fourteenth century there was no place for relativism; the conditions were so stern and difficult and exacting and catastrophic that no survival, no social discipline, would be possible without the absolutistic morals and faith.

For the same reason, it is comprehensible why, after the fifteenth century, relativism began to grow, and why, especially in the fat and safe and prosperous "Victorian age," it has made such enormous gains. These brief considerations perhaps explain that the lack of arithmetical balance in this case is good testimony of a real balance; among mortals inclined to indulgence and egotism, absolutism has to be stronger and greater arithmetically than relativism. Our data show this plainly.

Further, it hardly needs to be mentioned that in the main movements the curve of absolutism runs parallel with those of the ethics of principles, of the truth of faith (or providential indeterminism), of idealism, of Ideational art — in brief, parallel to the curve of the rise and fall of the Ideational and partly Idealistic culture — while the curves of relativism and singularism go in a tangible association with the ingredients of the Sensate culture — materialism, truth of the senses (science), determinism, ethics of happiness, and Visual or sensory art.

Thus the stream of thought in this field seems somehow to be, in *grosso modo*, also connected with the movements of the main types of culture and of their constituent elements. It seems also to comprise an organic part of the whole system of culture, and, having a degree of autonomy in its minor movements, in its main and long-time trends to change with the deep transformations of the whole system of the main types of culture.

II. PULSATION OF OPTIMISM AND PESSIMISM

Turn now to optimism and pessimism.[2] Here also we do not find an arithmetical balance between these two currents, either in separate periods or for the whole period considered. The figures in Table 34 give their relative strength for the times specified.

The lack of arithmetical balance there is about as great as in the relationship of absolutism and relativism. And yet, for similar reasons, it means rather the presence of a real balance. In order to live, one has to have a surplus of optimism over pessimism. Otherwise, one would be inclined to commit suicide. This is what is shown by the figures in Table 34. For different reasons, at one period for the Sensate reason of empirical enjoyment of life and the prevalence of pleasant experiences over the painful ones (Greece from the fifth to the first century A.D. and in modern times);

[2] Here again, for the sake of economy and in view of the uncertainty as to the validity of the results, I am giving, in Table 33 and Figure 18, only the table by century periods, and the chart which shows, by 20-year periods, the movement of the optimistic and pessimistic currents.

TABLE 33. INDICATORS OF FLUCTUATION OF PESSIMISM AND OPTIMISM
(on the basis of different values given from 1 to 12)

PERIOD	Pessimism		Optimism		Total	
	No.	Per cent	No.	Per cent	No.	Per cent
600–500 B.C.	12	60.0	8	40.0	20	100
500–400	21	33.3	42	66.7	63	100
400–300	23	15.4	126	84.6	149	100
300–200	11	10.2	97	89.8	108	100
200–100	0	0	35	100	35	100
100–0	0	0	82	100	82	100
0–100 A.D.	0	0	76	100	76	100
100–200	26	15.6	141	84.4	167	100
200–300	13	12.9	88	87.1	101	100
300–400	14	16.1	73	83.9	87	100
400–500	17	21.8	61	78.2	78	100
500–600	6	12.5	42	87.5	48	100
600–700	2	20.0	8	80.0	10	100
700–800	2	25.0	6	75.0	8	100
800–900	5	23.8	16	76.2	21	100
900–1000	1	25.0	3	75.0	4	100
1000–1100	8	25.0	24	75.0	32	100
1100–1200	9	20.0	36	80.0	45	100
1200–1300	19	22.9	64	77.1	83	100
1300–1400	24	27.0	65	73.0	89	100
1400–1500	3	15.0	17	85.0	20	100
1500–1600	92	50.5	90	49.5	182	100
1600–1700	132	43.3	173	56.7	305	100
1700–1800	75	23.7	242	76.3	317	100
1800–1900	272	28.8	673	71.2	945	100
1900–1920	92	24.9	278	75.1	370	100

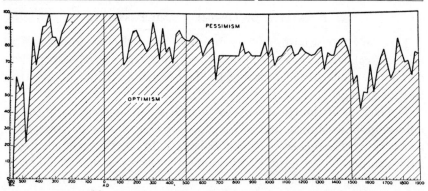

FIG. 18. MOVEMENTS OF OPTIMISM AND PESSIMISM

at another period for the Ideational reason of belief in everlasting happiness in the Kingdom of God, optimism has been prevalent over pessimism. The figures suggest further that the Graeco-Roman philosophical mood was more optimistic than that of any subsequent period; optimistic currents were then about seven times as strong as the pessimistic. The dawn of the Graeco-Roman culture and the morning of the Christian culture were also optimistic; the current of optimism (though for different reasons for the Pagan and the Christian thinkers) was almost five times as strong as that of pessimism. It is interesting to note, as the data at hand show, that optimism of the Pagan thought, *beginning with the fourth century* A.D. began decisively to decline, while it grew in the Christian thought. The optimistic current was about three times as strong as the pessimistic in the Middle Ages (optimism on account of belief in the Kingdom of God). Finally, it has been about twice as strong in the modern period.

TABLE 34. SUM OF INDICES FOR OPTIMISM AND PESSIMISM
FOR THE SPECIFIED PERIODS

Period	Optimism	Pessimism
580 B.C.–A.D. 100	466	67
100–600	405	76
600–1500	239	73
1500–1920	1456	663
Total	2566	879

So far as our own time is concerned, the end of the nineteenth and the beginning of the twentieth centuries have been marked by a rising wave of empirical optimism. The improvement of economic and social conditions in the Western World, especially in the second half of the nineteenth century; the progress of science, and other well-known facts, have "created" a "religion of progress," in the sense of a linear eternal trend toward the "bigger and better." The belief has become almost universal, and most of us have witnessed this optimistic credo spreading more and more, especially before the World War.

Since then the current has been somewhat weakened, as is shown in our indices (76.2 for 1880–1900 and 75.1 for 1900–1920); but it was still very strong during 1900–1920. After 1920 it has possibly declined.

Here, in contradistinction to the previous variables, one does not find any tangible correlation of pessimism or optimism with any of the main types of culture. The reason, as mentioned, is that pessimism, as well as optimism, has very different forms: Ideational and Sensate. In the Middle Ages, the ideology was optimistic in spite of the common conviction that this whole empirical life is but sorrow and sin. It was transcendental or Ideational optimism of belief in the Kingdom of God. And vice versa: the optimism of the most optimistic centuries, like the second and the first B.C., was rather Sensate, in the form of a belief that this life is worth living and that it is going to be bigger and better in the course of time.   Due to this, the figures do not, and cannot, give any special connection of pessimism or optimism with either Ideationalism, or Sensatism, or Idealism. If, however, the above fundamental distinction of the opposite types of pessimism, as well as those of optimism, is made, it is easy to see that in the predominantly Ideational culture optimism assumes also ideational (transcendental and "otherworldly") forms, while in the dominant Sensate culture it assumes the Sensate forms (earthly belief in progress and in empirical life, as having more positive than negative values).

As far as the quantitative "ups and downs" of pessimism are concerned (without the above distinction of its radically different forms), in many cases (whether by 20–year or century periods), but not in all, it tended to rise in the centuries of the "great turns," like the sixth and the fifth B.C. (when Greek culture passed from Ideational to Sensate form) ; in the fifth century A.D., which is again the end of the Sensate culture and the beginning of the new Ideational wave; the same is true of the eighth, the eleventh, and (partly) the fourteenth and especially the sixteenth centuries. When we take the 20-year periods, we note, however, that the eras of acute revolutions, like the French and others (see Chapter Thirteen of Volume Three, devoted to the movement of internal disturbances), are often characterized by a marked rise of optimism.   Pessimism does not rise in such periods of doing and acting (for which a belief in the optimistic goals is necessary) but in the period some twenty to forty years before such a great upheaval, when its forebodings begin to be felt, and then again after the acute stage of the practical remodeling is over. Its intoxication evaporated, and its prosaic aftermath — in form of a reality different from the expectations — arrived, an atmosphere of disillusion and disappointment increases and often manifests itself in a rise of pessimistic theories and, as Durkheim's and other studies of suicide show, in an increase of suicide cases.[3]

However, in view of the different nature of the Ideational and Sensate pessimism, as well as optimism, these conjectures are very uncertain and are mentioned as mere possibilities.

[3] See E. Durkheim, Le suicide (Paris, 1887) ; M. Halbwachs, Les causes du suicide (Paris, 1930).

Chapter Fifteen

FLUCTUATION OF ETHICOJURIDICAL MENTALITY IN CRIMINAL LAW [1]

I. INTRODUCTION

I have mentioned that not every culture necessarily develops up to the level consistent with the ethicophilosophical systems, in its ethical mentality, but every culture has some kind of division of the field of human actions and of other events into opposite classes : "the right and wrong," "approved and disapproved," "recommended and prohibited," "sacred and sinful," "moral and immoral," "lawful and unlawful," and the like.

This division of ethical values into the positive and negative classes (not to mention the neutral class) is found in practically every primitive tribe, as well as in more complex societies. It goes without saying that it is evident in the Graeco-Roman and Western cultures, beginning with the earliest period known up to their end, or to the present time.

The division being an "immanent trait" of every culture and group, inalienable from every essence of sociocultural life, the concrete content of each of the "right and wrong" classes differs widely from culture to culture, and even within the same culture or group, from period to period. Many a "right" form of conduct in one society or period is found to be "wrong" in other societies and periods, and vice versa. This enormous diversity should not be exaggerated, however ; in almost all cultures and societies a central set of the right and wrong forms of conduct in regard to its own members is similar.

It is to be mentioned further that not only do these categories — right and wrong (or their equivalents : sacred-profane, saintly-sinful, etc.) — exist in every group, but in practically all of them a further, more detailed ethical ranking of the forms of conduct from this standpoint is found along the lines, "most, more, and less right," and "most, more, and less wrong." Many an action is qualified as the "greatest crime," absolutely prohibited and the one most severely punished. The other wrong actions are regarded as lesser and lesser "felonies" up to the still slighter "misdemean-

[1] In co-operation with N. S. Timasheff.

ors" (*Verbrechen, Vergechen*, and *Übertrebungen* in German law; *Crime, délit*, and *contravention* in French law; *Prestuplenia, prostupki*, and *narushenia* in Russian law) beyond which there is a class of actions which, though also regarded as wrong and undesirable, are not punished in the criminal-law sense and are penalized only by "restitutive" — mainly fines — measures. Finally, beyond this class, lies a sphere of forms of conduct which are permitted and are regarded as neither criminal nor wrong nor undesirable. This is the region of normal, right conduct which is expected from the members of a group and is exercised by them most frequently. It is the field of the "right." However, it is the "right" of a so-to-speak normal, unelevated level. Beyond it lie the fields of behavior more qualified, nobler, more heroic and saintly and sublime — the "superright" recommended and praised but not demanded, and left entirely to the good will of the members. Such is a picture of the many-graded "right" levels, from a slightly above-the-plane right up to the "superright" of the very righteous.

In other words, we have in one form or another, in practically all societies, a many-graded series, beginning with the "most criminal and most severely punished" through many classes of the less and less criminal, up through the undesirable but unpunished activities; then we come into the realm of the "right" behavior, which, through many grades, ends at the highest peak of "superrighteousness." Thus, the highest crime (sin, sacrilege, etc.) and the highest superrighteousness (heroic, saintly, divine) are at the opposite poles between which many intermediary classes of conduct lie.[2] Practically every society has not only these differentiated ranks of forms of conduct, but a long list of the forms of conduct — specified activities and actions — which fall within each of these divisions. Especially long and detailed is the list of the specified forms of conduct which lie within the main classes of the "wrong" (criminal, prohibited though not punished, undesirable). Here detailed ranking is manifest, not only in the separation of the wrong forms of conduct into felony, misdemeanor, and various violations of legal and social rules, but in the most detailed and careful enumeration of exactly which actions fall within each class, and in a still more detailed description of the actions which, within each class, are punished differently, more or less severely, and in thousands of still more detailed rules, classifications, bylaws, and subsidiary specifications.

It goes without saying that this whole structure of the ethical differ-

[2] See P. Sorokin, *Crime and Punishment, Heroism and Reward* (in Russian) (St. Petersburg, 1913). See there the literature. See also G. Jellineck's work, quoted.

entiation and qualification of the forms of conduct does not remain unchanged in the course of existence of a given society. It does change, and
sometimes changes rapidly. Actions once regarded as most criminal,
later on become lawful or less criminal; actions once punished most
severely, later on become either unpunishable or less punishable; and
vice versa. In other words, the composition of each of the classes,
"criminal," "wrong," "right," "heroic," in regard to the specified forms
of action which compose it, changes in the course of time.

However, the velocity as well as the profundity of the change is not the
same in the course of time and in all specified forms of conduct. There
are societies and periods in which the change is very slow and practically
imperceptible, sometimes even during several hundreds of years. On the
other hand, there are societies and periods in which the profundity as well
as the tempo of the change is great; sometimes within the course of
several years the change is tangible. The same is true in regard to the
fields of conduct. As we shall see, there are several specified forms of
conduct — for instance, the murder of a member of the group — which in
practically all periods and societies remain in the same category of the
"wrong," "sinful," "prohibited," "criminal." Their ethical qualifications do not change, except in secondary details. And there are specified
forms of action — for instance, in the field of dress fashions, or in that of
forms of belief and religion, political convictions, and activities — which
change seemingly more rapidly and more radically, a given form being
now in one ethical class, and now being shifted into the opposite, from the
"wrong" to the "right," or vice versa.

The best source or "social mirror" of the ethical mentality and respective forms of conduct, or of the mores, is usually given by the totality of
the "official" laws of a given group, plus its "official" moral prescriptions.[3]

---

[3] I do not want to enter here into a discussion of what is the law and what is the moral code
of a given society. For the sake of brevity it is enough to say that by law is meant here the
totality of the imperative — attributive convictions of a given person or of the totality of
persons (two-sided convictions and experiences, ascribing a right to one party and a duty
to another: "the creditor has the right to demand the stipulated payment of debt from the
debtor, and the debtor has a duty to pay the debt when, where, and under the conditions of
the stipulation"). In contradistinction to that, the purely "moral" rules are only one-sided,
only imperative (not the imperative-attributive) rules which urge, recommend, advise to do
so and so; but do not ascribe to anybody the right to demand such actions. Such are, for
instance, most of the rules — for the Christian Western society — like: remain chaste and do
not marry; give all your property to the poor; sacrifice your life for your neighbor; and so
on. Finally, any action which transgresses or violates the rules of conduct as they are defined
by the totality of the imperative-attributive rules and respective convictions will be a "wrong"
— criminal, unlawful, sinful — action. The concrete forms of what actions are lawful, moral,
and wrong vary greatly from individual to individual, from group to group, from period to

Any enforced and functioning code of "official" law is the most authoritative, the most (comparatively) accurate, and most reliable reflection of the ethical mentality and ethical differentiation of the actions in the above classes. There is no doubt that such an "official code" does not reflect the totality of the real imperative-attributive convictions of the members of the society perfectly. There always is some discrepancy between the situation as it is depicted in the "official law" and in the psychosocial mentality of the members of the society. And the discrepancy is the greater, the quicker the socioethical life of the society changes. As the official laws cannot be changed incessantly, so to speak, while the social life is changing constantly, the discrepancy is inevitable.[4] However, the discrepancy should not be exaggerated, especially for the earlier centuries, when the tempo of the change of the ethicojuridical mentality, and of the respective forms of conduct, was slow. All in all, any functioning code of law which existed and was enforced for decades or centuries, and which has been the foundation for the activities of the courts and of the agencies of justice, does reflect the reality in essential parts fairly accurately, anyhow better than any other source. If in this or that special field it shows a discrepancy with the ethical mentality of the members, it does not do so in the greater part of the conduct covered by it. When the discrepancy becomes indeed considerable, such a code is revised or replaced by a new

---

period. The totality of the imperative-attributive rules of a communist differs from that of a monarchist and capitalist; of a slave from his master; of a "criminal gang" (which has also its own laws and morals, though different from the official law) from the honest citizens.

Such being the general definition of law and moral and wrong actions, one has to bear in mind that in any organized group, regardless of a variation of the content of each of these classes of actions from member to member, there always is an "official" code of law (and respectively of the moral and wrong forms of conduct) which by the powerful part of the group is regarded as "obligatory" for all its members, and as such is enforced. What generally is known as "law" represents exactly this specific "official" subclass of the general class of the law and moral phenomena.

Subsequently, I shall deal mainly with the codes of this "official" law, as the enforced and obligatory norms of a given group.

For details of this theory of law and morals, see the works of possibly the greatest theorizer on law and morals in the twentieth century, Leo Petrajitsky, *Introduction to the Theory of Law and Morals* (St. Petersburg, 1907), and also his *Theory of Law and Morals*, 2 vols. (in Russian) (St. Petersburg, 1910). See also P. Sorokin, *General Theory of Law* (in Russian) (Jaroslavle, 1919) and *Crime and Punishment*, quoted.

[4] See Leo Petrajitsky, *Theory of Law and Morals*, Vol. II, chap. V. This, in my opinion, gives a penetrating and deep analysis of this problem in the form of an analysis of the conflicts and discrepancies of the "official" and "intuitive" law. I am not giving here references to many other works on the subject, for the sake of economy of time and space; but a thorough knowledge of the literature in the field of general theory of law, and of criminal law particularly, mainly by European scholars, would be very helpful to an adequate understanding of many of my statements here.

"official" code. For these reasons a study of the codes of law in a given country in the course of its existence gives practically the best material for a study of the ethical mentality of a given society, as well as of its change. By carefully and accurately marking the main changes and the main differences of the preceding and subsequent codes, we can obtain knowledge, if not of a perfectly continuous change, then, anyhow, of the main landmarks of that change and of the main content of it from one period to the next, and so on through the whole set of centuries studied.

These remarks are sufficient to explain why, for grasping the main forms of change of the ethicojuridical mentality in its daily "routine" form, I am taking systematically the codes of law — the criminal, the civil, and others — instead of using any other material — from the incidental and partial testimonies of the contemporaries up to the fragmentary data of various kinds. These cannot give even remotely as good, as reliable, and as systematic material as that given by the codes. The testimonies and other material are almost always biased, fragmentary, uncertain, untypical, and incidental, while the code which has been "law" and has been enforced and followed for decades and centuries is an objective, super-individual and superfactional epitome of the main aspects of the respective ethicojuridical reality of the period of the code's validity. As such, it is the best and most impartial witness of the status and of the character of the "daily ethical and juridical mentality and conduct." So much for this point.

Having taken note of these generalities, we can turn now to the problem of our study. It consists of an elucidation of whether or not the ethico-juridical mentality on the level of the "daily routine conduct" fluctuates in the course of time. If so, how and what are some characteristics of this fluctuation? Do, for instance, the ethicojuridical rules and norms all change together, or do they change in one field of conduct independently of changes in other fields of action specified in the juridical official law and moral codes? In other words, is the totality of such norms and "laws" a unified organic system where a change in one field leads to that in the whole system, or is it a conglomeration of several clusters of norms, each of which has its own existence and therefore changes independently? Finally, are the changes in the field of the juridicoethical mentality, as it is reflected in the "official law" and moral norms, associated in a tangible way with the alternation of the Ideational and Sensate cultures, and if so, in what way and how?

In order that our study may be systematic, I shall proceed systematically in the investigation of the relevant material. In this chapter I shall consider the criminal law and codes; in other parts of this work, the other branches of law — namely, the civil, the constitutional, and the administrative laws — will be briefly touched upon, so far as they concern our main problem : the mode and the manner of association of the forms of ethicojuridical mentality with the main types of culture studied here. So much about the general plan of the study. I begin by paying particular attention to the criminal law for several reasons. First, it is connected more than any other branch of law or of moral codes with "wrong" conduct in its worst forms, according to the mentality of the respective society. More than any other source it tells us *what forms of conduct* are considered wrong in a given society, and not only this but also, How wrong? Which of the totality of the "wrong" actions is considered the "most wrong," and then "less and less wrong," giving thus a many-ranked gradation from the gravest crimes, punished most severely, up to the lightest misdemeanors and violations of the norms. The *gradation of the punishments is a fairly good indicator of the comparative gravity of the wrongfulness of the specified class of prohibited action, as it appears to the respective societies and culture mentalities. The greater the crime, the greater, usually, the punishment.* In this sense, the criminal law and codes make the best map of the ethicojuridical mentality of a given society, far better and more detailed and transindividual than any other source, especially for grasping which specified forms of action the "official ethicojuridical" mentality tries to inhibit, to bind by punishment, and to what extent. It is true that the totality of the actions prohibited and punished by the criminal codes does not exhaust the whole field of the actions regarded as undesirable and wrong; outside of the criminal actions there are others, also regarded as wrong and also inhibited, either by the sanctions of the civil, the disciplinary, the administrative law, or by sanctions of purely moral character; or, finally, "wrong actions" but not inhibited by any punishment in the strict sense of the word (*leges imperfecta*). But it is certain that all such wrong actions as lie outside of the actions punished by the criminal law compose much milder forms of "wrong" actions and many of them are just intermediary between the slightly wrong and the lower grades of permitted actions. As such, they are therefore much less important for our purposes and for this reason they can be passed by.[5] Subsequently, however, the most important

---

[5] See the details in Petrajitsky's and Sorokin's works, quoted. See also Jellineck's work, quoted. See also K. Binding, *Normen und ihre Uebertretung* (Leipzig, 1890), Vol. I; Binding, *Grundriss der deutschen Strafrechts* (Leipzig, 1907); for other literature, see P. Sorokin, "Structure of the Contemporary Dogmatics of Criminal Law," in the *Vestnik Psychologii, Kriminalnoi Antropologii i Pedologii*, Vol. XIII (1917); also P. Sorokin, "The Third School

cases of the prohibited actions by the norms of the civil and the administrative law will be touched upon briefly.

As to the *material* from which the problem is studied, it consists of practically all the important criminal codes (and laws) which have been functioning in the history of the five countries, France, Austria, Italy, Germany, and Russia, from the earliest "Barbaric" codes up to the codes of the present day. All in all, these codes give a picture of the main changes in the ethicojuridical mentality of Europe, with the exception of the Anglo-Saxon countries. Their "evolution" in this field has been similar to that of Europe, but since their laws are not codified, they have been omitted from our study. The names of the codes and of other sources are indicated in detail farther on.

As mentioned, the real process of change of the ethicojuridical mentality in the field of criminal law has been more continuous than is shown by the changes given by the codes, as we compare the preceding code with the one which replaced it in the history of each of these countries. The curve of the changes shown by such a study of the codes indicates only the "main points" through which it has passed, like the "points" of a diagram which mark the main positions through which a curve goes, but which do not indicate in detail the small fluctuations which the real course depicted by the curve had between the "points." There we usually draw a straight line, though in almost all cases there was not a straight line but a fluctuating line. Similar is the situation here. Some of the codes are separated from one another by a span of one or more centuries. There is no doubt that during such a long period many secondary changes took place in the ethicojuridical mentality of the society. But since we do not have the sources for their study, and since, in most cases, the changes are secondary (because when the change in the mentality is deep, it usually leads to a replacement of the out-of-date code or law by a new one which eliminates the discrepancy), the study of the comparative changes from one code to the following one gives indeed the main "points" through which the curve of the ethicojuridical mentality passed. For this reason, the "landmarks" given by all the codes in the history of each of these countries are the real landmarks of the main points through which the curve of the "evolution" of the mentality studied passed. They give a

---

and the Dispute between the 'Classical' and the Sociological School in Criminal Law," in *Yuridichesky Vestnik* (1915); K. Birkmeyer, *Studien zu dem Hauptgrundsatz* (Berlin, 1909); H. von Ferneck, *Die Rechtswirdigkeit*, 2 vols. (Leipzig, 1905); N. Timasheff, "*Le droit, l'éthique, le pouvoir*," in *Archives de philosophie de droit* (1936), nos. 1-2; P. Haesaert, *La forme et le fond du juridique* (Bruxelles, 1934).

firm basis on which to draw the configuration of the curve in accordance with the real movement of the process studied.

A. *Method of Procedure.* An investigator of the changes in the ethicojuridical mentality, as they are reflected in the main criminal codes in the history of a given country, can hardly grasp the important points of the changes by a mere general comparison of the codes in their succession. Such generalities can give something of value but they will miss many important points. Therefore, I choose the detailed way. It is more difficult; it requires incomparably more time and energy; but it yields results which are more solid, more verifiable, and which even lend themselves to a kind of quantitative treatment. The essence of the "detailed" way adopted here is as follows.[6]

In the first place, of all the criminal actions (*Tatbestände*) 104 main and typical crimes which embrace practically all the main forms of prohibited and punished *corpus delicti* are taken. These contain practically all the forms of crimes found in any criminal code of any time, as well as all the main crimes of a specific epoch or country under investigation. These crimes or the main forms of the prohibited actions are as follows.[7]

GROUP I. CRIMES AGAINST PHYSICAL PERSON

1. Murder
2. Suicide
3. Inducement to suicide; stimulation to it; facilitation to commit it; forcing it
4. Bodily injury (grave, resulting in the disturbance of the normal functioning of the organs of the body)
5. Assault and battery (violence not resulting in the disturbance of the normal functioning of the bodily organs)
6. Feticide and infanticide
7. Participation in duel
8. Challenge to duel
9. Leaving in danger (leaving in a situation dangerous to the life of the helpless person by a person who is obliged to take care of the helpless)
10. Causation of danger to life (putting another person in a situation dangerous to his life, by a person who is not juridically obliged to take care of him)
11. Causation of danger of infection by venereal disease
12. Nonrendering of help (noninterference in the course of events which are an evident danger to the life of another person)

[6] I hardly need to say that this detailed way has never been used, so far as I know, by any investigator, including the specialists in the history of criminal law. For this reason, the subsequent study may not be useless, even for these specialists.

[7] For the sake of brevity and economy of space the numbers given to each form of crime listed are systematically used throughout. No. 1, throughout the study, means "murder"; No. 2, "suicide," and so on.

Group II. Crimes against Moral Person

13. Enslavement (attempt against the *status libertatis*)
14. Deprivation of the freedom of locomotion (unlawful kidnaping and detention)
15. Coercion (violation of the freedom of choice by violence or threat of violence)
16. Unlawful medical treatment (without the consent of the patient or his representative)
17. Threat
18. Disturbance of the home peace (willful intrusion into the dwelling of another person or nonleaving it against the will of the person)
19. Violation of secrecy of mail and correspondence
20. Unlawful disclosure of a secrecy
21. Insult (utterance or writing of insulting and humiliating words)
22. Defamation and dishonoring (spreading ignominious information about another person)

Group III. Crimes against Property

23. Theft (secret taking or removing of another's property)
24. Larceny (open taking and removing of another's property, but without violence)
25. Robbery and brigandage (taking and removing property through use of compulsion, violence, and coercion)
26. Unlawful appropriation of a thing found
27. Unlawful appropriation of entrusted property
28. Removal of landmarks
29. Property damage (simple, not creating a general danger)
30. Dangerous property damage (through arson, explosion, flooding)
31. Swindle (taking property or removing it through fraud, deceit, cheat)
32. Extortion (coercion to disadvantageous business deal through threat of violence or by violence)
33. Blackmail (coercion to disadvantageous business deal through threat of disclosure of dishonoring or damaging information)
34. Misuse of trust (misuse of the rights entrusted in regard to another's property)
35. Misuse of trusting (misuse of another's weakness, inexperience, light-mindedness, or need, by involving him in disadvantageous deal of a noncreditable character)
36. Usury (misuse in the field of credit transactions)
37. Criminal bankruptcy
38. Buying stolen goods
39. Plagiarism (stealing or using another's literary or art or scientific work as one's own)

Group IV. Crimes against Religion and Religious Values

40. Blasphemy (cursing or reviling God)
41. Sacrilege
42. Hindering religious service
43. Religious coercion (by violence or threat of violence to perform or not to perform religious activities)
44. Apostasy

45. Heresy and schism
46. Conversion to another religion
47. Sorcery and witchcraft
48. Nonperformance of religious rites (prescribed by the official religion)
49. Performance of prohibited religious rites (prohibited by the state)
50. Abuse of a corpse
50a. Contact with Jews

Group v. Crimes against the Family

51. Substitution of children
52. Kidnaping of children
53. Abduction of women with their consent (but with violation of the rights of persons to whom they are subordinated)
54. Secret marriage (violating the rights of the persons to whom the married are subordinated)
55. Polygamy and bigamy
56. Adultery
57. Incest

Group vi. Sex Crimes

58. Fornication
59. Abduction of women against their consent
60. Rape (the carnal knowledge of a woman forcibly and without her consent)
61. Coercive lechery (coercion by force or threat of force to performance of actions of sexual character except the act of copulation)
62. Lewdness with the underaged
63. Seduction
64. Lewdness with a misuse of dependence
65. Panderage (facilitation of fornication and lechery without personal participation in it)
66. Financial exploitation of a prostitute
67. Sodomy
68. Sexual copulation with animals
69. Public indecency

Group vii. Crimes against the Certainty of the Evidential Means and Documents

70. Counterfeit of money
71. Forgery of documents
72. Intellectual forgery (false statement to an official for incorporation in the public official record)
73. Removal or annihilation of documents (which does not become either theft or property damage)
74. Perjury
75. False denunciation

GROUP VIII. CRIMES AGAINST SOCIOECONOMIC MORES

76. Attempt against existing social order (unlawful change of its foundations)
77. Attempts against the freedom of trade
78. Strike
79. Lockout
80. Unlawful disposal of dwelling
81. Unlawful gambling
82. Unlawful departure abroad
83. Wearing prohibited clothing, apparel, uniform
84. Tobacco smoking

GROUP IX. CRIMES AGAINST THE STATE AND POLITICAL ORDER

85. Attempt against the Constitution
86. Attempt against the supreme organs of the State (against the lawful discharge of the functions of the head of the State and its legislative organs)
87. Communication with the State's enemy (with the intention to involve it in war, or other inimical activities against the State)
88. Treason (helping the enemy, either through helping its military forces or by damaging the forces of one's own State)
89. Coercion in election (through force or threat of force to performance or non-performance of the electoral or voting functions)
90. Distortion of the results of election
91. Bribery in election
92. Attempts against friendly states (the same actions as in nos. 85 and 86, but directed against friendly States)
93. Violation of neutrality
94. Resistance of the state authorities
95. Coercion of the state authorities
96. Usurpation of authority (by persons who do not have it)
97. Participation in unlawful gathering
98. Participation in illegal political society
99. Liberation of prisoners
100. Self-liberation of prisoners
101. Libel and slander of the State (making false and inimical statements about the State and its agents)
102. Bribery of the officials
103. Nondenunciation of contemplated crimes

Such are the main crimes in regard to which the successive codes of the same country are compared. The essence of the comparison of each preceding code with the successive one consists in marking out the following points.

Having found out which of these 104 forms of activities (and their derivatives) are mentioned in the earliest code — that is, are qualified as criminal — we have studied: first, *which of the crimes of the earlier (or preceding) code are excluded from the subsequent code; such an exclusion means that from the class of criminal actions they are shifted to the non-criminal class of actions.* Second, *what new activities are given as criminal in the subsequent code, which were not mentioned in the preceding code. Such a change ordinarily means that the activities which were noncriminal from the standpoint of the earlier code are now shifted into the class of the criminal.* In this way, then, we obtain the main data concerning the change of the ethicojuridical mentality in regard to actions regarded as criminal and noncriminal. This change is supplemented further by a study of the changes in the estimation of the gravity of these actions. The point is that certain forms of activity may be regarded as criminal in two or all successive codes; it is present in all of them as criminal. This does not mean, however, that no change has taken place. Change may consist of a modification of the kind and degree of punishment for such a crime: in one code it may be punished by the qualified capital punishment; in another only by imprisonment for a short time or by a fine. The action remains criminal in both codes, but in one it is regarded as the gravest offense; in the other as a slight misdemeanor. Such a change of the mentality is often as important a fact as the exclusion of an action from the criminal class, or the inclusion of a hitherto noncriminal action in the criminal class. This explains why, thirdly, we have marked all the main changes from code to code in the punishments for all the crimes for which the criminal sanction (the kind of punishment) is modified.[8] The system of marking these changes is explained later. Such, then, are the main

---

[8] It must be clear that such a procedure gives a more adequate picture of the quantitative-qualitative change of the ethicojuridical mentality, as it is reflected in the law, than the mere enumeration of the number of crimes in the compared codes, or the mere number of the enactments and articles, without a real analysis of the kind of crimes enumerated. This last method is used, for instance, by R. Pound and F. Frankfurter. In *Criminal Justice in America* (New York, 1930), Dean Pound indicates that the successive relevant main criminal laws of Rhode Island ("Act to Reform the Penal Laws," 1822; Title XXX, of "Crimes and Punishments," in the General Statutes of 1872; and Title XXXIV "Of Crimes and Punishments," in the General Laws of 1923) show that in these sources are specifically mentioned: 50 crimes in the Act of 1822; 128 in that of 1872; and 212 in that of 1923. He indicates further that the Laws of 1923 do "not contain half of the offences" of the previous laws; and contain many new offenses in the fields of Labor and Industry, Factory Sanitary Conditions, Prohibition, Sale of Securities, and so on, which were absent in the Acts of 1822 and 1872 (see pp. 16–17 *et passim*).

Still more summary and less specified are the comparisons used by F. Frankfurter in his *The Public and the Government* (New Haven, 1930). He simply indicates that the Congress of 1789 passed only 26 Acts; that of 1790, 66; of 1791, 94; 1792, 38; 1793, 63; meanwhile the Seventieth Congress, in a single session, passed "993 enactments, contained in a mastodonic volume of 1014 pages, quarto, not octavo" (*ibid.*, p. 11). Both of these studies omit entirely a special enumeration either of the changes in the actions which are regarded as criminal or are excluded from this class; neither of them gives any real material about the

lines of the analysis of the codes pursued in this study. But two or three additional remarks need to be made here.

(1) The above 104 forms of crimes embrace not only the patterns of crimes typical for all times and societies, so to speak, but also those typical for only a certain period or society.

(2) In these 104 types are not included the auxiliary and intermediary forms of crimes, or merely some variation of the types given. The reason for the omission is that they do not give a fundamentally new type of "prohibited" action; for instance, in several codes there are many special varieties of counterfeiting and forgery; being such, they are embraced by the main crimes in that field and therefore need not be included as special types. In other cases, a crime not mentioned in the above 104 types — for instance, uprising, riot, or revolt — is not given special mention because an analysis of such a crime shows that it consists of a composite mixture or compounded conglomeration of the other simpler types of crimes already enumerated. Finally, a systematic analysis of even these 104 types is an exceedingly complicated matter. A further complication by the introduction into the list of thousands of varieties or composites of these types would make the analysis almost an impossible task.

(3) In this study we take the patterns of these crimes as purely "behavioristic" types of activities, without a specific analysis of their subjective aspects — such as "self-defense," "emergency situation," "vis absoluta et relativa," various motives, presence or absence of intention, the degree of sanity of the criminal during the perpetration of the crime, and many other subjective conditions which, in one form or another, have been relevant in the ethical qualification of the purely behavioristic patterns of the criminal actions, and in the gravity of their punishment. These "subjective" conditions are kept in mind, but the analysis of the composition (*Tatbestände*) of the criminal action is taken in its objective form, in the sense in which it has been especially well depicted by Beling,[9] and which is particularly fitted to the purposes of our study.

fluctuation of the punishment for the same crime from the earlier to the later code. Mere increase or decrease of the number of Acts or laws from code to code is somewhat misleading, because a mere enumeration of the varieties of the same crime may often lead to an increase in the number of "crimes," without introducing any really new one, and vice versa; a systematic generalization into one article of many "cases" and "varieties" of the same crime, which before were not systematized, may lead to a decrease either of the number of crimes in the Act, or the size and number of the Acts. For these reasons a real study of the change requires a study along the lines outlined above.

[9] See E. von Beling, *Die Lehre vom Verbrechen* (Tübingen, 1906).

B. *The Material and Codes Studied*. The material for the study is composed of the main criminal codes of the five European countries — France, Italy, Austria, Germany, and Russia, from the earliest codes or their substitutes up to the recent ones, and up to the modern projects of future criminal codes. Anglo-Saxon countries whose criminal law is still based largely upon the common law, and is therefore not codified, had to be omitted from the study. However, the evolution of the criminal law of these five countries represents fairly well the course for the whole of Europe and certainly reflects its main fluctuations, or "turning points," or "landmarks." Though each of these five countries, as well as the other European countries, has its own peculiar "twists" in the course of the change of their ethicojuridical mentality, as it is reflected in their successive criminal codes, nevertheless several traits, fundamental for our purpose, are fairly similar in each of them, if the essential turning points are considered. As for the sources and the main codes for each of these countries which have been studied and on which Tables 35, 36, and 37 and their conclusions are based, they may be summed up as follows.

In the *earliest period of the criminal law of the Germanic peoples* from the beginning of the Middle Ages to about the end of the eleventh or the twelfth century (according to the country), its general principles were about the same in the four European countries. The Criminal Laws of that period, incorporated later in the *Lex Alamannorum* or *Lex Ripuariorum* or *Lex Salica*, do not represent the criminal laws of the period completely. At the same time their foundations are so similar, and these foundations have been summed up and analyzed so well, that it has been found to be more satisfactory to use the best and most authoritative sources which have so excellently analyzed these criminal laws on the basis of all the main codes, instead of a specific analysis of each of these "Barbaric Law Collections." The works of Wilda, Brunner, and Hippel [10] give an excellent analysis and summary of the criminal law for all the Germanic or Teutonic peoples of the period when they came in contact with Christianity and the late Graeco-Roman culture. When the essentials of the Canon Law, as it is summed up from this standpoint by several excellent investigators,[11] are added to that, we have fairly adequate material from which to learn all the essentials of the ethico-

---

[10] W. E. Wilda, *Das Strafrecht der Germanen* (Halle, 1842); H. Brunner, *Deutsche Rechtsgeschichte* (Leipzig, 1906), Vol. II; R. von Hippel, *Deutsches Strafrecht* (Berlin, 1925), Vol. I.

[11] See especially P. Hinschius, *System des katholischen Kirchenrechts* (Berlin and Leipzig, 1869–1897), Vols. IV and V.

juridical mentality of the early Middle Ages, so far as it is reflected in the Criminal Law of these "Barbaric Codes."

As to the Russian Criminal Law of that period, the main source is the famous code "*Russkaia Pravda*" with some other subsidiary sources.[12]

For the subsequent feudal period (in the countries where feudalism existed as a special regime), or, roughly speaking, for the period from the twelfth century on, the main codes and sources for each specified country are as follows.

(1) *France.* For the "Barbaric period" *Lex Salica* (ed. by Hessels) and the mentioned summaries made by Wilda, Brunner, and others. For the feudal period possibly the most typical code of the thirteenth century : P. Beaumanoir's *Coutumes de Beauvoisis*,[13] with the supplementations of the Canon Law. For the subsequent period — from about the fifteenth to the eighteenth century — the court practice and many special *ordonnances* excellently summed up in the classical works of Muyart de Vouglans and Jousse.[14]

For the end of the eighteenth century and the beginning of the nineteenth (the period of the Revolution and the Restoration), the Law of July 20–22, 1791 ; the Criminal Code of October 6, 1791, with the supplementary enactments of the Criminal Code of the IVth year [15] and other revolutionary Acts. Then the Criminal Code of 1810 (*Code pénal du 12 février 1810*) in its initial form. For the later period, the same Code with the later — up to 1933 — modifications and supplementations.

(2) *Germany* (meaning the whole area of the Germanic peoples in Europe up to the seventeenth century, when Austria is taken separately). Barbarian law codes and their summaries by Wilda, Brunner, Hippel. For the feudal period, the *Sachsenspiegel* (thirteenth century),[16] supplemented by the provisions of the Canon Law as it is summarized by

---

[12] See about these in M. Vladimirsky-Boudanoff, *Obsor istorii Russkago prava* (Kiev, 1904).

[13] Edited by Comte Beugnot, Paris, 1842. It is styled the most typical law monument of the period. See J. Ortolan, *Éléments de droit pénal* (Paris, 1875), Vol. I, p. 43.

[14] For this period there existed no new codification of the laws and practice of criminal law. Therefore one has to use the excellent analyses and summaries made by several scholars. See especially Muyart de Vouglans, *Les lois criminelles de France* (Paris, 1780); D. Jousse, *Traité de la justice criminelle* (Paris, 1751), Vol. IX. Concerning the lack of codification of criminal laws of the period, see P. Garraud, *Traité théorique de droit pénal* (Paris, 1913), Vol. I, pp. 138–139.

[15] *Code pénal du 6. X. 1791; Code des délits et des peines du 3 brumaire au IV* (1795). Properly speaking, this Code is a codification of the criminal procedure mainly. In the field of the "material" (not processual) criminal law, it fills only some of the hiatuses of the previous enactments.

[16] Edited by K. von Amira (Leipzig, 1902). In the fourteenth century this law was regarded as the law of the Holy Roman Empire. See Hippel, *op. cit.*, p. 126.

Hinschius and others. For the sixteenth and seventeenth centuries *Constitutio Criminalis Carolina*, 1532,[17] with other special enactments (the Imperial *Polizei-Ordnungen* and other Acts), as they are summarized in the classic works of Liszt and Hippel.[18] For the end of the eighteenth century, the Prussian Code of 1794.[19] For the nineteenth century, the Prussian Criminal Code of 1851 [20]; then the German Criminal Code of 1871,[21] with the subsequent modifications. Finally, for postwar Germany, the Projects of the Criminal Code in the formulations of 1927 and 1935.

(3) *Austria*. The independent Criminal Law of Austria (separate from the Germanic Law) starts at the end of the eighteenth century with the Criminal Laws of Joseph II, 1787.[22] This code is taken, however, in its later edition of 1803,[23] because its original version had many omissions.[24] The next code is that of 1852.[25] With subsequent modifications, this code has been functioning practically up to the present time. However, for the twentieth century, the project of a new Criminal Code of 1912 is considered as the variant which incorporates the new tendencies and trends in that field. Of several independent projects of Austria, this project is possibly the most important.[26]

(4) *Italy*. For the earliest period the same sources as in other countries. For the feudal period (the twelfth and thirteenth centuries) the city ordinances of these centuries in the systematization of Kohler. For the fourteenth, fifteenth, sixteenth, and seventeenth centuries, similar statutes of the city states in the systematization by the same scholar.[27] Then comes the Criminal Code of 1786 of Toscana;[28] then the Code of 1839 of Sardinia,[29] replaced by the Italian Criminal Code of 1889.[30] The latest code is represented by the Fascist Code (*Codice Penale*) of October 22, 1930.

[17] Edited by J. Kohler and W. Sched (Halle, 1900–1904).

[18] F. von Liszt, *Lehrbuch der deutschen Strafrecht* (Berlin and Leipzig, 1927); Von Hippel, *op. cit.* See also R. His, *Das Strafrecht des deutschen Mittelalters* (Leipzig, 1920).

[19] *Allgemeines Landrecht für die Preussischen Staaten;* 20. Marz, 1791. (In force since 1794.)

[20] *Preussisches Strafgesetzbuch vom 14 April 1851.*

[21] *Reichsstrafgesetzbuch vom 15 Mai 1871.*

[22] *Gesetz über Verbrechen und deren Bestrafungs*, vom 13 Jan. 1787.

[23] *Strafgesetz vom 3 Sept. 1803.*

[24] See Hippel, *op. cit.*, pp. 271 and 377; Liszt, *op. cit.*, p. 61.

[25] *Strafgesetz vom 27 Mai 1852.*

[26] See Hippel, *op. cit.*, pp. 378–380.

[27] J. Kohler, *Das Strafrecht der italianischen Statuten* (Mannheim, 1895–1896).

[28] *Legge sul la riforma della legislazione penale*, in Toscana, 30 Nov. 1786.

[29] *Codice penale Albertino*, 1839.

[30] *Codice penale per il regno d' Italia*, June 30, 1889.

(5) *Russia*. For the earliest period the *Russkaia Pravda* in the third variant,[31] supplemented by the Canon Constitution (*Tzerkovny Oustav*) of the Grand Prince Jaroslav.[32] After that codification there was none fundamental, up to the Code of 1649 (*Sobornoie Ulojenie*). The next fundamental code is that of 1832, improved in the edition of 1845. With subsequent modifications, this code was valid up to the Russian Revolution, though it was replaced in part by the Code of 1903. Practically, in the last few years before the Revolution, three codes were functioning, each in its own field ; the Code of 1845, modified by the latest revision of 1916; the *Ustav o nakazaniakh* in the revision of 1914; and the Code of 1903 in the latest revision of 1916 (several parts enacted as the functioning law). Finally, the latest code is the Soviet Criminal Code of 1926. This code was enacted in the period of the New Economic Policy, later replaced by the new swing toward the planned Communist Society. In several parts it is in discrepancy with the Communist System started with the five-year plan in 1929.[33] In 1930 there was established a project for a new code, but it is not as yet given the status of a law.[34]

Such are the main "landmarks" in the evolution of the criminal laws of the countries studied. Table 35 gives a brief recapitulation of the above, useful for our purposes.

We can now pass to the study of the main changes in the criminal laws along the lines mentioned above. Several technical and methodological details not already explained are discussed at the beginning of each of the subsequent paragraphs.

II. FLUCTUATION IN THE SIZE OF THE CLASS OF CRIMINAL ACTIONS

I. NUMBER OF TYPES OF ACTIONS QUALIFIED AS CRIMINAL

The first task in our study of the ethicojuridical mentality as it is reflected in the criminal law consists in finding out which of the numerous types of activity are regarded as criminal in each period ; which of those given in the earlier period are excluded from the criminal class of later codes, and which types of actions not regarded as criminal in an earlier period are included in the criminal class in later laws. The elucidation

---

[31] In the edition of Sergeevitch (St. Petersburg, 1904).

[32] In the edition of Telberg (Harbin, 1921).

[33] See the details in A. Maklezow, "Das Strafrecht," in *Das Recht Sovietrusslands*, pp. 365–366 (Tübingen, 1925); N. Timasheff, "*L'evoluzione del diritto penale Sovietico*," in the *Rivista di driritto penale*, No. 2 (1932); P. Sorokin, "The New Soviet Codes," in *Michigan Law Review* (1924), Vol. XXIII, pp. 38–52.

[34] *Sovietskaia Iustitzia*, No. 19 (1930).

TABLE 35.   MAIN CODES AND SOURCES

Period	France	Germany	Austria	Italy	Russia
Up to about the twelfth century	Common Principles of Barbaric Law (summarized by Wilda, Brunner, and Hippel)				Russkaia Pravda and Jaroslav's Canon Statute
Twelfth to fourteenth century	Coutumes de Beauvoisis (thirteenth century)	Sachsenspiegel (thirteenth century)		City-statutes of the twelfth and thirteenth centuries (summarized by Kohler)	
	Supplemented by the norms of the Canon Law (summarized by Hinschius)				
Fourteenth to eighteenth century	Court practice and various statutes (summarized by Muyart de Vouglans and Jousse)	Constitutio Criminalis Carolina (supplemented by particular statutes and the Canon Law)		City statutes of the fifteenth, sixteenth, and seventeenth centuries	Code of 1649, plus other statutes
Eighteenth century	Act of 20–22 July, 1791 Codes of 1791 and 1795	Allgemeines Landrecht 1794	Code 1787–1803	Toscanian Code of 1786	
Nineteenth century	Code of 1810	Prussian Code of 1851 German Imperial Code of 1871	Code of 1852 with modifications up to 1880	Sardinian Code of 1839 Italian Code of 1889	Code of 1832 Code of 1845 with later modifications
Twentieth century	Code of 1810 with modifications up to 1933	Project of the Code in the revision of 1927 Project of the Code, 1935	Project of the Code in the revision of 1912	Fascist Code of 1930	Codes of 1903 Revisions of 1914 and 1916 Soviet Code of 1926 Project of 1930

of this problem means not only listing the kind of actions "excluded from" and "included in" the criminal class, but also noting any modification, extension, or narrowing of the varieties of a given type of action considered as criminal, from code to code. A proper knowledge of these changes gives us an idea of the extension and contraction of the size of the class of criminal actions as such. By size here is meant the total number of the types of criminal actions. In its totality the number gives an idea of the total volume of actions regarded as criminal.

In studying these changes from period to period, an investigator will easily notice several tendencies which in a sense unify and give meaning to numerous concrete changes of that specific type. In order that the subsequent enumeration of the types of actions excluded from and included in the criminal class, or modified in part from period to period, would not be fragmentary, devoid of deeper meaning, and not too burdensome to remember, it is advisable to mention briefly some of the relevant tendencies which unify the changes into something significant and permit us to reduce the multiplicity of the changes to a few classes of main trends from period to period. Some of these trends are as follows.

1. *Religious Ideational,* or
2. *Sensate Secular* (with various shades and varieties of these opposite tendencies)
3. *Authoritarian* or *Universalistic,* directed toward a reinforcement of the State's power
4. *Democratic* or *Singularistic,* directed toward weakening of the State's power in favor of the subjective "inalienable rights" of man and citizen
5. As a special variety of that, the *Étatistic* (from *l'état,* the State) or *Totalitarian* tendency, directed toward an expansion of governmental interference and governmental "planned" regulation of the social life and relationships of the citizens; and
6. *Liberal* trend, directed toward the limitation of this regulation, or toward the "*laissez faire, laissez passer.*"
7. *Humanistic,* directed toward protection and alleviation of the rights and interests of an individual generally and of the socially weaker groups and individuals in a given society particularly; and
8. *Anti-Humanistic,* directed to an elimination of the juridical protection and uplifting of these rights of a man generally and of the socially weaker elements.
9. *Innovating* trend, directed toward a destruction of the existing forms of social relationship and organization and toward replacement of these with new ones; and
10. *Restorative* tendency, directed toward restoration of the disrupted forms of social organization and relationships.

There are other tendencies, but it is unnecessary to mention them here. In a general way, it can be said that often not one only of the above tendencies is manifested, but several, and in a considerable number of cases the opposite trends are at work simultaneously. This fact shows, in passing, the complexity of social processes, their "not entirely rationalistic nature"; that the "*coincidentia oppositorum*" is present almost all the time in social life, where opposite tendencies and forces coexist and struggle against, or strive to limit, one another; and finally, it means also that any set of official laws is the result of many forces directed differently, and thus, in this sense, is almost always a kind of compromise which incorporates the pressure of these divergent forces, and therefore can rarely be quite consistent from a purely logical standpoint. This logical "nonconsistency" does not mean that a law is bad from the standpoint of the practical purposes which it serves. It means that here, as in many other compartments of the social values, the logic of intellect is not the only, and perhaps not even the main, criterion of the value of the law. Like beauty or goodness, law has its own criteria of value and they are often — and should be often — different from a purely intellectual, logical consistency. Such a consistency leads to the *Summum jus, summa injuria*, to blind fanaticism, dogmatism, formalism, and finally to "soulless, deadly intellectualism in law," whose bad effects were long ago formulated in the above statement: *Summum jus, summa injuria*.

Now we can proceed to mark the main changes in the successive codes from the standpoints outlined above.

Let us see whether the total size of the class of criminal actions fluctuated from period to period, and if so, how and to what extent. In which periods did the size tend to expand, and in which to contract? And what is the meaning of such expansions and contractions?

The results of this study are given in a series of summary tables commented on and explained in the text.

In order to answer the first problem as to whether in passing from period to period the size of the class of criminal actions expanded or contracted, we require a knowledge of what types of actions were considered criminal in the earliest period of the common Teutonic criminal law. Tables 36 and 37 give an enumeration of thirty-eight types of actions which fairly accurately sum up the situation as it is shown by the early "Barbaric" codes, and as a supplement to them, during the feudal time, by the main provisions of the Canon Criminal Law.

Having such a "size and composition" of the class of criminal actions as our starting point, we can now depict the main fluctuations, from period to period, in each country studied.

A. *France.* (1) Here the transition from the "Barbaric" criminal law — representing mainly the law of the pre-Christianized Teutonic

TABLE 36. COMMON TEUTONIC BASIS OF CRIMINAL LAW

Number in the List of 104 Crimes	Specification of Crime	Sources			Definition[4]	Intensity of Punishment (on a scale 1-10)[5]
		A[1]	B[2]	C[3]		
1	Murder	686–701	627–634	115		9
4	Bodily injury	729–775	634	115		1–7
5	Blows and violence	775–784	674–675	116	(1)	1–5
6	Feticide	718–723	634–637		(2)	5–7
13	Enslavement	797–798			(3)	7
14	Deprivation of freedom of movement and motion	794				7
18	Disturbance of home peace	781–783	651–654	115	(4)	3–9
21	Insult	785–793	671–674			1–3
22	Libel	785–793	671–674			1–3
23	Theft	854–906	637–647	115		1–9
24 / 25	Larceny } Robbery	907–917	647–649	115		1–5
26	Appropriation of a thing found					
27	Appropriation of the entrusted property	} 917–920	650–651	115		1–7
28	Removal of landmarks	923–926				
29	Property damage	926–934			(5)	1–9
30	Dangerous property damage	940–952	654–658	115–116	(6)	5–9
31	Swindle	937			(7)	
41	Sacrilege			117	(8)	
44	Apostasy	970			(9)	5–10
47	Sorcery and witchcraft	961–973	679–681	116	(10)	5–9
50	Abuse or distortion of a corpse	973–978	683–685	117	(11)	3–5
53	Abduction of woman	845–849	670–671			
55	Polygamy	852–855			(12)	
56	Adultery	821–829	662–664	116	(13)	5–9
57	Incest	855–858	664	116	(14)	7–9
58	Fornication	810–820	658–662	116	(15)	5–9
59	Kidnaping of women	839–845	661–671	116		5–7
60	Rape	829–839	664–667			7–9
67	Sodomy	} 858–859				7
68	Sex copulation with animals					
70	Counterfeit of money	938–939				7
74	Perjury	978–984	681–683	116–117		1–7
75	False denunciation	957–961	675–678	116		3–5
82	Unlawful departure abroad	686–687				9
86	Attempt against the supreme state authority	980–992	688–690	114	(16)	9
87 / 88	Facilitation of enemy } Treason	} 984–988	681–683	116–117		9

[1] A. Reference pages to Wilda, *op. cit.*

[2] B. Reference pages to Brunner, *op. cit.*

[3] C. Reference pages to Hippel, *op. cit.*

[4] (1) Blows, disarming, unsheathing of sword, putting hands upon one, violent grabbing, throwing down, pulling out one's hair, hindering one's passing, lifting woman's dress, tearing off woman's head apparel; (2) Feticide in the womb or abortion by artificial means; (3) Selling free man into slavery; (4) Violent breaking into another's house, with a company; (5) Slaughtering another's cattle, damaging his sown fields, woods, gardens, vegetable gardens; (6) Setting fire to a house, barn, shed, mill, forest, fence; (7) False measure and weight in trading; (8) Sacrilege of temples; (9) Giving up one's religion; (10) Sorcery, causing injury or damage, especially through poisoning; (11) Combined with robbery of the murdered; (12) Punishable with a consideration of the survival of the previous polygamy; (13) Punishable only to married woman and her corespondent; (14) Only with close relations punishable; (15) Meaning sex relation of a free woman with a man not free; (16) Invitation to an enemy, facilitation of their military operations, handing over fortified places to enemy; willful desertion of an army on the battlefield.

[5] See pages 581 to 583.

tribes — to the medieval criminal law, as it is reflected in the *Coutumes de Beauvoisis* and other criminal-law codifications of the thirteenth and fourteenth centuries, is marked by the following changes.

Of *thirty-eight types of criminal actions*, two — No. 26, appropriation of things found and No. 82, departure abroad — *cease to be crimes and are*

TABLE 37. CANON CRIMINAL LAW

Number in the List of 104 Crimes	Specification of the Crime [1]	Sources [2]	Definition [3]
2	Suicide	179	
9	Leaving in danger	183	(1)
14	Kidnaping	183	
18	Disturbing home peace	223–224	(2)
31	Swindle	209	(3)
36	Usury	196–199	(4)
40	Blasphemy	184	
42	Hindering religious service	207	
44	Apostasy	158	(5)
45	Heresy and schism	157–158	
47	Sorcery	160	(6)
48	Nonfulfillment of rites	205–206	(7)
50	Abuse of corpse	227	(8)
50a	Contact with Jews	159, 227	
53	Abduction	175	
55	Polygamy (polyandry)	170	(9)
56	Adultery	169–170	
57	Incest	173–175	(10)
58	Fornication	170–171	(11)
59	Kidnaping woman against her will .	175	
65	Panderage	176	(12)
67	Homosexuality (sodomy)	176	
68	Unnatural sexuality with animals . .	176	
70	Counterfeiting of money	} 199–201	(13)
71	Forgery of documents		
74	Perjury	184	
75	False denunciation	201–202	
102	Bribery	202	

[1] In the crimes listed above are included only those which complemented or supplemented the omissions of the simultaneously functioning secular law. The list does not contain the crimes included in all the Germanic secular criminal codes; nor the crimes which, neither before introduction of functioning nor after the termination of functioning of the Canon Law, were considered or mentioned in the secular criminal law.

[2] The figures in this column mean the respective pages in P. Hinschius, *op. cit.*

[3] (1) Exposure of infant; (2) Disturbing God's peace; (3) Nonreturn of receipt, with a purpose to demand a second payment of debt already paid; (4) Taking interest, except where it is permitted; (5) Abandonment of Christianity; (6) Superstition, sorcery, magic, divination, fortunetelling; (7) Neglect of church attendance on holy days, of the sacrament of the Eucharist and confession; (8) Connected with opening of grave; (9) Unlawful freeing of wife and subsequent marriage with another woman; (10) Marriage and sex relations with close relatives as well as between persons bound by spiritual kinship; (11) Sex relations of an unmarried with an unmarried or widow; (12) Coercion of one's daughter to prostitution; (13) The certificates and documents of the Pope and kings.

excluded from that class. Fifteen new types of actions are included in the class of criminal actions. The result is *an expansion of the size of the criminal acts from thirty-eight to fifty-one.* The fifteen new crimes are: No. 2, suicide; No. 9, exposure of child; No. 17, threat; No. 36, usury; No. 38, buying stolen goods; No. 40, blasphemy; No. 42, hindering religious services; No. 45, heresy and schism; No. 48, violation of the Fourth Commandment (in regard to Sundays and holy days); No. 50a, contact with Jews; No. 65, panderage; No. 71, forgery of documents; No. 99, liberation of prisoners (from the place of detention); No. 100, self-liberation of prisoners; No. 102, bribery.

Of the thirty-six types of crimes which passed to the new period from the preceding one, three are now interpreted in a wider sense, namely, No. 55, polygamy-polyandry, which is criminal in all varieties of such actions, in contradistinction to the previous period, where it was criminal in only a few specific forms; No. 56, adultery, which is now punishable for husbands as well as for wives, while before only wives were punished; No. 57, incest, which is now punishable for a much larger circle of relatives, and not only the relatives by blood (consanguinity and affinity) but also the spiritual relatives (godfather, godmother, etc.).[35]

Somewhat expanded also, and at the same time modified, is the definition of four other crimes, namely: No. 6, feticide, which is now punishable for perpetration by all means, while before it was punishable only when perpetrated by specific mechanical means; on the other hand, this action is punished now only when the fetus was alive. Likewise also widened is the concept of swindle (No. 31), which now embraces a much larger class of actions of deceit; the violation of the "home peace" (No. 18) is transformed into the wider concept of "God's peace." Finally, somewhat expanded and changed, is the concept of fornication, which now embraces all cases of sex relation of an unmarried man with an unmarried or widowed woman, while before only sex relation of a free woman with a man not free composed punishable fornication.

Such, in brief, are the main changes in the number as well as in the types of criminal actions which one finds on comparing the earliest with the subsequent periods of criminal law in France. A mere glance at these changes is sufficient to show their main and unmistakable trend. *It consists of a conspicuous swing toward Ideationalism*, as we pass from the pre-Christian stage of the people of Europe to their existence during the Middle Ages. Though the *Coutumes de Beauvoisis* is a monument of the thirteenth century, it codifies the norms and rules of the preceding centuries of the Middle Ages and not those of the thirteenth century only. Bearing this in mind, we see that the *main changes introduced by the medieval criminal law consisted of the inclusion in the criminal class of those actions not necessarily harmful from a narrow utilitarian or hedonistic or even eudaemonistic standpoint.* Not at all. But in *the "negativization" and "criminalization" of the actions which violate the Absolute Ideational values, regardless of their effects from the standpoint of the relativistic ethics of happiness. Most of the fifteen new crimes are such in their*

---

[35] Generally, Ideational moral mentality enlarges the circle of relatives among whom marriage is prohibited, and prohibits also marriage and sex relationships among the "spiritual relatives." This is a specific trait of the Ideational codes.

nature; and the expansion and modification of seven other crimes show the same earmarks.

Here, then, we see, unexpectedly, a perfect agreement with the results obtained in the preceding study of the fluctuation of the main ethical systems. The medieval period is marked by a sharp decline of all the branches of the ethics of happiness and by a monopolistic domination of the ethics of absolute (Ideational) principles. Here, on the lowest level of the ethicojuridical mentality, we find a swing of the same character; a more imperfect reflection of the same change in the moral mentality. Even on the level of the criminal law it cares now much less for the material comforts and pleasures, and rigorously demands a most vigorous suppression and inhibition of the actions (heresy, schism, blasphemy, nonobservance of the Sunday, hindering of religious services, suicide, usury; panderage, incest, adultery, and fornication in an expanded sense; and so on) which violate the absolute Ideational commandments, or the "nonmaterial" and "nonrelativistic" absolute values. It does not hesitate to declare criminal and most severely to punish many actions which, from the standpoint of the ethics of happiness, are possibly harmless or even enjoyable (especially in the field of sex relations).

In other words, in the field of criminal law, we see a swing of the same type that we have seen and shall see in all the main compartments of culture, namely, toward Ideationalism.

(2) Let us now observe what were the main changes in France in the transition from the thirteenth, fourteenth, and (partly) the fifteenth centuries to the subsequent ones — the sixteenth, seventeenth, and the first half of the eighteenth century — in the field of criminal law and the respective ethicojuridical mentality.

Of fifty-one types of criminal actions of the preceding period, one — contact with Jews — ceases to be criminal; twenty-three new types are added to the criminal class; thus we have seventy-three types of crimes in that period.

The twenty-three new actions now included in the criminal class are as follows: participation in duel; challenge to duel; appropriation of thing found; abuse of signature and receipt; premeditated bankruptcy; plagiarism; conversion into Protestantism; performance of Protestant services; substitution of infants; secret marriage; seduction; lewdness with the underaged; public indecency; elimination of documents; factual monopoly created by traders; exciting games; departure abroad; attempt against the Constitution; resistance to the officials; coercion of the state officials; appropriation of power and authority; participation in a society with unlawful objectives; nondenunciation of a plot or planned crime against the State.

Finally, of the fifty crimes which passed into this period from the previous one, six are expanded in their interpretation (Nos. 6, 71, 86, 87, 88, and 99); [36] two are narrowed (Nos. 27 and 58); and five are modified (Nos. 18, 29, 31, 44, and 65).

Again, a slight study of the changes is sufficient to show that the main trends were notably different from the changes in the preceding period. Here we do not find that the change is toward further Ideationalism. If anything, it is rather away from it. Some of the crimes of that character, like contact with Jews, motivated mainly by religious reasons, now cease to be crimes. No new "religious" crime is introduced. Instead, we have a "narrowing" of the previous religious crimes against Christianity into a crime against the Roman Catholic denomination only (the Protestant crimes). Likewise, the conception of some of the crimes, like the previous violation of God's peace, is now secularized into a disturbance of home tranquillity, without any reference to God.

The bulk of the new crimes are conspicuously of the secular character, being either a violation of the commercial and trade and property values (Nos. 26, 34, 37, 39, 51, 77, 81, and some others) or the actions undermining or dangerous to the grown-up monarchical power and authority (Nos. 7, 8, 46, 83, 94, 95, 98, and some others). The rest represents a mixture of the utilitarian-hedonistic and eudaemonistic and — only in a small part — purely Ideational motives and values. Even here, in several modifications, the hedonistic-utilitarian motive is perfectly dominant; for instance, now fornication is punishable only when it takes the form of a concubinate, that is, a lasting and durable sex relation between the unmarried parties; while before, any single sex relation was punishable. Expansion of other crimes is due partly to the same motive — a probable increase in the frequency of their perpetration and some danger (for instance, of venereal disease for the customers of the houses of ill fame) which made urgently necessary the inhibition, prevention, and suppression of such crimes.

In brief, here again, as in the movement of the main ethical systems studied, we are at the beginning of a recession of Ideationalism, and in the period of a rising tide of Sensate mentality. The trends are the same on both levels of the ethical mentality: on the highest, in the ethical systems; and on the lowest, in the field of crime.

Of other tendencies in the change studied we can mention: increasing

---

[36] Numeration is in accordance with previous list of 104 crimes.

power of the monarchy; an expansion of the State's interference in the relationships of its citizens; growth of authoritativeness and "totalitarianism"; the trend of secularization; that of commercialization; and, generally, a "materialistic tendency."

(3) When we pass to the criminal law of the end of the eighteenth century (the Revolutionary Criminal Law), we witness a most violent "earthquake" in the ethicojuridical mentality; it represents, however, an enormously exaggerated realization of the tendencies of the previous period, which, though tangible, were still mainly in a latent state.

First, out of seventy-three types of crimes of the previous period, thirty-five are made noncriminal actions and six new crimes are added, giving a net result of forty-four crimes. This looks like a real moral earthquake and the "sanctification" of a large number of actions previously considered criminal. Such a fact by itself is meaningful, but before elucidation of the meaning, let us see which actions previously regarded as criminal now are not so regarded. They are: suicide; participation in duel; challenge to duel; exposure of infant; enslavement; disturbance of home peace; removal of landmarks; misuse of signature; usury; plagiarism; blasphemy; apostasy and atheism; heresy and schism; religious conversion; sorcery; nonfulfillment of religious rites; abuse of corpse; abduction; secret marriage; adultery; incest; concubinage; lewdness with the underaged; seduction; panderage; homosexuality; sodomy (with animals); false denunciation; monopoly by the commercial people; departure abroad; coercion of the government; appropriation of government authority; self-liberation of prisoners; bribery; nondenunciation of crime. The new crimes added are: violation of the secrecy of correspondence; extortion; religious coercion; strikes of laborers and employees; coercion of voting in elections; night demonstrations and meetings.

Finally, of thirty-eight crimes of the previous period which passed into the Revolutionary Criminal Codes, six are widened in their scope (Nos. 5, 27, 30, 31, 69, 74); seven are narrowed in their content (Nos. 17, 21, 22, 73, 81, 85, 99); and three are changed in their interpretations (Nos. 29, 49, 98).

The meaning of the change is clear. It is a great triumph of sensual ethicojuridical mentality. It is a veritable outburst of it, and a great recession of the Ideational moral conscience.

This is shown by the almost wholesale exclusion of the previous religious crimes from the class of criminal actions; likewise such actions as suicide (whose punishment was motivated by religious considerations), as sorcery and magic operations based upon the belief in the existence of super-empirical forces.   In this respect, this code shows a thoroughly empirical and nonsuperstitious mentality which does not believe in, and cares little about, any superempirical Ideational reality.   On the other hand, the particularly hedonistic and utilitarian and even sensual ethicojuridical mentality of the period is excellently demonstrated by the almost whole-sale exclusion of forms of sex activities from the class of criminal actions, where they were formerly included.   Neither abduction, nor secret marriage, nor seduction, nor lewdness with children, nor concubinage, nor homosexuality, nor sodomy with animals, nor adultery, nor incest, nor abuse of a corpse, nor even exposure of an infant is punishable now. It is as though the lawgiver were saying: "Why?   If they give pleasure, and they certainly do, why prohibit them and punish them?   Let every-body enjoy as much as he can."   A mentality which is a mere reflection of the factual conduct in the time of the Revolution, and which is typical of conduct in the periods of great revolutions generally.[37]

Again this result agrees excellently with the conspicuous rise in the ethics of happiness at the end of the eighteenth century, as shown before, when it rose from 23 and 28 per cent for the periods 1660 to 1720, to 34, 52, and 35 per cent of all the systems of ethics for the periods 1740 to 1800 (see the preceding chapter).   It is interesting to note that in the field of the ethical systems, the rise of sensualism preceded slightly the manifestation of the same mentality in the form of the Criminal Laws of 1791 (which lag is comprehensible).

In passing, it is to be remarked that the period shows that there is no perpetual trend of increase of the types of actions qualified as criminal, in the course of time, as is often assumed to be the case by many (see above the quotations from Pound and Frankfurter).   From thirty-eight the types rose to fifty-one and then to seventy-three, in the three periods considered; and they fell to forty-four in the Revolutionary period.

(4) As it happens often (but not always [38]) and as has been noted several times, the *sharper the motion in one direction, the greater the chances for an acute reaction of some kind.*   This happens here when we pass from the Revolutionary Codes of 1791 to the Criminal Code of 1810.   *This Code is in many respects quite opposite to the tendencies of the Codes of 1791.*

First of all, it shifts back into the class of criminal actions most of the actions excluded therefrom by the Revolutionary Codes.   Of the previous

---

[37] See P. Sorokin, *Sociology of Revolution* (Philadelphia, 1925), pt. i, and especially chap. vi.

[38] It is only remotely analogous to Newton's law of action and reaction and has little to do with it.

forty-four types of crime, in the Code of 1810, only six are transferred to the class of noncriminal actions, but twenty-four new actions, which were non-criminal according to the Revolutionary Criminal Law, are included, or rather shifted back into the class of criminal actions. Thus the number of crimes in that code is sixty-two.

The six crimes dropped are: violation of secrecy of correspondence; prohibited manifestations of religion; kidnaping of women against their will; workers' strike; electional coercion; night demonstration.

The new crimes added (or rather reinstated) are: exposure of a child; coercion; disclosure of trusted secret; removal of landmarks; misuse of signature; misuse of trust; usury; plagiarism; abuse of corpse; kidnaping of children; abduction; adultery; compulsory lewdness; panderage; false denunciation; monopoly of trade; electional forgery and electional bribery; inimical activity against a friendly state; coercion of government; appropriation of governmental authority; self-liberation of prisoners; bribery; nondenunciation of planned crime against the State; and counterfeiting of money.

Of the remaining thirty-eight crimes which passed into the Code of 1810 from the previous one, nine crimes are expanded in their interpretation (Nos. 21, 22, 27, 29, 30, 31, 73, 85, 99); three are narrowed (Nos. 37, 41, 98); and two (Nos. 17 and 81) are modified.

The totality of the changes shows that there is a return to something which existed before the Revolution; namely, a return not to Ideationalism at all — there is little, if anything, of that; on the contrary, the whole list of the dropped, added, and modified crimes in the Code is thoroughly sensual: hedonistic, utilitarian, and eudaemonistic in its nature. But it is the realization of a more conservative, more "decent," and less wild utilitarianism, hedonism, and eudaemonism than was evident in the Revolutionary Codes. The Code of 1810 is the "practical moral" of a now balanced and moderate and "sensible" *bourgeoisie*, which has finished sowing its wild oats. In this respect, it adopted the code and morality of the pre-Revolutionary "nobility" but in a more prosaic and solid manner. The code stands with both feet upon purely empirical reality; it does not show much longing for or belief in the superempirical reality; therefore it is concerned entirely with this world; but it is the world of a man who wants to have solid comfort, a faithful wife, daughters safely married; himself a respectable citizen (with incidental and secret deviations from the path of sex faithfulness). It stands naturally for the sacredness of private property (often acquired by plunder and trickery in the Revolution), for economic security, for property protection. In brief, it is an incorporated epitome of the ethicojuridical mentality of the French Babbitts, the predecessors of the twentieth-century Babbitts, but more robust, more aggressive in their readiness to protect their own rights. Such, in brief, is the meaning of this change. It is a secondary reaction of a more conservative Sensate ("happiness") morality, of a balanced Jeremy Bentham type against an erratic sensual morality.

(5) Finally, if we take the Code of 1810 (France has not enacted any new criminal code since then) with all the changes during the nineteenth and twentieth centuries, its main modifications are as follows.

Two of the previous crimes (insulting the sacred object and nondenunciation of crime) were dropped. Ten new ones were introduced; giving thus the total number of the types of criminal actions as seventy. The added crimes are: reinstatement of violation of secrecy of correspondence; blackmail; participation in prohibited forms of religious processions and exhibition of the religious emblems outside of churches and dwellings, as well as prohibited teaching of the Bible and religious dogmas; incest; lewdness with the underaged; intellectual forgery; financial exploitation of prostitute; coercion to strike; electional coercion; and armed demonstration.

Of the previous sixty crimes which remain, three are expanded in their interpretation (Nos. 9, 17, and 65); two are narrowed (Nos. 22 and 86); and one is modified (No. 43).

These changes indicate only a further swing from religiosity and Ideationalism (even the remnants of the religious crimes are practically abolished) toward secularism and "conservative" but tolerant, balanced, liberal sensualism. They show also increasing liberal and "individualistic" trends; belief in Adam Smith's and the Classical school's "egotistic man" and his sensibleness, reasonableness, and "rationality." The law tries to give to man as much freedom and comfort as is necessary. However, if he is unreasonable, it is ready to punish him and to inhibit him in the name of "progress" and "the greatest happiness of the greatest number of men."

Such is the last "liberal" movement of the fluctuation of the French ethicojuridical mentality. Again, confronting these last steps in the fluctuation of the Criminal Law of France with the above data concerning the fluctuation of the main ethical systems, we see that they agree rather well; with a slight and temporary recession of the ethics of happiness in the period 1800–1820, it began to grow again from 28 per cent to 42 and 43 per cent for 1880–1920. France has not as yet had the "post-liberal" stage of its criminal law, as some other countries (Soviet Russia,

Italy, Germany) have had.   There is little doubt, however, that France is bound to follow in their footsteps and enact something along the line of the "newest trends" manifested by the postwar and postliberal codes of these other countries.

B. *Germany.*   (1) In Germany the passage from the earliest (pre-Christian) to the later (medieval) period, as it is reflected in the *Sachsenspiegel* (thirteenth century, but it incorporates practically the entire medieval law) is marked by the following changes in the field of criminal law.

Of the earlier thirty-eight types of crimes, eight are dropped and twelve new ones are added, which gives forty-two types of crimes for the period. The dropped crimes are : appropriation of the entrusted value ; removal of landmarks ; property damage ; apostasy ; departure abroad ; attempts against the supreme organs of the State ; and treason.   The newly added crimes are : suicide ; exposure of an infant ; usury ; blasphemy ; obstruction of performance of religious services ; heresy and schism ; nonperformance of religious rites ; contact with Jews ; panderage ; forgery of documents ; participation in a prohibited society ; bribery.

Of the thirty crimes which passed into the law of that period from the preceding one, three are expanded in their interpretation (polygamy or polyandry, adultery, incest) and four are expanded and modified (feticide, swindle, disturbing home peace, and fornication).

Without any extended comment, one can see that the character of the change was very similar to that in the French law, and its main feature consists of a swing toward strong religiosity and Ideationalism, with all the characteristics outlined in the case of the French Criminal Law.

(2) When the criminal law of the next period is considered — that represented by the *Constitutio Criminalis Carolina* (1532) and other statutes — the main differences with the preceding period are found to be as follows.

Of forty-two types of crimes of the Saxon Law period, four are dropped (sorcery, contact with Jews, participation in an unlawful society, and bribery) and sixteen new crimes are added, which gives a total of fifty-four crimes for that period.   The newly added crimes are : appropriation of the entrusted ; removal of landmarks ; property damage ; misuse of trust ; intentional bankruptcy ; buying stolen goods ; kidnaping of children ; unlawful agreement of traders ; wearing prohibited uniform and clothing ; attempts against the constitution of the State and the supreme organs ; communication with and helping the enemy ; treason ; resistance to and coercion of the government ; liberation of prisoners.

Of the other crimes which passed into the law of that period, three are expanded (Nos. 6, 56, and 71), three are narrowed (Nos. 13, 36, and 58), and two are modified (Nos. 18 and 65).

Here again we find a swing similar to that observed in the French law for the same period, namely, toward secularization, with its utilitarian, hedonistic, and eudaemonistic principles. In other words the tendency is away from the Ideational ethics of the absolute principles.[39] Of the trends, one notes the increase of interference by the State, the growth of secular authoritativeness, and several other similar changes.

(3) The criminal law of the second half of the eighteenth century represented by the *Preussische Landrecht*, 1794, gives the following changes, compared with the criminal law of the previous period. *It excludes four crimes, includes twenty-four new ones; thus giving seventy-four types of crimes.*

Those dropped are: nonobservance of holy days; abuse of a corpse; wearing prohibited apparel; and coercion of government.

Those added are: participation in and challenge to duel; putting in danger of infection of venereal disease; nonrendering help; coercion; threat; violation of secrecy of correspondence; extortion; misuse of trust; plagiarism; connection with a socially dangerous sect; substitution of children; lewdness with the underaged; public impudence; elimination of documents; lottery and other hazardous and exciting games; departure abroad; attempts against friendly states; appropriation of governmental authority; participation in riot and secret unlawful society; insult of the State; nondenunciation of a planned crime.

Of the remaining fifty crimes, three are expanded (Nos. 13, 30, 34); eight are limited (Nos. 40, 41, 47, 52, 57, 77, 85, 99); and four are modified (Nos. 18, 29, 59, 65).

A glance at the dropped crimes and also at the limited (which include blasphemy, sacrilege, sorcery, and incest) shows that the main trend here is a continuation of the movement away from Ideationalism, and toward secular utilitarianism, hedonism, and comfort, already clearly shown by the criminal law of the preceding period. And here again the

---

[39] Again it is to be noted that the results are in substantial agreement with the movement of the main ethical systems outlined in the preceding chapter. There, throughout the Middle Ages, the ethics of principles monopolistically dominates. Beginning with 1500, the ethics of happiness reappear and grow, with fluctuations. The same procedure is shown by the French as well as by the German Criminal Law and by the laws of other countries studied. Thus one set of data well supports the other set. And as they are different and even were collected by different persons, such an agreement is further evidence that the results are not misleading.

trend is similar to that shown by the French Criminal Law of that period (though not so pronounced), and it is again in agreement with the trend in the movement of the ethical systems already outlined. Side by side with the principal trend, others are noticeable. The main one of these is an increase of the power of the "enlightened absolutism," with its authoritarian tendencies toward the expansion of its regulation and control of social relationships, not to mention its stress on protective measures in regard to itself.

(4) The Prussian Criminal Code of 1851 exhibits the following differences with the criminal law of the preceding period. Seven crimes are dropped (Nos. 2, 11, 28, 35, 45, 47, 77); twelve new ones are added (Nos. 20, 43, 50, 61, 63, 72, 89, 90, 91, 95, 100, 102), giving thus seventy-nine types of punishable actions. In addition, ten crimes are broadened in their interpretation (Nos. 5, 9, 18, 29, 30, 57, 67, 69, 98, 99); eleven are limited (Nos. 15, 17, 32, 36, 37, 41, 59, 73, 81, 82, 97); and finally, six are modified in their meaning.

The essence of the change is very similar to that of the French Criminal Code of the nineteenth century. We are in a respectable utilitarian-hedonistic stream, going still farther away from religious and Ideational values, as is shown by exclusion from the crimes of the actions of suicide, heresy, sorcery; limitation of the punishable sacrilege; in brief, by banishment of the last traces of crimes against religion. The code tries to secure to citizens an orderly and respectable and enjoyable life of empirical comfort, security, and safety, with all the possible pleasures of a well-balanced Epicurean. All that has been said of the French Criminal Law of the nineteenth century is applicable to the Prussian law, with some slight modifications. Of other tendencies, those of individualism and singularism, democracy and liberalism, are to be mentioned.

(5) The essentials of this code are reproduced in the German Empire's Criminal Code of 1871. It excludes two crimes — usury and religious coercion; adds four new ones (Nos. 28, 33, 35, 78), giving a total of eighty-one crimes. It expands five in their interpretation (Nos. 9, 15, 17, 32, 37); limits three (Nos. 41, 89, 101); and somewhat modifies four. Exclusion of religious coercion and the limitation of slander of religious societies are signs of a movement still further away from Ideationalism and religiosity. Other trends are toward a more careful protection of purely economic interests; toward "freedom of the individual," toward liberalism, democracy, and "equality." We are at the "apex" of a liberal code of a purely utilitarian and hedonistic brand.

(6) Finally, when we take the projects of the postwar and post-liberal criminal codes (in the edition of 1927) and the project of the Nazi Criminal Code of 1935, we find in both some deviation from the liberal, individualistic, and similar tendencies shown in the codes for the preceding three centuries.

The project of 1927 (the period of the Weimar Constitution) drops five crimes from the preceding code (Nos. 13, 40, 78, 82, 103); it adds five new ones (Nos. 3, 16, 36, 66, 93), leaving the same number — eighty-one types of punishable actions — as before. In addition, it modifies the content of three crimes, expands that of eight, and limits four.

The total character of these changes shows that the code moves still in a purely anti-Ideational and antireligious stream; still is permeated by purely utilitarian and Sensate principles; perhaps even more so than the preceding code. But it deviates from it by its conspicuous "authoritarian" and "étatistic" tendencies toward expansion of governmental interference; by its anti-individualism. Being a creation of the pre-Nazi regime, it shows some signs of revolt against various trends of the preceding codes; but its program remains still, in a sense, that of the "capitalist" code, but stripped of liberalism and individualism. It longs for the autocratic discipline of a stern but paternalistic policeman.

These new tendencies and some other ones find much clearer expression in the project of the Nazi Criminal Code of 1935.[40]

---

[40] *Das Kommende deutsche Strafrecht. Bericht über die Arbeit der amtlichen Strafrechts-Kommission*, ed. by Dr. Franz Görtner, Reichjustizminister, 2 vols. (Berlin, 1934–1935). Also *National-sozialistische Leitsätze für ein neues deutsche Strafrecht*, ed. by Reichsrechtsamt der NSDAP (*Nation.-Sozial. Deutsche Arbeiter Partie*).

Minister of Justice, Franz Guertner, characterizes its main principles as follows (*Boston Evening Transcript*, November 5, 1936).

"1. The death penalty for murder and extortionary kidnaping.

"2. Prison sentences for 'publicly inciting the limitation of the number of offspring'; cornering the market, making insulting remarks about Adolf Hitler.

"3. Monetary fines or jail sentences for resurrecting the pasts of persons who have since proved worthy citizens, causing or ordering strikes or lockouts, and disclosing industrial secrets to foreign countries.

"The spirit of the code is summed up in its preface, which says in part:

"'The healthy feeling of the people for right and wrong determines the content and application of the penal code.

"'Atonement for wrong, the protection of our people as a whole . . . determine its meaning and purpose.

"'Its task is to safeguard honor and fidelity, race heredity, defensive powers of labor, discipline and order.

"'Its motto is "the common weal takes precedence over private advantage."'

"The new code is based on the Nazi principle that protection of the nation, rather than protection of the individual, is the paramount consideration in jurisprudence.

Compared with the Draft Code, 1927, the Code of 1935 adds eleven new types of criminal actions: namely, putting in a dangerous situation the life of another; infection of venereal disease; blasphemy; unpermitted marriage; slander of state authorities; strike; lockout; slandering marriage and the family; leaving the pregnant without help and support; squandering the resources of the family; slandering justice. Libel of the State is dropped, but it is replaced by additional crimes which specify more accurately the crimes of this type. The interpretation of fourteen crimes is widened: withholding help; threat; dangerous property damage; usury; sacrilege; hindering religious services; kidnaping woman without her consent; fornication; seduction; traffic (trade) of women; revolt; coercion of the authorities; self-liberation of prisoners; false denunciation. Five crimes are interpreted more narrowly.

Such are the main differences of this code from the previous ones. Its tendencies are: first, *totalitarian and authoritarian or antiliberal and anti-individualistic*. This is shown by the introduction of several new crimes and by widening the interpretation of several previous crimes — all against the State and its authorities. It is shown also by the interference of the State in such hitherto private matters (for the criminal law) as slandering marriage and the family; as squandering the family resources; as leaving without help the pregnant; as lockout, strike, and other labor crimes. In these and in several other fields of activity where, especially in the Code of 1871, the criminal law did not enter, it now enters unhesitatingly. The other side of the situation is the limitation of the freedom and autonomy of the individual, and of social

---

"Besides punishing murder and manslaughter strictly, the new code even makes the acquisition of instrument for killing punishable if intent to kill can be proved.

"Attempts at suicide, however, will go unpunished.

"Anyone speaking contemptuously of marriage or motherhood in public will be penalized.

"Abortion is considered a crime.

"Much space in the code is devoted to two phases: First, the protection of labor and industry, and second, the protection of German honor, both individual and national.

"Generally speaking anything calculated to interfere with the nation's will or capacity to work is punishable.

"This includes, among other things, the squandering of supplies or materials, because Nazi jurists said such acts might result in scarcity which would lead to the laying off of workers or the shutting down of plants.

"Personal honor is safeguarded to the extent that insults, delivered with no third party present, will be punished.

"The act of speaking disrespectfully of war deeds of the German army likewise will be penalized.

"Duels will be permitted, since they are held to enable a man to defend his honor."

groups other than the State. In all this the code definitely revolts against the liberal code of prewar Germany.

The second main tendency is, in a sense, Ideational. It manifests itself in the reinstatement of blasphemy as a crime; in an increase of punishment for, and in widening the interpretation of, sacrilege; in considering the hindrance of religious services punishable; also in protection of the value of the family, marriage, justice; and in the punishment of actions that ideationally and sensately display a lack of sociality, like withholding help, leaving the pregnant without help, and the like. In all this the code displays, if not a return to Ideationalism, at least some trend toward it. Here again it is opposite to the tendencies of the codes of the nineteenth century. In other respects, it is also anticapitalistic, and replaces several crimes that before resulted from contractual relationships, by crimes which are motivated by the transgression of the paternalistic, fraternalistic, and "familistic" relationships (for the meaning of these terms see Chapter One of Volume Three). It replaces a part of the contractual relationship by familistic and compulsory authoritarianism. In lieu of the "contractual man" — free employer and employee and free contractual parties generally — it attempts to set up, on the one hand, a benevolent policeman; on the other, a *bonus pater familias*, who demands that all members of his family behave and do their duty, regardless of whether or not it limits their freedom and comfort. In all these tendencies, the code turns in the opposite direction from that of the codes of the eighteenth and nineteenth centuries.

C. *Austria.* (1) Here the passage from the criminal law of the centuries preceding the eighteenth (for which period the law is the same as outlined for Germany) to the criminal law of the end of the eighteenth and the beginning of the nineteenth century (the Criminal Law of 1803) is marked by trends and characteristics quite similar to those in France and Germany. Of fifty-four crimes, six are dropped (Nos. 34, 47, 48, 50, 83, 95); nineteen new ones are added (Nos. 7, 8, 11, 17, 20, 32, 35, 46, 62, 63, 64, 78, 81, 96, 97, 98, 101, 102, 103), giving a total of sixty-seven types of punished actions. In addition, four crimes are expanded in their interpretation (Nos. 13, 27, 31, 100); four are limited (Nos. 5, 21, 4, 57); and four are changed in their content (Nos. 18, 29, 58, 65).

The totality of the changes manifests a tendency toward secularization, and side by side with it, toward authoritarianism of the monarchical power (the "Enlightened Despotism") and its trend to expand state interference.   The principal difference from the changes in the codes of France and Germany of that period is that in Austria the drift toward secularization is somewhat more moderate.

(2) The main changes introduced by the Code of 1852, with the subsequent modifications up to 1880, are: exclusion of three crimes (suicide, usury, and strike) and the addition of ten (Nos. 15, 19, 39, 45, 50, 51, 69, 90, 91, 92).   This gives a total of seventy-four crimes.   Five crimes are expanded in their scope; five are narrowed; three are changed. All in all, the code continues the secularization; introduces some limitation of authoritarianism of the State; favors the expansion of individualism, democracy, and liberalism.

(3) Finally, the project of 1912 reflects in a sense the climax of the utilitarian, antireligious, and liberal-democratic trends, representing the unrealized "swan song" of the nineteenth century.   As such, it is quite out of date with the postwar and postliberal conditions of Austria, and with her martial laws, which now have become normal for her.

It planned to drop heresy, religious seduction, abduction, sodomy (with animals), traders' strikes, and participation in criminal associations. It planned to add sixteen new crimes (Nos. 3, 10, 12, 16, 33, 34, 36, 49, 61, 66, 72, 73, 76, 93, 95, 100), giving thus eighty-four punishable types of activities.   In addition, it planned to expand the limits of fifteen, to narrow four, and to modify three crimes.

These contemplated changes show a continuation of the secularizing tendency; further growth of utilitarian principles; further expansion of liberalism; a trend toward the protection of the socially weak elements.   It is, perhaps, the most consistent expression of these tendencies in the eighteenth and nineteenth centuries.

As mentioned, the troubled conditions in postwar Austria have hindered the juridical introduction of this project and have forced a regime of martial law, of application of force on principles far different from those of this liberal code.   However, as this new factual situation is not codified as yet, it cannot be studied, as a code.

D. *Italy*.   Similar in essentials has been the fluctuation of the ethicojuridical mentality in Italy, as expressed in its criminal law.

(1) The passage from the "Barbaric" to the Feudal Criminal Law of the Middle Ages, as it is reflected in the city-state statutes of the twelfth and thirteenth centuries, is marked by dropping three and by adding twenty-one new crimes, which gives fifty-six types of punishable actions.   Those which are added are partly crimes against religion (Nos. 2, 40, 42, 45, 48, 50a); partly those against the State (Nos. 83, 85,

94, 97, 98, 99); partly those against the good mores (Nos. 9, 32, 36, 38 62, 65, 71, 81, 102). In addition, three crimes are expanded, three narrowed, and three modified. All in all, the change shows a movement toward religious and Ideational principles, with additional trends toward authoritarian, governmental interference and regulation. In essentials, it is similar to what we have noted in other countries.

(2) The criminal law of the statutes of the fifteenth, sixteenth, and seventeenth centuries introduces the following changes: four crimes are dropped, all of a religious nature (suicide, heresy and schism, abuse of a corpse, and contact with a Jew), and fifteen are added (Nos. 7, 8, 17, 19, 37, 51, 52, 54, 64, 72, 73, 77, 92, 96, 100); the total gives sixty-seven types of crimes. Three crimes are expanded and one modified in interpretation.

The total change shows a clear secular (antireligious and anti-Ideational) trend, with its satellites: utilitarianism, hedonism, and sensualism, moderated still, however, by the religious principles and by similar interests of the whole society. The authoritarian principle continues its progress, but is limited here and there by the rising tide of individualism and liberalism.

(3) The Criminal Code of Tuscany, 1786, excludes thirty of sixty-seven previous crimes, adds seven, and thus retains only forty-four types of crimes.[41] The crimes excluded are: Nos. 7, 8, 9, 13, 14, 17, 18, 19, 26, 27, 28, 32, 36, 38, 47, 48, 50a, 51, 52, 64, 72, 74, 77, 83, 87, 88, 92, 96, 97, 98. The new crimes introduced are Nos. 34, 35, 41, 46, 63, 69, 101. Of other crimes, six are expanded, five narrowed, and one changed in interpretation. All in all, the code remains in the secular current, trying, however, to cope with the materially dangerous and harmful activities. Of other trends, none is particularly conspicuous.

(4) The Sardinian Criminal Code of 1839 excludes two and adds thirty-five, increasing thus the number of punishable types of activities to seventy-seven. The dropped crimes are: secret marriage and slandering of the State. The new ones are Nos. 2, 7, 8, 9, 14, 15, 17, 18, 20, 26, 27, 28, 32, 36, 38, 39, 43, 50, 51, 52, 61, 72, 73, 74, 77, 78, 79, 87, 88, 92, 95, 96, 97, 98, 103. These are mainly crimes limiting the freedom of individuals, their economic interests, and finally the interests and safety of the State and its government. Of other crimes, four are expanded, eight limited, and four modified in their content.

---

[41] However, Article 56 of the code entitles the police to impose penalties in the cases not foreseen by the code. For this reason, the number of punishable actions might not be reduced at all, or reduced much less than the figures above show.

The totality of these changes shows that this code is also almost entirely in the secular utilitarian stream and has little religious or Ideational tendency. But within this empirical utilitarianism, it is "restorational" and "conservative." Its main preoccupation is the protection of the bodily integrity of an individual, of his freedom, of his economic interests, and of his comfort. In these traits it again is essentially similar to the codes of the nineteenth century of the other countries studied.

(5) The Italian Criminal Code of 1889 is a further development of these same trends. It excludes twelve, adds eleven, and gives thus seventy-six types of punishable actions. Those excluded are mainly the crimes against religion and decent mores, like suicide, blasphemy, religious coercion, religious seduction, concubinage, homosexuality, sodomy (with animals), the other activities being usury, lockout, and crimes against the State (Nos. 92, 97, and 103). The actions included in the criminal class are Nos. 3, 12, 13, 19, 33, 49, 64, 89, 90, 91, 101; that is, mostly crimes against the freedom of the individual and then against the State and the freedom of voting.

Of other crimes, seven are expanded, eight narrowed, and five modified in content and interpretation. All in all, here is a further step toward secularization, empirical utilitarianism, material comfort and protection — especially of the freedom of the individual — with democratic, liberal, and partly philanthropic tendencies. Like all the other European codes of the second part of the nineteenth century the Italian code is an incorporation of the same main tendencies of European culture: secularism, sensualism, utilitarianism, hedonism, individualism, indifference to religious and Ideational value, with a trend to protect the weak groups of society, and the respectability and sensibleness of a well-balanced Victorian.

(6) When finally we come to the Fascist Code of 1930, we see that it continues the secular and areligious and a-Ideational trend. But, like the Nazi Code of 1935, it shows evidences of a higher appreciation of these values; and then, in several other respects, it somewhat breaks the trend of the nineteenth century and introduces certain novelties (more accurately, it reintroduces the traits present in the codes before the nineteenth century, but effaced during this century of liberalism and individualism). It drops only one crime — performance of prohibited rites — but adds eight new ones, raising the total to eighty-three. The newly added crimes are: putting another's life in danger; usury; blasphemy; economic exploitation of a prostitute; attempts against the political and social order; lockout; participation in a riot; and nondenunciation

of contemplated crimes. Of other crimes fifteen are expanded in their content and interpretation; one is limited; and four are modified.

Summing up the main novelties, one can say that the code emphasizes the religious and Ideational values a little more than did the codes of the nineteenth century; but especially strongly it manifests the authoritarian, the disciplinarian, or somewhat antiliberal tendencies, expanding the power, prestige, and interference of the State and its government. In this sense, it is somewhat antiliberal and anti-individualistic. By its prohibition of lockouts and strikes it renounces also some forms of collective liberty and economic interests. By its enlargement of the interpretation of such actions as "leaving another's life in danger," misuse of dependence for the purpose of lewdness, panderage, and others, it tries to enforce decent mores and moral discipline. In these and in several other respects it breaks the traditions of the nineteenth century. In all its tendencies it is quite similar to the Nazi Code, and, with several exceptions, to the Soviet Code of 1926. Just as all the codes of the nineteenth century show similar characteristics, so the codes of the twentieth century display similar tendencies in Nazi Germany, Fascist Italy, and Soviet Russia.[42]

E. *Russia.* In contradistinction to the Barbarian Teutonic Criminal Law, more or less common to the four European countries studied, the early Russian Criminal Code (*Russkaia Pravda*) gives not thirty-eight types of punishable actions, but only twenty-one, namely, those crimes in the list of 104 which are numbered: 1, 4, 5, 13, 21, 23, 28, 29, 30, 47, 53, 55, 56, 57, 58, 59, 60, 68, 75, 87, 88. These crimes consist mainly of offenses against a person, his life, his bodily integrity, and his status as a free man; there are practically no crimes against religion, except that of sorcery; there are several crimes against sex mores, a few against property, and then treason against the State. It is an epitome of conciseness in the sense that it considers only the most essential violations which, as we shall see, are present in almost all criminal codes of all times, and dismisses the too conditional and too variable "superfluities."

(1) The Code of 1649 (*Sobornoie Ulojenie*) introduces the following differences. It drops seven of the preceding crimes (Nos. 13, 47, 53, 58, 68, 87, and 88); adds twenty (Nos. 9, 17, 18, 22, 24, 25, 31, 40, 42, 44, 45, 46, 48, 65, 70, 74, 82, 84, 97, 103); thus it contains thirty-four punishable types of actions.

---

[42] The newly created Latvia, Estonia, and Lithuania use the Russian Code of 1903, with later revisions. The changes made in this code by these countries show tendencies not dissimilar to the Nazi, Fascist, and Soviet codes.

Then it enlarges the content of four crimes and modifies one. The totality of these changes shows that while in Europe the codes and the statutes of the seventeenth century exhibited a trend away from religion and Ideationality, here a strong trend is maintained toward these tendencies. About half of the newly added crimes are of religious and Ideational nature (blasphemy, obstructing religious service, apostasy, heresy, and schism, religious seduction, nonfulfillment of religious duties, etc.), while a few others are also closely associated with them, like panderage and tobacco smoking. Of other trends the main one is a reinforcement of the protection of the political order and the state authorities. Thus in law, as in most of the other compartments of culture, like art and science, Russia shows a lag of some two hundred years in comparison with the "progress" of European countries.

(2) The Criminal Code of 1845 gives the following differences from the previous code. One crime — tobacco smoking — is dropped ; forty-nine new crimes are added ; the total number of the types of punishable actions reaches thus eighty-two. The newly added crimes are : Nos. 2, 3, 6, 7, 8, 13, 14, 19, 26, 27, 32, 34, 35, 36, 37, 38, 39, 41, 43, 47, 50, 51, 52, 53, 58, 59, 62, 63, 64, 67, 68, 69, 71, 73, 77, 78, 81, 85, 86, 87, 88, 91, 94, 95, 96, 98, 99, 100, and 101. Four other crimes are enlarged in their content, four are narrowed, and four are changed.

According to the totality of these changes, the code was approaching those of the other European countries at the beginning or in the middle of the nineteenth century, in all essential respects, with the exception that it did not drop a majority of the religious crimes, and thus did not show the same trend away from religious and Ideational values toward purely earthly utilitarianism. The utilitarian motives and principles enter into it as fully as into the European codes, but the religious principles are there also, coexisting side by side. Of other tendencies, that toward authoritarianism, moderated by some efforts to protect the weaker elements of society, is noticeable. The liberal and individualistic tendencies of the European codes are also less conspicuous in the Russian Code.

(3) Since the Code of 1903 never has been put into effect in its complete form and its role has consisted mainly in correcting the previous Code through replacement of some of its parts by the parts of the Code of 1903, we can pass to the Criminal Law of 1914, 1916, as it is given in the Code of Criminal Laws of Russia (*Svod Zakonov ugolovnykh*, ed. 1914 and 1916). It differs from the preceding code as follows : four crimes are dropped (apostasy, schism, sorcery, and nonperformance of religious

rites); seven new crimes are added (Nos. 20, 66, 76, 89, 90, 92, and 102). The total number is thus eighty-five. Of other crimes, six are enlarged, four are narrowed, and seven are modified in their content.

The totality of changes shows thus the same strong secular trend which was manifested in other European codes of the nineteenth century. But though lagging, the Code of 1914–1916 reaches in this respect the European codes of prewar time. Several trends in Russian culture lag some hundred to a hundred and fifty years behind the European situation, but in the second half of the nineteenth century these trends move so fast that they catch up and the lag thus disappears. This has been shown in Volume One in regard to painting and sculpture and literature; and this we see here also.

Of other tendencies are to be mentioned increasing utilitarianism, liberalism, individualism, and an increasing emphasis on the protection of the freedom and economic interests of an individual. In brief, the code is generally similar to that of European countries of the prewar period.

(4) Finally, the postwar and the Revolutionary Code of 1926, like the Fascist and the Nazi codes, discloses new lines and tendencies. Like the French Revolutionary Code of 1791, the Soviet Code drops thirty-three crimes, adds six new ones, and thus retains fifty-eight types of punishable actions.[43] The crimes dropped are: Nos. 2, 7, 8, 12, 13, 17, 18, 19, 20, 28, 35, 37, 40, 41, 46, 50, 53, 55, 56, 57, 58, 59, 63, 66, 67, 68, 69, 81, 89, 91, 92, 98, and 101. We see that these are mainly crimes against religion, which are entirely eliminated from the class of criminal actions (in a country of a militant atheism, this is no more than natural); crimes connected with sex: here again, almost all such crimes, from seduction, adultery, polygamy, polyandry, incest, sodomy, homosexuality, up to fornication, kidnaping women against their will, public indecency, etc., are shifted into the class of noncriminal actions. Such a change is again quite natural for a regime which regarded the family as the worst form of capitalism, and sexual limitations as prejudice.[44]

[43] But here, like most of the Revolutionary codes and Revolutionary justice, any action displeasing to the government can become punishable. That is indeed the practice. And Article 16 of this code authorizes an imposition of punishment by analogy. Therefore the total number of punishable actions may be and is rather greater than fifty-eight. Practically anything which displeases the Soviet Government can become punishable, and such actions have been punished most severely, even by capital punishment.

[44] *Regarded*, because, at the present time, some ten years after the enactment of this code, the policies of the Soviet Government in regard to the family, marriage, sex, even religion, are notably different. Many of these values which they tried to destroy, now they try to re-establish.

It is consistent with the objectives of the Soviet Government. The other crimes dropped are also meaningless in a country where there is no real election, where the governmental coercion in a quasi-election is an open principle of the Communist regime. The crimes added are: Nos. 10, 11, 33, 49, 79, and 80, most of which, like lockout on the part of private employers (not on the part of the Soviet Government, which is the main employer); danger of infection by venereal disease; disposal of floor space in a dwelling (a special crime in the Soviet regime); blackmail; participation in prohibited religious ceremonies, are again quite in agreement with such a form of government. Of other crimes, thirteen are enlarged, six narrowed, and six modified in their content.

The totality of these changes means a complete rupture with any religious principles and Ideational values; the Soviet Code is merely putting the finishing touch to the codes of the liberal *bourgeoisie* and professional classes of the nineteenth century. In this sense, the code is not a rupture from, but, on the contrary, the terminal point of the "capitalist codes" of the nineteenth century and of even the earlier codes of the liberal nobility. It expels Ideational values entirely and replaces them with frankly utilitarian, frankly material, principles. In all these respects it is a realization of the trends of the preceding period, but pushed now to the extreme possible point; consistently, logically, and "rationalistically" driven to the final stage without any inhibition by considerations of decency and other "superstitions." The same is to be said of the other groups of actions excluded from the criminal class in the Soviet Code. I mean the whole group of sex activities. The prewar codes of Europe more and more tended in the same direction, cutting off the Ideational and religious and transcendental ethical motives which placed seduction, sodomy, homosexuality, adultery, kidnaping of women, and so on, in the class of criminal actions. These prewar codes considered these acts more and more from the purely relativistic utilitarian standpoint; therefore they excluded many such "pleasant" and "hedonistically enjoyable" actions from the class of crime. But they did not dare to go up to the logically consistent terminal point of this road. The Soviet Code did that. In this respect again, it consistently pushed to the terminal point the principles introduced by liberalism, "enlightened scientism," "mental progress," "decay of superstitions," and other fashionable slogans of the nineteenth-century mentality. If the liberals are displeased with the Soviet radicalism along these lines, they must go farther back than Soviet cynicism, immorality, and so on, in their criticism. They must ask themselves whether their own principles, of which they were so proud in the nineteenth century, were all entirely sound. Whether, in their efforts to get away from religion and Ideationality (from superstitions and prejudices, in their terminology), they did not prepare the ground and sow the seed from which the above "poisonous Soviet flowers" have blossomed. If the question is honestly answered, the answer is "Yes." And if it is "Yes," then it means the need of return to the old criminal codes and the transfer of the whole ethico-juridical mentality to Ideationalism and religious bases. Until this is done, the Soviet flowers will continue to bloom. They are a mere realization of the seeds of Sensate mentality, and of the relativistic, purely utilitarian, and frankly hedonistic morality. In this sense, the Soviet Code is typical. It has the consistency of a sensual lunatic.

Of other tendencies, the conspicuous trend is toward autocratic despotism. *"Princeps legibus solutus est"; "Quod principi placuit legis habet vigorem,"* says the Soviet lawgiver through that code. It breaks with the individualistic, liberal, democratic tendencies of the nineteenth century, and it has something in common with the Fascist Code of 1930 and the Nazi Code of 1935, as well as with the practices of the factual functioning of criminal justice (with purgings, mass shootings, mass arrests, and so on) of many dictatorial countries of the present time. This practice, in fact, broke almost entirely with the nineteenth-century concept of the "inalienable rights of man and citizen," with its guarantees to an individual against maltreatment and unjust persecution on the part of the government. We are living in an age where citizens are "at the mercy of the governments," which are antihumanitarian, vigorous, cruel, and cynical, with some pseudo-Ideational aspirations poorly understood and poorly carried out. These governments are successfully "liquidating" the political, juridical, and cultural values of the nineteenth and preceding centuries; in this sense they are "grave worms" of the declining Sensate culture, that prepare the ground for possibly a new Ideational culture to come. Unconsciously, some of them seem even to aspire to something like Ideationalism. But wreckers are rarely the real builders. Like Cubists and Modernists in art, and other revolters against the overripe Sensate culture of the end of the nineteenth century, these Cubists in government are powerful destroyers and "cleansers," but they poorly see the port of destination of a new culture to come. Hence their above characteristics.

F. *Summary of the Above.* The preceding data entitle us to draw several conclusions of a fairly general nature concerning the fluctuation of the ethicojuridical mentality as it is reflected in the field of criminal law.

(1) There is no doubt that a fluctuation does take place in that field. We have seen that in each country the number of types of punishable actions, as well as the nature of such actions, changes. Passing from period to period, we have seen an invariable exclusion from the class of criminal actions of some so qualified by the criminal law of the preceding period, and an inclusion in the criminal class of actions that were non-criminal according to the previous criminal law. As a result, the total number of the types of punishable actions fluctuates from period to period. There is no single period or country which is an exception to this rule.

(2) Turning to the fluctuation of the number of the types of actions criminal from period to period in each of the countries studied, as well as the total for all the countries studied, the following conclusions are validated by the data.

It is untrue that the number of punishable actions tends to increase as we pass from the earlier to the later periods in the history of criminal law, either of the same country, or in that of all the countries studied. Many an investigator (see the quoted works of R. Pound and F. Frankfurter, for instance) has been claiming that such a trend exists. Their claims, however, confuse two different things; the number of the statutes issued and the number of the types of activity punished. They are very different, and should not be confused. The number of statutes or the pages of the statutes or the number of divisions, chapters, and paragraphs in it may increase; and yet the number of the punishable actions may decrease or may remain constant. One is a matter of editorial ability, so to speak; the other is the manifestation of the existing moral mentality. Even the number of the statutes or pages does not necessarily increase in the course of time, especially in the countries which, at intervals, undertake the systemization and codification of their laws and statutes, as do most countries except the Anglo-Saxon. The later codes of these countries are not necessarily more bulky nor larger, nor do they contain more pages than the earlier ones. Only in the Anglo-Saxon countries the situation may be different.

Anyhow, the claim that in the course of time the number of the types of actions punishable by criminal law increases is invalid. This is shown by Table 38, which summarizes the above data.

A glance at the figures in the second column is sufficient to show: first, that the number of the punishable types of actions fluctuates comparatively, narrowly, only between 33 and 76 when all the countries are taken together; and between 21 and 91 numerically, when each

TABLE 38. FLUCTUATION OF THE NUMBER OF TYPES OF CRIMINAL (PUNISHABLE) ACTIONS IN THE SPECIFIED COUNTRIES

COUNTRY AND PERIOD[1]	Number of Crimes Excluded by the Subsequent Code	Total Number of Criminal Types of Action in a Given Code	Of the Total		Of Those Retained from Previous Code			
			Newly added	Remained from previous code	Enlarged	Narrowed	Modified	Unchanged
France								
I		38						
II	2	51	15	36	3		4	29
III	1	73	23	50	6	2	5	37
IV	35	44	6	38	6	7	3	22
V	6	62	24	38	9	3	2	24
VI	2	70	10	60	3	2	1	54
Germany								
I		38						
II	8	42	12	30	3		4	23
III	4	54	16	38	3	3	2	30
IV	4	74	24	50	3	8	4	35
V	7	79	12	67	10	11	6	40
VI	2	81	4	77	5	3	4	65
VIIa	5	81	5	76	8	4	3	61
VIIb	1	91	11	80	14	5		60
Austria								
III		54						
IV	6	67	19	48	4	4	5	35
V	3	74	10	64	5	5	3	51
VII	6	84	16	68	15	4	3	46
Italy								
I		38						
II	3	56	21	35	3	3		29
III	4	67	15	52	3		1	48
IV	30	44	7	37	6	5	1	25
V	2	77	35	42	4	8	4	26
VI	12	76	11	65	7	8	5	45
VIIb	1	83	8	75	15	1	4	55
Russia								
I		21						
III	7	34	20	14	4		1	9
V	1	82	49	33	4	4	4	21
VIIa	4	85	7	78	6	4	7	61
VIIb	33	58	6	52	13	6	6	27
AVERAGE (Percentages) FOR THE FIVE COUNTRIES STUDIED								
I		33.8[2]						
II		49.7	32.2	67.8	6.1	2.0	5.3	54.4
III		69.0	37.3	62.7	5.8	3.3	4.4	49.2
IV		57.3	25.0	75.0	8.7	11.0	6.0	49.3
V		75.2	23.2	76.8	11.5	10.8	7.6	46.9
VI		75.7	13.9	86.1	7.5	7.0	5.9	65.7
VII		76.5	11.4	88.6	16.3	4.8	5.6	61.9

[1] Means each of the subsequent codes studied and the respective centuries of which each period is representative.

[2] The average in absolute number. For the computation of these percentages the Nazi Code is not included. In this average for the five countries the period I means the pre-Christian codes; the period II the codes of the Middle Ages; the period III embraces the codes of the fifteenth to the first part of the eighteenth century; the period IV, the codes of the end of the eighteenth century (the Enlightened Absolutism and the Revolutions); the period V, the codes of the first part of the nineteenth century; the period VI, the codes of the second part of that century; the period VII and VIIa, prerevolutionary codes of the end of the nineteenth or of the beginning of the twentieth century; VIIb, postwar and postrevolutionary codes.

country is taken separately.   Second, that whether for all the countries taken together or for each country separately (except perhaps the Germanic peoples) there is no perpetual trend toward an ever-increasing number of punishable actions.   After an increase for one or two periods, there comes a decrease.   If each subsequent code adds some new crimes, the same code excludes some actions which the preceding code regarded as criminal.   There seems to exist a kind of limit in tabooing or prohibiting the types of actions and stamping them as criminal.   So much for that point.

(3) Looking at the first column, we see that the French, the Italian, and the Russian codes enacted in the times of revolution (1791 and 1926), or of autocratic anticlerical reform (1786), exclude an abnormally high number of actions from the class of crime in which they were put by previous codes.   In France the number is thirty-five; in Italy, thirty; in Soviet Russia, thirty-three.   For each of these countries these numbers stand far above the respective numbers for other periods.   This shows once more that a great reconstruction effects not only a change in the political regime, but also an abnormally sharp change in the ethicojuridical mentality and in law — even in criminal law — not to mention changes in other compartments of sociocultural life.

(4) Looking at the column which shows the number of the newly added crimes from period to period, for the countries taken together we see that the most radical in innovation (that is, in the introduction of new crimes) were the second and third periods — roughly, the Middle Ages and the beginning of "modern times" (about the fifteenth to the seventeenth centuries).   They give a percentage respectively of 32.2 and 37.3 of new crimes from the total number of crimes in these periods. Subsequent periods give a smaller and smaller percentage of new crimes (25, 23, 13, 11 per cent respectively).   This indicates several things. First, that the Middle Ages and the late Middle Ages or the beginning of "modern times" tried to be more rigorous and more exacting in their efforts to uplift the conduct of man to a higher level, as they understood it, or to hinder an increased perpetration of several actions, which before were possibly of rare occurrence.   An increase of new crimes in the Middle Ages (second period) is in agreement with the theory that these were Ideational and Idealistic cultures which deemed sinful many actions before regarded as normal.   It means also a deeper moral revolution in the ethicojuridical mentality of the contemporaries or of the lawgivers. Only by such a revolution can one explain their courage in shifting a com-

paratively enormous number of actions hitherto noncriminal and not punishable into the class of crimes. An increase of new crimes in the third period (fifteenth to seventeenth centuries) may mean an urgent necessity to hinder an increased frequency of actions which have become socially dangerous and which possibly were more rare before. Such an hypothesis agrees with the great demoralization during these transitory centuries from Ideational to Sensate standards. The falling percentage of such innovations in the later periods may signify either a moral standardization of the new Sensate conduct, or an increasing moral laxity, or an exhaustion of man's limited possibilities to create new crimes out of human actions. However it may be, the figures show a decreasing "innovating" trend.

When each of the countries studied is taken separately, their data in this respect vary. All in all, however, they do not show any perpetual trend; the innovating tendency just erratically fluctuates in them, now increasing, now decreasing. This, together with the trend shown by the totality of the countries, is sufficient to dispel the widely accepted opinion that as we pass to our times, the innovations discussed progressively increase in the field of law, and in criminal law especially. Nothing of the kind is shown by the data. Most of the "new" crimes introduced by a certain code are but a reintroduction of the crimes excluded by previous codes and are therefore mere restorations of past "inventions" — even then we do not find any progressively increasing tendency to innovations in this field. So much for that theory here. Later on, I shall take the problem up again.

(5) If the later periods do not show any increase of an "innovating" ability, they do show such an increase in the slighter and less fundamental changes made in the content of the crimes, namely, in their enlargement, narrowing, and modifications. Examining the data for all the countries studied, taken together, we find that as we pass from the earlier to the later periods, the percentage of the enlarged — and partly of the narrowed — content of the crimes tends somewhat to increase, though even here the trend is not steady and consistent. This means that in mere variation and modification of the actions previously put into the criminal class, the modern times show a somewhat greater ingenuity than the earlier. But the earlier times, which made more extensive and deeper innovations, did not need the more superficial modifications as much as the modern times do.

(6) The next interesting problem is to what extent the countries and periods studied show similarity or homogeneity of the total class of

criminal actions. Is the composition of the class of crimes in the various countries equally homogeneous in all periods, or does its homogeneity vary, being higher in a given period, lower in another? The answer to this question is found in Table 39. Its indicators of homogeneity are computed in this way. Let us mark by N the number of the types of crimes in a given country at a given period. By P we mark the number of the countries which passed the same period, or stage of development, of criminal law. The product NP would then give the possible maximum of homogeneity of criminal law in the period; it would mean that all the crimes in all the countries studied are similar and the same. Such a complete identity (NP) we give the value of 100. In reality, such a complete identity is improbable, if not impossible. Some differences in the number and nature of the crimes of two or more countries are to be expected. Therefore, of the total number of crimes N, the number A_1 is punished in only one country; A_2 will be found in the lists of two countries; A_3 in those of three countries, and so on, up to the number AP, in the lists of all the countries studied. The sum of these: $S = A_1 + 2A_2 + 3A_3 \ldots pAP$ will always be smaller than the product NP. The coefficient of homogeneity therefore will be the result of $\dfrac{100\,S}{NP}$.

Computed according to this formula, the coefficient of homogeneity of the list of crimes in the countries studied for the main periods is given in Table 39.

TABLE 39. HOMOGENEITY OF THE TOTAL CLASS OF CRIMES

PERIOD [1]	Number of Types of Crimes Repeated in					The Proportion of the Number of the Factual Repetitions to the Possible Maximum	Indicator of Homogeneity
	Five Countries	Four Countries	Three Countries	Two Countries	One Country		
I				21	17	59 : 76	78%
II			43	7	10	153 : 180	85%
III		47	17	13	11	276 : 352	78%
IV	27	19	16	14	12	299 : 440	68%
V	49	24	7	5	6	378 : 445	83%
VI			62	14	10	224 : 258	87%
VII, a, b		46	31	14	4	309 : 380	81%

[1] See the notes to Table 38.

The figures in the last column show that most homogeneous were the second (the medieval and feudal) periods, and then the sixth period, which falls roughly within the nineteenth century — the period of liberalism, individualism, and respectable utilitarianism.

We can hardly be surprised by this result. After all, the medieval culture in its aspirations was very homogeneous throughout all Europe, having the same Ideational form, the same Canon Law, and the same "intelligentsia" and supreme moral body, the Church, which guided and controlled the ethicoreligious mentality of the whole of Europe.

In all centuries of the Middle Ages, Christendom, which in destiny is identical with Mankind, is set before us as a single universal Community, founded and governed by God himself. Mankind is one "mystical body"; it is one single and internally connected "people" or "folk"; it is an all-embracing corporation (*universitas*), which constitutes that Universal Realm, spiritual and temporal, which may be called the Universal Church (*ecclesia universalis*), or with equal propriety, the Commonwealth of the Human Race (*respublica generis humani*). Therefore, that it may attain its own purpose, it needs One Law (*lex*) and One Government (*unicus principatus*)."[45]

These words of O. von Gierke put the matter concisely and accurately. The mental, moral, and cultural unity of Europe of the Middle Ages was much greater than in many subsequent periods. And this unity shows itself also in the homogeneity of the criminal law.

The next homogeneous period is the nineteenth century — the period of triumphant liberalism, individualism, prosperity, utilitarianism, science, and capitalism. The ethicojuridical mentality and the criminal law of all the European countries became permeated by the same principles and by the same aspirations. Hence, a conspicuous homogeneity of the criminal law in all the countries studied. The other periods were those which split Europe into two or more parts, with different, sometimes even opposite, moral mentalities, as in the period of the Revolution, that of the "Enlightened Absolutism" of the postwar period, with Europe divided into liberal democracies and various dictatorships. In such periods, the homogeneity of law generally, and of criminal law particularly, naturally goes down.

These results would be still more conspicuous if we took only four European countries for such a study, omitting Russia, which lagged considerably behind the other countries and which had an initial foundation of criminal law different from theirs.

(7) Finally, and this is the most important point for us, the above data have shown clearly that the ethicojuridical mentality, as it is shown by criminal law, reflects very well the predominant — Ideational or Sensate — character of the culture. In the analysis of the criminal codes of the

---

[45] O. von Gierke, *Political Theories of the Middle Ages*, trans. by F. W. Maitland (Cambridge, 1900), p. 10.

five countries, it has been stressed and shown that the medieval innovations consisted in an introduction of many purely religious or Ideational crimes; they occupy the central place in the list of crimes of that period, not only in the Canon Law, but in the secular codes which were enacted then. And we shall see that the central place belongs to them, not only by reason of their large number, but also because of the severity of punishment they received. And then, as we passed to the codes of the fifteenth and sixteenth centuries, we saw how the number of such crimes against religion began to decrease, how more and more of them were shifted into the class of noncriminal actions. The process started then, with slight fluctuations, has continued up to the present time. In other words, in the period, roughly, from the beginning of the Christianization of the barbaric Teutonic peoples, their "Barbaric" codes began to undergo the process of ideationalization. The process continued, roughly, up to the fourteenth and fifteenth centuries. Since that time, the opposite process of "secularization" or rapid growth of purely utilitarian principles in the codes started. It has been continued up to the present time; and the latest codes of the nineteenth century as well as the postwar codes, especially the Soviet Code, put the final finishing touches to the process. In these it reached the point beyond which it is not possible to go. Only the Fascist and the new Nazi codes show the first signs of return to the Ideational-religious tendency.

In this great fluctuation, criminal law described practically the same curve which has been followed by all the main compartments of culture. This means that it is an inseparable part of an integrated culture; that when the latter experiences a great transformation, passes from dominant Ideationalism to Sensatism, or vice versa, criminal law reflects the process and also passes from one form to the other.

(8) Expressed in the quantitative form of the number of crimes included or excluded by any code, compared with the previous one, and noting the tendency or motive that lies at the basis of each exclusion or inclusion, the results of the rise and fall of various tendencies in various countries and periods are roughly shown by Table 40. It gives the averages for all the countries taken together in the form of percentages of crimes excluded or included to the total number of crimes of a given code.[46] The figures are only approximate; but they seem to reflect the real tendencies fairly well. The moral given by them can be summed up in a few propositions.

[46] For the sake of economy, the absolute figures for each country, as well as for all countries together, are not given.

TABLE 40. FLUCTUATIONS OF THE MAIN TENDENCIES IN THE CHANGE OF CRIMINAL LAW FROM PERIOD TO PERIOD (average for all five countries)

PERIOD	TENDENCIES							
	Religious	Secular	Authoritarian	Democratic	Totalitarian	Liberal	Humanitarian	Anti-Humanitarian
1. Medieval —feudal	12.7	1.0	3.7	0.0	0.7	0.0	4.7	1.3
2. Monarchical (XIV–XVIII century)	3.0	2.8	8.3	0.5	3.0	1.3	14.8	0.5
3. Enlightened absolutism and the Revolution (end of XVIII century)	1.0	8.0	3.5	5.3	2.3	2.3	9.5	0.8
4. Restorational (beginning of XIX century)	1.4	3.0	4.2	1.2	1.2	2.8	8.6	2.2
5. Liberal (XIX century)	0.0	4.7	0.3	2.0	1.3	2.7	7.7	0.7
6. Postliberal (postwar period) [1]	1.0	5.5	3.0	0.5	6.3	2.0	11.8	1.0

[1] Without the Nazi Code. If included, it will increase the authoritarian, totalitarian, and religious tendencies.

(*a*) In any change from one criminal code to another, several tendencies are at work simultaneously. Some of these are quite opposite. This is shown by all the horizontal rows of Table 40. But at various periods now one of the opposite tendencies, now the other, forges ahead, showing in this field also the principle of limits and of the immanent self-regulation of social processes.

(*b*) Of all the tendencies which motivated the changes in criminal law from period to period, the strongest, comparatively, have been:

(i) The *humanitarian* tendency, which even in the post-liberal period plays a prominent part in the innovations of the Fascist, Communist, and German codes. Its Golden Age, however, was the "monarchical" period. Specialists who are familiar with the "classic" criminal law of that period cannot fail to agree with that proposition. The codes enacted then are stamped with the objectives of protecting the individual and especially the weak elements of society against the oppression of the stronger groups and classes.

(ii) The *antihumanitarian* trend was, on the contrary, the strongest in the medieval, Restorational, and again in the modern post-war period, where the Communist and Fascist and Nazi codes threw aside many of the "rights of a man and a citizen" and likewise many "humanitarian" values present in the preceding codes.

(iii) The *religious* (*Ideational*) tendency was the strongest in the Middle Ages. Since then it has been steadily waning, until in the nineteenth century it ceased to play any role. The Fascist and Nazi codes of the twentieth century show some signs of its revival, but the signs are weak as yet; while the Communist and (partly) the German project of 1927 either leaned still farther away from the religious tendency or remained in the status of the nineteenth century.

(iv) The *secular* (*sensually utilitarian*) tendency grew rapidly after the Middle Ages up to the end of the eighteenth century, reaching its maximum in the period of the Revolution and the "enlightened absolutism." Then the reaction at the beginning of the nineteenth century pushed it down, after which, however, it resumed its growth, which it has continued up to the present time.

(v) The *authoritarian* tendency has also been one of the strongest. Its maximums were reached in the monarchical period, then in the period of the Restoration; and again it shows itself greatly revived in the postwar period. All the three codes of this latter time manifest it clearly and unmistakably.

(vi) The *democratic-singularistic* tendency was strongest in the eighteenth and in the second half of the nineteenth centuries. At the present time it is waning rapidly.

(vii) The tendencies *totalitarian and liberal* are closely connected with the previous authoritarian and democratic ones, but stress a specific angle of the bigger problem of singularism or universalism, of the state control or individual liberty. Their movement is similar in essentials to the movement of the authoritarian-democratic tendencies. The great days of totalitarianism in the past were, of course, the period of growth of the national monarchies and then of the enlightened absolutism and of the Revolution. The state interference in the control and regulation of the conduct of its citizens made great strides during these periods. Respectively the liberty and freedom of the individual were restrained. The end of the Revolution and then the nineteenth century were the heydays of limitation of this state control and of the blossoming of the freedom and liberty of a citizen. During that century, in fact, all these rights of man and citizen were enjoyed possibly more than at any other period of time studied. The postwar era presents a sharp change; the liberal tendency dimmed somewhat, while the totalitarian flared up to an unprecedented level. The Communism, the State Socialism, the Corporative State, the Nazi Reich, the Rooseveltian policy, the policies of other dictatorial states all are a manifestation of the same trend toward a totalitarianism of various shades and forms and away from liberalism. The same trend is well reflected in the criminal codes of our times.

(c) In regard to all these tendencies there is a lack of any definite perpetual trend. They just move erratically up and down. This means that the tendencies which are now faint, some day will be strong, and the trends which are now strong, some day will wane. The theory of limit is again vindicated here.

(d) These erratic fluctuations of the tendencies are not erratic, however, in their connection with the transformations of other main compartments of culture. As has already been mentioned, and as will be made clearer later, the tendency to erratic changes in criminal law well reflects similar tendencies of change in other compartments of culture. In this sense, the outlined "dynamics" of the tendencies of criminal law is harmonious with the tendencies in the other divisions of culture studied.

III. WHICH TYPES OF ACTIONS ARE CRIMINAL IN ALL CODES STUDIED AND WHICH ARE VARIABLE?

In the introductory notes to this chapter, I mentioned that the content of the class of actions qualified as criminal varies from period to period, and from country to country. I stated also that several types of actions are found to be criminal in practically all codes of all times and countries. Now we can go into this problem more thoroughly, and can, on the basis of the codes studied, quite definitely depict what types of actions tend to be viewed as criminal throughout all periods and all countries studied; what are variable and to what extent.

In order to make the analysis quite definite and detailed, let us divide the actions into several classes, beginning with those criminal in all codes studied, and ending with those which are found to be criminal only in one to three of all these codes. From this standpoint we can distinguish the following classes.

A. *Most Frequent Types of Criminal Actions*, which are qualified as criminal and punishable in all the codes studied, beginning with the earliest Barbaric codes and ending with those of the postwar time. They may be styled *absolute crimes*.

B. *Types of Actions Approaching the Absolute Crimes.* By these are meant the types which are found criminal in all the codes of all the countries and periods studied, minus no more than three codes. In other words, those which are less than the possible maximum by no more than three.

C. *Regularly Criminal Actions*, by which are meant the types of actions which were originally qualified as criminal in the Middle Ages, or at the end of the Middle Ages, and which since that time have been criminal in all subsequent codes.

D. *Types of Actions Approaching the Regularly Criminal Actions.* By these are meant the actions which originated in their criminal qualification in the Middle Ages, or in the late Middle Ages, and have since been included as crimes in all subsequent criminal codes except — the maximum — three.

E. *Types of Actions Criminal Only in Comparatively Modern Times.* By these are meant the actions which were not qualified as criminal until the seventeenth and eighteenth centuries, but which are found punishable in practically all the subsequent codes.

F. *Types of Actions Which Ceased to Be Criminal.* These are the actions considered before and in the Middle Ages, but which ceased to be so considered and were shifted into the class of noncriminal actions in the codes of the later periods.

G. *Types of Actions Sporadically Criminal.* Found criminal only in few codes (less than ten and mainly in one to four codes; they come in and drop out from period to period, or country to country).

Thus these classes, A to G, represent a descending scale from the absolute crimes in all the codes studied, up to those on the borderline of the criminal and noncriminal, which are qualified as criminal very rarely and for some very special reason. Such "incidentally criminal actions" are represented by the Class G.

If one wishes to give a positive and quite definite content to what in the past was styled "natural law" and respectively "natural crime," or "absolute crime," one can use the Class A actions as an example (within at least the universe of Europe and the period of some fifteen centuries studied).

Now let us see which actions compose each of these classes.

To *Class A* (absolute crimes) belong the following types of action: No. 1, murder; No. 4, bodily injury; No. 5, blows and violence; No. 6, feticide; No. 21, insult; No. 22, slander; No. 23, theft; No. 24, spoil and plunder and open unlawful appropriation of another's property; No. 25, robbery and brigandage; No. 30, publicly dangerous property damage; No. 31, swindle; No. 60, rape; No. 70, counterfeit of money; No. 75, false denunciation; No. 86, attempt against the supreme organs of the State; Nos. 86 and 87, treason.

The very existence of this class of crimes indicates why the relativists in morals, so fashionable up to the present time, have been overdrawing their argument of the extreme relativity of the "moral conventions," in claiming that there is no type of actions which would be criminal (or noncriminal) in all periods and countries. The above (within the social universe studied) shows that there is a kernel group of actions which — in application to a member of the group (not to an outsider or an enemy) — tends to be considered criminal in almost all societies and at all periods. So far the partisans of the "natural law," in the sense of the old Roman "*quod natura omnia animalia docuit,*" or in Cicero's sense of the "*aeturnum quiddam, quod universum mundum regeret imperandi prohibendique sapientia,*" are not essentially wrong if they do not insist upon the purely "instinctive" nature of such a constancy, or on a perfectly universal and eternal constancy of the above actions as criminal in all the past, present, and future codes of all peoples and all groups. Fairly universally and fairly perpetually most of the above actions are qualified as criminal or "wrong." And that is sufficient to throw out the one-sided exaggerations of the moral relativists and nihilists.[47]

To *Class B* belong these types of actions: No. 14, deprivation of freedom of movement; No. 18, disturbance of home peace; Nos. 26 and 27, appropriation of found object and of entrusted value; No. 28, removal of landmarks; No. 29, property damage; No. 41, slander of the sacred; No. 53, abduction; No. 55, polygamy; No. 56, adultery; No. 59, kidnaping of woman against her will; No. 74, perjury.

The more variable *Class C* is composed of these types of actions: No. 9, leaving in danger; No. 17, threat; No. 32, extortion; No. 38, buying stolen goods; No. 39, plagiarism; Nos. 51 and 52, substitution and kidnaping of children; No. 65, panderage; No. 71, forgery of documents; No. 85, attempt against the constitution; Nos. 94 and 96, resistance to and usurping the authority of government; No. 99, liberation of prisoners; No. 102, bribery.

Still more variable *Class D* actions include: Nos. 7 and 8, participation in and challenge to duel; No. 34, misuse of trust; No. 35, misuse of trustworthiness; No. 36, usury; No. 37, intentional bankruptcy; No. 42, hindering religious services; No. 62, lewdness with the underaged; No. 63, seduction; No. 64, lewdness with dependent persons; No. 73, removal of documents; No. 81, hazardous and exciting games; No. 97, riot; No. 98, participation in criminal society or group; No. 103, non-denunciation of contemplated crime.

To *Class E*, the actions qualified as criminal only in modern times, belong: No. 11, creation of danger of infection with venereal disease; No. 15, coercion; No. 20, disclosure of a secret; No. 33, blackmail; No. 61, compulsory lewdness; No. 66, economic exploitation of prostitute; No. 76, attempt against the social order; No. 89, coercion in voting; No. 90, electoral forgery.

To *Class F*, composed of the actions which ceased to be criminal in later periods, belong: No. 2, suicide; No. 44, atheism; No. 45, heresy and schism; No. 46, religious conversion; No. 47, sorcery; No. 48, nonperformance of religious rites; No. 50a, contact with Jews; No. 54, secret marriage; No. 83, wearing inappropriate apparel; No. 84, tobacco smoking.

Finally, to *Class G*, the somewhat "incidental" and "sporadic" crimes, belong the types of actions like No. 13, enslavement; No. 16, unlawful

---

[47] A comparatively recent example of such baseless criticism of the natural law is given by Pareto in his *Mind and Society*, Vol. I, chap. iv. Here, as well as in many other places, Pareto's speculative — and neither logical nor experimental — empiricism made him blind to the wood behind the trees.

medical treatment; No. 19, violation of secrecy of correspondence; No. 40, blasphemy; No. 50, abuse of a corpse; No. 57, incest; No. 58, fornication; No. 67, homosexuality; No. 68, sodomy with animals; No. 69, public impudence; No. 77, violation of freedom of trade; No. 78, strike of employees; No. 79, lockout; No. 80, disposal of floor space of dwelling (special Soviet crime); No. 93, violation of neutrality, and others.

Such, in brief, is the scale of frequency of various actions qualified as criminal. In this scale the actions are taken merely from the standpoint of how frequently they are so qualified in the codes studied. This analysis does not consider either the tendency of the specified types of action to be constant in their content as to criminal action, or their tendency to be interpreted more and more broadly in their content, or vice versa.

Thus the 104 types of actions can be divided into a few classes according to whether their content remains constant or tends to change.

To the *types of criminal actions whose content remains constant* in the codes studied belong: Nos. 1, 14, 23, 24, 25, 26, 33, 38, 51, 60, 61, 66, 70, 87, 88, 89, 90, 96, 102. From this, one can see that most of these actions are the ones listed in Class A, most frequently met as criminal.

To the types of actions which gradually become qualified as criminal, or, in other terms, the *actions with progressively enlarging content* in the course of time, are: Nos. 4, 5, 9, 15, 17, 18, 20, 27, 29, 30, 31, 32, 39, 62, 64, 71, 74, 75. If, for instance, No. 4 or No. 5, bodily injury and blows and violence. were, in the early codes, criminal only when they were given under specific conditions, in a specific way, and with specific consequences, in the later codes these narrow casuistic specifications were removed and bodily injury or blows were held to be criminal in all cases when the essence of these actions was given, regardless of whether the previous specific conditions were present or not. In the case of socially dangerous property damage, the early codes meant by this only damage caused by setting fire; the later codes add to that explosion and flooding and a few other causes, and in this way expand the content of the crime. The same is to be said of all the crimes enumerated in this class. Many of them belong to Class E, "modern crimes," in the above classification.

The class of actions opposite to the previous class is represented by those whose content has tended to become more and more narrowed in a later code. In other words, these are the *crimes with a regressive tendency* or *tendency to atrophy*. To this class belong mainly the crimes which were included in the earlier codes and which in later codes had their "criminal" content limited more and more by specific conditions and characteristics. Such are the actions: Nos. 7, 8, 13, 40, 41, 52, 53, 57, 58, 59, 67, 68. For instance, Nos. 7 and 8, participation in and challenge to duel, ceased to be crimes in the later codes of France and Russia; No. 40, blasphemy, followed the same course in several codes; in others it is punishable only under specific conditions; No. 53, abduction of woman with her consent, ceased to be a crime in several codes; in others it is limited to a specific case of abduction of the underaged; likewise, No. 57, incest, either ceased to be criminal or became limited to the closest relatives. And so on.

Finally, the *actions with somewhat indefinite tendency* — that is, whose criminal content does not show either a tendency to be constant, or to be enlarged progressively, or to be excluded from crimes, or to be narrowed — are given by the following: Nos. 6, 11, 19, 21, 22, 28, 35, 36, 37, 42, 50, 55, 56, 63, 65, 69, 73, 76, 78, 81, 85, 86, 92, 95, 97, 99, 100, 101, 103. For instance, No. 36, usury, at one time is included in the criminal class, at another excluded; now its content is enlarged, now narrowed; no definite tendency is shown. Similarly, No. 69, public indecency; its criminal content also fluctuates without any definite tendency. And so on.

The above gives an idea of the most and the least frequent types of actions qualified as criminal in the various periods and countries studied. It shows also which of these types are "modern" in their criminal qualifications; and which are "old" and tend to be qualified as noncriminal by the later codes.

The bearing of these results upon the problem of "moral relativity" or "moral absolutism," upon the "natural law," and finally, their connection with the predominant type of culture has already been indicated.

IV. FLUCTUATION OF INTENSITY OF PUNISHMENT

Up to the present moment, the other aspect of the problem, that of punishment, has been left without any consideration. Now we turn to a study of this aspect. Punishment is, in a sense, a measure of the gravity of the crime in the mentality of the creators and enforcers of the law. All in all, the graver the crime is considered, the greater the punishment assigned for it. For this and for several other reasons a serious analysis of the dynamics of punishment from code to code, from period to period, from country to country, represents a fascinating task, capable of throwing a great light upon many problems of the fluctuation and change of the ethicojuridical mentality of a given society.

Unfortunately an adequate investigation of the sanctions (punishments) of criminal law for the purposes of sociological analysis meets several obstacles, the main ones of which are : the punishments for various crimes in several codes are indeterminate, left to the decision of the judge ; they are directed against different values (life, freedom, property, social status, etc.), which, as such, are incommensurable. These and several other circumstances make it impossible to construct an accurate statistical index of the movement of punishment, its index of increase and decrease. However, these obstacles are not absolute, if one sets forth to obtain not a perfect index, but a roughly representative indicator of the fluctuation of the intensity and extension of punishment, as it is given in the criminal law.[48] With a few general rules, such an indicator seems possible to construct. The following are the assumptions made in the subsequent study.

It is assumed that in cases where the punishment is not absolutely indeterminate, the maximum of punishment for a given crime is a more adequate measure of comparison than the minimum, or some intermediary punishment between the maximum and the minimum. In the maximum punishment, the socioethical evaluation of a given crime in its abstract form finds a proper expression ; by the idea of the maximum the law creator tries to exert pressure upon the conduct of an individual while the middle and the minimum punishments represent, so to speak, the post-factum estimation of the criminal action with all its specific conditions.

Therefore, in Table 41 all the codes and sources are compared according to their maximum punishment for a given crime. However, the maximum of punishment may take different forms. There is the maximum for a given crime perpetrated in its "normal" form, and there is a still greater maximum for the same crime when perpetrated in a particularly aggravated — qualified — form. Therefore, subsequently, these two maximums are studied separately : the maximum for a normal and that for the qualified form of the same crime.

As to the incomparability of various punishments with one another and the impossibility of giving them quantitative value on a certain scale, without a somewhat arbitrary assumption, this has to be recognized without any questioning. What is possible to do here is to measure the relative gravity of the punishments on a certain arbitrary scale, by giving to each of the main types of punishment some certain value on such a scale. This may indeed be an arbitrary procedure, but hardly unsound

---

[48] Here again the intensity and extension of punishment as it is imposed by the codes and inflicted in reality do not always coincide. This problem is discussed later. Here we are studying the fluctuation of punishment in the codes only.

TABLE 41. VALUES ASSIGNED TO THE MAIN TYPES OF PUNISHMENT

Numerical Value	Capital Punishment and Bodily Punishments	Banishment and Hard Labor	Imprisonment Aggravated by Loss of Rights, or Bodily Punishment	Imprisonment in Pure Form	Deprivation of Honors and Rights	Economic Punishments
10	Qualified capital punishment					
9	Simple capital punishment					
8	Gravely mutilating bodily punishment	Hard labor and banishment for life	Imprisonment for life			
7	Less gravely mutilating corporeal punishments	The same for not more than 10 years	Imprisonment for more than 10 years	Detention for life		Confiscation of the whole property
6	Very painful bodily punishments	The same for 3 to 10 years	Imprisonment for 3 to 10 years	Detention for more than 10 years	Banishment from the country for life	
5		The same for less than 3 years	The same for 1 to 3 years	Detention for 3 to 10 years	Loss of all civil rights	Great public auction ("compositio")
4	Less painful bodily punishments		The same from 3 months to 1 year	Detention for 1 to 3 years	Exposure to the post	
3			The same for less than 3 months	Detention for 3 months to 1 year		Moderate public auction
2		For a short time to compulsory labor without imprisonment		Detention for less than 3 months		
1					Reprimand reproof	Fine

in its essence. The lawmakers themselves, in several codes, work on somewhat similar assumptions, ranking the punishments in a certain order, beginning with the greatest (capital punishment) and ending with a small fine, or merely a reprimand or the like, as the lightest punishment. Furthermore, some of them indicate how one kind of punishment may be replaced by another under certain circumstances. Since such a procedure is given in the codes, a more systematic application of it is not a subjective procedure. By making it more systematic, the investigator applies the same measuring stick to all the codes compared. Following this, a scale of values from 1 to 10 is applied for quantitative comparison of the various punishments. The value 10 denotes the gravest punishment (capital punishment); the value 1 a slight monetary fine (not involving confiscation of property) or a slight reprimand. In Table 41 each of the other crimes is given values intermediary between 10 and 1.

Table 41 shows what values are assigned to each of the types of punishment and thus gives the key to the subsequent figures which indicate the main changes in the movements of punishments from code to code and from period to period. So much for this point.

Based upon this scale of values, I am giving several other tables which in various ways show the main changes which the severity of punishment has undergone through the ages, for each country separately as well as for all the five countries taken together. Table 42 gives, in quantitative language, a description of the "dynamics" of punishment, when all the 104 types of crimes are taken under consideration. The fault in this table is that not all of these 104 types of crimes are given in all the codes compared; therefore the main results will be, at the best, only approximate, because the codes are not entirely comparable and the final results may not reflect the reality exactly. With this reservation, Table 42 follows.[49]

Taken at its face value, Table 42 shows, first, that the punishability of crime fluctuates much less than we usually think. From popular books and from stories we get the impression that the Middle Ages were terrible in this respect, and that with their tortures and pitiless punishments — usually the capital punishment applied most extensively — they were intensely cruel, while the modern times have been more and more human. Table 42 shows that though the severity of punishment has indeed fluctuated, the amplitude of the fluctuation has been narrow, from 4.6 to 5.8 for the normal forms for all the countries studied; from 5.6 to 6.9 for

[49] The Nazi Code is not included in the computation.

TABLE 42.   AVERAGE PUNISHABILITY OF 104 TYPES OF CRIMES

PERIOD	France		Germany		Austria		Italy		Russia		All Countries	
	Normal	Qualified	Normal	Qualified	Normal	Qualified	Normal	Qualified	Normal	Qualified	Normal	Qualified
Barbaric	4.4	7.2	4.4	7.2			4.4	7.2	5.1	6.1	4.6	6.9
Middle Ages	6.6	7.2	6.3	7.8			3.3	4.3	6.8	7.3	5.4	6.4
Monarchical, XV–XVIII centuries	6.3	7.7	7.8	8.2			4.3	6.1	6.8	7.3	5.8	6.9
Enlightened despotism and revolution, XVIII, end	5.3	6.4	4.6	6.0	4.3	5.5	6.7	7.7	4.6	5.7	5.2	6.4
XIX, first half	5.0	5.9	5.4	5.9	4.0	5.3	5.3	6.1	4.4	5.0	4.8	5.6
XIX, second half	4.8	5.7	5.1	5.6	4.6	5.4	4.9	5.7	4.4	5.0	4.9	5.6
Postwar period			5.5[1]	5.8[1]	4.6	5.4	4.9	5.6	4.8	5.6	5.0	5.6

[1] The Nazi Code of 1935 is not included in this computation. If it were, the figure would rise still more; that is, the increase of punishability and its severity in the latest code of Germany would still be greater than in the Code of 1927. The reason is that in the Code of 1935 the severity of punishment is increased in 33 crimes, while it is made milder in only one crime.

the qualified forms. Fairly near to those figures are the "coefficients" for each of the countries studied.

Viewed in the perspective of time, the figures show further that *there has not been any perpetual trend either toward an increase or decrease of punishment in the course of time.* Instead, we see that so far as the normal punishments are concerned, the Barbaric times were mildest; then the severity of punishment begins to grow in the medieval period and still more (with the exception of France) in the period of growth of the national monarchies, at the close of the late Middle Ages and at the beginning of the modern period, in the fourteenth, fifteenth, sixteenth, and seventeenth centuries. The end of the seventeenth century, the period of the Enlightened Absolutism, marks the downward turn of the severity of punishment. This trend continues, with a short-time rise at the very end of the eighteenth and the beginning of the nineteenth century (the period of the "Restoration") up to the end of the nineteenth century. The postwar period (in Russia, Germany, and Austria) shows signs of a new turn — toward a growth of severity of punishment. Such, in brief, are the main indications given by Table 42. If they are valid, we must drop our habitual idea that the evolution of criminal law and of penology shows a perpetual trend toward more and more human and milder treatment of criminals. Such a belief was but natural in the nineteenth century, in the period of the mildest punishments, but it is hardly tenable when the "evolution of punishment" is studied factually for the longer period, as is done here; and when we are in the postwar period, which has reversed the trends of the nineteenth century in so many a compartment of culture.[50] However, about that something more is to be said in a later part of this chapter. Now we continue our study of the main problem.

As mentioned, the above comparison of the codes along the line of 104 types of crimes is in several respects inadequate. Therefore, two other approaches to the problem have been used. These approaches are free, at least, from the main defect of the above comparison. The second approach is as follows. Of all the crimes included in the codes, after preliminary study, twenty-eight types are selected. These twenty-eight types are found in almost all the codes compared, beginning with the fifteenth century [51] (the Barbaric and the medieval periods had to be

[50] By these statements I am criticizing not only the theories of that kind set forth by many investigators, but also my own theory, developed in my youthful works: *Crime and Punishment, Heroism and Reward* (in Russian), and especially in my "Laws of Evolution of Punishment" in the *Novyie Idei v Pravovedenii* (St. Petersburg, 1915), No. 3.

[51] There are two or three cases where a few crimes are absent from two or three codes. Such a shortcoming, however, does not and cannot change appreciably the results.

omitted), and their content has remained essentially the same, without any notable enlargement, or narrowing, or modification.   In this way, we obtain twenty-eight types of crimes contained in practically all the codes; these embrace the most essential types of criminality (mostly belonging to classes A and B in the classification made); in other words, they are all comparable.   By comparing the punishments for these crimes from code to code, and from period to period, we can obtain somewhat more reliable results, as shown in Table 43.

TABLE 43. AVERAGE PUNISHABILITY OF 28 TYPES OF CRIMES FOR ALL THE COUNTRIES STUDIED BY THE MAIN PERIODS [1]

TYPE OF CRIME	Normal Punishment					Qualified Punishment				
	XV–XVIII Monarchical Period	XVIII, end Enlightened Despotism, and Revolution	The "Restoration" Beginning of XIX (1st half)	XIX (2d half)	Postwar Period	XV–XVIII	XVIII, end	XIX (1st half)	XIX (2d half)	Postwar Period
1. Murder	8.5	7.8	8	7.7	7.3	9.5	9.0	9.0	8.7	9.0
4. Bodily injury . . .	7.0	4.0	4.8	4.7	4.8	7.3	6.8	7.0	7.0	6.3
5. Blows, violence . .	3.0	2.5	5.2	3.7	3.8	3.0	5.6	5.4	5.3	4.3
6. Feticide	8.3	6.4	5.8	5.4	4.5	8.8	7.0	7.8	7.0	6.3
7. Participation in duel	4.0	5.7	3.5	3.5	5.0	7.7	6.7	4.5	6.0	6.0
8. Challenge to duel . .	2.7	4.7	4.0	2.0	3.3	5.3	5.0	4.3	2.5	3.7
13. Enslavement . . .	8.3	6.0	6.3	7.0	7.0	8.3	7.3	6.7	7.0	7.0
14. Deprivation of freedom of movement	5.5	4.5	4.6	6.0	5.3	7.5	5.8	6.8	7.7	5.8
23. Theft	3.8	4.4	5.0	5.7	5.0	8.3	6.8	7.0	6.7	6.3
24. Spoil	6.3	4.6	5.0	5.6	5.0	7.8	7.0	6.8	6.3	6.3
25. Robbery	8.3	6.6	6.8	6.7	6.0	9.0	8.0	7.4	7.7	7.5
26. Appropriation of the found value	2.7	3.0	3.0	4.3	4.8	4.7	4.0	4.8	4.3	5.3
27. Appropriation of the entrusted value	1.8	5.0	4.8	5.3	5.0	5.0	4.5	5.4	5.7	5.5
28. Removal of landmarks	4.7	2.7	4.5	5.0	2.7	5.3	4.3	5.3	5.3	4.7
37. Intentional bankruptcy	6.0	6.0	5.8	7.0	5.0	8.0	6.8	6.8	7.0	5.5
38. Buying stolen goods .	5.0	4.0	4.5	6.0	5.0	7.0	6.8	5.5	6.7	5.7
41. Sacrilege	6.5	5.2	4.8	3.3	5.0	8.0	6.0	6.2	4.0	5.0
51. Substitution of children	5.3	6.3	5.2	4.7	5.5	8.0	6.3	6.0	6.0	5.8
55. Polygamy	7.0	5.6	5.8	5.7	5.0	8.5	6.4	6.0	5.7	5.7
56. Adultery	5.5	4.3	3.4	3.0	3.7	7.5	4.3	4.2	4.3	4.0
60. Rape	8.3	7.0	6.2	6.3	6.0	8.8	7.6	7.6	7.7	6.5
61. Coercive lewdness . .			6.3	6.0	6.0			7.3	7.3	6.7
70. Counterfeit of money	9.7	6.5	7.5	7.3	7.0	9.7	8.5	8.0	7.3	7.5
74. Perjury	7.3	7.5	5.6	5.7	5.0	7.3	8.3	6.4	6.7	5.8
75. False denunciation .	4.3	4.0	4.5	5.3	5.5	5.0	6.7	5.5	5.7	6.3
87. Communication with enemy	9.3	8.5	7.6	6.7	6.8	9.5	8.7	8.8	7.3	8.3
88. Helping enemy . .	9.3	6.5	7.6	6.7	6.3	9.5	9.0	9.0	7.3	8.3
95. Coercion of government	8.5	5.3	5.0	4.7	5.3	8.8	6.4	6.4	6.0	5.5
Average for 28 crimes . .	6.2	5.3	5.4	5.4	5.6	7.4	6.7	6.6	6.3	6.1

[1] The Nazi Code is not included.   If included, it would raise the punishment index for the postwar period.

Within the period considered, roughly, beginning with the end of the Middle Ages, up to the present time, the indicators do not show any definite tendency in the punishments for all the twenty-eight crimes studied. In the field of normal punishment, there grows, in the course of time, a tendency toward the mitigation of punishment for some of the crimes, as for instance, feticide, or polygamy, or adultery. The punishments for other crimes, like appropriation of found value, tend to become more severe. But even here, the trend is not without exception, while in most of the crimes studied there is no unilinear trend at all; the punishment decreases from one period to another, in order to increase again; and vice versa. In other words, the data in Table 43 also show that there has not been evident any perpetual tendency toward either mitigation or increase of severity of punishment in the course of time. Punishment just erratically fluctuates. This is shown also by the averages for all the crimes taken together. Their series, 6.2, 5.3, 5.4, and 5.6, shows the same perpetually trendless movement of the sanctions. So far the results corroborate those given by Table 42.

Only in a very relative way is it possible to note that, all in all, the punishments for the crimes against the person have tended (not without exceptions) to become milder in the later periods, as compared with the earlier ones, while the punishments for the crimes against property tended rather to become sterner. This reflects in a way the tendency of the Sensate culture to underestimate man and overestimate wealth and other means of bodily comfort. But even here the trends are not clear cut.

Of other results, it is to be mentioned that in the field of normal punishment the early monarchical period was comparatively the sternest; next comes the postwar period; the epoch of the enlightened despotism (the very end of the seventeenth and the eighteenth centuries) was the mildest. It is to be noted that the postwar period shows signs of increasing the severity of punishments. Such are the results given by the dynamics of the normal punishments during the last five hundred years.

When we turn to the qualified punishments, most of what is said about the movement of the normal punishments is true also of this form of punishment. The only difference is that the trend to mitigate the punishments is more pronounced and fairly definite here. Most of them show such a trend, which is reflected in the averages for all the twenty-eight crimes; they systematically descend from 7.4 to 6.1, showing thus an approach to the level of the normal punishments. Considering that the qualified punishments are applied with comparative rarity, such a trend is hardly important in its bearing upon the real movement of the sanctions.

It is possibly a forerunner of the modern technique of criminal law, which has tended to leave it to the decision of the court to decide the exact amount and character of the punishment, within the limits of the law, and for this reason has paid less and less attention to a casuistic specification of the qualifying forms; the other aspect of the trend has been a comparative increase of punishment for normal forms of crime. So much for the results of this approach to the problem.

Finally, the problem is attacked in the third manner, shown in Table 44. Here, for each country separately, and then for all five countries together, is computed the change of punishment from one period to another, for the crimes which are present in both compared epochs and whose content in both epochs remains unchanged. Here the number of crimes compared in two adjacent periods is smaller than the number indicated for each of the epochs in Table 42. The smaller number here is due to the fact that the punishment for some of these crimes is indeterminate in some epochs or incomparable (for instance, depriving the culprit of Christian burial). All such crimes with indeterminate or incomparable punishments had to be omitted. Hence, the smaller number of crimes for each compared period in Table 44. The comparison of change in punishments is made in two forms in the table: on the one hand, from the total number of crimes compared in the form of the number of crimes whose punishment increased, decreased, or remained unchanged from one period to another; on the other hand, in the form of computation of the indicators of the punishments for normal and qualified form for both the periods compared.

In the computation of these changes, the punishment is considered as increased: (1) when it is higher for the normal form of crime, and remains the same for its qualified form; (2) when it is higher for the qualified form, remaining the same for the normal form; (3) when it is higher for the normal as well as for the qualified form; (4) when, in the later period, to the normal punishment is added a qualified punishment which was lacking in the preceding period. In the opposite cases, the punishment is considered lowered.

A. *France*. The data show that in France the severity of punishments becomes milder as we pass from the fifteenth and the sixteenth centuries to the end of the eighteenth (1791); then it increases from 1791 to 1810; and again decreases from 1810 to the present time. This is shown by the indicators as well as by the number of crimes punished more strongly and more mildly.

In comparison with the previous period, the Code of 1791 punishes more mildly seventeen crimes: murder; bodily injury; leaving in danger;

TABLE 44.   PUNISHMENT OF COMPARABLE CRIMES IN TWO ADJACENT PERIODS

Country and Period	Number of Compared Crimes	Punishment in Preceding Period		Subsequent Period		Of These Punished in the Subsequent Period		
		Normal	Qualified	Normal	Qualified	Number more severe	Number milder	Number the same
France								
From XV–XVII to the end of XVIII (1701)	21	8.0	8.7	6.2	7.2	1	17	3
From the Revolution to the Restoration (1810)	23	5.9	7.0	6.1	7.1	11	5	7
From the Restoration to 1933	47	5.2	6.1	5.0	5.8	3	9	35
Germany								
From 1532 to 1794	20	8.1	9.2	5.9	7.7	1	12	7
From 1794 to 1851	38	5.4	6.8	5.6	6.3	11	15	12
From 1851 to 1871	64	5.5	6.1	5.3	5.9	9	21	34
From 1871 to 1927 [1]	69	4.4	4.9	4.6	5.0	22	13	24
Austria								
From 1532 to 1803	23	8.2	8.7	5.8	7.0	1	22	
From 1803 to 1852	51	4.1	5.0	4.2	5.6	9	12	30
From 1852 to 1912	44	4.3	5.9	4.8	5.6	19	16	9
Italy								
From XVI to 1786	22	6.2	7.3	6.1	6.5	3	12	7
From 1786 to 1830	23	6.6	7.0	5.6	7.0	8	13	2
From 1839 to 1889	43	5.5	6.4	5.0	6.0	6	32	5
From 1889 to 1930	48	5.0	5.9	5.5	6.3	24	18	6
Russia								
From 1649 to 1845–1914	61	4.8	5.8	4.6	5.5	3	19	39
From 1914 to 1926	23	4.5	6.0	5.1	6.0	11	7	5

AVERAGE FOR FIVE COUNTRIES

Country and Period	Relationship of Indicators		In per cent		
	Normal	Qualified	Number more severe	Number milder	Number the same
From XVI to XVIII	− 1.5	− 1.4	7	73	20
From XVIII to middle XIX	− 0.7	− 0.1	21	33	46
From middle of XIX to XX	− 0.9	− 0.9	10	38	52
From prewar to postwar period	+ 0.8	+ 0.2	44	30	26

[1] The Nazi Code is not included.   If included, it would raise the figure.

theft; spoil; robbery; appropriation of the found value; intentional bankruptcy; sacrilege; substitution of children; polygamy; kidnaping of woman; rape; counterfeiting of money; forgery of documents; resistance to the government; attempts against the constitution. For one crime only — hindering religious services — punishment is increased.

In comparison with the Code of 1791, the Code of 1810 increases the punishments for eleven crimes (mostly the crimes for which the punishments were lowered in the Code of 1791) and decreases them for five crimes: bodily injury; hindering religious services; substitution of children; perjury and resistance to the government.

B. *Germany*. In Germany, the Code of 1794 shows a strong decrease of punishment in comparison with the previous code. The indicators fall from 8.1 to 5.9 and from 9.2 to 7.7. Of twenty crimes compared, only one is punished more severely, while twelve are punished more mildly than before. In comparison with this code, the Code of 1851 punishes the normal forms of crime slightly more, the qualified forms slightly less. Respectively, the number of crimes punished more severely and less severely than in the preceding code is nearly equal. The code of the later period (1871, with subsequent changes) gives a new mitigation of punishment, in comparison with the previous code. The indicators fall, and the number of crimes punished more mildly is more than twice as great as the number punished more severely.

Finally, even the pre-Nazi, postwar "socialist-republican-democratic" project of 1927 shows a definite tendency toward reinforcement of punishment, in the indicators as well as in the number of the crimes punished more severely (twenty-two) and less severely (thirteen) than before. The Nazi Code increases the severity still more.

C. *Austria*. Similar is the movement of punishment in Austria. The Code of 1803 indicates a great mitigation of punishment in comparison with the preceding criminal law (decrease from 8.2 to 5.8; from 8.7 to 7.0). Of twenty-three crimes compared, twenty-two are punished more mildly, and only one more severely than before. The Code of 1852 slightly increases the punishments for both normal and qualified forms. However, subsequent changes in that code somewhat reduced this increase. Finally the project of 1912 — and it is significant that this project was prepared before the war and the postwar changes — slightly increases the punishability of the normal forms of crime.

D. *Italy*. In Italy from the sixteenth century up to practically the Code of 1930 we have a fairly steady decrease of punishment for both the normal and qualified forms of crimes. The Code of 1930 breaks the trend and reverses it; like practically all the postwar codes, it increases the punishments.

E. *Russia.* In Russia the movement is very similar to that in Italy. From 1649 up to about 1916, punishments tend to decrease for both normal and qualified forms. The Code of 1926 changes the trend and shows a considerable increase of severity of punishment for normal crimes (the qualified punishments remain unchanged).

Finally, when the changes for the five countries are summed up together, they show a decrease of punishment from about the sixteenth century up to the prewar period. Especially marked is the change from the sixteenth to the end of the eighteenth century. It continues, but less noticeably, in the period from the eighteenth to about the middle of the nineteenth century; that period in France, Austria, and Germany is even marked by a slight increase in severity of punishment. The second part of the nineteenth century resumes the trend of humanization of punishment. And so it goes, up to the twentieth century. That century, especially in its postwar codes, sharply reverses the movement and so far — not only in reality, where executions, "purgings," and other mass extermination of human life have assumed extraordinary proportions, but even in its codes — points definitely, at least so far, to a trend of increased severity in punishment for crimes. The sentimental, soft, and "humanitarian" criminal law promulgated by Beccaria and other classical criminologists and penologists, especially of the eighteenth century, and developed by the criminal law of the end of the nineteenth century, has been rejected by the twentieth century and has been replaced by less sentimental, less soft, and less humanitarian criminal laws, not only in the countries studied, but in many other European countries.

Thus, all three approaches give results quite consistent with one another. This is good evidence that, in spite of the shortcomings mentioned above, the results are not misleading and do reflect the changes of the ethicojuridical mentality as it is embodied in criminal law rather accurately.

F. *Summary.* The totality of the data given entitle us to draw the following conclusions concerning the fluctuating movement of punishment as it is given in the criminal laws of the period studied.

(1) Beginning with the Barbaric codes and ending with the postwar criminal codes, there is no perpetual tendency either toward a progressive increase of severity of punishment, or toward its mitigation. Instead we have merely a fluctuation, with various ups and downs.

(2) The Barbaric Codes of the Germanic and Slavic peoples in their tribal stage, before their Christianization and "acculturation" by the Roman or Byzantine cultures, or before the separate but internally homogeneous tribes were thrown together into one medley with different mores and rules of conduct — the codes of such separate groups show comparatively mild forms of punishment. In Tables 42, 43, and 44, we have seen that these codes give practically the lowest indicators of punishability of any codes, even including those of the second half of the nineteenth century. Instead of the fairly common opinion shared by many specialists (see further in this chapter my criticism of E. Durkheim's theory) these Barbaric codes are the least cruel, so far as their system of punishment is concerned. Thus we find the mildest punishment not in our own times, but at the earliest period of our investigation.

(3) In the Middle Ages, when these tribes began to be Christianized and "ideationalized" (partly by the Romans and partly by Byzantines), when they were hastily thrown into one body politic, in the form of various Merovingian or Carlovingian empires, or the principalities of Kiev; when, in other words, they were compulsorily united into various (short-lived) bodies, we find a rapid growth in the severity of punishment — a growth which seems to have continued at least up to the thirteenth century, and then stayed on a high level throughout the next two or three centuries.

(4) With the end of the seventeenth century, and especially in the eighteenth, when the national bodies politic were already consolidated and crystallized, and when, as we shall see, the Ideational culture had already given way to Sensate culture, which was consolidated in that period, the severity of punishment sharply drops. It turns decidedly downward.

(5) With the temporary exception of the post-Revolutionary period — the Restoration and "Reaction" at the beginning of the nineteenth century, when the curve of severity of punishment takes a slight and short-lived upward movement — the curve continued to move down in severity throughout the nineteenth century, especially in its second part. In most countries the process continued up to the time of the World War.

(6) Finally, the postwar Europe shows a new inclination toward an increase — and a notable increase — in the severity of punishment in its postwar codes.

Thus there is no perpetual trend toward ever bigger and better "humanization" of punishment. Here we see the same erratic fluctuations, and a further example of the "principle of limit" and "self-regulation of socio-cultural processes." Having reached its point of saturation, the curve turns and moves in a direction either different or opposite from its previous course.

(7) Farther on, we see that the amplitude of the punishability fluctuates within a comparatively narrow limit.

(8) Very narrow also are the differences between various countries, on this point. We do not find either particularly "humanitarian" or particularly "cruel" nations. They are all about the same.

So much for the fluctuations of punishment, as they are given in the criminal codes. I mentioned that the real extension and intensity of the fluctuation of punishment deviates in social life, and sometimes very considerably, from the situation as given in the codes. Therefore, in the next section, I am going to say something about this discrepancy as well as about the causes or reasons and the amplitude of the fluctuation of punishment in real social life. This has to be said also, because it will connect these fluctuations with our main topic, the Ideational and the Sensate cultures and their fluctuations.

V. Fluctuation of Extension and Severity of Punishment in Social Life

The preceding analysis gives a fairly accurate idea of the movement of punishment, especially in its severity, in the criminal codes and laws. As mentioned, the severity or mildness of punishment in the codes is not identical with the real amount and severity of punishment in social life. The point is that punishment in the code, be it mild or severe, does not indicate *to how many persons it is applied.* The punishment in a certain code may be milder than in another, but it may be applied, say, to 20 per cent of the population, while the severer punishment may be imposed on 1 per cent of the population only.

Though in the second case the severity of the code punishment is greater, the total amount of it is smaller than in the first case. In other words, the severity or mildness of punishment in criminal law does not determine the real amount of it imposed upon the population. From the first we cannot conclude anything about the second. More than that. The code may continue to exist unchanged for some time; meanwhile the real punishment may increase enormously in its amount as well as in its severity, regardless of the code. Through special decrees of the government, in an administrative way — by declaring a state of siege or martial law, or by mere physical force, even without any proclamation of special decree or martial law — the government or the dominant dictatorial faction may impose upon its opponents hundreds, thousands, hundreds of thousands, even millions of executions, without changing the existing criminal law at all.   In such cases, it would be just brushed aside and the punishment for real or supposed offenses would be inflicted through many other channels and ways than criminal justice in a proper sense.   This means again that the amount and severity of real punishment in social life is not always conditioned by the code and sometimes depends upon it very little.   The cases of great revolutions give a good example of that.   In addition, even when and if the codes represent the severity of real punishment to some extent, they are often too far apart from one another to reflect all the changes which may take place between two codes separated from one another by the distance of a hundred or more years.

These reasons show that the problems of increase and decrease of severity of punishment in criminal codes and in social reality are different problems.   To some extent they may be connected, but this connection is in no way close, or such as to entitle us directly to conclude the movement of one curve from that of the other.   The criminal law is symptomatic of the changes in the ethicojuridical mentality; it may, to some extent, be indicatory of the movement of punishment in real social life, at least for the periods for which the criminal codes function.   But that is all that can be claimed for the codes.   The movement of the amount and severity of punishment in a given society in the course of time has to be studied and "plotted" upon bases other than the criminal law and the codes.   These may be at best only one of the many sources for that purpose.

However important and interesting is the problem of the movement, increase, and decrease of quantity (proportion of population upon which the punishment is imposed) and of severity of punishment in social life in the course of time, I am afraid it cannot be studied — so far as long periods of time are concerned — because the data are lacking.   What is possible in this respect is to try to formulate a hypothesis as to when and under what conditions the amount and severity of punishment (or one of these variables) are to be expected to increase or, on the contrary, to decrease; and then, assembling the relevant, historical, and statistical evidences, to try to test its validity or its inadequacy.   To be sure, each of such hypotheses, even when it stood the test successfully, would not, and cannot, account for all the ups and downs of the course of punishment, but it may account at least for some of them.

My object is to offer one such hypothesis which would seem to account for a number of the main swings of the curve of punishment in the course of time and which appears to be borne out by the facts to a considerable extent. A discussion of the hypothesis has additional reasons: if it be valid, it connects the movement of the curve of punishment with that of internal disturbances; it elucidates the problem to what extent the criminal codes reflect the real movement of punishment; and finally, it has some relationship to the theory of fluctuation of the Ideational and Sensate cultures. For all these reasons, at least, a brief formulation of it is not out of place.

Its essense was formulated by the author in his first book, *Crime and Punishment*, among several other "laws of evolution of punishment." Almost all the other "laws" which I believed at that time, and which are still believed by many, I find fallacious now. They are invalid and do not stand the test of real facts.[52] But one "law" as I styled it then, or some fairly general uniformity among these pseudo laws, I am inclined to support still; and perhaps now even more than before. Here it is, in its previous formulation:

"Each time when, in a given social group, the ethicojuridical heterogeneity and antagonism of its members increases — whatever may be the reasons for such an increase — the amount as well as the severity of punishment imposed by one part of the group upon the other tends to increase; and, other conditions being equal, the greater the heterogeneity and antagonism, the greater is the increase."

When the heterogeneity and antagonism decrease, the quantity and severity of the punishment tend to decrease also.[53]

Such is the essence of this hypothesis. By increase (or decrease) of ethicojuridical heterogeneity is meant increase (or decrease) of similarity of the law (imperative-attributive) and moral (purely imperative) convictions of the members. When all the members are convinced that "private property is sacred" and ascribe to the proprietor the *jus utendi* and *abutendi*, and to all the others the duty to abstain from interference in his right to use, to possess, and to dispose of the property as he pleases,

---

[52] Most of them were a reflection of the nineteenth-century theory of "bigger and better progress," according to which the primitive man was quite bad in all respects, and the modern man, especially the living generation, is an embodiment of the "last perfection" in all important respects, including the moral one. At that time I also subscribed to this linear — and most cheerful and gratifying — belief. Now I do not subscribe to it any more. See also Sorokin, "Laws of Evolution of Punishment," quoted, where I rather carefully put all these beliefs of my youthful "progressiveness."

[53] P. Sorokin, "Laws of Evolution of Punishment," in *Novyia Idei v Pravovedenii*, No. 3, pp. 147-148; P. Sorokin, *Crime and Punishment*, pp. 424 ff.

there is ethicojuridical homogeneity in the group.   When one part of it is convinced that "private property is sacred," while the other part contends that "private property is theft," the ethicojuridical homogeneity of the group is broken, and is replaced by ethicojuridical heterogeneity and antagonism.   When a similar split of the imperative-attributive and purely imperative convictions of the members of a group occurs in regard to any other cultural value, social relationship, institution, or social function, we have an increase of ethicojuridical heterogeneity and antagonism within the group.   When the split is replaced by unanimity of the convictions, we have a decrease of these.

Expressed in purely sociological terms, an increase of ethicojuridical heterogeneity means an increase of splitting, shattering, and falling into pieces of the network of social relationships and of the system of sociocultural values of a given society.   A decrease of ethicojuridical heterogeneity means a stabilization, crystallization, and unification of the society's network of social relationships and of the system of values.   Any law conviction (imperative-attributive) and any moral conviction (imperative) ascribes definite rights and duties to the members of the group; it indicates what they should do in each particular configuration of their relationship; what is expected from them as a norm, or as a "right" conduct.   If the ethicojuridical convictions of the masters and slaves are homogeneous, both groups ascribe certain rights and duties (imperatively and attributively) to the masters and certain other rights and duties to the slaves.   To one group, to command; to the other, to obey.   Under such circumstances, the network of their social relationships becomes not only definite but a spontaneous result of such a unanimity or homogeneity.   Though, like radio network, it is unseen physically, it is there, and guides and controls and conditions the relationships of the masters and slaves.   And when a master commands, the slave obeys, not out of fear, but willingly, motivated from within by his "imperative-attributive" psychology and convictions.   The same can be said of any other case of imperative-attributive conviction.   Each of them distributes in a certain way the rights, the duties, and, respectively, the social functions among the members of the society.   Each of them indicates and urges from within the proper form of conduct and relationship of every member of the group to the others under each definite set of circumstances.   If these convictions are homogeneous among the members,[54] their total network of social relation-

---

[54] Not in the sense that all members ascribe the identical rights and duties to all, but in the sense that they (say serfs, nobility, clergy) similarly ascribe the same duties and rights to a given person (say, king) or to a given group (say, nobility).   The rights and duties may

ship, their system of sociocultural values, and the functions and forms of conduct of each of them become not only clear, certain, definite, and unified, but the whole network of social relationship, the whole system of sociocultural values of such a group functions, so to speak, by itself, as a spontaneous outcome of the homogeneity of their imperative-attributive and imperative convictions.[55] It lives a full-blooded life, all the time sustained from within, reinforced from within, supported by the unanimity of the members. As such it appears to them absolute, sacred, unquestionable. As such it guides them, binds them, and controls their conduct most effectively. In other words, as soon as such a homogeneity of the ethicojuridical convictions of the members of the society is attained, a strong and most virile network of social relationships and a system of cultural values are established in such a society.

And vice versa. A split, increasing heterogeneity, and an antagonism of the imperative-attributive and imperative convictions of the members of a society mean the shattering, breaking, and disintegrating of its network of social relationship and of its system of sociocultural values. It is like a torn spider's web and, like such a broken web, it ceases to control innerly the conduct and relationships of the members of the society. They become "free"; they lose the clear "signposts" and guides, showing them what they should do in any special configuration of their relationship to one another and to the values of the society.

---

be different for each member, but all members are unanimous in ascribing the same set of duties or rights to A, another set to B, and so on.

[55] Each of such convictions, especially the imperative-attributive, is not merely an idea, an image, but at the same time psychologically has in itself one of the strongest emotions, with all its dynamic, urging, driving, pushing force. When we are fulfilling our "right" — no matter what it is concretely — we do not have the slightest hesitation in performing the respective action: to spend money which is "mine"; to enter one's own house, to arrest a man, and so on. When somebody tries to violate our right — to take our property, to threaten, to resist it and so on, we are most indignant and resist such actions most forcefully. When we are called to do our duty (which is duty according to our imperative-attributive convictions) we do it without any external compulsion, however unpleasant it may be in itself: pay taxes, care for children, sometimes spending many sleepless nights at the bedside of a sick child; obey the policeman who stops our car; go into battle, as soldiers, risking our lives, etc. In brief, the emotional drive of the attributive-imperative convictions is terrific; likewise enormous is the urging power of purely imperative convictions. This explains why, in an ethicojuridically homogeneous society — no matter how great is the inequality of the distribution of various rights and duties among its members — the total network of social relationship and of the system of values functions easily, spontaneously, propelled, so to speak, by the enormous emotional urge inherent in the imperative-attributive and imperative convictions of each member. About that urge and generally about the psychological composition of the law and moral experiences see the marvelous and deep analysis of L. Petrajitsky, in his works, quoted. Hardly anybody has given it as thoroughly, systematically, and scientifically as he.

Their conduct becomes like traffic in a city square with many corners, where no indication is given as to which direction cars must take, what is the right of way, and what is the order of entering and crossing the square. As a result, cars often collide, the air is full of curses of drivers accusing each other, traffic becomes stalled, a general tangle follows. Similar is the situation in a society with the ethicojuridical heterogeneity of its members, or, what is the same, with a split and shattered and tangled network of social relationships and sociocultural values.

Outlining the hypothesis in psychological as well as in sociological terms, a few words will show why an increase or decrease of punishment is to be expected with an increase or decrease of ethicojuridical homogeneity. If and when the "collective morality" of the group is homogeneous the members follow the "map of rights and duties" spontaneously, propelled to it from within by their convictions and emotions. Only through a set of exceedingly unfavorable combinations of circumstances would some of them be driven to crime. Therefore crimes themselves in such a society will be infrequent. Being infrequent, they do not put the society into a dangerous position, and do not decrease its chances for survival. Therefore, punishment will also be rare in such a society and it need not be severe or pitiless.[56] There is no urgent need for such severity. In a society of homogeneous angels, there is no need for a policeman or for an electric chair. Without these rude stimuli to law-abiding honesty, they would be law-abiding spontaneously, urged by their "imperative-attributive" forces. In brief, under such circumstances, the amount as well as the severity of the punishment should be expected to be low.

Quite different are the conditions in a society with a shattered and "relativized" and muddled system of social relationships and cultural values, with its concomitant ethicojuridical heterogeneity. Where a part of the members are convinced that it is their duty to protect the "sacredness of property" while the other members regard "property" as theft; where a part of the members consider bigamy, atheism, adultery, communism, kidnaping, as the greatest crimes, while the other part regard them as "perfectly normal mores" — in such a society we cannot expect "inner peace" and lack of antagonisms and conflicts, infrequent crime and mild punishments. One part of it is bound all the time to commit actions which the other part qualifies and feels as "crime," "sacrilege," "outrage," "impudence," "sin," and so on. As a result,

---

[56] As we shall see, here was one of the big blunders of Durkheim, who assumed that under such conditions punishment has to be pitiless. See further about Durkheim's theory.

one part would tend to punish the other: to stop this "outrageous perpetration of crime." Since it cannot stop the actions by preaching, it will try to stop them by the infliction of actions which are equivalent to punishments. Especially when such "sanctions" are applied by the existing government. It is but natural that the amount of punishment should greatly increase in such a society, and its severity also. If mild punishments applied only once in a while are insufficient to stop the enormous number of crimes committed continually by the other part of the society, a recourse has to be had to most severe punishments applied in supergenerous quantity to all the numerous violators. Such is the evident reason why the hypothesis has to be valid deductively. Is this deduction supported by the facts? It seems to me it is.

A. *Its first corroboration is given by the periods of revolutions and deep internal disturbances.* Viewed from this standpoint, any deep revolution in a given society is the period when the ethicojuridical homogeneity of the society is broken and replaced by a greatly increased heterogeneity and antagonism. It is so great that there is no possibility of peaceful agreement between the "revolutionary" and the "nonrevolutionary," or especially the "antirevolutionary," parts of the society. Hence revolution, that is, a violent attempt to change a set of important social relationships and social values by force. This being evident, we shall expect, according to the hypothesis, that the amount and severity of the punishment of the revolutionaries by the existing government or by the successful new revolutionary government, must increase. By this increase is meant not the phenomena of open battles and civil wars between the groups, but more narrowly the crimes and punishments of the perpetrators of the actions regarded as crimes by the opposite faction. Does such an increase take place? Undoubtedly, and usually upon a large scale, and the deeper and more radical the revolution is, the larger the scale. The increase has been so regular, and has occurred so invariably in practically all the great revolutions, that to mention here a long list of facts and evidences is rather superfluous. Instead, it is enough to enumerate briefly the set of ever-repeated uniformities in the field of punishment, in order to establish the unquestionable fact of the increase of amount of punishment.

(1) Prisons, jails, places of detention, and many other buildings temporarily converted to such uses, are literally filled up to their supercapacity by the arrested persons. This means an extraordinary increase of amount of punishment, measured by the number of people upon whom it is imposed.

(2) Confiscation of the properties and possessions of the opposite party likewise assumes invariably extraordinary proportions, far above any normal period, and has occurred in every revolution — not only in the Communist one. This means again an extraordinary increase in this form of punishment in its quantity.

(3) Ostracism, banishment, driving the opponents out of the country or from their locality near its borders, or sending them to places of confinement again increases inevitably.

(4) Infliction of bodily punishment, revival of various torturing and painful — psychologically and physically — punishment is again an invariable satellite of revolution.

(5) Instituting hostages and the revival of a "collective responsibility" and a "collective punishment," for a deed of one, of all those who are supposed to belong to his group, though they may not have any connection with the perpetration of the crime, is again an ordinary manifestation of an extraordinary increase of the amount of punishment.

(6) Terror, an invariable accompaniment of any revolution, "purgings," mass extermination of the enemies, of persons of "impure" blood, means the same.

(7) Capital punishment usually jumps to a level far above the normal, often unbelievably high.

(8) Introduction of martial law, a "state of siege," of extraordinary commissions for fighting the enemies (the Cheka and O G P U of the Russian Revolution, the Committee of Public Safety and Salvation of the French Revolution, and so on), who arrest, torture, kill without any trial; extraordinary decrees, which, in a summary manner, regardless of any guarantees of the law, entitle the agents of the government to dispose of its enemies, or supposed enemies, in any way they please, that is, to dispatch anybody to the next world if they find it advisable — and they usually do — these and many other uniformly repeated phenomena of the same kind do not leave the slightest doubt that in the time of revolutions the amount and severity of punishment rise to an exceedingly high level, the higher, the greater the revolution and the respective disintegration of the system of social relationships and values.

The uniformities have invariably been repeated in all the revolutions beginning with the Egyptian revolution, some 1600 or 2000 years before our era (described by Ipuver, and three other Egyptian sources), the earliest known revolutions in Greece (described by Theognis, Thucydides, Plato, Aristotle, and others), and ending with the Russian Revolution.[57]

[57] See the facts in P. Sorokin, *The Sociology of Revolution* (Philadelphia, 1925), chap. ix.

For a typical illustration of these statements, a few figures are given. In Russia the average annual number of capital punishments was as follows for the specified years.

1881–1885	15.4
1886–1890	18.0
1891–1895	9.6
1896–1900	15.5
1901–1905	18.6

Then comes the Revolution of 1905–1907. The curve of the executions (which hardly embrace absolutely all cases) at once begins to rise.

1906	547
1907	1139
1908	1340

Then, with the subsiding of the Revolution (in 1907) the figures fall.

1909	717
1910	129
1911	73
1912	126 [58]

However, the tragic story does not stop here. With the Revolution of 1917 and the subsequent years, the number of the executions (not counting those lives lost in the battles of the civil war) by the Communist Government flares up to perfectly fantastic heights, to such heights, indeed, that nobody has any exact statistics, because executions have been carried on by the wholesale — hundreds, thousands, tens of thousands.

According to the most conservative estimate, which certainly understates the real number, during the years 1917 to 1922, at least 600,000 (!) persons were executed. The executions during the subsequent years, especially from 1929 to 1935, have also to be counted by the tens of thousands.

Imprisonment? During the eighteen years of the Russian Revolution, at least 20 per cent of the grown-up population of Russia (many millions) were arrested and imprisoned. Banishment? During the years of the famous five-year plan alone, at least 2,000,000 peasants were uprooted and banished to the lumber camps and other places of slow death! Abroad now there are at least 1,500,000 Russians. Bodily punishment? Anybody who is really acquainted with the Soviet justice knows about the rooms with the corked walls, which slowly suffocate the victims, about the mutilation of suspected persons in the process of questioning and

[58] See M. Gernet, *Smertnaia Kasn* (*Capital Punishment*) (Moscow, 1915), pp. 57–76.

inquisition; about "beating up" to the loss of consciousness; about driving nails under the nails of the hand; about "psychological" tortures through infliction of punishment upon the parents, children, wife, or husband of the "criminal," and so on.   Property fines and confiscations? Well, almost all the population of Russia was dispossessed of almost everything, not the aristocracy and the well-to-do classes only.

It is perfectly useless to continue this catalogue of absolutely certain facts.

Perhaps other revolutions did not commit these deeds?   Perhaps few of them did to the same extent, but all of them did, to some degree. Who does not know of the terror of the French Revolution?   The September massacres?   Of three thousand guillotined in Paris and 17,000 (or 16,594)[59] in the whole of France, plus 12,000 executed without trial, during only two years of the Revolution?   Of two thousand slaughtered in Lyons in a few days; 382 in Toulouse; 1800 shot by Carrier in the stone quarries; 332 in Orange?   Of those thousands butchered in the Vendée, and so on and so forth?   Or of 400,000 prisoners in 1794, exclusive of persons confined to their communes? [60]

Or let us turn to the great Dutch Revolution of 1566 and the subsequent years.   Well, let anybody read a competent account of it, in any work of any authoritative historian.   That is enough.   The same can be said of the Cromwellian Revolution in England of the seventeenth century, or the Hussite Revolution, or the French Revolution of 1870–1871, or the European revolutions of 1848–1849; of the Russian Revolution of the seventeenth century, or the medieval revolutions in various countries. Or shall I remind the reader of the Greek and Roman revolutions, with their proscriptions, their terror, when even the nearest friends of the triumvirs, like Cicero, were not spared?   Of the mass executions, tortures, confiscations of the opponents of Marius, or of Sulla, or of the members of the first and second triumvirates?   Or shall I remind you of the typical revolutions of the Thirty and of the Ten Tyrants?   Of the revolution in Corcyra, so splendidly described by Thucydides?   Of other Greek revolutions so excellently analyzed by Plato in his *Republic* and *Laws* and so wonderfully dissected by Aristotle in the fifth book of his *Politics?*   Or shall I refer to the good historical descriptions of the great revolutions in Persia and India, in China and Syria?   Or, finally, shall

[59] D. Greer, *The Incidence of the Terror during the French Revolution* (Harvard University Press, 1935), pp. 26 and 37.   "It is probable that between 35,000 and 40,000 persons lost their lives as a consequence of terrorism.   Those condemned by the courts — less than 17,000 — constitute the minority."

[60] *Ibid.*, p. 27.

I recommend you to read carefully the old Egyptian *Admonitions of the Sage* by Ipuver, or three other surviving documents with their descriptions of the revolutions of those remote past millenniums? Everywhere the uniformity claimed will be found. It is unquestionable.[61]

Even in much more superficial internal disturbances, a similar trend almost always shows itself, only in much less pronounced degree. Already

Professor Garcon noticed an interesting fact in the movement of the number of capital punishments in France; namely, under any new political regime the number of the death penalty verdicts was greater at the beginning of the new regime, during the first years of its existence, than later on. Thus, the Consulate begins with 605 death verdicts in 1803, while in 1813 the number is only 325, that is, twice less; the Restoration in 1816 starts with 514 death penalties; later on this figure falls to 91. The July Monarchy makes its debut with 108 death penalties in 1831 and ends with 65 in 1847; the Napoleonic Monarchy (Napoleon III) had the greatest number of the death penalties in 1854 (79); in its last year of existence the number was only 11. Finally, the decrease of death penalties from 1871, when the Republic was established, to the end of the 19th century is evident.[62]

The beginning of any new political regime means a revolution or important internal disturbance. According to the hypothesis, such a year, and the first years of the new regime (because, the revolution being already over, the trials for the crimes perpetrated in the period of the revolution usually lag by some one, two, or even more years) had to show an increase of punishment. The above figures show it indeed. Subsequent years of the regime mean some unification and consolidation of the ethicojuridical homogeneity as well as of the system of social relationships and of social values. Hence, a decrease of the number of the death penalties in the later period of any of these regimes. What is said of capital punishment can be said also of the other forms of punishment.

What is said of the political crises can be said of any form of social crisis, whether it be religious, or moral, or economic, or familistic, or any other. Professor G. Richard has shown well that

Social milieu determines the formation of the penal system and criminality. When society is in a normal state, that is, in the state of slow, gradual and harmonious development, it spontaneously organizes the resistance to criminal

---

[61] See the facts and evidence in my *Sociology of Revolution*. See there also the literature.
[62] Quoted from M. Gernet, *op. cit.*, pp. 75–76.

tendencies; when it is in the state of crisis, it calls forth the rise of criminality [and of more abundant and severe punishment].[63]

G. Richard has well shown that the sharp social crises are uniformly followed by a sudden rise of mass bloody criminality and of bloody punishment imposed liberally; that the mild and fading social perturbations are followed by a slighter rise of individual and sly or cunning criminality (mainly against property in the way of theft, forgery, swindle, etc.) and respectively by only a slight increase of punishment, while the growing normalcy of the social life leads usually to a decrease of criminality and, respectively, of penalties.

Germany of the fifteenth century was economically and materially in good condition; but ethicojuridically and religiously it was split already into two opposed parts: the old Catholic and the new Protestant, the world of the Lollards, the Hussites, the predecessors of Luther. We see an enormous development of brigandage, murder, and other forms of bloody and brutal criminality, followed by a growth of the severest private and public punishments imposed liberally.

The continuation of this split, in the form of the Reformation, led not only to an increase in criminality, but to riots, uprisings, and revolutions in which punishment was used on a scale typical of revolutions and far above the level of punishment in normal times. Similar processes took place in the crisis at the end of the eighteenth and the beginning of the nineteenth century in India, in the period of struggle between Mohammedanism and Hinduism; in Indo-China at the end of the eighteenth century for the same reasons, and in several other places.

In Italy the number of murders decreased from 8000, about 1860, to 5418 in 1880, 4288 in 1885, and 3629 in 1895.[64]   Richard points out that

[63] G. Richard, "Les crises sociales et les conditions de la criminalité," in L'année sociologique (1900), p. 17.   I have several times called the attention of contemporary American criminologists to the fact that as long as the contemporary American (and also European) population is in the state of ethicojuridical heterogeneity, moral relativity, and moral anarchy, all the attempts to cope with criminality by change of the methods and technique of penology, of court procedure, of "ecological areas," of the contemporary backboneless (moral) education, of improvement of economic conditions and other similar factors can give but quite insignificant results.   Some of them recently seem to begin to understand this simple thing; but the majority of the penologists and politicians are still on the wrong road in their search for the "causes of crime" and the methods to combat criminality.   See my statements in Sorokin, Zimmerman, and Galpin, Source Book in Rural Sociology (Minneapolis, 1931), Vol. II, chap. xiii; P. Sorokin, Social Mobility (New York, 1927), chap. xxi.   One of the similar and sound works along this line is E. Sutherland and C. E. Gehlke's "Crime and Punishment," in Recent Social Trends (New York, 1933), chap. xxii.

[64] The trend continued after 1895; in 1906 the number of murders was still less than in 1895.   See M. Gernet, op. cit., p. 135.

the period after 1860 was that of a new life in Italy, in the form of a national state, regenerated after the crisis which occurred during the first part of the nineteenth century. Hence, the noticeable decline of bloody criminality, and, parallel to it, a decline in punishment; in 1890 the death penalty was abolished from the Italian penal system.

Similar parallelism is found in France, as already mentioned. The number of usual murders (not to mention the revolutionary and counter-revolutionary killings) here jumped in the time of crisis, like the period 1788–1801 or 1871, and fell in the period of pacification and order. Respectively, as we have seen, the number of death penalties imposed followed a parallel course.[65]

If need be, one can present a very large number of cases of the sharp and slight, sudden and gradual, social crises of various kinds, which uniformly are followed by an increase of criminality and of punishment.

The proposition is so sound and evident that one can test it in daily life, on the small scale of the inner relationship of a family, in a business enterprise, a trade union, a literary association, or even in a group of children. If, and when, in a family, the forms of conduct of the children and the parents clash (say, a small boy becomes naughty) the result is an increase of reprimand, the deprivation of a dessert, sending the child to his room, and often a spanking. What is that but the same phenomenon on a small scale?

Once in a while, unfortunately, the heterogeneity and smashed system of the family values lead to real tragedies: to the murder of one member of the family by another; to the infliction of serious bodily injury or other punishment; to disinheritance of the unruly, not to mention the cases of the disruption of the family (divorce, desertion, separation, running away, and so on).

With a corresponding modification, the same thing takes place in any association, organization, institution, when the ethicojuridical and sociological standards of its members become heterogeneous or opposed;

---

[65] See for details Richard's article, quoted. An explosion of looting, sacking, murder, and robbery in the cities and areas stricken by inundation, earthquake, fire, abandoned by the native army in war, is a phenomenon familiar to all and invariably repeated in the past as well as in the present. An introduction of martial law and a mass punishment is a usual satellite of such an explosion. Examples of this phenomenon were given in the spring of 1936 in many American cities (in Massachusetts, Connecticut, Pennsylvania, and in other states) that were flooded. Another example of the same phenomenon was given by the explosion of these criminal activities in the capital of Ethiopia after it was abandoned by the Ethiopian army and before the Italians entered it. These facts are but a special variety of the same generic fact of splitting and shattering of the system of social relationship and values, and as such they give an additional evidence for the proposition discussed.

when, in sociological terms, the network of social relationships and of the system of the values of the group is broken, shattered, split. The invariable result is either an increase of the penalties imposed by one section of the members upon the other (no matter what are their concrete forms) or the downfall of the organization — its split, its decline, its elimination.

These everyday occurrences, perhaps even more than the prominent cases of history, show the validity of the proposition.

The totality of the types of the phenomena of this category proves the hypothesis as strongly as any hypothesis in the field of the sociocultural phenomena can be proved.

B. What is said of revolutions as a particularly conspicuous type of the periods of increase of the ethicojuridical heterogeneity, and of the shattering and disintegration of social relationships and the system of social values, can be said, with corresponding modifications, of almost any type or period or case of such an increase of heterogeneity. In all such cases, no matter what their concrete forms may be, an increase of the amount and the severity of punishment can be expected. Here are some examples of such cases.

(1) When a certain area and its inhabitants are conquered and taken possession of by a people having very different mores, the punishments imposed upon the newly conquered population tend almost always to be more severe and more abundant than upon the population of the conquering country itself. Whether we take the punishments imposed upon new colonies and possessions, with a primitive people having an ethicojuridical mentality different from that of the incorporating, often so-called "civilized" people; or the case of a civilized population conquered, but still different from the conquerors — be the vanquished the Roman *peregrini* (and especially the *peregrini dediticii*); be they Indians conquered by the Spaniards; or the native populations of British India or of the Fiji Islands; or the Negroes of Martinique;[66] or the Ethiopians; or any other population with different ethicojuridical mores — an excess of the quantity and severity of punishment is almost always noticeable.

[66] As an example the Code Noir of 1685 enacted by the French Government and the verdicts of the Council of Martinique of 1674 and 1677 can serve. Article 4 of the decisions of the Council says: "All negroes who give a blow to the white will be either hanged or suffocated. If the white dies, they will be torn apart alive." And this at the end of the seventeenth century, when the French Criminal Law was already soft and humanitarian to a considerable degree. See Loiseleur, *Les crimes et les peines dans l'antiquité et dans les temps modernes* (Paris, 1863), chapter on the punishments in colonies and p. 327. The situation with many a native preliterate people, colonized by the European countries, is not much different. The lynching of Negroes in the United States is also somewhat related to this category of facts.

The reason? The same already given: the great heterogeneity of their morality from that of the dominant people; hence, the effort to bring it into similarity with the system of the dominant people through the instrumentality of punishment.

(2) Likewise, within the same nation, or state, or cultural system, when such a society or *state enters a period of rapid expansion through the conquest and incorporation of many new peoples and societies different in their morality from one another and from the kernel of the integrating nation, the ethicojuridical heterogeneity of such an expanded society rapidly increases through the rapid absorption of the different groups; therefore, according to the theory, such periods in such an empire have to be marked by an increase of the quantity and quality of punishment imposed upon the new as well as upon the old members.* The reason for such an expectation is that, in order for such an empire to hold together these different centrifugal elements and unite them into one sociocultural system with homogeneous relationships and values, it has to turn to an increased pressure of punishment and coercion. Until all the more important parts of the empire are "acculturated" homogeneously, the instrumentality of punishment and coercion must continue. When, and if, the uniform acculturation and homogeneity are accomplished, the curve of punishment can be lowered, and usually the severity does become mitigated. This process has recurred many times. It is especially conspicuous in the cases of very rapid creation of vast empires through conquest. Here are a few examples of that.

(a) The Empire of Jenghiz Khan was created very rapidly and embraced a large number of tribes and peoples with very different mores. Jenghiz Khan enacted his famous *Jassa* or Code of Law, the greater part of which can be styled Criminal Law. What is its leading motto? "Wise severity is the basis of the strength of the Empire." "Out of 36 fragments which survive, 13 impose the death penalty for violation of established rules," not only for theft, adultery, intentional lie, and similar crimes, but also for compassion to a prisoner; urination into water and ashes; lack of respect to elderly persons and beggars; gluttony in eating; and the like. In brief, the *Jassa* is severe, stern, pitiless.[67] And what is known from history of the methods of ruling the vast empire used by the great Khan, as well as by his immediate successors, testifies uniformly to a most extensive use of punishment in unlimited amount and of the highest severity.

[67] V. A. Riasanovsky, *The Mongolian Law* (in Russian) (Kharbin, 1931), pp. 12-20. See there chap. i.

(*b*) Not different was the situation in the empires or vast principalities created by the great successors of Jenghiz Khan, like Batiy and others; in the empires of Tamerlane, or of Alexander the Great; or of the first Merovingians and Carlovingians; or, as we shall see, in the expanded Roman Empire.

(*c*) In regard to more modern times, the special Colonial Law created by the European nations for their newly incorporated colonies, with their deeply different populations — whether of India, of Africa, of the West Indies, or of New Guinea or the Fiji Islands, or of the Congo, or of Java and so on — is an example of the phenomenon of the same sort, marked by a similar sternness of the law in regard to the newly incorporated people. The factual behavior of the "colonizers" has been still more conspicuous for its cruelty — quantitative and qualitative — of punishment.

Often, and in the preceding few centuries, as a rule, the factual treatment of the "natives," whether by the Spaniards or the British, or the French, or the Dutch, was simply the extermination of the native population through the imposition of an overabundant and most severe penalty.[68] In brief, the facts of that kind are so numerous that it is unnecessary to quote them extensively.

(3) *A further type of increase of ethicojuridical heterogeneity and disintegration of the existing network of social relationships, as well as the system of sociocultural values, is given by the periods of deep internal transformation of the culture of a given society, no matter what are the causes of such a transformation.*

[68] It is enough to remind the reader of the prodigious decrease of the native population under the regime of the "cultural" peoples, in order to prove the validity of the point. Of course the decrease has been due not only to the impossible regime and cruelty of the colonizers, but these cruelties and penalties imposed upon the natives for their deviation from the norms imposed upon them by the conquerors were certainly one of the main — direct and indirect — causes of such a decrease. In the conquests of the type of the Spanish adventurers, and similar others, this is quite certain and unquestionable. In other cases, the factor studied has been one of the most important, because if there were not imposed abundantly the most severe punishments for the violation of the rules commanded by the colonizers, the rules would not have been obeyed. Therefore, if they were to be enforced, their enforcement must be assured through a stern application of this "medicine" to the natives. Thus, directly and indirectly, severest punishment was one of the main factors which led to the decrease of the native population and to the process of their complete extermination. Here are a few figures:

"The native population of New Zealand was 104,000 in 1841; 55,467 in 1858; and no more than 47,000 in 1864. . . . At the time of Cook's visit the native population of Tahiti was between 150,000 and 200,000. In the sixties of the nineteenth century, it was only about 15,000. In the Fiji Islands, from 1875 to 1912, it decreased from about 150,000 to 75,000." P. Sorokin, *Social Mobility*, p. 31. See there the sources.

If the hypothesis is valid, we have to expect, in such periods, a quantitative and qualitative increase of the punishment imposed by one part of society upon the other, by the existing governments upon the subjects. We know that the cultural transformations have various concrete forms. But one of the deepest, possibly *the* deepest, transformation is from the *Ideational to the Sensate*, or vice versa.

The periods of transition from one form to the other mean an increase of the ethicojuridical heterogeneity and antagonism within the society, between those who remain in the morality of the culture hitherto existing and those who shift to the new form of culture and its morality. In large social bodies, it is a very rare occurrence when the transition is made simultaneously by all members. As a rule, a part shifts to the new standards, while the other part remains faithful to the old ones. Hence, increase of heterogeneity and disintegration of the previously unified system of relationships and values; and, if the hypothesis is right, the probability of increase of punishment in the society. Only when the new form of culture becomes dominant and the new morality homogeneous, the social relationships and the system of values crystallized and generally accepted, can the curve of punishment go down, and it usually does. The facts on a large historical scale, as well as on the scale of everyday occurrences, seem to corroborate this. As an example of the alternation of the Ideational and Sensate cultures, let us take the Roman, the medieval, and later evolution of punishment, as it is given in the codes as well as in the social reality.

However uncertain is the movement of the curve of punishment in Rome, in the course of its history, one thing seems to be certain enough, namely that the amount and the severity of punishment in normal times (except for the period of the Civil Strife at the end of the Republic) greatly increased, beginning with the end of the second century A.D. and up to the end of the Western Roman Empire.[69]

---

[69] Durkheim, and also the author, in his early work, *Crime and Punishment*, assumed that the early Roman law, as it is expressed by the Twelve Tables (according to the most accepted opinion enacted around 451 B.C.), *Leges XII tabularum*, was exceedingly severe and cruel. The basis for that belief is that the main form of punishment in the Tables is the death penalty, or, as T. Mommsen says: " *Die einzige gesetzliche Strafe des öffentlichen Verfahrens bleibt der Tod.*" Mommsen, *Römisches Strafrechts* (Leipzig, 1899), pp. 939 ff., and "*Die Geschichte der Todesstrafe im Römischen Staat,*" in his *Reden und Aufsätze* (Berlin, 1905), pp. 437–448. From this as well as from the prevalence of the repressive laws over the restitutive laws in the Code (assumed by Durkheim), it does not necessarily follow that the penalty was imposed liberally and was severe. The point is that, first of all, only exceedingly few forms of actions are considered as crime, and especially as crime punished by the death penalty in the laws. As the *delicta publica* punished by that penalty are: murder (*parricidium*);

While in the period of the Empire during its first two centuries the death penalties for Roman citizens are few, "in the time of Severus the death penalty becomes a usual punishment for felonies, and this tendency more and more grows in subsequent periods." "It more and more often begins to threaten and for less and less grave violations." [70] The persecution now does not depend upon the private initiative (*accusatio*); it is started by the officials also. The number of the forms of actions which began to be regarded as criminal and punishable greatly increased; the content of the previous crimes is notably enlarged. Punishable are now the *crimina legitima*, the *crimina extraordinaria*, and many of the previous *delicta privata*.

As to the system of punishment, there now develops, instead of a simple and comparatively mild system of penalty of the Republican period, a very complicated, very severe, often barbarian system of penalties. . . . The death penalty, which almost disappeared in the Republican period, now is reëstablished and often assumes the most qualified forms (burning, crucifixion, *poena culei*, etc.). . . . In addition, quite frequent becomes hard labor, imprisonment in the state mines (*condemnatio ad metallum*), followed by the loss of freedom and all rights (*capitis diminutio*), banishment, exile, fines and a vast system of torturing and painful bodily punishments.[71]

---

intentional arson (for which *vindictus verberatus igni necari jubetur*); removal of landmarks (*termini motio*), which was regarded as sacrilege violating the religious taboo; theft and extermination of sowing (*suspensum Cereri necari jubebant*); magic and sorcery in regard to the sowing; libel; treason. These forms almost exhaust the *delicta publica* for which *poena capitalis* or the somewhat equivalent *sacer esto* were imposed. For other violations, the penalty is either the equivalent talion ("*talio esto*") or just a fine. Even those are few comparatively, because most of the conflicts or violations of the mores were still the private matter of the parties involved, the *delicta privata*, at best. Such a small number of the actions regarded as crimes and so punished does not entitle us to view this code as a severe *criminal* code; still less does it give us a basis on which to assume that the punishment at that epoch was quantitatively and qualitatively severe.

As to the system of punishment for crime in the Republican period, it also does not strike us as severe. If anything, it was, in normal periods during the first half of the Republic, mild, with its principle of private initiative in accusation; with its mitigation of the death penalty by the introduction of the right of appeal (*provocatio*) to the people; in making it possible for a culprit to leave Rome and to go into exile (*jus exulandi* and *aquae et ignis interdictio*) and in the imposition of various fines, which tended to serve as a substitution for it. In the time of Pompey, the death penalty even for fratricide and murder of relatives, the latest of the crimes punished by capital punishment, was replaced by other forms of punishment. See the details in the above works of Mommsen. Also, J. Pokrovsky, *History of the Roman Law* (in Russian) (Riga, 1924), pp. 47–51, 113–117, and 166–169. As mentioned, in the periods of revolutions and internal strife, like that between Marius and Sulla, the members of the first and the second triumvirates, the real punishment greatly increased at the end of the Republic. But such periods are not the normal periods; besides, they themselves excellently support the thesis discussed.

[70] Mommsen, *Römisches Strafrecht*, pp. 942–943.   [71] J. Pokrovsky, *op. cit.*, pp. 225–227.

In brief, there can hardly be any doubt that the curve of punishment went up greatly — quantitatively and qualitatively — in the criminal law as well as in the social reality, during the centuries from the end of the second to the end of the fifth.

If we inquire what were the causes or reasons for such an increase, several hypotheses are possible answers. One of them is offered by E. Durkheim. Here is its essence: "The intensity of punishment is proportional to the degree of absolutism and unlimitedness of the central power. The more unlimited it is, the severer are the punishments."

As from the first to the fifth centuries A.D., absolutism grew, Durkheim sees in it the main factor of the growth of punishment.[72]

The reason for such a causal relationship is shown in Durkheim's distinction between the crimes directed against the collective or religious values, and those against the individual or human values (murder, theft, violence). The former, as insulting the whole collectivity, are punished more severely than the latter.[73]

As the growing absolutistic central government in Rome began to deify itself and be deified more and more by others, the violation of its laws and rules began to be regarded more and more as *criminalité religieuse*, therefore the sanctions naturally became more and more severe.

Here we have a conspicuous case of parallelism in the movement of two variables taken for a causal relationship between them. It is easy to point out the fallacy of Durkheim's theory. We may grant for a moment his assumption that crimes against the collectivity (*criminalité religieuse*) are punished more severely than crimes against an individual.[74] This,

---

[72] E. Durkheim, "*Deux lois de l'évolution pénale*," in *L'année sociologique*, Vol. IV, pp. 65 ff.

[73] *Ibid.*, pp. 86–94. This he developed also in his *De la division du travail social* (Paris, 1893).

[74] In Durkheim's theory this assumption is connected with another; namely, that the crime is punished in such cases not so much for the sake of vengeance, or intimidation, or redemption of the criminal, as for the sake of reinforcement of this unanimity of the collective consciousness and conscience. This is the main thesis in his *Division of Social Labor*. Respectively, he assumed that among the primitive peoples who have a slight division of labor, and whose morality is homogeneous, punishments are most cruel and terrible; and that as we move toward our society, with its enormous division of labor and heterogeneity of morality among its members, the penalties become quite mild and easy and are reduced purely to deprivation of freedom, which becomes more and more slight. See about this also in his *Deux lois de l'évolution pénale*, quoted, p. 78. These assumptions have to be taken now as fallacious, for the most part. First, he underestimated greatly the division of labor among the primitive people. He is wrong in assuming that the penalty system of primitive peoples generally is severe. On the contrary, in a great many cases it is mild. Even in the study of the Barbaric Codes, we saw that their system of punishment was, all in all, the mildest of all of the systems up to the present time. He is wrong also in assuming that at the present moment all forms of punishment except comfortable detention have disappeared. At the very end of the nineteenth century, when he was writing, such a delusion might have been

however, does not explain why crimes against the central government of the Roman Republic were punished more mildly than those against the Roman Principatus, because in both cases the crimes were in violation of the *leges* of the State.   If the reason is the deification of the Emperor in the later period, this deification did not necessarily mean that it was agreed to by the population.   As we shall see, during these centuries, there was not a growth of the unanimity of the ethicojuridical mentality of the citizens and all the population, but, on the contrary, its split and antagonism.   Therefore, according to Durkheim himself, the unanimity of the religious and ethicojuridical consciousness of the population was less than in the first part of the Republic.   Therefore, the *criminalité religieuse* was here weaker, and therefore the penalties had to be milder, according to Durkheim's own theory.   Meanwhile, they really were severer.   Furthermore, he himself claims (also a wrong claim) that with the evolution of society the *criminalité religieuse* tends to decrease, while the *criminalité humaine* (crimes against the individual) tends to increase. If this be so, then again we must expect in the post-Republican Rome an increase of the *criminalité humaine*, and therefore a decrease of punishment.   In brief, Durkheim's theory is internally quite inconsistent.   In addition, his generalization is factually fallacious.   There have been many republics whose penal systems have been more severe than those of the absolute monarchies.

Next, in the above we saw that the penal system of the Codes of the Absolute and Enlightened Despotism at their climax of absolutism and unlimited power became much milder than the system of feudal Europe with its kings and monarchs, who were often only *primus inter pares;* whose rule was much more limited than that of the absolute monarchs of the seventeenth and eighteenth centuries.   And yet, these seventeenth and eighteenth centuries were marked by the greatest mitigation of the penal system, which was milder, all in all, than the systems of the republics and constitutional monarchies of the beginning and the first part of the nineteenth century.

---

excusable; the subsequent decades, especially the postwar period, have shown such an orgy of executions, banishments, bodily punishments in so many countries that at the present moment there is not the slightest ground on which to maintain such an opinion.   We saw also that the twentieth-century codes increased punishment.   Likewise, the assumption that the stronger is the unanimity of the collective morality the severer have to be the punishments for its further reinforcement is also generalization of a case into a universal rule. As M. Kovalevsky rightly said: "It is not quite comprehensible why, for honest people to reinforce themselves in their righteousness, it is necessary to inflict the severest punishment upon the culprit."   M. Kovalesky, *The Contemporary Sociologists* (in Russian) (St. Petersburg, 1905), pp. 141 and 142.

We saw also, from the comparison of the codes, that the codes of Russia of the second half of the nineteenth century, with its unlimited absolutism of the Czars, were in no way more severe (were, if anything, milder) than the codes of France, Italy, and Austria, with their republican or limited-monarchy regimes. It is useless to pile up the evidence to the contrary. Durkheim's generalization is but a mere "derivation" or "rationalization" of the wishes and biases of the liberal and radical humanitarianism of the nineteenth century of which he was a typical representative.

Now let us try to approach the rise of the curve of the penalties in Rome from the standpoint of the hypothesis offered here. Up to the beginning of our era, Rome included in its empire large areas, with most heterogeneous populations. The culture, mores, and ethicojuridical mentality of these diverse groups were very different. During the subsequent centuries — the second, third, fourth, and fifth — heterogeneity continued to increase rather than decrease because during that period new Teutonic tribes — the Gauls, Helvetians, the Araviscians, the Treverians, the Nervians, the Vangiones, the Triboshians, the Nemetes, the Ubians, the Batavians, the Cattians, the Mattiaci, the Usipians, and so on [75] — and then the Asiatic groups, continued to enter the Roman Empire, and the contacts between such groups became closer and closer. In addition, the previously real Roman population, which had built up the Roman Empire, dwindled and almost disappeared. The population and even the aristocracy, beginning with the emperors, began to be increasingly recruited from the "barbarians," the Orientals, and other racial and ethnic groups quite unrelated to the previous Roman population.[76] Rome itself turned into "a meeting place of the globe," as Cicero puts it. "They have converged . . . from all parts of the globe," Seneca says. Pliny and Tacitus state the same thing in still stronger terms, talking of Rome as a place where all the dregs of the world are flowing and gathering.

This means that the balancing and digesting center of the population which could impose the Roman uniform culture upon the new groups and peoples incorporated disappeared or greatly weakened. But that is not all. Add to this the most fundamental process of the transformation of the Roman culture from the predominantly Sensate into the Ideational, which, in the form of the appearance and growth of Christianity, emerged and rapidly progressed. It split into absolutely irreconcilable parts the

[75] Tacitus, *De situ, moribus et populis Germaniae*, xxviii–xlvi.

[76] See about that in T. Frank, "Race Mixture of the Roman Empire," in *American Historical Review*, Vol. XXI, pp. 705 ff. Of 92 Roman emperors of these centuries, 42, or about 45 per cent, came from the groups different from the Roman population. See P. Sorokin, "Monarchs and Rulers," in *Social Forces*, Vol. IV, pp. 527 ff.

whole mentality — scientific, philosophic, religious, artistic, and ethico-juridical — of the population. This most fundamental process alone is sufficient to create the appearance and growth of the ethicojuridical heterogeneity and antagonism of the deepest possible kind. It means the most fundamental split, the shattering and disintegration of the whole network of social relationships and of the whole system of sociocultural values.

Add to this the ever-increasing restlessness and riots of the *coloni*, the slaves or the *serves*, the rapid growth, especially in the third century A.D., of the half-revolutionary, half-criminal bands of brigands, robbers, and rioters (the "bagaudi" and others).[77]

When all this is taken into consideration, the fact of an extraordinary increase of the heterogeneity of the mores, of the shattering and dis-integration of the previously existing Sensate culture, becomes certain and unquestionable. Shall we wonder, therefore, that the penalty sys-tem began rapidly to grow — quantitatively and qualitatively; that the number of punishments imposed upon the people began to increase, and grow more and more severe? In the light of this, it is not strange that increase of punishment and persecution of the Christians occurred and was strongly enforced by the best Roman emperors, like Trajan, Marcus Aurelius, Diocletian, and others. Being really the best of the emperors, they had to follow this course in their effort to preserve the unity and vitality of the Empire. This shows that the hypothesis fits the facts excellently. It shows also that in any period of such a deep transforma-tion of culture, as its passage from the Sensate to the Ideational form (and also, though not to the same extent, in its passage from the Ideational to the Sensate) the curve of crime must go up.

After the legalization of Christianity, the factors of heterogeneity and disorganization of the system of social relationships and social values continued to exist. The establishment and consolidation of a new system of relationships and values cannot be accomplished at once or even quickly. It needs a long time.

Politically and socially, the situation was, as Jordan (sixth century) puts it, such that

In that epoch all armed themselves for mutual protection. . . . Kingdoms fall into pieces; out of one body social come separate parts, and one part does

[77] See M. Rostovtzeff, *The Social and Economic History of the Roman Empire* (Oxford, 1926), *passim*. Of contemporary writers, Salvianus, in his *De gubernatione dei*, especially in Bk. V, 4–9, gives a particularly vivid characterization of the situation of the time. The work was written in the fifth century. Likewise, St. Augustine's *De civitate dei* serves the purpose excellently.

not feel the pains of the others, but after separation they continue to harm and fight one another. The strongest nations, unrivalled before, now tear themselves into pieces, deepening and enlarging their wounds mutually." [78]

Therefore the Theodosian Code and the practice of the time does not naturally show any mitigation or economy of penalty, but on the contrary, its quantitative and qualitative increase.

We can continue the interpretation further, for the next centuries. From the preceding pages, we have seen that in comparison with the Barbaric Codes, which reflect largely the ethicojuridical mores of the tribes in their pre-Christianized and pre-Romanized stage, subsequent codes, the medieval penal system, increased the severity of punishment, and the punishments probably increased also quantitatively. What are the reasons?

They remain the same. The great migration of the peoples which took place during the subsequent centuries increased the heterogeneity and broke into fragments the network of social relationships and values of the old Roman Empire. Many of the attempts to effect a rapid unification of these varied tribes and peoples into one social or political body, made either by Merovingians or Carlovingians, could be carried out only through the instrumentality of the severest punishments. And they were imposed and applied pitilessly, in great abundance, usually on a mass scale.

Furthermore, the rising Christianity (Ideationalism) had to "discipline" them and inhibit many of their traditional mores which were contradictory to the Ideational morality of Christianity, and engraft many others quite strange to them, whether in the field of marriage, or property, or religion, or in any other field. Such a task of creating and engrafting a new ethicojuridical mentality, of the organization of a new social and cultural system, especially when this new system happened to be Ideational — which called for the inhibition of many previous "natural" appetites, desires, proclivities, and pleasures — such an enormous work could hardly be done by mere sentimental preaching, or by orders, without the introduction of the "iron system of penalties," and without a growth in their quality as well as quantity. Hence, the increase of severity of the penal system of the Middle Ages, compared with that of the Barbaric Codes. To the "this-worldly" punishment the "otherworldly" ones had to be added to increase the pressure. Shall we wonder that in the codes of the Middle Ages generally, and of even the thirteenth and fourteenth centuries, we do not see any mitigation of the penal system?

[78] Jordan, *De Gothorum origine et rebus gestis*, L–LII.

Perhaps if the Ideational culture had been rooted deeply in the masses and had lasted for many centuries after the unification of the peoples into a homogeneous body social and politic, the curve of punishment would have gone down around the twelfth and thirteenth centuries. But if at that time the consolidation of the peoples into comparatively large national states only began to take place, the culture itself began to experience the transformation from the Ideational to the Sensate form, as we have seen. Such a transformation would mean again an increase of heterogeneity and the beginning of a new "revaluation of all sociocultural values"; therefore it would work in favor of at least the maintenance of the high level of the penalties. It is not incidental that exactly at that time the Church introduced the Inquisition, and with it a great reinforcement of the punishments imposed by and through the Church. The beginning of the Inquisition can be found either in the Decree of the Council of Verona, 1184, or in the edicts of Pope Innocence III, of 1203 and 1215, which appeared exactly at the time when the Ideational culture began to show the first signs of decline, and the Sensate the first indications of rise; when in the Church itself heresies and schisms occurred on a large scale and were increasing; when a new secular and "humanitarian" spirit made its first notable manifestation. Briefly, when in the systems of the values of the Ideational culture there appeared a split and a new heterogeneity. Hence, an increase of the cruelty of the penalties imposed through and by the Church; by the Canon Law; and also, if not an increase, then at least a maintenance of the previous high level of punishment in the secular Criminal Law.

When the consolidation of the national States progressed sufficiently, during the next few centuries, and established a new system of social relationships; when, during the same centuries, the new Sensate culture definitely crystallized, grew, and became the dominant system of sociocultural values; when, in other words, a new homogeneity was established, yes, then, from the sixteenth or seventeenth century, roughly, we had to expect a decline of the curve of punishment. And the codes studied reflected the decline. We have seen that practically all the codes of the seventeenth and eighteenth centuries registered a great decrease of punishment and an enormous mitigation of their severity; and, as sources show, the establishment of many guarantees (for normal times) against unlawful persecution, against too liberal imposition of punishment; and, briefly, favored a quantitative decrease of punishment.

Short-time jumps — due to the revolutions and other circumstances of the same type — of increase of heterogeneity excepted, the main trend of mitigation of punishment continued up to the end of the nineteenth century, throughout all the period of the crystallization and growth of the Sensate culture.   As was indicated above, in many forms, the nineteenth century represented the climax of the Sensate culture.   Also, in all the countries studied (not excluding Russia), the criminal law was essentially similar, permeated by the same principles, by the same system of values; and the culture of Europe of the nineteenth century was also one of the most homogeneous, in all its main countries.

The postwar period, as we have seen, is marked by many signs of the decline of the Sensate culture; by many new and deep movements; by the shattering of the previously existing social, political, economic, and other orders; by a most profound and radical revaluation of all values.[79]

---

[79] This is shown also by the data that of 100 per cent of the crimes identical in the prewar and postwar periods, only in 26 per cent did the punishment remain the same, while in 74 per cent of the crimes it was changed.   In previous periods, from the eighteenth century up to the twentieth, from 46 to 52 per cent of the crimes had their punishment unchanged. This shows that even in this particular field the change in the postwar period is greater and more radical than during the two preceding centuries.   See Tables 42, 43, and 44.   Similar results are shown by the data concerning the change in the criminal and noncriminal actions.

In passing, it is to be noted that though the history of the criminal law in Greece is little known, the few important facts established agree also with the hypothesis offered.   Here Draco's laws (*thesmoi*) issued *c.* 621 B.C. are notorious for their cruelty, punishing almost all crimes by capital punishment.   Then Solon's laws (*nomoi*), issued after 594 B.C., are milder, but still very stern and severe.   Both extended the interference of the State's criminal machinery enormously, allowing it to interfere by its own initiative in the relationship of the criminal and victim, without waiting for the complaint of the injured party.   Now the seventh and the beginning of the sixth century in Athens was the period of great social disturbance and revolution.   Some investigators, like Professor Calhoun, say, not without reason, that they were "class-war laws."   Thus the increase of punishment in that period fits the hypothesis.   The subsequent history of the criminal law in Greece is known too fragmentarily to give any basis for a solid verification of the hypothesis.   But what is known of this history, especially if one takes into consideration the cruelties and mass murders perpetrated in many Greek revolutions and disturbances, like that in Corcyra described by Thucydides, or that described by Theognis, or other accounts of other revolutions — in Athens, Miletus, Mitylene, Megara, Syracuse, and Argos — and then the " Bolshevist " revolutions with the Ten and Thirty Tyrants — these fragments again agree well with the theory presented.   See the data, the material, and the outline of the evolution of the Greek criminal law in L. Gernet, *Recherches sur le développement de la pensée juridique et moral en Grèce*, (Paris, 1917); G. Glotz, *La solidarité de la famille dans le droit criminel en Grèce* (Paris, 1904); G. M. Calhoun, *The Growth of Criminal Law in Ancient Greece* (Berkeley, 1927); S. Ranulf, *The Jealousy of the Gods and Criminal Law at Athens*, 2 vols. (London and Copenhagen) 1933–1934; J. H. Lipsius, *Das Attische Recht und Rechtsverfahren* (Leipzig, 1905–1915).   For the mass cruelties and murders in the Greek revolutions, see my *Sociology of Revolution*.   It is to be mentioned that practically all the main changes in the ethical mentality as well as in the criminal law of Greece can be explained much more satisfactorily by the theory of the Ideational and Sensate cultures (as this theory is given in this work, with a proper periodization of the domination of these cultures in the life history of Greek culture) and by the

Therefore we shall expect the curve of punishment to go up.   And indeed, it went up, as shown by the codes, and went up in the social reality still higher than the codes registered.   As a matter of fact, it flared into the "stratosphere" in the real social life.

Thus, this sketch shows that the hypothesis offered fits the main movements of the quantitative-qualitative curve of punishment, from the Roman times to the twentieth century.[80]

C. *Summary*.   The preceding analysis warrants the following conclusions.

(1) Though the quantitative-qualitative fluctuation of punishment in reality is not identical with the curve of punishment in the subsequent criminal codes, nevertheless, in a more conservative and limited way, the codes as a whole reflect the main ups and downs of the curve of severity (but not of amount) of punishment in real social life. Aside from the short-lived codes, like those enacted in the time of revolution which sometimes do not last even long enough to be included and enforced in the functioning of criminal courts and justice ; or are neglected in the time of revolution, when justice functions through other channels — with the exceptions of such codes and laws, the long-time functioning criminal codes reflect the main changes of the ethicojuridical mentality and of the penal system.   But the fluctuation of the composition of the actions of criminal class, as well as of the amount and severity of punishment, is narrower in the codes than it is in reality.   Codes in this respect remind us of an even and "averaged" curve from which the numerous erratic and wide fluctuations are eliminated.   The fluctuations of crime and punishment in social reality are likely to be much more violent and irregular.   Besides, the codes do not show all the fluctuations, sometimes enormous, which take place between two codes, especially when one of these codes is separated from its successor by decades and even centuries. Long-time functioning codes are enacted in normal times and intended for a long existence under normal conditions ; the periods of abnormal crises and their systems of "justice" and punishment are not reflected in them,

---

hypothesis discussed here as one of the details of the Ideational-Sensate culture theory, than by the theories of the above authors.   Some of them, like Ranulf's theory of envy and jealousy, explain hardly anything; because this theory is purely psychological, it does not explain why jealousy and envy appeared just in the sixth and fifth centuries; why it has to manifest itself in such particular forms, and so forth.   All the criticism which he directs against the other theories applies to his own.   Other theories either merely glide on the surface with their "positivistic-rationalistic-linear" presuppositions, or, if touching to some extent the real reasons, do not develop them far enough or deep enough.

[80] See several details in P. Sorokin, *Crime and Punishment*, chap. ix.

and when a "crisis code" is enacted, it usually reflects the reality in this field quite incorrectly.

With these reservations, codes, then, are roughly accurate indicators of the changes in the criminal and penal fields which take place in the course of time in the life history of a given social body.

(2) In the comparatively integrated cultures, the criminal and penal law also reflects the substantial changes in the inner nature of a given culture.   So far as we are following the fluctuation of Ideational and Sensate types of culture, we see that the codes reflect this fluctuation in the criminal as well as penal parts.   When a culture passes from the Sensate or even subcultural form to the Ideational form, the transformation manifests itself in the field of crime:

(a) by an increase of the actions qualified as criminal in the sense that a series of actions which were not regarded as criminal in Sensate or subcultural periods are now included in the criminal class;

(b) most of such newly created crimes are of Ideational nature, representing actions violating Ideational values.   Of these especially are the religious values.   Hence most of such newly created crimes represent, in usual terminology, crimes against religion and absolute moral principles. The consideration of mere individual or social utilitarianism, hedonism, eudaemonism, play little part in the creation of these new types of crimes;

(c) in the field of punishment, in the introduction of forms of punishment which have also a somewhat Ideational nature, like the deprivation of Christian burial, imposition of anathema, interdiction, and so on.   In Ideational crimes against religion there is a tendency to punish with particular severity in the criminal law of the Ideational culture.[81]

(3) Passage from the Ideational to the Sensate form of culture is marked by opposite characteristics in the Sensate criminal law, namely, by exclusion of almost all Ideational crimes from the class of criminal actions.   This means the elimination of almost all the crimes against religion and Ideational values as such.   If a few of them remain in the criminal class, they remain mainly because of some utilitarian effects which their perpetration may endanger.   Otherwise, almost all the actions

---

[81] This is well shown also by the lawbooks of India, whose culture has predominantly been Ideational.   Whether one takes the *Laws of Manu*, the *Instituts of Vishnu, Brihaspati, Gautama, Narada*, and other codes published in M. Müller's collection of the *Sacred Books of the East*, one can see this clearly.   The Ideational and Sensate codes differ also in their processual part; the Ideational codes use widely such evidences as "The Judgment of God," various ordeals, and similar supersensory evidences.   Sensate codes do not have them.   See the details in W. Robson, *Civilization and the Growth of Law* (New York, 1935), chap. x; A. S. Diamond, *Primitive Law* (London, 1935), chaps. xvii, xviii, and xxx.

considered criminal in such Sensate criminal codes are those which are thought of as socially dangerous, or dangerous to the governing part of the society, from the utilitarian, hedonistic, or eudaemonistic standpoints. If such dangers are not involved, the codes tend to regard all the actions which do not have such effects as normal and permitted, though from the Ideational standpoint many of them would appear as great crimes as the "unforgivable sin," "blasphemy," "sacrilege," "most outrageous profanity," and so on. On the other hand, such codes make a revaluation of the gravity of crimes, tending to regard as the gravest those actions which from the same hedonistic-utilitarian standpoint endanger the hedonistic-utilitarian values of a given society and especially of its commanding and controlling groups.

In accordance with this principle, the crimes against property values and against bodily comfort tend to increase in such codes.

As to the changes in the penal part, they consist in elimination of penalty for most Ideational crimes; in an enormous mitigation for the few Ideational actions that remain punishable; in the elimination of most of the punishments of purely Ideational nature, like anathema, deprivation of Christian burial, etc.

As to the comparative severity and amount of punishment in the Ideational and Sensate codes, there is hardly any ground to contend that, per se, one of these types is correlated with much greater or less punishment.[82] With some reservation, the comparative severity and amount of penalty depend not so much upon the predominant type of culture in which the code is enacted as upon how deeply it is rooted, settled, crystallized, and engrafted. When either one of these types is deeply rooted and settled, the punishment tends to be mild and moderate. When either one of them is in a state of transition, just being introduced or beginning to disintegrate, then the curve of penalty tends to go up, and the sharper the transition, the more pronounced the curve. This explains why the curve of penalty rose in the periods of transition from the Sensate to the Ideational form (in the centuries beginning with the third A.D., and following); or from the Ideational to the Sensate in the centuries beginning with the thirteenth, up to the seventeenth. If other disturbing factors are not present, each of these cultures, as it progresses in the crystallization of its network of social relationships and systems of values, tends to have a lesser and lesser penalty, quantitatively and qualitatively. An example

---

[82] With the exception of the "otherworldly" punishments (*in inferno* and the like) used by the Ideational mentality. But they hardly function in the codes. They are left to God. And, from the Sensate standpoint, they are unreal, anyhow.

of this is given by the centuries from the seventeenth to the beginning of the twentieth, when, short-time fluctuations excluded, the curve tended to decline.

Such is the general answer to this question. One reservation, however, should be made. All in all, it is possible that the Ideational Criminal Law tends generally to be somewhat more severe and stern than the normal Sensate criminal law (but not the Sensate law of the period of crisis, which tends to be outrageously rude, cruel, stern, and almost bestial in its real form in social life). There are several reasons for that : first, the requirements of Ideational culture, and its laws as to man's conduct, are generally more exacting and less loose and lenient than those of the Sensate law. The first aspires to a higher level of moral conduct, admits less opportunism, inhibits a greater number of the natural proclivities of sensate man than the opportunistic-utilitarian law. Therefore, the penal pressure of the Ideational criminal law should be, and is, somewhat greater than that of the purely Sensate criminal law. Without such pressure it can hardly reach even the minimum of its objective. Second, Ideational culture and law come usually after the disintegration of overripe Sensate culture and man, with appetites let loose, with hedonism, skepticism, sensualism rampant ; with the human personality deeply demoralized and disorderly. Under such circumstances, in order to discipline such a man and such a society ; in order successfully to bridle the rampant sensual appetites and passions, and engraft new forms of conduct inhibiting these tendencies, a culture and law cannot be too soft. One does not educate tigers not to touch a lamb by mere sermons and similar means. One needs a cage, sometimes a whip ; sometimes something still more severe and materially efficient. It is not my intention to claim that these rude and material ways and means have been the main and the most efficient means with which the newly coming Ideational culture disciplines man ; its other ways and means, of a nobler, more ingenuous, more "spiritual" nature, are certainly as efficient — nevertheless their work, especially in the initial stages of Ideational culture, has to be reinforced and supported by the ruder means of physical coercion and severe penalty. For these reasons, the average level of the Ideational penal system is likely to be more severe than that of the Sensate. This we see in the great expansion of punishable actions, as well as in an increase of penalty of the medieval codes in comparison with the Barbaric ; of the penal system of Rome in the centuries beginning with the third with that of preceding eras. As explained, the increase of punishment in these periods was due not only to the growth of Ideational culture, but also to the growth of the ethicojuridical heterogeneity of the population.

A further reservation to this reservation is that though Sensate law in normal society tends to be somewhat milder in its penal system than the Ideational penal system, nevertheless in the period of crisis, like revolution, when not only religious and inner moral control, generally weak in such a culture, ceases to regulate human behavior, but all the other inner — and often external — inhibitive factors cease to work, and man becomes like a little boat tossed aimlessly by the stormy passions of sensual nature — in such cases the real penal system of such a culture (not the fictitious one of the "revolutionary code") usually is incomparably more severe and cruel and blind than the system of Ideational culture. For in the Ideational culture, even in emergency crises, the inner inhibitions continue to work ; therefore they do not permit a purely cynical butchering and torturing of all the enemies of the ruling group, as is the case in the disintegrated Sensate culture in the periods of crisis. So much for this point.

(4) When one compares the essence of the hypothesis discussed with the main factor of social internal disturbances (see Part Three of Volume Three), one can easily see that the main reasons (or factors) for internal disturbances and crimes and penalty are practically the same. All of these are simultaneously the result, and at the same time a manifestation of a great or small, an extraordinary or ordinary, lack of perfect crystallization and unification of the system of social relationships and values. In psychological aspect, it is a great or small ethicocultural heterogeneity and antagonism. When this lack is small, and concerns only a small minority of the members of the society, it assumes the form of crime, that is a deviation from the accepted norms of conduct of only a small part of its members. When this lack becomes great and involves the deviation of conduct of the major part of the members, or even a considerable part, it becomes not crime, but riot, revolt, revolution. The violent appropriation of another's property by a few individuals is larceny, or robbery ; the same form of appropriation of another's property perpetrated by thousands and tens of thousands, becomes riot, revolt, revolution, or internal social disturbance. The same can be said of any other crime. When a few individuals refuse to obey the officials, they are guilty of a "crime against the State" ; when resistance to the government involves tens of thousands, the event changes its qualification and becomes again riot, revolt, revolution. Murder perpetrated by a few individuals is crime ; by many, "internal disturbance." And so on.

This shows that the crime and the disturbance phenomena are indeed of the same class, the main difference being the quantitative scale on which the respective form of conduct occurs.

Since they belong to the same class, to the same class belong their results. The main result is the increase of the intensity of the struggle between the parties and the use of rude and painful and physical means for inhibiting the conduct of the party which deviates from the norms backed and believed in by the opposite group. Physical force and painful coercion in the form of killing, arrest, confiscation of property, restriction of freedom of movement, and, generally, the infliction of various pains and deprivations upon the opposite party is the result. In the case of crime it is styled "penalty"; in the case of riots, revolutions, and so on, it also is often styled punishment (of the revolutionaries or counter-revolutionaries), vengeance, penalty, retribution, and so on; but more often it is styled more elegantly: "elimination of social parasites," "undeserved privileges," "annihilation of injustice and disfranchise-ments," "restoration of justice," "freedom," "liberty," and so on. The essence of the relationship between the struggling factions is, however, the same as that of the criminal and the public authority, namely, the use of violent and painful means toward the weaker party in the struggle: killing, torturing, infliction of bodily sufferings, deprivation and con-fiscation of property, banishment, imprisonment, deprivation of civil and other rights, detention, and so on. When these are inflicted upon a few criminals, they are punishment. When they are inflicted upon many, they are "instrumentalities and means of revolutionary struggle."

Since such is the situation, one can foresee what is to be the relationship between the curves of movement of the internal disturbances of crimes and of punishments. They have to go partly parallel, partly in opposite directions. If the mutual killings and other violent and painful forms of "internal warfare" inflicted by the opposite parties in the disturbances were not "swallowing" in their mass the cases of individual crimes and punishments; if, in addition, in all the disturbances the normal apparatus of justice (the codes, the laws, the courts, the trials, etc.) were not dis-organized and smashed, or brushed aside — under these conditions the three curves would all move parallel all the time. We know, however, that the real situation is often different; often the "swallowing" of the crimes by mass violence and the enormous number of actions of the same criminal type takes place; likewise, the normal special apparatus of justice is often brushed aside. Under these circumstances, the rise of crime and punishment can be lost in the internal disturbances, masked by them; therefore the rise may not show itself clearly in such periods. It is a well-established fact that a very large proportion of criminals enter, in the time of revolution, the army of the revolutionaries (or counterrevolutionaries) and do their killing, robbing, and other similar actions in the guise of revolutionary or counterrevolutionary conduct. Since there is a large river of mutual violent relationships, there is no need for little rivulets of the usual crimes; they become invisible in the large river of the disturbances. Hence, in such periods, the officially registered number of crimes may not show an increase. Since through special "extraordinary committees," through "martial laws," and so on, the dominant party may execute their opponents by hundreds and thousands, there is no need for the existing criminal codes to be made more severe. They are brushed aside; and the severest and greatest penalty is imposed through different channels. Therefore, the codes in such periods may not show any modification toward an increase in severity. On the contrary, as in the Code of 1791, which, being merely a Platonic code, exhibits what the dominant party would like to have as its ideal, but which does not hinder a practice quite opposite to it, they may even show a desire to shine in compassion, humanitarianism, mildness, and similar qualities — like Robespierre, who sent daily many persons to the guillotine and in the evenings read and cried over the sentimental writings of Bernardin St. Pierre. Such a code can afford to be humanitarian and noble and compassionate. Therefore, in itself, it would exhibit again a trend opposite to the real trend of punishment.

Thus in all such cases, outwardly the movement of crimes, punishments, and internal disturbances will be not parallel, but opposite, "compensatory."

Compensatory also is the relationship of these curves in the periods when the high tide of social disorganization and demoralization begins to fall, and socioethical order begins to be reinforced more and more. As the curve of social disturbances declines, the curve of crime and penalty may be rising, because now most of the crimes are not drowned in the ocean of mass violence; they begin to be more and more distinguishable from this ocean, as individual crimes. An improved and reinforced apparatus of justice now begins to treat them as crimes; begins to catch their perpetrators more and more successfully, and, mutual mass punishments of the disturbances declining, the severe individual punishments inflicted through the normal apparatus of justice are imposed. Being imposed in this way, they appear outwardly in the form of increase of the quantitative and qualitative punishments of the codes and criminal law.

Viewed as a whole, such periods mean that society, all in all, moves toward greater order and harmonious unity, in spite of the fact that crime and punishment of law show an increase. And vice versa. If and when the curve of disturbance begins to rise, while the curve of punishment and crime in the sense of criminal law remains static, or even goes down in the frequency of crimes and the severity of punishment, such periods may often indicate a rising tide of social disorganization and antagonism, in spite of the fact that the criminal law shows the opposite.

Under these circumstances, then, the movement of these three curves may be "compensatory," that is, outwardly either opposite or unrelated. When these and similar circumstances are absent, their movement may be parallel. Such is the explanation of this seeming inconsistency of the movement of the three curves.

(5) Turning to our other indicators of the movement of the internal disturbances (taken from Part Three of Volume Three), crimes, and punishments, we see this empirically. In Rome, the disturbances grew from the second to the fourth century A.D., from 267.92 to 475.79 in the third, and 368.95 in the fourth century. Then they fall sharply to 142.82 in the fifth century. We know that beginning with practically the same second century, the curve of penalty began to grow also. The punishments began to be more severe and more frequently imposed. Thus here we have a parallelism; all three curves indicate uniformly the progressing disorganization of the Roman society. In the fifth century the disturbances fall, but the punishments do not show such a movement. If anything, they probably have become more severe. The explanation is that the social order began to be more firmly established; the high tide of internal disturbances began to ebb; therefore, the small rivulets of the individual crimes and imposed punishments began to be more noticeable on the "beach" freed from the tide of disturbances. The process continued during the next few centuries, as the data for Byzantium and Italy show; the disturbances continued to decrease; the apparatus of normal criminal justice continued to function more and more vigorously and the penal system continued to grow in severity.

Turning to Europe, we see that the disturbances remain fairly low in the centuries from the ninth to the thirteenth; but the criminal justice was rather stern and severe during that period. During the thirteenth and fourteenth centuries the disturbances went up greatly. The penal system did not show any sign of mitigation. This means that the social disorganization of the previously existing system, its shattering and deepest transformations, were progressing also.

In the sixteenth, the seventeenth, and the eighteenth (up to its last quarter) centuries, the disturbances decreased, and during the same centuries we had the greatest mitigation of the penal system. All this testifies that the new social order began to be rooted in the fifteenth century and became stronger and more definite during the sixteenth, seventeenth, and eighteenth centuries.

At the end of the eighteenth century, the disturbances began to grow, though not very strongly at first. The penal system, however, continued (with the exception of the end of the eighteenth and of the first part of the nineteenth century) its process of mitigation. This means that at the end of the eighteenth century, a new process of disintegration of the social system of relationships and values entrenched during the previous centuries had already begun. But, short-lived violent outbursts excepted, it proceeded to progress slowly, but not deeply as yet, throughout the first part of the nineteenth century. In its second part it temporarily subsided. This is testified to by the fact that the indicator for the disturbances for that part of the century went down, and that the penal machinery did not become more severe.

(6) The twentieth century changes the picture. After the orderly last quarter of the nineteenth century, the curve of disturbances in the first quarter of the twentieth greatly rose; the severity of the penal system, especially of postwar criminal codes, increased also. This means that the process of disorganization started at the end of the eighteenth century and waveringly continued in the nineteenth century, gathered momentum, and greatly increased in the twentieth century, showing itself in the increase of the disturbances as well as the severity (and also amount) of punishment. Both "barometers" register "storm" in that century. Both indicate a great stride in the way of splitting and shattering of the previously existing social order, and entrance into a period of disorganization and demoralization.

Such is the interpretation of the data on disturbances and crime and punishments in the light of the hypothesis discussed. It elucidates why the relationship of the three curves sometimes is parallel, sometimes "compensatory"; in spite of the fact that all of them are the symptoms of the same phenomenon of increase of socioethical heterogeneity and disorganization of the system of social relationships and values. It explains also that, used as "barometers," these three classes of phenomena permit us to make the following diagnoses.

(a) When in a given society the curves of disturbances, crimes, and punishments all go up, it is a sure sign that the society is in a status of the sharpest disorganization of its system of relationships and social values. It is in the deepest crisis.

(b) When all these curves go down, it is the surest sign that the society is rapidly progressing toward the strongest stabilization of its socioethical mentality, social relationships and values. It is on the way to the strongest social and mental stability and order.

(c) When the curve of disturbances rises, but the curves of crimes and punishments do not rise, and even go down, this is a sign that the society is entering mildly and slowly the period of disorganization.

(d) When the curve of disturbances falls, but the curve of crimes and punishments goes up, this is a fairly definite sign that the society is beginning to move toward a consolidation of its social order, its system of relationships and values (including the ethicojuridical homogeneity).[83]

(7) In conclusion, it is to be noted again that the centuries from the second to the fifth A.D., and those from the twelfth to the fifteenth, and finally the twentieth, come out as the most disorganized periods, as the centuries of the deepest and greatest shattering of social orders and values. From the other parts of this work, we already know that these earlier centuries were the periods of the deepest transformations of culture, the centuries of the transition from the Sensate to the Ideational culture (from the second to the fifth A.D.) ; and from Ideational to Sensate (from the twelfth to the fifteenth). The data on the disturbances and the criminal law show that once more, in their own way, indicating the validity of our basic theory and, in the light of it, that of the above analysis and interpretation of disturbances, crimes, and punishments.

So this division of culture well fits into the whole picture painted in this study and gives an additional proof of its inner coherency, its consistent style, and its meaningfulness.[84]

[83] From this standpoint a relatively high level of criminality and punishment in a country which is relatively free from disturbances is by itself not a particularly disquieting symptom. On the contrary, it is rather reassuring that its social order is sufficiently strong; anyhow, stronger than in a society with low criminality and weak penal system, but with frequent riots, revolts, and other disturbances. From this standpoint the high level of crimes and partly even of penalty in the United States for the last century, coupled with the relatively infrequent and small social disturbances, with the exception of the Civil War which was a great internal disturbance, is a sign that the whole social order in the country was stronger than in many other countries. Here is, if one pleases, an apology for criminality and severity of the penal system versus social disturbances. The high criminality with seemingly increasing social disturbances of the present time is, on the contrary, a disquieting symptom.

[84] I had to omit several appendixes to this chapter, as they are very cumbersome and too extensive to print. They are deposited in the Sociology Library of Harvard University.

VI. Entr'acte : Coefficients of Correlation
between the Variables

Before passing to the next volume, let us pause and indicate briefly the movements of the Ideational and Sensate variables studied. I have mentioned many times that in the main movements all the Ideational variables have proceeded in a tangible parallelism with one another, while all the Sensate variables have done the same in regard to their movements. I pointed out also that this association is imperfect, how-ever, due first to the principle of the "margin of autonomy" and "internal self-regulation" possessed by any integrated system; and also to inter-ference of other (cosmic and biological) forces that may decrease or break the logically expected association (see about that principle in Chapter One of Volume One, and especially in Volume Four), to an incomplete-ness of the materials, and to other factors. How close is the association of the variables of each of the two types of culture and how large is the "margin of autonomy" within which each of these have independently moved is pictorially shown by Figures 19 and 20. Each of these depicts the movement of eight variables (eight Ideational, and eight Sensate) during the periods studied. Glancing at these, we can easily see: first, that for several centuries of the Middle Ages their association was prac-tically perfect; all the eight variables of Sensate culture coincide upon zero line; and seven of the eight Ideational variables coincide upon 100 per cent line.[85]

For other periods, the tidal trends of these variables are also similar, but imperfect. Their secondary movements rise and decline with a substantial degree of independence. Expressed in musical terms, their scores are not unisonic (as they are in the medieval centuries), but polyphonic. Likewise, their tempo and rhythm are not the same all the time. In many respects their total character reminds one of a complex fugue. It is, however, a fugue written not so much by the classic and

---

[85] Deviation of the line of Eternalism (Figure 19) for the centuries from the eighth to tenth is not a deviation in fact. As explained in Chapter Five of this volume, we put most of these theories of that period into the class of the "Equilibrium of Both." The thinkers put into this class recognize the reality of both aspects — temporalistic and eternalistic — and give the priority to the eternalistic aspect; but for formal reasons they were put not into the class of the "Eternalists" but in that of the "Equilibrium." Hence, decrease of the percentage for the Eternalists for that period, and the deviation discussed. That it is not a real devia-tion is supported by Figure 20, where the line of Temporalism for that period is zero line, that is, the period did not have at all purely or even predominantly temporalistic theories, and the whole field was occupied with either eternalistic or eternalistic-temporalistic mentality. Viewed in this light, the deviation becomes in fact much less significant than it appears in Figure 20.

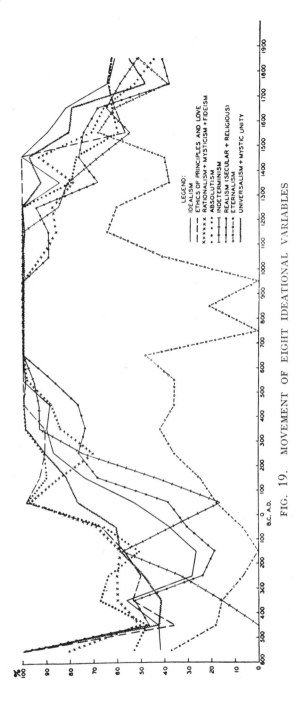

FIG. 19. MOVEMENT OF EIGHT IDEATIONAL VARIABLES

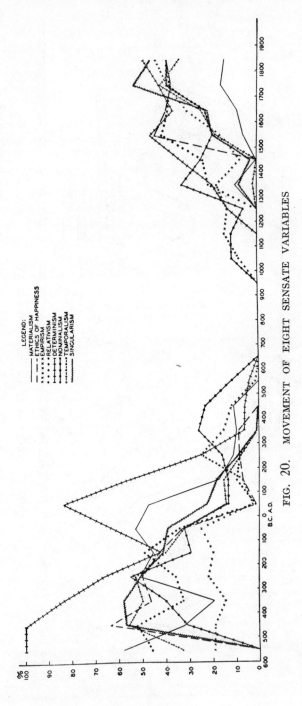

FIG. 20. MOVEMENT OF EIGHT SENSATE VARIABLES

puristic composers of the centuries from the fourteenth to the eighteenth, but one made by a composer of more modern times, who has infused into the grand fugue many dissonances, atonalities, and other complications.

And still, in spite of all this "modernistic complexity," the similarity of rising and declining tidal trends of all the eight variables of each type of culture is evident. It is evident also that in their autonomous movements, these variables do not exhibit any uniformity, in that some of them always change the first while the others always lag; or that they all move always parallel; or that there are no consonances or no dissonances in their movements. All this means a repudiation of many a fashionable theory in the social sciences about the existence of uniformity of "lag," of periodicity, and of many other opinions so uncritically and baselessly accepted by many.

Figures 19 and 20 show also that the cultures studied have indeed been integrated to a tangible degree, causally and functionally, but this integration, even within these variables, has not been perfect. For the present, these remarks are sufficient; in Volume Four, many of these problems will be analyzed more seriously.

In the elucidation of this problem, I have not, so far, used the language of statistical correlation, for reasons that must be clear to every competent statistician. However, several computations of the coefficients of the correlation, for the variables involved, for the specific periods of the whole twenty-five hundred years were made. They can hardly add anything new and important to what has already been shown; but for the satisfaction of many who think still that "all laws and prophets" are given in the coefficients of the correlation, a few of these coefficients may be given here. They only confirm what has been said above. Here are the samples.

A. Correlation coefficients between *idealism* and *all the non-empirical theories of truth* (rationalism, mysticism, fideism, skepticism, criticism).

(1) For the medieval centuries it is perfect; for the periods 580 B.C. to A.D. 160, r is .51; for 580 B.C.–A.D. 140, r is .52; for A.D. 180–520, .669; for A.D. 160–520, .51; for 1500–1900, .86. Thus the coefficients show the existence of a tangible positive correlation between these variables; but it is, though tangible and high (and if the perfect correlation for the medieval centuries is included, the coefficient will be still higher), not perfect. The variables have a tangible autonomy in their secondary movements. The relationship between idealism and empiri-

cism has shown a negative correlation : for instance, for the period 1500–1900, *r* is minus .832.

(2) If the nonempirical systems of truth are broken into their main currents, then the coefficients of the correlations between the specified periods and variables appear to be as follows.

(a) Between *rationalism* and *idealism:* 580 B.C.–20 B.C., .796 ; A.D. 0–520, .619.

(b) Between *mysticism* and *idealism:* 580 B.C.–A.D. 520, .77 ; 1500–1900, .73.

(c) *Skepticism* and *idealism:* 560 B.C.–A.D. 200, minus .44.

(d) *Fideism* and *idealism:* 400 B.C.–A.D. 260, minus .78 ; for 1500–1900, no correlation.

(e) *Absolutism* and *idealism:* 540 B.C.–A.D. 520, .67 ; 1500–1900, .33.

(f) *Materialism* and *relativism:* .43.

(g) *Ethics of happiness* and *idealism:* 540 B.C.–20 B.C., minus .59 ; A.D. 0–380, very insignificant ; A.D. 380–1480, perfect negative correlation ; 1500–1900, minus .41.

(h) *Ethics of happiness* and *materialism:* 440 B.C.–A.D. 380, very low positive correlation ; A.D. 580–1500 both are absent ; 1500–1900, .44.

(i) *Ethics of principles* and *idealism:* 540 B.C.–A.D. 340, .59 ; 1500–1900, .56 ; 600–1500, almost perfect positive correlation.

(j) *Ethics of happiness* and *empiricism:* 440 B.C.–A.D. 180, .62 ; for several centuries of the Middle Ages, both are absent ; for 1500–1900, .47 ; for 1600–1900, .73.

(k) *Ethics of principles* and *empiricism:* 540 B.C–A.D. 520, minus .28 ; for the Middle Ages, empiricism absent while the ethics of principles and love occupy almost 100 per cent (perfect negative relationship) ; for 1500–1900, minus .61 ; for 1600–1900, minus .92.

Without giving other coefficients of the correlations computed (some for the same variables, but for shorter periods ; some others for other variables), the above gives an idea of the relationship between these and other Sensate and Ideational variables when it is expressed in the terms of the correlation coefficients. A careful study of these hardly adds anything new to what has been said of their relationships in the preceding chapters ; they simply corroborate the verbal and pictorial characteristics given.

APPENDIXES

LIST OF THINKERS FOR EACH PERIOD, WITH THE VALUE GIVEN TO EACH ON A SCALE 1 TO 12

Graeco-Roman and European-Christian Cultures

RATIONALISM (560 B.C.–A.D. 1920)

B.C. 560–540   total 10
———— Anaximander 5, Xenophanes 5

540–520   total 18
———— Anaximander 5, Xenophanes 5, Pythagoras 8

520–500   total 20
———— Herakleitos 7, Xenophanes 5, Pythagoras 8

500–480   total 27
———— Herakleitos 7, Xenophanes 5, Parmenides 7, Pythagoras 8

480–460   total 20
Herakleitos 7, Hippasos 1, Parmenides 7, Zenon 5

460–440   total 17
———— Anaxagoras 5, Archelaos 1, Hippasos 1, Kratylos 2, Zenon 5, Melissos 3

440–420   total 22
———— Anaxagoras 5, Archelaos 1, Hippasos 1, Kratylos 2, Zenon 5, Melissos 3, Philolaos 5

420–400   total 22
———— Kratylos 2, Melissos 3, Philolaos 5, Simmias 1, Kebes 1, Lysis 1, Socrates 9

400–380   total 30
———— Kratylos 2, Eukleides 3, Phaidon 2, Philolaos 5, Simmias 1, Kebes 1, Lysis 1, Socrates 9, Aeschines 3, Eurytos 1, Archytas 1, Hiketas 1

380–360   total 24
———— Eukleides 3, Phaidon 2, Eubulides 1, Aeschines 3, Platon 12, Eurytos 1, Archytas 1, Hiketas 1

360–340   total 23
———— Phaidon 2, Eubulides 1, Aeschines 3, Hiketas 1, Ekphantos 2, Xenophilos 1, Phanton 1, Echekrates 1, Diokles 1, Polymnastos 1, Spensippos 3, Eudoxos 3, Herakleides 3

340–320   total 31
———— Eubulides 1, Diodoras 2, Stilpon 2, Aristotle 12, Xenophilos 1, Phanton 1, Echekrates 1, Diokles 1, Polymnastos 1, Speusippos 3, Eudoxos 3, Herakleides 3

320–300   total 38
———— Diodoros 2, Stilpon 2, Alexinos 1, Menedemos 2, Aristotle 12, Theophrastos 7, Eudemos 2, Xenophilos 1, Phanton 1, Echekrates 1, Diokles 1, Polymnastos 1, Herakleides 3, Polemon 2

300–280   total 23
———— Stilpon 2, Alexinos 1, Menedemos 2, Theophrastos 7, Eudemos 2, Asclepiades 2, Polemon 2, Krantor 4, Krates 1

280–260   total 11
———— Menedemos 2, Asclepiades 2, Polemon 2, Krantor 4, Krates 1

260–240   total 3
———— Lykon 1, Hieronymos 2

240–220   total 4
———— Lykon 1, Hieronymos 2, Prytanis 1

220–200   total 8
———— Ariston 3, Prytanis 1, Satyros 3, Hermippos 1

200–180   total 9
———— Ariston 3, Satyros 3, Hermippos 1, Sotion 2

NOTES TO ALL THE SUBSEQUENT APPENDIXES

Besides the works indicated in the text, the following sources were consulted: R. Schmidt, *Die Deutsche Philosophie der Gegenwart in Selbstdarstellungen* (Leipzig, 1920); J. H. Muirhead, *Contemporary British Philosophy*, 2 vols. (New York, 1924); *Contemporary American Philosophy*, 2 vols. (New York, 1930); V. Parrington, *Main Currents in American Thought* (NewYork, 1927–1930). All the volumes of F. Überweg's *Grundriss der Geschichte der Philosophie*, mentioned (Volumes IV (Berlin, 1923) and V (Berlin, 1928) re-edited by T. K. Oesterreich).

The Graeco-Roman and some of the medieval names are not uniformly standardized in view of an absense of any generally accepted transliteration of these names.

With few exceptions, the initials of the thinkers are not given: specialists can easily determine who of the thinkers is meant; if need be, one can easily find the initials in the dictionaries and works referred to.

A few names are put in the period after their death. The reason for this is either a publication of their posthumous works, or the founding of a journal or society for the propagation of the theories of such a thinker, or other similar reasons evidencing a continuation and resuscitation of the influence of the thinker.

180–160   total 6
——————— Sotion 2, Antisthenes 2, Kritolaos 2

160–140   total 5
——————— Antisthenes 2, Kritolaos 2, Herakleides 1

140–120   total 2
——————— Herakleides 1, Diodoros 1

120–100   total 2
——————— Diodoros 1, Erimnaeus 1

100–80   total 5
——————— Diodoros 1, Erimnaeus 1, Philon Lar. 3

80–60   total 16
——————— Andronikos 2, Xenarchos 1, Ariston 1, Philon Lar. 3, Antiochos 4, T. Varro 5

60–40   total 10
——————— Xenarchos 1, Ariston 1, Andronikos 2, T. Varro 5, Aristos 1

40–20   total 12
——————— Andronikos 2, Q. Sextius 2, T. Varro 5, Theomnetes 1, Derkylides 2

20–0   total 7
——————— Q. Sextius 2, Sextius Jr. 1, Nicolaus 2, Derkylides 2

A.D. 0–20   total 9
——————— Boethos 1, Sextius Jr. 1, Nicolaus 2, Sotion 2, Cornelius Celsus 1, L. Crassicius 1, Fabianus Papirius 1

20–40   total 5
——————— Sotion 2, Cornelius Celsus 1, L. Crassicius 1, Fabianus Papirius 1

40–60   total 2
——————— Alexandros 2

60–80   total 2
——————— Alexandros 2

80–100   total 2
——————— Ptolemaios Chennos 2

100–120   total 12
——————— Ptolemaios 2, Περὶ Κόσμον 4, Aspasios 2, Adrastos 2, Christian school 2

120–140   total 8
——————— Aspasios 2, Adrastos 2, Ptolemaios 2, Christian school 2

140–160   total 14
——————— Aspasios 2, Adrastos 2, Herminos 2, Klaudios 3, Iustinus Martyr 5

160–180   total 15
——————— Herminos 2, Klaudios 3, Aristokles 1, Iustinus Martyr 5, Minucius Felix 4

180–200   total 26
——————— Herminos 2, Klaudios 3, Aristokles 1, Alexandros (Aphr.) 6, Athenagoras 4, Minucius Felix 4, Theophilus (Ant.) 2, Irenaeus (Lugd.) 4

200–220   total 13
——————— Alexandros (Aphr.) 6, Irenaeus (Lugd.) 4, Hippolytus 3

220–240   total 9
——————— Alexandros (Aphr.) 6, Hippolytus 3

240–260   total 3
——————— Peripatetic school 1, Dionysius Magnus 2

260–280   total 3
——————— Peripatetic school 1, Dionysius Magnus 2

280–300   total 2
——————— Peripatetic school 1, Christian school 1

300–320   total 4
——————— Alexandros (Lykop.) 2, Methodius (Phil.) 2

320–340   total 16
——————— Chalcidius 4, Athanasius Magnus 4, Lactantius 4, Arius 4

340–360   total 12
——————— Chalcidius 4, Athanasius Magnus 4, Arius 4

360–380   total 16
——————— Themistios 3, Athanasius Magnus 4, Hilarius (Poit.) 3, Marius Victorinus 4, Aetios 2

380–400   total 16
——————— Themistios 3, Ambrosius Mediol. 3, Augustinus 10

400–420   total 20
——————— Hypatia 1, Domninos 1, Olympiodoros 2, Theodorus (Mops.) 1, Cyrillus (Alex.) 2, Iulian (Ekl.) 1, Pelagius 2, Augustinus 10

420–440   total 22
——————— Domninos 1, Olympiodoros 2, Hierakles 1, Theodorus (Mops.) 1, Cyrillus (Alex.) 2, Iulian (Ekl.) 1, Pelagius 2, Nestorius 2, Augustinus 10

440–460   total 14
——————— Domninos 1, Hierakles 2, Cyrillus (Alex.) 2, Nestorius 2, Eutyches 3, Others 4

460–480   total 11
——————— Ammonios Hermeion 2, Asklepios 1, Olympiodoros Jr. 2, Claudianus Mamertus 3, Eutyches 3

480–500   total 11
——————— Ammonios Hermeion 2, Asklepios 1, Olympiodoros Jr. 2, Elias 1, David 2, Aineas Gazensis 2, Acacius 1

500–520   total 16
——————— Ammonios Hermeion 2, Elias 1, David 2, Simplikios 5, Aineas Gazensis 2, Procopius Gaz. 3, Severus 1

520–540   total 24
——————— Simplikios 5, Aineas Gaz. 2, Procopius Gaz. 3, Boethius 6, Leontius (Byz.) 3, Ioannes Philop. 4, Severus 1

540–560   total 17
——————— Simplikios 5, Leontius (Byz.) 3, Ioannes Philop. 4, Zacharias (Myt.) 2, Cassiodorus 3

560–580   total 6
——————— Greek-Roman culture 1, Cassiodorus 3, Martinus Brac. 2

580–600   total 8
——————— Stephanos 2, Martinus Bracar. 2, Gregorius I, Magnus 4

600–620   total 10
——————— Stephanos 2, Isidorus Hispelevsis 4, Gregorius I, Magnus 4

620–640   total 6
——————— Stephanos 2, Isidorus Hispelevsis 4

640–660   total 3
——————— Stephanos 2, Samuel Tajus 1

660–680   total 2
——————— Adatho 2

680–700   total 2
——————— Adatho 2

700–720   total 3
——————— Beda Venerabilis 3

720–740   total 8
——————— Beda Venerabilis 3, Ioannes Damasc. 5

740–760   total 5
——————— Ioannes Damasc. 5

760–780   total 1
——————— Egbertus 1

780–800   total 4
——————— Alcuinus 4

800–820   total 6
——————— Alcuinus 4, Fredegisus 2

820–840   total 8
——————— Fredegisus 2, Hrabanus Maurus 4, Candidus 2

840–860   total 8
——————— Hrabanus Maurus 4, Servetus Lupus 2, Paschasius Radbertus 2

860–880   total 9
——————— Servetus Lupus 2, Paschasius Radbertus 2, Ratramnus 2, Photius 3

880–900   total 3
——————— Photius 3

900–920   total 2
——————— Arethas 2

920–940   total 2
——————— Arethas 2

940–960   total 1

960–980   total 1

980–1000   total 3
——————— Sylvester II (Gerbert) 3

1000–1020   total 6
——————— Notker Labeo 3, Sylvester II (Gerbert) 3

1020–1040   total 3
——————— Notker Labeo 3

1040–1060   total 8
——————— Berengarius T. 3, Anselmus (Bes.) 2, Lanfrancus 3

1060–1080   total 11
——————— Berengarius T. 3, Anselmus (Bes.) 2, Lanfrancus 3, Mich. Psellos 3

1080–1100   total 9
——————— Berengarius 3, Lanfrancus 3, Mich. Psellos 3

1100–1120   total 7
——————— Odo 1, Adelard of Bath 2, Bruno (Segni) 2, Guilelmus Camp. 2

1120–1140   total 17
——————— Adelard of Bath 2, Bruno (Segni) 2, Guilelmus Camp. 2, P. Abaelardus 4, Bernardus Carn. 2, Guilelmus de Conch. 2, Honorius Aug. 3

1140–1160   total 21
——————— P. Abaelardus 4, Robertus Melid. 2, Guilelmus de Conch. 2, Honorius Aug. 3, Joscellin 1, Gualterus de Maur. 1, Petrus Lombardus 4, Dominicus Gundiss 2, Bernardus Silv. 2

1160–1180   total 17
——————— Gualterus de Maur. 1, Robertus Melid. 2, Petrus Lombardus 4, Dominicus Gundiss 2, Gandulfus 2, Rolendus Band. 2, Petrus Comestor 2, Bernardus Silv. 2

1180–1200   total 6
——————— Rolendus Band. 2, Petrus Pictav. 2, Petrus Cantor 2

1200–1220   total 15
——————— Petrus Pictav. 2, Nicolaus Ambian. 2, Simon de Tornaco 1, Praepositinus 2, Robertus de Corcion 1, Guilelmus (Aux.) 2, Philippus Grevius 2, David Dinantensis 3

1220–1240   total 17
——————— Praepositinus 2, Guilelmus (Aux.) 2, Philippus Grevius 2, Guilelmus Alvernus 3, Robert Grosseteste 4, Alexander Halensis 4

1240–1260   total 29
——————— Guilelmus Alvernus 3, Robert Grosseteste 4, Alexander Halensis 4, Walter (Ch.–Th.) 1, Ioannes de Rupella 2, Hugo (St. Cher.) 2, Albertus Magnus 8, Guilelmus Shyreswood. 1, Nikephoros Blemmyd. 1, Vincentius Bellovac. 2, Richard Fischacre 1

1260–1280   total 44
——————— Siger (Brabant) 4, Boethius de Dacia 2, Hugo (St. Char.) 2, Albertus Magnus 8, Nikephoros Blemm. 1, Vincentius Bellovac. 2, Robert Kilward. 2, Thomas (York) 2, Thomas Aquinas 12, Ulricus 3, Petrus de Tarentas 2, Petrus Hispanus 2, Bombolognus de Bon. 1, Romanus de Rome 1

1280–1300   total 56
———————— Albertus Magnus 8, Ragmundus
Lullus 5, Witelo 2, Guilelmus de la Mere 1,
Henricus Gandav. 4, Gottfried (Font.) 3, Bernardus de Trilia 2, Aegidius (Lessines) 2, Remigio
di Ch. d. G. 2, Ioannes (Genua) 1, Ramberto dei
Prim. 1, Aegidius Romanus 3, Georgios Pachymeres 2, Sophonias 2, Hugo Ripelin 3, Matthaeus
ab Ag. 2, Nicolaus (Ockham) 1, Roger (Marston)
2, Guilelmus (Ware) 2, Guilelmus (Hothun) 1,
Richard (Clapwell) 1, Siger of Brabant 4, Boethius
de Dacia 2

1300–1320   total 53
———————— Ragmundus Lullus 5, Gottfried
(Font.) 3, Aegidius (Less.) 2, Remigio di Ch. d. G.
2, Ioannes (Genua) 1, Ramberto dei Prim. 1,
Aegidius Romanus 3, Georgios Pachym. 2,
Sophonias 2, Matthaeus ab Ag. 2, Guilelmus
(Ware) 2, Bernardus de Alv. 1, Jean Quidort 2,
Guilelmus P. de G. 2, Hervé Nédélec 3, Tolomeo
(Lucca) 2, Guilelmus Mackl. 1, Jacobus Capocci 2,
Gerbart (Bol.) 2, I. Duns Scotus 8, Jacobus
(Metz) 2, Thomas (Sutton) 2, Pietro d' Abano 1

1320–1340   total 30
———————— Guilelmus Petri de G. 2, Hervé
Nédélee 3, Tolomeo (Lucca) 2, Thomas (Sutton)
2, Siger (Courtrai) 2, Petrus de Palude 1, Jacobus
(Laus.) 1, Ioannes de Reg. 1, Ioannes Pic. de Luc.
2, Nicolaus Trivet 2, Guido Terreni 2, Siegbert
(Beck.) 2, Bartoldus de Mosb. 1, Antonius An-
dreas 1, Heinrich (Lübeck.) 1, Franciscus de
Mayronis 2, Walter Burleigh 1, Ioannes
(Baconth.) 2

1340–1360   total 13
———————— Thomas (Sutton) 2, Petrus de Palude
1, Guido Terreni 2, Walter Burleigh 1, Bernardus
Lomb. 1, Durandellus 1, Thomas (Strassb.) 2,
Ioannes (Baconth.) 2, Urban 1

1360–1380   total 4
———————— Marsilius (Inghen.)   2,   Heinrich
(Hainbuch) 2

1380–1400   total 4
———————— Marsilius (Inghen.)   2,   Heinrich
(Hainbuch) 2.

1400–1420   total 2
———————— Paulus (Venetia) 2

1420–1440   total 9
———————— Ioannes Capreolus 3, Heinrich (Gorkum) 1, Antonin 3, Paulus (Venetia) 2

1440–1460   total 9
———————— Ioannes Capreolus 3, Antonin 3,
Heimerich de Campo 1, Cajetanus Thiaencus 2

1460–1480   total 3
———————— Petrus Nigri 1, Cajetanus Thiaencus 2

1480–1500   total 3
———————— Petrus Nigri 1, Petrus Tartaretus 1,
Nicoletto Vernias 1

1500–1520   total 4
———————— Pico della Mirandola 4

1520–1540   total 4
———————— Pico della Mirandola 4

1540–1560   total 4
———————— Serveto 4

1560–1580   total 14
———————— Copernicus 8, Marsilius Ficinus 4,
Lever 1, Wilson 1

1580–1600   total 20
———————— G. Bruno 8, Suarez 6, Case 1, R. Scotus
2, Wilson 1, Sanderson 1, Lever 1

1600–1620   total 39
———————— Descartes 8, Galileo 8, G. Bruno 8,
Keppler 8, Harvey 4, Scotus 2, Sanderson 1

1620–1640   total 39
———————— Descartes 8, Keppler 8, Comenius 7,
Galileo 8, Regius 3, Mersenne 5

1640–1660   total 42
———————— Galileo 8, Descartes 8, Comenius 7,
J. van Helmont 4, E. Weigel 4, Harvey 4, Regius
3, Renery 1, De Raey 1, Culverwell 1, Brooke 1

1660–1680   total 74
———————— Rohault 1, De Raey 1, Pascal 7,
Malebranche 7, Nicole 4, Le Grand 1, Heereboord
1, De la Forge 1, Geulinex 6, Clauberg 3, H. Morus
4, Wilkins 1, Leibnitz 9, Spinoza 8, Thomasius 4,
Cudworth 5, Heidanius 1, Arnauld 4, Weigel 4

1680–1700   total 84
———————— Bossuet 6, Fénelon 6, Reynaud 2,
Toland 4, Cordemoy 2, Rohault 1, De la Forge 3,
Arnauld 4, Nicole 4, Leibnitz 9, Malebranche 7,
Benker 4, Wittich 1, Clauberg 3, Cudworth 5,
H. Morus 4, Lamy 1, Lanion 1, Volthaysen 1,
J. Tomasius 2, Thomassin 1, Pordage 1, J. Jelles 1,
De Vries 1, Wreen 4, Wallis 3, Tilletson 2, Olden-
burg 1

1700–1720   total 63
———————— Bossuet 6, Fénelon 6, Collier 5, Reg-
naud 1, Wittich 1, Malebranche 7, Tindal 2,
Fardella 2, Collins 2, Chubb 1, Boerhave 4,
Giovenale 2, Taylor 1, Thomassin 1, André 1,
Leibnitz 9, Wolf 7, Masonic "rationalistic
currents" 4, Leenhof 1

1720–1740   total 35
———————— J. J. Lange 2, Tindal 2, Billfinger
1, André 1, Buddaeus 2, Collins 2, Crousaz 2,
Wolf 7, Gottsched 2, Leibnitz 9 (posthumous
works), Boerhaave 3, Reinbeck 1, Boulinvillier 1

1740–1760   total 73
———————— Morgan 1, Edelmann 1, Polignac 4,
Crousaz 2, Vico 7, Wolf 7, Swedenborg 4, Kant
12, Fontenelle 2, Gerdil 2, Lomonosov 4, Lam-
bert 4, Reinbeck 1, Hollmann 1, Baumgarten 4,
M. Knutzen 4, Crusius 2, Gottsched 2, Davies 2,
Plouquet 4, Gellert 1

1760–1780   total 53
———— Kant 12, Boscovich 4, Baumgarten 4, Tetens 4, Swedenborg 4, Lomonosov 4, Plouquet 4, Euler 6, Lessing 6, Lambert 4, Ickstadt 1

1780–1800   total 68
———— Fichte Sr. 8, Schelling 8, Nithammer 2, Forberg 2, Laplace 8, Lessing 6, Mendelssohn 4, Eberhard 1, Garve 1, Hegel 8, Tittel 1, Schwab 1, Weisshaupt 4, Goethe 8, Bonnet 5, Feder 1

1800–1820   total 78
———— Windischmann 1, Fichte 8, Laplace 8, Schelling 8, Hegel 8, Rattenhofer 1, Stuzmann 1, Oken 3, Troxler 1, Ast 1, J. Wagner 1, Rixmann 1, Ehrenbeck 1, Steffens 2, Schad 2, Memel 1, Krause 4, Tennemann 2, Lamarque 8, Wronski 6, Vellansky 1, Pavlov 1, Goethe 8

1820–1840   total 78
———— V. Cousin 4, Whewell 6, Ampère 5, Fourier 5, Damiron 2, A. Franck 1, Sasset 1, Hegel 8, Goethe 8, Herbart 7, Galitch 2, Bolzano 6, Wronsky 6, Laplace 8, Palov 1, Herzen 4, Khomiakov 4

1840–1860   total 97
———— G. Biedermann 1, A. Biedermann 1, Carove 2, Češkovsky 1, Daub 1, J. E. Erdmann 4, Kuno Fischer 4, Gabler 1, Goeschl 1, Reiff 1, Rosmini 6, Boole 4, Lasson 3, Th. Vischer 4, Zeising 2, Kremer 4, Dombrovsky 1, Liebelt 4, Rosenkrantz 4, Schasler 1, H. Schwarz 1, Marheinecke 1, Cousin 4, Vatke 1, Gans 1, Čičerin 4, Vera 2, De Morgan 2, Zeller 5, Fechner 7, A. Smetana 4, Planck 1, Prantl 4, Herzen 4, Riemann 6

1860 1880   total 80
———— Kuno Fischer 4, Lassale 4, Čičerin 4, Vera 2, J. Erdmann 4, V. Cousin 4, Riemann 6, Paul Janet 4, Fr. Boullier 2, Strachov 3, Lioubimov 2, Fechner 7, Ravaisson 3, Remusat 3, Spaventa 4, Planck 1, Grassmann 4, B. Bauer 2, Zeller 5, Brentano 4, Vatke 1, Lasson 3, Cournot 5

1880–1900   total 90
———— Čičerin 4, Bradley 7, Bosanquet 4, Rehmke 7, Penjon 3, Schasler 2, Strachov 3, Fiorentino 2, Erkole 2, Debolsky 1, Jevons 5, Lasson 3, Michelet 2, Cantor 4, Dedekind 2, Zeller 5, K. Fischer 4, Cohen 7, Schröder 4, Edgeworth 4, Bakunin 2, Hamelin 4, McTaggart 5, Bugaiev 3, Vatke 1

1900–1920   total 107 [1]
———— Bradley, B. Croce, Rehmke, Cohen, Royce, Schuppe, B., Whitehead, Russell, Husserl, Peano, Heidegger, S. Frank, Frege, Hillebrand, Lalande, Milhaud, Hilbert, Einstein, Lessing, Helfmann, Belobřesky, Pfander, Couturat, Bunitzky, Geyger, Gentile, McTaggart, Birkhoff, Duhem

[1] For obvious reasons the values of the living contemporaries are not given. This note applies to all subsequent lists for the period 1900–1920.

MYSTICISM (360 B.C.–A.D. 1920)

B.C. 360–340   total 15
———— Platon (after 385 B.C.) 12, Xenokrates 3

340–320   total 5
———— Xenokrates 3, Philippos Op. 2

320–300   total 5
———— Xenokrates 3, Philippos Op. 2

300–280   total 1

280–260   total 1

260–240   total 1

240–220   total 1

220–200   total 1

200–180   total 1

180–160   total 1

160–140   total 1

140–120   total 1

120–100   total 1

100–80   total 1

80–60   total 1

60–40   total 4
———— Nigidius Figulus 4

40–20   total 1

20–0   total 2
———— Eudoros 2

A.D. 0–20   total 8
———— Philon Iud. 8

20–40   total 11
———— Philon Iud. 8, Thrasyllos 3

40–60   total 11
———— Philon 8, Thrasyllos 3

60–80   total 8
———— Apollonios from Tyana 5, Moderatus 3

80–100   total 16
———— Apollonios 5, Moderatus 3, Plutarchos 8

100–120   total 16
———— Apollonios 5, Plutarchos 8, Cerinthus 2, Saturnilus 1

120–140   total 32
———— Plutarchos 8, Theon 2, Sekundos 2, Nikomachos 1, Gaios 2, Cerinthus 2, Saturnilus 1, Cerdon 2, Marcion 4, Basilides 4, Valentinus 4

140–160   total 31
———— Theon 2, Sekundos 2, Nikomachos 1, Gaios 2, Herodes 2, Albinos 3, Kalvisios 2, Nigrinos 1, Saturnilus 1, Cerdon 2, Marcion 4, Karpokrates 1, Bazilides 4, Valentinus 4

160–180   total 31
————— Herodes 2, Albinos 3, Kalvisios 2, Nikostratos 2, Nigrinos 1, Apuleius 6, Numenios 4, Kronios 2, Marcion 4, Karpokratos 1, Valentinus 4

180–200   total 42
————— Apuleius 6, Numenios 4, Kronios 2, Attikos 2, Harpokration 1, Celsus 4, Maximos 5, Hierax 1, Severus 1, Clemens Alex. 6, Bardesanes 4, Apelles 2, Ptolomaeus 1, Heracleon 2, Marcus 1

200–220   total 33
————— Numenios 4, Hierax 1, Severus 1, Philostratos 5, Hermetic Literature 5, Ammonios Sakkas 3, Clemens Alex. 5, Bardesanes 4, Philippus 1, Heracleon 2, Marcus 1

220–240   total 29
————— Philostratos 5, Hermetic Literature 5, Ammonios Sakkas 3, Origenes 8, Bardesanes 4, Orphic books 4

240–260   total 36
————— Hermetic Literature 5, Ammonios Sakkas 3, Herennios 4, Plotinos 12, Origenes 8, Orphic books 4

260–280   total 23
————— Plotinos 12, Amelios 2, Anatolios 2, Cornelius Labeo 3, Orphic books 4

280–300   total 15
————— Amelios 2, Anatolios 2, Porphyrios 7, Cornelius Labeo 3, Pamphilus (Caes.) 1

300–320   total 15
————— Porphyrios 7, Jamblichos 7, Pamphilus (Caes.) 1

320–340   total 17
————— Jamblichos 7, Sopatros 2, Theodoros 1, Dexippos 2, Alexandros 2, Aidesios 2, Christian culture 1

340–360   total 11
————— Sopatros 2, Theodoros 1, Dexippos 2, Aidesios 2, Macarius Aegyp. 4

360–380   total 40
————— Aidesios 2, Julianus 7, Maximos 1, Sallustios 3, Eunapios 3, Vettius Agor. Praetextatus 2, Basilius Magnus 6, Gregorius Naz. 6, Gregorius Nyss. 6, Macarius Aegyp. 4

380–400   total 30
————— Vettius Agor. Praetextatus 2, Sallustios 3, Eunapios 3, Basilius Magnus 6, Gregorius Naz. 6, Gregorius Nyss. 6, Macarius Aegyp. 4

400–420   total 22
————— Plutarchos from Athens 1, Macrobius 4, Syrianos 1, Augustinus 10, Synesius 2, Nemesius 2, Pseudo Macarius 2

420–440   total 18
————— Plutarchos 1, Macrobius 4, Syrianos 1, Augustinus 10, Pseudo Macarius 2

440–460   total 13
————— Hermeias 3, Proclos 8, Diadochos (Fot.) 2

460–480   total 13
————— Hermeias 3, Proclos 8, Diadochos (Fot.) 2

480–500   total 14
————— Proclos 8, Asklepiodotos 2, Marinos 3, Christian culture 1

500–520   total 14
————— Isidoros 1, Doros 1, Damaskios 4, Dionysios Areop. 4

520–540   total 14
————— Doros 1, Damaskios 4, Priskianos 1, Dionysios Areop. 8

540–560   total 6
————— Damaskios 4, Priskianos 1, Christian culture 1

560–580   total 1
————— Priskianos 1

580–600   total 0

600–620   total 1

620–640   total 6
————— Maximus Confessor 6

640–660   total 6
————— Maximus Confessor 6

660–680   total 6
————— Maximus Confessor 6

680–840   total 0

840–860   total 8
————— John Scotus Erigena 8

860–880   total 8
————— John Scotus Erigena 8

880–900   total 2
————— Remigius (Alex.) 2

900–920   total 2
————— Remigius (Alex.) 2

920–1060   total 0

1060–1080   total 11
————— Anselmus Cant. 7, Symeon Th. Nov. 4

1080–1100   total 11
————— Anselmus Cant. 7, Symeon Th. Nov. 4

1100–1120   total 7
————— Anselmus Cant. 7

1120–1140   total 12
————— Bernardus Claraev. 5, Thierry (Chartres) 2, Hugo à S. Victore 5

1140–1160   total 16
————— Bernardus Claraev. 5, Thierry (Chartres) 2, Hugo à S. Victore 5, Richardus à S. Victore 4

1160–1180   total 8
————— Richardus à S. Victore 4, Isaak de Stella 2, Clarenbaldus 2

1180–1200   total 10
————— Alanus ab Insulis 2, Gualterus à S. Victore 2, Gottfried de Bret. 1, Radulfus Ardens 1, Ioachim de Floris 2, St. Francis 2

1200–1220   total 10
————— Alanus ab Insulis 2, Thomas Gallo 1, Ioachim de Floris 2, Amalrich de Bene 3, St. Francis 2

1220–1240   total 2
————— Thomas Gallo 1, Radulfus de Longo, 1

1240–1260   total 1

1260–1280   total 8
————— Ioannes Bonaventure 8

1280–1300   total 7
————— Ioannes Peckham 1, Walter of Bruges 2, Fr. Eustachius 2, Dietrich de Friberg 2

1300–1320   total 12
————— Walter of Bruges 2, Dietrich de Friberg 2, M. Eckehart 8

1320–1340   total 10
————— M. Eckehart 8, Thomas Bradw. 2

1340–1360   total 25
————— I. Tauler 4, H. Suso 5, Ruysbroeck 4, Gregorius Palam. 6, Nik. Kabas. 4, Thomas Bradw. 2

1360–1380   total 26
————— I. Tauler 4, H. Suso 5, Ruysbroeck 4, Gregorius Palam. 6, Nik. Kabas. 4, "Eine deutsche Theologie" 3

1380–1400   total 8
————— Ruysbroeck 4, Nik. Kabas. 4

1400–1420   total 4
————— Jean Charlier (Gerson) 4

1420–1440   total 4
————— Jean Charlier (Gerson) 4

1440–1460   total 12
————— Dionysius Cartusianus 4, Nicolaus Cusanus 8

1460–1480   total 16
————— Dionysius Cartus. 4, Nicolaus Cusanus 8, Thomas à Kempis 4

1480–1500   total 0

1500–1520   total 6
————— S. Franck 2, P. della Mirandola Sr. 4

1520–1540   total 11
————— P. della Mirandola Jr. 4, Agrippa 2, Seb. Franck 2, Faber 3

1540–1560   total 13
————— Paracelsus 4, Serveto 4, Seb. Franck 2, Leo Hebraeus 3

1560–1580   total 22
————— Jean de la Croix 4, G. Bruno 8, Paracelsus 4, Cardanus 6

1580–1600   total 24
————— Bruno 8, Paracelsus 4, St. Theresa 6, Jean de la Croix 4, Hannequin 2

1600–1620   total 17
————— Bruno 8, François de Sales 4, Fludd 2, V. Weigel 3

1620–1640   total 12
————— Jacob Boehme 6, Vincent de Paul 2, François de Sales 4

1640–1660   total 17
————— J. Boehme 6 (posthumous works), Comenius 7, J. Smith 1, Culverwell 1, Whichcote 2

1660–1680   total 42
————— Pordage 1, Renery 1, Brooke 1, Pascal 7, Spinoza 8, Law 2, Gale 2, H. Morus 4, Malebranche 7, Cudworth 5, Scheffler/Angelus Silesius/ 3, Bromley 1

1680–1700   total 44
————— Malebranche 7, Arnauld 4, Nicole 4, H. Morus 4, Cudworth 5, Pordage 1, Whichcote 1, Bourignon 2, Poiret 2, Lamy 2, Molinos 3, Guyon 2, Shaftesbury 5, Kuffeler 1, Jelles 1

1700–1720   total 39
————— Shaftesbury 5, Norris 2, Mairon 2, B. Lamy 2, F. Lamy 2, A. Collier 5, V. Helmont Jr 2, André 1, Malebranche 7, Molinos 3, Marinière 2, English Mystic Masons 4, Thomassin 1, Taylor 1

1720–1740   total 16
————— Mairan 2, Martinez Pasquelez 4, Marinière 2, Mme. Guyon 2, Norris 2. French Masons 4

1740–1760   total 14
————— Berkeley 8, J. Edwards 1, Swedenborg 4, Sam. Johnson 1

1760–1780   total 26
————— Mairan 1, S. Johnson 1, Rousseau 8, Swedenborg 4, English Masons 4, French Lodge "The Great East" 4, Russian Masons 4

1780–1800   total 58
————— Jacobi 6, Herder 6, Schelling 8, Goethe 8, Hemsterhuis 3, Hamann 3, Deschamps 1, Fr. Schlegel 4, Novalis 2, W. Blake 4, Martin 4, Schleiermacher 4, Masons 5

1800–1820   total 61
————— Fichte 8, Schelling 8, Schopenhauer 8, Hegel 8, Wronsky 6, Schleiermacher 4, Schlegel 4, St. Martin 4, Baader 5, Masons 4, Russian Masons 2

1820–1840   total 65
————— Schopenhauer 8, Hegel 8, Burdach 2, Steffens 1, Schleiermacher 4, George 2, Ritter 2, Vorländer 2, Wronsky 6, Fr. Baader 5, Toviansky 3, Krasinsky 4, Mizkiewicz 6, Khomiakov 4, Iv. Kireewsky 2, Shelley 6

1840–1860   total 93
———————— Schopenhauer 8, Weissenbaum 1, Ritter 1, Brandis 1, George 2, Frauenstädt 2, Romang 1, Fr. Baader 5, Rosenkranz 4, K. Fischer 4, Wronsky 6, Emerson 6, Toviansky 3, Mizkiewicz 6, Kireewsky 2, Khomiakov 4, Ruskin 6, Gioberti 6, Fournier 5, Allan Cardec 4, Dostoevski 8, Schubert 3, Perty 2, Thoreau 3]

1860–1880   total 74
———————— Schopenhauer 8, Hartmann 8, Wagner 8, Vl. Soloviev 6, A. J. Davies 4, Frauenstädt 2, Axakov 4, Emerson 6, Ruskin 6, Mainländer 4, J. Erdmann 4, K. Fischer 4, Michelet 2, Dostoevski 8

1880–1900   total 94
———————— Hartmann 8, Lipps 7, Bradley 7, V. Soloviev 6, Axakov 4, Blavatskaia 4, Steiner 4, Secretan 4, Schuppe 5, Wagner 8, Bergson 8, M. Eddy 4, J. Royce 4, Tolstoi 8, Nietzsche 9, Du-Prel 1, Hellenbach 2

1900–1920   total 101 [1]
———————— Hartmann, Bergson, Lossky, Royce, Hoppe, Bradley, Maeterlink, V. Soloviev, Unamuno, Richet, M. Eddy, Maxwell, R. Steiner, Keyserling, L. Tolstoi, Karsavin, Berdiaev, Losev, Jankelevič, Vyšeslavcev, S. Frank, Segond, Blavatskaia, O. Lodge.   "Psychic research"

FIDEISM (400 B.C.–A.D. 1920)

B.C. 400–380   total 5
———————— Antisthenes 5

380–360   total 5
———————— Antisthenes 5

360–340   total 5
———————— Diogenes 5

340–320   total 5
———————— Diogenes 5

320–300   total 11
———————— Monimos 1, Onesiaritos 2, Philiskos 1, Krates 4, Dikaearchos 3

300–280   total 20
———————— Monimos 1, Onesiaritos 2, Philiskos 1, Krates 4, Metrokles 1, Dikaearchos 3, Zenon 8

280–260   total 24
———————— Metrokles 1, Zenon 8, Bion 3, Ariston 5, Herillos 1, Dionysios 1, Kleanthes 5

260–240   total 22
———————— Bion 3, Ariston 5, Herillos 1, Persaios 2, Dionysios 1, Kleanthes 5, Menippos 5

240–220   total 40
———————— Bion 3, Ariston 5, Herillos 1, Persaios 2, Dionysios 1, Kleanthes 5, Chrysippos 7, Sphairos 1, Menippos 5, Teles 3, Menedemos 2, Kerkidas 5

[1] For obvious reasons values are not given for living authors.

220–200   total 20
———————— Chrysippos 7, Sphairos 1, Menippos 5, Menedemos 2, Kerkidas 5

200–180   total 6
———————— Sphairos 1, Zenon 1, Diogenes 1

180–160   total 6
———————— Diogenes 4, Antipatros 2

160–140   total 6
———————— Diogenes 4, Antipatros 2

140–120   total 6
———————— Panaitios 5, Q. Mucius Sc. 1

120–100   total 8
———————— Panaitios 5, Q. Mucius Sc. 1, Hekaton 1, Mnesarchos 1

100–80   total 12
———————— Hekaton 1, Mnesarchos 1, Meleagros 2, Apollodoros 1, Poseidonios 7

80–60   total 14
———————— Meleagros 2, Apollodoros 1, Poseidonios 7, Asclepiodotos 2, Geminos 2

60–40   total 30
———————— Poseidonios 7, Asclepiodotos 2, Geminos 2, Phainias 1, Dionysios 1, Antipatros 2, Jason 2, Athenodoros Kord. 1, Apollonides 1, Diodotos 1, Cato 2, Cicero 8

40–20   total 17
———————— Athenodoros Kord. 1, Apollonides 1, Diodotos 1, Apollonios 1, Athenodoros 3, Areios Didymos 2, Cicero 8

20–0   total 5
———————— Athenodoros 3, Areios Didymos 2

A.D. 0–20   total 5
———————— Areios Didymos 2, Herakleitos 3

20–40   total 6
———————— Herakleitos 3, Strabon 2, Attalos 1

40–60   total 16
———————— Strabon 2, Attalos 1, Seneca 8, L. Ann. Korn. 4, Demetrios 1

60–80   total 27
———————— Seneca 8, Chairemon 2, L. Ann. Korn. 4, Pers. Flaccus 3, Ann. Luc. 4, Muson. Ruf. 5, Demetrios 1

80–100   total 18
———————— Muson. Ruf. 5, Demetrios 1, Epiktetos 6, Dion Chrysostomos 6

100–120   total 12
———————— Epiktetos 6, Dion Chrysostomos 6

120–140   total 17
———————— Epiktetos 6, Arrianos 2, Hierokles 2, Kleomedes 2, Oinomaos 3, Demonax 2

140–160   total 14
———————— Arrianos 2, Hierokles 2, Kleomedes 2, Oinomaos 3, Demonax 2, Peregrinos Prot. 3

160–180   total 11
———————— Demonax 2, Peregrinos Prot. 3, Marcus Aurel. 6

180–200   total 8
————— Demonax 2, Marcus Aurel. 6

200–220   total 1
————— Stoic school 1

220–240   total 1
————— Stoic school 1

240–260   total 1
————— Stoic school 1

260–280   total 1
————— Stoic school 1

280–1040   total 0

1040–1060   total 5
————— Petrus Damiani 3, Otloh 2

1060–1080   total 5
————— Petrus Damiani 3, Otloh 2

1080–1100   total 3
————— Manegoldus 3

1100–1120   total 3
————— Manegoldus 3

1120–1380   total 0

1380–1400   total 4
————— Petrus d'Ailly 4

1400–1420   total 4
————— Petrus d'Ailly 4

1420–1440   total 4
————— Petrus d'Ailly 4

1500–1520   total 1

1520–1540   total 2
————— Agrippa 2

1540–1560   total 10
————— Agrippa 2, Loyola 8

1560–1580   total 8
————— Loyola 8

1580–1600   total 1

1600–1620   total 1

1620–1640   total 1

1640–1660   total 7
————— Pascal 7

1660–1680   total 7
————— Pascal 7

1680–1700   total 1

1700–1720   total 1

1720–1740   total 2
————— Turnboule 2

1740–1760   total 1

1760–1780   total 6
————— Reid 4, Beattie 2

1780–1800   total 16
————— Reid 4, Beattie 2, Jacobi 6, O.
Stuart 4

1800–1820   total 29
————— Jacobi 6, Beattie 2, Brown 3, O.
Stuart 4, Fichte 8, Fries 6

1820–1840   total 5
————— Lammenais 4, Bouterwek 1

1840–1860   total 4
————— Lammenais 4

1860–1880   total 21
————— Hamilton 6, Mansel 2, McCosh, 4,
Khomiakov 4, Gratry 1, Cousin 4

1880–1900   total 37
————— Sigwart 5, Balfour 4, Veitch 4,
Renouvier 7, Karinsky 4, Wwedensky 4, Milhaud
3, Elsenhans 2, Keibel 2, Hammerling 2

1900–1920   total 24 [1]
————— W. James, Unamuno, Nelson, Balfour,
Elsenhans, Keibel

SKEPTICISM (460 B.C.–A.D. 1920)

B.C. 460–440   total 13
————— Protagoras 8, Gorgias 5

440–420   total 13
————— Protagoras 8, Gorgias 5

420–400   total 36
————— Protagoras 8, Gorgias 5, Prodikos 5,
Hippias 4, Antiphon 4, Polos 2, Kallikles 2,
Kritias 3, Thrasymachos 3

400–380   total 29
————— Gorgias 5, Prodikos 5, Hippias 4,
Antiphon 4, Polos 2, Thrasymachos 3, Aristippos 6

380–360   total 16
————— Gorgias 5, Alkidamos 4, Metrodoros
1, Aristippos 6

360–340   total 14
————— Alkidamos 4, Aristippos 6, Metrodoros 1, Arete 1, Aithiops 1, Antipatros 1

340–320   total 5
————— Arete 1, Aithiops 1, Antipatros 1,
Aristippos (grandchild) 1, Anaxarchos 1

320–300   total 16
————— Theodoros 2, Hegesias 2, Annikeris 2,
Euhemeros 3, Anaxarchos 1, Pyrrhon 6

300–280   total 15
————— Theodoros 2, Hegesias 2, Annikeris 2,
Euhemeros 3, Pyrrhon 6

280–260   total 18
————— Theodoros 2, Hegesias 2, Annikeris 2,
Pyrrhon 6, Timon 3, Arkesilaos 3

260–240   total 6
————— Timon 3, Arkesilaos 3

240–220   total 9
————— Timon 3, Arkesilaos 3, Lakydes 3

[1] For obvious reasons values are not given for living
authors.

220–200   total 7
———— Lakydes 3, Telekles 2, Euandros 2

200–180   total 3
———— Euandros 2, Hegesinus 1

180–160   total 6
———— Hegesinus 1, Karneades 5

160–140   total 7
———— Karneades 5, Kleitomachos 2

140–120   total 9
———— Karneades 5, Kleitomachos 2, Charmadas 2

120–100   total 4
———— Kleitomachos 2, Charmadas 2

100–80   total 2
———— Charmadas 2

80–60   total 0

60–40   total 5
———— Ainesidemos 5

40–20   total 5
———— Ainesidemos 5

20–0   total 5
———— Ainesidemos 5

A.D. 0–100   total 0

100–120   total 2
———— Menodotos 2

120–140   total 6
———— Favorinus 4, Menodotos 2

140–160   total 6
———— Favorinus 4, Menodotos 2

160–180   total 6
———— Sextus Empir. 6

180–200   total 6
———— Sextus Empir. 6

200–220   total 6
———— Sextus Empir. 6

220–1300   total 0

1300–1320   total 3
———— Ioannes de Ianduno 3

1320–1340   total 7
———— I. de Ianduno 3, Nicolaus (Autr.) 4

1340–1360   total 4
———— Nicolaus (Autr.) 4

1500–1520   total 1

1520–1540   total 4
———— Pomponatius 4

1540–1560   total 2
———— Raymund Seb. 2

1560–1580   total 8
———— Raymund Seb. 2, translators and followers of Sextus Emp. 6

1580–1600   total 8
———— Sanchez 2, Montaigne 6

1600–1620   total 8
———— Sanchez 2, Charron 2, L. Vanini 4

1620–1640   total 1

1640–1660   total 1
———— La Rochefoucauld 1

1660–1680   total 2
———— Glanville 2

1680–1700   total 11
———— Glanville 2, De la Mozze le Vayer 1, Huet 1, Foucher 1, P. Bayle 6

1700–1720   total 7
———— Foucher 1, P. Bayle 6

1720–1740   total 1

1740–1760   total 19
———— D'Alembert 5, Diderot 6, Hume 8

1760–1780   total 19
———— D'Alembert 5, Diderot 6, Hume 8

1780–1800   total 2
———— Lichtenberger 2

1800–1820   total 3
———— Lichtenberger 2, Schalmeier 1

1820–1840   total 1
———— Schalmeier 1

1840–1860   total 18
————L. Feuerbach 6, J. St. Mill 8, Kirkegaard 4

1860–1880   total 20
———— Renan 6, Multatuli 4, Nietzsche 9, Bahnsen 1

1880–1900   total 21
———— Renan 6, Multatuli 4, Nietzsche 9, Bahnsen 1, Peirce 1

1900–1920   total 36 [1]
———— Poincaré, F. Schiller, Mauthner, Moebius, W. James, Vaihinger, Rensi, Spengler

EMPIRICISM (580 B.C.–A.D. 1500)

B.C. 580–560   total 4
———— Thales 4

560–540   total 4
———— Thales 4

540–520   total 2
———— Anaximenes 2

520–500   total 2
———— Anaximenes 2

500–480   total 2
———— Alkmaion 2

480–460   total 2
———— Alkmaion 2

[1] For obvious reasons values are not given for living authors.

460–440   total 11
———————— Diogenes 3, Empedokles 6, Hippon 2

440–420   total 13
———————— Leukippos 2, Diogenes 3, Empedokles 6, Hippon 2

420–400   total 18
———————— Leukippos 2, Demokritos 8, Hippon 2, Empedokles 6

400–380   total 9
———————— Demokritos 8, Nessas 1

380–360   total 16
———————— Demokritos 8, Nessas 1, Xenophon 7

360–340   total 9
———————— Nessas 1, Diogenes 1, Xenophon 7

340–320   total 1
———————— Diogenes 1

320–300   total 14
———————— Bion 1, Hekataios 1, Nausiphenes 2, Dikaearchos Mess. 3, Aristoxenos 4, Demetrios 3

300–280   total 24
———————— Bion 1, Hekataios 1, Nausiphenes 2, Dikaearchos Mess. 3, Aristoxenos 4, Demetrios 3, Straton 2, Epikuros 8

280–260   total 16
———————— Epikuros 8, Metrodoros 2, Polyainos 1, Demetrios 3, Straton 2

260–240   total 4
———————— Hermarchos 2, Kolotes 2

240–220   total 7
———————— Hermarchos 2, Kolotes 2, Polystratos 2, Hippokleides 1

220–200   total 3
———————— Polystratos 2, Hippokleides 1

200–180   total 4
———————— Polystratos 2, Hippokleides 1, Dionysios 1

180–160   total 2
———————— Dionysios 1, Basileides 1

160–140   total 3
———————— Basileides 1, Philonides 2

140–120   total 2
———————— Apollodoros 2

120–100   total 4
———————— Apollodoros 2, Zenon 2

100–80   total 7
———————— Amafinius 1, Apollodoros 2, Zenon 2, Phaidros 2

80–60   total 5
———————— Amafinius 1, Zenon 2, Phaidros 2

60–40   total 18
———————— Patron 1, Philodemos 5, Lucretius 8, Asclepiades 4

40–20   total 10
———————— Philodemos 5, Asclepiades 4, Boethos 1

20–0   total 1
———————— Boethos 1

A.D. 0–20   total 1
———————— Potamon 1

20–40   total 1
———————— Potamon 1

40–60   total 1
———————— Epicurean school 1

60–80   total 1
———————— Epicurean school 1

80–100   total 1
———————— Epicurean school 1

100–120   total 1
———————— Epicurean school 1

120–140   total 2
———————— Epicurean school 1, Celsus Ep. 1

140–160   total 3
———————— Epicurean school 1, Celsus 1, Diogenianus 1

160–180   total 10
———————— Epicurean school 1, Celsus 1, Diogenianus 1, Galenos 7

180–200   total 12
———————— Galenos 7, Epicurean school 1, Diogenianus 1, Diogenes 3

200–220   total 20
———————— Diogenes 3, Galenos 7, Theodotus 2, Noëtus 2, Tertullianus 6

220–240   total 12
———————— Epicurean school 1, Noëtus 2, Theodotus 2, Asklepiodotos 1, Tertullianus 6

240–260   total 11
———————— Epicurean school 1, Longinos 2, Artemas 1, Mani 4, Diogenes Laërtius 3

260–280   total 13
———————— Epicurean school 1, Longinos 2, Diogenes Laërtius 3, Artemas 1, Paulus (Samos) 2, Mani 4

280–300   total 9
———————— Epicurean school 1, Lucianus 2, Paulus 2, Mani 4

300–320   total 7
———————— Epicurean school 1, Eusebius 3, Lucianus 2, Manicheists 1

320–340   total 9
———————— Epicurean school 1, Eusebius 3, Eusthatius (Aut.) 1, Manicheists 1, Arnobius 3

340–360   total 6
———————— Epicurean school 1, Eusebius (Caes.) 3, Manicheists 2

360–380   total 3
———————— Eunomius 1, Manicheists 2

380–400   total 9
———————— Ioannes Chrysostomos 5, Eunomius 1, Manicheists 3

400–420   total 8
——————— Ioannes Chrysostomos 5, Manicheists 3

420–440   total 6
——————— Theodoretus (Cyr.) 3, Manicheists 3

440–460   total 4
———————Theodoretus (Cyr.) 3, Manicheists 1

460–480   total 4
——————— Theodoretus (Cyr.) 3, Manicheists 1

480–500   total 1
——————— Manicheists 1

500–520   total 1
——————— Manicheists 1

520–540   total 1
——————— Manicheists 1

540–1080   total 0

1080–1100   total 3
——————— Roscelinus 3

1100–1120   total 3
——————— Roscelinus 3

1120–1140   total 3
——————— Roscelinus 3

1140–1160   total 3
——————— Gilbertus Parred. 3

1160–1180   total 3
——————— Ioannes Saresberiensis 3

1180–1200   total 7
——————— Ioannes Saresberiensis 3, Alfredus Anglicus 2, Alexander Neckham 2

1200–1220   total 4
——————— Alfredus Anglicus 2, Alexander Neckham 2

1220–1240   total 4
——————— Rolendus Cremon. 2, Michael Scottus 2

1240–1260   total 4
——————— Bartholomaeus Anglicus 2, Thomas (Chantimpré) 2

1260–1280   total 10
——————— Bartholomaeus Anglicus 2, Thomas (Chantimpré) 2, Roger Bacon 6

1280–1300   total 9
——————— Roger Bacon 6, Richardus de Mediav. 3

1300–1320   total 5
——————— Richardus de Mediav. 3, Durandus de s. Porc. 2

1320–1340   total 12
——————— William of Ockham 8, Durandus de s. P. 2, Petrus Aureoli 2

1340–1360   total 16
——————— William of Ockham 8, Gregorius (Rimini) 2, Buridan 2, Adam Wodhem 2, Ioannes de Mirec. 2

1360–1380   total 7
——————— Buridan 2, Nicolaus (Oresme) 2, Albert de Saxonia 2, Brinkel 1

1380–1400   total 4
——————— Nicolaus (Oresme) 2, Albert de Saxonia 2

1400–1420   total 0

1420–1440   total 0

1440–1460   total 0

1460–1480   total 3
——————— Gabriel Biel 3

1480–1500   total 3
——————— Gabriel Biel 3

EMPIRICISM (1500–1920)

The indicators for empiricism for the period 1500–1920 are made up out of the indicators of "total materialism" plus those of "Mixed Philosophies" (without skepticism, criticism, and fideism), given further in the Appendix, of the representatives of Idealism, Materialism, and Mixed ontological systems. The list of the representatives of the "Mixed Philosophies" follows. Adding to it the indicators of weight of materialism (mechanistic and hylozoistic) the indicators of empiricism given in the tables result.

1500–1520   total 1

1520–1540   total 6
——————— B. Telesius 6

1540–1560   total 6
——————— B. Telesius 6

1560–1580   total 6
——————— Telesius 6

1580–1600   total 4
——————— Patricius 2, Ellinger 2

1600–1620   total 11
——————— Baco 7, Jungius 4

1620–1640   total 15
——————— Baco 7, Jungius 4, Cherbury 4

1640–1660   total 8
——————— Gorlaeus 4, Cherbury 4

1660–1680   total 8
——————— Gorlaeus 4, R. Boyle 4

1680–1700   total 34
——————— Newton 9, Locke 8, R. Boyle 4, Bould 2, Lowde 1, Leeuwenhoek 5, Hooke 5

1700–1720   total 30
——————— Claude Brunet 4, Locke 8, Newton 9, Burnet 2, Cockburn 2, Leeuwenhoek 5

1720–1740   total 22
——————— Newton 9, Clarke 1, Leeuwenhoek 5, Claude Brunet 4, Wollaston 2

1740–1760 total 27
——————— Buffon 6, Voltaire 7 (Locke's and Newton's popularizations), Montesquieu 6, Hutcheson 4, Richmann 3, Leroy 1

1760–1780 total 27
——————— Buffon 6, Condillac 6, Whitherspoon 2, Reid 4, Hume 8, Garve 1

1780–1800 total 40
——————— Garve 1, Tiedemann 2, E. Darwin 4, Franklin 4, Whitherspoon 2, Ethan Allen 2, Soave 2, Lesage 2, Reid 4, Beattie 2, Campe 2, Gioja 3, Condillac 6, Tetens 4

1800–1820 total 46
——————— Lesbios 1, Soave 2, Pestalozzi 4, Beattie 2, Brown 3, D. Stewart 4, Gauss 8, Gioja 3, Galuppi 3, Romagnosi 2, Bichat 6, Carnot 6, Hufeland 2

1820–1840 total 54
——————— Herbart 7, Gauss 8, James Mill 6, Bentham 6, Benecke 2, Leroux 1, S. Germain 2, Lesbios 1, Gioja 3, J. St. Hilaire 6, Cuvier 6, Burdach 2, Drobisch 4

1840–1860 total 70
——————— H. Spencer 8, J. S. Mill 8, A. Comte 8, J. Muller 6, Gauss 8, Drobisch 4, Purkinje 6, Durdik 1, Strümpell 2, Leroux 2, Littré 4, Herbart 7, Benecke 2, Fortlage 4

1860–1880 total 104
——————— H. Spencer 8, Buckle 5, Littré 4, Wyrubov 4, Exner 3, Lafitte 5, G. Grote 2, C. Bernard 5, C. Darwin 8, Liebig 4, Helmholtz 6, Bonatelli 5, Bonitz 2, Drobisch 4, Fortlage 1, Cornelius 1, Hirschmann 2, H. Struve 4, McCosh 4, Hamilton 6, Dressler 1, Lazarus 4, Steinthal 4, Strümpell 2, Waitz 4, Zimmermann 4, Oušinsky 3

1880–1900 total 164
——————— Lazarus 4, Steinthal 4, Cornelius 1, Lindner 1, Du Bois Reymond 5, H. Spencer 8, Lewes 5, Hertwig 3, Galton 6, Göring 1, Binet 4, Baldwin 5, Ziegler 1, De Roberty 3, Berthelot 2, S. Soldern 4, N. Grote 2, Brentano 4, Meinong 3, Rein 4, Geier 1, Meinert 2, Hoppe 2, Tönnies 4, Elsenhans 4, Croom Robertson 4, Karinsky 4, Volkmann 3, Hartenstein Jr. 2, Willmann 4, Zimmermann 4, Dressler 1, G. Gomperz 4, Troizky 2, Masaryk 4, Avenarius 6, Laas 4, Mach 6, Lobatchevsky 6, Tarde 4, Tannery Sr. 4, Hodgson 4, W. James 7, Brunschvicg 4, Mikhailovski 3

1900–1920 total 229 [1]
——————— Karstanjen, Petzold, Kleinpeter, Cornelius, Elsenhans, Jerusalem, Mareš, Masaryk, Rade, Brentano, Binet, Kozak, Tarde, Loisy,

Guignebert, Brunschvicg, C. L. Morgan, Tannery, Hodgson, Cyples, Levy-Bruhl, Adamson, Moore, Durkheim, Dewey, Drake, Spencer, Taylor, Ardigo, Karejev, Lehmann, Fiske, Browne, W. James, Lovejoy, Pratt, Rogers, Santajana, Callius, Berthelot, Poincaré, Sully, C. Read, Alexander, Baldwin, Galton, Woodbridge, Perry, H. Gomperz, Mach, Meinong, Carnap, Krause, De Roberty, S. Soldern, Kulpe, Dyroff, Messer, Sellers, Freud, J. A. Thomson, M. Petrovič, Meyerson, Delbet, H. Souple, Nordmann, Moch, Whitehead

CRITICISM (1780–1920)

1780–1800 total 41
——————— Kant 12, Reinhold 2, S. Maimon 4, S. Beck 3, Krug 2, J. Schultz 3, Tenneman 4, Nitch 1, Willich 1, Wigman 1, Kinker 1, K. E. Schmid 1, Abicht 1, Born 1, Mellin 1, Metz 1, M. Reis 1, O'Keffee 1

1800–1820 total 36
——————— Kant 12, Jäsche 2, L. Bendavid 1, Viller 1, Svabedissen 1, Kiesewetter 1, Tenneman 4, Fries 6, Schopenhauer 8

1820–1840 total 8
——————— Fries 6, Krug 2

1840–1860 total 11
———————Renouvier 7, Apelt 2, Testa 2

1860–1880 total 25
——————— Renouvier 7, F. A. Lange 7, O. Liebmann 5, Windelband 6

1880–1900 total 100
——————— Vaihinger 6, Liebmann 5, Riehl 5, Cohen 7, Stadler 2, Stallo 3, Watson 4, M. Muller 2, Windelband 6, Volkelt 2, Rickert 6, Wwedensky 4, J. Cohn 3, Münsterberg 4, Pillon 4, F. Schultze 1, Classen 1, Rokitansky 1, Lasswitz 2, Vorländer 4, Cantoni 4, Credaro 1, Caird, 3, Bosanquet 4, Ritchie 2, Palágyi 4, Land 2, Tocca 2, Harris 4, Turbiglio 2

1900–1920 total 121 [1]
——————— Vaihinger, Wwedensky, Liebmann, Riehl, Natorp, Cohen, Rickert, S. Hessen, Windelband, Koppelmann, Liebert, Stammler, Bauch, Hamelin, Pillon, A. Gurland, Buchenau, Kinkel, Paul Stern, N. Hartmann, Lasswitz, Krause, Stadler, Christiansen, Bosanquet, Lask, Ehrenberg, Palágyi, Harris, Cassirer, Cantoni, Ritchie, Staudinger, Pringle-Pattison, Evald, Simmel, Lewis

[1] For obvious reasons values are not given for living authors.

LIST OF THINKERS FOR EACH PERIOD, WITH THE VALUE GIVEN TO EACH ON A SCALE 1 TO 12

Graeco-Roman and Western Cultures

MECHANISTIC MATERIALISM
(440 B.C.–A.D. 1920)

B.C. 440–420   total 2
———— Leukippos 2

420–400   total 10
———— Leukippos 2, Demokritos 8

400–380   total 9
———— Demokritos 8, Nesaea (or Nessas) 1

380–360   total 9
———— Demokritos 8, Nesaea 1

360–340   total 2
———— Nesaea 1, Diogenes 1

340–320   total 1
———— Diogenes 1

320–300   total 4
———— Bion 1, Hekataios 1, Nausiphanes 2

300–280   total 12
———— Epicurus 8, Bion 1, Hekataios 1, Nausiphanes 2

280–260   total 11
———— Epicurus 8, Metrodorus 2, Polyainos 1

260–240   total 4
———— Hermarchus 2, Kolotes 2

240–220   total 7
———— Hermarchus 2, Kolotes 2, Polystratos 2, Hippokleides 1

220–200   total 3
———— Polystratos 2, Hippokleides 1

200–180   total 4
———— Polystratos 2, Hippokleides 1, Dionysios 1

180–160   total 2
———— Dionysios 1, Basileides 1

160–140   total 3
———— Basileides 1, Philonides 2

140–120   total 2
———— Apollodoros 2

120–100   total 4
———— Apollodoros 2, Zeno 2

100–80   total 7
———— Amatios 1, Apollodoros 2, Zeno 2, Phaidros 2

80–60   total 5
———— Phaidros 2, Amatios 1, Zeno 2

60–40   total 18
———— Petron 1, Philodemos 5, Lucretius 8, Asclepiades 4

40–20   total 9
———— Philodemos 5, Asclepiades 4

20–0   total 1
———— Epicurean school 1

A.D. 0–20   total 1
———— Epicurean school 1

20–40   total 1
———— Epicurean school 1

40–60   total 1
———— Epicurean school 1

60–80   total 1
———— Epicurean school 1

80–100   total 1
———— Epicurean school 1

100–120   total 1
———— Epicurean school 1

120–140   total 2
———— Epicurean school 1, Celsus 1

140–160   total 3
———— Epicurean school 1, Celsus 1, Diogenianos 1

160–180   total 3
———— Epicurean school 1, Diogenianos 1, Celsus 1

180–200   total 5
———— Epicurean school 1, Diogenianos 1, Diogenes 3

200–220   total 3
———— Diogenes 3

220–240   total 1
———— Epicurean school 1

240–260   total 1
———— Epicurean school 1

260–280   total 1
———— Epicurean school 1

280–300   total 1
———————— Epicurean school 1

300–320   total 1
———————— Epicurean school 1

320–340   total 1
———————— Epicurean school 1

*   *   *

1500–1520   total 1

1520–1540   total 1

1540–1560   total 1

1560–1580   total 1

1580–1600   total 4
———————— Lublin 2, Bodin 2

1600–1620   total 1
———————— Nicolaus Hill

1620–1640   total 1

1640–1660   total 13
———————— Hobbes 8, Bérigard 2, T. Browne 3

1660–1680   total 11
———————— T. Browne 3, Hobbes 8

1680–1700   Total 11
———————— T. Browne 3, Hobbes 8

1700–1720   total 4
———————— Mandeville 4

1720–1740   total 7
———————— Mandeville 4, Jean Meslier 3

1740–1760   total 17
———————— Hartley 4, Voltaire 7, Vaucanson 2, Morelly 2, Dumarsais 2

1760–1780   total 37
———————— Voltaire 7, Lambert 1, Helvetius 6, Hartley 4, Holbach 6, Priestley 6, Freret 3, Mably 2, Morelly 2

1780–1800   total 30
———————— Priestley 6, Voltaire 7, Holbach 6, Volney 2, Lambert 1, Condorcet 4, Destutt de Tracy 4

1800–1820   total 11
———————— Destutt de Tracy 4, Volney 2, Broussais 2, Borelli 1, Lâlande 2

1820–1840   total 4
———————— Destutt de Tracy 4

1840–1860   total 31
———————— A. Ruge 4, D. Strauss 6, Corove 1, Chernyshevsky 3, Biedermann 1, Herzen 4, C. Baur 4, Marx 8

1860–1880   total 66
———————— Chernyshevsky 3, Pisarev 1, Sechenov 5, Büchner 5, D. Strauss 6, Moleschott 4, Ribot 7, Vogt 4, Pouchet 1, Joly 1, Duehring 6, Bain 7, Herzen 4, Marx 8, Kropotkin 4

1880–1900   total 45
———————— H. Spitzer 1, Ribot 7, Duehring 6, Jodl 4, Lombroso 4, Bain 7, Kropotkin 4, Bender 1, Mosso 2, Marx 8, Mantegazza 1

1900–1920   total 110 [1]
———————— Ivan Pavlov, Bechterev, Loeb, Zeleny, Zehnder, Plessner, J. Schmidt, Verworn, Seman, Roux, Zur Strassen, Lewin, Jensen, Ostwald, Hering, Pierre Janet, Kautsky, Bychovecky, Lashley, Pieron, Ribot, Sollier, Menger, Gibbs, Kostyleff, Planck, Stumpf, Boltzmann, Plechanov, Deborin, Lenin, Bazarov, Russell, Kotarbinsky, J. Watson

---

HYLOZOISM (580 B.C.–A.D 1920.)

B.C. 580–560   total 4
———————— Thales 4

560–540   total 9
———————— Thales 4, Anaximander 5

540–520   total 7
———————— Anaximander 5, Anaximenes 2

520–500   total 9
———————— Anaximenes 2, Herakleitos 7

500–480   total 7
———————— Herakleitos 7

480–460   total 8
———————— Herakleitos 7, Hippasos 1

460–440   total 10
———————— Diogenes 3, Anaxagoras 5, Archelaos 1, Hippasos 1

440–420   total 20
———————— Diogenes 3, Anaxagoras 5, Archelaos 1, Empedokles 6, Hippasos 1, Kratylos 2, Hippon 2

420–400   total 11
———————— Hippon 3, Empedokles 6, Kratylos 2

400–380   total 7
———————— Kratylos 2, Antisthenes 5

380–360   total 5
———————— Antisthenes 5

360–340   total 5
———————— Diogenes 5

340–320   total 5
———————— Diogenes 5

320–300   total 11
———————— Monimos 1, Onemakritos 2, Philistos 1, Krates 4, Dikaiarchos 3

300–280   total 20
———————— Monimos 1, Onemakritos 2, Philistos 1, Krates 4, Metrokles 1, Dikaiarchos 3, Zeno 8

[1] For obvious reasons values are not given for living authors.

280–260 total 24
———————— Metrokles 1, Zeno 8, Bion 3, Aristo 5, Herilos 1, Dionysios 1, Kleanthes 5

260–240 total 22
———————— Bion 3, Aristo 5, Herilos 1, Dionysios 1, Kleanthes 5, Menippos 5

240–220 total 40
———————— Bion 3, Aristo 5, Herilos 1, Dionysios 1, Kleanthes 5, Chrysippos 7, Menippos 5, Teles 3, Menedemos 2, Kerkides 5

220–200 total 15
———————— Chrysippos 7, Sphairos 1, Menedemos 2, Kerkides 5

200–180 total 6
———————— Sphairos 1, Zeno 1, Diogenes 4

180–160 total 6
———————— Diogenes 4, Antipater 2

160–140 total 6
———————— Diogenes 4, Antipater 2

140–120 total 6
———————— Panaitios 5, F. Mucius Scaevola 1

120–100 total 8
———————— F. Mucius Scaevola 1, Hekato 1, Mnesarchos 1, Panaitios 5

100–80 total 12
———————— Hekato 1, Mnesarchos 1, Meleagros 2, Apollodoros 1, Poseidonios 7

80–60 total 14
———————— Meleagros 2, Apollodoros 1, Poseidonios 7, Asklepiodotos 2, Geminos 2

60–40 total 22
———————— Poseidonios 7, Asklepiodotos 2, Geminos 2, Phanias 1, Dionysios 1, Antipater 2, Jason 2, Athenagoros 1, Apollonios 1, Diodotos 1, Cato 2

40–20 total 9
———————— Athenagoros 1, Apollonios 1, Diodotos 1, Apollodoros 1, Athenodoros 3, Areios Didymos 2

20–0 total 5
———————— Athenodors 3, Areios Didymos 2

A.D. 0–20 total 5
———————— Areios Didymos 2, Herakleitos 3

20–40 total 6
———————— Herakleitos 3, Strabon 2, Attalos 1

40–60 total 16
———————— Strabon 2, Attalos 1, Seneca 8, L. Annaeus Cornutus 4, Demetrios 1

60–80 total 27
———————— Seneca 8, Chairemon 2, L. Annaeus Cornutus 4, A. Persius Flaccus 3, Annaeus Lucanus 4, Musonius Bufus 5, Demetrius 1

80–100 total 18
———————— Musonius Bufus 5, Demetrius 1, Epictetus 6, Dionysios Chrysostomos 6

100–120 total 12
———————— Epictetus 6, Dionysios Chrysostomos 6

120–140 total 17
———————— Epictetus 6, Arrian 2, Hierokles 2, Kleomedes 2, Oenomaos 3, Demonax 2

140–160 total 14
———————— Arrian 2, Hierokles 2, Kleomedes 2, Oenomaos 3, Peregrinus Proteus 3

160–180 total 11
———————— Demonax 2, Peregrinus Proteus 3, Marcus Aurelius 6

180–200 total 8
———————— Demonax 2, Marcus Aurelius 6

200–220 total 7
———————— Scholastic Stoic school 1, Tertullian 6

220–240 total 7
———————— Scholastic Stoic school 1, Tertullian 6

240–260 total 5
———————— Scholastic Stoic school 1, Mani 4

260–280 total 5
———————— Scholastic Stoic school 1, Mani 4

280–300 total 4
———————— Mani 4

300–320 total 1
———————— Manicheists 1

320–340 total 4
———————— Manicheists 1, Arnobius 3

340–360 total 6
———————— Manicheists 2, Macarius Aegyptus 4

360–380 total 6
———————— Manicheists 2, Macarius Aegyptus 4

380–400 total 7
———————— Manicheists 3, Macarius Aegyptus 4

400–420 total 8
———————— Manicheists 3, Pseudo Macarius 2, Cassianus 3

420–440 total 9
———————— Manicheists 3, Pseudo Macarius 2, Cassianus 3, Callestius 1

440–460 total 1
———————— Manicheists 1

460–480 total 3
———————— Manicheists 1, Faustus 1, Gennadius 1

480–500 total 3
———————— Manicheists 1, Faustus 1, Gennadius 1

500–520 total 1
———————— Manicheists 1

520–540 total 1
———————— Manicheists 1

540–1320 total 0

1320–1340 total 8
———————— William Ockham 8

1340–1360 total 13
———————— William Ockham 8, Adam Woodham 2, Richard Swineshead 1, John of Mirecourt 2

1360–1380 total 5
———————— Brinkel 1, Nicholas of Oresme 2, Albert of Saxony 2

* * *

1500–1520 total 1

1520–1540 total 1

1540–1560 total 1

1560–1580 total 1

1580–1600 total 1

1600–1620 total 6
————— Sennert 2, Gilbert 4

1620–1640 total 8
————— Sennert 2, Campanella 6

1640–1660 total 10
————— Gassendi 7, Magnenus 2, C. de Bergerac 1

1660–1680 total 13
———————— Gassendi 7, Sorbière 1, Glisson 3, Bernier 2

1680–1700 total 5
———————— Glisson 3, Bernier 2

1700–1720 total 1

1720–1740 total 1

1740–1760 total 21
———————— Lamettrie 5, Diderot 7, D'Alambert 5, Maupertuis 4

1760–1780 total 16
———————— Diderot 7, D'Alambert 5, Maupertuis 4

1780–1800 total 9
———————— Diderot 7, Radischtschev 2

1800–1820 total 1

1820–1840 total 6
————— Hershell 6

1840–1860 total 1

1860–1880 total 17
———————— Haeckel 6, Zöllner 4, Wundt 7

1880–1900 total 95
———————— Büchner 5, F. Schultze 4, Garlo 2, Nietzsche 9, Delboeuf 4, Wandermann 2, Wundt 7, Barat 1, Baldwin 5, Clifford 4, Naheli 3, Preyer 3, Morgan 3, Überweg 5, Romanes 4, Haeckel 6, Zollner 4, Ziehen 3, Paul Carus 4, Fouillée 5, Guyau 5, Espinas 4, Durand de Gros 2

1900–1920 total 100 [1]
———————— H. Maier, Wundt, Enriquez, Dantec, Rignano, Goeffding, B. Erdmann, Ziehen, Pauly, Bogdanov, Fouillée, Lazursky, Kandinsky, Wundt's school, Haeckel's followers (Monistenbund), W. Wagner

---

MONISTIC IDEALISM (560 B.C.–A.D. 1920)

B.C. 560–540 total 5
——————— Xenophanes 5

540–520 total 5
——————— Xenophanes 5

520–500 total 5
——————— Xenophanes 5

500–480 total 12
——————— Xenophanes 5, Parmenides 7

480–460 total 12
——————— Parmenides 7, Zeno 5

460–440 total 8
——————— Zeno 5, Melissos 3

440–420 total 8
——————— Zeno 5, Melissos 3

420–400 total 3
——————— Melissos 3

400–380 total 5
——————— Eukleides 3, Phaido 2

380–360 total 6
——————— Eukleides 3, Phaido 2, Eubulides 1

360–340 total 3
——————— Phaido 2, Eubulides 1

340–320 total 17
——————— Eubulides 1, Diodoros 2, Stilpo 2, Aristotle 12

320–300 total 35
——————— Diodoros 2, Stilpo 2, Alexinos 1, Menedemos 2, Aristotle 12, Theophrastos 7, Eudemos 2, Aristoxenos 4, Demetrios 3

300–280 total 30
——————— Stilpo 2, Alexinos 1, Menedemos 2, Theophrastos 7, Eudemos 2, Aristoxenos 4, Demetrios 3, Asclepiades 2, Theodulos 1, Klearchos 1, Phainias 1, Chamaileon 1, Praxiphanes 1, Straton 2

280–260 total 14
——————— Menedemos 2, Demetrios 3, Asclepiades 2, Theodulos 1, Klearchos 1, Phainias 1, Chamaileon 1, Praxiphanes 1, Straton 2

260–240 total 3
——————— Lykon 1, Hieronymos 2

240–220 total 4
——————— Lykon 1, Hieronymos 2, Prytanis 1

[1] For obvious reasons values are not given for living authors.

220–200   total 8
————— Ariston 3, Prytanis 1, Satyros 3, Hermippos 1

200–180   total 9
————— Ariston 3, Satyros 3, Hermippos 1, Sotion 2

180–160   total 6
————— Sotion 2, Antisthenes 2, Kritolaos 2

160–140   total 5
————— Antisthenes 2, Herakleides 1, Kritolaos 2

140–120   total 4
————— Herakleides 1, Boethos 2, Diodoros 1

120–100   total 4
————— Boethos 2, Diodoros 1, Erynneos 1

100–80   total 2
————— Diodoros 1, Erynneos 1

80–60   total 4
————— Andronikos 2, Xenarchos 1, Ariston 1

60–40   total 4
————— Ariston 1, Xenarchos 1, Andronikos 2

40–20   total 5
————— Andronikos 2, Boethos 1, Sextus 2

20–0   total 6
————— Boethos 1, Sextus 2, Sextus Jr. 1, Nikoleos 2

A.D. 0–20   total 10
————— Boethos 1, Sextus 1, Nikoleos 2, Sotion 2, Cornelius Celsus 1, L. Crassicius 1, Fabianus Papirius 1, Potamon 1

20–40   total 6
————— Sotion 2, Cornelius Celsus 1, L. Crassicius 1, Fabianus Papirius 1, Potamon 1

40–60   total 2
————— Alexander 2

60–80   total 2
————— Alexander 2

80–100   total 2
————— Ptolemaeus 2

100–120   total 10
————— Ptolomaeus 2, "Perikosm" 4, Aspasius 2, Adrastus 2

120–140   total 10
————— Aspasius 2, Adrastus 2, Ptolomaeus 2, Valentinus 4

140–160   total 13
————— Aspasius 2, Adrastus 2, Herminus 2, Claudius Ptol. 3, Valentinus 4

160–180   total 17
————— Herminus 2, Claudius Ptol. 3, Aristocles 1, Galenus 7, Valentinus 4

180–200   total 23
————— Herminus 2, Claudius Ptol. 3, Aristocles 1, Galenus 7, Alexander 6, Ptolemaeus 1, Heracleon 2, Marcus 1

200–220   total 16
————— Galenus 7, Alexander 6, Heracleon 2, Marcus 1

220–240   total 10
————— Alexander 6, "Pistis Sophia" 4

240–260   total 5
————— Peripatetic school 1, Orphic-Hermetic "Pistis Sophia" 4

260–280   total 5
————— Peripatetic school 1, "Pistis Sophia" 4

280–300   total 1
————— Peripatetic school 1

300–1200   total 0

1200–1220   total 6
————— Amalric de Bène 3, David Dinantensis 3

1220–1240   total 0

1240–1260   total 0

1260–1280   total 6
————— Siger of Brabant 4, Boethius de Dacia 2

1280–1300   total 6
————— Siger of Brabant 4, Boethius de Dacia 2

1300–1320   total 1
————— Pietro d'Abano 1

1320–1340   total 2
————— John of Baconthorp 2

1340–1360   total 3
————— John of Baconthorp 2, Urban 1

1360–1380   total 1
————— Averroism 1

1380–1400   total 1
————— Averroism 1

1400–1420   total 2
————— Paulus 2

1420–1440   total 2
————Paulus 2

1440–1460   total 2
————— Cajetan of Thiene 2

1460–1480   total 2
————— Cajetan of Thiene 2

1480–1500   total 3
————— Nicoletto Vernias 1, Leonardo da Vinci 2

1500–1520   total 6
————— Zimara 1, Achillini 1, Nifo 1, Faber 2, Fracastoro 1

1520–1540   total 8
————— Achillini 1, Nifo 1, Faber 2, Pomponazzi 4

1540–1560 total 11
———————— Faber 2, Leo Hebraeus 3, Serveto 4,
Dolet 2

1560–1580 total 6
———————— Cardanus 4, Supulveda 2

1580–1600 total 10
———————— G. Bruno 8, Lipsius 1, Cremonini 1

1600–1620 total 13
———————— G. Bruno 8, Vanini 4, Cesalpino 1

1620–1640 total 1

1640–1660 total 8
———————— Spinoza 8

1660–1680 total 15
———————— Spinoza 8, Rienverz 1, Balings 1,
S. Basso 2, Jorrig Jelles 1, Fédé 1, Oldenburg 1

1680–1700 total 19
———————— Spinoza (posthumous editions) 8,
Toland 4, Balings 1, S. de Vries 1, Pordage 1,
Rienverz 1, Kuffeler 1, Stosch 1, Jorrig Jelles 1

1700–1720 total 10
———————— Leenhof 1, Toland 4, Edelmann 1,
Boerhaave 3, Staalkopf 1

1720–1740 total 12
———————— Toland 4, Bolingbroke 2, Collins 1,
Chubb 1, Boerhaave 3, Boulinvillier 1

1740–1760 total 5
———————— Tindal 2, Morgan 1, Chubb 1, Edelmann 1

1760–1780 total 5
———————— Illuminates 3, Robinet 2

1780–1800 total 14
———————— Robinet 2, Deschamps 1, Fichte 8,
Heydenreich 2, Thorild 1

1800–1820 total 38
———————— Schelling 8, Hegel 8, Schopenhauer 8,
Cabanis 4, Goethe 8, Hölderlin 2

1820–1840 total 26
———————— Schopenhauer 8, Hegel 8, Feuerbach
6, Richter 4

1840–1860 total 21
———————— Schopenhauer 8, Feuerbach 6,
Frauenstädt 2, Lassale 4, F. Feuerbach 1

1860–1880 total 46
———————— R. Wagner 8, Hartmann 8, A. Spir 3,
Fiorentino 2, Feuerbach 6, Renan 6, Emerson 6,
Green 5, Frauenstädt 2

1880–1900 total 98
———————— Frauenstädt 2, L. Tolstoi 8, Rehmke
7, Bergson 8, Spir 3, Schuppe 5, Meis 1, Morselli 1,
Kreiči 4, Wallace 2, Hobhouse 4, E. Hartmann 8,
Ritchie 4, Störring 4, Lipps 7, Green 5, Bradley 7,
Bosanquet 4, W. Stern 4, Van Vloten 4, Brunsch-
vicg 4, W. Harris 2

1900–1920 total 110 [1]
———————— L. Tolstoi, Petronievič, Hartmann,
Schuppe, Lipps, Kreiči, Hobhouse, W. Stern,
Tauschinsky, Masci, Boelsche, Bradley, Rehmke,
Bergson, Bruno Willy, Haldane, Jones, Bosan-
quet, Gentile, Royce, Pringle-Pattison, Wallace,
Ritchie, Lasswitz, Benedetto Croce, Steudel,
Joachim, Segond

PLURALISTIC IDEALISM (nonreligious)
(540 B.C.–A.D. 1920)

B.C. 540–520 total 8
———————— Pythagoras 8

520–500 total 8
———————— Pythagoras 8

500–480 total 10
———————— Pythagoras 8, Alkmaion 2

480–460 total 2
———————— Alkmaion 2

460–440 total 1
———————— Ion 1

440–420 total 8
———————— Philolaos 5, Hippodamus 2, Ion 1

420–400 total 19
———————— Philolaos 5, Hippodamos 2, Simmias 1, Kebes 1, Lysis 1, Socrates 9

400–380 total 25
———————— Philolaos 5, Hippodamos 2, Sim-
mias 1, Kebes 1, Lysis 1, Sokrates 9, Aeschines 3,
Eurytos 1, Archytas 1, Hiketas 1

380–360 total 25
———————— Aeschines 3, Xenophon 7, Plato 12,
Eurytos 1, Archytas 1, Hiketas 1

360–340 total 42
———————— Aeschines 3, Xenophon 7, Plato 12,
Hiketas 1, Ekphantes 2, Xenophilos 1, Phanto 1,
Echekrates 1, Diokles 1, Polymnastos 1, Speus-
ippos 3, Xenokrates 3, Eudoxos 3, Herakleides 3

340–320 total 21
———————— Ekphantos 2, Xenophilos 1, Phanto 1,
Echekrates 1, Diokles 1, Polymnastos 1, Speus-
ippos 3, Xenokrates 3, Eudoxos 3, Herakleides 3,
Philippos 2

320–300 total 15
———————— Xenophilos 1, Phanto 1, Echekrates 1,
Diokles 1, Polymnastos 1, Xenokrates 3, Hera-
kleides 3, Philippos 2, Polemon 2

300–280 total 7
———————— Polemon 2, Krantor 4, Krates 1

280–260 total 7
———————— Polemon 2, Krantor 4, Krates 1

260–240 total 1

[1] For obvious reasons values are not given for living
authors.

240–220   total 1

220–200   total 1

200–180   total 1

180–160   total 1

160–140   total 1

140–120   total 1

100–80   total 3
————— Philo 3

80–60   total 12
————— Philo 3, Antiochos 4, T. Varro 5

60–40   total 18
————— T. Varro 5, Cicero 8, Aristo 1, Nigidius Figulus 4

40–20   total 16
————— Cicero 8, T. Varro 5, Theomnestos 1, Derkylides 2

20–0   total 4
————— Derkylides 2, Eudorus 2

A.D. 0–20   total 8
————— Philo Jud. 8

20–40   total 11
————— Philo Jud. 8, Thrasyllus 3

40–60   total 11
————— Philo Jud. 8, Thrasyllus 3

60–80   total 8
————— Apollonius 5, Moderatus 3

80–100   total 16
————— Apollonius 5, Moderatus 3, Plutarch 8

100–120   total 16
————— Plutarch 8, Apollonius 5, Cerinthus 2, Saturninus 1

120–140   total 28
————— Plutarch 8, Theo 2, Secundinus 2, Nicomachus 1, Gaius 2, Cerinthus 2, Saturninus 1, Cerdon 2, Marcion 4, Basileides 4

140–160   total 27
————— Theo 2, Secundinus 2, Nicomachus 1, Gaius 2, Herodes 2, Albinus 3, Calvicius 2, Nigrinus 1, Saturnilus 1, Cerdon 2, Marcion 4, Karpocrates 1, Basileides 4

160–180   total 27
————— Herodes 2, Albinus 3, Calvacius 2, Nicostratus 2, Nigrinus 1, Apuleius 6, Numenius 4, Cronius 2, Marcion 4, Karpocrates 1

180–200   total 35
————— Apuleius 6, Numenius 4, Cronius 2, Atticus 2, Karpocrates 1, Celsus 4, Maximus 5, Hierax 1, Severus 1, Bardesanes 4, Tatianus 3, Apelles 2

200–220   total 28
————— Numenius 4, Hierax 1, Severus 1, Philostratus 5, Hermetic literature 5, Ammonias Saccus 3, Bardesanes 4, Philippus 1, Theodotus 2, Noëtus 2

220–240   total 24
————— Philostratus 5, Hermetic literature 5, Ammonias Saccus 3, Bardesanes 4, Theodotus 2, Noëtus 2, Asclepiodotus 1, Sabellius 2

240–260   total 32
————— Hermetic Literature 5, Ammonias Saccus 3, Origines (Pagan) 2, Herennius 2, Longinus 2, Diogenes Laërtius 3, Plotinus 12, Sabelius 2, Artemus 1

260–280   total 27
————— Longinus 2, Diogenes Laërtius 3, Plotinus 12, Amelius 2, Anatolius 2, Cornelius Labeo 3, Artemus 1, Paulus 2

280–300   total 18
————— Amelius 2, Anatolius 2, Porphyry 7, Cornelius Labeo 3, Paulus 2, Lucianus 2

300–320   total 18
————— Porphyry 7, Alexander 2, Jamblichus 7, Lucianus 2

320–340   total 24
————— Jamblichus 7, Sopatros 2, Theodorus 1, Daxippos 2, Alexandros 2, Aidesios 2, Chalcidius 4, Arius 4

340–360   total 15
————— Sopatros 2, Theodoros 1, Daxippus 2, Aedesius 2, Chalcidius 4, Arius 4

360–380   total 27
————— Aedesius 2, Julianus 7, Maximus 1, Themistius 5, Sallustius 3, Eunapius 3, Vettius Agorius Praetextatus 2, Aetius 1, Ursacius 1, Valens 1, Eunomius 1

380–400   total 20
————— Themistius 5, Vettius Agorius Pretextatus 2, Sallustius 3, Eunapius 3, Eunomius 1, Augustine 6 (Pagan)

400–420   total 21
————— Plutarch 1, Hypatia 3, Macrobius 4, Dominus 3, Olympiodorus 4, Syrianus 1, Julian (Exlanum) 2, Pelagius 3

420–440   total 23
————— Plutarch 1, Macrobius 4, Domninus 3, Olympiodorus 4, Syrianus 1, Hierocles 2, Julian 2, Pelagius 3, Nestorius 3

440–460   total 22
————— Domninus 3, Hermias 3, Hierocles 2, Proclus 8, Nestorius 3, Eutyches 3

460–480   total 19
————— Hermias 3, Proclus 8, Ammonius Hermeion 2, Asclepios 1, Olympiadus Jr. 2, Eutyches 3

480–500   total 22
————— Proclus 8, Ammonius Hermeion 2, Asclepios 1, Olympiadus 2, Marinus 3, Elias 1, David 2, Acacius 1

500–520   total 17
————— Ammonius Hermeion 2, Elias 1, David 2, Diodorus 1, Doros 1, Damascius 4, Simplicius 5, Severus 1

520–540 total 12
————— Doros 1, Damascius 4, Simplicius 5,
Priscianus 1, Severus 1

540–560 total 11
————— Damascius 4, Simplicius 5, Priscianus
1, Themistius 1

560–580 total 1
————— Priscianus 1

580–600 total 2
————— Stephanus 2

600–620 total 4
————— Stephanus 2, Sergius 2

620–640 total 4
————— Stephanus 2, Sergius 2

640–660 total 3
————— Stephanus 2, Pyrrhus 1

660–1140 total 0

1140–1160 total 2
————— Bernardus Silvestris 2

1160–1180 total 2
————— Bernardus Silvestris 2

1180–1200 total 3
————— Joachim de Floris 3

1200–1220 total 3
————— Joachim de Floris 3

1220–1240 total 2
————— Michael Scotus 2

1240–1260 total 0

1260–1280 total 0

1280–1300 total 0

1300–1320 total 8
————— Master Eckhart 8

1320–1340 total 10
————— Master Eckhart 8, Thomas Bradwardine 2

1340–1360 total 13
————— Thomas Bradwardine 2, J. Buridan 2, J. Wycliffe 3, Petrarca 6

1360–1380 total 11
————— J. Buridan 2, J. Wycliffe 3, Petrarca 6

1380–1400 total 7
————— J. Wycliffe 3, Peter d'Ailly 4

1400–1420 total 4
————— Peter d'Ailly 4

1420–1440 total 4
————— Peter d'Ailly 4

1440–1460 total 0

1460–1480 total 0

1480–1500 total 0

II — 43

1500–1520 total 5
————— Erasmus 5

1520–1540 total 22
————— S. Franck 2, Vives 6, Reuchlin 4,
T. Morus 6, J. Pico della Mirandola Sr. 4

1540–1560 total 16
————— S. Franck 2, Vives 6, Paracelsus 4,
Servetus 4

1560–1580 total 22
————— Paracelsus 4, Copernicus 8, Wilson 3,
Lever 3, Telesius 4

1580–1600 total 25
————— Paracelsus 4, Case 2, Scotus 2,
Crackanthrop 1, Hixner 1, Wilson 1, Weigel 3,
Lever 3, Telesius 4, Sanderson 1, Ramists 4,
Arminius 1

1600–1620 total 36
————— Galileo 8, Keppler 8, Case 2, Crackan-
throp 1, Hixner 1, Scotus 2, Fludd 2, Weigel 3,
Tycho Brahe 8, Renery 1

1620–1640 total 69
————— Weigel 3, Regius 3, Fludd 2, Keppler
8, J. van Helmont 4, Galileo 8, Descartes 8,
Mersenne 4, Herrebord 1, Renery 1, Koxner 1,
Comenius 7, H. Grotius 6, H. Cherbury 4, Al-
stedius 3, Althusius 3, Lemaitre 1, R. Arnauld 2

1640–1660 total 61
————— Descartes 8, Galileo 8, Geulinex 6,
Comenius 7, Pascal 7, Regius 3, De Roy 1, H.
Morus 4, Culverwell 1, Heerebord 1, Mersenne 4,
Brooke 2, Whichcote 1, Smith 2, Th. White 2,
H. Cherbury 4

1660–1680 total 69
————— De Roy 1, Heerebord 1, Heydanus 1,
Comenius 7, Rohault 1, De la Forge 3, Nicole 4,
Arnauld 4, Geulinex 6, Malebranche 7, Clauberg 3,
H. Morus 4, Leibnitz 9, Puffendorf 3, Thomasius
4, Bourignon 2, Le Grand 2, Pascal 7

1680–1700 total 82
————— Rohault 1, Meier 3, Cordemoy 2,
De la Forge 3, Lanion 2, Lamy 2, Leibnitz 9,
Wittich 1, Heydanus 1, Arnauld 4, Nicole 4,
H. Morus 4, Puffendorf 3, Molinos 3, Fardella 2,
Guyon 2, Cudworth 5, Clauberg 3, Tomassin 1,
Fontenelle 2, Shaftesbury 5, Poiret 2, Th. Tay-
lor 3, Giovenale 2, Norris 2, Malebranche 7,
Bourignon 2

1700–1720 total 55
————— Cordemoy 2, Wittich 1, Norris 2,
Malebranche 7, Lamy 1, Leibnitz 9, Poiret 2,
M. van Helmont 2, Tomassin 1, Shaftesbury 5,
Berkeley 8, Clarke 2, Collier 5, Giovenale 2,
Fardella 2, André 1, Taylor 1, Guyon 2

1720–1740 total 38
————— Leibnitz 9, Berkeley 8, André 1,
C. Wolf 7, Billfinger 1, Thümmig 2, Reinbeck 1,
Heineccius 1, Joch. Lange 2, Budde 2, Rüdiger 2,
Creuz 2

1740–1760   total 81
——————— Berkeley 8, C. Wolf 7, Gottsched 2, Plouquet 4, Swedenborg 4, Vico 7, Martin Knutzen 4, Edelmann 1, Gerdil 2, Hutcheson 4, Fontenelle 2, Lomonosov 4, Kant 12, Polignac 4, Baumgarten 4, Daries 2, Crusius 4, Creuz 2, Richmann 3, Reinbeck 1

1760–1780   total 59
——————— Swedenborg 4, Baumgarten 4, Euler 6, Plouquet 4, Lambert 4, Kant 12, C. Wolf 7, Tetens 4, Lomonosov 4, Rousseau 8, Daries 2

1780–1800   total 73
——————— Kant 12, Rousseau 8, Eberhardt 1, Platner 1, Reinhold 2, S. Maimon 4, Tetens 4, Herder 6, Jacobi 6, Jacob 1, J. Schultz 3, Schwab 1, Schiller 8, Hamann 4, Pestalozzi 4, Krug 2, Tittel 1, Mendelssohn 4

1800–1820   total 100
——————— Fichte 8, Kant 12, Schelling 8, Goethe 8, Jäsche 2, Krug 2, Wellansky 3, Wronsky 6, Schleiermacher 4, Wittenbach 2, Kinker 1, Villers 1, Wirgmann 1, Jacob 1, Fries 6, M. de Biran 5, Hemert 2, Stutzmann 2, Krause 4, Mehmel 1, Fourier 5, St. Martin 4, Coleridge 4, Tennemann 4, W. Blake 4

1820–1840   total 123
——————— Weisse 1, V. Cousin 4, Schelling 8 Goethe 8, M. de Biran 5, Ampère 5, Whewell 6, Galitch 2, Bolzano 6, Krause 4, Fourier 5, Schleiermacher 4, A. Frank 1, Damiron 2, Saisset 1, Mizkiewicz 6, Rosmini 6, Lammenais 4, Chateaubriand 5, M. de Stael 4, Royer-Collard 2, Jouffroi 1, Benecke 2, Leroux 1, Wronsky 6, Khomiakov 4, Fichte Jr. 4, Harms 2, Bouterwek 1, V. Hugo 8, S. Sibbern 3, Galluppi 2

1840–1860   total 153
——————— Romer 1, Hermann 1, Steffens 1, Schaden 1, Carlyle 4, Baader 5, Harris 3, Khomiakov 4, Samarin 2, Deutinger 2, Schelling 8, Schmidt 1, Lotze 5, Carrière 3, Noack 1, Fechner 7, Minghetti 1, Chalybaeus 1, Michelet 4, Pagano 1, Zeller 5, J. Erdmann 4, Daub 2, Tomasseo 2, V. Cousin 4, Vacherot 3, Pavlov 1, Krause 4, Maglia 1, M. de Biran 5 (posthumous works), Saisset 1, Bouillier 2, Ravaisson 3, Amerling 1, Frank 3, A. Smetana 4, Weikenborn 1, Bolzano 6, Klocel 1, Manzoni 1, Rosmini 6, Gioberti 6,

Maniani 3, Benecke 2, Ampère 5, Paul Janet 4, Rosenkrantz 4, Secretan 4, V. Hugo 8, Allievo 1

1860–1880   total 163
——————— Carlyle 4, Hamilton 6, Mansel 2, Michelet 4, Zeller 5, P. Janet 4, Vacherot 3, Frank 3, V. Soloviev 6, M. Carrière 4, Lotze 5, Saisset 1, J. Erdmann 4, Bouillier 3, Mamiani 3, Ferri 3, Ravaisson 3, Remusat 3, Butlerov 2, Chaignet 2, Damiron 2, Brochard 2, Boutroux 4, G. Class 2, Zerteleff 1, Bahnsen 1, Sengler 1, Perty 1, Fichte Jr. 4, V. Cousin 4, Tyndall 4, Brace 2, Hickock 2, Fraser 3, Ruskin 6, Kavelin 3, A. J. Davies 4, Axakov 4, Lachelier 4, Ferrier 2, Brentano 4, Uphues 1, J. Simon 2, Jurkevic 1, Secretan 4, Teichmüller 2, Bergmann 2, J. Martineau 4, Upton 2, Owen 2, V. Hugo 8, W. Crookes 4, Du Paul 1

1880–1900   total 190
——————— Soloviev 6, Renouvier 7, Paul Janet 5, Martineau 4, Carpentier 2, Ruskin 6, Browning 4, Armstrong 2, Lopatine 4, S. Trubetzkoi 4, E. Trubetzkoi 3, Debolsky 2, Kozlov 2, Croll 1, Tait 2, Ladd 4, Sommer 1, Hauréau 4, Čičerin 4, Strachov 3, Radlov 2, N. Grot 3, Siebeck 2, Caird 3, Howison 2, R. Eucken 5, Drummond 4, Secretan 4, Ormond 1, Vacherot 3, Chaignet 2, Brochard 2, Naville 4, F. Brentano 4, Axakov 4, Lachelier 4, J. Simon 2, Teichmüller 2, Bergmann 2, Martineau 4, Upton 2, Amiel 4, E. Rod 2, Dauriac 3, Pillon 4, C. Read 2, Lutoslavsky 4, A. Seth 4, Jones 2, McTaggart 5, Mackenzie 3, Fairbairn 2, Crookes 4, Bugaiev 4, Bobrov 2, Novgorodzev 2, Owen 2, Du Pret 1, Ose 2, Ulrich 2, Muirhead 3

1900–1920   total 163 [1]
——————— Renouvier, Münsterberg, Max Scheler, S. Hessen, V. Soloviev, Lossky, Ambrosi, Petrone, Credaro, Howison, Vorovka, Alloway, R. Eucken, Oldendorf, Askoldov, McTaggart, S. Frank, Lasci, Heymans, Muirhead, Ormond, Novgorodzev, W. James, Ilyin, Lac´yzensky, Zenkovsky, Pelikan, Hoppe, Ladd, S. Trubetzkoi, Bulgakov, E. Trubetzkoi, Lopatine, Debolsky, Radlov, K. Groos, Joël, Falckenberg, H. Schwarz, Maritain, Becker, Tröltsch, Oesterreich, Schultz, Pfleiderer, E. Wyneken, W. Temple, McDougall

[1] For obvious reasons values are not given for living authors.

European-Christian Culture

PLURALISTIC IDEALISM (religious)
(A.D. 100–1920)

A.D. 100–120   total 3

120–140   total 3

140–160   total 8
——————— M. Aristides 3, Justin Martyr 5

160–180   total 15
——————— Justin Martyr 5, Melito 2, Apollinaris 1, Tatianus 3, Minucius Felix 4

180–200   total 23
——————— Melito 2, Apollinaris Hier. 1, Athenagoras 4, Minucius Felix 4, Theophilus Ant. 2, Jerenaeus Lugd. 4, Clement of Alexandria 6

200–220   total 13
——————— Jerenaeus Lugd. 4, Clement of Alexandria 6, Hippolitus 3

220–240 total 11
———————— Hippolitus 3, Origenes 8

240–260 total 12
———————— Origenes 8, Dionysius Magnus 2, Gregorius Thaumaturgus 2

260–280 total 5
———————— Dionysius Magnus 2, Gregorius Thaumaturgus 2, Theognostus 1

280–300 total 1
———————— Pamphilus (Caes.) 1

300–320 total 6
———————— Pamphilus (Caes.) 1, Eusebius (Caes.) 3, Methodius (Phil.) 2

320–340 total 13
———————— Eusebius (Caes.) 3, Athanasius Magnus 4, Lactantius 4, Eustethius (Ant.) 1, Alexander (Alex.) 1

340–360 total 11
———————— Eusebius (Caes.) 3, Athanasius Magnus 4, Didymus 1, I. Firm. Maternus 3

360–380 total 32
———————— Athanasius Magnus 4, Didymus 1, I. Firm. Maternus 3, Hilarius (Poit.) 3, Marius Victorinus 3, Basilius Magnus 6, Gregory Nazianzen 6, Gregory of Nyssa 6

380–400 total 32
———————— Didymus 1, Basilius Magnus 6, Gregory Nazianzen 6, Gregory of Nyssa 6, Johannes Chrys. 5, Ambrosius Mediol. 5, Apollinarius Laod. 3

400–420 total 24
———————— Johannes Chrysostomus 5, Augustinus 10, Synesius 2, Nemesius 2, Theodorus (Mops.) 2, Cyrillus Alex. 3

420–440 total 20
———————— Augustinus 10, Theodorus (Mops.) 2, Cyrillus (Alex.) 3, Theodoretus (Cyr.) 3, Ibass Edess. 2

440–460 total 10
———————— Diadochos (Fot.) 2, Cyrillus Alex. 3, Theodoretus (Cyr.) 3, Ibass of Edessa 2

460–480 total 8
———————— Diadochos (Fot.) 2, Claudius Mamertus 3, Theodoretus (Cyr.) 3

480–500 total 2
———————— Aeneas of Gaza 2

500–520 total 13
———————— Aeneas of Gaza 2, Procopius of Gaza 3, Dionysius Areopag. 8

520–540 total 26
———————— Aeneas of Gaza 2, Procopius of Gaza 3, Dionysius Areopag. 8, Boethius 6, Leontius 3, Joannes of Philopinus 4

540–560 total 14
———————— Leontius (Byr.) 3, Joannes of Philopinus 4, Zacharias (Myx.) 2, Joannes Lydos 2, Cassiodorus 3

560–580 total 7
———————— Joannes Lydos 2, Cassiodorus 3, Martinus (Bracar.) 2

580–600 total 6
———————— Martinus (Bracar.) 2, Gregorius Magnus 1st 4

600–620 total 8
———————— Isidorus Hispalensis 4, Gregorius Magnus 1st 4

620–640 total 10
———————— Isidorus Hispalensis 4, Maximus Confessor 6

640–660 total 6
———————— Maximus Confessor 6

660–680 total 8
———————— Maximus Confessor 6, Agatho 2

680–700 total 2
———————— Agatho 2

700–720 total 3
———————— Bede Venerable 3

720–740 total 8
———————— Bede Venerable 3, John Damascene 5

740–760 total 6
———————— John Damascene 5, Egbertus 1

760–780 total 1
———————— Egbertus 1

780–800 total 4
———————— Alcuin 4

800–820 total 6
———————— Alcuin 4, Fredegisus 2

820–840 total 10
———————— Fredegisus 2, Hrabanus Maurus 4, Agobard 2, Candidus 2

840–860 total 18
———————— Hrabanus Maurus 4, Agobard 2, Servetus Lupus 2, Paschasius Radbertus 2, John Scotus Erigena 8

860–880 total 21
———————— Servatus Lupus 2, Paschasius Radbertus 2, John Scotus Erigena 8, Ratramnus (of Corbie) 2, Photius 3, Godescale 2, Hincmar of Rheims 2

880–900 total 9
———————— Photius 3, Hincmar 2, Eric of Auxerre 2, Remigius of Auxerre 2

900–920 total 4
———————— Remigius of Auxerre 2, Arethas 2

920–940 total 2
———————— Arethas 2

940–960 total 1

960–980 total 1

980–1000   total 3
——————— Sylvester II (Gerbert) 3

1000–1020   total 8
——————— Sylvester II (Gerbert) 3, Fulbert 2, Notker Labeo 3

1020–1040   total 5
——————— Fulbert of Chartres 2, Notker Labeo 3

1040–1060   total 13
——————— Berengar of Tours 3, Peter Damian 3, Anselm (Bes.) 2, Otloh 2, Lanfrancus 3

1060–1080   total 31
——————— Berengar 3, Peter Damian 3, Anselm (Bes.) Otloh 2, Lanfrancus 3, Mich. Psellus 3, Symeon Th. Nov. 4, Anselm of Canterbury 7, Johannes Italus 2, Michael Ephes. 2

1080–1100   total 32
——————— Berengar T. 3, Lanfrancus 3, Mich. Psellos 3, Symeon Th. Nov. 4, Anselm Cant. 7, Johannes Italus 2, Michael Ephesus 2, Manegold 3, Eustratios 2, Roscelinus 3

1100–1120   total 22
——————— Anselm of Canterbury 7, Manegold 3, Eustratius 2, Roscelinus 3, Odo 1, Adelard of Bath 2, Bruno (Segni) 2, William of Champeaux 2

1120–1140   total 34
——————— Eustratius 2, Roscelinus 3, Adelard of Bath 2, Bruno (Segni) 2, William of Champeaux 2, Peter Abelard 4, Bernard Carn. 2, William of Conches 2, Honorius Aug. 3, Thierry of Chartres 2, Hugh of St. Victor 5, Bernardus Claraev. 5

1140–1160   total 40
——————— Peter Abelard 4, William of Conches 2, Bernard Claraev. 5, William of St. Theodoni 2, Honorius of Antim 3, Joscelin 1, Thierry of Chartres 2, Hugh of St. Victor 5, Gualterus de Mauret. 1, Robert of Melid. 2, Gilbert de la Porree 3, Richard of St. Victor 4, Peter Lombard 4, Dominicus Gundissalinus 2

1160–1180   total 26
——————— Gualterus de Mauretania 1, Robert of Melid. 2, Richard of St. Victor 4, Peter Lombard 4, Dominicus Gundissalinus 2, John of Salisbury 3, Isaac de Stella 2, Gandulfs 2, Clarenbaldus 2, (Alex. III) Roland Bandinelli 2, Petrus Comestor 2

1180–1200   total 22
——————— John of Salisbury 3, Roland Bandinelli (Alex. III) 2, Petrus Pichav. 2, Peter the Chanter 2, Alfredus Anglicus 2, Radulfus Ardens 1, Alan of Lille 3, Nicolaus Amb. 2, Gualterus of St. Victor 2, Gottfried de Bretenil 1, Alexander Neckham 2

1200–1220   total 21
——————— Petrus Pictaviensis 2, Alfredus Anglicus 2, Radulfus Ardens 1, Alan of Lille 3, Nicolaus Ambian. 2, Alexander Neckham 2, Simon of Tournai 1, Thomas Gallo 1, Praepositinus (Crom.) 2, Robertus de Corceon 1, Guilelmus (Aux.) 2, Philippus Grevius 2

1220–1240   total 22
——————— Thomas Gallo 1, Praepositinus (Cr.) 2, Guilelmus of Auxerre 2, Philippus Grevius 2, Radulfus de Longo Camps. 1, William of Auvergne 3, Robert Grosseteste 4, Alexander of Hales 4, Walter (Chateau-Thierry) 1, Roland Cremona 2

1240–1260   total 42
——————— William of Auvergne 3, Robert Grosseteste 4, Alexander of Hales 4, Walter (Chateau-Thierry) 1, Bartholomeus Anglicus 2, Johannes de Rupella 2, Adam de Marisco 2, Hugh of St. Caro 2, Robert Bacon 1, Albertus Magnus 8, William Shyreswood 1, Nicolaus (Methone) 3, Nicephorus Blemmydes 1, Vincent of Beauvais 2, Richard Fischacre 1, Lambert (Auxerre) 1, Nicolaus of Paris 2, Thomas (Chantimpré) 2

1260–1280   total 64
——————— Bartholomeus Anglicus 2, Hugh of St. Caro 2, Albertus Magnus 8, Nicolaus (Methone) 3, Nicephorus Blemmydes 1, Vincent of Beauvais 2, Thomas (Chantimpré) 2, Nicolaus of Paris 2, Robert Kilwardby 2, Johannes Bonaventura 8, Richard Rufus 1, Thomas (Torn) 2, Thomas Aquinas 12, Ulricus Engelberti 3, Petrus de Tarentasia (Johannes V) 2, Petrus Hispanus (Johannes XXI) 2, Roger Bacon 6, Hannibaldus de Hannibeldis 1, Bombolognus de Bononia 1, Romanus de Roma 1, Reginald (Piperno) 1

1280–1300   total 74
——————— Albertus Magnus 8, Roger Bacon 6, Reginald (Piperno) 1, Raymond Lully 5, Witelo 2, Heinrich Bates 2, John Peckham 1, William de la Mare 1, Walter (Brugges) 2, Henricus Gandavensis 4, Goffried (Fontaines) 3, Bernard of Trulio 2, Aegidius (Lessines) 2, Remigio di ch. dei Gir. 2, John of Ghent 1, Ramberto dei Primadirri 1, Aegidius Romanus 3, George Pachymeres 2, Sophonias 2, Hugo Ripelin 3, Matthew of Aquasparta 2, Fr. Eustachius 2, Nicolaus of Occam 1, Roger (Marston) 2, Richard de Mediavilla 3, William (Ware) 2, Peter John Olivi 3, William (Hothun) 1, Richard (Clapwell) Dietrich de Vriberg 2, Augustinus Triumphus 2

1300–1320   total 75
——————— Raymond Lully 5, Heinrich Bates 2, Walter (Brugges) 2, Goffried (Fontaines) 3, Aegidius (Lessines) 2, Remigio di ch. dei Gir. 2, John of Ghent 1, Ramberto dei Primedirri 1, Aegidius Romanus 3, George Pachymeres 2, Sophonias 2, Matthew of Aquasparta 2, Richard de Mediavilla 3, William (Ware) 2, Dietrich de Vriberg 2, Augustinus Triumphus 2, Maximus Plemides 2, Bernard of Auvergne 1, Jean Quidort 2, William Peter of Godino 2, Hervé Nédéllec 3, Tolomeo (Lucca) 2, William Macklesfield 1, Jacobus Capocci 2, Gerard (Bologna) 2, Dante 8, Duns Scotus 2, Durandus de S. Porciano 2, Thomas Sutton 2

1320–1340   total 42
————————— Augustinus Triumphus 2, William Peter God. 2, Hervé Nédéllec 3, Tolomeo (Lucca) 2, Dante 8, Durandus de S. Porciano 2, Thomas Sutton 2, Siger (Courtrai) 2, Petrus Aureolus 2, Petrus de Palude 1, Jacobus (Lausanne) 1, Johannes de Regina 1, Johannes Picardi de Lucid. 2, Nicolus Triveth. 2, Guido Terreni 2, Siegbert (Beek) 2, Bartoldus de Mosburch 1, Antonius Andreas 1, Heinrich (Lübeck) 1, Franciscus of Mayron 2, Walter Burleigh 1

1340–1360   total 36
————————— Thomas Sutton 2, Petrus de Palude 1, Guido Terreni 2, Walter Burleigh 1, Bernardus Lombardi 1, Durandelus 1, J. Tauler 4, H. Suso 5, Ruysbroeck 4, Robert Holkot 1, Thomas (Strassburg) 2, Gregorius (Rimini) 2, Gregorios Palames 6, Nicolaus Kabasilas 4

1360–1380   total 30
————————— J. Tauler 4, H. Suso 5, Ruysbroeck 4, Gregorius Palames 6, Nicolaus Kabasilas 4, "Eine Deutsche Theologie" 3, Marsilius (Inghen.) 2, Heinrich (Hainbuch) 2

1380–1400   total 12
————————— Ruysbroeck 4, Nicolaus Kabasilas 4, Marsilius (Inghen.) 2, Heinrich (Hainbuch) 2

1400–1420   total 4
————————— Jean Charlier (Gerson) 4

1420–1440   total 11
————————— Jean Charlier (Gerson) 4, John Capreolus 3, Heinrich (Gorkum) 1, Antonin 3

1440–1460   total 19
————————— John Capreolus 3, Antonin 3, Dionysius Cartusianus 4, Heimerick de Campo 1, Nicolaus Cusanus 8

1460–1480   total 20
————————— Dionysius Cartusianus 4, Nicolaus Cusanus 8, Petrus Nigri 1, Thomas à Kempis 4, Gabriel Biel 3

1480–1500   total 5
————————— Petrus Nigri 1, Gabriel Biel 3, Petrus Tartaretus 1

1500–1520   total 10
————————— Bembo 2, Bovillus 2, Mut. Rufus 2, Bessarion 4

1520–1540   total 12
————————— Bovillus 2, Pereira 4, Mut. Rufus 2, Agrippa 2, Bembo 2

1540–1560   total 20
————————— Loyola 8, Soto 2, Nizolius 3, Xaverius 3, Laynes 4

1560–1580   total 27
————————— St. Theresa 6, Jean de la Croix 4, Hurtado de Mendoza 2, Zamora 2, Ledesma 1, Gursky 1, Rodrigez 4, Salmeron 3, Laynes 4

1580–1600   total 47
————————— Jean de la Croix 4, Ledesma 1, Temple 2, Toletus 3, Fonseca 3, Molina 3, Suarez 6, Ribadeneira 3, St. Theresa 6, Cam. de Lelly 2, Mariana 3, Rodrigez 4, Salmeron 3, Goes 2, S. Conto 2

1600–1620   total 50
————————— Toletus 3, Bellarminus 4, Temple 2, Vallius 2, Herrera 1, Vasquez 4, Fr. Salesius 4, P. Hurtado de Mendosa 2, B. Pereira 2, Roselli 4, Molina 3, Grey de Valencia 4, Albergati 4, Caponus 2, Strizzi 2, Davy de Perrin 3, Berulle 4

1620–1640   total 49
————————— Fr. Salesius 4, Bellarminus 4, Lessius 4, Colombi 2, Pateanus 1, Pastorus 1, Maltesius 1, Scribonius 3, Escobard y Mendoza 6, Ruez de Mont 2, Tanner 3, V. Depaul 2, Busenbaum 4, Berulle 4, Duverger 3, Lemaitre 1, R. Arnauld 2, Reginaldius 2

1640–1660   total 29
————————— Bourdin 3, Morin 2, Escobard 6, Izambertus 2, Barbosa 3, Jacobus Ganz 1, J. De Sen Thoma 1, Martinez de Rip 1, Balthasar Grazian 4, Busenbaum 4, Reginaldius 2

1660–1680   total 38
————————— Voetius 2, Bourdin 3, Bernier 2, Lamy 2, Malebranche 7, Nicole 4, Arnauld 4, J. De Lago 3, Rodriquez 2, Pascal 7, Martinius 2

1680–1700   total 46
————————— Daniel 2, Buffier 2, Bossuet 6, Makovsky 2, Tournemine 2, Janyševsky 2, Tylkovsky 2, Mlodzinevsky 2, Moškovsky 2, Faydit 2, Voetius 2, Fardella 2, Fénelon 6, Thomassin 1, Pyrrhing 2, Mairus 2, Guillemin 2, Ortega 3, Sanucky 2

1700–1720   total 43
————————— Renodot 2, Heiffenstael 1, Merger 1, Duhamel 1, Bossuet 6, Fénelon 6, Buffier 2, Tournemine 2, Regnaut 1, Andola 1, Thomassin 1, Petau 1, Daniel 2, Giovenale 2, Lamy 2, Malebranche 7, André 1, Huet 1, Faydit 1, Fardella 2

1720–1740   total 24
————————— Petrus Mansi 2, Schallkovitch 2, Cordeyro 2, Montefortuno 2, Fénelon 6, Frassen 2, Dutertre 2, Miaskovsky 2, André 1, Podlesjecky 2, Huet 1

1740–1760   total 12
————————— Polignac 4, Radsky 2, Dobscievič 2, Dom Calmes 4

1760–1780   total 16
————————— Gutharoth 2, Menschenberger 2, Poliansky 1, Lechner 1, Bonotto 2, Guenée 4, Dom Calmes 4

1780–1800   total 17
————————— Holzelau 1, Muschka 1, Gero 2, Cortivo 1, Geuldus 1, Zanchi 1, Oetinger 1, Baader 5, De Bonald 4

1800–1820   total 22
————————— Molitor 1, Trebinsky 2, Kollataj 2, J. de Maistre 6, De Bonald 4, Baader 5, Pembridge 1, Bonafons 1

1820–1840   total 47
———————— Vinet 4, Goerres 5, Surovecky 2,
Lammenais 4, De Maistre 6, De Bonald 4,
Ferault 2, Molitor 1, Goluchovsky 2, Barruel 2,
Torre 1, Tchaadaiev 3, Pointer 1, Novinsky 2,
Szumavy 1, Mutter 1, Ganitch 1, Tomazzo 2,
Franceskino 1, Fournièr 2

1840–1860   total 52
———————— Dorgan 2, Hagel 1, Regaut 1, Richter
1, Menden 1, Dufour 1, Fitz 1, Gumpasin 1,
Barrau 1, Manosciaglio 1, Rosaunen 1, Goerres 5,
Scherer 3, Gioberti 6, Balmez 5, Vinet 4, Newmann 6, Nitsch 1, Miller 1, Krolikovsky 1, Gratry
1, Baader 5 (posthumous works), Kleutgen 2

1860–1880   total 44
———————— Kleutgen 2, Scherer 3, Sabatier 2,
Pécaut 3, Bois 2, Newmann 6, Gioberti 6, Bach 1,
Rittler 1, Lehmann 1, Hortling 1, Michelis 1,
Margot 1, Stoeckl 4, Hahn 1, Gordon 1, Spalding
1, Volzoger 1, Lacordaire 1, Mandrolle 1, Secchi 4

1880–1900   total 94
———————— Feldner 2, Kathrein 2, Hortling 1,
Schnitzler 2, Dressel 2, Schneid 1, Fischer 1,
Schneider 3, Lehmen 1, Schell 1, Rittler 1, Bach 1,
Hebinger 1, Kahn 2, Linsemann 2, Margot 1,
Hagemann 1, Stoeckl 4, Schwanz 1, Haffner 1,
Pfeiffer 1, Plancy 2, Ardouin 2, Merkle 2, Word 1,
Champigny 2, Probst 1, Moignot 2, Hildebrandt 1,
Boncant 1, Liberatore 1, Froschhammer 3, Luto-
slavsky 4, Gonzales 3, T. Pesch 4, C. Pesch 1,
Deschamps 1, Ollé-Laprune 4, Harper 4, Gruber
4, Otto Willmann 4, Wassmann 4, Sabatier 2,
Gutberlet 4, De-Verges 1, Ventura 1, Fontana 2

1900–1920   total 90 [1]
———————— Gutberlet, Piat, Schneider, Mercier,
Hartner, Lehmen, Hebinger, Hortling, Baur,
Schell, Lutoslavsky, S. Severino, Cordovaní,
Gemelli, Olgiati, Thierry, Caro, Baets, Cossena,
Bonillard, Duhem, Lapperent, Grasset, Thamin,
Dumesnil, Bros, Wassmann, Dunan, Maritain,
Gay, Blondel, Labertonnière, Hoppe, Isenkrahe,
Mausbach, Förster, Geyser, Willmann, Horvat,
Loisy

MIXED PHILOSOPHIES, plus Skepticism,
Agnosticism, Criticism, and others.
(460 B.C.–A.D. 1920)

B.C. 460–440   total 13
———————— Protágoras 8, Gorgias 5

440–420   total 13
———————— Protagoras 8, Gorgias 5

420–400   total 36
———————— Protagoras 8, Gorgias 5, Prodikos 5,
Hippias 4, Antiphon 4, Pollio 2, Kallikles 2,
Kritias 3, Thrasymachos 3

[1] For obvious reasons values are not given for living
authors.

400–380   total 29
———————— Gorgias 5, Prodikos 5, Hippias 4,
Antiphon 4, Polos 2, Thrasymachos 3, Aristippos 6

380–360   total 16
———————— Gorgias 5, Alkidamas 4, Metrodoros 1,
Aristippos 6

360–340   total 14
———————— Alkidamas 4, Aristippos 6, Metrodoros 1, Arete 1, Aithiops 1, Antipater 1

340–320   total 5
———————— Arete 1, Aithiops 1, Antipater 1,
Aristippos (grandchild) 1, Anaxarchos 1

320–300   total 16
———————— Theodoros 2, Hegesias 2, Annikeris 2,
Euhemeros 3, Anaxarchos 1, Pyrrho 6

300–280   total 15
———————— Theodoros 2, Hegesias 2, Annikeris 2,
Euhemeros 3, Pyrrho 6

280–260   total 18
———————— Theodoros 2, Hegesias 2, Annikeris 2,
Pyrrho 6, Timon 3, Arkesilaos 3

260–240   total 6
———————— Timon 3, Arkesilaos 3

240–220   total 9
———————— Timon 3, Arkesilaos 3, Lakydes 3

220–200   total 7
———————— Lakydes 3, Telekles 2, Euanoridas 2

200–180   total 3
———————— Euanoridas 2, Hegesinos 1

180–160   total 6
———————— Hegesinos 1, Karneades 5

160–140   total 7
———————— Karneades 5, Kleitomachos 2

140–120   total 9
———————— Karneades 5, Kleitomachos 2, Charmedas 2

120–100   total 4
———————— Kleitomachos 2, Charmedas 2

100–80   total 2
———————— Charmedas 2

80–60   total 0

60–40   total 5
———————— Ainesidemos 5

40–20   total 5
———————— Ainesidemos 5

20–0   total 5
———————— Ainesidemos 5

A.D. 0–100   total 0

100–120   total 2
———————— Menodotus 2

120–140   total 6
———————— Favorinus 4, Menodotus 2

140–160   total 6
——————— Favorinus 4, Menodotus 2

160–180   total 6
——————— Sextus Empiricus 6

180–200   total 6
——————— Sextus Empiricus 6

200–220   total 6
——————— Sextus Empiricus 6

220–1300   total 0

1300–1320   total 3
——————— Ioannes of Iandun 3

1320–1340   total 7
——————— I. of Iandun 3, Nicolaus (Autr.) 4

1340–1360   total 4
——————— Nicolaus (Autr.) 4

1380–1400   total 4
——————— Albert of Saxony 2, Nicolas of Oresme 2

1400–1500   total 0

1500–1520   total 1

1520–1540   total 10
——————— Telesius 6, Pomponatius 4

1540–1560   total 8
——————— Telesius 6, Raymundus Sab. 2

1560–1580   total 14
——————— Telesius 6, Raymundus Sab. 2, translators and followers Sextus Emp. 6

1580–1600   total 12
——————— Sanchez 2, Montaigne 6, Patricius 2, Ellinger 2

1600–1620   total 19
——————— Sanchez 2, Charron 2, L. Vanini 4, Bacon 7, Jungius 4

1620–1640   total 15
——————— Bacon 7, Jungius 4, Cherbury 4

1640–1660   total 8
——————— Cherbury 4, Gorlaeus 4

1660–1680   total 10
——————— Gorlaeus 4, Rob. Boyle 4, Glanville 2

1680–1700   total 45
——————— Glanville 2, De la Mozze le Vayer 1, Huet 1, Foucher 1, P. Bayle 6, Newton 9, Locke 8, R. Boyle 4, Lowde 1, Leeuwenhoek 5, Hooke 5

1700–1720   total 37
——————— Foucher 1, P. Bayle 6, Newton 9, Claude Brunet 4, Locke 8, Burnet 2, Cockburn 2, Leeuwenhoek 5

1720–1740   total 22
——————— Newton 9, Clarke 1, Leeuwenhoek 5, Claude Brunet 4, Wollaston 3

1740–1760   total 46
——————— D'Alembert 5, Diderot 6, Hume 8, Buffon 6, Voltaire 7 (as a popularizer of Locke and Newton), Montesquieu 6, Hutcheson 4, Richman 3, Leroi 1

1760–1780   total 38
——————— Buffon 6, Condillac 6, Witherspoon 2, Reid 4, Hume 8, Garve 1, D'Alembert 5, Diderot 6

1780–1800   total 72
——————— Garve 1, Tiedemann 2, E. Darwin 4, Franklin 4, Witherspoon 2, Ethan Allen 2, Soave 2, Reid 4, Beattie 2, Campe 2, Gioja 3, Condillac 6, Tetens 4, Lichtenberg 2, Kant 12, Reinhold 2, S. Maimon 4, Beck 3, Krug 2, J. Schultz 3, Tenneman 4

1800–1820   total 79
——————— Kant 12, Jäsche 2, Schopenhauer 8, Fries 6, Lesbios 2, Soave 2, Pestalozzi 4, Beattie 2, Brown 3, D. Stewart 4, Gauss 8, Gioja 3, Galluppi 3, Romagnosi 2, Bichat 6, Carnot 6, Hufeland 2, Lichtenberg 2, Schalmeier 1, Krug 2

1820–1840   total 63
——————— Herbart 7, Gauss 8, James Mill 6, Bentham 6, Beneke 4, Leroux 1, S. Germain 2, Lesbios 1, Gioja 3, J. St. Hilaire 6, Cuvier 6, Burdach 2, Drobisch 4, Fries 6, Krug 1

1840–1860   total 90
——————— H. Spencer 8, J. St. Mill 8, A. Comte 8, J. Muller 6, Gauss 8, Drobisch 4, Purkinje 6, Durdik 1, Strümpell 1, Leroux 1, Littré 4, Herbart 7, Beneke 4, Fortlage 4, Kirkegaard 4, L. Feuerbach 6, Renouvier 6, Apelt 2, Jesta 1

1860–1880   total 149
——————— H. Spencer 8, Buckle 5, Littré 4, Wyrubov 4, Exner 3, Lafitte 5, G. Grote 2, C. Bernard 4, C. Darwin 8, Liebig 4, Helmholtz 6, Bonatelli 5, Bonitz 2, Drobisch 4, Fortlage 3, Cornelius 1, Hirschmann 2, H. Struve 4, MacCosh 4, Hamilton 6, Dressler 1, Lazarus 4, Steinthal 4, Strümpell 2, Waitz 4, Zimmermann 4, Oušinsky 2, Nietzsche 9, Renan 6, Multatuli 4, Bahnsen 1, Renouvier 6, F. A. Lange 7, Windelband 6, O. Liebmann 5

1880–1900   total 261
——————— Lazarus 4, Steinthal 4, Cornelius 1, Lindner 1, Durdik 1, Drobisch 4, H. Spencer 8, Lewes 5, P. Carus 2, Galton 6, Göring 1, Binet 4, Baldwin 4, Ziegler 1, De Roberty 4, Berthelot 2, S. Soldern 4, N. Grote 2, Brentano 4, Meinong 3, Rein 4, Geijer 1, Meinert 2, Hoppe 2, Tönnies 4, Elsenhans 4, Croom Robertson 4, Karinsky 3, Volkmann 3, Cornelius 2, Hartenstein Jr. 2, Willmann 3, Zimmermann 4, Dressler 1, G. Gomperz 4, Durkheim 4, Troizky 2, Masaryk 5, Avenarius 5, Laas 4, Mach 6, Lobachevsky 6, Tarde 4, Tannery Sr. 4, Hodgson 4, W. James 7, Brunschvicg 4, Renan 6, Multatuli 4, Nietzsche 9, Bahnsen 1, Peirce 1, Vaihinger 6, Wwedensky 4, Liebmann 5, Riehl 5, Cohen 7, Rickert 6, Windelband 6, Pillon 4, Bosanquet 4, Münsterberg 4, Vorländer 4, Cantoni 4, Watson 4, Harris 4, Cyples 1, Adamson 2, Ritchie 2, Palágyi 4

1900–1920   total 328 [1]
———————— Karstanjen, Petzold, Kleinpeter, Cornelius, Elsenhans, Jerusalem, Mareš, Masaryk, Radl, Brentano, Binet, Kozak, Tarde, Loisy, Guignebert, Brunschvicg, Meierson, Tannery, Hodgson, Laird, Levy-Bruhl, D. Adamson, G. E. Moore, Durkheim, Dewey, Drake, Spencer, Taylor, Ardigo, Karejev, Lehmann, Fiske, Browne, W. James, Lovejoy, Pratt, Rogers, Santayana, Callius, Berthelot, Poincaré, Sully, Read, Alexander, Baldwin, Galton, Woodbridge, Perry, H. Gomperz, Mach, Meinong, Carus, Krause, De Roberty, S. Soldern, Külpe, Dyroff, Messer, Sellers, Freud, Vernadsky, M. Petrovič, Meyerson, Delbet, H. Souple, Nordmann, Pearson, Spengler, Vaihinger, Wwedensky, Liebmann, Riehl, Natorp, Cohen, Rickert, Windelband, Stammler, Hamelin, Pillon, N. Hartmann, Lasswitz, A. Gurland, Christiansen, Bosanquet, Harris, Cassirer, Cantoni, Ritchie, Pringle-Pattison, Whitehead

[1] For obvious reasons values are not given for living authors.

LISTS OF THINKERS FOR EACH PERIOD, WITH THE VALUE GIVEN TO EACH ON A SCALE 1 TO 12

Graeco-Roman Culture

ETERNALISM (500 B.C.– A.D. 1920)

B.C. 500–480   total 7
———— Parmenides 7

480–460   total 12
————Parmenides 7, Zenon 5

460–440   total 8
———— Zenon 5, Melissos 3

440–420   total 8
———— Zenon 5, Melissos 3

420–400   total 3
———— Melissos 3

400–380   total 3
———— Eukleides 3

380–360   total 3
———— Eukleides 3

360–0   total 0

A.D. 0–1500   total 0

1500–1520   total 0

1520–1540   total 5
———— S. Franck 2, Leo Hebraeus 3

1540–1560   total 5
———— S. Franck 2, Leo Hebraeus 3

1560–1580   total 1

1580–1600   total 1

1600–1620   total 8
———— Cervantes 8

1620–1640   total 12
———— J. Boehme 6, Jansenius 6

1640–1660   total 34
———— Pascal 7, Calderon 8, Balthasar du Verger 3, R. Arnaud 2, J. Boehme 6, B. Grazian 4, Jansenists 4

1660–1680   total 7
———— Pascal 7

1680–1700   total 1
———— Kuhlmann 1

1700–1720   total 1

1720–1740   total 1

1740–1760   total 1
———— K. Selivanov 1

1760–1780   total 4
———— K. Selivanov 1, Gamalei 1, Schwarz 2

1780–1800   total 1
———— Gamalei 1

1800–1820   total 21
———— Schelling 8, Schopenhauer 8, Baader 5

1820–1840   total 28
———— Schopenhauer 8, Schelling 8, Kirejevsky 2, Gamalei 1, Baader 5, Leopardi 4

1840–1860   total 30
———— Schopenhauer 8, Wagner 8, Schelling 8, Kireievsky 2, Kierkegaard 4

1860–1880   total 53
———— Tolstoi 8, Schopenhauer 8, Wagner 8, Peters 4, E. von Hartmann 8, H. von Stein 3, Zerteleff 2, Mainländer 4, Deussen 4, Plumacher 4

1880–1900   total 40
———— Tolstoi 8, Frauenstädt 2, E. von Hartmann 8, R. Wagner 8, Deussen 4, Turgenev 6, Feth 4

1900–1920   total 47 [1]
———— Hartmann, Drews, Peters, I. Tolstoi, Unamuno, Petronević, Weininger, Schneider, L. von Schröder, Feth

TEMPORALISM (520 B.C.–A.D. 1920)

B.C. 520–500   total 7
———— Herakleitos 7

500–480   total 7
———— Herakleitos 7

480–460   total 7
———— Herakleitos 7

460–440   total 1

440–420   total 10
———— Kratylos 2, Protagoras 8

[1] For obvious reasons values are not given for living authors.

[1] See footnote, p. 635.

420–400   total 29
——————— Kratylos 2, Protagoras 8, Prodicos 5, Hippias 4, Polos 2, Callicles 2, Critias 3, Thrasymachos 3

400–380   total 27
——————— Kratylos 2, Antisthenes 5, Prodicos 5, Hippias 4, Polos 2, Thrasymachos 3, Aristippos 6

380–360   total 15
——————— Antisthenes 5, Alcidamas 4, Aristippos 6

360–340   total 18
——————— Diogenes (Sinope) 5, Alcidamas 4, Aristippos 6, Arete 1, Aithiops 1, Antipatros 1

340–320   total 9
——————— Diogenes (Sinope) 5, Arete 1, Aithiops 1, Antipatros 1, Aristippos (grandson) 1

320–300   total 17
——————— Monimos 1, Onesicritos 2, Philiscos 1, Crates (Thebe) 4, Theodoros 2, Hegesias 2, Anniceris 2, Euhemeros 3

300–280   total 18
——————— Monimos 1, Onesicritos 2, Philiscos 1, Crates (Thebe) 4, Metrocles (Maron.) 1, Theodoros 2, Hegesias 2, Anniceris 2, Euhemeros 3

280–260   total 16
——————— Metrocles (Maron.) 1, Bion (Boristhenes) 3, Theodoros 2, Hegesias 2, Timon 3, Arcesilaos 3, Anniceris 2

260–240   total 14
——————— Bion (Boristhenes) 3, Menippos 5, Timon 3, Arcesilaos 3

240–220   total 27
——————— Bion (Boristhenes) 3, Menippos 5, Teles 3, Menedemos 2, Cercidas 5, Timon 3, Arcesilaos 3, Lakydes 3

220–200   total 14
——————— Menedemos 2, Cercidas 5, Lakydes 3, Teleclos 2, Euandros 2

200–180   total 3
——————— Euandros 2, Hegesinus 1

180–160   total 6
——————— Hegesinus 1, Karneades 5

160–140   total 7
——————— Karneades 5, Cleitomachos 2

140–120   total 9
——————— Karneades 5, Cleitomachos 2, Charmadas 2

120–100   total 4
——————— Cleitomachos 2, Charmadas 2

100–80   total 4
——————— Meleagros 2, Charmadas 2

80–60   total 2
——————— Meleagros 2

60–40   total 5
——————— Ainesidemos 5

40–20   total 5
——————— Ainesidemos 5

20–0   total 5
——————— Ainesidemos 5

A.D. 0–20   total 1
——————— Skeptics 1

20–40   total 1
——————— Skeptics 1

40–60   total 2
——————— Skeptics 1, Demetrios 1

60–80   total 2
——————— Skeptics 1, Demetrios 1

80–100   total 7
——————— Demetrios 1, Dion Chrysostomos 6

100–120   total 8
——————— Dion Chrysostomos 6, Menodotos 2

120–140   total 7
——————— Oinomaos 3, Demonax 2, Menodotos 2

140–160   total 7
——————— Oinomaos 3, Demonax 2, Menodotos 2

160–180   total 12
——————— Lukian 4, Demonax 2, Sextus Empiricus 6

180–200   total 12
——————— Lukian 4, Demonax 2, Sextus Empiricus 6

200–220   total 6
——————— Sextus Empiricus 6

220–1500   total 0

1500–1520   total 4
——————— Pomponazzi 4

1520–1540   total 4
——————— Pomponazzi 4

1540–1560   total 2
——————— Raymundus Sab. 2

1560–1580   total 8
——————— Raymundus Sab. 2, Followers of Sextus Empiricus 6

1580–1600   total 12
——————— Sanchez 2, Vanini 4, Montaigne 6

1600–1620   total 12
——————— Sanchez 2, Charron 2, Vanini 4, Shakespeare 4 (Hamlet, 1603)

1620–1640   total 1

1640–1660   total 1

1660–1680   total 6
——————— Glanville 2, Lobkovič 1, Hirnhaym 3

1680–1700   total 10
——————— Glanville 2, La Motte le Vayer 1, Foucher 1, P. Bayle 6

1700–1720   total 11
——————— Mandeville 4, Foucher 1, Bayle 6

1720–1740	total 3	
——————— Jean Meslier 3		
1740–1760	total 20	
——————— Hume 8, D'Alembert 5, Diderot 7		
1760–1780	total 20	
——————— Hume 8, Diderot 7, D'Alembert 5		
1780–1800	total 2	
——————— Lichtenberg 2		
1800–1820	total 1	
——————— Schalmaier 1		
1820–1840	total 7	
——————— Schalmaier 1, Feuerbach 6		

1840–1860   total 25
——————— Feuerbach 6, Stirner 6, Bakunin 4, Blanqui 1, J. S. Mill 8

1860–1880   total 25
——————— Renan 6, Nietzsche 9, Blanqui 1, J. S. Mill 8, Bahnsen 1

1880–1900   total 26
——————— Nietzsche 9, Multatuli 4, Renan 6, Vaihinger 6, Bahnsen 1

1900–1920   total 37 [1]
——————— W. James, Shiller, Mauthner, Moebius, Vaihinger, Rensi, Spengler, Schestov, Andreev, Omar-Khayyam Society, J. Gaultier

---

ETERNALISM–TEMPORALISM
(560 B.C.–A.D. 1920)

B.C. 560–540   total 10
——————— Xenophanes 5, Anaximander 5

540–520   total 10
——————— Xenophanes 5, Anaximander 5

520–500   total 5
——————— Xenophanes 5

500–480   total 5
——————— Xenophanes 5

480–460   total 1

460–440   total 1

440–420   total 1

420–400   total 1

400–380   total 2
——————— Phaidon 2

380–360   total 14
——————— Platon 12, Phaidon 2

360–340   total 20
——————— Platon 12, Speusippos 3, Xenocrates 3, Phaidon 2

340–320   total 10
——————— Speusippos 3, Xenocrates 3, Philippos Opuntios 2, Stilpon 2

[1] For obvious reasons values are not given for living authors.

320–300   total 6
——————— Philippos Opuntios 2, Polemon 2, Stilpon 2

300–280   total 9
——————— Polemon 2, Crantor 4, Crates (Athen.) 1, Stilpon 2

280–260   total 7
——————— Polemon 2, Crantor 4, Crates 1

260–60   total 0

60–40   total 4
——————— Nigidius Figulus 4

40–20   total 2
——————— Dercylides 2

20–0   total 4
——————— Dercylides 2, Eudoros 2

A.D. 0–20   total 8
——————— Philon Iudaeus 8

20–40   total 8
——————— Philon Iudaeus 8

40–60   total 8
——————— Philon Iudaeus 8

60–80   total 8
——————— Apollonios 5, Moderatos 3

80–100   total 8
——————— Apollonios 5, Moderatos 3

100–120   total 6
——————— Apollonios 5, Saturnilus 1

120–140   total 17
——————— Theon 2, Gaios 2, Saturnilus 1, Marcion 4, Basileides 4, Valentinus 4

140–160   total 21
——————— Theon 2, Gaios 2, Peregrinos Proteus 3, Saturnilus 1, Marcion 4, Karpocrates 1, Basileides 4, Valentinus 4

160–180   total 23
——————— Nicostatos 2, Numenios 4, Cronios 2, Peregrinos Proteus 3, Tatianus 3, Marcion 4, Karpocrates 1, Valentinus 4

180–200   total 21
——————— Numenios 4, Cronios 2, Atticos 2, Herpocration 1, Celsus 4, Theophilus 2, Tatianus 3, Apelles 2, Epiphanes 1

200–220   total 22
——————— Numenios 4, Philostratos 5, Hermetic literature 5, Epiphanes 1, Philippus 1, Tertullianus 6

220–240   total 20
——————— Philostratos 5, Hermetic literature 5, "Pistis Sophia" 4, Tertullianus 6

240–260   total 15
——————— Hermetic literature 5, Origenes (heathen) 2, "Pistis Sophia" 4, Mani 4

260–280   total 10
——————— Amelios 2, "Pistis Sophia" 4, Mani 4

280–300   total 13
——————— Amelios 2, Porphyrios 7, Mani 4

300–320   total 15
——————— Porphyrios 7, Iamblichos 7, Manicheists 1

320–340   total 18
——————— Iamblichos 7, Theodoros 1, Aidesios 2, Manicheists 1, Arnobius 3, Athanasius Magn. 4

340–360   total 14
——————— Theodoros 1, Aidesios 2, Manicheists 2, Macarius Aegypt. 4, Athanasius Magn. 4, Didymus 1

360–380   total 20
——————— Aidesios 2, Maximos 1, Eunapios 3, Manicheists 2, Macarius (Aeg.) 4, Athanasius Magn. 4, Didymus 1, Marius Victorinus 3

380–400   total 22
——————— Eunapios 3, Augustinus 6, Manicheists 3, Macarius Aegyptius 4, Didymus 1, Ambrosius Med. 5

400–420   total 16
——————— Syrianos 1, Manicheists 3, Pseudo Macarius 2, Augustinus 10

420–440   total 16
——————— Syrianos 1, Manicheists 3, Pseudo Macarius 2, Augustinus 10

440–460   total 12
——————— Hermeias 3, Proklos 8, Manicheists 1

460–480   total 12
——————— Hermeias 3, Proklos 8, Manicheists 1

480–500   total 12
——————— Proklos 8, Marinos 3, Manicheists 1

500–520   total 14
——————— Isidoros 1, Damaskios 4, Manicheists 1, Dionysius Areopag. 8

520–540   total 14
——————— Priskianos 1, Damaskios 4, Manicheists 1, Dionysius Areopag. 8

540–560   total 5
——————— Damaskios 4, Priskianos 1

560–580   total 1
——————— Priskianos 1

580–600   total 4
——————— Gregorius I Magnus 4

600–620   total 4
——————— Gregorius I Magnus 4

620–640   total 6
——————— Maximus Confessor 6

640–660   total 6
——————— Maximus Confessor 6

660–680   total 6
——————— Maximus Confessor 6

680–820   total 0

820–840   total 2
——————— Agobardus 2

840–860   total 4
——————— Agobardus 2, Paschasius Radbertus 2

860–880   total 6
——————— Paschasius Radbertus 2, Ratramnus 2, Godescale 2

880–1040   total 0

1040–1060   total 5
——————— Petrus Damiani 3, Otloh 2

1060–1080   total 16
——————— Petrus Damiani 3, Otloh 2, Symeon Th. Nov. 4, Anselmus Cant. 7

1080–1100   total 14
——————— Symeon Th. Nov. 4, Anselmus Cant. 7, Manegoldus 3

1100–1120   total 15
——————— Anselmus Cant. 7, Manegoldus 3, Odo 1, Bruno (Segni) 2, Guilelmus Camp. 2

1120–1140   total 21
——————— Bruno (Segni) 2, Guilelmus Camp. 2, Bernardus Carnot. 2, Honorius Augustod. 3, Bernardus Claraev. 5, Guilelmus s. Thod. rem. 2, Hugo à S. Victore 5

1140–1160   total 25
——————— Bernardus Claraev. 5, Guilelmus s. Thod. rem. 2, Honorius Augustod. 3, Robertus Melidun. 2, Hugo à S. Victore 5, Richardus à S. Victore 4, Petrus Lombardus 4

1160–1180   total 19
——————— Robertus Melidun. 2, Richardus à S. Victore 4, Petrus Lombardus 4, Ioannes Saresberiansis 3, Gandulfus 2, Clarenbaldus 2, Rolandus Band. (Alex. III) 2

1180–1200   total 14
——————— Ioannes Saresberiansis 3, Rolandus Band. (Alex. III) 2, Petrus Pictaviensis 2, Petrus Cantor 2, Gualterus à S. Victore 2, Ioachim de Floris 3

1200–1220   total 17
——————— Petrus Pictaviensis 2, Innocentius III 3, Simon de Tarnaco 1, Thomas Gallo 1, Praepositinus (Cr.) 2, Robertus de Corceon 1, Guilelmus (Aux.) 2, Philippus Grevius 2, Ioachim de Floris 3

1220–1240   total 16
——————— Thomas Gallo 1, Praepositinus (Crem.) 2, Guilelmus (Aux.) 2, Philippus Grevius 2, Radulphus de Longo Campo 1, Guilelmus Alvernus 3, Alexander Halensis 4, Walter (Chateau-Thierry) 1

1240–1260   total 18
——————— Guilelmus Alvernus 3, Alexander Halensis 4, Walter (Chateau-Thierry) 1, Ioannes de Rupella 2, Hugo (St. Cher.) 2, Robert Bacon 1, Vincentius Bellovacens. 2, Richard Fischacre 1, Thomas (Chantimpré) 2

1260–1280   total 37
——————— Hugo (St. Cher.) 2, Vincentius Bellovac. 2, Thomas (Chantimpré) 2, Robert Kilwardby 2, Ioannes Bonaventure 8, Ulricus Engelberti 3, Petrus de Tarenbasia (Innoc. V) 2, Petrus Hispanus (Ioann. XXI) 2, Bombolognus de Bononia 1, Romanus de Roma 1, Thomas Aquinas 12

1280–1300   total 36
——————— Raymundus Lullus 5, Ioannes Peckham 1, Guilelmus de la Mare 1, Walter of Brugges 2, Henricus Gandavensis 4, Bernardus de Trilia 2, Aegidius (Lessines) 2, Remigio di Ch. dei Gir. 2, Aegidius Romanus 3, Hugo Ripelin 3, Matthaeus ab Aquasparta 2, Fr. Eustachius 2, Roger (Marston) 2, Petrus Ioannis Olivi 3, Augustinus Triumphus 2

1300–1320   total 30
——————— Raymundus Lullus 5, Walter of Brugges 2, Aegidius (Lessines) 2, Remigio di Ch. dei Gir. 2, Aegidius Romanus 3, Matthaeus ab Aquasparta 2, Augustinus Triumphus 2, Bernardus de Alvernia 1, Guilelmus Petri de Godino 2, Hervé Nédélec 3, Iacobus Capocci 2, Gerhard (Bologna) 2, Thomas (Sutton) 2

1320–1340   total 14
——————— Augustinus Triumphus 2, Guilelmus Petri de Godino 2, Hervé Nédélec 3, Thomas (Sutton) 2, Ioannes de Regina 1, Ioannes Picardi de Lucid. 2, Thomas Bradwardine 2

1340–1360   total 30
——————— Thomas (Sutton) 2, Bernardus Lombardi 1, Durandellus 1, H. Suso 5, Ruysbroeck 4, Robert Holvot. 1, Thomas (Strasbourg) 2, Gregorios Palemos 6, Nicolaus Kabasilas 4, Thomas Bradwardine 2

1360–1380   total 24
——————— H. Suso 5, Ruysbroeck 4, Gregorios Palemos 6, Nicolaus Kabasilas 4, "Eine deutsche Theologie" 3, Heinrich (Hainbuch) 2

1380–1400   total 6
——————— Ruysbroeck 4, Heinrich (Hainbuch) 2

1400–1420   total 4
——————— Jean Charlier (Gerson) 4

1420–1440   total 7
——————— Jean Charlier (Gerson) 4, Ioannes Capreolus 3

1440–1460   total 7
——————— Ioannes Capreolus 3, Dionysius Cartusianus 4

1460–1480   total 9
——————— Dionysius Cartusianus 4, Petrus Nigri 1, Thomas à Kempis 4

1480–1500   total 3
——————— Petrus Nigri 1, Savonarola 2

1500–1520   total 36
——————— Thomas Morus 6, Melanchthon 5, Erasmus 5, Faber 2, Achillini 1, Zimara 1, Nifus 1, Agricola 4, Fracastor 1, Bovillus 2, M. Rufus 2, Bembo 2, Bessarion 4

1520–1540   total 53
——————— Achillini 1, Luther 8, Nifus 1, Melanchthon 5, Reuchlin 4, Zwingli 6, T. Morus 6, P. della Mirandola Jr. 4, Faber 2, Serveto 4, Bembo 2, Agrippa 2, M. Rufus 2, Pereira 4, Bovillus 2

1540–1560   total 39
——————— Melanchthon 5, Ramus 4, Faber 2, Paracelsus 4, Serveto 4, Loyola 8, Soto 2, Nizolius 3, Laynes 4, Xaverius 3

1560–1580   total 57
——————— Paracelsus 4, Wilson 3, Lever 3, Sepulveda 2, Cardanus 4, Chytraeus 1, Camerarius 1, Freigius 1, Fabricius 1, Schegk 1, Pfaffrad 1, Sturm 1, Strigel 2, Ramus 4, Carpentarius 1, St. Theresa 6, Rodrigez 4, Hurtado de Mendoza 2, Jean de la Croix 4, Ledesma 1, Gursky 1, Laynes 4, Zamora 2, Salmeron 3

1580–1600   total 84
——————— Gocklinenius 3, Ramists 4, Scotus 2, Case 2, Bodin 2, Wilson 3, Sanderson 1, Crackanthrop 1, Lever 1, V. Weigel 3, Hixner 1, Paracelsus 4, Sturm 2, Digly 4, Schegk 1, Fabricius 2, Freigius 1, Camerarius 1, Snellius 1, Scherbius 1, Jean de la Croix 4, Salmeron 3, Temple 2, Toletus 3, Fonseca 3, Ledesma 1, Molina 3, St. Theresa 6, Suarez 6, Ribadeneira 3, S. Conto 2, C. de Lelly 2, Rodrigez 4, Goes 2

1600–1620   total 66
——————— Crackanthrop 1, Fludd 2, Hixner 1, Scotus 2, V. Weigel 3, Harvey 4, Fortherby 2, Sanderson 1, Franciscus Salesius 4, Pereira 2, Roselli 4, Grey de Valencia 4, Molina 3, Berulle 4, Albergati 4, Strizzi 2, Caponus 2, Toletus 3, Davy de Perrin 3, Bellarmin 4, Temple 2, Vallius 2, Herrera 1, Hurtado de Mendoza 2, Vasquez 4

1620–1640   total 65
——————— Crackanthrop 1, Hixner 1, Cherbury 4, V. Helmont 4, Alstedius 3, Fludd 2, V. Weigel 3, Althusius 4, Fr. Salesius 4, Lessius 4, Bellarminus 4, Colomi 1, Pateanus 2, Pastorus 1, Maltesius 1, Tanner 3, Escobard y Mendoza 6, Ruez de Mont 2, Berulle 4, Scribonius 3, V. Depaul 2, Busenbaum 4, Reginaldius 2

1640–1660   total 46
——————— Smith 2, Fludd 2, Whichcote 1, Culverwell 1, White 2, Brooke 2, Cherbury 4, Spinoza 8, Bourdin 3, Morin 2, Escobard y Mendoza 6, Izambertus 2, Barbosa 3, Jacobus Ganz 1, De San Thoma 1, Busenbaum 4, Reginaldius 2

1660–1680   total 63
——————— La logique du Port Royal (1662) 4, Thomasius 4, H. Morus 4, Spinoza 8, Jelles 1, Clauberg 3, Balings 1, Rieuwertz 1, Geulynx 6, Oldenburg 1, De la Forge 3, Voetius 2, Bourdin 3, Malebranche 7, Nicole 4, Arnauld 4, Martinius 2, J. deLago 3, Bernier 2

1680–1700 total 89
——————— Tschirnhausen 2, Stahl 3, Thomasius 4, Meier 3, H. Morus 4, Stotch 1, Pordage 1, Cudworth 5, Lanion 2, Norris 2, Spinoza (posth.) 8, Rieuwertz 1, Clauberg 3, Cuffeler 1, Taylor 3, Giovenale 2, Poiret 2, Fénelon 4, Thomassin 1, Duhamel 2, Pyrrhing 2, Makovsky 2, Bossuet 6, Buffier 2, Mairan 2, Guillemin 2, Ortega 3, Tournemine 2, Malysevsky 2, Tylkovsky 2, Moškovsky 2, Mlodzinevsky 1, Faydit 1, Samucky 2, Voetius 2, Fardella 2

1700–1720 total 71
——————— Berkeley 8, Collier 5, Stahl 3, Norris 2, Poiret 2, Lange 1, M. van Helmont 2, Taylor 3, Marinière 2, Mme. Guyon 2, Renodot 2, Reiffenstael 1, Merger 1, Duhamel 1, Bossuet 6, Fénelon 6, Buffier 2, Tournemine 2, Andola 1, Thomassin 1, Petau 1, Lamy 2, Daniel 2, Giovenale 2, Malebranche 6, Faydit 1, Huet 1, André 1, Fardella 2

1720–1740 total 53
——————— Turnbull 2, Mairan 2, Stahl 3, Vico 7, Martinez Pasquales 4, Berkeley 8, French Masons 3, Petrus Monsi 2, Fraken 2, Schallkovič 2, Huet 1, Cordeiro 2, Fénelon 6, Montefortuno 2, André 1, Dutertre 2, Miaskovsky 2, Podlesecky 2

1740–1760 total 54
——————— Knutzen 4, Vico 7, Berkeley 8, Gerdil 2, Edelmann 1, Fontenelle 2, Swedenborg 4, Reimarus 4, Euler 6, Mendelssohn 4, Polignac 4, Radsay 2, Dobrinevič 2, Dom Calmes 4

1760–1780 total 64
——————— Reid 4, Euler 6, Beattie 2, Tetens 4, Jacobi 6, Lessing 6, Herder 6, Mairan 2, Swedenborg 4, Bonnet 4, Mendelssohn 4, Menschenberger 2, Polignac 1, Lechner 1, Bonotto 2, Gutharoth 2, Guenée 4, Dom Calmes 4

1780–1800 total 78
——————— Mendelssohn 4, Jacobi 6, Herder 6, Reid 4, Beattie 2, D. Stewart 4, Pestalozzi 4, Tittel 1, Hegel 8, St. Martin 4, Bonnet 5, Robinet 2, Novalis 3, Deschamps 1, Thorild 1, Schelling 8, Schleiermacher 4, Zanchi 1, Muschka 1, Holzelau 1, Gero 2, Cortivo 1, Gealdus 1, De Bonald 4

1800–1820 total 88
——————— Krause 4, Beattie 2, D. Stewart 4, Pestalozzi 4, M. de Biran 5, Brown 3, Fourier 5, Troxler 1, Ast 1, Rixner 1, Hegel 8, Silbern 1, Steffens 1, S. Martin 4, Kerner 1, Blasche 1, Jacobi 6, Coleridge 4, Wagner 1, Schleiermacher 4, Hölderlin 2, Wronsky 7, Vellansky 2, Molitor 1, Bonafons 1, Třebinsky 2, De Bonald 4, Kollatay 2, Pembridge 1, J. de Maistre 6

1820–1840 total 141
——————— Hegel 8, Herbart 7, Cousin 4, Brown 3, Ampère 5, Stahl 4, M. de Biran 5, D. Stewart 4, Pestalozzi 4, Cuvier 6, Galitch 2, Khomiakov 4, Bolzano 6, Ritter 1, Fichte Jr. 4, Gratry 3, Vorländer 1, Frank 1, Burdach 1, Steffens 1, Krause 4, Wronsky 6, Royer Collard 2, Towiansky 4, Jouffroy 4, Schleiermacher 4, Fournier 2, Molitor 1, Novinsky 1, De Bonald 4, Torre 1, Ferault 2,

Barruel 2, Goluchovsky 2, Pointer 1, Frančeskino 1, Mutter 1, Čăadajev 3, Szumavy 1, Ganič 1, Tomazzo 2, Vinet 4, Goerres 5, Surovecky 2, De Maistre 6, Lammenais 4

1840–1860 total 204
——————— Durdik 1, Herbart 7, Strümpell 2, Krause 4, Drobisch 4, V. Cousin 4, J. Erdmann 4, M. de Biran 5, A. Smetana 4, Maylin 1, Wassenborn 1, Rohmer 1, Schaden 1, Schmidt 1, Stahl 4, Lotze 5, Bolzano 6, Franck 3, Goeschel 1, Rosmini 6, Zeller 5, Trendelenburg 5, Noack 1, Carrière 3, Emerson 6, L. V. Stein 6, Mizkievicz 6, Ranke 4, Towiansky 3, Th. Vischer 4, Reiff 1, Mamiani 2, Minghetti 1, Rosenkrantz 4, Chalybaeus 1, Pagano 1, Michelet 4, K. Fischer 4, Harris 3, Wronsky 6, Daub 2, Khomiakov 4, Samarin 2, Mahreinecke 1, Vera 2, Schasler 1, Liebelt 4, Thieberghen 1, Prantl 4, Ahrens 1, Lasson 3, Amerling 1, Dorgan 1, Rosaunen 1, Fitz 1, Richter 1, Goerres 5, Hagel 1, Regnaut 1, Scherer 4, Balmez 5, Gioberti 6, Neumann 6, Nitsch 1, Dufour 1, Menden 1, Kralikovsky 1, Muller 1, Kleutgen 2, Gumparin 1, Barrou 1, Fabri 1

1860–1880 total 187
——————— Hamilton 6, Cousin 4, M. Carrière 4, Green 4, Jurkevič 2, Mansel 2, J. Simon 2, Chaignet 2, Paul Janet 4, Ranke 4, Fiorentino 3, A. Spir 4, Frauenstädt 2, McCosh 4, Michelet 4, Brochard 2, Zimmermann 4, Remusat 2, Franck 3, Lazarus 4, K. Fischer 4, Zeller 5, Strümpell 2, Teichmüller 2, Vera 2, Steinthal 4, Ravaisson 2, Bergmann 2, Soloviev 6, Erdmann 4, Lasson 3, Martineau 4, Spaventa 2, Ferri 3, Dressler 1, Strachov 3, Boutroux 4, Exner 2, Mamiani 3, Upton 2, Waitz 4, Lachelier 4, Čičerin 4, Kleutgen 2, Sabatier 2, Scherer 3, Pecaut 3, Bois 2, Newman 6, Hahn 1, Gioberti 6, Rittler 1, Michelis 1, Moryott 1, Bauch 1, Stöckl 4, Gordon 1, Spalding 1, Volzogen 1, Lacordaire 2, Secchi 6, Cornoldis 2

1880–1900 total 207
——————— Zimmermann 4, Rein 4, Lazarus 4, Veitch 4, Steinthal 4, Spir 4, Durdik 1, Sigwart 4, Karinsky 4, Chaignet 4, Schuppe 5, Palagyi 4, Muller 2, Bergson 8, Green 5, S. Trubetzkoi 4, E. Trubetzkoi 3, Ferrier 3, Howison 2, Debolsky 2, V. Lamy 2, V. Vloten 4, Bergmann 2, Hilarov 3, Seth 4, Čičerin 4, Martineau 4, Royce 5, Cantor 4, Drummond 4, J. Erdmann 4, Soloviev 6, Feldner 2, Moignot 2, Kathrein 4, Hortling 1, Schnitzler 2, Bach 1, Hebinger 1, Sabatier 2, D. de Vorges 2, C. Pesch 1, Dressel 2, Schned 1, Kahn 2, Hildebrandt 1, Liberatore 2, Linsemann 1, Boncant 1, Lutoslavsky 4, Moryott 1, Hagemann 1, Froschhammer 4, Gonzalez 3, Stöckl 4, Schwanz 1, Haffner 2, Ward 3, T. Pesch 2, Deschamps 1, Pfeffer 1, Olle-Laprune 4, Plancy 2, Ardouin 2, Probst 1, Harper 4, Gruber 4, Merkle 2, O. Willmann 4, Champigny 2, Wasmann 4, Gutberlet 4

1900–1920 total 268 [1]
——————— Schuppe, W. Stern, Tröltsch, Lipps,

[1] For obvious reasons values are not given for living authors.

Pfleiderer, Ladd, Max Scheler, Masci, Hobhouse, Bradley, Ladyžensky, Lasci, Soloviev, Pelikan, Ambrosi, Petrone, S. Trubetzkoi, E. Trubetzkoi, Boelsche, Hoppe, Zienkovsky, Iljin, Tauschinsky. Gredaro, Bergson, Howison, Rehmke, Lopatine, Royce, Vorovka, Jones, R. Eucken, Radlov, Falkenberg, Debolsky, Karsavin, Haldane, Oldendorf, K. Gross, H. Schwarz, Galloway, S. Frank, Br. Welly, Gentile, Bosanquet, Amaldov, Novgorodzev, Joachim, Heymans, Ben. Croce, Segond, Vyšeslavzev, Steudel, Wyneken, Laberthonnier, Munzbach, Caro, Isenkrahe, Geijer, Foerster, Bota, Cossena, Bonillard, Gay, Duhem, Lapparent, Grasset, Thamin, Bros, Dumesnil, Piat, Wasmann, Dunan, Maritain, Blondel, Gutberlet, Bach, Schneider, Lehmann, Hartner, Mercier, Hortling, Hebinger, Schell, Ventura, Taparelli, D'Ondes, Fontana, Gondero, Descrescencio, Capozza, Audisio, Lutoslavsky, Palmieri, Thierry, Sanseverino, Cornaldi, Horvath, Willmann

---

TEMPORALISM–ETERNALISM
(540 B.C.–A.D. 1920)

B.C. 540–520   total 2
——————— Anaximenes 2

520–500   total 2
——————— Anaximenes 2

500–480   total 2
——————— Alkmaion 2

480–460   total 3
——————— Alkmaion 2, Hippasos 1

460–440   total 10
——————— Diogenes 3, Anaxagoras 5, Hippasos 1, Archelaos 1

440–420   total 20
——————— Hippodamos 2, Leukippos 2, Diogenes 3, Anaxagoras 5, Archelaos 1, Empedocles 6, Hippasos 1

420–400   total 18
——————— Hippodamos 2, Leukippos 2, Democritos 8, Empedocles 6

400–380   total 11
——————— Hippodamos 2, Democritos 8, Nessas 1

380–360   total 16
——————— Xenophon 7, Democritos 8, Nessas 1

360–340   total 15
——————— Xenophon 7, Eudoxos (Gnidos) 3, Herakleides 3, Nessas 1, Diogenes (Smyrna) 1

340–320   total 10
——————— Eudoxos 3, Herakleides 3, Diodoros Cronos 2, Diogenes (Smyrna) 1, Anaxarchos 1

320–300   total 13
——————— Herakleides 3, Diodoros Cronos 2, Bion (Abdere) 1, Hekataios 1, Nausiphanes 2, Dikaiarchos (Messene) 3, Anaxarchos 1

300–280   total 17
——————— Straton (Lampsacos) 2, Bion (Abdera) 1, Hekataios 1, Nausiphanes 2, Epicuros 8, Dikaiarchos (Messene) 3

280–260   total 13
——————— Straton (Lampsacos) 2, Epicuros 8, Metrodoros 2, Polyainos 1

260–240   total 4
——————— Hermarchos 2, Kolotes 2

240–220   total 7
——————— Hermarchos 2, Kolotes 2, Polystratos 2, Hippokleides 1

220–200   total 3
——————— Polystratos 2, Hippokleides 1

200–180   total 4
——————— Polystratos 2, Hippokleides 1, Dionysios 1

180–160   total 2
——————— Dionysios 1, Basileides 1

160–140   total 3
——————— Basileides 1, Philonides 2

140–120   total 2
——————— Apollodoros 2

120–100   total 4
——————— Apollodoros 2, Zenon (Sidon) 2

100–80   total 7
——————— Apollodoros 2, Zenon (Sidon) 2, Amafinius 1, Phaidros 2

80–60   total 5
——————— Zenon (Sidon) 2, Amafinius 1, Phaidros 2

60–40   total 18
——————— Patron 1, Philodemos 5, Lucretius 8, Asclepiades 4

40–20   total 10
——————— Boethos (Sidon) 1, Philodemos 5 Asclepiades 4

20–0   total 2
——————— Boethos (Sidon) 1, Epicureans 1

A.D. 0–20   total 2
——————— Boethos (Sidon) 1, Epicureans 1

20–40   total 1
——————— Epicureans 1

40–60   total 1
——————— Epicureans 1

60–80   total 1
——————— Epicureans 1

80–100   total 1
——————— Epicureans 1

100–120   total 1
——————— Epicureans 1

120–140   total 1
——————— Celsus (Epicurean) 1

140–160   total 2
————— Celsus (Epicurean) 1, Diogenianos 1

160–180   total 2
————— Celsus (Epic.) 1, Diogenianos 1

180–200   total 4
————— Diogenianos 1, Diogenes 3

200–220   total 3
————— Diogenes 3

220–240   total 1
————— Epicureans 1

240–260   total 1
————— Epicureans 1

260–280   total 1
————— Epicureans 1

280–300   total 1
————— Epicureans 1

300–320   total 1
————— Epicureans 1

320–340   total 1
————— Epicureans 1

340–360   total 1
————— Epicureans 1

360–1320   total 0

1320–1340   total 4
————— Nicolaus (Autrecuria) 4

1340–1360   total 4
————— Nicolaus (Autrecuria) 4

1360–1500   total 0

1500–1520   total 6
————— Machiavelli 6

1520–1540   total 12
————— Machiavelli 6, Vives 6

1540–1560   total 6
————— Vives 6

1560–1580   total 1

1580–1600   total 15
————— Baco 7, Lublin 2, Campanella 6

1600–1620   total 32
————— Campanella 6, Baco 7, Jungius 4,
Hill 1, Gilbert 4, Sennert 2, Shakespeare 8 (*The
Tempest*, 1616)

1620–1640   total 27
————— Baco 7, Hobbes 8, Jungius 4, Sennert
2, Campanella 6

1640–1660   total 23
————— Hobbes 8, Gassendi 7, Magnenus 2,
Bergerac 1, Berigard 2, Brown 3

1660–1680   total 27
————— Brown 3, Gassendi 7, Hobbes 8,
Glisson 3, Sorbier 1, Bernier 1, R. Boyle 4

1680–1700   total 49
————— Glisson 3, Bernier 2, Newton 9,
Locke 8, S. Regis 2, R. Boyle 4, Bould 2, Lowde 1,
Leewenhoek 5, Hook 5, Toland 4, Dodwell 2,
Coward 2

1700–1720   total 39
————— Locke 8, Newton 9, Burnet 2, Cock-
burn 2, Leewenhoek 5, Toland 3, Boerhaave 4,
Clarke 2, Dodwell 2, S. Regis 2

1720–1740   total 48
————— Newton 9, Voltaire 7, Clarke 2,
Toland 4, Collins 1, Chubb 1, Bolingbrooke 2,
Johnson 6, Edwards 6, Buffon 6, Hutcheson 4

1740–1760   total 60
————— Voltaire 7, Hartley 4, Vaucanson 2,
Dumarsais 2, Morelli 2, Hutcheson 4, Montes-
quieu 6, Lamettrie 5, Leroy 1, Chubb 1, Burke 4,
Price 2, Tindall 2, Morgan 1, Edwards 6, Buffon 6,
A. Smith 5

1760–1780   total 82
————— Voltaire 7, Buffon 6, Lambert 1,
Condillac 6, Helvetius 6, Franklin 4, Paine 4,
Hartley 4, Holbach 6, Genovesi 2, Priestley 6,
Tucker 2, Freret 3, Ferguson 4, Mably 2, Burke 4,
Morelli 2, Turgot 4, A. Smith 5, Maupertuis 4

1780–1800   total 75
————— Bentham 6, Laplace 8, Soave 2,
Ethan Allen 2, Condillac 6, Gioja 3, Priestley 6,
Holbach 6, Volney 2, James Mill 6, Condorcet 4,
Lambert 1, E. Darwin 4, D. de Tracy 4, Rad-
itchtev 1, Paine 4, Jefferson 6, Burke 4

1800–1820   total 56
————— Laplace 8, Volney 2, D. de Tracy 4,
Gioja 3, Galluppi 3, Romagnosi 2, Broussais 2,
Cabanis 4, S. Simon 5, Soave 2, Bentham 6,
James Mill 6, Borelli 1, Lamarck 8

1820–1840   total 50
————— J. Mill 6, J. Bentham 6, Benecke 2,
S. Germain 2, S. Simon 5, Laplace 8, Gioja 3,
D. de Tracy 4, Hershel 6, A. Comte 8

1840–1860   total 71
————— Carové 1, A. Comte 8, Marx 8,
Pouchet 1, Joly 1, V. Considérant 4, H. Spencer 8,
Chr. Baur 1, Biedermann 1, Lewes 5, Cabet 2,
Engels 6, Littré 4, Helmholtz 6, Proudhon 5,
A. Ruge 4, Strauss 6

1860–1880   total 179
————— Moleschott 4, Maxwell 8, H. Spencer
8, Thomson 6, Laas 4, Černyševsky 3, Taine 8,
Grote 2, Ribot 7, Lewes 5, Galton 6, Vogt 4,
Troizky 2, Lavrov 4, Liebig 4, Herzen 4, D. Strauss
6, Oušinsky 3, Kropotkin 4, Pisareff 1, Setchenov
4, C. Bernard 4, Huxley 2, Darwin 8, Jevons
6, Austin 4, Duehring 6, Haeckel 6, Wundt 7,
Lafitte 5, Bain 7, Wyrubov 4, Zöllner 4, Marx 8,
Engels 6, Helmholtz 6

1880–1900   total 242
————— Überweg 5, Spencer 8, Darwin 8,
Ribot 7, Taine 7, Bain 7, Marx 8, Engels 6,

Lombroso 4, Haeckel 7, Wundt 7, Lewes 5, Duehring 6, Delboeuf 4, Kropotkin 4, Clifford 4, Peirée 1, Büchner 5, Guyau 5, Robertson 4, Fouillée 5, W. James 7, Göring 2, Pavlov 6, Menger 2, Binet 4, Bechterev 4, Galton 6, Baldwin 5, P. Carus 4, Nägeli 3, Romanes 3, Ziegler 1, Ziehen 3, Espinas 4, Mantegazza 1, Avenarius 6, Mach 6, Sully 4, Geier 1, Bender 1, Spitzer 1, Lavrov 4, Kautzky 4, Krejči 4, Edgeworth 2, Jevons 6, Lobačevsky 6, Tarde 4, Tannery 4, Laas 3, Troizky 2, Preier 2, De Roberty 4, Masaryk 6

1900–1920   total 382 [1]
————— Milhaud, Leub, Keibel, Delbet, Karinsky, Radl, Carstanjen, C. Read, Cornelius, Fiske, Petzold, Ribot, Kléinpeter, Roux, Lehmann, Masaryk, H. Souplé, Planck, Nordmann, Stumpf, Bolzmann, Lenin, Jerusalem, Brentano, Rogers, Einstein, Plechanov, Wundt, Kozak, Binet, Colleus, Zeleny, Tarde, Zahnder, Schmidt, P. Carus, Dyroff, Messer, Freud, Vernadsky, Petrovič, Berthelot, Plessner, Russell, Bazarov, Katarbinsky, H. Maier, Enriquez, Dantec, Rignano, Höffding, Quiquebert, Dewey, Brunschvicg, Külpe, Meyerson, Tannery, Dürkheim, Spencer, Cyples, Ardigo, Levy-Brühl, Perry, Poincaré, Baldwin, Verworn, Sully, M. Weber, Mach, Alexander, Simon, Zur Strassen, Galton, Woodbridge, Ostwald, Lewin, Jensen, Pierre Janet, Mach, Meinong, H. Gomperz, De Roberty, S. Soldern, Pauly, Hering, Pieron, Sollier, Menger, Kostyleff, B. Erdmann, Ziehen, Fouillée, Bogdanov, Lazursky, Kandinsky, Wundt's school, *Monistenbund*

EQUILIBRIUM OF BOTH
(540 B.C.–A.D 1920)

B.C. 540–520   total 8
————— Pythagoras 8

520–500   total 8
————— Pythagoras 8

500–480   total 8
————— Pythagoras 8

480–460   total 1

460–440   total 1
————— Ion 1

440–420   total 6
————— Philolaos 5, Ion 1

420–400   total 21
————— Philolaos 5, Simmias 1, Cebes 1, Lysis 1, Socrates 9, Antiphon 4

400–380   total 26
————— Philolaos 5, Simmias 1, Cebes 1, Lysis 1, Socrates 9, Aeschines 3, Eurytos 1, Archytas 1, Antiphon 4

[1] For obvious reasons values are not given for living authors.

380–360   total 5
————— Aeschines 3, Eurytos 1, Archytas 1

360–340   total 8
————— Aeschines 3, Xenophilos 1, Phanton 1, Echekrates 1, Diocles 1, Polymnastos 1

340–320   total 17
————— Xenophilos 1, Phanton 1, Echekrates 1, Diocles 1, Polymnastos 1, Aristoteles 12

320–300   total 35
————— Xenophilos 1, Phanton 1, Echekrates 1, Diocles 1, Polymnastos 1, Menedemos 2, Aristoteles 12, Theophrastos 7, Eudemos 2, Aristoxenos 4, Demetrios 3

300–280   total 26
————— Menedemos 2, Theophrastos 7, Eudemos 2, Aristoxenos 4, Demetrios 3, Zenon 8

280–260   total 25
————— Menedemos 2, Demetrios 3, Zenon 8, Ariston (Chios) 5, Herillos 1, Dionysios 1, Cleanthes 5

260–240   total 17
————— Lykon 1, Hieronymos 2, Ariston (Chios) 5, Herillos 1, Persaios 2, Dionysios 1, Cleanthes 5

240–220   total 26
————— Lykon 1, Hieronymos 2, Prytanis 1, Ariston (Chios) 5, Herillos 1, Persaios 2, Dionysios 1, Cleanthes 5, Chrysippos 7, Sphairos 1

220–200   total 16
————— Ariston (Keos) 3, Prytanis 1, Satyros 3, Hermippos 1, Chrysippos 7, Sphairos 1

200–180   total 15
————— Ariston (Keos) 3, Satyros 3, Hermippos 1, Sotion 2, Sphairos 1, Zenon (Tarsos) 1, Diogenes (Seleukeia) 4

180–160   total 12
————— Sotion 2, Antisthenes (Rhodos) 2, Kritolaos 2, Diogenes (Seleukeia) 4, Antipatros 2

160–140   total 11
————— Antisthenes (Rhodos) 2, Herakleides Lembos 1, Kritolaos 2, Diogenes (Seleukeia) 4, Antipatros 2

140–120   total 10
————— Herakleides Lembos 1, Boethos (Sidon) 2, Diodoros (Tyros) 1, Panaitios 5, Qu. Mucius Scaevola 1

120–100   total 12
————— Boethos (Sidon) 2, Diodoros (Tyros) 1, Erymneus 1, Panaitios 5, Qu. Mucius Scaevola 1, Hecaton 1, Mnesarchos 1

100–80   total 15
————— Philon (Larissa) 3, Diodoros (Tyros) 1, Erimneus 1, Hecaton 1, Mnesarchos 1, Apollodoros (Stoa) 1, Poseidonios 7

80–60   total 28
———— Philon (Larissa) 3, Antiochos (Asca-
lon) 4, T. Varro 5, Andronicos 2, Xenarchos 1,
Ariston 1, Apollodoros (Stoa) 1, Poseidonios 7,
Asclepiodotos 2, Geminos 2

60–40   total 40
———— T. Varro 5, Cicero 8, Aristos (Ascalon)
1, Xenarchos 1, Ariston 1, Andronicos 2, Posei-
donios 7, Asclepiodotos 2, Geminos 2, Phainios 1,
Dionysios 1, Antipatros 2, Iason 2 Athenodoros 1,
Apollonides 1, Diodotos 1, Cato 2

40–20   total 27
———— Cicero (43) 8, T. Varro 5, Theom-
nestos 1, Andronicos 2, Q. Sextius 2, Athenodoros
Kordylion 1, Apollonides 1, Athenodoros 3,
Areios Didymos 2

20–0   total 10
———— Sextius 2, Sextius (Jr.) 1, Nicolaus
(Damascos) 2, Athenodoros 3, Areios Didymos 2

A.D. 0–20   total 14
———— Sextius 1, Nicolaus (Damascos) 2,
Sotion 2, Cornelius Celsus 1, Fabianus Papirius 1,
L. Crassicius 1, Potamon 1, Areios Didymos 2,
Herakleitos 3

20–40   total 10
———— Sotion 2, Cornelius Celsus 1, Fa-
bianus Papirius 1, L. Crassicius 1, Potamon 1,
Herakleitos 3, Attalos 1

40–60   total 15
———— Alexandros (Aigai) 2, Attalos 1,
Seneca 8, L. Annaeus Cornutus 4

60–80   total 28
———— Alexandros 2, Seneca 8, L. Annaeus
Cornutus 4, Chairemon 2, A. Persius Flaccus 3,
Annaeus Lucanus 4, Musonius Rufus 5

80–100   total 21
———— Plutarchos 8, Ptolemaios Chennos 2,
Musonius Rufus 5, Epictetos 6

100–120   total 26
———— Plutarchos 8, Ptolemaios Chennos 2,
Περὶ Κόσμου 4, Aspasios 2, Adrastos 2, Epictetos
6, Cerinthus 2

120–140   total 35
———— Cerdon 2, Cerinthus 2, Plutarchos 8,
Nikomachos 1, Ptolemaios Chennos 2, Aspasios 2,
Adrastos 2, Epictetos 6, Arrianos 2, Hierocles 2,
Cleomedes 2, Favorinus 4

140–160   total 30
———— Nikomachos 1, Herodes 2, Albinos 3,
Calvisios Tauros 2, Nigrinos 1, Aspasios 2,
Adrastos 2, Herminos 2, Claudios Ptolem. 3,
Arrianos 2, Hierocles 2, Cleomedes 2, Favorinus
4, Cerdon 2

160–180   total 45
———— Herodes 2, Albinos 3, Calvisios
Tauros 2, Nigrinos 1, Apuleius 6, Herminos 2,
Claudios Ptolem. 3, Aristocles 1, Galenos 7,
Marcus Aurelius 6, Iustinus Martyr. 5, Melito 2,
Apollinarius 1, Minucius Felix 4

180–200   total 63
———— Apuleius 6, Maximos 5, Hierax 1,
Severus 1, Herminos 2, Claudios Pt. 3, Aristocles
1, Galenos 7, Alexandros (Aphr.) 6, Marcus
Aurelius 6, Melito 2, Apollinarius 1, Minucius
Felix 4, Athenagoras 4, Irenaeus Lugd. 4, Clemens
Alexandr. 6, Bardesanes 4

200–220   total 29
———— Hierax 1, Severus 1, Galenos 7,
Alexandros (Aphrodis.) 6, Stoics 1, Irenaeus
Lugd. 4, Clemens Alex. 6, Hippolytus 3

220–240   total 18
———— Alexandros (Aphrodisios) 6, Stoics 1,
Hippolytus 3, Origenes 8

240–260   total 30
———— Longinos 2, Diogenes Laërtius 3,
Plotinos 12, Stoics 1, Origenes 8, Dionysius
Magn. 2, Gregorius Thaumaturgus 2

260–280   total 24
———— Longinos 2, Diogenes Laërtius 3,
Cornelius Labeo 3, Dionysius Magnus 2, Gregor-
ius Thaumaturgus 2

280–300   total 5
———— Cornelius Labeo 3, Peripatetics 1,
Pamphilos (Caes.) 1

300–320   total 8
———— Alexandros (Lykopolis) 2, Pamphilos
(Caes.) 1, Eusebius (Caes.) 3, Methodius (Phil.) 2

320–340   total 18
———— Alexandros (Lykopolis) 2, Chalcidius
4, Arius 4, Eusebius (Caes.) 3, Lactantius 4,
Eusthatius (Ant.) 1

340–360   total 14
———— Chalcidius 4, Arius 4, Eusebius
(Caes.) 3, I. Firmicus Maternus 3

360–380   total 42
———— Iulian 7, Themistios 5, Sallustios 3,
Eunomius 1, Vett. Agorius Praetextatus 2,
I. Firmicus Maternus 3, Hilarius (Poit.) 3,
Basilius Magnus 6, Gregorius Naz. 6, Gregorius
Nyss. 6

380–400   total 37
———— Themistios 5, Vett. Agorius Prae-
textatus 2, Sallustios 3, Eunomius 1, Basilius
Magn. 6, Gregorius Naz. 6, Gregorius Nyss. 6,
Ioannes Chrys. 5, Apollinarius Laod. 3

400–420   total 33
———— Plutarchos 1, Hypatia 3, Macrobius 4,
Domninos 3, Iulian (Eklanum) 2, Pelagius 3,
Cassianus 3, Ioannes Chrys. 5, Synesius 2,
Nemesius 2, Theodorus (Mops.) 2, Cyrillus
Alex. 3

420–440   total 27
———— Plutarchos 1, Macrobius 4, Domninos 3, Hierokles 2, Iulian (Eklanum) 2, Pelagius
3, Cassianus 3, Caelestius 1, Theodorus (Mops.) 2,
Cyrillus (Alex.) 3, Theodoretus (Cyr.) 3

440–460 total 11
————— Domninos 3, Hierokles 2, Cyrillus
Alex. 3, Theodoretus (Cyr.) 3

460–480 total 13
————— Ammonios Hermeion 2, Asklepios
1 Olympiodorus Jr. 2, Faustus 1, Gennadius 1,
Claudianus Mamertus 3, Theodoretus (Cyr.) 3

480–500 total 10
————— Ammonios Hermeion 2, Asclepio-
dotos 2, Elias 1, David 1, Faustus 1, Gennadius 1,
Aeneas Gazensis 2

500–520 total 14
————— Ammonios Hermeion 2, Elias 1,
David 1, Simplikios 5, Aeneas Gazensis 2, Pro-
kopius Gazensis 3

520–540 total 23
————— Simplikios 5, Aeneas Gazensis 2,
Prokopius Gazensis 3, Boëthius 6, Leontius
(Byz.) 3, Ioannes Philoponus 4

540–560 total 17
————— Simplikios 5, Leontius (Byz.) 3,
Ioannes Philop. 4, Zacharias (Myt.) 2, Cassio-
dorus 3

560–580 total 5
————— Cassiodorus 3, Martinus Bracar. 2

580–600 total 4
————— Stephanos 2, Martinus Bracar. 2

600–620 total 8
————— Stephanos 2, Sergius 2, Isidorus
Hispal. 4

620–640 total 8
————— Stephanos 2, Sergius 2, Isidorus
Hispal. 4

640–660 total 3
————— Stephanos 2, Pyrrhus 1

660–680 total 2
————— Agatho 2

680–700 total 2
————— Agatho 2

700–720 total 3
————— Beda Venerabilis 3

720–740 total 8
————— Beda Venerabilis 3, Ioannes Damascenus 5

740–760 total 6
————— Ioannes Damascenus 5, Egbertus 1

760–780 total 1
————— Egbertus 1

780–800 total 4
————— Alcuinus 4

800–820 total 6
————— Alcuinus 4, Fredegisus 2

820–840 total 8
————— Fredegisus 2, Hrabanus Maurus 4,
Candidus 2

840–860 total 14
————— Hrabanus Maurus 4. Servatus Lupus
2, John Scotus Erigena 8

860–880 total 15
————— Servatus Lupus 2, John Scotus Erig.
8, Photius 3, Hincmarus 2

880–900 total 9
————— Photius 3, Hincmarus 2, Heiricus
(Aux.) 2, Remigius (Aux.) 2

900–920 total 4
————— Remigius (Aux.) 2, Arethas 2

920–940 total 2
————— Arethas 2

940–960 total 1

960–980 total 1

980–1000 total 3
————— Sylvester II (Gerbert) 3

1000–1020 total 8
————— Sylvester II (Gerbert) 3, Fulbert 2,
Notker Labeo 3

1020–1040 total 5
————— Fulbert 2, Notker Labeo 3

1040–1060 total 8
————— Berengarius T. 3, Anselmus (Besate)
2, Lanfrancus 3

1060–1080 total 15
————— Berengarius T. 3, Anselmus (Besate)
2, Lanfrancus 3, Mich. Psellos 3, Ioannes Italos 2,
Michael Ephes. 2

1080–1100 total 18
————— Berengarius T. 3, Lanfrancus 3,
Mich. Psellos 3, Ioannes Italos 2, Michael Ephes.
2, Eustratios 2, Roscelinus 3

1100–1120 total 8
————— Eustratios 2, Roscelinus 3, Adelard
of Bath 2, Raimbert (Lille) 1

1120–1140 total 15
————— Eustratios 2, Roscelinus 3, Adelard of
Bath 2, Petrus Abaelardus 4, Guilelmus de
Conches 2, Thierry de Chartres 2

1140–1160 total 16
————— Petrus Abaelardus 4, Guilelmus de
Conches 2, Thierry de Chartres 2, Gualterus de
Mauretania 1, Gilbertus Porretanus 3, Dominicus
Gundissalinus 2, Bernardus Silvestris 2

1160–1180 total 7
————— Gualterus de Mauretania 1, Domini-
cus Gundissalinus 2, Isaac de Stella 2, Bernardus
Silvestris 2

1180–1200 total 8
————— Alfredus Anglicus 2, Radulfus Ardens
1, Alanus ab Insulis 3, Alexander Neckham 2

1200–1220 total 14
————— Alfredus Anglicus 2, Radulfus Ardens
1, Alanus ab Insulis 3, Alexander Neckham 2,
Amalrich de Bene 3, David Diantanensis 3

1220–1240   total 8
———————— Robert Grosseteste 4, Rolandus Cremonensis 2, Michael Scotus 2

1240–1260   total 15
———————— Robert Grosseteste 4, Bartholomaeus Anglicus 2, Albertus Magnus 8, Nikephoros Blemmydes 1

1260–1280   total 26
———————— Bartholomaeus Anglicus 2, Albertus Magnus 8, Nikephoros Blemmydes 1, Thomas (York) 2, Siger of Brabant 4, Roger Bacon 6, Hannibaldus de Hannib. 1, Boetius de Dacia 2

1280–1300   total 36
———————— Albertus Magnus 8, Roger Bacon 6, Witelo 2, Heinrich Bate 2, Gottfried (Fontaines) 3, Georgios Pachymeres 2, Richardus de Mediaville 3, Guilelmus (Ware) 2, Dietrich de Vriberg 2, Siger of Brabant 4, Boetius de Dacia 2

1300–1320   total 50
———————— Heinrich Bate 2, Gottfried (Fontaines) 3, Georgios Pachymeres 2, Richardus de Mediavilla 3, Guilelmus (Ware) 2, Dietrich de Vriberg 2, Maximos Planudes 2, Jean Quidort 2, Tolomeo (Lucca) 2, Dante 8, Duns Scotus 8, Durandus de S. Porc. 2, M. Eckehart 8, Pietro d'Abano 1, Ioannes de Ianduno 3

1320–1340   total 47
———————— Tolomeo (Lucca) 2, Dante 8, Durandus de S. Porc. 2, Petrus Aureoli 2, Nicolaus Trivet 2, Guido Terreni 2, Siegbert (Beck.) 2, Bartoldus de Mosburch 1, Antonius Andreos 1, Heinrich (Lübeck) 1, Franciscus de Mayronis 2, Walther Burleigh 1, M. Eckehart 8, Ioannes (Baconthorp) 2, Ioannes de Ianduno 3, William Ockham 8

1340–1360   total 33
———————— Guido Terreni 2, Walther Burleigh 1, I. Tauler 4, I. Buridan 2, I. Wicklif 3, Petrarca 6, Ioannes (Baconthorp) 2, William Ockham 8, Adam Wodham 2, Richard Swineshead 1, Ioannes de Mirecuria 2

1360–1380   total 23
———————— I. Tauler 4, Marsilius (Inghen) 2, I. Buridan 2, I. Wicklif 3, Petrarca 6, Ioannes de Mirecuria 2, Nicolaus (Oresma) 2, Albert de Saxonia 2

1380–1400   total 13
———————— Marsilius (Inghen) 2, I. Wicklif 3, Petrus d'Ailly 4, Nicolaus (Oresma) 2, Albert de Saxonia 2

1400–1420   total 6
———————— Petrus d'Ailly 4, Paulus 2

1420–1440   total 9
———————— Antonin 3, Petrus d'Ailly 4, Paulus 2

1440–1460   total 14
———————— Antonin 3, Heimerick de Campo 1, Nicolaus Cusanus 8, Cajetanus Thiaeneus 2

1460–1480   total 13
———————— Nicolaus Cusanus 8, Gabriel Biel 3, Cajetanus Thiaeneus 2

1480–1500   total 7
———————— Gabriel Biel 3, Petrus Tartaretus 1, Nicoletto Vernias 1, Leonardo da Vinci 2

1500–1520   total 8
———————— Leonardo da Vinci 8

1520–1540   total 1

1540–1560   total 1

1560–1580   total 16
———————— Bruno 8, Copernicus 8

1580–1600   total 16
———————— Galileo 8, Keppler 8

1600–1620   total 34
———————— Bruno 8, Galileo 8, Keppler 8, Descartes 8, Reneri 1, Heereboord 1

1620–1640   total 38
———————— Descartes 8, Galileo 8, Keppler 8, Comenius 7, Mersenne 4, Reneri 1, Heereboord 2

1640–1660   total 36
———————— Descartes 8, Comenius 7, Galileo 8, Keppler 8, Mersenne 4, Heereboord 1

1660–1680   total 23
———————— Comenius 7, Leibnitz 9, Le Roy 2, Le Grand 2, Rohault 1, Clerselier 1, Heydanus 1

1680–1700   total 26
———————— Leibnitz 9, Shaftesbury 5, Cordemoy 3, Meier 3, Wittich 3, Heydanus 1, Fontenelle 2

1700–1720   total 25
———————— Leibnitz 9, Wolf 7, Wittich 1, Cordemoy 3, Shaftesbury 5

1720–1740   total 23
———————— C. Wolf 7, Thummig 1, Rudiger 2, Billfinger 1, Crouzas 1, Reinbeck 1, Heineccius 1, J. Lange 1, Buddaeus 2, Baumgarten 4, Cramer 2

1740–1760   total 39
———————— Kant 12, Wolf 7, Reinbeck 2, Crusius 4, Daries 2, Baumgarten 4, Plouquet 4, Boškovič 4

1760–1780   total 39
———————— Kant 12, Rousseau 8, Baumgarten 4, Ickstadt 1, Daries 2, Lomonosov 4, Plouquet 4, Lambert 4

1780–1800   total 55
———————— Kant 12, Goethe 8, Schiller 8, Kinker 1, Nitsch 1, Niethammer 1, Beck 1, Fichte 8, Tettens 4, Jacob 1, S. Maimon 4, Schultz 1, Schultze 3, Schwab 1

1800–1820   total 71
———————— Kinkel 1, Villers 1, Schultz 1, Schmid 1, Schad 2, Abicht 1, O'Keeffe 2, Born 1, Jäsche 2, Mellin 2, Goethe 8, Gauss 8, Fichte 8, Kant 12, Wirgmann 1, Fries 6, Nitsch 1, Willich 1, Krug 2, Beck 2, Reinhold 3, S. Maimon 4, Jacob 1

1820–1840 total 40
——————— Fichte 8, Krug 5, Fries 6, Damiron 2, B. de Moulin 1, Saisset 2, Jäsche 2, Goethe 8, Whewell 6

1840–1860 total 29
——————— Renouvier 7, Secrétan 4, Testa 2, Apelt 2, Saisset 1, P. Janet 4, Fechner 7, Boullier 2

1860–1880 total 53
——————— F. Lange 7, Renouvier 7, Liebmann 5, Cohen 7, Ruskin 6, Emerson 6, Saisset 1, G. T. Fechner 7, Dostoevsky 7

1880–1900 total 103
——————— Stallo 6, Wvedensky 4, Riehl 5, Natorp 5, Cohen 7, Rickert 6, Stadler 2, Watson 4, Windelband 6, M. Muller 2, Munsterberg 4, Credaro 1, Cohn 3, Pillon 4, Classen 1, Caird 3, Rokytansky 1, Vorländer 4, Bauch 2, Hamelin 4, Cantoni 4, Stammler 4, Renouvier 7, Koppelmann 1, Liebert 2, Harris 4, Turbiglio 2, Tocco 2, F. Schultz 1, Land 2

1900–1920 total 109 [1]
——————— Liebmann, Cohen, Rickert, Natorp, Windelband, Wvedensky, Hessen, Koppelmann, Liebert, Stammler, Hocking, Pillon, Hamelin, Kinkel, P. Stein, Gurland, Buchenau, Lasswitz, N. Hartmann, Christiansen, Krause, Stadler, Cantoni, Muirhead, Staudinger, Ewald, Pringle-Pattison, Gavronsky, Kistiakovsky, Cassirer, Lask, Lossky, Renouvier

[1] For obvious reasons values are not given for living authors.

Appendix to Chapter Six [1]

LIST OF THINKERS FOR EACH PERIOD, WITH THE VALUE GIVEN TO EACH ON A SCALE 1 TO 12

Graeco-Roman and Western Cultures

NOMINALISM (440 B.C.–A.D. 1920)

B.C. 440–420   total 8
———— Protagoras 8

420–400   total 27
———— Protagoras 8, Prodicos 5, Hippias 4, Polos 2, Callicles 2, Critias 3, Thrasymachos 3

400–380   total 25
———— Antisthenes 5, Prodicos 5, Hippias 4, Polos 2, Thrasymachos 3, Aristippos 6

380–360   total 15
———— Antisthenes 5, Alcidames 4, Aristippos 6

360–340   total 19
———— Diogenes (Sinope) 5, Alcidames 4, Aristippos 6, Metrodoros 1, Arete 1, Aithiops 1, Antipatros 1

340–320   total 10
———— Diogenes (Sinope) 5, Arete 1, Aithiops 1, Antipatros 1, Aristippos (grandson) 1, Anaxarchos 1

320–300   total 15
———— Monimos 1, Onesicritos 2, Phyliscos 1, Crates (Theb.) 4, Theodoros 2, Hegesias 2, Anniceris 2, Anaxarchos 1

300–280   total 23
———— Epicuros 8, Monimos 1, Onesicrotos 2, Phyliscos 1, Crates 4, Metrocles (Maron.) 1, Theodoros 2, Hegesias 2, Anniceris 2

280–260   total 23
———— Epicuros 8, Metrocles (Maron.) 1, Bion (Borysthenes) 3, Ariston (Chios) 5, Theodoros 2, Hegesias 2, Anniceris 2

260–240   total 17
———— Hermarchos 2, Colotes 2, Bion (Borysth.) 3, Ariston (Chios) 5, Menippos 5

240–220   total 28
———— Hermarchos 2, Colotes 2, Polystratos 2, Hippokleides 1, Bion (Borysth.) 3, Ariston (Chios) 5, Menippos 5, Teles 3, Cercidas (Kerkidas Megalopolis) 5

220–200   total 8
———— Polystratos 2, Hippokleides 1, Cercidas (Megalop.) 5

200–180   total 4
———— Polystratos 2, Hippokleides 1, Dionysios 1

180–160   total 2
———— Dionysios 1, Basilleides 1

160–140   total 3
———— Basilleides 1, Philonides 2

140–120   total 2
———— Apollodoros 2

120–100   total 2
———— Apollodoros 2

100–80   total 9
———— Amafinius 1, Apollodoros 2, Zenon (Sidon) 2, Phaidros 2, Meleagros 2

80–60   total 7
———— Phaidros 2, Amafinius 1, Zenon 2, Meleagros 2

60–40   total 18
———— Patron 1, Philodemos (Gadara) 5, Lucretius 8, Asclepiades (Bith.) 4

40–20   total 9
———— Philodemos 5, Asclepiades 4

20–0   total 1
———— Epicurean school 1

A.D. 0–20   total 1
———— Epicurean school 1

20–40   total 1
———— Epicurean school 1

40–60   total 1
———— Demetrios 1

60–80   total 1
———— Demetrios 1

80–100   total 7
———— Demetrios 1, Dion Chrysostomos 6

100–120   total 6
———— Dion Chrysostomos 6

120–140   total 6
———— Celsus (Epicur.) 1, Oinomaos 3, Demonax 2

140–160   total 7
———— Celsus (Epicur.) 1, Diogenianos 1, Oinomaos 3, Demonax 2

160–180   total 4
———— Celsus (Epicur.) 1, Diogenianos 1, Demonax 2

180–200   total 6
———— Demonax 2, Diogenianos 1, Diogenes (Oiksanda) 3

200–220 total 9
――――――― Diogenes (Oiksanda) 3, Tertullianus 6

220–240 total 7
――――――― Epicureans 1, Tertullianus 6

240–260 total 2
――――――― Epicureans 1, Arthemas 1

260–280 total 4
――――――― Epicureans 1, Arthemas 1, Paulus (Samos.) 2

280–300 total 5
――――――― Epicureans 1, Paulus (Samos.) 2, Lucianus (Samos.) 2

300–320 total 3
――――――― Epicureans 1, Lucianus (Samos.) 2

320–340 total 13
――――――― Epicureans 1, Arnobius 3, Lactantius 4, Eustathius (Antioch.) 1, Arius 4

340–360 total 5
――――――― Epicureans 1, Arius 4

360–380 total 2
――――――― Eunomius 1, Aetios 1

380–400 total 6
――――――― Eunomius 1, Ioannes Chrysostomos 5

400–420 total 5
――――――― Ioannes Chrysostomos 5

420–440 total 3
――――――― Nestorius 3

440–460 total 6
――――――― Nestorius 3, Eutyches 3

460–480 total 3
――――――― Eutyches 3

480–500 total 1
――――――― Acacius 1

500–520 total 1
――――――― Severus 1

520–540 total 5
――――――― Severus 1, Ioannes Philoponus 4

540–560 total 4
――――――― Ioannes Philoponus 4

560–1080 total 0

1080–1100 total 3
――――――― Roscelinus 3

1100–1120 total 4
――――――― Roscelinus 3, Raimbert (Lille) 1

1120–1140 total 7
――――――― Roscelinus 3, Petrus Abaelardus 4

1140–1160 total 4
――――――― Petrus Abaelardus 4

1160–1260 total 0

1260–1280 total 6
――――――― Roger Bacon 6

1280–1300 total 9
――――――― Roger Bacon 6, Richardus de Mediavilla 3

1300–1320 total 3
――――――― Richardus de Mediavilla 3

1320–1340 total 16
――――――― Petrus Aureoli 2, Guido Terreni (Perp.) 2, William Ockham 8, Nicolaus (Autricuria) 4

1340–1360 total 22
――――――― William Ockham 8, Robert Holcot 1, Gregorius (Rimini) 2, I. Buridan 2, Adam Wodham 2, Richard Swineshead 1, Ioannes de Mirecuria 2, Nicolaus (Autricuria) 4

1360–1380 total 13
――――――― Marsilius Inghen 2, I. Buridan 2, Adam Wodham 2, Richard Swineshead 1, Ioannes de Mirecuria 2, Nicolaus (Oresme) 2, Albert de Saxonia 2

1380–1400 total 10
――――――― Marsilius Inghen 2, Petrus d'Ailly 4, Nicolaus (Oresme) 2, Albert de Saxonia 2

1400–1420 total 4
――――――― Petrus d'Ailly 4

1420–1440 total 4
――――――― Petrus d'Ailly 4

1440–1460 total 1

1460–1480 total 3
――――――― Gabriel Biel 3

1480–1500 total 3
――――――― Gabriel Biel 3

1500–1520 total 6
――――――― Machiavelli 6

1520–1540 total 18
――――――― Pomponazzi 4, Luther 8, Machiavelli 6

1540–1560 total 2
――――――― Raymundus Sab. 2

1560–1580 total 8
――――――― Raymundus Sab. 2, Followers of Sextus Empiricus 6

1580–1600 total 28
――――――― Sanchez 2, Vanini 4, Montaigne 6, Lublin 12, Baco 7, Campanella 7

1600–1620 total 32
――――――― Sanchez 2, Charron 2, Vanini 4, Sennert 2, Gilbert 4, N. Hill 1, Baco 7, Jungius 4, Campanella 6

1620–1640 total 27
――――――― Baco 7, Jungius 4, Campanella 6, Hobbes 8, Sennert 2

1640–1660 total 23
――――――― Magnenus 2, Biergerne 1, Beregard 2, Brown 3, Hobbes 8, Gassendi 7

1660–1680   total 36
———————— Brown 3, Hobbes 8, Gassendi 7, Glanville 2, Glisson 3, Sorbière 1, Bernier 1, R. Boyle 4, Lobkovič 4, Hirnhaym 3

1680–1700   total 69
———————— Hobbes 8, Brown 3, Glanville 2, Foucher 1, La Motte Le Vayer 1, Huet 1, P. Bayle 6, Glisson 3, Bernier 2, Newton 9, Locke 8, R. Boyle 4, Bould 2, Lowde 1, Leeuwenhoeck 5, Hook 5, Toland 4, Dodwell 2, W. Coward 2

1700–1720   total 54
———————— Mandeville 4, Foucher 1, Bayle 6, Claude Brunet 4, Locke 8, Newton 9, Burnet 2, Cockburn 2, Leeuwenhoeck 5, Toland 4, Boerhaave 3, Clarke 2, W. Coward 2, Dudwell 2

1720–1740   total 51
———————— Voltaire 7, Newton 9, Clarke 2, Jean Meslier 3, Toland 4, Collins 1, Chubb 1, Bolingbrooke 2, Johnson 6, Edwards 6, Buffon 6, Hutcheson 4

1740–1760   total 82
———————— D'Alembert 5, Diderot 7, Hume 8, Maupertuis 4, Hartley 4, Voltaire 7, Vaucanson 2, Morelli 2, Dumarsais 2, Montesquieu 6, Lamettrie 5, Hutcheson 4, Burke 4, Leroy 1, Tindall 2, Morgan 1, Chubb 1, Edwards 6, Buffon 6, A. Smith 5

1760–1780   total 106
———————— Buffon 6, Condillac 6, D'Alembert 5, Diderot 7, Hume 8, Voltaire 7, Helvetius 6, Lambert 1, Franklin 4, Paine 4, Hartley 4, Holbach 6, Genovesi 2, Priestley 6, A. Tucker 2, Freret 3, Ferguson 4, Mably 4, E. Burke 4, Morelli 2, Turgot 4, Maupertuis 4, A. Smith 5, Quesnay 4

1780–1800   total 83
———————— Ethan Allen 2, Soave 2, Gioja 3, Condillac 6, Lichtenberg 2, Priestley 6, Holbach 6, Volney 2, James Mill 6, Lambert 1, E. Darwin 4, Destutt de Tracy 4, Condorcet 4, Radichtev 1, S. Simon 5, Paine 4, Jefferson 6, Aenesidemus 2, E. Burke 4, Bentham 6, Laplace 7

1800–1820   total 55
———————— Gioja 3, Galluppi 3, Romagnosi 2, Destutt de Tracy 4, Volney 2, Borelli 1, Lalande 2, Broussais 2, Laplace 8, Lichtenberg 2, Schalmeier 1, S. Simon 5, Cabanis 4, Aenesidemus 2, Bentham 6, J. Mill 6, Soave 2

1820–1840   total 69
———————— Herbart 7, J. Mill 6, Bentham 6, Benecke 2, S. Simon 5, S. Germain 2, Bazard 1, Gioja 3, J. St. Hilaire 6, Enfantin 1, Drobisch 4, Blanqui 1, D. de Tracy 4, Schalmeier 1, Herschel 6, A. Comte 8, Feuerbach 6

1840–1860   total 117
———————— Feuerbach 6, J. S. Mill 8, A. Comte 8, K. Marx 8, Joly 1, Pouchet 1, Considerant 4, Stirner 6, Spencer 8, Chr. Baur 4, Biedermann 1, De Morgan 2, Bakunin 4, G. Lewes 5, Engels 6, Cabet 2, Helmholtz 6, Benecke 2, Littré 4, Durdik

1, Strümpell 2, Proudhon 5, Blanqui 1, A. Ruge 4, Herzen 4, Strauss 6, Černyševsky 3, Drobisch 4, Carové 1

1860–1880   total 239
———————— J. S. Mill 8, Maxwell 8, Spencer 8, Thomson 6, Galton 6, Lavrov 4, Taine 7, Buckle 5, Černyševsky 3, Kreiči 4, Oušinsky 3, Pisarev 1, Setchenov 5, Cl. Bernard 4, Darwin 8, D. Strauss 6, Huxley 1, Austin 4, Jevons 6, Vogt 4, Troitzky 2, Moleschott 4, Ribot 7, Grote 2, Liebig 5, Lewes 5, Haeckel 6, Wundt 7, Bain 7, Duehring 6, Renan 6, McCosh 4, Zöllner 4, Engels 6, Marx 8, Nietzsche 9, Lazarus 4, Steinthal 4, Hamilton 6, Helmholtz 6, Herzen 4, Kropotkin 4, Zimmerman 4, Dressler 1, Lotti 4, Wyrubov 4, Exner 3, Lafitte 5, Strümpell 2, Waitz 4

1880–1900   total 275
———————— Spencer 8, Darwin 8, Ribot 7, Taine 7, Bain 7, Haeckel 7, Wundt 7, Renan 6, Lewes 5, Duehring 6, Marx 8, Engels 6, Zimmerman 4, Nietzsche 9, Delboeuf 4, Kropotkin 4, Clifford 4, Durdik 1, Peirce 1, Lazarus 4, Steinthal 4, Guyau 5, Cornelius 1, Fouillée 5, Lindner 1, Goring 2, Jodl 4, N. Grote 2, Pavlov 7, Binet 4, Bechterev 4, K. Menger 2, Galton 6, Baldwin 5, P. Carus 4, Nägeli 3, Preyer 3, Romanes 3, Ziehen 3, Ziegler 1, Büchner 5, Überweg 5, Lombroso 4, Pearson 4, Mantegazza 1, Rein 4, Avenarius 6, Mach 6, W. James 7, C. Robertson 4, Kreiči 4, Huxley 1, Jevons 6, Troizky 2, Lobačevsky 6, Tarde 4, Tannery 4, Laas 4, Geier 1, Bender 1, Spitzer 1, Edgeworth 2, Kautsky 4, Lavrov 3, Sully 4

1900–1920   total 322 [1]
———————— W. James, Vaihinger, Schiller, Mauthner, Moebius, Russell, Lewin, Hering, Mach, H. Gomperz, Freud, Nietzsche, Ostwald, Tarchanov, Kozlovsky, Wundt's school, "Monistenbund," Kandinsky, Pearson, Renzi, Pauly, Pierre Janet, Bogdanov, Kautsky, Carus, Vernadsky, Petrovič, B. Erdmann, Nordmann, Wundt, H. Souplé, H. Maier, Enriquez, Hoeffding, Dantec, Rignano, Ziehen, Mečnikov, Loeb, Zeleny, Zehnder, J. Schmidt, Plessner, Verworn, Roux, Seimon, Zur Strassen, Gibbs, Bychovsky, Carnap, Pieron, Sollier, Menger, Ribot, A. France, Planck, Boltzmann, Plechanov, Lenin, Bazarov, Kotarbinsky, Lunačarsky, Deborin, Kostyleff, Karstanien, Radl, Petzold, Kleinpeter, Cornelius, Jerusalem, Binet, Tarde, Guignebert, Sully, Galton, Dewey, Perry

---

CONCEPTUALISM (460 B.C.–A.D. 1920)

B.C. 460–440   total 5
———————— Anaxagoras 5

440–420   total 11
———————— Anaxagoras 5, Empedocles 6

[1] For obvious reasons values are not given for living authors.

420–400   total 14
——————— Democritos 8, Empedocles 6

400–380   total 8
——————— Democritos 8

380–360   total 8
——————— Democritos 8

360–340   total 1

340–320   total 1

320–300   total 1

300–280   total 8
——————— Zenon (Kition) 8

280–260   total 13
——————— Zenon (Kition) 8, Cleanthes 5

260–240   total 5
——————— Cleanthes 5

240–220   total 13
——————— Cleanthes 5, Chrysippos 7, Sphairos 1

220–200   total 8
——————— Chrysippos 7, Sphairos 1

200–180   total 6
——————— Sphairos 1, Zenon (Tarsos) 1, Diogenes (Sel.) 4

180–160   total 6
——————— Diogenes (Sel.) 4, Antipatros (Tarsos) 2

160–140   total 6
——————— Diogenes (Sel.) 4, Antipatros (Tarsos) 2

140–120   total 6
——————— Panaitios 5, Qu. Muc. Scaevola 1

120–100   total 8
——————— Panaitios 5, Qu. Muc. Scaevola 1, Hekaton 1, Mnesarchos 1

100–80   total 10
——————— Hekaton 1, Mnesarchos 1, Apollodoros (Athen.) 1, Poseidonios 7

80–60   total 12
——————— Apollodoros (Athen.) 1, Poseidonios 7, Asclepiodotos 2, Geminos 2

60–40   total 22
——————— Poseidonios 7, Asclepiodotos 2, Geminos 2, Pheinios 1, Dionysios (Cyren.) 1, Antipatros (Tyros) 2, Iason 2, Athenodoros 1, Apollonides 1, Diodotos 1, Cato 2

40–20   total 9
——————— Athenodoros (Kord.) 1, Apollonides 1, Diodotos 1, Apollonios 1, Athenodoros (Send.) 3, Areios Didymos 2

20–0   total 6
——————— Boethos (Sidon) 1, Athenodoros (Send.) 3, Areios Didymos 2

A.D. 0–20   total 3
——————— Boethos (Sidon) 1, Areios Didymos 2

20–40   total 1
——————— Stoics 1

40–60   total 12
——————— Seneca 8, L. A. Cornutus 4

60–80   total 19
——————— Seneca 8, Chairemon 2, L. A. Cornutus 4, Musonius Rufus 5

80–100   total 11
——————— Musonius Rufus 5, Epictetos 6

100–120   total 6
——————— Epictetos 6

120–140   total 12
——————— Epictetos 6, Arrianos 2, Hierocles 2, Cleomedes 2

140–160   total 6
——————— Arrianos 2, Hierocles 2, Cleomedes 2

160–180   total 6
——————— Marcus Aurelius 6

180–200   total 12
——————— Marcus Aureluis 6, Alexandros (Aphrod.) 6

200–220   total 7
——————— Alexandros (Aphrod.) 6, Stoics 1

220–240   total 7
——————— Alexandros (Aphrod.) 6, Stoics 1

240–260   total 1
——————— Stoics 1

260–280   total 1
——————— Stoics 1

280–1500   total 0

1500–1520   total 10
——————— Agricola 4, Fracastor 1, Melanchthon 5

1520–1540   total 11
——————— Melanchthon 5, Vives 6

1540–1560   total 15
——————— Vives 6, Ramus 4, Melanchthon 5

1560–1580   total 4
——————— Ramus 4

1580–1600   total 4
——————— Ramus 4

1600–1620   total 1

1620–1640   total 19
——————— Comenius 7, Descartes 8, Mersenne 4

1640–1660   total 26
——————— Pascal 7, Comenius 7, Mersenne 4, Descartes 8

1660–1680   total 39
——————— Pascal 7, Puffendorf 4, Leibnitz 9, La logique du Port Royal (1662) 4, Le Roy 1, Le Grand 2, Thomasius 4, Rohault 1, Comenius 7

1680–1700   total 15
——————— Leibnitz 9, Tschirnhausen 2, Thomasius 4

1700–1720   total 29
——————— Berkeley 8, Collier 5, Leibnitz 9, Wolf 7

1720–1740   total 26
——————— Turnbull 2, C. Wolf 7, Billfinger 1, Rudiger 2, Thümmig 2, Crouzas 1, Reinbeck 1, Heineccius 1, J. Lange 1, Buddaeus 2, Baumgarten 4, Cramer 2

1740–1760   total 45
——————— Kant 12, Wolf 7, Plouquet 4, M. Knutzen 4, Baumgarten 4, Crusius 4, Crouzas 2, Reinbeck 2, Daries 2, Reimarus 4

1760–1780   total 57
——————— Reid 4, Beattie 2, Kant 12, Rousseau 8, Euler 6, Tetens 4, Plouquet 4, Lambert 4, Baumgarten 4, Ickstadt 1, Daries 2, Jacobi 6

1780–1800   total 69
——————— Kinker 1, Nitsch 1, Nithammer 2, Beck 1, Kant 12, Reid 4, D. Stewart 4, Beattie 2, Jacobi 6, Tetens 4, Fichte 8, Salomon Maimon 4, Schultz 1, Schultze 3, Schwab 1, Schiller 8, Pestalozzi 4, Tittel 1

1800–1820   total 88
——————— Beattie 2, D. Stewart 4, Brown 3, Gauss 8, Pestalozzi 4, Metz 1, Maine de Biran 5, Reiss 1, Fichte 8, Kant 12, O. Keffel 1, Born 1, Wirgmann 1, Fries 6, Nitsch 1, Willich 1, Jäsche 2, Krug 2, Reinhold 3, Mellin 2, S. Maimon 4, Beck 2, Kinker 1, Villers 1, Jacob 1, Schultz 3, Tenneman 4, Schmid 1, Schad 1, Abicht 1

1820–1840   total 55
——————— Cousin 4, Ampère 5, Maine de Biran 5, Fries 6, Fichte 8, Krug 2, D. Stewart 4, Brown 3, Pestalozzi 4. Jäsche 2, Damiron 2, B. de Moulin 1, Saisset 1, Jacobi 6 (posthum. works), Joufroy 2

1840–1860   total 31
——————— V. Cousin 4, Renouvier 7, Maine de Biran 5, Secretan 4, Testa 2, Apelt 2, Saisset 1, P. Janet 4, Boullier 2

1860–1880   total 68
——————— Cousin 4, F. Lange 7, Liebmann 5, Renouvier 7, Cohen 7, Hamilton 6, Tolstoi 8, A. Spir 4, Mansel 2, Boullier 2, P. Janet 4, Ravaisson 3, Saisset 1, Brochard 2, Rémusat 2, J. Simon 2, Chaignet 2

1880–1900   total 157
——————— Veitch 4, Naville 4, J. Cohn 3, Koppelmann 1, Stammler 4, Liebert 2, Sigwart 4, Renouvier 7, Vvedensky 4, Karinsky 4, Chaignet 4, Masaryk 6, Rickert 6, Cohen 7, Liebmann 5, Turbiglio 2, Windelband 4, Riehl 5, Land 2, Tocca 2, Tolstoi 8, Münsterberg 4, Secretan 4, Frauenstädt 2, Palagyi 4, F. Schultze 2, Müller 2, Bosanquet 4, Deussen 4, Dauriac 3, Cantoni 4, Pillon 4, Staden 2, Vorländer 4, Watson 4, Natorp 5, Lasswitz 2, Rokytansky 1, W. Harris 4, J. Simon 2, Bauch 2, Caird 3, Credaro 1

1900–1920   total 173 [1]
——————— Caccirer, Lask, Ehrenburg, Cohen, Palagyi, Natorp, Christiansen, Simmel, Masaryk, Renouvier, Bosanquet, Vvedensky, Credaro, Pillon, Staudinger, Riehl, Rickert, Krause, Kistiakovsky, Saketti, Tolstoi, P. Stern, Windelband, Münsterberg, Kinkel, Liebmann, Liebert, Stammler, Cantoni, Koppelmann, Gavronsky, Stadler, Lasswitz, Buchenau, Girland, Novgorodcev, Pringle-Pattison, Fouillée, Einstein, Brentano, Stumpf, Teichmüller, Dyroff, Elsenhans, Messer, S. Soldern, Durkheim, M. Weber, De Roberty, Espinas

REALISM (540 B.C.–A.D. 1920)

B.C. 540–520   total 8
——————— Pythagoras 8

520–500   total 8
——————— Pythagoras 8

500–480   total 15
——————— Pythagoras 8, Parmenides 7

480–460   total 13
——————— Parmenides 7, Zenon El. 5, Hippasos 1

460–440   total 9
——————— Zenon El. 5, Melissos 3, Hippasos 1

440–420   total 14
——————— Philolaos 5, Zenon El. 5, Melissos 3, Hippasos 1

420–400   total 21
——————— Philolaos 5, Melissos 3, Socrates 9, Antiphon 4

400–380   total 27
——————— Philolaos 5, Socrates 9, Aeschines 3, Eukleides (Megar.) 3, Phaidon (Elis.) 2, Antiphon 4, Archytas 1

380–360   total 21
——————— Aeschines 3, Platon 12, Archytas 1, Eukleides (Megar.) 3, Phaidon (Elis.) 2

360–340   total 23
——————— Aeschines 3, Platon 12, Speusippos 3, Xenocrates 3, Phaidon (Elis.) 2

340–320   total 18
——————— Speusippos 3, Xenocrates 3, Aristoteles 12

320–300   total 29
——————— Xenocrates 3, Polemon 2, Aristoteles 12, Theophrastos 7, Eudemos (Rhodos) 2, Dikaiarchos (Messene) 3

300–280   total 19
——————— Polemon 2, Crantor 4, Crates (Athen.) 1, Theophrastos 7, Eudemos 2, Dikaiarchos (Messene) 3

[1] For obvious reasons values are not given for living authors.

280–260   total 7
———— Polemon 2, Crantor 4, Crates
(Athen.) 1

260–240   total 1
———— Lynon 1

240–220   total 2
———— Lynon 1, Prytanis 1

220–200   total 4
———— Prytanis 1, Ariston 3

200–180   total 3
———— Ariston 3

180–160   total 2
———— Kritolaos 2

160–140   total 2
———— Kritolaos 2

140–120   total 1
———— Diodoros (Tyros) 1

120–100   total 1
———— Diodoros (Tyros) 1

100–80   total 1
———— Diodoros (Tyros) 1

80–60   total 9
———— Antiochos (Ascalon) 4, T. Varro 5

60–40   total 17
———— T. Varro 5, Cicero 8, Nigidius
Figulus 4

40–20   total 13
———— Cicero 8, T. Varro 5

20–0   total 5
———— Eudoros 2, Q. Sextius 2, Sextius Jr. 1

A.D. 0–20   total 11
———— Philon 8, Sextius Jr. 1, Sotion 2

20–40   total 10
———— Philon 8, Sotion 2

40–60   total 10
———— Philon 8, Alexandros (Aigai) 2

60–80   total 5
———— Moderatos 3, Alexandros (Aigai) 2

80–100   total 11
———— Moderatos 3, Plutarchos 8

100–120   total 21
———— Plutarchos 8, Theon (Smyrna) 2,
Secundos 2, Nicomachos (Gerase) 1, Gaios 2,
Περὶ Κόσμον 4, Adrastos 2

120–140   total 25
———— Plutarchos 8, Theon 2, Secundos 2,
Nicomachos 1, Gaios 2, Adrastos 2, Basileides 4,
Valentinus 4

140–160   total 32
———— Theon 2, Secundos 2, Gaios 2,
Albinos 3, Calvisios 2, Adrastos 2, Herminos 2,
Claudios Ptolem. 3, Iustinus Martyr. 5, Basileides
4, Carpocrates 1, Valentinus 4

160–180   total 36
———— Albinos 3, Caloisios 2, Nicostratos 2,
Apuleius 6, Numenios 4, Cronios 2, Herminos 2,
Claudios Ptolem. 3, Aristocles 1, Galenos 7,
Carpocrates 1, Tatianus 3

180–200   total 48
———— Apuleius 6, Numenios 4, Cronios 2,
Atticos 2, Harpocration 1, Celsus 4, Maximos
(Tyros) 5, Hierax 1, Severus 1, Herminos 2,
Claudios Ptolem. 3, Aristocles 1, Galenos 7,
Tatianus 3, Clemens Alex. 6

200–220   total 32
———— Numenios 4, Hierax 1, Severus 1,
Philostratos 5, Hermetic Literature 5, Ammonios
Saccas 3, Galenos 7, Clemens Alex. 6

220–240   total 21
———— Philostratos 5, Hermetic Liter. 5,
Ammonios Saccas 3, Origenes 8

240–260   total 37
———— Hermetic Literature 5, Ammonios
Saccas 3, Amelios 2, Diogenes Laërtius 3, Ploti-
nos 12, Origenes 8, Gregorius Thaumaturgus 2,
Dionysius Magnus 2

260–280   total 22
———— Diogenes Laërtius 3, Plotinos 12,
Amelios 2, Dionysius Magnus 2, Gregorius Thau-
maturgus 2, Theognostus 1

280–300   total 10
———— Amelios 2, Porphyrios 7, Pamphylus
(Caes.) 1

300–320   total 18
———— Porphyrios 7, Iamblichos 7, Eusebius (Caes.) 3, Pamphylus (Caes.) 1

320–340   total 19
———— Iamblichos 7, Theodoros (Asine) 1,
Chalcidius 4, Athanasius Magnus 4, Eusebius
(Caes.) 3

340–360   total 12
———— Theodoros (Asine) 1, Chalcidius 4,
Eusebius (Caes.) 3, Athanasius Magnus 4

360–380   total 34
———— Iulian 7, Themistios 5, Athanasius
Magnus 4, Basilius Magnus 6, Gregorius Nazian-
zenus 6, Gregorius Nyssenus 6

380–400   total 28
———— Themistios 5, Basilius Magnus 6,
Gregorius Nazianzenus 6, Gregorius Nyssenus 6,
Ambrosius Mediol. 5

400–420   total 19
———— Macrobius 4, Syrianos 1, Augustinus
10, Synesius 2, Nemesius 2

420–440   total 20
———— Macrobius 4, Syrianos 1, Hierocles 2,
Augustinus 10, Theodoretus Cyrensis 3

440–460   total 13
———— Hierocles 2, Proclos 8, Theodoretus
Cyrensis 3

460–480   total 14
———————— Proclos 8, Theodoretus Cyrensis 3,
Claudianus Mamertus 3

480–500   total 13
———————— Proclos 8, Marinos 3, Aeneas Gazensis 2

500–520   total 21
———————— Isidoros 1, Doros 1, Dameseios 4,
Simplicios 5, Aeneas Gazensis 2, Dionysius
Areopagite 8

520–540   total 28
———————— Damascios 4, Simplicios 5, Aeneas
Gazensis 2, Dionysius Areopagite 8, Boethius 6,
Leontius (Byz.) 3

540–560   total 16
———————— Damascios 4, Simplicios 5, Leontius
(Byz.) 3, Zacharias (Mytilene) 2, Ioannes Lydos 2

560–580   total 2
———————— Ioannes Lydos 2

580–600   total 4
———————— Gregorius I Magnus 4

600–620   total 4
———————— Gregorius I Magnus 4

620–640   total 6
———————— Maximus Confessor 6

640–660   total 6
———————— Maximus Confessor 6

660–680   total 8
———————— Maximus Confessor 6, Agatho 2

680–700   total 2
———————— Agatho 2

700–720   total 3
———————— Beda Venerabilis 3

720–740   total 8
———————— Beda Venerabilis 3, Ioannes Damascenus 5

740–760   total 5
———————— Ioannes Damascenus 5

760–780   total 1

780–800   total 4
———————— Alcuinus 4

800–820   total 6
———————— Alcuinus 4, Fredegisus 2

820–840   total 6
———————— Fredegisus 2, Hrabanus Maurus 4

840–860   total 12
———————— Hrabanus Maurus 4, John Scotus
Erigena 8

860–880   total 11
———————— John Scotus Erigena 8, Photius 3

880–900   total 5
———————— Photius 3, Remigius Antissiodorensis 2

900–920   total 4
———————— Remigius Antissiodorensis 2, Arethas 2

920–940   total 2
———————— Arethas 2

940–960   total 1

960–980   total 1

980–1000   total 3
———————— Sylvester II (Gerbert) 3

1000–1020   total 5
———————— Sylvester II (Gerbert) 3, Fulbert
Carnotensis 2

1020–1040   total 2
———————— Fulbert 2

1040–1060   total 5
———————— Anselmus (Besate) 2, Lanfrancus 3

1060–1080   total 19
———————— Anselmus (Besate) 2, Lanfrancus 3,
Michael Psellos 3, Symeon Th. Nov. 4, Anselmus
Cant. 7

1080–1100   total 17
———————— Lanfrancus 3, Michael Psellos 3,
Symeon Th. Nov. 4, Anselmus Cant. 7

1100–1120   total 14
———————— Anselmus Cant. 7, Adelard of Bath 2,
Otto Cameracensis (odo from Cambrai) 1, Bruno
(Segni) 2, Guilelmus Campellensis 2

1120–1140   total 27
———————— Adelard of Bath 2, Bruno (Segni) 2,
Guilelmus Camp. 2, Bernardus Carnofensis 2,
Guilelmus de Conches 2, Bernardus Claraev. 5,
Guilelmus of St. Thierry 2, Honorius Augusto-
dunensios 3, Thierry (Chartres)-Theodoricus
Brito 2, Hugo à S. Victore 5

1140–1160   total 34
———————— Guilelmus de Conchos 2, Bernardus
Claraevalensis 5, Guilelmus s. Th. rem. 2, Hon-
orius Augustodun. 3, Ioscellin (Ganslenus) 1,
Thierry (Chartres) 2, Hugo à S. Victore 5,
Gilbertus Porretanus 3, Richardus à S. Victore 4,
Dominicus Gundissalinus 2, Bernardus Silvestris
2, Gualterus de Mauretania 1, Robertus Melidu-
nensis 2

1160–1180   total 15
———————— Gualterus de Mauret. 1, Robertus
Melidun. 2, Richardus à S. Victore 4, Dominicus
Gundissal. 2, Isaac de Stella 2, Clarenbaldus 2,
Bernardus Silvestris 2

1180–1200   total 12
———————— Alfredus Anglicus 2, Radulfus Ardens
1, Alanus ab Insulis 3, Nicolaus Ambianensis 2,
Gualterus à S. Victore 2, Alexander Neckham 2

1200–1220   total 24
———————— Alfredus Anglicus 2, Radulfus Ardens
1, Alanus ab Insulis 3, Nicolaus Ambian. 2, Alexander Neckham 2, Simon de Tornace 1, Thomas

Gallo 1, Praepositinus (Cremone) 2, Guilelmus (Auxerre) 2, Philippus Grevius 2, Amalrich de Bene 3, David Dinantenensis 3

1220–1240   total 19
———————— Thomas Gallo 1, Praepositinus (Cr.) 2, Guilelmus (Aux.) 2, Philippus Grevius 2, Radulphus de Longo Campo 1, Guilelmus Alvernus 3, Robert Grosseteste 4, Alexander Halensis 4

1240–1260   total 30
———————— Guilelmus Alvernus 3, Robert Grosseteste 4, Alexander Halensis 4, Bartholomaeus Angl. 2, Ioannes de Rupella 2, Albertus Magnus 8, Guilelmus Shyreswood 1, Lambert (Auxerre) 1, Vincentius Bellovacensis 2, Richard Fischacre 1, Nicolaus Parisiensis 2

1260–1280   total 52
———————— Bartholomaeus Anglicus 2, Albertus Magnus 8, Vincentius Bellovacensis 2, Nicolaus Parisiensis 2, Robert Kirwardby 2, Ioannes Bonaventura 8, Thomas (York) 2, Thomas Aquinas 12, Ulricus Engelberti 3, Petrus de Tarentasia (Inn. V) 2, Petrus Hispanus (Ioann. XXI) 2, Hannibaldus de Hannibaldis 1, Siger of Brabant 4, Boetius de Dacia 2

1280–1300   total 52
———————— Albertus Magnus 8, Raymundus Lullus 5, Witelo 2, Ioannes Peckham 1, Henricus Gandavensis 4, Gottfried (Fontaines) 3, Bernardus de Trilia 2, Aegidius (Lessines) 2, Remigio di Chiaro dei Gir. 2, Aegidius Romanus 3, Georgios Pachymeres 2, Matthaeus ab Aquasparte 2, Eustachius 2, Roger (Marston) 2, Petrus Ioannis Olivi 3, Guilelmus (Hothun) 1, Dietrich de Vriberg 2, Siger (Brabant) 4, Boetius de Dacia 2

1300–1320   total 51]
———————— Raymundus Lullus 5, Gottfried (Fontaines) 3, Aegidius (Lessines) 2, Remigio di Ch. dei Girol. 2, Aegidius Romanus 3, Georgios Pachymeres 2, Matthaeus ab Aquasparta 2, Dietrich de Vriberg 2, Bernardus de Alvernia 1, Jean Quidort 2, Guilelmus Petri de Godino 2, Hervé Nédélec (Herveus Natalis Brito) 3, Tolomeo (Lucca) 2, Duns Scotus 8, Durandus de s. Parciano 2, Thomas (Sutton) 2, M. Eckehart 8

1320–1340   total 32
———————— Guilelmus Petri de Godino 2, Hervé Nédélec 3, Tolomeo (Lucca) 2, Durandus de s. Porciano 2, Thomas (Sutton) 2, Ioannes de Regina 1, Ioannes Picardi de Lucidom. 2, Nicolaus Trivet 2, Bartoldus de Mosburch 1, Franciscus de Mayronis 2, Walter Burleigh 1, M. Eckehart 8, Thomas Bradwardine 2, Ioannes (Baconthorp.) 2

1340–1360   total 18
———————— Thomas (Sutton) 2, Walter Burleigh 1, Durandellus 1, H. Suso 5, Thomas (Strasbourg) 2, Thomas Bradwardine 2, I. Wiclif 3, Ioannes (Baconthorp.) 2

1360–1380   total 8
———————— H. Suso 5, I. Wiclif 3

1380–1400   total 3
———————— I. Wiclif 3

1400–1420   total 4
———————— Jean Charlier (Gerson) 4

1420–1440   total 11
———————— Jean Charlier (Gerson) 4, Ioannes Capreolus 3, Antonin 3, Heinrich (Gorkum) 1

1440–1460   total 19
———————— Ioannes Capreolus 3, Antonin 3, Dionysius Cartusianus 4, Heimerich de Campo 1, Nicolaus Cusanus 8

1460–1480   total 13
———————— Dionysius Cartusianus 4, Nicolaus Cusanus 8, Petrus Nigri 1

1480–1500   total 2
———————— Petrus Nigri 1, Petrus Tartaretus 1

1500–1520   total 16
———————— Zimara 1, Achillini 1, Nifus 1, Faber 2, Erasmus 5, Thomas Morus 6

1520–1540   total 34
———————— Frank 2, Serveto 4, Faber 2, Reuchlin 4, Paracelsus 4, T. Morus 6, P. della Mirandola Jr. 4, Zwingli 6, Achillini 1, Nifus 1

1540–1560   total 15
———————— Frank 2, Paracelsus 4, Serveto 4, Faber 2, Leo Hebraeus 3

1560–1580   total 43
———————— Paracelsus 4, Copernicus 8, Lever 3, Wilson 3, Cardanus 4, Sepulveda 2, Freigius 1, Camerarius 1, Fabricius 1, Chytraeus 1, Schegk 1, Pfaffrad 1, Sturm 2, Carpentarius 1, Bruno 8, Strigel 2

1580–1600   total 61
———————— Bodin 2, Case 2, Scotus 2, Paracelsus 4, Lever 1, Hixner 1, Crackanthrop 1, Wilson 3, Sanderson 1, V. Weigel 3, Galilei 8, Giordano Bruno 8, Schegk 1, Sturm 2, Camerarius 1, Freigius 1, Keppler 8, E. Digby 4, Fabricius 2, Snellius 1, Temple 1, Goclenius 3, Scherbius 1

1600–1620   total 45
———————— Bruno 8, Galilei 8, Case 2, Keppler 8, Hixner 1, Renery 1, Crackanthrop 1, Scotus 2, Fludd 2, V. Weigel 3, Harvey 4, Sanderson 1, Heerebord 2, Fotherby 2

1620–1640   total 50
———————— H. Cherbury 4, Helmont 4, Heerebord 1, Renery 1, Hixner 1, Alstedius 3, Weigel 3, Althusius 3, Galileo 8, Keppler 8, Fludd 2, J. Boehme 6, Jansenius 6

1640–1660   total 39
———————— Spinoza 8, Galileo 8, Keppler 8, Heerebord 1, Whichcote 1, Fludd 2, Smith 2, Culverwelle 1, White 2, Brooke 2, Cherbury 4

1660–1680   total 47
———————— Heerebord 1, Spinoza 8, Heydanus 1, Rienverz 1, Balings 1, De la Forge 3, Basso 2, Geulynx 6, Malebranche 7, Jelles 1, Arnauld 4, Nicole 4, Oldenburg 1, H. Morus 4, Clauberg 3

1680–1700   total 87
——————— Spinoza (posth.) 8, Stahl 3, Kuffeler 1, Pordage 1, Jelles 1, Rienverz 1, Storch 1, Arnauld 4, Nicole 4, H. Morus 4, Meier 3, Fardella 2, Cordemoy 3, B. Lamy 2, Cudworth 5, Clauberg 3, Lanion 2, Thomassin 2, Norris 2, Shaftesbury 5, Wittich 1, Heydanus 1, Malebranche 7, Bossuet 6, Fénelon 6, Fontenelle 2, Giovenale 2, Taylor 3, Poiret 2

1700–1720   total 51
——————— Bossuet (1704) 6, Cordemoy 3, Wittich 1, Stahl 3, Norris 2, Malebranche 7, Fénelon 6, Poiret 2, M. van Helmont 2, Lange 1, Thomassin 1, Shaftesbury 5, Giovenale 2, Fardella 2, André 1, Taylor 1, Mairan 2, B. Lamy 2, F. Lamy 2

1720–1740   total 26
——————— Mairan 2, Stahl 3, Morinière 2, Martinez Pasquales 3, Vico 7, Berkeley 8, André 1

1740–1760   total 34
——————— Berkeley 8, Swedenborg 4, R. Boškovič 6, Vico 7, Edelmann 1, Gerdil 2, Polignac 4, Fontenelle 2

1760–1780   total 22
——————— Swedenborg 4, Bonnet 4, Mairan 2, Lessing 6, Herder 6

1780–1800   total 53
——————— Robinet 2, Deschamps 1, Heydenreich 2, Thorild 1, W. Blake 4, Schleiermacher 4, St. Martin 4, Novalis 2, Schelling 8, Hegel 8, Bonnet 5, De Maistre 6, De Bonald 4, R. Price 2

1800–1820   total 90
——————— Troxler 1, Sibbern 1, Ast 1, Rixner 1, Schubert 1, Solger 1, Blasche 1, Hegel 8, Schopenhauer 8, Steffens 1, Schelling 8, Wagner 1, Kerner 1, Schleiermacher 4, Goethe 8, Hölderlin 2, Vellansky 2, Wronsky 6, Krause 4, Memel 1, Stuzmann 2, Wittenbach 2, Galitch 2, Fourièr 5, S. Martin 4, De Maistre 6, W. Blake 4, Coleridge 4

1820–1840   total 120
——————— Cuvier 6, F. J. Stahl 4, Goethe 8, Weisse 1, Schelling 8, Schopenhauer 8, Galitch 2, Bolzano 6, Krause 4, Whewell 6, Fichte Jr. 4, Sibbern 3, Franck 1, Mizkievicz 6, Lammenais 4, Chateaubriand 4, Baader 6, Royer-Collard 2, Wronsky 6, Towiansky 3, Jouffroy 1, Khomiakov 4, Kirejevsky 2, Gratry 3, Harms 3, Balmez 5, Burdach 2, Steffens 1, Schleiermacher 4, Ritter 2, Vorländer 1, Pavlov 1

1840–1860   total 175
——————— Schopenhauer 8, Wagner 8, J. Erdmann 4, Smetana 4, Krause 4, Melylin 1, Weissen-

born 1, Romer 1, Steffens 1, Schaden 1, Schmidt 1, Schelling 8, Lotze 5, Bolzano 6, Českovsky 1, Klacel 1, Gabler 1, Frank 3, Göschl 1, Fechner 7, Rosmini 6, Reiff 1, Mamiani 3, Minghetti 1, Rosenkranz 4, Chalybaeus 1, Pagano 1, Michelet 4, K. Fischer 4, Harris 3, Perty 2, Wronsky 6, Daub 2, Khomiakov 4, Samarin 2, Zeller 5, V. Carrière 3, Noack 1, Ranke 4, Towiansky 3, Mizkievicz 6, Kirejevsky 2, Emerson 6, L. Stein 6, Trendelenburg 5, Amerling 1, Lasson 3, Liebelt 4, T. Vischer 4, Ahrens 2, Schasler 1, Tieberghen 1, Vera 2, Prantl 4, Wahreinecke 1

1860–1880   total 142
——————— Schopenhauer 8, Ruskin 6, Hartmann 8, Emerson 6, Green 5, Fiorentino 3, Ferrier 2, Peters 3, H. von Stein 3, Wagner 8, Frauenstädt 2, Michelet 4, Ranke 4, Frank 3, K. Fischer 4, Zeller 5, Bergmann 2, Teichmüller 2, Soloviev 6, M. Carrière 4, Lotze 5, Jurkevič 2, J. Erdmann 4, Ferri 3, Mamiani 3, Vera 2, Fechner 7, Spaventa 2, Strachov 3, Lasson 3, Boutroux 4, Zerteleff 2, Lachelier 4, Upton 2, Martineau 4, Čičerin 4

1880–1900   total 160
——————— Bergson 8, Spir 4, Schuppe 5, Bulgakov 4, Lopatine 4, Lipps 7, Bradley 7, Hartmann 8, Hobhouse 3, Wallace 2, Stern 4, Eucken 5, Dilthey 4, Ose 2, Husserl 7, S. Trubetzkoi 4, E. Trubetzkoi 3, Debolsky 2, Strachov 3, Radlov 3, Čičerin 4, Ferrier 3, Howison 2, A. Seth 4, Cantor 4, R. Wagner 8, Drummond 4, J. Erdmann 4, Ranke 4, Royce 5, Lamy 2, Ruskin 6, Soloviev 6, Martineau 6, van Vloten 4, Bergmann 2

1900–1920   total 186 [1]
——————— Soloviev, Lossky, M. Scheler, Hessen, R. Eucken, Karsavin, K. Gross, Joël, Herbertz, Becher, Frank, Hartmann, H. Schwarz, Bergson, Maeterlink, Bradley, Spengler, Lasci, Iljin, Askoldov, Bulgakov, Vyšeslavcev, Petronievič, Heiđegger, Jankelevič, Ormond, Lopatine, E. Radlov, Vorovka, Pelikan, Hoppe, Losev, S. Trubetzkoi, E. Trubetzkoi, Maritain, Tröltsch, Ladyžensky, Oesterreich, Husserl, Gentile, Pfleiderer, B. Croce, Unamuno, Michaltchef

NOTE: — For Religious Realism for the period 1500–1920 see the names of the representatives of the Pluralistic Religious Idealism in the Appendix to Chapter Four.

——————
[1] For obvious reasons values are not given for living authors.

Appendix to Chapter Seven [1]

LIST OF THINKERS FOR EACH PERIOD, WITH THE VALUE GIVEN TO EACH ON A SCALE 1 TO 12

Graeco-Roman and Western Cultures

EXTREME SINGULARISM–INDIVIDUALISM (420 B.C.–A.D. 1920)

B.C. 420–400   total 10
——————— Polos 2, Callicles 2, Critias 3, Thrasymachos 3

400–380   total 11
——————— Polos 2, Thrasymachos 3, Aristippos 6

380–360   total 6
——————— Aristippos 6

360–340   total 9
——————— Aristippos 6, Arete 1, Aithiops 1, Antipatros 1

340–320   total 4
——————— Arete 1, Aithiops 1, Antipatros 1, Aristippos (grandson) 1

320–300   total 4
——————— Theodoros 2, Hegesios 2

300–280   total 12
——————— Epicuros 8, Theodoros 2, Hegesios 2

280–260   total 15
——————— Epicuros 8, Bion (Borysth.) 3, Theodoros 2, Hegesios 2

260–240   total 12
——————— Hermarchos 2, Colotes 2, Bion (Borysth.) 3, Menippos 5

240–220   total 23
——————— Hermarchos 2, Colotes 2, Polystratos 2, Hippokleides 1, Bion (Borysth.) 3, Menippos 5, Teles 3, Cercidas 5

220–200   total 8
——————— Polystratos 2, Hippokleides 1, Cercidas 5

200–180   total 4
——————— Polystratos 2, Hippokleides 1, Dionysios 1

180–160   total 2
——————— Dionysios 1, Basileides 1

160–140   total 3
——————— Basileides 1, Philonides 2

140–120   total 2
——————— Apollodoros (Ath.) 2

120–100   total 4
——————— Apollodoros (Ath.) 2, Zenon (Sidon) 2

100–80   total 7
——————— Apollodoros (Ath.) 2, Zenon (Sidon) 2, Amafinius 1, Phaidros 2

80–60   total 5
——————— Amafinius 1, Phaidros 2, Zenon (Sidon) 2

60–40   total 18
——————— Patron 1, Philodemos (Gadara) 5, Lucretius 8, Asclepiades 4

40–20   total 9
——————— Philodemos 5, Asclepiades 4

20–0   total 0.5

A.D. 0–20   total 0.5

20–40   total 0.5

40–60   total 0.5

60–80   total 0.5

80–100   total 0.5

100–120   total 0.5

120–140   total 1
——————— Celsus (Epicur.) 1

140–160   total 2
——————— Celsus (Epic.) 1, Diogenianos 1

160–180   total 6
——————— Diogenianos 1, Celsus (Epic.) 1, Lucian 4

180–200   total 8
——————— Diogenianos 1, Diogenes (Oinoanda) 3, Lucian 4

200–220   total 3
——————— Diogenes (Oinoanda) 3

220–240   total 0.5
——————— Epicureans

240–260   total 0.5
——————— Epicureans

260–280   total 0.5
——————— Epicureans

280–300   total 0.5
——————— Epicureans

300–320   total 0.5
——————— Epicureans

320–340   total 0.5
——————— Epicureans

340–360   total 0.5
———— Epicureans

360–1500   total 0

1500–1520   total 4
———— Pomponatius B. 4 (*Duplex veritas*)

1520–1540   total 6
———— Pomponatius B. 4, Rabelais 2 (Thélème)

1540–1560   total 2
———— Mennonites 1, Simonis 2

1560–1580   total 3
———— La Boecie 2, Mennonites 1

1580–1600   total 2
———— Mennonites 2

1600–1620   total 4
———— Vanini 4 (Aristocratic anarchism)

1620–1640   total 1

1640–1660   total 1

1660–1680   total 1

1680–1700   total 1

1700–1720   total 8
———— Claude Brunet 4, Mandeville 4

1720–1740   total 2
———— Defoe 2 (1732)

1740–1760   total 19
———— Lamettrie 5 (*L'école de la volupté*, 1751), Diderot 6 (Anarchie), Rousseau 8 (*Discours*, 1750)

1760–1780   total 10
———— Diderot 7, Meslier 3

1780–1800   total 12
———— Godwin 4, Anarchists among Jacobins 8

1800–1820   total 4
———— Godwin 4

1820–1840   total 4
———— Godwin 4

1840–1860   total 33
———— Proudhon 6, Bakunin 4, Stirner 6, Duehring 6, Harro Harring 1 (Anarchistic Utopia), C. Fourièr 5, Carlyle 5

1860–1880   total 29
———— Proudhon 6, Bakunin 4, Kropotkin 4, Nietzsche 9, Duehring 6

1880–1900   total 37
———— Tolstoi 8, Kropotkin 4, Nietzsche 9, Duehring 6, Brousse 1, Gode 1, Malot 1, Allemand 1, Mackay 2 (Anarchists), E. Reclus 4

1900–1920   total 37 [1]
———— Tolstoi, Kropotkin, Nietzsche, Duehring, G. Sorel, St. Taylor, P. Boncour. E. Reclus, Palant

[1] For obvious reasons values are not given for living authors.

SINGULARISTIC COLLECTIVISM
(1500 A.D.–A.D. 1920)

A.D. 1500–1520   total 6
———— Thomas More 6 (Anabaptists)

1520–1540   total 8
———— T. More 6, Johann Leyd. 2

1540–1560   total 2
———— Doni 1, Patritio 1 Anabaptists

1560–1580   total 1

1580–1600   total 1

1600–1620   total 6
———— Andreae 2, Bonifacio 2, The foundation of theocratic communistic state in Paraguay by Jesuits 2

1620–1640   total 7
———— Campanella 7

1640–1660   total 4
———— Peter Cornelius 1, John Hare 1, Hartlib 2

1660–1680   total 2
———— Vairasse 2

1680–1700   total 6
———— Fénelon 6

1700–1720   total 6
———— Fénelon 6

1720–1740   total 1

1740–1760   total 7
———— Mably 4, Morelli 3

1760–1780   total 6
———— Mably 4, Brissot de Warvilles 2

1780–1800   total 8
———— Mably 4, Babeuf 3, Buonarotti 1

1800–1820   total 8
———— Fichte 4 (*Der geschlossene Handelsstaat*, 1800), Saint-Simon 4

1820–1840   total 4
———— Rob. Owen 4

1840–1860   total 23
———— Cabet 3, Herzen 2, Weitling 1, K. Marx 8, Engels 6, L. Blanc 3

1860–1880   total 33
———— Marx 8, Engels 6, Herzen 2, Černyševsky 3, Lafargue 2, De Pape 2, Français 2, Blanqui 2, G. Gaide 2, L. Blanc 3

1880–1900   total 75
———— Marx 8, Engels 6, W. Morris 4, Guesde 2, Bourdeau 1, Lamprecht 4, Patten 2, Kautsky 4, Plechanov 4, Eveling 1, Tugan-Baranovsky 3, P. Struve 4, Labriola 3, R. Wipper 2, V. Adler 2, Bernstein 4, Jaurès 5, Bebel 4, S. Webb 4, Van der Velde 4, David 2, Hyndman 2

1900–1920 total 80 [1]
——————— A. France, (*Sur la pierre blanche*), Jaurès, Lenin, Pokrovsky, Van der Velde, Bebel, Liebknecht, Kl. Zetkin, R. Luxembourg, Labriola, Shaw, Braun, Elentheropulos, David, Plechanov, T. Baranovsky, Struve, Rezanov, Bazarov, S. Webb, V. Adler, Hyndman, B. Bax, Tschernoff, Singer, W. Heine, K. Schmidt, R. MacDonald, Lunačarsky, Deborin, Bogdanov

---

SINGULARISM–UNIVERSALISM
(460 B.C.–A.D. 1920)

B.C. 460–440 total 5
——————— Anaxagoras 5

440–420 total 19
——————— Anaxagoras 5, Empedocles 6, Protagoras 8

420–400 total 48
——————— Socrates 9, Democritos 8, Thucydides 8, Empedocles 6, Protagoras 8, Prodicos 5, Hippias 4

400–380 total 42
——————— Socrates 9, Aeschines 3, Democritos 8, Antisthenes 5, Prodicos 5, Hippias 4, Thucydides 8

380–360 total 23
——————— Aeschines 3, Xenophon 7, Democritos 8, Antisthenes 5

360–340 total 19
——————— Aeschines 3, Xenophon 7, Diogenes (Sinope) 5, Demosthenos 4

340–320 total 10
——————— Diogenes (Sinope) 5, Anaxarchos 1, Demosthenos 4

320–300 total 14
——————— Monimos 1, Onesicritos 2, Philiscos 1, Crates (Theb.) 4, Anniceris 2, Anaxarchos 1, Euhemeros 3

300–280 total 14
——————— Monimos 1, Onesicritos 2, Philiscos 1, Crates (Theb.) 4, Metrocles 1, Anniceris 2, Euhemeros 3

280–260 total 3
——————— Metrocles 1, Anniceris 2

260–240 total 2
——————— Hieronymos 2

240–220 total 4
——————— Hieronymos 2, Menedemos 2

220–200 total 2
——————— Menedemos 2

200–180 total 1

180–160 total 5
——————— Carneades 5

160–140 total 7
——————— Carneades 5, Cleitomachos 2

140–120 total 7
——————— Carneades 5, Cleitomachos 2

120–100 total 2
——————— Cleitomachos 2

100–80 total 5
——————— Philon (Larissa) 3, Meleagros (Gadara) 2

80–60 total 5
——————— Philon (Larissa) 3, Meleagros 2

60–40 total 1

40–20 total 8
——————— Horatius 6, Qu. Sextius 2

20–0 total 15
——————— Horatius 6, Ovidius 6, Qu. Sextius 2, Sextius (son) 1

A.D. 0–20 total 9
——————— Sextius (son) 1, Sotion 2, Ovidius 6

20–40 total 2
——————— Sotion 2

40–60 total 1
——————— Demetrios 1

60–80 total 1
——————— Demetrios 1

80–100 total 7
——————— Demetrios 1, Dion Chrysostomos 6

100–120 total 6
——————— Dion Chrysostomos 6

120–140 total 5
——————— Oinomaos 3, Demonax 2

140–160 total 5
——————— Oinomaos 3, Demonax 2

160–180 total 2
——————— Demonax 2

180–200 total 8
——————— Alexandros (Aphrodis.) 6, Demonax 2

200–220 total 6
——————— Alexandros (Aphrodis.) 6

220–240 total 6
——————— Alexandros (Aphrodis.) 6

240–1300 total 0

1300–1320 total 3
——————— Ioannes de Ianduno 3

1320–1340 total 11
——————— Ioannes de Ianduno 3, Marsilius (Padua) 4, Nicolaus (Autrecourt) 4

1340–1360 total 8
——————— Marsilius (Padua) 4, Nicolaus (Autrecourt) 4

1360–1400 total 0

1400–1420 total 0

1420–1440   total 0

1440–1460   total 2
——————— Laurentius Valla 2

1460–1500   total 0

1500–1520   total 1

1520–1540   total 6
——————— Machiavelli 6 (Discorsi)

1540–1560   total 0

1560–1580   total 1
——————— H. Donellus 1

1580–1600   total 1

1600–1620   total 1

1620–1640   total 1

1640–1660   total 2
——————— U. Horn 1, European Christian culture 1

1660–1680   total 8
——————— Locke 8

1680–1700   total 16
——————— Locke 8, D. Nort 2, P. Bayle 6

1700–1720   total 16
——————— Locke 8, Bayle 6, Clarke 2

1720–1740   total 19
——————— Hutcheson 4, Montesquieu 6, Voltaire 7, Forbonnais 2

1740–1760   total 47
——————— Hutcheson 4, A. Smith 6, Hume 8, Voltaire 7, Montesquieu 6, Helvetius 6, V. Gournay 2, Robertson 4, Burke 4

1760–1780   total 91
——————— Raynal 1, James Stewart 2, Ferguson 4, A. Smith 6, Weisshaupt 2, Holbach 6, Turgot 6, Thomas Payne 4, Galiani 2, Burke 4, Hume 8, Helvetius 6, Quesnay 6, Ethan Allen 4, Franklin 5, Voltaire 7, Robertson 4, Pothier 4, Condorcet 6, Mercier de la Rivière 4

1780–1800   total 47
——————— Ferguson 4, Gibbon 6, Bentham 6, Filangieri 4, Blakestone 5, B. Constant 6, Galiani 2, Weisshaupt 2, Pothier 4, Robertson 5, Mme de Staël 3

1800–1820   total 39
——————— Destutt de Tracy 4, Bentham 6, B. Constant 6, Charles Comte 3, Sismondi 4, Malthus 6, Ricardo 5, J. Adams 3, G. Romagniosi 2

1820–1840   total 70
——————— Destutt de Tracy 4, A. Comte 8, James Mill 6, J. Stuart Mill 8, Bentham 6, B. Constant 6, Michelet 4, Sismondi 4, Charles Comte 3, Ricardo 5, J. B. Say 3, Austin 4, Thières 4, Amédée Thierry 2, Augustin Thierry 3

1840–1860   total 64
——————— J. St. Mill 8, H. Spencer 8, Laboulaye 2, Buckle 5, Toqueville 2, Bastiat 4, Cairnes 2,

Austin 4, A. Comte 8, Augustin Thierry 3, Amédée Thierry 2, Thières 4, Michelet 4, Cobden 3, Grote 3, Royet-Collart 2

1860–1880   total 80
——————— J. St. Mill 8, Darwin 8 (*The Origin of Species*), Buckle 5, Laboulaye 2, Taine 7, Wyroubov 4, Littré 6, Bancroft 3, Bachofen 4, Ihering 5, Cobden 2, Austin 4, H. Spencer 8, Gobineau 4, Espinas 5, Baehr 5, K. Gerber 2

1880–1900   total 139
——————— Baldwin 4, Freud 4, Tarde 5, Le Bon 4, Lapouge 4, Gobineau 4, M. Kovalevsky 5, Lombroso 4, Simmel 5, Westermarck 4, Novikov 3, Lacombe 3, Mikhailovski 4, Ward 4, Kidd 2, Hauriou 4, Mougeolle 2, Letourneau 2, Ratzel 4, Ammon 4, Galton 6, Giddings 4, Schmoller 5, Avenarius 5, Korkunov 4, Maine 5, K. Menger 3, Edgeworth 3, Leroy-Beaulieu 4, Fouillée 5, Duguit 5, Lavrov 4, Maitland 5, G. de Greef 2, L. Brentano 4

1900–1920   total 111 [1]
——————— Xénopol, Tarde, Pavlov-Sylvansky, Pareto, Lapouge, Van-Genepp, Mendeleev, Lombroso, Le Bon, Kovalevsky, Simmel, MacDougal, Ellwood, Pearson, Ross, Baldwin, Niceforo, Ostwald, Petražicky, Frazer, Bortkievitch, Leroy-Beaulieu, Laband, W. Sumner, Hobhouse, Bouglé, Thomas, Freud, Jung, Palante

---

UNIVERSALISM–SINGULARISM
(540 B.C.–A.D. 1920)

B.C. 540–520   total 8
——————— Pythagoras 8

520–500   total 15
——————— Pythagoras 8, Herakleitos 7

500–480   total 15
——————— Pythagoras 8, Herakleitos 7

480–460   total 7
——————— Herakleitos 7

460–440   total 6
——————— Herodotus 6

440–420   total 11
——————— Philolaos 5, Herodotus 6

420–400   total 9
——————— Philolaos 5, Antiphon 4

400–380   total 10
——————— Philolaos 5, Archytas 1, Antiphon 4

380–360   total 5
——————— Archytas 1, Isocrates 4

360–340   total 10
——————— Speusippos 3, Xenocrates 3, Isocrates 4

[1] For obvious reasons values are not given for living authors.

340–320   total 22
————— Speusippos 3, Xenocrates 3, Aristoteles 12, Isocrates 4

320–300   total 32
————— Xenocrates 3, Polemon 2, Aristoteles 12, Theophrastos 7, Eudemos 2, Dikaiarchos (Messene) 3, Demetrios Phaler. 3

300–280   total 30
————— Polemon 2, Crantor 4, Crates 1, Theophrastos 7, Eudemos 2, Dikaiarchos 3, Zenon (Kition) 8, Demetrios Phal. 3

280–260   total 28
————— Ariston (Chios) 5, Polemon 2, Crantor 4, Crates 1, Zenon (Kition) 8, Cleanthes 5, Demetrios Ph. 3

260–240   total 10
————— Ariston (Chios) 5, Cleanthes 5

240–220   total 18
————— Ariston (Chios) 5, Cleanthes 5, Chrysippos 7, Sphairos 1

220–200   total 11
————— Chrysippos 7, Sphairos 1, Ariston (Keos) 3

200–180   total 9
————— Ariston (Keos) 3, Sphairos 1, Zenon (Tarsos) 1, Diogenes (Seleukeia) 4

180–160   total 8
————— Kritolaos (Phasel.) 2, Diogenes (Seleukeia) 4, Antipatros (Tarsos) 2

160–140   total 12
————— Kritolaos (Phasel.) 2, Diogenes (Seleukeia) 4, Antipatros 2, Polybios 4

140–120   total 12
————— Boethos (Sidon) 2, Polybios 4, Panaitios 5, Q. Muc. Scaevola 1

120–100   total 14
————— Boethos (Sidon) 2, Polybios 4, Panaitios 5, Qu. Muc. Scaevola 1, Hecaton (Rhodos) 1, Mnesarchos 1

100–80   total 10
————— Hecaton (Rhodos) 1, Mnesarchos 1, Apollodoros (Ath.) 1, Poseidonios 7

80–60   total 21
————— Antiochos 4, T. Varro 5, Apollodoros 1, Poseidonios 7, Asclepiodotos 2, Geminos 2

60–40   total 37
————— T. Varro 5, Nigidius Figulus 4, Poseidonios 7, Asclepiodotos 2, Geminos 2, Phainios 1, Dionysios 1, Antipatros 2, Iason 2, Athenodoros (Kord.) 1, Apollonides 1, Diodotos 1, Cato Utic. 2, Caesar 6

40–20   total 28
————— T. Varro 5, Vergilius 8, Athenodoros (Kord.) 1, Apollonides 1, Diodotos 1, Apollonios (Tyros) 1, Athenodoros 3, Areios Didymos 2, Caesar 6

20–0   total 19
————— Eudoros (Alexandreia) 2, Vergilius 8, Athenodoros 3, Areios Didymos 2, T. Livius 4

A.D. 0–20   total 17
————— Philo Iudaeus 8, Areios Didymos 2, Herakleitos 3, T. Livius 4

20–40   total 14
————— Philo Iudaeus 8, Herakleitos 3, Strabon 2, Attalos 1

40–60   total 17
————— Philo Iudaeus 8, Alexandros (Aigai) 2, Strabon 2, Attalos 1, Annaeus Cornutus 4

60–80   total 16
————— Moderatos 3, Alexandros (Aigai) 2, Chairemon 2, L. Annaeus Cornutus 4, Musonius Rufus 5

80–100   total 8
————— Moderatos 3, Musonius Rufus 5

100–120   total 10
————— Περὶ Κόσμον 4, Adrastos 2, Tacitus 4

120–140   total 21
————— Theon 2, Nicomachos 1, Gaios 2, Adrastos 2, Hierocles 2, Tacitus 4, Marcion 4, Valentinus 4

140–160   total 27
————— Hierocles 2, Theon 2, Nicomachos 1, Gaios 2, Herodes Atticos 2, Albinos 3, Calvisios Tauros 2, Adrastos 2, M. Aristides 3, Marcion 4, Valentinus 4

160–180   total 31
————— Herodes Atticos 2, Albinos 3, Calvisios T. 2, Apuleius 6, Numenios 4, Cronios 2, Aristocles 1, Tatianus 3, Marcion 4, Valentinus 4

180–200   total 49
————— Apuleius 6, Numenios 4, Cronios 2, Atticos 2, Celsus 4, Maximos (Tyros) 5, Hierax 1, Severus 1, Aristocles 1, Gaius 3, Athenagoras 4, Irenaeus Lugd. 4, Tatianus 3, Ptolemaeus 1, Heracleon 2, Clemens Alex. 6

200–220   total 32
————— Numenios 4, Hierax 1, Severus 1, Hermetic literature 5, Paulus 3, Papinian 3, Irenaeus Lugd. 4, Hippolytus 3, Heracleon 2, Clemens Alex. 6

220–240   total 11
————— Hermetic literat. 5, Ulpian 3, Hippolytus 3

240–260   total 13
————— Hermetic literature 5, Diogenes Laërtius 3, Tryphonianus 3, Dionysius Magnus 2

260–280   total 9
————— Diogenes Laërtius 3, Amelios 2, Florentinus 2, Dionysius Magnus 2

280–300   total 6
————— Amelios 2, Marcianus 3, Christian culture 1

300–320   total 4
————————— Alexandros (Lyk.) 2, Methodius
(Phil.) 2

320–340   total 11
————————— Theodoros (Asine) 1, Alexandros
(Lycop.) 2, Chalcidius 4, Athanasius Magnus 4

340–360   total 9
————————— Theodoros (Asine) 1, Chalcidius 4,
Athanasius Magnus 4

360–380   total 13
————————— Eunapios 3, Athanasius Magnus 4,
Hilarius (Poitiers) 3, Marius Victorinus 3

380–400   total 6
————————— Eunapios 3, Apollinarius (Laod.) 3

400–420   total 10
————————— Syrianos 1, Cyrillus Alex. 3, Pelagius
3, Cassianus 3

420–440   total 12
————————— Syrianus 1, Hierocles (Alex.) 2, Pelagius 3, Cyrillus Alex. 3, Cassianus 3

440–460   total 5
————————— Hierocles 2, Cyrillus Alex. 3

460–480   total 6
————————— Hermeias (Alex.) 3, Claudianus
Mamertus 3

480–500   total 4
————————— Marinos 3, Christian culture 1

500–520   total 17
————————— Isidoros 1, Simplicios 5, Procopius
Garensis 3, Dionysius Areopag. 8

520–540   total 21
————————— Simplicios 5, Priscianos 1, Procopius
Garensis 3, Ioannes Philoponus 4, Dionysius
Areopag, 8

540–560   total 14
————————— Ioannes Philoponus 4, Procopios
Caesariansis 4, Simplicios 5, Priscianos 1

560–580   total 5
————————— Procopios Caesariansis 4, Priscianos 1

580–600   total 6
————————— Gregorius I (Magnus) 4, Enagrios 2

600–620   total 8
————————— Isidorus Hispalensis 4, Gregorius I
(Magnus) 4

620–640   total 4
————————— Isidorus Hispalensis 4

640–660   total 1
————————— Christian culture 1

660–680   total 2
————————— Agatho (Pope) 2

680–700   total 2
————————— Agatho (Pope) 2

700–720   total 3
————————— Beda Venerabilis 3

720–740   total 3
————————— Beda Venerabilis 3

740–760   total 1
————————— Egbertus 1

760–780   total 1
————————— Egbertus 1

780–800   total 4
————————— Alcuinus 4

800–820   total 5
————————— Alcuinus 4, Smaragdus (abb. Castellion) 1

820–840   total 6
————————— Hrabanus Maurus 4, Smaragdus
(abb. Castellion) 1, Ionas (Orlean.) 1

840–860   total 6
————————— Hrabanus Maurus 4, Ionas (Orlean.)
1, Sedulius Scotus 1

860–880   total 4
————————— Photius 3, Sedulius Scotus 1

880–900   total 3
————————— Photius 3

900–920   total 2
————————— Arethas 2

920–940   total 2
————————— Arethas 2

940–960   total 2
————————— Konstantinus VII Porphyrogen-
netos 2

960–980   total 2
————————— Konstantinus VII Porphyr. 2

980–1000   total 3
————————— Sylvester II (Gerbert) 3

1000–1020   total 5
————————— Sylvester II (Gerbert) 3, Fulbert 2

1020–1040   total 2
————————— Fulbert 2

1040–1060   total 3
————————— Lanfrancus 3

1060–1080   total 6
————————— Lanfrancus 3, Michael Psellos 3

1080–1100   total 8
————————— Lanfrancus 3, Michael Psellos 3,
Eustretios (Nicca) 2

1100–1120   total 4
————————— Eustratios 2, Hugo (Fleury) 2

1120–1140   total 12
————————— Eustratios 2, Petrus Abaelardus 4,
Guilelmus de Conches 2, Hugo (Fleury) 2, Nice-
phoros Bryennios 2

1140–1160   total 12
————————— Petrus Abaelardus 4, Guilelmus de
Conches 2, Otto Freising (historian) 2, Arnold
(Breseia) 2, Anna Comnena 2

1160–1180   total 3
——————— Bulgarus 2, Stephan (Tournai) 2

1180–1200   total 3
——————— Radulfus Ardens 1, Stephan (Tournai) 2

1200–1220   total 5
——————— Stephan (Tournai) 2, Radulfus Ardens 1, Azo Porcius 2

1220–1240   total 4
——————— Azo Porcius 2, Accursius 2

1240–1260   total 4
——————— Accursius 2, Ioannes (Parma) 2

1260–1280   total 8
——————— Roger Bacon 6, Ioannes (Parma) 2

1280–1300   total 11
——————— Roger Bacon 6, Walter of Brugges 2, Petrus Ioannis Olivi 3

1300–1320   total 19
——————— Walter of Brugges 2, Jean Quidort (Ioannes Parisiensis) 2, Duns Scotus 8, Pierre Dubois 3, Ptolomacus (Lucca) 2, Engebrecht von Volkersdorf 2

1320–1340   total 18
——————— Ioannes Baconthorp. 2, William Ockham 8, Ubertinus de Casali 1, Pierre Dubois 3, Ptolomacus (Lucca) 2, Alvarius Pelagius 2

1340–1360   total 22
——————— William Ockham 8, Gregorius (Rimini) 2, I. Buridan 2, I. Wicklif 3, Ioannes Baconthorp. 2, Ubertinus de Casali 1, Lupold (Babenberg) 1, Petrarca 3

1360–1380   total 16
——————— I. Buridan 2, I. Wicklif 3, Nicolaus (Oresme) 2, Albert de Saxonia 2, Ioannes VI Cantacusenos 2, Petrarca 3, Baldus de Ubaldis 2

1380–1400   total 15
——————— I. Wicklif 3, Petrus d'Ailly 4, Nicolaus (Oresme) 2, Albert de Saxonia 2, Ioannes VI Cantacusenos 2, Fr. de Zabarellis 2

1400–1420   total 11
——————— Jean Charlier (Gerson) 4, Petrus d'Ailly 4, Heinrich (Hessen) 2, Matthaeus de Cracovia 1

1420–1440   total 12
——————— Jean Charlier (Gerson) 4, Petrus d'Ailly 4, Heinrich (Hessen) 2, N. Panormitanus 2

1440–1460   total 10
——————— Sir John Fortescue (Jurist) 1, Gregorius (Heimburg) 2, Dionysius Cartusianus 4, Petrus Chelčicky 3

1460–1480   total 15
——————— Sir John Fortescue 1, Gregorius (Heimburg) 2, Philippe Pot 1, Dionysius Cartusianus 4, Gabriel Biel 3, Petrus Chelčicky 3, Antonius de Rosellis 1

1480–1500   total 12
——————— Gabriel Biel 3, Petrus Tartaretus 1, Leonardo da Vinci 2, Comines (historian) 3, Philippe Pot 1, Franciscus Patricius Senensis 2

1500–1520   total 10
——————— Nilus Sorsky 4, Helčicky 4, Padilla 2 (*Letters to His Wife*)

1520–1540   total 10
——————— Calvin 6, Zwingli 4

1540–1560   total 14
——————— Calvin 6, Zwingli 4, Paynet 4

1560–1580   total 25
——————— A. Kurbsky 2, Calvin 6, Hotman 4, Languet 3, C. Seissel 1, Buchanan 4, Knox 4, Goodinan 1

1580–1600   total 22
——————— Buchanan 4, Althusius 4, Poinet Bishop of Winchester 4, Bruno 8, J. Faber 2

1600–1620   total 18
——————— Althusius 4, G. Grotius 6, Barklay 4, Bohemian Brothers 4

1620–1640   total 17
——————— Comenius 7 (*Labyrinth of Light*, 1623), H. Grotius 6, Barklay 4

1640–1660   total 35
——————— Milton 7, Harrington 4 (*Oceana*, 1656), John Hill 3, Comenius 7, Pascal 7 (1654), Selden 2, M. Needham 1, W. Petty 2, J. Cook 2

1660–1680   total 13
——————— Comenius 7, Cumberland 4, Klim 2

1680–1700   total 14
——————— Cumberland 4, Spinoza 8, Sidney 2

1700–1720   total 17
——————— Cumberland 4, Wachter 4, Thomasius 4, Shaftesbury 5

1720–1740   total 8
——————— Cumberland 4, Thomasius 4

1740–1760   total 12
——————— Rousseau 8 (*Contrat social*, 1762), Süssmilch 4

1760–1780   total 24
——————— Rousseau 8, Beccaria 6, Verri 2, Sonnenfeld 2, Süssmilch 4, D. Nettelbladt 2

1780–1800   total 38
——————— Sieyès 4, Jefferson 4, Herder 6, Kant 12, Schiller 8, Sonnenfeld 2, J. Müller 2

1800–1820   total 46
——————— Kant 12, Fichte 8, Fries 6, S. Simon 6, Fourier 5, Rotter 2, Wölcker 2, W. von Humboldt 5

1820–1840   total 43
——————— Lieber 4, Lammenais 4, Fries 6, S. Simon 6, Bazard 3 (Carbonaric Movement), Enfantin 3, Considérant 4, Fourier 5, Rotter 2, Wölcker 2, Macaulay 4

1840–1860   total 55
———————— A. Comte 8, Lassale 5, L. Blanc 4,
Rodbertus 4, Renouvier 7, Enfantin 3, Macaulay
4, George Sand 3 (socialistic novels before 1848),
Considérant 4, Quetelet 5, Wölcker 2, Emerson 6

1860–1880   total 103
———————— Cohen 6, Lassale 5, F. Lange 7,
Secretan 2, L. Blanc 4, Lorant 4, Renouvier 7,
Lavrov 4, Lafitte 5, Quetelet 5, Oettingen 2,
Karejev 2, Le Play 7, Fabian Society (Gobson,
etc.) 2, Beseler 2, Emerson 6, Gierke 6, Toynbee 1,
Fouillée 5, Lazarus 4, Steinthal 4, Fustel de
Coulanges 4, Macaulay 4, Renan 6

1880–1900   total 89
———————— Renouvier 7, Schäffle 3, Gumplo-
witcz 4, Masaryk 5, Lilienfeld 4, Tönnies 4, De
Roberty 4, Durkheim 5, Sombart 5, Stammler 5,
Cohen 7, Natorp 5, Gierke 6, Worms 3, Espinas
4, Izoulet 3, M. Weber 5, F. de Coulanges 4,
Blondel 3, Morgan 3

1900–1920   total 134 [1]
———————— Gierke, Tönnies, Cooley, Lapa-Dani-
levsky, Lilienfeld, Masaryk, Cohen, A. Tschu-
prov, Kistiakovsky, Maeterlink, Münsterberg,
Joël, Max Weber, Rickert, Mackenzie, Bern-
stein, Spann, Vorländer, Staudinger, Woltmann,
Rostovtzeff, Novgorodzeff, Cassirer, Sombart, L.
Duguit, De Roberty, Durkheim, Draghicesco,
Izoulet, Richard, Litt, Wiese, Worms

UNIVERSALISM (560 B.C.–1920 A.D.)

B.C. 560–540   total 5
———————— Anaximandros 5

540–520   total 5
———————— Anaximandros 5

520–500   total 1

500–480   total 7
———————— Parmenides 7

480–460   total 12
———————— Parmenides 7, Zenon 5

460–440   total 8
———————— Zenon 5, Melissos 3

440–420   total 10
———————— Zenon 5, Melissos 3, Hippodamos 2

420–400   total 5
———————— Melissos 3, Hippodamos 2

400–380   total 2
———————— Hippodamos 2

380–360   total 12
———————— Platon 12

360–340   total 14
———————— Platon 12, Ephorus 2

[1] For obvious reasons, values are not given for living
authors.

340–320   total 2
———————— Ephorus 2

320–0   total 0

A.D. 0–100   total 0

100–120   total 1
———————— Saturnilus 1

120–140   total 5
———————— Saturnilus 1, Basileides 4

140–160   total 6
———————— Saturnilus 1, Carpocrates 1, **Basi-**
leides 4

160–180   total 1
———————— Carpocrates 1

180–200   total 1
———————— Epiphanes 1

200–220   total 6
———————— Tertullianus 6

220–240   total 6
———————— Tertullianus 6

240–260   total 8
———————— (Pistis Sophia) 4,
Mani 4

260–280   total 8
———————— (Pistis Sophia) 4,
Mani 4

280–300   total 4
———————— Mani 4

300–320   total 1
———————— Manicheists 1

320–340   total 1
———————— Manicheists 1

340–360   total 4
———————— I. Firmicus Maternus 3, Manicheists 1

360–380   total 4
———————— I. Firmicus Maternus 3, Manicheists 1

380–400   total 11
———————— Ambrosius Mediolanensis 5, Augustinus 6

400–420   total 11
———————— Augustinus 10, Manicheists 1

420–440   total 11
———————— Augustinus 10, Manicheists 1

440–460   total 1
———————— Manicheists 1

460–480   total 1
———————— Manicheists 1

480–500   total 1
———————— Manicheists 1

500–520   total 1
———————— Manicheists 1

520–540   total 1
———————— Manicheists 1

540–860 total 0

860–880 total 4
——————— Hincmarus Remensis 2, Georgios Hamartolos 2

880–900 total 2
——————— Hincmarus Remensis 2

900–1000 total 0

1000–1020 total 1
——————— Leon Diaconos 1

1020–1040 total 0

1040–1060 total 5
——————— Petrus Damiani 3, Otloh (St. Emmeram) 2

1060–1080 total 12
——————— Petrus Damiani 3, Otloh (St. Emmeram) 2, Anselmus Cant. 7

1080–1100 total 18
——————— Manegoldus 3, Gregorius VII (Hildebrand) 6, Ivo (Chartres) 2, Anselmus Cant. 7

1100–1120 total 14
——————— Manegoldus 3, Irnerius (jurist) 2, Ivo (Chartres) 2, Anselmus Cant. 7

1120–1140 total 7
——————— Hugo à S. Victore 5, Irnerius 2

1140–1160 total 13
——————— Hugo à S. Victore 5, Richardus à S. Victore 4, Petrus Lombardus 4

1160–1180 total 21
——————— Richardus à S. Victore 4, Petrus Lombardus 4, Ioannes Saresberiensis 5, Gratian (canonist) 3, Pancapabea (jurist) 1, Rolandus Band. (Alex. III) 2, Ioannes Zonaras (historian) 2

1180–1200 total 14
——————— Ioannes Saresberiensis 5, Gualterus à S. Victore 2, Rufinus (jurist) 1, Rolandus Band. (Alex. III) 2, Ioannes Kinnamos (historian) 2, Ioannes Zonaras 2

1200–1220 total 11
——————— Innocentius III 6, Guilelmus (Auxerre) 2, Amalrich de Bene 3

1220–1240 total 9
——————— Guilelmus (Auxerre) 2, Guilelmus Alvernus 3, Alexander Halensis 4

1240–1260 total 22
——————— Guilelmus Alvernus 3, Alexander Halensis 4, Gregorius IX 3, Albertus Magnus 8, Vincentius Bellovacensis 2, Thomas (Chantimpré) 2

1260–1280 total 35
——————— Albertus Magnus 8, Vincentius Bellovacensis 2, Thomas Chantimpré 2, Ioannes Bonaventura 8, Thomas Aquinas 12, Petrus de Tarentasia (Inn. V) 2, Martinus Polonus (jurist) 1

1280–1300 total 27
——————— Albertus Magnus 8, Raymundus Lullus 5, Ioannes Peckham 1, Aegidius (Lessines)

2, Remigio di Chiarodei Girol. 2, Aegidius Romanus 3, Georgios Pachymeres 2, Matthaeus ab Aquasparte 2, Augustinus Triumphus 2

1300–1320 total 31
——————— Raymundus Lullus 5, Aegidius (Lessines) 2, Remigio di Chiarodei Girol. 2, Aegidius Romanus 3, Georgios Pachymeres 2, Matthaeus ab Aquasparte 2, Augustinus Triumphus 2, Hervé Nédeléc 3, Jacobus Capocci 2, Dante 8

1320–1340 total 21
——————— Augustinus Triumphus 2, Hervé Nédeléc 3, Dante 8, Ioannes de Regine 1, Ioannes Picardi de Lucid. 2, Nicolaus Trivet 2, Guido Terreni 2, Alvarus Pelagius (jurist) 1

1340–1360 total 7
——————— Guido Terreni 2, Thomas (Strasbourg) 2, Nicephoros Gregoras 2, Bartolus a Saxoferrato (jurist) 1

1360–1380 total 4
——————— Heinrich (Hainbuch) 2, Nicephoros Gregoras 2

1380–1400 total 2
——————— Heinrich (Hainbuch) 2

1400–1420 total 2
——————— Followers of Albertus Magnus and Thomas Aquinas in University of Cologne

1420–1440 total 7
——————— Ioannes Capreolus 3, Heinrich (Gorkum) 1, Antonin 3

1440–1460 total 6
——————— Ioannes Capreolus 3, Antonin 3

1460–1480 total 4
——————— Petrus Nigri 1, Pius II (Aeneas Sylvius Piccolomini) 2, Ioannes a Turrecremata 1

1480–1500 total 3
——————— Petrus Nigri 1, Savonarola 2

1500–1520 total 12
——————— Luther 8, Fr. Guicciardini 4

1520–1540 total 25
——————— Luther 8, Machiavelli 6 (*Il Principe*), Melanchthon 5, Oldendorf 2, Guicciardini 4

1540–1560 total 21
——————— Luther 8, Melanchthon 5, Loyola 8

1560–1580 total 19
——————— Melanchthon 5, Hemming 2, J. Bodin 4, Laines 4, Guicciardini 4 (posthumous works)

1580–1600 total 36
——————— Bodin 6, Suarez 6, Bellarmin 4, Baco 7, Campanella 7, Boucher 1, Hemming 2, Risseus 1, Stafford 2

1600–1620 total 42
——————— Winkler 3, J. Bodin 6, Bellarmin 4, Baco 7, Campanella 7, Suarez 6, Mariana 3, Brooke 2, Th. Mun 2, Raleigh 2

1620–1640   total 20
———— Winkler 3, Baco 7, Mariana 3, Campanella 7

1640–1660   total 14
———— Th. Hobbes 8, Erhard Weigel 4, Hippolites a Lapide 2 (*Bohuslav Chemnitz*)

1660–1680   total 31
———— Pufendorf 4, Child 2, Leibnitz 9, Filmer 2, Maevius 1, E. Weigel 4, Kryžanič 1, Hobbes (*Politica*) 8

1680–1700   total 45
———— Leibnitz 9, Bossuet 6, Alberti 2, Fénelon 6, Pufendorf 4, Seckendorf 2, Filmer (1680 — Patriarchia) 2, H. Coccei 4, E. Weigel 4, Thomasius 4, Praschius 1, Marius 1

1700–1720   total 35
———— Leibnitz 9, Bossuet 6, Fénelon 6, Vico 6, S. Coccei 1, Kaestner (1705) 2, Theophanes Prokopovič 2, Posořkov 3

1720–1740   total 24
———— Wolf 7, Vico 6, Ramsay (*Voyages of Cyrus*) 2, Abbé de Terrasson (Sethoss) 4, Theophanes Prokopovič 2, Posoškov 3

1740–1760   total 23
———— Wolf 7, Vico 6, Frederic the Great (*Antimachiavel*, 1740) 4, Pombal 4, J. Moser 2

1760–1780   total 17
———— Achenwahl 2, Le Grand 4 (utopic novels in form of biography), Pothier 2, Pombal 4, Scherbatov 2, J. Moser 2, K. Moser 1

1780–1800   total 23
———— De Maistre 6, De Bonald 4 (1799), Pombal 4 (*Mémoires*), Scherbatov 2, Gentz 1, J. Moser 2, J. Putter 2, K. Moser 1, J. Moeser 1

1800–1820   total 71
———— Arcillon 1, Savigny 4, De Maistre 6, Hegel 8, Schopenhauer 8, De Bonald 4, Haller 1, Schelling 8, Nibler (1805) 1, Loden (1811) 1, Putter 2, R. Wangenheim 1, Wagner 1, Baader 5, J. Moeser 1, A. Müller 1, A. Schlegel 2, Hugo 1, Ballanche 1, Krause 4, Schleiermacher 4, Niebur 4, Gentz 1, J. Müller 1

1820–1840   total 83
———— Savigny 5, Puchta 4, Fr. List 4, Radovitz 1, Zacharie 2, Schopenhauer 8, Schelling 8, Hegel 8, Troxler (1820) 1, Baader 5, Krause 4, Herbart 7, Guizot 4, De Bonald 4, Hello 2, Gioberti 6, Gentz 1, Arcillon 1, Niebur 4, Speransky (project) 2, Dalhmann 2

1840–1860   total 107
———— Schopenhauer 8, Carlyle 5, Savigny 5, Hildebrand 2, Leo 2, Radowitz 1, Schelling 8, Schmidthenner 1, Gioberti 6, Baader 5, Ahrens 2, Fr. List 4, Tieberghen 1, Waitz 1, Herbart 7, Stahl 4, Mohl 2, Niebuhr 4, Gneist 2, Guizot 4, Hartenstein 3, Bluntschli 4, J. Erdmann 4, Ranke 4, L. v. Stein 6, Rückert 4, Rossi 4, Fr. Romer 2, Dahlmann 2

1860–1880   total 83
———— Michelet 4, Ahrens 2, F. Walter 2, Ranke 5, Erdmann 4, Hartmann 8, Gabineau 4, S. Soloviev 4, V. Soloviev 6, Čičerin 4, Dostoevsky 7, Schlosser 4, Roscher 2, Schmoller 4, Schäffle 4, Stöcker 2, A. Wagner 2, Bluntschli 4, Hildebrand 2, Th. Carlyle 5, Leontiev 2, Etwesch 2

1880–1900   total 42
———— E. v. Hartmann 8, J. Erdmann 4, N. Danilevsky 4, Čičerin 4, Ranke 5, Schmoller 4, Leontiev 2, Kliučevsky 4, Dostoevsky 7

1900–1920   total 50 [1]
———— E. Hartmann, Čičerin, Spectorsky, Sellière, Liautey, Lalande, J. Chamberlain, Kjellen, Wundt, Schmoller, E. Richter, Kathrein, Kliučevsky, Imperialistic Racists, Spengler

---

MYSTICAL UNITY OF SINGULARISTIC PERSONS (60 B.C.–A.D. 1920)

B.C. 60–40   total 8
———— M. Tullius Cicero 8

40–20   total 8
———— M. Tullius Cicero 8

20–0   total 0

A.D. 0–20   total 0

20–40   total 0

40–60   total 8
———— Seneca 8

60–80   total 8
———— Seneca 8

80–100   total 14
———— Plutarchos 8, Epictetos 6

100–120   total 14
———— Plutarchos 8, Epictetos 6

120–140   total 16
———— Plutarchos 8, Epictetos 6, Arrianos 2

140–160   total 2
———— Arrianos 2

160–180   total 15
———— Marcus Aurelius 6, Justinus Martyr 5, Minucius Felix 4

180–200   total 10
———— Marcus Aurelius 6, Minucius Felix 4

200–220   total 5
———— Philostrates 5

220–240   total 13
———— Philostrates 5, Origenes 8

240–260   total 22
———— Plotinos 12, Origenes 8, Gregorius Thaumat. 2

[1] For obvious reasons values are not given for living authors.

260–280 total 14
————— Plotinos 12, Gregorius Thaumat. 2

280–300 total 8
————— Porphyrios 7, Pamphilus (Caesaria) 1

300–320 total 18
————— Porphyrios 7, Iamblichos 7, Pamphilus (Caesaria) 1, Eusebius (Caesaria) 3

320–340 total 16
————— Iamblichos 7, Sopatros 2, Eusebius (Caes.) 3, Lactantius 4

340–360 total 5
————— Sopatros 2, Eusebius (Caes.) 3

360–380 total 30
————— Iulian 7, Themistios 5, Basilius Magnus 6, Gregorius Naz. 6, Gregorius Nyssenus 6

380–400 total 28
————— Themistios 5, Basilius Magnus 6, Gregorius Naz. 6, Gregorius Nyss. 6, Ioannes Chrys. 5

400–420 total 11
————— Macrobius 4, Ioannes Chrysostomos 5, Synesius 2

420–440 total 7
————— Macrobius 4, Theodoretus Cyrensis 3

440–460 total 11
————— Proclos 8, Theodoretus Cyrensis 3

460–480 total 11
————— Proclos 8, Theodoretus Cyrensis 3

480–500 total 10
————— Proclos 8, Aeneas Gazensis 2

500–520 total 6
————— Damascios 4, Aeneas Gazensis 2

520–540 total 12
————— Damascios 4, Aeneas Gazensis 2, Boethius 6

540–560 total 7
————— Damascios 4, Cassiodorus 3

560–580 total 5
————— Cassiodorus 3, Martinus Bracarensis 2

580–600 total 2
————— Martinus Bracarensis 2

600–620 total 0

620–640 total 6
————— Maximus Confessor 6

640–660 total 6
————— Maximus Confessor 6

660–680 total 6
————— Maximus Confessor 6

680–700 total 0

700–720 total 0

720–740 total 5
————— Ioannes Damascenus 5

740–760 total 5
————— Ioannes Damascenus 5

760–840 total 0

840–860 total 8
————— John Scotus Erigena 8

860–880 total 8
————— John Scotus Erigena 8

880–1060 total 0

1060–1080 total 4
————— Simeon Theologus Novus 4

1080–1100 total 4
————— Simeon Theologus Novus 4

1100–1120 total 0

1120–1140 total 5
————— Bernardus Claraevalensis 5

1140–1160 total 5
————— Bernardus Claraevalensis 5

1160–1180 total 0

1180–1200 total 3
————— Ioachim de Floris 3

1200–1220 total 3
————— Ioachim de Floris 3

1220–1240 total 6
————— Franciscus (Assisi) 6

1240–1300 total 0

1300–1320 total 8
————— M. Eckehart 8

1320–1340 total 8
————— M. Eckehart 8

1340–1360 total 19
————— I. Tauler 4, H. Suso 5, Gregorios Palamas 6, Nicolaos Cabasilas 4

1360–1380 total 19
————— I. Tauler 4, H. Suso 5, Gregorios Palamas 6, Nicolaos Cabasilas 4

1380–1400 total 4
————— Nicolaos Cabasilas 4

1400–1420 total 3
————— Ioannes Hus 3

1420–1440 total 0

1440–1460 total 8
————— Nicolaus Cusanus 8

1460–1480 total 8
————— Nicolaus Cusanus 8

1480–1500 total 4
————— Nilus Sorsky 4

1500–1520 total 10
————— Nilus Sorsky 4, Thomas Morus 6

1520–1540	total 4	
———— Zwingli 4		
1540–1560	total 0	
1560–1580	total 0	
1580–1600	total 8	
———— Bruno 8		
1600–1620	total 0	
1620–1640	total 7	
———— Jan Amos Komensky 7		
1640–1660	total 13	
———— Jan Amos Komensky 7, Milton 6		
1660–1680	total 7	
———— Jan Amos Komensky 7		
1680–1700	total 0	
1700–1720	total 5	
———— Shaftesbury 5		
1720–1740	total 0	

1740–1760	total 8	
———— Rousseau 8		
1760–1780	total 20	
———— Rousseau 8, Kant 12		
1780–1800	total 20	
———— Kant 12, Schiller 8		
1800–1820	total 12	
———— Kant 12		
1820–1840	total 5	
———— Fourière 5		
1840–1860	total 5	
———— Emerson 5		
1860–1880	total 12	
———— Dostoevsky 7, Emerson 5		
1880–1900	total 7	
———— Dostoevsky 7		
1900–1920	total 0	

Appendix to Chapter Nine [1]

LIST OF THINKERS FOR EACH PERIOD, WITH THE VALUE GIVEN TO EACH ON A SCALE 1 TO 12

Graeco-Roman and European-Christian Cultures

DETERMINISM [2] (540 B.C.– A.D. 1920)

B.C. 540–520   total 8
———— Pythagoras 8

520–500   total 15
———— Herakleitos 7, Pythagoras 8

500–480   total 15
———— Herakleitos 7, Pythagoras 8

480–460   total 7
———— Herakleitos 7

460–440   total 1
———— Pythagoras's school 1

440–420   total 9
———— Leukippos 2, Kratylos 2, Philolaos 5

420–400   total 29
———— Leukippos 2, Demokritos 8, Kratylos 5, Sokrates 9, Philolaos 5, Simmias 1, Kebes 1, Lysis 1

400–380   total 41
———— Demokritus 8, Nessas 1, Kratylos 2, Antisthenes 5, Eukleides 3, Sokrates 9, Aeschines 3, Philolaos 5, Simmias 1, Kebes 1, Lysis 1, Eurytos 1, Archytas 1

380–360   total 42
———— Demokritos 8, Nessas 1, Antisthenes 5, Euklides 3, Eubulides 1, Aeschines 3, Xenophon 7, Platon 12, Eurytos 1, Archytas 1

360–340   total 47
———— Nessas 1, Diogenes 1, Diogenes (Kin.) 5, Eubulides 1, Aeschines 3, Xenophon 7, Platon 12, Speusippos 3, Xenokrates 3, Eudoxos 3, Herakleides 3, Xenophilos 1, Phanton 1, Echekrates 1, Diokles 1, Polymnastos 1

340–320   total 30
———— Diogenes 1, Diogenes (Kin.) 5, Eubulides 1, Diodoros 2, Stilpon 2, Speusippos 3, Xenokrates 3, Eudoxos 3, Herakleides 3, Philippos 2, Xenophilos 1, Phanton 1, Echekrates 1, Diokles 1, Polymnastos 1

320–300   total 34
———— Bion 1, Hekataios 1, Nausiphanas 2, Monimos 1, Onesikritos 2, Philiskos 1, Krates 4, Diodoros 2, Stilpon 2, Alexinos 1, Menedemos 2, Xenokrates 3, Herakleides 3, Philippos 2, Pole- mon 2, Xenophilos 1, Phanton 1, Echekrates 1, Diokles 1, Polymnastos 1

300–280   total 37
———— Bion 1, Hekataios 1, Nausiphanos 2, Monimos 1, Onesikritos 2, Philiskos 1, Krates 4, Metrokles 1, Zenon 8, Stilpon 2, Alexinos 1, Menedemos 2, Asclepiades 2, Straton 2, Polemon 2, Krantor 4, Krates 1

280–260   total 37
———— Metrokles 1, Zenon 8, Bion 3, Ariston 5, Herillos 1, Dionysios 1, Kleanthes 5, Menedemos 2, Asclepiades 2, Straton 2, Polemon 2, Krantor 4, Krates 1

260–240   total 22
———— Bion 3, Ariston 5, Herillos 1, Persaios 2, Dionysios 1, Kleanthes 5, Menippos 5

240–220   total 40
———— Bion 3, Ariston 5, Herillos 1, Persaios 2, Dionysios 1, Kleanthes 5, Chrysippos 7, Sphairos 1, Menippos 5, Teles 3, Menedemos 2, Kerkidas 5

220–200   total 20
———— Chrysippos 7, Sphairos 1, Menippos 5, Menedemos 2, Kerkidas 5

200–180   total 6
———— Sphairos 1, Zenon 1, Diogenes 4

180–160   total 6
———— Diogenes 4, Antipatros 2

160–140   total 6
———— Diogenes 4, Antipatros 2

140–120   total 8
———— Panaitios 5, Q. M. Scaevola 1, Boethos 2

120–100   total 10
———— Panaitios 5, Q. M. Scaevola 1, Hekaton 1, Mnesarchos 1, Boethos 2

100–80   total 12
———— Hekaton 1, Mnesarchos 1, Meleagros 2, Apollodoros 1, Poseidonios 7

80–60   total 23
———— Meleagros 2, Apollodoros 1, Poseidonios 7, Asclepiodotos 2, Geminos 2, Antiochos 4, T. Varro 5

[1] See footnote, p. 635.   [2] From 540 to 340 B.C. the theories are mixed.

60–40   total 40
————— Poseidonios 7, Asclepiodotos 2, Geminos 2, Phainias 1, Dionysios 1, Antipatros 2, Jason 2, Athenodoros 1, Apollonides 1, Diodotos 1, Cato 2, T. Varro 5, Cicero 8, Aristos 1, Nigid. Figulus 4

40–20   total 24
————— Athenodoros 1, Apollonides 1, Diodotos 1, Apollonios 1, Athenodoros 3, Areios Didymos 2, Q. Sextius 2, Cicero 8, T. Varro 5

20–0   total 10
————— Athenodoros 3, Areios Didymos 2, Q. Sextius 2, Sextius Jr. 1, Eudoros 2

A.D. 0–20   total 12
————— Areios Didymos 2, Herakleitos 3, Sextius Jr. 1, Sotion 2, Cornelius Celsus 1, L. Crassicius 1, Fab. Papirius 1, Potamon 1

20–40   total 15
————— Herakleitos 3, Strabon 2, Attalos 1, Sotion 2, Cornelius Celsus 1, L. Crassicius 1, Fab. Papirius 1, Potamon 1, Thrasyllos 3.

40–60   total 19
————— Strabon 2, Attaios 1, Seneca 8, L. Ann. Korn. 4, Demetrios 1, Thrasyllos 3

60–80   total 27
————— Seneca 8, Chairemon 2, L. Ann. Korn. 4, Persius Fl. 3, Ann. Luc. 4, Musonius Ruf. 5, Demetrios 1

80–100   total 26
————— Musonius Ruf. 5, Demetrios 1, Epictetos 6, Dionysios Chrysostomos 6, Plutarchos 8

100–120   total 23
————— Epictetos 6, Dionysios Chrysostomos 6, Plutarchos 8, Cerinthus 2, Saturnilus 1

120–140   total 47
————— Epictetos 6, Arrianos 2, Hierakles 2, Kleomedes 2, Oinomaos 3, Demonax 2, Plutarchos 8, Theon 2, Gaios 2, Nikomachos 1, Cerinthus 2, Basilides 4, Saturnilus 1, Cerdon 2, Marcion 4, Valentinus 4

140–160   total 38
————— Arrianos 2, Hierokles 2, Kleomedes 2, Oinomaos 3, Demonax 2, Peregrinos Prot. 3, Theon 2, Nikomachos 1, Gaios 2, Nigrinos 1, Kalvisios Taur. 2, Karpokrates 1, Basilides 4, Saturnilus 1, Cerdon 2, Marcion 4, Valentinus 4

160–180   total 31
————— Demonax 2, Peregrinus Prot. 3, Marcus Aurelius 6, Kalvisios Taur. 2, Nigrinos 1, Nikostratos 2, Numenios 4, Kronias 2, Karpokrates 1, Marcion 4, Valentinus 4

180–200   total 34
————— Demonax 2, Marcus Aurelius 6, Numenios 4, Kronios 2, Attikos 2, Harpokration 1, Celsus 4, Hierax 1, Maximos 5, Severus 1, Apelles 2, Ptolemaeus 1, Herakleon 2, Marcus 1

200–220   total 9
————— Numenios 4, Hierax 1, Severus 1 Herakleon 2, Marcus 1

220–240   total 5
————— Scholastic Stoic school 1, Orphic books 4

240–260   total 15
————— Origenes (heathen) 2, Longinos 2, Diogenes L. 3, Orphic books 4, Mani 4

260–280   total 13
————— Longinos 2, Diogenes L. 3, Orphic books 4, Mani 4

280–300   total 4
————— Mani 4

300–320   total 1
————— Manicheists 1

320–340   total 1
————— Manicheists 1

340–360   total 2
————— Manicheists 2

360–380   total 2
————— Manicheists 2

380–400   total 3
————— Manicheists 3

400–420   total 3
————— Manicheists 3

420–440   total 3
————— Manicheists 3

440–460   total 1
————— Manicheists 1

460–480   total 1
————— Manicheists 1

480–500   total 1
————— Manicheists 1

500–520   total 1
————— Manicheists 1

520–540   total 1
————— Manicheists 1

540–1220   total 0

1220–1240   total 3
————— Guilelmus Alvernus 3

1240–1260   total 3
————— Guilelmus Alvernus 3

1260–1280   total 6
————— Siger of Brabant 4, Boethius de Dacia 2

1280–1300   total 9
————— Siger of Brabant 4, Boethius de Dacia 2, Gottfried (Fontaines) 3

1300–1320   total 6
————— Gottfried (Fontaines) 3, Thomas (Sutton) 2, Pietro d'Abano 1

1320–1340   total 8
————————— Thomas (Sutton) 2, Siegbert (Beck) 2, Thomas Bradwardine 2, Ioannes (Baconthorp) 2

1340–1360   total 13
————————— Thomas (Sutton) 2, Robert Holkot 1, Thomas Bradw. 2, Ioannes (Baconth.) 2, Urban 1, Wicklif 3, Ioannes Assir. 2

1360–1380   total 6
————————— Wicklif 3, Brinkel 1, Albert de Sax. 2

1380–1400   total 5
————————— Wicklif 3, Albert de Sax. 2

1400–1420   total 2
————————— Paulus (Venetia) 2

1420–1440   total 2
————————— Paulus (Venetia) 2

1440–1460   total 2
————————— Cajetanus Thiaeneus 2

1460–1480   total 2
————————— Cajetanus Thiaeneus 2

1480–1500   total 7
————————— Nicoletto Vernias 1, Leonardo da Vinci 6

1500–1520   total 8
————————— Leonardo da Vinci 8

1520–1540   total 19
————————— Luther 8, Zwingli 6, Melanchthon 5

1540–1560   total 38
————————— Luther 8, Zwingli 6, Melanchthon 5, Calvin 6, Serveto 4, Nostradamus 4, Dolet 2, Leo Hebraeus 3

1560–1580   total 22
————————— Calvin 4, Sturm 2, Freigius 1, Camerarius 4, Fabricius 2, Schegk 1, P. Ramus 4, Chytraeus 1, Pfaffrad 1, Supolvedo 2

1580–1600   total 24
————————— Sturm 2, Camerarius 2, Schegk 1, Pfaffrad 1, Freigius 1, Ramus and his followers 4, Fabricius 2, G. Bruno 8, Scherbius 1, Hannequin 2

1600–1620   total 27
————————— Baco 7, Vanini 4, Keppler 8, Galilei 8

1620–1640   total 30
————————— Keppler 8, Galilei 8, Jansenius 6, Lemaitre 1, Baco 7

1640–1660   total 42
————————— Hobbes 8, Galileo 8, Keppler 8, Jansenius 6, Berigard 2, Brown 3, Pascal 7

1660–1680   total 38
————————— Brown 3, Pascal 7, Hobbes 8, Geulynx 6, Spinoza 8, Basso 2, Lemaitre 1, Morin 3 (Astrologia Gallica, 1661)

1680–1700   total 36
————————— Hobbes 8, Brown 3, Bekker 4, Spinoza 8 (1677), Toland 4, Boerhaave 3, Cuffeler 2, Rieuwertz 2, De Vries 1, Pordage 1

1700–1720   total 31
————————— Malebranche 7, Guyon 2, Toland 4, Mandeville 4, Boerhaave 3, Wollaston 2, Astrologers 2, Tschirnhausen 2, Leeuwenhoek 5

1720–1740   total 27
————————— Mandeville 4, D'Alembert 5, Bolingbroke 2, Voltaire 7, Boerhaave 2, Boulainvillier 1, Jean Meslier 3, Wollaston 2

1740–1760   total 40
————————— Tindale 2, Bolingbroke 2, Morgan 2, Lamettrie 5, Diderot 7, D'Alembert 5, Hume 8, Voltaire 7, Vaucanson 2

1760–1780   total 59
————————— Voltaire 7, Leroy 1, Hartley 4, Helvetius 6, Holbach 6, Priestley 6, Diderot 7, D'Alembert 5, Hume 8, Freret 3, Franklin 4, Morelli 2

1780–1800   total 52
————————— Diderot 7, Tetens 4, Leroy 1, Paine 4, Radischtschef 1, Kant 12, Priestley 6, Helvetius 6, Holbach 6, D. de Tracy 4, Lambert 1

1800–1820   total 79
————————— Volney 1, Lamarck 8, Beck 2, S. Maimon 4, Aenesidemus 2, Laplace 8, Fries 6, D. de Tracy 4, Schleiermacher 4, Broussais 2, Hegel 8, Schopenhauer 8, Lalande 2, James Mill 4, Herbart 7, Bentham 6

1820–1840   total 76
————————— Lamarck 8, Laplace 8, Hegel 8, Schopenhauer 8, Herbart 7, Bentham 7, J. Mill 6, A. Comte 8, L. Feuerbach 6, D. Strauss 4, Benecke 2, A. Ruge 4

1840–1860   total 100
————————— Carové 1, Biedermann 1, C. Baur 4, Feuerbach 6, K. Marx 8, Michelet 4, J. Erdmann 4, Br. Bauer 4, Fechner 7, A. Ruge 4, D. Strauss 6, Schopenhauer 8, Herzen 4, Fries 6, Herbart 7, A. Comte 8, H. Spencer 8, Engels 6, G. Grote 2, Vera 2

1860–1880   total 163
————————— K. Marx 8, Setschenoff 5, D. Strauss 6, Büchner 5, Kropotkin 4, Moleschott 4, K. Vogt 4, Haeckel 6, Zollner 4, Cournot 4, Wyrubov 4, Renan 6, Adickes 2, Ribot 7, Duehring 6, Pisarev 1, Bain 7, Poachet 1, Joly 1, A. Spir 4, Schopenhauer 8, F. Lange 7, H. Spencer 8, Fechner 7, Cl. Bernard 7, Taine 7, Littré 4, Galton 6, Cernysevsky 3, Engels 6, L. Tolstoi 8, Turgenev 3

1880–1900   total 186
————————— H. Spitzer 2, Lesshaft 2, Bain 7, Jodl 4, Spir 4, Frauenstädt 2, Tolstoi 8, Ferri 4, Lombroso 4, Duehring 6, Kropotkin 4, Marx 8, Mantegazza 1, Plechanov 4, Engels 6, Schuppe 5, S. Soldern 4, Nordau 4, Mach 6, Rehmke 7, Avenarius 6, Penjon 4, Bradley 7, Büchner 5, Ribot 7, Taine 7, Spencer 8, Baldwin 5, Romanes 4, Fouiller 5, Guyau 5, Ziehen 3, Ueberweg 5, Clifford 4, Riehl 6, Bunge 6, Meis 1

1900–1920   total 205 [1]
———— Pavlov, Loeb, Bechterev, Lipps, Hering, J. C. Fischer, Ostwald, Leuba, L. Tolstoi, Gibbs, Rohland, Schuppe, Zehnder, Rehmke, Bradley, J. Schmidt, Bosanquet, Verworn, Semon, Cohen, Roux, Zur Strassen, Natorp, Lewin, Boelsche, Jensen, Steudel, Planck, Bruno Wille, Boltzmann, Enriquez, Ziehen, Windelband, Haeckel, Petzold, Spencer, Pieron, Metschnikov, Tarkhanov, Royce, Krause, Müffelmann, Cassirer, Ehrenfels, Meinong, Kozlovsky, Lilienthal, Kohlrausch, Žižilenko, Liszt, Van Hamel, Ratzenhofer, Bernheim, Durkheim, Pearson, M. Weber, Pareto, Einstein, Bridgman, A. A. Tschuprov, Brunschvicg, Duhem, Heisenberg

---

INDETERMINISM (340 B.C.–A.D. 1920)

B.C. 340–320   total 12
———— Aristotle 12

320–300   total 21
———— Aristotle 12, Theophrastos 7, Eudemos 2

300–280   total 17
———— Epicuros 8, Theophrastos 7, Eudemos 2

280–260   total 11
———— Epicuros 8, Metrodoros 2, Polyainos 1

260–240   total 7
———— Hermarchos 2, Kolotes 2, Lykon 1, Hieronymos 2

240–220   total 11
———— Hermarchos 2, Kolotes 2, Polystratos 2, Hippokleides 1, Lykon 1, Hieronymos 2, Prytanis 1

220–200   total 11
———— Polystratos 2, Hippokleides 1, Ariston 3, Prytanis 1, Satyros 3, Hermippos 1

200–180   total 13
———— Polystratos 2, Hippokleides 1, Dionysios 1, Ariston 3, Satyros 3, Hermippos 1, Sotion 2

180–160   total 8
———— Dionysios 1, Basileides 1, Sotion 2, Antisthenes 2, Kritolaos 2

160–140   total 7
———— Basileides 1, Philonides 1, Antisthenes 2, Kritolaos 2, Herakleides 1

140–120   total 4
———— Apollodoros 2, Herakleides 1, Diodoros 1

120–100   total 6
———— Apollodoros 2, Zenon 2, Diodoros 1, Erymneos 1

[1] For obvious reasons values are not given for living authors.

100–80   total 9
———— Apollodoros 2, Zenon 2, Amafinius 1, Phaidoros 2, Diodoros 1, Erymneos 1

80–60   total 9
———— Phaidoros 2, Amafinius 1, Zenon 2, Ariston 1, Xenarchos 1, Andronikos 2

60–40   total 22
———— Patron 1, Philodemos 5, Lucretius 8, Asclepiades 4, Ariston 1, Xenarchos 1, Andronikos 2

40–20   total 12
———— Philodemos 5, Asclepiades 4, Andronikos 2, Boethos 1

20–0   total 1
———— Boethos 1

A.D. 0–20   total 9
———— Boethos 1, Philon Jud. 8

20–40   total 8
———— Philon Jud. 8

40–60   total 10
———— Alexandros 2, Philon 8

60–80   total 2
———— Alexandros 2

80–100   total 2
———— Ptolemaios Ch. 2

100–120   total 13
———— Ptolemaios Ch. 2, Περὶ κόσμον 4, Aspasios 2, Adrastos 2, Christianity 3

120–140   total 13
———— Celsus (Epicurean) 1, Oinomaos 3, Aspasios 2, Adrastos 2, Ptolemaios 2, Christianity 3

140–160   total 22
———— Celsus (Epicurean) 1, Diogenianos 1, Oinomaos 3, Herminos 2, Claudios Ptol. 3, Albinos 3, Justinus Martyr 5, Aspasios 2, Adrastos 2

160–180   total 36
———— Celsus (Epicurean) 1, Diogenianos 1, Herminos 2, Claudios 3, Galenos 7, Aristokles 1, Albinos 3, Apuleius 6, Justinus Martyr 5, Tatianus 3, Minucius Felix 4

180–200   total 50
———— Diogenianos 1, Diogenes 3, Herminos 2, Claudios 3, Galenos 7, Aristokles 1, Alexandros Aphr. 6, Apuleius 6, Minucius Felix 4, Irenaeus Lugd. 4, Clemens Alex. 6, Tatianus 3, Bardesanes 4

200–220   total 40
———— Diogenes from Oin. 3, Galenos 7, Alexandros Aphr. 6, Irenaeus Lugd. 4, Clemens Alex. 6, Hippolytus 3, Bardesanes 4, Philippus 1, Tertullianus 6

220–240   total 27
———— Alexandros Aphr. 6, Hippolytus 3, Origenes 8, Bardesanes 4, Tertullianus 6

240–260 total 25
———————— Ammonios 1, Plotinos 12, Origenes 8, Dionysius Magnus 2, Gregorius Thaumat. 2

260–280 total 22
———————— Ammonios 1, Plotinos 12, Amelios 2, Dionysius Magnus 2, Gregorius Thaumat. 2, Theognostos 1, Paulus (Samosate) 2

280–300 total 8
———————— Prosenos 1, Amelios 2, Pamphilus (Caes.) 1, Paulus (Samosate) 2, Lucianus (Samosate) 2

300–320 total 22
———————— Porphyrios 7, Iamblichos 7, Pamphilus (Caes.) 1, Eusebius (Caes.) 3, Methodius (Phil.) 2, Lucianus (Sam.) 2

320–340 total 27
———————— Iamblichos 7, Sopatros 2, Theodoros 1, Dexippos 2, Eusebius (Caes.) 3, Athanasius Magnus 4, Lactantius 4, Arius 4

340–360 total 20
———————— Sopatros 2, Theodoros 1, Dexippos 2, Eusebius (Caes.) 3, Athanasius Magnus 4, Arius 4, Macarius Aegipt. 4

360–380 total 36
———————— Themistios 5, Athanasius Magnus 4, Hilarius (Poit.) 3, Basilius Magnus 6, Gregorius Naz. 6, Gregorius Nyss. 6, Aetios 1, Eunomius 1, Macarius Aegipt. 4

380–400 total 41
———————— Themistios 5, Basilius Mag. 6, Gregorius Naz. 6, Gregorius Nyss. 6, Ioannes Chrysost. 5, Ambrosius Mediol. 5, Apollinarius Laod. 3, Eunomius 1, Macarius Aegipt. 4

400–420 total 33
———————— Syrianos 1, Ioannes Chrysost. 5, Augustinus 10, Nemesius 2, Theodorus (Mops) 2, Cyrillus Alex. 3, Iulian (Ekl.) 2, Pelagius 3, Pseudo Macarius 2, I. Cassianus 3

420–440 total 35
———————— Hierocles 2, Syrianos 1, Augustinus 10, Theodorus (Mops) 2, Cyrillus Alex. 3, Theodoretus Cyr. 3, Iulian (Ekl.) 2, Pelagius 3, Nestorius 3, Pseudo Macarius 2, I. Cassianus 3, Caelestius 1

440–460 total 24
———————— Hierocles 2, Proklos 8, Diodoros (Fot.) 2, Cyrillus Alex. 3, Theodoretus Cyr. 3, Nestorius 3, Eutyches 3

460–480 total 18
———————— Proklos 8, Diadochos (Fot.) 2, Theodoretus Cyr. 3, Eutyches 3, Faustus 1, Gennadius 1

480–500 total 12
———————— Proklos 8, Aeneas Gazensis 2, Faustus 1, Gennadius 1

500–520 total 7
———————— Simplikios 5, Aeneas Gazensis 2

520–540 total 16
———————— Simplikios 5, Aeneas Gazensis 2, Boethius 6, Leontius (Byz.) 3

540–560 total 11
———————— Simplikios 5, Leontius (Byz.) 3, Cassiodorus 3

560–580 total 3
———————— Cassiodoros 3

580–600 total 4
———————— Gregorius I (Magnus) 4

600–620 total 4
———————— Gregorius I (Magnus) 4

620–640 total 6
———————— Maximus Confessor 6

640–660 total 6
———————— Maximus Confessor 6

660–680 total 8
———————— Maximus Confessor 6, Agatho 2

680–700 total 2
———————— Agatho 2

700–720 total 1

720–740 total 5
———————— Ioannes Damascenus 5

740–760 total 5
———————— Ioannes Damascenus 5

760–780 total 0

780–800 total 4
———————— Alcuinus 4

800–820 total 4
———————— Alcuinus 4

820–840 total 4
———————— Hrabanus Maurus 4

840–860 total 14
———————— Hrabanus Maurus 4, Servetus Lupus 2, Erigena 8

860–880 total 15
———————— Servetus Lupus 2, Erigena 8, Photius 3, Hincmarus 2

880–900 total 5
———————— Photius 3, Hincmarus 2

900–920 total 2
———————— Arethas 2

920–940 total 2
———————— Arethas 2

940–960 total 0

960–980 total 0

980–1000 total 0

1000–1060 total 0

1060–1080 total 14
———————— Michael Psellos 3, Simeon Th. Nov. 4, Anselmus Cent. 7

1080–1100   total 21
———————— Michael Psellos 3, Simeon Th. Nov. 4,
Anselmus Cant. 7, Michael Ephens. 2, Mane-
goldus 3, Eustratios 2

1100–1120   total 12
———————— Anselmus Cant. 7, Manegoldus 3,
Eustratios 2

1120–1140   total 21
———————— Eustratios 2, Petrus Abaelardus 4,
Bernardus Claraev. 5, Guilelmus S. Th. rem. 2,
Honorius Augustod. 3, Hugo à S. Victore 5

1140–1160   total 27
———————— Petrus Abaelardus 4, Bernardus
Claraev. 5, Guilelmus S. Th. rem. 2, Honorius
Augustod. 3, Hugo à S. Victore 5, Richardus à
S. Victore 4, Petrus Lombardus 4

1160–1180   total 19
———————— Richardus à S. Victore 4, Petrus
Lombardus 4, Ioannes Saresber. 3, Isaac de
Stella 2, Gandulfus 2, Clarenbaldus 2, Rolandus
Band. 2

1180–1200   total 16
———————— Ioannes Saresberiensis 3, Rolandus
Bandinelli 2, Petrus Pictaviensis 2, Petrus
Cantor 2, Nicolaus Amb. 2, Gualternus à S.
Victore 2, Ioachim de Floris 3

1200–1220   total 13
———————— Petrus Pictaviensis 2, Nicolaus Ambian. 2, Prepositinus (Crem.) 2, Guilelmus (Aux.)
2, Philippus Grevius 2, Ioachim de Floris 3

1220–1240   total 14
———————— Prepositinus (Crem.) 2, Guilelmus
(Aux.) 2, Philippus Grevius 2, Robert Grosse-
teste 4, Alexander Halensis 4

1240–1260   total 17
———————— Robert Grosseteste 4, Alexander
Halensis 4, Albertus Magnus 8, Nikephoros
Blemmydes 1

1260–1280   total 31
———————— Albertus Magnus 8, Nikephoros
Blemmydes 1, Ioannes Bonaventure 8, Thomas
Aquinas 12, Petrus de Tarentesia 2

1280–1300   total 39
———————— Albertus Magnus 8, Raymundus
Lullus 5, Ioannes Peckham 1, Walter of Brugges 2,
Henricus Gondaven 4, Hugo Ripelin 3, Petrus I.
Olivi 3, Bernardus de Trilia 2, Aegidius Romanus
3, Remigio di Ch. d. G. 2, Georgios Pachymeres 2,
Sophonias 2, Matthaeus ab Aquasp. 2

1300–1320   total 54
———————— Raymundus Lullus 5, Walter of
Brugges 2, Remigio di Ch. d. G. 2, Aegidius
Romanus 3, Georgios Pachymeres 2, Sophonias 2,
Matthaeus ab Aquasp. 2, Bernardus de Albern. 1,
Jean Quidort 2, Guilelmus Petri de God. 2, Hervé
Nédélec 3, Tolomeo (Lucca) 2, Dante 8, Duns
Scotus 8, Durandus de S. Porc. 2, M. Eckehart 8

1320–1340   total 36
———————— Guilelmus Petri de God. 2, Hervé
Nédélec 3, Tolomeo (Lucca) 2, Dante 8, Durandus
de S. Porc. 2, Ioannes de Regine 1, Ioannes
Picardi 2, Nicol. Trivet 2, Guido Terreni 2,
Antonius Andreas 1, Franciscus de Mayronis 2,
Walter Burleigh 1, M. Eckehart 8

1340–1360   total 20
———————— Guido Terreni 2, Walter Burleigh 1,
Bernardus Lombard. 1, Durandellus 1, Suso 5,
Thomas (Strassb.) 2, Gregorios Papamas 6,
I. Buridan 2

1360–1380   total 14
———————— Suso 4, Gregorios Papamas 6,
Marsilius (Inghen.) 2, I. Buridan 2

1380–1400   total 2
———————— Marsilius (Inghen.) 2

1400–1420   total 4
———————— Jean Charlier (Gerson) 4

1420–1440   total 11
———————— Jean Charlier (Gerson) 4, Ioannes
Capreolus 3, Heinrich (Gorkum) 1, Antonin 3

1440–1460   total 14
———————— Ioannes Capreolus 3, Antonin 3,
Nicolaus Cusanus 8

1460–1480   total 11
———————— Nicolaus Cusanus 8, Gabriel Biel 3

1480–1500   total 4
———————— Gabriel Biel 3, Petrus Tartaretus 1

1500–1520   total 12
———————— F. P. de la Mirandola 4, Maffei 2,
Vives 6

1520–1540   total 16
———————— Erasmus 5, Reuchlin 4, Agrippa 2,
Bovillus 2, Xaverius 3

1540–1560   total 20
———————— Loyola 8, Agrippa 2, Soto 2, Nizolius 3, Pereira 4, Ledesma 1

1560–1580   total 28
———————— Loyola 8, Melanchthon 5, G. Pereira
4, Ledesma 1, Vittoria 2, Carpentarius 1, Gursky
1, Cardanus 6

1580–1600   total 37
———————— Taurellus 3, Cardanus 6, Vittoria 2,
St. Theresa 6, Temple 2, Molina 3, Suarez 6,
Toletus 3, Fonseca 3, M. Vasquez 3

1600–1620   total 30
———————— Campanella 6, Toletus 3, Fonseca 3,
Charron 2, Suarez 6, G. Vasquez 4, Consilium de
auxilibus gratiae (1598–1607) 6

1620–1640   total 28
———————— Campanella 6, Escobard 6, Mariana
3, Albergati 4, Gray de Valencia 4, Davy de
Perrin 4, Sa 1

1640–1660 total 27
———— Gassendi 7, Descartes 8, Regius 3, Escobard 6, De Raey 2, Heereboord 1

1660–1680 total 51
———— Arnauld 4, Cudworth 5, Gassendi 7, Leibnitz 9, Bernier 2, Glanville 2, Sorbière 2, Lamy 2, Molinos 3, Malebranche 7, Rohault 1, Clauberg 3, R. Boyle 4

1680–1700 total 73
———— Locke 8, Arnauld 4, Nicole 4, Leibnitz 9, H. Morus 4, Malebranche 7, Clauberg 3, Cudworth 5, Bossuet 6, Poiret 1, Fénelon 6, De Raey 2, Volthausen 2, Guyau 2, Glisson 3, De la Forge 3, Pappo 2, Giovenale 1, Wachter 1

1700–1720 total 57
———— Bold 1, Cockburn 1, Locke 8, Bossuet 6, Fénelon 6, Collins 5, Leibnitz 9, Berkeley 8, Giovenale 2, V. Helmont 2, Shaftesbury 5, André 1, Thomassin 1, Norris 2

1720–1740 total 42
———— Bold 1, Schultz 4, Lange 1, Cockburn 1, Clarke 2, Leibnitz 9 (posthumous works), C. Wolf 7, Berkeley 8, Billfinger 1, André 1, Baumgarten 4, Thümmig 1, Cramer 2

1740–1760 total 60
———— Kant 12, Berkeley 8, Wolf 7, Vico 9, J. Edwards 6, Billfinger 2, Baumgarten 4, M. Knutzen 4, Crusius 4, Daries 2, Schultze 4

1760–1780 total 47
———— Basedow 5, Reid 4, Rousseau 8, Condillac 6, Kant 12, Beattie 2, Baumgarten 4, Euler 5, Ickstadt 1

1780–1800 total 80
———— Kant 12, Condillac 6, Reid 5, Beattie 2, Mendelssohn 4, D. Stewart 4, Rousseau 8, Beck 2, Fichte 8, Schiller 8, Nithammer 2, Forberg 2, Kinker 1, Jacobi 6, Herder 6, Reinhold 2, Jacob 1, Schwarz 2

1800–1820 total 90
———— Rixner 1, Blasche 1, Troxler 1, D. Stewart 4, Goethe 8, M. de Biran 5, Fichte 8, Schelling 8, Jacobi 6, Herder 6, Schubert 1, Sibborn 2, Steffens 1, Solger 1, Nithammer 1, Schad 2, Krug 2, Kinker 1, Villers 1, Wirgmann 1, Reinhold 2, Pestalozzi 4, Jäsche 1, Hemert 2, E. Hermann 1, J. Wagner 2, Fourier 5, De Maistre 6, De Bonald 5

1820–1840 total 80
———— Galič 2, Bolzano 6, Krause 4, Whewell 6, Fichte Jr. 4, D. Stewart 4, V. Cousin 4, Ampère 5, M. de Biran 5, Harms 3, Schelling 8, Weisse 4, Rosmini 4, Damiron 2, Laromiguière 5, Lammenais 4, A. Franck 3, Khomiakov 4, Kireevsky 2, Bordat de Moulin 1

1840–1860 total 114
———— Fr. Baader 5, Schelling 8, K. Fischer 4, Carlyle 4, Krause 4, Saisset 1, Damiron 2, A. Franck 3, Bolzano 6, M. de Biran 5, Vacherot 3, Fichte Jr. 4, Lotze 5, Ravaisson 3, Rosmini 6, Gioberti 6, Quetelet 6, Renouvier 7, A. Smetana 4, Ampère 5, Schaden 1, V. Cousin 4, Whewell 6, Lassale 4, Harms 3, Vinet 4, Gratry, 1

1860–1880 total 105
———— Quetelet 6, Hartmann 8, V. Cousin 4, Hamilton 6, Mansel 2, Fechner 7, Renouvier 7, Dostoevsky 7, Pirogov 4, P. Janet 4, Fr. Bouillier 3, Damiron 2, A. Franck 3, Vacherot 3, Khomiakov 4, Kavelin 3, Strachov 3, Lotze 5, J. S. Mill 8, J. Erdmann 4, N. Grote 3, Mansel 2, Fonsegrive 5, Remusat 3, Ravaisson 3, Perty 1

1880–1900 total 157
———— Balfour 4, Veitch 4, Karinsky 4, Wwedensky 4, Lopatin 4, Kozlow 3, Eucken 5, E. Rod 2, Dauriac 3, Rickert 6, Lutoslavsky 4, S. Trubetzkoi 4, E. Trubetzkoi 3, Renouvier 7, Hartmann 7, W. James 7, Pillon 4, Wundt 7, Delboeuf 4, Dantec 4, Grote 4, Radlow 3, Liebman 5, Boussinesque 3, S. Kovalevskaja 4, Secretan 3, Lotze 5, L. Stephen 4, Brochard 4, Lachelier 4, Naville 4, Čičerin 4, Axakov 4, Strachov 3, Masaryk 6, Dostoevsky 7

1900–1920 total 185 [1]
———— Plessner, B. Selle, Uexcül, Wusker, Jellineck, Francé, Koelsch, Pauly, Reinke, K. C. Schneider, Ungern, V. Soloviev, Lossky, M. Scheler, Hessen, Renouvier, Vorovka, Pelikan, R. Eucken, W. James, Hoppe, Ladd, S. Trubetzkoi, E. Trubetzkoi, K. Groos, Joël, Falkenberg, Wertheimer, Dantec, Poincaré, O. Pfleiderer, Bergson, Jankelevitsch, Masaryk, Münsterberg, Gutberlet, Berdiaev, Unamuno, Delbet, Wwedensky, Blondel, M. Planck, Einstein, Duhem, Tchuproff, Brunschvicg, Heisenberg, Pearson, Bridgman

[1] For obvious reasons values are not given for living authors.

LIST OF THINKERS FOR EACH PERIOD, WITH THE VALUE GIVEN TO EACH ON A SCALE 1 TO 12

Graeco-Roman and European-Christian Cultures

ETHICS OF HAPPINESS
(440 B.C.–A.D. 1920.)

B.C. 440–420   total 13
———— Protagoras 8, Gorgias 5

420–400   total 53
———— Protagoras 8, Demokritos 8, Socrates 9, Gorgias 5, Prodikos 5, Hippias 4, Polos 2, Thrasymachos 3, Kallikles 2, Kritias 3, Antiphon 4

400–380   total 49
———— Demokritos 8, Socrates 9, Aeschines 3, Gorgias 5, Prodikos 5, Hippias 4, Antiphon 4, Polos 2, Thrasymachos 3, Aristippos 6

380–360   total 29
———— Demokritos 8, Aeschines 3, Xenophon 7, Gorgias 5, Aristippos 6

360–340   total 22
———— Aeschines 3, Xenophon 7, Eudoxos 3, Aristippos 6, Arete 1, Aethiops 1, Antipatros 1

340–320   total 8
———— Anaxarchos 1, Eudoxos 3, Arete 1, Aithiops 1, Antipatros 1, Aristippos Jr. 1

320–300   total 17
———— Nausiphanes 2, Menedemos 2, Theodoros 2, Anaxarchos 1, Pyrrhon 6, Hegesias 2, Annikeris 2

300–280   total 24
———— Nausiphanes 2, Epicuros 8, Menedemos 2, Theodoros 2, Megesias 2, Annikeris 2, Pyrrhon 6

280–260   total 35
———— Bion 3, Epicuros 8, Metrodoros 2, Polyainos 1, Dionysios 1, Menedemos 2, Theodoros 2, Hegesias 2, Annikeris 2, Pyrrhon 6, Timon 3, Arkesilaos 3

260–240   total 21
———— Bion 3, Hermarchos 2, Kolotes 2, Dionysios 1, Hieronymos 2, Menippos 5, Timon 3, Arkesilaos 3

240–220   total 32
———— Bion 3, Hermarchos 2, Kolotes 2, Polystratos 2, Menippos 5, Hippokleides 1, Dionysios 1, Hieronymos 2, Timon 3, Arkesilaos 3, Teles 3, Kerkides 5

220–200   total 8
———— Polystratos 2, Hippokleides 1, Kerkides 5

200–180   total 4
———— Polystratos 2, Hippokleides 1, Dionysios 1

180–160   total 7
———— Dionysios 1, Basileides 1, Karneades 5

160–140   total 10
———— Basileides 1, Philonides 2, Karneades 5, Kleitomachos 2

140–120   total 9
———— Apollodoros 2, Karneades 5, Kleitomachos 2

120–100   total 6
———— Apollodoros 2, Zenon 2, Kleitomachos 2

100–80   total 7
———— Apollodoros 2, Zenon 2, Amafinius 1, Phaidros 2

80–60   total 5
———— Zenon 2, Amafinius 1, Phaidros 2

60–40   total 23
———— Patron 1, Philodemos 5, Lucretius 8, Asclepiades 4, Ainisidemos 5

40–20   total 14
———— Philodemos 5, Asclepiades 4, Ainisidemos 5

20–0   total 6
———— Epicureans 1, Ainisidemos 5

A.D. 0–20   total 1
———— Epicureans 1

20–40   total 1
———— Epicureans 1

40–60   total 1
———— Epicureans 1

60–80   total 1
———— Epicureans 1

80–100   total 1
———— Epicureans 1

100–120   total 1
———— Epicureans 1

120–140   total 2
————— Epicureans 1, Celsus (Epic.) 1

140–160   total 3
————— Epicureans 1, Celsus 1, Diogenianos 1

160–180   total 9
————— Epicureans 1, Celsus 1, Diogenianos 1, Sextus Emp. 6

180–200   total 11
————— Epicureans 1, Diogenianos 1, Diogenes 3, Sextus Emp. 6

200–220   total 9
————— Diogenes 3, Sextus Emp. 6

220–240   total 1
————— Epicureans 1

240–260   total 1
————— Epicureans 1

260–280   total 1
————— Epicureans 1

280–300   total 1
————— Epicureans 1

300–320   total 1
————— Epicureans 1

320–340   total 1
————— Epicureans 1

340–360   total 1
————— Epicureans

360–380   total 5
————— Themistios 5

380–400   total 5
————— Themistios 5

* * *

1440–1460   total 3
————— L. Valla 3

1500–1520   total 10
————— Machiavelli 6, Pomponazzi 4

1520–1540   total 17
————— Pomponazzi 4, Vives 6, Machiavelli 6, Desperrières 1

1540–1560   total 16
————— Loyola 8, Luther 8

1560–1580   total 28
————— Raymundus 2, Cardanus 6, Telesius 6, Ledesma 1, Fonseca 3, Montaigne 6, Charron 4

1580–1600   total 45
————— Suarez 6, Toletus 2, Molina 3, Baco 7, Charron 4, Mariana 3, Bodin 4, Salmeron 3, G. Vasquez 3, C. Vasquez 3, Lublin 1, Montaigne 6

1600–1620   total 56
————— Baco 7, Shakespeare 8, Vanini 4, G. Vasquez 4, C. Vasquez 3, Belarminus 4, Toletus 3, Althusius 4, Molina 3, Berulle 4, Grey de Valencia 4, Albergati 4, Davy de Perrin 4

1620–1640   total 35
————— Baco 7, Bellarminus 4, Mariana 3, Magnenus 2, Shakespeare 8, Escobard Mendoza 4, Althusius 4, Cherbury 3

1640–1660   total 34
————— Gassendi 7, B. Grazian 4, LaRochefoucauld 4, Magnenus 2, Busenbaum 4, Hobbes 8, Brown 3, Maignan 2

1660–1680   total 32
————— Busenbaum 4, Gassendi 7, LaRochefoucauld 4, Huet 1, Bernier 2, C. de Bergerac 2, La Bruyère 2, Maignan 2, Hobbes 8

1680–1700   total 30
————— Locke 8, Bernier 2, Glanville 2, P. Bayle 6, Daniel 2, Makovsky 2, Hobbes 8

1700–1720   total 33
————— Locke 8, Huet 1, Mandeville 4, Faydit 1, Renodot 2, Merger 1, Buffier 2, Tournemine 2, Petau 1, Claude Brunet 4, Jean Meslier 3, Heiffenstael 1, Duhamel 1, Regnaut 1, Andola 1

1720–1740   total 35
————— Mandeville 4, Brown 2, Bolingbrooke 2, J. Meslier 3, D'Alembert 5, Maine 2, Montesquieu 8, Butler 3, Dutertre 2, Morelli 2, Dumarsais 2

1740–1760   total 56
————— Lamettrie 5, Diderot 7, Freret 3, D'Alembert 5, Hartley 4, Priestley 6, Radsky 2, Morelli 2, Mably 2, Montesquieu 8, Maupertuis 4, Dumarsais 2, Helvetius 6

1760–1780   total 82
————— Robinet 2, Priestley 6, Helvetius 6, Voltaire 7, Condillac 6, Condorcet 4, Franklin 4, Aenesidemus 2, Maupertuis 4, Bentham 6, D'Alembert 5, Beccaria 4, Turgot 4, Freret 3, Mably 2, Holbach 6, Morelli 2, Hume 8, Holzelau 1

1780–1800   total 61
————— Priestley 6, Helvetius 6, Holbach 6, Bentham 6, Aenesidemus 2, Filangieri 4, Volney 2, Lambert 1, Turgot 4, A. Ferguson 6, J. Mill 4, Condillac 6, Cabanis 4, Condorcet 4

1800–1820   total 54
————— L. von Galler 4, Třebinsky 2, Bonafons 1, Pembridge 1, Bentham 6, J. Mill 6, D. de Tracy 4, Paine 2, A. Ferguson 6, Saint-Simon 4, Baader 5, Goethe 8, Jefferson 2, Molitor 1, M. de Biran 2

1820–1840   total 60
————— D. Strauss 6, Bolzano 6, B. Constant 3, J. Austin 3, Goerres 5, L. von Galler 4, Bentham 6, Gratry 3, Herschel 6, Benecke 2, D. de Tracy 4, Scherer 3, Balmez 5, Richter 4

1840–1860   total 127
————— D. Strauss 6, J. S. Mill 8, Fr. Baader 5, Gratry 3, Goerres 5, Beyle 6, Marx 8, Engels 6, Ch. Baur 4, Newmann 6, Carove 1, Setchenov 5, Purkinje 3, Austin 3, Büchner 5, Černyševsky 3, Spencer 8, Littré 4, Lewes 5, Herschel 6, Buckle 5, Moleschott 4, Vogt 4, Duehring 6, A. Ruge 4, P. Proudhon 4

1860–1880 total 138
——————— H. Spencer 8, Ribot 7, Duehring 6, Taine 7, Büchner 5, Buckle 5, Haeckel 6, Renan 6, Fiorentino 4, Strauss 6, Černyševsky 3, Newmann 6, Littré 4, Fechner 7, Lewes 5, Huxley 2, Bain 7, Lavrov 4, Grote 2, Engels 6, Austin 4, Darwin 8, Marx 8, Wyrubov 4, J. S. Mill 8, Kleutgen 2, Sabatier 2

1880–1900 total 189
——————— Renan 6, Marx 8, Bain 7, Krejči 4, Kropotkin 4, Laas 4, Lutoslavsky 4, Dressel 1, Multatuli 4, Duehring 6, Newmann 6, Karstanjen 2, Lesevič 1, E. Ferri 4, A. France 6, Maupassant 4, Morgan 2, Büchner 5, Ribot 7, Haeckel 6, Dantec 4, Espinas 4, Willmann 4, Lombroso 4, Gonzales 4, Avenarius 6, Mach 6, Zola 4, Linsemann 1, Taine 7, Riehl 6, Nordau 4, Fouillée 5, Kahn 1, R. Steiner 4, Baldwin 5, Gruber 4, Drummond 4, Deschamps 1, T. Pesch 4, O. Pesch 1, Harper 4, Sabatier 2, Liberatore 3, Feldner 2, Kathrein 2, Schned 1

1900–1920 total 200 [1]
——————— Kautsky, Menger, Simmel, Baldwin, Claparede, H. Maier, R. Steiner, Alexander, H. Gomperz, Petzold, Freud, Plechanov, Kropotkin, Ostwald, Metschnikov, Boelsche, E. K. Capek, R. Willy, B. Kidd, Spengler, Dantec, Loeb, Dewey, Russell, Shiller, Pavlov, Pierre Delbet, Leuba, Pieron, Boltzmann, Planck, Pauly, Kostyleff, Fouillée, Nordau, B. Erdmann, Bogdanov, Ziehen, Rignano, Enriquez, Vaihinger, Mauthner, Ehrenfels, Deborin, Bazarov, Tarchanov, Poincaré, Lévi-Bruhl, Durkheim, Max Weber, Troeltsch, Perry, De Roberty, Westermarck

ETHICS OF LOVE
(A.D. 100–1920)

A.D. 100–120 total 3
——————— Christianity 3

120–140 total 3
——————— Christianity 3

140–160 total 6
——————— Iustin Martyr 5, Karpokrates 1

160–180 total 6
——————— Iustin Martyr 5, Karpokrates 1

180–200 total 10
——————— Irenaeus Lugd. 4, Clemens (Alex.) 6

200–220 total 10
——————— Irenaeus Lugd. 4, Clemens (Alex.) 6

220–240 total 8
——————— Origenes 8

240–260 total 10
——————— Origenes 8, Gregorius Thaum. 2

[1] For obvious reasons values are not given for living authors.

260–280 total 2
——————— Gregorius Thaum. 2

280–300 total 1
——————— Pamphilus (Caes.) 1

300–320 total 1
——————— Pamphilus (Caes.) 1

320–340 total 4
——————— Athanasius Magnus 4

340–360 total 8
——————— Athanasius Magnus 4, Macarius Aegyptius 4

360–380 total 26
——————— Athanasius Magnus 4, Basilius Magnus 6, Gregorius Naz. 6, Gregorius Nyss. 6, Macarius Aegyptius 4

380–400 total 32
——————— Basilius Magnus 6, Gregorius Naz. 6, Gregorius Nyss. 6, Ioannes Chrysost. 5, Ambrosius Med. 5, Macarius Aegyptius 4

400–420 total 20
——————— Ioannes Chrys. 5, Augustinus 10, Cyrillus Alex. 3, Pseudo Macarius 2

420–440 total 18
——————— Augustinus 10, Cyrillus Alex. 3, Theodoretus Cyr. 3, Pseudo Macarius 2

440–460 total 8
——————— Diodochos (Fot.) 2, Cyrillus Alex. 3, Theodoretus Cyr. 3

460–480 total 5
——————— Diodochos (Fot.) 2, Theodoretus Cyr. 3

480–500 total 2
——————— Aeneas Gez. 2

500–520 total 10
——————— Aeneas Gez. 2, Dionysius Areop. 8

520–540 total 10
——————— Aeneas Gez. 2, Dionysius Areop. 8

540–560 total 2
——————— Ioannes Lydos 2

560–580 total 2
——————— Ioannes Lydos 2

580–600 total 4
——————— Gregorius I (Magnus) 4

600–620 total 4
——————— Gregorius I (Magnus) 4

620–640 total 6
——————— Maximus Confessor 6

640–660 total 6
——————— Maximus Confessor 6

660–680 total 6
——————— Maximus Confessor 6

680–700 total 1

700–720 total 1

720–740   total 5
———— Ioannes Damascenus 5

740–760   total 5
———— Ioannes Damascenus 5

760–780   total ½

780–800   total 2
———— Alcuinus 2

800–820   total 2
———— Alcuinus 2

820–840   total 1

840–860   total 8
———— John Scotus Erigena 8

860–880   total 11
———— John Scotus Erigena 8, Photius 3

880–900   total 5
———— Photius 3, Remigius (Aux.) 2

900–920   total 2
———— Remigius (Aux.) 2

920–940   total 1

940–960   total ½

960–980   total ½

980–1000   total 1

1000–1020   total 2
———— Fulbert 2

1020–1040   total 2
———— Fulbert 2

1040–1060   total 3
———— Petrus Damiani 3

1060–1080   total 17
———— Petrus Damiani 3, Michael Psellos 3, Simeon Th. Nov. 4, Anselmus Cant. 7

1080–1100   total 17
———— Michael Psellos 3, Simeon Th. Nov. 4, Anselmus Cant. 7, Manegoldus 3

1100–1120   total 12
———— Anselmus Cant. 7, Manegoldus 3, Guilelmus Camp. 2

1120–1140   total 18
———— Guilelmus Camp. 2, Petrus Abaelardus 4, Bernardus Claraev. 5, Guilelmus Th. Rem. 2, Hugo à S. Victore 5

1140–1160   total 20
———— Petrus Abaelardus 4, Bernardus Claraev. 5, Guilelmus Th. Rem. 2, Hugo à S. Victore 5, Richardus à S. Victore 4

1160–1180   total 10
———— Rolandus Bandin. 2, Richardus à S. Victore 4, Isaac de Stella 2, Clerenbaldus 2

1180–1200   total 10
———— Radulfus Ardens 1, Alanus ab Insulis 3, Ioachim de Floris 3, Rolandus Bandin. 2, Gottfried de Bret. 1

1200–1220   total 8
———— Radulfus Ardens 1, Alanus ab Insulis 3, Thomas Gallo 1, Ioachim de Floris 3

1220–1240   total 5
———— Thomas Gallo 1, Radulfus de Longo 1, Guilelmus Alvernus 3

1240–1260   total 11
———— Guilelmus Alvernus 3, Albertus Magnus 8

1260–1280   total 28
———— Albertus Magnus 8, Ioannes Bonaventura 8, Thomas Aquinas 12

1280–1300   total 45
———— Raymundus Lullus 5, Albertus Magnus 8, Henricus Gandav. 4, Ioannes Peckham 1, Walter of Brugges 2, Eustachius 2, Dietrich de Friberg 2, Gottfried (Font.) 3, Bernardus de Trilia 2, Aegidius (Lessines) 2, Remigio di Ch. 2, Ioannes (Genua) 1, Ramberto dei Prim. 1, Aegidius Rom. 3, Mattheus ab Aqu. 2, P. I. Olivi 3, Guil. (Hothun) 1, Rich. (Clapwell) 1

1300–1320   total 58
———— Raymundus Lullus 5, Walter of Brugges 2, Gottfried (Font.) 3, Aegidius (Less.) 2, Remigio di Ch. 2, Ioannes (Genua) 1, Ramberto d. Pr. 1, Aegidius Roman. 3, Mattheus ab Aqu. 2, Dietrich de Vrieberg 2, Bernardus de Alveronia 1, Jean Quidort 2, Guilelmus Patride G. 2, Hervé Nedeléc 3, Tolomeo (Lucca) 2, Guilelmus (Mackl.) 1, Dante 8, I. Duns Scotus 8, M. Eckehart 8

1320–1340   total 30
———— Guilelmus P. de G. 2, Hervé Nedeléc 3, Tolomeo (Lucca) 2, Dante 8, Ioannes de Reg. 1, Ioannes Pic. de Luc. 2, Guido Terreni 2, Bertholdus de Mosb. 1, Antonius Andreos 1, M. Eckehart 8

1340–1360   total 28
———— Guido Terreni 2, Durandellus 1, I. Tauler 4, H. Suso 5, Ruysbroeck 4, Thomas (Strassb.) 2, Gregorius Palamas 6, Nicolaus Kabasiles 4

1360–1380   total 26
———— I. Tauler 4, H. Suso 5, Ruysbroeck 4, Gregorius Palamas 6, Nicolaus Kabas. 4, " Eine deutsche Theologie " 3

1380–1400   total 8
———— Ruysbroeck 4, Nicolaus Kabasiles 4

1400–1420   total 4
———— Jean Charlier (Gerson) 4

1420–1440   total 11
———— Jean Charlier (Gerson) 4, Ioannes Capreolus 3, Heinrich (Gorkun) 1, Antonin 3

1440–1460   total 18
———— Ioannes Capreolus 3, Antonin 3, Dionysius Cartus. 4, Nicolaus Cusanus 8

1460–1480   total 17
———— Dionysius Cartusianus 4, Nicolaus Cusanus 8, Thomas à Kempis 4, Petrus Nigri 1

1480–1500   total 2
———— Petrus Nigri 1, Petrus Tartaretus 1

1500–1520   total 1

1520–1540   total 1
———— St. Theresa 1

1540–1560   total 1
———— St. Theresa 1

1560–1580   total 4
———— Johannes del Dio 2, St. Theresa 2

1580–1600   total 14
———— C. Bruno 8, Jean de la Croix 4, Hannequin 2

1600–1620   total 12
———— Bruno 8, Franciscus Salesius 4

1620–1640   total 9
———— Comenius 7, Vincent de Paul 2

1640–1660   total 7
———— Comenius 7

1660–1680   total 7
———— Comenius 7

1680–1700   total 5
———— Shaftesbury 5

1700–1720   total 5
———— Shaftesbury 5

1720–1740   total 4
———— Hutcheson 4

1740–1760   total 12
———— Hutcheson 4, Rousseau 8

1760–1780   total 14
———— Rousseau 8, A. Smith 6

1780–1800   total 20
———— Rousseau 8, Jacobi 6, Herder 6

1800–1820   total 33
———— Schopenhauer 8, Herder 6, Jacobi 6, Fourier 5, Fichte 8 (*Anweisungen*, 1811)

1820–1840   total 36
———— Jacobi 6, Emerson 6, Feuerbach 6, Khomiakov 4, Fourier 5, Leroux 1, Schopenhauer 8

1840–1860   total 38
———— A. Comte 8, Schopenhauer 7, Feuerbach 6, Emerson 6, Fourier 5, Considérant 5

1860–1880   total 56
———— Ruskin 6, Mainländer 4, F. Lange 7, Lafitte 5, Harrison 3, Tolstoi 8, Feuerbach 6, Emerson 6, Soloviev 6, Congreve 3, Frey 2

1880–1900   total 64
———— Ruskin 6, Lafitte 5, Soloviev 6, Tolstoi 8, Dostoevsky 8, R. Wagner 8, Schuppe 5, Renouvièr 6, Secretan 4, Guyau 5, Radlov 3

1900–1920   total 74 [1]
———— Unamuno, Höffding, Ruskin, Soloviev, Schuppe, Maeterlink, Renouvier, S. Trubetzkoi, Secretan, Tolstoi, Lossky, Carpenter, M. Eddy

---

ETHICS OF PRINCIPLES
(540 B.C.–A.D. 1920)

B.C. 540–520   total 8
———— Pythagoras 8

520–500   total 15
———— Pythagoras 8, Herakleitos 7

500–480   total 15
———— Herakleitos 7, Pythagoras 8

480–460   total 7
———— Herakleitos 7

460–440   total 1
———— Ion 1

440–420   total 12
———— Empedokles 6, Philolaos 5, Ion 1

420–400   total 14
———— Empedokles 6, Philolaos 5, Simmias 1, Kebes 1, Lysis 1

400–380   total 18
———— Antisthenes 5, Eukleidos 3, Philolaos 5, Simmias 1, Kebes 1, Lysis 1, Eurytos 1, Archytas 1

380–360   total 22
———— Antisthenes 5, Eukleides 3, Platon 12, Eurytos 1, Archytas 1

360–340   total 28
———— Diogenes 5, Platon 12, Xenophilos 1, Phanton 1, Echekrates 1, Diokles 1, Polymnastos 1, Speusippas 3, Xenokrates 3

340–320   total 32
———— Diogenes 5, Stilpon 2, Aristotle 12, Xenophilos 1, Phanton 1, Echekrates 1, Diokles 1, Polymnastos 1, Speusippas 3, Xenokrates 3, Philippos 2

320–300   total 46
———— Monimos 1, Onesikritos 2, Philiskos 1, Krates 4, Stilpon 2, Aristotle 12, Theophrastos 7, Eudemos 2, Demetrios 3, Xenophilos 1, Phanton 1, Echekrates 1, Diokles 1, Polymnastos 1, Xenokrates 1, Philippos 2, Polemon 2

300–280   total 38
———— Monimos 1, Onesikritos 2, Phileskos 1, Krates 4, Metrokles 1, Zenon 8, Stilpon 2, Theophrastos 7, Eudemos 2, Demetrios 3, Polemon 2, Krantor 4, Krates 1

[1] For obvious reasons values are not given for living authors.

280–260   total 30
———— Metrokles 1, Zenon 8, Ariston 5, Herillos 1, Kleanthes 5, Demetrios 3, Polemon 2, Krantor 4, Krates 1

260–240   total 13
———— Ariston 5, Herillos 1, Persaios 2, Kleanthes 5

240–220   total 23
———— Ariston 5, Herillos 1, Persaios 2, Kleanthes 5, Chrysippos 7, Sphairos 1, Menedemos 2

220–200   total 13
———— Chrysippos 7, Sphairos 1, Menedemos 2, Ariston from Keas 3

200–180   total 9
———— Sphairos 1, Zenon 1, Diogenes 4, Ariston from Keas 3

180–160   total 8
———— Diogenes 4, Antipatros 2, Kritolaos 2

160–140   total 8
———— Diogenes 4, Antipatros 2, Kritolaos 2

140–120   total 9
———— Panaitios 5, Q. M. Scaevola 1, Boethos 2, Diodoros 1

120–100   total 11
———— Panaitios 5, Q. M. Scaevola 1, Hekaton 1, Mnesarchos 1, Boethos 2, Diodoros 1

100–80   total 16
———— Hekaton 1, Mnesarchos 1, Apollodoros 1, Poseidonios 7, Diodoros 1, Philon from Larissa 3

80–60   total 28
———— Meleagros 2, Apollodoros 1, Poseidonios 7, Asclepiodotos 2, Geminos 2, Andronikos 2, Philon from Larissa 3, Antiochos 4, Terentius Varro 5

60–40   total 37
———— Poseidonios 7, Asclepiodotos 2, Geminos 2, Phainias 1, Dionysios 1, Antipatros 2, Jason 2, Athenodoros 1, Apollonides 1, Diodotos 1, Cato 2, Andronikos 2, T. Varro 5, Cicero 8

40–20   total 15
———— Athenodoros 1, Apollonides 1, Diodotos 1, Apollonios 1, Athenodoros 3, Ar. Didymos 2, Andronikos 2, Q. Sextius 2, Eudoros 2

20–0   total 10
———— Athenodoros 3, Ar. Didymos 2, Q. Sextius 2, Sextius Jr. 1, Eudoros 2

0–20   total 20
———— Areios Didymos 2, Herakleitos 3, Sextius 1, Sotion 2, Corn. Celsus 1, L. Crassicius 1, Fav. Papirius 1, Potamon 1, Philon Iud. 8

20–40   total 12
———— Herakleitos 3, Attalos 1, Philon Iud. 8

40–60   total 22
———— Attalos 1, Seneca 8, L. Ann. Korn. 4, Demetrios 1, Philon Iud. 8

60–80   total 35
———— Seneca 8, Chairemon 2, L. Ann. Korn. 4, Persius Fl. 3, Ann. Lucanus 4, Mus. Rufus 5, Demetrios 1, Apollonios 5, Moderatos 3

80–100   total 34
———— Mus. Rufus 5, Demetrios 1, Epictetos 6, Dionysios Chrysost. 6, Apollonios 5, Moderatos 3, Plutarchos 8

100–120   total 38
———— Epictetos 6, Dionysios Chrys. 6, Περὶ κόσμον 4, Aspasios 2, Adrastos 2, Plutarchos 8, Theon 2, Sekundos 2, Nikomachos 1, Gaios 2, Cerinthus 2, Saturnilus 1

120–140   total 56
———— Epictetos 6, Arrianos 2, Hierokles 2, Kleomedes 2, Oinomaos 3, Demonax 2, Peregrinus Pr. 3, Aspasios 2, Adrastos 2, Plutarchos 8, Theon 2, Sekundos 2, Nikomachos 1, Gaios 2, Cerinthus 2, Saturnilus 1, Cerdon 2, Marcion 4, Basilides 4, Valentinus 4

140–160   total 54
———— Arrianos 2, Hierokles 2, Kleomedes 2, Oinomaos 3, Demonax 2, Peregrinus Pr. 3, Aspasios 2, Adrastos 2, Claudios Pt. 3, Theon 2, Sekundos 2, Nikomachos 1, Gaios 2, Herodes 2, Albinos 3, Kalvisios 2, Nigrinos 1, M. Aristides 3, Saturnilus 1, Cerdon 2, Marcion 4, Basilides 4, Valentinus 4

160–180   total 57
———— Demonax 2, Peregrinus Pr. 3, Marcus Aurelius 6, Claudios Pt. 3, Aristokles 1, Galenos 7, Herodes 2, Albinos 3, Kalvisios 2, Nigrinos 1, Apuleius 6, Numenios 4, Kronios 2, Valentinus 4, Tatianus 3, Minucius Felix 4, Marcion 4

180–200   total 68
———— Demonax 2, Marcus Aurelius 6, Claudios Pt. 3, Aristokles 1, Galenos 7, Alexandros Aphr. 6, Apuleius 6, Numenios 4, Kronios 2, Attikos 2, Harpokration 1, Celsus 4, Maximos 5, Hierax 1, Severus 1, Minucius Felix 4, Bardesanes 4, Tatianus 3, Apelles 2, Ptolemaeus 1, Herakleon 2, Marcus 1

200–220   total 49
———— Galenos 7, Alexandros Aphr. 6, Numenios 4, Hierax 1, Severus 1, Philostratos 5, Hermetic literature 5, Ammonios Sakkas 3, Hippolytus 3, Bardesanes 4, Philippos 1, Herakleon 2, Marcus 1, Tertulianus 6

220–240   total 36
———— Alexandros Aphr. 6, Philostratos 5, Hermetic literature 5, Ammonios Sakkas 3, Hippolytus 3, Bardesanes 4, Orphic books 4, Tertulianus 6

240–260   total 31
————— Hermetic literature 5, Ammonios Sakkas 3, Diogenes Laertius 3, Plotinos 12, Orphic books 4, Mani 4

260–280   total 27
————— Plotinos 12, Diogenes Laertius 3, Amelios 2, Anatolios 2, Orphic books 4, Mani 4

280–300   total 15
————— Amelios 2, Anatolios 2, Porphyrios 7, Mani 4

300–320   total 17
————— Porphyrios 7, Iamblichos 7, Methodius (ph.) 2, Manicheists 1

320–340   total 15
————— Iamblichos 7, Lactantius 4, Manicheists 1, Arnobius 3

340–360   total 6
————— Neo-Platonic school 1, Manicheists 2, I. Firm. Maternus 3

360–380   total 21
————— Iulian 7, Sallustrios 3, Eunapios 3, I. Firm. Maternus 3, Marius Victorinus 3, Manicheists 2

380–400   total 15
————— Sallustrios 3, Eunapios 3, Augustinus 7 (pagan), Manicheists 2

400–420   total 12
————— Macrobius 4, Syrianos 1, Synesius 2, Nemesius 2, Manicheists 3

420–440   total 13
————— Macrobius 4, Syrianos 1, Hierocles 2, Nestorius 3, Manicheists 3

440–460   total 17
————— Hierocles 2, Proklos 8, Hermeias 3, Nestorius 3, Manicheists 1

460–480   total 12
————— Hermeias 3, Proklos 8, Manicheists 1

480–500   total 12
————— Proklos 8, Marinos 3, Manicheists 1

500–520   total 18
————— Isidoros 1, Doros 1, Damaskios 4, Simplikios 5, Boethius 6, Manicheists 1

520–540   total 17
————— Daros 1, Damaskios 4, Simplikios 5, Boethius 6, Manicheists 1

540–560   total 14
————— Damaskios 4, Simplikios 5, Zacharius (Myt.) 2, Cassiodorus 3

560–580   total 5
————— Cassiodorus 3, Martinus Brac. 2

580–600   total 2
————— Martinus Bracer. 2

600–620   total 4
————— Isidorus Hispalensis 4

620–640   total 4
————— Isidorus Hispalensis 4

640–660   total 1

660–680   total 1

680–700   total 1

700–720   total 1

720–740   total 1

740–760   total 1

760–780   total 0

780–800   total 1

800–820   total 1

820–840   total 6
————— Hrabanus Maurus 4, Candidus 2

840–860   total 6
————— Hrabanus Maurus 4, Servetus Lupus 2

860–880   total 2
————— Servetus Lupus 2

880–900   total 1

900–920   total 1

920–940   total 1

940–960   total ½

960–980   total ½

980–1000   total 1

1000–1020   total 1

1020–1040   total 1

1040–1060   total 5
————— Berengarius T. 3, Anselmus (Bes.) 2

1060–1080   total 5
————— Berengarius T. 3, Anselmus (Bes.) 2

1080–1100   total 6
————— Berengarius T. 3, Roscelinus 3

1100–1120   total 3
————— Roscelinus 3

1120–1140   total 5
————— Roscelinus 3, Guilelmus de Conches 2

1140–1160   total 2
————— Guilelmus de Conches 2

1160–1180   total 2

1180–1200   total 2

1200–1220   total 2

1220–1240   total 4
————— Alexander Halensis 4

1240–1260   total 4
————— Alexander Halensis 4

1260–1280   total 10
————— Roger Bacon 6, Siger of Brabant 4

1280–1300   total 12
————— Siger of Brabant 4, Roger Bacon 6, Heinrich Bate 2

1300–1320   total 3
————— Pietro d'Abano 1, Heinrich Bate 2

1320–1340   total 4
————— Petrus Aureoli 2, Ioannes (Baconth.) 2

1340–1360   total 9
————— Petrarca 6, Ioannes (Baconth.) 2, Urban 1

1360–1380   total 6
————— Petrarca 6

1380–1400   total 1

1400–1420   total 2
————— Paulus (Venetia) 2

1420–1440   total 2
————— Paulus (Venetia) 2

1440–1460   total 2
————— Cajetanus Thiaeneus 2

1460–1480   total 2
————— Cajetanus Thiaeneus 2

1480–1500   total 1
————— Nicoletto Vernias 1

1500–1520   total 32
————— Erasmus 5, P. de Mirandola 4, S. Franck 2, Luther 8, Savonarola 6, Nifus 1, T. Morus 6

1520–1540   total 45
————— Luther 8, Zwingli 6, Calvin 6, Melanchthon 5, Erasmus 5, Agrippa 2, Reuchlin 4, S. Franck 2, Menno 2, Johannes de Leyd 5

1540–1560   total 31
————— Luther 8, Melanchthon 5, Loyola 8, Calvin 6, Serveto 4

1560–1580   total 35
————— Melanchthon 5, P. Ramus 4, Calvin 6, Schengk 1, Sturm 2, Wilson 1, Strigel 2, J. Knox 5, Pfaffrad 1, Lipsius 2, Freigius 1, Fabricius 1

1580–1600   total 27
————— Keppler 8, Freigius 1, Fabricius 1, Sturm 1, Digby 4, Oxlein 3, Lipsius 2, Snellius 1, Gocklenius 3, Case 2, Sanderson 1

1600–1620   total 48
————— Descartes 8, Mersenne 4, Keppler 8, Galileo, 8, Davies 2, Cervantes 8, Hereford 2, Campanella 6, Fotherby 2

1620–1640   total 54
————— Descartes 8, Campanella 6, H. Grotius 6, A. Arnauld 4, Keppler 8, Galileo 8, Jansenius 6, Mersenne 4, Regius 3, Alstedius 3

1640–1660   total 46
————— Pascal 7, Descartes 8, Heereboord 1, Regius 3, Jansenius 6, Geulynx 6, Malebranche 7, Spinoza 8

1660–1680   total 71
————— H. Morus 4, Pascal 7, Lamy 2, Duverré 1, Lemaitre 1, Spinoza 8, Arnauld 4, Cudworth 5, Leibnitz 9, De Raey 1, Clauberg 3, Rohault 1, Fardella 1, Nicole 4, Geulynx 6, Malebranche 7, De la Forge 3, Cherbury 4

1680–1700   total 94
————— John Sergeant 1, Leibnitz 9, Burthogge 1, Clauberg 3, H. Morus 4, Malebranche 7, Arnauld 4, Nicole 4, Bekker 1, Legrand 1, Fardella 2, Bossuet 6, Lamy 1, Lamon 1, De la Forge 3, Rohault 1, Pufendorf 3, Fénelon 4, Cudworth 5, Heereboord 1, Fontenelle 4, De Volder 1, Wittich 1, Heidanus 1, Jelles 1, De Vries 1, Lead 1, Bayle 6, Spinoza 8, Thomassin 1, Taylor 1, Whichcote 1

1700–1720   total 78
————— Berkeley 8, Boerhaave 3, Giovenale 2, Collier 5, Lamy 1, Norris 2, Thomassin 1, Bossuet 6, Fénelon 6, André 1, Gottfried Arnold 3, Leenhof 2, Leibnitz 9, Stahlkopf 1, Clarke 2, Taylor 1, Malebranche 7, Hutten 1, Buddaeus 1, Wittich 1, Edelmann 1, Toland 4, P. Bayle 6, Spener 4

1720–1740   total 64
————— Leibnitz 9, Wolf 7, Berkeley 8, André 1, Toland 4, Vico 7, Johnson 6, Edwards 6, Norris 2, Gottsched 1, Thümmig 1, Schultz 4, Baumgarten 4, John Lange 1, Wollaston 2, G. Cocceji 1

1740–1760   total 88
————— Berkeley 8, Wolf 7, Edwards 6, Tindall 2, Voltaire 6, Billfinger 2, Baumgarten 4, Knutzen 2, Hume 8, Lomonosov 3, Vico 7, Kant 12, Polignac 4, Morgan 1, Edelmann 1, Vauvenargue 4, Daries 1, Fr. Schultze 4, Cruzius 4, Crouzas 1, Gottsched 1

1760–1780   total 60
————— Reid 4, Beattie 2, Kant 12, Tetens 4, Lomonosov 4, Wolf (Works) 7, Lessing 6, Price 4, Warburton 2, Formey 1, Ickstadt 2, Nettelbladt 2, Baumeister 2, Baumgarten 4, Plouquet 4

1780–1800   total 93
————— Kant 12, D. Stewart 4, Beck 2, De Bonald 4, Chateaubriand 5, Fichte 8, Schiller 8, Schultz 3, Forberg 1, J. de Maistre 6, Hegel 8, Pestalozzi 4, Jacob 1, Krug 2, Mendelssohn 4, Willich 1, Reinhold 2, Weisshaupt 4, Cl. St. Martin 4, Blake 4, Nitsch 1, Schwarz 2, Kinker 1, Wirgmann 1, Wasiansky 1

1800–1820   total 102
————— Kant 12, Treviranus 1, De Bonald 4, J. de Maistre 6, Chateaubriand 5, Galitch 1, Abicht 2, Born 2, Wittenbach 1, Mellin 2, Kiesewetter 1, Reingold 2, Swabedissen 1, Forberg 1, Villers 1, Pestalozzi 4, G. M. Kleins 1, Windischmann 1, Jacob 1, Stuzmann 1, Fries 6, Ast 1, Wronsky 3, Krug 4, J. Wagner 1, M. de Biran 5, Kerner 1, Rixner 1, Schelling 8, Hemert 1, Schleiermacher 4, Nithammer 2, Herbart 7, Steffens 1, Krause 4, S. Maimon 4, Holsen 1

1820–1840   total 108
———————— Hegel 8, Herbart 7 Schelling 8, V. Cousin 4, Ampère 5, Brown 3, M. de Biran 5, Rosmini 6, Galluppi 3, Wronsky 3, De Bonald 4, Krause 4, Harms 2, A. Franck 3, Laromiguiere 4, Bouterweck 1, D. Stewart 4, Fichte (Jr.) 4, Schleiermacher 4, Fries 6, Bordat de Moulin 1, Whewell 6, Shelly 6, Khomiakov 3, Kirejevsky 2, Miror 2

1840–1860   total 150
———————— Schelling 8, Cousin 4, Krause 4, Ampère 5, M. de Biran 5, Harms 3, Whewell 6, Fichte (Jr.) 4, Damiron 2, Ranke 5, A. Franck 3, Vinet 4, Saisset 1, Lassale 6, Lotze 5, Carlyle 6, Wronsky 3, Rosmini 6, Gioberti 6, Ravaisson 3, Zeller 5, Čičerin 4, Exner 1, Strümpell 2, Fr. Bouiller 1, Vischer 4, Romer 1, Schaden 1, Michelet 4, V. Hugo 8, Strachov 3, Vacherot 3, Renouvièr 7, Galluppi 3, Mansel 2, Hamilton 6, Trendelenburg 4, Jurkievitch 2

1860–1880   total 166
———————— Damiron 2, Green 5, Renouvier 7, Samarin 5, Tscertelef 2, Brochard 2, Lachelier 4, Cohen 7, Boutroux 4, McCosh 4, Mansel 2, Liebmann 5, Plumacher 4, Taubert 3, Bahnsen 1, Windelband 6, A. Spir 4, Hartmann 8, V. Hugo 8, Čičerin 4, Carlyle 6, J. Fischer 3, V. Cousin 4, Naville 4, Bouillier 2, P. Janet 4,

Vera 2, Spaventa 4, Hamilton 6, Axakov 4, Butlerov 2, Khomiakov 4, Pillon 4, Laprade 2, Vischer 4, Davies 4, Ranke 5, Ravaisson 3, Kuno Fischer 4, Jurkievitch 2, Huet 2, Remusat 1

1880–1900   total 187
———————— Windelband 6, Natorp 5, Lotze 5, Brochard 2, Pillon 4, Lachelier 4, Balfour 4, Karinsky 4, Wwedensky 4, Boutroux 4, Liebmann 5, Cohen 7, Elsenhans 2, Bradley 7, Bosanquet 4, Petronievič 6, Drews 4, Green 5, Lopatin 4, A. Spir 4, Hartmann 8, Dilthey 5, Masaryk 5, Čičerin 4, B. Croce 7, C. Reid 2, Ibsen 4, Naville 4, Axakov 4, Lipps 7, Rehmke 7, James 7, Wundt 7, Amiel 4, Ed. Rod 2, Eucken 5, H. Sidgwick 4, Rickert 6, Stadler 2, J. Cohn 3

1900–1920   total 191 [1]
———————— Lipps, Cohen, Natorp, Milhaud, Hartmann, Windelband, Masaryk, Rehmke, B. Croce, Royce, Bradley, Bosanquet, N. Hartmann, Palmer, Michaltschef, Pillon, Cassirer, Rickert, Watson, Hobhouse, Balfour, Wwedensky, Novgorodzev, Petronievič, Karinsky, Kroner, Falckenberg, Schultze-Gewaernitz, R. Eucken, Bulgakov, S. Hessen, Münsterberg, James, Ascoldov, Pfleiderer, Ormund, Bergson, Brunschvicg, Tatarkevicz, Twardowsky, Brentano, Maritain

[1] For obvious reasons values are not given for living authors.

INDEXES

Index of Authors

All names given in the Appendixes, including those of the authors of reference and other works cited, are not included in the Index. For these names see the Appendixes.

715